INTRODUCTION

TO

JURISPRUDENCE

BY

LORD LLOYD OF HAMPSTEAD

Quain Professor of Jurisprudence
in the University of London

THIRD EDITION

LONDON
STEVENS & SONS
1972

First Edition	- -	1959
Second Impression	-	1960
Second Edition -	-	1965
Second Impression -		1969
Third Impression	-	1971
Third Edition	- -	1972

Published in 1972 by
Stevens & Sons Limited of
11 New Fetter Lane, London
and printed in Great Britain
by The Eastern Press Limited
of London and Reading

SBN   Hardback   420   42910   7
Paperback   420   42920   4

PREFACE TO THE THIRD EDITION

THAT there has been a reversal of attitude towards Jurisprudence in this country in the last fifteen years seems hardly open to doubt. When the first edition of this book appeared in 1959 Jurisprudence was still something of a "dirty word," certainly in the ranks of the practising profession and among most of the judiciary, and even be it admitted, in some academic circles. Re-reading the Preface to the First Edition there is detectable a faint note of apology, albeit combined with a hint of defiance. Since then, Jurisprudence in this country may be said to have come of age. This is not the place to attempt an exploration of the causes of these winds of change, but what has manifestly occurred is a change in the climate of opinion. Instead of regarding rules of law as simply something to be accepted as part of the natural order of society, every aspect of the legal system, the legislative and judicial processes, the working of the legal profession, the nature and functioning of law in all its aspects in relation to society, and its relevance to contemporary needs, are now recognised as legitimate and indeed pressing fields of study. These, it is widely acknowledged, concern not merely the remote legal theoretician residing totally outside or haunting only the fringes of legal activity, but each and every participant in the legal process, including the community as a whole and the individuals and sectional groups which are comprised within that community. It should also be added that this movement may be linked, though not necessarily in a causative sense, to the immense change in student attitudes from one of relatively passive reception to that of active participation. For, in a field of study such as law, the urge to understand and appraise the relevance of the subject-matter of what is studied must lead directly from the apparatus of the rules and principles of the law to jurisprudential exploration into their meaning and their effects in our society.

Again, the viewpoint rather hesitatingly adumbrated in the preface to the first edition, that the links between the law and other fields of study, such as sociology, psychology and anthropology, had an essential contribution to make to the deeper understanding of law, has now been overtaken by a situation where such inter-disciplinary study and research has been greatly developed and expanded. The recently announced establishment at Oxford of a centre of socio-legal studies sufficiently signalises this new approach, and many other developments on similar lines could be detailed as

v

occurring both in the newer and the older universities, as well as in
the sphere of government and elsewhere. In saying all this there
is no desire in any way to strike a complacent note, or to suggest that
all the work of this order that is being done is of equal or indeed of
substantial merit. Many such undertakings taking place in a burst
of understandable enthusiasm will doubtless prove futile or abortive,
though an optimistic view may remain justifiable so far as concerns
the general value of this new movement. Nor should it be overlooked that the new developments in analytical jurisprudence also
reflect the influence of this general change of attitude, as is emphasised in the appropriate place in this edition, where these new
developments are discussed and explained.

The prefaces to the previous two editions devoted a good deal of
space to discussing the form and purpose of the book and dealt with
certain criticisms which had been or might be expected to be
raised in regard to its structure and the character of its contents.
At the risk of appearing immodest it is felt that the book is now
sufficiently well-established and accepted for such discussion to be
omitted from the present preface, though the text of the preface to
the first edition has still been retained for the benefit of such readers
as may come upon the work in the present edition for the first time.
Accordingly the rest of this preface will be devoted to indicating
the main changes that have been brought about in the preparation
of the third edition. In the preface to the first edition I referred
to my efforts to keep the book within moderate proportions, and in
the preface to the second edition I stated proudly that, despite the
introduction of considerable new material, by a ruthless process of
weeding out earlier material, I had contrived to produce a new
edition slightly shorter than its predecessor. Very different is the
outcome of the present edition which the reader will ascertain,
perhaps with some sense of shock, is practically double the length
of the second edition. It need hardly be said that this is the
result of a conscious act of choice, since I have for some time been
aware that it is really not possible to do adequate justice to the
areas to which the book gives attention without a substantial
expansion of the material provided for study, as well as in the
introductory chapters and the annotations to the extracts. It is the
earnest hope of the author that any disadvantages entailed by this
attempt to cover the chosen field more comprehensively, and not
least the inevitable increase in cost of production and of sale price,
will be more than outweighed by affording the student more scope
for study in depth, and providing the teacher with an instrument
of greater flexibility. All the same I am only too well aware that it
is not possible in a field such as Jurisprudence to satisfy everyone,

or indeed anyone at all, including even oneself. The fact remains that a balance has to be struck at some point and the hope can only be expressed that a more effective balance has been attained than hitherto.

Some details can now be given as to the changes which have been effected in this new edition. To begin with, it should be pointed out that the new edition is approximately 400 pages longer than its predecessor. There have been included 66 new extracts not contained in the earlier edition, and from that earlier edition 16 extracts have been totally deleted and five others have been materially shortened. Of these new extracts 26 are of American origin, 18 come from English or Commonwealth sources, and 22 are European. Nor is it only in relation to the extracts that this edition materially differs from its predecessor. The introductory chapters have undergone substantial rewriting and received many extensive additions. In fact the overall increase in these introductory chapters amounts to some 100 additional pages. It will suffice here to refer merely to those sections where the most substantial additions or rewriting have occurred. New sections have been added on Recent Trends in Jurisprudence, on Lon Fuller, on Bentham, *Of Laws in General,* on Sociological Jurisprudence since Pound, on Lasswell and McDougal, on the Sociology of Law and Legal Sociology, on Judicial Behaviouralism, on Hägerström, on Recent Developments in Tribal Law, on English and American Judges as Lawmakers, on Rules of Precedent as Law or Practice, and on Prospective Overruling. Apart from such completely new sections there has been considerable rewriting in many of the previously existing sections, of which the following may be particularly singled out for mention, namely, the Legal Enforcement of Morality, Kelsen on the Basic Norm, Sanctions, International Law, the Legal Theories of A. Ross, Codification and Statutory Interpretation.

Turning now to the more important of the new extracts the following can be specially mentioned by way of stating the authors and the sources from which their respective extracts are derived:– Gunnar Myrdal, *Objectivity in Social Research* (1970), Thomas H. Kuhn, *The Structure of Scientific Revolutions* (1970), Judith N. Shklar, *Legalism* (1964), Julius Stone, *Legal System and Lawyers' Reasonings* (1964), *Law and the Social Sciences* (1966), and *The Ratio of the Ratio Decidendi* (1959), H. L. A. Hart, *Problems of Philosophy of Law* (1967), L. L. Fuller, *The Morality of Law* (1969), and *Human Interaction and the Law* (1969), Margaret Mead, *Some Anthropological Considerations Concerning Natural Law* (1961), Mark M. MacGuigan, *Obligation and Obedience* (1970), Jeremy Bentham, *Of Laws in General*, ed. H. L. A. Hart (1970), R. Summers

Scope of the New Analytical Jurisprudence (1966), H. Kelsen, *The Pure Theory of Law* (1967), and *Professor Stone and the Pure Theory of Law* (1965), B. Barry, *Political Argument* (1965), G. Sawer, *Law in Society* (1965), Harry C. Bredemeier, *Law as an Integrative Mechanism* (1962), P. Selznick, *The Sociology of Law* (1959), J. Dewey, *Logical Method and the Law* (1924), E. Cahn, *Confronting Injustice* (1967), K. Llewellyn, *The Common Law Tradition* (1960), H. Kalven, and H. Zeisel, *The American Jury* (1966), Underhill Moore and Gilbert Sussmann, *The Lawyer's Law* (1932), L. Loevinger, *Jurimetrics—The Next Step Forward* (1949), G. Schubert, *Mathematical Prediction of Judicial Behaviour* (1964), Reed C. Lawlor, *What Computers Can Do: Analysis and Prediction of Judicial Decision* (1963), A. Hägerström, *Inquiries into the Nature of Law and Morals* (1953), K. Olivecrona, *Legal Language and Reality* (1962), and *Law as Fact* (2nd ed. 1971), A. Ross, *Directives and Norms* (1968), and *Tu-Tu* (1957), R. David and J. Brierley, *Major Legal Systems of the World* (1968), P. Bohannan, *The Differing Realms of Law* (1965), R. Schwartz and J. Miller, *Legal Evolution and Societal Complexity* (1964), John P. Dawson, *The Oracles of the Law* (1968), H. Wechsler, *Towards Neutral Principles of Constitution of Law* (1959), L. Scarman, *Law Reform—The New Pattern* (1968). In addition a number of substantial extracts have been included from important new English and American cases of which examples are, *Conway* v. *Rimmer, Home Office* v. *Dorset Yacht Company, Madzimbamuto* v. *Lardner-Burke, Griswold* v. *Connecticut* and *Harper* v. *The Virginia Board of Education.* There have also been lengthy additions and amendments to the annotations to many of the extracts.

Apart from the foregoing, a substantial new chapter on the Marxist Theory of Law and Socialist Legality has been added. The first edition of this book did contain a short chapter on these topics, but it may be recollected that it was omitted from the second edition for reasons which were explained in the preface to that edition. My main reason for this omission was that it did not seem practicable to do adequate justice to the subject-matter in a single short chapter. This omission, however, proved to be the most criticised feature of the second edition, a criticism which the author took very much to heart and to which he gave considerable attention. As a result an endeavour has been made to deal far more thoroughly in the new chapter with these topics than had proved possible in the original chapter of the first edition. A substantially rewritten introduction containing many completely new sections has been included in the present edition, resulting in an increase from 5 to 25 pages. This comprises both new and rewritten sections covering the theoretical aspects of Marxism in relation to law as well as legal developments in the Soviet Union, Yugoslavia and Communist China. Whereas the brief extracts in the first edition covered no more than 11 pages, the extracts in the present edition, practically all of them new, extend to nearly 50 pages. These extracts in the new edition comprise not only material derived from the classical authors but much recent Soviet material not easily accessible elsewhere, as a perusal of the contents of the new chapter 10 will readily reveal. I am very glad to have been able to fill this lacuna in the second edition in a manner which I hope will be found to be a substantial improvement on the Marxist chapter in the first edition. It is indeed absurd, as I would readily acknowledge, to attempt a comprehensive survey of contemporary trends in Jurisprudence without taking a careful look at what is happening in that substantial area of the world's surface which remains deeply influenced by Marxist theory and ideology.

Last but not least, I would wish to place on record my deep indebtedness to my colleague Michael Freeman, LL.M., Lecturer in Law, at University College, London, without whose invaluable and devoted assistance the preparation of this new edition, especially in its greatly extended range, could scarcely have been undertaken or accomplished. He has brought youthful enthusiasm, extensive learning and careful reflection to bear upon the subject-matter of the work, from which it has greatly benefited. The responsibility however for the opinions expressed and for errors or omissions remains my own.

LLOYD OF HAMPSTEAD.

LONDON
April 1972.

PREFACE TO THE FIRST EDITION

THE aims of this book can be stated quite simply. They are, first, to provide the student of jurisprudence with a textbook which will enable him to become acquainted with the theories, attitudes, and insights of leading jurists from selected texts culled from their own writings. In the second place, an attempt is made to afford him a coherent picture of the subject, by means of a full commentary setting out the background and inter-connections between the differing approaches, and a critical appraisal of the viewpoints illustrated in the selected texts. This is done by means of introductory chapters to each section of the book, as well as by way of annotations to the texts themselves.

Present-day textbooks of jurisprudence, by attempting to summarise at second-hand the views of a great number of leading writers, tend not only to reduce themselves to a repertory of schools of thought, but inevitably to lose the distinctive flavour of the particular writers it is sought to epitomise. It is therefore hoped that a book in the present form will provide the student with the stimulation of sampling the actual style of those whose ideas he is studying. This is not to say of course that all the styles represented in this volume are admirable in themselves. Far from it. But at least they do afford the student first-hand contact with an author's own thoughts expressed in his own way. *Le style c'est l'homme.* And among the many authors whose viewpoints are contained in this volume it seems reasonable to suppose that a few students at least will find some passages which will strike a sufficient chord in their own minds to provoke them into reading more of the writings of authors to whom they have proved responsive. At least it seems to me that the existing plan may achieve more, in encouraging the serious student to range beyond the covers of his chosen textbook, than will a series of potted summaries. And for those who find themselves unable or unwilling thus to enlarge their range of reading, it is hoped that the fare contained in this volume will provide a more educative study of its subject-matter than the traditional approach.

As I have attempted to indicate, this is not a book of readings on the American pattern, though it obviously owes a good deal of inspiration to that familiar transatlantic aid to learning. Where it differs principally is in the fullness of the accompanying commentary, by which I have striven to give a coherence to the book as a whole, and thus enable it to be read through as a self-contained textbook, and not simply to be used as an ancillary aid to a course of lectures or seminars. Nevertheless it is hoped that it may also be found of service for that purpose too, particularly by affording scope for discussion of the actual writings of the authors quoted. Also I have tried to keep the book within moderate proportions, and not to let it exceed the accepted limits—vague though these may be—of standard students' textbooks in this country. The student is apt to reflect the view attributed to Callimachus that " a big book is a big evil," [1] and I dare to confess that I am not without sympathy for that opinion.

Yet by restricting the size of the present volume the task of selecting its contents has inevitably become a more anxious and searching one. Selection involves both a choice of authors and of the passages to be chosen from them, and although at least the choice of some of the authors may be self-evident, in all other respects the selection must necessarily be of a highly personal character. This I venture to think needs no excuse, for a book on jurisprudence which is devoid of such individuality would be nothing at all. At the same time when, within the limits of space, a firm choice had to be made, the author could not avoid both a wistful glance at the almost limitless size of some American compilations, and the feeling that the dictum of Callimachus is a hard saying. Yet all life is a series of choices, and to cultivate a disciplined and even rigorous approach to selection is not without its benefits. At any rate, though conscious that no selection can ever satisfy everyone or indeed anyone, least of all the selector himself, perhaps I may be permitted to hope that, within the limits of the available space, the reader is presented with a fair and representative collection, in one shape or another, of most of the dominant trends in modern legal thinking, as well as of certain developments which have contributed to these.

In making my selection I have been influenced by certain objectives which seemed to me desirable. Thus I have placed a particular emphasis on modern developments, while endeavouring at the same time to set these in their relationship to the main streams of Western legal thought. Again I have attempted to emphasise the more universal aspects of the subject by giving full space to the viewpoints of leading jurists in other Western countries, whether from the continent of Europe or of America. Harold Laski once wrote of English jurisprudence that it " still does little more than ring the changes on the ideas of Jeremy Bentham and Sir Henry Maine." [2] Such a view may seem not a little unjust at the present day, and though (as will be seen in the pages that follow), I am not

[1] *Fragments*, 359.
[2] *American Democracy* (1949), p. 66.

among those who desire to denigrate either Bentham or Austin, I do attempt to evaluate the contributions of those eminent writers for our modern atomic age. At the same time, while allowing foreign jurists to speak for themselves in their own context and sometimes at considerable length, I have not hesitated to essay an evaluation of those writers from the standpoint of an English lawyer desirous of seeing what fresh insights he may learn from them, and their relevance to his own legal community. Also in selecting passages I have aimed —though not consistently—at providing long extracts from a few authors rather than a series of short passages from a great many. In this way I feel the student is given the opportunity of coming more adequately to grips both with the style and approach and the extended argument of the writer in a way that cannot be provided by very short extracts. For this purpose, too, I have not sought to select what may be called " purple passages," but those which set forth the core or certain essential features of the writer's approach. In this connection I am very mindful of Holmes' saying: " I care nothing for the systems—only for the insights." [3] It is these which, more than sustained argument, often afford the most illumination, and we must always guard against a tendency to depreciate their originality when uttered, because they may since have become part of our current mental coinage. I have also quoted from leading judgments both English and American where these seemed effectively to illustrate or expound an important approach: only severe limitations of space have prevented me from doing this as often as I could have wished.

Throughout this volume signs will be found of the controversy —ancient in lineage but as vital as ever—between the positivists and the natural lawyers. In a recent essay on " The present position of Jurisprudence in the United States," [4] Professor Jerome Hall has written that " the most striking fact about current national developments is the rise of natural law philosophies almost everywhere. England, Sweden, and Denmark are among the few countries which do not participate in this world movement. The contrast is sharpest in England where, despite Maine and Pollock, Austin continues to reign. Indeed Austin's imperative theory has been subjected to logical positivism, and the product is a nominalist jurisprudence which reflects the view that logical analysis is the only function of jurisprudence." Despite these strictures I am not ashamed to affirm that my own allegiance is with the positivists, but lest it be thought that this implies acceptance of what Jerome Hall calls a " nominalist

[3] *Holmes-Laski Letters*, I, 300.
[4] (1958) 44 Virginia L.R. 321.

jurisprudence ". I feel called upon to say something here of my own position.

The recent emphasis on the linguistic nature of philosophical problems stems principally in England from the overwhelming influence of the Cambridge philosopher, Ludwig Wittgenstein.[5] His approach, which is often wrongly called logical positivism, was aimed at showing how philosophical puzzlement is frequently due to confusions of language. " Philosophy is a battle against the bewitchment of our intelligence by means of language." [6] And in answer to the question, What is your aim in philosophy?, the reply is given, " To show the fly the way out of the fly-bottle." [7] Wittgenstein's later developments, which have proved so pervasive in almost every field of thought, including even legal theory, mainly occurred in the 1930s, but owing to his unwillingness to publish his own writings, the details of his thought and method were little known at that time outside a small circle in Cambridge. It was my good fortune to meet Wittgenstein and attend his seminars when I was in Cambridge, during the years 1935 and 1936, on the introduction of my friend, Francis Skinner (one of Wittgenstein's closest associates and followers up till the time of Skinner's lamented early death in 1938). The force of Wittgenstein's thought and personality could hardly fail to make some impact even on one who, like myself, was quite unequipped to assess their significance. Certainly as a lawyer I was naturally intrigued with the implications of this approach for legal thinking. Soon after, however, legal practice and a long absence on war service took me far from these esoteric regions, though an article I published in the *Law Quarterly Review* in 1948 was a reflection of the continuing influence of this approach.[8] Since the war, and particularly with the posthumous publication of Wittgenstein's later works, the impact of his influence has spread very widely, and far beyond the field of purely philosophical speculation.

The present author writes as a lawyer and not as a philosopher, and is fully conscious of his lack of competence to evaluate philosophical theories. At the same time their impact on legal, as on other fields, cannot be altogether denied, as the contents of this volume sufficiently testify. It always seemed to me, from my Cambridge days, that the value of this new " Socratic " method, as strikingly demonstrated to us by Wittgenstein himself, was in its ability to clear up linguistic confusions, to get rid of " puzzlement,"

---

[5] But this itself is linked with the empirical tradition which has been dominant in English philosophical thought from Hume to Bertrand Russell.

[6] L. Wittgenstein, *Philosophical Investigations*, 47e.

[7] *Ibid.*, 103e.

[8] " Reason and Logic in the Common Law " (1948) 64 L.Q.R. 468; see *post*, p. 428.

as we were constantly told. Wittgenstein, so far as I could see, claimed no more than this, and it seemed to me that his method might well prove apt for showing how some of the more philosophical aspects of legal thinking, such as the concept of corporate personality,[9] as well as general thinking about law, might benefit from his " purgative " approach.[10]

Since the war, however, developments have taken place which, though derived from Wittgenstein, seem to me, to a greater or lesser extent, to distort his teaching, or seek to press it further than it will go. I have in mind here the tendency in some quarters to try to resolve all problems into purely linguistic ones, and to try to build up a positive body of knowledge by purely linguistic analysis. As I have said, I am a lawyer and not a philosopher, and I do not presume to embark on matters of high philosophy. I confess, however, that I am not persuaded, as a lawyer, that it is possible or desirable to resolve fundamental legal problems in purely linguistic or analytical terms. What is, however, of first importance is to avoid confusions or misunderstandings which have their roots in the misuse of language. For my part I am doubtful whether Wittgenstein's message goes beyond this, and certainly not for the lawyer, whatever may be the case for the purely speculative philosopher. But while, therefore, I agree with Jerome Hall that logical analysis is not enough—and with all respect to him, I take leave to doubt whether any English positivist would wish to take up so extreme a position [10a]—it seems to me that the natural law developments, which Hall discerns so widespread outside the purlieus of these benighted islands, will also benefit from a little of Wittgenstein's purgative method. At the same time I have endeavoured, within the limits of space of this volume, to give full scope to the natural law viewpoint, for its importance, whether we accept it or not, cannot be gainsaid. In this section of the book I have therefore given examples of natural law thinking at many different periods, and in particular quoted modern authors who have attempted to adapt this line of thought to modern conditions, with what success must be judged by the reader.

But Legal Positivism, it may still be said, is not enough. And certainly if reduced to mere verbal analysis, this may be so. But must it be treated so narrowly? Does it necessarily mean no more

---

[9] Chap. 1 of my *Unincorporated Associations* (1938) owes something to this approach.

[10] But it is as well to remember Holmes' admonition that " philosophising about the law does not amount to much until one has soaked in the details "—*Holmes-Laski Letters*, II, 1253.

[10a] *Pace* also E. McWhinney, who has referred to " some " (unspecified) English law schools as " bogged down in rather trivial problems of linguistic analysis ": (1958) McGill L.J. 213, 218.

than the arid study of linguistic forms? Certainly not for Bentham or Austin, who fully recognised the need to take account of human values and man's social and economic needs, though admittedly their approach, in accordance with their times, was far more abstract than would satisfy a modern sociological jurist. What, however, I desire to maintain is that there is nothing inconsistent or incompatible with a positivist outlook, in acknowledging the essential role of human values in law and human society. What the positivist rejects is neither valuations nor their effect on human institutions, but only the logical or practical possibility of establishing a scale of absolute values which govern mankind universally without distinction of time or place. Since, however, those who maintain this position regard it not so much as a question of logic or practice but of feeling or intuition, it is evident that the debate is likely to remain inconclusive. What matters, however, are the ideas which at different times are accepted and impel men to action, and if it is true that " the law is a museum of philosophical concepts which men not primarily interested in philosophy have found in practice to be valid," [11] one cannot ignore any operative concepts in that field, however much they may be open to question.

One result of the positivist school of law which derived from Bentham and Austin was that legal science became, both in the minds of practitioners and jurists, rigidly demarcated from other studies, and this led to the notion that legal problems could be solved purely in terms of legal analysis without regard to other fields of study and in rather lofty disregard of external considerations.[12] This certainly was very far from the aim of either Bentham or Austin,[13] nor was it by any means invariably reflected in the writings or judgments of many of the distinguished jurists and judges who broadly accepted the Austinian approach. The rise of the modern sociological school has restored much of the original objective (but not the dogmas) of the earlier utilitarians, and has made conspicuous—if not so far outstandingly successful—attempts to link legal thought with developments in other subjects, such as anthropology, psychology and sociology. This has been by no means a one-way traffic, for other branches of learning at the present day have found some fertile insights and illumination from the study of jurisprudence and the working of legal systems or institutions. Although, in a work of these limited proportions, there can be but little space for such sorties, I have

---

[11] Rebecca West, *Sunday Times*, May 25, 1958.

[12] It is this form of so-called legal positivism that has earned so many transatlantic strictures, from Pound's " Mechanical Jurisprudence " in 1908 (8 Col.L.R. 605) to McWhinney in *Canadian Jurisprudence* (1959), p. 10. It would almost seem that positivism is a " dirty " word in America, with overtones that it lacks in this country.

[13] *Cf. post*, 783.

where possible endeavoured to introduce occasional material from non-legal writings, where these can throw light on current trends of thought or the connection of legal thinking with related fields of study.

It should be observed that some of the original notes to the selected texts have been omitted wholly or in part where this seemed desirable for the present purpose. No indication has been given of particular omissions of such notes, as this would have been unduly cumbersome. Original notes to the selected texts which have been retained are clearly distinguishable from my own annotations to the texts, as the latter are always enclosed in square brackets.

Lastly I would like to express my gratitude, in no perfunctory sense, for the most helpful co-operation I have been accorded, at every stage of the production of this book, by the publishers, Messrs. Stevens & Sons, and especially by my friend Mr. Hilary Stevens himself. . . .

DENNIS LLOYD.

LONDON,
September, 1959.

ACKNOWLEDGMENTS

GRATEFUL acknowledgment is made for permission to reproduce from the undermentioned works:

AQUINAS, *Summa Theologica*, trans. J. G. Dawson, ed. d'Entrèves (Basil Blackwell).

ARISTOTLE, *Ethics*, trans. Sir D. Ross (Oxford Univ. Press).

ARISTOTLE, *Politics*, trans. Sir E. Barker (Oxford Univ. Press).

AUSTIN, J., *Lectures on Jurisprudence*, ed. H. L. A. Hart.

AUSTIN, J., " The Uses of the Study of Jurisprudence " (from *The Province of Jurisprudence Determined*, ed. H. L. A. Hart) (George Weidenfeld & Nicolson Ltd.).

BARRY, B., *Political Argument* (Routledge & Kegan Paul Ltd. and New York: Humanities Press, Inc.).

BENTHAM, J., *An Introduction to the Principles of Morals and Legislation* (ed. J. H. Burns and H. L. A. Hart, 1970) (The Athlone Press, Univ. of London).

BENTHAM, J., *Of Laws in General*, ed. H. L. A. Hart (The Athlone Press, Univ. of London, 1970).

BERMAN, H., *Justice in the U.S.S.R.* (Reprinted by permission of the publishers and the author: Harvard Univ. Press, copyright 1950, 1963, by the President and Fellows of Harvard College).

BODIN, *Six Books of the Republic*, trans. M. J. Tooley (Basil Blackwell).

BOHANNAN, PAUL, " The Differing Realms of The Law " from *Law and Warfare*, ed. Bohannan (Natural History Press).

BREDEMEIER, HARRY C., " Law as an Integrative Mechanism " from *Law and Sociology*, ed. W. M. Evan (Reprinted with permission of The Macmillan Company. Copyright by The Free Press of Glencoe, a Division of The Macmillan Company, 1962).

BRYCE, *Studies in History and Jurisprudence* (Oxford Univ. Press).

CAHN, E., *Confronting Injustice* (Little, Brown & Co.).

CARDOZO, *Nature of the Judicial Process* (Yale Univ. Press Library).

CASTBERG, F., *Problems of Legal Philosophy* (Oslo Univ. Press).

CICERO, *De Republica*, trans. C. W. Keyes (Loeb Classical Library).

DABIN, J., *General Theory of Law*, 2nd ed., trans. K. Wilk (1950).

DAVID, R. and BRIERLEY, J., *Major Legal Systems in the World To-day* (Stevens & Sons Ltd.).

DAWSON, JOHN P., *Oracles of the Law* (Michigan Legal Publications).

DENNING, RT. HON. LORD, " The Need for a New Equity " (1952) 5 *Current Legal Problems* 1 (Stevens & Sons, Ltd.).

DEWEY, J., " Logical Method and Law " from (1924) 10 *Cornell Law Quarterly* 17 (Cornell Law Review. Copyright 1924, by Cornell University).

DUGUIT, L., " The Law and the State " (1917) 31 Harv.L.Rev. 1–185 (Harvard Law Review Association).

EHRLICH, E., *Fundamental Principles of the Sociology of Law*, trans. L. W. Moll (Harvard Univ. Press, Copyright 1936, by The President and Fellows of Harvard College).

ENGELS, " Anti-Dühring " from *Social and Political Doctrines of Contemporary Europe*, M. Oakshott (Cambridge Univ. Press).

FRANK, J., *Law and the Modern Mind* (Stevens & Sons Ltd.).

FRIEDMANN, W., *Law and Social Change in Contemporary Britain* (Stevens & Sons Ltd.).

FULLER, L. L., " Human Interaction and the Law " from (1969) 14 Amer. J. of Jurisprudence 1 (American Journal of Jurisprudence).

FULLER, LON L., " Positivism and Fidelity to Law—A Reply to Professor Hart " (1958) 71 Harv.L.Rev. 630 (Harvard Law Review Association).

FULLER, L. L., *The Morality of Law* (Yale Univ. Press, Copyright 1964, by Yale University).

" Georgian Conference on Law," trans. from Jaworskyj, *Soviet Political Thought* (John Hopkins Press).

GLUCKMAN, M., *Judicial Process Among the Barotse* (Published on behalf of the Institute for Social Research, Univ. of Zambia, by Manchester Univ. Press. First published 1955; 2nd edition with corrections and two additional chapters 1967).

GOLUNSKII, S. A. and STROGOVICH, M. S., " The Theory of State and Law " (Reprinted by permission of the Publishers from *Soviet Legal Philosophy*, trans. by Hugh W. Babb, with an Introduction by John N. Hazard, Cambridge, Mass.: Harvard Univ. Press, Copyright 1951, by the President and Fellows of Harvard College).

GOODHART, A. L., " Ratio Decidendi of a Case " (1930) (Yale Law Journal).

GUTTERIDGE, H. C., *Comparative Law* (Cambridge Univ. Press).

HÄGERSTRÖM, AXEL, *Inquiries into the Nature of Law and Morals*, trans. C. D. Briad (Almqvist and Wiksell).

HART, H. L. A., " Definition and Theory in Jurisprudence " (1954) 70 L.Q.R. 37 (Stevens & Sons Ltd.).

HART, H. L. A., " Positivism and the Separation of Law and Morals " (1958) 71 Harv.L.Rev. 593 (Harvard Law Review Association).

HART, H. L. A., " Problems of Philosophy of Law: Substantive Law " (Reprinted with Permission of the Publisher from the *Encyclopedia of Philosophy*, Paul Edwards, Editor in Chief. Vol. 6, pp. 273–274. Copyright 1967, by Crowell Collier and Macmillan, Inc.).

HEGEL, *Philosophy of Right*, trans. T. M. Knox (Oxford Univ. Press).

HOEBEL, E. A., *Law of Primitive Man* (Harvard Univ. Press, Copyright 1954, by the President and Fellows of Harvard College).

HOHFELD, W. N., *Fundamental Legal Conceptions as Applied in Judicial Reasoning* (Yale Univ. Press).

HOLMES, O. W., " The Path of Law " (1897) 10 Harv.L.Rev. 457–478 (Harvard Law Review Association).

IOFFE, O. S. and SHARGORODSKII, M. D., " The Significance of General Definitions in the Study of Problems of Law and Socialist Legality," from *Soviet Law and Government*, Vol. IV, No. 4 (International Arts and Sciences Press Inc.).

JAMES, W., *Pragmatism* (Longmans, Green & Co. Inc.).

JHERING, R., VON, *Law as Means to an End*, trans. I. Husik.

JOLOWICZ, H. F., *Hist. Intro. to Roman Law* (Cambridge Univ. Press).

JOUVENEL, B. DE, *Sovereignty* (Cambridge Univ. Press).

JUSTINIAN, *Institutes*, trans. R. W. Lee (Oxford Univ. Press).

KALVEN, H., and ZEISEL, H., *The American Jury* (Little, Brown & Co.).

KELSEN, H., " Professor Stone and the Pure Theory of Law " originally from *Stanford Law Review*, Vol. 17, p. 1128 (Copyright 1965, by the Board of Trustees of the Leland Stanford Junior University).

KELSEN, H., " The Pure Theory of Law," trans. Max Knight (1934–35), Vols. 50 and 51 L.Q.R. (Originally published by the Univ. of California Press; reprinted by permission of the Regents of the Univ. of California).

KELSEN, H., *What is Justice?* (Originally published by the Univ. of California Press; reprinted by permission of the Regents of the Univ. of California).

KUHN, T. S., *The Structure of Scientific Revolutions* (Univ. of Chicago Press).

LAMONT, *Principles of Moral Judgment* (Oxford Univ. Press).

LAWLOR, REED C., "What Computers Can Do: Analysis and Prediction of Judicial Decisions" from 49 *American Bar Association Journal* 337 (Reprinted from Schubert, *Judicial Behaviour*, by Rand, McNally & Co.).

LENIN, "State and Revolution," from *Social and Political Doctrines of Contemporary Europe*, M. Oakshott (Cambridge Univ. Press).

LEVI, E. H., *An Introduction to Legal Reasoning* (Univ. of Chicago Press).

LI, VICTOR H., "The Role of Law in Communist China" from *China Quarterly* (1970), Pt. 4 (Contemporary China Institute).

LLEWELLYN, K. N., *The Common Law Tradition: Deciding Appeals* (Little, Brown & Co.).

LLEWELLYN, K. N., "On Reading and Using the Newer Jurisprudence" (1940) 40 Col.L.R. 581 (Columbia Law Review).

LLEWELLYN, K. N., "Some Realism about Realism—Responding to Dean Pound" (1931) 44 Harv.L.Rev. 1222–1256 (Harvard Law Review Association).

LLOYD, D., "Reason and Logic in the Common Law" (1948) 64 L.Q.R. 468 (Stevens & Sons Ltd.).

LOEVINGER, LEE, "Jurimetrics—The Next Step Forward," from 33 Minn. L.R. 455 (Minnesota Law Review).

LUNSTEDT, *Legal Thinking Revised* (Almqvist & Wiksell).

MACDONALD, M., "Natural Rights" (1948/8) Proc.A.S. (Aristotelian Society).

MACGUIGAN, M. R., "Obligation and Obedience" (Reprinted from J. Roland Pennock and John W. Chapman, editors, *Political and Legal Obligation*, Nomos XII (New York: Atherton Press, 1970, Copyright 1970, by Atherton Press. Reprinted by permission of the authors and Aldine Atherton, Inc.).

MAINE, SIR HENRY, *Ancient Law*, ed. Sir F. Pollock (J. M. Dent & Sons).

MARITAIN, J., *Man and the State* (Univ. of Chicago Press).

MARX, K., "German Ideology," trans. T. B. Bottomore, from *Karl Marx, Selected Writings in Sociology and Social Philosophy* (Pitman Publishing).

MARX, K., "Preface to Contribution to Critique of Political Economy," trans. T. B. Bottomore, from *Karl Marx, Selected Writings in Sociology and Social Philosophy* (Pitman Publishing).

MEAD, M., "Some Anthropological Considerations Concerning Natural Law," 6 *Naturae Law Forum* 51 (American Journal of Jurisprudence).

MOORE and SUSSMAN, "Lawyer's Law" from *The Yale Law Journal*, Vol. 41, pp. 566, 567, 568–573, 574 (Reprinted by permission of the Yale Law Journal Co. and Fred. B. Rothman & Co.).

MYRDAL, G., *Objectivity in Social Research* (Gerald Duckworth & Co. Ltd. and Random House Inc.).

OLIVECRONA, K., *Law as Fact* (Ejnar Monksgaard).

OLIVECRONA, K., "Legal Language and Reality" from *Essays in honour of Pound*, ed. Newman (Bobbs-Merrill Co., Inc.).

PASHUKANIS, E. B., "Theory of Law and Marxism" from *Soviet Legal Philosophy* (Harvard Univ. Press).

PLATO, *Republic*, trans. F. M. Cornford (Oxford Univ. Press).

PLUCKNETT, T. F. T., *Legislation of Edward I* (Oxford Univ. Press).

POPPER, K., *Poverty of Historicism* (Routledge & Kegan Paul, Ltd.).

POUND, R., *Contemporary Juristic Theory* (Claremont College).

POUND, R., *Outlines of Lectures on Jurisprudence* (Harvard Univ. Press, Copyright 1943, by the President and Fellows of Harvard College).

POUND, R., *Philosophy of Law* (Yale Univ. Press).

POUND, R., *Social Control Through Law* (Yale Univ. Press).

REES, W. J., "Theory of Sovereignty Re-stated" (from *Mind* (1950)).

Restatement of the Law of Tort (Copyright 1965. Reprinted with the permission of the American Law Institute).

ROSS, A., *Directives and Norms* (Routledge & Kegan Paul Ltd. and New York: Humanities Press, Inc.).

Ross, A., *On Law and Justice* (Stevens & Sons Ltd.).

Ross, A., " Tû-tû " from *Scandinavian Studies in Law* 1957 (Permission granted by Stockholm Institute for Scandinavian Law).

Rousseau, *Social Contract*, trans. G. D. H. Cole (J. M. Dent & Sons Ltd.).

Russell, B., " Dewey's New Logic " in *The Philosophy of John Dewey*, The Library of Living Philosophers (ed. P. A. Schilpp) (Tudor Publishing Co., New York).

Ryle, G., " Theory of Meaning " (from *British Philosophy in Mid-Century* (1957), ed. Mace) (George Allen & Unwin Ltd.).

Sawer, G., *Law in Society* (by permission of The Clarendon Press, Oxford).

Scarman, Sir L., *Law Reform—The New Pattern* (Routledge & Kegan Paul).

Schubert, G., " Mathematical Prediction of Judicial Behavior " from *Judicial Behavior, A Reader in Theory and Research* (Rand, McNally & Co.).

Schwartz, R., and Miller, J., " Legal Evolution and Societal Complexity " from 70 *American Journal of Sociology* 159 (Univ. of Chicago Press).

Selznick, P., " The Sociology of Law " from *Sociology Today*, ed. Robert K. Merton, Leonard Broom and Leonard S. Cottrell, Jr. (Copyright 1959 by Basic Books, Inc., Publishers, New York).

Shklar, J., *Legalism* (Reprinted by permission of the publishers from pp, 1–3, 8–13; Cambridge, Mass.: Harvard Univ. Press, Copyright 1964, by the President and Fellows of Harvard College).

Soviet Statutes and Decisions, " Fundamental Principles of Legislation of the U.S.S.R. and Union Republics on Marriage and the Family " from *Izvestia*, June 28, 1968, Vol. IV, No. 4 (Published by International Arts and Sciences Press Inc., White Plains, New York 10603).

Stalin, J., " Political Report of the Central (Party) Committee to the XVI Congress " from *Soviet Legal Philosophy* (Harvard Univ. Press).

Stammler, R., *Theory of Justice*, trans. I. Husik.

Stone, J., *Law and the Social Sciences*, The Second Half-Century (Univ. of Minnesota Press, Mpls. Copyright 1966, by Univ. of Minnesota).

Stone, J., *Legal System and Lawyers' Reasonings* (Stevens & Sons Ltd.).

Stone, J., " The Ratio of the Ratio Decidendi " from 22 M.L.R. 597 (Stevens & Sons Ltd.).

Strogovich, M. S., " Problems of Methodology in Jurisprudence " from *Soviet Law and Government*, Vol. IV, No. 4 (published by International Arts and Sciences Press Inc., White Plains, New York 10603).

Summers, R., " The New Analytical Jurists " (1966) 41 New York Univ. Law R. 861 (New York Univ. Law Review).

Tumanov, V. A., " Contemporary Anti-Marxism and The Theory of Law " from *Soviet Law and Government*, Vol. VIII, No. 1 (International Arts and Sciences Press Inc.).

Underhill, M., and Sussmann, G., " The Lawyer's Law " (Reprinted by permission of the Yale Law Journal Co. and Fred. B. Rothman & Co. from *The Yale Law Journal*, Vol. 41, pp. 566, 567, 568–573, 574).

Vyshinskii, A., " A ' New ' Approach to Socialist Law " from *The Fundamental Tasks of the Science of Soviet Socialist Law*, No. 8 (1938), pp. 12–17, trans. in *Soviet Legal Philosophy*, eds. Babb and Hazard (Harvard Univ. Press).

Wechsler, H., " Toward Neutral Principles of Constitutional Law " from *Principles, Politics and Fundamental Law*; Cambridge, Mass. (Harvard Univ. Press, Copyright 1961 by the President and Fellows of Harvard College).

Williams, G. L., " Controversy Concerning the Word 'Law' " (1945) 22 B.Y.I.L. (Oxford Univ. Press).

Williams, G. L., " Language and the Law " (1945) 61 L.Q.R. 71, 179, 293, 384 (Stevens & Sons Ltd.).

WISDOM, J., " Gods " (from 1944 Proc. A.S.) (Aristotelian Society).

WOLLHEIM, R., " Nature of Law" (from *Political Studies* (1954), Vol. 2) (Oxford Univ. Press).

Extracts from divers cases reported in the *Law Reports*, Inc. Council of Law Reporting for England and Wales; *Times Law Reports*, Times Publishing Co. Ltd.; and *Commonwealth Law Reports*, Law Book Co. of Australasia Pty. Ltd.

CONTENTS

TABLE OF CASES

*Figures in heavier type refer to pages on which an extract from
a case is to be found*

1

NATURE OF JURISPRUDENCE

*" You will not mistake my meaning or suppose that I depreciate
one of the great humane studies if I say that we cannot learn law
by learning law. If it is to be anything more than just a technique
it is to be so much more than itself: a part of history, a part of
economics and sociology, a part of ethics and a philosophy of life."*
—Lord Radcliffe, *The Law and Its Compass* (1961), pp. 92–93.

" Jurisprudence is as big as law—and bigger "—Karl Llewellyn,
Jurisprudence (1962), p. 372.

WHAT IS JURISPRUDENCE?

To ask this question is to be reminded of the old adage, *quot homines,
tot sententiae.*[1] For not only does every jurist have his own notion
of the subject-matter and proper limits of jurisprudence, but his
approach is governed by his allegiances, or those of his society, by,
what is commonly referred to nowadays as, his " ideology."[2] No
doubt such ideological factors are frequently implicit rather than
openly avowed; thus Holmes's description of them as " inarticulate
major premises."[3] Nonetheless, they are to be discerned in juristic
theories both past and present. At the present day little difficulty
may be felt in detecting some of the glaring ideological factors, as
we have grown familiar with the fundamental cleavages between the
basic outlook of the Soviet bloc and the West, as well as between
other countries or groups of countries.[4] But, equally, " traditional

---

[1] Terence, *Phormio*, II, 4, 14.

[2] *Cf.* Myrdal, *post*, 16. See also Harris, *Beliefs in Society* (Pelican 1971), and
Lichtheim, *The Concept of Ideology* (1969), the former for contemporary
relevance, the latter for an historical analysis of the development of the concept.
See further Plamenatz, *Man and Society* (1963), Vol. 2, pp. 344–347.

[3] *Collected Legal Papers*, 203, 209. This expression received judicial approval
from Schreiner, J.A. in *Daniels* v. *Daniels* (1958) 1 S.A. 513. " To be sure,
there are lawyers, judges and even law professors who tell us they have no legal
philosophy. In Law, as in other things, we shall find that the only difference
between a person ' without a philosophy ' and someone with a philosophy is
that the latter knows what his philosophy is, and is, therefore, more able to make
clear and justify the premises that are implicit in his statement of the facts of
his experience and his judgment about those facts " (F. C. S. Northrop, *The
Complexity of Legal and Ethical Experience* (1959), p. 6).

[4] There is, however, a body of opinion today represented by such figures as Daniel
Bell (*The End of Ideology* (1961)), S. M. Lipset (*Political Man* (1963)), Herbert
Marcuse (*One-Dimensional Man* (1964)) and Raymond Aron which has diag-
nosed the end of ideology. Their argument runs that all advanced industrial
societies are fundamentally similar. Technology, communication and propaganda

1

theories in jurisprudence reflect the old ideologies," [5] as we may readily see in such theories as those of natural law,[6] or of utilitarianism.[7] It may be, though, that lawyers, whatever their philosophical leaning, have through their training and environment more in common than divides them.[8] Contemporary jurisprudence, moreover, is often open in its espousal of a particular ideology: the jurisprudence of civil disobedience, which has mushroomed in the last decade, is in open response to what its protagonists see as the urban crisis, and to the Vietnam war.[9]

Nor is law unique in this tendency to reflect the ideologies of its place and time, for similar characteristics will be encountered in many other fields, in history, ethics, psychology and, indeed, probably in all those studies now designated as social sciences. Nor have the natural sciences escaped.[10] However, the close relation of law to the social structure [11] inevitably brings into prominence the ideological background of any form of basic legal theorising.

LEGAL IDEOLOGY

One striking illustration of the way in which ideological differences distinguish different legal systems may be readily found in the contrasts between modern systems of law based on the common law and those based on the civil law derived from the Continent of Europe and distilled through the medium of medieval, Roman and canon law. We shall have something to say later about the differences of tradition and outlook which animate these respective systems, but it hardly needs emphasis here that one of the links between countries within the Commonwealth is the tradition of the common law, while what may be called the spirit of the civil law is one of the factors which tends more than most to cross the frontiers of the nation-states of Europe. Thus the acceptance of the Rome Treaty setting up the Common Market has proved far easier in the case of European countries which already possess this cement of civil law thinking.[12]

together with welfare economics have eliminated conflict. The argument seems to ignore, for one thing, cultural factors. It may be, for example, that this trend is seen in the "bourgeoisisation" of Soviet law. See *post*, Chap. 10.
[5] Northrop, in *Journal of Legal Education* (1949), p. 791. For an illustration from Roman law, see Schulz, *Classical Roman Law*, pp. 545–546.
[6] See, *post*, Chap. 3.
[7] See, *post*, p. 153.
[8] *Cf.* Shklar, *post*, 35.
[9] See, for example, ed. Pennock and Chapman, *Political and Legal Obligation* (1970) (vol. XII of *Nomos*), and the excellent survey of recent trends in MacGuigan, *Democracy and Civil Disobedience* (1971) 49 Can.B.R. 222 and *post*, p. 147.
[10] *Cf.* Kuhn, *post*, 25.
[11] *Cf.* Schwartz and Miller, *post*, p. 622.
[12] On which see Donner, *The Role of the Lawyer in the European Communities* (1966), Chap. 1.

Yet another modern example which comes to mind is the position of Indian society, with its deep roots in a traditional and religious order based on a rigid caste-system, but now overlaid by a modern constitution laying down the system of the natural rights of man—including such matters as freedom of religion and expression—which were consecrated in the revolutions of eighteenth-century Europe, and fused in the later struggles of the Western world to achieve an egalitarian democracy. Here, then, one has built into the very fabric of the legal system a basic conflict of ideologies which can clearly give rise to acute legal controversy and must necessarily involve the courts in matters of choice and policy. Thus difficulties have arisen, to give only one example, in regard to excommunication, a power traditionally exercisable by the head of a religious community. Here courts have been involved in the complex problem of deciding what beliefs are essential to religion,[13] and how far conceding the right of excommunication may not infringe the fundamental constitutional freedom of religion. So far the courts have leaned in favour of treating practices such as ritual slaughter as secular acts not essential to religion and it has been pointed out that this might well eventually lead to the court treating as inessential all beliefs they regard as merely superstitious and not, therefore, deserving the court's protection. Such a result, however, could hardly be achieved without entrenching severely on the guarantee of freedom of religion so far as this entails the right to maintain the traditional order of beliefs.[14]

In view of the impossibility of excluding factors of this kind it would be idle to aspire to a formula which would establish, once and for all, objectively, the exact province and scope of such a study as jurisprudence.[15] Nevertheless, there remain certain general characteristics of such a study which can hardly be left out of view if a comprehensive picture is to be formed. This chapter, then, will confine itself to remarking upon certain of these characteristics.

JURISPRUDENCE AND SCIENCE

The noteworthy development of the natural sciences (both physical and biological) during the nineteenth century earned for them overwhelming prestige, and this produced marked effects upon other fields

---

13 Nor is this particular problem peculiar to Eastern societies. The United States courts have been faced with similar problems. See Kurland, *Religion and the Law* (1962). See also the recent English case, *R. v. Registrar-General, ex parte Segerdal* [1970] 2 Q.B. 697.

14 *Cf.* J. D. M. Derrett, *Religion, Law and State in Modern India* (1968), particularly Chap. 13. See also, Galanter (1968) 24 *Journal of Social Issues* 65, and Bottomore, *Sociology* (2nd ed. 1971), pp. 253–255.

15 The word " jurisprudence " is not generally used in other languages in the English sense. Thus in French it refers to something like our " case-law," *théorie générale du droit* being used to cover our meaning of jurisprudence.

of study, which sought to share in this prestige by claiming also to
be sciences, engaged in a similar pursuit of empirical knowledge
by similar procedures to those accepted as the acknowledged
methods of the physical sciences. Scientific method, as, for instance,
expounded by Mill, was based on determinism and causal laws, and
with the growth of Darwinism in the field of biology the belief grew
that similar causal laws could be shown to govern man in society
as well as the physical world of science. Indeed, so powerful was
this sentiment that it spread even to such improbable spheres as
art [16] and literature. Consider, for example, impressionist art and
naturalism in fiction. "Zola (for instance) tried to create a new
type of fiction ruled by scientific laws, based on scientific investigation
and written by scientific methods . . . 'Study men as simple elements
and note the reactions,' he said. Notebook in hand, he studied them
as if they were specimens in a biological laboratory." [17] With this
stimulus it is hardly surprising that every social study, whether
long established, as in the case of history or ethics, or recently
inaugurated, as with anthropology and sociology, clamoured to
establish its scientific credentials.

The natural sciences were long considered to proceed by the
method of induction, that is, by the observation of empirical facts,
the propounding of a hypothesis to explain those facts, and the subsequent verification or otherwise of that hypothesis by observing
further facts. Such a process was believed to result in scientific laws
of complete generality and uniformity, though admittedly Hume's
tormenting argument that there was no possibility of finding a *logical*
justification for induction,[18] continued to raise nagging doubts in the
minds of philosophers, if not of scientists. In the course of this
century, however, this rigidly mechanistic view of science has been
greatly departed from.[19] It is now generally recognised that induction
does not lead to the inference of absolutely rigid causal laws governing all phenomena and whose truth is unassailable but, on the
contrary, " all that the modern physicist claims for a theory is that it

---

[16] The realism of Courbet was influenced by the positivism of Comte. Courbet
regarded reality as only what is observed and can be expressed scientifically.
Again, the impressionist painters were concerned with the scientific theory of
vision, and Seurat sought to establish a scientific method of rendering light (see
B. Taylor, *The Impressionists and their World*, pp. 6–15). In 1836 John
Constable wrote, " Painting is a science, and should be pursued as an enquiry
into the laws of nature " (Leslie, *Life of Constable*, p. 323). Ruskin, too,
was persuaded that there was such a close connection between art and science
that he believed his aesthetic observations were as conclusive as those of a
scientist (see Quentin Bell, *Ruskin* (1963), pp. 16–17).
[17] M. Cowley, *Literary Situation in America* (1954), pp. 75–76.
[18] See *A Treatise of Human Nature*, Bk. I, sect. 6. See also Kolakowski, *Positivist
Philosophy* (1972), p. 52.
[19] See Friedmann, *Legal Theory* (5th ed.) Chap. 4, especially at pp. 50–53.

fits the known facts and therefore cannot at present be refuted." [20]
The cast-iron laws of nineteenth-century science are now looked upon
rather as "statistical regularities" which we assume will apply (as
with Newton's law of gravity) until we find that they do not, and,
indeed, there are good scientific reasons for believing that in any
event there remains in the physical world as it is, an element of
indeterminacy or "chance" such that it cannot be explained solely
in terms of predictable deterministic laws.[21] Moreover, an influential
modern view of induction treats it, not so much as a method of
arriving at final laws by inference from observed facts, but rather
as a procedure implying bold conjectures, which are capable of conflicting with possible observations, and which may be accepted so
long as they are not refuted by such observations.[22] All scientific
theories (or laws) are, therefore, tentative and provisional, and liable
to possible refutation in the future.

Furthermore, it was once assumed that a rigid distinction could
be drawn between facts and values in the natural sciences. It is,
however, becoming increasingly realised that this is a somewhat
idealistic, over-simplified picture. What Kuhn [23] has called "normal
science" has a moral or value base: as a system it classifies those
facts which are considered worthy of study, it has its own technology
and material apparatus, and carries the commitment of the community of scientists. It may have the organised support and direction
of government or industrial enterprise. Change from such existing
"world view" is slow and tortuous. "Scientists hang on to theories
long after they have been refuted in the sense of failing to square
with large numbers of facts, and the attractions of a 'good' theory
seem to depend a great deal on such extra-scientific qualities as its
aesthetic qualities, its coherence with religious attitudes and the
like." [24] New "world views" or "paradigms" evolve as increasing
anomalies in an existing pattern break down the resistance of the
old paradigm's adherents.

How far, then, can it be said that other studies, besides the
physical sciences, fit into this pattern? Now the mere fact that the

[20] B. Russell, *Portraits from Memory*, pp. 117–118. See also Nagel, *The Structure of Science* (1961), Chap. 10.
[21] A brief clarification of this point and its philosophic significance will be found in Passmore, *A Hundred Years of Philosophy* (1957), p. 332. Consider also the part played by intuition in scientific method. See Sir Peter Medawar's Jayne Lectures, *Induction and Intuition in Scientific Thought* (1969), particularly Lecture 3.
[22] See K. Popper, *post*, 22; *cf.* T. Kuhn, *post*, pp. 30–31.
[23] In *The Structure of Scientific Revolutions* (revised ed. 1970) and see *post*, 27–28. This thesis may do something to explain resistance to legal change as well. But here there is the additional factor of pressure groups. Kuhn's model has been used to explain the revolution in juvenile justice in California. See Lemert, *Social Action and Legal Change* (1970).
[24] Alan Ryan, *The Philosophy of the Social Sciences* (1970), p. 71.

so-called social sciences involve a more complex subject-matter than
that of inanimate bodies does not necessarily entail that there can
be no unity of method between them, since the complexity of
phenomena is only a matter of degree, and even in physical experiment certain ideal conditions are often postulated.[25] Moreover, in
some fields, such as psychology, there may be more scope for controlled experiments [26] than in others. All the same it seems incontestable that at the present day the social sciences can hardly be said
to aim so high as to seek for hypotheses of complete uniformity and
generality, comparable to those encountered in the physical sciences.
Put at its highest, they can be said to content themselves with trying
to detect certain patterns of regularity in human behaviour, whether
individual or social, which may help in our understanding, treatment,
and social control of human beings, but which may fall a long way
short even of the " statistical uniformities " encountered in the purely
physical sciences.[27] In this sense, indeed, it may well be that such
studies as psychotherapy,[28] or, indeed, medicine itself,[29] are not
sciences in quite the way in which physics is a science, for while they
may to some extent depend on the truths of physics and chemistry,
they are not themselves so much concerned with absolute uniformities,
but rather with clinical techniques whose results may show some
pattern of uniformity of effect. Again, all these studies are equally
concerned in the accumulation of factual data in their respective
fields and its appropriate classification. History, indeed, though
sometimes now treated as a social science, is primarily interested in
particular facts rather than in general causal laws, and though it may
also concern itself with the causes of those facts, which themselves
may involve general laws, these are for the most part trivial and of
little interest to historians.[30] Where, indeed, the historian does look

25 K. Popper, *Poverty of Historicism*, pp. 139–140.
26 In the United States controlled experiments have been introduced into the legal
process. The efficacy of pretrial conferences in New Jersey was so tested. See
Rosenberg, *The PreTrial Conference and Effective Justice: A Controlled Test
in Personal Injury Litigation* (1964). " Contrary to a widely held belief, obligatory pretrial did not save court time, but in fact wasted it. Persuaded by the
experiment . . . New Jersey forthwith changed its rule and made it optional "
per Zeisel, *The Law*, in *The Uses of Sociology* (1968) ed. Lazarsfield, Sewell and
Wilensky, p. 81 at 83–84. See also Zeisel's criticism of the non-controlled
methodology of an earlier experiment on impartial medical testimony. ((1956)
8 *Stanford Law Review* 730). But controlled experiments have made no headway
in this country due mainly to an almost legalistic insistence on equality of treatment as a supreme notion of law. See, for example, the report of the debate
between Hood and Cross at the British Association meeting in 1967, reported in
[1967] Crim.L.R. 554.
27 For a detailed discussion of the " scientific " character of social inquiries see
Quentin Gibson, *Logic of Social Enquiry* (1960).
28 *Cf.* P. Alexander, in " Proceedings of Arist. Soc.," Supp., vol. 29, pp. 27–42.
29 See the discussion in Nowell-Smith, *Ethics*, at p. 64.
30 See B. Russell, *op. cit.*, pp. 177–180; K. Popper, *Poverty of Historicism*, p. 143.
As Russell points out with studied understatement, " there is not so much
recurrence in history as in astronomy."

for general laws of development, as, for example, with Hegel, Spengler or Toynbee,[31] this process is likely to result in extravagant conjecture, incapable of verification or refutation, and bearing more resemblance to prophetic utterance than to scientific discovery.

It will be apparent that, in the limited sense in which one may speak of the social sciences, it is possible or perhaps not unreasonable to designate jurisprudence as a science.[32] For it may be said to concern itself with patterns of behaviour of man in society and to be engaged both in accumulating facts and clarifying them in this field, and with discerning regularities of human behaviour or establishing ways of bringing about or controlling such regularities. One facet of jurisprudence, judicial behaviouralism,[33] can claim unequivocally to be a child of the social sciences. Behaviourists using quantitative analysis of factual data and, such elaborate techniques as Guttman scaling,[34] increasingly insist that they can predict with as much as 90 per cent. certainty the results of legal decision-making.[35] In this way jurisprudence would be an empirical study, just as ethics, too, could be treated as such a study by basing it on an inquiry into observed facts, such as moral judgments found to be actually existing in human beings or human society.[36] Such an approach will inevitably lead to some measure of co-ordination with other social sciences, such as anthropology and sociology, for relevant empirical data must be considered wherever it may be found.[37] Moreover, this method, in jurisprudence [38] is likely to possess a powerful ideological

31 Although Toynbee claims that he employs the empirical method in constructing his laws of history, not only do these seem quite incapable of being subjected to any effective form of verification, but Toynbee himself concedes that his theory requires the existence of a Law of Love which he attributes to God's will, and the existence of which is based solely on personal intuition. The result is a curious amalgam of pseudo-science and mystic theology. See in particular Arnold J. Toynbee, *Study of History*, vol. 9, pp. 395–405; and vol. 12, pp. 239–242, and 650–677. See A. J. P. Taylor's comment in ed. Ashley Montagu, *Toynbee and History* (1956), p. 115: " This is not history."

32 Note that Continental writers often speak of " legal science," not in referring to jurisprudence, but as emphasising technical or professional legal method (sometimes also called " legal dogmatics "). See Kantorowicz, *Definition of Law*, p. 11; and *cf.* Schulz, *Roman Legal Science*, p. 1. See *Incorporated Council of Law Reporting* v. *Att.-Gen.* [1971] 3 W.L.R. 853 approving Pollock's comment that law is a science in the same sense as chemistry.

33 See *post*, p. 419.

34 Or " linear cumulative scaling," which is " a method of measuring differences in and the consistency of the attitudes of a group of persons toward a single shared value," Glendon Schubert, *Judicial Behaviour* (1964), p. 308. For example, studies have investigated the attitude of judges toward civil liberties or trade unions.

35 For an assessment of the success of behaviouralism, see Becker, *Political Behaviouralism and Modern Jurisprudence* (1964), Chap. 1.

36 *Cf.* Lamont, *Principles of Moral Judgement* (1946), pp. 12–19; see *post*, p. 32.

37 See further Barkun, *Law Without Sanctions* (1968), pp. 3–7, who comments " Lawyers who are anxious to apply a social scientific outlook often fail to take advantage of valuable categories that already are at work in other fields " (p. 4).

38 See more generally, Joan Robinson, *Freedom and Necessity* (1970).

background, since it will normally be animated by a reforming impulse, desirous of moulding the law in accordance with some pre-conceived pattern.

" Normative " Character of Law

The emphasis on the science of law or the study of factual patterns of behaviour is apt to lead to a neglect or even a denial of an aspect of law which is no less crucial. For human laws are not in themselves statements of fact,[39] but are rules or norms, which prescribe a course of conduct, and usually indicate what should happen (the sanction) if this norm is not complied with.[40] The sanction, however, is not usually connected in an empirical sense with the rule or its breach, but is merely indicative of what the rule itself prescribes, as the consequence of non-compliance. This is, therefore, a particular form or use of language different from that part of language concerned with propositions of fact, but it is a no less legitimate usage than factual statements, and, is, indeed, related to a whole group of similar " normative " usages, such as commands, exhortations, and moral, ethical, or religious codes or rules of conduct. Hence normative rules must be carefully distinguished from physical laws, which state causal connections. The latter are subject to verification,[41] that is, they can be true or false; but the notion of truth or falsity is inapplicable to normative rules. Such rules simply state what should or " ought to " happen. This is the distinction made by Kant between *sein* (being) and *sollen* (ought) which is so emphatically brought out by Kelsen,[42] and which tended to be obscured or even rejected in the earlier writings of the so-called Realists.[43] Of course, it must be borne in mind that the use of the word " ought " does not necessarily imply *moral* obligation, for in relation to a purely positive rule, such as a legal duty of care, the " ought " merely relates to the duty of compliance with the rule on pain of suffering the prescribed penalty.[44]

" Ought " and " Is "

The tendency to derive normative rules from physical or natural laws, or to analyse or define them in terms of physical qualities or

---

[39] Whether the norm *itself* is a correct statement within a particular legal system is another matter; this will depend not on factual verification but on whatever tests are afforded by that system.

[40] Austin endeavoured to stress this by his imperative theory of law as a command, but his actual analysis was not free from objection; see *post*, 108.

[41] *Cf.* Popper, *post*, 23.

[42] *Post*, 269.

[43] *Post*, 413.

[44] This is not to say that the *legal* " ought " may not, in some instances, correspond with the *moral* " ought "; *cf. post*, p. 47.

phenomena, has long been a pervasive one. Thus many of the attempts to base positive law on an immutably established natural law governing the universe have involved an attempt to link normative rules directly with what are really conjectural hypotheses of a factual character (*i.e.*, in the nature of physical laws). But long ago Hume pointed out the fallacy of trying, as he put it, to derive "ought" from "is," and that a normative statement could not be inferred from a purely factual one.[45] So, too, the efforts to define moral norms in terms of something else which can be ascertained or verified as a fact, such as pleasure or utility, involve a similar confusion which has been stigmatised in the well-known formula of G. E. Moore as "the naturalistic fallacy." [46] There is, in other words, an unbridgeable gap between "ought" and "is," or norm and fact, but this does not mean, as has sometimes been thought, that "ought" statements occupy a special world of existence of their own, distinct from physical reality.[47] In this century, the epoch-making work of the philosopher Wittgenstein on the uses of language as a solvent of many of the puzzles and paradoxes that have perplexed philosophers,[48] has also helped to bring out more clearly the distinction between normative and factual usages of language. In this connection close consideration has been given by moral philosophers and, more recently, jurists like Hart, the Scandinavians and Raz to the logical structure of the imperative and normative forms of language, and although finality of opinion is not by any means attained or perhaps attainable, much of this sort of analysis is illuminating not only in

---

[45] *Post*, 31. Hume's "law" or "hurdle" or "guillotine," as it has been variously called, has in recent years been challenged. Alistair MacIntyre alleged that Hume is being read out of context, that what Hume was attacking was "vulgar systems of morality," "a religious foundation for morality," that, in fact, moral judgments were being inferred from the wrong facts. (68 *Philosophical Review* 451, now reprinted in *Against the Self-Images of the Age* (1971).) In the last decade there has been an attempt by Zimmerman to avoid the dualism altogether by reducing ought-statements to is-statements (71 Mind 53). But this does not solve the problem of relating *descriptive* "is-statements" and *evaluative* is-statements, and Zimmerman stops short of doing this. Of greater interest and significance have been the many attempts, notably by John Searle, to show that one can derive an "is" from an "ought." (His latest formulation is in *Speech Acts: An Essay in Philosophy of Language* (1969), pp. 175 *et seq.*) His claim has not gone unchallenged, but his logical demonstration must convince even the sceptic that the truth of Hume's law is not totally incontestable, as has previously been assumed. A useful collection of essays on this theme is *The Is/Ought Question* (1969); ed. W. D. Hudson: the editor's lucid introduction is particularly recommended. See also L. Kolakowski, *Positivist Philosophy* (1972), pp. 42–59.

[46] For a discussion, see Toulmin, *An Examination of the Place of Reason in Ethics* (1950), Chap. 2 and G. J. Warnock, *Contemporary Moral Philosophy* (1967).

[47] *Cf. post*, 269. Moore, himself, to some extent landed into this difficulty by arguing that ethical terms, such as "good," though indefinable, represented a "quality" which we experience directly by intuition, analogous to a physical quality like "yellow." This led him to describe such qualities as "non-natural," which seemed to postulate a "non-natural" world of their own. For criticisms, see Nowell-Smith, *op. cit.*, p. 33 *et seq.*; *cf.* Ewing, *op. cit.*, p. 83 *et seq.*

[48] *Cf. post*, 39.

regard to ethics but also in relation to the nature and logic of legal rules.[49] Thus the notion that a statement that something ought (morally) to be done is not to give a factual description but to prescribe a course of conduct based on the implication that reasons exist for so acting, and also on the existence of standards and criteria of appraisal, by which those reasons may be judged. A rule of law, however, differs from this in that, though it does not state a fact but only prescribes a course of conduct, it does not necessarily imply that reasons for compliance could be sought and perhaps given, but rather that it is derived from a valid authority.[50] Such authority can, as both Hume and Kelsen have pointed out, only consist in another normative statement.[51]

FORM (OR STRUCTURE) AND CONTENT

Those jurists who have stressed the form or logical structure of legal and other normative propositions have not unnaturally been disposed to adopt a " conceptual " kind of jurisprudence, laying emphasis on the fundamental *form* of legal concepts without regard to their content. This was no doubt in the mind of Austin when he sought to lay down a universal definition of law, and to adumbrate the distinction between what he called general and particular jurisprudence. Austin, indeed, fell a good deal short of applying this notion with logical rigidity, since he sought to derive his ultimate source of law, *viz.*, sovereignty, from a basis of *fact*,[52] but his idea of general jurisprudence as concerned with the principles common to various systems of law, and which those systems *inevitably* involve, appears to recognise a structural identity which does not arise merely *de facto*, but is *logically* inherent. This distinction is applied a good deal more deliberately and consistently in the writings of Hans Kelsen.[53]

PHILOSOPHY OF LAW?

The choice between a philosophy or a science of law is no doubt to a large extent a matter of terminology. Philosophy was once the

---

49 Discussions include Toulmin *op. cit.*, Nowell-Smith *op. cit.*, Hare, *The Language of Morals* (1952). Recent juristic writings adopting a linguistic approach include Ross, *Directives and Norms* (1968), *post*, 549, Olivecrona, *Law As Fact* (2nd ed. (1971)), particularly Chaps. 8 and 9, *post*, 533, the writings of H. L. A. Hart, see, for example, *post*, 59, 254 and Raz's *The Concept of a Legal System.*
50 *Cf.* Nowell-Smith, *op. cit.*, Chap. 13. Many rules of law also, however, like moral rules, contain, so to speak, a built-in standard of appraisal, *e.g.*, a legal duty of care implies that reasons exist for taking such care, and criteria exist for appraising these reasons. Such criteria, however, need not necessarily coincide with those of morals in a comparable case. *Cf. post*, 47.
51 *Post*, 31, 294 ; but *cf.* 285.
52 *Post*, 163.
53 *Post*, 271.

fashionable word, when physics was known as " natural philosophy." [54]
But since that day science has become all the rage, and, as we have
seen, many studies beyond the physical sciences have sought shelter
under the comforting umbrella of science. Science, however, is
concerned with empirically observable facts and events, whereas
philosophy is concerned with certain ultimate questions of structure.
Bertrand Russell once put it rather neatly by saying that science is
what we know, philosophy what we don't know.[55] Nowadays the
emphasis in Anglo-Saxon countries [56] is rather on the structure of
language and logic than on a search for some ultimate metaphysical
reality beyond the realm of empirical fact. But be that as it may,
philosophers in one form or another are still seekers after, or at least
analysers of, what Whitehead calls " unifying concepts," [57] and in this
sense we may perhaps regard those jurists who study law in its
normative aspects, and who seek to identify and analyse the conceptual structure of all legal systems, as legal philosophers rather
than legal scientists. The latter, indeed, so far as they concern
themselves with general jurisprudence, might be expected to identify
and compare what may be the common elements of different legal
systems as a matter of *fact* rather than of logical necessity.[58] Austin,
though he does speak of the science of jurisprudence, also uses the
description " philosophy of positive law " [59]; Kelsen, on the other
hand, despite the philosophical character of his approach, insists that
his theory is a pure *science* of law. Yet what he apparently desires to
emphasise by this nomenclature is the elimination (as with Austin
before him) of all extraneous matter from the study of positive law,
such as natural law or ethics. Kelsen also insists that he has purged
his science of all ideological elements whatsoever,[60] but he hardly
seems to have been any more successful than other jurists in
achieving a total *catharsis* of this nature.

On the relation of philosophy to science, Northrop makes the

54 *Cf.* Ryle, in *British Philosophy in Mid-Century*, ed. Mace (1957), pp. 257–258.
55 B. Russell, *My Philosophical Development*, p. 276 In considering how argument
often arises over the sense of words, Perelman remarks that " From this I might
draw the conclusion—disrespectful though it may appear—that the proper object
of philosophy is the systematic study of confused ideas " (see C. Perelman,
The Idea of Justice and the Problem of Argument (1963), p. 4).
56 Unlike Continental countries: see Passmore, *100 Years of Philosophy* (1957),
pp. 459–460.
57 See A. N. Whitehead, *The Concept of Nature* (1920).
58 *Cf.* the distinction between political *science* as a general empirical study of
institutions involving the comparison of a great many systems, and political
philosophy, which is reflective rather than comparative, and concerned not so
much with a large number of states, but to think a great deal about a particular
kind of state or what a state ought to be: see Lindsay, *Modern Democratic
State*, p. 347.
59 See *post*, 20.
60 *Post*, 291.

following point: " Philosophy is the name for the basic methodological and theoretical assumptions of a subject. . . . Since every
science uses some method of investigation and any scientist who
reports its facts to his colleagues must express these facts in words,
and hence introduce concepts and theory, it follows that any science
whatever is also a philosophy. . . . When no facts arise, however, to
bring the traditional theories or methods of a subject into question
the problems are not philosophical. . . . But whenever any facts
arise in any subject which bring its traditional theory or methods
into question, at that moment its problems become philosophical." [61]
This can be related to what has happened to law in recent times.
Due to the rise of modern science man is faced with a new view of
the world and of his place in it, and this has thrown many of the
traditional attitudes into doubt and has called for some fundamental
re-thinking regarding law and its role in society. This process has
certainly been going on since the end of the nineteenth century and
is very far from having reached finality at the present day.

NEED FOR A SYNTHESIS

Although, therefore, both the law as a system of norms, and as a
form of social control based on certain patterns of human behaviour,
are equally legitimate fields of study and inquiry, it is suggested that
it is an unduly narrowing attitude to limit jurisprudence rigidly to one
approach derived from one or other of these viewpoints alone. Each
represents an equally vital aspect of the legal process, and any
attempt rigidly to exclude one in favour of the other must
inevitably result in an incomplete picture of the subject-matter of
jurisprudence. Nor does there appear to be any sufficient warrant
for treating these two approaches as quite distinct fields of study,
after the manner of Kelsen. To give an illustration, an adequate
presentation of the judicial process requires an examination not only
of the logical working of a system of norms but also a study of the
actual factors involved in the application and development of legal
materials by judges and to consider one without the other is to provide
a very imperfect and distorted view, whether the bias is normative, as,
for instance, with Kelsen, or factual, as with the so-called Realists.
This is not to say that jurists may not be entirely justified in con-
fining their particular study to some special aspect of the whole field
of jurisprudence. In this way, a writer such as Salmond may desire
to confine himself to what Austin called *particular* jurisprudence,
namely, " those more fundamental conceptions and principles which
serve as the basis of the concrete details " of a particular system,

[61] F. C. S. Northrop, *The Complexity of Legal and Ethical Experience* (1959), p. 20.

such as English law.[62] Indeed, even if a preference is felt for a more generalised form of jurisprudence, it must be borne in mind that the search for universal elements, whether in the realm of concepts or in that of actual patterns of social behaviour, may prove somewhat unrewarding. Moreover, jurisprudence, like other social studies, may well be just as interested in diversity as in uniformity.

Buckland tells us, perhaps not altogether justly, that for Austin, jurisprudence was the analysis of legal concepts. "That is what jurisprudence meant for the student in the days of my youth. In fact it meant Austin. He was a religion; today he seems to be regarded rather as a disease." [63] If this is an exaggeration it remains true that the whole attitude towards jurisprudence has undergone a sweeping change in the last half-century. During this period jurisprudence has seen some far-reaching changes. There was first a tendency to stress the sociological factors and forces which underlay legal systems and condition their development, and a consequent neglect of the conceptual aspects of legal method. Even so, the United States which produced Pound and Llewellyn also produced Hohfeld. More recently the pendulum has swung violently in both directions under increasing pressures of, what Summers [64] has called, " professionalisation."

RECENT TRENDS

On the one hand there has been a valuable revival of analytical jurisprudence. A glance at some of the innumerable periodicals, collections of symposia, or monographs which have mushroomed in the 'sixties should be enough to convince even the sceptic that analytical jurisprudence and contiguous studies loom large once again. Some of the reasons for this renaissance have been suggested by Summers.[65] Most significant of the sources of this revitalisation is the increasing interest and attention paid by professional philo-

---

[62] Salmond, *Jurisprudence*, 11th ed., pp. 2–3 (not in 12th ed.). Salmond, unlike Austin, regarded this as *general* jurisprudence, which was not the study of legal systems in general, but of the fundamental elements in a particular system. Jerome Hall (*Studies in Jurisprudence and Criminal Theory* (1958), pp. 7–24) distinguishes legal theory from jurisprudence on the basis of the level of generality. He points out that it is not the extent of the system or systems discussed but the generality of the concepts which determines the nature of the subject. Legal theory deals with the general principles involved in branches of positive law, *e.g.*, *mens rea*, mistake, etc., while jurisprudence describes the more universal concepts inherent in legal theory, *e.g.*, causation. "It includes the search for ultimate conceptions in terms of which all legal knowledge can be significantly expressed " (p. 24). See further King [1966] C.L.J. 106.

[63] *Reflections on Jurisprudence*, p. 2.

[64] In *Essays in Legal Philosophy* (1968), pp. 1, 17–21.

[65] *Ibid.* at pp. 17–21. Its characteristics and practical utility are further sketched by Summers in an article heralding " The New Analytical Jurists " in 41 N.Y.U.L. Rev. 861, *post*, p. 260.

sophers to legal concepts and problems. It has both stimulated the
jurist and made him more articulate. " Gone are the days when just
any lawyer or law teacher could venture into the field and hold
forth *merely* by virtue of being a lawyer or a law teacher . . . when
legal philosophy could be considered ' just another subject in law . . .'
it is . . . a *philosophical discipline* with its own distinctive types of
problems and methodology." [66] The writings of Professor H. L. A.
Hart are a further stimulus to this move towards cross-fertilisation,
as well as being some of the most distinguished products of it.[67]
Analytical jurisprudence today ranges over a wide complex of questions. " Jural relations," for so long the bedrock of the school, now
assume minor significance besides the judicial process, punishment
and responsibility, causation, civil disobedience and a host of other
problems. Summers has drawn an important distinction which can be
detected in these writings between conceptual analysis and revision
and rational justification, " where argument . . . is deployed distinctively to build up cases *for* or *against* general social institutions,
practices, choices." [68]

Typically the question asked in the course of the latter approach
is: what is the " case " for *stare decisis,* strict liability, civil disobedience, divorce by consent? Furthermore, analytical jurisprudence
is less positivist than it was and, methodologically, has attained a
level of sophistication unknown to the Austinian.

On the other hand, and equally significant, sociological and realist
jurisprudence have become totally professionalised and interdisciplinary. Of the former, Selznick has written that its " premises . . .
achieved a rather quick and general victory (in the United States—
in this country it has only just begun to attack). . . . This victory
. . . has had but little to do with actual researches of sociologists.
But research has been wanting. This is the kind of problem that
can be approached in many ways, but it surely demands both a
broad theoretical perspective and an emphasis on social needs and

---

[66] *Ibid.* p. 17.
[67] See, for example, *The Concept of Law* (1961) *post,* p. 168, *Causation in the Law*
(1959), *Punishment and Responsibility* (1968) and his seminal inaugural lecture,
Definition and Theory in Jurisprudence, post, 59, and 254. His editing of
Bentham's important legal works (particularly *Of Law in General* (1970), *post,*
p. 187) is a significant pointer, for Bentham is in many ways the spiritual
ancestor of the new movement. See Hart, *Bentham's " Of Laws in General "*
(1971), *Rechtstheorie,* p. 55.
[68] Summers, *op. cit.,* p. 6. Examples of this approach are legion. A number may
be found in Part 2 of *Summers.* Other examples may be found in *Nomos,* the
annual volume of the American Society for Political and Legal Philosophy,
which, in twelve years, has surveyed in depth such concepts as authority, responsibility, the public interest, rational decisions, equality and obligation. See also
Wasserstrom, *The Judicial Decision* (1961); Hodgson, *Consequences of Utilitarianism* (1967); Gottlieb, *The Logic of Choice* (1968); Hart, *Punishment and
Responsibility* (1968).

institutional potentialities." [69] His plea has not gone unanswered. So, Raab has called for a cybernetic approach to sociological jurisprudence,[70] Schwarz for field experimentation in socio-legal research,[71] there have been surveys [72] and controlled experiments.[73] Much of this is doing little else than carry out Roscoe Pound's programme,[74] but it is doing it using techniques and disciplines which were unknown to the jurists of classical sociological jurisprudence.

At the same time realist jurisprudence has been swallowed up in judicial behaviouralism and jurimetrics. The jurist has sold his soul to the statistician, the Boolean algebrist, the computer scientist. Jurisprudence is dead, according to Lee Loevinger, the prophet of this science. "The next step forward in the long path of man's progress must be from jurisprudence (which is mere speculation about law) to *jurimetrics*—which is the scientific investigation of legal problems." [75] A glance at *Jurimetrics Journal* (formerly *Modern Uses of Logic in Law*) will horrify the average lawyer but the jurimetricians claim some real coups in predictive analysis of court decisions. An opinion on the movement must be reserved until American Realism is considered.[76]

To summarise, recent trends in jurisprudence exhibit a variety of movements linked by an increasing awareness of the fruits of interdisciplinary cooperation, and buttressed by a more sophisticated methodology. It is apparent that, with its increasing professionalisation, jurisprudence has now moved, if belatedly, into the twentieth century.

---

[69] In "The Sociology of Law" in ed. Merton, Bloom and Cottrell, *Sociology Today* (1959), 115, 121.

[70] 17 *Journal of Legal Education* 397. An interesting illustration is Bredemeier's "Law as an Integrative Mechanism," in ed. Evan, *Law and Sociology* (1962), p. 73; also in ed. Aubert, *Sociology of Law* (1969), p. 52, and see *post*, p. 385.

[71] 13 *Journal of Legal Education* 401. See, for example, Schwarz's own researches on the development of legal controls ((1954) 63 Yale L.J. 471) and on motivational factors affecting compliance with income tax laws ((1967) 34 U.Chi.L. Rev. 274). Two other important studies on "living law" (*cf. post*, p. 359) and attitudes to legal regulations are Cohen, Robson and Bates, *Parental Authority: The Community and the Law* (1958) and Skolnick's *Justice Without Trial* (1966).

[72] The most famous example was the Chicago Jury Project, which culminated in *The American Jury* (1966), *post*, p. 465.

[73] For example, the many pieces of research in civil litigation carried out by the *Columbia Project for Effective Justice*. Its outstanding success has been its work on the New Jersey pretrial conference procedure, referred to *ante*, at note 26.

[74] *Post*, p. 366.

[75] (1949) 33 *Minnesota Law Review* 455, 483; *post*, p. 476.

[76] *Post*, Chap. 7.

G. MYRDAL

Objectivity In Social Research

(1970)

The ethos of social science is the search for " objective " truth. The faith of the student is his conviction that truth is wholesome and that illusions are damaging, especially opportunistic ones. He seeks " realism," a term which in one of its meanings denotes an " objective " view of reality.

The most fundamental methodological problems facing the social scientist are therefore, what is objectivity, and how can the student attain objectivity in trying to find out the facts and the causal relationships between facts? How can a biased view be avoided? More specifically, how can the student of social problems liberate himself from (1) the powerful heritage of earlier writings in his field of inquiry, ordinarily containing normative and teleological notions inherited from past generations and founded upon the metaphysical moral philosophies of natural law and utilitarianism from which all our social and economic theories have branched off; (2) the influences of the entire cultural, social, economic, and political milieu of the society where he lives, works, and earns his living and his status; and (3) the influence stemming from his own personality, as molded not only by traditions and environment but also by his individual history, constitution, and inclinations?

The social scientist faces the further problem: how can he be in this sense objective and, at the same time, practical? What is the relation between wanting to understand and wanting to change society? How can the search for true knowledge be combined with moral and political valuations? How can truth be related to ideals?

In our profession there is a lack of awareness even today that, in searching for truth, the student, like all human beings whatever they try to accomplish, is influenced by tradition, by his environment, and by his personality. Further, there is an irrational taboo against discussing this lack of awareness. It is astonishing that this taboo is commonly respected, leaving the social scientist in naïveté about what he is doing. To destroy this naïveté should be the object of the sociology of science and scientists, the least developed branch of social science. This is important, as these influences, if they are not controlled, are apt to cause systematic biases in research and thus lead to faulty knowledge.

Even if the influences conditioning research had already been exposed, so that the social scientist was more sophisticated about himself and his attitudes in searching for truth, there would still remain a problem of the philosophy of social science: are there logical means by which he can better assure objectivity in his research? . . .

As we shall find, the logical means available for protecting ourselves from biases are broadly these: to raise the valuations actually determining our theoretical as well as our practical [77] research to full

---

[77] I am using the words " theoretical " and " practical " (or " political ") with the meanings they have in philosophy: the former refers to thinking in terms of causes and effects, the latter to thinking in terms of means and ends.

awareness, to scrutinize them from the point of view of relevance, significance, and feasibility in the society under study, to transform them into specific value premises for research, and to determine approach and define concepts in terms of a set of value premises which have been explicitly stated. [pp. 3–5]

" Facts do not organize themselves into concepts and theories just by being looked at; indeed, except within the framework of concepts and theories, there are no scientific facts but only chaos. There is an inescapable *a priori* element in all scientific work. Questions must be asked before answers can be given. The questions are all expressions of our interest in the world; they are at bottom valuations. Valuations are thus necessarily involved already at the stage when we observe facts and carry on theoretical analysis, and not only at the stage when we draw political inferences from facts and valuations." [78] . . . [p. 9]

There are two types of conception held by people about reality: in their pure form I call these *" beliefs"* and *" valuations."* In people's *" opinions,"* beliefs and valuations are blended in a way that I shall discuss. Though there is not a hard and fast line in people's mental processes between these two types of conception, it is nevertheless useful for our analysis to distinguish between them, as their logical import is different. One of these types of conception is intellectual and cognitive; the other, emotional and volitive.[79] The beliefs express our ideas about how reality actually is, or was, while the valuations express our ideas of how it ought to be, or ought to have been.

A person's beliefs pretend knowledge. As a consequence, it should always be possible to judge the correctness of beliefs by applying the criterion of whether they are true or false and, in the latter case by gauging the extent and direction in which they deviate from truth. Another dimension is their relative completeness. Here, again, they may be objectively compared with more comprehensive knowledge, and the site of the deficiencies may be determined. A person's valuations, on the other hand—that a social situation is or was " just," " right," " fair," " desirable," or the opposite—cannot be judged and measured by the same objective criteria through comparison with true and fuller knowledge.

When valuations are held by an individual or group, however, they are, like beliefs, a part of reality that can be ascertained by research, though not without difficulty. One basic difficulty stems from the fact that a person's valuations are usually shifting and contradictory. Behind *behavior* there is not one homogeneous set of valuations but a mesh

---

[78] Gunnar Myrdal, *The Political Element in the Development of Economic Theory*, Preface to the English [language] Edition, pp. ix–xvi.

[79] To stress the subjectivity of the valuation process, I deliberately use the word " valuations " and avoid the term " values " that is so popular in all social science—except in the combination " value premises," where certain valuations have been defined and made explicit for use in research. The common use of the term " values " invites confusion between valuations in the subjective sense, the object of these valuations, and indeed the whole social setting of valuations. The use of the term " values," especially in sociological and anthropological literature, also usually contains a hidden value premise, that a " value " *eo ipso* is valuable in some objective sense ; this implies a bias of the *laissez-faire* variety. The term " values " finally gives the association of something solid, homogeneous, and stable while in reality valuations are contradictory and also unstable, particularly in modern society.

of struggling inclinations, interests, and ideals. Some of these are held consciously and some are suppressed for long intervals, but all of them work to move behavior in their particular direction.

There are no solid "attitudes," and *behavior normally becomes a moral compromise.* Valuations are, so to speak, located on different levels of the moral personality, in the main corresponding to various degrees of generality of moral judgments.

In our civilisation people ordinarily agree that, as an abstract proposition, the more general valuations—felt to be valid in relation to the whole nation or even to all human beings—are morally "*higher*" than those relating to particular individuals or groups. This is not an *a priori* assumption but a generalization founded on empirical observation. We all know that it is so.

In the course of actual day-to-day living, acting, thinking, and talking, a person will be found to focus attention on the valuations on one plane of his moral personality while leaving in the shadows for the time being, the often conflicting valuations on other planes. The basis of this selective focusing is plainly opportunistic.

We are imperfect beings, and it is most often the higher valuations that are pushed into the shadows in everyday living. They are preserved for expression on occasions that are more ceremonial in nature or that in one way or another are isolated from daily life where the "*lower*" valuations more often predominate. Taking a shorter view, these latter valuations are more narrowly selfish, more in the nature of economic, social, or sexual interests and jealousies in a particular setting and at a particular time, and less universally benevolent and humane.

A national trade union convention may, for instance, come out strongly against discrimination against Negroes on the labor market, reflecting valuations on the higher level. Meanwhile, in a narrow, local setting these higher valuations will be overshadowed by valuations on the lower level—"prejudices," as they are often called when viewed from the higher level—and these lower valuations express themselves in discriminatory practices. . . .

One difficulty in ascertaining valuations springs from the fact that people often try to conceal them *qua valuations,* particularly the operative ones on the lower level. They try to dress up these valuations as beliefs about reality. People, in their opinions, generally underplay valuations by stating their positions as if they were simply logical inferences from what they believe to be true about reality. They seek the "good reasons" which usually cannot qualify as "true reasons." Their opinions then become what we call "*rationalizations.*"

In this process valuations are "objectified" by being presented as beliefs or simple inferences from beliefs—which implies hiding them and thereby also keeping their lack of consistency out of sight. Through this process beliefs become distorted. People succeed in believing what they want to believe, what serves the "purposes" of the underlying valuation compromise. A scientific scrutiny of popular beliefs shows not only that they are often wrong but also that they are twisted in a systematic way. It also shows blind spots of unnecessary ignorance and, on the other hand, an astonishing eagerness to acquire knowledge when it is opportune for the urge to rationalize.

All ignorance, like all knowledge, tends thus to be opportunist. Every educational effort aimed at correcting distorted beliefs in a society meets strong resistance. People are interested in hiding their valuations and valuation conflicts or want at least to attempt to preserve an appearance of consistency and order in that sphere. . . . [pp. 15–19]

People's beliefs—unlike their valuations—can be directly judged by the objective criteria of correctness and completeness. This fact offers us a clue with which to analyze scientifically the patterns of internally inconsistent and often concealed valuations that exist in the minds of people. The direction and the degree of the deviation of their beliefs from objective, comprehensive knowledge will tell us how people are trying to escape a confrontation of the valuations held on the lower level (implicit in their daily behavior) with the more general valuations which are recognized as morally higher in our society.

From this point of view, it becomes important to chart quantitatively people's knowledge and ignorance on controversial issues. For this purpose certain of the questions in scientific opinion studies should be purged as far as possible of all explicit valuations; they should test only the respondents' conception of a particular part of reality. It should be fairly easy to prepare standard, lucid norms of what represents " objective " knowledge. (In the many problems in which we are ignorant or hesitant, consciousness of our limitations constitutes true knowledge.) For testing beliefs to determine their completeness—and to find the lacunae—some sort of graduated scales should be developed.

The hypothesis is that we almost never face a random lack of knowledge. Ignorance, like knowledge, is purposefully directed. An emotional load of valuation conflicts presses for rationalization, creating blindness at some spots, stimulating an urge for knowledge at others, and, in general, causing conceptions of reality to deviate from truth in determined directions.

If the degree of knowledge and ignorance and also their location and concrete character were analyzed in this way, the valuations and their conflicts could be recorded indirectly but quantitatively—as the heat of distant stars is measured by observing their spectra. The hypothesis behind such research is that ignorance and knowledge are generally not simple and haphazard but are opportunistic. If a major research program were undertaken with this purpose, opinion polls might prove far more valuable than they can be in their present journalistic role.

But, of course, the valuations should also be studied directly insofar as possible. For this purpose other questions should be selected relating to opinions that contain no reference to the more specific reality about which people have beliefs. Valuations are complex and ordinarily conflicting, and an individual focuses attention in his valuation sphere in an opportunist fashion—and his selection and presentation of valuations is probably different in a testing situation from what it is in real life. Hence, indirect analysis of the valuations, through the study of the deviations of beliefs from true and more complete knowledge, is likely to probe more deeply than direct analysis. Normally an individual feels an urge to arrange his valuations so that they may be presented in an orderly and acceptable form. In his beliefs concerning social reality— which are shaped to give the appearance of rational organization to his morals and his behavior—he reveals himself.[80]

---

[80] [For a discussion of some examples of judicial ideology see Friedmann, *Legal Theory* (5th ed.), pp. 436–439.]

When studying valuations by either method—or a combination of them—it is important to observe another distinction: namely that between a person's "*private*," or "*personal*" opinion and his "*public*," or "*political*," opinion on the same question. These do not necessarily agree; in fact, they seldom agree. Studying this distinction throws light on the dichotomy of (and usually the conflict between) valuations on different levels of generality.

In the Negro problem, for instance, there are often flagrant contradictions between people's valuations about how society ought to be and the valuations implicit in their daily behaviour. . . .[80a]   [pp. 28–30]

J. AUSTIN

The Uses of the Study of Jurisprudence [81]

(ed. H. L. A. Hart, 1954)

Proper subject of jurisprudence

The appropriate subject of Jurisprudence, in any of its different departments, is positive law: Meaning by positive law (or law emphatically so called), law established or "positum," in an independent political community, by the express or tacit authority of its sovereign or supreme government.

Considered as a whole, and as implicated or connected with one another, the positive laws and rules of a particular or specified community, are a system or body of law. And as limited to any one of such systems, or to any of its component parts, jurisprudence is particular or national.

Though every system of law has its specific and characteristic differences, there are principles, notions, and distinctions common to various systems, and forming analogies or likenesses by which such systems are allied.

Many of these common principles are common to all systems ;—to the scanty and crude systems of rude societies, and the ampler and maturer systems of refined communities. But the ampler and maturer systems of refined communities are allied by the numerous analogies which obtain between all systems, and also by numerous analogies which obtain exclusively between themselves. Accordingly, the various principles common to maturer systems (or the various analogies obtaining between them), are the subject of an extensive science: which science (as contradistinguished to national or particular jurisprudence on one side, and, on another, to the science of legislation) has been named General (or comparative) Jurisprudence, or the philosophy (or general principles) of positive law.

As principles abstracted from positive systems are the subject of general jurisprudence, so is the exposition of such principles its exclusive or appropriate object. With the goodness or badness of laws, as tried by the test of utility (or by any of the various tests which divide the opinions of mankind), it has no immediate concern. If, in regard to some of the

[80a] [This Myrdal characterised, in his classic study of racial tension in the U.S.A., *The American Dilemma.*]
[81] In volume entitled *The Province of Jurisprudence Determined Etc.*

principles which form its appropriate subject, it adverts to considerations of utility, it adverts to such considerations for the purpose of explaining such principles, and not for the purpose of determining their worth. And this distinguishes the science in question from the science of legislation: which affects to determine the test or standard (together with the principles subordinate or consonant to such test) by which positive law ought to be made, or to which positive law ought to be adjusted.

If the possibility of such a science appear doubtful, it arises from this; that in each particular system, the principles and distinctions which it has in common with others, are complicated with its individual peculiarities, and are expressed in a technical language peculiar to itself.

It is not meant to be affirmed that these principles and distinctions are conceived with equal exactness and adequacy in every particular system. In this respect different systems differ. But, in all, they are to be found more or less nearly conceived; from the rude conceptions of barbarians, to the exact conceptions of the Roman lawyers or of enlightened modern jurists.

I mean, then, by General Jurisprudence, the science concerned with the exposition of the principles, notions, and distinctions which are common to systems of law: understanding by systems of law, the ampler and maturer systems [82] which, by reason of their amplitude and maturity, are pre-eminently pregnant with instruction.

Of the principles, notions, and distinctions which are the subjects of general jurisprudence, some may be esteemed necessary. For we cannot imagine coherently a system of law (or a system of law as evolved in a refined community), without conceiving them as constituent parts of it.[83]   [pp. 1072–1073]

The word Jurisprudence itself is not free from ambiguity; it has been used to denote—

The knowledge of Law as a science, combined with the art or practical habit or skill of applying it; or, secondly,

Legislation;—the science of what *ought to be done* towards making good laws, combined with the art of doing it.

[82] [Note that Austin *expressly* excludes from his conception of law and jurisprudence immature systems, such as primitive customary and feudal law. *Cf. post*, 41–42.]

[83] [Austin proceeds to give as examples of such necessary principles, notions and distinctions, the following: the notions of duty, right, liberty, injury, punishment, redress; with their various relations to one another, and to law, sovereignty and independent political society; the distinction between written and unwritten law; the distinction beween rights availing against the world at large and variously restricted rights; the division of obligations into those arising from contract and from injuries, and from other sources; and the distinction between civil injuries and crimes.

Stone, *Legal System and Lawyers' Reasonings* (1964), pp. 82–85, sees here " Austin's tendency to straddle the particularist and universalist view." He believes that Austin makes unwarranted inferences from English and Roman law, the only two systems with which he was familiar.

Austin goes on to refer to other principles, notions and distinctions which are not " necessary " in the above sense, but which on grounds of utility occur very generally in mature systems of law, and, therefore, may be ranked with the general principles which are the subjects of general jurisprudence. He gives as an example, the distinction between the law of persons and the law of things, as a basis for a scientific arrangement of a body of law. *Cf.* Margaret Mead, *post*, 144.]

Inasmuch as the knowledge of what ought to be, supposes a know-ledge of what is, legislation supposes jurisprudence, but jurisprudence does not suppose legislation. What laws have been and are, may be known without a knowledge of what they ought to be. Inasmuch as a knowledge of what ought to be, is bottomed on a knowledge of antecedents *cognato genere*, legislation supposes jurisprudence.

With us, Jurisprudence is the science of what is essential to law, combined with the science of what it ought to be. It is particular or universal. Particular Jurisprudence is the science of any actual system of law, or of any portion of it. The only practical jurisprudence is particular.

The proper subject of General or Universal Jurisprudence (as distin-guished from Universal Legislation) is a description of such subjects and ends of Law as are common to all systems; and of those resemblances between different systems which are bottomed in the common nature of man, or correspond to the resembling points in their several positions.

And these resemblances will be found to be very close, and to cover a large part of the field. They are necessarily confined to the resem-blances between the systems of a few nations; since it is only a few systems with which it is possible to become acquainted, even imperfectly. From these, however, the rest may be presumed. And it is only the systems of two or three nations which deserve attention:—the writings of the Roman Jurists; the decisions of English Judges in modern times; the provisions of French and Prussian Codes as to arrangement.

[p. 1077]

K. POPPER

Poverty of Historicism

(1957)

Method of science

What is important is to realize that in science we are always concerned with explanations, predictions, and tests, and that the method of testing hypotheses is always the same. From the hypothesis to be tested—for example, a universal law—together with some other statements which for this purpose are not considered as problematic—for example, some initial conditions—we deduce some prognosis. We then confront this prognosis, whenever possible, with the results of experimental or other observations. Agreement with them is taken as corroboration of the hypothesis, though not as final proof; clear disagreement is considered as refutation or falsification.

The result of tests is the *selection* of hypotheses which have stood up to tests, or the *elimination* of those hypotheses which have not stood up to them, and which are therefore rejected It is important to realize the consequences of this view. They are these: all tests can be interpreted as attempts to weed out false theories—to find the weak points of a theory in order to reject it if it is falsified by the test. This view is sometimes considered paradoxical; our aim, it is said, is to establish theories, not to eliminate false ones. But just because it is our aim to establish theories as well as we can, we must test them as severely as we can ; that is, we must try to find fault with them, we must try to falsify them. Only if we cannot falsify them in spite of our best efforts can we say that they have stood up to severe tests.[84] This is the reason why the discovery of instances which confirm a theory means very little if we have not tried, and failed, to discover refutations. For if we are uncritical we shall always find what we want: we shall look for, and find, confirmations, and we shall look away from, and not see, whatever might be dangerous to our pet theories. In this way it is only too easy to obtain what appears to be overwhelming evidence in favour of a theory which, if approached critically, would have been refuted. In order to make the method of selection by elimination work, and to ensure that only the fittest theories survive, their struggle for life must be made severe.

This, in outline, is the method of all sciences which are backed by experience. But what about the method by which we *obtain* our theories or hypotheses? What about *inductive generalizations*, and the way in which we proceed from observation to theory? To this question . . . I shall give two answers.[85] (*a*) I do not believe that we ever make inductive generalizations in the sense that we start with observations and try to derive our theories from them. I believe that the prejudice that we proceed in this way is a kind of optical illusion, and that at no stage of scientific development do we begin without something in the nature of a theory, such as a hypothesis, or a prejudice, or a problem—often a technological one—which in some way *guides* our observations, and helps us to select from the innumerable objects of observation those which may be of interest.[86] But if this is so, then the method of elimination—which is nothing but that of trial and error . . . —can always be applied. However, I do not think that it is necessary for our present discussion to insist upon this point. For we can say (*b*) that it is irrelevant from the point of view of science whether we have obtained our theories by jumping to unwarranted conclusions or merely by stumbling over them (that is, by ' intuition ') [87] or by some inductive procedure. The question, ' How did you first *find* your theory? ' relates, as it were, to an entirely private matter, as opposed to the question, ' How did you *test* your theory? ' which alone is scientifically relevant. And the method of testing described here is fertile ; it leads to new observations, and to a mutual give and take between theory and observation.

Now all this, I believe, is not only true for the natural but also for the social sciences. And in the social sciences it is even more obvious than in the natural sciences that we cannot see and observe our objects before we have thought about them. For most of the objects of social

---

[84] [But many theories which nobody accepts today have never been falsified. Medawar, *Induction and Intuition in Scientific Thought* (1969), has commented : " Theories are repaired more often than they are refuted. . . . Sometimes theories meekly fade away. . . . More often they are merely assimilated into wider theories in which they rank as special cases. [Some theories] . . . have been trivialised " (p. 30).]

[85] [*Cf*. Medawar, *idem*, pp. 40–44 for a catalogue of the deficiencies of inductivism.]

[86] [It is interesting to note that so creative a scientific theorist as Darwin seems gradually to have changed his view from the idea that science consists in collecting facts from which general laws may be deduced, to the notion that observation of facts needs to be guided by theory: see *Autobiography of Charles Darwin* (ed. N. Barlow, 1958), especially pp. 70, 98, 119 and 157–164. See also J. O. Wisdom, *Foundations of Inference in Natural Science*.]

[87] [*Cf*. Medawar, *idem*, pp. 56 *et seq*. on the role of " luck " in scientific discovery.]

science, if not all of them, are abstract objects; they are *theoretical* constructions.[88] (Even 'the war' or 'the army' are abstract concepts, strange as this may sound to some. What is concrete is the many who are killed; or the men and women in uniform, etc.) These objects, these theoretical constructions used to interpret our experience, are the result of constructing certain *models* [89] (especially of institutions), in order to explain certain experiences [90]—a familiar theoretical method in the natural sciences (where we construct our models of atoms, molecules, solids, liquids, etc.). It is part of the method of explanation by way of reduction, or deduction from hypotheses. Very often we are unaware of the fact that we are operating with hypotheses or theories, and we therefore mistake our theoretical models for concrete things. This is a kind of mistake which is only too common.[91]   [pp. 132–136]

More especially the statement that we shall not, as a rule, be able 'to predict the precise result of any *concrete* situation' opens up the problem of the inexactitude of prediction. I contend that precisely the same may be said of the concrete physical world. In general it is only by the use of artificial experimental isolation that we can predict physical events. (The solar system is an exceptional case—one of natural, not of artificial isolation; once its isolation is destroyed by the intrusion of a foreign body of sufficient size, all our forecasts are liable to break down.) We are very far from being able to predict, even in physics, the precise results of a *concrete* situation, such as a thunderstorm, or a fire.

A very brief remark may be added here on the problem of complexity. There is no doubt that the analysis of any concrete social situation is made extremely difficult by its complexity. But the same holds for any concrete physical situation.[92] The widely held prejudice that social situations are more complex than physical ones seems to arise from two sources. One of them is that we are liable to compare what should not be compared; I mean on the one hand concrete social situations and on the other hand artificially insulated experimental physical situations. (The latter might be compared, rather, with an artificially insulated social situation—such as a prison, or an experimental community.) The other

---

88 [This applies with particular force to law; hence the oddity of the view of some of the Scandinavian Realists who seek to eliminate legal concepts as mere flights of fancy and therefore superfluous. *Cf. post*, 501.]

89 [Such as Hart's construction of a legal system in *The Concept of Law, post*, p. 168 or Dworkin's of positivism, *post*, 172. See also McBride, *The Essential Role of Models and Analogies in the Philosophy of Law*, 43 *N.Y.U.L. Rev.* 53.]

90 [*Sed quaere*, do not these ideas exist in the minds of people long before the social scientist arrives with his explanations? *Cf.* P. Winch, *The Idea of a Social Science* ((1958), p. 127).]

91 [" When we verify a model by testing how far it does or does not correspond to the phenomena, this is, of course, not an end in itself but only a means to an end. Our ulterior purpose is not to learn whether the model is or is not valid; it is to get a new insight into the structure and nature of Reality by applying a model that is valid and is therefore an effective tool." A. J. Toynbee, *A Study of History*, vol. 12, p. 160. *Cf.* p. 224: " Definitions . . . are frozen 'models'. . . . If definitions are to be used at all in the study of human affairs, they will be less hampering, if, instead of making them, *more mathematico*, at the beginning of our enquiry, we work them out retrospectively, as a check on the results we have obtained by the application of ill-defined and therefore flexible 'models.' " *Cf. post*, 59.]

92 [But for an argument that the complexity involved in introducing the human element results in a difference in kind both in the concepts used and the nature of the problems from those of natural science, see P. Winch, *op. cit.*, Chap. 3.]

source is the old belief that the description of a social situation should involve the mental and perhaps even physical states of everybody concerned (or perhaps that it should even be reducible to them). But this belief is not justified; it is much less justified even than the impossible demand that the description of a concrete chemical reaction should involve that of the atomic and sub-atomic states of all the elementary particles involved (although chemistry may indeed be reducible to physics). The belief also shows traces of the popular view that social entities such as institutions or associations are concrete natural entities such as crowds of men, rather than abstract models constructed to interpret certain selected abstract relations between individuals.[93]

[pp. 139–140]

T. S. KUHN

The Structure of Scientific Revolutions

(1970)

History, if viewed as a repository for more than anecdote or chronology, could produce a decisive transformation in the image of science by which we are now possessed. That image has previously been drawn, even by scientists themselves, mainly from the study of finished scientific achievements as these are recorded in the classics and, more recently, in the textbooks from which each new scientific generation learns to practice its trade. Inevitably, however, the aim of such books is persuasive and pedagogic; a concept of science drawn from them is no more likely to fit the enterprise that produced them than an image of a national culture drawn from a tourist brochure or a language text . . . we have been misled by them in fundamental ways. There follows a sketch of the quite different concept of science that can emerge from the historical record of the research activity itself.

Even from history, however, that new concept will not be forthcoming if historical data continue to be sought and scrutinised mainly to answer questions posed by the unhistorical stereotype drawn from science texts. Those texts have, for example, often seemed to imply that the content of science is uniquely exemplified by the observations, laws and theories described in their pages. . . . The result has been a concept of science with profound implications about its nature and development.

In recent years, however, a few historians of science have been finding it more and more difficult to fulfil the functions that the concept of development-by-accumulation assigns to them. As chroniclers of an incremental process, they discover that additional research makes it harder not easier, to answer questions like: When was oxygen discovered? Who first conceived of energy conservation? Increasingly, a few of them suspect that these are simply the wrong sorts of questions to ask. Perhaps science does not develop by the accumulation of individual discoveries and inventions. Simultaneously, these same historians confront

[93] [Consider here, *e.g.*, the Scandinavian Realist criticism of the command theory of law, which regards that theory as untenable in a modern state since it is impossible to attribute any command to particular determinate individuals. *Cf. post*, 523.]

growing difficulties in distinguishing the "scientific" component of past observation and belief from what their predecessors had readily labeled "error" and "superstition." The more carefully they study, say, Aristotelian dynamics, phlogistic chemistry, or caloric thermodynamics, the more certain they feel that those once current views of nature were, as a whole, neither less scientific nor more the product of human idiosyncrasy than those current today. If these out-of-date beliefs are to be called myths, then myths can be produced by the same sorts of methods and held for the same sorts of reasons that now lead to scientific knowledge. If, on the other hand, they are to be called science, then science has included bodies of belief quite incompatible with the ones we hold today. Given these alternatives, the historian must choose the latter. . . .

The result of all these doubts and difficulties is a historiographic revolution in the study of science, though one that is still in its early stages. Gradually, and often without entirely realising they are doing so, historians of science have begun to ask new sorts of questions and to trace different, and often less than cumulative, developmental lines for the sciences. Rather than seeking the permanent contributions of an older science to our present vantage, they attempt to display the historical integrity of that science in its own time. They ask, for example, not about the relation of Galileo's views to those of modern science, but rather about the relationship between his views and those of his group, *i.e.*, his teachers, contemporaries, and immediate successors in the sciences. Furthermore, they insist upon studying the opinions of that group and other similar ones from the viewpoint—usually very different from that of modern science—that gives those opinions the maximum internal coherence and the closest possible fit to nature. . . .

The early developmental stages of most sciences have been characterised by continual competition between a number of distinct views of nature, each partially derived from, and all roughly compatible with, the dictates of scientific observation and method. What differentiated these various schools was not one or another failure of method—they were all "scientific"—but what we shall come to call their incommensurable ways of seeing the world and of practising science in it. Obervation and experience can and must drastically restrict the range of admissible scientific belief, else there would be no science. But they cannot alone determine a particular body of such belief. An apparently arbitrary element, compounded of personal and historical accident, is always a formative ingredient of the beliefs espoused by a given scientific community at a given time.

That element of arbitrariness does not, however, indicate that any scientific group could practice its trade without some set of received beliefs. Nor does it make less consequential the particular constellation to which the group, at a given time, is in fact committed. Effective research scarcely begins before a scientific community thinks it has acquired firm answers to questions like the following: What are the fundamental entities of which the universe is composed? How do these interact with each other and with the senses? What questions may legitimately be asked about such entities and what techniques employed in seeking solutions? At least in the mature sciences, answers (or full substitutes for answers) to questions like these are firmly embedded in the educational initiation that prepares and licenses the student for professional practice. Because that education is both rigorous and rigid, these answers come to exert a deep hold on the scientific mind. That they can do so does much to account both for the peculiar efficiency of the normal research activity and for the direction in which it proceeds at any given time. . . .

Yet that element of arbitrariness is present and it too has an important effect on scientific development. . . . Normal science, the activity in which most scientists inevitably spend almost all their time, is predicated on the assumption that the scientific community knows what the world is like. Much of the success of the enterprise derives from the community's willingness to defend that assumption, if necessary at considerable cost. Normal science, for example, often suppresses fundamental novelties because they are necessarily subversive of its basic commitments. Nevertheless, so long as those commitments retain an element of the arbitrary, the very nature of normal research ensures that novelty shall not be suppressed for very long. Sometimes a normal problem, one that ought to be solvable by known rules and procedures, resists the reiterated onslaught of the ablest members of the group within whose competence it falls. On other occasions a piece of equipment designed and constructed for the purpose of normal research fails to perform in the anticipated manner, revealing an anomaly that cannot, despite repeated effort, be aligned with professional expectation. In these and other ways besides, normal science repeatedly goes astray. And when it does—when, that is, the profession can no longer evade anomalies that subvert the existing tradition of scientific practice—then begin the extraordinary investigations that lead the profession at last to a new set of commitments, a new basis for the practice of science. The extraordinary episodes in which that shift of professional commitments occurs are the ones known in this essay as scientific revolutions. They are the tradition-shattering complements to the tradition-bound activity of normal science.

The most obvious examples of scientific revolutions are those famous episodes in scientific development that have often been labeled revolutions before. . . . The major turning points in scientific development associated with the names of Copernicus, Newton, Lavoisier, and Einstein. More clearly than most other episodes in the history of at least the physical sciences, these display what all scientific revolutions are about. Each of them necessitated the community's rejection of one time honoured scientific theory in favour of another incompatible with it. Each produced a consequent shift in the problems available for scientific scrutiny and in the standards by which the profession determined what should count as an admissible problem or as a legitimate problem-solution. And each transformed the scientific imagination in ways that we shall ultimately need to describe as a transformation of the world within which scientific work was done. Such changes, together with the controversies that almost always accompany them, are the defining characteristics of scientific revolutions. . . .

A new theory, however special its range of application, is seldom or never just an increment to what is already known. Its assimilation requires the reconstruction of prior theory and the re-evaluation of prior fact, an intrinsically revolutionary process that is seldom completed by a single man and never overnight. No wonder historians have had difficulty in dating precisely this extended process that their vocabulary impels them to view as an isolated event.

Nor are new inventions of theory the only scientific events that have revolutionary impact upon the specialists in whose domain they occur. The commitments that govern normal science specify not only what sorts of entities the universe does contain, but also, by implication, those that it does not. It follows, . . . that a discovery like that of oxygen or X-rays does not simply add one more item to the population of the scientist's world. Ultimately it has that effect, but not until the professional community has re-evaluated traditional experimental procedures, altered its conception of entities with which it has long been familiar, and, in the process, shifted the network of theory through which it deals with the world. Scientific fact and theory are not categorically separable, except perhaps within a single tradition of normal-scientific practice. That is why the unexpected discovery is not simply factual in its import and why the scientist's world is qualitatively transformed as well as quantitatively enriched by fundamental novelties of either fact or theory. . . .

A theory of scientific inquiry, replace[s] the confirmation or falsification procedures made familiar by our usual image of science. Competition between segments of the scientific community is the only historical process that ever actually results in the rejection of one previously accepted theory or in the adoption of another. . . .

" Normal science " means research firmly based upon one or more past scientific achievements, achievements that some particular scientific community acknowledges for a time as supplying the foundation for its further practice. . . .

Their achievement was sufficiently unprecedented to attract an enduring group of adherents away from competing modes of scientific activity. Simultaneously, it was sufficiently open-ended to leave all sorts of problems for the redefined group of practitioners to resolve.

Achievements that share these two characteristics I shall henceforth refer to as " paradigms," a term that relates closely to " normal science." By choosing it, I mean to suggest that some accepted examples of actual scientific practice—examples which include law, theory, application, and instrumentation together—provide models from which spring particular coherent traditions of scientific research. . . .

The study of paradigms, including many that are far more specialised than those named illustratively above, is what mainly prepares the student for membership in the particular scientific community with which he will later practice. Because he there joins men who learned the bases of their field from the same concrete models, his subsequent practice will seldom evoke overt disagreement over fundamentals. Men whose research is based on shared paradigms are committed to the same rules and standards for scientific practice. That commitment and the apparent consensus it produces are prerequisites for normal science, *i.e.,* for the genesis and continuation of a particular research tradition. . . .

[pp. 1–11]

Discovery commences with the awareness of anomaly, *i.e.* with the recognition that nature has somehow violated the paradigm-induced expectations that govern normal science. It then continues with a more or less extended exploration of the area of anomaly. And it closes only when the paradigm theory has been adjusted so that the anomalous has become the expected. Assimilating a new sort of fact demands a more than additive adjustment of theory, and until that adjustment is completed—until the scientist has learned to see nature in a different way—the new fact is not quite a scientific fact at all. . . .   [pp. 52–53]

Once it has achieved the status of paradigm, a scientific theory is declared invalid only if an alternate candidate is available to take its place. No process yet disclosed by the historical study of scientific development at all resembles the methodological stereotype of falsification by direct comparison with nature. That remark does not mean that scientists do not reject scientific theories, or that experience and experiment are not essential to the process in which they do so. But it does mean—what will ultimately be a central point—that the act of judgment that leads scientists to reject a previously accepted theory is always based upon more than a comparison of that theory with the world. The decision to reject one paradigm is always simultaneously the decision to accept another, and the judgment leading to that decision involves the comparison of both paradigms with nature *and* with each other. . . . [p. 77]

If an anomaly is to evoke crisis, it must usually be more than just an anomaly. There are always difficulties somewhere in the paradigm-nature fit; most of them are set right sooner or later, often by processes that could not have been foreseen. The scientist who pauses to examine every anomaly he notes will seldom get significant work done. We therefore have to ask what it is that makes an anomaly seem worth concerted scrutiny, and to that question there is probably no fully general answer. The cases we have already examined are characteristic but scarcely prescriptive. Sometimes an anomaly will clearly call into question explicit and fundamental generalisations of the paradigm, as the problem of ether drag did for those who accepted Maxwell's theory. Or, as in the Copernican revolution, an anomaly without apparent fundamental import may evoke crisis if the applications that it inhibits have a particular practical importance, in this case for calendar design and astrology. . . .

When, for these reasons or others like them, an anomaly comes to seem more than just another puzzle of normal science, the transition to crisis and to extraordinary science has begun. The anomaly itself now comes to be more generally recognised as such by the profession. More and more attention is devoted to it by more and more of the field's most eminent men. If it still continues to resist, as it usually does not, many of them may come to view its resolution as *the* subject matter of their discipline. For them the field will no longer look quite the same as it had earlier. Part of its different appearance results simply from the new fixation point of scientific scrutiny. An even more important source of change is the divergent nature of the numerous partial solutions that concerted attention to the problem has made available. The early attacks upon the resistant problem will have followed the paradigm rules quite closely. But with continuing resistance, more and more of the attacks upon it will have involved some minor or not so minor articulation of the paradigm, no two of them quite alike, each partially successful, but none sufficiently so to be accepted as paradigm by the group. Through this proliferation of divergent articulations (more and more frequently they will come to be described as *ad hoc* adjustments), the rules of normal science become increasingly blurred. Though there is still a paradigm, few practitioners prove to be entirely agreed about what it is. Even formerly standard solutions of solved problems are called in question. . . .

All crises begin with the blurring of a paradigm and the consequent

loosening of the rules for normal research. In this respect research
during crisis very much resembles research during the pre-paradigm
period, except that in the former the locus of difference is both smaller
and more clearly defined. And all crises close in one of three ways.
Sometimes normal science ultimately proves able to handle the crisis-
provoking problem despite the despair of those who have seen it as the
end of an existing paradigm. On other occasions the problem resists
even apparently radical new approaches. Then scientists may conclude
that no solution will be forthcoming in the present state of their field.
The problem is labeled and set aside for a future generation with more
developed tools. Or, finally, . . . a crisis may end with the emergence of
a new candidate for paradigm and with the ensuing battle over its
acceptance. . . .

The transition from a paradigm in crisis to a new one from which a
new tradition of normal science can emerge is far from a cumulative process, one achieved by an articulation or extension of the old paradigm.
Rather it is a reconstruction of the field from new fundamentals, a reconstruction that changes some of the field's most elementary theoretical
generalisations as well as many of its paradigm methods and applications.
During the transition period there will be a large but never complete
overlap between the problems that can be solved by the old and by the
new paradigm. But there will also be a decisive difference in the modes
of solution. When the transition is complete, the profession will have
changed its view of the field, its methods, and its goals. . . .

Just because the emergence of a new theory breaks with one tradition
of scientific practice and introduces a new one conducted under different
rules and within a different universe of discourse, it is likely to occur
only when the first tradition is felt to have gone badly astray. That
remark is, however, no more than a prelude to the investigation of the
crisis-state, and, unfortunately, the questions to which it leads demand
the competence of the psychologist even more than that of the historian.
What is extraordinary research like? How is anomaly made lawlike?
How do scientists proceed when aware only that something has gone
fundamentally wrong at a level with which their training has not equipped
them to deal? Those questions need far more investigation, and it ought
not all be historical. . . .   [pp. 82–86]

Almost always the men who achieve these fundamental inventions
of a new paradigm have been either very young or very new to the
field whose paradigm they change. And perhaps that point need not have
been made explicit, for obviously these are the men who, being little
committed by prior practice to the traditional rules of normal science,
are particularly likely to see that those rules no longer define a playable
game and to conceive another set that can replace them.

The resulting transition to a new paradigm is scientific revolution. . . .
                                                                [p. 90]

If any and every failure to fit were ground for theory rejection, all
theories ought to be rejected at all times. On the other hand, if only
severe failure to fit justifies theory rejection, then the Popperians will
require some criterion of " improbability " or of " degree of falsification." . . .

Falsification, though it surely occurs, does not happen with, or simply
because of, the emergence of an anomaly or falsifying instance. Instead,
it is a subsequent and separate process that might equally well be called

verification since it consists in the triumph of a new paradigm over the old one. Furthermore, it is in that joint verification-falsification process that the probabilist's comparison of theories plays a central role. Such a two-stage formulation has, I think, the virtue of great verisimilitude, and it may also enable us to begin explicating the role of agreement (or disagreement) between fact and theory in the verification process. To the historian, at least, it makes little sense to suggest that verification is establishing the agreement of fact with theory. All historically significant theories have agreed with the facts, but only more or less. There is no more precise answer to the question whether or how well an individual theory fits the facts. But questions much like that can be asked when theories are taken collectively or even in pairs. It makes a great deal of sense to ask which of two actual and competing theories fits the facts *better.* . . .   [pp. 146–147]

The man who embraces a new paradigm at an early stage must often do so in defiance of the evidence provided by problem-solving. He must, that is, have faith that the new paradigm will succeed with the many large problems that confront it, knowing only that the older paradigm has failed with a few. A decision of that kind can only be made on faith. . . .

At the start a new candidate for paradigm may have few supporters, and on occasions the supporters' motives may be suspect. Nevertheless, if they are competent, they will improve it, explore its possibilities, and show what it would be like to belong to the community guided by it. And as that goes on, if the paradigm is one destined to win its fight, the number and strength of the persuasive arguments in its favour will increase.[94]   [pp. 158–159]

D. HUME

A Treatise of Human Nature

(ed. 1777)

'*Is*' and '*Ought*'

I cannot forbear adding to these reasonings an observation, which may, perhaps, be found of some importance. In every system of morality, which I have hitherto met with, I have always remark'd, that the author proceeds for some time in the ordinary way of reasoning, and establishes the being of a God, or makes observations concerning human affairs; when of a sudden I am surpriz'd to find, that instead of the usual copulations of propositions, *is* and *is not*, I meet with no proposition that is not connected with an *ought*, or an *ought not*. This change is imperceptible; but is, however, of the last consequence. For as this *ought*, or *ought not*, expresses some new relation or affirmation, 'tis necessary that it shou'd be observ'd and explain'd; and at the same time that a reason should be given, for what seems altogether inconceivable, how this new relation can be a deduction from others, which are entirely different from it. But as authors do not commonly use this precaution, I shall presume

---

[94] [Kuhn's model has been used to illustrate the reversal in juvenile justice policy in California in the 1960s. See Lemert, *Social Action and Legal Change* (1970).]

to recommend it to the readers; and am persuaded, that this small attention wou'd subvert all the vulgar systems of morality, and let us see,
that the distinction of vice and virtue is not founded merely on the
relations of objects, nor is perceiv'd by reason.[95]

LAMONT

Principles of Moral Judgement

(1946)

Ethics as Science of Moral Ideas

The central question of ethics, then . . . is: What are the principles on
which we base our moral judgements of right and wrong? We shall be
concerned here with the analysis of moral ideas, and particularly with
the analysis of moral judgements on conduct, in order to discover the
standards implied in those judgements; and I have described this as
the central problem in the 'science' of ethics.

The next question to be discussed is whether we are entitled to call
an inquiry of this sort a 'science'. Is ethics a science in the proper
sense of the word, or is it rather more appropriately described as a
particular branch of philosophy? In my view, the problems of ethics
are susceptible to scientific treatment in precisely the same sense as
problems in psychology or economics. If we can appropriately speak of
mental and social sciences at all, as I think we can, then ethics can be
classified as one of these.   [p. 12]

It will be noted that, in the use of scientific method all the reasoning
comes in, so to speak, between two sets of observations, the initial
observations on which we found our hypothesis, and the final observations by means of which we test it. So that the crucial question to be
decided in determining whether ethics can be a science is whether it
deals with observable facts. Limiting our attention to what I have called
the central problem of ethics, namely that of discovering the standards
or principles upon which our moral judgements are based, can we say
that we are here concerned with the correlation of 'observed facts'? . . .

Now it is true that facts observed by the external senses are, as a
general rule, the ones most easily brought within the sphere of scientific
treatment. But this is not invariably the case; and when we examine
the reasons why, in science, stress is laid upon 'observation', we shall see
that it is not 'sensible' observation which is the really important thing,
but 'objectivity' in the sense of verifiability independently of any particular person's testimony. All that we require is that our facts should

---

95 [This passage makes a point of great significance in distinguishing between " is "
and " ought," *i.e.*, propositions which state facts on the one hand, and which
prescribe norms on the other. The " logic " of these two types of statements is
different, with the result that we cannot properly infer norms from facts, or
translate one into the other, at least without a good deal of qualification. See
further on this, *ante*, 8, and *post*, 270, 509. For a detailed study of the historical
origins of the distinction between " is " and " ought," see A. Brecht, *Political
Theory* (1959), Chap. 5. Brecht minimises the influence of Hume, and attributes
much greater importance to later German philosophy. The early history of
positivism is also traced by L. Kolakowski, *Positivist Philosophy* (1972), Chap. 2.]

permit of the construction of hypotheses concerning them and of deductive prediction and verification. . . .

We come now to the specific application of scientific method to the study of moral ideas. Ethics is not a study of a mathematical type which, according to certain trends in current opinion, is a rigidly deductive system constructed on the basis of a number of postulates, the main condition governing the selection of postulates being that they shall be consistent with each other. Such a study of purely formal implications may be of very great value when we are dealing with a qualitatively homogeneous 'material' such as space, time, number, or motion. The essential nature of the material can be apprehended and indicated in a few carefully defined concepts without extensive empirical inquiry; and the mathematician can be confident that anything which he discovers in the manipulation of these concepts will illuminate the province of experience to which they refer. Ethics, however, is like the physical and biological sciences in that its field of inquiry is much more complex. To elicit concepts which are both precise and also adequate to the subject-matter is much more difficult. Certainly, if our concepts are not clear our reasoning will be confused. But, on the other hand, no matter how clearly we may define the concepts which we are to relate to each other, any conclusions to which we come with regard to them will be incapable of illuminating moral experience if those concepts are not properly tied to the facts of moral experience itself. Consequently purely formal methods of reasoning must be based upon a preliminary empirical investigation of the facts to be interpreted; and this empirical part of ethics should occupy at least as much attention as it does in biology or in one of the other social sciences.

What are these facts with which we shall be concerned? As has already been indicated, the facts on which we base any theory of the principles implied in moral judgement must be those judgements themselves. We shall be concerned not so much with the right and wrong behaviour of men as with judgements passed upon that behaviour with respect to its rightness and wrongness. We shall take these value judgements as our facts or data to be explained, assuming that they will have some kind of relation to each other, and looking for the standards which will make those relations plain.[96]   [pp. 15–19]

J. SHKLAR

Legalism

(1964)

Law and Ideology

What is legalism? It is the ethical attitude that holds moral conduct to be a matter of rule following, and moral relationships to consist of

[96] [This suggestion as to how a science of ethics may be constructed should be compared with similar proposals in regard to a science of law or jurisprudence, consisting of principles or hypotheses based on or related to a certain order of facts. *Cf. ante,* 3. Such a method in no way precludes a different approach to ethics or jurisprudence, whereby the normative propositions of morals or law are analysed, and their nature, meaning, purpose and value are inquired into. This approach may be more appropriately designated " philosophical."]

duties and rights determined by rules. Like all moral attitudes that are both strongly felt and widely shared it expresses itself not only in personal behavior but also in philosophical thought, in political ideologies, and in social institutions. As an historical phenomenon, it is, moreover, not something that can be understood simply by defining it. Such a morality must be seen in its various concrete manifestations, in its diverse applications, and in the many degrees of intensity with which men in different places and conditions have abided by it. It is in short, a complex of human qualities, not a quantity to be measured and labelled.

Legalism, so understood, is thus often an inarticulate, but nonetheless consistently followed, individual code of conduct. It is also a very common social ethos, though by no means the only one, in Western countries. To a great extent it has provided the standards of organization and the operative ideals for a vast number of social groups, from governmental institutions to private clubs. Its most nearly complete expression is in the great legal systems of the European world. Lastly, it has also served as the political ideology of those who cherish these systems of law and, above all, those who are directly involved in their maintenance—the legal profession, both bench and bar. The court of law and the trial according to law are the social paradigms, the perfection, the very epitome, of legalistic morality. They are, however, far from being its only expressions. Indeed, they are inconceivable without the convictions, mores, and ideologies that must permeate any society which wishes to maintain them. Yet the spirit of legalism is not now, and never has been, the only morality among men even in generally legalistic societies. The full implications of this moral and political diversity, though its existence is commonly acknowledged and often regretted, has rarely been thoroughly investigated. This is by no means surprising, since almost all those who have devoted themselves to the study of legalistic morality and institutions have been their zealous partisans and promoters, anxious to secure their moral empire.

Even though it is no sign of disaffection for legalism to treat it as but one morality among others, such a view has not been congenial to any of the traditional theories of law. These have been devised almost exclusively by lawyers and philosophers who agree in nothing but in taking the prevalence of legalism and of law for granted, as something to be simply defined and analysed. The consequences for legal theory have not been altogether fortunate. The urge to draw a clear line between law and non-law has led to the constructing of ever more refined and rigid systems of formal definitions. This procedure has served to isolate law completely from the social context within which it exists. Law is endowed with its own discrete, integral history, its own " science," and its own values, which are all treated as a single " block " sealed off from general social history, from general social theory, from politics, and from morality. The habits of mind appropriate, within narrow limits, to the procedures of law courts in the most stable legal systems have been expanded to provide legal theory and ideology with an entire system of thought and values. This procedure has served its own ends very well: it aims at preserving law from irrelevant considerations, but it has ended by fencing legal thinking off from all contact with the rest of historical thought and experience.

As an alternative to this unsatisfactory situation, it is suggested here that one ought not to think of law as a discrete entity that is " there," but rather to regard it as part of a social continuum. At one end of the scale of legalistic values and institutions stand its most highly articulate and refined expressions, the courts of law and the rules they follow; at the other end is the personal morality of all those men and women who think of goodness as obedience to the rules that properly define their duties and rights. Within this scale there is a vast area of social beliefs and institutions, both more and less rigid and explicit, which in varying degrees depend upon the legalistic ethos. This would provide an approach suitable to law as an historical phenomenon, and would replace the sterile game of defining law, morals, and politics in order to separate them as concepts both " pure " and empty, divorced from each other and from their common historical past and contemporary setting. . . . [pp. 1–3]

Lastly, there is legalism itself. To say that it is an ideology is to criticise only those of its traditional adherents who, in their determination to preserve law from politics, fail to recognise that they too have made a choice among political values. In itself this would hardly be a new accusation, nor a very important one. What does matter is again the intellectual consequences of this denial, and the attendant belief that law is not only separate from political life but that it is a mode of social action superior to mere politics. This is what will later be discussed as " the policy of justice," for legalism as an ideology does express itself in policies, in institutional structures, and in intellectual attitudes. As a social ethos which gives rise to the political climate in which judicial and other legal institutions flourish, legalism is beyond reproach. It is the rigidity of legalistic categories of thought, especially in appraising the relationships of law to the political environment within which it functions, that is so deleterious. This is the source of the artificiality of almost all legal theories and is what prevents its exponents from recognising both the strengths and weaknesses of law and legal procedures in a complex social world.

Legalism as an ideology is the common element in all the various and conflicting modes of legal thinking. . . . It is what gives legal thinking its distinctive flavour on a vast variety of social occasions, in all kinds of discourse, and among men who may differ in every other ideological respect. Legalism is, above all, the operative outlook of the legal profession, both bench and bar. Moreover, most legal theory, whether it be analytical positivism or natural law thinking, depends on categories of thought derived from this shared professional outlook. The tendency to think of law as " there " as a discrete entity, discernibly different from morals and politics, has its deepest roots in the legal profession's views of its own functions, and forms the very basis of most of our judicial institutions and procedures. That lawyers have particularly pronounced intellectual habits peculiar to them has often been noticed, especially by historians and other students of society whose views differ sharply from those of the legal profession. As one English lawyer has put it, " A lawyer is *bound* by certain habits of belief . . . by which lawyers, however dissimilar otherwise, are more closely linked than they are separated. . . . A man who has had legal training is never quite the same again . . . is never able to look at institutions or administrative practices or even social or political policies, free from his legal habits or beliefs. It is not easy for a lawyer to become a political scientist. It is very difficult for him to become a sociologist or a historian. . . . He is interested in relationships, in rights in something and against somebody, in relation to others. . . . This is what is meant by the legalistic approach. . . . [A lawyer] will fight to the death to defend legal rights against persuasive arguments based on expediency or the public interest or the social good. . . . He distrusts them. . . . He believes, as part of his mental habits, that they are dangerous and too easily used as cloaks for arbitrary action.[97]

These remarkable observations come from an academic lawyer, forced perhaps by the demands of scholarly objectivity and daily contacts with non-lawyerly teachers to look at his profession from the outside. Another academic lawyer has noted in a similar vein that " it is possible for the commercial lawyer and the economist, for the family lawyer and the sociologist to regard one area of social activity from standpoints so far apart that contact becomes infrequent and indeed almost fortuitous." [98] A practising lawyer might not rest with noting the difference between himself and others; he would insist that his was simply the right and true view. That is the meaning of legalism as an ideology.

The dislike of vague generalities, the preference for case-by-case treatment of all social issues, the structuring of all possible human relations into the form of claims and counter-claims under established rules, and the belief that the rules are " there "—these combine to make up legalism as a social outlook. When it becomes self-conscious, when it challenges other views, it is a full-blown ideology. Since lawyers are engaged in their daily lives with political or social conflicts of some kind, they are bound to run up against perspectives radically different from their own. As law serves ideally to promote the security of established expectations, so legalism with its concentration on specific cases and rules is, essentially, conservative. It is not, however, a matter of " masking " a specific class and economic interest. Not only do lawyerly interests often differ from those of other conservative social groups, businessmen's, for example, but legalism is no mask for anything. It is an openly, intrinsically, and quite specifically conservative view, because law is itself a conservatizing ideal and institution. In its epitome, the judicial ethos, it becomes clear that this is the conservatism of consensus. It relies on what appears already to have been established and accepted. When constitutional and social changes have become inevitable and settled, the judiciary adapts itself to the new order. The " switch in time " from 1937 onward, after all, involved the whole federal bench eventually, not just one Supreme Court justice. For the judiciary to remain uncontroversial is the mark of neutral impartiality. Adjustment is therefore its natural policy, whenever possible.

The limits to such adaptation are to be found not in judicial attitudes but in society itself, when no consensus prevails to allow the judiciary to appear neutral. When a consensus does emerge, as it rarely does, adjustment is easier. The ease with which the English judiciary not only accommodated itself to socialist legislation, but even bent backward to facilitate its enforcement, shows how the belief in statute law as " there " can help an immensely conservative set of lawyers to adapt

---

[97] J. A. G. Griffith, " The Law of Property " in ed., Ginsberg, *Law and Opinion in the 20th Century* (1959), pp. 117–119.
[98] de Smith, *Lawyers and the Constitution* (1960), p. 5.

itself to political *force majeure*.[99] Yet in 1911 Winston Churchill had said in Parliament that it was impossible for trade unionists to expect fairness or understanding of the nature of social conflicts from the judiciary. Even before turning to Marxism, Harold Laski assumed that no amount of personal impartiality could save the English judiciary from its upper-class outlook.[1] That English barristers have not as a group been drawn to the cause of socialism remains true. It is not likely that the judiciary is now composed of ardent Labour sympathizers. Far from it. However, men live up to the expectations that their own ideology imposes upon them and to the demands of public office. Faced with the consensus that supported the reforming legislation of the first years after the war, the judiciary demonstrated its neutrality by adapting to the new order as it had supported the old.[2]

Aloofness from politics and impartiality depend upon avoidance of conflict with other, more powerful political agents. The politics of judicial legislation is exposed as such only when there is conflict. As long as there is no opposition to them, decisions seem to be not choices but accepted necessities. There is no reason to suspect the "legal caste" of using the "thereness" of law as a cover in order to exercise politicial power irresponsibly.[3] Ideology is rarely so rational or so purposefully designed a Machiavellian scheme. Neither natural law nor positivism is "there" to hide anything. They are not contrived to protect the judiciary or the bar. They are ideas that correspond, each in its way, to the professional experiences and necessities of bench and bar, and that help to maintain their identity, their social place, and their sense of purpose. However, both natural law theories and analytical positivism allow judges to believe that there always is a rule somewhere for them to follow. The consensus of society or of its wise men, a statute (however broadly interpreted), a precedent (however twisted in meaning), all are somehow present to serve as rationalizations to which a judge must resort if his decisions are to meet the demands that a legalistic conscience and his office make upon him.

If many lawyers, in America especially, do recognize that the courts do legislate and make basic social choices, this is less true and even less accepted in other countries. Even in the United States, moreover, the public at large and important sections of the bar do not perceive their functions thus. The courts are expected to interpret the law, not to alter it. Professional ideology and public expectations, in fact, do mold the conduct of the judiciary and its perception of its role. To seek rules, or at least a public consensus that can serve in place of a rule, must be the judge's constant preoccupation, and it affects his choices in ways that are unknown to less constrained political agents. To avoid the appearance of arbitrariness is a deep inner necessity for him. The trouble is that the possibility of aloofness does not depend on the judge's behavior alone, but also on the public responses to it. In England, given the acceptance of Parliamentary sovereignty, the judiciary is not exposed to controversy as extensive as that in America. Here both the nature of the issues placed before the courts and the greater scope of choice available put the judiciary inevitably into the very

---

[99] Griffith, *op. cit.*, p. 120.
[1] Laski, *Studies In Law and Politics* (1932), pp. 163–180, 230.
[2] [But see O'Higgins and Partington, 32 M.L.R. 53 and *post*, 402, n. 17.]
[3] Watkins, *The State As A Political Concept* (1934), pp. 51–56.

midst of the great political battles of the nation. Elective state judiciaries, moreover, are bound to remain subject to public scrutiny, which the English judiciary is spared.

In any case, no basic social decision, whether made by court or legislature, can ever meet with unanimous approval in a heterogeneous society. Without consensus the appearance of neutrality evaporates. Every offended party characteristically responds to a decision by accusing the judges of " legislating." It is not the law, which is clearly far from self-evident, but the judge, who is at fault, and an erring judge is a legislating judge, since the losing party begins its case by presenting its version of the true law. The result is that, as denunciations of " lawmaking " multiply, the legalistic ethos is reinforced and the likelihood of judges satisfying it becomes increasingly rare. As long as substantial interests and expectations are disappointed by judicial decisions, there can be no realization of legalistic hopes for a neutral judicial process. Law exists to satisfy legally argued expectations, and the loser is sure to feel that the judge, not the law, has arbitrarily deprived him of " his own." The easiest resort, under such circumstances, is for judges to escape into formalism when they can. For American judges this is frequently not possible. In England it is. As for analytical legal theory, it is more than anything an effort to enhance the formalism that is already a built-in feature of legal discourse. Modern legal theory would be incomprehensible if it were forgotten that its creators are themselves lawyers and that professional habits of mind exercise a real influence upon them as they strive to extract the formal essence of law from the confusion of its historical reality.[4]   [pp. 8–13]

---

4 [Shklar's book formed the focus of a symposium to which Shklar herself, Shuman, Coons and Jones contributed. See (1966) 19 *Journal of Legal Education* 49 *et seq.* One telling illustration of legalism is described by Coons, *ibid.*, p. 67, as the " cult of winner-take-all." " For any given dispute submitted to adjudication " he rightly remarks, " only two solutions exist: for plaintiff or defendant; it makes litigation what the game theorists describe as a zero-sum game. On this theme see Coons, further, in (1964) 58 *Northwestern University Law Review* 50. Arnold, *The Symbols of Government* (1935), pp. 10–15 is also critical.]

2

MEANING OF LAW

"Omnis definitio in jure civili periculosa est."
—Iavolenus, D. 50.17.202.

"Obviously, 'law' can never be defined. With equal obviousness, however, it should be said that the adherents of the legal institution must never give up the struggle to define law, because it is an essential part of the ideal that it is rational and capable of definition. . . . Hence the verbal expenditure necessary in the upkeep of the ideal of 'law' is colossal and never ending. The legal scientist is compelled by the climate of opinion in which he finds himself to prove that an essentially irrational world is constantly approaching rationality. . . ."
—Thurman Arnold, *The Symbols of Government* (1935), pp. 36–37

THE NATURE OF DEFINITIONS

SINCE much juristic ink has flown in an endeavour to provide a universally acceptable definition of law, but with little sign of attaining that objective, it may be as well here to take a glance at the general nature and scope of the process of defining.[1] Two confusions need here to be dispelled.

"Naming a Thing"

One approach with a long history has been to regard the act of giving the meaning or defining a word as equivalent to naming or "denoting" the thing for which it stands.[2] This leads to somewhat odd results in many cases, for instance, those of *classes* of things, non-existent things, or fictitious creations. These difficulties have caused many philosophers, especially those associated with the so-called "linguistic" philosophy initiated by Wittgenstein,[3] to reject this theory of meaning, save in relation to proper names, and to treat the meaning or definition of a word as given not so much by denoting what it stands for, but by showing the ways in which a word is used in the context of a particular language.[4] Such usage may indeed

---

[1] Parkinson, *The Theory of Meaning* (1968), is a useful reader surveying contemporary problems of definition.
[2] See Ryle, *post*, 56.   [3] *Cf. ante*, 9, and *post*, 57.
[4] "For a large class of statements—though not all—in which we employ the word 'meaning' it can be defined thus: the meaning of a word is its use in the language": L. Wittgenstein, *Philosophical Investigations*, p. 43. And *cf.* Ryle, *post*, 57.

vary even within the same language, and it may therefore be necessary to distinguish between the " logical grammar " of a word as it
may be used in different contexts.[5] A useful analogy here, and one
much favoured by Wittgenstein himself, is that of various games, so
that, for instance, it is said that the " meaning " of a knight is given
by the part it plays in the game of chess. Wittgenstein commonly
employed the phrase " language games " to describe how we develop
a conventional usage of words within the four corners of a particular
type of activity,[6] and it may readily be seen how this approach affords
an insight into the manner in which lawyers give words a special and
conventional use as " counters," so to speak, in the " game " of
operating a legal system.

One great benefit of this new attitude is that it acts as a kind of
" Ockham's razor," [7] eliminating the need to postulate fictitious or
non-existent *entities* to correspond with the meaning of particular
conceptual words.[8] Thus the fact that we have and frequently use
words such as the state, the law, sovereignty and so on, does not
necessarily imply the existence of a mysterious " entity " denoted by
such words.[9] At the same time, this viewpoint has not itself been
without its dangers, as I shall attempt to show.

" *Essentialism* " [10]

Essentialism, by no means unconnected with the previous confusion,
is one that has a history stretching back to Plato's notion of ideal
universals, namely, the notion that every class or group of things
has an essential or fundamental nature, common to every member of
the class, and that the process of defining consists in isolating and
identifying this common nature or intrinsic property. In this way,
to define a class expression, such as " law," is to state an inherent
fact about the world as it is. This attitude may be detected in such
legal writers as Austin, who seeks to define law " properly so called,"

---

5 See D. Pole, *The Later Philosophy of Wittgenstein* (1958), p. 31.
6 See, especially, his *Philosophical Investigations* (1953) *passim*. His influence is
  reflected in Hart, 70 L.Q.R. 37, Dworkin, *Essays in Legal Philosophy* ed. Summers (1968), p. 25. On the difference between the models, see Hughes in *Law,
  Reason and Justice* ed. Hughes (1969), at pp. 104–107. See, also, the recent
  introduction to this facet of Wittgenstein's philosophy in Part II of Pears,
  Wittgenstein (1971).
7 See B. Russell, *A History of Western Philosophy*, pp. 494–495.
8 See the discussion of this by Prof. H. L. A. Hart, in " Definition and Theory
  in Jurisprudence " (1954) 70 L.Q.R. 37.
9 *Pace* the Scandinavian Realists, as to which, see *post*, 509.
10 So called by Popper, in *Poverty of Historicism* (1957), see pp. 26–34. In the
   Middle Ages the conflict was between nominalists and realists, the former regarding the class designation as a mere name or label, the latter treating it as
   denoting a " universal object," which really enjoyed a distinct existence over
   and above the single members of the class.

or Kelsen, who aims at identifying the essential logical structure of a legal system. Some of those who follow the linguistic approach, have perhaps been rather too eager in rejecting this confusion, and have not limited themselves to demonstrating that this doctrine of " essentialism " is another futile search for a metaphysical entity, the " essence " of a thing. One of the strongest critics of this approach, Hart, has, it has been suggested, succumbed to it himself.[11] What is also suggested by way of *riposte* is that definition is only a matter of choice of criteria, and that this choice cannot be right or wrong, for it is simply *arbitrary* and, therefore, a mere matter of words; another way of putting it is to say that a definition is a " linguistic recommendation " to be accepted or rejected, but which, being put forward as an axiom, cannot be proved or disproved.[12] This assertion really proves too much, for while it may be correct to say that truth or falsity are inapplicable to definitions, what it overlooks is that these may be good or bad in the very real sense that they may or may not be appropriately correlated to the nature of the facts or phenomena which are being described.[13]

Thus suppose we desire to frame a definition of " law," we are surely obliged to study the phenomena of legal activities to which this word is usually appropriated.[14] In addition there may be borderline or peripheral matters which are for some purposes differentiated, but which possess some features in common with or bear a close analogy to the matter generally accepted without question as being legal. Examples are customs in a tribal society or informal controls in a small, well-integrated community such as the *kibbutz* described by Schwartz,[15] or the former practice in this country whereby collective industrial bargains were not legally enforceable.[16] Here, certainly, our definition may be said to be arbitrary in the sense that we may, for

---

[11] *Cf.* Stone, *Legal System and Lawyers' Reasonings* (1964), p. 166.

[12] See Glanville Williams, *post*, 58.

[13] *Cf.* J. Wisdom, *post*, 798 *et seq.*; it should be noted in considering the passages referred to that Prof. Wisdom is himself one of the late Ludwig Wittgenstein's closest followers. As Weldon points out (*Vocabulary of Politics*, pp. 156, 170) a definition of something like " law " is a kind of appraisal; it is not merely arbitrary or based on mere prejudice, but resembles rational judgment, one which can be supported by good reasons.

[14] Little help can be derived from dictionaries in so complex a matter as this, *e.g.*, *Webster* describes law as " rules of conduct enforced by a controlling authority."

[15] See (1954) 63 Yale L.J. 471. The Kibbutz is a collective community in Israel in which informal controls operate with sufficient effectiveness to obviate the necessity for the development of distinctively legal institutions.

[16] On the former English practice, see Kahn-Freund (1969) 1 *Current Legal Problems*, 6–28. The introduction of legal sanctions was condemned by the Royal Commission on Trade Unions and Employers' Associations 1965–1968 (The Donovan Report) Cmnd. 3623, Chap. 8, but subsequently implemented, though not without considerable opposition, in the Industrial Relations Act 1971 (s. 34). Collective agreements are now legally binding, unless the parties expressly stipulate to the contrary.

instance, like Austin, choose so to frame it as to exclude primitive law, and no one can say that we are *wrong*. Yet even here the matter is not one *purely* of words, since we may legitimately inquire into the factual background in order to compare the character and function of law in stateless societies with that of developed law, and reach our choice as to whether the concept law may be suitably extended to comprise both types on a reasoned consideration of the facts to be described.[17] It may even be that our understanding of law in the more developed complex systems will be furthered if we focus our attention upon simpler societies and systems.[18] To describe such a proceeding as necessarily arbitrary is thus highly misleading. The requirements of a " good " definition of law should therefore (a) include what is generally accepted as properly within this sphere; (b) exclude which is universally regarded as not being " law " (*e.g.*, the rules of a robber band); and (c) include or exclude borderline cases in the light of a reasoned comparison of the phenomena in question. As has been pointed out, a good definition is, therefore, one framed with a close eye on the nature of things; for even statements true by definition may be said " to feel the pressure of facts " and we may re-echo the sentiment that it is " extraordinary that we should need to be reminded that definitions are concerned with the nature of things! "[19] This, it may be suggested, is a legitimate assertion without in any way recreating the old bogey of a metaphysical " essence."

ANALYSIS OF WORDS OR FACTS

The limits of defining should also be considered from a further viewpoint. To define is strictly to substitute a word or words for another set of words, and these further words may and generally will stand in need of additional explanation. It must, therefore, be borne in mind that when what is to be discussed is a highly complex concept such as " law " the vital and illuminating feature is not so much the form of words chosen as a definition, but the accompanying elucida-

---

[17] *Cf.*, for instance, the question whether Neanderthal man is " properly " described as an ape or a man. This is no mere sterile verbal discussion for it involves the examining, classifying and comparing of many facts before the choice is made, and though in a sense the definition itself is arbitrary, so far as we apply words to established facts in one way or another, a " good " definition will be conditioned by the accepted results flowing from the survey of the facts described.

[18] See, for example, the approach of Barkun, *Law Without Sanctions* (1968), where the thesis is presented that the " essence " of law (custom, conflict and mediation) can be seen clearly in societies based upon kinship (segmentary lineage societies), and international systems. But note the author's starting point, itself an *a priori* " definition " of law. See also Bohannan, *The Differing Realms of Law* in *Law and Warfare* ed. Bohannan (1967), pp. 43–56 and see, *post*, 619 and Fuller, *post*, 598.

[19] See Harvey, in " Proceedings of Aristotelian Society," Suppl., vol. 29, pp. 5–6. *Cf.* also B. Russell, *My Philosophical Development*, pp. 14, 148–151.

tion of the manner in which those words are to function in all the diverse contexts in which they may be used. Thus, in Professor Hart's *Concept of Law* no definition of law is posited. Instead we are treated to a description of a working model of a standard legal system. His concern is with the conditions which are necessary and sufficient for the existence of a legal system. Quoting J. L. Austin, he claims that he is "using a sharpened awareness of words to sharpen our perception of phenomena," and on this basis, perhaps somewhat dubiously, proffers *The Concept of Law* as "an essay is descriptive sociology." [20]

ARE DEFINITIONS UNNECESSARY?

Does this imply, as some have contended, that to define our concepts is really a waste of time? [21] Sometimes this view is put forward as a form of hard-headed practicality: let's ignore generalities and get down to cases! Or again, definitions may be rejected as a misleading substitute for concrete examples in sentences showing the actual function or use of the word in question.[22] The former view can really only be met by a demonstration that even in practical life clarity is often attained, and futile dispute avoided, by a careful defining of our terms, and equally the scientist knows that little advance would be possible without a rigorously defined terminology. Admittedly, such precision may not always be attainable, but an attempt at an approximation is not necessarily futile. As to the latter view, we may concede that we can only adequately understand our terms by seeing how they function in the particular linguistic or logical framework of their use, but this does not necessarily condemn general definitions as worthless, for though in complex matters they cannot afford complete explanations in themselves, they may help in the light of the functional exposition, to provide an overall picture and to emphasise certain key criteria.[23] They may thus serve to illuminate our understanding, provided we avoid the confusions

---

[20] *Cf.* A. J. Ayer, *The Problem of Knowledge* (1956), particularly at pp. 2–3, 26: "Inquiry into the use of words can equally be regarded as inquiring into the nature of the facts which they described." As Moore remarked, we all know quite well that hens lays eggs, but we differ about the "ultimate analysis" of this proposition. See Passmore, *A Hundred Years of Philosophy* (1968), p. 364.
[21] Professor Stone is of the opinion that quite the reverse may be the case, that those who seek for definitions are seeking mnemonics, "short cut(s) or even substitute(s) for exposition. . . . It is this [he argues] which is the gravest sense in which *omnis definitio periculosa est.*" *Legal System and Lawyers' Reasonings* (1964), p. 185 and *post*, 64.
[22] *Cf.* Hart, *op. cit., ante*, 40, n. 8.
[23] *Cf.* the discussion between Prof. Hart and Cohen, in "Proc. of Arist. Soc.," Suppl., vol. 29, p. 213 *et seq.* Cohen not only argues in favour of the need for criteria to distinguish "legal" from "non-legal" but also that juristic definitions should take account of the politico-moral factors which are entailed in the construction of legal rules. As to these, *cf. post*, 47.

to which reference has been made, and provided also they are treated as more in the nature of a summing-up of the discussion than as a series of axioms from which all subsequent conclusions may logically be inferred. This, indeed, is the cardinal weakness of such an approach as Austin's, which begins by postulating the " nature " of law and then goes on to deduce conclusions from such postulates, instead of first discussing and analysing the relevant phenomena and then providing a definition not as a logically deduced conclusion, but as a rational generalisation [24] in relation to the subject-matter so analysed.

IDEOLOGICAL FACTORS

Apart from the foregoing considerations, it must also be remembered that choices will be influenced by the ideology or attitudes of the chooser; whether, for instance, he favours capitalism or socialism, or whether his general outlook is idealist or positivist. Thus linguistic recommendations may be activated, consciously or subconsciously, by such underlying premises.[25] It must always be borne in mind that beneath even the most apparently technical of rules there may lurk deeply held social or political philosophies. Thus, the doctrine of " *caveat emptor* "—the rule that it is for the purchaser to take the risk whether he has made a good or bad bargain—is certainly no mere legalistic technicality but involves the whole philosophy of *laisser faire*, which has played such an influential part in the classical theory both of the common and of the civil law of property and contract. Moreover, words themselves contain many emotional overtones and the choice of language may act as what have been termed " persuasive definitions," [26] inducing practical and psychological consequences or effects on the part of those to whom they are offered. Accordingly, although a state may be an " organism unknown to biology " it may make a considerable difference whether we define it in a legalistic way as a contract between the citizens or as a type of " moral person," and much of the conflict between political theorists may be traceable to this source.[27] So again, we may recall that the most bitter attacks on the Austinian scheme were by those who rejected his classification of international law as not being law; nor is this a merely verbal question, even from this point of view, since much might turn, so far as the influence

---

[24] *Cf.* W. L. Morison, 68 Yale L.J. 212, who argues that Austin's jurisprudence was an empirical science, though Stone (*op. cit.*, p. 66) sums up his empiricism as no more than that of " any thinker [who] approaches his problems on the basis of his own experience and knowledge."

[25] *Cf. ante*, 1, 16, 33. See further Friedmann, *Legal Theory* (5th ed.), Chap. 6.

[26] See C. L. Stevenson, in (1937) *Mind*, p. 47, and Glanville Williams, *Philosophy, Politics and Society* ed. Laslett (1956), 1st series, p. 134.

[27] See M. Macdonald, in *Logic and Language*, 1st series (1955), p. 167 *et seq.*

of international law itself is concerned, on people generally linking it with the emotional associations normally induced by the very word "law," as something which must be unquestionably obeyed, in contrast with morality, compliance with which may depend on the individual conscience.

CRITERION OF VALIDITY

Wollheim has pointed out that much of the confusion in defining law has also been due to the different type of purpose sought to be achieved, and in particular that jurists have not clearly distinguished between three types of question, *viz.* (1) a definition, in the sense of an elucidation of meaning; (2) a criterion for the validity of law; and (3) a general scheme for the criterion of validity of *any* legal system whatever. As to the second, this must be relative to a particular legal system; the third, on the other hand, involves a search for a perfectly general criterion of a purely formal kind.[28] It is this latter that Bentham and Austin in the nineteenth century and Kelsen and Hart in this have tried to attain, with varying degrees of success.[29] A serious limitation of this method is that there is no guarantee that the criteria selected can be shown to be applicable to the actual content of particular legal systems, since these have empirical characteristics not necessarily capable of being confined within the particular strait-jacket it is desired to impose upon them.[30] But it is no coincidence that the problem of content is one which has little exercised those jurists who have sought to construct a model of a legal system.[31] Content, the problem of whether systems must satisfy any minimal requirements,[32] is no further explicated in the two most recent forays into the " grand theory "[33] of legal systems. For Fuller's " internal moral structure," whilst an exemplary code of legality, shows no awareness of any relationship between this and laws so processed,[34] and Raz's searching analysis of the writings of these earlier jurists merely treads the path well worn by them.[35]

---

[28] R. Wollheim, " Nature of Law," in 2 *Political Studies* (1954), p. 128 ; see *post*, 62.
[29] See *post*, Chaps. 4 and 5 and the account in Joseph Raz, *The Concept of a Legal System* (1970).
[30] A difficulty encountered by Austin and Kelsen, *post*, 162, and 289. Both wrote against the backgrounds of particular systems and hoped to structure a logically self-contained formal skeleton with general, if not universal, validity upon knowledge culled from such sources.
[31] With the notable exception of Hart. *Cf. post*, 84, 130.
[32] *Cf.* Raz, *op. cit.* p. 2.
[33] The phrase is C. Wright Mills', *The Sociological Imagination* (1959), Chap. 2.
[34] *Post*, 138.
[35] Hence, not only his relative lack of interest in the problem of content, but also his failure to consider the social, moral and cultural factors that act upon a legal system, a concentration on what he calls " momentary legal systems " (pp. 34, 189), and his rule-centred definition of law with its oversimplified model of the legal process. *Cf.* Dworkin, *post*, 172.

And the three other criteria which Raz believes a theory of a legal system must adequately tackle, *viz. existence* (how can we distinguish between existing systems and those which no longer exist or are fragments of the imagination? [36]); *identity* and *membership* (how do we know to which system a given law belongs?) and *structure* (are there types of system or are certain patterns of relations common to all?) [37] will be found in the writings of leading analytical jurists, albeit not expressed with such precision or emphasis.[38]

LAW AND REGULARITY

Law also seems to require a certain minimum degree of regularity and certainty, for without this it would be impossible to assert that what was operating in a given territory amounted to a legal *system.* Clearly, however, no exact criterion can be applied for determining what degree of regularity or certainty is necessary to achieve this aim, and states may vary from arbitrary tyrannies where all are subject to the momentary caprices of a tyrant, to the elaborate and orderly governed states associated with Western democracies. Pollock urged that the exercise of a merely capricious power, according to the whim of the moment, is not law, and criticised Austin on the ground that, on his theory, the capricious orders of a crazy despot would still be law until revoked.[39] It is not, of course, an answer to this to say that the tyrant's whims would, to satisfy Austin's theory, at least have to be expressed in general terms, for it is by no means inconceivable or beyond the experience of actual tyrannies, that the whims of despots have been embodied in formal legislation.

It goes without saying, however, that a system pivoted on the caprice of a despot could not long function effectively. But this goes no way towards substantiating the very different thesis of some naturalists that commands issuing from such a source could not be described as law, any more than their source would merit the description as a "legal system." [40] Lon Fuller, for example, has posited eight *sine qua non* of a legal system: the laws issued from such a source must be promulgated, intelligible, prospective, non-contradictory, general, avoid impossible demands and frequent change, and official actions must be congruent with promulgated

---

[36] *Cf.* Plato, *post*, 89.
[37] See, pp. 1–2. Raz's own conclusions are expressed in a number of theses (pp. 155, 156, 164, 169, 170, 171).
[38] *Post*, Chaps. 4, 5.
[39] *Jurisprudence and Legal Essays*, ed., A. L. Goodhart, pp. 18, 162–163: Others, on the contrary, have seen this as a positive merit of Austinian or Kelsenian jurisprudence *viz.* its ability to embrace all institutional set-ups. See, for example, McBride, 43 N.Y.U.L. Rev. 53, 62.
[40] See *post*, Chap. 3.

rules.[41] But, as Friedmann [42] has pointed out, the laws of the Nazi régime for one were consonant with these requirements. Furthermore, in spite of being subject to the whims of Hitler, the legal system of the Third Reich did not operate in a total vacuum. A large structure of laws and customs continued to operate with some measure of regularity. The question in all such cases will be whether the degree of capricious intervention is so far reaching as to deprive the citizenry of any expectation of the orderly and regular application of even that (possibly large) segment of rules which is outside the probable sphere of the tyrant's particular interest. It is one thing to deny that such a system is a legal system: quite another to prophesy that its inefficacy will lead to its eventual downfall.

LAW AND MORALS

We have already seen how the normative structure of the language of the law resembles that of ethics, a point that is brought out by their common use of "ought," "obligation" and "duty." [43] Even linguistically, however, there may be no coincidence, for it has been argued that logically you lay yourself open to a request for reasons for asserting a moral duty, whereas legal obligation is more in the nature of a command, depending not on reason but on *authority*.[44] In this respect law resembles religion more closely than ethics, for religion also appeals to authority in the shape of what is decreed by God.[45] Some ethical approaches, however, such as that of certain natural law thinkers, have reduced morals to a series of imperatives comparable to rules of law,[46] but these have often involved a close interconnection between religion and moral obligation.

Apart from differences in the *language* of law and morals, attempts have long been made to detect distinctions of *substance* between these two closely related spheres.[47] Thus even the natural lawyers have recognised that the two do not altogether coincide, and

41 See *The Morality of Law* (1969), Chap. 2 and *post*, 138.
42 *Legal Theory* (5th ed.), p. 19 with, he admits, the exception to some extent of promulgation. *Cf.* Grunberger, *A Social History of the Third Reich* (1971), Chap. 8.
43 *Ante*, 8.
44 See Nowell-Smith, *Ethics*, pp. 190–198. But it is now regarded as of the essence of a *judicial* decision that reasons should be given. *Cf. post*, 729.
45 *Cf.* Kantorowicz, *Definition of Law* (1958), p. 34.
46 *Post*, 78.
47 Thus Hart has pointed out that the main differences between moral and legal responsibility is due to substantive differences between the content of legal and moral rules and principles, rather than in semantic distinctions, *e.g.* there may be important differences in the criteria applied, as, for instance, where the law may rely upon concepts of strict or even absolute liability, which are hard, if not impossible, to reconcile with our present concept of morality. See 83 L.Q.R. 346, 358–9, also in *Punishment and Responsibility* (1968), pp. 224–225. See also *The Concept of Law* (1961), pp. 163–176.

that there is a field of positive law not deducible from any pre-existing or presupposed system of natural law and, therefore, morally neutral.[47a] Certainly one of the firmest tenets of the positivist jurists from Bentham and Austin onwards has been that positive law is quite distinct from and its validity in no way dependent upon morals. This is not put forward as a purely logical or formal contrast, but as asserting a distinction *de facto* between two normative systems to be found side by side in human society. As a matter of social fact there may be many reasons why these two systems should fail to correspond in particular instances, even though a broad measure of coincidence between them may be essential to the working of human society. Moral sentiments on some matters may be insufficiently developed or mobilised to be translated into law,[48] as witness the comparatively recent legal prohibition of cruelty to children or animals in England, or, more recently still, the abolition of capital punishment or the prohibition of racial discrimination. Or law may be too cumbersome an instrument to justify legal prohibition in some spheres, and might thus do more harm than good, as in the case of some sexual irregularities,[49] or it may be felt that certain moral duties are best left to the individual conscience, as, for instance, the duty to rescue a drowning man.[50] Again,

---

[47a] *Post*, 91.

[48] The question whether the passing of legislation in such a case actually affects morality has come in for a lot of recent discussion and socio-legal research. The views of the Scandinavians, notably Olivecrona, are considered *post*, 510. But particularly interesting are the findings of Berkowitz and Walker. " There appears to be a comparatively small but nevertheless significant tendency for some people to alter their views of the morality of some actions in accord with laws specifying that these actions are legal or illegal. Knowledge of the existence of these laws, however, does not have as much effect in changing the moral judgments as knowledge of the consensus of opinions among one's peers " ((1967) 30 Sociometry 410, 418). These conclusions were based on the testing and retesting of some 87 English university students, hardly, therefore, a representative sample. Furthermore, as the authors of the survey admit, the dichotomy between the impact of the law and the attitudes of one's peers whilst distinguishable in a laboratory setting, does not exist in the " real world." See also Colombotos's article showing the change in doctors' attitudes to *Medicare* before the passage of legislation, after this but before its operation, and after six months of operation. Whilst 38 per cent. were in favour of compulsory health insurance through social security to cover hospitalisation of the over-sixty-fives before the law, the figures were 70 per cent. and 81 per cent. at the later times. See (1969) 34 Amer. Soc Rev. 318.

[49] The success rate for the legislation of morality depends upon a number of variables. The chances of success are greatest where violation of the new law involves a *victim* who can act as a " plaintiff " and where the arena for the occurrence of the offence is *visible*. " Laws which affect both the public arena and concern victimisation will be most effective in changing the existing moral order. Thus civil rights legislation is placed in a new light. . . . It is at the exact opposite pole of discussions about moral legislation on prostitution and drug addiction." *Per* Troy Duster, *The Legislation of Morality* (1970), p. 26.

[50] Not a legal duty by the common law, though some systems, *e.g.*, French law, take a different view. On which see Radcliffe, *The Good Samaritan and the Law* (1966) and Linden, 34 M.L.R. 241. A survey conducted by Kaufman found that where the law required aid, failure to intervene was considered significantly

many legal questions are morally indifferent, for instance, the rule of the road, and others are afforded no certain guide by appeal to moral considerations, for example where a choice is to be made whether a loss is to fall on one or other of two innocent persons.[51]

Is it then possible to point to any distinction of substance which can enable us to differentiate legal from moral norms? The more philosophical approach has generally been to follow or adapt the thought of Kant by regarding laws as prescribing *external* conduct whereas morals prescribe *internal* conduct, that is, morals alone are concerned with subjective factors, such as motive.[52] Thus it is said that law, even when purporting to deal with motive, is really only concerned with its external manifestations,[53] on the well-known principle that " the thought of man is not triable, for the devil himself knoweth not the thought of man." [54] Yet for the lawyer this is really a matter of difficulty of proof, and it is hardly possible to draw a precise line at the point where law can be said to ignore subjective considerations.[55] Lawyers have, therefore, tended to put their faith rather in the element of *sanctions* as the characteristic feature differentiating law from morals. Yet even morals is not without a sanctioning element, if only in the form of incurring the disapprobation of one's fellows, which may indeed be the most powerful of all pressures in human society. This difficulty it is sought to overcome by asserting that law calls for a regularised, if not a specific sanction. More will be said of this in later sections of this book, but it should be pointed out here that the sanctionists do not rely upon this as a merely *formal* characteristic of legal rules, but appeal to the history of human society as bearing out the indispensability of regular sanctions as part of any recognised legal system.[56]

---

less moral than where the law did not require one to intervene. See *Legality and Harmfulness of a Bystander's Failure to Intervene as Determinants of Moral Judgment* in *Altruism and Helping*, ed. Macaulay and Berkowitz (1969), p. 77.

[51] *e.g.*, an innocent purchaser, as against the lawful owner of stolen goods. And see Hughes, *The Existence of a Legal System*, 35 N.Y.U.L. Rev. 1001.

[52] See H. Kantorowicz, *op. cit.*, pp. 41–51. *Cf.* pp. xxi–xxiii.

[53] *Cf.* Holmes J. in *Collected Legal Papers* (1920), p. 177. The much-criticised decision in *D.P.P.* v. *Smith* [1961] A.C. 290, was based on this philosophy.

[54] *Per* Brian C.J. in Y.B. 17 Edw. IV, 1.

[55] Thus, the courts balanced subjective and objective factors in the old concept of cruelty: conduct had to be " grave and weighty," the respondent's intention was relevant, though not decisive, and above all the courts looked to " this man and this woman " *per* Lord Reid in *Gollins* v. *Gollins* [1964] A.C. 644. It is thought that the same balancing is likely to be found in the concept of " intolerable conduct " in the Divorce Reform Act 1969. See Freeman (1971) 178 C.L.P. 192. This interpretation is supported by *Ash* v. *Ash* [1972] 2 W.L.R. 347.

[56] So Kelsen, at least; see *post*, 274. Equally, if all peoples were found to obey the rules laid down by constituted authority without sanction, no one would suggest sanctions as the criterion of law.

MORALS AS PART OF LAW

The controversies do not, however, end here, for there are some who assert that even if law and morals are distinguishable it remains true that morality is in some way an integral part of law or of legal development, that morality is, so to speak " secreted in the interstices " of the legal system, and to that extent is inseparable from it. There are various ways in which this viewpoint has been put forward. Thus it has been said that law in action is not a mere system of rules, but involves the use of certain principles, such as that of the equitable and the good (*aequum et bonum*). By the skilled application of these principles to legal rules the judicial process distils a moral content out of the legal order, though it is admitted that this does not permit the rules themselves to be rejected on the general ground of their immorality.[57] Another approach would go much further and confer upon the legal process an inherent power to reject immoral rules as essentially non-legal; this seems to resemble the older natural law mode of thought, but, it is urged, the difference is that according to the present doctrine it is a matter of the *internal* structure of the legal system, which treats immoral rules as inadmissible rather than as being annulled by an external law of nature.[58] At any rate, it should not be overlooked that even the positivist does not deny that many factors, including morality, may and do concur in the development of a legal rule, and that where there is a gap or a possible choice within the legal system, moral or other extra-legal pressures may cause that gap to be filled or the choice to be determined in one way rather than another.[59] What the positivist insists is, that once the rule is laid down or determined, it does not cease to be law because it may be said or shown to be in conflict with morality.

THE LEGAL ENFORCEMENT OF MORALS

A good deal of controversy has arisen in recent years as to whether the fact that conduct is, by common standards, regarded as immoral, in itself justifies making that conduct punishable by law. This controversy was set off by the opinion expressed in the Wolfenden Committee Report on Prostitution and Homosexuality,[60] which in

---

[57] Lamont, *Value Judgment*, p. 292 *et seq.* Lamont also argues as to the structural similarity between legal and moral systems, the main difference being that in the latter the individual can balance a rule against other rules or principles, and retains autonomy to decide according to his own judgment.
[58] See L. L. Fuller, referred to *ante*, 46–47, and see extracts *post*, 138.
[59] *Cf.* Lloyd, *Public Policy* (1953), Chaps. 1 and 7.
[60] Cmnd. 247 (1957). *Cf.* the Report by the Advisory Committee on *Drug Dependence: Cannabis* (1968), paras. 13–18. The Committee refer to Mill's dictum, but go on to say that while the force of his argument is appreciated, " it has to be recognised that no hard and fast line can be drawn between actions that are purely self-regarding and those that involve wider social consequences. If,

effect re-asserted the answer given by John Stuart Mill, that legal coercion can only be justified for the purpose of preventing harm to others.[61] Mill's thesis had been attacked by the great Victorian judge, Stephen, in his *Liberty, Equality and Fraternity*,[62] and the issue was now rekindled by Lord Devlin's [63] critique of *Wolfenden* [64] in a lecture called "The Enforcement of Morals" delivered in 1959. Lord Devlin has subsequently returned to this theme a number of times.[65] He has argued that there is a public morality which provides the cement of any human society, and that the law, especially the criminal law, must regard it as its primary function to maintain this public morality. Whether in fact in any particular case the law should be brought into play by specific criminal sanctions must depend upon the state of public feeling. Conduct which arouses a widespread feeling of reprobation, a mixture of "intolerance, indignation and disgust," deserves to be suppressed by legal coercion in the interests of the integrity of society. For this purpose, Lord Devlin has recourse to the common law jury idea, the notion that the "man in the jury-box" supplies an adequate standard of current morality for the purpose of assessing the limits of legal intervention. The juryman after all does not give a snap judgment; his verdict is the outcome of argument and deliberation after, perhaps, listening to expert evidence and receiving guidance from an experienced judge. And

generally speaking, everyone is entitled to decide for himself what he will eat, drink or smoke, the fact remains that those who indulge in gross intemperance of almost any kind will nearly always become a burden to their families, the public authorities or both. Indeed, examples of actions which never in any circumstances involve social repercussions are by no means easy to find. Nor can it be said that any consistent principle dictates the occasion on which the law at present intervenes to protect the individual from himself. . . ." The Committee also assert that account must be taken of public attitudes, as well as the difficulty and dangers of enforcement. "We have to recognise that there comes a point at which public pressures becomes so powerful that it is idle to keep up attempts to resist them, the classic example in this context being the American prohibition of the consumption of alcohol." On the latter see Sinclair, *Prohibition: The Era of Excess* (1962), pp. 179–214.

[61] For a discussion of Mill's stand see Samek, 49 Can.Bar Rev. 188, 197–200. According to Berlin there are two concepts of liberty telescoped in Mill's account. That described here is negative liberty: its concomitant, positive liberty, is "that men should seek to *discover* the truth, or to develop a certain type of character of which Mill approved—fearless, original, imaginative, independent, non-conforming . . . and that truth can be found, and such character bred only in conditions of freedom," in *Two Concepts of Liberty* (1969), p. 128.

[62] See edition edited by R. S. White, 1967. Samek, *op. cit.* discusses Stephen's attack on Mill and concludes that he did not intend "to depart from a utilitarian position," nor did he advocate, as Hart has suggested he did (*Law, Liberty, and Morality*, p. 48) enforcement of morals as an end in itself. His gravest sin was "to accept too readily conventional moral values . . . as satisfying the principle of utility" (pp. 200–208). One of the dangers of the Stephen-Devlin thesis is that the positive morality of a society may be deemed beyond criticism. *Cf.* Glanville Williams [1966] Crim.L.R. 132, 135–136.

[63] Now the first essay in a collection called *The Enforcement of Morals* (1965). The Preface and essays 6 and 7 are particularly germane to this issue.

[64] *Idem*, and see also discussion reported in *The Listener*, June 18, 1964.

[65] *Idem*, pp. 86, 102, 124.

as for reliance upon feeling, this was the ordinary man's best guide where a choice had to be made between a number of reasonable conclusions.[66] He therefore stigmatises as an "error of juris-prudence" the view in the Wolfenden Report that there is some single principle explaining the division between crime and sin, such as that based upon Mill's notion of what may lead to harmful consequences to third persons.

Devlin concluded that if vice were not suppressed society would crumble: "The suppression of vice is as much the law's business as the suppression of treason." [67]

Such a thesis appears to have received some support from the remarkable decision of the House of Lords in the so-called *Ladies' Directory Case*,[68] but has been strenuously opposed by Professor Hart.[69] Hart has outlined,[70] in the first place, "the types of evidence that might conceivably be relevant to the issue." One could examine "crude historical evidence," look at disintegrated societies and enquire whether disintegration was preceded by a malignant change in their common morality, considering further any "causal connection." Such a survey would have formidable diffi-culties for, even supposing, which is most unlikely, that moral decadence was responsible for the decline of Rome,[71] would such evidence be persuasive in considering modern technological societies? Hart puts his faith rather in the evidence of social psychology.[72] Depending on one's ideology, the way of viewing the alternatives to the maintenance of a common morality, this could take one of two forms. One view would be *permissiveness*: one would show how this led to a weakening of individual capacity for self-control and contributed to an increase in violence and dishonesty. But the other side of the coin is *moral pluralism*. Would this lead to antagonism, to a society in the state of nature depicted by Hobbes,[73] or rather to mutual tolerance, to co-existence of divergent moralities? What evidence there is comes down firmly in favour of co-existence.[74] Having removed the foundations of Devlin's thesis, Hart then sets about to demolish the structure erected upon them. He dismisses as

---

[66] *Idem*, p. ix.
[67] In 35 *University of Chicago Law Review*, 1, 11–13. For some empirical evidence on the impact of erotica and its relation to anti-social and criminal behaviour, see the U.S. Government's *Commission on Obscenity and Pornography* (1970) (Bantam edition), pp. 169–309.
[68] See *post*, 69.
[69] See especially, H. L. A. Hart, *Law, Liberty and Morality* (1963).
[70] *Idem*, p. 11.
[71] For the view that moral decadence was not among the causes of the decline of the Roman Empire, see A. H. M. Jones, *The Decline of the Ancient World* (1966), Chaps. 24 and 26.
[72] *Op. cit.* pp. 12–13.
[73] See *post*, 178.
[74] Hart believes rightly that modern Britain exemplifies this trend.

fantastic the notion that all morality forms " a single seamless web " so that deviation from any one part will almost inevitably produce destruction of the whole. The mere fact that conventional morality may change in a permissive direction does not mean that society is going to be destroyed or subverted.[75] Again, Lord Devlin assumes a degree of moral solidarity in society, which may have existed in mid-Victorian England, but is hardly discernible at the present time.[76] Hart goes on to point out that the real solvent to social morality is not the failure of the law to endorse its restrictions, but rather the operation of free critical discussion, and he goes on to point out the dangers to democracy which might flow from the notion that free discussion should be prohibited on account of its impact on prevalent social morality. That the moral notions of the majority are matters to which the legislature must pay close account seems beyond question, but what Mill had in mind was that at all costs the idea that the majority had a moral right to dictate how everyone else should live, was something which needed to be resisted. It is essential, therefore, from a libertarian point of view, that public indignation, while given due weight, should be subject to the overriding tests of rational and critical appraisal.[77]

Nevertheless, Hart accepts the need for the law to enforce some morality and the real area of dispute is where the line should be drawn. Mill drew it at harm to others. Hart extends the role of the law by his acceptance of " paternalism," in addition to Mill's

---

[75] *Op. cit.* pp. 9–10.

[76] But *cf.* Marcus, *The Other Victorians* (1967). Ranulf's view that the middle classes have a monopoly of moral indignation may be the key. (See *Moral Indignation and Middle Class Psychology* (1938), pp. 1–95 or Gusfield, *Symbolic Crusade* (1963).)

[77] For further viewpoints in this controversy see E. V. Rostow, " The Enforcement of Morals " [1960] C.L.J. 174; G. B. J. Hughes, " Morals and the Criminal Law " (1962) 71 Yale L.J. 662; Robert S. Summers, in (1963) New York University L.R., p. 1201; R. Wollheim, " Crime, Sin and Mr. Justice Devlin," *Encounter*, November, 1959, p. 34. See also H. L. A. Hart, " Immorality and Treason," *The Listener*, July 30, 1959, p. 162. In a discussion reported in *The Listener*, June 18, 1964, Lord Devlin emphasised that he was not seeking to say that the law must automatically punish in the case of offences against morality, but rather that there are no circumstances in which you can say that the law may not punish in such cases. Also, while reiterating his test about conduct which arouses emotions of intolerance, indignation and disgust, he emphasised that he regards this merely as a " supreme factor " in deciding whether the law should be invoked, but recognises that there are also other important factors, such as whether the law is likely to be effective in reducing vice, or likely to produce more harm than good, *e.g.*, by encouraging blackmail. This seems to leave as the main point of difference between the controversialists that Lord Devlin would look primarily to the state of public indignation in deciding whether the law should intervene or not, and would not regard this as necessarily overridden by any critical and scientific appraisal of social consequences, though he would agree that public opinion and moral belief are more important in maintaining social morality than the law itself. See also, P. Devlin, *The Enforcement of Morals* (1965), especially Chaps. 6 and 7.

reliance on harmful consequences to others.[78]   So, where Devlin justified *R. v. Donovan*[79] as enforcement of morality, Hart sees the decision as a concession to paternalism. Hart never defines paternalism and Devlin has been critical of its vagueness. "What, also, I did not foresee was that some of the crew who sail under Mill's flag of liberty would mutiny and run paternalism up the mast."[80] Although Devlin is unable to distinguish paternalism and the enforcement of morals, there is a distinction which centres on the decision-making process of those who are subject to the law. Paternalism thus may intervene to stop self-inflicted harm or euthanasia, not because of a wish to enforce conventional morality, but because of doubts as to the capacity of the "victim" to make a rational decision where, as usually, he is mentally disturbed (according to conventional morality[81]) or physically ill.[82]

But Hart goes further than this. He admits, with Devlin, that some shared morality is essential to society, what he calls "universal values."[83] If *any* society is to survive, if any legal system is to function, then there must be rules prohibiting, for example, murder. But is abortion or euthanasia murder?[84] The standard case remains uncontroversial, the marginal situation is no nearer solution. Hart further argues, in a later formulation,[85] that rules essential for a *particular* society (monogamy might be an example) might also be enforced. "For any society there is to be found . . . a central core of rules or principles which constitutes its pervasive and distinctive style of life." And he continues: "it then becomes an open and empirical question whether any particular moral rule is so organically connected with the central core that its preservation is

---

[78] *Law, Liberty and Morality* (1963), pp. 30–34.

[79] [1934] 2 K.B. 498 in which it was held that consent negatives the crime of assault. See *The Enforcement of Morals*, pp. 6–7; *Law, Liberty and Morality*, pp. 30–34. See also Glanville Williams [1962] Crim.L.R. 74, 154.

[80] *Op. cit.*, p. 132.

[81] *Cf.* Laing, *The Divided Self* (1960); Goffman, *Asylums* (1961).

[82] *Cf.* C. L. Ten, 32 M.L.R. 648, 660–661. There is also the difficulty as to whether "harm" covers only physical harm, or whether it can extend to psychological harm as well. Hart thinks it can extend to psychological harm, but not to purely moral harm. It must be conceded, however, that it is extremely difficult to draw the line between these different kinds of potential harm in the case of some legal systems generally recognise as criminal, *e.g.* the performance of sexual acts in public, and various other forms of indecency. See, further, Mitchell, *op. cit.*, pp. 57–59.

[83] *Op cit.*, p. 71; *cf. The Concept of Law* (1961) and "the minimum content of natural law" (pp. 189–195) and see *post*, 130.

[84] *Cf.* Basil Mitchell, *Law, Morality and Religion in a Secular Society* (1967), pp. 119 *et seq.* Mitchell's approach is more sympathetic to Devlin than most commentators. In his view the law may be used to support an institution like monogamy for moral reasons, even though it could not be shown that specific harmful consequences of any kind would result from the abandonment of that form of marriage.

[85] The Chicago article referred to *op. cit.* at p. 10.

required as a vital bastion." [86] At this stage a point has been reached where there is not much to choose between the two main contestants.[87] It is only perhaps the recent " backlash " against permissiveness which keeps the legal enforcement of morality as a live issue.[88]

LAW AND VALUE JUDGMENTS [89]

Some positivists, such as Kelsen, have desired to banish any element of value judgments from the juristic study of law, on the ground that these are purely subjective and, therefore, cannot be admitted into the scientific study of law as an objective phenomenon.[90] Yet, if value judgments, such as moral factors, form an inevitable feature of the climate of legal development, as is generally admitted, it is difficult to see the justification for this exclusive attitude. For not only, even in the realm of pure science, are valuations almost inescapable,[91] but also the value judgments which enter into law, such as consideration of what would be a just rule or decision, even though not " objective " in the sense of being based on absolute truth, may, nevertheless, be relatively true, in the sense of corresponding to the existing moral standards of the community. Certain standards of conduct, for instance, if not patterns laid up in heaven, may be at least part of what have been called the " operative ideals " of a particular society,[92] a part of its accepted system of values, and whether this is so or not is a matter of objective social fact. And if lawyers and legislators do in fact have regard to such values in the working of the legal system, this is just as much a part of the legal system in action as rules contained in a statute, and can no more be ignored by the jurist than by the legal practitioner advising his client, or the judge determining a case. So that whether it is convenient or not to define law without reference to subjective factors,[93] when we come to observe the phenomena with which law is concerned and to analyse

---

[86] *Idem*, p. 11.
[87] For further viewpoints in this controversy see E. Rostow [1960] C.L.J. 174, reprinted in *The Sovereign Prerogative* (1962); Hughes, 71 Yale L.J. 662, reprinted in Summers, *Essays in Legal Philosophy* (1968), p. 183 ; Summers (1963) 38 N.Y.U.L. Rev. 1201 ; Henkin (1963) 63 Col.L.Rev. 393 ; Samek, 49 Can. Bar Rev. 188.
[88] Consider, for example, the successful prosecutions under the Obscene Publications Act of *The Little Red School Book, The Times,* July 8, 1971, and *Oz No. 28, The Times,* July 30, 1971, the first successful conviction under the Theatres Act 1968, *R.* v. *Brownson and others* [1971] Crim.L.R. 551–552, *R.* v. *Knuller* [1971] 3 All E.R. 314, and the unofficial commission set up by Lord Longford.
[89] *Cf. post,* 165.
[90] *Post,* 270.
[91] *Cf.* Kuhn, *ante,* 25.
[92] *Cf.* R. Pound, *post,* 379.
[93] For a recent argument as to the desirability of importing subjective factors into the definition of law, see H. Kantorowicz, *op. cit.,* pp. 72–73.

the meaning and use of legal rules in relation to such phenomena, it will be found impossible to disregard the role of value judgments in legal activity, and we cannot exorcise this functional role by stigmatising such judgments as merely subjective or unscientific.

G. RYLE

The Theory of Meaning

(1957) [94]

Let me briefly mention some of the consequences which successors of Mill actually drew from the view, which was not Mill's, that to mean is to denote, in the toughest sense, namely that all significant expressions are proper names, and what they are the names of are what the expressions signify.

First, it is obvious that the vast majority of words are unlike the words 'Fido' and 'London' in this respect, namely, that they are general. 'Fido' stands for a particular dog, but the noun 'dog' covers this dog Fido, and all other dogs past, present and future, dogs in novels, dogs in dog breeders' plans for the future, and so on indefinitely. So the word 'dog', if assumed to denote in the way in which 'Fido' denotes Fido, must denote something which we do not hear barking, namely, either the set or class of all actual and imaginable dogs, or the set of canine properties which they all share. Either would be a very out-of-the-way sort of entity. Next, most words are not even nouns, but adjectives, verbs, prepositions, conjunctions and so on. If these are assumed to denote in the way in which 'Fido' denotes Fido, we shall have a still larger and queerer set of nominees or *denotata* on our hands, namely, nominees whose names could not even function as the grammatical subjects of sentences. . . .

Whenever we construct a sentence, in which we can distinguish a grammatical subject and a verb, the grammatical subject, be it a single word or a more or less complex phrase, must be significant if the sentence is to say something true or false. But if this nominative word or phrase is significant, it must, according to the assumption, denote something which is there to be named. So not only Fido and London, but also centaurs, round squares, the present King of France, the class of albino Cypriots, the first moment of time, and the non-existence of a first moment of time must all be credited with some sort of reality. They must *be*, else we could not say true or false things of them. We could not truly say that round squares do not exist, unless in some sense of 'exist' there exist round squares for us, in another sense, to deny existence of. Sentences can begin with abstract nouns like 'equality' or 'justice' or 'murder' so all Plato's Forms or Universals must be accepted as entities. Sentences can contain mentions of creatures of fiction, like centaurs and Mr. Pickwick, so all conceivable creatures of fiction must be genuine entities, too. Next, we can say that propositions

94 [*From British Philosophy in Mid-Century* (1957), ed. Mace, p. 239.]

are true or false, or that they entail or are incompatible with other propositions, so any significant 'that'-clause, like 'that three is a prime number' or 'that four is a prime number', must also denote existent or subsistent objects. It was accordingly, for a time, supposed that if I know or believe that three is a prime number, my knowing or believing this is a special relation holding between me on the one hand and the truth or fact, on the other, denoted by the sentence 'three is a prime number'. If I weave or follow a romance, my imagining centaurs or Mr. Pickwick is a special relation holding between me and these centaurs or that portly old gentleman. I could not imagine him unless he had enough being to stand as the correlate-term in this postulated relation of being imagined by me.

Lastly, to consider briefly what turned out, unexpectedly, to be a crucial case, there must exist or subsist classes, namely, appropriate *denotata* for such collectively employed plural descriptive phrases as 'the elephants in Burma' or 'the men in the moon'. It is just of such classes or sets that we say that they number 3,000, say, in the one case, and 0 in the other. For the results of counting to be true or false, there must be entities submitting to numerical predicates; and for the propositions of arithmetic to be true or false there must exist or subsist an infinite range of such classes.

At the very beginning of this century Russell was detecting some local unplausibilities in the full-fledged doctrine that to every significant grammatical subject there must correspond an appropriate *denotatum* in the way in which Fido answers to the name 'Fido'. The true proposition 'round squares do not exist' surely cannot require us to assert that there really do subsist round squares. The proposition that it is false that four is a prime number is a true one, but its truth surely cannot force us to fill the Universe up with an endless population of objectively existing falsehoods. . . .

It was, however, not Russell but Wittgenstein who first generalized or half-generalized this crucial point. In the *Tractatus Logico-Philosophicus*, which could be described as the first book to be written on the philosophy of logic, Wittgenstein still had one foot in the denotationist camp, but his other foot was already free. . . .

. . . It was only later still that Wittgenstein consciously and deliberately withdrew his remaining foot from the denotationist camp. When he said 'Don't ask for the meaning, ask for the use,'[95] he was imparting a lesson which he had had to teach to himself after he had finished with the *Tractatus*. The use of an expression, or the concept it expresses, is the role it is employed to perform, not any thing or person or event for which it might be supposed to stand. Nor is the purchasing power of a coin to be equated with this book or that car-ride which might be bought with it. The purchasing power of a coin has not got pages or a terminus. Even more instructive is the analogy which Wittgenstein now came to draw between significant expressions and the pieces with which are played games like chess. The significance of an expression and the powers or functions in chess of a pawn, a knight or the queen have much in common. To know what the knight can and cannot do, one must know the rules of chess, as well as be familiar with various kinds of chess-

[95] [Cf. ante, 39, n. 4.]

situations which may arise. What the knight may do cannot be read out of the material or shape of the piece of ivory or boxwood or tin of which this knight may be made. Similarly to know what an expression means is to know how it may and may not be employed, and the rules governing its employment can be the same for expressions of very different physical compositions. The word ' horse ' is not a bit like the word ' cheval '; but the way of wielding them is the same. They have the same role, the same sense. Each is a translation of the other. Certainly the rules of the uses of expressions are unlike the rules of games in some important respects. We can be taught the rules of chess up to a point before we begin to play. There are manuals of chess, where there are not manuals of significance. The rules of chess, again, are completely definite and inelastic. Questions of whether a rule has been broken or not are decidable without debate. Moreover, we opt to play chess and can stop when we like, where we do not opt to talk and think and cannot opt to break off. Chess is a diversion. Speech and thought are not only diversions. But still the partial assimilation of the meanings of expressions to the powers or the values of the pieces with which a game is played is enormously revealing. There is no temptation to suppose that a knight is proxy for anything, or that learning what a knight may or may not do is learning that it is a deputy for some ulterior entity.

[pp. 250-255]

G. WILLIAMS

International Law and the Controversy Concerning the Word ' Law ' [96]

(Revised version 1956)

It will be seen . . . that the error as to the ' proper ' meaning of words and as to ' true ' definitions is still widespread. . . .

. . . Arising out of the proper-meaning fallacy is the idea that words have not only a proper meaning but a single proper meaning. This involves a denial of the fact that words change their meanings from one context to another. To illustrate the difficulties into which this idea lands one: we commonly speak of ' early customary law ', yet a municipal lawyer refuses to say that all social customs at the present day are law. Conventions of the constitution, for instance, are not usually called ' law ' by the modern lawyer. Now it is a fact that it is practically impossible to frame a definition of ' law ' in short and simple terms that will *both* include early customary law *and* exclude modern conventions of the constitution. If it includes the one it will include the other, and if it excludes the one it will exclude the other. This leads the single-proper-meaning theorists to argue among themselves whether conventions are to be put in or early custom to be left out. The misconception again comes from supposing that there is an entity suspended somewhere in the universe called ' law ', which cannot truthfully be described as both including custom and excluding custom. When we get rid of the entity

[96] [From (1945) 22 B.Y.B.I.L. 146, and reprinted in a revised version in *Philosophy, Politics and Society* (1956), ed. Laslett, p. 134, to which present page references are given.]

idea and realize that we are defining words, we see also that there is no absolute need to use words consistently. The word ' law ' has one meaning in relation to early customary law and a different meaning in relation to municipal law. . . .

Closely connected with the last misconception is the idea that there are natural differences of ' kind ' quite independent of human classification. Thus, Leslie Stephen, in a discussion of Austin, asks whether the fact that Austin's ' laws improperly so called ' do not conform to his definition of law ' corresponds to a vital difference in their real nature. Is he simply saying, " I do not call them laws ", or really pointing out an essential and relevant difference of " kind "?' And again: ' The question then arises whether the distinction between laws and customs is essential or superficial—a real distinction of kinds or only important in classification.' [97] This language is misleading because it overlooks the fact that the concept of kind results from the process of classification, and that all classification is a man-made affair. An inquiry into whether a given difference is one of kind or of degree is a verbal, not a scientific, inquiry.

This error as to the existence of natural kinds is again closely connected with, if not simply an aspect of, the error as to the existence of natural essences. The latter error consists in the idea that the search for ' essences ' or ' fundamental features ' is in some way a factual investigation, and not merely an inquiry into the meaning of words.
[pp. 148–153]

Must these dusty disputes last for ever? They will unless we bring ourselves to realize that definitions have no importance in themselves, no importance apart from the expression and ascertainment of meaning. The only intelligent way to deal with the definition of a word of multiple meaning like ' law ' is to recognize that the definition, if intended to be of the ordinary meaning, must itself be multiple. [p. 155]

When jurisprudence comes to disembarrass itself of verbal controversies . . . there will still be some questions that may usefully be saved for discussion on their own account. Thus a comparison of international law with *municipal law* would be a factual, not a verbal, discussion.
[p. 156]

H. L. A. HART

Definition and Theory in Jurisprudence [98]

In law as elsewhere, we can know and yet not understand. Shadows often obscure our knowledge which not only vary in intensity but are cast by different obstacles to light. These cannot all be removed by the same methods and till the precise character of our perplexity is determined we cannot tell what tools we shall need.

The perplexities I propose to discuss are voiced in those questions of analytical jurisprudence which are usually characterised as requests for definitions: What is law? What is a State? What is a right? What is possession? I choose this topic because it seems to me that the common mode of definition is ill-adapted to the law and has

---

97 *The English Utilitarians* (1900), iii, pp. 322, 324.
98 [(1954) 70 L.Q.R. 37. See, also, H. L. A. Hart, *The Concept of Law*, pp. 14–17.]

complicated its exposition ; its use has, I think, led at certain points to a divorce between jurisprudence and the study of the law at work, and has helped to create the impression that there are certain fundamental concepts that the lawyer cannot hope to elucidate without entering a forbidding jungle of philosophical argument. I wish to suggest that this is not so ; that legal notions however fundamental can be elucidated by methods properly adapted to their special character. Such methods were glimpsed by our predecessors but have only been fully understood and developed in our own day.

Questions such as those I have mentioned "What is a State?" "What is law?" "What is a right?" have great ambiguity. The same form of words may be used to demand a definition or the cause or the purpose or the justification or the origin of a legal or political institution. But if, in the effort to free them from this risk of confusion with other questions, we rephrase these requests for definitions as "What is the meaning of the word 'State'?" "What is the meaning of the word 'right'?," those who ask are apt to feel uneasy as if this had trivialised their question. For what they want cannot be got out of a dictionary and this transformation of their question suggests it can. This uneasiness is the expression of an instinct which deserves respect : it emphasises the fact that those who ask these questions are not asking to be taught how to use these words in the correct way. This they know and yet are still puzzled. Hence it is no answer to this type of question merely to tender examples of what are correctly called rights, laws, or corporate bodies, and to tell the questioner if he is still puzzled that he is free to abandon the public convention and use words as he pleases. For the puzzle arises from the fact that though the common use of these words is known it is not understood ; and it is not understood because compared with most ordinary words these legal words are in different ways anomalous. Sometimes, as with the word "law" itself, one anomaly is that the range of cases to which it is applied has a diversity which baffles the initial attempt to extract any principle behind the application, yet we have the conviction that even here there is some principle and not an arbitrary convention underlying the surface differences ; so that whereas it would be patently absurd to ask for elucidation of the principle in accordance with which different men are called Tom, it is not felt absurd to ask why; within municipal law, the immense variety of different types of rules are called law, nor why municipal law and international law, in spite of striking differences, are so called.

But in this and other cases, we are puzzled by a different and more troubling anomaly. The first efforts to define words like "corporation," "right" or "duty" reveal that these do not have the straightforward connection with counterparts in the world of fact which most ordinary words have and to which we appeal in our definition of ordinary words. There is nothing which simply "corresponds" to these legal words and when we try to define them we find that the expressions we tender in our definition specifying kinds of persons, things, qualities, events, and processes, material or psychological, are never precisely the equivalent of these legal words though often connected with them in some way. This is most obvious in the case of expressions for corporate bodies and is commonly put by saying that a corporation is not a series or aggregate of persons. But it is true of other legal words. Though one

who has a right usually has some expectation or power the expression
" a right " is not synonymous with words like " expectation " or " power "
even if we add " based on law " or " guaranteed by law." And so, too,
though we speak of men having duties to do or abstain from certain
actions the word " duty " does not stand for or describe anything as
ordinary words do. It has an altogether different function which makes
the stock form of definition, " a duty is a . . . ," seem quite inappropriate.

These are genuine difficulties and in part account for something
remarkable: that out of these innocent requests for definitions of fundamental legal notions there should have arisen vast and irreconcilable
theories so that not merely whole books but whole schools of juristic
thought may be characterised by the type of answer they give to
questions like "What is a right?" or "What is a corporate body?"
This alone, I think, suggests that something is wrong with the approach
to definition; can we really not elucidate the meaning of words which
every developed legal system handles smoothly and alike without
assuming this incubus of theory? And the suspicion that something is
amiss is confirmed by certain characteristics that many such theories
have. In the first place they fall disquietingly often into a familiar triad.
Thus the American Realists striving to give us an answer in terms of
plain fact tell us that a right is a term by which we describe the
prophecies we make of the probable behaviour of courts or officials; the
Scandinavian jurists after dealing the Realist theory blows that might
well be thought fatal (if these matters were strictly judged) say that a
right is nothing real at all but an ideal or fictitious or imaginary power,
and then join with their opponents to denigrate the older type of theory
that a right is an " objective reality "—an invisible entity existing apart
from the behaviour of men. These theories are in form similar to the
three great theories of corporate personality, each of which has dealt
deadly blows to the other. There, too, we have been told by turn that
the name of a corporate body like a limited company or an organisation
like the State is really just a collective name or abbreviation for some
complex but still plain facts about ordinary persons, or alternatively that
it is the name of a fictitious person, or that on the contrary it is the
name of a real person existing with a real will and life, but not a body
of its own. And this same triad of theories has haunted the jurist even
when concerned with relatively minor notions. Look, for example, at
Austin's discussion of status [99] and you will find that the choice lies for
him between saying that it is a mere collective name for a set of special
rights and duties, or that it is an " ideal " or " fictitious " basis for these
rights and duties, or that it is an " occult quality " in the person who
has the status, distinguishable both from the rights and duties and from
the facts engendering them.

Secondly. Though these theories spring from the effort to define
notions actually involved in the practice of a legal system they rarely
throw light on the precise work they do there. They seem to the lawyer
to stand apart with their head at least in the clouds; and hence it is
that very often the use of such terms in a legal system is neutral
between competing theories. For that use " can be reconciled with any
theory, but is authority for none." [1]

[99] *Jurisprudence*, 5th ed., pp. 699–700.
[1] P. W. Duff, *Personality in Roman Private Law*, p. 215.

Thirdly.   In many of these theories there is often an amalgam of issues that should be distinguished.   It is, of course, clear that the assertion that corporate bodies are real persons and the counter-assertion that they are fictions of the law were often not the battle cries of analytical jurists.   They were ways of asserting or denying the claims of organised groups to recognition by the State.   But such claims have always been confused with the baffling analytical question " What is a corporate body?" so that the classification of such theories as Fiction or Realist or Concessionist is a criss-cross between logical and political criteria.   So, too, the American Realist theories have much to tell us of value about the judicial process and how small a part deduction from predetermined premises may play in it, but the lesson is blurred when it is presented as a matter of definition of " law " or " a right " ; not only analytical jurisprudence but every sort of jurisprudence suffers by this confusion of aim.

Hence though theory is to be welcomed, the growth of theory on the back of definition is not.   Theories so grown indeed represent valuable efforts to account for many puzzling things in law ; and among these is the great anomaly of legal language—our inability to define its crucial words in terms of ordinary factual counterparts.   But here, I think, they largely fail because their method of attack commits them all, in spite of their mutual hostility, to a form of answer that can only distort the distinctive characteristics of legal language.   [pp. 37–41]

R. WOLLHEIM

The Nature of Law

(1954) [2]

The question, What is the nature, or essence, of law? has long perplexed legal and political philosophers. . . .   Perhaps the failure to produce a conclusive answer in this matter is to be ascribed not so much to the difficulty of the question as to the ambiguity of it.   And perhaps many of the traditional answers are to be seen not as incompatible answers to the same question but as compatible answers to different questions : and the various ' schools of jurisprudence ' not as the champions of conflicting views but as the reflections of divergent yet complementary lines of research.   And this supposition is further confirmed by the way the question is phrased : What is the nature, or essence, of law?   For questions of the form, What is the nature of X? or What is the essence of X? are notoriously equivocal.   Indeed the unsatisfactory condition of political philosophy can largely be attributed to the dominating position occupied within it by questions posed in this form.

1. The first and the simplest interpretation that can be put on the formula What is the nature, or essence, of law? is to see it as raising the question, *What is the definition of ' law '*?   That is to say, the question might be a linguistic question : not a question about the phenomenon of law at all but a question about the word ' law '—this distinction between

[2] [From 2 *Political Studies* (1954), p. 128.]

questions about phenomena and questions about words being well brought out by the use of inverted commas in the formulation of the latter. Such linguistic questions can be answered in one or more of three possible ways. In the first place they can be answered by giving an *explicit* or *equipollent definition*, i.e., by giving a word or set of words that can in any sentence be substituted for any occurrence of the word to be defined so as to yield a new sentence equivalent in meaning to the old. Or they can be answered by giving a *definition in use*, i.e., by giving a series of equivalences each consisting of one sentence in which the word to be defined occurs and one sentence in which the word to be defined does not occur and that also differs from the first sentence in some further respect. From such a series we gather the use of the original word. Or finally such linguistic questions can be answered by giving an *elucidation* of the word, by giving a general characterization of what we mean by it. Such elucidations can, however, be very misleading, for the fact that they are generally couched in the material mode of speech may make us forget or overlook their essentially verbal character. We say 'Law is . . .' rather than 'The word "law" means . . .', and in saying the first may well forget that we are saying nothing that we could not say if we said the second.

But once we have recognized the purely linguistic character of these elucidations, we may easily come to question their value or importance. For how, we might ask, can a question that is merely verbal be anything but trivial? Certainly the extreme claims put forward by philosophers, either for the process of elucidation in general or for their own particular elucidation, cannot be admitted. But setting aside these exaggerated claims, can we not establish a more moderate case for the utility of these elucidations? Some philosophers will no doubt want to deny even this on the grounds that we know perfectly well how to use the words in question and that any further effort to instruct us in this matter can only result in barren scholasticism. Such an attitude is certainly congenial in its impatience with futile word-chopping. And there seems to me to be at least this much truth in it: that the value of such elucidations lies not so much in revealing to us senses of words hitherto unsuspected but in separating the real meaning of a word from accretions due to association and custom. But this in itself is no mean or otiose task.

[pp. 128–130]

2. A second question that the formula, What is the nature or essence of law? can be used to raise is the question that we could express more precisely by asking *What is the criterion of validity of law*? Now though Analytical Jurisprudence has done much to dispel many of the confusions that perplex legal philosophers, it has made little or no attempt to differentiate clearly between a definition and a criterion of validity. I think that the best way of exhibiting the distinction I have in mind is this: when we define the word 'law', we aim at producing or eliciting a rule for the use of the word that applies equally well whether we are talking about English, French, Swiss, or Bantu social life. But a criterion of validity is necessarily relative to the particular legal system. It may, of course, be the case that two legal systems employ the same criterion of validity, but this would only be coincidental. Before we can justifiably declare that a certain law is valid we must know, first, of which system it purports to be an element, and secondly what is the operative criterion

for that system. A definition is relative to a language, a criterion of validity is relative to a legal system.

Now to talk of a criterion of validity in respect of legal systems may well sound artificial. And of course it is, and intentionally so. Lawyers, judges, use the law, present cases, produce decisions, and their activity seems at first sight chaotic and without principle. However, we find that there is a permanent effort made to distinguish between statements that are statements of law and statements that are not statements of law. A task that confronts the jurist is to elicit the general principles on which this is done. We may profitably compare this activity to that of the logician who, confronted by the apparently irregular and 'natural' linguistic behaviour of people, makes a 'rational reconstruction' of a language: and, having done so, can talk about the criterion of significance of that language. Such a 'rational reconstruction' of a language does not imply that people consciously use only statements permitted by this criterion or consciously refrain from making statements prohibited by this criterion. Linguistic discrimination of this sort is intuitive and unconscious. The logician's task is to draw up the principles that logically justify such an activity—not those that psychologically prompt it. Even in such a rigorous language-system as a logical calculus, we may well have little difficulty in determining, in an intuitive fashion, whether certain formulae are or are not theorems of that calculus: and only later attempt to formalize what we have been doing by laying down the decision-procedure for that calculus.

3. However, there also exists an important and interesting line of inquiry which has been almost universally misunderstood—and certainly no less by its practitioners than by its critics. Let us look at this. As we have seen, a criterion of legal validity is necessarily relative to a legal system; each system has its own criterion, and to ask for a criterion without specifying the system is analogous to asking for the method of scoring without specifying the game. But, it has been felt, perhaps what we can give is, not a general criterion of validity for all systems, but *a general schema for the criterion of validity of any system*; a skeleton, as it were, that any criterion must satisfy if it is to fulfil its proper task— just as we might hope to give, not a general method of scoring, but a schema that any method must satisfy.[3]   [pp. 131–132]

J. STONE

Legal System and Lawyers' Reasonings

(1964)

. . . It can be said that juristic thought, from Austin to the present, though with individual variations, has tended to converge on a definition of law which we immediately state in seven cumulative steps. . . .

First, by definitional fiat, law is recognised as a complex whole of many phenomena. What precisely this predication of unity can

---

[3] [This, in Wollheim's view, was what Austin's theory of sovereignty aimed at achieving (see *op cit.*, pp. 133–137). But it should be borne in mind that Austin was expressly limiting his criterion to developed systems: see *ante*, 21.]

mean, and what are the factors working to make it a reality, are questions which no mere definition can answer; but their elaboration is a main concern of the present work.[4]

Second, these phenomena within this whole include <u>norms regulating behaviour</u>, that is, <u>prescribing what the behaviour ought to be, forbidding what it ought not to be, or declaring what it is permitted to be</u>.[5] The function of a norm, be it noted, is not only to guide the main behaviour envisaged but also to guide those who make decisions about the standing of that behaviour.[6] The term " norm " tends to be selected in preference to " rule " because this more familiar English term " rule " may have associations limited to a prescription of a course of behaviour as distinct from conduct on a particular occasion, a distinction indeed made much of by Austin and his followers.[7] A definitional fiat excluding the prescription of behaviour for a particular occasion is difficult to justify to lawyers, much of whose activity is increasingly concerned not only with judicial decisions but with the effect of administrative action in particular concrete situations.

While it scarcely needs expressing that the behaviour in question is of human beings,[8] it should perhaps be said that it includes " internal " behaviour. It should be added that the term " behaviour " seems preferable to " conduct," insofar as the latter is associated in usage with behaviour which is willed, and it seems best not to conclude, by mere definition whether a norm can prescribe that a man ought or ought not to do what he cannot, by an act of will, do or refrain from doing. It is debatable whether the rational and humane maxim *lex non cogit ad impossibilia*[9] represents today a boundary of the concept of law for most lawyers. Even if we ignore such arbitrary phenomena as the language or similar tests practised even in some democratic States to ensure the exclusion of undesired immigrants, or voters from voting, all lawyers are aware that much of the legal regulation of the modern State has objectives to which it is irrelevant whether behaviour is willed or not.

Third, <u>the norms which law embraces in a complex unity are *social norms*</u>, that is, they generally regulate behaviour of a member of society

---

4 See esp. Ch. 1, §§ 1 *et seq.*; *infra* this Chapter, §§ 7 *et seq.*; Ch. 6, §§ 1 *et seq.* And see the fourth *proprium* listed *infra*.

5 See, however, M. Villey, " Une Définition du Droit " (1959) 4 Arch. de Phil. du Droit 47, at p. 50, who says that law consists of an activity and (p. 52) that the sources of the juridical art are not reducible to rules. The former statement is, as the author himself expects, " *pénible à digérer* ". The latter statement can be accepted with the observation that for the " juridical art " there may be several sources, only one of which is law.

6 *Cf.* Pound, 3 *Jurisprudence* 5, according to whom " law in the sense of the legal order has for its subject-matter relations of individual human beings with each other and the conduct of individuals so far as they affect others or affect the social or economic order. Law in the sense of the body of authoritative grounds of . . . judicial decision and administrative action has for its subject-matter the expectations or claims or wants held or asserted by individual human beings or groups of human beings which affect their relations or determine their conduct."

7 See Austin, *Province Determined*, p. 19; [*The Concept of*] *Law*, p. 9: " . . . to say that a rule exists means . . . that . . . people . . . behave ' as a rule ', *i.e.*, generally in a specified similar way. . . ."

8 Hence the definition here envisaged is not useful in relation to the legal orders of primitive people, the norms of which refer also to the putative behaviour of putative entities such as gods, demons, and angels, as well as to the behaviour of animals.

9 See I. Tammelo, Book Review (1960–61) 13 J.Leg.Ed. 550.

vis-à-vis others, and only exceptionally, as in the rules against suicide, in relation only to himself. Conceivably, there need only be two persons involved to satisfy the present point, even if one of them himself issues the norms, for there is nothing in the present approach to definition, as there was in Austin's sovereign command theory, which prevents the law being reflexive in this way.

The next step, the fourth, on which a wide degree of convergence is apparent, is that the complex "whole" of phenomena which "law" comprises is an orderly whole, that is, one whose parts are not merely chaotically thrown together. It is in short a "legal order." And while this correctly emphasises that the relations between the parts are not of mere arbitrary conglomeration, it also stops short of claiming that the relations are entirely orderly, i.e. that they are strictly systematic. Clearly there are many points at which even the most systematic law falls short of orderliness in whatever terms this be conceived; and it may indeed be that certain antinomies are inescapable in any legal order which actually functions.

Fifth, the order of social norms, of which law consists, is now widely seen to be characteristically a coercive order. "Coercive" means that the authority of law is supported, where required, by acts of external compulsion such as deprivation of life, health, liberty, or property, or the withholding of benefits of these kinds. While troublesome confusions still occur,[10] it seems clear that Austin's attempt to require each legal norm to be coercively supported, has been abandoned in favour of the view that it is the "order" as a whole, and not each particular norm comprised in it, that must be so qualified; so that many *leges imperfectae* may still be included in a legal order.[11] Moreover, again steering away from Austinian rigidity, it is recognised that self-help of the injured subject may, under given conditions, satisfy the requirement that the order be coercive, thus leaving open the standing of the international legal order. The *proprium* of being supported by coercion is particularly aimed to set off a legal from a moral order, reliance on external coercion to support the latter not being essential; though of course some moral norms may be enforced by coercion even to the point that they also become embodied in the legal order. Coerciveness as a mark of a legal order does not, of course, mean that this is the only factor pressing to secure law-observance.

Also not fatal to this *proprium*, if properly understood, are the reminders given by social and legal historians and anthropologists that noncoercive "legal" orders can be found in a number of societies. The instances vouched fall usually into two categories. In one category, though there is no coercive enforcement of the legal order in Austin's sense of emanating from determinate sovereign superiors, there may

---

[10] See, *e.g.*, as to A. Ross's recent work *On Law and Justice* (1958) on this matter, P. Stone "Social Engineers and Rational Technologists" (1961), 13 Stan. L.R. 670, 681.

[11] See for an unusual modern problem, *National Trustees Exors. Case* (1954) 91 C.L.R. 540, esp. Dixon C.J. and the majority at pp. 558, 571–572, 584–587. The question was whether estate duty was leviable on the statutory benefit of distribution (not yet made at death) under a wool scheme. The statutory benefits were deemed not to be "rights" since unenforceable and inalienable, as contrasted with the identical benefits when these restraints are wholly or partly removed, which might be "rights." Presumably, however, the conferring rules were in either case "law."

still be institutionalised coercion in the present sense. In the other category of instances, probably a very small one, it seems sensible to acknowledge that the maxim *ubi societas ibi ius* may not have universal validity, particularly not for the simpler undeveloped societies. The fact that it seems necessary to include the element of coercion as a basis for explaining what a legal order is, is no reason for refusing to admit that there may be normative orders whose authority rests on brotherly love, fear of supernatural forces, or even some sort of enlightened understanding of what is expedient, right and proper.[12]

By a similar token, the inclusion of the element of coercion as a mark of a legal order, does not necessarily import any denial that observance may in part proceed from the supposed force of "natural law" with which the legal order is assumed to coincide. And even insofar as the supposed provinces of natural law do not coincide with those of the coercive legal order, so that this part of the definition is not useful for the explication of natural law, the latter still remains a matter of deep jurisprudential concern, at least on the present view that jurisprudence is "the lawyer's extraversion." For it is clearly a most important medium, historically, through which men's socio-ethical convictions, as well as their speculations concerning justice, morals and human dignity, have penetrated all social life and activity, including legal orders.

Sixth, as we have already presaged, the coercion by which the order of social norms is supported is an institutionalised coercion,[13] that is, the coercion itself is brought to bear according to established norms, even when it consists of the self-help of the aggrieved party. The coercion is not merely spontaneous and capricious, as in a lynching, or an act of vengeance.

Seventh, this institutionalised coercive order of social norms should have a degree of effectiveness sufficient for the order to maintain itself. The legal order must, in other words, by and large regulate in fact the behaviour of its subjects, and not merely purport to do so. If the purpose of the definition of law which is here being sketched were to enable a lawyer (or for that matter the ordinary citizen) to decide whether a particular norm is a legal norm, the inclusion of the present requirement would quite destroy its value. For clearly the present requirement, of "effectiveness by and large" is quite indeterminate, at any particular time, and also variable from time to time. Legal officials will scarcely suspend action until they have investigated how many people conform their behaviour to how many norms and how often; moreover, even if they could make this calculation the definition gives them no quantitative guide for measuring the result.

But in the present view the purpose of definition is not to provide a

---

12 *Cf.* J. Salmond, *Jurisprudence* (7th ed., 1954), p. 51, who takes the view that primitive law may be regarded as "the primeval substitutes for law."
13 Thus the institutionalist theory of law centred on the law as a product of, or indeed (in the case of Romano) as identical with, the institutionalised structure of the making, application and enforcement of rules. This led to recognition of the plurality of "legal orders" within an inclusive society ranging from that of the State through even to those of organised gangs, even though these were "outlawed" by the State. It is strange to find this being presented in 1961 as a discovery made by A. Ross in 1958, when it was fully developed by Romano in 1918. (See Hughes, "The Existence of a Legal System," 35 N.Y.U.L.R. 1001, 1029.) And see Stone, *Social Dimensions*, Ch. 11.

test for declaring that a particular norm is or is not law; the *propria* attributed to law by the definition are rather rubrics which serve as an outline, or index, or table of contents, of the matters which most clearly call for explication in connection with the notion of law in general. From this point of view, to omit any reference to effectiveness as a going order would certainly be to overlook an aspect of all legal orders which both lawyers and citizens generally tend always to regard as essential. Conversely, to include it, even though its indeterminacy leaves it open to a degree of variable subjective judgment, does at least ensure that those who offer these variable judgments are talking about the same phenomenon—that (for instance) one side is not talking about normative orders operative in society, while the other is talking about an order consisting merely of symbols on paper.[14]

Whether, eighthly, we must add with Kantorowicz, as a *differentia specifica* of law, that the institutionalised effective coercive order of social norms must be considered to be judicially cognisable by the "judicial organs" and by the subjects[15] who obey them, is more debatable. As A. L. Goodhart observes, Kantorowicz did not have the opportunity to develop this concept in full. One thing he had in mind was, no doubt, that the norms "must be sufficiently precise and defined to furnish a possible basis of decision."[16] But he also appears to have had in mind that norms "considered fit" for judicial determination would display a twin tendency towards "justice and impartiality," and the growth of a "multiform class of professional lawyers."[17] On this basis "justiciability" might indeed be a desirable further *proprium*. For without it it could be argued that institutionalised coercive orders of social norms of groups like Chicago gangs, or the Mafia, are usefully regarded as legal orders, though neither "judicial organs," nor lawyers nor people generally habitually so regard them.

[14] It should perhaps be added that on the present threefold division of the tasks of jurisprudence, reference to conformity by and large may be relevant in three ways. (1) It may be said as a sociological observation that a majority of subjects *do* conform to the law. (2) It may be mentioned as a *proprium* of the *concept* of law that for "law" to be present it must be possible to say this; and this is all that is at present intended. (3) It may be said that subjects or particular subjects *should* conform to the law. But the questions whether and in what conditions this last (3) can be said (on which see R. A. Wasserstrom and R. D. Lumb, 10 U.C.L.A.L.Rev. 780, and in Summers, *Essays in Legal Philosophy* (1968) and Tammelo, Blackshield and Campbell, *Australian Studies In Legal Philosophy* (1963), pp. 195–218) are *moral* questions on which both (1) and (2) above are quite inconclusive, if not simply irrelevant. As for (1), it might at most be *relevant* to the moral question as bringing law-conformity into the range of "what one does." See Stone, *Social Dimensions*, Ch. 12. As for (2), even apart from the indeterminacy stressed in the text, it obviously does not equate "law" as a concept with "that which is to be obeyed." However, it might conceivably (especially when conjoined with the second *proprium* mentioned in the text) equate "law" as a concept with "that which by its mere existence raises the *question* of obedience or disobedience as a relevant question"; and this may be more meaningful than the claim that we are "*prima facie*" obliged to obey, which Wasserstrom (pp. 783–784 and *passim*) rightly criticises. [*Cf. post*, 283.]

[15] He speaks of the "element of being 'considered fit' for 'some kind of procedure,'" and says that "'considered' should be used with regard to those who actually apply the rules or wish them to be applied," *op. cit.*, p. 73. And see generally pp. 76–77 where he admitted his formula to be "vague" and open to "doubts" and "uncertainty."

[16] *Idem*, xxiv.

[17] *Idem*, 77.

As already observed, the phrases " judicially cognisable," " justiciable," " judicial courts," " judicial organs," are to be taken to refer to " any definite authority concerned with a certain kind of ' casuistry,' to wit, the application of principles to individual cases of conflict between parties." [18] Clearly the essence here is not personnel or form of organisation, but the characteristics of the activity of the institution, impartial third-party settlement, deliberation in the course of settlement, and application of methods of juristic reasoning, in applying rules to cases. Nor is the reference limited to courts of law, for this (as Kantorowicz himself points out) would involve a circularity.[19]

Here again, it must be apparent that a definition of which this would be a requirement cannot serve as more than an outline, or index, or table of contents, for an explication of those matters which require to be discussed for an understanding of " law." [20] In particular, it cannot serve as a touchstone of whether a particular norm is a legal norm under a particular legal order. For many volumes have to be read, and as many still to be written, really to convey what is meant by " justiciable"; and even then resorts would also be necessary to ostensive definition by observing the bodies themselves in which these activities are performed. Kantorowicz, indeed, thought the " subjective ingredient " imported into the notion of law by this requirement was a great advantage, since (he thought) the failure to include " a subjective criterion " was a main defect of most definitions of law offered up to his time.[21]

[pp. 179–183]

SHAW v. DIRECTOR OF PUBLIC PROSECUTIONS [22]

[1962] A.C. 220

The appellant published a booklet, the Ladies' Directory, most of which was taken up with the names and addresses of prostitutes ; the matter published left no doubt that the advertisers could be got in touch with at the telephone numbers given and were offering their services for sexual intercourse and, in some cases, for the practice of sexual perversions. The appellant's avowed purpose in publication was to assist prostitutes to ply their trade when as a result of the Street Offences Act, 1959, they were no longer able to solicit in the street. The prostitutes paid for the advertisements and the appellant derived a profit from the publication.

. . . *Held* (Lord Reid dissenting), that a conspiracy to corrupt public morals was a common law misdemeanour and that there was evidence fit to be left to the jury on which the appellant could be found guilty of this offence.

---

[18] *Idem*, 69.
[19] See esp. 77.
[20] Accordingly, we would say that the worthwhile response to an offered definition is not so much " a practical assent " as a *recognition* and consequential *insight*.
[21] See H. Kantorowicz [*The Definition of Law*], p. 72. [See also *ante*, 49.]
[22] [For some recent decisions in which the relationship of law to morality forms a crucial feature of the judgment, see *Weatherley* v. *Weatherley* [1947] A.C. 628; *Baxter* v. *Baxter* [1948] A.C. 274; *Fender* v. *St. John-Mildmay* [1937] A.C. 1; *Williams* v. *Williams* [1964] A.C. 698; and *Gollins* v. *Gollins* [1964] A.C. 644; *Mohammed* v. *Knott* [1969] 1 Q.B. 1.]

LORD SIMONDS. . . .

. . . My Lords, as I have already said, the first count in the indictment is " Conspiracy to corrupt public morals," and the particulars of offence will have sufficiently appeared. I am concerned only to assert what was vigorously denied by counsel for the appellant, that such an offence is known to the common law, and that it was open to the jury to find on the facts of this case that the appellant was guilty of such an offence. I must say categorically that, if it were not so, Her Majesty's courts would strangely have failed in their duty as servants and guardians of the common law. Need I say, my Lords, that I am no advocate of the right of the judges to create new criminal offences? I will repeat well-known words: " Amongst many other points of happiness and freedom which your Majesty's subjects have enjoyed there is none which they have accounted more dear and precious than this, to be guided and governed by certain rules of law which giveth both to the head and members that which of right belongeth to them and not by any arbitrary or uncertain form of government." These words are as true today as they were in the seventeenth century and command the allegiance of us all. But I am at a loss to understand how it can be said either that the law does not recognise a conspiracy to corrupt public morals or that, though there may not be an exact precedent for such a conspiracy as this case reveals, it does not fall fairly within the general words by which it is described. I do not propose to examine all the relevant authorities. . . . The fallacy in the argument that was addressed to us lay in the attempt to exclude from the scope of general words acts well calculated to corrupt public morals just because they had not been committed or had not been brought to the notice of the court before. It is not thus that the common law has developed. We are perhaps more accustomed to hear this matter discussed upon the question whether such and such a transaction is contrary to public policy. At once the controversy arises. On the one hand it is said that it is not possible in the twentieth century for the court to create a new head of public policy, on the other it is said that this is but a new example of a well-established head. In the sphere of criminal law I entertain no doubt that there remains in the courts of law a residual power to enforce the supreme and fundamental purpose of the law, to conserve not only the safety and order but also the moral welfare of the State, and that it is their duty to guard it against attacks which may be the more insidious because they are novel and unprepared for. That is the broad head (call it public policy if you wish) within which the present indictment falls. It matters little what label is given to the offending act. To one of your Lordships it may appear an affront to public decency, to another considering that it may succeed in its obvious intention of provoking libidinous desires it will seem a corruption of public morals. Yet others may deem it aptly described as the creation of a public mischief or the undermining of moral conduct. The same act will not in all ages be regarded in the same way. The law must be related to the changing standards of life, not yielding to every shifting impulse of the popular will but having regard to fundamental assessments of human values and the purposes of society. Today a denial of the fundamental Christian doctrine, which in past centuries would have been regarded by the ecclesiastical courts as heresy and by the common law as blasphemy, will no longer be an offence if the decencies of controversy are observed. When Lord Mansfield, speaking long after the Star Chamber had been abolished, said [23] that the Court of King's Bench was the *custos morum* of the people and had the superintendency of offences *contra bonos mores*, he was asserting, as I now assert, that there is in that court a residual power, where no statute has yet intervened to supersede the common law,[24] to superintend those offences which are prejudicial to the public welfare. Such occasions will be rare, for Parliament has not been slow to legislate when attention has been sufficiently aroused. But gaps remain and will always remain since no one can foresee every way in which the wickedness of man may disrupt the order of society. Let me take a single instance to which my noble and learned friend, Lord Tucker, refers. Let it be supposed that at some future, perhaps early, date homosexual practices between adult consenting males are no longer a crime. Would it not be an offence if even without obscenity, such practices were publicly advocated and encouraged by pamphlet and advertisement? Or must we wait until Parliament finds time to deal with such conduct? I say, my Lords, that if the common law is powerless in such an event, then we should no longer do her reverence. But I say that her hand is still powerful and that it is for Her Majesty's judges to play the part which Lord Mansfield pointed out to them. . . .[25]

. . . I will say a final word upon an aspect of the case which was urged by counsel. No one doubts—and I have put it in the forefront of this opinion—that certainty is a most desirable attribute of the criminal and civil law alike. Nevertheless, there are matters which must ultimately depend on the opinion of a jury. In the civil law I will take an example which comes perhaps nearest to the criminal law—the tort of negligence. It is for a jury to decide not only whether the defendant has committed the act complained of but whether in doing it he has fallen short of the standard of care which the circumstances require. Till their verdict is given it is uncertain what the law requires. The same branch of the civil law supplies another interesting analogy. For, though in the Factory Acts and the regulations made under them, the measure of care required of an employer is defined in the greatest detail, no one supposes that he may not be guilty of negligence in a manner unforeseen and unprovided for. That will be a matter for the jury to decide. There are still, as has recently been said, "unravished remnants of the common law." [26]

So in the case of a charge of conspiracy to corrupt public morals the uncertainty that necessarily arises from the vagueness of general words can only be resolved by the opinion of twelve chosen men and women. I am content to leave it to them.

The appeal on both counts should, in my opinion, be dismissed.

[pp. 266–269]

[23] *Rex* v. *Delaval* (1763) 3 Burr. 1434, 1438, 1439.

[24] [So, in a recent case accepting *Shaw* the House of Lords distinguished the instant case upon the basis that Parliament had, indeed, legislated. See *D.P.P.* v. *Bhagwan* [1970] 3 All E.R. 97, 104–105.]

[25] [The removal of homosexual offences between consenting male adults was accomplished by the Sexual Offences Act 1967 and following Viscount Simonds' prediction it has recently been held by the Court of Appeal (Criminal Division) that the common law is not powerless in such an event. See *R.* v. *Knuller & Others* [1971] 3 W.L.R. 633.

[26] Lord Radcliffe, *The Law and its Compass*, p. 53.

LORD REID. . . .

    . . . There are two competing views. One is that conspiring to corrupt public morals is only one facet of a still more general offence, conspiracy to effect public mischief; and that, like the categories of negligence, the categories of public mischief are never closed. The other is that, whatever may have been done two or three centuries ago, we ought not now to extend the doctrine further than it has already been carried by the common law courts. Of course, I do not mean that it should only be applied in circumstances precisely similar to those in some decided case. Decisions are always authority for other cases which are reasonably analogous and are not properly distinguishable. But we ought not to extend the doctrine to new fields. . . .

    . . . Even if there is still a vestigial power of this kind it ought not, in my view, to be used unless there appears to be a general agreement that the offence to which it is applied ought to be criminal if committed by an individual. Notoriously, there are wide differences of opinion today as to how far the law ought to punish immoral acts which are not done in the face of the public. Some think that the law already goes too far, some that it does not go far enough. Parliament is the proper place, and I am firmly of opinion the only proper place, to settle that. When there is sufficient support from public opinion, Parliament does not hesitate to intervene. Where Parliament fears to tread it is not for the courts to rush in. . . .

    . . . But in argument more stress was put on words which are reported to have been used by the judges than on the actual decisions, and in particular on the statement by Lord Mansfield and others that the Court of King's Bench was custos or censor morum. It was said that they thereby decided or recognised that any conspiracy to corrupt morals or, as the learned trial judge put it in the present case, " to lead morally astray " was an indictable offence. I do not think so. As the reports of those days are not full reports of the judgments, we do not have the precise context, but I think it much more probable that those judges were intending to say that they then had power to create new offences, that this power extended to the moral field, and that the acts in these particular cases should be held to be punishable. It must be observed that these references to the court being censor or custos morum occur equally in decisions in cases of conspiracy and in cases against individuals. In the eighteenth century courts created new offences in the field of morals both against individuals (see, for example, *Curl's* case [27]) and against combinations. So if, contrary to my view, the references established a general offence of conspiring to corrupt public morals, then surely they must also have established that it is a general offence for an individual to act so as to corrupt public morals or to attempt to do so. If it was established in the eighteenth century that there was a general offence of conspiring to corrupt public morals (or to lead members of the public morally astray) then, as the essence of criminal conspiracy is doing or agreeing to do an unlawful act, it must follow that for two centuries every act which has tended to lead members of the public astray morally has been an unlawful act, and the respondent's argument would apply equally to make unlawful every act which tends to lead a

[27] (1727) 2 Stra. 788.

single individual morally astray. In the unending controversy about the proper relationship between law and morals no one seems to have suspected that. Hitherto, I think, there has been a wide measure of agreement with Professor Kenny's view that only _certain_ acts which are _outrageously_ immoral are unlawful in this sense. . . .

. . . Finally I must advert to the consequences of holding that this very general offence exists. It has always been thought to be of primary importance that our law, and particularly our criminal law, should be certain: that a man should be able to know what conduct is and what is not criminal, particularly when heavy penalties are involved. Some suggestion was made that it does not matter if this offence is very wide: no one would ever prosecute and if they did no jury would ever convict if the breach was venial. Indeed, the suggestion goes even further: that the meaning and application of the words " deprave " and " corrupt " (the traditional words in obscene libel now enacted in the 1959 Act [28]) or the words " debauch " and " corrupt " in this indictment ought to be entirely for the jury, so that any conduct of this kind is criminal if in the end a jury think it so. In other words, you cannot tell what is criminal except by guessing what view a jury will take, and juries' views may vary and may change with the passing of time. Normally the meaning of words is a question of law for the court. For example, it is not left to a jury to determine the meaning of negligence: they have to consider on evidence and on their own knowledge a much more specific question—Would a reasonable man have done what this man did? I know that in obscene libel the jury has great latitude but I think that it is an understatement to say that this has not been found wholly satisfactory. If the trial judge's charge in the present case was right, if a jury is entitled to water down the strong words " deprave," " corrupt " or " debauch " so as merely to mean lead astray morally, then it seems to me that the court has transferred to the jury the whole of its functions as censor morum, the law will be whatever any jury may happen to think it ought to be, and this branch of the law will have lost all the certainty which we rightly prize in other branches of our law.[29]

[pp. 274–282]

---

28 [Obscene Publications Act 1959, s. 1.]
29 [This decision has aroused a good deal of criticism in so far as it appears to suggest that the courts are custodians of morality, and, therefore, have an unspecified discretion to extend the ambit of the criminal law by recognising new types of offences against morality. Apart from introducing a considerable element of uncertainty in the administration of the law, this also seems to be contrary to the fundamental principle of Western criminal jurisprudence, that there should be no criminal sanction without a prior established law (_nulla poena sine lege_). Moreover, there seems to be a departure from the principles of the rule of law acknowledged in democratic countries, and a tendency to blur the basic contrasts between the canons of Western and of totalitarian legal systems, under which courts have sometimes been given a discretion to punish what is contrary to " sound national feeling." The main impact of the *Shaw* decision has been in the area of obscene publications. When difficulty was encountered with the Obscene Publications Act 1959 (and later 1964) *Shaw* was frequently invoked to circumvent its problems. More recently the Obscene Publications Acts have resulted in successful prosecutions (*e.g.*, *The Little Red School Book*, and *Oz No. 28*, and in the latter an attempt to use *Shaw* failed), so it may be that its future use will be limited.]

3

NATURAL LAW

NATURAL law thinking has occupied a pervasive role in the realms of ethics, politics, and law from the earliest times. Indeed, so numerous are its forms and so varied its disguises that many an empiricist may end by resignedly applying to it the Horatian tag: *furca expellas tamen usque recurret*. At some periods its appeal may have been essentially religious or supernatural, but in modern times it has formed an important weapon in political and legal ideology. Essentially it has afforded a valuable aid to the powers that be, desirous of justifying the existing law, and the social and economic system it embodied, for by regarding positive law as based on a higher law ordained by God or by divine or natural reason, the actual legal system thus acquired a sanctity it would not otherwise possess.[1] And though the possibility of conflict existed between the two laws, this rarely, if ever, arose in practice and was usually met by a presumption in favour of existing law. The idea of natural rights similarly had its origin in conservative forces anxious to sanctify property (symbol of the existing order) as the fundamental human right overriding even the right to life itself.[2] Yet there lurked behind this notion an equally revolutionary factor in its emphasis on human equality, which was already in evidence in the American Declaration of Rights and became fully manifest with the outbreak of the French Revolution. The reaction which this provoked, coupled with other factors which will be mentioned later, resulted in a diminished respect for natural law theories as such during the nineteenth century. During the present century there are signs of a revival, though these are not easy to evaluate.

IDEALISM AND POSITIVISM [3]

Any attempt to split human thought into rigid categories is bound to fail. But certain broad trends or attitudes are nevertheless discernible, and although the division may be as suspect as the belief expressed in Gilbert's *Iolanthe* that everyone is born a little Conser-

---

[1] *Cf.* Kelsen, *What is Justice?*, p. 137 *et seq.*; also V. Gordon Childe, *What Happened in History*, pp. 211–217; and Ross, *On Law and Justice* (1958), pp. 258–262.

[2] Kelsen, *op. cit.*, p. 153.

[3] *Cf. post*, 164, note 66.

vative or a little Liberal, it remains a useful starting point to emphasise how certain minds have leaned towards idealism, while others have heartily rejected this in favour of positivism or empiricism. This cleavage is to be observed in most, if not all, forms of human thought, of which philosophy, history and ethics afford useful illustrations. Indeed it is even to be found in the arts and literature, whose exponents may be segregated into adherents of either the romantic or the classical approach.[4] The idealist attitude received its most famous and influential exposition in Plato's theory of ideas. On this theory the physical phenomena of the world are mere manifestations of a superior order laid up in heaven and should be studied only in order to gain insight into the ultimate pattern. Those whose eyes are fixed on the " apparent " facts of this world are likened to dwellers in a cave studying but the shadows on the wall of the real events happening outside.[5] Incidentally this attitude is also associated with another unfortunate consequence of Platonism, namely, the belief that words have an intrinsic meaning which can be ascertained by proper inquiry and which thereby leads us to the immutable essence of the things for which they stand.[6] It also tends to look for absolutes, such as absolute justice.

Positivism,[7] on the other hand, prefers observable facts to metaphysics, and although not averse to abstractions, such as sense-data, does not look for or accept a higher reality over and above the external world of the senses. It therefore tends to be secular, empirical, and relativist, and concentrates on things as they are rather than as they might or ought to be.[8]

At first sight natural law would seem to be essentially an idealist conception, and it is true that this has indeed been its characteristic in many phases of its long history. Thus natural law has often been pictured as an ideal system laid up in heaven of which positive law can be but an imperfect simulacrum. Yet positivist and empirical thinkers have also at times deployed natural law ideas. When they have done so, however, they have tended to associate it with the physical laws of nature (including human nature itself) rather than with an ideal system of law. Hence natural law has been envisaged

---

[4] The classical artist seeks to discover some universal order behind the individual phenomena, whereas the romantic artist is more empirical, relying rather on the emotional experience of the individual.

[5] See, *Republic*, vii, 514.

[6] *Cf. ante*, 40.

[7] The word we owe to Comte; but English philosophy, except for a brief period at the end of the nineteenth century, has long been associated with empiricism.

[8] The literature abounds currently with attempts at reconciliation. The best examples are Jenkins (1959–60) 12 *Journal of Legal Education* 1 and D'Entrèves, *Natural Law* (1970), Additional Essays B and C. Also of interest, though simplifying the problem, is Dias, *A Temporal Approach to Natural Law* (1970) C.L.J. 75.

as a mere law of self-preservation,[9] or as an operative law of nature (either man's or the universe's) constraining him to a certain pattern of behaviour, though without necessarily any belief in any higher purpose inherent in such a law.

Also it should be observed that juristic, like other theories, sometimes cut across this division. Thus the approach of the sociological jurist, such as Pound, is basically empirical, yet by its reliance on a pre-established canon of values it seems to partake of idealist natural law thinking, so that Friedmann even feels justified in calling it sociological idealism.[10] Yet this approach is markedly secular and also relativist in its emphasis on *changing* values. So, too, Bentham was fundamentally a positivist whose *bêtes noires* were natural law and metaphysics; yet, in some ways, his principle of utility was a canon of value not susceptible of proof but only justifiable if at all by a metaphysical argument,[11] and therefore idealist in character.

No real categorisation is therefore possible, yet it may assist clarity of thought if we recognise as idealists only those jurists who believe in some higher system to which mere positive law should conform.

GREEK ORIGINS

If there are traces to be discerned of the conception of natural law among almost all peoples,[12] it is nevertheless to the Greeks that we must look for the primary source of western allegiance to this pervasive notion. Whether the law of nature was first conceived as governing the cosmos and thence applied to man or society, or whether (as Kelsen contends) the idea of universal law was a projection of the law of the state into the physical universe, may well be disputed. Certainly the notion of divine retribution operating in human affairs [13] tended to create confusion between natural law as a norm prescribing conduct and physical law compelling it, and Kelsen even suggests that it was not till Hume that the idea of causality as a norm directed at nature by the divine will was substantially abandoned.[14]

---

[9] As in Hobbes, see *post*, 178. Or in Hart, *post*, 130. See D'Entrèves, *op. cit.* pp. 193–194.

[10] *Legal Theory*, 5th ed., Chap. 27.

[11] This was admitted by Bentham himself: see *Principles of Morals and Legislation*, Chap. I, § 11.

[12] See, *e.g.*, as to China, J. Needham, *Science and Civilisation in China*, vol. 2 (1956), Chap. 18, p. 518 *et seq.*; and for Hebraic civilisation see H. Silving (1953) 28 N.Y.U.L.Rev. 1129, and Lloyd, *The Idea of Law* (1964), pp. 48–51.

[13] For an attempt to derive natural law thinking from an " approach to life compounded of magic, religion and metaphysics," see A. Ross, *Law and Justice* (1958), p. 227 *et seq.*

[14] Kelsen, *op. cit.*, p. 314 *et seq.*

The Greeks themselves, though comparatively uninterested in the technical development of law, were much concerned in exploring its philosophical foundations, and in doing so evolved many fundamental concepts, of which natural law was one of the most important. In the classical period, however, little attention was paid to the idea of universal law, though it was current doctrine that there was in each city-state a body of law (νόμος), fundamental and unchangeable and often unwritten, and which it was a usurpation to override, though the assembly might pass decrees changing the law in matters of less moment.[15] Plato, by his idealist philosophy, laid the foundations for much of subsequent speculation on natural law themes, but he had nothing to say on natural law as such in the sense of a normative and overriding system of rules. Indeed his *Republic* was based on the substitution for law of the philosopher-king, who could attain absolute justice by consulting the mystery locked in his own heart, which partook of the divine wisdom but remained uncommunicable to lesser mortals. And even Aristotle, for whom nature played a cardinal role in the unfolding of man's social development, was so little interested in natural law in the form of normative rules that he contented himself with a passing reference to the distinction between natural and conventional justice, while immediately qualifying this by pointing out that, among men, even natural justice is not necessarily unchanging.[16]

It is with the decline of the city-state and the rise of large empires and kingdoms in the Greek world, associated with the conquests of Alexander, that natural law as a universal system comes to the fore, and for this the stoic philosophers were particularly responsible. They stressed the ideas of individual worth, moral duty and universal brotherhood, and though in the early days theirs was a philosophy of withdrawal enjoining conformity to the universal law upon the select few of wise men alone, in its later development, especially under Panaetius of Rhodes, in the second century B.C., stress was placed on its universal aspects as laying down a law not only for the wise, but for all men.[17]

---

[15] See Aristotle, *Politics* (ed. E. Barker), pp. 127–128. The odium attached to legislative innovation is dramatically illustrated by the fact that the existing law had to be arraigned in a prosecution and that among the Locrians, the "prosecutor" had to appear with a halter round his neck, which was drawn tight if his proposal was rejected. *Cf.* Ehrenberg, *The Greek State* (1969), 2nd ed., pp. 56–58.

[16] See *post*, 91. This was put forward as a counter-blast to the Sophist view of law as purely conventional (see *Republic*, Bk. II). For a defence of the positive humanist viewpoint of the Sophists, see A. Ross, *op. cit.*, pp. 240–241. For Sophist views on natural law and the equality of all men thereunder, see also Lesky, *History of Greek Literature* (1966), p. 359.

[17] The rival and less important school of Epicurus was typically positivist, equating morality with expediency.

Jus Gentium

It was in this form, especially through the Greek-loving Scipionic circle, that Stoicism passed over to and influenced Roman thought. But the more pragmatic mind of the Roman jurist was little interested in " higher law " and regarded it as more suitable for oratorical rhetoric.[18] The opening sentence of Gaius's *Institutes* (c. A.D. 160) may be regarded in this light,[19] as can Ulpian's " what nature has taught all animals," [20] though the latter was taken at face-value by Aquinas, and vestiges plague even contemporary polemics.[21]

But conquest and commerce necessitated the development of law which could be applied to foreigners, *peregrini. Jus Gentium,* the *jus civile* stripped of formalities and with cosmopolitan trimmings, was the result. Against the intellectual background of stoicism, the Roman jurists can be forgiven the fact that they confused the law they applied universally with the law of nature which stoicism had taught was of universal validity. In truth, this was but an early example of the " naturalistic fallacy," [22] a confusion of " is " and " ought," of what Jolowicz called " practical " and " theoretical " *jus gentium.*[23]

Medieval Period

Throughout the Middle Ages, the theology of the Catholic Church set the tone and pattern of all speculative thought. As Gierke has pointed out, two vital principles animated medieval thought: *unity,* derived from God, and involving one faith, one Church, and one empire, and the *supremacy of law,* not merely man-made, but conceived as part of the unity of the universe.[24] Yet, until Aquinas in the thirteenth century, Christian thought [25] was also bedevilled by the notion of law and human dominion being rooted in sin. It was not the least of Aquinas's contributions that, in his synthesis of Aristotelian philosophy and Catholic faith in a universal divine law, he

---

[18] See Cicero, *post,* p. 92. D'Entrèves, *Natural Law* calls them " ornamental commonplaces " (p. 28).

[19] *Viz.* " That law which a people establishes for itself is peculiar to it, and is called *jus civile* (civil law) as being the special law of that *civitas* (state), while the law that natural reason establishes among all mankind is followed by all peoples alike, and is called *jus gentium* (law of nations, or law of the world) as being the law observed by all mankind," as translated by De Zulueta, *The Institutes of Gaius,* Part 1.

[20] See Justinian's *Institutes post,* p. 93.

[21] See, for example, the recent Papal Encyclical, *Humanae Vitae* in Harris, *et al., On Human Life* (1968). The essay by Keane, p. 27, is particularly instructive.

[22] *Ante,* p. 9.

[23] *Post,* p. 93. D'Entrèves, *Natural Law* provides a glowing account of natural law in Roman writings and a panegyric of its heritage. See Chap. 1.

[24] *Political Theories of the Middle Age* (ed. Maitland), p. 9 *et seq.*; p. 73 *et seq.*

[25] See, for example, the 5th chapter of St. Augustine's *Civitas Dei.*

rejected the idea that civil government was necessarily tainted with original sin and argued for the existence of a hierarchy of law derived ultimately from God, and in which human or positive law had a rightful though lowly place and was worthy for its own sake.[26]

The difference between practice and theory was never more manifest than in the medieval period, with its high-sounding moral doctrine combined with barbarous usages and strong-arm justice. Thus the universal recognition that civil law was subordinate to natural law and invalid if infringing it (though Aquinas distinguished between primary and secondary natural law, the latter being to some extent destructible [27]) had little significance in practice, as witness the attitude to usury prescribed by natural law, yet indulged in by the Popes themselves.[28] Sometimes an English court would declare that a statute contrary to natural law or reason would be void,[29] but as Pollock remarked, " in England it was never a practical doctrine "[30]; to use Maitland's phrase, "little came of it."[31]

SIXTEENTH TO EIGHTEENTH CENTURIES

The Renaissance led to an emphasis on the individual and a rejection of the universal collective society of medieval Europe in favour of independent national states, and, where the Reformation followed, separate national Churches.[32] Thought begins to take a secular cast, as exemplified by Machiavelli, who examined human institutions without regard for divine prescriptions, and in the light of naked expediency. Natural law survived, and indeed was used by Grotius

---

26 See T. Gilby, *Principality and Polity*, p. 146 *et seq.*

27 *Post*, 100. Aquinas is not specific on the question *when* a secondary precept can change. The general opinion of theological commentators seems to be that this happens upon the occurrence of social, economic or technological upheaval. The Renaissance was the watershed that hit the prohibition on usury; perhaps the population explosion and world food shortage, together with the changed status of woman, will lead to a change in the ban on birth control and non-acceptance of divorce. Or are these prohibitions primary rules and therefore unchangeable? On the proper classification of rules of private property and commerce see McLaren, *Private Property and the Natural Law* (1948) (Aquinas papers no. 8).

28 *Cf.* T. Gilby, *op. cit.*, pp. 183–184. The prohibition of usury was recognised (by Cardinal Cajetan in the sixteenth century) as a secondary precept and, therefore, capable of change. (O'Connor, *Aquinas and Natural Law* (1967), p. 78.)

29 A final attempt was Coke C.J.'s in *Bonham's* Case (1610) 8 Rep. 114, 118, on which see Gough, *Fundamental Law in English History* (1955), pp. 30–38. He maintains that by " adjudg[ing] them to be utterly void " Coke meant interpreting strictly so that the case fell outside the statute. Both Plucknett (40 Harv.L.R. 30) and Thorne (54 L.Q.R. 543) suggest that Coke's *authorities* do not support any doctrine of higher law. See also Lewis, 84 L.Q.R. 330 where Coke's pronouncement is dismissed as " mere rhetoric."

30 *Expansion of the Common Law*, pp. 121–122.

31 *Select Legal Essays*, p. 124.

32 Even in some Catholic countries, especially France, the Church adopted a distinctively nationalist attitude. In France this was known as Gallicanism.

and others as the foundation of a new international law to regulate the affairs and warfare of the rising national states, but it became distinctly secular,[33] and more lawyer-like and indeed Romanist in character. At the same time it was used, together with the more popular though not in itself novel [34] theory of the social contract, either to bolster up,[35] or in some cases to restrain,[36] the new-found weapon in the lawyers' and politicians' armoury of legal sovereignty. By the eighteenth century it had become identified with universal reason,[37] but it was dealt severe blows both by that age's supreme rationalist, David Hume, who rejected the existence of natural law and the social contract as contrary to empirical truth, and also indirectly by that most irrational of thinkers, Rousseau, who emphasised the revolutionary aspect of the doctrine by his arguments in favour of inalienable sovereignty vested in the " general will," as opposed to any individual ruler or oligarchy. By the end of the century the French Revolution had shown how what was primarily a conservative doctrine justifying existing law could be turned into a dangerous weapon of subversion, and the philosopher Kant had in any event reduced it to a bloodless category, a categorical imperative of a purely formal kind of universal application but without material content.

NINETEENTH CENTURY

The time had come to explore other paths, and two of these became dominant during the succeeding century. Rousseau, by his emphasis on the mystic collective power of the " general will" which he attributed to every political society, paved the way for the more extreme idealist position of Hegel, who ended by deifying the state as a higher reality implicit in the laws of history and the consciousness of the people, whose individual wills only attain full realisation in this form. The state was an end-in-itself and absolutely sovereign, a

---

[33] Thus Grotius asserted that human nature is the mother of natural law, and that it would operate even if God did not exist. See *De Jure Belli ac Pacis*, proleg. 11.

[34] This idea can be traced at least as far back as the Greek Sophists; see *per* Glaucon in Plato's *Republic*, Bk. II. Silving *op. cit.* sees the seeds of social contract in God's covenant with man as reported in the Old Testament. On social contract theories, generally, see Gough, *The Social Contract* (1957) and Barker's introduction to the World Classics edition of *The Social Contract* (1947).

[35] As in Hobbes.

[36] As in Locke, whose doctrine of natural rights was later embodied in the United States Declaration of Independence and Constitution. *Cf. post*, 113.

[37] The eighteenth century has been called the Age of Reason by its excessive faith in rationalism. Thus whole systems of natural law were expounded as derivable from pure reason, though they strongly bore the influence of Roman law, which was believed to embody the *ratio juris*. *Cf.* Schulz, *Principles of Roman Law*, pp. 38–39, 100.

product of the laws of history but not otherwise subject to an external natural law. Later in the century, the rise of Darwinism led to an attempt to see the law of evolution and natural selection as a sociological phenomenon automatically regulating man's relations in society.[38] Both attitudes involved the rejection of a normative natural law in favour of a causal law dominating the actual course of events.

The other and equally important movement was positivist in approach, and sought to relegate natural law to the sphere of morals and religion, and to segregate man-made law as a distinct phenomenon whose validity did not rest on divine or supernatural sanctions. Such was the doctrine of the influential Utilitarians, followers of Bentham. Austin gave this approach its classic expression in his imperative theory.[39]

TWENTIETH CENTURY [40]

Yet the idea of an overriding law expressing a higher truth and a higher justice than that embodied in man-made law is not easily extinguished.[41] On the one hand some detect signs of this doctrine even among those who reject it, as, for instance, in the principle of utility of Bentham. Lundstedt asserts that all schools of jurisprudence (except his own) adopt the natural law approach, by admitting what he terms the " method of justice," whereby the law is developed according to what is deemed objectively just in accordance with an imaginary " material " law underlying the positive legal rules.[42] Apart from this, the decline in social and economic stability in the present century, with the resulting expansion in governmental activity,[43] coupled with reviving doubts as to the method of the empirical sciences affording the sole avenue to truth, have led to some reaction in favour of natural law thinking. In England, positivism still remains dominant, and natural law or justice is but rarely invoked (and then usually with a sneer or an apology) by the

---

[38] Herbert Spencer exemplified this approach.

[39] But the analytical jurisprudence of Austin resembled that of the natural lawyers in being primarily conceptual; also Austin interpreted both natural and positive law in terms of command; God's and the sovereign's respectively.

[40] For an attempt to appraise the question whether the doctrine of natural law, either in its traditional or modern dress, has anything useful to contribute to the problem of justice in the modern world, see Dennis Lloyd, " Legal and Ideal Justice ", in *Legal Essays to Castberg* (1963), p. 111.

[41] *Cf.* H. J. Laski to Holmes J.—" The truth is that we are witnessing a revival of ' natural ' law and natural is the purely inductive statement of certain minimum conditions we can't do without if life is to be decent " (*Holmes-Laski Letters*, I, 116–117).

[42] *Post*, 512.

[43] *Cf.* Carl Friedrich, *The Philosophy of Law in Historical Perspective* (1963), pp. 178–179.

judge or practising lawyer.[44] This, however, is not to say that it may not occasionally reappear in a disguised form,[45] as well as being dressed up for formal occasions.[46] In the United States the existence of fundamental rights in the Constitution has given more scope for the natural lawyer,[47] and the Universal Declaration of Human Rights is essentially a natural law document. On the Continent, idealism has long remained the dominant philosophy,[48] and natural law thinking is by no means as alien among Continental lawyers (especially in Catholic countries) as in those of common law countries.

In the realm of theory, first, there are the neo-scholastics who follow and further refine the doctrines of Aquinas, officially adopted as part of the teaching of the Catholic Church since 1879.[49] Then there are the formal idealist schools, who seek to set up a formal structure of just law and then strive, however unsuccessfully, to give it a material content, such as Stammler in Germany, and del Vecchio in Italy. Lastly, there are empirical and sociological lawyers, such

---

[44] There may be occasional references to natural law in such matters as parental relations (see, *e.g.*, *Re Carroll* [1931] 1 K.B. 717; for a recent Canadian case on this topic placing far greater emphasis on natural law, see *Chabot* v. *Lamorandière* [1957] Q.B. 707, and notes thereon in (1958) 36 Can.B.R. 248, and (1958) 4 McGill L.R. 279 *et seq*.); and where foreign law is involved (see, *e.g.*, *National Bank of Greece* v. *Metliss* [1958] A.C. 509, 525: see also *Adams* v. *National Bank of Greece* [1961] A.C. 255). See further *Chaplin* v. *Boys* [1971] A.C. 356, on which Graveson has written (85 L.Q.R. 505, 507–508): " the only matter which four of them [Law Lords] used as a positive factor, while a fifth found it unnecessary to mention, was the factor of justice " (to Graveson, justice is the underlying rationale of the whole of conflict of laws). Other illustrations are *Starkowski* v. *A.-G.* [1954] A.C. 155; *Formosa* v. *Gray* [1963] P. 259; *Middleton* v. *Middleton* [1967] P. 62, and most recently *Meyer* v. *Meyer* [1971] 1 All E.R. 378. Also natural justice is invoked in some cases, *e.g.*, in quasi-contract (see *Holt* v. *Markham* [1923] 1 K.B. at p. 513, where Scrutton L.J. stigmatised this as " well-meaning sloppiness of thought "). And see the recent developments in administrative law, *e.g.*, *Anisminic* v. *Foreign Compensation Commission* [1969] 2 A.C. 147 of which Yardley has written: [it is] " conclusive that *every* breach of natural justice makes a decision void." (*Source Book of Administrative Law* (1970), p. 97); and P. J. Fitzgerald, " Crime, Sin and Negligence " (1963) 79 L.Q.R. 351, on *mala in se*. For natural justice in African territories, see *post*, 569.

[45] *e.g.*, under the concepts of reasonableness, and of public policy: see Sir F. Pollock, *Jurisprudence and Legal Essays* (ed. A. L. Goodhart), pp. 142, 149.

[46] Thus in welcoming the American Bar Association to London in 1957, Lord Kilmuir L.C. referred to " the doctrine which we share with a wider community even than that of the Common Law but which has for various reasons become a little dusty and old-fashioned in recent years and which I myself would like to see refurbished and restored to the position which it once used to occupy. I refer to the doctrine of the law of nature, one of the noblest conceptions in the history of jurisprudence " (*The Times*, July 25, 1957).

[47] Though for the most part the higher law envisaged was, as Judge Arnold has pointed out, little more than " the folklore of capitalism ": see Thurman Arnold, *Folklore of Capitalsm* (1937). Bodenheimer, *Jurisprudence* (1962) gives a useful résumé of post-war natural law writings in the United States. The rekindling of naturalism in the United States is seen in the development of the *American Journal of Jurisprudence* (formerly *Natural Law Forum*). The Vietnam war has done much to keep up interest in idealistic jurisprudence. See the discussion on civil disobedience, *post*, 147.

[48] See Passmore, *100 Years of Philosophy*, pp. 318–321, 459–461.

[49] Encyclical, *Aeterni Patris*, 1879.

as Gény; among these also may be reckoned Duguit, who, while rejecting a metaphysical natural law, seeks to re-establish overriding principles in the name of social solidarity. Among common lawyers there are also signs in some quarters of a desire to establish or recognise, as an inner core of the law itself, a moral standard which must accept or reject individual rules according as they conform to what is believed to be objective justice.

FULLER AND THE MORALITY OF LAW

Outstanding among such attempts are the urbane writings of Lon Fuller.[50] His Harvard Law Review [51] debate with Professor Hart is well-known. More recently he has developed themes from this in *The Morality of Law*, which, in its turn, has led to an ongoing debate with a number of leading positivists.[52]

For Fuller the connection between law and morality is a necessary one. But, unlike earlier naturalists, he does not argue that the rules of a legal system must conform to any substantive requirements of morality, or to any other external standard; rather, he postulates the need for rules of law to comply with " internal morality."

He draws a distinction, initially, between the morality of duty and the morality of aspiration. The former corresponds to an external morality of law. It consists in those fundamental rules without which society could not exist.[53] But Fuller's demands go further. He sees law as a " purpose activity "; the morality of aspiration exhorts mankind to strive for ideals, to fulfil their potentialities in a Platonic way.[54] So Fuller lists eight typical ideals or formal virtues to which a legal system should strive.[55] These principles of legality are not basic conditions which every system necessarily fulfils, but constant

---

[50] See " Positivism and Fidelity to Law " (71 Harv.L.R. 630) *post*, 243, *The Morality of Law* (revised edition 1969), *Anatomy of the Law* (1968) and *Human Interaction and the Law* in (1969), 14 *American Journal of Jurisprudence*, 1.

[51] *Post*, 243.

[52] See, for example, Hart (1965) 78 Harv.L.R. 1281, Summers (1965) 18 *Journal of Legal Education* 1, and in ed. Summers, *More Essays in Legal Philosophy* (1971), p. 101, and see the symposium in 10 *Villanova Law Review*, pp. 631–678 (Murray, Dworkin, Cohen and a reply by Fuller at pp. 655–666). The fifth chapter of *The Morality of Law* (revised edition) is an extended reply to critics, in which Fuller develops his thesis that the legal system is not a unidirectional exercise of authority (" managerial direction ") but an interactional process. See also his treatment of custom in (1969) 14 *American Journal of Jurisprudence* 1, referred to in note 50, and see *post*, 598.

[53] *Cf.* Hart's " minimum content of natural law " *post*, 84, 130.

[54] *Cf. ante*, 77 and *post*, 89.

[55] *Viz.* " generality, promulgation, absence of retroactive legislation and certainly no abuse of retrospective legislation, no contradictory rules, congruence between rules as announced and their actual administration, clarity, avoidance of frequent change, absence of laws requiring the impossible." See *Morality of Law*, Chap. 2.

polestars guiding its progress. The greater its success, the more fully
legal such a system would be.

Implicit in this analysis is a rejection of a finite definition of
law. Fuller is critical, for example, of Dworkin's [56] assertion that,
whilst baldness is a matter of degree, a line can be drawn between
law and non-law, that, to quote Fuller, "law does not just fade
away, but goes out with a bang." [57]

Fuller does not develop the relationship between the form in
which legal rules are expressed and their content. As was suggested
earlier,[58] the Nazi legal system was faithful, with one possible
exception, to Fuller's canons, yet it was able to promulgate the
Nuremberg racial laws, laws utterly offensive to all human values.
Fuller must surely believe that form has a direct bearing on content,
for otherwise his principles would be nothing more than the tools
of an efficient craftsman. But no such relationship is delineated
by him. Until this gap is filled it is difficult to disagree with critics
who argue that Fuller's account betrays confusion between efficacy
and morality. One can accept the need for legality, as most of Fuller's
critics do,[59] and yet, to quote Hart, still object " to the designation
of these principles of good legal craftsmanship as morality, in spite
of the qualification ' inner,' [as] perpetrat[ing] a confusion between
two notions that it is vital to hold apart: the notions of purposive
activity and morality." [60] Is there a lapse in morality when an
assassin forgets to load his gun? [61, 62]

HART ON NATURAL LAW

One of the most significant contemporary characteristics of jurisprudence is the coming together of positivism and natural law.[63] In
the last section Fuller's mild, some might even think, shallow version
of naturalism was presented, and it was seen how Hart, among

---

[56] In 10 *Villanova Law Review* at pp. 677–678.
[57] *Morality of Law*, p. 199.
[58] *Ante*, 47.
[59] See, *e.g.*, *The Concept of Law*, p. 202 or Dworkin, *op. cit.* p. 609. But Kelsenian doctrine of identity of Law and State would render any such principles
utterly superfluous (*post*, 324). Hart's acceptance of the value of Fuller's canons
seems to commit him to a utilitarian ideology (see 78 Harv.L.R. 1281, 1291).
[60] 78 Harv.L.R. 1281, 1285.
[61] A question asked by Maxwell Cohen, 10 *Villanova Law Review*, pp. 640, 651.
[62] An interesting recent attempt to restate Fuller, has been made by Lyons (1971)
Proc.Aristot.Soc. 105. He reduces Fuller's principles to one of " followability "
i.e. a legal requirement that cannot be followed is defective. He then argues
that what we regard as unjust is not such defective rules themselves but " the
way individuals who run afoul of unfollowable requirements are treated. Were
they not penalised we would not call their treatment unjust " (p. 114). The
dichotomy drawn between law-making and law-enforcement seems to ignore
another of Fuller's principles, *viz.* the necessity for congruence between declared
rule and official action.
[63] See note 8 *ante*, and *post*, 130.

others, had been severely critical of Fuller's formulation. But positivists today are less positivistic than they were a very few years ago,[64] and Hart himself, in many ways the leader of contemporary positivism, has himself attempted to restate a natural law position from a semi-sociological point of view.[65] Hart points out that there are certain substantive rules which are essential if human beings are to live continuously together in close proximity. "These simple facts constitute a core of indisputable truth in the doctrines of natural law."[66] Hart places primary emphasis here on an assumption of survival as a principal human goal. We are concerned, he says, with social arrangements for continued existence, and not with those of a suicide club. There are, therefore, certain rules which any social organisation must contain, and it is these facts of human nature which afford a reason for postulating a "minimum content" of natural law.

In fact, however, Hart does not go on to state the actual minimum universal rules, but certain facts of the "human condition" which must lead to the existence of some such rules (but not necessarily rules with any specific content). These facts of the human condition Hart describes as consisting of human vulnerability; approximate equality; limited altruism; limited resources; and limited understanding and strength of will. What he argues is, that in the light of these inevitable features of the human condition, there follows[67] a "natural necessity" for certain minimum forms of protection for persons, property and promises. "It is in this form that we should reply to the positivist thesis 'law may have *any* content'."[68]

However, Hart does not seek to suggest that, even if this analysis of human society is accepted, this must inevitably lead to a system of even minimal justice within a given community. On the contrary, he accepts the fact, as indeed is hardly to be denied, that human societies at all periods of history have displayed a melancholy record of oppression and discrimination in the name of security and legal order, as, for instance, in the case of systems based on slavery, or

---

[64] Nuremberg and Hiroshima, Sharpeville and Vietnam must be in some measure responsible for this. Dworkin himself is an interesting case in point, for, whilst his earlier writings are undoubtedly of positivist character, there are now signs of a naturalist trying to break out. See his critique of Hart's reductionist impulse, *post*, 172, and his discussion of the Chicago Conspiracy trial, *The Listener*, October 8, 1970, pp. 485–487, and his "On Not Prosecuting Civil Disobedience," *New York Review of Books*, June 6, 1968.

[65] *The Concept of Law*, pp. 189–195 and see *post*, 130.

[66] p. 176.

[67] Is Hart attempting to derive a value from a fact, thus transgressing Hume's law (*ante*, 31)? See Sir Isaiah Berlin for a suggestion that Hart is doing this, in *Does Political Theory still Exist?* in, *inter alia, Philosophy, Politics and Society*, 2nd series, ed. Laslett and Runciman (1962), p. 27.

[68] p. 195.

systems based on positive religious or racial discrimination, all too familiar in the modern world.

A number of comments seem called for upon this approach to a minimum content for natural law. In the first place, it must be clear that this approach must not be confused with an attempt to establish some kind of "higher law" in the sense of overriding or eternally just moral or legal principles, but is merely an attempt to establish a kind of sociological foundation for a minimum content for natural law. The justification for the use of the term natural law here is that regard is paid to what is suggested to be the fundamental nature of man as indicated in Hart's five facts of the human condition. It must be pointed out, however, that these "facts," apart from being extremely vague and uncertain in most respects, do not depend upon sociological investigation, but are really an intuitive appraisal of the character of the human condition.[69]

Moreover, it is difficult to see how any real minimum content whatever can be based upon such principles as those formulated. For example, the factor of human vulnerability seems necessarily to restrict the use of violence. But the need for human survival has not prevented the acceptance in many societies of the exposure of infants or the killing of slaves or children by those exerting power over them. Moreover, a society may actually base its survival upon the need for human slaughter. Thus the ancient Mexican civilisation possessed a religious and state system which required the perpetual propitiation of the gods by continuous human sacrifice on a massive scale. In relation to such a society, which attained in other respects a high measure of civilisation, it seems difficult to talk in terms of individual human vulnerability as it might be conceived in a developed modern state, which acknowledges as a fundamental principle the value of individual life and security.[70]

Again, although Hart refers to the implications of what he calls the approximate equality between human beings, he himself recognises that no universal system of natural law or justice can be based upon the principle of impartiality, or that of treating like cases alike.[71] For the essential question here is by what criteria we are to determine which cases are to be treated as alike, and no such feature of the physical or psycho-somatic condition of human beings as embodied in the idea of approximate equality can indicate how a society may decide which cases are alike for this purpose. Hindu

---

[69] For a discussion of this point, and a comparison with the method of Hobbes, see D'Entrèves, *Natural Law* (1970), p. 194.

[70] Though developed modern states accept killing in war, execute criminals, abort foetuses. No modern society has abolished the motor car. Minimum content based on human vulnerability will always be culturally-biased, or a general principle with stated exceptions. *Cf.* Mead, *post*, 144.   [71] *Cf. post*, 732.

society may justify distinguishing between categories of persons on the footing of the caste system, and other societies may regard as essentially unlike, slaves and freemen, or black and white, and so forth. The rule of equality, therefore, cannot be derived from any formal principle of impartiality, any more than it can be derived from the physical or psychic nature of human beings or from the character of human practice and experience in this or other ages. The idea of equality or non-discrimination is essentially a value-judgment which cannot be derived from any assertions or speculations regarding the nature of man. No insistence, therefore, on the idea of impartiality, or the rules of natural justice, or the " inner morality " of the law in the sense used by Professor Fuller [72] can afford a basis for arriving at such a principle as that of non-discrimination. This, indeed, is fully recognised by Hart himself, when he remarks that the idea of impartiality is " unfortunately compatible with very great iniquity." [73]

D'Entrèves,[74] a sympathetic critic of Hart's minimum content, has pointed to yet another gap in his treatment of natural law. For, whilst Hart unequivocally accepts the key positivist tenet that the validity of a legal norm " does not depend in any way on its equity or iniquity," [75] he tells us that natural law contains " the elementary principles which men must respect as long as men are what they are and propose to set up a viable society." [76] " Are we," D'Entrèves asks, " to conclude that natural law is a central and privileged sphere of morality distinguished by its sacred and inviolable character?" [77] Does this mean that outside the area of the minimum content laws of any iniquity may stand? And, even within it, what is the status of laws which flagrantly violate that minimum protection for which Hart's natural law stands? Are such laws laws and, if so, what, if any, is the right of resistance? To what extent can " evil laws " permeate a system before that set-up becomes no more than a suicide club? D'Entrèves is clearly right to ask for clarification.[78]

CONCLUSION

Behind all these attempts [79] to find a place for a higher law may be discerned a feeling of discontent with justice based on positive

[72] See *ante*, 83, and *post*, 138.
[73] p. 202. *Cf.* Barry, *Political Argument*, *post*, 373.
[74] See *Natural Law*, Appendix C. [75] *Idem*, p. 199.
[76] *Idem*. [77] *Idem*.
[78] D'Entrèves makes a number of other pertinent comments on Hart's approach. See pp. 198–203. *Cf.* also *post*, 133.
[79] The search continues. Among recent attempts to construct universal principles are Northrop's thesis of " first-order " facts (see *The Complexity of Legal and Ethical Experience* (1959) Chap. 21 and see comments in Lloyd, *Introduction to Jurisprudence* (2nd ed.) pp. 64–66), Arnold Brecht's introspective empiricism (*Political Theory* (1959) Chaps. 9 and 10), Jerome Hall's synthesis of positivism

law alone, and a strenuous desire to demonstrate that there are objective moral values which can be given a positive content and expressed in normative form, and that law which denies or rejects these values is self-defeating and nugatory. How, for instance, can we honour with the name of law many of the inhuman decrees of the Nazi state? [80] With this feeling we may sympathise, but the belief in objective moral values is easier to assert than to justify rationally. Hume long ago pointed out the logical objection to any attempt to transmute " ought " into " is " (*i.e.*, to attempt to derive normative statements from statements of *fact*) [81] and it may be questioned whether recent attempts to bridge this gulf succeed in overcoming this basic obstacle.[82] Value judgments do not state *facts* but indicate choices or preferences, though it may be acknowledged that such choices are not necessarily completely arbitrary or random, but may be based on rational argument and persuasion,[83] and in this sense therefore, need not be characterised, *pace* Kelsen and Lundstedt, as purely subjective. But it is difficult to avoid the reflection that even if a universally acknowledged set of values could be established, so that in this qualified sense it could be said that such a code " exists " as a *fact*,[84] its content would be likely to be so vague and subject to so much qualification, as to be vacuous.[85]

---

and natural law in what he calls " integrative jurisprudence " ((1964) 33 *Cincinnati Law Review* 153). Though neo-Thomism still flourishes (see, *e.g.* Brown's restatement of Aquinian thought, 31 Tul.L.Rev. 491), natural law today is but a pale reflection of its former strength. This is perhaps reflected in the belief current among a number of prominent naturalists that natural law has but a limited role to play and that there is some value in positivism. So, O'Meara (5 Natural L.F. 83) wrote that he did not " envisage natural law as the arbiter of legal validity," and D'Entrèves has pressed that natural law must become less abstract, must respect the integrity and autonomy of the legal order. Thus, whilst D'Entrèves is critical of the " statist " theory of positivism (*cf.* Hart, *post*, p. 164), and its ideology, he approves of its method. It " certainly contains an answer to the question *quid iuris*." (p. 176.) See also the attempts to build natural law on an existentialist approach to the human person in John XXIII's Encyclical, *Pacem in Terras* (1963), or Rodes, 2 *Natural Law* Forum 88.

[80] *Cf.* Fuller, op. *cit.*, p. 650 *et seq.*; and J. Hall, who raises the issue whethe̦ there can be said to be " law " in Soviet Russia, *op. cit.*, p. 142; but *cf.* H. J. Berman, " Soviet Law and Government," in (1958) 21 M.L.R. 19. But where is the line to be drawn? How is one to distinguish law so offensive to human values as to be null and void and law which is objectionable (*e.g.* apartheid) and yet accepted among many countries. The dilemma is well described by Friedmann in ed. Hook, *Law and Philosophy* (1964), pp. 144, 148–149, 151–154.

[81] *Ante*, 31.

[82] *Cf. post*, 83. See also W. H. Whyte, *The Organisation Man* (1951), pp. 28–30, on the attempt to determine ethics " scientifically " through the concept of " equilibrium," one of those " murky words so serviceable to obscuring contradiction " (p. 29). Moore's theory that " good " is a simple unanalysable " non-natural " quality like " yellow," which we know directly by intuition is a form of objectivism, but even if accepted (which few philosophers do) it does not solve the problem of reconciling conflicting intuitions. *Cf. ante*, 9, and Nowell-Smith, *Ethics*, Chap. 3, and p. 237.

[83] See *post*, 729.   [84] *Cf. ante*, 55.

[85] *Cf. per* Lord Shaw in *L. G. B.* v. *Arlidge* [1915] A.C. at p. 138; Weldon *Vocabulary of Politics*, p. 128.

PLATO

Republic [86]

[The " Idealist " philosophy of Plato] [87]

Now we said that ignorance must correspond to the unreal, knowledge to the real. So what he is believing cannot be real nor yet unreal.

True.

Belief, then, cannot be either ignorance or knowledge.

It appears not.

Then does it lie outside and beyond these two? It is either more clear and certain than knowledge or less clear and certain than ignorance?

No, it is neither.

It rather seems to you to be something more obscure than knowledge, but not so dark as ignorance, and so to lie between the two extremes?

Quite so.

Well, we said earlier that if some object could be found such that it both *is* and at the same *is not*, that object would lie between the perfectly real and the utterly unreal; and that the corresponding faculty would be neither knowledge nor ignorance, but a faculty to be found situated between the two.

Yes.

And now what we have found between the two is the faculty we call belief.

True.

It seems, then, that what remains to be discovered is that object which can be said both to be and not to be and cannot properly be called either purely real or purely unreal. If that can be found, we may justly call it the object of belief, and so give the intermediate faculty the intermediate object, while the two extreme objects will fall to the extreme faculties.

Yes.

On these assumptions, then, I shall call for an answer from our friend who denies the existence of Beauty itself or of anything that can be called an essential Form of Beauty remaining unchangeably in the same state for ever, though he does recognize the existence of beautiful things as a plurality—that lover of things seen who will not listen to anyone who says that Beauty is one, Justice is one, and so on. I shall say to him, Be so good as to tell us: of all these many beautiful things is there one which will not appear ugly? Or of these many just or righteous actions, is there one that will not appear unjust or unrighteous?

No, replied Glaucon, they must inevitably appear to be in some way both beautiful and ugly; and so with all the other terms your question refers to. . . .

It seems, then, we have discovered that the many conventional notions of the mass of mankind about what is beautiful or honourable or just and so on are adrift in a sort of twilight between pure reality and pure unreality.

[86] Translated, F. M. Cornford.
[87] *Cf. ante*, 74. See also Lloyd, *The Idea of Law* (1964), pp. 74–77. For a recent, and rare, attempt to restate idealism see Iris Murdoch, *The Sovereignty of Good* (1970).

We have.

And we agreed earlier that, if any such object were discovered, it should be called the object of belief and not of knowledge. Fluctuating in that half-way region, it would be seized upon by the intermediate faculty.

Yes.

So when people have an eye for the multitude of beautiful things or of just actions or whatever it may be, but can neither behold Beauty or Justice itself nor follow a guide who would lead them to it, we shall say that all they have is beliefs, without any real knowledge of the objects of their belief.

That follows.

But what of those who contemplate the realities themselves as they are for ever in the same unchanging state? Shall we not say that they have, not mere belief, but knowledge? [88]

That too follows. [pp. 182–184; v. 478–479]

ARISTOTLE

Politics [89]

Because it is the completion of associations existing by nature, every polis [90] exists by nature, having itself the same quality as the earlier associations from which it grew. It is the end or consummation to which those associations move, and the 'nature' of things consists in their end or consummation; for what each thing is when its growth is completed we call the nature of that thing, whether it be a man or a horse or a family. Again [and this is a second reason for regarding the state as natural] the end, or final cause, is the best. Now self-sufficiency [which

---

[88] [Thus for Plato justice is not to be attained by a legal system, but by the unfettered rule of the philosopher-king who has attained knowledge of absolute justice. It is usually supposed that Plato turned to a second-best alternative in his *Laws* when an attempt to put the *Republic* into practice in Dionysian Sicily proved an abject failure. (See Barker, *Greek Political Theory*, pp. 113–116.) But as T. A. Sinclair points out (*A History of Greek Political Thought* (1951), p. 182): "there could never have been any question of establishing in Syracuse the Ideal State of the *Republic*. . . . None of the conditions needed for its establishment was to be had and he was given no thirty years in which to train Guardians. . . . Plato never imagined any mortal man in [the] exalted role except himself; and he was offered no such post at Syracuse." This has persuaded some (*e.g.* Hall, *Studies in Jurisprudence and Criminal Theory* (1958), Chap. 3) that Plato viewed this second-best as the best *actual* state. For a rather different interpretation, see G. R. Morrow, *Plato's Cretan City* (1960), Chap. 12. Morrow argues that though in founding the ideal city the lawgiver is entirely free to follow reason in establishing its laws and institutions, after these have been established, the rulers become "guardians of law" and are bound by it. However, Morrow concedes that in the ideal state of the *Republic*, as against that of the *Laws*, the guardians are only morally and not legally bound.

Plato's *Laws*, in which the blueprint of a Spartan totalitarian society is spelt out in minute detail, have been condemned successively as irrational, militarist, totalitarian, racialist, and reactionary by such writers as Popper, *The Open Society and its Enemies*, and Crossman, *Plato Today*. But, see the spirited defence in Wild, *Plato's Modern Enemies and the Theory of Natural Law* (1953).]

[89] [Translated, Sir Ernest Barker.]   [90] [*i.e.*, city-state.]

it is the object of the state to bring about] is the end, and so the best; [and on this it follows that the state brings about the best, and is therefore natural, since nature always aims at bringing about the best].

From these considerations it is evident that the polis belongs to the class of things that exist by nature, and that man is by nature an animal intended to live in a polis.[91] He who is without a polis, by reason of his own nature and not of some accident, is either a poor sort of being, or a being higher than man. . . .

. . . We may now proceed to add that [though the individual and the family are prior in the order of time] the polis is prior in the order of nature to the family and the individual. The reason for this is that the whole is necessarily prior [in nature] to the part.[92] If the whole body be destroyed, there will not be a foot or a hand, except in that ambiguous sense in which one uses the same word to indicate a different thing, as when one speaks of a ' hand ' made of stone ; for a hand, when destroyed [by the destruction of the whole body], will be no better than a stone ' hand '. All things derive their essential character from their function and their capacity ; and it follows that if they are no longer fit to discharge their function, we ought not to say that they are still the same things, but only that, by an ambiguity, they still have the same names.[93]

[pp. 5–6; 1253 a, §§ 9, 12, 13]

ARISTOTLE

Nicomachean Ethics [94]

Natural and legal justice

Of political justice part is natural,[95] part legal—natural, that which everywhere has the same force and does not exist by people's thinking this or that; legal, that which is originally indifferent, but when it has been laid down is not indifferent, e.g. that a prisoner's ransom shall be a mina, or that a goat and not two sheep shall be sacrificed, and again all the laws that are passed for particular cases, e.g. that sacrifice shall be made in honour of Brasidas, and the provisions of decrees. Now some think that all justice is of this sort, because that which is by nature is unchangeable and has everywhere the same force (as fire burns both here and in Persia), while they see change in the things recognized as just. This, however, is not true in this unqualified way, but is true in a sense ; or rather, with the gods it is perhaps not true at all, while with us there is something that is just even by nature, yet all of it is changeable [96];

---

91 [This is the meaning of the phrase, " a political animal." ($\zeta\tilde{\omega}ov$ $\pi o\lambda\iota\tau\iota\kappa\acute{o}v$).]

92 [For Aristotle, the nature of a thing is conditioned by its end or purpose: the form of the oak is potentially in the acorn which determines every stage of its development. As a biologist, Aristotle applies the same notion to man in society.]

93 [Words in square brackets are added by the translator.]

94 [Translated, Sir David Ross.]

95 [Cf. the discussion on the nature of justice in Plato, *Republic*, 367 (Cornford's translation, pp. 51–52).]

96 [As a biologist Aristole could not contemplate an unchanging nature; but beyond the sub-lunary region all was eternal and unchangeable: see Popper, *The Open Society*, II, p. 271.]

but still some is by nature, some not by nature. It is evident which sort of thing, among things capable of being otherwise, is by nature; and which is not but is legal and conventional, assuming that both are equally changeable. And in all other things the same distinction will apply; by nature the right hand is stronger, yet it is possible that all men should come to be ambidextrous. The things which are just by virtue of convention and expediency are like measures; for wine and corn measures are not everywhere equal, but larger in wholesale and smaller in retail markets. Similarly, the things which are just not by nature but by human enactment are not everywhere the same, since constitutions also are not the same, though there is but one which is everywhere by nature the best.[97]   [p. 124; 1134 b; 18–1135 a. 5]

CICERO

De Re Publica [98]

[The stoic view of natural law seen through the eyes of a Roman orator] [99]

True law is right reason in agreement with nature; it is of universal application, unchanging and everlasting; it summons to duty by its commands, and averts from wrongdoing by its prohibitions. And it does not lay its commands or prohibitions upon good men in vain, though neither have any effect on the wicked. It is a sin to try to alter this law, nor is it allowable to attempt to repeal any part of it, and it is impossible to abolish it entirely. We cannot be freed from its obligations by senate or people, and we need not look outside ourselves for an expounder or interpreter of it. And there will not be different laws at Rome and at Athens, or different laws now and in the future, but one eternal and unchangeable law will be valid for all nations and all times, and there will be one master and ruler, that is, God, over us all, for he is the author of this law, its promulgator, and its enforcing judge. Whoever is disobedient is fleeing from himself and denying his human nature, and by reason of this very fact he will suffer the worst penalties, even if he escapes what is commonly considered punishment.[1]   [p. 211; III, 22]

---

[97] [The doctrine of natural justice is an attempt to justify philosophically the Greek belief in a fundamental law (*cf. ante*, 77) but it played little part in Aristotle's ethics, *e.g.*, he does not say that positive law which conflicts with natural justice is invalid. *Cf.* Kelsen, *What is Justice?*, p. 384.]

[98] [*Cf.* Marcus Aurelius, *Meditations:* " If our intellectual part is common, the reason also, in respect of which we are rational beings, is common: if this is so, common also is the reason which commands us what to do, and what not to do; if this is so, there is a common law also; we are fellow-citizens; we are members of some political community; the world is in a manner a state. For of what other common political community will anyone say that the whole human race are members? And from thence, from this common political community, comes also our very intellectual faculty and reasoning faculty and our capacity for law . . . ." (Book IV, para 4).] [See also Cicero, *Laws* I, 6.]

[99] [Translated, C. W. Keyes.] [But *not* of a lawyer; and the remark of Gallus: " Nihil hoc ad ius; ad Ciceronem," see F. Schultz, *Classical Roman Law*, p. 198.]

[1] [This passage was cited with approval by Walsh J. in the Supreme Court of New York in 1945 (*Sodero* v. *Sodero*, 56 N.Y.S. 2d. 823)].

JUSTINIAN

Institutes [2]

Of the Law of Nature, Universal Law and the Civil Law

The law of nature is the law which nature has taught all animals. This law is not peculiar to the human race, but belongs to all living creatures, birds, beasts and fishes. This is the source of the union of male and female, which we called matrimony, as well as of the procreation and rearing of children ; which things are characteristic of the whole animal creation.

The civil law is distinguished from universal law as follows. Every people which is governed by laws and customs uses partly a law peculiar to itself, partly a law common to all mankind. For the law which each people makes for itself is peculiar to itself, and is called the civil law, as being the law peculiar to the community in question. But the law which natural reason has prescribed for all mankind is held in equal observance amongst all peoples and is called universal law, as being the law which all peoples use. Thus the Roman People uses a law partly peculiar to itself, partly common to all mankind.

The civil law takes its name from the country to which it belongs. . . . But universal law is common to the whole human race. For under the pressure of use and necessity the peoples of mankind have created for themselves certain rules. Thus, wars arose and captivity and slavery, which is contrary to natural law, for by natural law from the beginning all men were born free. From this universal law almost all contracts are derived, such as sale, hire, partnership, deposit, loan and countless others.

The laws of nature which are observed amongst all people alike, being established by a divine providence, remain ever fixed and immutable, but the laws which each State makes for itself are frequently changed either by tacit consent of the people, or by a later statute. [pp. 41–43 ; 1. 2.]

H. F. JOLOWICZ

Historical Introduction to Roman Law

(2nd ed., 1954)

Jus gentium and Jus naturale

In any case there did grow up, through the edicts of the *praetor peregrinus* and the provincial governors, a system which was neither the Roman *ius civile* nor a code of " private international law ", but a general system of rules governing relations between free men as such, without reference to their nationality. Much of this system of law, seeing that it was based on the edicts of Roman magistrates, was Roman in origin, but it was Roman law stripped to a great extent of its formal elements, and influenced by other, especially Greek, ideas. Thus the Roman contract of

[2] [Translated, R. W. Lee.]

stipulation was one of the institutions extended in this way to foreigners, i.e. a foreigner can be bound and entitled under it,[3] and it is not difficult to see why, for although the stipulation is what we call a formal contract,[4] the forms required are the simplest imaginable, and the contract is useful for all manner of purposes. Mancipation, on the other hand, with its elaborate ceremony, involving the use of scales and copper and the speaking of set words, remains exclusively a transaction of the *ius civile*. It must also be noticed that the rules of which we are speaking refer almost exclusively to transactions *inter vivos*; matters of family law and of succession remain under the personal law of each particular man.[5]

That the phrase *ius gentium* was ever applied to these rules developed in the peregrine and provincial edicts cannot be shown, but it is clear that they were of great importance in leading up to the conception of the *ius gentium*, for, once established, they in their turn influenced the development of the law as applied between citizens, especially in the direction of making it less formal, and thus there came into existence the *ius gentium*, in its practical sense, i.e., " that part of the law which we apply both to ourselves and to foreigners ". In this sense there is a great deal of law which is *iuris gentium*, e.g., not only the stipulation among contracts, but all the informal contracts, both " real " and " consensual " (the consensual at least being probably importations from the rules developed for foreigners), and much of the law of delict, which is extended from the civil law to apply where foreigners are concerned by the " fiction " that the foreigner is a citizen.

In the sources this " practical " sense of the phrase *ius gentium* is not always clear, because the Roman writers themselves do not distinguish it from a rather different sense which is not practical but derived from Greek philosophical theories. Aristotle, speaking of law in general, had divided it into two parts, that which was " natural " ($\phi\nu\sigma\iota\kappa\acute{o}\nu$) and that which was man-made ($\nu o\mu\iota\kappa\acute{o}\nu$), and he asserted that natural law was the same everywhere and had equal validity everywhere; as well as being " natural " it was " common " ($\kappa o\iota\nu\acute{o}\nu$). This idea became a commonplace, especially among the Stoics, with whose ideal of a " life according to Nature " it, of course, fitted admirably. Cicero repeats lofty sentiments about the law of Nature in a similar strain; he does not, any more than the Greeks, get beyond elementary moral rules when he gives instances of the precepts of this law, but it is clear that for him, as for Aristotle, the universality of a principle is a proof of its naturalness and hence of its validity, for the law of Nature is no mere ideal, it is a binding law and no enactment of the people or senatus-consult can prevail against it.[6] The argument, though not put in these words, is obvious: if all races of mankind acknowledge a practice it must be because it has been taught

---

[3] Provided he did not use the word *spondeo*, which was reserved for citizens; Gai. III. 93.

[4] *i.e.*, a particular form, in this case an oral question and answer concluded in corresponding terms, is necessary for its validity.

[5] *e.g.*, the question of *patria potestas* can only arise if both father and child are Roman citizens. No foreigner can take under a Roman will; whether a Roman can take under a foreign will is a question for the foreign law.

[6] *Cf.* Blackstone, *Commentaries*, I. 41: " This law of nature, being coeval with mankind, and dictated by God himself, is, of course, superior in obligation to any other . . . no human laws are of any validity if contrary to this."

them by their universal mother, Nature. Cicero thus identifies the law of Nature with the *ius gentium* in the sense of law common to all peoples, and draws the inference that what is part of the *ius gentium* should also be part of the *ius civile*, i.e., of the law of each particular state, although what is *ius civile* is not necessarily *ius gentium*, for, as in Aristotle's view, there are matters on which Nature is indifferent and each community can lay down rules for itself. This theoretical view of the *ius gentium* as law common to all mankind became current coin among the jurists. Gaius begins his Institutes almost in the words of Aristotle, " All peoples who are governed by laws and customs apply partly their own law, partly law which is common to all mankind ; for the law which each people has made for itself is peculiar to that people and is called its *ius civile*, the special law of the state ; but that which natural reason has appointed for all men is in force equally among all peoples, and is called *ius gentium*, being the law applied by all races. Thus the Roman people applies partly its own law, partly that common to all men ".

The difference between this " theoretical " meaning and the " practical " meaning of which we spoke above, is best seen when we consider the correlative term to *ius gentium*. In each case it is *ius civile*, but in translating this phrase into English we have to differentiate. Where the " practical " meaning is in question, we say " civil law " ; meaning " Roman law ", e.g., the answer to the question whether *mancipatio* is an institution of the *ius gentium* is " No ; it is an institution of the civil law ". But where the theoretical meaning is in question, as in the passage from Gaius above, we have to refer to the particular state in question, e.g., if we ask, " Is the rule that a husband or son must authorise a woman's contract part of the *ius gentium*?" the answer would have to be: " No ; it is a rule of Bithynian civil law ". Justinian makes this quite clear. " If ", he says, " a man wishes to call the laws of Solon or Draco Athenian civil law, he will not be wrong."

It is true that this distinction is not made by the Romans themselves— they did not in fact succeed in distinguishing morals from law in theory —but it is there all the same and must be grasped if we are to understand the different senses in which an institution can be said to be part of the *ius gentium*. The sense in which the stipulation, for instance, can be so classified has been explained ; it is part of the *ius gentium* because an Athenian or a Gaul or a Junian Latin, who has no state, may be bound or entitled under it. But when the Romans say that slavery and manumission or the right of capturing things in war (*occupatio bellica*) is part of the *ius gentium* they mean something different. They mean that these institutions are common to all systems of law which they know, not that they will be recognised in a Roman court. A person who alleges that he has been manumitted by a foreigner cannot claim to be free by Roman law ; whether he is free or not will depend on the law of his manumitter's state. It is true that all states know manumission, but the rules on the subject differ greatly from state to state ; whereas when a stipulation is mentioned the Roman institution of that name is meant, and any rules there may be in the systems of other states with regard to some similar contract do not matter in the least. It is this latter sort of *ius gentium* alone which really concerns the practical lawyer ; the rest is philosophical ornament.

As appears from what has already been said the law of Nature is only another name for the (theoretical) *ius gentium.* Not only does Cicero identify them, but the lawyers generally use the two phrases indiscriminately. Only one refinement which occasionally appears needs mention. If there was one institution which was really common to all peoples of antiquity it was slavery, which consequently is always reckoned as *iuris gentium.* According to Aristotle it was also natural, for some men were slaves by nature, but other Greek philosophers had different views ; man was by nature free, and we thus find slavery defined occasionally as an institution of the *ius gentium* contrary to Nature and resulting from war. But this is the only case in which a discrepancy between the two systems can be found. An identification, ascribed to Ulpian, of the law of Nature with the instincts which men share with animals is unfortunately given prominence by appearing in Justinian's Institutes, but it is an isolated opinion in legal literature and was never made the basis of any consistent theory.[7]   [pp. 102–105]

AQUINAS

Summa Theologica[8]

Law in General

(Qu. 90.)

The Nature of Law (Art. 1, concl.)

Law is a rule or measure of action in virtue of which one is led to perform certain actions and restrained from the performance of others. The term " law " derives [etymologically] from " binding," because by it one is bound to a certain course of action. But the rule and measure of human action is reason, which is the first principle of human action: this is clear from what we have said elsewhere. It is reason which directs action to its appropriate end; and this, according to the philosopher,[8a] is the first principle of all activity.

Reason and Will in Law (Ibid. ad 3um.)

Reason has power to move to action from the will, as we have shown already: for reason enjoins all that is necessary to some end, in virtue of the fact that that end is desired. But will, if it is to have the authority of law, must be regulated by reason when it commands. It is in this sense that we should understand the saying that the will of the prince has the power of law.[9] In any other sense the will of the prince becomes an evil rather than law.

The Object of the Law is the Common Good (Ibid. Art. 2, concl.)

Since every part bears the same relation to its whole as the imperfect to the perfect, and since one man is a part of that perfect whole which

---

[7] The idea appears to have been developed in the Greek schools of rhetoric. [Another useful discussion of the role played by natural law in Rome will be found in Schulz, *Roman Legal Science* (1946), see particularly pp. 70–71, 136– 137.]

[8] [Translated, J. G. Dawson.]

[8a] [*i.e.* Aristotle. See *ante*, 78.]

[9] The reference is to the text in the Roman law: " *Quod principi placuit legis habet vigorem.*" (*Dig.*, I, iv, 1, Ulpianus.)

is the community, if follows that the law must have as its proper object the well-being of the whole community. So the Philosopher, in his definition of what pertains to law, makes mention both of happiness and of political union. He says (*Ethics* V. chap. 1): "We call that legal and just which makes for and preserves the well-being of the community through common political action ": and the perfect community is the city, as is shown in the first book of the *Politics* (chap. 1).

Who has the right to promulgate Law (Ibid. Art. 3, concl.)

Law, strictly understood, has as its first and principal object the ordering of the common good. But to order affairs to the common good is the task either of the whole community or of some one person who represents it. Thus the promulgation of law is the business either of the whole community or of that political person whose duty is the care of the common good. Here as in every other case it is the one who decrees the end who also decrees the means thereto.

(Ibid. ad 2um.)

A private person has no authority to compel right living. He may only advise; but if his advice is not accepted he has no power of compulsion. But law, to be effective in promoting right living must have such compelling force; as the Philosopher says (X *Ethics,* chap. 9). But the power of compulsion belongs either to the community as a whole, or to its official representative whose duty it is to inflict penalties, as we shall see later. He alone, therefore, has the right to make laws.

(Ibid. ad 3um.)

Just as one man is a member of a family, so a household forms part of a city: but a city is a perfect community, as is shown in the first book of the *Politics*. Similarly, as the well-being of one man is not a final end, but is subordinate to the common good, so also the well-being of any household must be subordinate to the interests of the city, which is a perfect community. So the head of a family may make certain rules and regulations, but not such as have, properly speaking, the force of law.

Definition of Law (Ibid. Art. 4, concl.)

From the foregoing we may gather the correct definition of law. It is nothing else than a rational ordering of things which concern the common good; promulgated by whoever is charged with the care of the community.

The Various Types of Law

(Qu. 91)

The Eternal Law [10]

As we have said, law is nothing else but a certain dictate of the practical reason 'in the prince' who rules a perfect community. It is

---

[10] [Aquinas' fourfold classification also comprised what was called " Divine Law." This is distinguished from natural law as being " revealed " rather than discovered by reason, for instance, the code of law given by God to the Hebrews, or the rules given through Scripture; *cf. op. cit.,* pp. 115–117; G. H. Sabine, *A History of Political Theory*, 3rd ed., revised, p. 222.]

clear, however, supposing the world to be governed by divine providence
. . . that the whole community of the Universe is governed by the divine
reason. Thus the rational guidance of created things on the part of
God, as the Prince of the universe, has the quality of law. . . . This we
can call the eternal law.[11]

The Natural Law. (Art. 2, concl.)

Since all things which are subject to divine providence are measured
and regulated by the eternal law—as we have already shown—it is clear
that all things participate to some degree in the eternal law; in so far as
they derive from it certain inclinations to those actions and aims which
are proper to them. But, of all others, rational creatures are subject to
divine providence in a very special way; being themselves made par-
ticipators in providence itself, in that they control their own actions and
the actions of others. So they have a certain share in the divine reason
itself, deriving therefrom a natural inclination to such actions and ends
as are fitting. This participation in the eternal law by rational creatures
is called the natural law.

Human Law. (Art. 3, concl.)

Just as in speculative reason we proceed from indemonstrable principles, naturally known, to the conclusions of the various sciences, such
conclusions not being innate but arrived at by the use of reason; so also
the human reason has to proceed from the precepts of the natural law, as
though from certain common and indemonstrable principles, to other
more particular dispositions. And such particular dispositions, arrived at
by an effort of reason, are called human laws: provided that the other
conditions necessary to all law, which we have already noted, are
observed.

The Natural Law [12]

(Qu. 94)

Precepts of the Natural Law. (Art. 2, concl.)

The order of the precepts of the natural law corresponds to the order
of our natural inclinations. For there is in man a natural and initial
inclination to good which he has in common with all substances; in so
far as every substance seeks its own preservation according to its own
nature. Corresponding to this inclination, the natural law contains all
that makes for the preservation of human life, and all that is opposed
to its dissolution. Secondly, there is to be found in man a further inclination to certain more specific ends, according to the nature which man
shares with other animals. In virtue of this inclination there pertains to
the natural law all those instincts 'which nature has taught all animals,' [13]

---

[11] [The Scholastic approach to natural law was in a sense a form of rationalism
in that from its own premises, it claimed to reason with rigorous logic, but it
must not be overlooked that these premises themselves were derived from certain
theological dogmas and traditions which it was forbidden to deny or even doubt.
These, therefore, form fundamental presuppositions of the system which were not
open to rational refutation. (*Cf.* G. G. Coulton, *Medieval Panorama*, pp. 113–
114.)]

[12] See, generally, O'Connor, *Aquinas and Natural Law* (1967) particularly Chap. VII.

[13] [*Cf. ante*, 93.]

such as sexual relationship, the rearing of offspring, and the like. Thirdly, there is in man a certain inclination to good, corresponding to his rational nature: and this inclination is proper to man alone. So man has a natural inclination to know the truth about God and to live in society. In this respect there come under the natural law, all actions connected with such inclinations: namely, that a man should avoid ignorance, that he must not give offence to others with whom he must associate and all actions of like nature.

The Universality of the Natural Law. (Art. 4, concl.)

As we have just said, all those actions pertain to the natural law to which man has a natural inclination: and among such it is proper to man to seek to act according to reason. Reason, however, proceeds from general principles to matters of detail, . . . The practical and the speculative reason, however, go about this process in different ways. For the speculative reason is principally employed about necessary truths, which cannot be otherwise than they are; so that truth is to be found as surely in its particular conclusions as in general principles themselves. But practical reason is employed about contingent matters, into which human actions enter: thus, though there is a certain necessity in its general principles, the further one departs from generality the more is the conclusion open to exception.

So it is clear that as far as the general principles of reason are concerned, whether speculative or practical, there is one standard of truth or rightness for everybody, and that this is equally known by every one. With regard to the particular conclusions of speculative reason, again there is one standard of truth for all; but in this case it is not equally known to all: it is universally true, for instance, that the three interior angles of a triangle equal two right angles; but this conclusion is not known by everybody. When we come to the particular conclusions of the practical reason, however, there is neither the same standard of truth or rightness for every one, nor are these conclusions equally known to all. All people, indeed, realize that it is right and true to act according to reason. And from this principle we may deduce as an immediate conclusion that debts must be repaid. This conclusion holds in the majority of cases. But it could happen in some particular case that it would be injurious, and therefore irrational, to repay a debt; if, for instance, the money repaid were used to make war against one's own country. Such exceptions are all the more likely to occur the more we get down to particular cases: take, for instance, the question of repaying a debt together with a certain security, or in some specific way. The more specialized the conditions applied, the greater is the possibility of an exception arising which will make it right to make restitution or not.

So we must conclude that the law of nature, as far as general first principles are concerned, is the same for all as a norm of right conduct and is equally well known to all. But as to more particular cases which are conclusions from such general principles it remains the same for all only in the majority of cases, both as a norm and as to the extent to which it is known. Thus in particular instances it can admit of exceptions: both with regard to rightness, because of certain impediments, (just as in nature the generation and change of bodies is subject to accidents caused by some impediment), and with regard to its knowability. This can happen because reason is, in some persons, depraved by passion or by some evil habit of nature; as Caesar relates in *De Bello Gallico* (VI, 23), of the Germans, that at one time they did not consider robbery to be wrong; though it is obviously against natural law.

The Immutability of Natural Law. (Art. 5.)

There are two ways in which natural law may be understood to change. One, in that certain additions are made to it. And in this sense there is no reason why it should not change. Both the divine law and human laws do, in fact, add much to the natural law which is useful to human activity.

Or again the natural law would be understood to change by having something subtracted from it. If, for instance, something ceased to pertain to the natural law which was formerly part of it. In this respect, and as far as first principles are concerned, it is wholly unchangeable. As to secondary precepts, which, as we have said, follow as immediate conclusions from first principles, the natural law again does not change; in the sense that it remains a general rule for the majority of cases that what the natural law prescribes is correct. It may, however, be said to change in some particular case, or in a limited number of examples; because of some special causes which make its observation impossible, as we have already pointed out.

Human Law

(Qu. 95.)

The Necessity for Human Laws. (Art. 1, concl.)

From the foregoing it is clear that there is in man a natural aptitude to virtuous action. But men can achieve the perfection of such virtue only by the practice of a "certain discipline."—And men who are capable of such discipline without the aid of others are rare indeed.—So we must help one another to achieve that discipline which leads to a virtuous life. There are, indeed, some young men, readily inclined to a life of virtue through a good natural disposition or upbringing, or particularly because of divine help; and for such, paternal guidance and advice are sufficient. But there are others, of evil disposition and prone to vice, who are not easily moved by words. These it is necessary to restrain from wrongdoing by force and by fear. When they are thus prevented from doing evil, a quiet life is assured to the rest of the community; and they are themselves drawn eventually, by force of habit, to do voluntarily what once they did only out of fear, and so to practise virtue. Such discipline which compels under fear of penalty is the discipline of law. Thus the enactment of laws was necessary to the peaceful and virtuous life of men. And the Philosopher says (I *Politics,* 2): "Man, when he reaches the perfection of virtue is the best of all animals: but if he goes his way without law and justice he becomes the worst of all brutes." For man, unlike other animals, has the weapon of reason with which to exploit his base desires and cruelty.

Human Law

(Qu. 95)

The Subordination of Human Laws to the Natural Law. (Art. 2, concl.)

Saint Augustine says (I *De Lib. Arbitrio,* 5): 'There is no law unless it be just.' So the validity of law depends upon its justice. But in human affairs a thing is said to be just when it accords aright with the rule of reason: and, as we have already seen, the first rule of reason is the natural law. Thus all humanly enacted laws are in accord with reason to the extent that they derive from the natural law. And if a human law is at variance in any particular with the natural law, it is no longer legal, but rather a corruption of law.[14]

But it should be noted that there are two ways in which anything may derive from natural law. First, as a conclusion from more general principles. Secondly, as a determination of certain general features. The former is similar to the method of the sciences in which demonstrative conclusions are drawn from first principles. The second way is like to that of the arts in which some common form is determined to a particular instance: as, for example, when an architect, starting from the general idea of a house, then goes on to design the particular plan of this or that house. So, therefore, some derivations are made from the natural law by way of formal conclusion: as the conclusion, 'Do no murder,' derives from the precept, 'Do harm to no man.' Other conclusions are arrived at as determinations of particular cases. So the natural law establishes that whoever transgresses shall be punished. But that a man should be punished by a specific penalty is a particular determination of the natural law.

Both types of derivation are to be found in human law. But those which are arrived at in the first way are sanctioned not only by human law, but by the natural law also ; while those arrived at by the second method have the validity of human law alone.[15]

The Difference Between Legal and Moral Obligation

(Qu. 100)

Law and the Practice of Virtue (Art. 9.)

As we have shown above, a precept of law has power to compel: thus whatever is obliged by law may be said to fall directly under the precept of law. But the compulsion of law obtains through fear of penalty, as is shown in the tenth book of the *Ethics*; for those matters may be said to come strictly under the precept of law for which a legal penalty is inflicted. Hence divine law differs from human law in the imposition of its penalties. For a legal penalty is inflicted only for those matters about which the law-giver is competent to judge, since the law punishes in view of a judgment passed. Now man, the maker of human law, can pass judgment only upon external actions, because " man seeth those things that appear," as we are told in the first book of *Kings*. God alone, the divine Law-giver, is able to judge the inner movements of the will, as the Psalmist says, " The searcher of hearts and reins is God."

---

14 [Aquinas, at any rate in his later works, was very guarded about rebellion. There was no effective power to coerce the prince and obedience was desirable to avoid scandal or disturbance. " This situation has proved a perpetual embarrassment to those scholastic moralists whose tenet has been that all rebellions are wrong— until they succeed ": T. Gilby, *Principality and Polity*, p. 289.]

15 [Natural law is not a complete body of precepts but needs to be supplemented by positive law. The latter are *justified* by natural law, but for the most part not *deduced* from it.]

In view of this we must conclude that the practice of virtue is in one respect subject both to human and to divine law, while in another respect it is subject to divine but not to human law. Again there is a third sense in which it is affected neither by divine nor by human law. Now the mode of the practice of virtue consists, according to Aristotle (II *Ethics,* 4), in three things. The first of these is that a person should act knowingly. And this is subject to judgment both by divine and by human law. For whatever a man does in ignorance he does accidentally, and in consequence both human and divine law must consider the question of ignorance in judging whether certain matters are punishable or pardonable.

The second point is that a man should act voluntarily, deliberately chosing a particular action for his own sake. This involves a two-fold interior action of the will and of intention, and of these we have already spoken above. Divine law alone is competent to judge of these, but not human law. For human law does not punish the man who meditates murder but does not commit it, though divine law does punish him, as we are told by *St. Matthew* (V, 22): " Whosoever is angry with his brother shall be in danger of the judgement."

The third point is that a man should act upon a firm and unchanging principle; and such firmness proceeds strictly from habit, and obtains when a man acts from a rooted habit. In this sense the practice of virtue does not fall under the precept either of divine or of human law for no man is punished for breaking the law, either by God or by man, if he duly honours his parents, though lacking the habit of filial piety.

[pp. 109–149]

LOCKE

Civil Government

But though this be a state of liberty,[16] yet it is not a state of licence; though man in that state have an uncontrollable liberty to dispose of his person or possessions, yet he has not liberty to destroy himself, or so much as any creature in his possession, but where some nobler use than its bare preservation calls for it. The state of Nature has a law of Nature to govern it, which obliges every one, and reason, which is that law, teaches all mankind who will but consult it, that being all equal and independent, no one ought to harm another in his life, health, liberty or possessions; for men being all the workmanship of one omnipotent and infinitely wise Maker; all the servants of one sovereign Master, sent into the world by His order and about His business; they are His property, whose workmanship they are made to last during His, not one another's pleasure. And, being furnished with like faculties, sharing all in one community of Nature, there cannot be supposed any such subordination among us that may authorise us to destroy one another, as if we were made for one another's uses, as the inferior ranks of creatures are for ours. Every one as he is bound to preserve himself, and not to quit his station wilfully, so by the like reason, when his own preservation comes not in competition, ought he as much as he can to preserve the rest of mankind, and not unless it be to do justice on an offender, take away or

---

[16] [*i.e.,* the state of nature, as described by Locke.]

impair the life, or what tends to the preservation of the life, the liberty, health, limb, or goods of another.

7. And that all men may be restrained from invading others' rights, and from doing hurt to one another, and the law of Nature be observed, which willeth the peace and preservation of all mankind, the execution of the law of Nature is in that state put into every man's hands, whereby every one has a right to punish the transgressors of that law to such a degree as may hinder its violation. For the law of Nature would, as all other laws that concern men in this world, be in vain if there were nobody that in the state of Nature had a power to execute that law, and thereby preserve the innocent and restrain offenders; and if any one in the state of Nature may punish another for any evil he has done, every one may do so. For in that state of perfect equality, where naturally there is no superiority or jurisdiction of one over another, what any may do in prosecution of that law, every one must needs have a right to do.

8. And thus, in the state of Nature, one man comes by a power over another, but yet no absolute or arbitrary power to use a criminal, when he has got him in his hands, according to the passionate heats or boundless extravagancy of his own will, but only to retribute to him so far as calm reason and conscience dictate, what is proportionate to his transgression, which is so much as may serve for reparation and restraint. For these two are the only reasons why one man may lawfully do harm to another, which is that we call punishment. In transgressing the law of Nature, the offender declares himself to live by another rule than that of reason and common equity, which is that measure God has set to the actions of men for their mutual security, and so he becomes dangerous to mankind; the tie which is to secure them from injury and violence being slighted and broken by him, which being a trespass against the whole species, and the peace and safety of it, provided for by the law of Nature, every man upon this score, by the right he hath to preserve mankind in general, may restrain, or where it is necessary, destroy things noxious to them, and so may bring such evil on any one who hath transgressed that law, as may make him repent the doing of it, and thereby deter him, and, by his example, others from doing the like mischief. And in this case, and upon this ground, every man hath a right to punish the offender, and be executioner of the law of nature.[17]   [Bk. II, cap. 2]

Man being born, as has been proved, with a title to perfect freedom and an uncontrolled enjoyment of all the rights and privileges of the law of Nature,[18] equally with any other man, or number of men in the world, hath by nature a power not only to preserve his property [19]—that is, his life, liberty, and estate, against the injuries and attempts of other men, but to judge of and punish the breaches of that law in others, as he is persuaded the offence deserves, even with death itself, in crimes where the

[17] [For the views on natural law of Bodin, Hobbes and Rousseau, see *post*, 177 *et seq.*]

[18] [It may be asked how Locke reconciled his belief in natural rights with his general empirical philosophy, which rejected "innate ideas." Locke seems to have believed in a demonstrative science of ethics based on rationalism, though as an empiricist he derived knowledge (including ideas) only from the senses. See Sabine, *History of Political Theory*, 3rd ed., pp. 448–449.]

[19] [The so-called Whig theory of government was primarily aimed at the preservation of private property, even against the ruler himself. Life and liberty are characteristically treated as mere aspects of the fundamental property right.]

heinousness of the fact, in his opinion, requires it. But because no
political society can be, nor subsist, without having in itself the power to
preserve the property, and in order thereunto punish the offences of all
those of that society, there, and there only, is political society where every
one of the members hath quitted this natural power, resigned it up into
the hands of the community in all cases that exclude him not from
appealing for protection to the law established by it.[20] And thus all
private judgment of every particular member being excluded, the community comes to be umpire, and by understanding indifferent rules and
men authorised by the community for their execution, decides all the
differences that may happen between any members of that society concerning any matter of right, and punishes those offences which any
member hath committed against the society with such penalties as the law
has established; whereby it is easy to discern who are, and are not, in
political society together. Those who are united into one body, and have
a common established law and judicature to appeal to, with authority to
decide controversies between them and punish offenders, are in civil
society one with another; but those who have no such common appeal, I
mean on earth, are still in the state of Nature, each being where there is
no other, judge for himself and executioner; which is, as I have before
showed it, the perfect state of Nature.   [Bk. II, cap. 7]
    Though the legislative, whether placed in one or more, whether it be
always in being or only by intervals, though it be the supreme power in
every commonwealth, yet, first, it is not, nor can possibly be, absolutely
arbitrary over the lives and fortunes of the people. For it being but the
joint power of every member of the society given up to that person or
assembly which is legislator, it can be no more than those persons had
in a state of Nature before they entered into society, and gave it up to
the community. For nobody can transfer to another more power than
he has in himself, and nobody has an absolute arbitrary power over
himself, or over any other, to destroy his own life, or take away the life
or property of another. A man, as has been proved, cannot subject
himself to the arbitrary power of another; and having, in the state of
Nature, no arbitrary power over the life, liberty, or possession of another,
but only so much as the law of Nature gave him for the preservation of
himself and the rest of mankind, this is all he doth, or can give up to the
commonwealth, and by it to the legislative power, so that the legislative
can have no more than this. Their power in the utmost bounds of it is
limited to the public good of the society.[21] It is a power that hath no
other end but preservation, and therefore can never have a right to
destroy, enslave, or designedly to impoverish the subjects; the obligations
of the law of Nature cease not in society, but only in many cases are
drawn closer, and have, by human laws, known penalties annexed to them
to enforce their observation. Thus the law of Nature stands as an eternal

---

[20] [This is Locke's version of the social contract.]
[21] [There is a mere delegation of authority on trust to act for the common good.
Locke states in detail those limitations natural law imposes on the legislator:
laws only for the public good, no arbitrary decrees, no taxes without consent,
and no delegation of the law-making power. See *op. cit.*, Chap. 11. But
Laslett has shown that Locke's work was not written after 1689 for the purpose
of sanctifying the settlement of that year, but was written some years earlier
with the aim of demanding a revolution. See Laslett, *Locke's Two Treatises
of Government* (1960).]

rule to all men, legislators as well as others. The rules that they make for other men's actions must, as well as their own and other men's actions, be conformable to the law of Nature—*i.e.*, to the will of God, of which that is a declaration, and the fundamental law of Nature being the preservation of mankind, no human sanction can be good or valid against it. [Bk. II, cap. 11]

L. DUGUIT

The Law and the State [22]

. . . The doctrine of solidarity was urged to show that the jural principle (*la règle de droit*) does not rest on the metaphysical and self-contradictory conception of rights of the individual anterior to society but is directly derived from the same elements which constitute the social bond. What are these elements? An analysis which seems decisive has been attempted by M. Durkheim in his excellent book, *La division du travail social*, 1895,[23] many of the detailed solutions of which are quite contestable, but the underlying principles of which seem sound.

In every grouping two elements constitute the social bond; two elements that may appear in infinitely variable forms, but the basis of which, reduced to its simplest terms, is always the same. They are (1) the similarity of needs, which is the basis of solidarity either through mechanical interdependence or through similitude; (2) the difference in needs and in aptitudes which produces and makes necessary an exchange of services, and which founds solidarity either by organic interdependence or by divisions of labor.

Thence is derived the following formula for the jural principle (*la règle de droit*) imposing itself on all the individuals of a social group, both great and small, both strong and weak, as well as the governing and the governed: Do nothing which can possibly infringe upon social interdependence, either through similitude or through division of labor; do all that is within your power, within your given situation and within your aptitudes, to insure and increase social interdependence both by similitude and by division of labor. . . .[24] [p. 178]

. . . With respect to the serious objections made to the doctrine of the jural principle founded on the theory of social solidarity, it may be said that, although they are very different in form, in the last analysis they all come to this: In admitting, it is said, that the law is a social standard (*une règle sociale*) and not the power of an individual will, in

22 [From (1917) 31 Harv.L.R., pp. 1–185, copyright 1917, by the Harvard Law Review Association. On Duguit, see R. Pound, *Jurisprudence*, Vol. 1, pp. 184–189. And Laski in ed. Jennings, *Modern Theories of Law*, pp. 52–67.]
23 [See translation by Simpson (1947), published by Free Press of Glencoe.]
24 [One implication that might be anticipated from Duguit's theory, would be the vesting in the courts of a power of judicial review of statute law. Duguit did come to favour this and claimed to discern an increasing tendency towards such a development even on the Continent. Indeed, he even went so far as to favour the creation of a tribunal to judge the "legality of law," that is, not whether the law conformed to a written constitution, but whether any particular enactment could be said to promote social solidarity. In a democratic society, however, this would appear to be the function rather of the elected parliamentary assembly (see *Law in the Modern State* (1921), trans. F. & H. Laski, pp. 83–94).]

admitting that social interdependence is the fundamental element of social integration, one is simply admitting a fact. But a fact can not be the foundation of a rule, of a precept of conduct, any more than it can be the basis for a jural principle (*une règle de droit*) or moral principle; and thus, it is said, the whole system gives way.[25] . . .

My answer is that this reasoning is true as regards the moral rule, but that it is not true as regards the jural principle (*la règle de droit*). To establish a rule of morals it is necessary in fact to establish a criterion of good and of evil. The moral rule compels us to do one thing because it is good, and forbids us to do another because it is bad. The rule of morality bases its precept on a certain value inherent in the very act which it commands; and we may maintain that such a rule is not truly imperative, except when the criterion of what is forbidden and of what is commanded is outside the facts and superior to the facts.

To act in conformity to law on the contrary, is to act in conformity to what is social. The jural principle (*la règle de droit*) says: Do such a thing because it is social; refrain from doing such and such a thing because it is anti-social. A juridical obligation is not an obligation to do what is good in itself but an obligation to do what has a social value, that is, not to do what is anti-social. It finds its proof in the fact that the whole world agrees in recognizing that the criterion of the jural principle is the social reaction which is caused by a violation of the principle; a reaction capable of being socially organized. Let us not say, then, that the jural principle can not be founded on a fact, since it is nothing more than a precept to conform one's self to facts. The fact is the true foundation of the jural principle, if such fact is truly the social, irreducible, and essential fact; and the whole question is resolved into determining whether or not social interdependence is that fact. It seems to us that it can scarcely be contested. Personally, the more I think of it, the more convinced I become. This fact alone is capable of giving to law a foundation at once positive and solid. . . .[26]   [pp. 180–181]

R. STAMMLER

Theory of Justice [27]

The universal standard of Law.—The various theories of the law of nature all undertake by their own method of argument to outline an

---

[25] [Duguit is presumably here thinking of the distinction between *is* and *ought*; *cf. ante*, 8. His answer, in the next paragraph, overlooks the fact that law, as well as morals, is normative in character.]

[26] [Duguit thought of himself as a sociological jurist desirous of basing law on fact and not on metaphysics. Hence his attack on the sovereignty of the state. The state is merely an instrument for performing the function of promoting social solidarity. Duguit's sympathy for syndicalism also led him to stress the autonomy of all groups even as against the state itself. Social solidarity, however, is in itself a metaphysical idea involving values, so that Duguit, who starts as a positivist, seems to return to the point where natural law in another form is reintroduced at the back door. Yet social solidarity seems hardly more than a slogan, which can give no more specific guidance to the judge than natural law itself, *e.g.*, does it enable one to say that workmen have a right to strike?]

[27] [Translated, I. Husik.]

ideal legal code whose content shall be unchangeable and absolutely valid. Our purpose, on the other hand, is to find merely a universally valid formal method, by means of which the necessarily changing material of empirically conditioned legal rules may be so worked out, judged, and determined that it shall have the quality of objective justice.[28]

The attempt of the law of nature was foredoomed to failure. For the content of law has to do with the regulation of human social life, which aims to satisfy human wants. But everything that has reference to human wants and to the manner of satisfying them is merely empirical and subject to constant change. There is not a single rule of law whose positive content can be fixed a priori.[29] [pp. 89–90]

. . . We must proceed as follows. Every legal investigation may be carried on from two points of view. We may regard the standpoint of the individual *qua* individual as the center of our investigation, or we may emphasize the community of individuals and their common aims. It is self-evident that in a complete union under the law both of these aspects are necessarily contained. For as such a union implies at least two members (unlike the problem of ethics), we can not possibly get away from this twofold aspect of considering the matter. . . .

In our investigation here we are not interested in following out further the system of positive law as thus built up, but in trying to see in what way the twofold aspect above mentioned may be made significant for the general application of the concept of a just legal content. Now it appears on closer observation that the twofold manner of thinking from which we started is already contained in the formula of the social ideal. This idea conceives of the persons united under the law as men who follow their particular aims in so far as they accord with justice. It follows therefore that every individual absolutely respects the other and is respected by him. For the social ideal demands that the individual should not be forced in his legal relations to renounce his justified interests. The principle here used as a standard requires that there shall be mutual respect of each other on the part of those united in the law. . . .

As on the other hand the principle of social investigation aims at the idea of living and working together as a unit, and finds its conclusion in the absolute solidarity of interests, we must also emphasize the social members in their unity. Here we think of the individual as a member of the whole, in which all must, for better or for worse, have their necessary share. The first lays stress upon the *respect* due to the individual in his specific right volition, whereas the second insists on the idea of social community and mutual *participation*. So we say, "Every man must carry his own burden"; and yet, without contradicting the prior warning, that "one should bear the burden of the other." . . .

[28] [Before embarking on the study of Continental philosophical jurists it is well for the English lawyer to bear in mind what Prof. Passmore has written in regard to philosophy. "The fact that we have to live with is that if most British philosophers are convinced that Continental metaphysics is arbitrary, pretentious, and mind-destroying, Continental philosophers are no less confident that British empiricism is philistine, pedestrian and soul-destroying": *Hundred Years of Philosophy*, pp. 459–460.]

[29] [Stammler's search for a natural law of *form* rather than *content* has resulted in his theory being described as "natural law with a changing content." The idea is as old as Aristotle, *ante*, 91.] A certain similarity with Fuller may also be detected, *ante*, 83 and *post*, 138.]

We have accordingly *four principles of just law*, which may be treated in two corresponding pairs.

The Principles of Respect.—1. The content of a person's volition must not be made subject to the arbitrary desire of another. 2. Every legal demand must be maintained in such a manner that the person obligated may be his own neighbor.

Both of these principles aim at enabling the individual member of a legal community to determine his own volition in freedom that accords with justice. The first principle starts from the idea of an existing duty and limits the extent to which the members of a legal community are bound one by the other. The second is concerned with the measure in which a legal demand is to be imposed, and restricts in systematic fashion the manner and the scope of the service demanded. The first refers to the *maintenance* of legal relations, the second to their *execution*. They are derived directly from the highest aim of the law, whose formula is the social ideal. As the concept of a just legal content is based upon the idea of a community of free men, it follows necessarily that in every external regulation the person subject to it always has the possibility of choosing the right. A legal command must not be understood to mean that the individual shall give up everything for the conditioned subjective purposes of another; that he must have the obligation, and is bound to regard those personal aims of the other as his own final aim.[30] . . .

The Principles of Participation.—1. A person under a legal obligation must not be arbitrarily excluded from a legal community. 2. Every ability of disposing that is granted by law may be exclusive only in the sense that the person excluded may be his own neighbor.

These propositions aim to carry out the idea of *community*. They express the thought that the legal command which unites the individuals to carry on the struggle for existence in common, must not become untrue to itself. But it would be guilty of a contradiction if it subjected the individual by compulsion to the social union, and at the same time treated him in a given case as a person who had nothing but legal duties. This would be a caricature of the idea of *co-operation*. The desire to avoid the logical contradiction which would result between the fundamental idea of just law and the particular illustration thereof, leads to the principles of *participation*.   [pp. 158–163]

J. MARITAIN

Man and the State

Since I have not time here to discuss nonsense (we can always find very intelligent philosophers, not to name Mr. Bertrand Russell, who defend it most brilliantly) I take it for granted that we admit that there is a

---

[30] [A large part of Stammler's work is devoted to showing how problems taken from German civil law may be solved by this method, though an English lawyer will probably sympathise with Friedmann's conclusion that it is incomprehensible how Stammler can maintain the illusion that a purely formal idea of law is capable of material guidance to the lawyer (*Legal Theory* 5th ed. p. 185), and it may indeed be doubted whether Stammler succeeds in bridging the gap between a formal structure and the social ideal of justice.]

human nature, and that this human nature is the same in all men.[31] I take it for granted that we also admit that man is a being who is gifted with intelligence, and who, as such, acts with an understanding of what he is doing, and therefore with the power to determine for himself the ends which he pursues. On the other hand, possessed of a nature, of an ontological structure which is a locus of intelligible necessities, man possesses ends which necessarily correspond to his essential constitution and which are the same for all—as all pianos, for instance, whatever their particular type and in whatever place they may be, have as their end the production of certain attuned sounds. If they do not produce these sounds they must be tuned, or discarded as worthless. But since man is endowed with intelligence and determines his own ends, it is for him to attune himself to the ends that are necessarily demanded by his nature. This means that there is, by force and virtue of human nature itself, an order or disposition which human reason can discover and according to which the human will must act in order to attune itself to the essential and necessary ends of the human being. The unwritten law, or natural law, is nothing more than that. . . .   [p. 78]

Natural law is not a written law. Men know it with greater or less difficulty, and in different degrees, here as elsewhere being subject to error. The only practical knowledge all men have naturally and infallibly in common as a self-evident principle, intellectually perceived by virtue of the concepts involved, is that we must do good and avoid evil. This is the preamble and the principle of natural law; it is not the law itself. Natural law is the ensemble of things to do and not to do which follow therefrom in *necessary* fashion. That every sort of error and deviation is possible in the determination of these things merely proves that our sight is weak, our nature coarse, and that innumerable accidents can corrupt our judgement. Montaigne maliciously remarked that, among certain peoples, incest and theft were considered virtuous acts. Pascal was scandalized by it. All this proves nothing against natural law, any more than a mistake in addition proves anything against arithmetic, or the mistakes of certain primitive peoples, for whom the stars were holes in the tent which covered the world, prove anything against astronomy.

Natural law is an unwritten law. Man's knowledge of it has increased little by little as man's moral conscience has developed. The latter was at first in a twilight state. Anthropologists have taught us within what structures of tribal life and in the midst of what half-conscious magic it was first formed. This proves merely that the knowledge men have had of the unwritten law has passed through more diverse forms and stages than certain philosophers or theologians have believed. The knowledge that our own moral conscience has of this law is doubtless still imperfect, and very likely it will continue to develop and to become more refined as long as mankind exists. Only when the Gospel has penetrated to the very depths of our human substance will natural law appear in its full flower and its perfection.

So the law and the knowledge of the law are two different things. Yet the law has force of law only when it is promulgated. It is only insofar as it is known and expressed in affirmations of practical reason that natural law has the force of law.

[31] [But see, on this facile generalisation, M. Macdonald, *post*, 133.]

At this point let us stress that human reason does not discover the regulations of natural law in an abstract and theoretical manner, as a series of geometrical theorems. Nay more, it does not discover them through the conceptual exercise of the intellect, or by way of rational knowledge. I think that Thomas Aquinas' teaching, here, needs to be understood in a much deeper and more precise fashion than is common. When he says that human reason discovers the regulations of natural law through the guidance of the *inclinations* of human nature, he means that the very mode or manner in which human reason knows natural law is not rational knowledge, but knowledge *through inclination*. That kind of knowledge is not clear knowledge through concepts and conceptual judgments; it is obscure, unsystematic, vital knowledge by connaturality or affinity, in which the intellect, in order to form its judgment, consults and listens to the inner melody that the vibrating strings of abiding tendencies awaken in us.   [pp. 81–83]

. . . *Positive Law*, or the body of laws (either customary law or statute law) in force in a given social group, deals with the rights and duties which are connected with the first principle, but in a *contingent* manner, by virtue of the determinate ways of conduct prescribed by the reason and the will of man when they institute the laws or mould the customs of a particular society, thus stating of themselves that in the particular group in question certain things will be good and permissible, certain other things bad and not permissible.

But it is by virtue of natural law that the law of Nations and positive law take on the force of law, and impose themselves upon the conscience. They are a prolongation or an extension of natural law, passing into objective zones which are less and less able to be adequately determined by the essential inclinations of human nature. For it is *natural law itself which requires that whatever it leaves undetermined shall subsequently be determined*, either as a right or a duty existing for all men, and of which they are made aware, not by knowledge through inclination but by conceptual reason—that is the *jus gentium*,[32]—or—and this is positive law— as a right or a duty existing for certain men by reason of the human and contingent regulations proper to the social group of which they are a part. Thus there are imperceptible transitions (at least from the point of view of historical experience) between Natural Law, the Law of Nations, and Positive Law. There is a dynamism which impels the unwritten law to show forth in human law, and to render the latter ever more perfect and just in the very field of its contingent determinations. It is in accordance with this dynamism that the rights of human persons take political and social form in the community.

Man's right to existence, to personal freedom, and to the pursuit of perfection in his moral life, belongs, strictly speaking, to natural law.

The right to the private ownership of material goods pertains to natural law, in so far as mankind is naturally entitled to possess for its own common use the material goods of nature; it pertains to the law of Nations, or *jus gentium*, in so far as reason necessarily concludes in the light of the conditions naturally required for their management and for human work that for the sake of the common good those material

---

[32] [This refers to " the common law of civilization " which can be " rationally inferred " from a principle of natural law. But what are the criteria of " rational inference "?]

goods must be privately owned. And the particular modalities of the right to private ownership, which vary according to the form of a society and the state of the development of its economy, are determined by positive law.[33]   [pp. 90–91]

J. DABIN

General Theory of Law [34]

Characteristics of Natural Law : A Norm That Issues from Nature, Universal and Immutable. . . . as the adjective "natural" indicates without too great ambiguity, the rule of human conduct that is called natural law is deduced from the nature of man as it reveals itself in the basic inclinations of that nature under the control of reason, independently of any formal intervention by any legislator whatsoever, divine or human. Natural law is thus distinguished from another law, which is called "positive" (or "voluntary," or "arbitrary") and is supposed to have been established by the will of God or of men. Natural law, furthermore, dominates positive law in the sense that, while positive law may add to natural law or even restrict it, it is prohibited from contradicting it.[35] How could the legislator, or at least the human legislator,[36] have the power to rebel against the "given" of human nature?

From the characteristics of human nature flow the characteristics of natural law. As human nature is identical in all men and does not vary,[37] its precepts have universal and immutable validity, notwithstanding the diversity of individual conditions, historical and geographical environments, civilizations and cultures. As, on the other hand, nature cannot deceive itself nor deceive us, its precepts, inasmuch as they are authentic, have a validity that is certain, suffering neither doubt nor discussion.

[33] [One may pertinently ask how the natural law character of private ownership is vouchsafed to us; also does this merely refer to the abstract concept, since the particular modalities rest with positive law?]

[34] [These extracts come from the second edition, translated by K. Wilk (1950). The third edition was published recently and has not yet been translated. There is, however, a discussion of it, bringing out the differences between the two editions, in Milhollin, 15 *American Journal of Jurisprudence* 116.]

[35] [But what is the effect of such a contradiction? Is it the duty of the judge, official or ordinary citizen to disregard such a law? Suppose a law abolishes the crime of abortion and that this contradicts natural law; must the courts still convict offenders, contrary to positive law? In the second edition Dabin ventured the open-ended comment that such a law should be "condemned." In the new edition he discusses what condemnation involves. Like Aquinas (*cf. ante* footnote 14 but see Milhollin, *idem*) he distinguishes a logical answer from a prudent one. Logically, moral rules must be preferred to legal ones and an immoral law is void. But one must predict and weigh the social consequences of so declaring it for the legislator and the image of the law itself, for even an immoral law contains an element of legality and merits reasonable respect. So both considerations must be weighed with "public good," the ultimate arbiter. Dabin's thoughts seem very close to the American school of "civil disobedience" writers, *e.g.* Wasserstrom, in ed. Summers, *Essays In Legal Philosophy*, p. 274. See also MacGuigan, *post*, 147.]

[36] For the divine legislator, the question is disputed whether God Himself could change or abrogate a law of nature whose author He is. In Catholic theology the answer is negative.

[37] [But see *post*, 133.]

Moral and Political But No Juridical Natural Law. To sum up. First, there exists a moral natural law which is fundamental to the moral conduct of individuals as well as to the positive moral rule, and in every domain including the social domain (social morals) and without distinction between outward and inner acts. This rule of itself obliges only in the internal forum [38] and not before the state, its police and its courts. Second, there also exists a political natural law which, based upon the political instinct of man, establishes political society and all that is essential to it, especially the public authority and the civil law, the latter being considered not in its concrete dispositions but in its principle and its method of elaboration. This political natural law is undoubtedly dependent upon moral natural law because morals govern everything human. But it is in turn the starting point of a new system of properly social (indeed, societal) institutions and rules, inspired by the idea of the public good (at once moral, utilitarian and technical) and governing only the outward acts of man as a member of the group. Third, there exists no juridical natural law in the sense of solutions or even mere directives given in advance to the authority charged with the establishment of the civil law according to the public good. No doubt there are principles commonly accepted in the laws of the countries of the same level of civilization: *Jus gentium* or " general principles of law." But one could not without ambiguity and danger credit natural law with principles which, on the one hand, are very heterogeneous, since one finds there commingled rules of morals, of common sense, and of social utility —and which, on the other hand, lack the characteristics of necessity and universally inherent in the idea of nature. The practice of civilized countries, even supported by wisdom and experience, is not synonymous with natural inclination.

The Dualism of " Natural law—Positive Law" Replaced by " Morals —Law." If these views are correct, they yield an important result concerning the statement of the problem here under discussion. One must no longer speak of relationships between natural law and positive law (at least when by positive law one understands, as is customary, the law of the jurists, the civil law, and not the positive moral law or rule). One must speak of relationships between morals, not only natural but also positive, and the civil law, that is to say, the law. This statement does correspond to reality. On the one hand, what makes its appearance throughout natural law is indeed morals. On the other hand, the law has relationships with kinds of values other than the ethical values. By comparison, the traditional statement errs both by lack of precision and by confusion. It does not bring out with precision that natural law above all signifies morals. At the same time, that statement leads us to believe that natural law covers all values whatever of interest to the jurist.[39]   [pp. 430–431]

---

[38] [*Cf. post*, 179, note 14.]

[39] [On this view, natural law seems no more than another name for morals; this would hardly be contested by a positivist (*cf. post*, 213) though differences would remain as to the nature of moral precepts. Nonetheless, similar ideas are to be found in many contemporary natural lawyers, such as Fuller and D'Entrèves. See also O'Meara, 5 Natural L.F. at p. 83: " Natural law fruitfully may be regarded as the contribution which ethics can make to law " or Utz, 3 Natural L.F. at p. 17: " Natural law is essentially normative ethics."]

THE UNITED STATES' CONSTITUTION

ARTICLE VI

SECTION 2

This Constitution, and the laws of the United States which shall be made in pursuance thereof ; and all treaties made, or which shall be made, under the authority of the United States, shall be the supreme law of the land ; and the Judges in every State shall be bound thereby, anything in the Constitution or laws of any State to the contrary notwithstanding.[40]

AMENDMENT I

Congress shall make no law respecting an establishment of religion, or prohibiting the free exercise thereof ; or abridging the freedom of speech or of the press ; or the right of the people peaceably to assemble, and to petition the government for a redress of grievances.

AMENDMENT V

No person shall be held to answer for a capital, or otherwise infamous crime, unless on a presentment or indictment of a grand jury, except in cases arising in the land or naval forces, or in the militia, when in actual service in time of war or public danger ; nor shall any person be subject for the same offense to be twice put in jeopardy of life or limb ; nor shall be compelled in any criminal case to be a witness against himself, nor be deprived of life, liberty or property, without due process of law ; nor shall private property be taken for public use without just compensation.

AMENDMENT VI

In all criminal prosecutions, the accused shall enjoy the right to a speedy and public trial, by an impartial jury of the State and district wherein the crime shall have been committed, which district shall have been previously ascertained by law, and to be informed of the nature and cause of the accusation ; to be confronted with the witnesses against him ; to have compulsory process for obtaining witnesses in his favor, and to have the assistance of counsel for his defense.[41]

---

[40] [This article shows that the intention of the framers of the U.S. Constitution was that the Constitution should be not only supreme, but be treated as law, *i.e.*, that it should be binding on and administered by the courts. This provision enabled Marshall C.J. to develop later the judicial doctrine laid down in *Marbury* v. *Madison* (1 Cranch 237) to the effect that the court had the power to declare laws of Congress unconstitutional. Even today the interpretation of this power is disputed. Judge Learned Hand, for example, maintained that judicial review was interpolated into the text so as " to prevent the defeat of the venture at hand " (see *The Bill of Rights* (1958)). But Wechsler, on the other hand, believes that " the power of the courts is grounded in the language of the constitution and is not a mere interpolation," that this article is " a mandate to all of officialdom including courts (see *Principles, Politics and Fundamental Law* (1961), pp. 5–6).]

[41] [The first ten Amendments constitute the so-called Bill of Rights, 1791. See also the American Declaration of Independence of 1776, of which the most memorable passage is as follows : " . . . We hold these truths to be self-evident —That all men are created equal ; that they are endowed by their Creator with certain inalienable rights ; that among these are life, liberty and the pursuit of happiness . . . ."]

AMENDMENT IX

The enumeration in the Constitution of certain rights, shall not be construed to deny or disparage others retained by the people.

AMENDMENT XIV

Section I

All persons born or naturalized in the United States, and subject to the jurisdiction thereof, are citizens of the United States and of the State wherein they reside. No State shall make or enforce any law which shall abridge the privileges or immunities of citizens of the United States; nor shall any State deprive any person of life, liberty or property, without due process of law; nor deny to any person within its jurisdiction the equal protection of the laws.[42]

---

[42] [Whilst the United States is the oldest example of a country with courts testing legislation by reference to fundamental law, their experience is no longer unique. See, for example, the developments in post-war Federal Germany. By means of a Basic Law fundamental human rights are given an overriding constitutional priority, and the strong naturalist tone of the constitution results in fundamental rights being regarded as not so much valid because they are in the framework of the law, but rather laws are treated as valid only in the framework of fundamental rights. The approach is typified by a decision in 1968, in which it was held that a Nazi Citizenship Law of 1941, purporting to deprive persons of nationality on grounds of race and religion, was not only in conflict with the Basic Law, but its inconsistency with justice had reached such intolerable proportions that it had to be considered void *ab initio* (see (1968) 9 Journal of I.C.J. 129–130). See, generally, Muller (1965) 6 Journal of I.C.J. 191 and Lewan, (1968) 17 I.C.L.Q. 571. Developments in Canada (see *R.* v. *Drybones* [1970] S.C.R. 282, on which see Smith 49 Can.Bar Rev. 163), Italy (see Evans, 17 I.C.L.Q. 602 and the 1970 decision of the Constitutional Court upholding the legality of the advocacy of birth control which led to the Italian Parliament immediately repealing legislation making this illegal), France and Israel may also be noted. On Israel see Albert, 82 Harv.L.Rev. 1245 and Nimmer, 70 Col.L.Rev. 1217, the latter discussing *Bergman* v. *Minister of Finance*, in which the Supreme Court declared an Act of the Knesset (the Israeli Parliament) void despite the fact that Israel has not yet adopted a constitution. Bergman complained that the Financing Law unfairly discriminated against new political parties in election campaigns by providing public money for existing parties, but not new parties. He asked the Supreme Court to invalidate the Financing Law by reason of section 4 of the Basic Law of the Knesset which provided for (*inter alia*) " equal " elections. According to Nimmer (p. 1225), " there is some language in the *Bergman* opinion which suggests that it was simply the court's own view of natural law requirements that prevailed over the stated intent of the Knesset in the Financing Law of 1969. He quotes the Court which said that the general principle of equality before the law *" can also stand on its own,* without being sustained by a section of a written law that expressly prescribes the principle of the equality of all before the law. We possess no such express section, neither in a written constitution, nor in an " entrenched " section of a Basic Law. *Nevertheless, this principle that is nowhere inscribed breathes the breath of life into our whole . . . system."* But this sweeping dictum is limited by the following sentence which states that " in the borderline case, when the provision of the enacted Law is open to two interpretations, we should prefer that which preserves the equality of all before the law and does not set it at nought." So, as Nimmer comments, " once again, natural law is used merely for interpretation, and not as a firm barrier to legislative omnipotence." (p. 1226).]

ADAMSON v. CALIFORNIA

(United States Supreme Court)

332 U.S. 46, 91 L. ed. 1903 (1946) [43]

Frankfurter J. . . .

Indeed, the suggestion that the Fourteenth Amendment incorporates the first eight Amendments as such is not unambiguously urged. Even the boldest innovator would shrink from suggesting to more than half the States that they may no longer initiate prosecutions without indictment by grand jury, or that thereafter all the States of the Union must furnish a jury of twelve for every case involving a claim above twenty dollars. There is suggested merely a selective incorporation of the first eight Amendments into the Fourteenth Amendment.[44] Some are in and some are out, but we are left in the dark as to which are in and which are out. Nor are we given the calculus for determining which go in and which stay out. If the basis of selection is merely that those provisions of the first eight Amendments are incorporated which commend themselves to individual justices as indispensable to the dignity and happiness of a free man, we are thrown back to a merely subjective test. The protection against unreasonable search and seizure might have primacy for one judge, while trial by a jury of twelve for every claim above twenty dollars might appear to another as an ultimate need in a free society. In the history of thought " natural law " has a much longer and much better founded meaning and justification than such subjective selection of the first eight Amendments for incorporation into the Fourteenth. If all that is meant is that due process contains within itself certain minimal standards which are " of the very essence of a scheme of ordered liberty,"

---

[43] [The issue in this case was whether a comment by the prosecutor in a state court to the effect that the accused's failure to testify amounted to an admission of guilt was contrary to the 14th Amendment. The 5th Amendment provided that no one should be compelled to be a witness against himself, but this applied to federal trials only. Did the 14th impliedly entail a similar prohibition? *Twining (post*, 116) and *Adamson* have been overruled in part by *Malloy* v. *Hogan*, 375 U.S. 1 (1964), where the Supreme Court, while still upholding the view that the 14th Amendment did not as such incorporate the Bill of Rights into the procedure of state trials, nevertheless held that the privilege against self-incrimination laid down in the 5th Amendment was safeguarded by the 14th Amendment, and, therefore, availed in state as well as federal proceedings: Brennan J. said : " It would be incongruous to have different standards determine the validity of a claim of privilege based on the same feared prosecution, depending on whether the claim was asserted in a state or federal court. . . . The same standards must determine whether an accused's silence in either a federal or state proceeding is justified " (p. 11). On the privilege against self-incrimination generally see Heydon (1971) 87 L.Q.R. 214.

The case law emphasises how conceptions may change over a comparatively brief period. This point is further illustrated by the omission in this edition of *Palko* v. *Connecticut*, 302 U.S. 319, as many of Cardozo's arguments have fallen under the axe in later cases.

Indeed, leading constitutional lawyers now agree that there is very little left of the " non-incorporation " doctrine. See, for example, Black, *Perspectives in Constitutional Law* (1970), pp. 76–77.

Of course, even without a fundamental law framework ideas on fundamental human rights may change rapidly ; witness the swing against the Judges' Rules in Lord Widgery C.J.'s address to the A.B.A. in 1971. (121 New L.J. 631).]

[44] [It was argued that the 14th Amendment (*ante*, 114), necessarily implied that each state of the Union was henceforth subject to these requirements of the earlier Amendments which laid down certain specific features to be embodied in *federal* trials.]

Palko v. Connecticut, 302 US 319, 325, 82 L ed 288, 292, 58 S Ct 149, putting upon this Court the duty of applying these standards from time to time, then we have merely arrived at the insight which our predecessors long ago expressed. We are called upon to apply to the difficult issues of our own day the wisdom afforded by the great opinions in this field. . . . This guidance bids us to be duly mindful of the heritage of the past, with its great lessons of how liberties are won and how they are lost. As judges charged with the delicate task of subjecting the government of a continent to the Rule of Law we must be particularly mindful that it is " a *constitution* we are expounding," so that it should not be imprisoned in what are merely legal forms even though they have the sanction of the Eighteenth Century.

. . . And so, when, as in a case like the present, a conviction in a State court is here for review under a claim that a right protected by the Due Process Clause of the Fourteenth Amendment has been denied, the issue is not whether an infraction of one of the specific provisions of the first eight Amendments is disclosed by the record. The relevant question is whether the criminal proceedings which resulted in conviction deprived the accused of the due process of law to which the United States Constitution entitled him. Judicial review of that guaranty of the Fourteenth Amendment inescapably imposes upon this Court an exercise of judgment upon the whole course of the proceedings in order to ascertain whether they offend those canons of decency and fairness which express the notions of justice of English-speaking peoples even toward those charged with the most heinous offenses. These standards of justice are not authoritatively formulated anywhere as though they were prescriptions in a pharmacopoeia. But neither does the application of the Due Process Clause imply that judges are wholly at large. The judicial judgment in applying the Due Process Clause must move within the limits of accepted notions of justice and is not to be based upon the idiosyncrasies of a merely personal judgment. The fact that judges among themselves may differ whether in a particular case a trial offends accepted notions of justice is not disproof that general rather than idiosyncratic standards are applied. An important safeguard against such merely individual judgment is an alert deference to the judgment of the State court under review.[45]

Mr. Justice Black, dissenting.

This decision reasserts a constitutional theory spelled out in Twining v. New Jersey, 211 US 78, 53 L ed 97, 29 S Ct 14, that this Court is endowed by the Constitution with boundless power under " natural law " periodically to expand and contract constitutional standards to conform to the Court's conception of what at a particular time constitutes " civilized decency " and "fundamental liberty and justice." Invoking this Twining rule, the Court concludes that although comment upon testimony in a federal court would violate the Fifth Amendment, identical comment in a state court does not violate today's fashion in civilized decency and fundamentals and is therefore not prohibited by the Federal Constitution as amended.

The Twining Case was the first, as it is the only, decision of this Court, which has squarely held that states were free, notwithstanding the

---

[45] [Held, accordingly, by the majority, that the appeal failed.]

Fifth and Fourteenth Amendments, to extort evidence from one accused of crime. I agree that if Twining be reaffirmed, the result reached might appropriately follow. But I would not reaffirm the Twining decision. I think that decision and the "natural law" theory of the Constitution upon which it relies degrade the constitutional safeguards of the Bill of Rights and simultaneously appropriate for this Court a broad power which we are not authorized by the Constitution to exercise. Furthermore, the Twining decision rested on previous cases and broad hypotheses which have been undercut by intervening decisions of this Court. See Corwin, The Supreme Court's Construction of the Self-Incrimination Clause, 29 Mich L Rev 1, 191, 202. . . .

I cannot consider the Bill of Rights to be an outworn 18th Century "strait jacket" as the Twining opinion did. Its provisions may be thought outdated abstractions by some. And it is true that they were designed to meet ancient evils. But they are the same kind of human evils that have emerged from century to century wherever excessive power is sought by the few at the expense of the many. In my judgment the people of no nation can lose their liberty so long as a Bill of Rights like ours survives and its basic purposes are conscientiously interpreted, enforced and respected so as to afford continuous protection against old, as well as new, devices and practices which might thwart those purposes. I fear to see the consequences of the Court's practice of substituting its own concepts of decency and fundamental justice for the language of the Bill of Rights as its point of departure in interpreting and enforcing that Bill of Rights. If the choice must be between the selective process of the Palko decision applying some of the Bill of Rights to the States, or the Twining rule applying none of them, I would choose the Palko selective process. But rather than accept either of these choices, I would follow what I believe was the original purpose of the Fourteenth Amendment— to extend to all the people of the nation the complete protection of the Bill of Rights. To hold that this Court can determine what, if any, provisions of the Bill of Rights will be enforced, and if so to what degree, is to frustrate the great design of a written Constitution.[46]

46 [Two general problems of great practical importance arise in connection with a guarantee of fundamental rights in a written constitution. In the first place there is the question how far such rights are to be taken to be unqualified. Thus the American Constitution guarantees freedom of speech, but this cannot mean that a person is absolutely entitled to incite others to criminal conduct, or to defame other citizens with impunity. As regards the problem of the extent to which those publicly advocating subversion may be restrained without infringement of the Constitution, Holmes J. in *Schenck* v. *U.S.*, 249 U.S. 47 (1919), formulated the celebrated test that there must be "a clear and present danger" to public security, to justify encroachment on the right of free speech. This test, while generally accepted, has given great difficulty in regard to its application. Thus in *Dennis* v. *U.S.*, 341 U.S. 494 (1951), it was held that the advocacy of Communist doctrine could be rendered criminally punishable without violation of the Constitution, on the ground that such doctrine contemplated the forcible overthrow of the existing form of government. (See, however, the later case of *Yates* v. *U.S.*, 353 U.S. 346 (1957), where the court adopted a far more liberal approach towards this type of question). Two Supreme Court judges, Black and Douglas J.J., vigorously dissented on the ground that the grant of free speech in the Constitution, must be regarded as virtually absolute, even if its exercise may incite to illegal action (see *per* Black J. in *Yates* v. *U.S.* at p. 340). While accepting the "clear and present danger" test, Black J. insists that this only refers to a situation where actual violence is in immediate contemplation, as for instance where a person seeks to persuade others to embark

Conceding the possibility that this Court is now wise enough to improve on the Bill of Rights by substituting natural law concepts for the Bill of Rights, I think the possibility is entirely too speculative to agree to take that course. I would therefore hold in this case that the full protection of the Fifth Amendment's proscription against compelled testimony must be afforded by California. This I would do because of reliance upon the original purpose of the Fourteenth Amendment.

It is an illusory apprehension that literal application of some or all of the provisions of the Bill of Rights to the States would unwisely increase the sum total of the powers of this Court to invalidate state legislation. The Federal Government has not been harmfully burdened by the requirement that enforcement of federal laws affecting civil liberty conform literally to the Bill of Rights. Who would advocate its repeal? It must be conceded, of course, that the natural-law-due-process formula, which the Court today reaffirms, has been interpreted to limit substantially this Court's power to prevent state violations of the individual civil liberties guaranteed by the Bill of Rights. But this formula also has been used in the past, and can be used in the future, to license this Court, in considering regulatory legislation, to roam at large in the broad expanses of policy and morals and to trespass, all too freely, on the legislative domain of the States as well as the Federal Government.

Since Marbury v. Madison, 1 Cranch (US) 137, 2 L ed 60, was decided, the practice has been firmly established, for better or worse, that courts can strike down legislative enactments which violate the Constitution. This process, of course, involves interpretation, and since words can have many meanings, interpretation obviously may result in contraction or extension of the original purpose of a constitutional provision thereby affecting policy. But to pass upon the constitutionality of statutes by looking to the particular standards enumerated in the Bill of Rights and other parts of the Constitution is one thing; to invalidate statutes because of application of "natural law" deemed to be above and undefined by the Constitution is another. "In the one instance, courts proceeding within clearly marked constitutional boundaries seek to execute policies written into the Constitution; in the other, they roam

upon immediate violent and/or illegal courses (*cf. Roth* v. *U.S.*, 354 U.S. 476 (1957). Black J. has repeatedly asserted that the distinction is a fundamental one in the approach to the Constitution, but, with respect, it may be suggested that once one recognises that there must inevitably be certain accepted limitations on any fundamental right, however unqualified the language granting that right may be, it would seem that the distinction is really one of degree. For a recent lucid exposition of the "clear and present danger" test see Strong, 1969 *Supreme Court Review*, pp. 41–80.

The second problem is how a balance is to be struck between different rights guaranteed by the Constitution, where these may possibly come in conflict. Here again, Justices Black and Douglas have become associated with the so-called doctrine of "preferred freedoms," under which it is suggested that certain freedoms, especially associated with personal liberty and freedom of speech, are to be given priority over other freedoms, such as economic freedoms connected with property or contract. This view has been strongly contested by others, especially by Frankfurter J., and still remains a highly controversial issue. Undoubtedly, courts having to administer a written constitution will tend to lean at times in favour of one class of rights rather than another, but it seems unlikely that courts will abandon their flexible approach for a rigid categorisation of values in order of priority, without regard to the particular circumstances in which such conflicts may arise from time to time. (See further on these matters S. Hook, *Paradoxes of Freedom* (1962) Chap. 2.)]

at will in the limitless area of their own beliefs as to reasonableness and actually select policies, a responsibility which the Constitution entrusts to the legislative representatives of the people." Federal Power Commission v. Natural Gas Pipeline Co., 315 US 575, 599, 601, note 4, 86 L ed 1037, 1056, 1057, 62 S Ct 736.

ROCHIN v. *CALIFORNIA*

(*United States Supreme Court*)

342 U.S. 165, 96 L. ed. 183 (1951)

Frankfurter J. . . . Due process of law, "itself a historical product," Jackman v. Rosenbaum Co. 260 US 22, 31, 67 L ed 107, 112, 43 S Ct 9, is not to be turned into a destructive dogma against the States in the administration of their systems of criminal justice.

However, this Court too has its responsibility. Regard for the requirements of the Due Process Clause "inescapably imposes upon this Court an exercise of judgment upon the whole course of the proceedings [resulting in a conviction] in order to ascertain whether they offend those canons of decency and fairness which express the notions of justice of English-speaking peoples even toward those charged with the most heinous offenses." Malinski v. New York (324 US at 416, 417, 89 L ed 1039, 65 S Ct 781). These standards of justice are not authoritatively formulated anywhere as though they were specifics. Due process of law is a summarized constitutional guarantee of respect for those personal immunities which, as Mr. Justice Cardozo twice wrote for the Court, are " so rooted in the traditions and conscience of our people as to be ranked as fundamental," Snyder v. Massachusetts, 291 US 97, 105, 78 L ed 674, 677, 54 S Ct 330, 90 ALR 575, or are " implicit in the concept of ordered liberty." Palko v. Connecticut, 302 US 319, 325, 82 L ed 288, 292, 58 S Ct 149.[47]

The Court's function in the observance of this settled conception of the Due Process Clause does not leave us without adequate guides in subjecting State criminal procedures to constitutional judgment. In dealing not with the machinery of government but with human rights, the absence of formal exactitude, or want of fixity of meaning, is not an unusual or even regrettable attribute of constitutional provisions. Words being symbols do not speak without a gloss. On the one hand the gloss may be the deposit of history, whereby a term gains technical content. Thus the requirements of the Sixth and Seventh Amendments for trial by jury in the Federal courts have a rigid meaning. No changes or chances can alter the content of the verbal symbol of " jury "—a body of twelve men who must reach a unanimous conclusion if the verdict is to go against the defendant. On the other hand, the gloss of some of the verbal symbols of the Constitution does not give them a fixed technical content. It exacts a continuing process of application.

[47] What is here summarized was deemed by a majority of the Court, in Malinski v. New York, 324 U.S. 401, 412 and 438, 89 L ed 1029, 1036, 1050, 65 S. Ct. 781, to be " the controlling principles upon which this Court reviews on constitutional grounds a state court conviction for crime." They have been applied by this Court many times, long before and since the Malinski Case.

When the gloss has thus not been fixed but is a function of the process of judgment, the judgment is bound to fall differently at different times and differently at the same time through different judges. Even more specific provisions, such as the guaranty of freedom of speech and the detailed protection against unreasonable searches and seizures, have inevitably evoked as sharp divisions in this Court as the least specific and most comprehensive protection of liberties, the Due Process Clause.

The vague contours of the Due Process Clause do not leave judges at large. We may not draw on our merely personal and private notions and disregard the limits that bind judges in their judicial function. Even though the concept of due process of law is not final and fixed, these limits are derived from considerations that are fused in the whole nature of our judicial process. See Cardozo, The Nature of the Judicial Process; The Growth of the Law; The Paradoxes of Legal Science. These are considerations deeply rooted in reason and in the compelling traditions of the legal profession. The Due Process Clause places upon this Court the duty of exercising a judgment, within the narrow confines of judicial power in reviewing State convictions, upon interests of society pushing in opposite directions.

Due process of law thus conceived is not to be derided as resort to a revival of " natural law." To believe that this judicial exercise of judgment could be avoided by freezing " due process of law " at some fixed stage of time or thought is to suggest that the most important aspect of constitutional adjudication is a function for inanimate machines and not for judges, for whom the independence safeguarded by Article 3 of the Constitution was designed and who are presumably guided by established standards of judicial behavior. Even cybernetics has not yet made that haughty claim. To practice the requisite detachment and to achieve sufficient objectivity no doubt demands of judges the habit of self-discipline and self-criticism, incertitude that one's own views are incontestable and alert tolerance toward views not shared. But these are precisely the presuppositions of our judicial process. They are precisely the qualities society has a right to expect from those entrusted with ultimate judicial power.

Restraints on our jurisdiction are self-imposed only in the sense that there is from our decisions no immediate appeal short of impeachment or constitutional amendment. But that does not make due process of law a matter of judicial caprice. The faculties of the Due Process Clause may be indefinite and vague, but the mode of their ascertainment is not self-willed. In each case " due process of law " requires an evaluation based on a disinterested inquiry pursued in the spirit of science, on a balanced order of facts exactly and fairly stated, on the detached consideration of conflicting claims (see Hudson County Water Co. v. McCarter, 209 US 349, 355, 52 L ed 828, 831, 28 S Ct 529, 14 Ann Cas 560), on a judgment not ad hoc and episodic but duly mindful of reconciling the needs both of continuity and of change in a progressive society.

Applying these general considerations to the circumstances of the present case, we are compelled to conclude that the proceedings by which this conviction was obtained do more than offend some fastidious squeamishness or private sentimentalism about combating crime too energetically. This is conduct that shocks the conscience. Illegally breaking into the privacy of the petitioner, the struggle to open his mouth and remove what was there, the forcible extraction of his stomach's contents—this course of proceeding by agents of government to obtain evidence is bound to offend even hardened sensibilities. They are methods too close to the rack and the screw to permit of constitutional differentiation.[48]

BROWN v. BOARD OF EDUCATION OF TOPEKA

(United States Supreme Court)

347 U.S. 483 ; 98 L. ed. 873 (1953)

The plaintiffs, Negro children, were denied admission to state public schools attended by white children under state laws requiring or permitting segregation according to race. There were findings below that the Negro and white schools involved had been equalized, or were being equalized, with respect to buildings, curricula, qualifications and salaries of teachers, and other tangible factors.

In an opinion by Warren, Ch. J., the Supreme Court unanimously held that the plaintiffs, by reason of the segregation complained of, were deprived of the equal protection of the laws guaranteed by the Fourteenth Amendment. The " separate but equal " doctrine announced in Plessy v. Ferguson, 163 US 537, 41 L ed 256, 16 S Ct 1138, involving equality in transportation facilities, under which equality of treatment is accorded by providing Negroes and whites substantially equal, though separate, facilities, was held to have no place in the field of public education.

Warren C.J. . . . In approaching this problem, we cannot turn the clock back to 1868 when the Amendment was adopted, or even to 1896 when Plessy v. Ferguson was written. We must consider public education in the light of its full development and its present place in American life throughout the Nation. Only in this way can it be determined if segregation in public schools deprives these plaintiffs of the equal protection of the laws.

Today, education is perhaps the most important function of state and local governments. Compulsory school attendance laws and the

---

[48] [See also *Fikes* v. *Alabama*, 352 U.S. 191, 199 (1957), where it was said that state court judgments are not to be set aside "where the practices of the prosecution, including the police as one of its agencies, do not offend what may fairly be called the civilised standards of the Anglo-American world." *Cf.* *Bartkus* v. *Illinois*, 359 U.S. 121 (1959), concerning the so-called "double jeopardy rule "; and *Gideon* v. *Wainwright*, 372 U.S. 335 (1963), on the right to counsel in criminal cases ; *Miranda* v. *Arizona* 384 U.S. 436 (1966) on a suspect's right to remain silent, his right to the presence of a lawyer, the knowledge that saying anything may incriminate him, and the right to have a lawyer appointed for him if he cannot afford one ; *Mapp* v. *Ohio* 367 U.S. 643 (1961) on the inadmissibility in a state court of evidence obtained by search and seizure in violation of the 4th amendment (such a principle already existed in federal courts) ; and *Berger* v. *New York* 388 U.S. 41 (1967), which held legislation invalid which permitted police eavesdropping without providing judicial supervision or other protective procedures. See also *Duncan* v. *Louisiana* 391 U.S. 145 (1968), *Witherspoon* v. *Illinois* 391 U.S. 510 (1968). The Supreme Court has gone further in the last ten years to protect the criminal than it had in the previous hundred: a backlash against " coddling criminals " is expected by many commentators.]

great expenditures for education both demonstrate our recognition of the importance of education to our democratic society. It is required in the performance of our most basic public responsibilities, even service in the armed forces. It is the very foundation of good citizenship. Today it is a principal instrument in awakening the child to cultural values, in preparing him for later professional training, and in helping him to adjust normally to his environment. In these days, it is doubtful that any child may reasonably be expected to succeed in life if he is denied the opportunity of an education. Such an opportunity, where the state has undertaken to provide it, is a right which must be made available to all on equal terms.

We come then to the question presented: Does segregation of children in public schools solely on the basis of race, even though the physical facilities and other " tangible " factors may be equal, deprive the children of the minority group of equal educational opportunities? We believe that it does. . . .   [pp. 492–493]

. . . We conclude that in the field of public education the doctrine of " separate but equal " has no place. Separate educational facilities are inherently unequal. Therefore, we hold that the plaintiffs and others similarly situated for whom the actions have been brought are, by reason of the segregation complained of, deprived of the equal protection of the laws guaranteed by the Fourteenth Amendment.[49]   [p. 495]

GRISWOLD v. CONNECTICUT

(United States Supreme Court)

381 U.S. 479

(1965)

DOUGLAS J. . . .

We are met with a wide range of questions that implicate the Due Process Clause of the Fourteenth Amendment. Overtones of some

---

[49] [The school board was accordingly ordered to desegregate its schools " with all deliberate speed." This vague standard permitted a number of recalcitrant authorities to delay inordinately and, often, indefinitely. However, in *Alexander* v. *Holmes County Board of Education*, 396 U.S. 19 (1969), the schools were ordered to desegregate " at once," the Supreme Court refusing additional time for 33 Mississippi school districts to submit their desegregation plans. Of course, " at once " is almost as vague as " with all deliberate speed " since certain arrangements have to be made and these cannot be programmed instantaneously. See, further, 84 Harv.L.Rev. 32–46. This saga illustrates the judicial dilemma: the Supreme Court is possessed of no enforcement mechanism. As Frankfurter J. said in *Baker* v. Carr, 369 U.S. 186 (1962) the Court's authority is nourished neither by purse nor sword, but rests on " sustained public confidence in its moral sanction." Even more resistance is expected to the Supreme Court's ruling that private racial discrimination in housing is illegal, (*Jones* v. *Mayer*, 392 U.S. 409 (1968)) for here the practice of the entire nation, not just a few Southern states, as in *Brown*, is at stake. See Denenberg [1971] C.L.J. 134, 140–141.

See also *Shelley* v. *Kramer*, 334 U.S. 1 (1948), holding that the judicial enforcement by state courts of racial covenants restricting the use or disposition of property, violates the equal protection clause of the 14th amendment. But compare *Evans* v. *Ebney*, 396 U.S. 435 (1970) where the court refused application of the *cy-près* doctrine to a gift to the town of Macon, Georgia of land for use as a park, where the testator's intent was that such park should be for whites only. This decision thus backfires: the heirs get an unlooked-for windfall and the negroes of Macon, who needed park facilities more than anyone, get no park.]

arguments suggest that *Lochner* v. *New York,* 198 US 45,[50] should be our guide. But we decline that invitation as we did in *West Coast Hotel Co.* v. *Parish,* 300 US 379. . . . We do not sit as a super-legislature to determine the wisdom, need, and propriety of laws that touch economic problems, business affairs, or social conditions. This law,[51] however, operates directly on an intimate relation of husband and wife and their physician's role in one aspect of that relation.

The association of people is not mentioned in the Constitution nor in the Bill of Rights. The right to educate a child in a school of the parents' choice—whether public or private or parochial—is also not mentioned. Nor is the right to study any particular subject or any foreign language. Yet the First Amendment has been construed to include certain of those rights.

By *Pierce* v. *Society of Sisters,* the right to educate one's children as one chooses is made applicable to the States by the force of the First and Fourteenth Amendments. By *Meyer* v. *Nebraska,* the same dignity is given the right to study the German language in a private school. In other words, the State may not, consistently with the spirit of the First Amendment, contract the spectrum of available knowledge. The right of freedom of speech and press includes not only the right to utter or to print, but the right to distribute, the right to receive, the right to read (*Martin* v. *Struthers,* 319 US 141) and freedom of inquiry, freedom of thought, and freedom to teach (see *Wieman* v. *Updegraff,* 344 US 183) —indeed the freedom of the entire university community. *Sweezy* v. *New Hampshire,* 354 US 234; *Barenblatt* v. *United States,* 360 US 109; *Baggett* v. *Bullitt,* 377 US 360. Without those peripheral rights the specific rights would be less secure. And so we reaffirm the principle of the *Pierce* and the *Meyer* cases.

In *NAACP* v. *Alabama* 357 US 449, we protected the "freedom to associate and privacy in one's association," noting that freedom of association was a peripheral First Amendment right. Disclosure of membership lists of a constitutionally valid association, we held, was invalid "as entailing the likelihood of a substantial restraint upon the exercise by petitioner's members of their right to freedom of association." Ibid. In other words, the First Amendment has a penumbra where privacy is protected from governmental intrusion. In like context, we have protected forms of "association" that are not political in the customary sense but pertain to the social, legal, and economic benefit of the members. *NAACP* v. *Button,* 371 US 415. In *Schware* v. *Board of Bar Examiners,* 353 US 232, we held it not permissible to bar a lawyer from practice, because he had once been a member of the Communist Party. The man's "association with that Party" was not shown to be "anything more than a political faith in a political party" and not action of a kind proving bad moral character. . . . [pp. 481–483]

The foregoing cases suggest that specific guarantees in the Bill of Rights have penumbras, formed by emanations from those guarantees that help give them life and substance. . . . Various guarantees create zones of privacy. The right of association contained in the penumbra of the First Amendment is one, as we have seen. The Third Amendment in its prohibition against the quartering of soldiers "in any house" in

---

[50] [*Post,* 432.]

[51] [*Viz.* a Connecticut statute forbidding the use of contraceptives].

time of peace without the consent of the owner is another facet of that
privacy. The Fourth Amendment explicitly affirms the "right of the
people to be secure in their persons, houses, papers, and effects against
unreasonable searches and seizures." The Fifth Amendment in its Self-
Incrimination Clause enables the citizen to create a zone of privacy
which government may not force him to surrender to his detriment. The
Ninth Amendment provides: "The enumeration in the Constitution, of
certain rights, shall not be construed to deny or disparage others retained
by the people."

The Fourth and Fifth Amendments were described in *Boyd* v. *United
States,* 116 US 616, as protection against all governmental invasions " of
the sanctity of a man's home and the privacies of life." We recently
referred in *Mapp* v. *Ohio,* 367 US 643, to the Fourth Amendment as
creating a "right of privacy, no less important than any other right
carefully and particularly reserved to the people. . . ."

We have had many controversies over these penumbral rights of
" privacy and repose." See e.g. *Breard* v. *Alexandria,* 341 US 622; *Public
Utilities Comm'n* v. *Pollak,* 343 US 451; *Monroe* v. *Pape,* 365 US 167;
Lanza v. *New York,* 370 US 139; *Frank* v. *Maryland,* 359 US 360;
Skinner v. *Oklahoma,* 316 US 535. These cases bear witness that the
right of privacy which presses for recognition here is a legitimate one.

The present case, then, concerns a relationship lying within the zone
of privacy created by several fundamental constitutional guarantees. And
it concerns a law which, in forbidding the *use* of contraceptives rather
than regulating their manufacture or sale, seeks to achieve its goals by
means having a maximum destructive impact upon that relationship.
Such a law cannot stand in light of the familiar principle, so often applied
by this Court, that a "governmental purpose to control or prevent
activities constitutionally subject to state regulation may not be achieved
by means which sweep unnecessarily broadly and thereby invade the
area of protected freedom." *NAACP* v. *Alabama,* 377 US 288. Would
we allow the police to search the sacred precincts of marital bedrooms
for telltale signs of the use of contraceptives? The very idea is repulsive
to the notions of privacy surrounding the marriage relationship.

We deal with a right of privacy older than the Bill of Rights—older
than our political parties, older that our school system. Marriage is a
coming together for better or for worse, hopefully enduring, and intimate
to the degree of being sacred. It is an association that promotes a way of
life, not causes; a harmony in living, not political faiths; a bilateral
loyalty, not commercial or social projects. Yet it is an association for
as noble a purpose as any involved in our prior decisions.

Reversed.   [pp. 484–486]

*Mr. Justice Goldberg, whom The Chief Justice and Mr. Justice
Brennan join, concurring:*

I agree with the Court that Connecticut's birth control law unconstitutionally intrudes upon the right of marital privacy, and I join in its
opinion and judgment. Although I have not accepted the view that " ' due
process ' as used in the Fourteenth Amendment incorporates all of the
first eight Amendments," . . . I do agree that the concept of liberty
protects those personal rights that are fundamental, and is not confined
to the specific terms of the Bill of Rights. My conclusion that the concept
of liberty is not so restricted and that it embraces the right of marital

privacy though that right is not mentioned explicitly in the Constitution is supported both by numerous decisions of this Court, referred to in the Court's opinion, and by the language and history of the Ninth Amendment. In reaching the conclusion that the right of marital privacy is protected, as being within the protected penumbra of specific guarantees of the Bill of Rights, the Court refers to the Ninth Amendment. . . . I add these words to emphasize the relevance of that Amendment to the Court's holding.

The Court stated many years ago that Due Process Clause protects those liberties that are " so rooted in the traditions and conscience of our people as to be ranked as fundamental." *Snyder* v. *Massachusetts,* 291 US 97. In *Gitlow* v. *New York,* 268 US 652, the Court said:

> For present purposes we may and do assume that freedom of speech and of the press—which are protected by the First Amendment from abridgment by Congress—are among the *fundamental* personal rights and " liberties " protected by the due process clause of the Fourteenth Amendment from impairment by the States. (Emphasis added.)

And, in *Meyer* v. *Nebraska,* 262 US 390, 399, the Court, referring to the Fourteenth Amendment, stated:

> While this Court has not attempted to define with exactness the liberty thus guaranteed, the term has received much consideration and some of the included things have been definitely stated. Without doubt, it denotes not merely freedom from bodily restraint, but also [for example] the right . . . to marry, establish a home and bring up children. . . .

This Court, in a series of decisions, has held that the Fourteenth Amendment absorbs and applies to the States those specifics of the first eight amendments which express fundamental personal rights. The language and history of the Ninth Amendment reveal that the Framers of the Constitution believed that there are additional fundamental rights, protected from governmental infringement, which exist alongside those fundamental rights specifically mentioned in the first eight constitutional amendments.

The Ninth Amendment reads, " The enumeration in the Constitution, of certain rights, shall not be construed to deny or disparage others retained by the people." . . . It was proffered to quiet expressed fears that a bill of specifically enumerated rights could not be sufficiently broad to cover all essential rights and that the specific mention of certain rights would be interpreted as a denial that others were protected. . . .
[pp. 486–488]

Statements of Madison and Storey make clear that the Framers did not intend that the first eight amendments be construed to exhaust the basic and fundamental rights which the Constitution guaranteed to the people.

While this Court has had little occasion to interpret the Ninth Amendment, " [i]t cannot be presumed that any clause in the constitution is intended to be without effect." *Marbury* v. *Madison,* 1 Cranch 137, 174, 2 L Ed. 60, 72. In interpreting the Constitution, " real effect should be given to all the words it uses." *Myers* v. *United States,* 272 US 52. The Ninth Amendment to the Constitution may be regarded by some as a recent discovery and may be forgotten by others, but since 1791 it has been a basic part of the Constitution which we are sworn to uphold. To hold that a right so basic and fundamental and so deep-rooted in our society as the right of privacy in marriage may be infringed because that right is not guaranteed in so many words by the first eight amendments to the Constitution is to ignore the Ninth Amendment and to give it no effect whatsoever. Moreover, a judicial construction that this fundamental right is not protected by the Constitution because it is not mentioned in explicit terms by one of the first eight amendments or elsewhere in the Constitution would violate the Ninth Amendment, which specifically states that "[t]he enumeration in the Constitution, of certain rights, shall not be *construed* to deny or disparage others retained by the people." (Emphasis added.)

A dissenting opinion suggests that my interpretation of the Ninth Amendment somehow "broaden[s] the powers of this Court." With all due respect, I believe that it misses the import of what I am saying. I do not take the position of my Brother Black in his dissent in *Adamson* v. *California*, 332 US 46,[52] that the entire Bill of Rights is incorporated in the Fourteenth Amendment, and I do not mean to imply that the Ninth Amendment is applied against the States by the Fourteenth. Nor do I mean to state that the Ninth Amendment constitutes an independent source of rights protected from infringement by either the States or Federal Government. Rather, the Ninth Amendment shows a belief of the Constitution's authors that fundamental rights exist that are not expressly enumerated in the first eight amendments and an intent that the list of rights included there not be exhaustive. As any student of this Court's opinions knows, this Court has held, often unanimously, that the Fifth and Fourteenth Amendments protect certain fundamental personal liberties from abridgment by the Federal Government or the States. . . . The Ninth Amendment simply shows the intent of the Constitution's authors that other fundamental personal rights should not be denied such protection or disparaged in any other way simply because they are not specifically listed in the first eight constitutional amendments. I do not see how this broadens the authority of the court; rather it serves to support what this Court has been doing in protecting fundamental rights. . . .   [pp. 490–493]

In determining which rights are fundamental, judges are not left at large to decide cases in light of their personal and private notions. Rather, they must look to the "traditions and [collective] conscience of our people " to determine whether a principle is " so rooted [there] . . . as to be ranked as fundamental." *Snyder* v. *Massachusetts,* 291 US 97. The inquiry is whether a right involved " is of such a character that it cannot be denied without violating those ' fundamental principles of liberty and justice which lie at the base of all our civil and political institutions.' . . ." *Powell* v. *Alabama,* 287 US 45. " Liberty " also " gains content from the emanations of . . . specific [constitutional] guarantees " and " from experience with the requirements of a free society." *Poe* v. *Ullman,* 367 US 497.

I agree fully with the Court that, applying these tests, the right of privacy is a fundamental personal right, " emanating from the totality of the constitutional scheme under which we live." Mr. Justice Brandeis,

[52] [*Ante,* 115.]

dissenting in *Olmstead* v. *United States,* 277 US 438, comprehensively summarized the principles underlying the Constitution's guarantees of privacy:

> The protection guaranteed by the [Fourth and Fifth] Amendments is much broader in scope. The makers of our Constitution undertook to secure conditions favorable to the pursuit of happiness. They recognized the significance of man's spiritual nature, of his feelings and of his intellect. They knew that only part of the pain, pleasure, and satisfactions of life are to be found in material things. They sought to protect Americans in their beliefs, their thoughts, their emotions and their sensations. They conferred as against the Government, the right to be let alone—the most comprehensive of rights and the right most valued by civilized men. [pp. 493–494]

The entire fabric of the Constitution and the purposes that clearly underlie its specific guarantees demonstrate that the rights to marital privacy and to marry and raise a family are of similar order and magnitude as the fundamental rights specifically protected.

Although the Constitution does not speak in so many words of the right of privacy in marriage, I cannot believe that it offers these fundamental rights no protection. The fact that no particular provision of the Constitution explicitly forbids the State from disrupting the traditional relation of the family—a relation as old and as fundamental as our entire civilization—surely does not show that the Government was meant to have the power to do so. Rather, as the Ninth Amendment expressly recognizes, there are fundamental personal rights such as this one, which are protected from abridgment by the Government though not specifically mentioned in the Constitution.

My Brother Stewart, while characterizing the Connecticut birth control law as " an uncommonly silly law," would nevertheless let it stand on the ground that it is not for the courts to "'substitute their social and economic beliefs for the judgment of legislative bodies who are elected to pass laws.'" Elsewhere, I have stated that " [w]hile I quite agree with Mr. Justice Brandeis that . . . 'a . . . state may . . . serve as a laboratory; and try novel social and economic experiments,' *New State Ice Co.* v. *Liebmann,* 285 US 262, I do not believe that this includes the power to experiment with the fundamental liberties of citizens. . . ." The vice of the dissenters' views is that it would permit such experimentation by the States in the area of the fundamental personal rights of its citizens. I cannot agree that the Constitution grants such power either to the States or to the Federal Government.

The logic of the dissents would sanction federal or state legislation that seems to me even more plainly unconstitutional than the statute before us. Surely the Government, absent a showing of a compelling subordinate state interest, could not decree that all husbands and wives must be sterilized after two children have been born to them. Yet by their reasoning such an invasion of marital privacy would not be subject to constitutional challenge because, while it might be " silly," no provision of the Constitution specifically prevents the Government from curtailing the marital right to bear children and raise a family. While it may shock some of my Brethren that the Court today holds that the Constitution protects the right of marital privacy, in my view it is far more shocking to believe that the personal liberty guaranteed by the

Constitution does not include protection against such totalitarian limitation of family size, which is at complete variance with our constitutional concepts. Yet, if upon a showing of a slender basis of rationality, a law outlawing voluntary birth control by married persons is valid, then by the same reasoning, a law requiring compulsory birth control also would seem to be valid. In my view, however, both types of law would unjustifiably intrude upon rights of marital privacy which are constitutionally protected.

In a long series of cases this Court has held that where fundamental personal liberties are involved, they may not be abridged by the States simply on a showing that a regulatory statute has some rational relationship to the effectuation of a proper state purpose. "Where there is a significant encroachment upon personal liberty, the State may prevail only upon showing a subordinating interest which is compelling," *Bates* v. *Little Rock*, 361 US 516. The law must be shown "necessary, and not merely rationally related, to the accomplishment of a permissible state policy." *McLaughlin* v. *Florida*, 379 US 184. . . .

Although the Connecticut birth control law obviously encroaches upon a fundamental personal liberty, the State does not show that the law serves any " subordinating state interest which is compelling " or that it is " necessary . . . to the accomplishment of a permissible state policy." The State, at most, argues that there is some rational relation between this statute and what is admittedly a legitimate subject of state concern —the discouraging of extra-marital relations. It says that preventing the use of birth control devices by married persons helps prevent the indulgence by some in such extra-marital relations. The rationality of this justification is dubious, particularly in light of the admitted widespread availability to all persons in the State of Connecticut, unmarried as well as married, of birth control devices for the prevention of disease, as distinguished from the prevention of conception, see *Tileston* v. *Ullman*, 129 Conn. 84, 26 A2d 582. But, in any event, it is clear that the State interest in safeguarding marital fidelity can be served by a more discriminately tailored statute, which does not, like the present one, sweep unnecessarily broadly, reaching far beyond the evil sought to be dealt with and intruding upon the privacy of all married couples. . . . Here, as elsewhere, " [p]recision of regulation must be the touchstone in an area so closely touching our most precious freedoms." *NAACP* v. *Button.* The State of Connecticut does have statutes, the constitutionality of which is beyond doubt, which prohibit adultery and fornication. See Conn Gen Stat §§ 53–218, 53–219 et seq. These statutes demonstrate that means for achieving the same basic purpose of protecting marital fidelity are available to Connecticut without the need to " invade the area of protected freedoms. . . ."   [pp. 495–498]

BLACK J. [dissenting]. . . .

My Brother Goldberg has adopted the recent discovery that the Ninth Amendment as well as the Due Process Clause can be used by this Court as authority to strike down all state legislation which this Court thinks violates " fundamental principles of liberty and justice," or is contrary to the " traditions and collective conscience of our people." He also states, without proof satisfactory to me, that in making decisions on this basis judges will not consider " their personal and private notions." One may ask how they can avoid considering them.

Our Court certainly has no machinery with which to take a Gallup Poll. And the scientific miracles of this age have not yet produced a gadget which the Court can use to determine what traditions are rooted in the " collective conscience of our people." Moreover, one would certainly have to look far beyond the language of the Ninth Amendment to find that the Framers vested in this Court any such awesome veto powers over lawmaking, either by the States or by the Congress. Nor does anything in the history of the Amendment offer any support for such a shocking doctrine. The whole history of the adoption of the Constitution and Bill of Rights points the other way, and the very material quoted by my Brother Goldberg shows that the Ninth Amendment was intended to protect against the idea that " by enumerating particular exceptions to the grant of power " to the Federal Government, " those rights which were not singled out, were intended to be assigned into the hands of the General Government [the United States], and were consequently insecure." That Amendment was passed, not to broaden the powers of this Court or any other department of " the General Government," but, as every student of history knows, to assure the people that the Constitution in all its provisions was intended to limit the Federal Government to the powers granted expressly or by necessary implication. If any broad, unlimited power to hold laws unconstitutional because they offend what this Court conceives to be " the collective conscience of our people " is vested in this Court by the Ninth Amendment, the Fourteenth Amendment, or any other provision of the Constitution, it was not given by the Framers, but rather has been bestowed on the Court by the Court. This fact is perhaps responsible for the peculiar phenomenon that for a period of a century and a half no serious suggestion was ever made that the Ninth Amendment, enacted to protect State powers against federal invasion, could be used as a weapon of federal power to prevent state legislatures from passing laws they consider appropriate to govern local affairs. Use of any such broad, unbounded judicial authority would make of this Court's members a day-to-day constitutional convention.

I repeat so as not to be misunderstood that this Court does have power, which it should exercise, to hold laws unconstitutional where they are forbidden by the Federal Constitution. My point is that there is no provision of the Constitution which either expressly or impliedly vests power in this Court to sit as a supervisory agency over acts of duly constituted legislative bodies and set aside their laws because of the Court's belief that the legislative policies adopted are unreasonable, unwise, arbitrary, capricious or irrational. The adoption of such loose, flexible, uncontrolled standard for holding laws unconstitutional, if ever it is finally achieved, will amount to a great unconstitutional shift of power to the courts which I believe and am constrained to say will be bad for the courts and worse for the country. Subjecting federal and state laws to such an unrestrained and unrestrainable judicial control as to the wisdom of legislative enactments would, I fear, jeopardize the separation of governmental powers that the Framers set up and at the same time threaten to take away much of the power of States to govern themselves which the Constitution plainly intended them to have.

I realize that many good and able men have eloquently spoken and written, sometimes in rhapsodical strains, about the duty of this Court

to keep the Constitution in tune with the times. The idea is that the
Constitution must be changed from time to time and that this Court
is charged with a duty to make those changes. For myself, I must
with all deference reject that philosophy. The Constitution makers
knew the need for change and provided for it. Amendments suggested
by the people's elected representatives can be submitted to the people or
their selected agents for ratification. That method of change was good
for our Fathers, and being somewhat old-fashioned I must add it is
good enough for me. And so, I cannot rely on the Due Process Clause
or the Ninth Amendment or any mysterious and uncertain natural law
concept as a reason for striking down this state law. The Due Process
Clause with an " arbitrary and capricious " or " shocking to the conscience " formula was liberally used by this Court to strike down
economic legislation in the early decades of this century, threatening,
many people thought, the tranquility and stability of the Nation.
. . . That formula, based on subjective considerations of " natural
justice," is no less dangerous when used to enforce this Court's views
about personal rights than those about economic rights. I had thought
that we had laid that formula, as a means for striking down state
legislation, to rest once and for all in cases like *West Coast Hotel Co.* v.
Parrish, 300 US 379. . . .   [pp. 518–522]
    The late Judge Learned Hand, after emphasizing his view that judges
should not use the due process formula suggested in the concurring
opinions today or any other formula like it to invalidate legislation
offensive to their " personal preferences," made the statements, with
which I fully agree, that:
        For myself it would be most irksome to be ruled by a bevy of
    Platonic Guardians, even if I knew how to choose them, which
    I assuredly do not.
    So far as I am concerned, Connecticut's law as applied here is not
forbidden by any provision of the Federal Constitution as that
Constitution was written, and I am therefore to affirm.   [pp. 526–527]

H. L. A. HART

Problems of Philosophy of Law

(1967) [53]

. . . **Substantive law.** The purposes which human beings pursue in
society and for the realization of which they employ law as an instrument are infinitely various, and men may differ in the importance
they attach to them and in their moral judgments about them. But
the simplest form of the argument that there are certain constant
criteria for the evaluation of a legal system consists in the elaboration
of the truth that if law is to be of any value as an instrument for the
realization of human purposes, it must contain certain rules concerning
the basic conditions of social life.[54] Thus it is not only true that the
legal system of any modern state and any legal system which has

---

53 [From ed. Edwards, *Encyclopaedia of Philosophy*, Vol. 6, p. 264.]
54 [Hart has elsewhere referred to these as a " minimum content of natural law."
See *The Concept of Law*, pp. 189–195. See *ante*, 84.]

succeeded in enduring have contained rules restricting the use of violence, protecting certain forms of property, and enforcing certain forms of contract; it is also clear that without the protections and advantages that such rules supply, men would be grossly hampered in the pursuit of any aims. Legal rules providing for these things are therefore basic in the sense that without them other legal rules would be pointless or at least would operate only fitfully or inefficiently. Criticism of a legal system on the grounds that it omitted such rules could be rebutted only by the demonstration that in the particular case they were unnecessary because the human beings to which the system applied or their natural surroundings were in some way quite extraordinary, that is, that they lacked certain of the salient characteristics which men and things normally have. This is so because the need for such rules derives from such familiar natural facts as that men are both vulnerable to violence and tempted to use it against each other; that the food, clothes, and shelter necessary to existence do not exist naturally in limitless abundance but must be grown or manufactured by human effort and need legal protection from interference during growth and manufacture and safe custody pending consumption; and that to secure the mutual cooperation required for the profitable development of natural resources, men need legal rules enabling them to bind themselves to future courses of conduct.

Argument along these lines may be viewed as a modest empirical counterpart to the more ambitious teleological doctrine of natural law, according to which there are certain rules for the government of human conduct that can be seen by men endowed with reason as necessary to enable men to attain the specifically human optimum state or end (*finis, telos*) appointed for men by Nature or (in Christian doctrine) by God. The empirical version of this theory assumes only that, whatever other purposes laws may serve, they must, to be acceptable to any rational person, enable men to live and organize their lives for the more efficient pursuit of their aims. It is, of course, possible to challenge this assumption and to deny that the fact that there are certain rules necessary if fundamental human needs are to be satisfied has any relevance to the criticism of law. But this denial seems intelligible only as a specifically religious doctrine which regards law as the expression of a divine will. It may then be argued that men's lives should be regulated by the law not in order to further any secular human purposes but because conformity to God's will is in itself meritorious or obligatory.

A more serious objection to the empirical argument conducted in terms of human needs for protection from violence to the person and property and for cooperation is the contention that although these are fundamental human needs, the coercive rules of a legal system need not provide for them. It may be said that the accepted morality of all societies provides a system of restraint which provides adequately for these needs, and that the vast majority of men abstain from murder, theft, and dishonesty not from fear of legal sanctions but for other, usually moral, reasons. In these circumstances it may be no defect in a legal system that it confines itself to other matters in relation to which the accepted morality is silent.

It seems clear, however, that social morality left to itself could not provide adequately for the fundamental needs of social life, save in the simplest forms of society. It may well be that most men, when they believe themselves to be protected from malefactors by the punishments, threats of punishment, and physical restrains of the law, will themselves voluntarily submit to the restraints necessary for peaceful and profitable coexistence. But it does not follow that without the law's protections, voluntary submission to these restraints would be either reasonable or likely. In any case, the rules and principles of social morality leave open to dispute too many questions concerning the precise scope and form of its restraints. Legal rules are needed to supply the detail required to distinguish murder and assault from excusable homicide and injury, to define the forms of property to be protected, and to specify the forms of contract to be enforced. Hence, the omission of such things from the legal system could not be excused on the ground that the existence of a social morality made them unnecessary.

Procedural law. Laws, however impeccable their content, may be of little service to human beings and may cause both injustice and misery unless they generally conform to certain requirements which may be broadly termed procedural (in contrast with the substantive requirements discussed above). These procedural requirements relate to such matters as the generality of rules of law, the clarity with which they are phrased, the publicity given to them, the time of their enactment, and the manner in which they are judicially applied to particular cases. The requirements that the law, except in special circumstances, should be general (should refer to classes of persons, things, and circumstances, not to individuals or to particular actions); should be free from contradictions, ambiguities, and obscurities; should be publicly promulgated and easily accessible; and should not be retrospective in operation are usually referred to as the principles of legality.[55] The principles which require courts, in applying general rules to particular cases, to be without personal interest in the outcome or other bias and to hear arguments on matters of law and proofs of matters of fact from both sides of a dispute are often referred to as rules of natural justice. These two sets of principles together define the concept of the rule of law to which most modern states pay at least lip service.

These requirements and the specific value which conformity with them imparts to laws may be regarded from two different points of view. On the one hand, they maximize the probability that the conduct required by the law will be forthcoming, and on the other hand, they provide individuals whose freedom is limited by the law with certain information and assurances which assist them in planning their lives within the coercive framework of the law. This combination of values may be easily seen in the case of the requirements of generality, clarity, publicity, and prospective operation. For the alternative to control by general rules of law is orders addressed by officials to particular individuals to do or to abstain from particular actions; and although in all legal systems there are occasions for such particular official orders, no society could efficiently provide the number of officials required to make them a main form of social control.

Thus, general rules clearly framed and publicly promulgated are the most efficient form of social control. But from the point of view

---

[55] [*Cf.* Fuller, *ante*, 83, and *post*, 138.]

of the individual citizen, they are more than that: they are required if he is to have the advantage of knowing in advance the ways in which his liberty will be restricted in the various situations in which he may find himself, and he needs this knowledge if he is to plan his life. This is an argument for laws which are general in the sense of requiring courses of action and not particular actions. The argument for generality in the sense of applicability to classes of persons is different: it is that such rules confer upon the individual the advantage of knowing the restrictions to which the conduct of others besides himself will be subject. Such knowledge in the case of legal restrictions which protect or benefit the individual increases the confidence with which he can predict and plan his future.

The value of the principles of natural justice which concern the process of adjudication are closely linked to the principles of legality. The requirement that a court should be impartial and hear arguments and proofs from both sides of a dispute are guarantees of objectivity which increase the probability that the enacted law will be applied according to its tenor. It is necessary to insure by such means that there will be this congruence between judicial decisions and the enacted law if the commitment to general rules as a method of government is taken seriously.

Care must be taken not to ascribe to these arguments more than they actually prove. Together they amount to the demonstration that all men who have aims to pursue need the various protections and benefits which only laws conforming to the above requirements of substance and procedure can effectively confer. For any rational man, laws conferring these protections and benefits must be valuable, and the price to be paid for them in the form of limitations imposed by the law on his own freedom will usually be worth paying. But these arguments do not show, and are not intended to show, that it will always be reasonable or morally obligatory for a man to obey the law when the legal system provides him with these benefits, for in other ways the system may be iniquitous: it may deny even the essential protections of the law to a minority or slave class or in other ways cause misery or injustice. . . .   [pp. 273–274]

M. MACDONALD

Natural Rights

(1948) [56]

[After citing Maritain's view on the common nature of man (*ante*, 108) Miss Macdonald comments as follows.]

And men's rights depend upon this common nature and end by which they are subject to the natural or 'unwritten' law. But this seems to me a complete mistake. Human beings are not like exactly similar bottles of whisky each marked 'for export only' or some device indicating a common destination or end. Men do not share a fixed nature, nor, therefore, are there any ends which they must necessarily pursue in

[56] [Reprinted from 1947/48 Proc. Arist. Soc., in *Philosophy, Politics and Society* (1956) ed. Laslett, to which page references are here given.]

fulfilment of such nature. There is no definition of ' man '.[57] There is a more or less vague set of properties which characterize in varying degrees and proportions those creatures which are called ' human '. These determine for each individual human being what he *can* do but not what he *must* do. If he has an I.Q. of 85 his intellectual activities will be limited ; if he is physically weak he cannot become a heavyweight boxer. If a woman has neither good looks nor acting ability she is unlikely to succeed as a film star. But what people may do with their capacities is extremely varied, and there is no one thing which they must do in order to be human. . . . There is no end set for the human race by an abstraction called ' human nature '. There are only ends which individuals choose, or are forced by circumstances to accept. There are none which they *must* accept. Men are not created for a purpose as a piano is built to produce certain sounds. Or if they are we have no idea of the purpose.

It is the emphasis on the individual sufferer from bad social conditions which constitutes the appeal of the social contract theory and the ' natural' origin of human rights. But it does not follow that the theory is true as a statement of verifiable fact about the actual constitution of the world. The statements of the Law of Nature are not statements of the laws of nature, not even of the laws of an ' ideal' nature. For nature provides no standards or ideals. All that exists, exists at the same level, or is of the same logical type. There are not, by nature, prize roses, works of art, oppressed or unoppressed citizens. Standards are determined by human choice, not set by nature independently of men. Natural events cannot tell us what we ought to do until we have made certain decisions, when knowledge of natural fact will enable the most efficient means to be chosen to carry out those decisions. Natural events themselves have no value, and human beings

---

[57] [For an interesting recent fictional attempt to emphasise the difficulty in drawing the line between man and the animal world, see Vercours, *Les Animaux Dénaturés* (1952). On the question, what criterion can be adopted to draw the distinction, it is suggested at one point that the vital criterion of humanity may be that man is not so much in accord with nature, but rather that he possesses the ability of regarding himself as separate from, and as confronting nature (see pp. 322–323, ed. Livre de Poche). On the other hand, the anthropologist, Lévi-Strauss, has argued that a capacity for symbolic thought through the medium of language is the distinctive human attribute, and that although, theoretically, the symbolic categories of human thought need not necessarily develop universally, in practice the human brain is so constructed that it is predisposed to follow certain similar paths. (See E. Leach, *Lévi-Strauss* (1969), pp. 36–44.) Such a line of thought might provide a basis for an argument in favour of universal moral categories, though Lévi-Strauss's emphasis is on common structure, rather than the actual content of particular categories. On the other hand, on more traditional lines, Sir Isaiah Berlin has argued for the factual existence of at least a minimum of common moral ground as intrinsic to human communication. In his view objectivity of moral judgment seems to depend on the degree of constancy in human responses, and though he agrees that moral categories are by no means as clear and firm as perception of the material world, nor are they as relative or fluid as some writers have tended to assume. But his argument that the possibility of ultimate or basic human values, as between different cultures and periods, is reinforced by the degree of communication and historical knowledge we are able to achieve, does seem to beg the question what degree of actual communication and knowledge we are in fact able to attain (see *Four Essays on Liberty* (1969), pp. xxxi–xxxiii. and lii–lvii.)]

as natural existents have no value either, whether on account of possessing intelligence or having two feet.

One of the major criticisms of the doctrine of natural rights is that the list of natural rights varies with each exponent. For Hobbes, man's only natural right is self-preservation. More 'liberal' theorists add to life and security; liberty, the pursuit of happiness and sometimes property. Modern socialists would probably include the right to 'work or adequate maintenance'. M. Maritain enumerates a list of nine natural rights which include besides the rights to life, liberty, and property [58] of the older formulations, the right to pursue a religious vocation, the right to marry and raise a family, and, finally, the right of every human being to be treated as a person and not as a thing.[59] It is evident that these ' rights' are of very different types which would need to be distinguished in a complete discussion of the problem. . . .

. . . When the lawyers said that a slave had a right in natural law to be free, they thought of a legal right not provided for by any existing statute, enactment or custom and to whose universal infringement no penalties attached. But this, surely, is the vanishing point of law and of legal right? It indicates that there just wasn't a law or legal right by which a slave might demand his freedom. But perhaps there was a moral right and a moral obligation. The slave ought to be free and maybe it was the duty of every slave-holder to free his slaves and of legislators to enact laws forbidding slavery. But until this happened there was no law which forbade a man to keep slaves. Consequently, there is no point in saying there was 'really' a natural law which forbade this. For the natural law was impotent. Statements about natural law were neither statements of natural fact nor legal practice.

So, does it follow that a 'natural' right is just a 'moral' right? Kant said, in effect, that to treat another human being as a person, of intrinsic worth, an end in himself, is just to treat him in accordance with the moral law applicable to all rational beings on account of their having reason. But this is not quite the sense in which the term 'natural rights' has been historically used. Declarations of the Rights of Man did not include his right to be told the truth, to have promises kept which had been made to him, to receive gratitude from those he had benefited, etc. The common thread among the variety of natural rights is their *political* character. Despite their rugged individualism, no exponent of the Rights of Man desired to enjoy them, in solitude, on a desert island. They were among the articles of the original Social Contract; clauses in Constitutions, the inspiration of social and governmental reforms. But 'Keep promises'; 'Tell the truth'; 'Be grateful' are not inscribed on banners carried by aggrieved demonstrators or circulated among the members of an oppressed party. Whether or not morality can exist without society, it is certain that politics cannot. Why then were

[58] [The right to compensation where the Crown in wartime requisitions or destroys private property for the public benefit has recently been upheld as a form of natural justice: see *Burmah Oil Co.* v. *Lord Advocate* [1965] A.C. 75. But this was immediately reversed by the legislature. See War Damage Act 1965.]

[59] [In the middle of the nineteenth century in the U.S.A., the belief in the natural equality of Man even led to the remarkable doctrine that any responsible citizen of full age had a natural right to follow any professional calling without any qualification. This was applied to the legal profession, as for instance, in 1893, by the Supreme Court of Indiana (See Erwin N. Griswold, *Law and Lawyers in the United States* (1964), pp. 16–18).]

'natural rights' conceived to exist independently of organized society and hence of political controversies? I suggest that they were so considered in order to emphasize their basic or fundamental character. For words like freedom, equality, security, represented for the defenders of natural rights what they considered to be the fundamental moral and social values which should be or should continue to be realized in any society fit for intelligent and responsible citizens.[60] . . .   [pp. 44–47]

HARPER v. VIRGINIA STATE BOARD OF EDUCATION

(*United States Supreme Court*)

383 U.S. 663, 16 L. ed. 2d 169

(1966)

DOUGLAS J. . . .[61]

We agree, of course, with Mr. Justice Holmes that the Due Process Clause of the Fourteenth Amendment " does not enact Mr. Herbert Spencer's Social Statics " (Lochner v. New York, 198 US 45 [62]). Likewise, the Equal Protection Clause is not shackled to the political theory of a particular era. In determining what lines are unconstitutionally discriminatory, we have never been confined to historic notions of equality, any more than we have restricted due process to a fixed catalogue of what was at a given time deemed to be the limits of fundamental rights. See Malloy v Hogan, 378 US 1, 5–6. Notions of what constitutes equal treatment for purposes of the Equal Protection Clause *do* change. This Court in 1896 held that laws providing for separate public facilities for white and Negro citizens did not deprive the latter of the equal protection and treatment that the Fourteenth Amendment commands. Plessy v. Ferguson, 163 US 537. Seven of the eight Justices then sitting subscribed to the Court's opinion, thus joining in expressions of what constituted unequal and discriminatory treatment that sound strange to a contemporary ear. When, in 1954—more than a half-century later—we repudiated the " separate-but-equal " doctrine of Plessy as respects public education [63] we stated: " In approaching this problem, we cannot turn the clock back to 1868 when the Amendment was adopted, or even to 1896 when Plessy v Ferguson was written." . . .

In a recent searching re-examination of the Equal Protection Clause, we held, as already noted, that " the opportunity for equal participation by all voters in the election of state legislators " is required. Reynolds v Sims, 377 US at 566. We decline to qualify that principle by sustaining this poll tax.

Our conclusion, like that in Reynolds v Sims, is founded not on what we think governmental policy should be, but on what the Equal Protection Clause requires.

We have long been mindful that where fundamental rights and liberties are asserted under the Equal Protection Clause, classifications

---

[60] [For a discussion of some of the values underlying the legal systems of Western democracy, see Dennis Lloyd, *The Idea of Law* (1964), Chap. 7. And Dias, *Jurisprudence*, Chap. 7.]

[61] [The court had to decide whether Virginia's poll-tax, which made voting dependent on the payment of taxes, was constitutional.]

[62] [*Post*, 432.]

[63] [In *Brown* v. *Board of Education, ante*, 121.]

which might invade or restrain them must be closely scrutinized and carefully confined. See, e.g., Skinner v Oklahoma, 316 US 535, 541; Reynolds v Sims, 377 US 533, 561–562.

Those principles apply here. For to repeat, wealth or fee paying has, in our view, no relation to voting qualifications; the right to vote is too precious, too fundamental to be so burdened or conditioned.
[pp. 174–175]

Black J. dissenting. . . .

. . . The Court's judgment and opinion . . . seems to be using the old " natural-law-due-process formula " [64] to justify striking down state laws as violations of the Equal Protection Clause. I have heretofore had many occasions to express my strong belief that there is no constitutional support whatever for this Court to use the Due Process Clause as though it provided a blank check to alter the meaning of the Constitution as written so as to add to it substantive constitutional changes which a majority of the Court at any given time believes are needed to meet present-day problems.[65] Nor is there in my opinion any more constitutional support for this Court to use the Equal Protection Clause, as it has today, to write into the Constitution its notions of what it thinks is good governmental policy. If basic changes as to the respective powers of the state and national governments are needed, I prefer to let those changes be made by amendment as Article V of the Constitution provides. For a majority of this Court to undertake that task, whether purporting to do so under the Due Process or the Equal Protection Clause amounts, in my judgment, to an exercise of power the Constitution makers with foresight and wisdom refused to give the Judicial Branch of the Government. I have in no way departed from the view I expressed in Adamson v California, 332 US 46, 90, that the " natural-law-due-process formula " under which courts make the Constitution mean what they think it should at a given time " has been used in the past, and can be used in the future, to license this Court, in considering regulatory legislation, to roam at large in the broad expanses of policy and morals and to trespass, all too freely, on the legislative domain of the States as well as the Federal Government."

The Court denies that it is using the " natural-law-due-process formula." It says that its invalidation of the Virginia law " is founded not on what we think governmental policy should be, but on what the Equal Protection Clause requires." I find no statement in the Court's opinion, however, which advances even a plausible argument as to why the alleged discriminations which might possibly be effected by Virginia's poll tax law are " irrational," " unreasonable," " arbitrary," or " invidious " or have no relevance to a legitimate policy which the State wishes to adopt. The Court gives no reason at all to descredit the long-standing beliefs that making the payment of a tax a prerequisite to voting is an effective way of collecting revenue and that people who pay their taxes are likely to have a far greater interest in their government. The Court's failure to give any reasons to show that these purposes of the poll tax are " irrational," " unreasonable," " arbitrary," or " invidious " is a pretty clear indication to me that none

64 [*Cf.* Black's dissenting opinion in *Adamson* v. *California, ante,* 116.]
65 [*Cf. Griswold* v. *Connecticut, ante,* 122.]

exist. I can only conclude that the primary, controlling, predominate, if not the exclusive reason for declaring the Virginia law unconstitutional is the Court's deep-seated hostility and antagonism, which I share, to making payment of a tax a prerequisite to voting.

The Court's justification for consulting its own notions rather than following the original meaning of the Constitution, as I would, apparently is based on the belief of the majority of the Court that for this Court to be bound by the original meaning of the Constitution is an intolerable and debilitating evil; that our Constitution should not be "shackled to the political theory of a particular era," and that to save the country from the original Constitution the Court must have constant power to renew it and keep it abreast of this Court's more enlightened theories of what is best for our society. It seems to me that this is an attack not only on the great value of our Constitution itself but also on the concept of a written constitution which is to survive through the years as originally written unless changed through the amendment process which the Framers wisely provided. Moreover, when a "political theory" embodied in our Constitution becomes outdated, it seems to me that a majority of the nine members of this Court are not only without constitutional power but are far less qualified to choose a new constitutional political theory than the people of this country proceeding in the manner provided by Article V.   [pp. 177–179]

L. L. FULLER

The Morality of Law

(Revised edition, 1969)

The Substantive Aims of Law

The two principal distinctions . . . are . . . the distinction between the moralities of duty and of aspiration and the distinction between the internal and external moralities of law.[66]

The Neutrality of the Law's Internal Morality toward Substantive Aims

In presenting my analysis of the law's internal morality I have insisted that it is, over a wide range of issues, indifferent toward the substantive aims of law and is ready to serve a variety of such aims with equal efficacy. One moral issue in lively debate today is that of contraception. Now it is quite clear that the principles of legality are themselves incapable of resolving this issue. It is also clear that a legal system might maintain its internal integrity whether its rules were designed to prohibit or to encourage contraception.[67]

But a recognition that the internal morality of law may support and give efficacy to a wide variety of substantive aims should not mislead us into believing that *any* substantive aim may be adopted without compromise of legality. Even the adoption of an objective like the legal suppression of contraception may, under some circum-

---

[66] [On which see *ante*, 83, and *The Morality of Law*, Chaps. 1 and 2.]
[67] [See, for example, *Griswold* v. *Connecticut*, *ante*, 122, and see, generally, N. St. J. Stevas, *The Agonising Choice* (1971).]

stances, impair legal morality. If, as sometimes seems to be the case, laws prohibiting the sale of contraceptives are kept on the books as a kind of symbolic act, with the knowledge that they will not and cannot be enforced, legal morality is seriously affected. There is no way to quarantine this contagion against a spread to other parts of the legal system. It is unfortunately a familiar political technique to placate one interest by passing a statute, and to appease an opposing interest by leaving the statute largely unenforced.

One of the tasks of the present chapter is to analyze in general terms the manner in which the internal and external moralities of law interact. . . .

. . . The internal morality of the law is not something added to, or imposed on, the power of law, but is an essential condition of that power itself. If this conclusion is accepted, then the first observation that needs to be made is that law is a precondition of good law. A conscientious carpenter, who has learned his trade well and keeps his tools sharp, might, we may suppose, as well devote himself to building a hangout for thieves as to building an orphans' asylum. But it still remains true that it takes a carpenter, or the help of a carpenter, to build an orphans' asylum, and that it will be a better asylum if he is a skillful craftsman equipped with tools that have been used with care and kept in proper condition.

If we had no carpenters at all it would be plain that our first need would be, not to draft blueprints for hospitals and asylums or to argue about the principles of good design, but to recruit and train carpenters. It is in this sense that much of the world today needs law more than it does good law. . . .

Legal Morality and Laws Aiming at Alleged Evils That Cannot Be Defined

The simple demand that rules of law be expressed in intelligible terms seems on its face ethically neutral toward the substantive aims law may serve. If any principle of legal morality is, in Hart's words, " compatible with very great iniquity," this would seem to be it. Yet if a legislator is attempting to remove some evil and cannot plainly identify the target at which his statute is directed, it is obvious he will have difficulty in making his laws clear. I have already tried to illustrate this point by a reference to statutes designed to prevent " a return of the old saloon." [68] In that case, however, we have to do with legislative foolishness, rather than with anything touching on iniquity.

It is quite otherwise with laws attempting to make legal rights depend on race. It is common today to think of the government of South Africa as combining a strict observance of legality with the enactment of a body of law that is brutal and inhuman. This view could only arise because of the now inveterate confusion between deference for constituted authority and fidelity to law. An examination of the legislation by which racial discrimination is maintained in South Africa reveals a gross departure from the demands of the internal morality of law.

[68] [See *The Morality of Law*, pp. 89–91.]

The following extracts are taken from a careful and objective study of the racial laws enacted by the Union of South Africa.

> The Legislation abounds with anomalies and the same person may, in the result, fall into different racial categories under different statutes . . . the Minister of the Interior on the 22nd March 1957, stated that approximately 100,000 race classification cases were then pending before the Director of Census and Statistics which were regarded as " borderline cases " . . . As the present study has revealed, the absence of uniformity of definition flows primarily from the absence of any uniform or scientific basis of race classification. . . . In the final analysis the legislature is attempting to define the indefinable.[69]

Even the South African judge who in his private life shares the prejudices that have shaped the law he is bound to interpret and apply, must, if he respects the ethos of his calling, feel a deep distaste for the arbitrary manipulations this legislation demands of him.

It should not be supposed it is only in South Africa that statutes attaching legal consequences to differences in race have given rise to serious difficulties of interpretation. In 1948 in *Perez* v. *Sharp* [70] the Supreme Court of California held unconstitutional a statute providing that " no license may be issued authorizing the marriage of a white person with a Negro, mulatto, Mongolian or member of the Malay race." The holding that the statute was invalid was rested in part on the ground that it did not meet the constitutional requirement " that a law be definite and its meaning ascertainable by those whose rights and duties are governed thereby."

Our naturalization laws now expressly provide that the " right of a person to become a naturalized citizen . . . shall not be denied . . . because of race." [71] The Supreme Court is thus now safe from the danger of getting itself entangled in its own interpretations as it did in 1922 and 1923. In *Ozawa* v. *United States* [72] the Court had to give some meaning to a provision restricting naturalization to " white persons." The court observed, " Manifestly, the test afforded by the mere color of the skin of each individual is impracticable as that differs greatly among persons of the same race." In an attempt to achieve something like scientific exactitude the Court declared that " white person " should be interpreted to mean a person of the Caucasian race. In a case argued a few months after this decision, the applicant for citizenship was a high-caste Hindu.[73] His counsel introduced rather convincing proof that among anthropologists employing the term " Caucasian," he would be assigned to that race. The Court observed that the term Caucasian was unknown to those who drafted the statute in 1790, and that " as used in the science of ethnology, the connotation of the word is by no means clear and the use of it in its scientific sense as an equivalent for the words of the statute . . . would simply

---

[69] Suzman, " Race Classification and Definition in the Legislation of the Union of South Africa, 1910–1960," *Acta Juridica* (1960), pp. 339–367; the extracts quoted in the text are taken from pp. 339, 355, and 367.

[70] 32 Cal. 2d 711.

[71] USCA, Tit. 8 §1422.

[72] 260 U.S. 178 (1922).

[73] *United States* v. *Thind*, 261 U.S. 204 (1923).

mean the substitution of one perplexity for another. . . . The words of familiar speech, which were used by the original framers of the law, were intended to include only the type of man whom they knew as white."

Finally, by a bitter irony the Israeli High Court of Justice has encountered well-nigh insoluble problems in trying to give some simple and understandable interpretation to the Law of Return granting citizenship automatically to immigrants who are "Jews." On December 6, 1962, a divided Court held that a Roman Catholic monk was not a Jew for purposes of this law. His counsel argued that, being of Jewish parentage, he was by rabbinical law still a Jew. The Court conceded that this was true, but said that the question was not one of religious law but of the secular law of Israel. By that law he was no longer a Jew because he had embraced the Christian religion.[74]

The View of Man Implicit in Legal Morality

I come now to the most important respect in which an observance of the demands of legal morality can serve the broader aims of human life generally. This lies in the view of man implicit in the internal morality of law. I have repeatedly observed that legal morality can be said to be neutral over a wide range of ethical issues. It cannot be neutral in its view of man himself. To embark on the enterprise of subjecting human conduct to the governance of rules involves of necessity a commitment to the view that man is, or can become, a responsible agent, capable of understanding and following rules, and answerable for his defaults.

Every departure from the principles of the law's inner morality is an affront to man's dignity as a responsible agent. To judge his actions by unpublished or retrospective laws, or to order him to do an act that is impossible, is to convey to him your indifference to his powers of self-determination. Conversely, when the view is accepted that man is incapable of responsible action, legal morality loses its reason for being. To judge his actions by unpublished or retrospective laws is no longer an affront, for there is nothing left to affront—indeed, even the verb "to judge" becomes itself incongruous in this context; we no longer judge a man, we act upon him.

Today a whole complex of attitudes, practices, and theories seems to drive us toward a view which denies that man is, or can meaningfully strive to become, a responsible, self-determining center of action. The causes of this development are of the most varied sort; in their motivation they seem to run the gamut from the basest to the most noble. . . .

[pp. 153–163]

The Problems of the Limits of Effective Legal Action

. . . It is now time to turn to the limits of legal morality and to an analysis of the situations in which an application of this morality may be inappropriate and damaging.

But first note must be taken of a confusion that threatens our subject. Let me give an historical instance of this confusion. In his essay *On Liberty* Mill had written:

[74] See the *New York Times* for Dec. 7, 1962, pp. 1 and 15, and Dec. 8, 1962, p. 13.

The object of this Essay is to assert one simple principle, as
entitled to govern absolutely the dealings of society with the
individual by way of compulsion and control, whether the means
used be physical force in the form of legal penalties, or the moral
coercion of public opinion. That principle, that . . . the only
purpose for which power can be rightfully exercised over any
member of a civilized community, against his will, is to prevent
harm to others. His own good, either physical or moral, is not a
sufficient warrant.[75]

In his famous reply to Mill, James Fitzjames Stephen sought to
refute Mill's " one simple principle " by pointing out that the British
citizen has power exercised over him to extract taxes which go in
support of the British Museum, an institution obviously designed, not
to protect the citizen from harm, but to improve him.[76]

What is illustrated here is a confusion between law in the usual
sense of rules of conduct directed toward the citizen, and governmental
action generally. Mill was arguing that " physical force in the form of
legal penalties " should not itself be used as a direct instrument for
improving the citizen. Certainly he did not intend to assert that the
government should never use funds raised through taxes—enforced, if
necessary, by coercive measures—to provide facilities that will enable
the citizen to improve himself.

The confusion Stephen introduced in his controversy with Mill
represents a fairly subtle representative of its class. A more thorough
piece of obfuscation is found in the following passage from a famous
anthropologist:

> Law has been often used as an instrument of legislative omni-
> potence. There was an attempt to make a whole nation sober by
> law. It failed. [At this point we may say, so far, so good.] In Nazi
> Germany a whole nation is being transformed into a gang of
> bloodthirsty world-bandits through the instrumentality of law, among
> others. This, we hope, will fail again. The Italian dictator is trying
> to make his intelligent, cynical, and peace-loving people into cour-
> ageous heroes. The fundamentalists have tried in some states of
> this Union to make people God-fearing and bibliolatric by law. A
> great communistic Union has tried to abolish God, marriage, and
> the family, again by law.[77] . . .   [pp. 168–169]

The Minimum Content of a Substantive Natural Law

In seeking to know whether it is possible to derive from the morality of
aspiration anything more imperative than mere counsel and encouragement, I have then so far concluded that, since the morality of aspiration
is necessarily a morality of human aspiration, it cannot deny the human
quality to those who possess it without forfeiting its integrity. Can we
derive more than this?

75 The quoted passage appears in Ch. I. [And see *ante*, 51.]
76 *Liberty, Equality, Fraternity* (1873), p. 16. " To force an unwilling person to
contribute to the support of the British Museum is as distinct a violation of
Mr. Mill's principle as religious persecution."
77 Malinowski, " A New Instrument for the Interpretation of Law—Especially
Primitive," 51 *Yale Law Journal* 1237–1254, at p. 1247 (1942).

The problem may be stated in another form. . . . I treated what I have called the internal morality of law as itself presenting a variety of natural law. It is, however, a procedural or institutional kind of natural law, though, as I have been at pains in this chapter to show, it affects and limits the substantive aims that can be achieved through law. But can we derive from the morality of aspiration itself any proposition of natural law that is substantive, rather than procedural, in quality?

In his *Concept of Law* H. L. A. Hart presents what he calls " the minimum content of natural law " (pp. 189–195). Starting with the single objective of human survival, conceived as operating within certain externally imposed conditions, Hart derives, by a process I would describe as purposive implication, a fairly comprehensive set of rules that may be called those of natural law. What is expounded in his interesting discussion is a kind of minimum morality of duty.

Like every morality of duty this minimum natural law says nothing about the question, Who shall be included in the community which accepts and seeks to realize cooperatively the shared objective of survival? In short, who shall survive? No attempt is made to answer this question. Hart simply observes that " our concern is with social arrangements for continued existence, not with those of a suicide club."

In justifying his starting point of survival Hart advances two kinds of reasons. One amounts to saying that survival is a necessary condition for every other human achievement and satisfaction. With this proposition there can be no quarrel.

But in addition to treating survival as a precondition for every other human good, Hart advances a second set of reasons for his starting point—reasons of a very different order. He asserts that men have properly seen that in " the modest aim of survival " is " the central indisputable element which gives empirical good sense to the terminology of Natural Law." He asserts further that in the teleological elements that run through all moral and legal thinking there is " the tacit assumption that the proper end of human activity is survival." He observes that " an overwhelming majority of men do wish to live, even at the cost of hideous misery."

In making these assertions Hart is, I submit, treading more dubious ground. For he is no longer claiming for survival that it is a necessary condition for the achievement of other ends, but seems to be saying that it furnishes the core and central element of all human striving. This, I think, cannot be accepted. As Thomas Aquinas remarked long ago, if the highest aim of a captain were to preserve his ship, he would keep it in port forever.[78] As for the proposition that the overwhelming majority of men wish to survive even at the cost of hideous misery, this seems to me of doubtful truth. If it were true, I question whether it would have any particular relevance to moral theory.

Hart's search for a " central indisputable element " in human striving raises the question whether in fact this search can be successful. I believe that if we were forced to select the principle that supports and infuses

---

[78] *Summa Theologica*, Pt. I–II, Q. 2, Art. 5. " Hence a captain does not intend as a last end, the preservation of the ship entrusted to him, since a ship is ordained to something else as its end, *viz.* to navigation."

all human aspiration we would find it in the objective of maintaining communication with our fellows.

In the first place—staying within the limits of Hart's own argument—man has been able to survive up to now because of his capacity for communication. In competition with other creatures, often more powerful than he and sometimes gifted with keener senses, man has so far been the victor. His victory has come about because he can acquire and transmit knowledge and because he can consciously and deliberately effect a coordination of effort with other human beings. If in the future man succeeds in surviving his own powers of self-destruction, it will be because he can communicate and reach understanding with his fellows. Finally, I doubt if most of us would regard as desirable survival into a kind of vegetable existence in which we could make no meaningful contact with other human beings.

Communication is something more than a means of staying alive. It is a way of being alive. It is through communication that we inherit the achievements of past human effort. The possibility of communication can reconcile us to the thought of death by assuring us that what we achieve will enrich the lives of those to come. How and when we accomplish communication with one another can expand or contract the boundaries of life itself. In the words of Wittgenstein, "The limits of my language are the limits of my world."

If I were asked, then, to discern one central indisputable principle of what may be called substantive natural law—Natural Law with capital letters—I would find it in the injunction: Open up, maintain, and preserve the integrity of the channels of communication by which men convey to one another what they perceive, feel, and desire. In this matter the morality of aspiration offers more than good counsel and the challenge of excellence. It here speaks with the imperious voice we are accustomed to hear from the morality of duty. And if men will listen, that voice, unlike that of the morality of duty, can be heard across the boundaries and through the barriers that now separate men from one another. . . .   [pp. 184–186]

MARGARET MEAD

Some Anthropological Considerations Concerning Natural Law [79]

(1961)

. . . In asking what conceptions of human rights are universal to all known cultures, it is, of course, necessary to recognize that we can only ask this question about the assemblage of societies that have been observed and recorded. Inevitably, our universe excludes all cultures that have vanished without leaving any record, and the steadily shrinking number of existing cultures that exist in the present but have not yet been studied. The culturally regulated relationship among persons within a given environment is characterized both by certain persistent regularities, due to the species-specific characteristics of human beings, and a wide variety of forms having historical uniqueness. It is only those areas of human life which are most closely based in our common

[79] [From 6 *Natural Law Forum* 51.]

biological heritage in which we may not expect still to find, among existing cultures, instances which alter existing generalizations.[80]

Nevertheless, the systematic observations of constancies among all known cultures make it highly probable that the kinds of cultural behavior found in all of them have been an integral part of their survival system up to the present time. Among such constancies we may note the distinction between the sacredness of human life within and without the group, or the existence of a category of murder—a type of killing that is different from all other killings, falling in specified ways within the circle of protected persons.[81] The distinctions vary from one group to another; a newborn infant may be excluded, or an adulterer caught in *flagrante delicto*; expected revenge may even take the form of a man's obligation to kill the foster father, who once killed his father, married his mother, and reared him from childhood. But the categories of justified versus unjustified killing remain for all known societies. As human beings, to survive, must live in aggregations of more than one biological family, this distinction can be regarded as a vital one for the development of a viable society. The extension of the category of those whose killing constitutes murder, in contradistinction to legitimate vengeance, or conventional head hunting or warfare, has been a conspicuous marker of the evolution of civilizations in spite of its carrying with it the inescapable corollary of increasing the number of those who become at one stroke—as with a declaration of war— legitimate victims.

With the same universality we find incest rules governing the three primary incest relationships—mother-son, father-daughter, and brother-sister—occurring in all known societies. Although in special cases they may be occasionally waived, as in royal marriages between brother and sister, or in cases of small in-marrying groups in which there are no possible mates, such exceptions are treated as exceptions, marking royalty off from commoners or signaling a desperate population emergency. The circumstance that the taboo is frequently broken—especially in the father-daughter form—under conditions of cultural breakdown, only serves to demonstrate that its maintenance is socio-cultural rather than instinctive. Clinical and anthropological evidence suggests that the attraction and repulsion of members of a biological family are such that social regulation has been necessary. The function of the incest taboo may be seen as preventing competition among members of the same sex within the family group during the long period when human young are not mature enough to fend for themselves, and as providing

---

[80] As an example of the borderline between present possibilities of extrapolation from known instances, we may take the question of kinship forms, all of which involve descent of offspring from parents of two sexes. In 1931 it was possible to catalogue the known forms of emphasis upon descent from father to son, from mother to daughter, from father to children of both sexes, from mother to children of both sexes, and to construct the possible but not yet recorded type of a society in which descent was patterned as father to daughter to daughter's son, to daughter's son's daughter, a form which had not been recorded and which, while possible, seemed inherently unstable. Several variations in this form have since been found, all unstable as predicted. Where such constant features as sex and descent are absent, the possibility that human invention has transcended our present powers of extrapolation is very high.

[81] Edward Westermarck, The Origin and Development of the Moral Ideas. 2 vols. (London: Macmillan, Vol. I, 1906; Vol. II, 1908).

forms in which the search for mates outside the immediate family strengthens ties within families.[82]

It is in those instances where incest rules have been elaborated to include large numbers of persons, all members of one clan, all members of one village or district, etc., that the compensatory need for religio-legal devices for breaking a rule that has become too onerous is found, and the complementary right to find a mate is brought into relief. Again those instances in which marriage is denied require strong cultural elaborations or religious and ethical sanctions, in which individuals become completely dedicated to a religious life.

Finally, in spite of the widespread notions of primitive communism, there is no known culture without some institution of private property. The forms in which this is expressed may appear bizarre—the right to a name, or the right to certain forms of privacy such as the right to sleep without being awakened, or to eat without being spoken to—but the association of social identity with rights against the invasion of others is universal.[83] Practices such as the destruction or interment of an individual's personal possessions, weapons, tools, dress and adornment, etc., combined with ownership of camping sites and hunting territories by larger corporate groups, have misled some observers into thinking that no property was held by individuals. Experience with attempts to impose modern ideas of state capitalism or collective ideologies upon " communistic " primitive people very rapidly exposes the error of this assumption.

Effective use of case studies from primitive cultures requires a recognition that no matter how primitive the people under discussion are, rules concerning the sacredness of life (under some circumstances), rules concerning the prohibition of incest in the primary familial relationships in most circumstances, and rules governing an individual's rights over some differentiated physical or cultural items will be found. That such recognitions have been universal in the past does not, however, argue conclusively for their necessary continuance in the future. But they appear to have provided a minimal culturally transmitted ethical code without which human societies were not viable. The English geneticist C. H. Waddington has argued persuasively,[84] on purely naturalistic grounds, that the capacity to accept a division of behavior into that which is right and that which is wrong, is a distinctively human species-specific type of behavior which has played an essential part in the evolution of culture.

" Natural law " might thus be defined as those rules of behavior which had developed from a species-specific capacity to ethicalize as a

---

[82] Robert H. Lowie, Primitive Society (New York: Boni & Liveright, 1920); George Peter Murdock, Social Structure (New York: Macmillan, 1949); Reo F. Fortune, *Incest*, in 7 The Encyclopaedia of the Social Sciences 620 (1932); Maurice J. Barry, Jr. & Adelaide M. Johnson, *The Incest Barrier*, 27 The Psychoanalytic Quarterly 485 (1958); Margaret Mead, Male and Female (New York: Morrow, 1949; London: Victor Gollancz, 1950; New York: The New American Library—a Mentor Book—1955).

[83] Lawrence K. Frank, *The Concept of Inviolability in Culture*, in Society as the Patient 143–150 (New Brunswick: Rutgers U. Press, 1948).

[84] C. H. Waddington, The Ethical Animal (London: George Allen & Unwin, 1960). See also Thomas H. & Julian Huxley, Evolution and Ethics, 1893–1943 (London: The Pilot Press, 1947). American edition, Touchstone For Ethics, 1893–1943 (New York: Harper, 1947).

feature of those examples of such ethicalizing that appear in all known societies.[85]   [pp. 51–54]

We have seen that recognition of natural rights, to life, property, and reproduction, is found in all societies, although with profound variations in interpretation. However, when Western law and traditional law or primitive custom have confronted each other, it is rather the question of sanctions, authority, order which have constituted the aspects of the law which have become salient. It would be worthwhile to undertake a series of intensive explorations of societies on the verge of intensive modernization who are at the moment attempting to formulate their legal systems, relying variously upon British, American, Swiss, French, Soviet models and others. In each such case two sets of cultural envelopes are involved, the culturally embedded system of the donor or model country, and the culture of the receiver or model-seeking country. If such situations were analyzed with a view to finding a minimal set of legal principles which might be regarded as stripped universals, the creation of new legal systems might be effectively streamlined—in contrast to the present attempt to tinker with models which are hoary with specific traditional accretions, many of which are inappropriate in the new situation. Is it possible to regard law as having such a set of universals, which can in any way be compared with scientific principles such as govern nutrition, or can we only arrive at a scientific study of the law by way of the study of comparative legal systems, each seen as part of a particular culture and one link in a long historical chain of legal inventions?[86]   [p. 64]

M. R. MACGUIGAN

Obligation and Obedience [87]

(1970)

. . . The question of whether or not to disobey a particular law is in most philosophies a separate question from the judgment that it is an immoral or bad law. A decision to disobey a particular law will be made after weighing (1) the worth of the whole legal order, (2) the role of the particular law in the legal order, (3) the degree of iniquity of the law, and (4) the seriousness of the consequences of disobedience. The internal incoherence of the Nazi legal system, as described by Professor Fuller in his dialogue with Professor Hart,[88] would be an important

---

[85] To argue this position fully it is necessary to circumscribe the definition of a viable human society by including survival over a generation span, which excludes both the nonviable Nazi experiment in mass murder, which lacked ethical sanctions, and such bizarre experiments as religious cults like the Oneida Community or experimental cult communities in which all sex relations are forbidden. . . .

[86] [Anthropological evidence is only part of the answer to what is natural, for even where an indisputable case is established, this says nothing about its moral rectitude. Slavery might exist everywhere but this would not prove it was a just ordering of society. Attempts to deny this look to a second meaning of nature, nature as an ideal standard. See further Lloyd, in *Essays to Castberg* p. 111.]

[87] [*From Political and Legal Obligation* ed. Pennock and Chapman (Nomos XII) (1970). See, further, MacGuigan, *Democracy and Civil Disobedience*, 49 Can. Bar Rev. 222 (1971).]

[88] Lon L. Fuller, *Positivism and Fidelity to Law—A Reply to Professor Hart* (1958) 71 Harv.L.Rev. 630. [And *post*, 243.]

factor in the decision whether or not to obey a particular Nazi edict. On the other hand, a bad law might be morally binding on a particular person at a particular time for the sake of the preservation of the whole system, if the degree of iniquity were not great and the degree of potential scandal (bad example) through disobedience were great.

Perhaps the most difficult case of disobedience is where the citizen does not regard the law which he disobeys as illegal, but takes the view that he may nevertheless disobey it in good conscience as an incident of his protest against some other law. Such indirect disobedience, as it may appropriately be called in contradistinction to direct disobedience where the law disobeyed is the very one against which the protest is being made, frequently involves trespass against land, and is sufficiently controversial to be worth separate consideration below. . . .

The validity of the whole legal system is a highly relevant factor in the determination of what means are morally right for the purpose of disobeying a particular law. Potential means of disobedience range from purely passive nonresistance through demonstrations, noncooperation, and physical confrontations to outright revolution. The more violent means are less likely to be justifiable, not only in small matters, but also in democratic societies where there are legally established methods of changing public policy.

Consequently, even though he adopts a position of the primacy of morals over law, the citizen is not, in such a situation, compelled to choose between showing that the whole system is unjust or that the particular prescription is not part of the legal system; his most likely alternative is simply to say, " Despite the presumption in favor of the legitimacy of legislation, this rule is morally wrong and I will not obey it." In that case, of course, he may be subjected to certain sanctions by the state, but this is a price which a morally sensitive and courageous citizen will be prepared to pay.

The orthodox legal position is that disobedience to law, however justifiable it may be on moral grounds, cannot have a legal justification, for it manifests an express refusal to conform to the commands of the law, through reliance on an appeal to nonlegal norms.[89] The classical natural-law tradition would take sharp issue with legal orthodoxy on the question of what constitutes legality,[90] and it is apparent that the orthodox legal position is nothing other than the legal expression of the philosophical doctrine of legal positivism. Natural-law thought recognized a legal justification for disobedience to bad laws. Not even natural-law theory, however, required disobedience to every unjust law, but left this determination to an ultimate practical judgment, so that there is a certain indefiniteness even in a natural-law context about the legality of disobedience. Few have gone so far as Professor Harrop Freeman in arguing that disobedience is completely legal if it is nonviolent,[91] but many would agree at least that civil disobedience is not opposed to the

---

[89] The orthodoxy is illustrated by *Walker* v. *Birmingham* (1967), 388 U.S. 307 [see also President Kennedy's oft-quoted remarks in, *inter alia*, Wasserstrom, in *Essays in Legal Philosophy*, ed. Summers at pp. 277–278.]

[90] See, for example, St. Thomas Aquinas, *Summa Theologica*—I, II, Q. 90, Art. 1, ad 3. [And *ante* 96. See also 101, n. 14.]

[91] Harrop Freeman, " Civil Disobedience and the Law," (1966) 21 *Rutgers Law Review* 17; " The Right of Protest and Civil Disobedience," (1966) 41 *Indiana Law Journal* 228, 238.

spirit of the law. If we define [92] civil disobedience as a public, non-violent [93] act of illegality, performed for a moral purpose, with a willingness to accept the legal penalty attached to the breach of the law,[94] perhaps it would be useful to think of it as *paralegal* rather than as either legal or illegal. Civil disobedience is directed toward justice and is not oriented so much against law as beyond the letter of the law. The facts that the violation of the law is open, that only nonviolent means are used, and that legal penalties are willingly accepted express a fundamental respect for the legal system even while demonstrating a refusal to accept a particular law. Civil disobedience is thus neither fully legal nor completely illegal. It is a benign illegality marked by a concern for the legal order.

But whatever the legal status of disobedience to law, its moral status is secure provided that it is a proportionate response to injustice. Even violence may be a proportionate response to some injustices, though within a framework of democratic government it is hard to conceive of circumstances, short of direct governmental compulsion of a minority to perform unconscionable acts, in which violent action would be an apt reaction to inadequacy or injustice in the laws. Direct civil disobedience, on the other hand, appears to be almost universally accepted as an appropriate moral response to governmental iniquity, even by authors who deny it legal validity. There may even be general agreement respecting its moral bounds as delimited by Dr. Adams' norms of civil disobedience, on the analogy of the norms of a just war.

But there is no such unanimity with regard to indirect civil disobedience. Dr. Mortimer Adler, for example, has forcefully declared: " Breaking laws for the sake of making public demonstrations against general injustice in society—against segregation or an unjust war—is criminal, not civil disobedience. . . . Those who act in this way cannot claim any of the protection that is and should be accorded to civil disobedience." [95] Mr. Fortas has taken a similar position: " In my judgment civil disobedience—the deliberate violation of law—is never justified in our nation, where the law being violated is not itself the focus or target of the protest." [96] Such disobedience is " morally as well as politically unacceptable." [97]

Such a limitation on civil disobedience would disallow the possibility of symbolic means of resistance. Ghandi,[98] for example, distilled salt from the sea, thus violating a specific law, in order to show the injustice not of that law but of the whole British rule of India. He justified such disobedience where the breach of law " does not involve moral turpitude

---

[92] [Adams in ed. Pennock and Chapman *op. cit.*, at pp. 294–295 gives an eight-point definition of civil disobedience culled from the literature. In addition to MacGuigan's criteria he adds (1) that the conduct is usually justified by some presumed higher authority than the law in question (2) that it is undertaken as a last resort (3) that there is intention to accept the penalty which the prevailing law imposes. Clearly the more careful and detailed the definition the more it restricts the concept.]

[93] [*Cf.* MacCallum in ed. Pennock and Chapman, *op. cit.* pp. 371–376.]

[94] [*Cf.* Greenawalt, in ed. Pennock and Chapman, *op. cit.* pp. 360–363.]

[95] Mortimer Adler, " Is there a Jurisprudence of Civil Disobedience?" (1966) 5 *Illinois Continuing Legal Education*, 71, 86.

[96] Abe Fortas, *Concerning Dissent and Civil Disobedience* (New York: Signet 1968), p. 124.

[97] *Ibid.*

[98] [On Gandhi and Civil Disobedience see MacGuigan, *op. cit.* at pp. 242–244.]

and is undertaken as a symbol of revolt against the State." [99] It would indeed seem that a necessary condition of the justification of indirect disobedience would be the closeness of the relationship, whether symbolic or conventional, between the object of protest and the law disobeyed, over and above the requisites for moral standing in the case of direct disobedience. A symbolic relationship might take its significance from its location (an appropriate government office) or its time (an anniversary) or its nature or purpose (a draft card). The more remote the relationship, the weaker the moral justification. If the connection is purely arbitrary, it will be entirely without justification.

To take a hypothesis which Mr. Justice Fortas himself cites, based upon *Brown* v. *Louisiana*,[1] we can see an unreasonableness in resting the morality of an act upon the resolution of a marginal illegality. In the Brown case, five Negroes sat in, in a public library to protest against the fact of its segregation and were arrested, tried, and convicted of disorderly conduct under a Louisiana statute. On appeal the United States Supreme Court decided by a 5–4 vote to set aside the conviction. The majority judges apparently took the view that a peaceful protest held in a library is protected by the First Amendment if it does not interfere with others and if it takes place when the protesters have a right to be present; whereas the minority judges believed that the Negroes were expressing their protest in an inappropriate and unauthorized place. Mr. Justice Fortas suggests that a majority of the court might have held against the protesters on the hypothesis that they had stayed in the library after its regular closing hour; possibly there might again have been dissenting opinions.

Now just as it is reasonable that the judicial judgment should relate back to the library sit-in to determine the legality of that action, it is equally reasonable that such relation back should not determine the morality of the protesters' action, which surely falls to be determined at the time of their action according to the best objective perception of the circumstances, including the relevant law. The law in existence at the time of the act, even if it is crystal clear, may be subsequently changed by the court through its power of reversal, but surely the morality of act cannot thus be reversed by a judicial change of mind. The point is that some acts of disobedience to law (e.g., minor forms of trespass) involve such marginal disobedience that the decisive question should not be whether or not they are in fact illegal—with the consequence that if they are illegal, they turn the act into one that is morally wrong—when even the courts may have difficulty in deciding their illegality. Of course, not all acts of indirect disobedience are of such marginal illegality, but I would suggest that the proper test ought to be whether such acts are on balance more coercive than persuasive.

Violence is a form of coercion, but coercion is a broader concept than violence, since it includes types of nonviolent action. The concept to be contrasted with coercion is persuasion, with the essential difference between the two indicated by the reaction of the opponent. If the opponent is induced to act favorably because he has become convinced by the disobeyer's case, he has been persuaded; but if he acts favorably only in order to avoid trouble, while continuing to hold a contrary

[99] M. K. Gandhi, *Non-Violent Resistance*, p. 175. It should be noted that Gandhi himself thought such resistance justified only in a corrupt or tyrannical state.
[1] (1966), 383 U.S. 131.

position to the disobeyer, he has been coerced rather than persuaded. Coercion, even when nonviolent, is analogous to violence, for it employs force even if it is of the nonphysical variety. Coercion manipulates the opponent as an object, while persuasion respects him as a person. In a democratic society, with its commitment to rationality in government and in political dialogue, persuasion must be the moral technique, since it makes its appeal to reason and to love.

Almost all techniques of civil disobedience combine both persuasion and coercion. Often the coercive aspect is the more arresting, but it is also the more socially disruptive. In my opinion, unless a particular tactic inconveniences only the people heavily involved in the injustice, it passes beyond the permissible limits of civil disobedience when the coercive aspect assumes more importance than the persuasive aspect. Ideally it should put the major burden of the suffering it causes upon the shoulders of the protesters themselves and not upon innocent bystanders. It will not always achieve the ideal, but it must achieve a due proportion.

Thus disruptive tactics like bridge stall-ins or building sit-ins which prevent the normal flow of traffic are invalid means of civil disobedience because of the inconvenience they cause to innocent members of society, in addition to the fact that they have a purely arbitrary relationship to the injustice whose correction is sought. There is no doubt that in concrete circumstances it may be difficult to decide whether the persuasive or the coercive element is predominant (or is likely to be, if the decision is being made in advance), but I believe this must be the ultimate test of indirect disobedience in a democracy. As an example of the principle of persuasion, it is an acceptable form of the political process which is the heart of democracy. But as a tool of violence, it has no place in a society dedicated to the rule of law. . . .   [pp. 49–54]

4

POSITIVISM, ANALYTICAL JURISPRUDENCE AND THE CONCEPT OF LAW

SOVEREIGNTY AND ITS ORIGINS

THE modern doctrine of sovereignty derived essentially from two lines of development which heralded the end of the medieval period.[1] On the one hand there was the rise of new national states anxious to assert their total independence in a new age of economic expansion and to reject all feudal notions of overlordship or papal interference; on the other, a departure from the medieval idea of law as being fundamentally custom, and legislation as merely a form of declaring the existence of new customs.[2] On the contrary each national territory was now recognised as constituting both a self-sufficient unit and an independent legal entity, so that the notion naturally followed that, within each such nation-state, there must be located some supreme power, the decisive feature of which was its virtually unlimited capacity to make new law. This doctrine was more than a reassertion of the earlier theory that *rex est imperator in regno suo*.[3] For it emphasised in a way that to the earlier theorists would have been unacceptable the idea of unfettered legislative capacity. The new approach was essentially secular and positivist, and though lip-service continued to be paid to a notional subjection to overriding natural law,[4] the supporters of legal sovereignty tended increasingly to whittle down natural law from a system of norms either to a mere statement of human impulses explaining the need for a sovereign power in human society, as with Hobbes, or to a mere formal

---

[1] In the Middle Ages, sovereignty in the sense of unfettered power of legislation, was more easily associated with the Pope than with secular rulers. For the latter were regarded not only as bound by feudal law, but also as coming within the ecclesiastical jurisdiction, whereas the Pope was regarded as outside and even above the Church. (See W. Ullman, *Principles of Government and Politics in the Middle Ages* (1961), pp. 72, 139, 150; and *A History of Political Thought in the Middle Ages* (1965), pp. 103 *et seq*.)

[2] See *post*, 613. The declaratory theory of precedent is a survival of this thinking. See *post*, 702.

[3] The maxim employed by French lawyers in the fourteenth century to resist imperial pretensions: *cf.* McIlwain, *Growth of Political Thought in the West*, p. 268; and by Henry VIII in his dispute with the Pope regarding Royal supremacy over a national Church. See J. J. Scarisbrick, *Henry VIII* (1968), pp. 267–273 and see, in particular, the preamble to the Act in Restraint of Appeals 1533: ". . . this realm of England is an empire. . . ." (*ibid.*, pp. 309–310).

[4] *Cf.* Bodin, *post*, 177.

category to justify a belief in inalienable sovereignty, as in Rousseau's theory of the general will. But as became apparent in the writings of Hume, true empiricism really involved the rejection of natural law as a system of norms since, as Hume argued, the validity of normative rules cannot logically be treated as an objective fact, but depends on the relative viewpoint of those who apply them.[5] On the other hand, *positive* law, in the sense of the law of the state, is something ascertainable and valid without regard to subjective considerations. Hence it must be regarded as separate from morals (which were equated with natural law, if this term was still used at all), although it might correspond in many respects to current moral standards and be subject to their influence.

[handwritten margin note: "ought" cannot be derived from "is"]

BENTHAM AND THE UTILITARIANS [6]

Did this entail that, for the positivist, mankind was thrown upon a sea of conflicting moralities with no metewand by which he might legitimately choose to follow or reject these? If natural law was dethroned, could some scientific or rational standard be found? Hume himself asserted that only utility could supply the answer,[7] but it was left to Bentham to expound in detail the significance and working of the principle of utility. Bentham, though he gave credit to Priestley as " the first who taught my lips to pronounce this sacred truth," [8] gave currency to its formulation as the principle of the greatest happiness of the greatest number, and sought to make himself the Newton of the legal and moral world by establishing the principles of an experimental science governing that sphere, much as Newton had formulated the fundamental laws of the physical world. To this end Bentham began with a savage but well-directed attack upon the traditional *clichés* of natural law and the social contract

[5] See *A Treatise of Human Nature* (ed. Selby-Bigge), pp. 516–534.
[6] The student may be referred to a new critical biography of Bentham, the first volume of which has been published, *viz. Jeremy Bentham: An Odyssey of Ideas, 1748–1792,* by Mary P. Mack (1962). This draws on a mass of unpublished materials deposited in the library of University College London, and is of value in removing many misconceptions about Bentham. Letwin's *The Pursuit of Certainty* (1965) is useful for the same reason. A massive project is under way for the publication of the majority of these unpublished materials. The first five volumes containing his correspondence, as well as *Of Law in General,* his main exercise in expository jurisprudence, and a new critical edition of *Principles of Morals and Legislation,* have already been published.
[7] See *Enquiry concerning the Principles of Morals,* Chap. V.
[8] *Works,* Vol. 10, p. 142. It may in fact derive originally from Beccaria: " La massima felicità divisa nel maggior numero," as Bentham himself admitted. See *A Fragment on Government* (ed. W. Harrison), p. xx. Letwin comments: " It had been suggested to him by everyone, or at any rate, he attributed his inspiration to different authors—Beccaria, Helvetius, Bacon, Hume. In fact, from each of them Bentham drew only what he was looking for. He borrowed phrases but the principle of utility as he came to understand and use it was entirely his own invention " (*The Pursuit of Certainty* (1965), p. 139).

as embodied in Blackstone's complacent and uncritical panegyric on the British Constitution.[9] This was followed by <u>an attempt to analyse the springs of human actions in terms of pleasures and pains,</u> and to reduce human needs to a " calculus of felicity " where different " lots " of happiness could be weighed by certain quantitative tests, in order to ascertain what utility decreed.[10]

The somewhat crude psychology of the Utilitarians, though plausible to contemporaries, has long been jettisoned, as has the notion of utility as the philosophical justification of ethics.[11] Nevertheless, Bentham, despite his occasional naïvetés, was a profound thinker, an acute social critic, and an untiring campaigner for the reform of antiquated law, and he became and, has indeed remained, one of the cardinal influences on modern society. By rejecting both natural law and subjective values and replacing these by standards based on human advantages, pleasures and satisfactions, he provided what may be, as many think, an insufficient substitute for ethics or aesthetics, but was at least a valuable signpost by which men in society might direct the external welfare of that society. Bentham himself was a believer in *laisser-faire* once the antiquated legal system had been renovated, but ironically, <u>his emphasis on reform and social welfare has made him one of the creators of the modern collectivist welfare state.</u>[12]

[9] Contained in the introduction to Blackstone's *Commentaries*. Bentham described natural rights as nonsense—" nonsense upon stilts." See *Anarchical Fallacies,* Works, Vol. 2, p. 501. Bentham argued that " the real object of one who asserts natural rights was to engage others to join with him in applying force, for the purpose of putting things into a state in which he would actually be in possession of the right of which he thus claims to be in possession " (quoted in Burns (1965), 16 Royal Hist.Soc.Transac. 95, 111–112). For Bentham's view that abuse of language, treating a claim as if it were a recognised right, is the fallacy at the root of the case for natural rights, see the illuminating discussion in Manning, *The Mind of Jeremy Bentham* (1968), pp. 42–43. It is all too easily forgotten that Bentham employed the phrase " securities against misrule " to fulfil the same function as " natural rights " did for contemporaries he castigated. See Letwin, *op. cit.*, p. 142.

[10] See *Principles of Morals and Legislation*, Chap. 4. Hazlitt's comment is not without justice. " He turns wooden utensils in a lathe for exercise, and fancies he can turn men in the same manner " (*Spirit of the Age*, World's Classics ed., p. 18).

[11] Attempts are still made to salvage something of value. Hence the growth of so-called " <u>rule-utilitarianism</u> " whereby a *practice*, rather than an isolated incident is tested by reference to utility. Instead of asking whether hanging *this* innocent man has good consequences it asks whether the practice of hanging *the* innocent is beneficial. See, particularly, the writings of Rawls in, for example, Foot, *Theories of Ethics* (1967). Bentham himself may have hinted as much. (See Hart, Bentham, 48 Proc. of Br.Acad. 297, 302–303, and in Summers, *More Essays in Legal Philosophy* (1971), 16, 23–24). Another curious survival of Benthamism is the " games theory " popular among sociologists and political and international theorists.

[12] See D. Lloyd, " Law of Associations," in *Law and Opinion in England in the Twentieth Century* (ed. Ginsberg, 1959), p. 99. A contrasting picture of Bentham's vision of governmental activity is given in Manning, *op. cit.*, at pp. 53, 86–97. Bentham believed in reducing law to a minimum; (" In France, where they have so much less liberty than we have, they have much more law ") in

Bentham was mainly interested in law reform and he distinguished what he called censorial jurisprudence, or the science of legislation, from expository jurisprudence. The latter was concerned with law as it is, without regard to its moral or immoral character. The science of legislation, however, was for him really a branch of morals, being the principles upon which men's actions were to be directed to the greatest quantity of possible happiness [13] by rules of a permanent kind, as distinguished from private morals, which are directed only to oneself.[14]

Bentham's writings of expository jurisprudence are only just beginning to see the light of day. It is now becoming apparent that these are no mere appendage to the Bentham canon. Nor are they mere chips from which Austin was able to build. On the contrary, there is little of Austin, or, indeed, a century of later jurists, which is not foreseen in Bentham. It is apparent from Raz,[15] for example, that no subsequent writer developed a formal concept of a legal system with such ingenuity. No doubt lawyers will still read Austin as the fount of nineteenth century positivism. He appeals to lawyers because he was a lawyer and Austinian jurisprudence is full of painstaking searching legal analysis. But there is no doubt who is the master, who the student.

BENTHAM'S " OF LAWS IN GENERAL "

Of Laws in General is Bentham's main contribution to analytical jurisprudence. Yet, it was not until 1970 that we had an authoritative

economic matters he believed that the governmental watchword should be " Be quiet." He, however, calibrated the degree of intervention with opulence, the greater the opulence, the less was the need of governmental interference. But " the problem in England was . . . one of growing unemployment and visible poverty. And in this circumstance, Bentham did gradually commit himself, by degrees, to an increasing measure of state intervention in the life of the individual. . . . There is nothing in Bentham . . . to suggest that he could not have been a supporter of Fabian Socialism had he lived a hundred years later " (pp. 91, 97). For a full discussion of matter see J. Stone, *Human Law And Human Justice* (1965), Chap. 4.

[13] It has been pointed out, however, that the greatest happiness of the greatest number might, on Bentham's calculations, require the greatest misery of the few. This is well brought out in Bentham's scheme for prison reform by way of his celebrated " Panopticon." It is clear that Bentham's ideas for a modern prison involved the infliction of appallingly inhuman conditions, and making the conditions of gaol a terror for all prisoners actual and potential, in the interests of the greatest number, who presumably were never to experience the torments of the Panopticon. Burke's comment on the keeper of the Panopticon as " the spider in the web " is far from inapt. (See G. Himmelfarb, " The Haunted House of Jeremy Bentham," *Victorian Minds* (1968), Chap. 2.)

[14] *Op. cit.*, Chap. 17, § 1. Bentham did not offer a systematic theory of ethics based on exact calculation, but a series of prudential rules addressed to legislators and judges based on a new vocabulary and a new logic. He was not concerned to describe every conceivable species of human behaviour, but only those with social consequences, the public and observable kinds the judge might have to estimate in court (see Mack, *op. cit.*, p. 18).

[15] *Ante*, 46, and Chap. 4 *passim*.

edition.[16] Its editor has remarked, with justification, that "had it been published in his lifetime, it, rather than John Austin's later and obviously derivative work, would have dominated English jurisprudence." [17] Nor must it be thought that it stands in isolation from Bentham's censorial jurisprudence. Bentham was a life-long law-reformer, but he believed (and Austin was his disciple in this as well) that no reform of the substantive law could be effectuated without a reform of its form and structure. A thoroughly scientific conceptual framework was thus but a prelude to reform.[18]

In the extracts which follow the reader may gain some insight into Bentham's contribution to analytical jurisprudence.[19] Like Austin's theory, Bentham's is an imperative theory of law, in which the key concepts are those of sovereignty and command. But, whilst their respective definitions of these concepts are closely related,[20] Bentham, to quote his editor again, "expounds these ideas with far greater subtlety and flexibility than Austin and illuminates aspects of law largely neglected by him." [21] A few illustrations of Bentham's originality are sketched in this section.

Austin's sovereign was postulated as an illimitable, indivisible entity: Bentham's is neither. There may be sound practical reasons for having one all-powerful sovereign, but Bentham saw the distinction, as Austin did not, between social desirability and logical necessity. From a conceptual standpoint there is no necessity for a sovereign to be undivided and unlimited. Indeed, in the complex societies that have developed since Bentham's day, particularly the modern collectivist states and federal systems, quite the reverse is true. Bentham thus accepts divided and partial sovereignty.[22] Furthermore, he discussed the legal restrictions that may be imposed upon sovereign power. "The business of the ordinary sort of laws is to prescribe to the people what *they* shall do: the business of this transcendent class of laws is to prescribe to the sovereign what *he* shall do." [23] Bentham believes a sovereign may bind his successors, explaining that "if by accident a sovereign should in fact come to the throne with a determination not to adopt the covenants of his

[16] The first edition of Bentham's manuscripts was published by their discoverer, Professor Everett in 1945 under the title *The Limits of Jurisprudence Defined.* The present definitive edition by Professor Hart, makes considerable changes of substance and arrangement to the earlier edition.
[17] H. L. A. Hart, *Rechtstheorie* (1971), pp. 55, 57. The discussion of Bentham's *Of Laws in General* which follows is largely based on Hart's article, which provides an invaluable introduction to that work.
[18] *Cf.* Stone, *Legal System and Lawyers' Reasonings* (1964), pp. 64–69. Bentham himself brings out the relationship in Chap. XIX of *Of Laws in General.*
[19] See *post*, 187.
[20] *Post*, 187 and 208.
[21] Hart, *op. cit.*, p. 58.
[22] *Of Laws in General*, p. 18, fn. 6.
[23] *Idem*, p. 64 and *post*, 196.

predecessors, he would be told that he had adopted them notwithstanding." [24] Without spelling it out Bentham comes close to concept-
ualising a doctrine of judicial review,[25] for, though he thought that
enforcement would be extra-legal (moral or religious), he did not rule
out the use of legal sanctions.

Sanctions generally play a less prominent part in Bentham's theory
than they do in Austin's. And Bentham, perhaps for this reason, is
prepared to undertake a more detailed, less crude, taxonomy of
motivating forces than Austin was. Thus, Bentham thought a sovereign's commands would be law even if supported only by religious
or moral sanctions.[26] Further, Bentham's account admits " alluring
motives," the concept of rewards. Bentham accepts that, what he
calls " praemiary or invitative laws," [27] are likely to be rare. " By
reward alone," he contends, " it is most certain that no material
part of that business [of government] could be carried on for half
an hour." [28] It is on " punishments " that " everything turns." [29]

But " what chiefly differentiates Bentham from Austin and makes
him so interesting a philosopher of law is that he was a conscious
innovator of new forms of enquiry into the structure of law, and
that he makes explicit his method and general logic of enquiry in a
way in which no other writer on these topics does." [30] This contrast
comes out when Austin's definition of law is compared with Bentham's. On the surface they are strikingly similar: both are framed
in terms of superiority and inferiority,[31] in terms of conduct to be
adopted by those in a habit of obedience to a sovereign. But there
the similarity ceases. Austin's " model," consciously or unconsciously,
was the criminal statute. Bentham, anticipating a trend in modern
analytical jurisprudence, has undertaken " rational reconstruction," [32]
wider than Austin's " model " and current usage. With his ultimate
goal the erection of a structure within which law reform could take
place, Bentham was prepared to " fix the meaning of terms," [33] so
as not to be restricted by contemporary patterns. Thus, in his
definition of law as an expression of volition, he covers not only
general laws made by legislatures (supreme and subordinate), but
also judicial, administrative and even domestic orders, such as those
given by a parent to a child: declaratory laws [34] are also within its

---

[24] *Idem,* p. 66 and *post,* 196.
[25] See Hart, *op. cit.,* p. 59. See also 2 *Irish Jurist* 327.
[26] *Idem,* p. 70.
[27] *Idem,* p. 136.
[28] *Idem,* p. 135.
[29] *Idem,* p. 136.
[30] Hart, *op. cit.,* p. 59.
[31] On which see Raz's comments, *The Concept of a Legal System* (1970), pp. 13–14.
[32] On this trend see Summers, *post,* 265 and his introduction to *Essays in Legal Philosophy* (1968), pp. 4–6. See also Wollheim, *ante,* 64.
[33] *Op. cit.,* p. 10.   [34] *Cf. The Province of Jurisprudence Determined,* p. 27.

ambit. One reason why Bentham prefers this "model" of a law as
a tool of analysis is clear, for a statute will usually only contain part
of a law and, indeed, will frequently contain parts of different laws.
　　Another difference between Austin's concept of law and Bentham's
is that, for Bentham, a command is only one of four "aspects"
which the legislator's will may bear to the acts concerning which
he is legislating. Bentham believes that an understanding of the
structure of law entails an appreciation of the "necessary relations"
of "opposition and concomitancy" [35] between these four aspects
of the legislator's will. To demonstrate these relationships, Bentham
developed, what modern jurists and logicians call, "deontic" logic,
the logic of imperatives.[36] Bentham can rightly claim to be the
discoverer of this pattern of thought.
　　Without discussing this in detail [37] it may be said to commit
Bentham to the view that there are no laws which are neither
imperative nor permissive. All laws command or prohibit or permit
some form of conduct. Bentham recognised, however, that the imperative character of law is often concealed, that law is expressed
descriptively ("whoever steals shall be sentenced to five years of
imprisonment"), or, further, that reference to any offence or sanction
is often hidden "in the course of many sentences or even pages or
even volumes." [38] An example of the latter approach is an area such
as the law of property. Every developed legal system sets out the
requirements of a valid title, explains what conditions must be
fulfilled to make a person an owner or vest in him some lesser
form of proprietary right, and explains what an owner must do to
divest himself of his property. One of the most interesting sections
of *Of Laws in General* is Bentham's reconciliation of such provisions,
which are indisputably law, with his thesis that all laws other than
merely permissive ones are *in part* imperative and penal. Title to
property is nothing more than a rationalisation of a particular
permission taken out of a general prohibition. The prohibition relates
to the act of "meddling" [39] with, for example, a piece of land, but
the owner is excepted from this prohibition. So the acts or events
which confer proprietary title are merely exceptions limiting the
scope of the basic prohibitory law. It follows from Bentham's analysis
that those laws he regarded as civil laws (that is laws which do not

---

[35] *Op cit.*, p. 97.
[36] See, for example, Ross, *Directives and Norms*; Raz, *The Concept of a Legal
System*; Von Wright, *Norm and Action*.
[37] A fuller discussion will be found in Hart, *op. cit.*, pp. 60–63 and Raz, *op. cit.*,
pp. 54–59.
[38] *Op. cit.*, p. 106.
[39] See *post*, 203.

impose obligations or duties or provide sanctions for them [40]) were not "complete laws," but only parts of laws. Convenience of exposition dictated that we detached such civil laws into separate codes, but there was nothing inherent in the laws themselves which made such division necessary.[41]

Bentham's analysis, it will be noticed, steers clear of a number of the pitfalls into which Austin fell. We are not forced into postulating nullity as a sanction, nor into rejecting laws in common usage as "law improperly so-called," nor into setting up fictions like "tacit command." Bentham's *Of Laws in General* is undoubtedly the best defence of the imperative theory. Where it fails and where modern jurisprudence picks up the strands is in a failure to develop the concept of a rule. Bentham, like Austin, is rooted to the concepts of sovereignty and the habit of obedience which as Hart and other leading contemporary jurists have demonstrated are deficient in aim and unsatisfactory in scope.

AUSTIN

Following Bentham's lead Austin attempted to work out what he believed to be the legal and logical implications of sovereignty as viewed by a legal positivist. There are few,[42] if any, at the present day, who regard him as either wholly successful in this undertaking or as being altogether clear-minded in his basic aims, but, nevertheless, Austin's thought still remains worthy of examination not only on account of his widespread influence, especially in common law countries,[43] but also by reason of his penetrating powers of applying analysis to jurisprudence.

As a positivist Austin sought to show what law really is, as opposed to moral or natural law notions of what it ought to be. It has been pointed out that there is no necessary logical connection

---

[40] So "penal" in Bentham's terminology is much wider than the accepted use of "criminal" and includes such civil wrongs as torts, breaches of contract and breaches of trust. Much property legislation (*cf. ante*, 158) and constitutional law would be classified as "civil" and, therefore, "incomplete." It should be added that *Of Laws in General* is the outcome of Bentham's pursuit of the difference, if any, between "penal" and "civil" law. See, on this, *Principles of Morals and Legislation*, p. 299. Bentham's analysis fails to characterise legal techniques other than the penal and the civil, for example, the administrative regulatory technique. See, further, Summers (1971) 59 Calif.L.R. 733.

[41] *Op. cit.*, p. 192.

[42] Rare defences of Austin may be found in Manning, *Modern Theories of Law* ed. Jennings (1933), pp. 180 *et seq.* and Morison (1958) 68 Yale L.J. 212.

[43] See, for example, the conceptual approach adopted in *N.P.B.* v. *Ainsworth* [1965] A.C. 1175; *Pettitt* v. *Pettitt* [1970] A.C. 777 or recently in *Tesco* v. *Nattrass* [1971] 2 All E.R. 127, or the attitude to the judicial role in *Scruttons* v. *Midland Silicones* [1962] A.C. 446 or *Myers* v. *D.P.P.* [1965] A.C. 1001.

between positivism and the command theory,[44] and it is certainly true that we are logically free to insist on the separation of law from morals, while rejecting the command theory. Yet to the Benthamites positivism seemed to require some simple empirical explanation of law devoid of metaphysics or mysticism. Bentham, ever critical of " judge-made " law, once compared this to the way of teaching conduct to one's dog,[45] by waiting till it has done something objectionable and then beating it. What was rationally needed was merely some prior command, so that law was really no more than a series of orders given to human beings, with penalties or sanctions attached for disobedience. Whether this was an over-simplification, or in what sense the word " command " was here used, were questions not fully explored by those to whom this approach seemed so obvious an explanation of the essence of law; to Austin [46] the problem was merely to link this logically with the universally recognised and esteemed doctrine of legal sovereignty.

CRITICISMS

In the ensuing pages Austin must be left to expound his own doctrines. I shall confine what follows to a brief examination of weaknesses, actual or alleged, in the Austinian doctrine. Much of the criticism directed at Austin has been concerned not unnaturally with the deductions that Austin made from his fundamental positions, such as the illimitable and indivisible nature of sovereignty, or that international and constitutional law and also custom are mere positive morality,[47] with the object thereby of casting doubt on the correctness of Austin's own definitions and assumptions. Of the validity and significance of a choice of a definition we have already written in an earlier chapter,[48] so that it is only necessary here to discuss the more specific points of criticism.

---

[44] See H. L. A. Hart, " Positivism and the Separation of Law and Morals " (1958) 71 Harv.L.R. 593; and in *Encyclopaedia of Philosophy* ed. Edwards (1967). Olivecrona (*Law As Fact* (2nd ed.), pp. 50–62) prefers to reserve the expression " legal positivism " to its " original and traditional sense of the German *Rechtspositivismus* " (p. 61). This connotes that all law is positive in the sense of being an expression of the will of a supreme authority.

[45] See *Works*, V, p. 235. *Cf.* De Jouvenel, *Sovereignty*, p. 242. Nor was Bentham any more laudatory of the organic development of Roman law: " It has no more pretensions to the title of a system, than the contents of a quarry or mason's yard have to that of a palace " (quoted in Letwin, *op. cit.*, pp. 164–165).

[46] This does not, of course, mean that Austin's sovereignty and imperative theories cannot stand independently of each other. See Stone, *Legal System and Lawyers' Reasonings* (1964), pp. 75–76: " They are independent starting points both of which Austin adopts : one is not deduced from the other."

[47] As to Austin's view regarding international law and custom, see *post*, 216, 284, 574.

[48] *Ante*, 39.

Law as a Command

A fundamental objection sometimes raised against the command theory is that the idea of a command presupposes the order of a determinate person, and that as law emanates from the ever-changing multitude which comprise the political machinery of the state, it cannot be treated as the command of anyone in particular. Curiously enough, Austin himself insisted on a determinate person or body as the source of a command, presumably on the footing that a command is an exercise of will of some particular person or persons. But the justification for calling law a command is really quite different, namely, that it refers to the *logical* classification of legal propositions as " imperatives," that is, they are normative statements laying down rules to guide human conduct as distinguished from statements of fact.[49] Hence it is a mere matter of terminology whether the word " command " is appropriate to bring out this distinction, or whether it should be confined to such specific instances as the order of a sergeant-major rapped out on the barrack square. Olivecrona, who raises this objection, in effect recognises that Austin is, nonetheless, warranted in classifying legal rules as imperative statements, and suggests the term " independent imperatives." [50] Perhaps the word " command " is undesirable for its psychological associations, and it is frequently replaced nowadays by the more colourless designation of " imperatives " or " directives."

Others, such as Duguit, asserted that the notion of command is in any event inapplicable to modern social legislation, which binds the state itself rather than the individual. To the suggestion that there is here no command at all, Austin's reply is that there can be a command where some organ of the sovereign, as against the sovereign itself—(Austin avoids the word " state ")—is commanded, and this would certainly cover most legislation of the type envisaged. But it must be admitted that the whole notion of the state or sovereign being unable to command itself is a wholly unrealistic one, in the ambit of the highly complex web of modern public law. This unreality is underlined, for instance, by Austin's treatment of constitutional law as not being positive law, since it is either mere question of fact as to who is habitually obeyed, or it consists of commands to the sovereign by itself. This is grotesque in relation to

---

[49] *Cf. ante,* 8.

[50] See *post,* 523, 538. Similarly, Kelsen insists that the word " command " can only be used here in an impersonal and anonymous way, and divested of any psychological association, such as the " will " of the legislator. In this sense it has hardly anything in common with a command properly so called: H. Kelsen, *General Theory of Law and State,* pp. 33–36.

modern conditions,[51] but the point can be met if "command" is regarded merely as denoting the logically imperative form of legal rules, for there is nearly always legal machinery for enforcing public law rules against some person or body within the state.[52] And to say that the state cannot bind itself is merely to assert that the sovereign may be able to change the law. Yet it can only do so by observing the procedure constitutionally laid down, and in the meantime existing imperatives remain law.

Sovereignty

Much of the keenest criticism is directed against Austin's rather rigid views as to the nature of sovereignty. Thus his notion that sovereignty is indivisible is falsified by federal constitutions, and certainly Austin's attempt to locate the sovereign in the United States was a singularly unhappy venture.[53] The mistake here was to assume that sovereignty has an inherent "nature" (though whether as a matter of logic or physical fact is far from clear) which it cannot avoid. Thus any attempt by the sovereign to divide itself can, on Austin's view, owing to the nature of sovereignty itself, be counter-manded and the original sovereign resume its former powers. The same argument applied to establish its illimitability. Here Austin was taking over, and seeking to justify logically, the notions of sovereignty propounded by his predecessors such as Bodin, Hobbes and Rousseau. The fallacy is that sovereignty is not a metaphysical entity with an ineradicable logical structure. On the contrary it is a practical device of law and politics whereby effect is given to the practical need in any political community for some final or ultimate legal authority. But there is no logical or any other compulsion to make this authority indivisible. Ultimate authority may be vested in different matters in various bodies, though a need will then be felt to have a tribunal to resolve conflicts. This does not mean, however, that the tribunal is thus constituted the Austinian sovereign, for in this setting there is no such animal. Sovereignty is divided [54] and the

---

51 But *cf.* David and de Vries, *French Legal System*, p. 61, pointing out that parts of the 1946 French Constitution are essentially "a statement of political aspiration."

52 See for example, *R. v. Criminal Compensation Board, ex parte Lain* [1967] 2 Q.B. 864, where certiorari was issued to enforce an *ex gratia* payment which was being denied by a non-statutory authority.

53 See *post*, 220.

54 In *Ex p. Mwenya* [1960] 1 Q.B. 241, the question was whether an English court could issue a writ of *habeas corpus* in regard to detention of an individual in a protectorate. The argument against this power was that a protected state was nevertheless independent and sovereign and, therefore, Great Britain could not exert any authority within such a territory except over British subjects. Evershed M.R. pointed out that according to W. E. Hall on "Foreign Jurisdiction of the British Crown" (1894) this view was really based on the Austinian theory of the indivisibility of sovereignty. However, Lord Evershed went on to point out

constitutional court is itself subject to or controlled by the legal
system. Nor need a sovereign's power be unlimited, and, indeed,
many constitutions impose entrenched clauses, so that to that extent
no change is possible without a change of constitution.[55] Unlimited
sovereignty, therefore, can properly only refer to a body being without a superior in the structure of the state, but this implies nothing
either logically or legally as to the degree of its freedom of action.

That these questions are by no means purely theoretical, but have
a distinctly practical implication, is sufficiently indicated by the
problems that have arisen in interpreting the effect of the Statute of
Westminster of 1931 on Dominion constitutions and currently the
question whether the United Kingdom government could resume
direct rule over Northern Ireland and whether the United Kingdom
can (constitutionally) join the European Communities.[56] For instance,
how far can the Imperial Parliament bind itself not to legislate in a
certain way for the future? [57] And to what extent can a sovereign
Parliament effectively define its own structure so as to constrain itself
to comply with a particular procedure for legislative purposes, *e.g.*, to
sit in two separate bodies? Such questions have arisen in
an acute form in the courts of South Africa, which have displayed a
laudable unwillingness to be tied to any rigid formula.[58] Indeed, it
is sometimes overlooked in this sort of discussion, that Austin himself based sovereignty on habitual obedience. There is no doubt whom
the people of South Africa habitually obey and thus no doubt on
Austin's test where sovereignty lies. But, in a revolutionary setting,
a military takeover, a revolution, a secession,[59] Austin's test of
habitual obedience is too open-textured to be useful as a criterion.
One must keep in mind Austin's failure to distinguish *de jure*
sovereignty (authority to make law) from *de facto* sovereignty (power
to enforce obedience).[60]

that it is now recognised that the meaning of a protectorate is both indefinite
and variable and the jurisdiction of the English courts may depend upon the
extent to which control is actually exercised by the Crown in the particular
territory.

[55] The provision in the U.S. Constitution whereby no state can be deprived of its
equal representations in the Senate without its consent is usually cited in this
connection (Art. 5).

[56] *Cf. post*, 236. See also the debates in the House of Commons on April
6, 1971 (H.C. Vol. 815, cols. 259 *et seq.*) wherein it was admitted that the
previous government had drafted a bill to reintroduce direct rule over Ulster.

[57] Hence the uneasy debate over the irrevocable step of commitment to the Treaty
of Rome. [58] See *post*, 232.

[59] Examples such as Pakistan (see *State* v. *Dosso* (1958) 2 P.S.C.R. 180), Uganda
(*Uganda* v. *Commissioner of Prisons* (1966) E.A.L.R. 514), Nigeria (*Lakanmi and
K. Ola* v. *A.G.* (*Western State*), discussed by Ojo in 20 I.C.L.Q. 117), Ghana
(*Sallah* v. *A.-G.*, discussed by Date-Bah in I.C.L.Q. 315) or, most notably,
Southern Rhodesia (*Madzimbamuto* v. *Lardner-Burke* [1969] 1 A.C. 645). See
post, 327 and, generally, Harris [1971] C.L.J. 103.

[60] *Cf.* Bryce, *post*, 224 and see Raz, *The Concept of a Legal System*, pp. 41–43.
Bentham saw the distinction (see Manning, *op cit.*, Chap. XI).

The attempt by Austin to base sovereignty on habitual obedience has been strongly criticised, as confusing the legal with the *de facto* or political sovereign. It has been suggested in answer, that Austin was looking for neither of these, but for the logically presupposed ultimate source of law in any state, viewed as an abstract concept. Thus his sovereign would be comparable to Rousseau's general will.[61] It seems certain, however, that this was not Austin's aim. Austin was a lawyer, and what he sought to provide was an unfailing test for locating legal sovereignty in the state.[62] He recognised, however, like Kelsen, that law cannot itself be based on law but must be based on something outside law. He, therefore, sought to base it upon fact,[63] *viz.*, the habitual obedience of the mass of the population. This was certainly not a confusion with a *de facto* sovereign. Indeed this latter concept is really meaningless, for the location of actual power in a modern state whether attributed to a power élite,[64] a pressure group, a social class, or different categories of individuals, is a sociological inquiry entirely distinct from locating the legal sovereign. Austin, for instance, never imagined that the body of electors was in itself the *de facto* power of the state, or was not subject to all the force of pressure of those able to direct it. That something was wrong with Austin's invocation of fact in the form he used it is, however, sufficiently shown by his refusal to accept the King in Parliament as England's legal sovereign. But to avoid repetition, the further examination of this point will be reserved until Kelsen's theory has been reviewed.[65]

Law and Morals

The positivist aspect of Austinianism is most in evidence in the rigid separation of law and morals.[66] Most of the critics of this approach

---

[61] C. W. Manning, in *Modern Theories of Law* (1933), p. 180 *et seq.* See also J. Stone, *Legal System and Lawyers' Reasoning* (1964), who argues that Austin is merely putting forward a formal theory, to enable the legal order to be seen as a coherent system of norms. But Stone admits that he is not always consistent on this plane (see pp. 73–88).

[62] *Cf.* W. L. Morison, " Some Myths about Positivism " (1958) 68 Yale L.J. 212.

[63] Ignoring the difficulty raised by Hume, that a norm (or system of norms) cannot be derived from existential propositions alone. On this account Kelsen relies on an ultimate norm outside the legal system, *cf. post,* 269.

[64] As in C. Wright Mills, *Power Elite* (1956). See also Milliband, *The State in Capitalist Society* (1969), and Dahrendorf, *Class and Class Conflict in Industrial Society* (1963). See also the Soviet approach in Chap. 10, *post.*

[65] *Post,* 269.

[66] Hart usefully identifies five different meanings of " positivism " :
　(1) The contention that laws are commands of human beings.
　(2) The contention that there is no necessary connection between law and morals or law as it is and ought to be.
　(3) The contention that the analysis (or study of the meaning) of legal concepts is (a) worth pursuing and (b) to be distinguished from historical inquiries into the causes or origins of laws, from sociological inquiries into the relation

may be classified in one way or another as supporters of an external natural law, which has already been discussed above.[67] Another approach, which appeals to some modern thinkers, is to claim that law is a kind of order which has an *internal* moral structure to which it must conform in order to be law.[68] Much of this sort of thinking is animated by the strong aversion to recognising some of the frenzied output of the Nazi legal system as " law." This is to set up some sort of an objective moral law as part of the universe and involves a rejection of Hume's distinction between objective existential propositions (" is ") and valuations (" ought "), and implies that the truth of value judgments at least in morals is as ascertainable as the truth of physical fact. Yet until some criteria are established for this purpose comparable to those available in the realm of fact it seems to add little to the argument to conceive the moral order as part of the inner structure of the legal order, rather than as an external system.[69] The approach remains essentially an idealist search for absolute truth in the realm of values, curiously enough at

of law and other social phenomena, and from the criticism or appraisal of law whether in terms of morals, social aims, " functions," or otherwise.

(4) The contention that a legal system is a " closed logical system " in which correct legal decisions can be deduced by logical means from predetermined legal rules without reference to social aims, policies, moral standards.

(5) The contention that moral judgments cannot be established or defended, as statements of facts can, by rational argument, evidence, or proof. (See (1958) 71 Harv.L.R. 601–602.)

For an extended list, see Summers, 41 N.Y.U.L.Rev. 861, 889. There is a good deal of truth in Summers' remark that " it would be best in legal philosophy to drop the term ' positivist,' for it is now radically ambiguous and dominantly pejorative " (in *Essays in Legal Philosophy,* p. 16). Olivecrona believes that much confusion over the meaning of " positivism " has been caused by failure to distinguish twin-origins of the concept: in the sense of law by position " *positum,*" it designates a theory on the nature of law, and, as a philosophy, it stands for a particular approach to legal problems, the " separation of positive law from morals, mores, religion . . ." (Hall, 33 U.Cinc.L.R. at p. 29). See Olivecrona, *Law As Fact* (2nd ed.), pp. 50–62.

The so-called " positivist school " in criminal law, though not referring to positivism in any of the above specific senses, is clearly related to several of them. The essence of this school is the rejection of the idea of moral guilt as the basis of legal responsibility, and the proposal to substitute for it the concept of social responsibility or accountability. The view of Barbara Wootton that the concept of responsibility in criminal law should be allowed gradually to " wither away," reflects this approach. See B. Wootton, " Diminished Responsibility " (1960) 76 L.Q.R. 224 and *Crime and Criminal Law* (1963), Chap. 2. See also M. Ancel, " Social Defence " (1962) 78 L.Q.R. 491 and *Social Defence* (1965).

[67] *Ante,* 74 *et seq.*

[68] See the writings of Lon Fuller, *ante,* 83, and 138 and *post,* 243.

[69] For an attempt to attain what some may regard as inherently unattainable, see F. S. C. Northrop, *The Complexity of Legal and Ethical Experience* (1959), Chap. 21. It may be said that the positivist looks at the actual *decision,* and says this is law, good or bad; the moralist looks at the process, and says morality has been taken into account. But a court is not *bound* to take account of moral factors, and even if it were, this would not establish a pre-existing objective ethical standard.

the very time when this search has virtually been abandoned in the field of scientific fact.[70]

Sanctions [71]

Austin's insistence on sanctions as a mark of law has frequently been objected to as concealing or distorting the real character and functions of law in a community. Sanctions, it is said, do not explain why law is changed and place an undue emphasis on fear. The essence of a legal system is the inherent fact, based on various psychological factors, that law is accepted by the community as a whole as binding, and the element of sanction is not an essential, or perhaps even an important, element in the functioning of the system.[72] " It is because a rule is regarded as obligatory that a measure of coercion may be attached to it; it is not obligatory because there is coercion." [73] But two misconceptions seem to be entailed here. First, the question is not the precise psychological [74] explanation why people obey the law. This is a matter of social psychology, not law. What it is sought to attain by invoking sanctions is some characteristic *formal* feature of legal systems, which differentiate them from others. Moreover, the fact that no sanction may actually exist to enforce a particular rule is not necessarily vital if one has regard to the fact that the legal system *as a whole* does provide sanctions.[75] But it may be doubted whether

---

[70] *Cf. ante*, 5. Note that this position also resembles the Kantian view that the absolute is only attainable in the moral sphere (the category of " essence ") and not in the sphere of human knowledge; *cf.* Mackinnon, *Ethical Theory* (1957), Chap. 3. For recent attempts to bridge this gap in the realm of phenomenology, see the lucid exposition in Friedmann, *Legal Theory* (5th ed.), pp. 197–208.

[71] For an account of the inconsistencies and ambiguities underlying Austin's discussion of sanctions, see Tapper [1965] C.L.J. 271.

[72] *Cf.* A. L. Goodhart, " An Apology for Jurisprudence," in *Interpretations of Modern Legal Philosophy* (ed. Sayre), p. 283. Goodhart restated his case in (1967) 41 Tul.L.R. 769. See also Hart, *The Concept of Law* (1961), for the view that sanctions play the secondary role of ensuring that " those who would voluntarily obey shall not be sacrified to those who do not " (p. 193).

[73] A. L. Goodhart, *English Law and the Moral Law*, p. 17.

[74] A recent socio-legal study undertaken to determine why people (in this case taxpayers) obeyed the law found that " the threat of sanction can deter people from violating the law, perhaps in important part by inducing a moralistic attitude toward compliance." See Schwartz and Orleans (1967) 34 U.Chi.L.R. 274, 300.

[75] In this way can be avoided those highly pedantic discussions as to whether sanctions can be spelt out in certain individual cases such as enabling statutes, imperfect obligations, duties of judges and juries, etc. *Cf.* also such " duties " as are laid down in s. 3 (1) of the Television Act, 1964. For the extent to which the Commissioner of Police or any chief constable can be treated as under a legal duty to enforce the law of the land, and the measure to which such officers have a discretion with which the law will not interfere, see *R. v. Metropolitan Police Commissioner, ex parte Blackburn* [1968] 2 Q.B. 118. This is but one illustration of the impracticability, though not any logical impossibility, of regulating effectively " by the imposition of sanctions the behaviour of high-ranking law-applying and law-creating organs." Austin's problem may be surmounted by looking, as Hart does, not for a sanction, but for " critical reactions," which may, or may not, include sanctions. See the useful discussion in Raz, *op. cit.*, pp. 152–154.

Austin would have agreed with this defence. He is not very explicit about the structure of a legal system. Is there any internal relationship between commands or are they, as in Cardozo's phrase, nothing more than "isolated dooms?"[76] Raz maintains that "the fact that every law is a command entails that every law can be an independent unit, the existence, meaning or application of which is not logically affected by other laws."[77] It is indeed difficult to find any distinctive feature of all legal systems other than the existence of some kind of sanctioning procedure.[78] Admittedly sanctions may exist in non-legal systems, such as codes of morals or etiquette, but these are not usually specific or governed by specific procedures; if they are, as in canon law, we seem justified in calling such rules "law." Certainly the notion of general acceptance lacks any distinctive character enabling us to distinguish law from the rules of a club, or of a robber gang, as well as being a fiction comparable to the old social contract theory.[79] The second objection is that although any particular individual may obey the law without thought of sanctions, it is practically certain that if the law ceased to apply sanctions *as a whole* society would disintegrate, for the recalcitrant minority would otherwise tyrannise over the majority. Indeed, the probable consequence would be simply a power movement within the state prior to a reaffirmation of a sanctioning legal system in favour of those who have seized control in defiance of previous law. It is, therefore, quite realistic to regard the policeman as the ultimate mark of the legal process, and the experience of Tolstoyan [80] or other seekers

---

[76] *The Nature of the Judicial Process* (1921), p. 126.
[77] *The Concept of a Legal System* (1970), p. 26. Raz makes no reference to *The Lectures*, in which Tapper, *op. cit.*, pp. 284–287, finds oblique equivocal evidence that Austin accepted legal rules without sanctions, provided they were part of a chain of obligations with ultimate infliction of an evil. It is as if Austin has seen the problem but has been unable to grasp fully its implications or work out its logical ends.
[78] It has recently come to be thought by some that the impression conveyed in the text results from adopting municipal legal systems in Western democracies as the norm and that, if, for example, we were to widen our horizon and look at law in stateless societies, colonial law, international relations or, indeed, areas of our law where sanctions are very much in the background, such as industrial relations or the family, then we might find some other distinctive feature in social control than the existence of sanctions. (See, for example, Bohannan's *The Differing Realms of Law*, in ed. Bohannan, *Law and Warfare* (1967) and *post*, 619 or Barkun, *Law Without Sanctions* (1968).)
[79] As pointed out by Castberg, *Problem of Legal Philosophy* (2nd. ed., 1957), p. 50.
[80] See Aylmer Maude's *Life of Tolstoy*, II, Chap. 8. *Cf.* the movements for an alternative society which have taken root in the last decade. The best general account of the mood is Roszak, *The Making of A Counter Culture* (1968). See, for example, his discussion of the writings of Paul Goodman (Chap. vi), and note Roszak's comment: " It is only a society possessing the elasticity of decentralised communities that can absorb the inevitable fallibilities of men " (p. 200).

after a society containing justice without force, show these to be Utopian seekers of an ideal world.[81]

Hart's "Concept of Law" and Austin

By far the most searching criticism of the Austinian position in recent years has come from Professor Hart, who has linked this criticism with his own original concept of law viewed from the positivist standpoint. Hart rejects any model of law based simply on coercive orders, on the ground that this is derived too exclusively from the criminal pattern of law and is really inapplicable to that large section of a modern legal system which confers public and private legal *powers*, for instance, in the case of the law relating to wills, contracts, marriage, the jurisdiction of the courts, or the powers of the legis- lature. Moreover, Hart points out that to try and extend the notion of a sanction to cover nullity of a transaction, as Austin did,[82] is really absurd, for in criminal law the purpose of a sanction is to *discourage* conduct, whereas the purpose of legal rules conferring power is to provide for the implementation of certain acts-in-the-law.

In place, then, of Austin's monolithic model, Hart suggests a dual system consisting of two types of rules.[83] These he describes as "primary" and "secondary" rules. The primary rules are those

[81] English courts have shown a recent tendency to extend the range of enforce- ability in the case of certain bodies which are not vested with legal powers or duties, and of relationships, which are not legal in the strict sense. In *Pharmaceutical Society of Great Britain* v. *Dickson* [1970] A.C. 403 a resolu- tion which was not legally binding or enforceable was nevertheless declared by the court to be in unlawful restraint of trade and an injunction was granted. Lord Morris pointed out that even though professional rules of a particular society might be binding only in honour and not subject to legal sanctions as such, since failure to comply with such rules might be treated as misconduct, it was open to an aggrieved member to apply to the court for a declaration and injunction on the ground that a particular rule was not one which it was within the powers of the society to impose (see pp. 429–430). Again in *R.* v. *Criminal Injuries Compensation Board* [1967] 2 Q.B. 864, in the case of a non-statutory scheme for *ex gratia* payments to be made subject to a quasi-judicial inquiry, it was held that the court had jurisdiction to grant certiorari where a case had been determined contrary to the terms of the scheme. See also *Nagel* v. *Feilden* [1966] 2 Q.B. 633. The court took cognisance of the rules of a purely voluntary body where an aggrieved person, who was not a member, claimed that she had been refused a licence by the Jockey Club to act as a trainer of racehorses, on the arbitrary ground that no such licences were granted to females. This case was followed in *Edwards* v. *SOGAT* [1970] 3 All E.R. 689. These and other cases illustrate the point that a norm which does not derive, directly or indirectly, from some law-making source, may nevertheless have conferred upon it a legal, or at least quasi-legal character, by its subsequent recognition by a court of law as a foundation upon which to grant a legal remedy.

[82] See *Lectures on Jurisprudence*, 5th edition (1885), p. 505. Raz remarks that Austin did not need this doctrine: "It is introduced to explain private powers which can be completely accounted for by his doctrine of capacity" (p. 22). Austin also regarded inconvenience and a declaration of infamy as sanctions, but, unlike Bentham, was careful to exclude rewards from their ambit, which seems odd for a utilitarian.

[83] H. L. A. Hart, *The Concept of Law* (1961), Chap. 5.

which lay down standards of behaviour and are rules of obligation, that is, rules that impose duties. The secondary rules, on the other hand, are ancillary to and concern the primary rules in various ways; for instance, they specify the ways in which the primary rules may be ascertained, introduced, eliminated or varied, and the mode in which their violation may be conclusively determined. These secondary rules are, therefore, mainly procedural and remedial and include, but go far beyond, the rules governing sanctions. For instance, they extend to the rules of judicial procedure and evidence,[84] as well as the rules governing the procedure by which new legislation may be introduced. It is conceivable that a society might have a legal system consisting solely of primary rules, and indeed, it may be that such a system is to be found in certain primitive societies.[85] However, as a society develops and becomes more complex the need for secondary rules will inevitably become manifest, and these will grow in complexity as the society develops. Indeed, Hart takes the view that a society which is legally so undeveloped as to have no secondary rules but only primary rules of obligation, would not really possess a legal system at all but a mere " set " of rules. For Hart, therefore, it is the union of primary and secondary rules which constitute the core of a legal system. For it is only in this condition that we may speak of officials, and it is in the relationship of citizens and officials to primary and secondary rules that Professor Hart finds his criteria for the existence of a legal system.

The " Internal Aspect " of Law

It is at this stage that reference needs to be made to Professor Hart's illuminating discussion of what he calls the " internal aspect " or " inner point of view " that human beings take towards the rules of a legal system.[86] Law, Hart points out, depends not only on the external social pressures which are brought to bear on human beings to prevent them deviating from the rules, but also on the inner point of view that human beings take towards a rule conceived as imposing an

---

[84] *Cf.* Austin's remark, *op. cit.*, p. 249: " All laws or rules determining the practice of the courts, or all laws or rules determining judicial procedure, are purely subsidiary to the due execution of others." Tapper comments with some justice: " This passage anticipates a whole body of later thought, and most strikingly the analysis of primary and secondary rules to be found in Hart's *The Concept of Law*," *op. cit.*, p. 285. It should be noted that it seems unlikely that Austin envisaged a court being liable to sanctions if it contravened procedural requirements, much less for exercising any judicial power wrongly.

[85] Hart is more correctly setting up a model of a primitive system. He admits that no such primitive society has ever existed. And his analysis of a legal system in a mature, stable society is no less a model. On the value and danger of models see Popper, *ante*, 22.

[86] Raz, *op. cit.*, p. 148, n. 3 substitutes for " internal aspect " " critical reactions," believing correctly that Hart uses the former expression somewhat ambiguously.

obligation. In the case of a society which has no more than a set of primary rules, it would be necessary for the citizens not only generally to obey the primary rules but also consciously to view such rules as common standards of behaviour, violations of which were to be criticised. In other words, in such a primitive order an internal point of view on the part of the members of the society would be necessary for the society to be held together in terms of obligation.

For a legal system " to exist," there must be general obedience by the citizens to the primary rules of obligation, but it would not be necessary for the citizens to possess " an internal point of view." In such a case, according to Hart, the importance of the internal point of view relates not to a body of citizens but to the officials of the system. These officials must not merely " obey " the secondary rules but must take an " inner view " of these rules, and this is a necessary condition for the existence of a legal system.[87] Official compliance with the secondary rules must, therefore, involve both a conscious acceptance of these rules as standards of official behaviour, and a conscious desire to comply with these standards. Whether this appropriate state of mind exists or not is for Hart a question of fact. Hart concedes that there will necessarily be a number of borderline cases, such as governments in exile, or countries subject to military occupation, but he insists that to establish the existence of a legal system in the full sense, the two types of rules and the view taken of the secondary rules by the officials are essential ingredients.

Hart on Sovereignty

Hart also has some pertinent criticisms to make on the Austinian view of sovereignty. Thus he points out that a mere " habit of obedience " cannot explain the *continuity* of law, that is to say, the fact that obedience is rendered not merely to the initial ruler, but to his successor upon the demise of that ruler.[88] This cannot, therefore, be explained in terms merely of " habit," but involves the acceptance of a *rule* and, as we have seen, on Hart's analysis, a rule as to the authoritative operation of legislation both past and present, is a secondary rule of the system which requires, among other things, the

---

[87] *Cf.* A. Ross, *post*, 323, and see Hughes, 25 M.L.R. 319, 329–332. Is it correct to see just one dimension behind official behaviour? Is it not possible that officials do the right thing for the wrong reasons? For example, comply with rules to get promotion or through bribery.

[88] For Raz, Austin only explains a momentary legal system, but not a legal system : " According to [Austin's] theory two different momentary legal systems which in fact belong to one system may turn out to belong to different systems," *op. cit.*, p. 35, and see also Chap. VIII, 1 and 2. Austin thus explains, for example, whether a valid contract is part of a legal system, but fails to explain the problem of continuity where there has been a revolution.

" internal aspect " towards it by the appropriate officials who operate the system.

As to the question of legal limitations upon the sovereign, Hart points out that it is a misconception to view these as legal duties on the Austinian pattern. They are in fact legal disabilities, *i.e.*, they involve an absence of legal power, with the consequence that legislation which infringes such limitations is treated as void.[89]

Nor is there any logical necessity in regarding a sovereign as being either able or unable to bind his successors. The problem really involves the way in which we are to interpret legal omnicompetence in accordance with whatever may be the secondary rules of the particular system. Here, as Hart points out, we are faced with a choice between either a continuing omnicompetence or one which is self-embracing, *i.e.*, can only be exercised once, the problem being comparable to that of the theologian faced with the choice between a God who always enjoys the same powers, or a God whose powers include a power to destroy his own omnipotence.[90]

Some Comments on Hart's Approach

Hart's description of a developed legal system in terms of a union of primary and secondary rules is undoubtedly of value, as Hart himself contends, as a tool for analysis of much that has puzzled both the jurist and the political theorist. At the same time one may be permitted to wonder whether too much is not claimed for this new view of some of the old problems which have assailed jurists since the time of Austin. Professor Hart himself seems to recognise that this system is not necessarily as comprehensive as he appears to indicate since he suggests that there are other elements in a legal system, and in particular, the " open texture " [91] of legal rules, as well as the distinctive relationship of law to morality and justice.[92]

More fundamental than this, however, is the question whether it is possible to reduce all the rules of the legal system to rules which impose duties and to rules which confer powers. This seems something of an oversimplification. For instance, it can be said that many of the so-called rules of recognition [92a] do not so much confer power but specify criteria which are to be applied in particular cases, such as rules of procedure and of evidence. Also, it is doubtful whether all the so-called secondary rules can properly be treated as a unified class, for there seems little in common between a rule

---

[89] *Cf.* Raz, *op. cit.*, pp. 27–33.
[90] *Cf.* Bentham's solution discussed, *ante*, 156, and see *post*, 195.
[91] See *post*, 730. See *post*, 797. But this concession has not satisfied critics, such as Dworkin and Hughes, who attack Hart's reduction of law to rules. See *post*, 172.
[92] *Cf. post*, 211, note 41.　　　　　　　　　　　　　　　[92a] See *post*, 285.

governing the formal validity of a will. and a rule governing the constitutional limitations of a legislature.[93] Professor Hart himself seems to recognise this when he concedes that a "full detailed taxonomy of the varieties of law . . . still remains to be accomplished." [94]

This has led to the criticism being levelled against Hart's analysis that by expressing law in terms of binding rules,[95] it fails to take into account the existence of all those various and miscellaneous principles and policies which affect judicial decisions, such as the principle that no man may benefit by his own wrong.[96] Professor Dworkin has argued that any attempt to bring such principles or policies under the same category as rules which are legally binding upon the Courts will create logical difficulty for the positivist model of law. For principles and policies clearly accord a broad discretion to a judge, and, therefore, cannot be binding upon a judge, in the same sense that rules are (*viz.,* that he must follow the rule if it applies). A way out of this dilemma may then be sought by saying that such principles and policies are not really part of the law at all, but are merely extra-legal standards of which the courts may, and do on occasions, make use. The difficulty that then arises is that this would involve treating *all* discretionary principles as outside the ambit of strict law and would extend, for example, to the principle that courts have discretion generally to overrule past precedents and thereby change established rules. This would have the effect of depriving the rules themselves of the character of binding law.[97]

Nor, Professor Dworkin contends, can some ultimate test of legitimacy, such as Austin's sovereignty, or Hart's rules of recognition, restore the legal status of principles and policies. For the origin of these as legal principles rests not upon particular decisions[98] or

---

[93] See, also, Raz's interesting suggestion that rules of recognition should be conceived as duty-imposing, rather than power-conferring, that they are addressed to officials, directing them to apply or act on certain laws, *op. cit.,* pp. 197–200.

[94] p. 32.

[95] See Dworkin, *The Model of Rules,* 35 U.Chi.L.R. 14, and republished in *Essays in Legal Philosophy,* ed. Summers (1968), p. 25, and in *Law, Reason and Justice,* ed. Hughes (1969), p. 3. See also Hughes (1968) 77 Yale L.J. 411, republished in ed. Hughes *idem,* p. 101 and Weiler, 46 Can.Bar Rev. 406, 428 *et seq.*

[96] *Cf. post,* 173, note 99.

[97] Apart from the conceptual problem, there is also a political obstacle, for a lawyer would in effect be telling a client that *in law* he had a perfectly good claim but a judge had used his *discretion* to deprive him of, for example, a legacy.

[98] As against this it may be said that many of the *rules* of law are hardly less vague than Dworkin's principles and derive not so much from particular decisions as from a whole line of case-law, *e.g.* the rule in tort liability governing the circumstances in which a duty of care may be owed which can found an action for negligence if damage results from its breach, or the rule invalidating transactions in unreasonable restraint of trade. Dworkin himself describes the latter as operating logically as a rule, substantially as a principle. Perhaps he rather overplays the distinction between rules, principles and policies, for this purpose.

enactments, but rather in the sense of appropriateness developed in the profession and public over a long period of time. They cannot, therefore, be referred to any particular institutional support such as Austinian or Hart's positivist criteria of legitimacy seems to demand. Such arguments point to the shortcomings not only of an analysis of law purely in terms of rules, but of any attempt to expand such an analysis in terms of rules coupled with discretionary principles and policies. Dworkin stops short of offering a fresh solution, and contents himself with calling for a reappraisal of some of the basic assumptions of the positivist thesis.

In defence of Hart it may be said that Dworkin's criticism of him is based on a model of positivism which pays scant regard to the sophistication of Hart's thought. Models are dangerous constructions, for their necessary over-simplification reveals just as much as the inventor wishes. It would be just as easy to reduce Dworkin's thoughts to a simple model, which would see his picture of the judicial process as a two-level procedure, wherein the role of rules was dominant yet not exclusive, and a generous application of principles was added to iron out the difficult case. Clearly the judicial process works neither in this way, nor in the way that Dworkin postulated that positivists thought it did. Dworkin has not destroyed Hart's elucidation of a concept of law. What he has done is rekindle our interest in looking at the concept of law from the angle of the judicial process.[99]

Moreover, revealing though Hart's view of the inner aspect of law may be, it is difficult to avoid the feeling that here, too, there is

That the distinction between a rule and a discretionary principle is far from clear-cut emerges sufficiently from the example of human rights, *e.g.*, freedom of speech, as guaranteed under the U.S. Constitution. Is this a principle or a rule? It is certainly nothing if not discretionary in its application, yet it enjoys clear institutional support.

[99] It is rare that judges articulate their decision-making process in terms of rules and principles, but three recent cases will illustrate the foregoing debate. In *R.* v. *Warner* [1969] 2 A.C. 256, Lord Reid was of the opinion that the requirement of *mens rea* was a principle in the area of "true crimes," but not a rule. Indeed, there was a somewhat ill-defined exception in public welfare offences. "In cases of this kind the question is not what the words mean but whether there are sufficient grounds for inferring that Parliament intended to exclude the general rule that *mens rea* is an essential element in every offence. And the authorities show that it is generally necessary to go behind the words of the enactment and take other factors into consideration" (p. 279). In *Burns* v. *Edman* [1970] 2 Q.B. 541 *ex turpi causa non oritur actio* was applied to knock down a widow's fatal accident claim for loss of her breadwinner husband where it was not proved that he had earned his living honestly and where he was known to have several convictions for dishonesty, and damages for loss of expectation of life were reduced on the basis that a criminal's life is not a happy one. In *Re C. L. Nye Ltd.* [1969] 2 All E.R. 587 (subsequently overruled by the Court of Appeal), Plowman J. held that a charge created by a company in favour of a bank was void against liquidators and creditors of the company on the principle that no man could take advantage of his own wrong: the company had, however, fully complied with statutory requirements including that of registration.

some oversimplification. For instance, is it really possible to identify the precise viewpoint which necessarily animates officials towards the so-called secondary rules of recognition? Officials are human beings like others, and are influenced by all the many conflicting and mixed motives which move humanity, and it seems excessive to qualify the existence of a legal system on such a comparatively tenuous criterion as the exact mental attitude of officials towards their own legal system.

Yet another observation which may be made on Hart's general approach is one which can be related to many of the attempts to express legal systems and relationships in analytical terms, but it is a criticism to which Hart is particularly susceptible as he claims his analysis to be " an essay in descriptive sociology." The attempt to reduce legal systems to nothing more than a congeries of rules, linked to the society in which they operate solely by the facts that the primary rules are habitually obeyed and the secondary rules are recognised as such by the officials, seems to ignore certain of the sociological foundations of legal systems without which the conception of law itself may be incapable of being fully grasped. Thus it has been pointed out with some force that one feature of a legal system which appears to be missing from Hart's analysis is the concept of an institution.[1] A leading American realist, Llewellyn, has stressed that one of the most important features of a legal system is " the way the law-jobs " get done.[2] It is not just the rules which reveal this but the institutional framework within which those rules operate. Thus a legal system contains not only rules, but also a mass of institutions, such as a legal profession, a set of law courts, a judicial hierarchy, various types of law-making bodies, administrative officials divided between different Ministries and so forth, and the structure of the legal rules comprising the system cannot be adequately grasped save in relation to the institutional framework.

This point may be brought out by referring once again to Hart's argument regarding the continuity of law, which he rightly points out cannot be explained purely in terms of a habit of obedience. It seems doubtful, however, whether his attempt to explain this purely in terms of the acceptance of a rule of recognition by officials is sufficient. In this connection reference may be made to the very revealing exposition of legal domination propounded by the German legal sociologist, <u>Max Weber</u>.[3] Weber pointed out that authority in

---

[1] See R. S. Summers, " Prof. H. L. A. Hart's Concept of Law " (1963) 4 *Duke Law Journal*, 629, 643.
[2] *Cf. post*, 407.
[3] See M. Weber, *Law and Economy in Society* (1954), ed. M. Rheinstein, Chaps. XII and XIII. For a discussion of *charisma* see Reinhard Bendix, *Max Weber: An Intellectual Portrait* (1959), Chap. X.

human society may take one of three forms, namely, charismatic, traditional or legal. The word "charismatic" comes from the Greek *charisma* meaning "grace," and is used to refer to that peculiar form of personal ascendancy which individuals may acquire in a particular society, and which confers an indisputable aura of legitimacy over all their acts. Such charisma may be associated, for instance, with the founder of a dynasty, but when the founder dies the question arises whether his legitimate authority will pass to his descendants, though these persons as individuals may be entirely lacking in any charismatic quality. If such legitimate authority is inherited, then the original charisma may become "institutionalised," and so embodied in permanent institutions to be formed largely by traditional usages. An instance of this would be an established monarchy in a feudal order of society.

A further stage may develop into what Weber calls "legal domination." In this situation the legitimate domination becomes impersonal and legalistic, and the institutional character of authority largely displaces the personal one. For instance, in a modern democratic state an institutionalised legislature, administration and judiciary operate impersonally under the legal order to which is attached a monopoly of the legitimate use of force.

It may be suggested that this institutional view of the continuity of law provides a more objective criterion for the continuance or persistence of law in a state governed by legal domination, in Weber's sense, than any attempt to scrutinise the particular psychological motivation of officials who operate the system. Nor does it seem practicable to qualify in purely general terms, based on juristic analysis, the exact type of motivation which is to be inevitably associated with the attitudes of officialdom. In this respect, too, Professor Hart does seem to give some hostages to fortune, by apparently insisting that what he is laying down in his analysis amounts to the "necessary and sufficient" conditions for the existence of a legal system. This seems to impose a degree of rigidity, which is more familiar in the writings of Austin and of Kelsen, than in the far more flexible approach to be encountered in most of Professor Hart's own writings.

EVALUATION

Any attempt to evaluate Austin's contribution for the present day must stress both the strength and the weaknesses of the analytical approach. On the one hand the determination to see things as they are, to resist metaphysical allurements, and to probe analytically and with vigour into the fundamental concepts of law on which so much confused thinking existed, has had a lastingly beneficial effect in persuading lawyers in common law countries that, as Holmes J. put it, "the common law is not a brooding omnipresence in the sky "[4] but a phenomenon susceptible of scientific analysis and investigation.[5] Austin's aims were to establish the autonomy of jurisprudence as a separate field of study, and to place it on a factual and scientific basis. The fundamental and general concepts of law that Austin explored were not regarded by him as *a priori* concepts, but were regarded as facts to be derived from experience.[6] At the same time this approach did tend, especially among Austin's followers, to induce a rather coldly logical and analytical approach to law as a set of rules existing separately and in its own right, and containing within itself the seeds of its own development.[7] Austin himself, as a Benthamite reformer, was certainly not unmindful of the social element in law and of the need to relate it to the needs of society, and he took a distinctly progressive view on judicial legislation,[8] which has been repeatedly overlooked subsequently by his followers and his critics. Even Austin, however, displayed some strong leanings in favour of conceptual thinking, especially in regard to sovereignty. But the suggestion that the positivist insistence on distinguishing law and morals has been instrumental in leading to dictatorship seems fanciful in the extreme,[9] for if Nazi Germany is cited in support of this contention, this not only ignores the role of German idealism and Hegelianism, but also leaves totally unexplained why England, with

---

[4] See *Holmes-Laski Letters*, II, p. 822.

[5] Outstanding among modern contributors to the analytical aspect of positivism are Hohfeld in America, and Hart in this country. For samples of their respective approaches to the " right-duty " concept, see *post*, 248 *et seq.* The last decade has witnessed a renaissance of analytical jurisprudence. Summers notes that this has been characterised by a watering down of the positivistic element, an increased awareness of philosophical technique and a widening of the net to take in a vast range of conceptual studies, such as punishment and responsibility, civil disobedience, causation in the law, vicarious responsibility and many others. See *post*, 260.

[6] This accounts for Austin's somewhat bizarre statement that Bentham belonged to the historical school of jurisprudence. For the historical school, the synthetic method of natural law, using *a priori* concepts and rules derived from these, was to be rejected in favour of studying law as based on the experience of a people. Austin thus regarded his approach as based on the inductive method, that is, on the observation of fact. Hence his claim to explain the derivation both of law and sovereignty from the fact of habitual obedience. *Cf.* A. Agnelli, *John Austin* (1959). Mill relates that Austin, on his return from Germany, " professed great respect for what he called ' the universal principles of human nature of the political economists ' and insisted on the evidence which history and daily experience afford of the ' extraordinary pliability of human nature.' " (J. S. Mill, *Autobiography*, p. 151.) A modern critic points out that Austin was a curious case. He both knew and admired the work of Savigny, but continued himself to write as a purely analytical jurist. (See J. W. Burrow, *Evolution and Society* (1966), p. 65.) See aso Schwarz (1934) 1 *Politica* 178.

[7] For a severe criticism of the conceptual approach to jurisprudence, see Felix S. Cohen, *The Legal Conscience* (1960), especially pp. 33–94.

[8] See *post*, 407.

[9] This view is urged by Prof. Fuller in 71 Harv.L.R., pp. 657–661, and denied by Prof. Hart, *ibid.*, p. 616 *et seq.*

its strong leaning to empiricism, and the United States, home of pragmatism, have not gone much further along this particular road. It may be ventured that experience shows that muddled metaphysical speculation rather than clear thinking and refusal to allow reason to be overborne by emotional considerations, is far more likely to result in totalitarianism. Indeed the natural outcome (if there is one) of the positivist position (as patterned by Bentham and Austin) is really the democratic welfare state.

J. BODIN

Six Books of the Republic [10]

. . . it is the distinguishing mark of the sovereign that he cannot in any way be subject to the commands of another, for it is he who makes law for the subject, abrogates law already made, and amends obsolete law. No one who is subject either to the law or to some other person can do this. That is why it is laid down in the civil law that the prince is above the law, for the word *law* in Latin implies the command of him who is invested with sovereign power. . . .

If the prince is not bound by the laws of his predecessors, still less can he be bound by his own laws. One may be subject to laws made by another, but it is impossible to bind oneself in any matter which is the subject of one's own free exercise of will. . . . It follows of necessity that the king cannot be subject to his own laws. Just as, according to the canonists, the Pope can never tie his own hands, so the sovereign prince cannot bind himself, even if he wishes. For this reason edicts and ordinances conclude with the formula 'for such is our good pleasure', thus intimating that the laws of a sovereign prince, even when founded on truth and right reason, proceed simply from his own free will.

It is far otherwise with divine and natural laws. All the princes of the earth are subject to them, and cannot contravene them without reason and rebellion against God. His yoke is upon them, and they must bow their heads in fear and reverence before His divine majesty. The absolute power of princes and sovereign lords does not extend to the laws of God and of nature. He who best understood the meaning of absolute power, and made kings and emperors submit to his will, defined his sovereignty as a power to override positive law; he did not claim power to set aside divine and natural law. . . . [pp. 28–29]

A distinction must . . . be made between right and law, for one implies what is equitable and the other what is commanded. Law is nothing else than the command of the sovereign in the exercise of his sovereign power. A sovereign prince is not subject to the laws of the Greeks, or any other alien power, or even those of the Romans, much less to his own laws, except in so far as they embody the law of nature which, according to Pindar, is the law to which all kings and princes are subject. Neither Pope nor Emperor is exempt from this law, though certain flatterers say they can take the goods of their subjects at will.

[10] [Translated, M. J. Tooley.]

But both civilians and canonists have repudiated this opinion as contrary to the law of God. They err who assert that in virtue of their sovereign power princes can do this. It is rather the law of the jungle, an act of force and violence. For as we have shown above, absolute power only implies freedom in relation to positive laws, and not in relation to the law of God. God has declared explicitly in His Law that it is not just to take, or even to covet, the goods of another. Those who defend such opinions are even more dangerous than those who act on them. They show the lion his claws, and arm princes under a cover of just claims. The evil will of a tyrant, drunk with such flatteries, urges him to an abuse of absolute power and excites his violent passions to the pitch where avarice issues in confiscations, desire in adultery, and anger in murder. . . .

Since then the prince has no power to exceed the laws of nature which God Himself, whose image he is, has decreed, he cannot take his subjects' property without just and reasonable cause, that is to say by purchase, exchange, legitimate confiscation, or to secure peace with the enemy when it cannot be otherwise achieved. Natural reason instructs us that the public good must be preferred to the particular, and that subjects should give up not only their mutual antagonisms and animosities, but also their possessions, for the safety of the commonwealth.[11] . . .

[p. 35]

Before going any further, one must consider what is meant by *law*. The word law signifies the right command of that person, or those persons, who have absolute authority over all the rest without exception, saving only the law-giver himself, whether the command touches all subjects in general or only some in particular. To put it another way, the law is the rightful command of the sovereign touching all his subjects in general, or matters of general application. . . .

The first attribute of the sovereign prince therefore is the power to make law binding on all his subjects in general and on each in particular. But to avoid any ambiguity one must add that he does so without the consent of any superior, equal, or inferior being necessary. If the prince can only make law with the consent of a superior he is a subject; if of an equal he shares his sovereignty; if of an inferior, whether it be a council of magnates or the people, it is not he who is sovereign. . . .

[p. 43]

HOBBES

Leviathan

Of the Naturall Condition of Mankind

. . . Whatsoever therefore is consequent to a time of Warre, where every man is Enemy to every man; the same is consequent to the time, wherein men live without other security, than what their own strength, and their own invention shall furnish them withall. In such condition,

---

11 [The prince is sovereign, but sovereignty for Bodin is not absolute and unfettered since it is limited by natural law. But in the hands of later writers, such as Hobbes and Rousseau, natural law becomes a mere device for producing and justifying absolute sovereignty, though Rousseau, unlike Hobbes, regards this as the inalienable property of the common will (*volonté générale*).]

there is no place for Industry; because the fruit thereof is uncertain: and consequently no Culture of the Earth, no Navigation, nor use of the commodities that may be imported by Sea; no commodious Building; no Instruments of moving, and removing such things as require much force; no Knowledge of the face of the Earth; no account of Time; no Arts; no Letters; no Society; and which is worst of all, continuall feare, and danger of violent death; And the life of man, solitary, poore, nasty, brutish, and short.[12]   [Pt. I, Chap. 13]

Of the first and second NATURALL LAWES

And because the condition of Man, (as hath been declared in the precedent Chapter) is a condition of Warre of every one against every one; in which case every one is governed by his own Reason; and there is nothing he can make use of, that may not be a help unto him, in preserving his life against his enemyes; It followeth, that in such a condition, every man has a Right to every thing; even to one anothers body. And therefore, as long as this naturall Right of every man to every thing endureth, there can be no security to any man, (how strong or wise soever he be,) of living out the time, which Nature ordinarily alloweth men to live. And consequently it is a precept, or generall rule of Reason, *That every man, ought to endeavour Peace, as farre as he has hope of obtaining it; and when he cannot obtain it, that he may seek, and use, all helps, and advantages of Warre*. The first branch of which Rule, containeth the first, and Fundamentall Law of Nature; which is, *to seek Peace, and follow it*. The Second, the summe of the Right of Nature; which is, *By all means we can, to defend our selves*.[13]

From this Fundamentall Law of Nature, by which men are commanded to endeavour Peace, is derived this second Law; *That a man be willing, when others are so too, as farre-forth, as for Peace, and defence of himselfe he shall think it necessary, to lay down this right to all things; and be contented with so much liberty against other men, as he would allow other men against himselfe*. For as long as every man holdeth this Right, of doing any thing he liketh; so long are all men in the condition of Warre. But if other men will not lay down their Right, as well as he; then there is no Reason for any one, to devest himselfe of his: For that were to expose himselfe to Prey, (which no man is bound to) rather than to dispose himselfe to Peace. This is that Law of the Gospell; *Whatsoever you require that others should do to you, that do ye to them*. And that Law of all men, *Quod tibi fieri non vis, alteri ne feceris*.[14]   [Pt. I, Chap. 14]

[12] [Modern psychology, ethology and anthropology have all demonstrated the essential truth of Hobbes's hypothesis about the innate nature of man. Nor would the elimination of aggressive instinct be all to the good, for it enables the child to develop, to break his ties of dependency and achieve personal autonomy, whilst at the same time enabling the great artist to work creatively and imaginatively. But aggression must be regulated, otherwise the species will destroy itself. Hence the need for conventional competition. See, further, A. Storr, *Human Aggression* (1968), particularly Chaps. 4–6.]

[13] [Hobbes's reduction of natural right to the law of self-preservation seems to confuse natural laws of a physical kind, such as those evidenced in human instincts, with normative rules. This confusion he shared with Ulpian: see *ante*, 93.]

[14] [Hobbes distinguishes between natural *law* and natural *right*. For Hobbes, all law, including natural law, only creates binding obligations when there is a power capable of enforcing them, and, therefore, natural law itself is only

Of the Causes of a COMMON-WEALTH

... Lastly, the agreement of these creatures [15] is Naturall; that of men, is by Covenant only, which is Artificiall: and therefore it is no wonder if there be somwhat else required (besides Covenant) to make their Agreement constant and lasting; which is a Common Power, to keep them in awe, and to direct their actions to the Common Benefit.

The only way to erect such a Common Power, as may be able to defend them from the invasion of Forraigners, and the injuries of one another, and thereby to secure them in such sort, as that by their owne industrie, and the fruites of the Earth, they may nourish themselves and live contentedly; is, to conferre all their power and strength upon one Man, or upon one Assembly of men, that may reduce all their Wills, by plurality of voices, unto one Will: which is as much as to say, to appoint one Man, or Assembly of men to beare their Person; and every one to owne, and acknowledge himselfe to be Author of whatsoever he that so beareth their Person, shall Act, or cause to be Acted, in those things which concerne the Common Peace and Safetie; and therein to submit their Wills, every one to his Will, and their Judgements, to his Judgement. This is more than Consent, or Concord; it is reall Unitie of them all, in one and the same Person, made by Covenant of every man with every man, in such manner, as if every man should say to every man, *I Authorise and give up my Right of Governing my selfe, to this Man, or to this Assembly of men, on this condition, that thou give up thy Right to him, and Authorise all his Actions in like manner.*[16] This done, the Multitude so united in one Person, is called a COMMON-WEALTH, in latine CIVITAS. This is the Generation of that great LEVIATHAN, or rather (to speake more reverently) of that *Mortall God*, to which wee owe under the *Immortall God*, our peace and defence. For by this Authoritie, given him by every particular man in the Common-Wealth, he hath the use of so much Power and Strength conferred on him, that by terror thereof, he is inabled to forme the wills of them all, to Peace at home, and mutuall ayd against their enemies abroad. And in him consisteth the Essence of the Common-wealth; which (to define it,) is *One Person, of whose Acts a great Multitude, by mutuall Covenants one with another, have made themselves every one the Author, to the end he may*

binding when civil society has been constituted by the social contract. Prior to this, natural law really only amounts to maxims of prudence which should govern man in his natural state, because it is in his interest to accept these, so as to attain a state of peace and security. This is why Hobbes declares that the laws of nature applied only *in foro interno* (see *Leviathan*, Book I, Chap. 15). Natural *right*, on the other hand, does apply in the state of nature, for it is no more than the right of every man to use such power as he has to preserve his own person. It is this natural right that the individuals transfer to the sovereign under the social contract, and thereby bring civil society into being (see Plamenatz, *Man and Society*, Vol. I, Chap. 4).]

[15] [*i.e.*, bees and ants, which Hobbes contrasts with men.]

[16] [Some writers, especially those, *e.g.*, Althusius, who favoured popular sovereignty, argued for two contracts, a *pactum unionis*, between individuals to create a unity in which sovereignty was vested, and a *pactum subjectionis*, between the unit and ruler. The latter contract could then contain restrictions on the ruler's powers and even a right of withdrawal. Hobbes would have none of this. His single contract both created the absolute sovereign and divested the individual of all vestige of pre-existing natural right. For a full account of the history of the social contract, see J. W. Gough, *Social Contract* (2nd ed., 1957).]

use the strength and means of them all, as he shall think expedient, for their Peace and Common Defence.

And he that carryeth this Person, is called SOVERAIGNE, and said to have *Soveraigne Power*; and every one besides, his SUBJECT.

The attaining to this Soveraigne Power, is by two wayes. One, by Naturall force; as when a man maketh his children, to submit themselves, and their children to his government, as being able to destroy them if they refuse; or by Warre subdueth his enemies to his will, giving them their lives on that condition. The other, is when men agree amongst themselves, to submit to some Man, or Assembly of men, voluntarily, on confidence to be protected by him against all others. This later may be called a Politicall Common-wealth, or Common-wealth by *Institution*; and the former, a Common-wealth by *Acquisition*.   [Pt. II, Chap. 17]

Of CIVILL LAWES

... I define Civill Law in this manner. CIVILL LAW, *Is to every Subject, those Rules, which the Common-wealth hath Commanded him, by Word, Writing, or other sufficient Sign of the Will, to make use of, for the Distinction of Right, and Wrong; that is to say, of what is contrary, and what is not contrary to the Rule.*

In which definition, there is nothing that is not at first sight evident. For every man seeth, that some Lawes are addressed to all the Subjects in generall; some to particular Provinces; some to particular Vocations; and some to particular Men; and are therefore Lawes, to every of those to whom the Command is directed; and none else. As also, that Lawes are the Rules of Just, and Unjust; nothing being reputed Unjust, that is not contrary to some Law. Likewise, that none can make Lawes but the Common-wealth; because our Subjection is to the Common-wealth only: and that Commands, are to be signified by sufficient Signs; because a man knows not otherwise how to obey them. And therefore, whatsoever can from this definition by necessary consequence be deduced, ought to be acknowledged for truth. Now I deduce from it this that followeth.

1. The Legislator in all Common-wealths, is only the Soveraign,[17] be he one Man, as in a Monarchy, or one Assembly of men, as in a Democracy or Aristocracy. For the Legislator, is he that maketh the Law. And the Common-wealth only, præscribes, and commandeth the observation of those rules, which we call Law: Therefore the Common-wealth is the Legislator. But the Common-wealth is no Person, nor has capacity to doe any thing, but by the Representative, (that is, the Soveraign;) and therefore the Soveraign is the sole Legislator. For the same reason, none can abrogate a Law made, but the Soveraign; because a Law is not abrogated, but by another Law, that forbiddeth it to be put in execution.

2. The Soveraign of a Common-wealth, be it an Assembly, or one Man, is not Subject to the Civill Lawes. For having power to make, and repeale Lawes, he may when he pleaseth, free himselfe from that subjection, by repealing those Lawes that trouble him, and making of new; and consequently he was free before. For he is free, that can be free

---

[17] [Hobbes did in fact recognise certain limits on sovereignty (see Pt. II, Chap. 21), *e.g.*, a command to a man to kill or maim himself, for the right of self-preservation could not be transferred by covenant.]

when he will: Nor is it possible for any person to be bound to himselfe; because he that he can bind, can release; and therefore he that is bound to himselfe onely, is not bound. . . .

4. The Law of Nature, and the Civill Law, contain each other, and are of equall extent. For the Lawes of Nature, which consist in Equity, Justice, Gratitude, and other morall Vertues on these depending, in the condition of meer Nature (as I have said before in the end of the 15th Chapter,) are not properly Lawes, but qualities that dispose men to peace, and to obedience. When a Common-wealth is once settled, then are they actually Lawes, and not before; as being then the commands of the Common-wealth; and therefore also Civill Lawes: For it is the Soveraign Power that obliges men to obey them. For in the differences of private men, to declare, what is Equity, what is Justice, and what is morall Vertue, and to make them binding, there is need of the Ordinances of Soveraign Power, and Punishments to be ordained for such as shall break them; which Ordinances are therefore part of the Civill Law. The Law of Nature therefore is a part of the Civill Law in all Common-wealths of the world. Reciprocally also, the Civill Law is a part of the Dictates of Nature. For Justice, that is to say, Performance of Covenant, and giving to every man his own, is a Dictate of the Law of Nature. But every subject in a Common-wealth, hath covenanted to obey the Civill Law, (either one with another, as when they assemble to make a common Representative, or with the Representative it selfe one by one, when subdued by the Sword they promise obedience, that they may receive life;) And therefore Obedience to the Civill Law is part also of the Law of Nature. Civill, and Naturall Law are not different kinds, but different parts of Law; whereof one part being written, is called Civill, the other unwritten, Naturall. But the Right of Nature, that is, the naturall Liberty of man, may by the Civill Law be abridged, and restrained: nay, the end of making Lawes, is no other, but such Restraint; without the which there cannot possibly be any Peace. And Law was brought into the world for nothing else, but to limit the naturall liberty of particular men, in such manner, as they might not hurt, but assist one another, and joyn together against a common Enemy.[18]   [Pt. II, Chap. 26]

ROUSSEAU

The Social Contract [19]

The Limits of the Sovereign Power

From whatever side we approach our principle, we reach the same conclusion, that the social compact sets up among the citizens an equality

---

[18] [Hence Hobbes arrives at the remarkable doctrine that law and morals are one, for obedience to the civil law is part of the law of nature. Yet it should not be overlooked that Hobbes did not contemplate his sovereign as a universal legislator controlling all men's activities. As Plamenatz points out, in Hobbes' day legislation was infrequent, and within the limits of a country's laws, it was assumed that each man governed himself (*English Utilitarians*, p. 110). *Cf.* Olivecrona's views on the relation of law to morality, *post*, 528. Rousseau's views were remarkably similar to those of Hobbes. In *Rousseau's Social Contract* (1968), Crocker notes (p. 54) that in Rousseau: "justice is identified with the Law, which creates it, and from that law there is no moral appeal, for the Law is morality." Rousseau in fact suppressed this passage.]

[19] [Translated, G. D. H. Cole.]

of such a kind, that they all bind themselves to observe the same conditions and should therefore all enjoy the same rights.[20] Thus, from the very nature of the compact, every act of Sovereignty, i.e. every authentic act of the general will,[21] binds or favours all the citizens equally; so that the Sovereign recognizes only the body of the nation, and draws no distinctions between those of whom it is made up. What, then, strictly speaking in an act of Sovereignty? It is not a convention between a superior and an inferior, but a convention between the body and each of its members. It is legitimate, because based on the social contract, and equitable, because common to all ; useful, because it can have no other object than the general good, and stable, because guaranteed by the public force and the supreme power.[22] So long as the subjects have to submit only to conventions of this sort, they obey no one but their own will ; and to ask how far the respective rights of the Sovereign and the citizens extend, is to ask up to what point the latter can enter into undertakings with themselves, each with all, and all with each.

We can see from this that the sovereign power, absolute, sacred, and inviolable as it is, does not and cannot exceed the limits of general conventions, and that every man may dispose at will of such goods and liberty as these conventions leave him ; so that the Sovereign never has a right to lay more charges on one subject than on another, because, in that case, the question becomes particular, and ceases to be within its competency.[23]   [p. 26; Bk. II, Chap. 4]

J. BENTHAM

A Fragment on Government

When a number of persons (whom we may style *subjects*) are supposed to be in the *habit* of paying *obedience* to a person, or an assemblage of persons, of a known and certain description (whom we may call *governor* or *governors*) such persons altogether (*subjects* and *governors*) are said to be in a state of *political* SOCIETY. . . .

---

[20] [Like Hobbes, Rousseau prefers to achieve his object by a single contract; *cf. ante*, 180. By this time the social contract had become little more than an attempted *a priori* justification of the legal state. It was an attempt to justify law by law. Positive law derived from a social contract, which in turn was validated by natural law. Crocker, *op. cit.*, p. 60, has described Rousseau's Social Contract as " not really a contract at all, but a covenant, in the Old Testament sense." His reasoning is that it is entered into by people who trust each other, and is completely open-ended. Furthermore it involves " a commitment to future decisions yet unknown." The covenant is entered into " between the people and the *moi commun*, or the general will."]

[21] [*Volonté générale*, which is generally interpreted as implying a mystic unity distinct from the will of the individual persons themselves (*volonté de tous*). But see J. Plamenatz, *Man and Society*, I, pp. 403–413.]

[22] [Note the influence on Rousseau of Calvinistic Geneva and ancient Sparta. The citizen " was one who identified himself with the community, and was tied to it by a spiritual bond " (Crocker, *op. cit.*, p. 48). Rousseau thus placed a premium on indoctrination in the community ethic. *Cf.* Berman on parental law in Soviet doctrine, *post*, 687 or Huxley's *Brave New World* jingle : " Ford, we are twelve; oh, make us one, like drops within the Social River " (p. 95).]

[23] [Rousseau regards " generality " as of the essence of an act of sovereignty; hence a decree not binding all citizens equally is invalid, as not being an expression of *la volonté générale*. But Rousseau accepts that the law may establish several classes of citizens (see Bk. II, Chap. 6). See Crocker, *op. cit.*, p. 82.]

A *parole expression of will* is that which is conveyed by the *signs* called *words*. . . .

A *parole* expression of the will of a superior is a *command*.

When a *tacit* expression of the will of a superior is supposed to have been uttered, it may be styled a *fictitious command*.

Were we at liberty to coin words after the manner of the Roman lawyers, we might say a *quasi*-command.

The STATUTE LAW is composed of commands. The COMMON LAW, of *quasi*-commands.   [Chap. 1]

. . . As to the LAW *of Nature*, if (as I trust it will appear) it be nothing but a phrase; if there be no other medium for proving any act to be an offence against it, than the mischievous tendency of such act; if there be no other medium for proving a law of the *state* to be contrary to it, than the *inexpediency* of such law, unless the bare unfounded disapprobation of any one who thinks of it be called a proof; if a test for distinguishing such laws as would be *contrary* to the LAW *of Nature* from such as, *without* being contrary to it, are simply *inexpedient*, be that which neither our Author, nor any man else, so much as pretended ever to give; if, in a word, there be scarce any law whatever but what those who have not liked it have found, on some account or another, to be repugnant to some text of scripture; I see no remedy but that the natural tendency of such doctrine is to impel a man, by the force of conscience, to rise up in arms against any law whatever that he happens not to like. What sort of government it is that can consist with such a disposition, I must leave to our Author to inform us.

It is the principle of *utility*, accurately apprehended and steadily applied, that affords the only clue to guide a man through these straits. It is for that, if any, and for that alone to furnish a decision which neither party shall dare in *theory* to disavow. It is something to reconcile men even in theory. They are at least, *something* nearer to an effectual union, than when at variance as well in respect of theory as of practice. . . .   [Chap. 4]

J. BENTHAM

An Introduction to the Principles of Morals and Legislation

(Edited by J. H. Burns and H. L. A. Hart, 1970)

Of the Principle of Utility

Nature has placed mankind under the governance of two sovereign masters, *pain* and *pleasure*. It is for them alone to point out what we ought to do, as well as to determine what we shall do. On the one hand the standard of right and wrong, on the other the chain of causes and effects, are fastened to their throne. They govern us in all we do, in all we say, in all we think: every effort we can make to throw off our subjection, will serve but to demonstrate and confirm it. In words a man may pretend to abjure their empire: but in reality he will remain subject to it all the while. The *principle of utility* [24] recognises this

---

[24] To this denomination has of late been added, or substituted, the *greatest happiness* or *greatest felicity* principle: this for shortness, instead of saying at length *that principle* which states the greatest happiness of all those whose interest is in question, as being the right and proper, and only right and proper and universally desirable, end of human action: of human action in every situa-

subjection, and assumes it for the foundation of that system, the object of which is to rear the fabric of felicity by the hands of reason and of law. Systems which attempt to question it, deal in sounds instead of sense, in caprice instead of reason, in darkness instead of light.

But enough of metaphor and declamation: it is not by such means that moral science is to be improved.

The principle of utility is the foundation of the present work: it will be proper therefore at the outset to give an explicit and determinate account of what is meant by it. By the principle of utility is meant that principle which approves or disapproves of every action whatsoever, according to the tendency which it appears to have to augment or diminish the happiness of the party whose interest is in question: or, what is the same thing in other words, to promote or to oppose that happiness. I say of every action whatsoever; and therefore not only of every action of a private individual, but of every measure of government.[25]

By utility is meant that property in any object, whereby it tends to produce benefit, advantage, pleasure, good, or happiness, (all this in the present case comes to the same thing) or (what comes again to the same thing) to prevent the happening of mischief, pain, evil, or unhappiness to the party whose interest is considered: if that party be the community in general, then the happiness of the community: if a particular individual, then the happiness of that individual.

The interest of the community is one of the most general expressions that can occur in the phraseology of morals: no wonder that the meaning of it is often lost. When it has a meaning, it is this. The community is a fictitious *body*, composed of the individual persons who are considered as constituting as it were its *members*. The interest of the community then is, what?—the sum of the interests of the several members who compose it.

tion, and in particular in that of a functionary or set of functionaries exercising the powers of Government. The word *utility* does not so clearly point to the ideas of *pleasure* and *pain* as the words *happiness* and *felicity* do: nor does it lead us to the consideration of the *number*, of the interests affected; to the *number*, as being the circumstance, which contributes, in the largest proportion, to the formation of the standard here in question; the *standard of right and wrong*, by which alone the propriety of human conduct, in every situation, can with propriety be tried. This want of a sufficiently manifest connexion between the ideas of *happiness* and *pleasure* on the one hand, and the idea of *utility* on the other, I have every now and then found operating, and with but too much efficiency, as a bar to the acceptance, that might otherwise have been given, to this principle. [For a spirited though not uncritical defence of Bentham's utilitarianism, see D. Baumgardt, *Bentham and the Ethics of Today* (1952). Bentham did not invent the principle of utility but he was the first to accept it unqualifiedly and to work out its consequences with precision (see Baumgardt, pp. 59–61). Popper has suggested that the utility principle might be more defensible if for " maximising happiness " we substitute " minimising suffering ": see *The Open Society and its Enemies*, Vol. I, p. 235. See also Freud's " Pleasure principle," which provides some support for Bentham's hedonism. (Wollheim, *Freud* (1971), pp. 225–226.)

For recent explorations of the limits of utilitarianism as a system of moral and legal justification, see D. B. Lyons, *Forms and Limits of Utilitarianism* (1965), and D. H. Hodgson, *Consequences of Utilitarianism* (1967).]

25 [The analysis of what is good in terms of happiness, which in turn is based on the amount of pleasure or pain resulting from any course of action, can be traced back to Aristippus, a Greek philosopher of the 4th century B.C. (see Diogenes Laertius, *Lives of Eminent Philosophers*, vol. II, pp. 86–88) (Loeb ed., vol. 1, pp. 217–221).]

It is in vain to talk of the interest of the community, without understanding what is the interest of the individual.[26] A thing is said to promote the interest, or to be *for* the interest, of an individual, when it tends to add to the sum total of his pleasures: or, what comes to the same thing, to diminish the sum total of his pains.

An action then may be said to be conformable to the principle of utility, or, for shortness sake, to utility, (meaning with respect to the community at large) when the tendency it has to augment the happiness of the community is greater than any it has to diminish it.

A measure of government (which is but a particular kind of action, performed by a particular person or persons) may be said to be conformable to or dictated by the principle of utility, when in like manner the tendency which it has to augment the happiness of the community is greater than any which it has to diminish it.[27] . . .　　　　[pp. 11–13]

Of the Four Sanctions or Sources of Pain and Pleasure

1. It has been shown that the happiness of the individuals, of whom a community is composed, that is their pleasures and their security, is the end and the sole end which the legislator ought to have in view: the sole standard, in conformity to which each individual ought, as far as depends upon the legislator, to be *made* to fashion his behaviour. But whether it be this or any thing else that is to be *done*, there is nothing by which a man can ultimately be *made* to do it, but either pain or pleasure. Having taken a general view of these two grand objects (*viz.* pleasure, and what comes to the same thing, immunity from pain) in the character of *final* causes; it will be necessary to take a view of pleasure and pain itself, in the character of *efficient* causes or means.

2. There are four distinguishable sources from which pleasure and pain are in use to flow: considered separately, they may be termed the *physical*, the *political*, the *moral*, and the *religious*: and inasmuch as the pleasures and pains belonging to each of them are capable of giving a binding force to any law or rule of conduct, they may all of them be termed *sanctions*.

3. If it be in the present life, and from the ordinary course of nature, not purposely modified by the interposition of the will of any human being, nor by any extraordinary interposition of any superior invisible being, that the pleasure or the pain takes place or is expected, it may be said to issue from or to belong to the *physical sanction*.

4. If at the hands of a *particular* person or set of persons in the

---

[26] (Interest, etc.) Interest is one of those words, which not having any superior *genus*, cannot in the ordinary way be defined.

　　[See the attempts to do so in American Restatement on Torts *post*, 363 and Barry, *post*, 375.]

[27] [The problem of dealing with the psychopath from the point of view of diminished responsibility in criminal law has some bearing on the utilitarian argument. As Dr. Fox points out, there might be utilitarian arguments from the point of view of social welfare in treating such persons *more* severely than normal offenders, and this seems to be one of the cases where humanitarian considerations are allowed to overrule what might be the severely utilitarian point of view. (See R. Fox, "Psychopathy and the Law" in (1964) 27 M.L.R. 196.) Further problems surrounding the application of utilitarian ethics to punishment are considered in Hart, *Punishment and Responsibility* (1968).]

community, who under names correspondent to that of *judge,* are chosen for the particular purpose of dispensing it, according to the will of the sovereign or supreme ruling power in the state, it may be said to issue from the *political sanction.*

5. If at the hands of such *chance* persons in the community, as the party in question may happen in the course of his life to have concerns with, according to each man's spontaneous disposition, and not according to any settled or concerted rule, it may be said to issue from the *moral* or *popular sanction.*

6. If from the immediate hand of a superior invisible being, either in the present life, or in a future, it may be said to issue from the *religious sanction.*

7. Pleasures or pains which may be expected to issue from the *physical, political,* or *moral* sanctions, must all of them be expected to be experienced, if ever, in the *present* life: those which may be expected to issue from the *religious* sanction, may be expected to be experienced either in the *present* life or in a *future.*[28]   [pp. 34–35]

J. BENTHAM

Of Laws in General

(ed. Hart (1970))

A Law Defined and Distinguished

A law may be defined as an assemblage of signs declarative of a volition conceived or adopted by the *sovereign* in a state, concerning the conduct to be observed in a certain *case* by a certain person or class of persons, who in the case in question are or are supposed to be subject to his power: such volition trusting for its accomplishment to the expectation of certain events which it is intended such declaration

---

[28] [Bentham never claimed that the principle of utility was a scientific law. It combined his opinion as to the proper end of government with the fact that men always seek to maximise pleasure and minimise pain. Therefore, the value of the Greatest Happiness Principle could not be measured by utility in prediction; it had a different logical status from scientific laws. Still, though his system began and ended with an ultimate value-judgment, in almost every other respect his new art-and-science conformed to the method of the natural sciences (see Mack, *op. cit.,* pp. 143–144). The principle of utility was Bentham's single initial axiom, the one extra-empirical assumption underlining the conditions or means of his new science, but everything in the system depended upon it. "If it be denied me, I must confess I shall be altogether at a loss to prove it . . . nor shall I easily be brought to think it necessary" (Bentham quoted, *op. cit.,* pp. 204–205). Manning (*op. cit.,* p. 12) suggests Bentham's "blunder" followed from [his] "belief that the truth is manifest in sense experience and available to all who will free their minds from the shackles of received opinion." Taken alone, the principle of utility is empty, or is too general to be applied to practice. Its value really depends on its middle level "laws" or subordinate principles. Thus to take his example in relation to sexual freedom, by his rule, evil was measured by the number of people affected. It was not utilitarian to punish sexual offences, for they usually took place in private and had no public consequences. As to the calculus, he offered this, not as a dogma of ethics, but as a useful rule of thumb. The legislator must become an impartial calculator, a moral mathematician for whom each man had a numerical value of one. To answer what he should do, the legislator was given evidence and forced to estimate its reliability and consequences, and to help him Bentham

should upon occasion be a means of bringing to pass, and the prospect of which it is intended should act as a motive upon those whose conduct is in question.

According to this definition, a law may be considered in eight different respects.

(1) In respect to its *source*: that is in respect to the person or persons of whose will it is the expression.

(2) In respect to the quality of its *subjects*: by which I mean the persons and things to which it may apply.

(3) In respect to its *objects*: by which I mean the *acts*, as character- ized by the *circumstances*, to which it may apply.

(4) In respect to its *extent*, the generality or the amplitude of its application: that is in respect to the determinateness of the persons whose conduct it may seek to regulate.

(5) In respect to its *aspects*: that is in respect to the various manners in which the will whereof it is the expression may apply itself to the acts and circumstances which are its objects.

(6) In respect to its *force*: that is, in respect to the *motives* it relies on for enabling it to produce the effect it aims at, and the laws or other means which it relies on for bringing those motives into play: such laws may be styled its *corroborative appendages*.

(7) In respect to its *expression*: that is in respect to the nature of the *signs* by which the will whereof it is the expression may be made known.

(8) In respect to its *remedial appendages*, where it has any: by which I mean certain other laws which may occasionally come to be subjoined to the principal law in question; and of which the design is to obviate the mischief that stands connected with any individual act of the number of those which are made offences by it, in a more perfect manner than can be done by the sole efficacy of the subsidiary appendages to which it stands indebted for its force.

The latitude here given to the import of the word *law* is it must be confessed rather greater than what seems to be given to it in common [29]: the definition being such as is applicable to various objects which are not commonly characterized by that name. Taking this definition for the standard it matters not whether the expression of

tried to establish a rudimentary calculus based on external observable phenomena that could be measured. Bentham regarded the science of legislation as a practical science. He gradually sought to replace the word " science " with the phrase " art-and-science." Science was concerned with theory; art with practice. Bentham wanted to substitute the word " discipline " to include both. He regarded law and morals as essentially a practical discipline with a particularly close analogy with chemistry and more particularly with medicine. " The art of legislation is but the art of healing practised upon a large scale " (p. 264). Experience, observation and experiment are the foundations of well-grounded medical practice as they are of legislative practice. Bentham had no illusions about the practical possibility of an effective science of legislation, before the science of social statistics had been developed. For this reason he concentrated mainly on penal law, where he considered that adequate material already existed upon which conclusions could be based. For Bentham's suggestions as to how the " value of a lot of pleasure or pain " might be measured, see *Principles and Morals and Legislation*, Chaps. 4–6. At the present day, a stronger defence of Bentham's " moral arithmetic " might be adduced in the light of such develop- ments as psychological and personality tests; the use of computers; and of opinion-polls and similar sociological techniques. *Cf. post*, 415.]

[29] [On Bentham's attitude and approach, see *ante*, 157.]

will in question, so as it have but the authority of the sovereign to back
it, were his by immediate conception or only by adoption: whether
it be of the most public or of the most private or even domestic
nature: whether the sovereign from whom it derives its force be an
individual or a body: whether it be issued *propter quid* as the phrase
may be, that is on account of some particular act or event which is
understood to warrant it (as is the case with an order of the judicial
kind made in the course of a cause); or without the assignment of
any such special ground: or whether it be susceptible of an indefinite
duration or whether it be *suâ naturâ* temporary and undurable: as is
most commonly the case with such expressions of will the uttering
of which is looked upon as a *measure of administration*: whether it be a
command or a countermand: whether it be expressed in the way of
statute, or of customary law. Under the term 'law' then if this
definition be admitted of, we must include a judicial order, a military
or any other kind of executive order, or even the most trivial and
momentary order of the domestic kind, so it be not illegal: that is,
so as the issuing of it be not forbidden by some other law.

Judging however from analogy, it would naturally be expected that
the signification given to the word *law* should be correspondent to that
of its conjugates *legislation* and *legislative power*: for what, it will be
said, is legislation but the act of making laws? or legislative power
but the power of making them? that consequently the term *law* should
be applied to every expression of will, the uttering of which was an act of
legislation, an exertion of legislative power; and that on the other
hand it should not be applied to any expression of will of which those
two propositions could not be predicated. Accordingly in the former
of these points it does indeed quadrate with these two expressions:
but it can not be said to do so in the latter. It has all the amplitude
which they have, but the import of it is not every where confined
within the bounds which limit theirs. This will be seen in a variety of
examples.

(1) In the first place, according to the definition, the word *law*
should be applicable to any the most trivial order supposing it to be not
illegal, which a man may have occasion to give for any of the most
inconsiderable purposes of life: to any order which a master may
have occasion to give to his servant, a parent to his child, or (where
the request of a husband assumes the harsh form of a command) of a
husband to his wife. Yet it would seem a strange catachresis to speak
of the issuing of any such order as an act of legislation, or as an
exercise of legislative power. Not but that in cases like these the word
law is frequently enough employed: but then it is in the way of figure.
Even where there is no strict legal superiority, a man may say to another
out of compliment, 'your commands are laws to me': but on occasions
like these the impropriety of the expression is the very reason of its
being chosen.

(2) With equal propriety (according to the definition) would the
word *law* be applicable to a temporary order issued by any magistrate
who is spoken of as exercising thereby a branch of *executive* power,
or as exercising the functions belonging to any department of *administration*. But the executive power is continually mentioned as distinct
from the legislative: and the business of administration is as constantly
opposed to that of legislation. Let the Board of Treasury order a

sum of money to be paid or issued to such or such a person, let the Commander in chief order such or such a body of troops to march to such a place, let the Navy Board order such or such a ship to be fitted out, let the Board of Ordnance order such or such a train of artillery to be dispatched to such a destination—Who would ever speak of any of these orders as acts of legislative power, as acts of legislation?

(3) With equal propriety again would the word law according to the definition be applicable to any *judicial* order, to any order which in the course of a cause of any kind a man might have occasion to issue in the capacity of a judge. Yet the business of judicature is constantly looked upon as essentially distinct from the business of legislation and as constantly opposed to it: and the case is the same between the judicial and the legislative power. Even suppose the order to have been ever so general, suppose the persons to whom it is addressed to be ever so numerous and indeterminate, and the duration of it ever so indefinite, still if issued in the course of a forensic contestation, the act of issuing it would not be looked upon in general as coming under the notion of an act of legislation, or as an exercise of legislative power. The fate of a province may be determined by a judicial decree: but the pronouncing of the decree will not on that account be looked upon as being capable with any sort of propriety of being termed an act of legislation. . . .   [pp. 1–5, footnotes omitted]

Such then are the various sorts of expressions of will to which men would be apt for one reason or other to deny the appellation of *a* law: such therefore are the points in which the definition here given of that important word outstretches the idea which common usage has annexed to it. And these excluded objects have in every point except that of the manner of their appertaining to the sovereign, in every point in short except their immediate *source*, the same nature with those whose title to the appellation stands clearest of dispute. They are all referrable *ultimately* to one common source: they have all of them alike their subjects and their objects, their local extent and their duration: in point of logical extent as it may be called they must all of them be either general or particular, and they may in most instances be indifferently either the one or the other: they are all of them susceptible of the same diversities with respect to the *parties* whom they may affect, and the *aspects* which they may present to the acts which are their objects: they require all of them the same *force* to give them effect, and the same *signs* to give them utterance.   [p. 9]

Source of a Law

First then with respect to its *source*. Considered in this point of view, the will of which it is the expression must, as the definition intimates, be the will of the sovereign in *a* state. Now by a sovereign I mean any person or assemblage of persons to whose will a whole political community are (no matter on what account) supposed to be in a disposition to pay obedience: and that in preference to the will of any other person.[30] Suppose the will in question not to be the will of *a*

30 [But note Bentham's omission of any negative condition such as is found in Austin's description of sovereignty. Austin commented: " Mr. Bentham has forgotten to notice the necessity of a negative condition " (*Province*, p. 212). See, further, Raz, *op. cit.*, pp. 6–8.]

sovereign, that is of some sovereign or other; in such case, if it come backed with motives of a coercive nature, it is not a law, but an illegal mandate: and the act of issuing it is an offence.

If the person of whose will it is the expression be a sovereign, but a sovereign to whose power in the case in question a person of the description in question happens not to be subject, it is a law, which as to that person indeed has no force, yet still it is a law. The law having no force, the not obeying it is either no offence or an offence which cannot be punished. Yet still it cannot here be said that the issuing it is an offence: because the person from whom it issues is one whose act, as such, cannot be invested with the character of an offence. Were the Lord High Treasurer of Great Britain to issue of his own authority an order for laying a tax on all the inhabitants of Great Britain the issuing of that order would indeed be an offence: since the Lord High Treasurer of Great Britain is no more a sovereign in Great Britain than he is anywhere else. But were the King of France to issue an order to the same effect addressed to the same persons, such law would indeed be of no force, but yet it would hardly be looked upon as coming under the name of an offence: why?—because the King of France, though not sovereign in Great Britain is sovereign elsewhere; to wit in France: on his part then it would be an act not of delinquency but of hostility.

Now a given will or mandate may be the will or mandate of a given person in either of two ways: in the way of *conception* as it may be called (that is of original conception) or 2. in the way of *adoption*. A will or mandate may be said to belong to a sovereign in the way of conception when it was he himself who issued it and who first issued it, in the words or other signs in which it stands expressed: it may be said to belong to him by adoption when the person from whom it immediately emanes is not the sovereign himself (meaning the sovereign for the time being) but some other person: insomuch that all the concern which he to whom it belongs by adoption has in the matter is the being known to entertain a will that in case such or such another person should have expressed or should come to have expressed a will concerning the act or sort of act in question, such will should be observed and looked upon as his.

Where a mandate appertains to the sovereign only by adoption, such adoption may be distinguished in several respects: 1. in respect of the *time* in which the mandate adopted appears with reference to that of the adopting mandate: 2. in respect of the persons whose mandates are thus adopted. 3. in respect of the *degree* in which the adoption is performed: fourthly in respect of the *form* of expression by which it may be performed.

(1) First then, with regard to *time*, the mandate which the sovereign in question is supposed to adopt may be either already issued, or not: in the former case it may be said to be his by *susception*; in the latter by *pre-adoption*. Where the sovereign holds himself thus in readiness to adopt the mandates of another person whensoever they shall happen to have been issued, he may thereby be said to invest that person with a certain species of power, which may be termed a *power of imperation*. Examples of this distinction we shall see immediately.

(2) As to the *persons* whose mandates the sovereign may have occasion to adopt, it would be to little purpose here, and indeed it

would be premature, to attempt reducing the enumeration of them to an analytic method. In the way of susception, the sovereign for the time being adopts as well the mandates of former sovereigns as those of subordinate *power-holders*: in the way of pre-adoption, he can adopt the last mentioned mandates only: for to pre-adopt the mandates of subsequent sovereigns would be nugatory, since whatever actual force there is in sovereignty rests in the sovereign for the time being: in the living, not in the dead. As the propensity to obedience may admit of every imaginable modification, it is just conceivable indeed that the people should in certain points obey the mandates of a deceased sovereign in preference to those of his living successor. Lycurgus, if the story be a true one, found means by a trick, thus to reign after his death: but it is a trick that would hardly succeed a second time: and the necessity he found himself under of having recourse to that expedient would be a sufficient proof, if there required any, how little need the sovereign who is recognized as such for the time being has to be beholden for his power to his departed predecessors.

As to the subordinate power-holders whose mandates the sovereign pre-adopts, these are of course as many and as various as the classes of persons to whom the law gives either powers of *imperation* or the contrary powers of *de-imperation*, if such is the name that may be given to the power of undoing what by imperation has been done. These powers it may give to the power-holder on his own account, in which case the power is beneficial, or on that of another; in which case it is fiduciary: and in this latter case, on account of an individual, or on account of the public at large; in which latter case again the power is of the public or constitutional kind. It is thus that every mandate that is issued within the limits of the sovereignty and that is not illegal, is in one sense or the other the mandate of the sovereign. Take any mandate whatsoever, either it is of the number of those which he allows or it is not: there is no medium: if it is, it is his; by adoption at least, if not by original conception: if not, it is illegal, and the issuing it an offence. Trivial or important makes no difference: if the former are not his, then neither are the latter. The mandates of the master, the father, the husband, the guardian, are all of them the mandates of the sovereign: if not, then neither are those of the general nor of the judge. Not a cook is bid to dress a dinner, a nurse to feed a child, an usher to whip a school boy, an executioner to hang a thief, an officer to drive the enemy from a post, but it is by his orders. If anyone should find a difficulty in conceiving this, he has only to suppose the several mandates in question to meet with resistance: in one case as well as in another the business of enforcing them must rest ultimately with the sovereign. Nor is there anything of fiction in all this: if there were, this is the last place in which it should be found.

To continue the laws of preceding sovereigns, and the powers of the various classes of magistrates, domestic as well as civil, is (in every tolerably well settled commonwealth at least) a matter of course. To suffer either of those systems of institutions to perish, and not to establish anything in their stead, would be to suffer the whole machine of government to drop to pieces. The one course no sovereign was ever yet mad enough, the other none was ever yet industrious enough, to pursue. If the adoption be not declared in words, it is because the fact is so notorious, that any express form of words to signify it would be unnecessary. It is manifested by means not less significant than words, by every act of government, by which the enforcement of the mandates in question is provided for. If it be alleged that the trivial transactions that pass in the interior of a family are not specifically in the contemplation of the sovereign: (trivial as they may be termed when individually considered, though in their totality they are the stuff that human life is made of) the same may be said of the transactions of fleets and armies: of those which become the objects of the mandates issued by the general or the judge. The same may even be said of those laws which emane directly from the very presence of the sovereign. It is only by the general tenor of their effects and not by any direct specification that individual acts of any kind can be comprised under extensive and general descriptions.

It is in this very way that conveyances and covenants acquire all the validity they can possess, all the connection they have with the system of the laws: adopted by the sovereign, they are converted into mandated laws. If you give your coat to a man, and the gift is valid, and nobody else has a right to meddle [31] with your coat, it is because a mandate subsists on the part of the sovereign, commanding all persons whatever to refrain from meddling with it, he to whom you gave it alone excepted, upon the event of your declaring such to be your pleasure. If a man engages or covenants to mend your coat for you, and such an engagement is valid, it is because on the part of the sovereign a mandate hath been issued, commanding any person upon the event of his entering into any engagement, (exceptions excepted) and thereby that particular person in consequence of his having entered into that particular engagement, (it not being within the exceptions) to perform it: in other words to render you that particular service which is rendered to you by performance of the act which he has engaged for.

Thus then in all cases stands the distinction between the laws which belong to the legislator in the way of conception, and those which belong to him in the way of pre-adoption. The former are the work of the legislator solely: the latter that of the legislator and the subordinate power-holder conjunctively, the legislator sketching out a sort of imperfect mandate which he leaves it to the subordinate power-holder to fill up. In the first case there are no other mandates in the case than those which emane from the legislator *immediate*: in the latter case whatever mandates there are emane from the subordinate power-holder *immediate*, and whenever they happen to be issued can only be said to emane *potestative* from the legislator. In the former case there are mandates from the first that exist *in actu*: in the latter until issued by the subordinate power-holder, whatever mandates there may be conceived to be exist only *in potentia*. In the former case the law will more readily than in the other be perceived to be occupied in issuing or repeating commands: In the other case it will be apt to appear as if it were employed solely in giving descriptions: for example of the *persons* by whom powers shall be possessed: of the *things* over which, or persons over whom, such powers shall be possessed: of the *acts* to which such power shall extend; that is of which the performance shall be deemed an exercise of such power: of the *place* in which and

---

[31] [For Bentham's concept of "meddling" see *post*, 203.]

the *time* during which such powers shall be exercised, and so on. Yet still such descriptions have so much in them of the nature of a command or what stands opposed to it, that whenever the power which they confer or limit comes to be exercised, the expression of will whereby it is exercised may, without any alteration made in the import of it, be translated into the form and language of a mandate: of a mandate issuing from the mouth of the lawgiver himself.

Next as to the degree in which the mandate of a subordinate power-holder may be adopted by the sovereign: or in other words the degree of force which such mandate acquires by the adoption. Take any single manifestation of the sovereign's will, and all the assistance that the mandate of a subordinate power-holder can receive from it consists in a bare permission: this is the first step that the sovereign takes towards the giving validity to subordinate mandates: the first and least degree of assistance or rather countenance that the inferior can receive from the superior: the not being made the subject of a law commanding him not to issue the subordinate mandate which is in question. The part thus far taken by the sovereign is, we see, merely a negative one. Nor would it be worthwhile, or indeed proper, to notice him as taking any part at all, since it is no more than what is taken by every the merest stranger, were it not for its lying so much in his way to take the contrary part; a part which he actually does take in relation to the greater number of the other members of the community. If any further degree of countenance is shewn it must be by another law or set of laws: a law permitting the subordinate power-holder to punish with his own hand the party who is made subject to the mandate in case of disobedience, by a law permitting others to assist in the administering such punishment, by a law commanding others to assist; and so on. Such ulterior corroborative laws however are not to be reckoned as exclusively necessary to the particular business of adoption: for a set of subsidiary laws like these are equally necessary, as will be seen hereafter, to the giving *force* and efficacy to such laws as emane from the sovereign himself in the most immediate manner.

Next as to the form or manner in which the adoption may be performed. We have already intimated that it may be done by permission: that is by a legislative permission: but it may also be done by mandate, by a legislative mandate: by a permission addressed in the first instance to the power-holder; a permission to issue the mandates which it is proposed to adopt; or by a mandate addressed immediately to those whom it is meant to subject to his power; a mandate commanding them to obey such and such mandates whensoever, if at all, he shall have thought fit to issue them. In the former case the mandate of the subordinate power-holder whenever it comes to be issued, is a *primordial* one: in the latter case it is *superventitious*, the mandate of the sovereign being the primordial one, of which this which is superventitious is *reiterative*. These terms should they appear obscure, will hereafter be explained.[32] Whichever be the form, it comes exactly to the same thing: and the difference lies rather in the manner in which we may conceive the inclination of the sovereign to be expressed, than in the inclination itself. In both cases the mandate depends for its force upon a further set of mandates, as hath been already intimated

[32] [Chap. X, at pp. 93 *et seq.*]

and will be shewn more particularly further on. Whether these subsidiary mandates be annexed to a mandate on the part of the sovereign *ab initio*, or to the mandates of the subsidiary power holder when they arise, is a matter of indifference.

The mandate of a subordinate powerholder, when it has the requisite degree of permanency and generality, to constitute it according to common speech *a law* is in the language of the English jurisprudence in many cases termed a *by-law*. It was first applied to the laws made by the governing body in corporate towns, being so much as to say a *town-law*. In process of time it has been extended to laws made by any other bodies corporate; although they had nothing to do with the government of particular towns: such as the trading, banking and insurance companies. It might with equal propriety and convenience be extended to any subordinate laws whatever. . . .   [pp. 18–28]

Parties Affected by a Law

. . . There yet remain a class of laws which stand upon a very different footing from any of those that have hitherto been brought to view. The laws of which we have hitherto been speaking have for their passible subjects not the sovereign himself, but those who are considered as being subject to his power. But there are laws to which no other persons in quality of passible subjects can be envisaged than the sovereign himself. The business of the ordinary sort of laws is to prescribe to the people what *they* shall do: the business of this trans-cendent class of laws is to prescribe to the sovereign what *he* shall do: what mandates *he* may or may not address to *them*; and in general how he shall or may conduct himself towards them. Laws of this latter description may be termed, in consideration of the party who is their passible subject, laws *in principem*: in contradistinction to the ordinary mass of laws which in this view may be termed laws *in subditos* or *in populum*.

These laws *in principem* may be of either of two sorts according to the party from whom they emane and the party whose conduct they are designed to influence. This latter party may be the individual sovereign himself from whom they emane, or any future sovereign or sovereigns his successor or successors: in the former case they are what are strictly and properly termed pacts or covenants: and to distinguish them from the ordinary covenants entered into by subjects, they may be styled *pacta regalia* or *royal covenants*: in the latter case, they have not as yet acquired any separate denomination. In the common way of speaking these indeed are likewise termed pacts or covenants, one man being considered as having covenanted in virtue of a covenant actually entered into by another: the succeeding sovereign in virtue of the covenant actually entered into by his predecessor. But this way of speaking, familiar as it is, is improper: it is inaccurate, inconsistent and productive of confusion: to obviate which, acts of this sort may be styled *recommendatory mandates*. When a reigning sovereign then in the tenor of his laws engages for himself and for his successors he does two distinguishable things. By an expression of will which has its own conduct for its object, he enters *himself* into a covenant: by an expression of will which has the conduct of his successors for its object, he addresses to *them* a recommendatory mandate. This mandate the successor whenever the sovereignty devolves to him will probably adopt: and then and not till then it is his covenant.

The causes which originally produced the original covenant and the considerations of expediency which justified the engaging in it on the part of the predecessor will in general subsist to produce and justify the adoption of it on the part of the successor. In most instances therefore it will have happened that upon any change taking place in the sovereignty such adoption shall have taken place: it will have become customary for it so to do: the people, influenced partly by the force of habit and partly by the consideration of the expediency of such adoption, will be expecting it as a thing of course: and this expectation will add again to the motives which tend to produce such effect in any given instance. So great in short is the influence of all these causes when taken together, that in any tolerably well settled government the successor is as much expected to abide by the covenants of his predecessor as by any covenants of his own: unless where any change of circumstances has made a manifest and indisputable change in the utility of such adherence. This expectation may even become so strong, as to equal the expectation which is entertained of the prevalence of that disposition to obedience on the part of the people by which the sovereignty *de facto* is constituted: insomuch that the observance of the covenant on the one part shall be looked upon as a condition *sine qua non* to the obedience that is to be paid on the other. Things are most apt to be upon this footing in those governments in which the sovereignty is ascribed nominally to a single person, who in reality possesses only a part, though perhaps the most conspicuous part, in it. But in all governments where either the whole or a principal part of the sovereignty is in the hands of a single person, the exercise of the sovereignty and the observance of the covenants entered into by preceding sovereigns are looked upon as being in such a degree connected that upon taking upon him the former a man is universally understood to have taken upon him the latter: understood, not only by the people, but by the sovereign himself. This notion is so universal and deep-rooted that if by accident a sovereign should in fact come to the throne with a determination not to adopt the covenants of his predecessors, he would be told that he had adopted them notwithstanding: adopting them tacitly by taking upon him those powers to the exercise of which the obligation of adopting those covenants, stood annexed. Nor would this way of speaking, how untrue soever it may be by the very supposition, seem mis-applied: since it has become the habit among men of law to speak of the matter of right in the same terms in which they would speak of the matter of fact: that which, according to the general opinion, *ought* to be done being spoken as if it *were* done.

It appears then that there are two distinct sorts of laws, very different from each other in their nature and effect: both originating indeed from the sovereign, (from whom mediately or immediately all ordinances in order to be legal must issue) but addressed to parties of different descriptions: the one addressed to the sovereign, imposing an obligation on the sovereign: the other addressed to the people, imposing an obligation on the people. Those of the first sort may again be addressed either to the sovereign himself who issues them, (the sovereign for the time being) or to his successors, or (what is most common) to the one as well as to the other. It is evident then

that in the distinction between these two classes of laws it is the quality
of the parties who are respectively bound by them that is the essential
and characteristic feature.

Here it may naturally enough be asked what sense there is in a
man's addressing a law to himself? and how it is a man can impose
an obligation upon himself? such an obligation to wit as can to any
purpose be effectual. Admit indeed we must that for a man to address
a law to himself, is what indeed there would be little sense in, were
there no other *force* in the world but his: nor can a man by his own
single unassisted force impose upon himself any effectual obligation:
for granting him to have bound himself, what should hinder him on any
occasion from setting himself free? On the other hand, take into
account an exterior force, and by the help of such force it is as easy
for a sovereign to bind himself as to bind another. It is thus, as was
seen in a former chapter, that in transactions between subject and
subject a man binds himself by the assistance of that force which
is at the disposal of the sovereign. Nor is the assertion we make in
speaking of a man's binding himself so wide from the literal truth as at
first sight might appear. The force which binds, depends indeed upon
the will of a third person: but that will itself waits to receive its
determination from the person who is said to bind, from the person
who is the promulgator of the law. Without the covenantor, there
would be no law at all: without the *guarantee*, as he is called, none
that can be effectual. The law then may in strictness be considered
as the work of both: and therefore in part, of either: but the share
which the covenantor takes in it is by much the more conspicuous.
It is this at all events that is taken first: it is seen to be taken while the
other perhaps is expected only: it is certain; while the other perhaps
is but contingent. In short the part which the sovereign for the time
being has in the establishment of a *pactum regium* whereby he binds
himself and his successors may be as considerable, and as independent of the part which may come to be taken by those to whom
belongs the enforcement of such covenant, as the part which is taken
by the legislator in the case of a law of the ordinary stamp *in populum*
is of the part which may come to be taken by the judge.

By what means then can a law *in principem* be enforced and
rendered efficacious: what force is there in the nature of things that
is applicable to this purpose? To answer this question, we have nothing
to do but to resort to the enumeration, that has been already given on a
former occasion, of the several sorts of forces by which the human
will is liable to be influenced. The forces and the only forces by
which the human will is influenced are *motives*: these, when considered
in the mass, may be distinguished according to the sources from whence
they issue: to these sources we set out with giving the name of
sanctions. Of these sanctions that which we termed the *physical* is out
of the question: for the force in the case in question is supposed to be
directed *by design*. There remain the political, the religious and the
moral. The force of the political sanction is inapplicable to this
purpose: by the supposition within the dominion of the sovereign
there is no one who while the sovereignty subsists can judge so as to
coerce the sovereign: to maintain the affirmative would be to maintain
a contradiction.[32a] But the force of the religious sanction is as applicable

[32a] [See Bentham's footnote, omitted here, but in an appendix at p. 854.]

to this purpose as to any other: and this is one of the great and beneficial
purposes to which the religious sanction, where it happens to have an
influence, is wont to be applied. The same may be said of the force
of the moral sanction. Now the force of the moral sanction as
applied to the purpose in question may be distinguished into two
great branches: that which may be exerted by the subjects of the state
in question acting without, and perhaps even against, the sanction of
political obligations, acting in short as in a state of nature; and that
which may be exerted by foreign states. When a foreign state stands
engaged by express covenant to take such a part in the enforcement
of such a law as that in question, this is one of the cases in which
such foreign state is said to stand with reference to such law in the
capacity of a guarantee. Of a covenant of this sort many examples are
to be met with in the history of international jurisprudence.

To all or any of these forces may a law *in principem* stand indebted
for its efficacy. Of all these forces even when put together the efficacy
it must be confessed is seldom so great as that of the political. How
should it? when it is in the nature of the political sanction to draw
with it in most instances a great part if not the whole of the force of
the other two? But to deny them all efficacy would be to go too far
on the other side. It would be as much as to say that no privileges
were ever respected, no capitulation ever observed. It would be as
much as to say, that there is no such system in Europe as the
Germanic body: that the inhabitants of Austrian Flanders are upon
no other footing than the inhabitants of Prussia: those of the *pays
d'états* in France than those of the *pays d'élection*: that no regard
was ever paid to the American charters by the British Parliament:
and that the Act of Union has never been anything but a dead
letter . . .   [pp. 64–71]

Force of a Law

. . . With respect to the *force* of the law: that is, with respect to the
motives it relies upon for enabling it to produce the effects it aims at.
Motives of some sort or other to trust to it evidently must have:
for without a cause, no such thing as an effect: without a motive, no
such thing as action. What then are motives? We have seen that they
are but the expectations of so many lots of pain and pleasure, as
connected in a particular manner in the way of causality with the
actions with reference to which they are termed *motives*. When it is in
the shape of pleasure they apply, they may be termed *alluring* motives:
when in the shape of pain, *coercive*. It is when those of the alluring
kind are held up as being connected with an act, that a *reward* is said
to be offered: it is when those of the coercive kind are thus held up,
that a *punishment* is said to be denounced.

The next question is from what source these motives may issue.
Now it has already been observed, that of the four sources from
whence pain and pleasure may be said to take their rise, there are
three which are under the influence of intelligent and voluntary agents;
viz: the political, the moral, and the religious sanctions. The legislator
then may, in the view of giving efficacy to his laws take either of two
courses: he may trust altogether to the auxiliary force of the two
foreign sanctions, or he may have recourse to motives drawn from
that fund which is of his own creation. The former of these courses is
what has sometimes been taken with success: there seem even to be

cases in which it is to be preferred to any other. These cases however are in comparison but rare. For the most part it is to some pleasure or some pain drawn from the political sanction itself, but more particularly, as we shall see presently, to pain that the legislator trusts for the effectuation of his will.

This punishment then, or this reward, whichever it be, in order to produce its effect must in some manner or other be announced: notice of it must in some way or other be given, in order to produce an expectation of it, on the part of the people whose conduct it is meant to influence. This notice may either be given by the legislator himself in the text of the law itself, or it may be left to be given, in the way of customary law by the judge: the legislator, commanding you for example to do an act: the judge in his own way and according to his own measure punishing you in case of your not doing it, or, what is much less frequent, rewarding you in case of your doing it. . . .

But the most eligible and indeed the most common method of giving notice is by inserting a clause on purpose: by subjoining to that part of the law which is expressive of the legislator's will, another part of the office of which is to indicate the motive he furnishes you with for complying with such will.

In this case the law may plainly enough be distinguished into two parts: the one serving to make known to you what the inclination of the legislator is: the other serving to make known to you what motive the legislator has furnished you with for complying with that inclination: the one addressed more particularly to your understanding; the other, to your will. The former of these parts may be termed the *directive*: the other, the *sanctional* or *incitative*.

As to the incitative this it is evident may be of two kinds: when the motive furnished is of the nature of punishment, it may be termed the *comminative* part, or *commination*: when it is of the nature of reward, the *invitative* part, or *invitation*.

Of the above two methods of influencing the will that in which punishment is employed is that with which we are chiefly concerned at present. It is that indeed of which we hear the most and of which the greatest use is made. So great indeed is the use that is made of it, and so little in comparison is that which is made of reward, that the only names which are in current use for expressing the different aspects of which a will is susceptible are such as suppose punishment the motive. Command, prohibition, and permission, all of them point at punishment: hence the impropriety we were obliged to set out with, for want of words to remedy it.

The case is that for ordinary use punishment is beyond comparison the most efficacious upon the whole. By punishment alone it seems not impossible but that the whole business of government might be carried on: though certainly not so well carried on as by a mixture of that and reward together. But by reward alone it is most certain that no material part of that business could ever be carried on for half an hour.[33]

---

[33] The reasons why the principal part of the business of government cannot be carried on any otherwise than by punishment are various: among which there are several which would each of them be abundantly sufficient of itself.

1. In the first place, any man can at any time be much surer of administering pain than pleasure.

2. The law (that is, the set of persons employed for this purpose by the legislator) has it still less in its power to make sure of administering pleasure

The sense of mankind on this head is so strong and general, however confused and ill developed, that where the motives presented to the inclination of him whose conduct it is proposed to influence are of no other than the alluring kind, it might appear doubtful perhaps whether the expression of the will of which such conduct is the object could properly be styled a law. The motives which the law trusts to are in most cases of a coercive nature: hence the idea of coercion shall in their minds have become inseparably connected with that of a law. Being then an invitation, that is an expression of will trusting for its efficacy to motives not coercive, they will conclude that it can not with propriety be styled a law.

The conclusion however seems not to be a necessary one. For as these invitations are as much the expressions of the will of a lawgiver as commands themselves are, as they issue from the same source, tend to the same ends, are susceptible of the same aspects, applicable to the same objects, and recorded indiscriminately in the same volumes with those expressions of will which beyond dispute are entitled to the appellation of a law, it should seem that without any great incongruity,

than particular persons have: since the power of administering pleasure depends upon the particular and ever-changing circumstances of the individual to whom it is to be applied: (See Ch. (Sensibility) of which circumstances the law is not in any way of being apprised. In short the law seems to have no means of administering pleasure to any man by its own immediate operation: all it can do is to put the instrument in his way, and leave him at liberty to apply it himself for that purpose if he thinks proper: this is accordingly what the law does when it is said to give a man a pecuniary reward.

3. The scale of pleasure supposing it actually applied is very short and limited: the scale of pain is in comparison unlimited.

4. The sources of pleasure are few and soon exhausted: the sources of pain are innumerable and inexhaustible. It has already been observed that the only means the law has of administering pleasure to a man is by placing the instruments of it within his reach. But the number and value of these instruments is extremely limited. Any object in nature may be converted into an instrument of pain: few in comparison and rare are those which are calculated to serve as instruments of pleasure.

5. The law has no means of producing pleasure without producing pain at the same time: which pleasure and which pain being considered by themselves apart from their effects, the pain is more than equivalent to the pleasure. For, an instrument of pleasure before it can be given to one man must have been taken from another: and since *ceteris paribus* it is more painful to lose a given sum than it is pleasurable to gain it, the pain produced by the *taking* is upon an average always more than equivalent to the pleasure produced by the *giving*.

6. The insufficiency of rewards is more particularly conspicuous when applied to acts of the negative kind. The acts of a positive kind of which it is necessary to enjoin the performance are always made referable to some definite possible subject, and included within a definite portion of time: such as to pay money on a certain occasion to a certain person: to lend a hand to the repair of a certain road for such a number of days; and so forth. But acts of a negative kind are commonly comprised under no such limitations. Take for instance the not stealing, and the not doing damage to the roads. Now by not stealing is meant the not stealing from any person any stealable articles at any time: but persons are numerous, stealable articles still more so, and time indefinitely divisible. If then Paul for example were to be rewarded for not stealing it must be in some such way as this: for not stealing from Peter a farthing at 12 o'clock, one shilling: for not stealing another farthing from the same Peter at the same time, another shilling: for not stealing another farthing from the same Peter at a moment after 12, another shilling: for not stealing from John a farthing at such a place at 12 o'clock, another shilling: the same sums to be given also to Peter and John for not stealing from Paul: and so on for everlasting.

they might be established in the possession of the same name. To distinguish, however, a law of this particular kind from the other, it should never be mentioned but under some particular name, such as that of an *invitative* or *praemiary* law; or it might be styled a *legislative invitation*, or a *bounty*.

As a law may have sometimes a penal sanction to back it, sometimes a sanction of the praemiary kind, so may it, (as is obvious) be provided with two opposite sanctions, one of the one kind, the other of the other. A law thus provided may be styled *a law with an alternative sanction*. In this case the mode of conduct with which the one of these sanctions is connected is the opposite to that with which the other is connected. If the one sanction is connected with the positive act, the other sanction is connected with the correspondent negative act. Take the following example. Whosoever comes to know that a robbery has been committed, let him declare it to the judge: if he declares it accordingly, he shall receive such or such a reward: if he fails to declare it, he shall suffer such or such a punishment.

We are now arrived at the notion of an object which might in a certain sense admit of the appellation of a law. It may even be looked upon as constituting a law and something more: since there are to be found in it two distinguishable parts: the directive part, which must of itself be a complete expression of will, and an article of a different nature, a *prediction*. But nothing hath as yet been brought to view by which the efficacy of the directive part, or the verity of the predictive can have been established upon any solid footing. Let the law stop here, and let the influence of the two auxiliary sanctions be for a moment set aside, what has been done by the law as yet amounts to nothing: as an expression of will, it is impotent; as a prediction, it is false. The will of the legislator concerning the matter in question has indeed been declared: and punishment has been threatened in the case of non-compliance with such will: but as to the means of carrying such threats into execution, nothing of this sort hath as yet been made appear.

What course then can the legislator take? There is but one, which is to go on commanding as before: for as to taking upon himself the infliction of the punishment with his own hands, this, were it practicable in every case which it manifestly can not be, would be overstepping the bounds of his own function and exercising a different sort of power. All he can do then in his capacity of legislator is to issue a second law, requiring some person to verify the prediction that accompanied the first. This secondary law being issued in aid of the primary may with reference thereto be termed the *subsidiary* law: with reference to which the primary law may on the other hand be termed the *principal*.

To whom is it then that this subsidiary law should be addressed? It can never be the same person to whom the principal law was addressed: for a man *can* not reward himself; nor *will* he punish himself. It must therefore be to some other person: a circumstance which of itself is sufficient to shew that the principal and subsidiary are two distinct laws, and not parts of one and the same law. It may be any other person indefinitely. Commonly however it is to some particular class of persons, who occupying some particular station or civil condition instituted for the purpose, such as that of judge, are presumed on the one hand to be properly qualified, on the other hand to be previously disposed, to execute or cause to be executed any such commands when issued by the legislature.

But neither can the hand nor the eye of the judge reach everywhere: to be in a condition to discharge his functions he must be provided with a variety of assistants: which assistants must for certain purposes be of various ranks, occupations and descriptions: witnesses, registers, court-keepers, jail-keepers, bailiffs, executioners, and so forth. Of these there are many who must begin to act in their respective characters even before the matter is submitted to his cognizance: consequently before they can be in a way to receive any commands from him. On this and other accounts they too must have their duties prescribed to them by the law itself: and hence the occasion for so many more subsidiary laws or sets of subsidiary laws, of which they are respectively the agible subjects, and their acts the objects.

It is evident that the number and nature of the subsidiary laws of this stamp will be determined by the number and nature of the different sorts of acts which on the part either of the same person or of different persons it is thought proper should be performed or abstained from in the course of the *procedure*. Now by the procedure is meant on the present occasion the suite of steps which are required to be taken in the view of ascertaining whether a man has or has not done an act of the number of those which stand prohibited by some principal law: and thereby of ascertaining whether he is or is not of the number of those persons, on whom a punishment of the sort denounced by the principal law in question is required to be inflicted.

Amidst this various train of laws subsidiary, that which is addressed to the judge and contains the command to punish, may for distinction's sake be termed the punitive or *punitory* law: and with reference to the rest the *proximate* subsidiary law: the rest may indiscriminately be termed *remote*. Where the principal law is of the praemiary kind, the proximate subsidiary law may be termed *remunerative*.

Now it is evident that in like manner as a principal law must have its subsidiary laws, so also must each of those subsidiary laws have a train of subsidiary laws to itself, and that for the same reason. This is a circumstance that belongs alike to every law which takes its support from the political sanction. *A* commits an offence: it is thereupon rendered the duty of *B* to contribute in such or such a way to the bringing of him to punishment in the event of his proving guilty: and a particular process is appointed to be carried on for ascertaining whether he be or no. In the course of that process such and such steps are required to be taken by *C* in such and such contingencies: such and such others by *D* and *E* and *F*: and so on indefinitely. But what if *B* also proved refractory? a similar process must thereupon be carried on and a similar provision made by the law for the bringing of him also to punishment: and so on if any failure should arise on the part of *D* or *E* or *F*. In this way must commands follow upon commands: if the first person called does not obey, the second may: if the second should not, yet a third may: if even the third should fail, yet there may be hopes of a fourth.[34] If it is not

---

[34] [It was from arguments such as these that Petrazycki argued that a sanction of any kind cannot be essential to a rule of law, for the transgression of a rule with a sanction would bring another rule and sanction into play and so on *ad infinitum*. But, as Stone points out (*Legal System, op. cit.* pp. 77–78), though

expected that anyone will obey, the law is plainly impotent and falls to the ground: but let obedience be but expected from any one of the persons addressed, at whatever distance he stands from him who was addressed first, this expectation may prove sufficient to keep all the intermediate persons to their duty. If an offence then be committed, until obedience takes place on the part of some one person or other of the persons thus connected, the law is as it were asleep, and the whole machine of government is at a stand: but let any one law in the whole penal train meet with obedience, let punishment take place in any quarter, the law awakens out of its trance, and the whole machine is set agoing again: the influence of that law which has met with obedience flows back as it were through all the intermediate laws till it comes to that principal one to which they are all alike subsidiary. . . . [pp. 133–141]

Idea of a Complete Law

. . . The laws relative to property may be considered in various points of view. To apprehend the nature of them, the relation they bear to the rest of the system, and how they are reducible to the nature of a mandate or its opposite, we must call back to mind what was said of the offences relative to property in the preceding chapter.[35] Let us begin with that sort of property which is the most simple. . . . The most simple case is where the proprietary subject as we may call it is corporeal, determinate and single. . . .

To understand the nature of the laws of property it will be requisite to recur to the enumeration we had occasion to make in the last chapter of the possible offences relative to property. It will also be necessary to recollect that an offence and the law whereby that offence is created are a sort of correlatives; so that for every offence there is a law: viz: a law of the mandative or imperative kind, and for every law of the imperative kind there is an offence: and that accordingly the offence being given the law is given also, or the law being given, the offence. Now in the list of the offences against property the radical one seems to be that which we have styled *wrongful occupation of property*: it is to that offence that the law, by which the most simple and elementary species of proprietary right is created, corresponds. This is the leading offence by reference to which the nature of those other offences may most commodiously be explained.

But without the idea of some particular sort of corporeal object before our eyes it will be difficult to reason clearly. Let the proprietary subject then be a certain piece of land, a field, the offence which consists in the wrongful occupation of this property will be any act in virtue of which the agent may be said to meddle with this field. But the name of the offence reflects the act which is the object of the law: now the offence is that of meddling with the field. But that object when represented by the name of the offence is represented just as natural objects are represented in certain mirrors, in an inverted position. The offence then being the act of meddling with the field, the act

logically sound, in sociological terms the support given by public opinion and power to the law renders the chance of violation of the first rule relatively small and the chance of violation of subsequent rules less and less likely.]

35 The reference intended is to Ch. XVI, para. 35 of *An Introduction to the Principles* (in *CW*, 226–232). [*CW* refers to Collected Works 1968–: the edition by Hart and Burns.]

which is the object of the law, the act commanded is the negative act of not meddling with the field. Annexing then the expression of will to the act thus expressed, we have the whole substance of the law; which amounts to this, 'Let no one, Rusticus excepted,' (so we will call the proprietor) 'and those whom he allows meddle with such or such a field.' Here then we have an example of one form in which the substance of a law of property creating property may be expressed.

But in this law we see there is an exceptive clause. Now every law in which there is an exceptive clause may be resolved into two provisions. These provisions where the law is, as it is here, of the negative or prohibitive kind are 1. a primordial mandate of the prohibitive kind, the more extensive of the two: 2. a superventitious mandate of the permissive kind which is the least extensive of the two, being revocative but revocative *pro tanto* only and not *pro toto* of the former. No man shall meddle with the field (describing it): Praetextatus and such other persons as he allows may meddle with the field.

Viewing the matter in this light it is not to be wondered if a man should be alarmed at first at the multitude of the laws to which the head of property may give occasion. To that multitude it must be acknowledged there are no bounds. In the first place we have a different law for every distinct proprietary subject: and matter is infinitely divisible. In the next place we have a new law every time the subject changes hands, and that may happen fifty times a day. But we are as yet got but a very little way in the enumeration of the circumstances which may give occasion to different laws relative to the same individual subject. In the example above exhibited it is taken for granted that the subject belongs solely to one person, that it is his not only for a certainty but at present, and not only for the present but for ever, that when he chooses to make use of it, he may make what use of it he pleases, and that he may make use of one part of it as well as of another, and that to warrant him in making use of it he has no need to wait for any particular event or for the consent of any other person. . . .

The laws then to which any one single proprietary subject may give occasion being infinite, how is it possible, it may be asked, to comprise the collection of the whole body of the laws relative to property within the limited compass of a code? Certainly to draw them out at length and conceived in the imperative form is not possible. But the modes of expressing imperation as there hath already been occasion to observe are indefinitely numerous. Of these many are indirect and have nothing of imperation upon the face of them; bearing the form not of imperative but of common assertive propositions: as if they were the words not of the lawgiver but of some one else who was giving an account of what the lawgiver had done. Now as in the imperative form the laws relative to this head would swell to an infinite degree of expansion: so in the narrative or assertive form they may be reduced to an almost infinite degree of compression. To describe and distinguish the several contrivances by which in different cases this concentration may be effected, would require a volume. All that can be done here is to give notice to the reader: inasmuch that being aware of the metamorphoses, he may be master of a thread which will conduct him at any time from the artificial and super-induced, to the native and primeval form of the several provisions of the law. To exhibit in this latter form all these provisions collectively is impossible, but it is no more than what a man must be able to do with regard to each of them taken separately, ere he can possess any accurate comprehension either of the nature and operation of such provision taken by itself, or of the relation it bears towards the other parts of the system. For a law of any kind or any part of the law of any kind to have any effect, a man must be punishable in case of his disobeying it: but to have an idea of a case in which a man is punishable for any act is to have the idea of an offence: and to have the idea of an offence, the signification of the will of him who makes it such being added, is to have the idea of a command.

It hath already been observed on a former occasion that private conveyances in as far as they are legal, that is adopted by the legislator, are so many laws or assemblages of laws. This being admitted, a body of the laws to be complete must be understood as including *inter alia* the whole body of conveyances: a complete body of the laws taken at any given period will therefore include a complete collection of the several conveyances which within the dominion of the state are in force at the instant of that period. Not that conveyances are on this account to be reckoned laws in any other sense than that in which any other commands issued in the exercise of powers are laws; those not excepted which are issued by parents, masters and other domestic power-holders for any the most trivial purposes of a private family. For the legislator then to take any separate notice of them is impossible. All that he can do, and all that it is requisite he should do is to describe in general terms such as he thinks proper to adopt, and thereupon explicitly or implicitly such others as he thinks proper not to adopt: in other words such as are deemed *good* or *valid*, and such as are to be deemed *void*. Now those are good or valid which are made in such *form* as it is thought proper to acknowledge for good form, by him who has a good title, or to speak shortly a title to convey, in favour of him who has a good title to take or receive: those bad or void which are made in such form as it is thought proper to hold for bad, by one who has no good title, or as the phrase is no title to convey, or in favour of one who has no good title or no title to take or receive. But an event which is allowed to give a man a title to one sort of proprietary subject may not perhaps be allowed to give him a title to a proprietary subject of another sort: and an individual event which gives a man title to an individual proprietary subject does not thereby give him a title to another individual proprietary subject. Moreover an event which is allowed to give to a person one sort of proprietary subject, may not be allowed to give a title to a proprietary subject of that sort to a man of another sort. Also as to events that depend upon the act of man, an event which if it resulted from the act of a person of one sort would be allowed to give to a person of a given sort a title as to a proprietary subject of a given sort, may not be allowed to produce that effect where it results from the act of a person of another sort, as in the case of minors, prodigals, trust-holders and the like. Hence the whole branch of the law relative to conveyances may be comprised in the exposition of a few such words as proprietary, proprietary subject, proprietary rights, proprietor or right-holder, title, conveyance, and the like: of which exposition every distinguishable clause by being applied to any particular conveyance that came into controversy might be translated into a command.

It is thus that by being applied to and combined in a manner with the expression of the wills of individual power-holders that branch of the law which concerns conveyances is transformable into and carries the effect of a command. But there is another branch of the law, still referable to the offence of wrongful occupation in which the matter of the command is furnished by the legislator solely and immediately without needing to be applied to the mandate of any private power-holder. This includes the cases where the title of him in whose favour the law is made is constituted either by an event which is altogether in his own power or by an event of any other kind in which, in as far at least as concerns the effect thus given to it, no other person's will has any participation: as is the case for instance with the title derived from occupancy, improvement, natural increment and succession *ab intestato*. In this latter sort of case the connection between the assertive matter of the law and the idea of a command emaning from the legislator will not be quite so remote as in the former. In the one case we may have a complete law, in the other case we can not without descending to that degree of minuteness and particularity as to take in the mandates of individuals. Thus it is that in one or other of these ways a good part of the matter of law is naturally and in a manner necessarily thrown into the assertive form constituting a kind of exposition of some such word as the word *title*.

This word then we see is a word that will be wanted to make part of the definition of the offence entitled wrongful occupation of property. But this same word or what is equivalent to it will be equally stood in need of for completing the several definitions of the several other acts which are ranked under the head of offences concerning property. Thus wrongful non-investment of property is the forbearing to render a man that sort of service which consists in the conveying to him or investing him with a title to a certain proprietary subject, he having a title to such service: wrongful investment of property, in the doing of any of those acts which are deemed by the law to divest a man of such a title, the wrongdoer having no title so to do: and so on in a manner that may be easily imagined.

We have shewn how it is that to the single offence of wrongful occupation, considering the matter in a certain point of view, there may belong an infinite multitude of laws. But such as the offence is such is the law: therefore if the offence is *one*, the law considered in a certain point of view, must be *one* also. Considered in this point of view the law when expressed in the imperative form will run in this wise, 'Let no man perform' or 'let no man commit wrongful occupation, that is an act of wrongful occupation understood of property.' This law then as we have shewn already will in order to be explicit enough stand in need of ample, and those very ample, expositions: out of which expositions and the several distinguishable clauses in them may be constructed, by a proper method of translation, as many laws as there may be occasion for to match with the several individual offences that may come under this title.

In the formulary just exhibited the law may be considered as being couched in the conditional form; the epithet *wrongful* prefixed to the term occupation being expressive of a specificant circumstance:

viz: the *wrongfulness* of the act of occupation. But a law in the conditional form may always be converted into an unconditional provision with exceptive clauses and with exceptions taken out of it. This accordingly is the case with the law in question. Omitting in the first instance the conditionalizing or limitative epithet *wrongful*, the law in the unconditional form will stand thus, ' Let no man perform any act of occupation ': or to express the same meaning with less stiffness: ' Let no man occupy any proprietary subject.' After that come the several exceptions, which may be all included under some such single formulary as this, except he have a title so to do: and then in order to accommodate the general proposition to the particular case of each proprietary right-holder, will come the exposition of the word title and of the other leading terms, such as proprietary subject, proprietary right, proprietary right-holder, proprietary right-giver, proprietary right-taker, form of conveyance, and so forth, as above.

Of the several forms above-mentioned perhaps this latter is the clearest, and that which places the station which the fundamental law of property occupies in the most satisfactory point of view. Upon this plan the leading provision is one simple mandate: a mandate which is the primordial work of the law itself without needing the co-operation of individuals, which contains what there is universal in the law of property and what must necessarily be applicable to every *corpus juris* whatsoever.

Thus much in the way of description: a word or two here may not be amiss in the way of caution. It is not enough that the law be really complete: to have the effect of a complete law it should be made to appear such in the eyes of those who are concerned in it: to the citizen who is to take it, that is to take the whole of it together, for the measure of his conduct; to the judge who is to take it for the measure of his decision: and to the legislator, who in order to know whether anything that is requisite remains to be done should be able to see at a moment's glance what it is he hath done. It ought accordingly to be consigned to paper, and that in such a form that anyone who opens a volume of the code may lay his finger upon it and say this is one law: and that is another: here the first of these begins, and there ends: here are all the parts, and these together are what make the whole of it.

This being the description of a complete law, where then it may naturally be asked is there a specimen of such a law to be met with? I answer—nowhere. . . .   [pp. 176–183]

J. AUSTIN

The Province of Jurisprudence Determined

(ed. Hart (1954))

The Definition of a Law

The matter of jurisprudence is positive law: law, simply and strictly so called: or law set by political superiors to political inferiors. But positive law (or law, simply and strictly so called) is often confounded with objects to which it is related by resemblance, and with objects to which it is related in the way of analogy: with objects which are also signified, properly and improperly, by the large and vague expression law.

A law, in the most general and comprehensive acceptation in which the term, in its literal meaning, is employed, may be said to be a rule laid down for the guidance of an intelligent being by an intelligent being having power over him. In this the largest meaning which it has, without extension by metaphor or analogy, the term law embraces the following objects:—Laws set by God to his human creatures, and laws set by men to men.

The whole or a portion of the laws set by God to men is frequently styled the law of nature, or natural law: being, in truth, the only natural law of which it is possible to speak without a metaphor, or without a blending of objects which ought to be distinguished. But, rejecting the appellation Law of Nature as ambiguous and misleading, I name those laws or rules, as considered collectively or in a mass, the *Divine law*, or the *law of God*.

Laws set by men to men are of two leading or principal classes. Some are established by *political* superiors, sovereign and subject: by persons exercising supreme and subordinate government, in independent nations, or independent political societies. The aggregate of the rules thus established, or some aggregate forming a portion of that aggregate, is the appropriate matter of jurisprudence, general or particular. To the aggregate of the rules thus established, or to some aggregate forming a portion of that aggregate, the term law, as used simply and strictly, is exclusively applied. But, as contradistinguished to natural law, or to the law of nature (meaning, by those expressions, the law of God), the aggregate of the rules, established by political superiors, is frequently styled positive law, or law existing *by position*. As contradistinguished to the rules which I style positive morality, and on which I shall touch immediately, the aggregate of the rules, established by political superiors, may also be marked commodiously with the name of positive law. For the sake, then, of getting a name brief and distinctive at once, and agreeably to frequent usage, I style that aggregate of rules, or any portion of that aggregate, positive law: though rules, which are not established by political superiors, are also positive, or exist by position, if they be rules or laws, in the proper signification of the term.

Though some of the laws or rules, which are set by men to men, are established by political superiors, others are not established by political superiors, or are not established by political superiors in that capacity or character.

Closely analogous to human laws of this second class, are a set of objects frequently but improperly termed laws, being rules set and enforced by *mere opinion*, that is, by the opinions or sentiments held or felt by an indeterminate body of men in regard to human conduct. Instances of such a use of the term *law* are the expressions—' The law of honour'; 'The law set by fashion'; and rules of this species constitute much of what is usually termed ' International law.'

The aggregate of human laws properly so called belonging to the second of the classes above mentioned, with the aggregate of objects improperly but by close analogy termed laws, I place together in a common class, and denote them by the term *positive morality*. The name morality severs them from positive law, while the epithet positive disjoins them from the law of God. And to the end of obviating confusion, it is necessary or expedient that they should be disjoined from the latter by that distinguishing epithet. For the name morality (or morals), when standing unqualified or alone, denotes indifferently either of the following objects: namely, positive morality *as it is*, or without regard to its merits; and positive morality, *as it would be*, if it conformed to the law of God, and were, therefore, deserving of approbation.[36]

Besides the various sorts of rules which are included in the literal acceptation of the term law, and those which are by a close and striking analogy, though, improperly, termed laws, there are numerous applications of the term law, which rest upon a slender analogy and are merely metaphorical or figurative. Such is the case when we talk of laws observed by the lower animals; of laws regulating the growth or decay of vegetables; of laws determining the movements of inanimate bodies or masses.[37] For where intelligence is not, or where it is too bounded to take the name of reason, and, therefore, is too bounded to conceive the purpose of a law, there is not the will which law can work on, or which duty can incite or restrain.[38]

Having suggested the purpose of my attempt to determine the province of jurisprudence; to distinguish positive law, the appropriate matter of jurisprudence, from the various objects to which it is related by resemblance, and to which it is related, nearly or remotely, by a strong or slender analogy: I shall now state the essentials of *a law* or *rule* (taken with the largest signification which can be given to the term *properly*).

Every *law* or *rule* (taken with the largest signification which can be given to the term *properly*) is a *command*. Or, rather, laws or rules, properly so called, are a species of commands.

Now, since the term command comprises the term law, the first is the simpler as well as the larger of the two. But, simple as it is, it

---

[36] [*Cf.* Pollock and Maitland on the position of villein tenure, whose sole protection in medieval law was in the court of the villein's lord in accordance with manorial custom. "As a matter of fact, tenure in villeinage is protected, and if we choose to say that it is protected by 'positive morality' rather than by 'law properly so called,' we are bound to add that it is protected by a morality which keeps a court, which uses legal forms, which is conceived as law, or as something akin to law. The lord has a court; in that court the tenant in villeinage, even though he be personally unfree, appears as no mere tenant at will, but as holding permanently, often heritably, on fairly definite terms. He is a customary tenant . . . he holds according to the custom of the manor." (*History of English Law*, Vol. 1, p. 361).]

[37] [This suggests that normative law is the basic idea and is extended to physical law by metaphor. For the view that the actual development was the other way, see *ante*, 77.]

[38] The classification may be arranged in tabular form:

Laws properly so called   Laws improperly so called

| Laws of God | Human Laws | | Laws by analogy | Laws by metaphor |

| Positive Laws or Laws strictly so called. | Laws set by men, not as political superiors (nor in pursuance of legal right). |

Positive Morality

admits of explanation. And, since it is the key to the sciences of jurisprudence and morals, its meaning should be analysed with precision.

Accordingly, I shall endeavour, in the first instance, to analyse the meaning of ' command ': an analysis which, I fear, will task the patience of my hearers, but which they will bear with cheerfulness, or, at least, with resignation, if they consider the difficulty of performing it. The elements of a science are precisely the parts of it which are explained least easily. Terms that are the largest, and, therefore, the simplest of a series, are without equivalent expressions into which we can resolve them concisely. And when we endeavour to define them, or to translate them into terms which we suppose are better understood, we are forced upon tedious circumlocutions.

If you express or intimate a wish that I shall do or forbear from some act, and if you will visit me with an evil in case I comply not with your wish, the expression or intimation of your wish is a command.[39] A command is distinguished from other significations of desire, not by the style in which the desire is signified, but by the power and the purpose of the party commanding to inflict an evil or pain in case the desire be disregarded. If you cannot or will not harm me in case I comply not with your wish, the expression of your wish is not a command, although you utter your wish in imperative phrase. If you are able and willing to harm me in case I comply not with your wish, the expression of your wish amounts to a command, although you are prompted by a spirit of courtesy to utter it in the shape of a request. ' Preces erant, sed quibus contradici non posset.' Such is the language of Tacitus, when speaking of a petition by the soldiery to a son and lieutenant of Vespasian.

A command, then, is a signification of desire. But a command is distinguished from other significations of desire by this peculiarity: that the party to whom it is directed is liable to evil from the other, in case he comply not with the desire.

Being liable to evil from you if I comply not with a wish which you signify, I am *bound* or *obliged* by your command, or I lie under a *duty* to obey it. If, in spite of that evil in prospect, I comply not with the wish which you signify, I am said to disobey your command, or to violate the duty which it imposes.

Command and duty are, therefore, correlative terms: the meaning denoted by each being implied or supposed by the other. Or (changing

---

[39] [For Austin only a command which obliges *generally* to acts or forbearances of a *class* is a law or rule (*ibid.*, p. 93). He does not, like Blackstone, insist on generality as to *persons*. Hence *privilegia, i.e.*, laws passed in regard to an individual, are laws so far as they enjoin or forbid generally acts of a class (*ibid.*, p. 519). Thus a private divorce Act, though directed only to two persons, has general legal consequences which bring it within the category of a law. *Cf.* the recent cases of *Liyanage* v. *R.* [1967] 1 A.C. 259 and *Kariapper* v. *Wijesinha* [1968] A.C. 717. Tapper [1965] C.L.J. 271, 276, believes that Austin's motive was " to remove judgments in particular cases from the category of law." He remarks that if this was so Austin chose " a singularly blunt " instrument to achieve his objective. Why did he not limit his exclusion " to commands to do particular acts addressed to particular persons "? Tapper's suggestion is that Austin may have tried to achieve a pattern like Blackstone's ; for " persons commanded," read " acts commanded." " The demands of an Augustan balance," he comments, " seem to have outweighed those of clarity and accuracy."]

the expression) wherever a duty lies, a command has been signified; and whenever a command is signified, a duty is imposed.

The evil which will probably be incurred in case a command be disobeyed or (to use an equivalent expression) in case a duty be broken, is frequently called a *sanction*, or an *enforcement of obedience*. Or (varying the phrase) the command or the duty is said to be *sanctioned* or *enforced* by the chance of incurring the evil.[40]

Accordingly, I distribute laws proper, with such improper laws as are closely analogous to the proper, under three capital classes.

The first comprises the laws (properly so called) which are set by God to his human creatures.

The second comprises the laws (properly so called) which are set by men as political superiors, or by men, as private persons, in pursuance of legal rights.

The third comprises laws of the two following species: 1. The laws (properly so called) which are set by men to men but not by men as political superiors, nor by men, as private persons, in pursuance of legal rights: 2. The laws, which are closely analogous to laws proper, but are merely opinions or sentiments held or felt by men in regard to human conduct.—I put laws of these species into a common class, and I mark them with the common name of positive morality or positive moral rules.[41]

Positive Law and Morality

My reasons for using the two expressions ' *positive* law' and ' *positive* morality,' are the following:

There are two capital classes of human laws. The first comprises the laws (properly so called) which are set by men as political superiors, or by men, as private persons, in pursuance of legal rights. The second comprises the laws (proper and improper) which belong to the two species above mentioned.

As merely distinguished from the second, the first of those capital classes might be named simply *law*. As merely distinguished from the first, the second of those capital classes might be named simply *morality*. But both must be distinguished from the law of God: and, for the purpose of distinguishing both from the law of God, we must qualify the names *law* and *morality*. Accordingly, I style the first of those capital classes 'positive law': and I style the second of those capital classes 'positive morality.' By the common epithet *positive*, I denote that both classes flow from human sources. By the distinctive names *law* and *morality*, I denote the difference between the human sources from which the two classes respectively emanate.

---

[40] [*Cf.* H. Eysenck, who argues that the reward of criminal activity comes almost immediately, whereas the infliction of punishment, if it occurs at all, occurs at a much later time. Since the nearer a consequence is, the more powerful will be its influence, a potential thief is likely to be far more strongly motivated by the immediate satisfaction of possessing the desired object, than by the fear of ultimate retribution (*Fact and Fiction in Psychology* (1965), pp. 258–259).]

[41] [By treating " law " as an aggregate of nothing but rules, Austin fails to take into account the extent to which it consists of principles or standards such as " good faith," " reasonableness," etc. These cannot be reduced to rules, and they represent one of the main points of contact between law and the " operative " values of society (*cf. ante*, 39) and see Dworkin's criticisms of Hart, discussed *ante*, 172.]

Strictly speaking, every law properly so called is a positive law. For it is put or set by its individual or collective author, or it exists by the position or institution of its individual or collective author.

But, as opposed to the law of nature (meaning the law of God), human law of the first of those capital classes is styled by writers on jurisprudence ' positive law.' [42] This application of the expression ' positive law' was manifestly made for the purpose of obviating confusion ; confusion of human law of the first of those capital classes with that Divine law which is the measure or test of human.

And, in order to obviate similar confusion, I apply the expression ' positive morality' to human law of the second capital class. For the name *morality*, when standing unqualified or alone, may signify the law set by God, or human law of that second capital class. If you say that an act or omission violates morality, you speak ambiguously. You may mean that it violates the law which I style ' positive morality,' or that it violates the Divine law which is the measure or test of the former.

From the expression *positive law* and the expression *positive morality*, I pass to certain expressions with which they are closely connected.

The science of jurisprudence (or, simply and briefly, jurisprudence) is concerned with positive laws, or with laws strictly so called, as considered without regard to their goodness or badness.

Positive morality, as considered without regard to its goodness or badness, *might* be the subject of a science closely analogous to jurisprudence. I say ' *might* be:' since it is only in one of its branches (namely, the law of nations or international law) that positive morality, as considered without regard to its goodness or badness, has been treated by writers in a scientific or systematic manner.—For the science of positive morality, as considered without regard to its goodness or badness, current or established language will hardly afford us a name. The name *morals*, or *science of morals*, would denote it ambiguously: the name *morals*, or *science of morals*, being commonly applied (as I shall show immediately) to a department of ethics or deontology. But, since the science of jurisprudence is not unfrequently styled ' the science of positive law,' the science in question might be styled analogically ' the science of positive morality.' . . .

The science of ethics (or, in the language of Mr. Bentham, the science of deontology) may be defined in the following manner.—It affects to determine the test of positive law and morality. In other words, it affects to expound them as they should be ; as they would be if they were good or worthy of praise ; or as they would be if they conformed to an assumed measure.

The science of ethics (or, simply and briefly, ethics) consists of two

---

[42] [Positivism is generally associated with a secular approach and accordingly a total rejection of the idea of a higher law. This was certainly true in the case of Bentham, who was probably an atheist and certainly disbelieved in all " higher laws " (see Baumgardt, *op. cit.*, pp. 167, 483). (Though Letwin believes that, " if pressed, he would have revealed no very shocking moral beliefs—he generally accepted the standards of his society " (*op. cit.*, p. 139).) But positivism was not irreconcilable with a deistic approach. Austin accepted the existence of a Law of God, but he regarded this latter as only knowable by human beings through the rational principle of utility. Austin regarded this as a moral principle distinct from positive human law, and not affecting the legal validity of such law, though, nevertheless, providing a criterion of its moral desirability (see J. Austin, *Lectures on Jurisprudence*, Lecture II).]

established by men living in the negative state which is styled a state of nature or a state of anarchy: that is to say, by men who are *not* members, sovereign or subject, of any political society: others are established by sovereign individuals or bodies, but not in the character of political superiors.

Of laws properly so called which are set by subjects, some are set by subjects as subordinate political superiors; others are set by subjects as private persons: Meaning by 'private persons,' subject not in the class of subordinate political superiors, or subordinate political superiors not considered as such.—Laws set by subjects as subordinate political superiors, are positive laws: they are clothed with legal sanctions, and impose legal duties. They are set by sovereigns or states in the character of political superiors, although they are set by sovereigns circuitously or remotely. Although they are made directly by subject or subordinate authors, they are made through legal rights granted by sovereigns or states, and held by those subject authors as mere trustees for the granters. Of laws set by subjects as private persons, some are not established by sovereign or supreme authority. And these are rules of positive morality: they are not clothed with legal sanctions, nor do they oblige legally the parties to whom they are set.—But of laws set by subjects as private persons, others are set or established in pursuance of legal rights residing in the subject authors. And these are positive laws or laws strictly so called. Although they are made directly by subject authors, they are made in pursuance of rights granted or conferred by sovereigns in the character of political superiors: they legally oblige the parties to whom they are set, or are clothed with legal sanctions. They are commands of sovereigns as political superiors, although they are set by sovereigns circuitously or remotely.[44]

A law set by a subject as a private person, but in pursuance of a legal right residing in the subject author, is either a positive law purely or simply, or it is a positive law as viewed from one aspect, and a rule of positive morality as viewed from another. The person who makes the law in pursuance of the legal right, is either legally bound to make the law, or he is not. In the first case, the law is a positive law purely or simply. In the second case, the law is compounded of a positive law and a positive moral rule.

For example, A guardian may have a right over his pupil or ward, which he is legally bound to exercise, for the benefit of the pupil or ward, in a given or specified manner. Now if, in pursuance of his right, and agreeably to his duty or trust, he sets a law or rule to the pupil or ward, the law is a positive law purely or simply. It is properly a law which the state sets to the ward through its minister or instrument the guardian. It is not made by the guardian of his own spontaneous movement, or is made in pursuance of a duty which the state has imposed upon him. The position of the guardian is closely analogous to the position of subordinate political superiors; who hold their delegated powers of direct or judicial legislation as mere trustees for the sovereign granters.

44 [*Cf. Carl-Zeiss* v. *Rayner* [1967] 1 A.C. 853 where it was held that a *de jure* sovereign cannot disclaim responsibility for the acts of a subordinate body which it has set up, where those acts have been carried out with either the express or implied consent of the sovereign.]

Again: the master has legal rights, over or against his slave, which are conferred by the state upon the master for his own benefit. And, since they are conferred upon him for his own benefit, he is not legally bound to exercise or use them. Now if, in pursuance of these rights, he sets a law to his slave, the law is compounded of a positive law and a positive moral rule. Being made by sovereign authority, and clothed by the sovereign with sanctions, the law made by the master is properly a positive law. But, since it is made by the master of his own spontaneous movement, or is not made by the master in pursuance of a legal duty, it is properly a rule of positive morality, as well as a positive law. Though the law set by the master is set circuitously by the sovereign, it is set or established by the sovereign at the pleasure of the subject author. The master is not the instrument of the sovereign or state, but the sovereign or state is rather the instrument of the master.

Laws which are positive law as viewed from one aspect, but which are positive morality as viewed from another, I place simply or absolutely in the first of those capital classes. If, affecting exquisite precision, I placed them in each of those classes, I could hardly indicate the boundary by which those classes are severed without resorting to expressions of repulsive complexity and length.

It appears from the foregoing distinctions, that positive moral rules which are laws properly so called are of three kinds.—1. Those which are set by men living in a state of nature. 2. Those which are set by sovereigns, but not by sovereigns as political superiors. 3. Those which are set by subjects as private persons, and are not set by the subject authors in pursuance of legal rights.

To cite an example of rules of the first kind were superfluous labour. A man living in a state of nature may impose an imperative law: though, since the man *is* in a state of nature, he cannot impose the law in the character of sovereign, and cannot impose the law in pursuance of a legal right. And the law being *imperative* (and therefore proceeding from a *determinate* source) is a law properly so called: though, for want of a sovereign author proximate or remote, it is not a positive law but a rule of positive morality.

An imperative law set by a sovereign to a sovereign, or by one supreme government to another supreme government, is an example of rules of the second kind. Since no supreme government is in a state of subjection to another, an imperative law set by a sovereign to a sovereign is not set by its author in the character of political superior. Nor is it set by its author in pursuance of a legal right: for every legal right is conferred by a supreme government, and is conferred on a person or persons in a state of subjection to the granter. Consequently, an imperative law set by a sovereign to a sovereign is not a positive law or a law strictly so called. But being imperative (and therefore proceeding from a determinate source), it amounts to a law in the proper signification of the term, although it is purely or simply a rule of positive morality.

If they be set by subjects as private persons, and not in pursuance of legal rights, the laws following are examples of rules of the third kind: namely, imperative laws set by parents to children; imperative laws set by masters to servants: imperative laws set by lenders to borrowers; imperative laws set by patrons to parasites. Being imperative (and therefore proceeding from determinate sources), the laws foregoing are laws properly so called: though, if they be set by subjects as private persons, and be not set by their authors in pursuance of legal rights, they are not positive laws but rules of positive morality.

Again: a club or society of men, signifying its collective pleasure by a vote of its assembled members, passes or makes a law to be kept by its members severally under pain of exclusion from its meetings. Now if it be made by subjects as private persons, and be not made by its authors in pursuance of a legal right, the law voted and passed by the assembled members of the club is a further example of rules of the third kind.

The positive moral rules which are laws improperly so called, are *laws set* or *imposed by general opinion*: that is to say, by the general opinion of any class or any society of persons. For example, some are set or imposed by the general opinion of persons who are members of a profession or calling: others, by that of persons who inhabit a town or province: others, by that of a nation or independent political society: others, by that of a larger society formed of various nations.

A few species of the laws which are set by general opinion have received appropriate names.—For example, There are laws or rules imposed upon gentlemen by opinions current amongst gentlemen. And these are usually styled *the rules of honour*, or *the laws* or *law of honour*. —There are laws or rules imposed upon people of fashion by opinions current in the fashionable world. And these are usually styled *the law set by fashion*.—There are laws which regard the conduct of independent political societies in their various relations to one another: Or, rather, there are laws which regard the conduct of sovereigns or supreme governments in their various relations to one another. And laws or rules of this species, which are imposed upon nations or sovereigns by opinions current amongst nations, are usually styled *international law*.

Now a law set or imposed by general opinion is a law improperly so called. It is styled a *law* or *rule* by an analogical extension of the term. When we speak of a law set by general opinion, we denote, by that expression, the following fact.—Some intermediate body or uncertain aggregate of persons regards a kind of conduct with a sentiment of aversion or liking. In consequence of that sentiment or opinion, it is likely that they or some of them will be displeased with a party who shall pursue or not pursue conduct of that kind. And, in consequence of that displeasure, it is likely that *some* party (*what* party being undetermined) will visit the party provoking it with some evil or another.

The body by whose opinion the law is said to be set, does not command, expressly or tacitly, that conduct of the given kind shall be forborne or pursued. For, since it is not a body precisely determined or certain, it cannot, *as a body*, express or intimate a wish. As a body, it cannot signify a wish by oral or written words, or by positive or negative deportment. The so-called law or rule which its opinion is said to impose, is merely the sentiment which it feels, or the opinion which it holds, in regard to a kind of conduct.

A determinate member of the body, who opines or feels with the body, may doubtless be moved or impelled, by that very opinion or sentiment, to command that conduct of the kind shall be forborne or pursued. But the command expressed or intimated by that determinate party is not a law or rule imposed by general opinion. It is a law properly so called, set by a determinate author.—For example, The so-called law of nations consists of opinions or sentiments current among nations generally. It therefore is not law properly so called. But one supreme government may doubtless command another to forbear from a kind of conduct which the law of nations condemns. And, though it is fashioned on law which is law improperly so called, this command is a law in the proper signification of the term. Speaking precisely, the command is a rule of positive morality set by a determinate author. For, as no supreme government is in a state of subjection to another, the government commanding does not command in its character of political superior.[45] If the government receiving the command were in a state of subjection to the other, the command, though fashioned on the law of nations, would amount to a positive law. . . .[46]

. . . In consequence of the frequent coincidence of positive law and morality, and of positive law and the law of God, the true nature and fountain of positive law is often absurdly mistaken by writers upon jurisprudence. Where positive law has been fashioned on positive morality, or where positive law has been fashioned on the law of God, they forget that the copy is the creature of the sovereign, and impute it to the author of the model.

For example: Customary laws are positive laws fashioned by judicial legislation upon pre-existing customs. Now, till they become the grounds of judicial decisions upon cases, and are clothed with legal sanctions by the sovereign one or number, the customs are merely rules set by opinions of the governed, and sanctioned or enforced morally: Though, when they become the reasons of judicial decisions upon cases, and are clothed with legal sanctions by the sovereign one or number, the customs are rules of positive law as well as of positive morality. But, because the customs were observed by the governed before they were clothed with sanctions by the sovereign one or number, it is fancied that customary laws exist *as positive laws* by the institution of the private persons with whom the customs originated.[47]

Again: The portion of positive law which is parcel of the *law of nature* (or, in the language of the classical jurists, which is parcel of the *jus gentium*) is often supposed to emanate, even as positive law, from a Divine or Natural source. But (admitting the distinction of positive law into law natural and law positive) it is manifest that law natural, considered as a portion of positive, is the creature of human sovereigns, and not of the Divine monarch. To say that it emanates, as positive law, from a Divine or Natural source, is to confound positive law with law whereon it is fashioned, or with law whereunto it conforms. . . .[48]

---

[45] [Habitual obedience cannot be founded on one law. *Cf.* Raz, *op. cit.*, pp. 15–16.]

[46] [From Lecture V.]

[47] [Austin here accepts a similar theory to Bentham's on delegated legislation *ante*, 194. But Austin himself has a very much more satisfactory explanation of delegated legislation in terms of what Raz calls " obedience laws " (pp. 21–22, 166–167), *i.e.*, " laws imposing a duty to obey a certain person, if he commands." So, for example, where a local authority imposes traffic restrictions in exercise of a power conferred by the sovereign, then the sovereign wishes citizens to obey the local authority, and the local authority wishes citizens to, say, drive only one way up a particular street. As Raz remarks, " their wishes are not identical, though practically they amount to the same thing " (p. 21).]

[48] [From Lecture V.]

The existence of law is one thing; its merit or demerit is another. Whether it be or be not is one inquiry; whether it be or be not conformable to an assumed standard, is a different inquiry. This truth, when formally announced as an abstract proposition, is so simple and glaring that it seems idle to insist upon it.[49] But simple and glaring as it is, when enunciated in abstract expressions, the enumeration of the instances in which it has been forgotten would fill a volume.[50]

. . . For example: The commons delegate their powers to the members of the commons' house, in the second of the above-mentioned modes. During the period for which those members are elected, or during the parliament of which those members are a limb, the sovereignty is possessed by the king and the peers, with the members of the commons' house, and not by the king and the peers, with the delegating body of the commons. The powers of the commons are delegated so absolutely to the members of the commons' house, that this representative assembly might concur with the king and the peers in defeating the principal ends for which it is elected and appointed. It might concur, for instance, in making a statute which would lengthen its own duration from seven to twenty years; or which would annihilate completely the actual constitution of the government, by transferring the sovereignty to the king or the peers from the tripartite body wherein it resides at present.

But though the commons delegate their powers in the second of the above-mentioned modes, it is clear that they might delegate them subject to a trust or trusts. The representative body, for instance, might be bound to use those powers consistently with specific ends pointed out by the electoral: or it might be bound, more generally and vaguely, not to annihilate, or alter essentially, the actual constitution of the supreme government. Where such a trust is imposed by a sovereign or supreme body (or by a smaller body forming a component part of it), the trust is enforced by legal, or by merely moral sanctions. The representative body is bound by a positive law or laws: or it is merely bound by a fear that it may offend the bulk of the community, in case it shall break the engagement which it has contracted with the electoral.

And here I may briefly remark, that this last is the position which really is occupied by the members of the commons' house. Adopting the language of most of the writers who have treated of the British Constitution, I commonly suppose that the king and the lords, with the members of the commons' house, form a tripartite body which is sovereign or supreme. But, speaking accurately, the members of the commons' house are merely trustees for the body by which they are elected and appointed: and, consequently, the sovereignty always resides in the king and the peers, with the electoral body of the commons. That a trust is imposed

---

[49] [After referring to a passage in Blackstone to the effect that no human law which conflicts with divine law is binding, Austin makes the following comment: " Now, to say [this] is to talk stark nonsense. The most pernicious laws, have been, and are continually enforced as laws by judicial tribunals. Suppose an act innocuous, or positively beneficial, be prohibited by the sovereign under the penalty of death; if I commit this act I shall be tried and condemned, and if I object to the sentence, on the ground that it is contrary to the law of God, . . . the Court of Justice will demonstrate the inconclusiveness of my reasoning by hanging me up ": J. Austin, *Lectures on Jurisprudence* (ed. Campbell), I, p 215.]

[50] [Appended to Lecture V, p. 214.]

by the party delegating, and that the party representing engages to discharge the trust, seems to be imported by the correlative expressions *delegation* and *representation*. It were absurd to suppose that the delegating empowers the representative party to defeat or abandon any of the purposes for which the latter is appointed: to suppose, for example, that the commons empower their representatives in parliament to relinquish their share in the sovereignty to the king and the lords.—The supposition that the powers of the commons are delegated absolutely to the members of the commons' house probably arose from the following causes. 1. The trust imposed by the electoral body upon the body representing them in parliament, is tacit rather than express: it arises from the relation between the bodies as delegating and representative parties, rather than from oral or written instructions given by the former to the latter. But since it arises from that relation, the trust is general and vague. The representatives are merely bound, generally and vaguely, to abstain from any such exercise of the delegated sovereign powers as would tend to defeat the purposes for which they are elected and appointed. 2. The trust is simply enforced by moral sanctions. In other words, that portion of constitutional law which regards the duties of the representative towards the electoral body, is positive morality merely. Nor is this extraordinary. For (as I shall show hereafter) all constitutional law in every country, whatever, is, as against the sovereign, in that predicament. . . .[51]

. . . In the case of a *composite state,* or a *supreme federal government*, the several united governments of the several united societies, together with a government common to those several societies, are jointly sovereign in each of those several societies, and also in the larger society arising from the federal union. Or, since the political powers of the common or general government were relinquished and conferred upon it by those several united governments, the nature of a composite state may be described more accurately thus. As compacted by the common government which they have concurred in creating, and to which they have severally delegated portions of their several sovereignties, the several governments of the several united societies are jointly sovereign in each and all.

It will appear on a moment's reflection, that the common or general government is not sovereign or supreme. A government supreme and federal, and a government supreme but not federal, are merely distinguished by the following difference. Where the supreme government is not federal, each of the several governments, considered in that character, is purely subordinate: or none of the several governments, considered in that character, partakes of the sovereignty. But where the supreme government is properly federal, each of the several governments, *which were immediate parties to the federal compact,* is, in that character, a limb of the sovereign body. Consequently, although they are subject to the sovereign body of which they are constituent members, those several governments, even considered as such, are not purely in a state of subjection.—But since those several governments, even considered as such, are not purely in a state of subjection, the common or general govern-

---

[51] [For, as against the sovereign itself, there is no political superior who has laid it down. From Lecture VI.]

ment which they have concurred in creating is not sovereign or supreme. . . .

. . . Now since the political powers of the common or general government are merely delegated to it by the several united governments, it is not a constituent member of the sovereign body, but is merely its subject minister. Consequently, the sovereignty of each of the united societies, and also of the larger society arising from the union of all, resides in the united governments *as forming one aggregate body*: that is to say, as signifying their joint pleasure, or the joint pleasure of a majority of their number, agreeably to the modes or forms determined by their federal compact. By that aggregate body, the powers of the general government were conferred and determined: and by that aggregate body, its powers may be revoked, abridged, or enlarged.—To that aggregate body, the several united governments, though not merely subordinate, are truly in a state of subjection.

The supreme government of the United States of America, agrees (I believe) with the foregoing general description of a supreme federal government. I believe that the common government, or the government consisting of the congress and the president of the United States, is merely a subject minister of the United States' governments. I believe that none of the latter is properly sovereign or supreme, even in the state or political society of which it is the immediate chief. And, lastly, I believe that the sovereignty of each of the states, and also of the larger state arising from the federal union, resides in the states' governments as *forming one aggregate body* : meaning by a state's government, not its ordinary legislature, but the body of its citizens which appoints its ordinary legislature, and which, the union apart, is properly sovereign therein. . . .[52]

The Definition of Sovereignty

The superiority which is styled sovereignty, and the independent political society which sovereignty implies, is distinguished from other superiority, and from other society, by the following marks or characters.—1. The *bulk* of the given society are in a *habit* of obedience or submission to a *determinate* and *common* superior: let that common superior be a certain individual person, or a certain body or aggregate of individual persons. 2. That certain individual, or that certain body of individuals, is *not* in a habit of obedience to a determinate human superior. Laws (improperly so called) which opinion sets or imposes, may permanently affect the conduct of that certain individual or body. To express or tacit com-

---

[52] The Constitution of the United States, or the constitution of their general government, was framed by deputies from the several states in 1787. It may (I think) be inferred from the fifth article, that the sovereignty of each of the states, and also of the larger state arising from the federal union, resides in the states' governments *as forming one aggregate body*. It is provided by that article, that " the congress, whenever two-thirds of both houses shall deem it necessary shall propose amendments to this constitution: or, on the application of the legislatures of two-thirds of the several states, shall call a convention for proposing amendments: which amendments, in either case, shall be valid to all intents and purposes, as part of this constitution, *when ratified by the legislatures of* three-fourths *of the several states, or by convention in* three-fourths *thereof.*" See also the tenth section of the first article: in which section, some of the disabilities of the several states' governments are determined expressly.

one of two positions. If the bulk of each of the parties be in a habit of obedience to its head, the given society is broken into two or more societies, which, perhaps, may be styled independent political societies.—If the bulk of each of the parties be not in that habit of obedience, the given society is simply or absolutely in a state of nature or anarchy. It is either resolved into its individual elements, or into numerous societies of an extremely limited size: of a size so extremely limited, that they could hardly be styled societies independent and political. For, as I shall show hereafter, a given independent society would hardly be styled political, in case it fell short of a number which cannot be fixed with precision, but which may be called considerable, or not extremely minute.

(3) In order that a given society may form a society political, the generality or bulk of its members must habitually obey a superior *determinate* as well as common.

On this position I shall not insist here. For I have shown sufficiently . . . that no indeterminate party can command expressly or tacitly, or can receive obedience or submission: that no indeterminate body is capable of corporate conduct, or is capable, as a body, of positive or negative deportment.

(4) It appears from what has preceded, that, in order that a given society may form a society political, the bulk of its members must be in a habit of obedience to a certain and common superior. But, in order that the given society may form a society political and independent, that certain superior must *not* be habitually obedient to a determinate human superior. He may render occasional submission to commands of determinate parties. But the society is not independent, although it may be political, in case that certain superior habitually obeys the commands of a certain person or body.

Let us suppose, for example, that a viceroy obeys habitually the author of his delegated powers. And, to render the example complete, let us suppose that the viceroy receive habitual obedience from the generality or bulk of the persons who inhabit his province. The viceroy is not sovereign within the limits of his province, nor are he and its inhabitants an independent political society. The viceroy, and (through the viceroy) the generality or bulk of its inhabitants, are habitually obedient or submissive to the sovereign of a larger society. He and the inhabitants of his province are therefore in a state of subjection to the sovereign of that larger society. He and the inhabitants of his province are a society political but subordinate.

A natural society, or a society in a state of nature, is composed of persons who are connected by mutual intercourse, but are not members, sovereign or subject, of any society political. None of the persons who compose it lives in the positive state which is styled a state of subjection: or all the persons who compose it live in the negative state which is styled a state of independence.

Considered as entire communities, and considered in respect of one another, independent political societies live, it is commonly said, in a state of nature. The expression, however, is not perfectly apposite. Since all the members of each of the related societies are members of a society political, none of the related societies is strictly in a state of nature: nor can the larger society formed by their mutual intercourse be styled strictly a natural society. Speaking strictly, the sovereign and subject members of each of the related societies form a society political: but the sovereign portion of each of the related societies lives in the negative condition which is styled a state of independence.

Society formed by the intercourse of independent political societies, is the province of international law, or of the law obtaining between nations. For (adopting a current expression) international law is conversant about the conduct of independent political societies considered as entire communities: *circa negotia et causas gentium integrarum.* Speaking with greater precision, international law, or the law obtaining between nations, regards the conduct of sovereigns considered as related to one another.

And hence it inevitably follows, that the law obtaining between nations is not positive law: for every positive law is set by a given sovereign to a person or persons in a state of subjection to its author. As I have already intimated, the law obtaining between nations is law (improperly so called) set by general opinion.[55] The duties which it imposes are enforced by moral sanctions: by fear on the part of nations, or by fear on the part of sovereigns, of provoking general hostility, and incurring its probable evils, in case they shall violate maxims generally received and respected. . . .[56]

The Limits of Sovereign Power

. . . Every positive law, or every law simply and strictly so called, is set, directly or circuitously, by a sovereign person or body, to a member or members of the independent political society wherein that person or body is sovereign or supreme. It follows that the power of a monarch properly so called, or the power of a sovereign number in its collegiate and sovereign capacity, is incapable of *legal* limitation.[57] A monarch or sovereign number bound by a legal duty, were subject to a higher or superior sovereign: that is to say, a monarch or sovereign number bound by a legal duty, were sovereign and not sovereign. Supreme power limited by positive law is a flat contradiction in terms.

Nor would a political society escape from legal despotism, although the power of the sovereign were bounded by legal restraints. The power of the superior sovereign immediately imposing the restraints, or the power of some other sovereign superior to that superior, would still be absolutely free from the fetters of positive law. For unless the imagined restraints were ultimately imposed by a sovereign not in a state of subjection to a higher or superior sovereign, a series of sovereigns ascending to infinity would govern the imagined community which is impossible and absurd.[58]

. . . In short, when we style an act of a sovereign an unconstitutional

---

[55] [The distinction drawn by Aquinas between the coercive and the directive authority of law seems to be of some value here. (See Aquinas, *Selected Political Writings*, ed. A. P. D'Entreves, pp. 136–141.) International law may be said to have a directive force upon sovereign states bound by that law, even in the absence of a coercive authority.]

[56] [From Lecture VI.]

[57] [*Cf.* Bentham, *ante,* 195.]

[58] [*i.e.,* absurd on Austin's assumption that law is a derivative of sovereignty, rather than that sovereignty is itself a product of law.]

act (with that more general import which is sometimes given to the epithet), we mean, I believe, this: That the act is inconsistent with some given principle or maxim: that the given supreme government has expressly adopted the principle, or, at least, has habitually observed it: that the bulk of the given society, or the bulk of its influential members, regard the principle with approbation: and that, since the supreme government has habitually observed the principle, and since the bulk of the society regard it with approbation, the act in question must thwart the expectations of the latter, and must shock their opinions and sentiments. Unless we mean this, we merely mean that we deem the act in question generally pernicious: or that, without a definite reason for the disapprobation which we feel, we regard the act with dislike.

The epithet unconstitutional as applied to conduct of a sovereign, and as used with the meaning which is more special and definite, imports that the conduct in question conflicts with constitutional *law*. And by the expression *constitutional law*, I mean the positive morality, or the compound of positive morality and positive law, which fixes the constitution or structure of the given supreme government. I mean the positive morality, or the compound of positive morality and positive law, which determines the character of the person, or the respective characters of the persons, in whom, for the time being, the sovereignty shall reside: and, supposing the government in question an aristocracy or government of a number, which determines moreover the mode wherein the sovereign powers shall be shared by the constituent members of the sovereign number or body.[59]

J. BRYCE

Studies in History and Jurisprudence

(1901, vol. 2)

Legal Sovereignty (De Iure)

For the purposes of the lawyer a more definite conception is required. The sovereign authority is to him the person (or body) to whose directions the law attributes legal force, the person in whom resides as of right the ultimate power either of laying down general rules or of issuing isolated rules or commands, whose authority is that of the law itself. It is in this sense, and in this sense only, that the jurist is concerned with the question who is sovereign in a given community. In every normal modern State there exist many rules purporting to bind the citizen, and many public officers who are entitled, each in his proper sphere, to do certain acts or issue certain directions. Who has the right to make the rules? Who has the right to appoint and assign functions to the officers? The person or body to whom in the last resort the law attributes this right is the legally supreme power, or Sovereign, in the State. There may be intermediate authorities exercising delegated powers. Legal sovereignty evidently cannot reside in them; the search for it must be continued till the highest and ultimate source of law has been reached.[60]   [pp. 51–52]

---

[59] [From Lecture VI.]
[60] [*Cf.* Kelsen's hierarchy of norms, *post*, 271.]

J. Bryce

Practical Sovereignty (De Facto)

We may now turn back to the more popular meaning in which the Sovereignty is used by others than lawyers. Even to the ordinary laym. it generally seems to convey some sort of notion of legal right, yet it may be, and sometimes has been, used to denote simply the strongest force in the State, whether that force has or has not any recognised legal supremacy. This strongest force may be a king, or an assembly, or an oligarchic group controlling a king or an assembly, or an army, or the chief or chiefs of an army. It may be and ought to be the legal sovereign, or it may be quite distinct from the legal sovereign and possess no admitted status in the Constitution. The expression is perhaps most frequent in the phrase 'Sovereign Power,' which carries with it the idea of its being, whether legal or not, at any rate irresistible. We may define this dominant force, whom we may call the Practical Sovereign, as the person (or body of persons) who can make his (or their) will prevail whether with the law or against the law. He (or they) is the *de facto* ruler, the person to whom obedience is actually paid. [pp. 59–60]

The Relations of Legal to Practical Sovereignty

The Sovereign *de iure* may also be the sovereign *de facto*. He ought to be so ; that is to say, the plan of a well-regulated State requires that Legal Right and Actual Power should be united in the same person or body. Right ought to have on its side, available for its enforcement, physical force and the habit of obedience. Where Sovereignty *de facto* is disjoined from Sovereignty *de iure*, there will not necessarily be a collision, because the former power may act through the latter. But there is always a danger that the laws will be overridden by the Practical Sovereign and disobeyed by the citizens. [p. 64]

W. J. REES

The Theory of Sovereignty Restated [61]

1. The word ['sovereign'] has been used by some as equivalent to a *supreme legal authority*. Those who have used the word in this way have not usually thought it necessary to define what they mean by authority, or to say how authority is to be distinguished from power or influence. It is clear, however, from the way in which they have written, that they have meant to draw some important distinction between these concepts. 'Let us notice in the first place', writes Lord Lindsay, 'that the doctrine of sovereignty is properly concerned with the question of authority. It is not properly concerned with questions of force or power as such'.[62] This is predominantly the sense in which the word was used by John Austin, and by the lawyers of the Austinian school. I shall call this, sovereignty in the legal sense.

2. The word 'sovereign' has been used by others to mean a *supreme legal authority in so far as it is also a completely moral authority*. This is sovereignty as understood by Rousseau and the Hegelians. 'The

[61] [Reprinted from *Mind* (1950) in *Philosophy, Politics and Society* (1956), ed. Laslett, to which page references are here given.]
[62] *The Modern Democratic State*, vol. 1, pp. 217–218.

overeign ', says Rousseau, ' merely by virtue of what it is, is always what
it should be '. ' Sovereignty ', says Bosanquet, ' is the exercise of the
General Will ', which ' is expressed in law, in so far as law is what it
ought to be '.[63] It is, therefore, a species of sovereignty in the previous
sense. For that reason, it is not always clear that a person who uses the
word in this way is using it necessarily in a way which is different from
the previous one. But we can, in fact, be sure that a different sense is
involved wherever there is clear evidence that the writer would, in
addition, deny the title of sovereign to a supreme legal authority which
is not, in his opinion, a completely moral authority. When the word is
used in this way, I shall say that it is used in the moral sense.

3. For another group of philosophers the word has meant *a supreme
coercive power exercised by a determinate body of persons possessing a
monopoly of certain instruments of coercion.* They have not usually
defined what they mean by coercive power, nor clearly stated how it is
to be distinguished from legal authority or political influence. But it has
been generally understood that power in this sense is to be distinguished
from legal authority at least in one respect, namely, that its exercise may
sometimes be extra-legal. In this sense, the sovereign is a determinate
body of persons capable of *enforcing* decisions against any likely opposition, no matter who *makes*, or *otherwise carries out*, those decisions.
Usually such a body consists of a professional police or a standing
army ; usually, too, the decisions which it enforces are those of Parlia-
ments, Ministries and Courts, but they may be the analogous decisions of
persons who have no legal authority to make such decisions, although
such persons may acquire such legal authority in virtue of their decisions
being enforced, e.g., the dissolution of the Long Parliament by Cromwell,
or the overthrow of the Directory by Napoleon. This use of the word
' sovereign ' is implied in Lord Bryce's concept of the Practical Sovereign,
which he defined as ' the strongest force in the State, whether that force
has or has not any recognised legal supremacy '.[64] T. H. Green also
wrote as if he thought the word should ordinarily be used in this or
some similar sense: ' the term " sovereign " is best kept to the ordinary
usage in which it signifies a determinate person or persons charged
with the supreme coercive function of the state '.[65] I shall call this,
sovereignty in the institutionally coercive sense.

4. The word has again been used by some as equivalent to a *supreme
coercive power exercised habitually and co-operatively by all, or nearly
all, the members of a community.* Locke speaks variously of this kind of
supreme coercive power as ' the force of the community ', ' the force of
the majority ', and ' all the force of all the people ', in such a way as to
imply a distinction between this and the coercive power of a professional
police or a standing army.[66] T. H. Green, although he did not favour the
usage, held that the word *could* be used in this, or a very similar, way.
' A majority of citizens *can* be conceived as exercising a supreme coercive power. . . . But as the multitude is not everywhere supreme, the
assertion of its sovereignty has to be put in the form that it is sovereign
" *de jure* ".' (p. 109.) This is also a meaning of the word which has

[63] *The Philosophical Theory of the State*, pp. 232 and 107.
[64] *Studies in History and Jurisprudence*, p. 511.
[65] *Lectures on the Principles of Political Obligation*, p. 103.
[66] For examples, see *Treatise*, Book II, paras. 3, 88, 96, 130, 131.

gainst Bodin as follows: ' The government which acts as its (Professor Laski means the state's) sovereign organ never, as a matter of history, has the prospect of permanence if it consistently seeks to be absolute. Civil War and Revolution in the England of the seventeenth century, 1789 in France, 1917 in Russia, are all of them footnotes to the problem of sovereignty '.[69] I shall call this, sovereignty in the permanent sense.

We are now in a position to answer the first of the traditional questions about sovereignty, namely, Is it necessary that there should be a sovereign in every state?

1. If we are using the word ' sovereign ' in the legal sense, it is not *logically* necessary that there should exist a sovereign in every state, on any of the three definitions of the word ' state ',[70] since it is clearly not self-contradictory to say that there does not exist in a state a supreme legal authority. But it is, however, *causally* necessary that there should exist a sovereign in every state, on any of our three definitions. I am now using the word ' cause ' in the sense in which it is normally used in the practical sciences, and which has been defined by Collingwood to mean ' an event or state of things which it is in our power to produce or prevent, and by producing or preventing which we can produce or prevent that whose cause it is said to be '. In this sense it is causally necessary that a sovereign should exist in every state, since, in practice, government can only be carried on by means of laws, and laws can only be effectively administered if there exists some final legal authority beyond which there is no further legal appeal. In the absence of such a final legal authority no legal issue could ever be certainly decided, and government would become impossible.

2. If, however, we take the word ' sovereign ' in the moral sense, and if, in addition, we use the word ' state ' in its second, or Hegelian, sense, then it is *logically* necessary that there should exist a sovereign in every state. For if the supreme legal authority which exists in a ' state ' is not a completely moral authority, that ' state ' is not an ideally organised society, that is, it is not a state on the present definition. This is an analytical proposition derived solely from the definitions of the terms used. But on any other use of the word ' state ', of course, it is neither logically nor causally necessary that there should exist in any state a sovereign in this sense.

3. It is not *logically* necessary that there should exist in a state, on any of the three definitions, a sovereign in the coercive sense, since again, it is not self-contradictory to say that there does not exist in a state a supreme coercive power. But it is, nevertheless, *causally* necessary, in the present state of society, that there should exist in the state—senses (1) and (2)—a sovereign either in the socially coercive or in the institutionally coercive sense. Since it is a fact that many men in their present state are prone to disobey the law, it is necessary, if laws are to be effective, that they should be capable of being enforced. But laws can only be enforced in one of two ways: either by the habitual and co-operative exercise of coercive power in support of the law by indeterminate but exceedingly numerous persons in society, or else by the exercise of

---

[69] *Grammar of Politics*, p. 49.

[70] [The three definitions given are:—a politically organised society; a politically organised society in so far as it is ideally organised; government as an institution.]

ued, where the actions of those who exercise the authority, in those
aspects in which they do exercise it, are not subject to any exercise by
other persons of the kind of authority which they are exercising . . .

. . . the definitions now given differ in two respects from the definitions
given by Austin: (1) the definition of law is wider and designed to include
customary law as well as case law and statute law, and (2) legal
sovereignty is defined in terms of law rather than vice versa. The latter
point has important implications, in that it enables us to reduce constitutional law, as it exists in either the United States or in Great Britain,
to positive law. This is theoretically important, since it enables us to
bring the theory of legal sovereignty into line with the more fundamental
aspects of constitutional and federal government. Moreover, it enables
us to do this without necessarily abandoning the command theory of
law . . . [pp. 68–69]

HARRIS AND OTHERS v. DÖNGES AND ANOTHER

Supreme Court of South Africa

[1952] 1 T.L.R. 1245

By s. 152 of the South Africa Act, 1909 (an Act of Parliament of the
United Kingdom), the Parliament of the Union of South Africa may by
law repeal or alter any of the provisions of that Act provided that certain
sections (the "entrenched" sections), including s. 152, can only be
repealed or altered by two-thirds of both Houses of Parliament sitting
together.

By s. 2 (2) of the Statute of Westminster, 1931, no law made after the
commencement of that Act by the Parliament of a Dominion (including
the Union) shall be void or inoperative on the ground that it is repugnant
to the provisions of any existing Act of Parliament of the United
Kingdom.

A law made by "the Parliament" of a Dominion in that provision
means, in relation to the Union of South Africa, a law made by the
Union Parliament functioning either bicamerally or unicamerally in
accordance with the requirements of the South Africa Act; the
sovereignty of the Union Parliament is divided between Parliament as
ordinarily constituted (sitting bicamerally) and as constituted under the
proviso to s. 152 of the South Africa Act. While the Statute of Westminster conferred new powers on the Parliament of the Union, it in no
way prescribes how that Parliament must function in exercising those
powers. Accordingly, the Union Parliament sitting bicamerally has no
power to repeal or alter any of the entrenched sections of the South
Africa Act.[74]

CENTLIVRES C.J. . . .

Mr. Beyers then contended that no country which, like the Union,

74 [Austin's theory of unlimited sovereignty answered this question, what constitutes
the sovereign, by treating this as a mere issue of *fact*. Few are prepared to go
with him on this point. The present South African cases raise, in an acute form,
what constitutes an act of sovereignty. Is a sovereign Parliament free to adopt
any procedure it likes? Can, *e.g.*, the English Parliament, without a prior Act
authorising this, pass legislation at a joint session of Lords and Commons?
Most would agree with Centlivres C.J. (*post*, 234) that it cannot.]

ATTORNEY-GENERAL FOR THE STATE OF NEW SOUTH WALES AND OTHERS v. TRETHOWAN AND OTHERS

High Court of Australia

Commonwealth L.R. (1931), Vol. 44, p. 394

Sec. 7A of the *Constitution Act*, 1902–29 (N.S.W.) provided:—" 7A (1) The Legislative Council shall not be abolished nor, subject to the provisions of sub-section 6 of this section, shall its constitution or powers be altered except in the manner provided in this section. (2) A Bill for any purpose within sub-section 1 of this section shall not be presented to the Governor or for His Majesty's assent until the Bill has been approved by the electors in accordance with this section. . . . (6) The provisions of this section shall be extended to any Bill for the repeal or amendment of this section."

Held, by *Rich, Starke* and *Dixon* JJ. (*Gavan Duffy* C.J. and *McTiernan* J. dissenting), that a repeal of this provision cannot be enacted unless it is submitted to and approved by a majority of the electors because it requires a manner and form in which a law shall be passed respecting powers of the Legislature within the meaning of sec. 5 of the *Colonial Laws Validity Act*, 1865; and, further, by *Rich* J. because, *quoad* the power to abolish the Legislative Council, it introduced into the legislative body a new element, namely, the electorate.

STARKE J. . . .

. . . Because of the supremacy of the Imperial Parliament over the law, the Courts merely apply its legislative enactments and do not examine their validity, but because the law over which the Imperial Parliament is supreme determines the powers of a legislature in a Dominion, the Courts must decide upon the validity as well as the application of the statutes of that legislature. It must not be supposed, however, that all difficulties would vanish if the full doctrine of parliamentary supremacy could be invoked. An Act of the British Parliament which contained a provision that no Bill repealing any part of the Act including the part so restraining its own repeal should be presented for the royal assent unless the Bill were first approved by the electors, would have the force of law until the Sovereign actually did assent to a Bill for its repeal.[81] In strictness it would be an unlawful proceeding to present such a Bill for the royal assent before it had been approved by the electors. If, before the Bill

---

heads while they are passing an Act if they like." For to sit (or stand on their heads) bicamerally where the law requires a joint session is to act as a body which is not Parliament for this purpose. See, further, Heuston in Guest, *Oxford Essays in Jurisprudence* (1961), Chap. 8.]

[81] [This raises the question how far procedural fetters may impose rigidity even on a sovereign Parliament. Suppose, *e.g.*, the English Parliament abolished the Upper House, or required a referendum before certain legislation could be passed. Could the original Parliament still continue to legislate in disregard of these developments? Dicey suggested that nothing short of *destruction* of the old constitution would suffice, *sed quaere*, what amounts to destruction? The New Zealand Constitutional Reform Committee of 1952 certainly was of opinion that if an Act required a referendum before abolishing a second Chamber, a later Act could still effect such abolition without a referendum. *Cf.* the discussion on the then projected Canadian Bill of Rights, in [1959] 37 Can.B.R. pp. 130–132.]

received the assent of the Crown, it was found possible, as appears to have been done in this appeal, to raise for judicial decision the question whether it was lawful to present the Bill for that assent, the Courts would be bound to pronounce it unlawful to do so. Moreover, if it happened that, notwithstanding the statutory inhibition, the Bill did receive the royal assent although it was not submitted to the electors, the Courts might be called upon to consider whether the supreme legislative power in respect of the matter had in truth been exercised in the manner required for its authentic expression and by the elements in which it had come to reside. But the answer to this question, whether evident or obscure, would be deduced from the principle of parliamentary supremacy over the law. This principle, from its very nature, cannot determine the character or the operation of the constituent powers of the Legislature of New South Wales which are the result of statute.[82] It is true that these constituent powers were meant to give to the constitution of New South Wales as much of the flexibility which in Great Britain arises from the supremacy of Parliament as was thought compatible with the unity of the Empire, the authority of the Crown and the ultimate sovereignty of the Imperial Parliament. But this consideration, although generally of importance, affords small help in a question whether the constituent authority of a legislature in a Dominion suffices to enable it to impose a condition or a restraint upon the exercise of its power. The difficulty of the supreme Legislature lessening its own powers does not arise from the flexibility of the constitution. On the contrary, it may be said that it is precisely the point at which the flexibility of the British constitution ceases to be absolute. Because it rests upon the supremacy over the law, some changes which detract from that supremacy cannot be made by law effectively. The necessary limitations upon the flexibility of the constitution of New South Wales result from a consideration of exactly an opposite character. They arise directly or indirectly from the sovereignty of the Imperial Parliament. But in virtue of its sovereignty it was open to the Imperial Parliament itself to give, or to empower the Legislature of New South Wales to give, to the constitution of that State as much or as little rigidity as might be proper.   [pp. 426–427]

BLACKBURN v. ATTORNEY-GENERAL

Court of Appeal, Civil Division

Lord Denning MR, Salmon and Stamp LJJ

[1971] 2 All E.R. 1380

The plaintiff brought two actions against the Attorney-General seeking declarations to the effect that on entry into the Common Market, signature of the Treaty of Rome by Her Majesty's government would be in breach of the law because the government would thereby be surrendering in part the sovereignty of the Crown in Parliament for ever. No agreement had yet been reached to sign the treaty but it was accepted by the court that signature of the treaty would be irreversible and would limit the sovereignty of the United Kingdom. Further, it was assumed by the court that on signing the treaty many regulations made by the European Economic Community would auto-

---

[82] [*Cf. Harper v. Secretary of State for Home Department* [1955] Ch. 238, 253.]

matically become binding on the United Kingdom, and that the courts would have to follow decisions of the European Court in certain defined respects such as the construction of the treaty.[83] The plaintiff appealed from orders striking out his statements of claim and dismissing the actions as showing no reasonable cause of action.   [p. 1380]

Lord Denning MR

. . . In this case Mr Blackburn—as he has done before [84]—has shown eternal vigilance in support of the law. This time he is concerned about the application of Her Majesty's government to join the Common Market and to sign the Treaty of Rome. He brings two actions against the Attorney-General, in which he seeks declarations to the effect that, by signing the Treaty of Rome, Her Majesty's government will surrender in part the sovereignty of the Crown in Parliament and will surrender it for ever. He says that in so doing the government will be acting in breach of the law. The Attorney-General has applied to strike out the statements of claim on the ground that they disclose no reasonable cause of action. The master and the judge have struck them out. Mr Blackburn, with our leave, appeals to this court. He thinks it is important to clear the air.

Much of what Mr Blackburn says is quite correct. It does appear that if this country should go into the Common Market and sign the Treaty of Rome, it means that we will have taken a step which is irreversible. The sovereignty of these islands will thenceforward be limited. It will not be ours alone but will be shared with others. Mr Blackburn referred us to a decision by the European Court of Justice, *Costa* v. *ENEL* [85] in February 1964, in which the court in its judgment said:

'. . . the member-States, albeit within limited spheres, have restricted their sovereign rights and created a body of law applicable both to their nationals and to themselves.'

Mr Blackburn points out that many regulations made by the European Economic Community will become automatically binding on the people of this country; and that all the courts of this country, including the House of Lords, will have to follow the decisions of the European Court in certain defined respects, such as the construction of the treaty.

I will assume that Mr Blackburn is right in what he says on those matters. Nevertheless, I do not think these courts can entertain these actions. Negotiations are still in progress for us to join the Common Market. No agreement has been reached. No treaty has been signed. Even if a treaty is signed, it is elementary that these courts take no notice of treaties as such. We take no notice of treaties until they are embodied in laws enacted by Parliament, and then only to the extent that Parliament tells us. That was settled in a case about a treaty between the Queen of England and the Emperor of China. It is *Rustomjee* v. *Reginam.*[86] . . .

---

83 [On this see G. Bebr, 34 M.L.R. 481 ; Wade, 88 L.Q.R. 1.]
84 [See *R.* v. *Commissioner of Police, ex parte Blackburn* [1968] 2 Q.B. 118, referred to *ante,* 166.]   85 [1964] C.M.L.R. 425 at p. 455.
86 (1876) 2 Q.B.D. 69. [But Community treaties are not like ordinary treaties : they create a new legal order. See Bebr, *op. cit.,* at pp. 497–498 on the recent judgment of the Belgian *Cour de Cassation* of May 27, 1971. De Smith (34 M.L.R. 597, 604) comments: " It is too early to advance such an argument before a U.K. court with any prospect of success."]

Mr Blackburn acknowledged the general principle, but he urged that this proposed treaty is in a category by itself, in that it diminishes the sovereignty of Parliament over the people of this country. I cannot accept the distinction. The general principle applies to this treaty as to any other. The treaty-making power of this country rests not in the courts, but in the Crown; that is, Her Majesty acting on the advice of her Ministers. When her Ministers negotiate and sign a treaty, even a treaty of such paramount importance as this proposed one, they act on behalf of the country as a whole. They exercise the prerogative of the Crown. Their action in so doing cannot be challenged or questioned in these courts.

Mr Blackburn takes a second point. He says that, if Parliament should implement the treaty by passing an Act of Parliament for this purpose, it will seek to do the impossible. It will seek to bind its successors. According to the treaty, once it is signed, we are committed to it irrevocably. Once in the Common Market, we cannot withdraw from it. No Parliament can commit us, says Mr Blackburn, to that extent. He prays in aid the principle that no Parliament can bind its successors, and that any Parliament can reverse any previous enactment. He refers to what Professor Maitland said about the Act of Union between England and Scotland. Professor Maitland in his Constitutional History of England, wrote [87]:

> 'We have no irrepealable laws; all laws may be repealed by the ordinary legislature, even the conditions under which the English and Scottish Parliaments agreed to merge themselves in the Parliament of Great Britain.'

We have all been brought up to believe that, in legal theory, one Parliament cannot bind another and that no Act is irreversible. But legal theory does not always march alongside political reality. Take the Statute of Westminster 1931, which takes away the power of Parliament to legislate for the dominions. Can anyone imagine that Parliament could or would reverse that statute? Take the Acts which have granted independence to the dominions and territories overseas. Can anyone imagine that Parliament could or would reverse those laws and take away their independence? Most clearly not. Freedom once given cannot be taken away. Legal theory must give way to practical politics. It is as well to remember the remark of Lord Sankey LC in *British Coal Corpn.* v. *Regem.*[88]

> ' . . . the Imperial Parliament could, as a matter of abstract law, repeal or disregard s. 4 of the Statute [of Westminster]. But that is theory and has no relation to realities.'

What are the realities here? If Her Majesty's Ministers sign this treaty and Parliament enacts provisions to implement it, I do not envisage that Parliament would afterwards go back on it and try to withdraw from it. But, if Parliament should do so, then I say we will consider that event when it happens. We will then say whether Parliament can lawfully do it or not.

Both sides referred us to the valuable article by Professor H. W. R.

---

[87] [At p. 332; *cf.* Bentham's attitude, *ante*, 195.]
[88] [1935] A.C. 500 at 520; [1935] All E.R. Rep. 139 at 146. [*Cf. Ibrablebbe* v. *R.* [1964] A.C. 900, 918, 924.]

Wade in the Cambridge Law Journal [89] in which he said that ' sovereignty
is a political fact for which no purely legal authority can be constituted.'
That is true. We must wait to see what happens before we pronounce
on sovereignty in the Common Market.

So, whilst in theory Mr Blackburn is quite right in saying that no
Parliament can bind another, and that any Parliament can reverse
what a previous Parliament has done, nevertheless so far as this court
is concerned, I think we will wait until that day comes. We will not
pronounce on it today.

A point was raised whether Mr Blackburn has any standing to
come before the court. That is not a matter which we need rule on
today. He says that he feels very strongly and that it is a matter in
which many persons in this country are concerned. I would not myself
rule him out on the ground that he has no standing. But I do rule him
out on the ground that these courts will not impugn the treaty-making
power of Her Majesty, and on the ground that insofar as Parliament
enacts legislation, we will deal with that legislation as and when it arises.

I think the statements of claim disclose no cause of action, and I
would dismiss the appeal.

Salmon LJ

Whilst I recognise the undoubted sincerity of Mr Blackburn's views,
I deprecate litigation the purpose of which is to influence political
decisions. Such decisions have nothing to do with these courts. These
courts are concerned only with the effect of such decisions if and when
they have been implemented by legislation. Nor have the courts any
power to interfere with the treaty-making power of the Sovereign. As
to Parliament, in the present state of the law, it can enact, amend and
repeal any legislation it pleases. The sole power of the courts is to
decide and enforce what is the law and not what it should be—now,
or in the future.

I agree that this appeal should be dismissed.

Stamp L.J.

I agree that the appeal should be dismissed; but I would express no
view whatsoever on the legal implications of this country becoming a
party to the Treaty of Rome. In the way Mr. Blackburn put it I think
he confused the division of the powers of the Crown, Parliament and
the courts. The Crown enters into treaties; Parliament enacts laws; and
it is the duty of this court in proper cases to interpret those laws when
made; but it is no part of this court's function or duty to make declarations in general terms regarding the powers of Parliament, more
particularly where the circumstances in which the court is asked to
intervene are purely hypothetical. Nor ought this court at the suit of
one of Her Majesty's subjects to make declarations regarding the
undoubted prerogative power of the Crown to enter into treaties.[90]

[pp. 1381–1383]

Appeals dismissed.

[89] [1955] C.L.J. 171.]
[90] [The judgments of Salmon and Stamp L.JJ. invoke, what is called in the United
States, the " political question " doctrine, under which certain areas of policy-
making are declared the exclusive province of, for example, the executive, and
hence are not " justiciable."]

H. L. A. HART

Positivism and the Separation of Law and Morals [91]

The third [92] criticism of the separation of law and morals is of a very different character; it certainly is less an intellectual argument against the Utilitarian distinction than a passionate appeal supported not by detailed reasoning but by reminders of a terrible experience. For it consists of the testimony of those who have descended into Hell, and, like Ulysses or Dante, brought back a message for human beings. Only in this case the Hell was not beneath or beyond earth, but on it; it was a Hell created on earth by men for other men.

This appeal comes from those German thinkers who lived through the Nazi regime and reflected upon its evil manifestations in the legal system. One of these thinkers, Gustav Radbruch, had himself shared the " positivist " doctrine until the Nazi tyranny, but he was converted by this experience and so his appeal to other men to discard the doctrine of the separation of law and morals has the special poignancy of a recantation. What is important about this criticism is that it really does confront the particular point which Bentham and Austin had in mind in urging the separation of law as it is and as it ought to be. These German thinkers put their insistence on the need to join together what the Utilitarians separated just where this separation was of most importance in the eyes of the Utilitarians; for they were concerned with the problem posed by the existence of morally evil laws.

Before his conversion [93] Radbruch held that resistance to law was a matter for the personal conscience, to be thought out by the individual as a moral problem, and the validity of a law could not be disproved by showing that its requirements were morally evil or even by showing that the effect of compliance with the law would be more evil than the effect of disobedience. Austin, it may be recalled, was emphatic in condemning those who said that if human laws conflicted with the fundamental principles of morality then they cease to be laws, as talking " stark nonsense." [94] These are strong . . . words, but we must remember that they went along—in the case of Austin and, of course, Bentham— with the conviction that if laws reached a certain degree of iniquity then there would be a plain moral obligation to resist them and to withhold obedience. We shall see, when we consider the alternatives, that this simple presentation of the human dilemma which may arise has much to be said for it.

Radbruch, however, had concluded from the ease with which the Nazi regime had exploited subservience to mere law—or expressed, as he thought, in the " positivist " slogan " law as law " (*Gesetz als Gesetz*)— and from the failure of the German legal profession to protest against the enormities which they were required to perpetrate in the name of law, that " positivism " (meaning here the insistence on the separation of

[91] [From (1958) 71 Harv.L.R. pp. 593–629, copyright 1958, by the Harvard Law Review Association.]

[92] [Prof. Hart had earlier dealt with other criticisms: the confusion between the " command " theory and the separation of law and morals; and the linking of that separation with " formalism."]

[93] [Cf. E. Wolf (1958) 3 Natural L.F. 1, who suggests that the seeds of post-war Radbruch were clearly detectable in his pre-Nazi-era writings.]

[94] [Cf. ante, 218.]

law as it is from law as it ought to be) had powerfully contributed to the horrors. His considered reflections led him to the doctrine that the fundamental principles of humanitarian morality were part of the very concept of *Recht* or Legality and that no positive enactment or statute, however clearly it was expressed and however clearly it conformed with the formal criteria of validity of a given legal system, could be valid if it contravened basic principles of morality. This doctrine can be appreciated fully only if the nuances imported by the German word *Recht* are grasped. But it is clear that the doctrine meant that every lawyer and judge should denounce statutes that transgressed the fundamental principles not as merely immoral or wrong but as having no legal character, and enactments which on this ground lack the quality of law should not be taken into account in working out the legal position of any given individual in particular circumstances. The striking recantation of his previous doctrine is unfortunately omitted from the translation of his works, but it should be read by all who wish to think afresh on the question of the interconnection of law and morals.

It is impossible to read without sympathy Radbruch's passionate demand that the German legal conscience should be open to the demands of morality and his complaint that this has been too little the case in the German tradition. On the other hand there is an extraordinary naïveté in the view that insensitiveness to the demands of morality and subservience to state power in a people like the Germans should have arisen from the belief that law might be law though it failed to conform with the minimum requirements of morality. Rather this terrible history prompts inquiry into why emphasis on the slogan "law is law," and the distinction between law and morals, acquired a sinister character in Germany, but elsewhere, as with the Utilitarians themselves, went along with the most enlightened liberal attitudes. But something more disturbing than naïveté is latent in Radbruch's whole presentation of the issues to which the existence of morally iniquitous laws gives rise. It is not, I think, uncharitable to say that we can see in his argument that he has only half digested the spiritual message of liberalism which he is seeking to convey to the legal profession. For everything that he says is really dependent upon an enormous overvaluation of the importance of the bare fact that a rule may be said to be a valid rule of law, as if this, once declared, was conclusive of the final moral question: "Ought this rule of law to be obeyed?" Surely the truly liberal answer to any sinister use of the slogan "law is law" or of the distinction between law and morals is, "Very well, but that does not conclude the question. Law is not morality; do not let it supplant morality."

However, we are not left to a mere academic discussion in order to evaluate the plea which Radbruch made for the revision of the distinction between law and morals. After the war Radbruch's conception of law as containing in itself the essential moral principle of humanitarianism was applied in practice by German courts in certain cases in which local war criminals, spies, and informers under the Nazi regime were punished. The special importance of these cases is that the persons accused of these crimes claimed that what they had done was not illegal under the laws of the regime in force at the time these actions were performed. This plea was met with the reply that the laws upon which they relied were invalid as contravening the fundamental principles of morality. Let me cite briefly one of these cases.[95]

In 1944 a woman, wishing to be rid of her husband, denounced him to the authorities for insulting remarks he had made about Hitler while home on leave from the German army. The wife was under no legal duty to report his acts, though what he had said was apparently in violation of statutes making it illegal to make statements detrimental to the government of the Third Reich or to impair by any means the military defense of the German people. The husband was arrested and sentenced to death, apparently pursuant to these statutes, though he was not executed but was sent to the front. In 1949 the wife was prosecuted in a West German court for an offense which we would describe as illegally depriving a person of his freedom (*rechtswidrige Freiheitsberaubung*). This was punishable as a crime under the German Criminal Code of 1871 which had remained in force continuously since its enactment. The wife pleaded that her husband's imprisonment was pursuant to the Nazi statutes and hence that she had committed no crime. The court of appeal to which the case ultimately came held that the wife was guilty of procuring the deprivation of her husband's liberty by denouncing him to the German courts, even though he had been sentenced by a court for having violated a statute, since, to quote the words of the court, the statute "was contrary to the sound conscience and sense of justice of all decent human beings." [96] This reasoning was followed in many cases which have been hailed as a triumph of the doctrines of natural law and as signalling the overthrow of positivism. The unqualified satisfaction with this result seems to me to be hysteria. Many of us might applaud the objective—that of punishing a woman for an outrageously immoral act—but this was secured only by declaring a statute established since 1934 not to have the force of law, and at least the wisdom of this course must be doubted. There were, of course, two other choices. One was to let the woman go unpunished; one can sympathize with and endorse the view that this might have been a bad thing to do. The other was to face the fact that if the woman were to be punished it must be pursuant to the introduction of a frankly retrospective law and with a full consciousness of what was sacrificed in

---

[95] Judgment of July 27, 1949, Oberlandesgericht, Bamberg.

[96] [It would seem, however, that this case discussed by Hart and Fuller was not in fact decided on the basis that the earlier Nazi laws were to be treated as invalid. For a full discussion of this and later German cases see H. O. Pappe, "On the Validity of Judicial Decisions in the Nazi Era" (1960) 23 M.L.R. 260. See also R. B. Schlesinger, *Comparative Law*, 3rd ed. (1970), pp. 500–505. Schlesinger also refers to a case before the Federal Supreme Court in 1955 where it was held that Art. 826 of the German Civil Code which renders actionable acts done *contra bonos mores*, "served to implement a law of a higher order and permits the court to consider the postulates of true justice not dependent on positive laws." See also E. Bodenheimer, *Jurisprudence* (1962), at pp. 226–227, who cites decisions of the West German Federal Supreme Court holding that totally obnoxious and unreasonable commands of the State would not be treated as involving a legal duty to obey such mandates. Thus he cites a decision of 1951 in which the principle was affirmed that a statute may cease to be valid where "the contrast between positive law and justice becomes so unbearable that the positive law, being 'false law' must yield to justice." See further *ante*, 114, as to the position under the Basic Law of the German Federal Republic.]

securing her punishment in this way. Odious as retrospective [97] criminal legislation and punishment may be, to have pursued it openly in this case would at least have had the merits of candour. It would have made plain that in punishing the woman a choice had to be made between two evils, that of leaving her unpunished and that of sacrificing a very precious principle of morality endorsed by most legal systems. Surely if we have learned anything from the history of morals it is that the thing to do with a moral quandary is not to hide it. Like nettles, the occasions when life forces us to choose between the lesser of two evils must be grasped with the consciousness that they are what they are. The vice of this use of the principle that, at certain limiting points, what is utterly immoral cannot be law or lawful is that it will serve to cloak the true nature of the problems with which we are faced and will encourage the romantic optimism that all the values we cherish ultimately will fit into a single system, that no one of them has to be sacrificed or compromised to accommodate another. . . .

It may seem perhaps to make too much of forms, even perhaps of words, to emphasize one way of disposing of this difficult case as compared with another which might have led, so far as the woman was concerned, to exactly the same result. Why should we dramatize the difference between them? We might punish the woman under a new retrospective law and declare overtly that we were doing something inconsistent with our principles as the lesser of two evils; or we might allow the case to pass as one in which we do not point out precisely where we sacrifice such a principle. But candour is not just one among many minor virtues of the administration of law, just as it is not merely a minor virtue of morality. For if we adopt Radbruch's view, and with him and the German courts make our protest against evil law in the form of an assertion that certain rules cannot be law because of their moral iniquity, we confuse one of the most powerful, because it is the simplest, forms of moral criticism. If with the Utilitarians we speak plainly, we say that laws may be law but too evil to be obeyed. This is a moral condemnation which everyone can understand and it makes an immediate and obvious claim to moral attention. If, on the other hand, we formulate our objection as an assertion that these evil things are not law, here is an assertion which many people do not believe, and if they are disposed to consider it at all, it would seem to raise a whole host of philosophical issues before it can be accepted. So perhaps the most important single lesson to be learned from this form of the denial of the Utilitarian distinction is the one that the Utilitarians were most concerned to teach: when we have the ample resources of plain speech we must not present the moral criticism of institutions as propositions of a disputable philosophy.   [pp. 615–621]

LON L. FULLER

Positivism and Fidelity to Law—a Reply to Professor Hart [98]

Most of the issues raised by Professor Hart's essay can be restated in terms of the distinction between order and good order. Law may be

---

[97] [Both Fuller and Radbruch would have preferred retrospective legislation.]
[98] [From (1958) 71 Harv.L.R., pp. 630–672, copyright 1958, by the Harvard Law Review Association.]

said to represent order *simpliciter*. Good order is law that corresponds to the demands of justice, or morality, or men's notions of what ought to be. This rephrasing of the issue is useful in bringing to light the ambitious nature of Professor Hart's undertaking, for surely we would all agree that it is no easy thing to distinguish order from good order. When it is said, for example, that law simply represents that public order which obtains under all governments—democratic, Fascist, or Communist—the order intended is certainly not that of a morgue or cemetery. We must mean a functioning order, and such an order has to be at least good enough to be considered as functioning by some standard or other. A reminder that workable order usually requires some play in the joints, and therefore cannot be too orderly, is enough to suggest some of the complexities that would be involved in any attempt to draw a sharp distinction between order and good order.

For the time being, however, let us suppose we can in fact clearly separate the concept of order from that of good order. Even in this unreal and abstract form the notion of order itself contains what may be called a moral element. Let me illustrate this "morality of order" in its crudest and most elementary form. Let us suppose an absolute monarch, whose word is the only law known to his subjects. We may further suppose him to be utterly selfish and to seek in his relations with his subjects solely his own advantage. This monarch from time to time issues commands, promising rewards for compliance and threatening punishment for disobedience. He is, however, a dissolute and forgetful fellow, who never makes the slightest attempt to ascertain who have in fact followed his directions and who have not. As a result he habitually punishes loyalty and rewards disobedience. It is apparent that this monarch will never achieve even his own selfish aims until he is ready to accept that minimum self-restraint that will create a meaningful connection between his words and his actions.

Let us now suppose that our monarch undergoes a change of heart and begins to pay some attention to what he said yesterday when, today, he has occasion to distribute bounty or to order the chopping off of heads. Under the strain of this new responsibility, however, our monarch relaxes his attention in other directions and becomes hopelessly slothful in the phrasing of his commands. His orders become so ambiguous and are uttered in so inaudible a tone that his subjects never have any clear idea what he wants them to do. Here, again, it is apparent that if our monarch for his own selfish advantage wants to create in his realm anything like a system of law he will have to pull himself together and assume still another responsibility.

Law, considered merely as order, contains, then, its own implicit morality. This morality of order must be respected if we are to create anything that can be called law, even bad law. Law by itself is power-less to bring this morality into existence. Until our monarch is really ready to face the responsibilities of his position, it will do no good for him to issue still another futile command, this time self-addressed and threatening himself with punishment if he does not mend his ways.

There is a twofold sense in which it is true that law cannot be built on law. First of all, the authority to make law must be supported by moral attitudes that accord to it the competency it claims. Here we are dealing with a morality external to law, which makes law possible. But this alone is not enough. We may stipulate that in our monarchy the accepted " basic norm " designates the monarch himself as the only possible source of law. We still cannot have law until our monarch is ready to accept the internal morality of law itself.

In the life of a nation these external and internal moralities of law reciprocally influence one another ; a deterioration of the one will almost inevitably produce a deterioration in the other. . . .

What I have called " the internal morality of law" seems to be almost completely neglected by Professor Hart. He does make brief mention of " justice in the administration of the law," which consists in the like treatment of like cases, by whatever elevated or perverted standards the word " like " may be defined. But he quickly dismisses this aspect of law as having no special relevance to his main enterprise.

In this I believe he is profoundly mistaken. It is his neglect to analyze the demands of a morality of order that leads him throughout his essay to treat law as a datum projecting itself into human experience and not as an object of human striving. When we realize that order itself is something that must be worked for, it becomes apparent that the existence of a legal system, even a bad or evil legal system, is always a matter of degree. When we recognize this simple fact of everyday legal experience, it becomes impossible to dismiss the problems presented by the Nazi regime with a simple assertion: " Under the Nazis there was law, even if it was bad law." We have instead to inquire how much of a legal system survived the general debasement and perversion of all forms of social order that occurred under the Nazi rule, and what moral implications this mutilated system had for the conscientious citizen forced to live under it.

It is not necessary, however, to dwell on such moral upheavals as the Nazi regime to see how completely incapable the positivistic philosophy is of serving the one high moral ideal it professes, that of fidelity to law. Its default in serving this ideal actually becomes most apparent, I believe, in the everyday problems that confront those who are earnestly desirous of meeting the moral demands of a legal order, but who have responsible functions to discharge in the very order toward which loyalty is due.

Let us suppose the case of a trial judge who has had an extensive experience in commercial matters and before whom a great many commercial disputes are tried. As a subordinate in a judicial hierarchy, our judge has of course the duty to follow the law laid down by his supreme court. Our imaginary Scrutton has the misfortune, however, to live under a supreme court which he considers woefully ignorant of the ways and needs of commerce. To his mind, many of this court's decisions in the field of commercial law simply do not make sense. If a conscientious judge caught in this dilemma were to turn to the positivistic philosophy what succor could he expect? It will certainly do no good to remind him that he has an obligation of fidelity to law. He is aware of this already and painfully so, since it is the source of his predicament. Nor will it help to say that if he legislates, it must be " interstitially," or that his contributions must be " confined from molar to molecular motions." [99]

[99] *Southern Pac. Co.* v. *Jensen*, 244 U.S. 205, 221 (1917) (Holmes J., dissenting), paraphrasing *Storti* v. *Commonwealth*, 178 Mass. 549, 554, 60 N.E. 210, 211 (1901) (Holmes C.J.), in which it was held that a statute providing for electro-

This mode of statement may be congenial to those who like to think of law, not as a purposive thing, but as an expression of the dimensions and directions of state power. But I cannot believe that the essentially trite idea behind this advice can be lifted by literary eloquence to the point where it will offer any real help to our judge; for one thing, it may be impossible for him to know whether his supreme court would regard any particular contribution of his as being wide or narrow.

Nor is it likely that a distinction between core and penumbra [1] would be helpful. The predicament of our judge may well derive, not from particular precedents, but from a mistaken conception of the nature of commerce which extends over many decisions and penetrates them in varying degrees. So far as his problem arises from the use of particular words, he may well find that the supreme court often uses the ordinary terms of commerce in senses foreign to actual business dealings. If he interprets those words as a business executive or accountant would, he may well reduce the precedents he is bound to apply to a logical shambles. On the other hand, he may find great difficulty in discerning the exact sense in which the supreme court used those words, since in his mind that sense is itself the product of a confusion.

Is it not clear that it is precisely positivism's insistence on a rigid separation of law as it is from law as it ought to be that renders the positivistic philosophy incapable of aiding our judge? Is it not also clear that our judge can never achieve a satisfactory resolution of his dilemma unless he views his duty of fidelity to law in a context which also embraces his responsibility for making law what it ought to be?

The case I have supposed may seem extreme, but the problem it suggests pervades our whole legal system. If the divergence of views between our judge and his supreme court were less drastic, it would be more difficult to present his predicament graphically, but the perplexity of his position might actually increase. Perplexities of this sort are a normal accompaniment of the discharge of any adjudicative function; they perhaps reach their more poignant intensity in the field of administrative law.

One can imagine a case—surely not likely in Professor Hart's country or mine—where a judge might hold profound moral convictions that were exactly the opposite of those held, with equal attachment, by his supreme court. He might also be convinced that the precedents he was bound to apply were the direct product of a morality he considered abhorrent. If such a judge did not find the solution for his dilemma in surrendering his office, he might well be driven to a wooden and literal application of precedents which he could not otherwise apply because he was incapable of understanding the philosophy that animated them. But I doubt that a judge in this situation would need the help of legal positivism to find these melancholy escapes from his predicament. Nor do I think that such a predicament is likely to arise within a nation where both law and good law are regarded as collaborative human achievements in need of constant renewal, and where lawyers are still at

cution as a means of inflicting the punishment of death was not cruel or unusual punishment within the Massachusetts Declaration of Rights, Mass. Const. pt. First, Art. XXVI, simply because it accomplished its object by molecular, rather than molar, motions.

[1] [*Cf. post*, 730, 796.]

least as interested in asking " What is good law?" as they are in asking
" What is law?" . . . .   [pp. 644-648]

. . . Professor Hart castigates the German courts and Radbruch, not
so much for what they believed had to be done, but because they failed
to see that they were confronted by a moral dilemma of a sort that
would have been immediately apparent to Bentham and Austin. By the
simple dodge of saying, " When a statute is sufficiently evil it ceases to
be law," they ran away from the problem they should have faced.

This criticism is, I believe, without justification. So far as the courts
are concerned, matters certainly would not have been helped if, instead
of saying, " This is not law," they had said, " This is law but it is so
evil we will refuse to apply it." Surely moral confusion reaches its
height when a court refuses to apply something it admits to be law, and
Professor Hart does not recommend any such " facing of the true issue "
by the courts themselves. He would have preferred a retroactive statute.
Curiously, this was also the preference of Radbruch. But unlike Professor
Hart, the German courts and Gustav Radbruch were living participants
in a situation of drastic emergency. The informer problem was a pressing one, and if legal institutions were to be rehabilitated in Germany it
would not do to allow the people to begin taking the law into their own
hands, as might have occurred while the courts were waiting for a
statute.

As for Gustav Radbruch, it is, I believe, wholly unjust to say that
he did not know he was faced with a moral dilemma. His postwar
writings repeatedly stress the antinomies confronted in the effort to
rebuild decent and orderly government in Germany. . . .

. . . The situation is not that legal positivism enables a man to know
when he faces a difficult problem of choice, while Radbruch's beliefs
deceive him into thinking there is no problem to face. The real issue
dividing Professors Hart and Radbruch is: How shall we state the
problem? What is the nature of the dilemma in which we are caught?

I hope I am not being unjust to Professor Hart when I say that I
can find no way of describing the dilemma as he sees it but to use
some such words as the following: On the one hand, we have an amoral
datum called law, which has the peculiar quality of creating a moral
duty to obey it. On the other hand, we have a moral duty to do what
we think is right and decent. When we are confronted by a statute we
believe to be thoroughly evil, we have to choose between those two
duties.

If this is the positivist position, then I have no hesitancy in rejecting
it. The " dilemma " it states has the verbal formulation of a problem,
but the problem it states makes no sense. It is like saying I have to
choose between giving food to a starving man and being mimsy with the
borogoves. I do not think it is unfair to the positivistic philosophy to
say that it never gives any coherent meaning to the moral obligation of
fidelity to law. This obligation seems to be conceived as sui generis,
wholly unrelated to any of the ordinary, extralegal ends of human life.
The fundamental postulate of positivism—that law must be strictly
severed from morality—seems to deny the possibility of any bridge
between the obligation to obey law and other moral obligations. No
mediating principle can measure their respective demands on conscience,
for they exist in wholly separate worlds.

While I would not subscribe to all of Radbruch's postwar views—especially those relating to "higher law"—I think he saw, much more clearly than does Professor Hart, the true nature of the dilemma confronted by Germany in seeking to rebuild her shattered legal institutions. Germany had to restore both respect for law and respect for justice. Though neither of these could be restored without the other, painful antinomies were encountered in attempting to restore both at once, as Radbruch saw all too clearly. Essentially Radbruch saw the dilemma as that of meeting the demands of order, on the one hand, and those of good order, on the other. Of course no pat formula can be derived from this phrasing of the problem. But, unlike legal positivism, it does not present us with opposing demands that have no living contact with one another, that simply shout their contradictions across a vacuum. As we seek order, we can meaningfully remind ourselves that order itself will do us no good unless it is good for something. As we seek to make our order good, we can remind ourselves that justice itself is impossible without order, and that we must not lose order itself in the attempt to make it good.[2]　　　　　　　　　　　　　　[pp. 655–657]

W. N. HOHFELD

Fundamental Legal Conceptions as Applied in Judicial Reasoning [3]

One of the greatest hindrances to the clear understanding, the incisive statement, and the true solution of legal problems frequently arises from the express or tacit assumption that all legal relations may be reduced to "rights" and "duties," and that these latter categories are therefore adequate for the purpose of analyzing even the most complex legal interests, such as trusts, options, escrows, "future" interests, corporate interests, etc. Even if the difficulty related merely to inadequacy and ambiguity of terminology, its seriousness would nevertheless be worthy of definite recognition and persistent effort toward improvement; for in any closely reasoned problem, whether legal or non-legal, chameleon-hued words are a peril both to clear thought and to lucid expression. As a matter of fact, however, the above mentioned inadequacy and ambiguity of terms unfortunately reflect, all too often, corresponding paucity and confusion as regards actual legal conceptions. That this is so may appear in some measure from the discussion to follow.

The strictly fundamental legal relations are, after all, *sui generis*; and thus it is that attempts at formal definition are always unsatisfactory, if not altogether useless. Accordingly, the most promising line of procedure seems to consist in exhibiting all of the various relations in a scheme of "opposites" and "correlatives," and then proceeding to exemplify their individual scope and application in concrete cases. An effort will be made to pursue this method:

Jural Opposites	{	right	privilege	power	immunity
	{	no-right	duty	disability	liability
Jural Correlatives	{	right	privilege	power	immunity
	{	duty	no-right	liability	disability

[2] [See also *The Morality of Law* (1969), *ante*, 83, and 138.]
[3] [Ed. Cook, Yale University Press (1923), Chap. 1.]

Rights and Duties. As already intimated, the term "rights" tends to be used indiscriminately to cover what in a given case may be a privilege, a power, or an immunity, rather than a right in the strictest sense. . . .

Recognizing, as we must, the very broad and indiscriminate use of the term "right," what clue do we find, in ordinary legal discourse, toward limiting the word in question to a definite and appropriate meaning? That clue lies in the correlative "duty," for it is certain that even those who use the word and the conception "right" in the broadest possible way are accustomed to thinking of "duty" as the invariable correlative.[4] As said in *Lake Shore & M. S. R. Co.* v. *Kurtz*[5]:

"A duty or a legal obligation is that which one ought or ought not to do. 'Duty' and 'right' are correlative terms. When a right is invaded, a duty is violated."[6]

In other words, if X has a right against Y that he shall stay off the former's land, the correlative (and equivalent) is that Y is under a duty toward X to stay off the place. If, as seems desirable, we should seek a synonym for the term "right" in this limited and proper meaning, perhaps the word "claim" would prove the best. The latter has the advantage of being a monosyllable. . . .[7]

Privileges and "No-Rights."[8] As indicated in the above scheme of jural relations, a privilege is the opposite of a duty, and the correlative of a "no-right." In the example last put, whereas X has a *right* or *claim* that Y, the other man, should stay off the land, he himself has the *privilege* of entering on the land; or, in equivalent words, X does not have a duty to stay off. The privilege of entering is the negation of a duty to stay off. As indicated by this case, some caution is necessary at this point; for, always, when it is said that a given privilege is the mere negation of a *duty*, what is meant, of course, is a duty having a content or tenor precisely *opposite* to that of the privilege in question. Thus, if, for some special reason, X has contracted with Y to go on the former's own land, it is obvious that X has, as regards Y, both the privilege of entering and the *duty of entering*. The privilege is perfectly consistent with this sort of duty,—for the latter is of the

---

4 [A useful illustration of the practical value of Hohfeldian analysis may be found in J. W. Harris, 87 L.Q.R. 31. Harris distinguishes four concepts of duty and finds a failure to appreciate that the concept can be used differently at the root of the confusion between trusts and powers.]

5 (1894) 10 Ind.App. 60.

6 See also *Howley Park Coal, etc., Co.* v. *L. & N. W. Ry.* [1913] A.C. 11, 25, 27 (*per* Viscount Haldane L.C.: "There is an obligation (of lateral support) on the neighbour, and in that sense there is a correlative right on the part of the owner of the first piece of land"; *per* Lord Shaw: "There is a reciprocal right to lateral support for their respective lands and a reciprocal obligation upon the part of each owner. . . . No diminution of the right on the one hand or of the obligation on the other can be effected except as the result of a plain contract. . . .").

7 [Hart has shown that claims can be defined as a power to enforce a duty coupled with the power to abolish the duty. See *Definition and Theory in Jurisprudence*, p. 16.]

8 [See further Glanville Williams, *The Concept of a Legal Liberty* in ed. Summers, *Essays in Legal Philosophy* (1968), p. 121. Williams, and many contemporary writers, prefer "liberty" to "privilege" as they believe the latter is tinged with political connotation of something specially granted, whereas in fact most "rights" are privileges or liberties.]

same content or tenor as the privilege ;—but it still holds good that, as regards Y, X's privilege of entering is the precise negation of a duty *to stay off*. Similarly, if A has not contracted with B to perform certain work for the latter, A's privilege of *not* doing so is the very negation of a duty of *doing* so. Here again the duty contrasted is of a content or tenor exactly opposite to that of the privilege.

Passing now to the question of " correlatives," it will be remembered, of course, that a duty is the invariable correlative of that legal relation which is most properly called a right or claim. That being so, if further evidence be needed as to the fundamental and important difference between a right (or claim) and a privilege, surely it is found in the fact that the correlative of the latter relation is a " no-right," there being no single term available to express the latter conception. Thus, the correlative of X's right that Y shall not enter on the land is Y's duty not to enter ; but the correlative of X's privilege of entering himself is manifestly Y's " no-right " that X shall not enter.

In view of the considerations thus far emphasized, the importance of keeping the conception of a right (or claim) and the conception of a privilege quite distinct from each other seems evident ; and, more than that, it is equally clear that there should be a separate term to represent the latter relation. No doubt, as already indicated, it is very common to use the term " right " indiscriminately, even when the relation designated is really that of privilege ; and only too often this identity of terms has involved for the particular speaker or writer a confusion or blurring of ideas. . . .

. . . On grounds already emphasized, it would seem that the line of reasoning pursued by Lord Lindley in the great case of *Quinn* v. *Leathem* [9] is deserving of comment:

"The plaintiff had the ordinary *rights* of the British subject. He was *at liberty* to earn his living in his own way, provided he did not violate some special law prohibiting him from so doing, and provided he did not infringe the rights of other people. This *liberty* involved *the liberty* to deal with other persons who were willing to deal with him. *This liberty* is *a right* recognized by law ; its *correlative* is the general *duty* of every one not to prevent the free exercise of this *liberty* except so far as his own liberty of action may justify him in so doing. But a person's *liberty* or *right* to deal with others is nugatory unless they are at liberty to deal with him if they choose to do so. Any interference with their liberty to deal with him affects him."

A " liberty " considered as a legal relation (or " right " in the loose and generic sense of that term) must mean, if it have any definite content at all, precisely the same thing as *privilege* ; and certainly that is the fair connotation of the term as used the first three times in the passage quoted. It is equally clear, as already indicated, that such a privilege or liberty to deal with others at will might very conceivably exist without any peculiar concomitant rights against " third parties " as regards certain kinds of interference.[10] Whether there should be such concomitant rights (or claims) is ultimately a question of justice and policy ; and it should be considered, as such, on its merits. The only correlative logically implied by the privileges or liberties in question are

9 [1901] A.C. 495, 534.
10 Compare *Allen* v. *Flood* [1898] A.C. 1.

the " no-rights " of " third parties." It would therefore be a *non sequitur* to conclude from the mere existence of such liberties that " third parties " are under a *duty* not to interfere, etc. Yet in the middle of the above passage from Lord Lindley's opinion there is a sudden and question-begging shift in the use of terms. First, the " liberty " in question is transmuted into a " right " ; and then, possibly under the seductive influence of the latter word, it is assumed that the " correlative " must be " the general duty of every one not to prevent," etc.

Another interesting and instructive example may be taken from Lord Bowen's oft-quoted opinion in *Mogul Steamship Co.* v. *McGregor.*[11]

" We are presented in this case with an apparent conflict or antinomy between two rights that are equally regarded by the law—the right of the plaintiffs to be protected in the legitimate exercise of their trade, and the right of the defendants to carry on their business as seems best to them, provided they commit no wrong to others."

As the learned judge states, the conflict or antinomy is only apparent ; but this fact seems to be obscured by the very indefinite and rapidly shifting meanings with which the term " right " is used in the above quoted language. Construing the passage as a whole, it seems plain enough that by " the right of the plaintiffs " in relation to the defendants a legal right or claim in the strict sense must be meant ; whereas by " the right of the defendants " in relation to the plaintiffs a legal privilege must be intended. That being so, the " two rights " mentioned in the beginning of the passage, being respectively claim and privilege, could not be in conflict with each other. To the extent that the defendants have privileges the plaintiffs have no rights ; and, conversely, to the extent that the plaintiffs have rights the defendants have no privileges (" no-privilege " equals duty of opposite tenor).   [pp. 35–44]

. . . *Powers and Liabilities.* As indicated in the preliminary scheme of jural relations, a legal power (as distinguished, of course, from a mental or physical power) is the opposite of legal disability, and the correlative of legal liability. But what is the intrinsic nature of a legal power as such? Is it possible to analyze the conception represented by this constantly employed and very important term of legal discourse? Too close an analysis might seem metaphysical rather than useful ; so that what is here presented is intended only as an approximate explanation, sufficient for all practical purposes.

A change in a given legal relation may result (1) from some superadded fact or group of facts not under the volitional control of a human being (or human beings) ; or (2) from some superadded fact or group of facts which are under the volitional control of one or more human beings. As regards the second class of cases, the person (or persons) whose volitional control is paramount may be said to have the (legal) power to effect the particular change of legal relations that is involved in the problem.

This second class of cases—powers in the technical sense—must now be further considered. The nearest synonym for any ordinary case seems to be (legal) " ability,"—the latter being obviously the opposite of " inability," or " disability." The term " right," so frequently and loosely used in the present connection, is an unfortunate term for the purpose,—

[11] (1889) 23 Q.B.D. 59.

a not unusual result being confusion of thought as well as ambiguity of expression. The term "capacity" is equally unfortunate; for, as we have already seen, when used with discrimination, this word denotes a particular group of operative facts, and not a legal relation of any kind.

Many examples of legal powers may readily be given. Thus, X, the owner of ordinary personal property "in a tangible object" has the power to extinguish his own legal interest (rights, powers, immunities, etc.) through that totality of operative facts known as abandonment; and—simultaneously and correlatively—to create in other persons privileges and powers relating to the abandoned object,—e.g., the power to acquire title to the latter by appropriating it. *Similarly*, X has the power to transfer his interest to Y,—that is, to extinguish his own interest and concomitantly create in Y a new and corresponding interest. So also X has the power to create contractual obligations of various kinds. Agency cases are likewise instructive. By the use of some *metaphorical* expression such as the Latin, *qui facit per alium, facit per se*, the true nature of agency relations is only too frequently obscured. The creation of an agency relation involves, *inter alia*, the grant of legal powers to the so-called agent, and the creation of correlative liabilities in the principal. That is to say, one party, P, has the power to create agency powers in another party, A,—for example, the power to convey P's property, the power to impose (so-called) contractual obligations on P, the power to discharge a debt owing to P, the power to "receive" title to property so that it shall vest in P, and so forth. In passing, it may be well to observe that the term "authority," so frequently used in agency cases, is very ambiguous and slippery in its connotation. Properly employed in the present connection, the word seems to be an abstract or qualitative term corresponding to the concrete "authorization,"—the latter consisting of a particular group of operative facts taking place between the principal and the agent. All too often, however, the term in question is so used as to blend and confuse these operative facts with the powers and privileges thereby created in the agent. A careful discrimination in these particulars would, it is submitted, go far toward clearing up certain problems in the law of agency. . . .

. . . Passing now to the field of contracts, suppose A mails a letter to B offering to sell the former's land, Whiteacre, to the latter for ten thousand dollars, such letter being duly received. The operative facts thus far mentioned have created a power as regards B and a correlative liability as regards A. B, by dropping a letter of acceptance in the box, has the power to impose a potential or inchoate obligation *ex contractu* on A and himself; and, assuming that the land is worth fifteen thousand dollars, that particular legal quantity—the "power *plus* liability" relation between A and B—seems to be worth about five thousand dollars to B. The liability of A will continue for a reasonable time unless, in exercise of his power to do so, A previously extinguishes it by that series of operative facts known as "revocation." These last matters are usually described by saying that A's "offer" will "continue" or "remain open" for a reasonable time, or for the definite time actually specified, unless A previously "withdraws" or "revokes" such offer. While, no doubt, in the great majority of cases no harm results from the use of such expressions, yet these forms of statement seem to represent a blending of non-legal and legal quantities which, in any problem requiring careful reasoning, should preferably be kept distinct. An offer, considered as a series of physical and mental operative facts, has spent its force and become *functus officio* as soon as such series has been completed by the " offeree's receipt." The real question is therefore as to the *legal effect*, if any, at that moment of time. If the latter consist of B's power and A's correlative liability, manifestly it is those *legal relations* that " continue " or " remain open " until modified by revocation or other operative facts. What has thus far been said concerning contracts completed by mail would seem to apply, *mutatis mutandis*, to every type of contract. Even where the parties are in the presence of each other, the offer creates a liability against the offerer, together with a correlative power in favor of the offeree. The only distinction for present purposes would be in the fact that such power and such liability would expire within a very short period of time. . . .

. . . In view of what has already been said, very little may suffice concerning a *liability* as such. The latter, as we have seen, is the correlative of power, and the opposite of immunity (or exemption). While no doubt the term " liability " is often loosely used as a synonym for " duty," or " obligation," it is believed, from an extensive survey of judicial precedents, that the connotation already adopted as most appropriate to the word in question is fully justified. . . .

. . . *Immunities and Disabilities.* As already brought out, immunity is the correlative of disability (" no-power "), and the opposite, or negation, of liability. Perhaps it will also be plain, from the preliminary outline and from the discussion down to this point, that a power bears the same general contrast to an immunity that a right does to a privilege. A right is one's affirmative claim against another, and a privilege is one's freedom from the right or claim of another. Similarly, a power is one's affirmative " control " over a given legal relation as against another; whereas an immunity is one's freedom from the legal power or " control " of another as regards some legal relation.

A few examples may serve to make this clear. X, a landowner, has, as we have seen, power to alienate to Y or to any other ordinary party. On the other hand, X has also various immunities as against Y, and all other ordinary parties. For Y is under a disability (i.e., has no power) so far as shifting the legal interest either to himself or to a third party is concerned; and what is true of Y applies similarly to every one else who has not by virtue of special operative facts acquired a power to alienate X's property. If, indeed, a sheriff has been duly empowered by a writ of execution to sell X's interest, that is a very different matter: correlative to such sheriff's power would be the *liability* of X,—the very opposite of immunity (or exemption). It is elementary, too, that as against the sheriff, X might be immune or exempt in relation to certain parcels of property, and be liable as to others. Similarly, if an agent has been duly appointed by X to sell a given piece of property, then, as to the latter, X has, in relation to such agent, a liability rather than an immunity. . . .

. . . In the latter part of the preceding discussion, eight conceptions of the law have been analyzed and compared in some detail, the purpose having been to exhibit not only their intrinsic meaning and scope, but also their relations to one another and the methods by which they are applied, in judicial reasoning, to the solution of concrete problems of litigation. Before concluding this branch of the discussion a general suggestion may be ventured as to the great practical importance of a clear appreciation of the distinctions and discriminations set forth. If a homely metaphor be permitted, these eight conceptions,—rights and duties, privileges and no-rights, powers and liabilities, immunities and disabilities,—seem to be what may be called "the lowest common denominators of the law." Ten fractions (1-3, 2-5, etc.) may, *superficially*, seem so different from one another as to defy comparison. If, however, they are expressed in terms of their lowest common denominators (5-15, 6-15, etc.), comparison becomes easy, and fundamental similarity may be discovered. The same thing is of course true as regards the lowest generic conceptions to which any and all "legal quantities" may be reduced.

Reverting, for example, to the subject of powers, it might be difficult at first glance to discover any essential and fundamental similarity between conditional sales of personalty, escrow transactions, option agreements, agency relations, powers of appointment, etc. But if all these relations are reduced to their lowest generic terms, the conceptions of legal power and legal liability are seen to be dominantly, though not exclusively, applicable throughout the series. By such a process it becomes possible not only to discover essential similarities and illuminating analogies in the midst of what appears superficially to be infinite and hopeless variety, but also to discern common principles of justice and policy underlying the various jural problems involved. An indirect, yet very practical, consequence is that it frequently becomes feasible, by virtue of such analysis, to use as persuasive authorities judicial precedents that might otherwise seem altogether irrelevant. If this point be valid with respect to powers, it would seem to be equally so as regards all of the other basic conceptions of the law. In short, the deeper the analysis, the greater becomes one's perception of fundamental unity and harmony in the law.[12]   [pp. 50–64]

H. L. A. HART

Definition and Theory in Jurisprudence [13]

Long ago Bentham issued a warning that legal words demanded a special method of elucidation and he enunciated a principle that is the beginning of wisdom in this matter though it is not the end. He said we must never take these words alone, but consider whole sentences in which they play their characteristic role. We must take not the *word* "right" but the sentence "You have a right" not the *word* "State" but the sentence "He is a member or an official of the State." His warning has largely been disregarded and jurists have continued to hammer away at single words. This may be because he hid the product

[12] [For a critical but sympathetic appraisal of Hohfeld's scheme, see M. Radin, "A Restatement of Hohfeld" (1938) 51 Harv.L.R. 1141.]
[13] [(1954) 70 L.Q.R. 37.]

of his logical insight behind technical terms of his own invention
" Archetypation," " Phraseoplerosis," and the rest; it may also be
because his further suggestions were not well adapted to the peculiarities
of legal language which as part of the works of " Judge & Co" was
perhaps distasteful to him. But in fact the language involved in the
enunciation and application of rules constitutes a special segment of
human discourse with special features which lead to confusion if neglected. Of this type of discourse the law is one very complex example
and sometimes to see its features we need to look away from the law
to simpler cases which in spite of many differences share these features.
The economist or the scientist often uses a simple model with which to
understand the complex ; and this can be done for the law. So in what
follows I shall use as a simple analogy the rules of a game which at
many vital points have the same puzzling logical structure as rules of
law. And I shall describe four distinctive features which show, I think,
the method of elucidation we should apply to the law and why the
common mode of definition fails.

   1. First, let us take words like " right " or " duty " or the names of
corporations not alone but in examples of typical contexts where these
words are at work. Consider them when used in statements made on a
particular occasion by a judge or an ordinary lawyer. They will be
statements such as " A has a right to be paid £10 by B." " A is under
a duty to fence off his machinery." " A & Company, Ltd. have a
contract with B." It is obvious that the use of these sentences silently
assumes a special and very complicated setting, namely the existence of
a legal system with all that this implies by way of general obedience,
the operation of the sanctions of the system, and the general likelihood
that this will continue. But though this complex situation is assumed
in the use of these statements of rights or duties they do not *state* that
it exists. There is a parallel situation in a game. " He is out " said
in the course of a game of cricket has as its proper context the playing
of the game with all that *this* implies by way of general compliance
by both the players and the officials of the game in the past, present, and
future. Yet one who says " He is out " does not *state* that a game is
being played or that the players and officials will comply with the rules.
" He is out " is an expression used to appeal to rules, to make claims,
or give decisions under them ; it is not a statement *about* the rules to
the effect that they will be enforced or acted on in a given case nor any
other kind of statement *about* them. The analysis of statements of
rights and duties as predictions ignores this distinction, yet it is just as
erroneous to say that " A has a right " is a prediction that a court or
official will treat A in a certain way as to say that " He is out " is a
prediction that the umpire is likely to order the batsman off the field or
the scorer to mark him out. No doubt, when someone has a legal right
a corresponding prediction will normally be justified, but this should not
lead us to identify two quite different forms of statement.

   2. If we take " A has a right to be paid £10 by B " as an example,
we can see what the distinctive function of this form of statement is.
For it is clear that as well as presupposing the existence of a legal
system, the use of this statement has also a special connection with a
particular rule of the system. This would be made explicit if we asked
" Why has A this right? " For the appropriate answer could only con-

sist of two things: first, the statement of some rule or rules of law (say those of Contract), under which given certain facts certain legal consequences follow; and secondly, a statement that these facts were here the case. But again it is important to see that one who says that " A has a right " does not *state* the relevant rule of law; and that though, given certain facts, it is correct to say " A has a right " one who says this does not state or describe those facts. He has done something different from either of these two things: he has drawn a conclusion from the relevant but unstated rule, and from the relevant but unstated facts of the case. " A has a right " like " He is out " is therefore the tail-end of a simple legal calculation: it records a result and may be well called a conclusion of law. It is not therefore used to predict the future as the American Realists say; it refers to the present as their opponents claim but unlike ordinary statements does not do this by describing present or continuing facts. This it is—this matter of principle—and not the existence of stray exceptions for lunatics or infants that frustrates the definition of a right in factual terms such as expectations or powers. A paralysed man watching the thief's hand close over his gold watch is properly said to have a right to retain it as against the thief, though he has neither expectation nor power in any ordinary sense of these words. This is possible just because the expression " a right " in this case does not describe or stand for any expectation, or power, or indeed anything else, but has meaning only as part of a sentence the function of which as a whole is to draw a conclusion of law from a specific kind of legal rule.

3. A third peculiarity is this: the assertion " Smith has a right to be paid £10 " said by a judge in deciding the case has a different status from the utterance of it out of court, where it may be used to make a claim, or an admission and in many other ways. The judge's utterance is official, authoritative and, let us assume, final; the other is none of these things, yet in spite of these differences the sentences are of the same sort: they are both conclusions of law. We can compare this difference in spite of similarity with " He is out " said by the umpire in giving his decision and said by a player to make a claim. Now of course the unofficial utterance may have to be withdrawn in the light of a later official utterance, but this is not a sufficient reason for treating the first as a prophecy of the last for plainly not all mistakes are mistaken predictions. Nor surely need the finality of a judge's decision either be confused with infallibility or tempt us to *define* laws in terms of what courts do, even though there are many laws which the courts must first interpret before they can apply. We can acknowledge that what the scorer says is final; yet we can still abstain from defining the notion of a score as what the scorer says. And we can admit that the umpire may be wrong in his decision though the rules give us no remedy if he is and though there may be doubtful cases which he has to decide with but little help from the rules.

4. In any system, legal or not, rules may for excellent practical reasons attach identical consequences to any one of a set of very different facts. The rule of cricket attaches the same consequence to the batsman's being bowled, stumped, or caught. And the word " out " is used in giving decisions or making claims under the rule and in other verbal applications of it. It is easy to see here that no one of these different

ways of being out is more essentially what the word means than the others, and that there need be nothing common to all these ways of being out other than their falling under the same rule, though there *may* be some similarity or analogy between them. But it is less easy to see this in those important cases where rules treat a *sequence* of different actions or states of affairs in a way which unifies them. In a game a rule may simply attach a single consequence to the successive actions of a set of different men—as when a team is said to have won a game. A more complex rule may prescribe that what is to be done at one point in a sequence shall depend on what was done or occurred earlier: and it may be indifferent to the identity of the persons concerned in the sequence so long as they fall under certain defining conditions. An example of this is when a team permitted by the rules of a tournament to have a varying membership is penalised only in the third round—when the membership has changed—for what was done in the first round. In all such cases a sequence of action or states of affairs is unified simply by falling under certain rules; they *may* be otherwise as different as you please. Here can be seen the essential elements of the language of legal corporations. For in law, the lives of ten men that overlap but do not coincide may fall under separate rules under which they have separate rights and duties and then they are a collection of individuals for the law; but their actions may fall under rules of a different kind which make what is to be done by any one or more of them depend in a complex way on what was done or occurred earlier. And then we may speak in appropriately unified ways of the sequence so unified, using a terminology like that of corporation law which will show that it is *this* sort of rule we are applying to the facts. But here the unity of the rule may mislead us when we come to define this terminology. It may cast a shadow: we may look for an identical continuing thing or person or quality *in* the sequence. We may find it—in " corporate spirit." This is real enough; but it is a secret of success not a criterion of identity.

These four general characteristics of legal language explain both why definition of words like " right," " duty," and " corporation " is baffled by the absence of some counterpart to " correspond " to these words, and also why the unobvious counterparts which have been so ingeniously contrived—the future facts, the complex facts or the psychological facts —turn out not to be something in terms of which we can define these words although to be connected with them in complex or indirect ways. The fundamental point is that the primary function of these words is not to stand for or describe anything but a distinct function ; this makes it vital to attend to Bentham's warning that we should not, as does the traditional method of definition, abstract words like " right " and " duty," " State," or " corporation " from the sentences in which alone their full function can be seen, and then demand of them so abstracted their genus and differentia.

Let us see what the use of this traditional method of definition presupposes and what the limits of its efficacy are, and why it may be misleading. It is of course the simplest form of definition, and also a peculiarly satisfying form because it gives us a set of words which can always be substituted for the word defined whenever it is used ; it gives us a comprehensible synonym or translation for the word which puzzles us. It is peculiarly appropriate where the words have the straightforward function of standing for some kind of thing, or quality, person, process, or event, for here we are not mystified or puzzled about the general characteristics of our subject-matter, but we ask for a definition simply to locate within this familiar general kind or class some special subordinate kind or class. Thus since we are not puzzled about the general notions of furniture or animal we can take a word like " chair " or " cat " and give the principle of its use by first specifying the general class to which what it is used to describe belongs, and then going on to define the specific differences that mark it off from other species of the same general kind. And of course if we are *not* puzzled about the general notion of a corporate body but only wish to know how one species (say a college) differs from another (say a limited company) we can use this form of definition of single words perfectly well. But just because the method is appropriate at this level of inquiry, it cannot help us when our perplexities are deeper. For if our question arises, as it does with fundamental legal notions because we are puzzled about the general category to which something belongs and how some general type of expression relates to fact, and not merely about the place within that category, then until the puzzle is cleared up this form of definition is at the best unilluminating and at the worst profoundly misleading. It is unilluminating because a mode of definition designed to locate some subordinate species within some familiar category cannot elucidate the characteristics of some anomalous category ; and it is misleading because it will suggest that what is in fact an anomalous category is after all some species of the familiar. Hence if applied to legal words like " right," " duty," " State," or "corporation " the common mode of definition suggests that these words like ordinary words stand for or describe some thing, person, quality, process, or event ; when the diffi-culty of finding these becomes apparent, different contrivances varying with tastes are used to explain or explain away the anomaly. Some say the difference is that the things for which these legal words stand are real but not sensory, others that they are fictitious entities, others that these words stand for plain fact but of a complex, future, or psycho-logical variety. So this standard mode of definition forces our familiar triad of theories into existence as a confused way of accounting for the anomalous character of legal words.

How then shall we define such words? If definition is the provision of a synonym which will not equally puzzle us these words cannot be defined. But I think there is a method of elucidation of quite general application and which we can call definition, if we wish. Bentham and others practised it, though they did not preach it. But before applying it to the highly complex legal cases, I shall illustrate it from the simple case of a game. Take the notion of a trick in a game of cards. Some-body says " What is a trick?" and you reply " I will explain: when you have a game and among its rules is one providing that when each of our players has played a card then the player who has put down the highest card scores a point, in these circumstances that player is said to have ' taken a trick '." This natural explanation has not taken the form of a definition of the single word " trick ": no synonym has been offered for it. Instead we have taken a sentence in which the word " trick " plays its characteristic role and explained it first by specifying the conditions under which the whole sentence is true, and secondly by showing how it is used in drawing a conclusion from the rules in a particular case. Suppose now that after such an explanation your questioner presses on: " That is all very well, that explains ' taking a trick '; but I still want to know what the word ' trick ' means just by itself. I want a definition of ' trick '; I want something which can be substituted for it whenever it is used." If we yield to this demand for a single word definition we might reply: " The trick is just a collective name for the four cards." But someone may object: " The trick is not just a name for the four cards because these four cards will not always constitute a trick. It must therefore be some entity to which the four cards belong." A third might say: " No, the trick is a fictitious entity which the players pretend exists and to which by fiction which is part of the game they ascribe the cards." But in so simple a case we would not tolerate these theories, fraught as they are with mystery and empty of any guidance as to the use made of the word within the game: we would stand by the original two-fold explanation; for this surely gave us all we needed when it explained the conditions under which the statement " He has taken a trick " is true and showed us how it was used in drawing a conclusion from the rules in a particular case.

If we turn back to Bentham we shall find that when his explanation of legal notions is illuminating, as it very often is, it conforms to this method though only loosely. . . .

. . . They are not paraphrases but they specify some of the conditions necessary for the truth of a sentence of the form " You have a right." Bentham shows us how these conditions include the existence of a law imposing a duty on some other person; and moreover, that it must be a law which provides that the breach of the duty shall be visited with a sanction if you or someone on your behalf so choose. This has many virtues. By refusing to identify the meaning of the word " right " with any psychological or physical fact it correctly leaves open the question whether on any given occasion a person who has a right has in fact any expectation or power; and so it leaves us free to treat men's expectations or powers as what in general men will have if there is a system of rights, and as part of what a system of rights is generally intended to secure. Some of the improvements which should be made on Bentham's efforts are obvious. Instead of characterising a right in terms of punishment many would do so in terms of the remedy. But I would prefer to show the special position of one who has a right by mentioning not the remedy but the choice which is open to one who has a right as to whether the corresponding duty shall be performed or not. For it is, I think, characteristic of those laws that confer rights (as distinguished from those that only impose obligations) that the obligation to perform the corresponding duty is made by law to depend on the choice of the individual who is said to have the right or the choice of some person authorised to act on his behalf.

I would, therefore, tender the following as an elucidation of the expression " a legal right ": (1) A statement of the form " X has a right " is true if the following conditions are satisfied:

(a) There is in existence a legal system.

(b) Under a rule or rules of the system some other person Y is, in the events which have happened, obliged to do or abstain from some action.

(c) This obligation is made by law dependent on the choice either of X or some other person authorised to act on his behalf so that either Y is bound to do or abstain from some action only if X (or some authorised person) so chooses or alternatively only until X (or such person) chooses otherwise.

(2) A statement of the form " X has a right " is used to draw a conclusion of law in a particular case which falls under such rules.[14]

[pp. 41–49]

R. SUMMERS

The New Analytical Jurists
(1966) [15]

Scope of the New Analytical Jurisprudence

The new jurists are performing a wider variety of analytical activities than did most of their predecessors. These activities can be divided into four main types (a good philosophical number): (1) analysis of the existing conceptual framework of and about law; (2) construction of new conceptual frameworks with accompanying terminologies; (3) rational justification of institutions and practices, existing and proposed; and (4) " purposive implication "—tracing out what the acceptance of social purposes " implies " in terms of social arrangements and social ordering.

---

[14] This deals only with a right in the first sense (correlative to duty) distinguished by Hohfeld. But the same form of elucidation can be used for the cases of " liberty," " power," and " immunity " and will, I think, show what is usually left unexplained, *viz.*: why these four varieties, in spite of differences, are referred to as " rights." The unifying element seems to be this: in all four cases the law specifically recognises the *choice* of an individual either negatively by not impeding or obstructing it (liberty and immunity) or affirmatively by giving legal effect to it (claim and power). In the negative cases there is no law to interfere if the individual chooses to do or abstain from some action (liberty) or to retain his legal position unchanged (immunity); in the affirmative cases the law gives legal effect to the choice of an individual that some other person shall do or shall abstain from some action or that the legal position of some other person shall be altered. Of course, when we say in any of these four senses that a person has a right we are not referring to any *actual* choice that he has made but either the relevant rules of law are such that *if* he chooses certain consequences follow, or there are no rules to impede his choice *if* he makes it. If there are legal rights which cannot be waived these would need special treatment.

[A. W. B. Simpson, in " The Analysis of Legal Concepts " (1964) 80 L.Q.R. 535, criticises Hart's suggestion that the meaning of legal concepts can be given by showing how they function in particular sentences where conclusions are drawn from rules. Simpson argues that this form of elucidation is of very limited value because it is very far from exhaustive of the type of questions which may be legitimately asked in relation to legal concepts. However, some of the questions which he regards as unanswered by this method, hardly seem to be matters of great seriousness for jurisprudence, such as the question why we use the word " possession " rather than the expression " old cheese." Other questions, such as the fact that Hart's elucidation does not enable us to see the common ground between, *e.g.*, possession in English and Roman law, seem misconceived, since there is no reason why both the similarities and also the differences in the concept of possession as employed in Roman and English law should not be expounded on the lines indicated by Hart.] [*Cf. post*, 556.]

[15] [From 41 New York Univ.Law R. 861.]

All analytical jurists have been interested in the first of the foregoing activities—conceptual analysis. In fact, conceptual analysis has been a main, if not the primary, interest of analytical jurists, old and new. But, compared to most of the older analysts, the new are analyzing a wider range of concepts and performing a wider variety of analytical activities. These represent significant differences of scope.

Analysis of the Conceptual Status Quo

At least to philosophers, conceptual analysis is important because clarity and insight are important.[16] Concepts, and their interrelations, often turn out to be far more complex than is supposed. Through analysis, it is often possible to achieve better understanding. But this is not all that analysis accomplishes. As the philosopher J. L. Austin was fond of observing, a sharpened awareness of the uses of words can sharpen our awareness of phenomena.[17] This is not, by any means, a new idea. Plato, in the *Cratylus*, had Socrates ask of Cratylus: "What is the force of names, and what is the use of them?" To this, Cratylus replied: "The use of names, Socrates, as I should imagine, is to inform: the simple truth is, that he who knows names knows also the things which are expressed by them." [18]

What is conceptual analysis? Whether we speak of "conceptual analysis" or of "analyzing the *uses* of words," it all comes to much the same. The phrase "linguistic analysis," though often used, is less appropriate. It implies that language itself is the relevant subject matter, and this is not so. The relevant subject matter consists of concepts or ideas currently used by either laymen or professionals in dealing with law. Language, of course, is necessary, but only as the means by which, and the medium in which, concepts or ideas are dealt with.[19] It is possible to hint meaningfully at the range and variety of relevant concepts or ideas for conceptual analysis. Consider the following inexhaustive list:

[16] What is insight? There is, of course, no Platonic "form" of insight, and what is insight for one person may be old hat to another. An insight may be presented in such forms as (1) a sharpened awareness, (2) an exposed presupposition, (3) a novel line of argument, (4) a new distinction, (5) a relationship or a similarity or a contrast not previously seen, (6) a new technique or method, (7) an unseen implication, (8) an exemplification of something more general.

[17] See J. L. Austin, A Plea for Excuses, 57 Proceedings of the Aristotelian Soc'y 1, 8 (1956).

[18] 1 Dialogues of Plato 224 (Jowett transl. Random House 1937). H. L. A. Hart has made this point similarly:

> The question "Is analytical jurisprudence concerned with words or with things?" incorporates a most misleading dichotomy. Perhaps its misleading character comes out in the following analogy. Suppose a man to be occupied in focusing through a telescope on a battleship lying in the harbor some distance away. A friend comes up to him and says, "Are you concerned with the image in your glass or with the ship?" Plainly (if well advised) the other would answer "Both. I am endeavouring to align the image in the glass with the battleship in order to see it better." It seems to me that similarly in pursuing analytical inquiries we seek to sharpen our awareness of what we talk about when we use our language. There is no clarification of concepts which can fail to increase our understanding of the world to which we apply them.

Hart, Analytical Jurisprudence in Mid-Twentieth Century: A Reply to Professor Bodenheimer, 105 U.Pa.L.Rv. 953, 967 (1957).

[19] This is not to say that idioms of language may not be useful as "pointers" to important distinctions or ideas. See Warnock, English Philosophy Since 1900, at 149–152 (1958).

(1) Concepts used in formulating theories of law, *e.g.,* sources of law, adjudication, minimum efficacy, sanctions.

(2) Concepts used in characterizing theories of law, *e.g.,* imperative positivist.

(3) Concepts that are more or less creatures of law, *e.g.,* ownership, corporation.

(4) Concepts widely used in formulations of substantive laws, *e.g.,* intention, causation, possession.

(5) Concepts used to demarcate basic legal relations, *e.g.,* right-duty, power-liability.

(6) Concepts central to the administration of law, *e.g.,* interpretation, *ratio decidendi,* discretion, stare decisis, justification.

(7) Concepts used in classifying laws, *e.g.,* criminal, civil, substantive, procedural, public, private.

(8) Concepts used in criticism of law and its administration, *e.g.,* justice, freedom, equality, morality, natural law, " the rule of law."

So much for subject matter. What activities are involved in the " analysis " of this subject matter? Like most cover words, " analysis " suggests more unity than exists. For analysis is not a single activity, but rather a family of related activities. It includes breaking down concepts, differentiating related concepts, correlating and/or unifying related concepts, classifying them in some way, and charting their implications—their " logical bearings." [20] Perhaps " analysis " is not an ideal word,[21] but in the interest of brevity some cover word is essential, and " analysis " seems better than any other. . . .

Because of vague similarities, conceptual analysis is not uncommonly confused with legal interpretation.[22] But when the jurist engages in conceptual analysis he is simply not doing the kind of work that the lawyer does when he interprets a statute or some other authoritative text. Although there are many differences, three will suffice for illustration. First, the sources of their problems are very different. The lawyer's interpretational problem arises because, for example, there is inconsistent usage of the same word in the text, syntactical ambiguity, or evidence of a difference between what the authority intended and the usual meanings of the words used. The conceptual analyst's problem does not arise in this manner. Instead, it may arise because he is genuinely puzzled or confused about what is involved in the general content of some concept or about how it contrasts with and relates to other concepts. Alternatively, his problem may arise not because he is antecedently puzzled or in a fog, but rather because he simply wants to articulate a clear analysis of something he has set out to investigate.[23]

---

[20] In the course of these activities, various methodological techniques, distinctions, or ideas may come into play. For discussion of some of these as they figure in Hart's work see Summers, Professor H. L. A. Hart's Concept of Law, 1963 Duke L.J. 629, 661.

[21] For those familiar with jurisprudence, it should be plain that " analysis," as used here, does not mean the formulation of logically equivalent definitions à la Russell and Moore. (The uninitiated would not know of and therefore not worry about this possible meaning anyway.)

[22] See, *e.g.,* Bodenheimer, Modern Analytical Jurisprudence and the Limits of Its Usefulness, 104 U.Pa.L.R. 1080, 1085 (1956); Dunlop, Developments in English Jurisprudence 1953–1963, 3 Alberta L. Rev. 63, 72 (1963); Jones, A View From the Bridge, Law & Society, Summer 1965, pp. 39, 40.

[23] See Warnock, English Philosophy Since 1900, at 147–157 (1958).

Second, the lawyer can almost always frame his issue in terms of a choice between two alternative interpretations each of which he readily grasps and fully understands. This cannot be true of the jurist whose problem arises because of antecedent confusion or puzzlement. Moreover, the jurist's analysis—his " solution," if it can be called that—can hardly be described in terms of a choice between alternatives. The complexity of the activities involved in analysis defies such simplicity of description. Third, the lawyer will use techniques in his " analysis " that are hardly appropriate for the analytical jurist. Thus, interpreting a statute, the lawyer can be expected to invoke canons of statutory construction, canons obviously foreign to conceptual analysis. Also, the lawyer might involve himself in the old methodological dispute between purposive and literal interpretation.[24] But the jurist, qua analyst, could not even be a party to this dispute if he is analyzing the conceptual *status quo,* or, indeed, even if he is recommending the adoption of a better conceptual framework for representing reality.[25] In both cases, he is plainly not trying to determine what a specific person on a particular occasion meant by a specific use of a term. Furthermore, the lawyer, in interpreting a statute, may quite rightly marshal and rely on relevant arguments of public policy. But it would be inappropriate, indeed, for a jurist to try to establish a *conceptual* connection between, say, the concept of law and the concept of general rules, by invoking considerations of " public policy." Similarly, it would be queer, indeed, for him to differentiate the concepts of purposive and reckless behavior " as a matter of public policy." It is proper that within *the substantive law's* own conceptual scheme, connections and distinctions be influenced by specific policies and purposes of duly constituted authorities. But it does not follow, in fact it is surely false, that all connections and distinctions within the conceptual scheme are exclusively creatures of specific human policies or purposes of the moment.[26] Whether or not there is a conceptual connection between the concept of law and the concept of

---

24 See generally Heydon's Case, 3 Coke 7a, 76 Eng.Rep. 637 (Ex. 1584). Every article on jurisprudence must include a citation to at least one case, for, as Holmes is supposed to have said, " Philosophising about the law does not amount to much until one has soaked in the details," quoted in J. Stone, Legal System and Lawyers' Reasonings 287 (1964).

25 Professor Lon L. Fuller appears to think the contrary. Thus, he has recently said that Professor Hart, in giving an account of judicial interpretation, is really " proposing " literal as opposed to purposive interpretation. See Fuller, Positivism and Fidelity to Law—A Reply to Professor Hart, 71 Harv.L.R. 630, 661–669 (1958). Professor Hart, however, is not in the relevant passages, proposing a theory of judicial interpretation at all. Rather, he is indicating his preference for one conceptual schema over another for the purpose of representing the nature of the process of judicial interpretation, and this he is doing in the context of conveying what he thinks is of value in the work of legal realists. Of course, he might be wrong in his preference, but this would be to adopt a framework that misrepresents reality, and not to adopt an indefensible theory of judicial interpretation. See Hart, Positivism and the Separation of Law and Morals, 71 Harv.L.R. 593, 606–608 (1958).

26 From the tenor of Professor Fuller's article, it appears he believes that the very existence of any distinction between law " as it is " and law " as it ought to be " must ultimately turn somehow on the relevance of some specific and practical purpose. He suggests that the only " real " reason Professor Hart might have for insisting on this distinction is not conceptual in nature. Rather, it is a more specific and practical reason, namely, that Professor Hart believes strongly in " fidelity to law." Fuller, Positivism and Fidelity to Law—A Reply to Professor Hart, 71 Harv.L.R. 630 (1958).

general rules, and whether or not the general concepts of purposive or reckless behavior can be differentiated, are *not,* as such, questions arising within the conceptional scheme of the substantive law. Moreover, while over the long run such connections and distinctions are influenced by general human purposes, they have a reality of their own [27] which is not governed by short-run, transitory, practical policies or purposes of the moment. Of course, whether or not these connections and distinctions are to be recognized and embodied in the substantive law, and thus made subject to such policies and purposes, is an entirely different question, and itself one of policy.

With respect to conceptual analysis, how do the old analysts differ from the new? The new are methodologically more sophisticated, a point that will be developed later in this article.[28] Of equal, if not greater, importance is the fact that the new analysts are engaged in analyzing a wider range of concepts than their predecessors. John Austin very broadly defined the range of concepts jurists might investigate.[29] But most of his successors actually worked within far narrower bounds. This is especially true of analytical jurists in the United States, who by the mid-1930's had become almost exclusively preoccupied with analyzing concepts of "jural relations" such as "right," "duty," "power," and "liability." [30] In 1937, the then leading American analytical jurist, Albert Kocourek, proclaimed that "the jural relation is the central theme of analytic jurisprudence." [31] And so it was. This myopic narrowness contrasts strikingly with the wide-ranging interests of the new jurists. Already they have published studies of such varied subjects

---

[27] For a useful general discussion of the "theory of distinctions" in which the interplay between purposes and less transient factors is perceptively analyzed see Crawshay-Williams, Methods and Criteria of Reasoning 103–127 (1957).

[28] See pp. 877–887, *infra.*

[29] He said their study encompassed "principles, notions, and distinctions" that are "necessary" to law, and others not necessary but which, because of their "utility," "extend through all communities." Austin, The Province of Jurisprudence Determined 367–369 (Library of Ideas ed. 1954) [and *cf.* Mead, *ante,* 144.]

[30] See Hohfeld, Fundamental Legal Conceptions (1923); Kocourek, Jural Relations (1927); Cook, Hohfeld's Contributions to the Science of Law, 28 Yale L.J. 721 (1919); Cook, The Utility of Jurisprudence in the Solution of Legal Problems, 5 Lectures on Legal Topics 337 (1928); Corbin, Jural Relations and Their Classification, 30 Yale L.J. 226 (1921); Corbin, Legal Analysis and Terminology, 29 Yale L.J. 163 (1919); Corbin, Rights and Duties, 33 Yale L.J. 501 (1924); Corbin, What Is a Legal Relation?, 5 Ill.L.Q. 50 (1922); Goble, Affirmative and Negative Legal Relations, 4 Ill.L.Q. 94 (1922); Goble, Negative Legal Relations Re-examined, 5 Ill.L.Q. 36 (1922); Goble, A Redefinition of Basic Legal Terms, 35 Colum.L.R. 535 (1935); Goble, The Sanction of a Duty, 37 Yale L.J. 426 (1928); Goble, Terms for Restating the Law, 10 A.B.A.J. 58 (1924); Radin, A Restatement of Hohfeld, 51 Harv.L.R. 1141 (1938); Terry, The Arrangement of the Law (pts. 1, 2), 17 Column.L.R. 291, 365 (1917); Terry, Duties, Rights and Wrongs, 10 A.B.A.J. 123 (1924).

For explicit statements of the scope of analytical jurisprudence as Hohfeld and Kocourek saw it see their remarks as quoted in Hall, Readings in Jurisprudence 336–339 (1938).

One brilliant American analytical jurist who was not preoccupied with the topic of jural relations during this period was John Dickinson. See, in particular, the following articles: The Law Behind Law (pts. 1, 2), 29 Column.L.R. 113, 285 (1929); Legal Rules—Their Application and Elaboration, 79 U.Pa.L.R. 1052 (1931).

[31] Kocourek, The Century of Analytic Jurisprudence Since John Austin, in 2 Law, A Century of Progress: 1835–1935, at 195, 216 (1937).

as justice,[32] discretion,[33] strict liability,[34] imperatives,[35] responsibility,[36] causation,[37] and the nature of law itself.[38]

Construction of a Conceptual Framework or Schema

If the analytical jurist is to provide the illumination and insight of which he is capable, he must commonly go beyond the conceptual *status quo*. He must go beyond analyzing concepts within our conceptual scheme as it is, and devise improved ways of more adequately representing reality.[39] The necessity for such creative and constructive effort stems from two sources. First, our existing conceptual framework does not always have things right initially. Second, things change, and our concepts sometimes lag behind, thus becoming outmoded. Just as the nineteenth century concept of travel is outmoded today, so too is its concept of law.

Not all concepts, not all ideas, are about things. But some are, and we sometimes have the wrong *idea* of a thing. Thus, some do not have the right idea of what it is to have an obligation, or what it is to exercise discretion, or what constitutes punishment, or what morality involves. Instead, they have *misconceptions*. Usually, misconceptions such as these can be cleared up by someone who has " got things right." But it is conceivable that no one has yet got some things right. Some things none of us yet understands. Our puzzlement exists not because we do not have enough facts about these things; rather, it is that our existing conceptual framework is inadequate—it does not take satisfactory account of what we are puzzled about. A different schema or framework is needed. While providing this involves going beyond the conceptual *status quo,* it does not necessarily involve introducing wholly new concepts or devising new terminologies in which to express these concepts. Frequently, it will involve combining old ideas or old and new ideas. Sometimes a new word or phrase will be invented, or an old word or phrase will be put to a new use. . . .

It is essential to stress that conceptual lag, as well as the failure to get things right in the beginning gives rise to the necessity of constructing conceptual frameworks. To illustrate: One of the central problems of jurisprudence is the problem of explicating the nature of law itself. Law—the phenomenon of law—unlike elephants or triangles, is a mode of social organization and therefore is itself subject to some change, even fundamental change over long periods. Because of this, our understanding of law, our conceptions of it, may ultimately require revision.[40] Hence, in criticizing a theory such as John Austin's that law consists of sovereign commands, there are two possible dimensions of criticism. It is not

---

[32] Fried, Justice and Liberty, 6 Nomos (Justice) 126 (1963).
[33] Dworkin, Judicial Discretion, 60 J. Philosophy 624 (1963).
[34] Wasserstrom, Strict Liability in the Criminal Law, 12 Stan.L.R. 731 (1960).
[35] Morris, Imperatives and Orders, 26 Theoria 183 (1960).
[36] Hughes, Book Review, 16 Stan.L.R. 470 (1964).
[37] Hart and Honoré, Causation in the Law (1959).
[38] Hart, The Concept of Law (1961) [a selection of essays illustrating Summers's theme is found in his *Essays in Legal Philosophy* (1968).]
[39] On the general nature of this task see Hall, Conceptual Reform—One Task of Philosophy, 61 Proceedings of the Aristotelian Soc'y 169 (1961); Nowell-Smith, Philosophical Theories, 48 Proceedings of the Aristotelian Soc'y 165 (1948).
[40] See generally Corbett, Innovation and Philosophy, 68 Mind 289 (1959). See also note 48, *supra*.

merely that Austin might have gotten it wrong in the first place back in 1828. It is also possible that some features of his theory might need to be revised specifically to account for basic developments since that date.[41] For example, any account of the nature of law in modern industrial societies must make a place for the pervasive impact of new administrative institutions with their varied structures and paraphernalia of orders, rulings, and regulations.

This, then, explains in a general way what is involved in constructing a conceptual framework, and explains what occasions this kind of creative analytical activity. With respect to this activity, how do the old and the new analysts compare? It cannot be said that old analysts did not engage in this activity. John Austin certainly did. His lectures are filled with formulations which he apparently thought more faithfully represented the nature of law than any framework theretofore devised.[42] But it can be said that, to date, conceptual revision, that is, the construction of new conceptual frameworks, appears to be a far more central interest of the new analysts as a whole than it was of their predecessors. Hart and all of the other principal analysts have been concerned with it, at one time or another.[43] Furthermore, since the nature of this kind of analytical work is much better understood today, it should be performed more perspicaciously.

Rational Justification

Rational justification is a third main type of activity that is, in its own way, analytical. Consider the following illustrative questions: What, if any, is the rational justification—the " case "—for civil disobedience? What, if any, is the rational justification—the " case "—for punishment as such? What, if any, is the rational justification—the " case "—for stare decisis? Questions of this type call upon the jurist to " make out a general case " —to marshal and articulate general justifying arguments, rather than to analyze the conceptual *status quo* or construct new conceptual schemes with their accompanying terminologies. Rational justification differs in two ways from the familiar day-to-day practical justification employed by the man of action. First, the analytical jurist works on a general type of question, *e.g.*, what, if any, is the rational justification—the " case "— for civil disobedience? The man of action, however, addresses himself to a more immediate and specific form of this general question, *e.g.*, is it justified to disobey the local ordinance against mixing races in public hotels? Second, the man of action, in the nature of things, takes a stand on the merits of his specific question, whereas the analytical jurist need not take a stand at all. His job is completed when he has formulated and marshalled the revelant arguments. While this task necessarily requires that he evaluate the *rational* plausibility of possible arguments, it does not *call* on him to take a stand on the ultimate

---

41 See generally Hexner, The Timeless Concept of Law, 52 J. Politics 48, 62–63 (1943).
42 See Austin, The Province of Jurisprudence Determined (Library of Ideas ed. 1954).
43 See, *e.g.* Hart, The Concept of Law (1961); Wasserstrom, The Judicial Decision: Toward a Theory of Legal Justification (1961); Dworkin, Judicial Discretion, 60 J. Philosophy 624 (1963); Fried, Moral Causation, 77 Harv.L.R. 1258 (1964); Williams, Concept of Legal Liberty, 56 Colum.L.R. 1129 (1956); Hughes, Book Review, 16 Stan.L.R. 470 (1964); Morris, Book Review, 13 Stan.L.R. 185 (1960).

question or to grind an axe of any kind. Rational justification is analytical at least in the positive respect that it involves differentiating, constructing, and marshalling rational arguments.

While rational justification does not appear to have engaged the old analytical jurists to any significant extent, it is a main interest of the new. Hart has written on the justification of punishment as a social practice,[44] Wasserstrom on the justification of judicial decisions,[45] and Dworkin on justified and unjustified uses of law to enforce morality.[46] This broadening of interests to include rational justification is a welcome development in an age incessantly plagued by forces fostering irrationalism.[47] It is simply not true that just anything can serve as a reason for anything else, nor is it true that all reasons are fungible, that one is always just as good as any other. Also, reasons count. They are seldom rationalizations.

Purposive Implication

Though of less significance than the activities already discussed, "purposive implication"[48] is another kind of analytical endeavor that has interested some of the new jurists. There is little or no evidence, however, that it occupied any of their predecessors. Its general character can be briefly explained. Consider the following illustrative questions: Given a purpose to have an effective system of law, does it *follow* that, in general, there must be rules? Known rules? Rules that are prospectively applicable? Given man's purpose to survive, his nature, and the conditions under which he lives, does it *follow* that he must have rules proscribing theft and violence? Given a purpose to have a humane and liberal society, does it *follow* that the legal system in such a society must recognize some version of the doctrine of *mens rea*? Questions of this nature call for work different from rational justification. In addressing such questions, the jurist does not build up a general case for or against some general proposition, institution, practice, or idea; instead, he traces what the acceptance of social purposes, aims, or values *commits* us to in terms of social arrangements and social ordering.[49] This activity is "analytical" at least in the positive respect that it involves tracing implications of what may be called "social premises."[50]

---

[44] See Hart, Prolegomenon to the Principles of Punishment, 60 Proceedings of the Aristotelian Soc'y 1 (1960).

[45] See Wasserstrom, The Judicial Decision: Toward a Theory of Legal Justification (1961).

[46] Dworkin, Lord Devlin and the Enforcement of Morals, 75 Yale L.J. 986 (1966).

[47] For the record, it is worth identifying some of these forces. First, the tag end, at least, of logical positivism remains. Some positivists thought rational justification was not even possible. Second, there is misplaced libertarianism: "A man is *free* to adopt any position." Third, there is misplaced egalitarianism: "One man's view is just as good as any other man's." Fourth, Freud gets into the act: "We don't know what our *real* reasons are, so they cannot be all that important." And, just to end this particular list, we have the alarming result-orientation of a few modern political scientists: "It's the result that counts, not the reasons; reasons have little to do with results anyway."

[48] This phrase was very recently introduced into the literature by Professor Lon L. Fuller. See Fuller, The Morality of Law 184 (1964). While Professor Fuller's book and his other works are full of insights of interest to analytical jurists, he would probably not want to be considered one of them.

[49] Actually, the most outstanding contemporary example of this kind of work appears in Fuller, The Morality of Law 33–94 (1964). But see Hart, The Concept of Law 189–195 (1961), for an apt example from the work of an avowed analyst.

---

[50] For footnote, see p. 268.

Thus, in addition to conceptual analysis, some or all of the new jurists are interested in what we have called the construction of conceptual frameworks, rational justification, and purposive implication, each of which may be plausibly characterized as analytical in nature. In these latter three types of work, most earlier analytical jurists displayed little or no interest. In summary, it can be said that the concerns of the new analytical jurists are broader in at least two important respects—they are performing a wider variety of analytical activities and, in doing conceptual analysis, always a major concern of analytical jurists, they are focusing on a much wider range of problems.   [pp. 865–877]

---

50 While this work is in one sense deductive, it differs from strictly formal deduction. It would be inappropriate to say that valid conclusions of purposive implication derive their validity—their " necessity "—from compliance with formal rules of logical inference. It is better to say, simply, that our shared purposes, our knowledge or assumptions concerning relevant facts, and our practical wisdom " demand " these conclusions. *Cf.* Hart, The Concept of Law 195 (1961), where the author discusses the concept of " natural " as opposed to " definitional " or " formal " necessity.

5

PURE THEORY OF LAW

KANT V. HUME

THERE is, perhaps, no single legal writer in this century who has made a more illuminating analysis of the legal process than Hans Kelsen. And certainly whether we accept or not all his positions, it cannot be denied that he has done as much as anyone, by his lucid exposition and his tenacious defence of them, to stimulate thought and provoke further inquiry in this controversial field. Yet some of the controversy that has resulted from his writings has undoubtedly been due to misunderstandings caused, for all his general clarity of thought, by the use of language which, to Anglo-Saxons at least, is apt to prove deceptive.[1] For although Kelsen is the very antithesis of those whom, rightly or wrongly, English lawyers may regard as the typical continental legal philosopher dealing in wordy abstractions unrelated to reality, it must be admitted that, especially in his earlier writing, a certain fondness for Kantian terminology may have resulted in confusions which have, however, been to some extent cleared up in his later writings.[2]

Kelsen has undoubtedly shown a leaning towards the Kantian approach to the theory of knowledge, according to which the objective world is transmuted by certain formal categories applied to it by the mind of the onlooker. This lies at the root of his search for the formal elements, as concepts of the human mind, which enable us to grasp the inherent structure of any legal system, and also to his acceptance of monism, a single " world of law." [3] Also Kelsen follows Kant in distinguishing between the two categories of existence and of normative relations (" is " and " ought "). But in reality Kelsen is a positivist of positivists, whose real spiritual father is Hume, rather

---

1 Also by a failure to appreciate the political and intellectual background, against which Kelsen developed his *Rechtswissenschaft*. The influence of Freud, The " Vienna Circle " of philosophy, and the remaking of central Europe after World War I are described by Stone, *Legal System and Lawyers' Reasonings* (1964), pp. 98–100. See also the philosophical controversies described by McBride (1968) 43 N.Y.U.L.Rev. 53, 66–70.

2 *Cf. post*, 217. Some of Kelsen's most lucid expositions will be found in the essays contained in *What is Justice?* (1957).

3 See also Harris's criticism of Kelsen's assumption that there is only one field of normative meaning to which scientific discourse can refer when it uses the concept of validity. The " unfortunate metaphysical gloss " to which Harris refers is yet another legacy of Kelsen's Kantian background ([1971] C.L.J. 103, 115–116).

than Kant. For while Kant regarded knowledge of the physical world as necessarily imperfect, for him moral truth was an absolute which could be directly understood *a priori* by reason, and which could be expressed in the form of a categorical imperative or unshakable natural law.[4] For Hume, on the other hand, the moral order could not be deduced from the physical world (or as he said, " ought " could not be inferred from " is "[5]) and moral or normative rules were merely relative to the subjective opinions of human beings. This, indeed, is precisely Kelsen's position. For him legal or moral statements are purely normative and must not be confused with physical facts. Moreover, a norm cannot be derived from facts, but only from other norms. In occasional unguarded language Kelsen seems to have suggested, on Kantian lines, that these correspond to two separate orders of existence.[6] In fact, however, what we have here is two different uses of language, or two different types of propositions.[7] This is brought out by Kelsen's later distinction between causality and what he calls " imputation." [8] Natural science is concerned with causal explanations of the physical world, whereas normative science, such as law or ethics, is concerned with conduct as it ought to take place, determined by norms. " Under certain conditions a certain consequence ought to take place. This is the grammatical form of the principle of imputation." [9] The old natural law is, therefore, rejected, as it was by Hume, on the ground that it is an illogical attempt to establish the objective character of what is necessarily normative. Where norms contain value judgments, as in ethics, these are subjective and relative and cannot be proved true or false, since they depend only on personal feeling or opinion, and not on objective fact.[10] Natural law, according to Kelsen, was nothing but an attempt to justify existing law, and give sanctity to the property system that it enshrined. Attempts in this century to revive it, by arguing that

---

[4] For an account of the Kantian attitude to moral law, see Mackinson, *Study of Ethical Theory* (1957), Chap. 3, or Paton, *The Moral Law* (1949).

[5] *Ante,* p. 31.

[6] Thus the Kantian morality compels us to think of ourselves as having a " real existence " *outside* the causal system: see Passmore, *100 Years of Philosophy,* p. 95.

[7] *What is Justice?*, p. 269. Though Kelsen was the first legal philosopher since Bentham to concern himself with the problems of legal language.

[8] See *What is Justice?*, p. 324 *et seq.* Kelsen's preference for " imputation " rather than " causality " has an ideological as well as a philosophical basis. He believes in individual responsibility (the German *Zurechnung,* translated as " imputation " is associated with the concept of accountability in the sense of responsibility; causality, on the other hand, connotes determinism). See, further, Ebenstein, 59 Calif.L.Rev. 617, 635–637 and *post,* 306.

[9] See *What is Justice?*, p. 349.

[10] Kelsen asserts that *legal* norms contain *legal* values which are objective in the sense that their existence depends on objectively verifiable *facts, i.e.,* the effectiveness of the legal system as a whole, and the facts which create those norms (*e.g.,* legislation, custom, etc.). Cf. *ibid.,* p. 224 *et seq.*; also *post,* 304.

values do exist in the same way as facts, are spurious, since the "existence" of a norm simply means that it is *valid* within a particular context, but not that it can be described as a *fact*.[11]

Norms and the Basic Norm

The pure theory thus desires, in a positivist and scientific spirit, to analyse the concept of positive law, its structure and typical forms, excluding all elements foreign to it, such as justice or sociology. Norms are regulations setting forth how men are to behave, and positive law is simply a normative order regulating human conduct in a specific way. A norm is an "ought" proposition; it expresses not what is, or is done, or must be, but what ought to be, given certain conditions [12]; its existence can only mean its *validity*,[13] and this refers to its connection with a system of norms of which it forms a part. It cannot be proved to exist factually, but simply to be derivable from other norms, and is, therefore, valid in that sense.

But if a norm can only be derived from another norm, does this mean one can continue this derivation *ad infinitum*? Theoretically, yes, but, in practice, as norms are concerned with human conduct, there must be some ultimate norm postulated on which all the others rest. This is the basic norm. So far as the legal system is concerned

---

11 See especially, *ibid.*, p. 174 *et seq.*

12 "Ought" here does not refer to moral obligation but simply to the normative form of legal propositions. For Kelsen these are mainly differentiated by the fact that the reaction of law consists in a measure of coercion enacted by the legal order and socially organised. Morality works by direct motivation, *i.e.*, it regulates the behaviour of one individual. Law is indirect as involving not only the person whose conduct is in question but also the one who is to apply the sanction. Religious norms are nearer to law than morals, as providing for supernatural sanctions. See H. Kelsen, *What is Justice?*, pp. 235–244. In his later writings, notably *The Pure Theory of Law* (English translation, 1967), Kelsen has indicated that "ought" covers such other modalities as "can" and "may" (see pp. 5, 16). So a norm "permits the use of force in self-defence" (p. 16); another allows the institution of court proceedings (pp. 134 *et seq.*). This goes some way towards countering the type of criticism that Hart makes of Austin's command concept as failing to explain the "variety of laws" (*The Concept of Law*, Chap. 3) and answers Bobbio's point (in Hughes, *Law, Reason and Justice* (1969), p. 189 *et seq.*) that Kelsen's theory fits the nineteenth century negative liberal state but not the contemporary social welfare ideal. See further the discussion of some of the practical implications of Kelsen's new standpoint in Clark (1969) 22 J.Legal Ed. 170, 177–179.

13 A concept with various meanings and one not used with any consistency by Kelsen. Harris demonstrates that there are four, possibly five, senses in which validity is used to qualify a legal norm. It may suggest conformity to a higher norm ("is not *ultra vires*, is not void"); or that it "is a consistent part of a normative field of meaning"; or correspondence with social reality; or that it "has inherent claim to fulfilment." As Harris points out, Kelsen himself uses "valid" primarily [in the second sense], but sometimes without recognising the distinction [in the first]. The third and fourth uses of the concept are alien to Kelsenian thought: the third equates validity and effectiveness and Kelsen specifically distinguishes them, *post*, n. 51: the fourth suggests that a rule has political or moral value and is thus inconsistent with the pure theory of law, *post*, 291. See *op. cit.*, pp. 112–116 and Christie (1964) 48 Minn.L.R. 1049.

this basic norm must be extra-legal, since *ex hypothesi* it does not rest upon another legal norm. But Kelsen is at pains to point out that the choice of the basic norm [14] is not arbitrary. On the contrary it must be selected by the legal scientist on the principle of efficacy, that is to say that the legal order as a whole must rest on an assumption that is by and large efficacious, in the sense that in the main people do conduct themselves in conformity with it.[15] The basic norm is non-positive and so is not the concern of legal science, but it is really purely formal in giving unity to the legal system and marking the limits of those norms which are the subject of legal science.[16] The choice of the basic norm may also have important implications in determining the relation of national state law to international law. For if the basic norm is in conformity to the constitution of each state, there will be a pluralistic congeries of independent legal systems, while if that norm is taken in relation to international law, there will be a monistic world order, from which each national law will derive. Kelsen does not, however, make very clear how far this choice is predetermined by the principle of effectiveness,[17] though the fact that all states purport to regard themselves as bound by international law (subject to their own construction of what may be its particular rules), may perhaps bring the choice of a monistic system, unquestionably favoured by Kelsen himself, within this principle.

Kelsen, as a true positivist, spurns all metaphysical entities, such as the state or rights and duties. Thus, the imputation of acts to the state is a figure of speech, which, in a legal context, merely refers to norms of the legal order.[18] But the term "legal order" is wider than that of the state, since it is only a relatively centralised order which is termed a state, and this would exclude, for instance, primitive societies and the present international legal order.[19] Again rights and duties are not entities existing in themselves, but merely the expression of legal norms related to the concrete conduct of individuals.

HIERARCHY OF NORMS AND LAW-MAKING PROCESS

Kelsen's description of the legal process as a hierarchy of norms, the validity of each norm (apart from the basic norm) resting upon a

[14] Kelsen's clearest formulation of this is his answer to Professor Stone's critique. See 17 Stan.L.R. 1128, 1140–1151 and see *post*, 309.
[15] *Ibid.*, p. 268.   [16] pp. 360–361.
[17] *Cf.* Benn, in *Political Philosophy* ed. Quinton (1967), pp. 75–77.
[18] According to Goodhart, Pollock's statement that law is enforced by the state because it is law; it is not law because the state enforces it; is Pollock's most important statement. (Pollock, *Jurisprudence and Legal Essays*, ed., A. L. Goodhart, pp. XXV and 15). This would certainly not be endorsed by Kelsen.
[19] *Ibid.*, p. 293, *post*, *cf.* Barkun, *ante*, 42. Kelsen refers to the animistic tendency to imagine a spirit behind phenomena, as Helios and the sun, and explains the idea of "the State" as an entity on the same basis.

higher norm, and each level in the hierarchy representing a movement from complete generality to increasing individualisation, has
sometimes been misunderstood as suggesting that the interpretation
and application of general rules are of a purely mechanical character.
This is far from being Kelsen's view. On the contrary, he points out
that though law has the peculiarity of regulating its own creation, a
higher norm can determine the creation and content of another norm
only to a certain extent. In so far as there is a discretion or a choice
as to the applicable rule, the norm-creating function takes on a
political character.[20] This is obvious in the case of the American
Supreme Court applying the general provisions of the constitution,
but it is the same with the application of law by any legal authority.
And the function does not cease to be legal on this account, for it
still takes place within the framework of norms.[21]

Kelsen does not deny the validity of the sociological viewpoint,
whose object is not the study of norms but of the actual legal
behaviour of men. This stands side by side with normative jurisprudence and neither can replace the other. The latter deals with
validity and the former with efficacy, but the two are inter-connected,
since the sociology of law presupposes the normative concept of
law.[22] But Kelsen makes a curious distinction between the role of
the legal scientist and of a law-making authority, such as a judge.
The former can only describe and not prescribe, and, therefore, he
cannot exercise any choice open to the latter. The legal scientist
must, therefore, accept any decision as valid, since it is outside his
competence to say whether it is within the framework of the general

---

[20] Kelsen would not approve of the development in the United States in recent
years of the " political question " doctrine under which the Supreme Court
(or, indeed, any lower court) refuses to hear a case on the grounds that the
decision is not within its competence but is the responsibility of another organ
of government. So, the Supreme Court has refused to decide upon the legality
of the Vietnam war (*Mora* v. *McNamara*, 398 U.S. 934 (1967); *U.S.* v. *Mitchell*,
386 U.S. 972 (1967): in both the Court merely denied certiorari, so gave no
reasons). On the doctrine see Gottlieb (1967) *Annual Survey of American Law*,
p. 699 and Frankfurter J.'s dissent in *Baker* v. *Carr*, 369 U.S. 186, 267 (1962).
Nor is the problem unique to the United States. See the endeavours of the
Constitutional Court in the German Federal Republic to limit its competence
in political matters by declaring, for example, that it will not review questions
of expediency nor assail the discretion of the legislator. (Muller (1965) 6 Journal
of I.C.L. 191.) *Cf. Blackburn* v. *A.-G.*, *ante*, 239. For a general survey of the
question of justiciability, see Marshall, in ed. Guest, *Oxford Essays in Jurisprudence*, p. 265, and for a recent discussion of some of its problems in connection
with administrative justice and the expulsion of an undesirable alien, see Hepple
(1971) 34 M.L.R. 501, 502–503, 513–518.

[21] *Ibid.*, pp. 372–373. The emphasis on the political element in the work of the
judge is most common in connection with constitutional interpretation. For
example, Rostow asserts that this function requires a judge to be thoroughly
steeped in the history and public life of his country. (See Eugene V. Rostow,
The Sovereign Prerogative (1962), p. 93.) For the place of policy considerations
in the international judicial process, see R. Higgins (1968) 17 I.C.L.Q. 58.

[22] pp. 267–271.

norm in question. And though he can point out possible interpretations he must leave it to the law-making authority to make the choice, for to try to influence this authority is to exercise a political and not a legal function.[23] This seems to involve an act of renunciation on the part of legal science which it is hardly likely to acquiesce in, and apparently treats the advocate arguing a case as a politician, rather than a lawyer.[24]

SANCTIONS

For Kelsen, every system of norms rests for its motivation on some type of sanction, though this may be of an undifferentiated kind, such as disapproval [25] by a group. The essence of law is an organisation of force, and law thus rests on a coercive order designed to bring about certain social conduct. The law attaches certain conditions to the use of force, and those who apply it act as organs of the community. Kelsen bases this view on the historical fact (as he asserts) that there has never been a " large " community which was not based on a coercive order. This applies equally to primitive and international [26]

---

[23] *Ibid.*, pp. 367–368. This is discussed more fully in *The Pure Theory of Law* (1967). The distinction in this later work is not so much between respective roles as between the products of the actors in each: law-making authorities issue *norms*; a jurist describes *normative statements*. See pp. 72–75, and Raz's discussion, *The Concept of a Legal System*, pp. 45–47. *Cf.* Hart's contrast of an external observer who can observe signs and predict accordingly but does not know the reasons for a pattern of behaviour, with the official who has a critical reflective attitude. (*The Concept of Law*, pp. 54–59.) Hart discussed Kelsen's distinction in 10 U.C.L.A.L.R. 709, 710–711.

[24] In a number of recent cases judges have failed to appreciate Kelsen's dichotomy between the respective roles of jurist and judge. For example, Udoma C.J. in *Uganda* v. *Commissioner of Prisons, ex p. Matovu* (1966) E.A. 514 said: " Applying the Kelsenian principles . . . our view is that the 1966 Constitution is a legally valid Constitution and the supreme law of Uganda . . . the 1962 Constitution abolished as a result of victorious revolution does no longer exist." But Kelsenian dogma is not really helpful to him. He had a practical decision to take which he did by weighing up relevant considerations, such as peace and stability. The pure science of law could not assist in this task. All it can do is to declare upon the new reality, one of the primary factors of which is judicial recognition. This interpretation is not supported by Harris (*op. cit.*, pp. 125–127) who, whilst admitting that there is no direct justification for his thesis in Kelsen's writings, has suggested that " judges in developed legal systems do act as legal scientists," so that, for example, they, as well as jurists, are capable of presupposing the grundnorm. His premise is that legal science " is a socially useful activity " (p. 119) and " can only continue to be socially useful so long as judges also indulge in it " (p. 126). It is difficult to see how the latter statement would have Kelsen's support, though its sentiment is one with which one would readily agree.

[25] Woozley (77 *Mind* 461, 475) points out that Kelsen fails to distinguish " disapproval " from " expressions of disapproval." The latter depends on " the supposed gravity of the infringement, the extent to which the society was a conformist society and the degree of tolerance which members of the society extended to each others' failings." Unlike legal sanctions, " they are the likely, not the necessary consequences of the infringement."

[26] The sanctions of international law are, for Kelsen, war and reprisals, comparable to self-help in primitive law: see *General Theory of Law and the State* (1946), p. 328 *et seq.* This is cogently criticised by Herz in ed. Engel and Metail, *Law, State and International Legal Order*, p. 108 (1968).

society, which simply lack the elements of specific centralised organs for law-creating and law-applying. The notion of a social order requiring no sanctions either looks back to a Golden Age or forward (as with Marxism) to a Utopian society. It is in fact the " negation of society," based on the illusion of the natural goodness of man.[27]

Kelsen commits himself to the view that every norm to be " legal " must have a sanction, though this may be found, as for instance in constitutional law, by taking it together with other norms with which it is inter-connected.[28]

Kelsen treats any breach of a legal norm as a " delict," whether this would normally be described in traditional terms as falling within the criminal or the civil law. For Kelsen, to be legally obligated to a certain behaviour means that the contrary behaviour is a delict and as such is the condition of a sanction stipulated by a legal norm.[29] Since Kelsen also regards a sanction as an essential characteristic of law, no conduct can amount to a delict unless a sanction is provided for it. This view has been criticised,[30] with some warrant, on the ground that though the absence of a sanction may make law ineffective, this is not the same as its being invalid, nor does the absence of a sanction necessarily entail invalidity. It is true that Kelsen does recognise that a legislature could make laws without considering it necessary to attach sanctions for violations.[31] He still objects, however, that although, under such a system it would be possible to decide whether a norm was legal or not by determining whether it had emanated from the appropriate authority, we would even so not be able to provide thereby a criterion by which law could be distinguished from other social norms. But, as has been pointed out, even if sanctions were essential to law, it is the legality of legal sanctions, not their character as coercive acts, which would contribute to the essence of law, since other social norms may also have coercive acts attached to them as sanctions.[32]

A further feature of Kelsen's analysis of the sanctionist view of law is that legal norms are stated in the form that, if a person does not comply with a certain prohibition, then the consequence is that the courts ought to inflict a penalty, whether criminal or civil. It follows that for Kelsen the content of legal norms is not primarily

---

[27] See especially, *What is Justice?*, pp. 231–256. *Cf.* Cowan's plea for Kelsen to substitute for force the notion of " control " (1971) 59 Calif.L.R. 683, 693–694.
[28] *General Theory*, pp. 29, 143–144.
[29] *General Theory of Law and State*, p. 59, *The Pure Theory of Law*, pp. 34, 115.
[30] By A. D. Woozley (1968) 77 *Mind* 461, 463–465 and Raz, *The Concept of a Legal System*, pp. 78 *et seq.*
[31] *General Theory of Law and State*, p. 122.
[32] *Cf.* Raz, *op. cit.*, p. 82 where lynching, vendetta (in " certain positive moral systems "), or the imposition of corporal punishment by parents and teachers are pointed to as examples of non-legal agencies of social control employing coercion to enforce non-legal norms.

to impose duties on the subject to conform, but rather to lay down
what judges or officials are expected to do in the event of a delict.
Accordingly, for Kelsen the norm which lays down the sanction,
involving a direction to the judge, is the primary norm, though he
recognises that there is a secondary norm which stipulates the
behaviour which the legal order endeavours to bring about by
announcing the sanction. This conflicts with the orthodox view
that legal duties set standards of conduct and accordingly
impose obligations on society as a whole. Moreover, as Woozley
points out,[33] although the officials ought to impose the sanction on a deviant, they may not have a legal duty to do so.
Whether they have will depend on further conditions. For if the
judge has such a legal duty, it can be only because there is a higher
norm prescribing a sanction against him for failing to apply the
lower-order norm. And such a hierarchy can lead to a " vicious
regress." "The stop is provided by having as a last norm one
' such that the sanction which it stipulates is not a legal duty in
the sense defined,' *i.e.*, the last norm is itself a sanctionless norm,"
of the permissive or power-conferring kind. Woozley justifiably
comments: "This is a serious watering-down . . . the proposition
that an organ of the state ought to act in a certain way may mean
nothing more than that, if it does not, its actions (legislative, judicial,
or administrative) have no validity." [34]

A further criticism of the sanctionist view, whether, indeed, that
of Kelsen or Austin, is that not only does it blur the distinction
between criminal and civil law,[35] but also makes it difficult to
distinguish between penal and administrative coercion. Thus, Kelsen
seeks to exclude cases of administrative enforcement, such as the
compulsory evacuation of buildings threatened by fire, or enforced
isolation of a person suffering from a contagious disease, from the
ambit of legal sanctions, on the ground that it is circumstances
other than human conduct which lead to the application of coercion,
whereas sanctions are always the consequent of human conduct.[36]
This distinction seems somewhat unrealistic, as it fails to take
account of the fact that many forms of administrative coercion,

---

[33] *Op. cit.*, pp. 470–474.
[34] *Idem*, p. 473, *cf.* the predictive view of Ross, *post*, 554.
[35] *Cf.* Bentham, *Of Laws in General*, Chap. 16.
[36] *General Theory of Law and State*, pp. 278–279. *The Pure Theory of Law*, pp.
40–42. For a detailed taxonomy of coercion in terms of their dominant purpose
or effect, see Packer, *The Limits of the Criminal Sanction* (1969), pp. 23–31,
251–257. His rough classification of coercion is into four categories; compensation, regulation, punishment and treatment. Both treatment and compensation
are also the consequent of human conduct, and neither are explained by a
sanctionist view of law. Packer's work draws particular attention to the neglect
of the concept of sanction, which is strange bearing in mind its prominence
in so many jurisprudential writings.

such as a compulsory purchase order on an owner unwilling to sell, or taxation, are the consequent of human conduct.[37] Perhaps the difficulty could be avoided by conceding that administrative coercion is just as much penal as any other coercion, if it is buttressed in any particular case by one form of penalty or another.

KELSEN AND AUSTIN

Kelsen has recognised the broad similarities between the pure theory and the imperative theory, but has equally emphasised the difference.[38] These may be summarised as follows:

Norm and Command

Austin, by relying on the idea of command as an expression of will, ignores the normative character of legal rules. A legal norm may bear an analogy to command but it does not rest on any active will (which is a fact, or perhaps here, a fiction) but on a higher norm, and is itself merely a proposition regarding human conduct in a particular form.[39]

Sanctions

Kelsen agrees with Austin that coercion is one essential feature of law but he rejects Austin's reliance on motivation by fear. Even if Austin is right as to this, which he probably is not,[40] the question is a sociological one. The science of law is solely concerned with coercive measures, directed under definite conditions, as part of the legal norm. Moreover, so far as legal science is concerned, the sanction is not the actual imprisonment operating on the mind of the wrongdoer, but is simply part of the rules forming the legal system. The application of the penalty represents the final individualisation of a set of legal norms.

Legal Dynamics

Austin ignores (so Kelsen says [41]) the dynamic process of law-creating which occurs throughout the hierarchy of norms, and which derive

---

[37] Nor could Kelsen extricate himself by defining a sanction as a consequent of " socially undesired behaviour," for " this is precisely an element which Kelsen considers to be excluded from the juristic definition of delict," *per* Hart, 10 U.C.L.A.L.R. 709, 720–721. Apart from which much administrative coercion is directed against " socially undesired behaviour " (*e.g.*, the high rates of purchase tax on luxury items and alcoholic beverages).

[38] See his detailed analysis, in *What is Justice?*, p. 271 *et seq.* Also it should be remembered that for Austin morality was to be measured by the objective criterion of utility, whereas for Kelsen, moral values are necessarily subjective and irrational. *Cf.* J. Hall, " Reason and Reality in Jurisprudence," in 7 Buffalo L.R. (1958), pp. 361, 369, 371.

[39] *Cf. ante*, 161. *Cf. The Pure Theory of Law*, 4–10, where Kelsen distinguishes the norm from " the act of will whose meaning the norm is: the norm is an *ought*, but the act of will is an *is* " (p. 5). See also 17 Stan.L.R. 1128, 1138–1139.

[40] For many other motives are involved.

[41] But Austin did not altogether overlook this. *Cf.*, *e.g.*, his view of judicial decision as a quasi-command of the sovereign and his general view as to the

from the constitution, whether written or unwritten. At each level of the hierarchy the *content* of norms may be developed on the basis of higher norms, and this, says Kelsen, is a "thoroughly dynamic principle." [42]

Basic Norm

Austin creates a dualism between the sovereign (or state) and the legal order. But the state is merely the "personification" of the legal order, and the sovereign merely that order's highest organ. Sovereignty is intended to imply that no higher order is assumed, such as an international order, but within the system of norms there is nothing stipulating that the sovereign must be free from legal limitation. Moreover, Austin makes the cardinal error of basing the validity of his legal order (or sovereignty) on a factual situation, *viz.*, habitual obedience, and ignores the logical objection to basing the validity of a norm on anything but another norm.

CRITIQUE

Kelsen's analysis of the formal structure of law as a hierarchical system of norms,[43] and his emphasis on the dynamic character of this process, is certainly illuminating and avoids some, at any rate, of the perplexities of the Austinian system. But is it not unduly rigid in its desire to make precise lines of demarcation between the legal scientist or the legal sociologist, and between the legal and political function? A legal system is not an abstract collection of bloodless categories but a living fabric in a constant state of movement. Is it enough simply to recognise, for instance, the discretionary process of courts as a dynamic function and then to hand over to an entirely different inquirer in order to ascertain the scope and significance of this function? Kelsen himself recognises that to call a judge's function "political" [44] as he does, does not deprive it of its legal quality. Then what is the virtue of this highly misleading description? There is a great danger that if we take the watch to pieces, and analyse each part separately, we shall never attain the overall picture which shows us how it works. And it is no answer to

creative role of the judiciary (*post*, 783). Bentham also recognised administrative acts as law-creating: see *Of Laws in General* ed. Hart (1970), pp. 3–4 (*ante*, 189).

42 *What is Justice?*, p. 280. See also *The Pure Theory of Law*, p. 198, where Kelsen is at pains to point out that this process involves creation, not merely the deductivism that he associates with Austinian jurisprudence. What is true is that many of Austin's successors and imitators did succumb to formalism and mechanical jurisprudence. This is almost a case of the sins of children being visited upon the father.

43 See *ante*, 8, for a further discussion as to the normative basis of law; also *post*, 497 as to the view of the Scandinavian Realists.

44 Alf Ross also speaks of "legal politics," though, unlike Kelsen, he contends that the doctrinal study of law cannot be detached from the sociology of law: see *On Law and Justice* (1958), pp. 19–24, and Chaps. 14–16.

say that we cannot criticise Kelsen, since this is his own chosen territory, as delimited by himself. For if he insists on occupying so narrow a platform this is no reason why we should be persuaded to join him there.

There are certain more specific points that need to be answered.

The Basic Norm ~TRANSCEDENTAL -LOGICAL PRESUPPOSITION

This is a very troublesome feature of Kelsen's system. We are not clear what sort of norm this really is, nor what it does, nor, indeed, where we find it. Part of the problem lies in Kelsen's own oblique-ness. In his latest formulation [45] he tells us that it is not " positive " (which means for Kelsen that it is *not* a norm of positive law, *i.e.*, created by *a real* act or will of a legal organ, but is *presupposed in juristic thinking*).[46] Hence, he argues, it is " meta-legal "; but, it is " legal " " if by this term we understand anything which has legally relevant functions." And, since it enables anyone to interpret a command, permission or authorisation as an objectively valid legal norm,[47] its legal functions are not in doubt. Nonetheless, we are told it is purely formal, is a juristic value judgment, and has a hypothetical character [48]; yet it forms the keystone of the whole legal arch (it is . . . " at the top of the pyramid [49] of norms of each legal order " [50]). Professor Goodhart was doubtful of the value of an

---

[45] In 17 Stan.L.R. 1130, 1140–1142.

[46] *Idem*, p. 1141, Kelsen reiterates in German terminology that the basic norm is not *gesetzt* by a real will, but *vorausgesetzt* in juristic thinking. Though Kelsen apparently now believes that the basic norm is a *fictitious norm* presupposing a *fictitious act of will* that lays down this norm. See in Olivecrona, *Law As Fact* (2nd ed., 1971), p. 114, and 1 Israel L.R. 1, 6–7. This shift is consistent with his new thinking on the concept of a norm. *Cf.* note 12, *ante*.

[47] Though, according to Harris, *op. cit.*, pp. 112–113, " the citizen or lawyer who distinguishes [for example] the tax officer's demand from the gangster's demand as ' valid ' or ' lawful ' does not need to presuppose a basic norm, unless he is a legal scientist seeking to show that the contents of the tax officer's directive form part of a unified field of meaning constituted by it and all other valid legal norms " [*cf. General Theory of Law and State*, p. 437]. The citizen or the lawyer need only go as far as the *particular* act of Parliament: he need not question Parliament's authority: only a legal scientist need do that.

[48] *What Is Justice?*, pp. 224–225, and see note 45.

[49] In *Legal System and Lawyers' Reasonings* (1964), Stone asserts that " the commonplace figure of a pyramid for the norms of a legal order is acceptable, with perhaps the modification (in view of the fact that the highest norms—those of the constitution—may themselves be numerous and complex) that the top of the figure may be a plateau rather than a point. . . . Indeed, since after all the norms of the pyramid are constructs out of the actual words of the constitutional and other laws, no harm is done by representing the constitution as a single point in the model, and in words, as a basic (or rather apex) norm. All that the logical theory of the structure of a legal order tells us is that the apex norm of any legal order, *i.e.*, its constitution, ought to be obeyed " (pp. 203–204). Stone here fuses, and thus confuses, the basic norm and ultimate constitutional norms. If there is only one basic norm, as is suggested in the text, then the figure will be a point, not a plateau, though Stone's term " apex norm," if the idea of a pyramid is retained, would appropriately describe this. [50] See 1 Israel L.R. 1.

analysis which did not explain the existence of the basic norm on which the whole legal system was founded.[51] However, it may be argued that we have reached the point where it is pointless to look for further *legal* justification. And this is what Kelsen recognises. Accordingly, he refers us to the principle of effectiveness. Kelsen tells us that every jurist assumes this to be the basis of the legal order (which is, surely, a fiction); and that it merely means that the legal order is as a whole effective (*i.e.*, that people do in fact behave according to the norms of this order), and that it may be stated in the form that men ought to behave in conformity with the legal order only if it is as a whole effective.[52] This seems to invoke either a totally unnecessary fictitious hypothesis, on the one hand, or, on the other, a statement of fact, dressed up in the shape of a general norm, but which is not unlike Austin's much-condemned reliance on habitual obedience.

Moreover, the basic norm is propounded as the means of giving unity to the legal system, and enabling the legal scientist to interpret all valid legal norms as a non-contradictory field of meaning.[53] Presumably, therefore, there can be only one basic norm. But is this so? And, if so, how is it related, if at all, to the constitution

---

[51] *English Law and Moral Law* (1953), p. 16. *Cf.* Toulmin, *Reason in Ethics*, p. 204 *et seq.* The same applies to giving reasons. "We can give people reasons for doing a thing in one way rather than another, so long as their ultimate proclivities are the same as our own; but the process must come to an end. And if this end being reached, we still differ, then there can be no more that we can do." D. Pole, *The Later Philosophy of Wittgenstein* (1958), p. 51. But *cf.* p. 56. Kelsen distinguishes carefully between validity and efficacy. The validity of the legal order as a whole, as well as of any particular norm within the legal order, depends on conformity with the basic norm. The efficacy of the legal order on the other hand is no more than the *condition* of validity, and not validity itself. The validity is conditioned by efficacy in the sense that a legal order as a whole, just as a single norm, *loses* its validity if it does not become by and large effective. "A legal order does not lose its validity by the fact that a single legal norm loses its efficacy, that is to say that this legal norm is not at all or in some particular cases not applied. A legal order is considered to be valid if its norms are *by and large* effective, that is, actually obeyed and applied." See Kelsen's reaffirmation of his views in "Professor Stone and the Pure Theory of Law" (1965) 17 Stan.L.Rev., pp. 1139–1140. It should be noted, further, that effectiveness is only one "condition" of validity. So, for example, a court which applies a statute immediately after promulgation—before the statute had a chance to become effective—applies a valid legal norm. (*Cf. The Pure Theory of Law*, p. 11.) See *The Pure Theory of Law*, pp. 211–214.

[52] *Ibid.* I do not know whether Kelsen has been influenced by the "coherence theory" of truth once propounded by the so-called Vienna Circle of logical positivists, but the resemblance is striking. According to this the criterion whether a statement is true, is its *consistency* with other statements. Since incompatible systems might each be internally consistent, we are told that we should accept that system *actually accepted* by scientists of our cultural circle: see *Revolution in Philosophy* (1956), p. 83. For Kelsen's association with the Vienna Circle, see Jerome Hall, *Studies in Jurisprudence and Criminal Theory* (1958), p. 35. Stone (*Legal System and Lawyers' Reasonings* (1964), p. 98) thinks Kelsen was influenced by the Vienna Circle.

[53] *Cf. The Pure Theory of Law*, p. 72. See also Harris, *op. cit.*, pp. 106–108.

of a given country? These questions are complicated by a lack of clarity in Kelsen's thought.

Kelsen has recently distinguished between what he calls the constitution in a legal-logical sense (what we have called the basic norm) and the constitution in a positive legal sense, which contains those rules governing the process of government which we call the constitution.[54] In the majority of countries this latter is usually contained in a document, but Kelsen admits that reduction to such a form is not necessary.[55] How are the basic norm and constitution in a positive legal sense related? Kelsen's answer is that we must trace back the existing constitution to a historically first constitution, which cannot be traced back to a positive norm created by a legal authority: " we arrive, instead, at a constitution that became valid in a revolutionary way, that is, either by breach of a former constitution, or for a territory that formerly was not the sphere of validity of a constitution and of a national legal order based on it." [56] The presupposition that this first constitution is valid is the basic norm. Furthermore, Kelsen has argued that this initial hypothesis is not a vague abstraction, but is based on objectively ascertainable facts, *viz.,* effectiveness.[57] We must, therefore, draw a distinction between the basic norm and the ultimate constitutional norms. There is necessarily only one basic norm, but the number of ultimate constitutional norms need not be so limited. Indeed, one of the functions of the basic norm is to resolve any conflict or seeming contradiction between different constitutional norms.[58]

The difficulty in relating this structure to a national legal order like that of the United Kingdom is that we have never had a constitution [59] and our ultimate constitutional norms have been established by custom. It is, nevertheless, possible, as Harris has recently demonstrated, to express our national legal order in Kelsenian terms. He suggests that the basic norm of the United Kingdom legal order is that " coercive acts ought to be applied only under conditions and in the ways customarily recognised as constitutional from time to time by the population at large," [60] and that there are two, possibly three,[61] ultimate constitutional norms. So, we

54 *Op. cit.,* note 45, at p. 1141, 1143.
55 See *The Pure Theory of Law,* p. 222 (the distinction between rules and a document).
56 *The Pure Theory of Law,* p. 200.
57 *Cf. What is Justice?,* pp. 262–263, 17 Stan.L.R. at p. 1141.
58 *General Theory of Law and State,* pp. 401, 406; *The Pure Theory of Law,* pp. 74, 195. See also Raz, *op. cit.,* p. 96.
59 In the sense of a single document.
60 *Op. cit.,* p. 111.
61 Is custom an independent source of law today? See Cross, *Precedent in English Law* (2nd ed.), pp. 155–162 and *post,* 573.

should obey the courts, for example, because of an ultimate constitutional norm that "coercive acts ought to be applied in accordance with judge-made rules established in conformity to the doctrine of binding precedent." [62] Is this to suggest that one should conform to an unwritten customary rule of the constitution? And, if so, is this additional hypothesis merely superfluous?

There is little doubt that in the majority of cases, certainly where stable democracies such as the United Kingdom are in issue, the basic norm is needless reduplication. But, if it can be shown that the basic norm is a positive guide in countries torn by revolution or other upheaval, then it may prove a valuable construct after all. Certainly, in the aftermath of such cataclysmic change, lawyers have believed that Kelsen's theory of the change of the basic norm was the key to unlock the mystery of the validity of pre- and post-revolutionary laws.[63] If it can be shown that their faith in Kelsen is well-placed, then there may be some justification for Kelsen's setting up of an additional extra-legal hypothesis. But, in deciding whether their expectations are legitimate ones, we must again return to Kelsen's curious distinction between the role of the legal scientist and the law-making authority.[64] For, it may be argued that Kelsen's theory, being descriptive of legal science, can only indicate the role of the jurist and can in no way assist the judge.[65] This would suggest that those judges who relied upon Kelsen's theory to solve post-revolution legal problems were labouring under the self-deception that Kelsen could assist them. But, this would in no way detract from any assistance that a legal scientist might seek in Kelsenian analysis.

Harris, however, goes further and, implying from Kelsen that a judge is a legal scientist, takes the view that the judges in Pakistan, Uganda and Southern Rhodesia were acting properly. "It is true," he argues, "that Kelsen's theory does not directly authorise a judge to make any particular decision. But indirectly it suggests that, when legal science gives a clear solution to a case, the judge ought to accept that solution, and this is true when, soon after the occurrence of a revolution, the question arises: has the grundnorm changed? The reason why it has this suggestive force for a judge is that the

---

[62] *Op. cit.,* pp. 109, 111.
[63] See *The State* v. *Dosso* (1958) 2 Pakistan S.C.R. 180, 185–186, 195, *Uganda* v. *Commissioner of Prisons, ex p. Matovu* (1966) E.A. 514, 535–536, *Madzimbamuto v. Lardner-Burke* (1968) 2 S.A. 284, 315, *Lakanmi and Kikelomoola* v. *A.-G.* (Western State), in 20 I.C.L.Q. 117, 127–128; *cf. Sallah* v. *A.-G.,* in 20 I.C.L.Q. 315, 320–321 where Sowah J.A. declared: "It seems to me we will not derive much assistance from the foreign theories." (Plato and Marx were also quoted!)
[64] *Cf. ante,* p. 273.
[65] See, for example, F. M. Brookfield, *The Courts, Kelsen, and the Rhodesian Revolution* (1969) 19 *University of Toronto Law Journal,* pp. 326, 342–344; *cf.* Harris, *op. cit.,* pp. 125–127.

theory assumes that legal science is a socially useful activity, which it could not be if it were not an essential part of the role of a judge to act as a legal scientist and to apply the conclusions of legal science." [66]

It is doubtful whether Harris is justified in drawing this conclusion from Kelsen and it may be that Kelsenian analysis of the change of a basic norm can only help the legal scientist pronouncing dispassionately after the event.[67] So, we must ask; what does Kelsen mean by "effective," for his basic norm is based upon this? How satisfactory a test is efficacy? What is meant by saying that norms, to be effective, must be obeyed or applied " by and large? " [68] How does one compute the number of opportunities to obey the law? What of "dead-letter" laws or laws only selectively enforced? [69] How many times is the law disobeyed by a motorist who drives for ten miles through a built-up area exceeding the speed-limit throughout his journey? [70] How many opportunities not to murder or steal does one get in a given period? Is motive for disobedience relevant? Are some laws more important than others? A man, for example, may never break a contract, pay all his taxes, heed the highway code but murder the head of state. Questions such as these suggest that effectiveness is a crude, unscientific test and yet it is crucial to Kelsen. Are we, therefore, to dismiss Kelsen's basic norm or can a more meaningful test be formulated? Harris's reformulation would relate the number of commands, permissions and authorisations issued by a legislator to the number of occasions that stipulated sanctions have been or are likely to be applied: "if there is a socially significant ratio between the official acts and the acts of disobedience, and it can be predicted that this ratio will continue to obtain for a reasonable length of time, the meaning-contents of the commands, permissions and authorisations are by and large effective norms." [71] But "socially significant" is vague, perhaps, purposely so. Would it involve, for example, attributing different weight to different "offences"? Would greater importance be attached to significant constitutional laws? [72] And, there are further difficulties: on this test, as indeed on Kelsen's, one might argue that the legal system in Southern Rhodesia today is the pre-U.D.I. system, for the majority of norms remain in force and there may be a certain amount

---

[66] *Op. cit.*, p. 132.
[67] See Dias [1968] C.L.J. 233; *cf.* Harris, *op. cit.*, p. 123.
[68] *The Pure Theory of Law*, p. 214, 17 Stan.L.R. at p. 1142.
[69] See, for example, the study by La Fave, *Arrest: The Decision to take a Suspect into Custody* (1965).
[70] *Cf.* Raz., *op. cit.*, p. 203.
[71] *Op. cit.*, p. 124; *cf.* Raz, *op. cit.*, pp. 203–205.
[72] See Hart, *The Concept of Law*, pp. 109–110.

of disobedience to those newly instituted, leaving on a ratio test the balance in favour of the pre-U.D.I. system.[73]

This analysis has raised some of the difficulties inherent in Kelsen's theory of the basic norm. It may be thought to demonstrate that Kelsen is only useful to the legal scientist, and not the judge and only in a residual case, and, further, that the kingpin of the whole structure rests upon the shaky foundation of a loose concept, *viz.*, effectiveness. It may be asked whether in this respect Kelsen really furthers our understanding of the legal order.[74]

International Law

We have seen how Austin relegated international law to the realm of positive morality, contrary to the universally accepted usage of modern states and lawyers.[75] Kelsen seeks to overcome this difficulty by demonstrating how state laws can [76] be dovetailed into the international order of norms so as to form one monistic system.[77] There is no logical reason why monism should not postulate the superiority of municipal law, but for ideological reasons Kelsen is not prepared to countenance this. But, quite apart from any possible objection as to the application of the principle of effectiveness,[78] this approach seems to be based on an illusory search for unity,[79] and to disregard the realities of the situation. Furthermore, it has led Kelsen to modify national basic norms. "The reason for the validity of the national legal order . . . is no longer a norm presupposed in juristic thinking but a positive norm of international law," [80] and the "presupposed norm" now becomes one of international law. But does international law need a basic norm? We have seen that, in spite of its difficulties, and within a limited

---

73 *Cf.* Raz's suggestion, *op. cit.*, p. 205.
74 For a very searching if inconclusive exploration of the problems and obscurities relating to the basic norm, see Julius Stone, " Mystery and Mystique in The Basic Norm " (1963) 26 M.L.R. 34 and, further, *Legal System and Lawyers' Reasonings*, pp. 123–131. Kelsen's *Stanford Law Review* article is an attempted answer to some of the problems posed by Stone. See *post*, 309.
75 *Ante*, 216.
76 *What is Justice?*, pp. 283–287; *The Pure Theory of Law*, pp. 328–344, and (1960) 48 Geo.L.J. 627.
77 Kelsen is well aware that in existing society a dualistic pattern is still retained. He is, however, hopeful that monism will prevail: it is, thus, merely a heuristic suggestion. From the point of view of legal science the choice is irrelevant (it is a political question outside the purview of the pure theory of law), but " from the point of view of political ideology the choice is important " (*General Theory of Law and State*, p. 398). See McBride, 43 N.Y.U.L.R. 53, 70–71, and Hughes, 59 Calif.L.R. 695, 711–713.
78 *Cf. ante*, 283.
79 Thus Kelsen states that the task of natural science is to describe reality in one system of the laws of nature, and that of the jurist is to comprehend all human laws in one system of rules of law: *What is Justice?*, p. 287. Note the influence of Kantian philosophy, *ante*, 269.
80 *The Pure Theory of Law*, p. 215.

sphere, the basic norm did serve a useful function in a national legal context. It was argued that in a post-revolutionary situation the basic norm might provide guidance to a legal scientist. Can it really be supposed though, that similar guidance is needed in international society? Can international society undergo a revolution? It is difficult to conceive of circumstances in which this could happen, short of one state or bloc capturing world power so conclusively that it could dictate new rules of international law to the rest of the subjugated world.[81] But practical realities do not seem to interest Kelsen as much as scientific unity and logical precision, and he accordingly postulates the basic norm of international law as " coercion of state against state ought to be exercised under the conditions and in the manner that conforms with the custom constituted by the actual behaviour of states." [82] What does this add to the positive norms of international law? To quote Professor Hart, " it says nothing more than that those who accept certain rules must also observe a rule that the rules ought to be observed," [83] a wholly unnecessary, if not spurious, assumption.

Why does Kelsen insist upon the need for monism? The answer follows from Kelsen's view of the logical impossibility of more than one basic norm. In a dualistic system there would be as many basic norms as systems. There would be an insoluble *logical* contradiction,[84] which could only be resolved by some norm higher than the collective basic norms of the national legal orders, *viz.*, an international legal order. So France and Germany might both claim to legislate for Alsace-Lorraine, and only international law could provide a solution. However, this is not a logical question at all, but simply one of how legal systems are in fact constructed. There is no reason why the basic norm of a national legal order should not take account of the international obligations accepted by that order. Is it not true, for example, that international obligations are in the United Kingdom " customarily recognised as constitutional from time to time " ? [85]

The Rules of Recognition

At this point it is relevant to refer again to Hart's analysis of the concept of law as divisible into two types of rules, namely, primary

[81] *Cf.* the systems theory popular in international relations today, whereby patterns of interaction between states lead to a self-regulating system which lasts so long as it can handle conflict and then gives way to successive self-regulating systems. See, for example, Rosecrance, *Action and Reaction in World Politics* (1963).
[82] *The Pure Theory of Law*, p. 216, *cf. post*, 305.
[83] *The Concept of Law*, p. 230 and *post*, 287.
[84] See *What is Justice?* pp. 284–285.
[85] *Ante*, 281.

and secondary rules.[86] According to Hart, the secondary rules cover, *inter alia*, what he calls " rules of recognition." [87] These rules provide authoritative criteria for identifying the primary rules and are often referred to as " norms of competence " in Continental law.[88] How then are these rules of recognition to be ascertained? Hart points out that such rules are often not expressly stated, but can be *shown* by the way in which particular primary rules are identified by the courts and other legal officials. Whether a primary rule is " valid " really amounts to saying no more than that it passes all the tests provided by the appropriate rules of recognition.

But in what sense can the rules of recognition themselves be regarded as " valid "? Hart appears to recognise that such rules may themselves be formed on a hierarchical pattern and that, therefore, the validity of one or more of these rules may depend upon some higher rule of recognition, but this still leaves open the Kelsenite question as to the status of any ultimate rule or rules of recognition. Hart's answer to this is that there is really no question of validity of any such ultimate rule since the only point is whether it is accepted as such by those who operate the system. There is, therefore, no assumption of validity but its acceptance is simply factual. Should we then call the basic norm of the system either law or fact? In a sense, says Hart, it is really both. The rule does provide criteria of validity within the system and, therefore, it is worth calling such a rule, law; there is, however, also a case for calling it fact in so far as it depends for its existence upon actual acceptance. This fact of acceptance may be looked upon from two points of view, namely, from the point of view of the external statement of the fact that the rule exists in the actual practice of the system, and also from the internal statements of validity which may be made by those in an official capacity who actually use it to identify the law.

Hart also points out that although the notions of efficacy and validity may be closely related in a legal system they are by no means identical. The relation of these two ideas is shown by the fact that if there is so little efficacy in a whole so-called system of law, it would really be pointless to attempt to assess what actual rights and duties might exist thereunder or the validity of particular rules.

As to the question whether every system of law must be referable to some basic norm, Hart rejects the idea of Kelsen that this is an essential presupposition of all legal systems.[89] All that it means, where a system lacks a basic norm, is that there will then be no way of demonstrating the validity of individual rules by reference to some ultimate rule of the system. Hart points out that this is not so much

---

[86] *Cf. ante*, 169.
[87] See *The Concept of Law*, Chaps. 5 and 6.
[88] *Cf. post*, 504.
[89] *Cf. ante*, 271.

a necessity as a *luxury* found in advanced social systems. In simpler forms of society we may have to wait and see whether a rule gets accepted as a rule or not. This does not mean that there is some mystery as to why rules in such a society are binding, which a basic rule, if only we could find it, would resolve. The rules of a simple society, like the rules of recognition of more advanced systems, are binding if they are accepted and function as such.[90]

Thus, says Hart, there is no reason at all why we should insist that international law as a legal system must have a basic norm; such an assertion really depends upon a false analogy with municipal law. International law may simply consist of a *set*[91] of separate primary rules of obligation which are not united in this particular way. Indeed the insistence upon the need for a basic norm, within the context of such a system as modern international law, often leads to a rather empty repetition of the mere fact that society does observe certain standards as obligatory. Thus, Hart refers to the rather empty rhetorical form of the so-called basic norm of international law to the effect that " states should behave as they have customarily behaved." This seems to be no more than an involved way of asserting the fact that there is a set of rules which are accepted by states as binding rules. As for the rule regarding the binding force of treaties, this is merely one of the " set " of rules accepted as binding. Of course, if the rule was generally recognised that treaties might bind not merely the parties thereto but other states, then treaties would have a legislative operation and the established form of treaty-making might have to be recognised as in itself one of the criteria of validity. It seems difficult to say, however, that international law has as yet attained this particular stage.

International Law and Sanctions

Professor Hart has some further very pertinent observations to make about the present status of international law.[92] He does not accept

---

[90] The position in medieval law provides an illustration. Thus Pollock and Maitland, after asserting that law may be taken to be the sum of the rules administered by courts of justice, proceed as follows: " We have not said that it must be, or that it always is, a sum of uniform and consistent rules (as uniform and consistent, that is, as human fallibility and the inherent difficulties of human affairs will permit) administered under one and the same system. This would, perhaps, be the statement of an ideal which the modern history of law tends to realise rather than of a result yet fully accomplished in any nation. Certainly it would not be correct as regards the state of English legal institutions, not only in modern but in quite recent times. Different and more or less conflicting systems of law, different and more or less competing systems of jurisdiction, in one and the same region, are compatible with a high state of civilisation, with a strong government, and with an administration of justice well enough liked and sufficiently understood by those who are concerned." (*History of English Law*, Vol. 1, p. xcv.)

[91] *Cf. ante*, 168.   [92] See *The Concept of Law*, Chap. 10.

the contention that this status is a mere matter of words in any trivial sense, for, as he points out, the extension of general terms may involve a question of principle whose credentials need to be inspected.

In the first place, Hart makes the valuable point that the role of coercion or sanction may be entirely different in the field of municipal law as compared with that of international relations. In the municipal sphere, in a reasonably well-regulated state, such is the position of individual human vulnerability, and the approximate equality of the citizen, that physical sanctions are generally likely to prevail, and no combination of malefactors is likely to be so strong as to be able to resist the organised power of the state. It may be said in answer to this that, in many countries, the operation of the law is exceedingly inefficient, and the over-powerful citizen or corporation or other organisation may be able to evade or resist or secure the perversion of actual legal rules. Moreover, in some instances, such as the Mafia in Sicily, the actual legal system may be virtually controlled by a secret or private organisation. These points, however valid, really only go to the actual existence of particular legal systems; they do not alter the fact that experience shows that within developed social communities it is quite possible to apply legal sanctions with considerable regularity and consistency with very small risks to the peace and order of the community. This situation, however, by no means holds in regard to international relations, for since sanctions would have to be applied to whole nations rather than to individuals, there may be fearful risks involved, and the effect of applying sanctions, even on a limited scale—as, for instance, if limited to so-called economic sanctions—might in fact provoke the holocaust of war rather than preserving peace and order in the international community. It is, therefore, obvious that the question of sanctions cannot be approached in the international sphere in the same way as they have been in municipal law. There thus seems to be a certain fallacy involved in the reasoning which regards international law as a kind of primitive system destined ultimately to develop on the same lines as municipal law has done in advanced communities, with a virtually self-operating impersonal acceptance of enforcement by way of physical sanctions in the last resort.[93]

---

[93] For a contrasting view see Barkun, *Law Without Sanctions* (1968), and see *ante*, 42. See also Schwartz and Miller, *post*, 622, where the interesting suggestion is made that damages and mediation nearly always precede the introduction of police in legal history because of " the need to build certain cultural foundations . . . before a central régime of control, as reflected in a police force, can develop " and they argue that " compensation by damages and the use of mediators might well contribute to the development of such a cultural foundation." Hence the need to stress " compensatory damages and mediation as pre-conditions for the growth of a world rule of law."

Nevertheless, this does not mean that the fact that sanctions may not be capable of being invoked in the same manner as in national affairs renders it futile to attempt to regulate international affairs by systematic legal rules. Such rules may be and are regarded as obligatory; there is a general pressure upon states for conformity to these rules; and actual claims are based upon them. These facts sufficiently show that there is value in attributing the title of law to the rules governing the international community.

Moreover, any attempt to identify international law with the rules of morality can lead to considerable confusion. Thus, claims in this sphere are not couched in moral terms but are put forward by reference to precedents, juristic writings and so forth. Moreover, a clear distinction is always drawn in the role of modern international affairs between assertions which are regarded as legal in character, and reproaches or blame cast upon states in purely moral terms. In truth then, there is a very close analogy with municipal law and one which, therefore, fully warrants the use of the term international " law." This analogy exists not so much in the sphere of form as of function and content. As to function, this sufficiently emerges by showing how international law differs both in its character and operation from principles of morality; as to content, there is a range of principles, concepts and methods [93a] which are common to both types of system which justifies us in treating the quality of the rules of international law as being essentially juristic in character.

Law and Fact

The relation of Kelsen's logical structure to the actual facts of particular states is by no means clear. Certainly Kelsen aims at presenting necessary form divorced from content, but, nevertheless, his whole argument is clearly aimed at a structure [94] which can be shown to fit the facts. Does this mean that his structure represents the form that any legal system *must* take, without being condemned to outer darkness as not being a legal order at all? Kelsen does seem to imply the universality of his system, yet much of it, such as his hierarchy of norms, as he himself admits,[95] is not relevant to anything but an advanced political state. Does it really apply to primitive society, or to an absolute theocratic monarchy, or to medieval feudal

[93a] For a good example of analogy of technique see Nelson (1972) 35 M.L.R. 52 on custom in international law.
[94] On the general difficulty of distinguishing structure and content, see Ayer, *Problem of Knowledge*, pp. 234–236.
[95] See *What is Justice?*, p. 246. *Cf.* McBride, 43 N.Y.U.L.R. 53, 70: " Kelsen's theory is most plausible against the background reality of the modern state, perhaps most especially the modern state of Continental Europe, with its legal systems built upon the principle of codification " and, one may add, written constitutions.

society?   Moreover, it is very hard to grasp exactly to what extent
Kelsen admits the relevance of fact at all.   We are not concerned
with how any particular system works, but with the ultimate fabric of
any system.   So that whether a judge individualises a statutory norm
does not rest on examining English or German law, but on a consideration of the general logic of the situation.   But then in deciding
whether this *is* the general structure, must one not compare it with
actual systems?   And if the fact of effectiveness is relevant to the
choice of the basic norm, why are facts irrelevant at other stages of
the analysis?   Kelsen, unfortunately, nowhere examines specifically
the link between fact and law [96] save to say, somewhat darkly, that
the relation of an act to a norm is that between an act and its
meaning, and that the legal norm is the specific *meaning* of a
norm-creating act.[97]

Non-Legal Norms

Kelsen tells us, truly enough, that even if racketeers enforce a " tax "
on night-clubs by coercion, this is not a legal norm.   The reason he
gives is that this can only be created by persons who are considered
legal authorities under the constitution.   In other words to be legal a
norm must form part of the official hierarchy of norms.[98]   But what
of bodies like trade associations, which possess rules and inflict
sanctions, and which the legal hierarchy neither prohibits nor
enforces?   These also are presumably not legal norms, yet they not
only resemble them closely but may be said to be lawful in so far
as the state does not prohibit them.   Must the lawyer pass over to the
sociologist the study of such important phenomena? [99]

Laski once remarked that " granted its postulates I believe the
pure theory to be unanswerable, but . . . its substance is an exercise
in logic, not in life." [1]   To some extent, as I have indicated, there
is truth in this dictum, but it certainly does less than justice to the
impressive display of learning, searching analysis, and striking
insights ranging over the whole vast field of law, which characterise

---

[96] By this I mean that he fails to clarify the relation of his general theory to the
facts of actual legal systems.   Of course, in other respects, Kelsen frequently
discusses fact and law, *e.g.*, acts creating norms (*General Theory*, p. 114); the
principle of effectiveness (p. 118); judicial ascertainment of facts (p. 135), etc.

[97] *What is Justice?*, p. 214. *Cf. The Pure Theory of Law*, p. 102.

[98] *Ibid.*, pp. 219–221.

[99] The same point arises with collective labour agreements which in some countries
lack legal sanctions.   See especially an article by J. de Givry, " Comparative
Observations on Legal Effects of Collective Agreements," in (1958) 21 M.L.R.
501. *Cf.* A. Adlercreutz, " Rise and Development of the Collective Agreement,"
in *Scandinavian Studies in Law* (1958), vol. 2, pp. 12–18 and O. Kahn-Freund
(1969) C.L.P. 1. See now Industrial Relations Act 1971, s. 34.

[1] *Grammar of Politics*, 4th ed., p. vi.

such books as Kelsen's *General Theory of Law and the State* and *The Pure Theory of Law.*[2]

H. KELSEN

The Pure Theory of Law

(1934–35) [3]

I

The Pure Theory of Law is a theory of positive law. As a theory it is exclusively concerned with the accurate definition of its subject-matter. It endeavours to answer the question, What is the law? but not the question, What ought it to be? [4] It is a science [5] and not a politics of law.

That all this is described as a ' pure ' theory of law means that it is concerned solely with that part of knowledge which deals with law, excluding from such knowledge everything which does not strictly belong to the subject-matter law. That is, it endeavours to free the science of law from all foreign elements. This is its fundamental methodological principle.[6] It would seem a self-evident one. Yet a glance at the traditional science of law in its nineteenth and twentieth century developments shows plainly how far removed from the requirement of purity that science was. Jurisprudence, in a wholly uncritical fashion, was mixed up with psychology and biology, with ethics and theology. There is to-day hardly a single social science into whose province jurisprudence feels itself unfitted to enter, even thinking, indeed, to enhance its scientific status by such conjunction with other disciplines. The real science of law, of course, is lost in such a process.

The Pure Theory of Law seeks to define clearly its objects of knowledge in these two directions in which its autonomy has been most endangered by the prevailing syncretism of methods. Law is a social phenomenon. Society, however, is something wholly different from nature, since an entirely different association of elements. If legal science is not to disappear into natural science, then law must be distinguished in the plainest possible manner from nature. The difficulty about such a distinction is that law, or what is generally called law, belongs with at

---

2 The *California Law Review* has recently published an excellent symposium of essays in tribute to Kelsen. (See 59 Calif.L.R. 609–819 (May, 1971).) This was unfortunately published too late for account to be taken of it in the text (though brief references have been made where possible).

3 [From Vols. 50 and 51 L.Q.R.]

4 [*Cf.* Austin, *ante*, 213.]

5 [On Kelsen's use of the word " science," see *ante*, 11.]

6 [Some supporters of Kelsen argue for the scientific character of his approach on the ground that his theory consists of generalisations based on juridical experience. The theory is therefore scientific because empirical, and " pure " because it disregards value-judgments, in common with all the sciences. (See, *e.g.*, N. Bobbio, *Teoria Generale del Diritto* (1955), pp. 46–48.) But this latter remark seems less applicable to the social than to the physical sciences, and in any event it does not seem beyond question why the science of *law* should not deal with *actual* values, as opposed at any rate to *a priori* values.]

least a part of its being to nature and seems to have a thoroughly natural existence. If, for instance, we analyse any condition of things such as is called law—a parliamentary ruling, a judicial sentence, a legal process, a delict—we can distinguish two elements. The one is a sensible act in time and place, an external process, generally a human behaviour; the other is a significance attached to or immanent in this act or process, a specific meaning. People meet together in a hall, make speeches, some rise from their seats, others remain seated; that is the external process. Its meaning: that a law has been passed. A man, clothed in a gown, speaks certain words from an elevated position to a person standing in front of him. This external process means a judicial sentence. One merchant writes to another a letter with a certain content; the other sends a return letter. This means they have concluded a contract. Someone, by some action or other, brings about the death of another. This means, legally, murder. . . .

These external circumstances, since they are sensible, temporospatial events, are in every case a piece of nature and as such causally determined. But as elements of the system nature, they are not objects of specifically juristic knowledge, are, indeed, not legal matter at all. That which makes the process into a legal (or illegal) act is not its factuality, not its natural, causal existence, but the objective significance which is bound up with it, its meaning. Its characteristically legal meaning it receives from a norm whose content refers to it. The norm functions as a schema of meaning. It itself is born of a legal act which in its turn receives its meaning from another norm. That a certain condition of fact is the execution of a death sentence and not a murder, this quality, which is not perceptible to the senses, is arrived at only by a mental process: by confronting the act with the penal statute book and penal administration. That the above-mentioned correspondence meant the conclusion of a contract resulted solely from the fact that this circumstance fell under certain rulings in the civil statute book. That an assembly of persons is a parliament and that the result of their activities is a law is only to say that the whole condition of fact corresponds to definite prescriptions in the constitution. That is to say, the content of some factual occurrence coincides with the content of some norm which is presupposed as valid. . . .

In defining the law as norm, and in restricting legal science (whose function is different from that of the legislative and executive organs) to knowledge of norms, we at the same time delimit law from nature and the science of law, as a normative science, from all other sciences which aim at explaining causal, natural processes. In particular, we delimit it from one science which sets itself the task of examining the causes and effects of these natural processes which, receiving their designation from legal norms, appear as legal acts.[7] If such a study be called sociology, or sociology of law, we shall make no objection. Neither shall we say anything here of its value or its prospects. This only is certain, that such legal-sociological knowledge has nothing to do with the norms of the law as specific contents. It deals only with certain processes without reference to their relation to any valid or assumed norms. It relates the

---

[7] [Thus though Kelsen would not deny that legal rules may have an actual causal effect on the minds of human beings and so affect their behaviour, he regards this as a sociological and not a juristic matter. *Cf. ante,* 272.]

circumstances to be examined not to valid norms but to other circumstances, as causes to effects. It inquires by what causes a legislator is determined in constituting these and not other norms, and what effects his ordinances have had. It inquires in what way economic facts and religious views actually influence the activities of the Courts, and for what motives men make their behaviour conform to the law or not. For such an inquiry law is only a natural reality, a fact in the consciousness of those who make, or of those subject to, the norms. The law itself, therefore, is not properly the subject of this study, but certain parallel processes in nature. In the same way the physiologist, examining the physical or chemical processes which condition or which accompany certain emotions, does not comprehend the emotions themselves. The emotions are not comprehensible in chemical or physiological terms. The Pure Theory of Law, as a specific science of law, considers legal norms not as natural realities, not as facts in consciousness, but as meaning-contents. And it considers facts only as the content of legal norms, that is, only as determined by the norms. Its problem is to discover the specific principles of a sphere of meaning.

. . . What is here chiefly important is to liberate law from that association which has traditionally been made for it—its association with morals. This is not of course to question the requirement that law ought to be moral, that is, good. That requirement is self-evident. What is questioned is simply the view that law, as such, is a part of morals and that therefore every law, as law, is in some sense and in some measure moral. . . .

II

To free the theory of law from this element is the endeavour of the Pure Theory of Law. The Pure Theory of Law separates the concept of the legal completely from that of the moral norm and establishes the law as a specific system independent even of the moral law. It does this not, as is generally the case with the traditional theory, by defining the legal norm, like the moral norm, as an imperative, but as an hypothetical judgment expressing a specific relationship between a conditioning circumstance and a conditioned consequence. The legal norm becomes the legal maxim—the fundamental form of the statute law. Just as natural law links a certain circumstance to another as cause to effect, so the legal rule links the legal condition to the legal consequence. In the one case the connecting principle is causality: in the other it is imputation. The Pure Theory of Law regards this principle as the special and peculiar principle of law. Its expression is the Ought. The expression of the causality principle is Necessity. The law of nature runs: If A is, then B must be. The legal rule says: If A is, then B ought to be. And thereby it says nothing as to the value, the moral or political value of the relationship. The Ought remains a pure *a priori* category for the comprehension of the empirical legal material. In this respect it is indispensable if we are to grasp at all the specific fashion in which positive law connects circumstances with one another. For it is evident that this connexion is not that of cause and effect. Punishment does not follow upon a delict as effect upon a cause. The legislator relates the two circumstances in a fashion wholly different from causality. Wholly different, yet a connexion as unshakeable as causality.[8] For in the legal system the punishment follows always and invariably on the delict even when in fact, for some reason or other, it fails of execution. Even though it does not so fail, it still does not stand to the delict in the relation of effect to cause. When we say: If there is tort, then the consequence of tort (punishment) shall (*i.e.* ought to) follow, this Ought, the category of law, indicates only the specific sense in which the legal condition and the legal consequence are held together in the legal rule. The category has a purely formal character. Thereby it distinguishes itself in principle from any transcendental notion of law. It is applicable no matter what the content of the circumstances which it links together, no matter what the character of the acts to which it gives the name of law. No social reality can be refused incorporation in this legal category on account of its contentual structure. . . .   [Vol. 50, pp. 477–485]

IV

The law, or the legal order, is a system of legal norms. The first question we have to answer, therefore, is this: What constitutes the unity in diversity of legal norms? Why does a particular legal norm belong to a particular legal order? A multiplicity of norms constitutes a unity, a system, an order, when validity can be traced back to its final source in a single norm. This basic norm constitutes the unity in diversity of all the norms which make up the system. That a norm belongs to a particular order is only to be determined by tracing back its validity to the basic norm constituting the order. According to the nature of the basic norm, *i.e.* the sovereign principle of validity, we may distinguish two different kinds of orders, or normative systems. In the first such system the norms are valid by virtue of their content, which has a directly evident quality compelling recognition. This contentual quality the norms receive by descent from a basic norm to whose content their content is related as particular to universal. The norms of morals are of this character. Thus the norms: Thou shalt not lie, Thou shalt not deceive, Thou shalt keep thy promise, etc. derive from a basic norm of honesty. From the basic norm: Thou shalt love thy fellow-men, we can derive the norms: Thou shalt not injure thy fellow, Thou shalt accompany him in adversity, etc. The question as to what, in a particular system of morals, is the basic norm, is not here under consideration. What is important is to recognize that the many norms of a moral system are already contained in its basic norm, exactly as particulars in a universal, and that all the individual norms can be derived from the basic norm by an operation of thought, namely, by deduction from universal to particular.

With legal norms the case is different. These are not valid by virtue of their content. Any content whatsoever can be legal; there is no human behaviour which could not function as the content of a legal norm. A norm becomes a legal norm only because it has been con-

---

[8] [This statement has been much criticized. Thus Olivecrona says of it ironically: " A mystery it is and a mystery it will remain for ever " (*Law as Fact* (1939), p. 21). It will be seen from what follows in this paragraph that Kelsen is here involved in the language of Kantian metaphysics. A rather more acceptable account of the normative proposition will be found in Kelsen's *General Theory of Law and State* (1946), quoted *post*, p. 300. *Cf.* also *ante*, p. 271. *Cf. post*, 306.]

stituted in a particular fashion, born of a definite procedure and a definite rule. Law is valid only as positive law, that is, statute (constituted) law. Therefore the basic norm of law can only be the fundamental rule, according to which the legal norms are to be produced; it is the fundamental condition of law-making. The individual norms of the legal system are not to be derived from the basic norm by a process of logical deduction. They must be constituted by an act of will, not deduced by an act of thought. If we trace back a single legal norm to its source in the basic norm, we do so by showing that the procedure by which it was set up conformed to the requirements of the basic norm. Thus, if we ask why a particular act of compulsion—the fact, for instance, that one man has deprived another of his freedom by imprisoning him—is an act of law and belongs to a particular legal order, the answer is, that this act was prescribed by a certain individual norm, a judicial decision. If we ask, further, why this individual norm is valid, the answer is, that it was constituted according to the penal statute book. If we inquire as to the validity of the penal statute book, we are confronted by the State's constitution, which has prescribed rules and procedure for the creation of the penal statute book by a competent authority. If, further, we ask as to the validity of the constitution, on which repose all the laws and acts which they have sanctioned, we come probably to a still older constitution and finally to an historically original one, set up by some single usurper or by some kind of corporate body. It is the fundamental presupposition of our recognition of the legal order founded on this constitution that that which the original authors declared to be their will should be regarded as valid norm. Compulsion is to be exercised according to the method and conditions prescribed by the first constitutional authority, or its delegated power. This is the schematic formulation of the basic norm of a legal order. . . .

(a) This analysis of the function of the basic norm brings to light also a special peculiarity of the law—the law regulates its own growth and its own making. The unity of the legal order is a law-*making* unity. The law is not a system of equal, side-by-side norms: it is a hierarchy with different layers. Its formal pattern is roughly the following.

At the highest point of the individual State's legal order is the constitution—in the material sense—the essential function of which is to determine the organs and procedure for the setting up of general law, to determine legislation. The next stage consists of the general norms, set up by legislation, whose function, in turn, is to determine not only the organs and procedure (Courts and administrative tribunals) for the individual norms, but also the content of the latter. The general norm, which links an abstract condition of fact to an equally abstract consequence, if it is to have any meaning, needs to be individualized. It must be known definitely whether there is present *in concreto* [9] a condition of fact which the general norm *in abstracto* regulates, and for this concrete case a concrete act of compulsion must be prescribed and carried out—

[9] [Hence the phrase, the "concretisation" of law. Ebenstein claims that this enables Kelsen to overcome "traditional weaknesses of both continental and Anglo-American legal theories, and to provide, perhaps, for the first time, the structure of a unified legal theory that integrates legal phenomena of diverse legal systems into a whole" (59 Calif.L.R. 617, 644). But this is to underestimate the contribution of Bentham.]

this also according to the abstract general norm. The agent in this is the judicial decision, the judicial power. The judicial power is by no means of a purely declaratory nature, such as the terms 'laying down' and 'ascertaining' the law suggest, as if in the statute, that is, the general norm, the law were already prepared and complete, simply waiting for the Courts to find it. The function of laying down the law is a properly constitutive one, it is a making of law in the real sense of the word. The relationship between the concrete condition of fact (and the discovery of its correspondence with the abstract condition) and the concrete legal consequence is specifically set up by the judicial decision. Just as at the general stage condition and consequence are joined by the statute, so at the individual stage they are joined by the judicial decision. The judicial decision is itself an individual legal norm.[10] It is the individualization or concretization of the general, abstract norm, the individual stage of the law-making process. This conclusion is hidden only from those who see in the general norm the repository of all law, wrongly identifying law with statute.

(b) Administration, no less than judicial decision, can be shown to be concretization of statute law. Indeed, a considerable part of that which we normally call administration is not to be distinguished functionally at all from that which we call judicial decision or finding of the Courts,[11] in so far as public policy is pursued technically, in both cases, in an identical fashion, namely, achieving the desired condition of affairs by attaching to its contradictory an act of compulsion, in short, by making the desired social behaviour legally obligatory. It makes no essential difference whether honour is protected by the assessment of damages in Court, or whether safety in the streets is ensured by the punishment of recklessness in administrative tribunals. To speak in the one case of the judiciary and in the other of the administration is to emphasize only a technical difference, the purely historical position of the Judge, namely, his independence—a characteristic generally, though by no means always, lacking to the administrative organ. Essential identity, however, is evident in this, that in each case public policy is realized indirectly. A functional distinction between judiciary and administration is present only when the State organ realizes the purposes of the State directly, as, for instance, when it itself builds the schools, drives the trains, administers hospitals. This kind of direct administration is indeed essentially different from

---

[10] [The ascertainment of the facts by the tribunal is part of the constitutive process by which the norm is created, for in the world of law there are no "absolute" facts, but only facts as ascertained by a competent organ: see H. Kelsen, *General Theory of Law and State*, pp. 135–136.]

[11] [This statement is criticised by E. Bodenheimer (see *Jurisprudence*, p. 240) on the ground that administration involves the discretionary exercise of power, whereas law is a limitation upon the exercise of such power. But this criticism seems misconceived, in so far as it ignores the further point in Kelsen's analysis, that such administrative exercise of power may itself be referable to higher norms in the legal hierarchy, and which may, therefore, control the norms on a lower level. It is in this way that one legal norm may operate as a limitation upon another such norm. There is nothing in Kelsen's view, therefore, which prevents the administrative activity of the Government taking place within a framework of rules or legal standards, if the legal system in fact provides such operative framework. This may be done either by means of the ordinary courts, or by means of a special administrative court or tribunal, such as the French *Conseil d'Etat*, or by means of an official such as the Scandinavian Ombudsman or the British Parliamentary Commissioner for Administration.]

judicial administration which is by its nature committed to an indirect pursuit of its, that is to say the State's, ends. If administration and judiciary, then, are to rank as fundamentally different, it can only be on the basis of the direct character of the former. This is to say that a correct view of the system of legal functions must draw a different line of demarcation from the customary one, which, legislation apart, breaks up the legal apparatus into a number of relatively isolated groups of tribunals which exercise for the most part similar functions. The correct view of the difference in function, the substitution for judiciary and administration of direct and indirect administration, would not be without its effects on the organization itself.

(c) In certain spheres of law, as for instance in civil law, the con-cretization of the general norms does not follow directly from the act of an official State instrument, such as is the judicial decision. In the case of the civil law, which the Courts have to apply, there is interposed between the statute and the decision the legal transaction, which with respect to the conditioning circumstance, has an individualizing function. Directed by the statute, the parties set up concrete norms for their mutual behaviour,[12] an offence against which constitutes the condition of fact to be determined by the judicial decision. To this condition the judicial decision attaches the penal consequence.

The final stage of this law-making process, which began with the formation of the constitution, is the carrying out of the compulsive act, the penal consequence. . . . [Vol. 51, pp. 517–522]

H. KELSEN

General Theory of Law and State
(1946)

Law as a Coercive Order

The evil applied to the violator of the order when the sanction is socially organized consists in a deprivation of possessions—life, health, freedom, or property. As the possessions are taken from him against his will, this sanction has the character of a measure of coercion. This does not mean that in carrying out the sanction physical force must be applied. This is necessary only if resistance is encountered in applying the sanction. This is only exceptionally the case, where the authority applying the sanction possesses adequate power. A social order that seeks to bring about the desired behavior of individuals [13] by the enactment of such measures of coercion is called a coercive order. Such it is because it threatens socially harmful deeds with measures of coercion, decrees such measures of coercion. As such it presents a contrast to all other possible social orders—those that provide reward rather than punishment as sanctions,

---

[12] [Thus a contract is a legal norm, an individualisation of the more general norm under which it is made.]

[13] [Kelsen has shifted his ground in *The Pure Theory of Law* (see p. 10). As Raz (*op. cit.*, p. 62) notes: " the intention to affect someone's behaviour is replaced by the intention to create a norm which presupposes the existence of norms and conventionalised activities, and cannot serve as their ultimate explanation." Hence, Raz argues " Kelsen's doctrine applies only to legislation within *the* framework of normative system."]

and especially those that enact no sanctions at all, relying on the technique of direct motivation. In contrast to the orders that enact coercive measures as sanctions, the efficacy of the others rests not on coercion but on voluntary obedience. Yet this contrast is not so distinct as it might at first sight appear. This follows from the fact that the technique of reward, as a technique of indirect motivation, has its place between the technique of indirect motivation through punishment, as a technique of coercion, and the technique of direct motivation, the technique of voluntary obedience. Voluntary obedience is itself a form of motivation, that is, of coercion, and hence is not freedom, but it is coercion in the psychological sense. If coercive orders are contrasted with those that have no coercive character, that rest on voluntary obedience, this is possible only in the sense that one provides measures of coercion as sanctions whereas the other does not. And these sanctions are only coercive measures in the sense that certain possessions are taken from the individuals in question against their will, if necessary by the employment of physical force.

In this sense, the law is a coercive order.

If the social orders, so extraordinarily different in their tenors, which have prevailed at different times and among the most different peoples, are called legal orders, it might be supposed that one is using an expression almost devoid of meaning. What could the so-called law of ancient Babylonians have in common with the law that prevails today in the United States? What could the social order of a negro tribe under the leadership of a despotic chieftain—an order likewise called " law "—have in common with the constitution of the Swiss Republic? Yet there is a common element, that fully justifies this terminology, and enables the word " law " to appear as the expression of a concept with a socially highly significant meaning. For the word refers to that specific social technique of a coercive order which, despite the vast differences existing between the law of ancient Babylon and that of the United States of today, between the law of the Ashantis in West Africa and that of the Swiss in Europe, is yet essentially the same for all these peoples differing so much in time, in place, and in culture: the social technique which consists in bringing about the desired social conduct of men through the threat of a measure of coercion which is to be applied in case of contrary conduct. What the social conditions are that necessitate this technique, is an important sociological question. I do not know whether we can answer it satisfactorily. Neither do I know whether it is possible for mankind to emancipate itself totally from this social technique. But if the social order should in the future no longer have the character of a coercive order, if society should exist without " law," then the difference between this society of the future and that of the present day would be immeasurably greater than the difference between the United States and ancient Babylon, or Switzerland and the Ashanti tribe. [pp. 18–19]

THE LEGAL NORM

Legal Norm and Rule of Law in a Descriptive Sense

If " coercion " in the sense here defined is an essential element of law, then the norms which form a legal order must be norms stipulating a coercive act, i.e. a sanction. In particular, the general norms must be

norms in which a certain sanction is made dependent upon certain conditions, this dependence being expressed by the concept of "ought."
This does not mean that the law-making organs necessarily have to give
the norms the form of such hypothetical " ought " statements.   The
different elements of a norm may be contained in very different products
of the law-making procedure, and they may be linguistically expressed in
very different ways.   When the legislator forbids theft, he may, for
instance, first define the concept of theft in a number of sentences which
form an article of a statute, and then stipulate the sanction in another
sentence, which may be part of another article of the same statute or
even part of an entirely different statute.   Often the latter sentence does
not have the linguistic form of an imperative or an " ought " sentence
but the form of a prediction of a future event.   The legislator frequently
makes use of the future tense, saying that a thief " will be " punished in
such and such a way. He then presupposes that the question as to who
is a thief has been answered somewhere else, in the same or in some
other statute.   The phrase " will be punished " does not imply the prediction of a future event—the legislator is no prophet—but an " imperative " or a " command," these terms taken in a figurative sense.   What
the norm-creating authority means is that the sanction " ought " to be
executed against the thief, when the conditions of the sanction are
fulfilled.

It is the task of the science of law to represent the law of a community, i.e. the material produced by the legal authority in the
law-making procedure, in the form of statements to the effect that " if
such and such conditions are fulfilled, then such and such a sanction
shall follow." These statements, by means of which the science of law
represents law, must not be confused with the norms created by the
law-making authorities.   It is preferable not to call these statements
norms, but legal rules. The legal norms enacted by the law creating
authorities are prescriptive ; the rules of law formulated by the science
of law are descriptive.   It is of importance that the term " legal rule "
or " rule of law " be employed here in a descriptive sense.[14]

---

[14] [It is clear that there is a distinction between legal norms as laid down by
law-creating authorities, and rules of law as formulated by the juristic science
of law.   The former can be said to be prescriptive, and the latter descriptive.
Some confusion, however, has been caused by Kelsen's description of the statements of the science of law as being " rules of law in a descriptive sense."
Ross criticises Kelsen as putting forward the view that it is possible to conduct
a science of law as being itself normative, *i.e.*, that its conclusions will be
normative statements and not descriptive statements.   (See *On Law and Justice*,
p. 10.) Hart, however, has pointed out that though Kelsen's curious terminology
is not beyond criticism, it does take account of an important distinction
which is worth preserving.   This is the fact that the statements of a jurist in
relation to the laws of the legal system he is dealing with, do not have a
" simple one-to-one correspondence," with the laws of the system in question.
The jurist's exposition may have a consistency and order not present in the
original, for the jurist does not just interpret the rules of the law-creating
authorities, but seeks in effect a rational reconstruction of the law of a
particular system.   This is why Kelsen regards the science of law as being
in a sense both normative and descriptive.   (See H. L. A. Hart, " International
Symposium on Jurisprudence : Kelsen Visited " (1963) 10 U.C.L.A. Law Review,
p. 709.) Kelsen has returned to this theme in *The Pure Theory of Law* (see
pp. 71 *et seq.*). " Legal norms," he writes, " are not judgments, that is, they
are not statements about an object of cognition. According to their meaning
they are commands ; they may also be permissions and authorisations." Norms

Rule of Law and Law of Nature

The rule of law, the term used in a descriptive sense, is a hypothetical judgment attaching certain consequences to certain conditions. This is the logical form of the law of nature, too. Just as the science of law, the science of nature describes its object in sentences which have the character of hypothetical judgments. And like the rule of law, the law of nature, too, connects two facts with one another as condition and consequence. The condition is here the " cause," the consequence the " effect." The fundamental form of the law of nature is the law of causality. The difference between the rule of law and the law of nature seems to be that the former refers to human beings and their behavior, whilst the latter refers to things and their reactions. Human behavior, however, may also be the subject-matter of natural laws, insofar as human behavior, too, belongs to nature. The rule of law and the law of nature differ not so much by the elements they connect as by the manner of their connection. The law of nature establishes that if A is, B is (or will be). The rule of law says: If A is, B ought to be. The rule of law is a norm (in the descriptive sense of that term). The meaning of the connection established by the law of nature between two elements is the " is," whereas the meaning of the connection between two elements established by the rule of law is the " ought." [15] The principle according to which natural science describes its object is causality ; the principle according to which the science of law describes its object is normativity. [16]

Usually, the difference between law of nature and norm is characterized by the statement that the law of nature can have no exceptions, whereas a norm can. This is, however, not correct. The normative rule " If someone steals, he ought to be punished," remains valid even if in a given case a thief is not punished. This fact involves no exception to the ought statement expressing the norm ; it is an exception only to an " is " statement expressing the rule that if someone steals, he actually will be punished. The validity of a norm remains unaffected if, in a concrete instance, a fact does not correspond to the norm. A fact has the character of an " exception " to a rule if the statement establishing the fact is in a logical contradiction to the rule. Since a norm is no statement of reality, no statement of a real fact can be in contradiction to a norm. Hence, there can be no exceptions to a norm. The norm is, by its very nature, inviolable. To say that the norm is " violated " by certain behavior is a figurative expression ; and the figure used in this statement is not correct. For the statement says nothing about the norm : it merely characterizes the actual behavior as contrary to the behavior prescribed by the norm.

can be valid or invalid (p. 73) ; normative statements convey information and consequently can be true or false. But Kelsen has added little about the structure or function of normative statements, though explorations along these lines have been carried out by Von Wright in *Norm and Action* and Ross in *Directives and Norms* (see *post*, 549). See also Raz, *op. cit.*, pp. 45–49.]

[15] [*Cf. ante*, 270.]

[16] [Where Kelsen speaks of two different *principles*, we may if we like refer to two types of propositions used for different purposes, *i.e.*, to assert facts or to prescribe conduct.]

The law of nature, however, is not inviolable.[17] True exceptions to a law of nature are not excluded. The connection between cause and effect established in a law of nature describing physical reality has the character of probability only, not of absolute necessity, as assumed by the older philosophy of nature. If, as a result of empirical research, two phenomena are considered to be in a relation of cause and effect, and if this result is formulated in a law of nature, it is not absolutely excluded that a fact may occur which is in contradiction to this law, and which therefore represents a real exception to the law. Should such a fact be established, then the formulation of the law has to be altered in a way to make the new fact correspond to the new formula. But the connection of cause and effect established by the new formula has also only the character of probability, not that of absolute necessity. Exceptions to the law are not excluded.

If we examine the way in which the idea of causality has developed in the human mind, we find that the law of causality has its origin in a norm. The interpretation of nature had originally a social character. Primitive man considers nature to be an intrinsic part of his society. He interprets physical reality according to the same principles that determine his social relations. His social order, to him, is at the same time the order of nature. Just as men obey the norms of the social order, things obey the norms emanating from superhuman personal beings. The fundamental social law is the norm according to which the good has to be rewarded, the evil punished. It is the principle of retribution which completely dominates primitive consciousness. The legal norm is the prototype of this principle. According to this principle of retribution, primitive man interprets nature. His interpretation has a normative-juristic character. It is in the norm of retribution that the law of causality originates and, in the way of a gradual change of meaning, develops. Even during the nineteenth century, the law of causality was conceived of as a norm, the expression of the divine will. The last step in this emancipation of the law of causality from the norm of retribution consists in the fact that the former gets rid of the character of a norm and thereby ceases to be conceived of as inviolable.[18]   [pp. 45–47]

The Basic Norm of a Legal Order

The Basic Norm and the Constitution

The derivation of the norms of a legal order from the basic norm of that order is performed by showing that the particular norms have been created in accordance with the basic norm. To the question why a certain act of coercion—e.g., the fact that one individual deprives another individual of his freedom by putting him in jail—is a legal act, the answer is: because it has been prescribed by an individual norm, a judicial decision. To the question why this individual norm is valid as part of a definite legal order, the answer is: because it has been created in conformity with a criminal statute. This statute, finally, receives its

[17] William A. Robson, *Civilisation and the Growth of Law* (1935) 340, says: "Men of science no longer claim for natural laws the inexorable, immutable, and objective validity they were formerly deemed to possess." [*Cf. ante*, 5 and Mead, *ante*, 144.]

[18] *Cf.* H. Kelsen, *Society and Nature*, pp. 233 *ff.* [and *ante*, 76.]

validity from the constitution, since it has been established by the competent organ in the way the constitution prescribes.

If we ask why the constitution is valid, perhaps we come upon an older constitution. Ultimately we reach some constitution that is the first historically and that was laid down by an individual usurper or by some kind of assembly. The validity of this first constitution is the last presupposition, the final postulate, upon which the validity of all the norms of our legal order depends. It is postulated that one ought to behave as the individual, or the individuals, who laid down the first constitution have ordained. This is the basic norm of the legal order under consideration. The document which embodies the first constitution is a real constitution, a binding norm, only on the condition that the basic norm is presupposed to be valid. Only upon this presupposition are the declarations of those to whom the constitution confers norm-creating power binding norms. It is this presupposition that enables us to distinguish between individuals who are legal authorities and other individuals whom we do not regard as such, between acts of human beings which create legal norms and acts which have no such effect. All these legal norms belong to one and the same legal order because their validity can be traced back—directly or indirectly—to the first constitution. That the first constitution is a binding legal norm is presupposed, and the formulation of the presupposition is the basic norm of this legal order. The basic norm of a religious norm system says that one ought to behave as God and the authorities instituted by Him command. Similarly, the basic norm of a legal order prescribes that one ought to behave as the " fathers " of the constitution and the individuals—directly or indirectly—authorized (delegated) by the constitution command. Expressed in the form of a legal norm: coercive acts ought to be carried out only under the conditions and in the way determined by the " fathers " of the constitution or the organs delegated by them. This is, schematically formulated, the basic norm of the legal order of a single State, the basic norm of a national legal order.[19] It is to the national legal order that we have here limited our attention. Later, we shall consider what bearing the assumption of an international law has upon the question of the basic norm of national law.

The Specific Function of the Basic Norm

That a norm of the kind just mentioned is the basic norm of the national legal order does not imply that it is impossible to go beyond that norm. Certainly one may ask why one has to respect the first constitution as a binding norm. The answer might be that the fathers of the first constitution were empowered by God. The characteristic of so-called legal positivism is, however, that it dispenses with any such

---

[19] [Cross asserts that the English legal system has two basic norms, namely, statutes and the rule that judicial decisions have the force of law. These, he says, are separate rules because the latter is not derived from the rule conferring legal validity on statute-law, even though a statute can reverse the effect of a judicial decision. (See, R. Cross, *Precedent in English Law* (2nd ed.), pp. 205–207.) Cross, however, seems to use the word " derived " in a historical sense, whereas Kelsen is thinking in terms of logical ultimacy. In the latter sense, judicial decisions under the English constitution are not ultimate: they do not have the last word. *Cf., ante,* 281.]

religious justification of the legal order. The ultimate hypothesis of positivism is the norm authorizing the historically first legislator. The whole function of this basic norm is to confer law-creating power on the act of the first legislator and on all the other acts based on the first act. To interpret these acts of human beings as legal acts and their products as binding norms, and that means to interpret the empirical material which presents itself as law as such, is possible only on the condition that the basic norm is presupposed as a valid norm. The basic norm is only the necessary presupposition of any positivistic interpretation of the legal material.

The basic norm is not created in a legal procedure by a law-creating organ. It is not—as a positive legal norm is—valid because it is created in a certain way by a legal act, but it is valid because it is presupposed to be valid; and it is presupposed to be valid because without this presupposition, no human act could be interpreted as a legal, especially as a norm-creating act.

By formulating the basic norm, we do not introduce into the science of law any new method. We merely make explicit what all jurists, mostly unconsciously, assume when they consider positive law as a system of valid norms and not only as a complex of facts, and at the same time repudiate any natural law from which positive law would receive its validity. That the basic norm really exists in the juristic consciousness is the result of a simple analysis of actual juristic statements. The basic norm is the answer to the question: how—and that means under what condition—are all these juristic statements concerning legal norms, legal duties, legal rights, and so on, possible?

[pp. 116–117]

Change of the Basic Norm [20]

It is just the phenomenon of revolution which clearly shows the significance of the basic norm. Suppose that a group of individuals attempt to seize power by force, in order to remove the legitimate government in a hitherto monarchic State, and to introduce a republican form of government. If they succeed, if the old order ceases, and the new order begins to be efficacious, because the individuals whose behavior the new order regulates actually behave, by and large, in conformity with the new order, then this order is considered as a valid order. It is now according to this new order that the actual behavior of individuals is interpreted as legal or illegal. But this means that a new basic norm is presupposed. It is no longer the norm according to which the old monarchial constitution is valid, but a norm according to which the new republican constitution is valid, a norm endowing the revolutionary government with legal authority. If the revolutionaries fail, if the order they have tried to establish remains inefficacious, then, on the other hand, their undertaking is interpreted, not as a legal, a law-creating act, as the establishment of a constitution, but as an illegal act, as the crime of treason, and this according to the old monarchic constitution and its specific basic norm.

[20] [This passage was relied upon in a number of the so-called "Grundnorm" cases. See note 63, *ante*, 282 and *cf. post*, 327.]

The Principle of Effectiveness

If we attempt to make explicit the presupposition on which these juristic considerations rest, we find that the norms of the old order are regarded as devoid of validity because the old constitution and, therefore, the legal norms based on this constitution, the old legal order as a whole, has lost its efficacy; because the actual behavior of men does no longer conform to this old legal order. Every single norm loses its validity when the total legal order to which it belongs loses its efficacy as a whole. The efficacy of the entire legal order is a necessary condition for the validity of every single norm of the order. A *conditio sine qua non*, but not a *conditio per quam*. The efficacy of the total legal order is a condition, not the reason for the validity of its constituent norms. These norms are valid not because the total order is efficacious, but because they are created in a constitutional way. They are valid, however, only on the condition that the total order is efficacious; they cease to be valid, not only when they are annulled in a constitutional way, but also when the total order ceases to be efficacious. It cannot be maintained that, legally, men have to behave in conformity with a certain norm, if the total legal order, of which that norm is an integral part, has lost its efficacy. The principle of legitimacy is restricted by the principle of effectiveness.   [pp. 118–119]

The Reason of Validity of National and International Law

In order to answer the question whether international and national law are different and mutually independent legal orders, or form one universal normative system, in order to reach a decision between pluralism and monism, we have to consider the general problem of what makes a norm belong to a definite legal order, what is the reason that several norms form one and the same normative system. . . .

. . . If the national legal order is considered without reference to international law, then its ultimate reason of validity is the hypothetical norm qualifying the " Fathers of the Constitution " as a law-creating authority. If, however, we take into account international law, we find that this hypothetical norm can be derived from a positive norm of this legal order: the principle of effectiveness. It is according to this principle that international law empowers the " Fathers of the Constitution " to function as the first legislators of a State. The historically first constitution is valid because the coercive order erected on its basis is efficacious as a whole. Thus, the international legal order, by means of the principle of effectiveness, determines not only the sphere of validity, but also the reason of validity of the national legal orders. Since the basic norms of the national legal orders are determined by a norm of international law, they are basic norms only in a relative sense. It is the basic norm of the international legal order which is the ultimate reason of validity of the national legal orders, too.

A higher norm can either determine in detail the procedure in which lower norms are to be created, or empower an authority to create lower norms at its own discretion. It is in the latter manner that international law forms the basis of the national legal order. By stipulating that an individual or a group of individuals who are able to obtain permanent obedience for the coercive order they establish are to be considered as a legal and legitimate authority, international law " delegates " the national legal orders whose spheres of validity it thereby determines.[21]

[pp. 366–368]

The Basic Norm of International Law

Since national law has the reason of its validity, and hence its " source " in this sense, in international law, the ultimate source of the former must be the same as that of the latter. Then the pluralistic view cannot be defended by the assumption that national and international law have different and mutually independent " sources." It is the " source " of national law by which that law is united with international law, whatever may be the " source " of this legal order. Which is the source, then, that is, the basic norm of international law?

To find the source of the international legal order, we have to follow a course similar to that which led us to the basic norm of the national legal order. We have to start from the lowest norm within international law, that is, from the decision of an international court. If we ask why the norm created by such a decision is valid, the answer is furnished by the international treaty in accordance with which the court was instituted. If, again, we ask why this treaty is valid, we are led back to the general norm which obligates the States to behave in conformity with the treaties they have concluded, a norm commonly expressed by the phrase *pacta sunt servanda*. This is a norm of general international law, and general international law is created by custom constituted by acts of States. The basic norm of international law, therefore, must be a norm which countenances custom as a norm-creating fact, and might be formulated as follows: " The States ought to behave as they have customarily behaved." Customary international law, developed on the basis of this norm, is the first stage within the international legal order.[22] The next stage is formed by the norms created by international treaties. The validity of these norms is dependent upon the norm *pacta sunt servanda*, which itself is a norm belonging to the first stage of general international law, which is law created by custom constituted by acts of

---

[21] [The attitude of the municipal courts of a state towards a particular norm of international law is not decisive for the question of the validity of that norm in the international sphere. Thus, if an English court holds that a provision in a treaty binding the U.K., is not valid in England because contrary to some provision of an English statute, this will have the effect of involving a violation of international law by the U.K. In other words, there will here be a conflict between the two types of law, but the state authorities in the international sphere will still be obliged to recognise the validity of the international norm notwithstanding this conflict. From this point of view, international law is not directly concerned with the method by which a state fulfils international obligations. Some states apply the method of transformation, which means that international norms are not accepted within the local legal system unless transformed into parallel municipal norms by local legislation. Other states employ the method of adoption, whereby provisions of international law are directly accepted as such. (See as to this I. Seidl-Hohenveldern, " Transformation or Adoption of International Law into Municipal Law," in [1963] I.C.L.Q. 88.) English law adopts the method of transformation; for the more complex position under Australian law, see C. H. Alexandrowicz, " International Law in the Municipal Sphere according to Australian Decisions," in [1964] I.C.L.Q. 78.]

[22] [*Cf.* Lauterpacht, *Development of International Law by International Court* (1958), 2nd ed., Chap. 28. See the *Franconia* case (*R.* v. *Keyn* (1876) 2 Ex.D. 63; but *cf. Chung Chi Cheung* v. *R.* [1939] A.C. 160). *Cf.* Nelson, 35 M.L.R. 52.]

States. The third stage is formed by norms created by organs which are themselves created by international treaties, as for instance decisions of the Council of the League of Nations, or of the Permanent Court of International Justice. [pp. 369–370]

H. KELSEN

Causality and Imputation [23]

. . . If there is a social science different from natural science, it must describe its object according to a principle different from that of causality. Society is an order of human behavior. But there is no sufficient reason not to consider human behavior as an element of nature, that is, as determined by the law of causality; and, so far as human behavior is conceived as determined by causal laws, a science which deals with the mutual behavior of men, and for this reason is classed as a social science, is not essentially different from physics or biology. However, if we analyze our propositions concerning human behavior, we find that we connect acts of human beings with one another and with other facts not only and exclusively according to the principle of causality, that is, as cause and effect, but according to another principle quite different from that of causality, a principle for which science has not yet established a generally recognized term. Only if it is possible to prove the existence of this principle in our thinking, and its application in sciences dealing with human behavior, are we entitled to consider society as an order or system different from that of nature and the sciences concerned with society as different from natural sciences.

Law is a most characteristic and highly important social phenomenon; and the science of law is probably the oldest and most developed social science. In analyzing juristic thinking, I have shown [24] that a principle different from that of causality is indeed applied in the rules by which jurisprudence describes the law, either the law in general or a concrete legal order, such as the national law of a definite state or international law. This principle has, in the rules of law, a function analogous to that which the principle of causality has in the natural laws by which natural science describes nature. A rule of law is, for instance, the statement that, if a man has committed a crime, a punishment ought to be inflicted upon him; or the statement that, if a man does not pay a debt contracted by him, a civil execution ought to be directed against his property. Formulated in a more general way: If a delict has been committed, a sanction ought to be executed. Just as a law of nature, a rule of law connects two elements with each other. But the connection described by the rule of law has a meaning totally different from that of causality. For it is evident that the criminal delict is not connected with the punishment, and that the civil delict is not connected with the civil execution, as a cause is connected with its effect. The connection between cause and effect is independent of the act of a human or superhuman being. But the connection between a delict and a legal sanction is established by an act, or acts, of human beings, by a law-creating act, that is, an act whose meaning is a norm.

---

[23] [From *What is Justice?* (1957), an essay originally published in 1950.]
[24] See my *General Theory of Law and State* (1945), pp. 45 *et seq.*, 92.

This distinction cannot be made within a religious-metaphysical view of the world according to which the connection of cause and effect is established by an act analogous to a law-creating act: by the act of God creating nature. Consequently, the laws of nature, as manifestation of the will of God, have the character of norms prescribing nature a definite behavior. This the basis on which a metaphysical doctrine of the law asserts that it is possible to find in nature a natural law. From the point of view of a scientific interpretation of the world, however, within which only a positivistic doctrine of law is possible, the distinction between law of nature and rule of law must emphatically be maintained.

The act of human behavior whose meaning is a norm may be performed in different ways: by a gesture; by spoken or written words; by a symbol or by a series of acts constituting a complicate legislative procedure; or by a custom. Using a figure of speech, we say that by such an act (or acts) a norm is " made " or " created "; in other words: the meaning of the act (or acts) is a norm. A norm " created " by an act of human behavior is a " positive " norm. Its existence consists in its validity. We describe its meaning by saying that something is " prescribed " or " permitted "; or, using a term comprising both, that something " ought (or, for the negative, ought not) to be done." If we presuppose a norm prescribing or permitting certain human behavior, we may characterize behavior which is in conformity with the pre-supposed norm as correct (right, good) and behavior which is not in conformity with the presupposed norm as incorrect (wrong, bad). If these statements are value judgments, the presupposed norm constitutes the value. If we presuppose a norm prescribing or permitting certain human behavior, we may define correct behavior as behavior which is in conformity with the presupposed norm; and incorrect behavior as behavior which is not in conformity with the presupposed norm. Then, we may say of a concrete human behavior that it does or does not fall under the definition of correct behavior and is, therefore, correct or incorrect behavior. But it falls under the definition only if it is in conformity with the presupposed norm. Only the statement whose meaning is that the behavior is or is not in conformity with the pre-supposed norm is a value judgment; not the statement that concrete behavior does or does not fall under the definition. Hence, the norm is not, as is sometimes said,[25] a definition; the norm is part of the content of a definition, the definition of correct or incorrect behavior. Definition is the meaning of an act of cognition. The acts whose meaning is a norm are not acts of cognition; they are acts of will. The function of the legal authorities is not to know and to describe law but to prescribe or permit human behavior and thus to make law. To know and to describe the law is the function of the legal science. The distinction between the function of the legal authority and that of the legal science, between legal norms and rules of law, is of great importance.

Since the connection between delict and sanction is established by a prescription or a permission—a " norm "—the science of law describes its object by propositions in which the delict is connected with the sanction by the copula " ought." I have suggested designating this

[25] Felix Kaufmann, *Methodology of the Social Sciences* (1944) pp. 48 *et seq.*

connection "imputation." [26] This term is the English translation of
the German *Zurechnung.* The statement that an individual is *zurech-
nungsfähig* (" responsible ") means that a sanction can be inflicted upon
him if he commits a delict. The statement that an individual is
unzurechnungsfähig (" irresponsible ")—because, for instance, he is a
child or insane—means that a sanction cannot be inflicted upon him
if he commits a delict. Formulating this idea more precisely, we may
say that in the first case a sanction is connected with certain behavior
as a delict, whereas in the second case a sanction is not connected
with such behavior. The idea of imputation (*Zurechnung*) as the specific
connection of the delict with the sanction is implied in the juristic
judgment that an individual is, or is not, legally responsible (*zurech-
nungsfähig*) for his behavior. Hence we may say: The sanction is
imputed to the delict; it is not caused by the delict. It is evident that
the science of law does not at all aim at a causal explanation of
phenomena, that in the propositions by which the science of law describes
its object the principle of imputation, not the principle of causality, is
applied. . . .

The grammatical form of the principle of causality as well as that
of imputation is a hypothetical judgment (proposition) connecting something as a condition with something as a consequence. But the meaning
of the connection in the two cases is different. The principle of causality
states: If there is A, there is (or will be) B. The principle of imputation states: If there is A, there ought to be B. As to the application
of the principle of causality to the laws of nature, I refer to the example
. . . the law describing the effect of heat on metallic bodies: If a metallic
body is heated, it is (or will be) expanding. Examples of the principle
of imputation as applied in social laws are: If somebody has done
you a favor, you ought to be grateful to him; or, if a man sacrifices his
life for his nation, his memory ought to be honored (moral laws). If
a man commits a sin, he ought to do penance (religious law). If
a man commits theft, he ought to be imprisoned (legal law). The
difference between causality and imputation is that the relation between
the condition, which in the law of nature is presented as cause, and the
consequence, which is here presented as effect, is independent of a
human or superhuman act; whereas the relation between condition and
consequence which a moral, religious, or legal law asserts is established
by acts of human or superhuman beings. It is just this specific meaning of the connection between condition and consequence which is
expressed by the term " ought."

Another difference between causality and imputation is that each
concrete cause must be considered as the effect of another cause and
each concrete effect as the cause of another effect; so that the chain of
causes and effects is, by definition, infinite. Further, each concrete
event is the intersection of an infinite number of lines of causality.
The condition to which the consequence is imputed in a moral or
religious or legal law, as, for instance, death for the sake of the nation,
to which honor of memory is imputed; benefaction, to which gratitude is
imputed; sin, to which penance is imputed; theft, to which imprisonment is imputed, are not necessarily at the same time consequences
imputable to some other condition. And the consequences, as, for

26 [*Cf. ante,* 270.]

instance, honor of memory imputed to the death for the sake of the nation, gratitude imputed to benefaction, penance imputed to sin, imprisonment imputed to theft, are not necessarily at the same time a condition to which another consequence is imputable The line of imputation has not, as the line of causality, an infinite number of links, but only two links. If we say that a definite consequence is imputed to a definite condition, for instance, a reward to a merit, or a punishment to a delict, the condition, that is to say the human behavior which constitutes the merit or the delict, is the end point of the imputation. But there is no such thing as an end point of causality. The assumption of a first cause, a *prima causa*, which is the *analogon* to the end point of imputation, is incompatible with the idea of causality, at least with the idea of causality implied in laws of classical physics. The idea of a first cause, too, is a relic of that stage of thinking in which the principle of causality was not yet emancipated from that of imputation. . . .

[pp. 324–327, 331–333]

H. KELSEN

Professor Stone and the Pure Theory of Law
(1965) [27]

. . . I have always and not only in the second edition of my *Reine Rechtslehre* [28] clearly distinguished between the basic norm presupposed in juristic thinking as the constitution in a legal-logical sense and the constitution in a positive legal sense, and I have always insisted that the basic norm as the constitution in a legal-logical sense—not the constitution in a positive legal sense—is *not* a norm of positive law, that it is not a norm "posited," *i.e.*, created by a real act of will of a legal organ, but a norm *presupposed in juristic thinking.*[29] . . .

It is as a norm presupposed in juristic thinking that the basic norm (*if* it is presupposed) is "at the top of the pyramid of norms of each legal order." It is "meta-legal" if by this term is understood that the basic norm is not a norm of positive law, that is, not a norm created by a real act of will of a legal organ. It is "legal" if by this term we understand everything which has legally relevant functions, and the basic norm presupposed in juristic thinking has the function to found the *objective* validity of the subjective meaning of the acts by which the constitution of a community is created. In this respect the theory of the basic norm is—to a certain extent—similar to the natural-law doctrine according to which a positive legal order is valid if it corresponds to the natural law. The natural law is not considered to be "meta-legal," though it is not *positive* law. But there are also essential differences between the doctrine of the basic norm and the natural-law doctrine. . . .

[27] [From 17 Stan.L.R. 1130. The article is written in reply to Stone's writings on Kelsen, notably his "Mystery and Mystique in the Basic Norm" in 26 M.L.R. 34, and his chapter in *Legal System and Lawyers' Reasonings*.]

[28] [Now translated as *The Pure Theory of Law* (1967), by Max Knight.]

[29] [By which Kelsen means that the basic norm is not the ought propositions "*of* the constitution, but rather an ought proposition *about* the constitution. As such it is not a legal norm in the usual sense of being the construct of an organ of the system; rather, it is a construct of juristic thought which is necessary if we are to regard the system as giving rise to valid norms" (*per* G. Hughes, 59 Calif.L.R. 695, 704.]

The main difference is that the *content* of the positive legal order is completely independent of the basic norm from which only the *objective validity* of the norms of the positive legal order, not the content of this order, can be derived; whereas according to the natural-law doctrine a positive legal order is valid only if and insofar as its content corresponds to the natural law. Hence there can be no conflict between a positive legal order and its basic norm, whereas from the point of view of a positivistic theory of law a conflict between positive law and what is supposed to be natural law is quite possible. . . .

I do not maintain that the basic norm " guarantees " the efficacy of the legal order to which it refers. What I say is that the basic norm refers only to a coercive social order which is by and large effective. That means: we presuppose the basic norm only if there exists a coercive social order by and large effective. I say in my *Reine Rechtslehre*: " [The] basic norm refers only to a constitution which is the basis of an effective coercive order. Only if the actual behavior of men corresponds, by and large, to the subjective meaning of the acts directed at this behavior, their subjective meaning is considered also as their objective meaning." [30] And I say further: " The reason for the objective validity of a legal order is . . . the presupposed basic norm according to which one ought to obey a constitution which actually is established and by and large effective; and consequently one ought also to obey the norms created in conformity with the constitution and by and large effective." [31] Since—according to my theory—the basic norm refers only to a coercive order which is by and large effective, and since the basic norm is adapted to this coercive order and not the coercive order to the basic norm, it is *in this sense* that in the basic norm the actual establishment of the norms of the coercive order by real acts of will and the efficacy of these norms are made the condition of the objective validity of the coercive order. Hence the basic norm does not " guarantee " the efficacy of the legal order; it does nothing to make this order effective. . . .

In view of the specific function of the basic norm presupposed in juristic thinking I call it " constitution in a legal-logical sense " in contradistinction to the " constitution in the sense of positive law." It is to the constitution in the sense of positive law that the basic norm refers. I distinguish these two concepts as clearly as possible. . . .

An essential point of my theory of the basic norm . . . is that it is not necessary to presuppose the basic norm, that only *if* we presuppose it can we consider a coercive order which is by and large effective as a system of *objectively valid* norms. Consequently, the foundation of the objective validity of the legal norms is conditional, conditioned by the presupposition of the basic norm. . . .

The problem that leads to the theory of the basic norm—as I explained in my *Reine Rechtslehre*—is how to distinguish a legal command which is considered to be objectively valid, such as the command of a revenue officer to pay a certain sum of money, from a command which has the same subjective meaning but is not considered to be objectively valid, such as the command of a gangster. The difference consists in that we do not consider the subjective meaning of the

---

30 [*Cf. The Pure Theory of Law*, pp. 46–47.]
31 [*Cf. The Pure Theory of Law*, pp. 212–213.]

command of a gangster—as we consider the subjective meaning of the
legal command of a revenue officer—as its objective meaning because
we do not presuppose in the former case—as we presuppose in the
latter case—a basic norm. A Communist may, indeed, not admit that
there is an essential difference between an organization of gangsters
and a capitalistic legal order which he considers as the means of ruthless
exploitation. For he does not presuppose—as do those who interpret
the coercive order in question as an objectively valid normative order
—the basic norm. He does not deny that the capitalistic coercive order
is the law of the State. What he denies is that this coercive order, the
law of the State, is objectively valid. The function of the basic norm
is not to make it possible to consider a coercive order which is by and
large effective as law, for—according to the definition presented by
the Pure Theory of Law—a *legal* order is a coercive order by and
large effective; the function of the basic norm is to make it possible
to consider this coercive order as an *objectively* valid order. . . .

Professor Stone again attacks my theory of the basic norm in a
chapter entitled, " Mystery and Mystique in the ' Basic Norm.' " What he
means he explains in seven questions; and my answers to these questions
will show that there is nothing " mysterious " at all in the theory which
arouses such an anger in Professor Stone's mind. He asks:

> 1. When Kelsen refers variously to " basic norm " (*Grundnorm*),
> " origin norm " (*Ursprungsnorm*) and " constitution in the legal-
> logical sense " (*Verfassung im rechtslogischen Sinne*), is he naming
> the same entity? If so, are these names semantically appropriate
> for the same entity? [32]

My answer: That these terms refer to the same entity Professor Stone
himself seems to suppose by formulating his question. That they are
semantically appropriate for the same thing is indeed my opinion; otherwise I would not use them in this way.

> 2. Does Kelsen offer the " basic norm " as merely an intellectual
> construct to aid cognition by jurisprudents of a legal order as a
> whole? Or does he offer it as the *Ursprungsnorm,* the source to
> which lawyers too must trace the validity of all the norms of the
> legal system? In his own language, is it a " legal-logical " (" trans-
> cendental-logical ") or is it a " legal " concept? [33]

The answer is: The basic norm is not an intellectual " construct "
because—as I mentioned before—it is not " created " by juristic thinking, but *presupposed* in it, if we consider—without referring to a meta-
legal authority such as God or nature—the subjective meaning of the
acts by which the constitution (in the positive-legal sense of the word)
is established and the subjective meaning of the acts established on the
basis of this constitution to be their objective meaning, and if we thus
consider these meanings (which are norms) as objectively valid. Because
this function is of legal importance, and because the question how is it
possible to consider the subjective meaning of the acts concerned
as their objective meaning is analogous to the question characterized by
Kant as transcendental-logical (how is it possible to have a nonmeta-

[32] *Legal System, op. cit.,* p. 124.
[33] *Idem.*

physical interpretation of the facts ascertained in the laws of nature by which the science of nature describes its object)—for these reasons is the basic norm at the same time a transcendental-logical *and* a legal concept.

> 3. In part consequentially on the above, does he say that the "basic norm" is not a part of the legal order (in our word, "extra-systemic") but a mere presupposition of the legal order directing obedience to the "constitution in the legal sense"? Or does he say it is a part of the legal order (in our word, "intra-systemic"), the apex norm of the system of norms? [34]

This question I have answered in the preceding explanations.

> 4. Again in part consequently, are Kelsen's formulations of the "basic norm" intended to express a uniform "basic norm" for all legal orders, of the pattern—"The constitution in the legal sense ought to be obeyed"? Or are they intended to be a statement matrix with a blank to be separately filled for each legal order, in the pattern "The constitution in the legal sense of (Legal Order A, or Legal Order B, etc.) ought to be obeyed"? (The latter would yield a different "basic norm" for each legal order, A, B, etc.) Or does he mean that the blank is in each case to be filled in with the actual norm or norms constituting the particular legal order's "apex norm"? [35]

Nobody who has read what I have said about the basic norm can have any doubt about my view that for each positive legal order a *specific* basic norm referring to the constitution (in the positive legal sense) of *this* legal order is to be presupposed if the subjective meaning of the acts by which *this* constitution is established, and the subjective meaning of the acts established on the basis of this constitution, creating positive legal norms, are to be interpreted as their objective meaning. Since different legal orders are based on different constitutions, different basic norms are to be presupposed. Each of these different basic norms refers to a different positive constitution. What is common to all these basic norms is that they refer to a positive legal constitution on the basis of which a positive normative coercive order is established which is by and large effective. All this stands to reason and has been questioned *only* by Professor Stone, though the same Professor Stone, presenting my theory, says: "[T]he difference between different systems of legal norms (English, for example, as opposed to American or Soviet) lies in their respective apex norms. . . ." [36]

> 5. What does Kelsen mean by calling the "basic norm" a "hypothesis" or "a hypothetical norm"? Are these the same thing? Or are they only related but not identical notions? Or the same notion applied to different entities? Or both of these? [37]

This question is answered in the preceding explanations. In addition, I call the attention of Professor Stone again to the fact that if I call the basic norm a "hypothesis" or "hypothetical" I am using the term in

[34] *Idem.*
[35] *Idem,* at pp. 124–125.
[36] *Idem,* at p. 108.
[37] *Idem,* at p. 125.

its literal meaning: pre-supposition=*Voraus-Setzung*. The term " hypo-thetical," it is true, I am using in some connection—*not with respect to the basic norm, but with respect to positive general legal norms*—in the sense in which Kant uses the term when he speaks of " hypothetical " in contradistinction to " categorical " *imperatives*. This too is evident to an attentive reader.

6. When Kelsen says that the " validity " of the " basic norm " is presupposed, does he mean that though its validity is to be estab-lished by reference to other norms, these latter are not the concern of the jurisprudent or lawyer? Or does he mean that its validity is to be established by reference to criteria which are factual, and not normative, and also not the concern of the jurisprudent or lawyer? Or does he mean both? Or that it is immaterial which?[38]

There cannot be the slightest doubt about my view that the basic norm —*if* presupposed to be valid—refers to the norms of a *legal* order and that a condition of their positivity is that they are by and large effective. When Professor Stone imputes to me—without quoting a statement of my writings which could justify it—as possible the stupid opinion that the positive legal norms are " not the concern of the jurisprudent or lawyer," I am forced to doubt the objectivity of his criticism. This doubt is confirmed also by other passages in Professor Stone's chapter on my theory. For instance, concerning the relationship between the Pure Theory of Law and logic, I have rejected the view expressed by some writers that this theory is merely a juristic logic. I have declared that it is not a juristic logic but a general theory of law which contains certain logical considerations. Professor Stone quite correctly quotes this state-ment on page 134. My own view concerning the nature of the Pure Theory of Law is for everybody a sufficient reason why this theory is not mentioned in A. G. Conte's " Bibliografia di Logica Giuridica."[39] But Professor Stone, in spite of quoting my statement, explains the omission of my work from Conte's *Bibliografia* by the fact that my use of basic terms of formal logic is—as Professor Stone thinks—" often loose."

7. What is the bearing, if any, of Kelsen's " purity " thesis on these and other aspects of the " basic norm "? Is the method of cognition of the " basic norm " intended to be " pure "? If so, in what sense? Or does Kelsen's recent re-emphasis that the " basic norm " stands " outside " the legal system imply that he recognises that the matters affecting the " basic norm " are also " outside " his requirement of juristic purity of method?"[40]

It stands to reason that the postulate of purity refers to the entire *theory* of law including the theory of the basic norm, and that there is no particular " bearing " of the " purity thesis " on any aspect of the basic norm. In which sense the principle of purity is to be understood Pro-fessor Stone has quite correctly formulated on page 101 of his book. That I have recently " re-emphasised " that the basic norm stands outside the legal system is simply not true. I have always, and from the very first time I spoke of the basic norm, maintained that this norm is not

[38] *Idem.*
[39] (1961) 38 *Rivista Internazionale de Filosofia del Diritto* 120.
[40] *Legal System, op. cit.,* p. 125.

a positive norm, that is, not a norm created by an act of will of a legal authority but presupposed in juristic thinking. Whether it " stands outside or inside " the legal system depends—as I said before—on the definition of the concept of " legal system." It is difficult to believe that Professor Stone cannot answer all these questions himself, and not to believe that he is unwilling to understand what I say.

The Hierarchy
International and National Law

The main objection which Professor Stone advances against my theory of the relationship between the national and international legal order concerns my view that even if one proceeds from the sovereignty, *i.e.,* the primacy of one's own national legal order, a monistic interpretation of this relationship results.[41] Professor Stone says: " He [Kelsen] pronounces that it is ' logically impossible to interpret the world of law by proceeding from the sovereignty of different States.' " [42] He refers to a " *tertium quid* " which I—as he says—" ruled out as ' logically impossible.' " " This *tertium quid* is that, as between the international legal order and a particular national order, primacy may simply be determined by the legal order which has the question before it." [43] But Professor Stone ignores the fact that if a national legal order presents itself as sovereign it cannot recognize the other national legal orders as sovereign because the sovereignty of one State or national legal order. . . . —is incompatible with the sovereignty of the other States. The chapter of my *General Theory of Law and State* in which I formulated the thesis which Professor Stone rejects is entitled " Sovereignty as Exclusive Quality of Only One Order." And, what is even more important, in my *General Theory of Law and State* to which Professor Stone refers in this connection, I did not say, as Professor Stone quotes, " that it is ' logically impossible to interpret the world of law by proceeding from the sovereignty of different States.' " On the contrary! I actually said:

> It is, however, logically possible that different theorists interpret the world of law by proceeding from the sovereignty of different States. Each theorist may presuppose the sovereignty of his own State. . . . Then he has to consider . . . these national legal orders [of the other States] as parts of the legal order of his own State, conceived as a universal legal order. . . .[44]

Professor Stone says: " It is only if the jurist is completely blind to the existence of any national legal order but his own in relation to the international, that the choice of the national order can be said to yield a monistic hypothesis." [45] That it is not necessary to be " blind " to the existence of the national legal orders which are not the starting point of the construction is shown by the statement on page 385 of the *General Theory of Law and State* (and the analogous statement on page 335 of the *Reine Rechtslehre*) that " the other national legal orders . . . have to be considered as inferior to the legal order of the State which first is, and which therefore alone can be, presupposed to be sovereign."

41 *Idem,* pp. 118–120.
42 *Idem,* p. 119.
43 *Idem.*
44 *General Theory,* p. 386.
45 *Legal System,* p. 119.

In my *General Theory of Law and State* [46] and in my *Reine Rechtslehre* [47] I have analyzed very carefully the relationship between international and national law. But Professor Stone ignores all the arguments I advocated in these works for the doctrine he rejects. In the same connection Professor Stone says:

> And it also becomes clear that one main source of Kelsen's confusion on this matter is his use of the term " national law " (or " national legal order ") as if, because it is *one phrase,* it must also be *one " law "* (or " legal order "). This is either the crudest nominalism, or it is an abstraction from the multiplicity of national legal orders. And while abstraction from the multiplicity is no sin, it becomes a rather serious one when the theorist then purports to base on it an assertion of logical impossibility which depends precisely on ignoring the elements left out by the abstraction. [48]

This objection is so completely untenable that it hardly needs a reply. It is above any reasonable doubt that my use of the term " national law " (or " national legal order ") has nothing to do with " nominalism," that it is an abstract concept comprehending all the national laws or national legal orders. To say that " I ignore " the multiplicity of national legal orders, that I use the term " national law " as if, because it is one phrase, it must be *one* " law " is an inexcusable misinterpretation in view of the fact that I repeatedly refer to the national legal orders (in the plural)—for instance, in my above quoted statement and especially in the chapter to which Professor Stone's critique refers.

[pp. 1141–1144, 1147–1153]

H. KELSEN

The Pure Theory of Law
(1967)

Norm and Norm Creation [49]

Those norms, then, which have the character of legal norms and which make certain acts legal or illegal are the objects of the science of law. The legal order which is the object of this cognition is a normative order of human behavior—a system of norms regulating human behavior. By " norm " we mean that something *ought* to be or *ought* to happen, especially that a human being ought to behave in a specific way. This is the meaning of certain human acts directed toward the behavior of others. They are so directed, if they, according to their content, command such behavior, but also if they permit it, and—particularly—if they authorize it. " Authorize " means to confer upon someone else a certain power, specifically the power to enact norms himself. In this sense the acts whose meaning is a norm are acts of will. If an individual by his acts expresses a will directed at a certain behavior of another, that is to say, if he commands, permits, or authorizes such behavior—then the meaning of his acts cannot be described by the statement that

---

[46] *General Theory,* pp. 328–388.
[47] [*Cf. The Pure Theory of Law,* pp. 318–320.]
[48] *Legal System,* pp. 119–120.
[49] [Translated by Max Knight from the second edition of *Reine Rechtslehre* (1960).]

the other individual *will* (future tense) behave in that way, but only
that he *ought* to behave in that way. The individual who commands,
permits, or authorizes *wills*; the man to whom the command, permission,
or authorization is directed *ought to*. The word " ought " is used here
in a broader than the usual sense. According to customary usage,
" ought " corresponds only to a command, while " may " corresponds to
a permission, and " can " to an authorization. But in the present work
the word " ought " is used to express the normative meaning of an act
directed toward the behavior of others; this " ought " includes " may "
and " can." If a man who is commanded, permitted, or authorized to
behave in a certain way asks for the reason of such command, permission, or authorization, he can only do so by saying: Why " ought " I
behave in this way? Or, in customary usage: Why may I or why can I
behave in this way?

   " Norm " is the meaning of an act by which a certain behavior is
commanded, permitted, or authorized. The norm, as the specific meaning
of an act directed toward the behavior of someone else, is to be carefully
differentiated from the act of will whose meaning the norm is: the
norm is an *ought*, but the act of will is an *is*. Hence the situation
constituted by such an act must be described by the statement: The
one individual wills that the other individual ought to behave in a
certain way. The first part of this sentence refers to an *is*, the existing
fact of the first individual's act of volition; the second part to an *ought*,
to a norm as the meaning of that act. Therefore it is incorrect to
assert—as is often done—that the statement: " An individual ought "
merely means that another individual wills something; that the *ought*
can be reduced to an *is*.

   The difference between *is* and *ought* cannot be explained further.
We are immediately aware of the difference. Nobody can deny that the
statement: " something is "—that is, the statement by which an existent
fact is described—is fundamentally different from the statement: " something ought to be "—which is the statement by which a norm is described.
Nobody can assert that from the statement that something is, follows
a statement that something ought to be, or vice versa.

   This dualism of is and ought does not mean, however, that there
is no relationship between *is* and *ought*. One says: an *is* conforms to
an ought, which means that something is as it ought to be; and one
says: an *ought is* " directed " toward an is—in other words: something
ought to be. The expression: " an is conforms to an ought " is not
entirely correct, because it is not the is that conforms to the ought, but
the " something " that one time is and the other time ought to be—it is
the " something " which figuratively can be designated as the content
of the is or as the content of the ought.

   Put in different words, one can also say: a certain something—
specifically a certain behavior—can have the quality of is or of ought.
For example: In the two statements, " the door is being closed " and
" the door ought to be closed," the closing of the door in the former
statement is pronounced as something that is, in the latter as something
that ought to be. The behavior that is and the behavior that ought to
be are not identical, but they differ only so far as the one is and the
other ought to be. Is and ought are two different modi. One and the
same behavior may be presented in the one or the other of the two
modi. Therefore it is necessary to differentiate the behavior stipulated by

a norm as a behavior that ought to be from the actual behavior that corresponds to it. We may compare the behavior stipulated by the norm (as content of the norm) with the actual behavior; and we can, therefore, judge whether the actual behavior conforms to the norm, that is, to the content of the norm.

The behavior as it actually takes place may or may not be equal to the behavior as it ought to be. But equality is not identity. The behavior that is the content of the norm (that is, the behavior that ought to be) and the actual behavior (that is, the behavior that is) are not identical, though the one may be *equal* to the other. Therefore, the usual way to describe the relation between an actual behavior and a norm to which the behavior corresponds: the actual behavior is the behavior that—according to the norm—ought to be, is not correct. The behavior that is cannot be the behavior that ought to be. They differ with respect to the modus which is in one case the is, in the other the ought.

Acts whose meaning is a norm can be performed in various ways. For example, by a gesture: The traffic policeman, by a motion of his arms, orders the pedestrian to stop or to continue; or by a symbol: a red light constitutes a command for the driver to halt, a green light, to proceed; or by spoken or written words, either in the imperative form— be quiet!—or in the form of an indicative statement—I order you to be silent. In this way also permissions or authorizations may be formulated. They are statements about the act whose meaning is a command, a permission, an authorization. But their meaning is not that something is, but that something ought to be. They are not—as they linguistically seem to be—statements about a fact, but a norm, that is to say, a command, a permission, an authorization.

A criminal code might contain the sentence: Theft is punished by imprisonment. The meaning of this sentence is not, as the wording seems to indicate, a statement about an actual event; instead, the meaning is a norm: it is a command or an authorization, to punish theft by imprisonment. The legislative process consists of a series of acts which, in their totality, have the meaning of a norm. To say that acts, especially legislative acts, "create" or "posit" a norm, is merely a figure of speech for saying that the meaning or the significance of the act or acts that constitute the legislative process, is a norm. It is, however, necesssary to distinguish the subjective and the objective meaning of the act. "Ought" is the subjective meaning of every act of will directed at the behavior of another. But not every such act has also objectively this meaning; and only if the act of will has also the objective meaning of an "ought," is this "ought" called a "norm." If the "ought" is also the objective meaning of the act, the behavior at which the act is directed is regarded as something that *ought* to be not only from the point of view of the individual who has performed the act but also from the point of view of the individual at whose behavior the act is directed, and of a third individual not involved in the relation between the two. That the "ought" is the objective meaning of the act manifests itself in the fact that it is supposed to exist (that the "ought" is valid) even if the will ceases to exist whose subjective meaning it is--if we assume that an individual ought to behave in a certain way even if he does not know of the act whose meaning is that he ought to behave in this way. Then the "ought," as the objective meaning of an act, is a valid *norm* binding

upon the addressee, that is, the individual at whom it is directed. The
ought which is the subjective meaning of an act of will is also the
objective meaning of this act, if this act has been invested with this
meaning, if it has been authorized by a norm, which therefore has the
character of a " higher " norm.

The command of a gangster to turn over to him a certain amount of
money has the same subjective meaning as the command of an income-
tax official, namely that the individual at whom the command is directed
ought to pay something. But only the command of the official, not that
of the gangster, has the meaning of a valid norm, binding upon the
addressed individual. Only the one order, not the other, is a norm-positing
act, because the official's act is authorized by a tax law, whereas the
gangster's act is not based on such an authorizing norm. The legislative
act, which subjectively has the meaning of *ought*, also has the objective
meaning—that is, the meaning of a valid norm—because the constitution
has conferred this objective meaning upon the legislative act. The act
whose meaning is the constitution has not only the subjective but also
the objective meaning of " ought," that is to say, the character of a
binding norm, if—in case it is the historically first constitution—we
presuppose in our juristic thinking that we ought to behave as the
constitution prescribes. . . .   [pp. 4–8]

Positive and Negative Regulations:
Commanding, Authorizing, Permitting

The behavior regulated by a normative order is either a definite action
or the omission (nonperformance) of such an action. Human behavior,
then, is either positively or negatively regulated by a normative order.
Positively, when a definite action of a definite individual or when the
omission of such an action is commanded. (When the omission of an
action is commanded, the action is forbidden.) To say that the behavior
of an individual is commanded by an objectively valid norm amounts to
the same as saying the individual is obliged to behave in this way. If the
individual behaves as the norm commands he fulfills his obligation—he
obeys the norm; if he behaves in the opposite way, he " violates " the
norm—he violates his obligation. Human behavior is positively regulated
also, when an individual is authorized by the normative order to bring
about, by a certain act, certain consequences determined by the order.
Particularly an individual can be authorized (if the order regulates its
own creation) to create norms or to participate in that creation; or
when, in case of a legal order providing for coercive acts as sanctions,
an individual is authorized to perform these acts under the conditions
stipulated by the legal order; or when a norm permits an individual to
perform an act, otherwise forbidden—a norm which limits the sphere
of validity of a general norm that forbids the act. An example for the
last-mentioned alternative is self-defense: although a general norm
forbids the use of force of one individual against another, a special
norm permits such use of force in self-defense. When an individual
acts as he is authorized by the norm or behaves as he is permitted by
a norm, he " applies " the norm. The judge, authorized by a statute
(that is, a general norm) to decide concrete cases, applies the statute to
a concrete case by a decision which constitutes an *individual* norm.
Again, authorized by a judicial decision to execute a certain punishment,

the enforcement officer "applies" the individual norm of the judicial decision. In exercising self-defense, one applies the norm that permits the use of force. Further, a norm is also "applied" in rendering a judgment that an individual does, or does not, behave as he is commanded, authorized or permitted by a norm.

In the broadest sense, any human behavior determined by a normative order as condition or consequence, can be considered as being authorized by this order and in this sense as being positively regulated. Human behavior is regulated negatively by a normative order if this behavior is not forbidden by the order without being positively permitted by a norm that limits the sphere of validity of a forbidding norm, and therefore is permitted only in a negative sense. This merely negative function of permitting has to be distinguished from the positive function of permitting—"positive," because it is the function of a positive norm, the meaning of an act of will. The positive character of a permission becomes particularly apparent when the limitation of the sphere of validity of a norm that forbids a certain conduct is brought about by a norm that permits the otherwise forbidden conduct under the condition that the permission has to be given by an organ of the community authorized thereto. The negative as well as positive function of permitting is therefore fundamentally connected with the function of commanding. A definite human behavior can be *permitted* only within a normative order that *commands* different kinds of behavior.

"To permit" is also used in the sense of "to entitle (*berechtigen*)." If *A* is commanded to endure that *B* behaves in a certain way, it is said that *B* is permitted (that is, entitled) to behave in this way. And if *A* is commanded to render a certain service to *B*, it is said that *B* is permitted (that is, entitled) to receive the service of *A*. In the first example, then, the sentence "*B* is permitted to behave in a certain way" says the same as the sentence: "*A* is commanded to endure that *B* behaves in a certain way." And in the second example, the sentence: "*B* is permitted to receive a certain service from *A*" says the same as the sentence: "*A* is commanded to render a service to *B*." The quality of *B's* behavior "to be permitted" is merely the reflex of the quality of *A's* behavior "to be commanded." This kind of "permitting" is not a function of the normative order different from its function of "commanding." [pp. 15–17]

The Reason for the Validity of a Legal Order

The norm system that presents itself as a legal order has essentially a dynamic character. A legal norm is not valid because it has a certain content, that is, because its content is logically deducible from a presupposed basic norm, but because it is created in a certain way—ultimately in a way determined by a presupposed basic norm. For this reason alone does the legal norm belong to the legal order whose norms are created according to this basic norm. Therefore any kind of content might be law. There is no human behavior which, as such, is excluded from being the content of a legal norm. The validity of a legal norm may not be denied for being (in its content) in conflict with that of another norm which does not belong to the legal order whose basic norm is the reason for the validity of the norm in question. The basic norm of a legal order is not a material norm which, because its content

is regarded as immediately self-evident, is presupposed as the highest
norm and from which norms for human behavior are logically deduced.
The norms of a legal order must be created by a specific process. They
are posited, that is, positive, norms, elements of a positive order. If by
the constitution of a legal community is understood the norm or norms
that determine how (that is, by what organs and by what procedure—
through legislation or custom) the general norms of the legal order that
constitute the community are to be created, then the basic norm is that
norm which is presupposed when the custom through which the constitution has come into existence, or the constitution-creating act consciously performed by certain human beings, is objectively interpreted as
a norm-creating fact; if, in the latter case, the individual or the assembly
of individuals who created the constitution on which the legal order
rests, are looked upon as norm-creating authorities. In this sense, the
basic norm determines the basic fact of law creation and may in this
respect be described as the constitution in a logical sense of the word
(which will be explained later) in contradistinction to the constitution
in the meaning of positive law. The basic norm is the presupposed starting
point of a procedure: the procedure of positive law creation. It is itself
not a norm created by custom or by the act of a legal organ; it is not
a positive but a presupposed norm so far as the constitution-establishing
authority is looked upon as the highest authority and can therefore not
be regarded as authorized by the norm of a higher authority.

If the question as to the reason for the validity of a certain legal
norm is raised, then the answer can only consist in the reduction to the
basic norm of this legal order, that is, in the assertion that the norm
was created—in the last instance—according to the basic norm. . . .

The question of the reason for the validity of a legal norm belonging
to a specific national legal order may rise on the occasion of a coercive
act; for example, when one individual deprives another of his life by
hanging, and now the question is asked why this act is legal, namely
the execution of a punishment, and not murder. This act can be
interpreted as being legal only if it was prescribed by an individual
legal norm, namely as an act that " ought " to be performed, by a
norm that presents itself as a judicial decision. This raises the questions:
Under what conditions is such an interpretation possible, why is a
judicial decision present in this case, why is the individual norm created
thereby a legal norm belonging to a valid legal order and therefore
ought to be applied? The answer is: Because this individual norm was
created in applying a criminal law that contains a general norm according
to which (under conditions present in the case concerned) the death
penalty ought to be inflicted. If we ask for the reason for the validity
of this criminal law, then the answer is: the criminal law is valid
because it was created by the legislature, and the legislature, in turn,
is authorized by the constitution to create general norms. If we ask for
the reason of the validity of the constitution, that is, for the reason of
the validity of the norms regulating the creation of the general norms,
we may, perhaps, discover an older constitution; that means the validity
of the existing constitution is justified by the fact that it was created
according to the rules of an earlier constitution by way of a constitutional
amendment. In this way we eventually arrive at a historically first constitution that cannot have been created in this way and whose validity,
therefore, cannot be traced back to a positive norm created by a legal

authority; we arrive, instead, at a constitution that became valid in a revolutionary way, that is, either by breach of a former constitution or for a territory that formerly was not the sphere of validity of a constitution and of a national legal order based on it. If we consider merely the national order, not international law, and if we ask for the reason of the validity of the historically first constitution, then the answer can only be (if we leave aside God or " nature ") that the validity of this constitution—the assumption that it is a binding norm—must be *presupposed* if we want to interpret (1) the acts performed according to it as the creation or application of valid general legal norms; and (2) the acts performed in application of these general norms as the creation or application of valid individual legal norms. Since the reason for the validity of a norm can only be another norm, the presupposition must be a norm: not one posited (i.e. created) by a legal authority, but a presupposed norm, that is, a norm presupposed if the subjective meaning of the constitution-creating facts and the subjective meaning of the norm-creating facts established according to the constitution are interpreted as their objective meaning. Since it is the basic norm of a legal order (that is, an order prescribing coercive acts), therefore this norm, namely the basic norm of the legal order concerned, must be formulated as follows. Coercive acts sought to be performed under the conditions and in the manner which the historically first constitution, and the norms created according to it, prescribe. (In short: One ought to behave as the constitution prescribes.) The norms of a legal order, whose common reason for their validity is this basic norm are not a complex of valid norms standing coordinatedly side by side, but form a hierarchical structure of super- and subordinate norms. . . .

The Basic Norm as Transcendental-logical Presupposition

To understand the nature of the basic norm it must be kept in mind that it refers directly to a specific constitution, actually established by custom or statutory creation, by and large effective, and indirectly to the coercive order created according to this constitution and by and large effective; the basic norm thereby furnishes the reason for the validity of this constitution and of the coercive order created in accordance with it. The basic norm, therefore, is not the product of free invention. It is not presupposed arbitrarily in the sense that there is a choice between different basic norms when the subjective meaning of a constitution-creating act and the acts created according to this constitution are interpreted as their objective meaning. Only if this basic norm, referring to a specific constitution, is presupposed, that is, only if it is presupposed that one ought to behave according to this specific constitution—only then can the subjective meaning of a constitution-creating act and of the acts created according to this constitution be interpreted as their objective meaning, that is, as objectively valid legal norms, and the relationships established by these norms as legal relations. . . .[50]

---

[50] [By insisting that the validity of the basic norm is a presupposition Kelsen excludes it from the category of propositions that may be verified. By investing his rules of recognition with the criterion of acceptance, Hart clothes his concept of the ultimate source of law with more meaningful purpose and reality. See, further, Hughes, 59 Calif.L.R. 695, 699–703.]

The Hierarchical Structure of the Legal Order

The Constitution

The peculiarity of the law that it regulates its own creation. . . . This can be done by a norm determining merely the procedure by which another norm is to be created. But it can be done also by a norm determining, to a certain extent, the content of the norm to be created. Since, because of the dynamic character of law, a norm is valid because, and to the extent that, it had been created in a certain way, that is, in a way determined by another norm, therefore that other norm is the immediate reason for the validity of the new norm. The relationship between the norm that regulates the creation of another norm and the norm created in conformity with the former can be metaphorically presented as a relationship of super- and subordination. The norm which regulates the creation of another norm is the higher, the norm created in conformity with the former is the lower one. The legal order is not a system of coordinated norms of equal level, but a hierarchy of different levels of legal norms. Its unity is brought about by the connection that results from the fact that the validity of a norm, created according to another norm, rests on that other norm, whose creation in turn, is determined by a third one. This is a regression that ultimately ends up in the presupposed basic norm. This basic norm, therefore, is the highest reason for the validity of the norms, one created in conformity with another, thus forming a legal order in its hierarchical structure. . . .

Considering, only a national legal order, the constitution represents the highest level of positive law. "Constitution" is understood here in its material sense, that is, we understand by constitution the positive norm or norms which regulate the creation of general legal norms. The constitution may be created by custom or by a specific act performed by one or several individuals, that is, by a legislative act. In the latter case it is always formulated in a document and hence called a "written" constitution, in contradistinction to the "unwritten" constitution brought about by custom. The material constitution may consist partly of norms of written and partly of unwritten law. The unwritten norms of the constitution may be codified; and if this codification is the work of a law-creating organ and therefore acquires binding force, it becomes a written constitution.

The constitution in the material sense must be distinguished from the constitution in the formal sense, namely a document called "constitution," which, as written constitution, may contain not only norms regulating the creation of general norms (that is, legislation), but also norms concerning other politically important subjects; and, besides, regulations according to which the norms contained in this document may be abolished or amended—not like ordinary statutes, but by a special procedure and under more rigorous conditions. These regulations represent the constitutional form, and the document to whose content these regulations refer, represents the constitution in a formal sense, which may include any desired content. The purpose of the regulations which render more difficult the abolition or amendment of the content of the constitution in a formal sense is primarily to stabilize the norms designated here as "material constitution" and which are the positive-legal basis of the entire national legal order.

In a modern legal order, the creation (regulated by the material constitution) of general legal norms has the character of legislation. The constitutional regulation of legislation determines the organs authorized to create general legal norms—statutes and ordinances. If the courts should be regarded as authorized to apply customary law also, they must be authorized by the constitution to do so in the same way as they must be authorized to apply statutes. In other words: the constitution must institute as a law-creating fact the custom constituted by the habitual behavior of the individuals subject to the national legal order—the " subjects." If the application of customary law by courts is considered to be legitimate although the written constitution contains no such authorization, then the authorization cannot be considered to proceed from an unwritten custom-created constitution [51] but must be *presupposed,* in the same way that it must be presupposed that the written constitution has the character of an objectively binding norm if the statutes and ordinances issued in accordance with it are regarded as binding legal norms. Then the basic norm (the constitution in the transcendental-logical sense) institutes not only the act of the legislator, but also custom as law-creating facts.

The constitution of the state, as a written constitution, can appear in the specific form of a constitution, that is, in norms that may not be abolished or amended as ordinary statutes but only under more rigorous conditions. But this need not be so. It is not so if there is no written constitution, if the constitution is created by custom and is not codified; then, even norms which have the character of a material constitution may be abolished or amended by simple statutes or by customary law.

It is possible that the organ specifically and formally authorized to create, abolish, or amend statutes having the character of a constitution is different from the organ authorized to create, abolish, or amend ordinary statutes. For example, the former function may be rendered by an organ different from the latter organ in composition and electoral procedure, such as a constituent national assembly. But usually both functions are performed by the same organ.   [pp. 221–223]

Public and Private Law

Until this day it has not been possible to achieve an entirely satisfactory definition of the difference. According to the majority view we are confronted here with a classification of legal relationships: private law represents a relationship between coordinated, legally equal-ranking subjects; public law, a relationship between a super- and a subordinated subject, that is, between two subjects of whom one has a higher legal value as compared with that of the other. The typical public-law relationship is that between state (or government) and subject (in German, characteristically, *Untertan*). Private-law relationships are called simply " legal relationships " in the narrower sense of the term, to juxtapose to them the public-law relationships as " power relationships " or relationships of " dominion." In general, the differentiation between private and public law tends to assume the meaning of a difference between law and a nonlegal, or at least a half legal, power, and, particularly, between law and state. A closer analysis of the higher value

[51] [*Cf. The Pure Theory of Law,* p. 226.]

attributed to certain subjects, of their superordination over others, discloses that we are confronted here with a differentiation between law-creating facts. And the decisive difference is the same as that which is the basis for the classification of forms of government. The legal plus-value assigned to the state—that is, to its organs in relation to the subjects—consists in that the legal order concedes to individuals qualified as officials (or at least to some of them) the power to obligate the subjects by a unilateral expression of their will (commands). A typical example of a public-law relationship is the one established by an administrative order, that is, an individual norm issued by an administrative organ obligating legally the addressee to behave in conformity with the order. A typical example of a private-law relationship is the one established by a legal transaction, especially the contract (that is, the individual norm created by the contract), by which the contracting parties are legally obligated to a mutual behavior. Whereas here the subjects participate in the creation of the norm that obligates them—this is, indeed the essence of contractual law creation—the subject obligated by the administrative order under public law has no part in the creation of the norm that obligates him. It is the typical case of an autocratic norm creation, whereas the private-law contract represents a typically democratic method of law-making. Therefore the sphere of legal transactions is characterized as the sphere of private autonomy.

The Ideological Character of the Dualism of Public and Private Law
If the decisive difference between private and public law is comprehended as the difference between two methods of creating law; if the so-called public acts of the state are recognized as legal acts just as the private legal transaction; if, most of all, it is understood that the acts constituting the law-creating facts are in both cases only the continuations of the process of the creation of the so-called will of the state, and that in the administrative order just as much as in the private legal transaction only the individualization of general norms are effected—then it will not seem so paradoxical that the Pure Theory of Law, from its universalistic viewpoint, always directed toward the whole of the legal order (the so-called will of the state), sees in the private legal transaction just as much as in an administrative order an act of the state, that is, a fact of law-making attributable to the unity of the legal order. By doing so, the Pure Theory of Law " relativizes " the contrast between private and public law " absolutized " by the traditional science of law, changes it from an extra-systematic difference, that is, a difference between law and nonlaw or between law and state, to an intra-systematic one. The Pure Theory proves to be a true science by dissolving the ideology connected with the absolutizing of the difference in question.[52] . . .

[pp. 280–282]

The Identity of State and Law
The State as a Legal Order
A cognition of the state free of ideology, and hence of metaphysics and mysticism, can grasp its essence only by comprehending this social structure as an order of human behavior. It is usual to characterize the state as a political organization. But this merely expresses the idea that the state is a coercive order. For the specifically " political " element

[52] [For the Marxist attitude see *post*, 639.]

of this organization consists in the coercion exercised by man against man, regulated by this order—in the coercive acts prescribed by this order. These are precisely the coercive acts which the legal order attaches to certain conditions stipulated by it. As a political organization, the state is a legal order. But not every legal order is a state. Neither the pre-state legal order of primitive society, nor the super- (or inter-) state international legal order represents a state. To be a state, the legal order must have the character of an organization in the narrower and specific sense of this word, that is, it must establish organs who, in the manner of division of labor, create and apply the norms that constitute the legal order; it must display a certain degree of centralization. The state is a relatively centralized legal order.

This centralization distinguishes the state as a legal order from the primitive pre-state order and the super-state order of general international law. In neither order are the general legal norms created by a central legislative organ but by way of custom, which means that the creation of general legal norms is decentralized. Neither the pre-state nor the super-state legal order establishes courts authorized to apply the general norms to concrete cases, but authorizes the individuals subjected to the legal order themselves to render this function and, particularly, to execute, by way of self-help, the sanctions prescribed by the legal order. According to primitive law, it is the members of the murdered man's family who take blood revenge against the murderer and his family, which means, they are authorized to carry out the primitive punishment; it is the creditor himself who can satisfy his claim against the debtor by taking some property of the debtor and holding it in pawn. It is the government of the individual state which, according to general international law, is authorized to resort to war or take reprisals against a law-violating state, which means: against the subjects of the state whose government has violated the law. True, the individuals who in the pre-state and in the super-state community create (by custom) or apply the law and execute the sanctions, are legal organs and thus organs of the legal community; but they are not functioning in the manner of division of labor and therefore not centralized organs like a government, a legislature, and courts under a national legal order. The legal order of primitive society and the general inter-national law order are entirely decentralized coercive orders and therefore not states. If, the state is comprehended as a social community, it can be constituted only by a normative order. Since a community can be constituted by only *one* such order (and is, indeed, identical with this order), the normative order constituting the state can only be the relatively centralized coercive order which is the national legal order.

In traditional theory the state is composed of three elements, the people of the state, the territory of the state, and the so-called power of the state, exercised by an independent government. All three elements can be determined only juridically, that is, they can be comprehended only as the validity and the spheres of validity of a legal order.

The state's population is the human beings who belong to the state. If it is asked why an individual together with other individuals does belong to a certain state, no other criterion can be found than that he and the others are subject to a certain, relatively centralized, coercive order. All attempts to find another bond that holds together and unites in one unit individuals differing in language, race, religion, world concept, and separated by conflicts of interests, is doomed to failure. It is particularly impossible to demonstrate the existence of some sort of psychic interaction which, independent of any legal bond, unites all individuals belonging to a state in such a way that they can be distinguished from other individuals, belonging to another state, and united by an analogous-interaction as two separate groups. It is undeniable that no such interaction exists uniting all individuals belonging to one state, and only them; and it is undeniable that individuals belonging to different states may be connected spiritually much closer than those belonging to the same state. For they belong to this state only legally. They certainly may have a psychic relation to their state, as the saying goes; they may love it, even deify it, and be prepared to die for it. But they belong to it even if they do not feel that way, if they hate it, even betray it, or are indifferent to it. The question whether an individual belongs to a state is not a psychological but a legal question. The unity of individuals constituting a state's population can only be seen in the fact that the same legal order is valid for these individuals, that their behavior is regulated by the same legal order. The state population is the personal sphere of validity of the national legal order.

The state territory is a certain delimited space. It is not a delimited piece of the earth's surface, but a three-dimensional space which includes the space below the ground and the space above the territory enclosed by the so-called frontiers of the state. It is obvious that the unity of this space is not a natural, geographic one. The same state territory may include areas separated by the ocean, which is not the territory of *one* state, or by the territory of another state. No natural science, but only legal cognition can answer the question what criteria determine the frontiers of the space which is that of one state territory, what constitutes its unity. The so-called state territory can only be defined as the spatial sphere of validity of a national legal order. . . .

It is almost self-evident that the so-called state power which is exercised by a government over a state's population within a state territory is not simply the power which some individual actually has over another individual consisting in the former's ability to induce the latter to behave as the first one desires. Many such actual power relationships exist without the one who has such power over another being regarded as an organ of the state. The relationship designated as state power is distinguished from other power relationships by the fact that it is legally regulated, which means that the individuals who exercise this power in their capacity as members of a state government are authorized by a legal order to exercise this power by creating and applying legal norms—that the state power has normative character. The so-called state power is the validity of an effective national legal order. That the government exerting the state power must be independent means that it must not be bound by any other national legal order; that the national legal order is inferior, if to any other legal order at all, only to the international legal order.

In the exercise of the state's power one usually sees the manifestation of a power which one considers as such an essential attribute of the state that one speaks of states as of " powers," even if they are not so-called " great powers." The " power " of a state can show itself only in the specific means of power which are at the disposal of a government; in the fortresses and prisons, the guns and gallows, the individuals uniformed as policemen and soldiers. But these fortresses and prisons, these guns and gallows, are dead objects; they become tools of state power only so far as they are used by a state government or by individuals according to orders directed to them by the government, only so far as the policemen and soldiers obey the norms that regulate their behavior. The power of the state is no mystical force concealed behind the state or its law; it is only the effectiveness of the national legal order.

Thereby the state whose essential elements are population, territory, and power is defined as a relatively centralized legal order, limited in its spatial and temporal sphere of validity, sovereign or subordinated only to international law, and by and large effective.   [pp. 286–290]

MADZIMBAMUTO v. LARDNER-BURKE [53]

Judicial Committee of the Privy Council
[1969] 1 A.C. 645

LORD REID

. . . (1) What was the legal effect in Southern Rhodesia of the Southern Rhodesia Act 1965, and the Order in Council which accompanied it? (2) Can the usurping government now in control in Southern Rhodesia be regarded for any purpose as a lawful government? (3) If not, to what extent, if at all, are the courts of Southern Rhodesia entitled to recognise or give effect to its legislative or administrative acts?

If The Queen in the Parliament of the United Kingdom was Sovereign in Southern Rhodesia in 1965, there can be no doubt that the Southern Rhodesia Act 1965, and the Order in Council made under it were of full legal effect there. Several of the learned judges have held that Sovereignty was divided between the United Kingdom and Southern Rhodesia. Their Lordships cannot agree. So far as they are aware it has never been doubted that, when a colony is acquired or annexed, following on conquest or settlement, the Sovereignty of the United Kingdom Parliament extends to that colony, and its powers over that colony are the same as its powers in the United Kingdom. So, in 1923, full Sovereignty over the annexed territory of Southern Rhodesia was acquired. That Sovereignty was not diminished by the limited grant of self government which was then made. It was necessary to pass the Statute of Westminster 1931, in order to confer independence and Sovereignty on the six Dominions therein mentioned, but Southern Rhodesia was not included. Section 4 of that Act provides:

[53] [The recent situation in Southern Rhodesia has provided a striking test for Kelsen's theory, but at the same time shown that it may tend to over-simplify complex constitutional issues. In 1965 the government of Mr. Smith declared a unilateral declaration of independence from British control. In the instant case the Rhodesian courts sought to interpret the change of régime in terms of the Kelsenian principle that a revolution may effect a change in the basic norm and, therefore, render a usurping régime valid (see *ante*, 282). The Rhodesian courts hesitated to say that the revolution had been completely successful, and therefore provided an acceptable basis for holding that the new usurping constitution was valid. They limited themselves to holding that the régime enjoyed *de facto* status, but was not yet a new constitution *de jure*. But they accordingly upheld the detention without trial of Madzimbamuto under regulations made in a state of emergency declared by the Smith régime.]

" No Act of Parliament of the United Kingdom passed after the commencement of this Act shall extend, or be deemed to extend, to a Dominion as part of the law of that Dominion, unless it is expressly declared in that Act that that Dominion has requested, and consented to, the enactment thereof."

No similar provision has been enacted with regard to Southern Rhodesia. . . .

The learned judges refer to the statement of the United Kingdom Government in 1961, already quoted, setting out the convention that the Parliament of the United Kingdom does not legislate without the consent of the Government of Southern Rhodesia on matters within the competence of the Legislative Assembly. That was a very important convention but it had no legal effect in limiting the legal power of Parliament.

It is often said that it would be unconstitutional for the United Kingdom Parliament to do certain things, meaning that the moral, political and other reasons against doing them are so strong that most people would regard it as highly improper if Parliament did these things. But that does not mean that it is beyond the power of Parliament to do such things. If Parliament chose to do any of them the courts could not hold the Act of Parliament invalid. It may be that it would have been thought, before 1965, that it would be unconstitutional to disregard this convention. But it may also be that the unilateral Declaration of Independence released the United Kingdom from any obligation to observe the convention. Their Lordships in declaring the law are not concerned with these matters. They are only concerned with the legal powers of Parliament.

Finally on this first question their Lordships can find nothing in the 1961 Constitution which should be interpreted as a grant of limited Sovereignty. Even assuming that that is impossible under the British system, they do not find any indication of an intention to transfer Sovereignty or any such clear cut division between what is granted by way of Sovereignty and what is reserved as would be necessary if there were to be a transfer of some part of the Sovereignty of The Queen in the Parliament of the United Kingdom. They are therefore of opinion that the Act and Order in Council of 1965 had full legal effect in Southern Rhodesia.

With regard to the question whether the usurping government can now be regarded as a lawful government much was said about de facto and de jure governments. Those are conceptions of international law and in their Lordships' view they are quite inappropriate in dealing with the legal position of a usurper within the territory of which he has acquired control. As was explained in *Carl Zeiss Stiftung* v. *Rayner & Keeler Ltd.* (*No.* 2) [54] when a question arises as to the status of a new régime in a foreign country the court must ascertain the view of Her Majesty's Government and act on it as correct. In practice the Government have regard to certain rules, but those are not rules of law. And it happens not infrequently that the Government recognise a usurper as the de facto government of a territory while continuing to recognise the ousted Sovereign as the de jure government. But the position is quite

[54] [1967] 1 A.C. 853.

different where a court sitting in a particular territory has to determine the status of a new régime which has usurped power and acquired control of that territory. It must decide. And it is not possible to decide that there are two lawful governments at the same time while each is seeking to prevail over the other.

It is an historical fact that in many countries—and indeed in many countries which are or have been under British Sovereignty—there are now régimes which are universally recognised as lawful but which derive their origins from revolutions or coups d'état. The law must take account of that fact. So there may be a question how or at what stage the new régime became lawful.

A recent example occurs in *Uganda* v. *Commissioner of Prisons, Ex parte Matovu.*[55] On February 22, 1966 the Prime Minister of Uganda issued a statement declaring that in the interests of national stability and public security and tranquillity he had taken over all powers of the Government of Uganda. He was completely successful, and the High Court had to consider the legal effect. In an elaborate judgment Sir Udo Udoma C.J. said [56]:

> "we hold, that the series of events, which took place in Uganda from February 22 to April, 1966, when the 1962 Constitution was abolished in the National Assembly and the 1966 Constitution adopted in its place, as a result of which the then Prime Minister was installed as Executive President with power to appoint a Vice-President could only appropriately be described in law as a revolution These changes had occurred not in accordance with the principle of legitimacy. But deliberately contrary to it. There were no pretensions on the part of the Prime Minister to follow the procedure prescribed in the 1962 Constitution in particular for the removal of the President and the Vice-President from office. Power was seized by force from both the President and the Vice-President on the grounds mentioned in the early part of this judgment."

Later he said [57]:

> ". . . our deliberate and considered view is that the 1966 Constitution is a legally valid constitution and the supreme law of Uganda; and that the 1962 Constitution having been abolished as a result of a victorious revolution in law does no longer exist nor does it now form part of the Laws of Uganda, it having been deprived of its de facto and de jure validity"

Pakistan affords another recent example. In *The State* v. *Dosso* [58] the President had issued a proclamation annulling the existing Constitution. This was held to amount to a revolution. Muhammed Munir C.J. said [59]:

> "It sometimes happens, however, that a Constitution and the national legal order under it is disrupted by an abrupt political change not within the contemplation of the Constitution. Any such

[55] [1966] E.A. 514 [and *ante*, 274.]
[56] *Idem*, p. 535.
[57] *Idem*, p. 539.
[58] [1958] 2 P.S.C.R. 180; (1958) P.L.D. 1 S.C. (PAK) 533 [and *ante*, 282.]
[59] [1958] 2 P.S.C.R. 180, 184.

change is called a revolution, and its legal effect is not only the destruction of the existing Constitution but also the validity of the national legal order."

Their Lordships would not accept all the reasoning in these judgments but they see no reason to disagree with the results. The Chief Justice of Uganda (Sir Udo Udoma C.J.) said [60]: "The Government of Uganda is well established and has no rival." The court accepted the new Constitution and regarded itself as sitting under it. The Chief Justice of Pakistan (Sir Muhammed Munir C.J.) said [61]: "Thus the essential condition to determine whether a Constitution has been annulled is the efficacy of the change." It would be very different if there had been still two rivals contending for power. If the legitimate Government had been driven out but was trying to regain control it would be impossible to hold that the usurper who is in control is the lawful ruler, because that would mean that by striving to assert its lawful right the ousted legitimate Government was opposing the lawful ruler.

In their Lordships' judgment that is the present position in Southern Rhodesia. The British Government acting for the lawful Sovereign is taking steps to regain control and it is impossible to predict with certainty whether or not it will succeed. Both the judges in the General Division and the majority in the Appellate Division rightly still regard the "revolution" as illegal and consider themselves sitting as courts of the lawful Sovereign and not under the revolutionary Constitution of 1965. Their Lordships are therefore of opinion that the usurping Government now in control of Southern Rhodesia cannot be regarded as a lawful government. . . .

The last question involves the doctrine of "necessity" and requires more detailed consideration. The argument is that, when a usurper is in control of a territory, loyal subjects of the lawful Sovereign who reside in that territory should recognise, obey and give effect to commands of the usurper in so far as that is necessary in order to preserve law and order and the fabric of civilised society. Under pressure of necessity the lawful Sovereign and his forces may be justified in taking action which infringes the ordinary rights of his subjects but that is a different matter. Here the question is whether or how far Her Majesty's subjects and in particular Her Majesty's judges in Southern Rhodesia are entitled to recognise or give effect to laws or executive acts or decisions made by the unlawful régime at present in control of Southern Rhodesia.

There is no English authority directly relevant but much attention was paid to a series of decisions of the Supreme Court of the United States as to the position in the states which attempted to secede during the American Civil War. Those authorities must be used with caution by reason of the very different constitutional position in the United States. It was held that during the rebellion the seceding states continued to exist as states, but that, by reason of their having adhered to the Confederacy, members of their legislatures and executives had ceased to have any lawful authority. But they had continued to make laws and carry out executive functions and the inhabitants of those states could

60 [1966] E.A. 514, 533.
61 [1958] 2 P.S.C.R. 180, 185.

not avoid carrying on their ordinary activities on the footing that these laws and executive acts were valid. So after the end of the war a wide variety of questions arose as to the legal effect of transactions arising out of that state of affairs.

The first case decided by the Supreme Court was *Texas* v. *White*.[62] The court laid down the principle to be applied in these terms.[63]

" . . . it is an historical fact that the government of Texas, then in full control of the state, was its only actual government; and certainly if Texas had been a separate state, and not one of the United States, the new government, having displaced the regular authority, and having established itself in the customary seats of power, and in the exercise of the ordinary functions of administration, would have constituted, in the strictest sense of the words, a de facto government, and its acts, during the period of its existence as such, would be effectual, and, in almost all respects, valid. And, to some extent, this is as true of the actual government of Texas, though unlawful and revolutionary, as to the United States. It is not necessary to attempt any exact definitions, within which the acts of such a state government must be treated as valid, or invalid. It may be said, perhaps with sufficient accuracy, that acts necessary to peace and good order among citizens, such for example, as acts sanctioning and protecting marriage and the domestic relations, governing the course of descents, regulating the conveyance and transfer of property, real and personal, and providing remedies for injuries to person and estate, and other similar acts, which would be valid if emanating from a lawful government, must be regarded in general as valid when proceeding from an actual, though unlawful government; and that acts in furtherance or support of rebellion against the United States, or intended to defeat the just rights of citizens, and other acts of like nature, must, in general, be regarded as invalid and void."

In *Hanauer* v. *Woodruff*[64] Field J. said [65]

" The difference between the two cases is the difference between submitting to a force which could not be controlled, and voluntarily aiding to create that force."

. . . Their Lordships would make three observations about this series of cases. In the first place there was divided sovereignty in the United States, the United States only being sovereign within defined limits: that is reflected in the first part of the above quotation from *Texas* v. *White*.[63] Secondly, the decisions were concerned with the legal effect, as regards the civil claims of individuals, after the end of the civil war, of acts done during it. None of them were cases of courts called upon, during the rebellion, to pass upon the legality of the governments of the rebelling states or of their legislation. And thirdly the Congress of the United States did not, and perhaps under the Constitution could not, make laws similar to the Southern Rhodesia Act, and Order

---

62 (1868) 7 Wallace 700 (74 U.S.).
63 *Ibid.* 733.
64 (1872) 15 Wallace 439 (82 U.S.).
65 *Ibid.* 449.

in Council of 1965, providing what the legal position was to be in the seceding States during the war. None of the cases cited conferred any validity upon Acts of the Confederate States which were contrary to the United States Constitution.

References were also made by the judges in Southern Rhodesia to the writings of civilians and jurists. It will be sufficient to quote from Grotius De Jure Belli ac Pacis, Bk. I, Ch. IV, Sect. XV, as translated in an English edition of 1738. [Hugo Grotius, " De Jure Belli ac Pacis." Translated by J. Barbeyrac (1738), 1st ed., p. 121.]

> " XV. We have treated of him, who has now, or has had a right to govern; it now remains, that we say something of him that usurps the government; not after he has either by long possession, or agreement obtained a right to it, but so long as the cause of his unjust possession continues. The acts of sovereignty exercised by such an usurper may have an obligatory force, not by virtue of his right (for he has none), but because it is very probable that the lawful sovereign, whether it be the people themselves, or a king, or a senate, chooses rather that the usurper should be obeyed during that time, than that the exercise of the laws and justice should be interrupted, and the state thereby exposed to all the disorders of anarchy."

It may be that there is a general principle, depending on implied mandate from the lawful Sovereign, which recognises the need to preserve law and order in territory controlled by a usurper. But it is unnecessary to decide that question because no such principle could override the legal right of the Parliament of the United Kingdom to make such laws as it may think proper for territory under the Sovereignty of Her Majesty in the Parliament of the United Kingdom. Parliament did pass the Southern Rhodesia Act, 1965, and thereby authorise the Southern Rhodesia (Constitution) Order in Council, 1965. There is no legal vacuum in Southern Rhodesia. Apart from the provisions of this legislation and its effect upon subsequent " enactments " the whole of the existing law remains in force. . . .

Her Majesty's judges have been put in an extremely difficult position.[66] But the fact that the judges among others have been put in a very difficult position cannot justify disregard of legislation passed or authorised by the United Kingdom Parliament, by the introduction of a doctrine of necessity which in their Lordships' judgment cannot be reconciled with the terms of the Order in Council. It is for Parliament and Parliament alone to determine whether the maintenance of law and order would justify giving effect to laws made by the usurping Government, to such extent as may be necessary for that purpose.

66 [It has been urged that the more appropriate course for the judiciary, faced with this dilemma, is to tender its resignation (see S. A. de Smith (1968) 7 W. Ontario L.R. 93). But the problem may also be raised at a later stage, at a time when the revolution is held to be totally successful and a judge is accordingly asked to attribute legal validity to the new revolutionary constitution. It may be urged that judges appointed to uphold an earlier constitution ought, as a matter of constitutional propriety, to resign rather than lend themselves to treating the new régime as enjoying legal validity. Positivistic philosophy would require a judge to accept the laws of a successful revolutionary régime. See, further, Harris (1971) 29 C.L.J. 103, 127. In fact two Southern Rhodesian judges resigned in 1968.]

The issue in the present case is whether Emergency Powers Regulations made under the 1965 Constitution can be regarded as having any legal validity, force or effect. Section 2 (1) of the Order in Council of 1965 provides:

" It is hereby declared for the avoidance of doubt that any instrument made or other act done in purported promulgation of any Constitution for Southern Rhodesia except as authorised by Act of Parliament is void and of no effect."

The 1965 Constitution, made void by that provision, provides by section 3 that " There shall be an Officer Administering the Government in and over Rhodesia "—an office hitherto unknown to the law. The Emergency Powers Regulations which were determined by the High Court to be valid were made by " the Officer Administering the Government." For the reasons already given their Lordships are of opinion that that determination was erroneous. And it must follow that any order for detention made under such regulations is legally invalid.

Their Lordships will therefore humbly advise Her Majesty that it should be declared that the determination of the High Court of Southern Rhodesia with regard to the validity of Emergency Powers Regulations made in Southern Rhodesia since November 11, 1965, is erroneous, and that such regulations have no legal validity, force or effect.[67]

[pp. 721–731]

LORD PEARCE delivered the following dissenting judgment.

. . . I agree that the United Kingdom Parliament can legislate for Rhodesia. . . .

The legal tie was not yet cut. . . .

In legal terms Rhodesia was still a colony over which the United Kingdom Parliament had Sovereignty. That Parliament still had the legal power to cut down the 1961 Constitution and alter the status of Rhodesia to that of a colony governed from the United Kingdom through a Governor. While I appreciate the careful reasoning of the learned Chief Justice [Beadle C.J.], by which he seeks to say that the United Kingdom Parliament had no such power, I cannot accept its validity.

Likewise I cannot accept his argument that the de facto control by the illegal government gave validity to all its acts as such so far as they did not exceed the powers under the 1961 Constitution. The de facto status of sovereignty cannot be conceded to a rebel government as against the true Sovereign in the latter's courts of law. The judges under the 1961 Constitution therefore cannot acknowledge the validity of an illegal government set up in defiance of it. I do not agree with the view of Macdonald J.A. that their allegiance is owed to the rebel government in power. It follows that the declaration of emergency and the regulations under which it is sought to justify the detention of Daniel Madzimbamuto are unlawful and invalid. The appeal therefore must be allowed unless the emergency and the regulations can be acknowledged by the courts as valid on some other ground than that they are the acts of a de facto government simpliciter.

---

67 [In *Adams* v. *Adams* [1970] 3 All E.R. 572 it was accordingly held that a divorce granted by a judge appointed *post*-U.D.I. was not entitled to recognition in this country. On the *Madzimbamuto* ruling there was no reason to distinguish the time factor: the time of the judge's appointment should be irrelevant.]

It is at this stage that I feel compelled to part company with their Lordships.

I accept the existence of the principle that acts done by those actually in control without lawful validity may be recognised as valid or acted upon by the courts, with certain limitations namely (*a*) so far as they are directed to and reasonably required for ordinary orderly running of the State, and (*b*) so far as they do not impair the rights of citizens under the lawful (1961) Constitution, and (*c*) so far as they are not intended to and do not in fact directly help the usurpation and do not run contrary to the policy of the lawful Sovereign. This last, i.e. (*c*), is tantamount to a test of public policy. . . .

This principle whether one calls it necessity or implied mandate, can in my opinion be extracted from the cases in the Supreme Court of the United States when dealing with the aftermath of the unsuccessful rebellion of the Southern States. These cases have been much canvassed in the able argument on both sides. They present a helpful analogy. So far as the decisions may have a slight quasi-international flavour derived from the sovereignty of the various states subject only to the obligation to the Union, that flavour is not out of place in dealing with the peculiar position of Rhodesia. I do not accept the argument that because the cases all took place *after* the rebellion had failed, and were therefore concerned only with retrospective acknowledgment of unlawful acts, their principle cannot be applied *during* a rebellion. If acts are entitled to some retrospective validity, there seems no reason in principle why they should not be entitled to some contemporaneous validity. It is when one comes to assess the question of public policy that there is a wide difference between the retrospective and contemporaneous. For during a rebellion it may be harmful to grant any validity to an unlawful act, whereas, when the rebellion has failed, such recognition may be innocuous.   [pp. 731–733]

. . . Perhaps one may emphasise, what should be obvious, that no question as to " the merits " of the main contest between the lawful ruler and the illegal government have any relevance whatever to the arguments in this case. Questions of martial law do not depend on the merits of an invasion. When a state of rebellion or invasion exists the law must do its best to cope with the resulting problems that beset it.[68]   [p. 745]

---

[68] [Subsequent to the Privy Council ruling the Rhodesian courts have treated the new régime as having attained sufficient success in its revolution to be given *de jure* recognition by Rhodesian courts. See *R.* v. *Ndhlorn* (1968) 4 S.A. 515, 531 *per* Beadle C.J., 542 *per* Quiènet J.P. and 554 *per* MacDonald J.A. This case, particularly the Southern Rhodesian judgments, has attracted a good deal of critical comment. See, particularly, Dias (1968) 26 C.L.J. 233 ; Harris (1971) 29 C.L.J. 103 ; Eekelaar (1967) 30 M.L.R. 156; (1969) 32 M.L.R. 19 and Brookfield (1969) 19 U. of Toronto L.J. 326.]

6

SOCIOLOGICAL SCHOOL

BACKGROUND: AUGUSTE COMTE

THE first serious attempt to apply the scientific method to social phenomena was made by Auguste Comte (1798–1857), who invented the term "sociology."[1] This was part of the powerful emphasis in the nineteenth century on science as the royal road to progress. Comte urged that there are four means of social investigation, namely, observation, experiment, comparison, and the historical method; and that it is the last which is peculiar to and of special value to sociology. The data of this latter method were to be taken from observation[2] and tested against the known laws of human nature. This involved some advance on Bentham who confined his attention to the laws of human nature as a foundation of social science to the virtual neglect of history. John Stuart Mill at any rate, so regarded it, and considered that, by means of this method, empirical generalisations could attain the status of laws and sociology thus become a science.

Unfortunately, Comte did not remain true to his own scientific approach, and in his later years deserted the empirical method for sweeping *a priori* affirmations, such as his view that there were invariable natural laws operating in the field of social activity. He laid down that mankind inevitably passes through three stages, *viz.,* the theological (where phenomena are explained in terms of superior

---

[1] It is no longer thought, as it once was, that Comte was the founder of sociology, any more than Bentham by coining the words "international law" and "codification" founded respectively that discipline or that method. See Runciman *Sociology in its Place* (1970), p. 1. As far as sociological jurisprudence is concerned, a case can be made for Montesquieu (see Ehrlich, 29 Harv.L.R. 582 and Stone, *Social Dimensions of Law and Justice* (1966), pp. 36–37; *Law and the Social Sciences* (1966), pp. 8–9). Nor should the influence of historical jurisprudence be passed over, for, in showing that law was intimately related to the social context, and in challenging the adequacy of logical analysis and *a priori* speculation on justice, the historical jurists paved the way for sociological jurisprudence. "Historical jurisprudence . . . not only led the jurists towards the promised land; it also reduced the main forts of its existing occupants. It played the role of Moses and, in part at least, of Joshua as well. But it was to be not under its own banner [the *Volksgeist*, see *post*, 562], but under that of sociological jurisprudence that the promised land was to be conquered and occupied" (Stone, *Social Dimensions*, p. 36). In view of this relationship between Savigny and Maine (*post*, 561 and 565) and the sociological school, Runciman's comment (*idem*, p. 2) that "'sociology' cannot be usefully distinguished in content from either anthropology or history" is particularly interesting.

[2] So law not being observable as a phenomenon was but a passing phase in civilisation and would disappear with the firm establishment of scientific positivism.

335

beings), the metaphysical (where abstract entities like nature are held responsible) and the scientific or positive (at which stage man is content to observe phenomena). Such was his final dogmatism that he was led to formulate an authoritarian conception of the character of " positive society," [3] and also to put forward a new Religion of Humanity, with an elaborate ritual aimed at achieving an effective means of social cohesion. On this, Mill made the comment: " Others may laugh, but we would rather weep at this melancholy decadence of a great intellect." [4]

LAISSEZ FAIRE AND HERBERT SPENCER

The dissemination of the Darwinian evolutionary theory of natural selection gave a further impetus to this development, and enabled it to be linked with the contemporary fondness for *laissez faire* in economic and social affairs. Thus, for Herbert Spencer (1820–1903), evolution was the key to the understanding of human progress and legal and social development could best be left to evolve by a natural selection parallel to that operating in the sphere of biology. [5] Such a conclusion was regarded as in the highest sense scientific [6] and not a reason for reliance on the historical and racial myths of Hegel or Savigny.

It should be borne in mind that *laissez faire* [7] was both an economic theory and a philosophy of action. In the narrow sense, it was developed as a reaction against the previously prevailing mercantilist theory by which it was thought that the state was under a duty to promote the economic welfare of a country by closely regulating its foreign and colonial trade. Adam Smith, on the other hand, argued that only harm could result from governmental inter-

---

[3] In this society sociologists would impose their solutions on the " uneducated " (roughly, everybody else). Berger tells of " some transatlantic disciples of Comte " who " seriously suggested in a memorandum to the president of Brown University that all departments of the latter should be reorganised under the department of sociology " (*Invitation to Sociology* (Penguin edition (1966), p. 17).

[4] See D. G. Carlton, *Positivist Thought in France During the Second Empire* (1959), especially pp. 28 *et seq.* *Cf.* R. Aron, *Main Currents In Sociological Thought* Vol. 1 (Penguin edition 1968), who explains that by humanity Comte means the best deeds of the greatest men, and as such his Religion of Humanity bears comparison with all the world's greatest religions. (See pp. 107–109.)

[5] Hence the state existed only to further individual freedom: Comte, on the other hand, favoured a highly collectivist programme. *Cf.* Kelsen, *What is Justice?*, pp. 137–173 and Aron *op. cit.*, pp. 73–74.

[6] But Darwin himself had a poor opinion of Spencer's airy generalisations. " They partake more of the nature of definitions than of laws of nature. They do not aid me in predicting what will happen in any particular case. Anyhow they have not been of any use to me " (*Autobiography of Charles Darwin* (ed. N. Barlow, 1958), p. 109). *Cf.* G. Himmelfarb, *Darwin and the Darwinian Revolution* (1959), pp. 412–431.

[7] For *laissez faire*, see Becker and Barnes, *Social Thought from Lore to Science*, Vol. II, pp. 518–524; on Spencer, see *op. cit.*, pp. 671–672; on Ward, Vol. III, p. 973.

ference in economic affairs, and that the highest prosperity and benefit to mankind would be achieved by leaving the economy to the operation of the natural laws controlling human economy. It was a fundamental part of this doctrine that there existed a natural order in the working of the universe, so that anything which conformed to these natural laws was destined to succeed, whereas whatever ran counter to them was bound to be handicapped and ultimately to end in failure. The function of the state, therefore, was limited to the protection of citizens against foreign states; the administration of law and justice; and the establishment and maintenance of public works. Thus both Malthus and Ricardo argued that it was useless to try to improve the lot of the poor by remedial legislation for this would only render their plight worse.

Spencer's contribution was to apply the organic evolutionary idea in relation to *laissez faire*.[7] He believed that by the great process of biological evolution, social evolution would arise as part of an automatic and independent process. Contrary to Bentham, Spencer desired to impress upon society the very small part that conscious direction could hope to achieve in altering the process of social evolution.[8] Quoting Hamlet's question, " Do you think I am easier to be played on than a pipe?", Spencer asks whether humanity could be more readily straightened than an iron plate. The grain of wisdom in Spencer's warning was that mankind should not fall into the fatal error of thinking that progress could necessarily be manufactured by legislation. But he entirely failed to perceive both the direction in which society in his own day was moving, and that that development was in fact, whatever abuses it might lead to, one which was essential if orderly social progress was to be achieved.[9] This latter point was fully grasped by the American sociologist, Ward. Though a follower of Spencer in accepting that social evolution begins as a spontaneous development, Ward, nevertheless, asserted that a point is reached in civilized society where the human mind is

---

[8] " But the world of Spencer's ' Industrial Society ' is a world bare of sociological furniture; a society with nothing but its naked economic bones showing. Man having become perfectly adapted to the social state, almost all the institutions in which his social life has clothed itself in its dangerous pilgrimage have become redundant and . . . can be cast off with a vote of thanks for past services. . . . It is essentially a new ' State of Nature,' founded on the division of labour and akin to the Utopia of the older utilitarians; only, for Spencer, instead of men being brought to it by rational perception of the laws of nature, or of the ultimate identity of interest, or coerced into it by a utilitarian legislator, it is the product of a long evolutionary process, in which conflict and the protective influences of irrational practices and taboos have been major factors " (J. W. Burrow, *Evolution and Society* (revised ed. 1970), p. 223).

[9] Spencer is apparently coming back into fashion. Donald Macrae (see his introduction to *The Man versus The State* (1969)) attributes this to a backlash against the increasing power of the bureaucracy and " over-criminalisation " of the citizen by constant addition of regulative offences.

capable of appreciating, and of comprehending, the trend of such evolution, and also of controlling it, and thereby artificially to some extent directing and speeding up social progress. This opinion has, on the whole, been the one that has prevailed with modern sociologists, and it is clear that this approach is one which exerted a marked influence upon American legal sociology, especially in the person of Roscoe Pound.

The modern sociological approach, however, has entirely rejected the comfortable belief in natural selection achieved through *laissez faire*, in favour of man's capacity to play a conscious role in directing his social evolution. Hence the preponderant emphasis on law reform. Indeed, it may be said that the modern school's principal debt is to Bentham, and those earlier thinkers upon whom he rested, in developing his theory of utility as applied to man in society. It is in Hobbes that we see a picture of a sovereign whose primary task is not to protect property or promote the good life, but forcibly to produce that harmony of interests which is the only way in which each may pursue effectively his own selfish pleasures without disrupting society itself. A different emphasis was given to this doctrine in the field of economics when Mandeville [10] argued that the very multitude of man's selfish wants obliged him to serve his fellows, and so promoted a natural harmony of interests which would result in the most effective production and distribution of goods. This was the notion which lay at the root of the theory of economic *laissez faire* embraced by the classical economists, such as Adam Smith and Ricardo. Bentham involved himself in some contradiction by attempting to ride both these horses at once. Thus, in economic affairs he followed Smith in favouring *laissez faire* and the removal of all restraints, while his juristic thought favoured Hobbes' notion of an artificial restraint, as exemplified in the criminal law. Some attempt to reconcile these conflicting approaches is to be found in Bentham's belief that by developing representative government the principle of the artificial identity of interests would tend to approach the natural identity, insofar as the former would command an ever larger majority.[11] Indeed Bentham at least, despite his enthusiasm for

[10] In *The Fable of the Bees* (1714).

[11] What William H. Whyte has termed the "social ethic" affords an interesting parallel in modern American society. According to this *ethic*, now (according to Whyte) dominant in America, man attains his worth as part of the group, and there is no real conflict between man and society, only misunderstandings which science, applied to human relations, can eliminate: see *The Organisation Man* (1957), pp. 6–8, 32–46. Spencer's comment on Bentham's contradiction was: ". . . a marvellous piece of legerdemain! . . . Surely, among metaphysical phantoms the most shadowy is this which supposes a thing to be obtained by creating an agent, which creates the thing, and then confers the thing on its own creator" (see *The Man Versus The State* (Penguin edition), pp. 162–163)).

law reform, remained a supporter of *laissez faire*, being wedded to the idea that once the legal system was overhauled and renovated there would be little need for further legislative interference.[12] He failed altogether to envisage the basic social and economic conflicts that were inherent in modern society and which required the continuous vigilance of the legislator. Yet Bentham's notion of the sovereign as engaged in the reconciling of conflicting interests is not (as with Hobbes) for the promotion of each man's selfish ends but for the better attainment of the greatest possible amount of general happiness, and his strong emphasis on law reform as the primary means of inducing the common good was destined to bear rich fruit in the course of the nineteenth century and underlies much of the sociological foundations of the modern democratic welfare state. For it was later realised, despite the fulminations of Spencer, that future progress lay with the movements for legislative reform, as exemplified by Shaftesbury and Chadwick, and not with those who said: " Let us fold our hands and allow natural evolution to work out for us the scientifically best solution." [13]

JHERING (1818–1892)

The Benthamite analysis was taken up by the eminent jurist, Jhering, who placed greater emphasis on the function of law as an instrument for serving the needs of human society. In society there is an inevitable conflict between the social interests of man and each individual's selfish interests.[14] To reconcile this conflict the state employs both the method of reward, by enabling economic wants to be satisfied, and also the method of coercion. There may be unorganised coercion, as in the case of social conventions or etiquette, but law is specifically that form of coercion which is organised by the state. Jhering did not deny the existence of

---

[12] Comte provides a striking contrast both with Bentham and with the early Socialists such as Saint-Simon. For whereas these believed that as the reforms they advocated were introduced, the need for coercion and an elaborate legal system would become far less compelling, since enlightened reason would tend to make men comply with what was understood to be in the common interest, Comte, on the other hand, moved steadily towards an increasingly authoritarian conception of the new society in a scientific age. Certainly it cannot be said that the predictions of Comte in this respect have been falsified by the subsequent current of events. For early Socialist thought, see Plamenatz, *Man and Society* (1963), Vol. II, Chap. 2, and for its relationship with early sociology, see Gouldner, *The Coming Crisis in Western Sociology* (1970), particularly Part 1, Chap. 4.

[13] For a fuller discussion of this aspect of Benthamism, see Dennis Lloyd, " Law of Associations," in *Law and Opinion in England in the 20th Century* (ed. Ginsberg, 1959), p. 99 *et seq. Cf. ante*, 154.

[14] The point is well brought out in the story of the man swinging a stick in a crowded street who, when reproached, said, " It's a free country." " Yes," said the remonstrator, " but your freedom ends where my nose begins."

altruistic impulses, but recognised that these would not suffice without the coercive form of social control provided by law. The success of the legal process was to be measured by the degree to which it achieved a proper balance between competing social and individual interests. Jhering, however, gave very little indication of a scale of values with which to achieve this balance.

WEBER (1864–1920) AND EHRLICH (1862–1922)

Further impetus was given to exploring the sociological foundations of law by the writings of Weber and Ehrlich. Weber began his career [15] as a lawyer, both as teacher and practitioner, but social science and economics became his dominating interests. His important contributions to general sociological theory cannot be discussed here,[16] and, it must suffice to state that, in the field of the sociology of law, his studies of legal institutions as produced by economic and social conditions proved very influential in their method as well as their emphasis on the factors which underlie legal development.[17]

Ehrlich, on the other hand, was an eminent jurist who was primarily concerned to expound the social basis of law. For him law is derived from social facts and depends not on state authority but on social compulsion. Law, he said, differs little from other forms of social compulsion, and the state is merely one among many associations, though admittedly it possesses certain characteristic means of compulsion. The real source of law is not statutes or reported cases but the activities of society itself.[18] There is a " living law " underlying the formal rules of the legal system and it is the task of judge and jurist to integrate these two types of law. Commercial law, for instance, as embodied in statutes and cases, involves a constant attempt to try to keep up with commercial usage,

---

15 For a summary of the more important events and features of Max Weber's career, see M. Weber, *Sociology of Religion*, appendix 1, pp. 275 *et seq.*

16 See R. Bendix, *Max Weber, An Intellectual Portrait.*

17 For Weber's very illuminating account of the role and nature of authority or " domination," see M. Weber, *Law and Economy in Society* (1954) (ed. M. Rheinstein), Chaps. XII and XIII. *Cf. ante*, 174.

18 Ehrlich did not automatically assume that the " law for decision " should be invariably based upon " living law." There might well be instances where the living law did not meet the real social need, *e.g.*, he criticised the German Civil Code for adopting the idea of " Husband managership " in the matrimonial property régime, even though this represented the living law of actual marriage relations, because he thought that this was only relevant to matrimonial relations while peace existed between the spouses, but that once litigation arose there was a dispute which required a different approach. (See G. Sawer, *Law in Society*, pp. 174–177.) Ehrlich however seemed to have in mind that appropriate solutions could only be arrived at by a full understanding and evaluation of both kinds of law. To this extent, Sawer's criticisms in the passage referred to seem excessive.

for the "centre of legal gravity lies . . . in society itself." [19] Hence great emphasis is placed on fact-studies, as against analytical jurisprudence, in exploring the real foundations of legal rules, their scope and meaning and potential development.[20]

Ehrlich thus minimises the place of legislation as such as a formative factor in law, and in some ways may be regarded as a Savigny denuded of the Hegelian *mystique*.[21] But there is far more in his approach than this, for he emphasised how law is, so to speak, distilled out of the interplay of social forces and activities. That there is much truth in this viewpoint can hardly be denied. Thus the practices of the commercial world are often found to be gradually embodied in commercial law, especially in the formative stage. Ehrlich recognised, however, that a legal system has an impetus of its own, a professional tradition which may operate for good or ill, and accordingly stressed the need for lawyers and judges to understand the social foundations of legal rules and thereby develop them on the right lines. So, too, by insisting on the fact that law was not a unique phenomenon,[22] he enabled us to attain a better grasp

[19] E. Ehrlich, *Fundamental Principles of Sociology of Law* (1936), foreword. Thus, Macaulay has demonstrated that in business conducted between manufacturers in Wisconsin relatively little attention is paid to detailed planning or legal sanctions and that the functions of contract are served by other devices. Two of the most effective norms, which are widely accepted, are the honouring of commitments and the "duty" to produce a good product and stand behind it. Not only is contract law not needed in many situations but its use is thought to have undesirable consequences. For, apart from the delay and possible loss of business, a carefully worked out relationship indicates a lack of trust and blunts the demands of friendship, "turning a co-operative venture into an antagonistic horse trade." There is, furthermore, a resulting loss of flexibility and the exposure to the costs of litigation. ((1963) 28 Amer.Sociol.Rev. 55.) See, also, Nussbaum, in *Essays on Jurisprudence from the Columbia Law Review*, p. 184, and the writings of Underhill Moore. Moore "felt that the degree of deviation in the behaviour of the litigants from regular, overt, institutional behaviour provides the crucial index in terms of which decisions could be predicted. The grosser the deviation, the more likely it is that the claims of the deviant litigant will not be judicially allowed. For this reason Moore insisted that the focus of scientific legal analysis should be the comparison of the behaviour of the litigants with patterns of institutional behaviour." (Rumble, *American Legal Realism*, p. 163.) A study of banking practices confirmed the hypothesis that the court in fact used as its standard the degree which litigants deviated from the institutional patterns of behaviour. Gross deviations were "not accorded by the court a legal consequence conforming to the institutional consequences which would have followed had the standard device been used " (50 Yale L.J. at p. 1250).

[20] In addition to this theoretical perspective, Ehrlich was one of the first to undertake empirical surveys to substantiate his thesis. Living in part of the Austro-Hungarian Empire where there were no less than nine different ethnic and religious groups, "he had his students investigate the 'practices and attitudes of nearby communities, using an original but rather primitive personal interview questionnaire.'" (Littlefield (1967) 19 Maine L.R. 1, 2). Partridge suggests that Ehrlich may have drawn an overgeneralised conclusion from a culturally diversified society which is not present in a more homogeneous one. ((1961) 39 Australian J.of Phil. 201, 217).

[21] *Cf.*, note 1, *ante* and *post*, 561.

[22] Nor are lawyers. See Johnstone and Hopson, *Lawyers and their Work* (1967), Chaps. 5–10.

of those large spheres of activity which are becoming increasingly widespread in the modern state, where autonomous associations apply private " legal systems " of their own almost independently of the ordinary legal process of the courts, as, for instance, in the case of trade or professional associations or trade unions exercising disciplinary powers.[23] And if it is said that Ehrlich failed to indicate how we are to distinguish such " quasi-law " from real law, his answer would surely have been that the common features rather than analytical distinctions were of primary importance. Yet one cannot deny that Ehrlich unduly belittled the primary role of legislation in creating new law, both in the public and the private sector, as well as the fact that a grasp of underlying social phenomena may not in itself point the way to appropriate solutions, either in new legislation or decisions of the courts. The legal process may need to be invoked as in itself an educative factor, as, for instance, in the attempt in the United States to impose de-segregation by judicial decree and so, it is hoped, set the educative forces in motion which might ultimately produce a *change* in the social climate, rather than yielding to existing social pressures. So, too, with such reforms as town planning, or the abolition of capital punishment, which may have to be forced by a progressive minority upon a, for the time being, recalcitrant majority.

ROSCOE POUND (1870–1964)

The sociological approach to law struck a particularly responsive chord in the United States in the early part of the twentieth century. The expansive character of American society, its endless material wealth, and its devotion to scientific technology, all encouraged the belief that the basic problem was merely one of adequately controlling and distributing that wealth, and that the solution could best be attained by the application of the developing social sciences to the problems of man in society, just as man's physical environment could be harnessed by the proper use of the physical sciences. Hence, law as a form of social control, to be adequately employed in enabling just claims and desires to be satisfied, must be developed in relation to existing social needs, and must not be chary of relying upon the social sciences in studying the place of law in society, and the means of making it most effective in action. Here, it is suggested, lies the royal road to future progress, rather than the dry art of legal analysis, the mystical faith of the historical school, or the cult of the human will, pursued by nineteenth-century Continental legal philosophers.

[23] See " The Right to Work " by D. Lloyd in (1957) 10 *Current Legal Problems*, 36 ; and see now *Nagle* v. *Feilden* [1966] 2 Q.B. 633, and *Edwards* v. *S.O.G.A.T.* [1971] Ch. 354, and Rideout (1967) 30 M.L.R. 389.

It is in the writings of Roscoe Pound that the main exposition of the American sociological viewpoint is to be encountered.[24] Leaning heavily on Jhering, Pound has none the less contrived to impart to the American approach a distinctive flavour which brought it into harmony with contemporary trends in the United States. Space will only permit here a brief reference to a few of these particular features:

Social engineering

For Pound, jurisprudence is not so much a social science as a technology, and the analogy of engineering is applied to social problems.[25] Emphasis is laid on the need to accumulate factual information and statistics (much beloved by Americans in all fields of research) and to this end Pound has put forward a practical programme,[26] in which the establishment of an adequately equipped Ministry of Justice [27] looms large. Little attention is paid to conceptual thinking regarding such matters as sovereignty and rights and duties, dear to the hearts of analysts. The creative role of the judiciary, on the other hand, is in the forefront, and the need for a new legal technique directed to social needs. The call is for a new functional approach to law based on sound theorising as to its purpose in our present age.

Pound has taken over Jhering's view of the law as a reconciler of conflicting interests, but at the same time has given it certain distinctive features. For Pound the law is an ordering of conduct so as to make the goods of existence and the means of satisfying claims go round as far as possible with the least friction and waste. Pound regards these claims as interests which exist independently of the

---

[24] "Of Pound's many contributions . . . not the least was to make jurisprudence respectable in the United States": Jerome Hall, *Studies in Jurisprudence and Criminal Theory* (1958), p. 119.

[25] This conception has played a part in the social sciences generally, see, *e.g.*, K. Popper, *Poverty of Historicism*, pp. 42–44, 64–67, 86–87; for ethics, see Toulmin, *Reason in Ethics*, pp. 172–174; for anthropology, *Man and Culture* (ed. R. W. Firth) (1957), pp. 245–246, 257 and see also Llewellyn, *Jurisprudence* (1962), Chap. 18. See also the remark by Edwin Patterson, *Law in a Scientific Age* (1963), " that the scientific analogy has . . . led some non-lawyers, especially scientists, to expect too much of law, and it has led to the over-confident emulation, or the despair, of jurists and legal philosophers " (pp. 3–4).

[26] See *post*, 366.

[27] In common law countries; civil law countries usually possess one. In England the Lord Chancellor's Department performs some of the functions of such a Ministry, and others are performed by other Ministries, such as the Home Office. These, of course, do not add up to a fully staffed and equipped Ministry continuously seised of the overall problem of the working of the legal system and the reform of the law. The proposal to set up a Ministry of Justice is at least as early as Brougham who could cite " a thousand reasons " (*per* Edwards, *The Law Officers of the Crown* (1964), pp. 2–3) for its establishment. A positive step was taken in 1965 when the Law Commission was set up. Its first Chairman, Sir Leslie Scarman, reviewing some of the Commission's problems, has suggested that " a Ministry of Justice could bridge the gap between the Law Commission and Parliament." (*Law Reform—The New Pattern* (1968), p. 41 and see *post*, 848).

law and which are " pressing for recognition and security." The
law recognises some of these, giving them effect within defined
limits, and Pound has attempted to expound and classify the
categories of interests which are thus acknowledged in a modern
democratic society.[28] In this approach Pound rather recalls
the method of Aristotle's distributive justice,[29] with no doubt
the added modern notion of " fair shares for all." This seems to
ignore the extent to which existing law is based on giving effect to
vested rights; however, the legislature is a vital factor in modern
society in overriding these to produce a fairer balance, and even
the courts can, by enlightened decisions, adjust losses and distribute
risks among those most able to bear them.[30] Further, it has been
pointed out by Stone [31] that in this age of mass communication
and mass persuasion considerable difficulty may be experienced in
distinguishing what are the actual desires of the public in particular
groups, in view of the operation of so many organised professional
persuaders, both open and hidden. The public as a whole may
both lack the means of articulating its desires, or their expression
may be manipulated in a variety of ways, if regard is to be paid to
genuine and not " phoney " interests.[32]

In what way, it may be asked, does Pound *locate* his interests?
Social psychologists might look for basic drives or instincts and
initially, this was the approach favoured by Pound. But the inadequacy of this method soon became apparent, for the social
psychologists themselves could reach no unanimity on what the
basic instincts were, and, further, it was clear that instinctual
behaviour could not be eliminated from its environmental source.[33]
Sociologists, on the other hand, might undertake empirical research
designed to elicit the wants of society. But this too has problems.

---

28 Lundstedt has attacked this thinking as open to the same objection as a belief
   in an objective natural law. See *Legal Thinking Revised* pp. 342–370 and *post*,
   513. See also Charles Fried, " Two Concepts of Interests " 76 Harv.L.R. 755,
   who distinguishes claims from interests on the basis that the latter involves " an
   assertion of competence to determine how much weight exactly to give the
   want." (p. 770). One must see " a litigant's reference to freedom of speech [as]
   not simply a claim for immediate satisfaction [but as] the assertion of an interest
   which can be understood only as a reference to systematic ways of doing things,
   to roles, institutions and practices." (p. 769).
29 The weakness of this was the absence of criteria as to the relevance of factors
   to be considered : see Kelsen, *What is Justice?*, pp. 127–128, and *cf.* De
   Jouvenel, *Sovereignty*, p. 151 *et seq.* and *post*, 377.
30 Thus many aspects of modern tort law, *e.g.*, vicarious and strict liability, can be
   explained on this basis.
31 See *Human Law and Human Justice*, pp. 278–279, 282–284.
32 For interesting analyses of the meaning of interests, see Ross, *On Law and
   Justice* (1958), Chap. 17 and Barry, *Political Argument* (1965), pp. 174–186 and
   post, 375. See also the definition in the U.S. Restatement of the Law of Torts,
   § 1, and *post*, 363.
33 Pound deferred to Dewey's advice. See, further, Dewey, *Human Nature And
   Conduct* (1922), Pt. II, secs. V, VI.

How should the questions be phrased? Should one ask for attitudes or, in an effort to assimilate norms of decision with "living law," should one question behaviour? or should one ask for opinions on existing law or frame questions in such a way as to elicit personal "injustices"? [34] And how should one weigh up expressions of wants against the practicalities of legal administration? [35] There are limits to effective legal action.

Pound's own approach was somewhat less fertile. He looks to actual assertions of claims in a particular society, especially as manifested in legal proceedings and legislative proposals, whether accepted or rejected.[36] As to the former, however, it may be said these will depend very much on the state of the law, and the extent to which the costs system may discourage litigation on doubtful new points.[37] The different way in which the law on privacy has developed in England and in the United States emphasises this distinction.[38] The failure of English law to develop more than a rudimentary corpus of social security case-law is a further example.[39] Patterson,[40] with some justice, has described Pound's catalogue of interests as a rationalisation of the actual. It must also be said that there are interests not only in the sense of what people want

---

[34] *Cf.* Barton and Mendlovitz, *The Experience of Injustice as a Research Problem* (1960) 13 J.Legal Ed. 24.

[35] These questions are suggested by a reading of Cohen, Robson and Bates's *Parental Authority: The Community and the Law* (1958), perhaps the only scientific attempt by lawyers and sociologists to find out the wants of a particular society (in this case appropriately enough Nebraska). They did this by posing questions to a carefully selected sample on parental authority and the law: should a parent be able to disinherit his child completely, was a typical question. Finding the law out of touch with community ethic on 10 out of 17 issues, they suggested three reasons for the lack of congruence: *viz.*, the built-in professional conservatism of lawyers and judges, the lack of pressure for change, and the "inadequacy of prevailing techniques utilised by law-makers for ascertaining the moral sense of the community" (at p. 195). The first of these reasons is acknowledged by Pound (*cf.* his "tenacity of the taught tradition" (1940) 56 Harv.L.R. 365) and must demonstrate the inadequacy of his own approach, *post*, 358, n. 82.

[36] See R. Pound, *Jurisprudence*, vol. 3, pp. 287–291.

[37] There may also be difficulty in securing legal aid to litigate a new point.

[38] See Westin, *Privacy and Freedom* (1967).

[39] *Cf.* the paucity of materials on the underprivileged and the law in this country with the comparative wealth of them in the United States. See, for example, Carlin and Howard, 12 U.C.L.A.L.R. 381 (in Aubert, *Sociology of Law*, p. 332), who point out the absence of a "one-to-one relationship between the *existence* of a legal problem and the recognition and exercise of legal rights" (p. 340) and the different forms of property which are characteristic forms of economic wealth for the poor (*e.g.*, job rights, social security, unemployment compensation). "The fact that these interests may not always be recognised as property may well be the result of the failure of the poor to establish or pursue their legal rights in these areas" (p. 341). The *locus classicus* on this "new property" is Charles Reich (1964) 73 Yale L.J. 778, on which see Joel Handler, in ed. ten Broek, *The Law of the Poor* (1966).

[40] *Jurisprudence: Men and Ideas of the Law* (1953), p. 518.

but in the sense of what may be good for them regardless of their actual desires. A good deal of social, and almost the whole of penal legislation, may be of this character.[41]

As to Pound's classification of interests, though this purports to be an objective statement of those existing desires which Western society, at least, wishes to protect, there is some force in the contention that it reads rather like a political manifesto in favour of a liberal and capitalist society, as well as suffering from excessive vagueness. Moreover it cannot be suggested that these categories of interests have ever been proved to exist, *de facto*, by scientific research; what they amount to really are no more than common-sense inferences deduced from different branches of the legal system itself, as symbolising the social purposes of the community. And the further question remains, what happens when these so-called interests conflict? or, in other words, how do we evaluate them in due order of priority? [42]

Values

Pound's answer here is that every society has certain basic assumptions upon which its ordering rests, though for the most part these may be implicit rather than expressly formulated.[43] Certain of these assumptions may be identified as the jural postulates of the legal system; as embodying its fundamental purposes. Pound has endeavoured to state what these are for existing Western society,[44] while recognising that they are not static, but may change as society develops new needs and new tensions. Some of these postulates may indeed conflict,[45] but the success of any particular society will depend on the degree to which it is socially integrated and so accepts as common ground its basic postulates. It is sometimes objected that here again we have natural law creeping in by the back door, but there is undoubtedly a distinction between maintaining the objective

---

[41] A striking example is the Obscene Publications Act 1959 (and, similarly, the Theatres Act 1968). Obscenity can be justified " as being for the *public good* " if it is in the interests of science, literature, art, etc., when it is quite clear that the majority of people would not wish these to be advanced.

[42] Another problem is that interests often cannot be secured unless they are able to depend on values. For example, if one regards racial equality as an interest, it is difficult to see how it can be made to work until integration and non-discrimination are accepted as postulates. See Barry, *post*, 373.

[43] In this connection, Pound had recourse especially to the ideas of Josef Kohler; see R. Pound, *Interpretations of Legal History*, Chap. 7.

[44] Some have detected the genius of American politics in the American's habit of taking his own premises and values for granted and not to be thought about: see D. Boorstein, *Genius of American Politics* (1953). For attempts to list the American value system, *cf.* Max Lerner, *America as Civilisation* (1958), p. 67. On Pound's method in reaching his postulates see, Stone, *Human Law and Human Justice* (1965), pp. 264–269.

[45] Though none of Pound's do. See, *e.g.*, Pound's careful rationalisation of the nascent postulate of " job-security," *post*, 380.

validity of ethical rules and simply ascertaining the operative values that exist, *de facto*, in a given society. These are value judgments that may affect our choices and conduct[46] and should, as Pound urges, be factors which weigh in determining the current of judicial decisions. Also their relative value may be assessed, after the manner of the Utilitarians, by regard for the consequences, and though these cannot be exactly predicted, social studies may provide some clues in this direction.

Pound does not give much detailed attention to the way one conflicting interest is to be compared with another, but he does indicate that if such an interest is stated in its social aspect then so, too, must the other interests, for otherwise there will be a built-in bias in favour of the social as against the private view. Thus, suppose a court is considering whether a factory, which is operating in a residential area, constitutes a nuisance. If the court is here considering the discomfort inflicted on adjoining residents, this must be weighed against the private interest of the factory-owner and not against the social interest which there may be in the factory, for instance, if this factory is contributing to the prosperity of the community. Some support for this view may be found in the English nuisance cases where it is held that the fact that the defendant factory-owner is a public benefactor is irrelevant. This might have been all very well in an individualist age, but it seems doubtful how far the social interests ought to be ignored at the present day. Ought, for instance, a court to ignore the fact that closing down the factory might well cause unemployment in the area?[47] Perhaps the appropriate answer at the present day is that private interests should always be balanced one against the other and then social interests should be evaluated separately, before a final balance is sought between both types of factor.[48]

[46] Castberg, *Problems of Legal Philosophy*, p. 100, objects that a belief in social welfare is itself metaphysical. Bentham accepted this in regard to his principle of utility, *Principles of Morals*, cap. I, § 11, but this does not imply an adoption of natural law, but merely that such a belief is a value judgment not susceptible of objective proof.

[47] See the Canadian case of *Bottom* v. *Ontario Leaf Tobacco Co.* [1935] 2 D.L.R. 699; and see also B. Wilson in (1961) *Canadian Bar Journal*, pp. 455–456. *Cf. Re Craven Insurance* [1968] 1 All E.R. 1140, where Pennycuick J. refused to take into consideration the factor of unemployment in exercising his discretion not to wind up an insurance company (see p. 1144). This case also throws an interesting light on the English courts' attitude to Brandeis briefs (*post*, 424) for the court read an affidavit submitted by the local M.P. arguing the case on the dangers of unemployment and using non-legal argumentation.

[48] For Pound's view that in " weighing " interests, the comparison must be made " on the same plane," whether this be private, public, or social, see R. Pound, *Jurisprudence*, Vol. 3, pp. 328–331 and *cf.* G. Sawer, *post*, 382. See also Kurland, *Religion and the Law* (1962), p. 58. For some constructive criticisms of Pound's interest theory, from the view of one who is in broad agreement with this approach, see J. Stone, *Human Law and Human Justice*, pp. 279–280.

SOCIOLOGICAL JURISPRUDENCE SINCE POUND

Roscoe Pound died in 1964, and, although his writings span sixty years, his seminal influence dates from the movement he helped to create in the early part of this century. It is all too easy to identify sociological jurisprudence with Pound: there is little in this field that does not get its inspiration and initiative from his writings. But sociological jurisprudence neither begins nor ends with Pound, and it is valuable to identify some recent trends in sociological thought.

Selznick, a leading American sociologist, has pin-pointed three stages in legal sociology.[49] Pound, together with his continental progenitors, belongs to the first stage, wherein the pioneer, the prophet in the wilderness communicates a perspective. So, Pound identified the task of the lawyer as " social engineer," formulated a programme of action, attempted to gear individual and social needs to the values of Western democratic society. The early Realist writings convey similar orientation.[50] Pound, and Holmes[51] for that matter, was a " generaliser," [52] a purveyor of " grand theory ": he provides the theoretical context for an understanding of law in society. But he did little or no empirical research, though such work was undertaken by contemporaries in the " twenties " and " thirties." Their writings are characterised by a concern for substantive legal problems rather than the working of legal institutions, and by a penchant for law reform, doubtless inherited from Pound and, indeed, the Realists. Furthermore, the initiative for this early empirical research was taken by lawyers, not sociologists, and often by practitioners rather than academic jurists. Perhaps, as a result, conclusions and implications were framed in grandiose terms.[53]

The second stage, which Selznick, writing in 1959, believed was that reached by contemporary writers was characterised by a concern for method. The skills of the academic lawyer and sociologist were synthesised: the jurist often suggested the field of activity and posed the questions: the sociologist collaborated in the research, adapting his techniques from the mainstream of sociological inquiry.

[49] See *post*, 390.
[50] *Cf. post*, 399.
[51] *Post*, 400.
[52] See Jerome Hall, *Methods of Sociological Research in Comparative Law* in *Legal Thought in the United States of America under Contemporary Pressures* ed. Hazard and Wagner (1970), p. 149, 152.
[53] So, Underhill Moore and Charles Callahan's research on traffic and parking regulations were described as contributions to psychological learning theory. See 53 Yale L.J. 1.

The Chicago jury project was the result of one such collaboration.[54] At the same time the jurist trained himself in the techniques of sociology, the mechanics of social surveys, the use of statistics and other necessary technological skills including those of cybernetics. On the whole, the jurists of this second generation have been content to survey narrower problems and achieve less far-reaching conclusions.

Lasswell and McDougal

But " grand theory " by no means died with Pound. In the writings of Lasswell and McDougal [55] we find the same broad generalisations, the same " grand prospectus," [56] though, it must be admitted, neither the same clarity nor urgency. Their theory is one of decision-making. There are, they postulate, a number of " desired events," catalogued under such vague headings as power, enlightenment, wealth, respect for human dignity, health and well-being, skill, affection and rectitude. For each of these categories they ask whether the legal process, in the context of the social system, is achieving a maximum sharing of the particular value. So, on health and well-being, it is asked whether " the legal system succeed[s] in stimulating and sustaining progress toward safety, health and comfort in every community," [57] and so on. Such a value-laden priority as " progress " can be explained by the articulated democratic and utilitarian aim of the philosophy.

Although the theory has been used for a stimulating plan for legal education,[58] it has a number of imponderables. The generalities of the values may be precise enough for a political scientist (which Lasswell is), but the lawyers' concepts, however fact-based and individualised, are apt to be submerged under them. Further, they are not ranked in any order and no provision is made for a likely clash of values. Nor are they detailed enough to be any positive guidance to a judge or legislator. It is not, therefore, surprising

---

[54] See *post*, 465. Other examples are the Columbia Project for Effective Justice, see *ante*, 6, and the study of the economics of personal injury litigation in (1961) 61 Colum.L.R. 1; empirical research on the legal profession (Carlin, *Lawyers on their Own* (1962); Smigel, *The Wall Street Lawyer* (1964), and see the contributions in Part 5 of Aubert, *Sociology of Law* (1969), particularly those by Rueschemeyer and Dahrendorf); work on the police (Skolnick, *Justice Without Trial* (1966)) and arrest (La Fave, *Arrest: The Decision to Take a Suspect into Custody* (1965)) and many other subjects. A number of readers have been published which give a conspectus of the work being done. The best of these is Friedman and Macaulay, *Law and the Behavioural Sciences* (1969). See also Aubert, *Sociology of Law* (1969); Simon, *The Sociology of Law* (1968); Schwartz and Skolnick, *Society and the Legal Order* (1970).

[55] See (1943) 52 Yale L.J. 203; (1952) 61 Yale L.J. 915; 21 Rutgers L.R. 645, also in ed. Haber and Cohen, *The Law School of Tomorrow* (1968), p. 87.

[56] See Kalven in *The Law School of Tomorrow op. cit.*, at p. 161.

[57] *Idem*, p. 90.

[58] See (1943) 52 Yale L.J. 203.

that the Lasswell-McDougal model has not had much impact on law or lawyers. The feeling is, and rightly, that it has all been said before—by Pound. So Kalven, a leading legal sociologist, has written that "the prospectus strategy does not work," that "something more concrete, something more specific, something more puzzling than the grand question of how American democracy is performing is needed to move one to research." [59]

This is not to dismiss theoretical models out of hand. What is required is a judicious blending of theory and empirical research, for research must have an integral reference. Critics of Lasswell and McDougal believe they have failed to achieve this.

Professor Stone is representative of modern sociological jurisprudence in arguing for theory to enable us to see the social and economic order in its complex unity.[60] One of the main faults of classical sociological jurisprudence was, he believes, its *ad hoc* approach, the treatment of particular problems in isolation. "The sociological jurist of the future will generally have to approach his problems through a vast effort at understanding the wider social context." [61] Stone indicates that, in spite of its difficulties and faults, the Parsonian "social system" is the type of model to which sociological jurists must aspire.[62] A common malaise in sociological jurisprudence is its prevalent methodology of working outwards from legal problems to the relevant social science. Instead, what is needed is "a framework of thought receptive of social data which will allow us to see 'the social system' as an integrated equilibration of the multitude of operative systems of values and institutions embraced within it." [63]

It may be that when this is achieved Selznick's third stage will be reached. Selznick admits this is in the future. It is the time when sociological jurisprudence will develop an "intellectual autonomy and maturity," when having learnt the necessary skills, the jurists can return to some of the theoretical questions posed at the outset, the function of law, the role of legality, the meaning of justice, and be ready to tackle them empirically. Selznick himself has begun to analyse legality from sociological premises.[64] It is difficult to assess this development which is barely out of its chrysalis stage, but it is not easy to see how empirical studies can answer, for example, the question whether the Nuremberg laws should be regarded as laws,

59 Kalven, *op. cit.*, p. 161.
60 See *Social Dimensions of Law and Justice* (1960); (1966) 1 Israel L.R. 173.
61 1 Israel L.R. 173, 176–177 *cf. Social Dimensions*, pp. 26–27.
62 See his discussion of Parsons in *Social Dimensions*, pp. 13–28 and also in *Law and The Social Sciences* (1966), pp. 29–49.
63 *Law and the Social Sciences* p. 27.
64 See *post*, 394 and, more particularly, in *Law, Society and Industrial Justice* (1969), an extract of which is found in Schwartz and Skolnick, *ante*, note 54.

though a proper question for empirical investigation might be whether disobedience to an "immoral" law is more likely to result from calling it a law or not.

It must not be thought that any of these strands are entirely independent, or that sociological jurisprudence presents a single face to the world. Much of the writings of contemporary realists and behaviourists and a good deal of anthropological research cannot really be distinguished from sociological jurisprudence. Sociological jurisprudence has, indeed, come some way since Pound, when bitter disputes raged with the Realists.[65]

SOCIOLOGICAL JURISPRUDENCE, SOCIOLOGY OF LAW AND LEGAL SOCIOLOGY

With the development of a distinctively sociological approach to law, there has been some discussion as to whether a distinction should be drawn between the sociology of law and legal sociology and between these and sociological jurisprudence.

It has been doubted whether such a field of study as legal sociology is capable of existence.[66] Generally speaking, when reference is made to sociology [67] in connection with law, what is intended is some aspect of a sociology of law, in the sense of established principles and techniques of the science of sociology being applied to legal fields, such as the effect of different forms of enforcement of debts,[68] or a study of the way in which hire-purchase laws affect the ordinary consumer. On the other hand, the term "legal sociology" would imply the existence of a body of learning peculiar to those situations in which legal rules operate, or where the behaviour of persons in relation to legal rules or institutions is particularly in question. Of course, the general body of sociological learning, such as Parsons's "social system" with its "pattern variables," [69] is quite independent of the legal field, since it operates generally over the whole area of social relations. This is not to say, however, that the law, and human behaviour in legal contexts, may not have certain characteristic features, and these features and the special interests of lawyers may have particular consequences in the realm of sociological thought and technique. It may, therefore, be that there is room for a specialised field of legal sociology, at least as a department of sociology in general,

---

[65] *Post*, 441, 443.

[66] See Sawer, *Law in Society* (1965), pp. 9–15. See also Stone, *Social Dimensions*, pp. 28–35.

[67] One of the problems with this speculation is that the nature of sociology itself is doubtful, and methodological questioning is far from quiescent.

[68] See "Report of the Committee on the Enforcement of Judgment Debts" (1969), Cmnd. 3909.   [69] Stone, *op. cit.*, note 66, at pp. 21–23.

which would then be related to general or pure sociology, just as one of the applied sciences would correspond to the field of pure science. Equally, however, it is probably true to say that developments in the field either of legal sociology or the sociology of law in its ordinary sense, have not yet been carried sufficiently far to justify any such theoretical distinction, though later developments may conceivably warrant a distinction of this kind as a body of theoretical knowledge accumulates and becomes more readily accessible.

The distinction between sociology of law and sociological jurisprudence is less specious and more readily acceptable, though the boundary is often not easy to draw.[70] Sociological jurisprudence is a branch of the normative sciences. Its concern is with making legal principle and administration more effective in action. Its values, as with Bentham's utility or Pound's jural postulates, are usually openly avowed. Sociological jurists frequently eschew objectivity: they are unashamedly political animals. They attack a "jurisprudence of concepts," formalism, legalism.[71] They believe the law can and must be developed to keep up with social change. Doubtless, sociologists of law believe this as well, and few today accept the Weberian myth of a value-free sociology.[72] But the sociology of law is in essence one of the descriptive sciences, its technique is empirical, not juridical. When practised by lawyers it is practised by them as sociologists looking at the working of legal institutions from the outside. Of course, they start with a suspicion that something is wrong (this governs their choice of field to survey) and they know what conclusions they would like to reach. They are sceptics and reformers, yet successful legal sociology must retain at least a veneer of objectivity. In many respects this distinction corresponds to Selznick's first two stages.[73] Sociological jurisprudence is stage one; the sociology of law stage two. It may be that the promised arrival of stage three will see the development of legal sociology.

The sociological approach has the merit of attacking the problems of our day in an empirical fashion and with due regard to the social purposes of the legal system,[74] though it is, perhaps, over-optimistic as to the extent to which the social sciences can point the way clearly

---

70 See Sawer, *op. cit.*, Chap. 2, Pound, 5 U. of Toronto L.J. 1 (1943).
71 *Cf.* Shklar, *ante*, 33.
72 See Gouldner, 9 *Social Problems*, 199–213.
73 *Ante*, 348, and *post*, 390.
74 The similarity of result produced in different legal systems by quite different paths of reasoning also points to the value of the sociological approach for the full understanding of legal phenomena. *Cf.* D. Lloyd, *Public Policy: A Comparative Study in English and French Law* (1953).

to acceptable solutions.[75] Also the notion that the law was ever developed as a purely analytical exercise without regard to social consequences is really quite fanciful, the main difference being the extent to which this process remains an "inarticulate premise" or is openly avowed. However, the open acceptance of this attitude by many influential lawyers can eventually serve to infuse a new spirit into the practical working of the law, and this has already led to practical consequences, especially in America. It may be that if legal education continues to emphasise the social function of law, and the need for a broader and more informed approach to legal development, the more conservative traditions of the professionally-taught common law may gradually be overborne even in the land of its origin.[76]

Unfortunately, however, there are certain factors which still tend to divert attempts to secure better knowledge of the functioning of the law. There is first of all the traditional and unfounded belief on the part of lawyers that participation in the legal process in some way gives unique access to an understanding of the working of society itself. In fact, law is only a very imperfect mirror of society and we know very little of the part that it actually plays in securing social cohesion.

Then, again, there is a certain fear of the law which is encouraged by the tendency to emphasise its ritualistic aspects, and the magic potency attributed to such ritual. How far such ritual aspects are still necessary in a developed civilisation may be regarded as an open question, but even if the answer is affirmative, the question still presses for an answer as to whether we have the right kind of magic. Lastly, it may be mentioned that any exploration into the inner workings of a society, and more particularly perhaps, its legal system, is apt to be regarded as something in the nature of a subversive activity and, therefore, one which does not always recommend itself either to officials or to the legal profession.

---

[75] *Cf.* W. H. Whyte, *The Organisation Man* (1957), where he discusses the role of "scientism" in modern America, the belief that "with the same techniques that have worked in the physical sciences we can eventually create an exact science of man" (p. 23). Whyte gives a particularly striking illustration of the fallacies in this approach in his description of "personality tests," which seek to measure the immeasurable (Chs. 14 and 15). For ways in which social science can assist in legal problems, see J. Hall, *op. cit.*, pp. 155–156; and, more particularly, the excellent summary in Rose, "The Social Scientist As an Expert Witness in Court Cases" in ed. Lazarsfeld, Sewell and Wilensky, *The Uses of Sociology* (1968). See also Patterson, *Law in a Scientific Age* (1963); but it must not be forgotten that the validity of our interpretation of human conduct cannot be proved by statistics: *cf.* P. Winch, *Idea of a Social Science* (1958), p. 113.

[76] In recent years there has been a gradual infiltration of these ideas in this country, particularly at some of the newer universities. See 9 J.S.P.T.L. 328–370 for some report of the progress made. Note also the work being undertaken by the new Institute of Judicial Administration in Birmingham.

At the same time we must also guard against the false idea that sociology can in some way eliminate or has eliminated the need for jurisprudence. For important though it may be as an aid to legal thinking and law reform, it is no substitute for jurisprudence itself. As Mr. Justice Frankfurter once said " sociologists should be on tap, but not on top." [77]

R. von JHERING

Law as Means to an End [78]

The decisive position which I shall constantly keep in mind in the following consideration is that of the *security* of the satisfaction of human wants; it shall be the standard by which I intend to measure all the phenomena of commerce.

Want is the band with which nature draws man into society, the means by which she realizes the two principles of all morality and culture, " Everybody exists for the world," and " the world exists for everybody." Dependent as he is upon his fellowmen through his need, and the more so as his need grows, man would be the most unhappy being in the world if the satisfaction of his need depended upon accident, and he could not count with all security upon the co-operation and assistance of his fellowmen. In that case the animal would be an object of envy to him, for the animal is so made by nature that when it comes into possession of the powers destined for it by nature it needs no such support. The realization of the mutual relations of man for her purpose; the elimination of accident; the establishment of the security of the satisfaction of human need as a basal form of social existence; the regulated, assured and substantial system of actions and methods which minister to this satisfaction, keeping equal step with the need—that is *commerce*.

The simplest form of satisfaction of a need, in man as in the animal, lies in his own power. But whereas in the animal, need and power coincide, this is not the case in man. It is this very disproportion between the two, this insufficiency of his own power, which is the cause by means of which nature forces him to be a man; namely, to look for man, and in association with others to attain those purposes to which he is alone unequal. In his necessity she refers him to the outside world and his fellows.   [pp. 75–76]

. . . we finally come upon the vital point in the whole organization of right. This consists in the preponderance of the *common* interest of *all* over the *particular* interests of one *individual; all* join for the common interests, only the *individual* stands for the particular interest. But the power of all is, the forces being equal, superior to that of the individual; and the more so the greater their number.[79]

[77] As quoted in Patterson, *Law in a Scientific Age*, p. 56.
[78] [Translated, I. Husik (1924).]
[79] [Although a follower of Bentham, Jhering criticised his individualistic approach. Jhering insisted on the primacy of social purposes, and based this on the fact that men in their mutual relations gradually perceive that they will best further their own purposes by co-operation. Jhering referred to " social mechanics," as

We thus have the formula for social organization of force, *viz.*, preponderance of the force which is serviceable to the interests of all over the amount at the disposition of the individual for his own interest; the power being brought over to the side of the interest common to all.

The form in private law of a combination of several persons for the pursuit of the same common interest is *partnership*, and although in other respects the State is very different from partnership, the formula in reference to regulating force by interest is quite the same in both. Partnership contains the prototype of the State, which is indicated therein in all its parts. Conceptually as well as historically, partnership forms the transition from the unregulated form of force in the individual to its regulation by the State. Not merely in the sense that it contains a combination of several for the same purpose, and thereby makes possible the pursuit of aims which were denied to the power of the individual . . . but in an incomparably greater measure in the sense that it solves the problem of creating the preponderance of power on the side of right. It does this by putting in place of the opposition of two particular interests fighting one another without an assured prospect of the victory of right, that between a common interest and a particular, whereby the solution comes of itself. In partnership all partners present a united front against the one who pursues his own interests at the expense of these common interests assigned by the contract, or who refuses to carry out the duties undertaken by him in the contract; they all unite their power against the one. So the preponderance of power is here thrown *on the side of right*, and partnership may therefore be designated as the mechanism of the *self-regulation of force according to the measures of right.*[80]

[pp. 220–221]

EHRLICH

Principles of the Sociology of Law [81]

The impulses to create law which result from the distribution of power in society have their source in society. The frequently used word *Machtverhältnisse* (distribution of power) indeed is not available as a

the means by which society achieved its social purposes. These means were divided between law, involving the use of organised coercion, and the voluntary processes of social life, which rely upon reward and the satisfaction of human needs etc. Justice is achieved by the measure to which the common purposes of society are fulfilled. Unfortunately, however, as Stone points out, Jhering did not really provide an adequate criterion of justice. Indeed his arguments seem to lead to the inevitable conclusion that individual purposes must always yield to social purposes. But this hypothesis depends on the rather naïve assumption that in any case of conflict there will always be an acceptable consensus as to what the common interest requires. Moreover, it appears to ignore those areas where individual interests, such as freedom of speech, may possess a higher value than some common social purpose which would favour the suppression of discordant voices (*cf.* J. Stone, *Human Law and Human Justice*, Chap. 5. Stone refers to Jhering's approach under the useful designation of " Social Utilitarianism." Pound also uses this expression, *post*, 361).]

80 [It should be pointed, however, that for Jhering the task of bringing the legal order into closer touch with actual human needs was a matter for the legislature rather than part of the judicial function. See as to this, I. Jenkins, " Jhering," in (1960–1961) 14 Vanderbilt L.R., 169, at pp. 184–185.]

81 [Translated, W. L. Moll (1936). For a sympathetic critique and detailed discussion of Ehrlich's thought see Littlefield (1967), 19 Maine L.R. 1.]

scientific term because of its indefiniteness; we are using it here as referring to the distribution of power which is based on position in the state, on economic or on social position. Furthermore the legal proposition does not owe its existence to any consideration of the interests of individual classes or ranks, but of those of all social strata; and it is immaterial whether actual general interests are involved or merely imagined ones, as in the case of the superstitious belief in the existence of witches. Under this head comes the defense against external enemies and elemental forces. In the last analysis, at least in the judgment of those that act, the interests of individual strata of the population are general interests when popular opinion does not regard the interests of the other strata as worth taking into account, e.g. the interests of the slaves in Rome; up to the nineteenth century, quite generally, the interests of the unfree peasantry; in the Polish republic, and in ancient Hungary, usually, the interests of those who were not members of the nobility; and until late in the nineteenth century, the interests of the non-propertied classes. And for most modern men and women the interest of the utterly neglected (*Verwahrlosten*) and submerged (*Verlorenen*) perhaps is but little more than something to be protected against. In their opinion, the general interest includes protection of the social order against individuals who are beyond the pale of society. This protection may be effected by means of a part of the criminal law, police law, and procedural law. In reality all of this is a matter of the distribution of power. A decision rendered for the protection of the general interest may be said to be a decision based solely upon considerations of expedience. Wherever there is no doubt as to where the power lies in a state, or where the voice of popular consciousness speaks in no uncertain tones, the task of the jurist is a merely technical one. The content of the legal proposition is given by society. His function is merely to provide the wording of it and to find the means whereby the interests which are to be secured can be secured most effectively. This technical function however must not be underrated . . .

The decision as to the interests involved in a dispute is entrusted by the state to the jurist when it is clearly indicated neither by the general interest nor by the distribution of power in society as a whole. This situation may be brought about by various causes. In the first place very often the parties to the dispute are quite unaware of the great social interests involved in the decision; very often the latter are distributed among the various classes and ranks in such a manner as to place them above the struggles of class and rank; in many cases these social interests are too inconsiderable and insignificant to become involved in the dispute. Very often, too, the possessors of power, who are called upon to render the decision, are not at all involved in the conflict of interests. The most important cause however is the fact that the powers that are engaged in the struggle in behalf of the different interests counterbalance one another or that the influences that proceed from the groups that are most powerful politically, economically, or socially, are checked or thwarted by other social tendencies, which are based on religious, ethical, scientific, or other ideological convictions.

When the jurist is asked to draw the line between the conflicting interests independently, he is asked, by implication, to do it according to justice. This implies, in the first place, something negative. He is asked to arrive at a decision without any consideration of expediency and uninfluenced by the distribution of power. In recent times, it is true, it has often been said that justice, too, is a matter involving questions of power. If the writer means to say that the idea of justice, on which the decision is based, must have attained a certain power in the body social at the time when it influences the judicial finding of norms or the activity of the state, he is indeed stating a truth, but it is a self-evident truth; and a self-evident truth does not require statement. But if he means to say that, under the cloak of justice, effect is always being given to the influence of political, social, or economic position, the statement is manifestly incorrect. A legal norm whose origin can be traced to such influences is usually stigmatized by that very fact as something unjust. Justice has always weighted the scales solely in favor of the weak and the persecuted. A just decision is a decision based on grounds which appeal to a disinterested person; it is a decision which is rendered by a person who is not involved in the conflict of interests, or which, even though it be rendered by a person involved in this conflict, nevertheless is such as a disinterested person would render or approve of. It is never based on taking advantage of a position of power. When a person who is in a position of power acts justly, he acts against his own interest, at any rate against his immediate interest, prompted by religious, ethical, scientific, or other ideological considerations; perhaps merely by considerations of prudent policy. The parties of political and social justice, e.g. the doctrinaire liberals, the English Fabians, the German Social-political or National-Socialist parties, the French Solidarists, find their adherents chiefly among ideologists who are not personally interested in the political and social conflicts of interests. In this fact lies their strength and also their weakness.

But all of these are negative characteristics. Which are the positive characteristics of justice? The catch phrase about balancing of interests which is so successful at the present time is not an answer to this question; for the very question is: What is it that gives weight to the interests that are to be balanced? Manifestly it is not the balancing jurist, writer or teacher, judge or legislator, but society itself. The function of the jurist is merely to balance them. There are trends caused by the interests that flourish in society which ultimately influence even persons that are not involved in these conflicting interests. The judge who decides according to justice follows the tendency that he himself is dominated by. Justice therefore does not proceed from the individual, but arises in society.

The rôle of the person rendering the decision is of importance only inasmuch as, within certain limitations, he can select the solution which corresponds most nearly to his personal feelings. But in doing this, he cannot disregard the social basis of the decision. If a Spartacus, favored by fortune, had abolished slavery in antiquity, or if the socialists should abolish private property, let us say in a beleaguered city, as was done in Paris during the days of the Commune, these facts would have nothing to do with justice. And a judge who, in a decision which he renders, recognizes private property in means of production in spite of the fact that he is a socialist, or who admits the defense that the debt sued upon in a stock-exchange transaction is a gaming debt although in his opinion the setting-up of this plea is a breach of good faith, does not thereby contradict himself. In doing these things he is merely being guided by social tendencies against his own individual feeling in the matter. A rebellious slave, the government of a beleaguered city, like that of Paris during the Commune, can indeed proceed according to their individual feelings, but they can do so only because they have been removed from social influences by the force of circumstances. Justice is a power wielded over the minds of men by society.[82]

It is the function of juristic science, in the first place, to record the trends of justice that are found in society, and to ascertain what they are, whence they come, and whither they lead; but it cannot possibly determine which of these is the only just one. In the forum of science, they are all equally valid. What men consider just depends upon the ideas they have concerning the end of human endeavor in this world of ours, but it is not the function of science to dictate the final ends of human endeavor on earth. That is the function of the founder of a religion, of the preacher, of the prophet, of the preacher of ethics, of the practical jurist, of the judge, of the politician. Science can be concerned only with those things that are susceptible of scientific demonstration. That a certain thing is just is no more scientifically demonstrable than is the beauty of a Gothic cathedral or of a Beethoven symphony to a person who is insensible to it. All of these are questions of emotional life. Science can ascertain the effects of a legal proposition, but it cannot make these effects appear either desirable or loathsome to man. Justice is a social force, and it is always a question whether it is potent enough to influence the disinterested persons whose function it is to create juristic and statute law.

But although science can teach us nothing concerning the ends, once the end is determined, it can enlighten us as to the means to that end. The practical technical rules that perform this function are based on the results of pure science. There is no science that teaches men that they ought to be healthy, but practical medical science teaches men who desire to be healthy what they can do, according to the present state of the natural sciences, to bring about that result. Practical juristic science is concerned with the manner in which the ends may be attained that men are endeavoring to attain through law, but it must utilize the results of the sociology of law for this purpose. The legal proposition is not only the result, it is also a lever, of social development; it is an instrumentality in the hands of society whereby society shapes things within

---

[82] [Yet a society may be so organised that justice according to law favours unduly the dominant section, and the judiciary, by being drawn from that section, consciously or unconsciously, will tend to favour the needs of that section to the detriment of the rest of society. But, on the view that a conservative judiciary will always favour the employers against the working classes (note the statistical survey of O'Higgins and Partington (1969) 32 M.L.R. 53), see Pound's insistence that the rule in *Priestley* v. *Fowler*, usually cited as a typical example of this emphasis, was not the product of a " tribunal consciously expressing in legal doctrine the self-interest of a dominant social or economic class " but that it was the result of a " conception of liability " in the " taught tradition " and that no court, however composed, would have decided otherwise ((1940) 53 Harv.L.R. 365). Pound's thesis is highly speculative since a judiciary from a working class background has never emerged. Nor is it thought that the doctrine, whatever its origin, could have lasted as long were it not for the nourishment it received from the ideology of a laissez-faire capitalism. See, further, Schubert, *Judicial Behaviour* (1964), pp. 187–300.]

its sphere of influence according to its will. Through the legal proposition man acquires a power, limited though it be, over the facts of the law; in the legal proposition a willed legal order is brought face to face with the legal order which has arisen self-actively in society.   [pp. 198–203] The sociology of law then must begin with the ascertainment of the living law. Its attention will be directed primarily to the concrete, not the abstract. It is only the concrete that can be observed. What the anatomist places under the microscope is not human tissue in the abstract but a specific tissue of a specific human being; the physiologist likewise does not study the functions of the liver of mammals in the abstract, but those of a specific liver of a specific mammal. Only when he has completed the observation of the concrete does he ask whether it is universally valid, and this fact, too, he endeavors to establish by means of a series of concrete observations, for which he has to find specific methods. The same may be said of the investigator of law. He must first concern himself with concrete usages, relations of domination, legal relations, contracts, articles of association, dispositions by last will and testament. It is not true, therefore, that the investigation of the living law is concerned only with "customary law" or with "business usage." If one does any thinking at all when one uses these words—which is not always the case—one will realize that they do not refer to the concrete, but to that which has been universalized. But only the concrete usages, the relations of domination, the legal relations, the contracts, the articles of association, the dispositions by last will and testament, yield the rules according to which men regulate their conduct. And it is only on the basis of these rules that the norms for decision that the courts apply and the statutory provisions that alone have hitherto occupied the attention of jurists arise. The great majority of judicial decisions are based on the concrete usages, relations of possession, contracts, articles of association, and dispositions by last will and testament, that the courts have found to exist. If we would comprehend the universalizations, the reductions to unity, and the other methods of finding norms that the judge and the lawgiver employ, we must first of all know the basis upon which they were carried out. The more we know of the Roman banking system, the better shall we understand *receptum* and *litteris contrahere*. Does this not hold true for the law of our day? To this extent Savigny was right when he said that the law—and by law he means above all the legal proposition—can be understood only from its historical connection; but the historical connection does not lie in the hoary past, but in the present, out of which the legal proposition grows.

But the scientific significance of the living law is not confined to its influence upon the norms for decision which the courts apply or upon the content of statutes. The knowledge of the living law has an independent value, and this consists in the fact that it constitutes the foundation of the legal order of human society. In order to acquire a knowledge of this order we must know the usages, relations of domination, legal relations, contracts, articles of association, declarations by last will and testament, quite independently of the question whether they have already found expression in a judicial decision or in a statute or whether they will ever find it. The provisions contained in the new German Commercial Code regulating stock exchanges, banks, publishing houses, and other supplementary provisions were full of gaps when they were enacted and, for the most part, have become antiquated today. Modern commerce, especially the export trade, has meanwhile created an enormous number of new forms, which ought to be the subject matter of scientific study as well as those that have been enumerated in the statute. Very much that is of genuine value can be found on this point in the literature on the science of commerce that is blossoming forth so abundantly. A part of the order in the sphere of mining and navigation has been made accessible to legal science through mining law, maritime law, and the law of inland navigation, but for the most part this has long since become antiquated. The factory, the bank, the railroad, the great landed estate, the labor union, the association of employers, and a thousand other forms of life—each of these likewise has an order, and this order has a legal side as well as that of the mercantile establishment, which is being regulated in detail only by the Commercial Code. In addition there are countless forms in which the activity of these associations manifests itself outwardly, above all the contracts. In studying the manufacturing establishment, the legal investigator must pursue the countless, highly intricate paths that lead from the acceptance of the order to the delivery of the finished products to the customer, to wit the position of the representative and of the commercial traveller, the three departments that are to be found in every manufacturing establishment (the sales department, the technical department, and the manufacturing department), the arrival of the orders, the preparation and the preservation of drawings, the computation of the cost of the undertaking, the sale price, the calculation for the purpose of checking up, the execution of the order on the basis of the drawings, the functions of the manufacturing department, of the master workman, the management of the warehouse, the computation of wages by the piece and by time, the distribution of wages among the individual workmen, the importance of the certificate showing that material has been handed over, the price list, the supervision at the gates by porters. Of equal importance for the legal side of the order of the undertaking is the keeping of books, the taking of inventories, the supervision over the warehouse, the preservation of drawings and models, the employment of workmen and of apprentices, the working regulations, and the committees of the workmen.[83]   [pp. 501–503]

R. POUND

Philosophy of Law
(Revised ed. 1954)

The End or Purpose of Law

At the end of the last and the beginning of the present century, a new way of thinking grew up. Jurists began to think in terms of human wants or desires or expectations rather than of human wills.[84] They began to think

---

[83] [Ehrlich's concern is with the actual sociological and economic background to legal norms rather than with the mere statements of legal rules by legislators or courts. This savours more of the later Realist movement (though lacking some of its doctrinal extravagances) than of Pound's *a priori* catalogues of human interests and values.]   [84] [*Cf.* Jhering, *ante*, 354.]

that what they had to do was not simply to equalize or harmonize wills, but, if not to equalize, at least to harmonize the satisfaction of wants. They began to weigh or balance and reconcile claims or wants or desires or expectations, as formerly they had balanced or reconciled wills. They began to think of the end of law, not as a maximum of self-assertion, but as a maximum satisfaction of wants. Hence for a time they thought of the problem of ethics, of jurisprudence, and of politics as chiefly one of valuing ; as a problem of finding criteria of the relative value of interests. In jurisprudence and politics they saw that we must add practical problems of the possibility of making interests effective through governmental action, judicial or administrative. But the first question was one of the wants to be recognized—of the interests to be recognized and secured. Having inventoried the wants or claims or interests which are asserting and for which legal security is sought, we were to value them, select those to be recognized, determine the limits within which they were to be given effect in view of other recognized interests, and ascertain how far we might give them effect by law in view of the inherent limitations upon effective legal action. This mode of thinking may be seen, concealed under different terminologies, in more than one type of jurist in the present century.

Three elements contributed to shift the basis of theories as to the end of law from wills to wants, from a reconciling or harmonizing of wills to a reconciling or harmonizing of wants. The most important part was played by psychology which undermined the foundation of the metaphysical will philosophy of law. Through the movement for unification of the social sciences, economics also played an important part, especially indirectly through the attempts at economic interpretation of legal history, reinforcing psychology by showing the extent to which law had been shaped by the pressure of economic wants. Also the differentiation of society, involved in industrial organization, was no mean factor, when classes came to exist in which claims to a minimum human existence, under the standards of the given civilization, became more pressing than claims to self-assertion. Attention was turned from the nature of law to its purpose, and a functional attitude, a tendency to measure legal rules and doctrines and institutions by the extent to which they further or achieved the ends for which law exists, began to replace the older method of judging law by criteria drawn from itself. In this respect the thought of the present is more like that of the seventeenth and eighteenth centuries than that of the nineteenth century. French writers have described this phenomenon as a " revival of juridical idealism." But in truth the social utilitarianism of today and the natural-law philosophy of the seventeenth and eighteenth centuries have only this in common: Each has its attention fixed upon phenomena of growth ; each seeks to direct and further conscious improvement of the law.

In its earlier form social-utilitarianism, in common with all nineteenth-century philosophies of law, was too absolute. Its teleological theory was to show us what actually and necessarily took place in lawmaking rather than what we were seeking to bring about. Its service to the philosophy of law was in compelling us to give over the ambiguous term " right " and to distinguish between the claims or wants or demands, existing independently of law, the legally recognized or delimited claims or wants or demands, and the legal institutions, which broadly go by the name of legal rights, whereby the claims when recognized and delimited are secured. Also it first made clear how much the task of the lawmaker is one of compromise. . . . Conflicting individual wills were to be reconciled absolutely by a formula which had ultimate and universal authority. When we think of law as existing to secure social interests, so far as they may be secured through an ordering of men and of human relations through the machinery of organized political society, it becomes apparent that we may reach a practicable system of compromises of conflicting human desires here and now, by means of a mental picture of giving effect to as much as we can, without believing that we have a perfect solution for all time and for every place. . . .[85]

. . . Social utilitarianism has stood in need of correction both from psychology and from sociology. It must be recognized that lawmaking and adjudication are not in fact determined precisely by a weighing of interest. In practice the pressure of wants, demands, desires will warp the actual compromises made by the legal system this way or that. In order to maintain the general security we endeavor in every way to minimize this warping. But one needs only to look below the surface of the law anywhere at any time to see it going on, even if covered up by mechanical devices to make the process appear an absolute one and the result a predetermined one. We may not expect that the compromises made and enforced by the legal order will always and infallibly give effect to any picture we may make of the nature or ends of the process of making and enforcing them. Yet there will be less of this subconscious warping if we have a clear picture before us of what we are seeking to do and to what end, and if we build in the image thereof so far as we consciously build and shape the law.

Difficulties arise chiefly in connection with criteria of value. If we say that interests are to be catalogued or inventoried, that they are then to be valued, that those which are found to be of requisite value are to be recognized legally and given effect within limits determined by the valuation, so far as inherent difficulties in effective legal securing of interests will permit, the question arises at once, How shall we do this work of valuing? Philosophers have devoted much ingenuity to the discovery of some method of getting at the intrinsic importance of various interests, so that an absolute formula may be reached in accordance wherewith it may be assured that the weightier interests intrinsically shall prevail. But I am skeptical as to the possibility of an absolute judgment. We are confronted at this point by a fundamental question of social and political philosophy. I do not believe the jurist has to do more than recognize the problem and perceive that it is presented to him as one of securing all social interests so far as he may, of maintaining a balance or harmony among them that is compatible with the securing of all of them. The last century preferred the general security. The present century has shown many signs of preferring the individual moral and social life.[86] I doubt whether such preferences can maintain themselves.

Social utilitarians would say, weigh the several interests in terms of

---

[85] [Sociological jurisprudence relies on " valuations " but these are relative, not absolute in character.]

[86] [This seems to contradict the trend towards " collectivism " in twentieth-century society.]

the end of law. But have we any given to us absolutely? Is the end of law anything less than to do whatever may be achieved thereby to satisfy human desires? Are the limits any other than those imposed by the tools with which we work, whereby we may lose more than we gain, if we attempt to apply them in certain situations? If so, there is always a possibility of improved tools. The Greek philosopher who said that the only possible subjects of lawsuit were " insult, injury, and homicide " was as dogmatic as Herbert Spencer, who conceived of sanitary laws and housing laws in our large cities as quite outside the domain of the legal order. Better legal machinery extends the field of legal effectiveness as better machinery has extended the field of industrial effectiveness. I do not mean that the law should interfere as of course in every human relation and in every situation where someone chances to think a social want may be satisfied thereby. Experience has shown abundantly how futile legal machinery may be in its attempts to secure certain kinds of interests. What I do say is, that if in any field of human conduct or in any human relation the law, with such machinery as it has, may satisfy a social want without a disproportionate sacrifice of other claims, there is no eternal limitation inherent in the nature of things, there are no bounds imposed at creation to stand in the way of its doing so . . .

. . . For the purpose of understanding the law of today I am content with a picture of satisfying as much of the whole body of human wants as we may with the least sacrifice. I am content to think of law as a social institution to satisfy social wants—the claims and demands and expectations involved in the existence of civilized society—by giving effect to as much as we may with the least sacrifice, so far as such wants may be satisfied or such claims given effect by an ordering of human conduct through politically organized society. For present purposes I am content to see in legal history the record of a continually wider recognizing and satisfying of human wants or claims or desires through social control ; a more embracing and more effective securing of social interests; a continually more complete and effective elimination of waste and precluding of friction in human enjoyment of the goods of existence—in short, a continually more efficacious social engineering.[87]   [pp. 42–47]

AMERICAN RESTATEMENT OF TORTS
(2nd edition, 1965)
§ 1. *Interest*

The word " interest " is used throughout the Restatement of this Subject to denote the object of any human desire.

Comment :

a. As defined in this Section, the word " interest " is used to denote anything which is the object of human desire. It carries no implication that the interest is or is not given legal protection, that is, that the realization of the desire is regarded as of sufficient social importance to

---

[87] [Here Pound displays his attachment to the nineteenth-century belief in evolutionary progress; nor is this surprising since the sociological creed is essentially an optimistic one which puts its faith in human perfectibility, especially in social relations.]

lead the law to protect the interest by imposing liability on those who thwart its realization. Thus, emotional tranquillity, for which the great mass of mankind feels a keen desire, is as much an " interest," as " interest " is defined in this Section, as is the interest in the possession of land or the security of one's person. While these are all " interests," they differ in that the former is given relatively little or no protection, while the common law from its very beginning has given the fullest protection to these latter interests.

The object of desire must be distinguished from the thing in respect to which the desire is entertained. Thus, everyone desires that his body shall be free from material harm. The object of this desire is the security of the body and not the body itself. The body, the security of which is desired, is the subject of the desire and not its object.

b. " Interest " as distinguished from " right." In so far as an " interest," as defined in this Section, is protected against any form of invasion, the interest becomes the subject matter of a " right " that either all the world or certain persons or classes of its inhabitants shall refrain from the conduct against which the interest is protected or shall do such things as are required for its protection.

c. " Interest " and " desire." Society may regard a particular desire as improper and may, therefore, by common law or by statute impose criminal responsibility or civil liability upon an effort to satisfy the desire by realizing its object. On the other hand, society may recognize the desire as so far legitimate as to make criminally punishable or civilly liable those who defeat its realization. Between these two extremes there are two other types of desire: (1) those which are recognized as so far legitimate that one who acts for the purpose of satisfying them is protected from criminal responsibility or civil liability which would otherwise attach to his conduct, but which are not recognized as so important as to make the interference with their realization a criminal offense or a civil wrong; (2) those as to which the law stands completely neutral, neither protecting the interest nor recognizing it as creating a privilege to satisfy it without liability, nor on the other hand, imposing criminal responsibility or civil liability upon one who seeks to gratify the desire of which the interest is the object.

d. Legally protected interests. If society recognizes a desire as so far legitimate as to make one who interferes with its realization civilly liable, the interest is given legal protection, generally against all the world, so that everyone is under a duty not to invade the interest by interfering with the realization of the desire by certain forms of conduct. Thus the interest in bodily security is protected against not only intentional invasion but against negligent invasion or invasion by the mischances inseparable from an abnormally dangerous activity. Every man has a right, as against every other, not to have his interest in bodily security invaded in any of these manners. On the other hand, the interest in freedom from mere offensive bodily contacts is protected only against acts done with the intention stated as necessary in that part of the Restatement which deals with liability for such contacts. Therefore, there is a right to freedom from only such contacts as are so caused, and there is no duty other than a duty not to cause offensive touchings by acts done with the intention there described.

e. Rationale. The entire history of the development of tort law shows a continuous tendency to recognize as worthy of legal protection interests which previously were not protected at all. Naturally, this tendency is not uniform in every common law jurisdiction. The interest of a wife in the consortium of her husband was not recognized at common law as worthy of protection even against acts intended to deprive the wife of such consortium.[88] On the other hand, this interest was protected against intentional invasion in Ohio during the latter part of the last century and within a few years thereafter substantially every American jurisdiction joined in so protecting it. In several recent decisions this interest has even been given protection against negligent conduct.

It is altogether unlikely that this tendency to give protection to hitherto unprotected interests and to extend a greater protection to those now infrequently protected has ceased. In the Restatement of Torts the word " interest " as defined in this Section readily lends itself to an analysis of tort liability which indicates the extent to which the law at present protects the realization of the desires of human beings. Because of the probability that the tendency to give legal protection to interests now unprotected and to increase the protection given to those now imperfectly protected will continue, the Restatement of this Subject contains numerous " Caveats." These call attention to the fact that the Institute takes no position as to whether the protection given to a particular interest by the rule stated in the Section to which the Caveat applies should or should not be extended to other analogous situations which have not been the subject of judicial consideration.

f. The word " interest " is used in the various Restatements in two senses: the one the sense here defined, the other denoting the beneficial side of legal relations, both generically to include the aggregate of " rights," " powers," " privileges," and " immunities," and distributively to mean any one of them. There is this fundamental difference between the two usages. As the word " interest " is used in this Restatement, it carries no implication as to whether it is legally recognized or not. When used in the second sense, the word " interest " denotes advantages which are legally recognized as incident to the possession or ownership of property and the like. Indeed " rights," " powers," " privileges," and " immunities " are not only recognized but created by law. For the reasons given in Comment *e*, it is necessary in restating the law of Torts to use the word " interest " in the sense here defined. In the Restatement of other Subjects, it is more convenient to use the word " interest " in the latter of the two senses. Occasionally it is necessary in the Restatement of this Subject to use the word " interest " in the sense of an aggregate of rights, powers, privileges, and immunities or any one of them. When the word is used in this sense, it is preceded by the adjective " legal " or the adjective " proprietary." The adjective " proprietary " is not used unless it is desired to emphasize the fact that the person having the " interest " is a person commonly spoken of as owner of the thing in relation to which the interest exists. . . .

[pp. 2–4]

---

[88] [It is not recognised in England today. See *Best* v. *Samuel Fox Ltd.* [1952] A.C. 716.]

R. POUND

Outlines of Jurisprudence
(5th ed. 1943) [89]

THE PROGRAMME OF THE SOCIOLOGICAL SCHOOL

Sociological jurists insist upon eight points:

(1) Study of the actual social effects of legal institutions, legal precepts and legal doctrines.[90]

(2) Sociological study in preparation for law-making.

(3) Study of the means of making legal precepts effective in action.[91]

(4) Study of juridical method.

(5) A sociological legal history; study of the social background and social effects of legal institutions, legal precepts, and legal doctrines, and of how these effects have been brought about.[92]

(6) Recognition of the importance of individualized application of legal precepts—of reasonable and just solutions of individual cases.

(7) In English-speaking countries, a Ministry of Justice.

(8) That the end of juristic study, toward which the foregoing are but some of the means, is to make effort more effective in achieving the purposes of law.

CHARACTERISTICS OF RECENT LEGAL SCIENCE

(1) The functional attitude.[93]

(2) Study of law in relation to and as part of the whole process of social control.

(3) The movement for preventive justice.

(4) The movement for individualization.

(5) The movement for team work with the other social sciences.

THE PROBLEMS OF JURISPRUDENCE TODAY

(1) The valuing of interests.

(2) The relation of law to administration.

(3) The limits of effective legal action.[94]

---

[89] [The programme in fact dates from 1911.]

[90] [Pound's numerous references to legal writings under each of these points are omitted.]

[91] [The working of the legal aid scheme would be most relevant here. See also the criticism levelled at the inadequacy of the Factories Act; Carson (1970) 33 M.L.R. 396; (1970) 10 Br.J. of Criminology 383: or the county court as a forum for small claims. See *Justice Out of Reach* (1970), and the experimental small claims tribunal set up in Manchester, *The Guardian*, July 6, 1971; McGregor, 121 New L.J. 624, 627. Problem discussed in Ison, 35 M.L.R. 18 (1972).]

[92] [Of which the outstanding contemporary examples are the writings of Willard Hurst. See, particularly, his *Law and Economic Growth* (1964), discussed by Stone, *Social Dimensions*, pp. 52–54.]

[93] [Functionalism is "the doctrine that all institutions and practices in society subserve needs of which the actors in society are not themselves necessarily aware nor capable of describing correctly. These needs may be biological, psychological, or social." (D. MacRae, *Ideology and Society* (1961), p. 34). See, also, the recent trenchant criticism of functionalism in Gouldner, *The Coming Crisis in Western Sociology*.]

[94] [The recent controversy as to the legal prohibition of homosexuality between consenting male adults in private and the control of prostitution, discussed in

(4) The means of informing judges, jurists and law-makers as to the social facts involved in legislation and in the judicial finding, shaping, and application of legal precepts.[95]

(5) Improvement in the form of the law—" restatement," [96] codification. [pp. 16–19]

R. POUND

Contemporary Juristic Theory
(1940)

A Measure of Values

Since Jhering showed us the difference between the legal institution we set up to secure a recognized claim or demand and the claim or demand itself, as it exists apart from the law,[97] we have known the claim or demand by the name of interest. The term has occasioned some confusion because it has easily been confused with an idea of advantage; the more so since Jhering's social utilitarianism made social advantage the criterion of value and treated it as something given, as something we know exactly as we know that a certain claim or demand exists *de facto* and is pressed upon lawmakers and courts for recognition. Everyone has an interest in, that is, makes a claim to the satisfaction of his desires. They are his interests as he sees it, and his view of the matter cannot be ignored by telling him it is not to his advantage to want what he feels he wants and insists he ought to have. Very likely we can't give him what he claims or all that he claims, but it is because we have to consider the conflicting or overlapping claims of others, not because we decide he does not want it. We must, therefore, as I have said, begin by ascertaining what are the claims or demands which press upon lawmakers and judges and administrative agencies for recognition and securing.

In the inventory with which we must begin it is convenient to classify the interests of which the legal order must take account as individual or public [98] or social. All interests are those of individual human beings

the Wolfenden *Report on Homosexuality and Prostitution* (1957), Cmd. 247, would come under this head. For example *cf.* dangerous drugs legislation and prohibitions on racial discrimination. See Duster, *The Legislation of Morality* (1970), pp. 23–28, and see *ante*, 48.]

[95] [Typical examples, it may be suggested, where the law is much in need of such background information, but where it has arrived at solutions in seeming disregard of the problems of modern life, are cases involving abuse of rights; the right to privacy; the restitution of property resulting from unjust enrichment; and rights of property between spouses. On the last-mentioned, see especially, Otto Kahn-Freund's Unger Lecture, *Matrimonial Property, Where Do We Go From Here?* (1971).]

[96] [*Cf.* a typical early Realist attitude which described restatements as " the last long-drawn-out gasp of a dying tradition " and declared that " the more intelligent of our younger law teachers and students are not interested in ' restating ' the dogmas of legal theology," in Felix Cohen, *The Legal Conscience* (1960), p. 59. However, Llewellyn was a prime mover of the *Uniform Commercial Code, post*, 408.] [97] [See *ante*, 354; but *cf.* 344.]

[98] [Stone has rejected the division of *public* interests on the ground that they are really a particular form of social interest. See J. Stone, *Social Dimensions*, pp. 171–175, where the author maintains a point he made in 1946, which he suggests Pound himself has showed some disposition to accept (in *Jurisprudence*, Vol. 3, p. 236).]

asserted by individuals. But some are claims or demands or desires involved in the individual life and asserted in title of that life. Others are claims or demands or desires involved in life in the politically organized society and asserted in title of that society. Others or the same in other aspects are claims or demands or desires involved in social life in civilized society and asserted in title of that life. Every claim does not necessarily go once and for all in one of these categories. The same claim may be asserted and may have to be looked at from different standpoints; it may be asserted in title of more than one aspect of life. Thus my claim to my watch may be asserted as an individual interest of substance when I sue someone, who walks off with it without my consent, either to recover possession of it or to obtain the money value as damages for converting it. But it may be looked at also as a social interest in the security of acquisitions and asserted as such when I persuade the district attorney to prosecute for larceny someone who has stolen it from me.

A mere sketch in broad lines of the scheme of interests which have pressed upon the legal order in the past will suffice for our purposes.[99] Individual interests are interests of personality or interests in the domestic relations or interests of substance. Interests of personality are those involved in the individual physical and spiritual existence; in one's body and life, i.e. security of his physical person and his bodily health, in free exertion of one's will, i.e. freedom from coercion, and from deception as to what one is tricked into doing by false representations, in free choice of location, in one's reputation, in freedom to contract and of entering into relations with others, in free industry, i.e. in freely employing himself or gaining employment in any occupation or activity for which he is or is considered qualified, and in free individual belief and opinion. It is enough to point out in passing that the interests in freedom of contract and in freedom of industry overlap or come into competition with claims of laboring men asserted through trade unions and have raised typically difficult questions for the courts for a generation.

Like difficult questions are raised by individual interests in the domestic relations. It is obvious that husband and wife have each a claim or demand which they make against the whole world that outsiders shall not interfere with the relation. Yet on a weighing of all the interests involved California and many other states have been impelled to abrogate the action for alienation of affections by which that interest had been secured. The interest is still recognized but effective security is now denied. It is obvious too that the relation involves reciprocal claims or demands which each asserts against the other. The claims of the husband to the society of the wife and to her services for the benefit of the household, formerly well secured, are now deprived of all substantial security on a weighing in comparison with the individual interest of the wife in individual free self-assertion. But the claim or demand of the wife for support and maintenance is not only recognized but is secured in a variety of ways which make it one of the best secured interests known to the law. So it is with the interests involved in the relation of parent and child. Formerly

[99] [For a very full discussion of the classification and the content of the various interests which compete in a modern legal system, see especially, R. Pound, *Jurisprudence*, Vol. 3. See also J. Stone, *Social Dimensions of Law and Justice*, pp. 175–176.]

the claims of the parent were given effect by privileges of correction, by control of the child's earnings, and by a wide authority of shaping the training and bringing up of the child in every phase. Everywhere today individual interests of the child and a social interest in dependents have been weighed against the claims of parents, and juvenile courts, courts of domestic relations, and family courts in our large cities have greatly changed the balance of these interests.

By interests of substance we mean the claims or demands asserted by individuals in title of the individual economic existence. Claims with respect to property involve too many questions to make it worth while to do more than mention them in the present connection. It will be more useful for our immediate purpose to look at a group of interests in economically advantageous relations with others. Such relations may be social or domestic or official or contractual. If a man is wrongfully and maliciously expelled from a social club the injury to his social standing in the community may have a serious economic effect upon him. Yet other claims have to be considered and the courts cannot compel the members of the club to associate with him if they persist in refusing to do so. In one case where the courts ordered the expelled member restored to membership the club reinstated him and then dissolved and formed a new club, leaving him out. We have noted already how claims of the husband to the services of the wife in the household are no longer effectively secured either against outside interference with the relation or against the wife's refusal to perform. As to official relations, public interests have to be weighed and the older conception of property in a profitable office has been given up. But the most significant questions have arisen with respect to contractual relations. If A has a contract with B he makes a claim against the whole world that third persons shall not interfere to induce B to break the contract. Yet the third person may assert claims which have to be taken account of in this connection, and some of the hardest questions in labor law have turned on recognition of claims of labor organizations to induce breaking of contracts of employment and what should be regarded as giving a privilege to interfere with such contracts.

As to public interests, it will be enough to instance one type of question where difficult problems of weighing have arisen. How far is the dignity of the political organization of society an interest to be taken into account? When the political organization was struggling with kin organization and religious organization for the primacy in social control, the dignity of the state was a very serious matter. Hence it was settled that the state could not be sued without its consent, that its debts could not be set off against its claims, that it was not estopped by what was done by its officials, and that its claims were not lost by official neglect to assert them nor barred by limitation. Other public interests, e.g. a claim to unimpaired efficiency of the political organization, entered into the reckoning. But the extent to which the rules just mentioned secure no more than the dignity of the state and the weight to be given to that interest today are controversial subjects in public law.

One could devote a whole lecture to a catalogue of social interests. First we may put the general security, including claims to peace and order, the first social interest to obtain legal recognition, the general safety, long recognized under the maxim that the public safety is the highest law, the general health, the security of acquisitions and the security of transactions. The two last afford an excellent example of the overlapping and conflict of recognized interests. From the standpoint of the security of acquisitions a thief or one who wrongfully holds another's property should not be able to transfer to a third person a better title than he has. But from the standpoint of the security of transactions, people generally who have no knowledge or notice of the owner's claim and, acting in good faith, part with value in a business transaction with one in possession of the property ought to be protected. Possession ought to give a power of business transactions as to the thing possessed and apparently owned. This question as to the limits of what is called negotiability has been coming up all over the world and recent legislation has been giving greater effect to the security of transactions in comparison with the security of acquisitions. Closely related, and scarcely less important is the social interest in the security of social institutions, domestic, religious, political, and economic. According as one gives the chief weight to the individual claims of husband and wife or to the social interest in marriage as a social institution, he arrives at different results on the vexed questions of divorce legislation. According as he gives more weight to individual interests in free belief and opinion or to the social interest in the security of political institutions, he will reach different results as to legislation against and prosecutions for sedition. Other important social interests are an interest in the general morals, an interest in the use and conservation of social resources, and an interest in general progress, social, political, economic and cultural. Finally and by no means least there is the social interest in the individual life, the claim or demand asserted in title of social life in civilized society that each individual be secure in his freedom, have secured to him opportunities, political, social and economic, and be able to live at least a reasonably minimum human life in society. Here again all manner of overlappings and conflicts are continually encountered. But perhaps enough has been said to bring out that every item in the catalogue requires to be weighed with many others and that no one can be admitted to its full extent without impairing the scheme as a whole.[1]   [pp. 60–67]

---

[1] [The cases in which courts can be seen to be consciously balancing various interests, are too innumerable to be cited here, but such a case as *Fender* v. *St. John-Mildmay* [1937] A.C. 1, is of particular interest. See also *Webb* v. *Times Publishing Co. Ltd.* [1960] 2 Q.B. 537, where the issue was whether qualified privilege as a defence to libel would attach to the report of a foreign trial. In the course of his judgment, Pearson J. said: " Most important, there is what may be called the balancing operation—balancing the advantage to the public of the reporting of judicial proceedings against the detriment to individuals of being incidentally defamed " (at p. 561; and see pp. 561–563, 568–570). See also the instructive case of *Eastham* v. *Newcastle United* [1964] Ch. 413; and see, recently, *Home Office* v. *Dorset Yacht Co. Ltd.* [1971] A.C.; *Conway* v. *Rimmer* [1968] A.C., particularly Lord Reid at p. 940; *Re Pergamon Press Ltd.* [1971] Ch. 388; *Langbrook Properties* v. *Surrey C.C.* [1970] 1 W.L.R. 161; *Re W (an Infant)* [1971] 2 All E.R. 49; *S* v. *S, W* v. *Official Solicitor* [1970] 3 All E.R. 107.

Perhaps the most deliberate application of the balancing process is seen in the American decisions on the " proper law " of a tort, where the interests of competing jurisdictions must be weighed. See, for example, *Babcock* v. *Jackson* [1963] 2 Lloyd's Rep. 286; *Reich* v. *Purcell* [1967] 432 P. 2d 727; *cf. Chaplin* v. *Boys* [1969] 3 W.L.R. 322; and *Sayers* v. *International Drilling Co. N.V.* [1971] 3 All E.R. 163.

For a discussion of the way in which law reform may proceed on a balance

After interests have been recognized and delimited there still remains how to secure them and the problem of a measure of values is decisive here also. One way is to confer a legal right, that is a capacity of influencing others through invoking the force of politically organized society. My interest of substance is secured in one of its aspects by a legal right of possession of my watch. If someone takes it I can regain possession by an action in the courts. My interest of substance is secured in another of its aspects by a legal right of excluding others from my garden. All others are under a legal duty of keeping out and can be sued in court if they do not and are under a legal liability if in anything they do they cast an unreasonable risk of injury upon it and injury results. I can go into the courts and enforce that liability. Another way is to confer a legal power. A wife has an interest in support by the husband. If he does not provide her with necessaries, she can pledge his credit at the grocer's and he can be held by the grocer as if he had bought them himself. Again recognized interests may be secured legally by privileges. You have a recognized interest in the integrity of your physical person. I have a recognized interest in the exclusive enjoyment of my garden. If a lunatic chases you with a hatchet, the law confers on you a privilege in that emergency of running across my garden to safety. Or finally, recognized interests may be secured by a liberty, by a condition of legal hands off, as for instance what is called the right to pursue a lawful calling. The law leaves your natural liberty in that respect unrestrained. You may choose what calling you like. It will be seen that an adjustment of claims to a measure of values governs here as in every other step in the legal adjustment of relations and ordering of conduct. . . .

. . . What then is the practical measure of values which the law has been using where theories have failed it? Put simply it has been and is to secure as much as possible of the scheme of interests as a whole as may be with the least friction and waste [2]; to secure as much of the whole inventory of interests as may be with the least impairment of the inventory as a whole.[3] No matter what theories of the end of law have prevailed, this is what the legal order has been doing, and as we look back we see has been doing remarkably well.   [pp. 73–76]

of human interest, see the article by F. E. Dowrick, " Lawyers' Values for Law Reform " (1963) 79 L.Q.R. 556. In this article Dowrick studies the recommendations of the Lord Chancellor's Law Reform Committee, and his conclusion is that this Committee has to a remarkable degree been implementing parts of the programme advocated by the sociological school of jurists.]

[2] [Recently, Pound has expressed a preference for stating the task of law not in terms of satisfying human demands, but of " providing as much as we may of the total of man's reasonable expectations in life in civilised society." One of such expectations he regards as " free self-determination " (see (1954) 68 Harv.L.R. 1, at p. 19). But the precise distinction between a demand and an expectation for this purpose is hardly clear.]

[3] [The problem here is to determine by what standard it is to be judged that one interest is to prevail over another. Social utility, for instance, may decree the extinction of criminal lunatics, but our sense of justice or morality may demand their preservation. Aristotle's theory of distributive justice breaks down because it fails to provide a standard of reference (*cf.* H. Kelsen, *What is Justice?*, pp. 127–128); Pound seems to consider that a ready test can be found, by assessing the resultant " friction and waste " involved in different solutions. But these are very intangible and even subjective conceptions as applied to human society. See also De Jouvenel, *post*, 377.]

It is too much to expect that the results achieved by long experience of administering justice according to law can be achieved independently by even the wisest of men acting on single cases with nothing but their personal judgment to guide them. If a court in one of our large cities, with one hundred and fifty thousand cases a year before it, had to work out a balancing or harmonizing or adjustment of interests in each case as something unique for the single case, there could not be judges enough provided to do the work. An architect may use formulas of the strength of materials although he could not work out one of them independently. A judge may use a formula of law, embodying long experience of deciding cases, although he personally has had little or none of the experience formulated and would not know how to reach the formula independently.

While philosophers are debating whether a scheme of values is possible, lawyers and courts have found a workable one which has proved as adequate to its tasks as any practical method in any practical activity. Without putting it in that way they have treated the task of the legal order as an engineering task of achieving practical results with a minimum of friction and waste. We must not forget that law is not the only agency of social control. The household, the church, the school, voluntary organizations such as trade associations, professional associations, social clubs and fraternal organizations, each with their canons of conduct, do a greater or lesser part of the task of social engineering. But the brunt of the task falls on the legal order. The increasing secularization of social control, the disintegration of kin organization, loosening of the discipline of the household, loss of ground by the church and secularizing of education, have added immeasurably to what we expect of the law. It is the more idle to expect its task to be performed by some off-hand system of personal discretion applied to single cases as unique.

There is at any rate an engineering value in what serves to eliminate or minimize friction and waste. It may be that an ethical value may be found in what gives the most effect to human demand with the least sacrifice. At any rate William James thought so. It may be that this adjustment of competing interests with a minimum of waste makes for civilization and has a philosophical value.

I am not offering this idea of social engineering as a cure-all to be taken over by political and juristic theory and used to solve all the difficult problems of the science of law in the world of today.[4] What I have set forth is no more than a description of how the legal order actually functions.　　　　　　　　　　　　　　　　[pp. 79–80]

---

4 [I am tempted here to quote Mr. J. B. Priestley's remarks arising out of a trip across the United States. "People load themselves with anxiety and grief because they will discuss their lives as if they were engineers on a job . . . Nice people talk like this and then worry themselves sick, for here are the 'problems' but where are the neat solutions, settling them once for all ? They forget that human relationships don't belong to engineering, mathematics, chess, which offer problems which can be perfectly solved . . . But this is what happens . . . in a mechanistic society. And when they have turned away in despair from these 'problems,' they begin asking for more and better 'machinery' where in fact there cannot be any machinery at all." J. B. Priestley and Jacquetta Hawkes, *Journey Down a Rainbow* (1955), p. 88.]

B. BARRY

Political Argument

(1965)

. . . The Fourteenth Amendment guarantees citizens of the USA the
'equal protection of the laws'. This is clearly the language of distributive judgments.[5] How then does it apply to segregation? The two
most interesting cases here are *Plessy* v. *Ferguson* (163 US 537) and
Brown v. *Topeka Board of Education* (347 US 483).[6] The first held
that segregated schools are 'equal' provided they have equal facilities
and the second rejected this. The court's opinion in the second case
did not however say that segregation is always and under all circumstances unequal, but that it always is in public education—and the
famous 'sociological' evidence was then brought in.[7] Although the
opinion is apparently limited in this way, the decision in *Brown* v.
Board of Education has subsequently been cited as the authority for
per curiam decisions in fields other than education: declaring, for
example, legally segregated transport facilities unconstitutional.

This is an awkward situation and it arises, I suspect, from the court's
trying to fit its own ideal-regarding principles into the constitutional
mould of distributive want-regarding principles. Thus, in the *Brown*
case, it could be claimed (whether correctly or not) that 'segregation
with the sanction of law . . . has a tendency to retard the educational
and mental development of Negro children and to deprive them of
some of the benefits they would receive in a racially integrated school
system'. Segregation can thus be called 'unequal' because it causes
an actual loss (of educational advancement) to the Negro children. But
what effects analogous to this do segregated buses have? Here, surely,
one could only say that the segregation itself was 'unequal', given the
context of white political supremacy.

Wechsler has questioned this line of thought: he asks whether
making racial segregation a denial in principle of equality to the group
that is not dominant politically does not involve

> an inquiry into the motive of the legislature, which is generally
> foreclosed to the courts? Is it alternatively defensible to make the
> measure of validity of legislation the way it is interpreted by those
> who are affected by it? In the context of a charge that segregation
> *with equal facilities* is a denial of equality, is there not a point in
> *Plessy* in the statement that if 'enforced separation stamps the
> colored race with a badge of inferiority' it is solely because its
> members choose 'to put that construction upon it'? Does enforced
> separation of the sexes discriminate against females merely because
> it may be the females who resent it and it is imposed by judgements
> predominantly male? Is a prohibition of miscegenation a discrimi-
> nation against the colored member of the couple who would like
> to marry?[8]

5 [*Cf. ante*, 344.]
6 [*Ante*, 121.]
7 [This is discussed *post*, 426, note 93.]
8 Wechsler, 'Toward Neutral Principles of Constitutional Law', 73 *Harvard Law
Review* 1, 26–35 (1959). [Now in *Principles, Politics and Fundamental Law*,
p. 3, and see *post*, 800.]

We can point the question further by asking whether segregation would still be unequal in a context of political equality if, in addition, the bulk of each race approved of the segregation? Or, again, what if the state law provided only that there must be facilities open only to Negroes but that there must not be facilities open only to whites? [9] Wechsler himself wishes to make the rejection of segregation turn on the denial by states of 'freedom to associate',

> a denial that impinges in the same way on any groups or races that may be involved. I think, and I hope not without foundation, that the Southern white also pays heavily for segregation, not only in the sense of guilt that he must carry but also in the benefits he is denied.
>
> Does not the problem of miscegenation show most clearly that it is the freedom of association that at the bottom is involved, the only case, I may add, where it is implicit in the situation that association is desired by the only individuals involved.

The difficulty of this is, as he recognizes, that

> if the freedom of association is denied by segregation, integration forces an association upon those for whom it is unpleasant or repugnant.

From the constitutional angle, the problem is then:

> Given a situation where the state must practically choose between denying the association to those individuals who wish it or imposing it on those who would avoid it, is there a basis in neutral principles for holding that the Constitution demands that the claims for association should prevail? I should like to think there is, but I confess I have not yet written the opinion. To write it is for me the challenge of the school-segregation cases.

Let us widen this: is there *any* principle (not just a constitutional principle) which condemns segregation where facilities are genuinely equal? 'Freedom of association', as Wechsler in effect admits, is a broken reed because if we are simply balancing want-satisfactions we have to take into account wants for non-association.[10] Wherever we are not willing to accept the conclusions of a want-regarding appraisal we must turn to ideal-regarding considerations. The reason for preferring the 'freedom' of those who wish to associate with members of other races can then be simply that they are a more desirable type of human being, and their number should be swelled as much as possible.

[pp.124–126]

---

[9] This example is not as fanciful as it may sound. Although there are some bus stations in the South where the writ of the ICC does not run and restaurants are still fully segregated, there are others (especially in larger towns) where the two restaurants are still kept going but the ex-white one is desegregated while the ex-Negro one remains wholly confined to Negroes. Since the Negro has, in these circumstances, a choice of non-segregated and segregated facilities, where is the 'inequality' here?

[10] It does not appear that we can dodge this problem by ruling out the wants for non-association as publicly-oriented wants. The desire not to live, work, eat or travel with a person of another race must surely be counted as a privately-oriented want.

The Definition of 'Interest'

Three Definitions Rejected. . . . While the word 'interest' no doubt has different meanings, the expression 'in so-and-so's interests' is neither equivocal nor vague. The explications of the phrase which have been offered are correspondingly clear, although, I think, incorrect. There seem to be three available. The first makes '*x* is in *A's* interests' equivalent to '*A* wants *x*'.[11] This rules out one's being able to ask '*A* wants *x* but is it in his interests?' Another makes '*x* is in *A's* interests' equivalent to '*x* would be a justifiable claim on the part of *A*'.[12] This rules out asking '*x* is in *A's* interests but would it be justifiable for him to claim it?' Since these two questions are perfectly sensible and one can easily think of situations where the answer would be 'No', these two suggestions as to the meaning of 'in so-and-so's interests' are obviously wrong.[13] The third explication of its meaning equates '*x* is in *A's* interests' with '*x* will give *A* more pleasure than any alternative open to him'.[14] There are two objections to this. One is that a person can be said without self-contradiction to find pleasure in advancing the interests of others—where this means something quite different from 'in pursuing his own interest he unavoidably has to advance those of others'. The other is that a solicitor can be retained to 'look after *A's* interests while he is away' and can make a good job of it without knowing what gives *A* pleasure. Conversely, an arrangement calculated to provide one with enjoyable conversation may well be described as giving pleasure but would hardly be described as being 'in one's interests'. However, these objections are slight compared to those I had to make of the other two explications, and the connection between 'interest' and 'pleasure' is indirect rather than non-existent.

'*Interest*' *Defined.* We can approach a precise characterization of what it is about an action or policy that makes it in someone's interests, in two stages. As a first approximation let us say that an action or policy is in a man's interests if it increases his opportunities to get what he wants.

Wealth and power . . . are potential means to any ultimate ends. . . .
It is primarily these generalized means to any ultimate ends, or

[11] C. B. Hagan, 'The Group in Political Science', in R. Young (ed.), *Approaches to the Study of Politics* (London, 1958).

[12] S. I. Benn, 'Interests in Politics', *Aristotelian Society* (1960); John Plamenatz, 'Interests', *Political Studies*, II (1954). Benn supposes that one asks a farmer 'What are your interests?' (This strikes me as a peculiarly phrased question to start with. 'Would it be in your interests for [say] Britain to enter the Common Market?' is surely a more natural kind of question.) He then says that the farmer would not give a vast sum of money as the answer to the question; but this is not because getting a large sum of money would not be in his interests but because it so obviously is. Indeed, I shall suggest that it is a paradigm of something that is in a person's interests. [*Cf.* Sawer, *post*, 382.]

[13] I add the point about the answer's sometimes being 'No' to cover the objection that one can also perfectly sensibly ask, 'Is a bachelor an unmarried man?' It is not the only way of disposing of the objection, but it seems to me the simplest.

[14] This is a common sense identification, though seldom offered as an explicit definition. Bishop Butler and Hume seem to treat 'interest' and 'pleasure' as interchangeable, as when Butler says, 'interest, one's own happiness, is a manifest obligation' (Preface to *Sermons on Human Nature*, ed. W. R. Matthews (London, 1914)).

generalized immediate ends of rational action, to which Pareto
gives the name ' interests '.[15]

Civil interests I call life, liberty, health and indolence of body; and
the possession of outward things such as money, lands, houses,
furniture and the like.[16]

The necessary qualifications to this first approximation can best be
introduced by thinking of wealth and power as assets. They can be
saved (i.e. held ready for future committal) or committed. If committed,
they can be either invested (i.e. tied up in a way not desired intrinsically
in hopes of having *more* to commit in the future), or transferred to the
use of another to do with as he thinks fit, or consumed. If consumed,
they may be used to satisfy one's own wants or those of someone else.
Under what circumstances would it be rational in a man to wish his
possession of these assets to be less than it might be? If he takes as his
point of departure a reference-group including others beside himself
he will almost certainly conclude that it would be better (from the
point of view of the group) for the disposal of some assets to be in
the hands of other members of the group.[17] He would thus be led to
favour a diminution of his own assets if this were necessary to provide
the amount for others which he thinks they ought to have. But although
one could say that under such circumstances the man *wants* his assets
to be reduced, this does not in the least entail that he thinks *it is in his
interests* for them to be reduced. Rather, it is to be described as a
case where he allows his principles to override his interests. To take
care of this we must say that, in the phrase ' if it increases his opportunities to get what he wants ', wants for *others* to have their share of
assets are not included.

However, even if a man takes as his reference group himself alone,
he may still, if he is rational, want to reduce either his assets or at
least his opportunities for committing them. He will do this not (*ex
hypothesi*) out of any regard for the interests of others but because he
knows he is likely to be irrational in the future and it will therefore
pay him to take precautions in advance. A man who knows he is
carried away by the gambling spirit will avoid going to the races with
more money in his pocket than he can afford to lose; a homicidal
maniac in his lucid moments, a somnambulist in his waking hours, and
an alcoholic or drug-addict when able to think clearly may all welcome
restraint. And if someone isn't himself able to make the rational calculation others can try to think their way into the man's value system, or
impute what seem reasonable values to him (based largely on the value

---

15 T. Parsons, *The Structure of Social Action* (Glencoe, Ill., 1949), p. 262.
16 John Locke, *The Second Treatise of Civil Government and A Letter Concerning
   Toleration*, ed. J. W. Gough (Oxford, 1948), p. 126 [and see *ante*, 102.]
17 It is not *necessary* to arrive at this conclusion by taking other people into consideration. You might, for example, wish for the happiness of others, but believe
   that this was more likely to be achieved if you obtained power or money and
   used it on their behalf. (*Cf.* Philip Wicksteed, *The Common Sense of Political
   Economy* (London, 1910) on ' non-tuism '). There are, however, many reasons
   for wanting others to have resources to use as they think fit; reasons of an
   ideal-regarding kind (independence develops character), of a distributive kind
   (each person has a right to a certain amount or proportion of the assets available) and of an aggregative kind (people want the chance to exercise initiative
   and are likely to know what is best for them).

systems of more rational people) and prevent him from doing things he will regret later or make him do things he will be pleased later to have done.[18]

This applies to any committal of opportunities, whether investment, transfer or consumption—not only to consumption.[19] Here we have a genuine qualification to the assertion which I put forward as a first approximation, that an increase in one's assets is always something which is in one's interests; but its status as something exceptional is often indicated by the use of a special expression ' best interests ', 'real interests ', ' true interests ', etc.   [pp. 174–178]

B. DE JOUVENEL

Sovereignty (1957)

The Notion of Relevance

This notion of relevance is fundamental to all problems of justice. If I have to effect a distribution of something among a series of individuals, I must, if I am to be just, found my classification and proportions on the serial order of these individuals in another plane; this serial order is my standard of reference. And if my final share-out does not conform to the serial order of reference, I show myself unjust. But, in addition, the serial order which I make my standard of reference must be relevant to the final share-out. If, for instance, it is a case of leaving my goods at death and I take as my standard for their share-out the serial order of degrees of relationship with myself, this standard of reference will be thought relevant; but if, as head of a government, I take the serial order of degrees of relationship as my standard for nominating to high office, my choice will be thought scandalous, because the standard of reference is irrelevant for the purpose.

There is injustice whenever the mind is scandalised by false proportions —a thing which happens either when the serial order laid down is not respected or when that serial order is clearly irrelevant. Let us take a concrete case. An industrialist, compelled by a falling off in orders to discharge several members of his staff, dismisses not the most recently engaged but those who are the least useful to him in his business; this

[18] An example is provided by a conversation (published in *The Observer*, March 10, 1963) between Kenneth Harris and a barrister. Defending the division between solicitors and barristers the latter said :

(Barrister): ' As things are, the barrister can concentrate on winning his case; he doesn't have to consider conducting the case in a manner which will satisfy " the gallery ", or his client.'

(Harris): ' But might a client want his case conducted in a way which would increase his chances of losing it? '

(Barrister): ' Indeed he might. He might, for instance, be so splenetic that he would much rather bring out in public his view that the other party is a blackguard and a cad and lose the case than stay quiet and win it. As it is, a barrister's whole training from his earliest years, both in advising and in fighting cases, is to think of nothing whatever but the client's real interest.'

In this passage the barrister assumes that a litigant's ' real interest ' lies in winning the case rather than in giving vent to his feelings; by preventing him from being able to influence the barrister, it is suggested, the system increases rationality.

[19] *Cf.* Lamont, *Principles of Moral Judgment*, pp. 106–107.

choice may seem just to him and unjust to his employees, who consider that he ought to apply the seniority rule, under which he would discharge those who had least service with him—the latest arrivals. There is in this case a clash between two conceptions of the just. Now let us suppose is to assure to each his due. On the other hand, there is a problem contract laying down the rule of seniority; in this case the conduct of the employer is unjust because it does not conform to the rule laid down. Lastly, let us suppose that the employer himself enunciated the rule of seniority, which he claims to apply but in fact violates; in this case there is injustice of a radical and absolute kind.

Analogous instances to the last two cases frequently occur in social life, and cause reactions which are as violent as they are legitimate; they involve, however, no intellectual problem. The intellectual problem is directly posed by whatever has affinity with the first case; for here there is a clash between two conceptions of the just, each of which is solidly founded.

The Problems of Justice [20]

There is no problem of justice when those who have to make a share-out know by reference to what serial order, whether agreed or by common consent relevant, this share-out must be made. The just share-out is that which conforms to the relevant serial order, and the man who aims at applying it conscientiously displays the virtue of justice, since his purpose that the employer acts in the same way but that there is a general of justice when there is doubt or dispute as to the serial order relevant to the occasion. More than that, and this is what makes for trouble, two or more men may be in conflict as to what is just in a case in which each of them displays the virtue of justice, each being determined to apply conscientiously the serial order which he thinks relevant. So we see that the thorny problems are those concerned with the choice of a criterion relevant to the occasion.   [pp. 153–154]

. . . Thus, the amount of resources which it will be thought just to devote to an end will turn on the importance attached to that end. But men are very unevenly taken up with distant ends necessitating collective action; thus a minority of promoters with a lively sense of ends requiring action, who therefore regard resources as first and foremost means of action, is naturally bound to come into conflict with a majority whose nature it is to regard resources as means of existence. The result is that tension underlies every process of share-out; it is the more serious with every rise in importance of the blocks of resources to be divided. That is the reason why it is wise to break up the general process of share-out into as many small, disconnected share-outs as possible. The more comprehensive the process the more serious the tension.[21]   [p. 157]

---

[20] [Cf. the discussion in A. Ross, *On Law and Justice* (1958), Chap. 12 and in Ch. Perelman, *The Idea of Justice and the Problem of Argument* (1963), Chaps. 1 and 2.]

[21] In reality the conflict is threefold: in what proportions should resources be regarded as means of action or as means of existence; how to distribute the means of existence; how to share out the means of action among different ends as to the relative importance of which there is disagreement.

R. POUND

Social Control through Law
(1942)

Jural Postulates

But the practical process of the legal order does not stop at finding by experience—by trial and error and judicial inclusion and exclusion—what will serve to adjust conflicting or overlapping interests. Reason has its part as well as experience. Jurists work out the jural postulates, the presuppositions as to relations and conduct, of civilized society in the time and place, and arrive in this way at authoritative starting points for legal reasoning. Experience is developed by reason on this basis, and reason is tested by experience. Thus we get a second method, namely, valuing with reference to the jural postulates of civilization in the time and place. Newly arising claims are measured by these postulates when they push for recognition. When recognized they are adjusted to other recognized interests by this measure. When they are delimited with reference to other interests the means of securing them are determined by this same measure.

A generation ago I sought to formulate the jural postulates [22] of civilized society in our time and place, for the purposes of systematic exposition of private law (i.e., the law governing individual interests and relations of individuals with their fellows) in five propositions, with certain corollaries. For the present purpose we need not look at the corollaries. What I sought to do was to formulate what was presupposed by the law as to possession, as to property, as to legal transactions and resulting relations, and as to wrongs. As I should put them now they read:

1. In civilized society men must be able to assume that others will commit no intentional aggressions upon them.

2. In civilized society men must be able to assume that they may control for beneficial purposes what they have discovered and appropriated to their own use, what they have created by their own labor, and what they have acquired under the existing social and economic order.

3. In civilized society men must be able to assume that those with whom they deal in the general intercourse of society will act in good faith and hence

(a) will make good reasonable expectations which their promises or other conduct reasonably create;

(b) will carry out their undertakings according to the expectations which the moral sentiment of the community attaches thereto;

(c) will restore specifically or by equivalent what comes to them by mistake or unanticipated or not fully intended situation whereby they receive at another's expense what they could not reasonably have expected to receive under the circumstances.

4. In civilized society men must be able to assume that those who are engaged in some course of conduct will act with due care not to cast an unreasonable risk of injury upon others.

[22] [The latest form of these postulates is found in Pound, *Jurisprudence* Vol. 3, pp. 8–10, quoted in Stone, *Human Law and Human Justice* (1965), p. 280.]

5. In civilized society men must be able to assume that those who maintain things likely to get out of hand or to escape and do damage will restrain them or keep them within their proper bounds. . . . [23]

. . . But it has been becoming more and more evident that the civilization of the time and place presupposes some further propositions which it is by no means easy to formulate, since the conflict of interests involved has by no means been so thoroughly adjusted that one may be reasonably assured of the basis upon which the adjustment logically proceeds.

In general, a postulated claim of the job holder to security in his job is becoming recognized. But exactly in what sort of job holders and in what sorts of jobs a right is to be recognized is far from clear. Moreover, the regime of collective bargaining with organizations commanding a majority of votes in a plant seems to involve a proposition that the minority are not to have a recognized right to their jobs as against the prevailing majority organization. The most that can be said at present is that the employer-employee relation is being removed from the domain of contract and is coming to involve a security of tenure not depending upon agreement.

Another emerging jural postulate appears to be that in the industrial society of today enterprises in which numbers of men are employed will bear the burden of what might be called the human wear and tear involved in their operation. Some such postulate is behind workmen's compensation laws. But in the administration of those laws there is much to suggest a wider proposition. There are also other indications of a third proposition, which may come to include the second, namely, that the risk of misfortune to individuals is to be borne by society as a whole. Some such postulate seems to be behind what has been called the insurance theory of liability and is behind much social security legislation.

[pp. 112–116]

E. A. HOEBEL

The Law of Primitive Man [24]
(1954)

. . . The basic postulates of legal significance for the Ifugao [25] as they may be abstracted from the Ifugao data are as follows:

---

[23] [On these postulates H. J. Laski (*American Democracy* (1949), p. 443), commented: " After his long journeys through the immense literature of legal theory he arrives at a framework of principles which are the obvious outcome of his affection for the country town of Lincoln, Nebraska . . . they are framed, that is to say, for a community of small owners such as the Middle West knew in the epoch first following the Civil War." There is nothing to suggest (adds Laski) that Pound has considered the implications of the giant corporation, labour relations, the effect of a market economy, the dependence of industry on business, and so on (p. 444). Pound's further postulates may seem a very timorous attempt to sound the fundamentals of the new collectivist society.

Sawer has suggested that these should be called *social* rather than jural postulates, since they are much too vague to provide starting points upon which legal reasoning can be based, but rather correspond to widely held assumptions as to social claims which the law should enforce (*Law in Society* (1965), pp. 147–150), *cf.* Hoebel, *post*, 380. Sawer also makes suggestions as to postulates that Pound has omitted: " the long-standing but now weakening postulate of the sexually based monogamous family " (*cf.* Toffler, *Future Shock* (1970), Chap. 11), the right of association, the rule of law, (*idem.*)]

[24] [See also *post*, 584.]

[25] [The Ifugao are described by Hoebel at pp. 100–103. They are a Philippino people who practise wet-rice husbandry in the rugged mountain terrain of Luzon.]

Postulate I.[26] The bilateral kinship group is the primary social and legal unit, consisting of the dead, the living, and the yet unborn.

Corollary 1. An individual's responsibility to his kinship group takes precedence over any self-interest.

Corollary 2. The kinship group is responsible for the acts of its individual members.

Corollary 3. The kinship group shall provide protection for its members and punish outside aggression against them.

Corollary 4. The kinship group shall control all basic capital goods.

Corollary 4'. Individual possession of rice lands and ritual heirlooms is limited to trust administration on behalf of the kin group.

Corollary 5. Marriage imposes strict and limiting reciprocal obligations on husband and wife, but the obligations of each to his own kinship group take priority.

Corollary 5'. Sex rights in marriage are exclusive between husband and wife.

Corollary 6. Because children provide the continuity essential to the perpetuation of the kinship group, the small family exists primarily for its child members.

Postulate II. Men and women are of equal social and economic worth.

Postulate III. Supernatural forces control most activities, and the actions of human beings are either compatible or incompatible with the predilections of the supernaturals.

Corollary 1. Compatibility should be determined for the most important activities by means of divination.

Corollary 2. The supernaturals may be controlled to some extent by magic and influenced to a considerable degree by extensive sacrifice and appeasement.

Corollary 3. The taking of enemy heads is religiously and magically necessary.

Corollary 3'. A record of successful head-hunting gives a man (and his kinship group) power and social prestige.

Postulate IV. Capital goods may be lent at interest.

Corollary 1. Control of wealth gives power and social prestige: property is important.

Corollary 1'. A debt never dies.

Postulate V. Rice is the one *good* food.

Corollary 1. Ownership of rice lands is the most important means for control of wealth.

Corollary 2. Since water is necessary for the growing of good rice, control of water is essential to useful ownership of rice lands.

Postulate VI. Propinquity of residence ameliorates the absoluteness of the primacy of kinship ties and, conversely, outside the kinship group responsibility to others diminishes with distance.

---

[26] [Note Sawer's comment: "The corollaries are given as if implied from the postulates, but clearly it is the corollaries which correspond to actually observed uniformities of behaviour or accorded statements of obligation, and the postulates are afterthoughts, attempts at constructing a general principle under which the more detailed statements can be subsumed." (*Law In Society*, p. 149.) Unlike Pound's statements, of which Sawer is critical (*ante*, note 23), he accepts the Hoebel statements as "statements of social claims . . . which could be expected to affect legal development."]

Corollary 1. People should avoid quarrels and quickly settle disputes with non-related neighbors.

Corollary 2. A person may ordinarily kill a distant stranger on sight.
[pp. 103–105]

G. SAWER

Law in Society

(1965)

. . . All Pound's ' individual ' claims are also social. Thus the private landlord will fight for his common-law right to levy distress for rent, without first applying to a court, on behalf of himself and all such landlords against his tenant and all such tenants. Is there a wider ' interest ' which can be distinguished from these class claims? The landlord may argue that unless he and all landlords have a right to distrain, they will not be prepared to put capital into building and buying houses for purposes of rental, so that the provision of housing will fall entirely on public housing authorities, if there are any; otherwise individuals lacking the money to buy houses will be left without shelter. This, then, appears to assert a general interest in the provision of shelter which is best served by being kind to landlords. Or the matter may be expressed even more generally by mentioning the advantages of a private enterprise economy. On the other hand, the tenant will argue that landlords with right to distraint may make an unreasonable use of the power, which many tenants will be too poor to question or resist, that such a power tends to provoke resistance and cause social insecurity, and that landlords can be adequately protected by ability to obtain judgment in a court and issue execution. This points to an interest in social order, served by being kind to tenants, with perhaps more general remarks about the advantages of private enterprise placed under a degree of ' welfare state ' control. The landlord can mention that one day his tenant may become a landlord, and the tenant can retort that landlords are sometimes reduced to becoming tenants. Yet there seems artificiality in asserting that behind the landlord interest and the tenant interest is a general interest which both share in the provision of shelter, and still more if the ' interest ' asserted is an interest in social order or in a general social policy such as private enterprise or collectivism. The artificiality is greatest in the case of ' social interests ' so vague as ' general security ', ' general morals ', and ' general progress '. Here we move from the sphere of actual claims actually made to that of speculations in the field of social philosophy; statements of the consequences for social development of having a legal system at all, or social ideals which all good men will acknowledge but which are likely to figure in the reasoning and speech of legislators and judges mainly as literary ornament. ' Conservation of social resources ' may be an aim of government policy, but as a social interest it has no higher standing than ' maximization of use of social resources ', which Pound does not include, and both so far as specific are reducible to claims of groups.

The ' interests ' concept has been discussed extensively by political scientists and social philosophers, since politics has long been considered as the organized pursuit and defence of interests, and the State as a means of reconciling the conflict of such interests and in doing so achieving a unified or ' highest ' interest of all. These discussions are summarized and criticized and the literature cited in S. L. Benn's paper, ' " Interests " in Politics ';[27] the distinctions made by these writers are relevant to legal sociology, though the legal case also brings out special difficulties. First, the behaviour associated with an interest needs to be distinguished from the discourse concerning it. Next, in the discourse concerning it there is a slide from description of the behaviour to arguments in which evaluation and ' ought ' statements become increasingly important. Next, it is necessary to distinguish two ways in which the interest may be regarded, namely the ' internal ' and the ' external ' view. The internal view is that of the persons asserting the interest, the claimants; how they actually see their own interest. The external view is that of other people—especially, in legal contexts, a legislator or court—who have examined the position. The external observer may think that the claimants mistake their interest or misdescribe it or fail to express it in the argumentative setting which is most advantageous. The claimants, on the other hand, may think they are better informed about their own interest and about the best way of relating it to the social system. Or the external and internal sides may learn from each other. Pound's ' social interests ' are most likely to be an exterior and normative account of a situation, and the felt ' artificiality ' in such statements arises because such a way of putting the matter corresponds so little to the motives and purposes of particular, identifiable claimants. In the landlord and tenant case, the landlord wants to get his overdue rent by the cheapest and most expeditious method, while the tenant wants to put him to as much trouble as possible. A powerful determining factor in the actual development of the law on distraint has been the contrast between the general common-law position of creditors, who have to obtain a court judgment before they can issue execution, and the position of landlords at common law; in that legal setting, the landlord position is seen as an anomalous historical survival, a special privilege, something more appropriate to an age when self-help was more common. But to try to translate these propositions into a social interest in legal consistency falsifies the actual course of the argument. Tenants would not themselves make too much of the consistency issue, since they want in various ways to establish a better position than that of most ' hirers ', for example by restricting the landlord's power to evict. As far as they are concerned, then, consistency is not an interest; it is an *argument* which they will use for what it is worth and abandon when it becomes inconvenient. This does not mean, however, that the argument as to consistency, equal protection of laws, due process, and so on, is unimportant nor that it will fail to be felt and understood as a main issue by someone. The point is that the ' someone ' is likely to be an official of the State whose social task it is to take account of such ' interests '. Social interests are in a sense the interests of everyone, but they are also the interests of no one in particular, and may be better stated not as interests but as values served by social leaders.

The interest theorists have said that interests must be stated at the same level before they can fairly be compared; otherwise the problem

27 *Aristotelian Society Proceedings*, vol. lx (1959–60), pp. 123–40. [For another example, see Barry, *ante*, 375.]

of deciding between them will be begged by the way in which they
are described. Such reduction or elevation to a common level is always
theoretically possible, though the 'highest' level interests can turn out
to be identical, so that the conflict is only at a 'lower' level. The
assumption made in this view about levels is that an interest asserted in
Poundian terms as social must prevail over one which is stated as
public, and both social and public must prevail over an interest stated
as individual. But in practice interests at various levels of statement are
commonly pitted against each other and there is no *a priori* reason why
social interests should prevail over the others, nor public over private,
either in fact or as a matter of evaluation. On the contrary, one of the
problems of social organization is to obtain a fair hearing for the more
general social interests as against the more specific interests of a
definable group. The political scientists see this as the problem of the
pressure group whose organization and power enable it to overcome
the more diffuse, less well organized claims of 'the public'. But there
is a similar difficulty in judicial administration, arising not from power
and organization but from the combination of logical and emotional
impact on judicial minds which some types of claim may make as
compared with others. Generally speaking, the most effective interest
from the point of view of impact is neither the claim peculiar to an
individual or small group, nor the very diffuse social interest, but an
intermediate range of group interests or aggregated individual interests
which concern large numbers. The interests of the very few are easily
assumed (not always justifiably) to be too selfish for legal protection;
the very general social interest is too diffuse for its precise significance
to be grasped in a particular context, and there is usually a good deal
of room for argument as to the course which will best secure that
interest. In between come the interests which can be illustrated in
behavioural terms, intuitively apprehended and satisfactorily managed.[28]

[pp. 156–160]

---

[28] [Unlike Jhering, who assumed that social and private interests should always be
directly compared, Pound insists that a fair balancing of interests can only be
achieved by examining a conflict of interests on the same plane or level, so that,
for example, interests as they affect the individual landlord should be compared
with those which affect the individual tenant, while the social interests of landlords, so far as they affect society generally, should be compared with the social
interests of tenants as these are relevant to the welfare of the community as a
whole. Even, however, if these distinctions are practicable, and are carefully
maintained, it seems unlikely that the court today would decide an issue between
litigants, which involves a new development of the law, purely on the plane of
a conflict of private interests, to the disregard of the social aspects of those
interests. So, in *Stringer* v. *Minister of Housing* [1971] 1 All E.R. 65, the
question arose whether the interests of science in the amenities of the Jodrell
Bank telescope should prevail over the interest in erecting housing which might
interfere with the efficient running of the telescope. Cooke J. refused to restrict
himself to balancing two private interests and said he " should feel considerable
hesitation in holding that the operation of the telescope was not a public, as
opposed to a private, interest ". (p. 77–78) See also the note by Howells on
Beckett v. *Kingston Bros.* in (1970) 33 M.L.R. 562 (*Cf.* now *Tesco* v. *Nattrass*
[1971] 2 All E.R. 127) and the note by Dworkin in (1970) 33 M.L.R. 552 (on
Woollerton and Wilson v. *Richard Costain Ltd.* [1970] 1 All E.R. 483).
   The difficulty in differentiating public and private interests is well-illustrated
by the restraint of trade cases. The court, in looking to the interest of the parties
has regard to the interest of the public, since it is consideration of the public
interests involved which determine what is an interest of the private party which
he has a right to have protected. For instance, it is for the reason that it is

HARRY C. BREDEMEIER
Law as an Integrative Mechanism [29]
(1962)

The function of the law is the orderly resolution of conflicts. As this implies, 'the law' (the clearest model of which I shall take to be the court system) is brought into operation after there has been a conflict. Someone claims that his interests have been violated by someone else.[30] The court's task is to render a decision that will prevent the conflict—and all potential conflicts like it—from disrupting productive cooperation. In order to do this, the court needs three things—or, in the language of Parsons and his colleagues, the court is dependent upon three kinds of ' inputs '.

In the first place, the court needs an analysis of cause-and-effect relationships. It needs a way of ascertaining both the *past* relationship between the alleged act of the defendant and the alleged injury of the plaintiff, and the probable *future* relationship between the decision and the activities of defendant and plaintiff (and all persons similarly situated). I suggest that this input comes from the adaptive system, in return for an immediate output of ' organic ' as distinguished from ' mechanical ' solidarity.

In the second place, as is implied by the phrase ' productive coopera- tion ', the court needs a conception of what the division of labor is *for*; what the goals of the system are, what state of affairs is to be created or maintained by the exercise of power. In other words, it needs standards by which to *evaluate* the conflicting claims and the anticipated effects of a decision on the role structure. I suggest that this is the primary input from the goal-pursuance or political system, in exchange for which the court's primary output is ' interpretation ' of the meaning in a particular case of the abstract language of legislation, or the even more abstract language of the society's ' ideals '.

Finally, in order to perform its function the court needs a willingness on the part of potential litigants to *use* the court as a conflict-resolving mechanism. This motivation to accept the court and abide by its decisions is an input from the pattern-maintenance or socialization system, and the court's' immediate return output is what is termed ' justice '. [pp. 74–75]

The Law and Adaptive Processes

. . . When the courts receive a signal, in the shape of a lawsuit, that there has been a clash of interests, the first requirement is ' to understand

regarded as potentially prejudicial to the public interest that a private individual is not considered to be entitled to protection against competition *per se*. Again, in considering the extent to which an employer may protect himself against the misuse of confidential information by his former servant, the law has regard to the effect that particular agreements may have upon the wider public interest. (See *Petrofina Ltd.* v. *Martin* [1966] Ch. 146, *per* Diplock L.J. at pp. 182–183).]

[29] [From W. M. Evan, *Law and Sociology* (1962), p. 73.]

[30] Whether it is a district attorney claiming that the " public interest " he " represents " has been violated by an alleged " criminal," or a citizen claiming (for example) that his interest in esteem has been violated by a libel or slander, the court's procedure is essentially the same.

it '. This means two things. First, it means discovering the factual connexion between the alleged harm and the event alleged to have caused
it. Second, it means discovering the functional context of the action of
plaintiff and defendant—that is to say, (a) the roles they are performing,
(b) the functional significance for the system of those roles, and (c) the
necessity (for efficient performance) of playing the roles in the manner
in which the litigants had in fact been playing them.

These 'discoveries' are made on the basis of certain cognitive
generalizations, beliefs, and theories concerning cause-and-effect relationships; and they are made with the aid of techniques for ascertaining
'truth.' The elaborate equipment and techniques of crime-detection
laboratories; the statistics contained in a 'Brandeis-type'[31] brief; the
mortality tables used in calculating potential earning power in order to
assess the 'damages' of a death; psychiatric examinations; public
opinion polls showing the amount of confusion existing between trade-
marks or brand-names—all those are examples of inputs to the legal
system from the adaptive system of the society.

Not only technique and factual knowledge are involved in this input,
but also cognitive theories regarding the necessity of certain kinds of
behavior if certain functions are to be efficiently performed. An important example of such an input is the use by the courts of classical
economic theory.

The very fact that Justice Holmes found it necessary to admonish his
colleagues on the Supreme Court that the Fourteenth Amendment 'does
not enact Mr. Herbert Spencer's social statics'[32] is evidence that in
fact the Fourteenth Amendment had, for all practical purposes, done
precisely that. In interpreting concepts such as 'property' and 'due
process' the Court for a very long time based its reasoning about
economic conflicts of interest on a specific theory of what was necessary
to achieve productive co-ordination of economic activities. . . .

The court utilizes these inputs of knowledge (together with the other
inputs that will be discussed below) to make a decision. The decision,
which will of course be binding on all persons in the same class or
category as the particular litigants at bar, is an output to the adaptive
system of the society. It is an output of *organization* or structure. . . .

[pp. 75–77]

The Law and the Polity

In modern democratic societies the prototype of the sovereign may be
taken to be the legislature. Legislative determination of policy—the actual
uses to which power is put—is one of the primary sources of the law's
conception of goals, or standards for evaluating the 'efficiency' of a
given or anticipated role structure.

The legislature's primary input into the legal system is, in other
words, a description of the ideal state of affairs for which social resources
are to be mobilized through the exercise of power. The immediate
corresponding output of the legal system is the *application* of general
policy statements to the specific conflict at hand. This, of course, means
that the courts can by no means be passive or mechanical 'implementers'
of the legislative policy; the statute must be interpreted, and its interpretation is a creative act, giving real effect to the abstract language of the

---

31 [On which see *post*, 424.]
32 *Lochner* v. *New York*, 198 U.S. 45, at p. 75 (1905) [and *post*, 433.]

legislature. It is an indispensable adjunct to the legislative exercise of power. In return for the output of interpretation, the legal system receives from the polity a secondary input, the sanction of *enforcement*. Judicial decisions become binding on the litigants through the power of the state; and—also to be included in the concept of enforcement— it is by the legislature that the courts are *empowered* to resolve disputes and are given the facilities for doing so: courthouses, judgeships, salaries, and so on.

These interchanges, of course, do not occur in any automatic or inevitable way. The transactions between the legal system and the polity may break down. Courts may 'interpret' the life out of legislative policies; or they may even ignore a statute. In turn, the polity may refuse to enforce legal decisions, and may fail to give any clear indication of public policy as a guide to judicial action. These interchanges are often precariously balanced, just as are the interchanges between the output of consumers' goods by business firms and the spending of money by households. The point is that when the exchanges are not completed smoothly, some re-adjustment is likely to occur, in the first place; and in the second place there will be repercussions in other subsystems of the society.

The exchange of policy directives for interpretation of such policies is especially susceptible to disruption because the legislature, subject to the influence of whimsical shifts in public opinion and to the private demands of various interest groups, often enacts contradictory policies. The court in such cases must choose between different policies of the state. . . .

That the courts must choose between conflicting policies means they have a secondary kind of output to make the polity in exchange for the secondary input of enforcement. In a sense, the court becomes a legitimator of legislative decisions; and this adds to the polity's dependence on a successful completion of the exchange.

This adds significance to the sociological problem of locating extra-legislative sources of the court's own goal conceptions. The social origins of judges and law professors probably point to one such source; another is the socialization received by lawmen in the traditions of the law, both formally in the law schools and informally in interaction with peers and clients. Further, the mechanisms by which lawmen maintain some degree of insulation from the fluctuating pressures to which legislators are exposed, and the process of reinforcement of an independent legal self-image, are problems to which sociologists could profitably direct their attention. . . . [pp. 79–81]

The Law and Pattern Maintenance

Presupposed by all that I have said so far, a third condition is necessary if the legal system is to contribute to integration through the resolution of conflicts. This is the obvious fact that conflicts must be brought to the courts' attention. People must be motivated to turn to the law for protection of their interests, and this implies that they must feel that the law will in fact give them justice. It is thus in the offer of 'justice' that the legal system makes its major output, in exchange for the input of motivations to accept the court as a problem-solving structure.

To do the proverbial rushing in, I want to define 'justice' for present purposes simply as the subjective feeling that one has got what's

coming to him, that one has received his 'due.' This amounts to saying
that internalized expectations have been met.

It is perhaps in connexion with these interchanges between the legal
system and the pattern-maintenance system that there are the most
familiar breakdowns. On the side of the pattern-maintenance system, one
reason for the breakdown, it is sometimes suggested, is that no one
really wants what the courts offer. As political boss Martin Lomassey
put it to Lincoln Steffens, in a remark revitalized in Merton's discussion
of the political machine, what people often want is simply *help*—' Help,
you understand; none of your law and justice, but help.' [33]

This dislike of justice may be put in other terms. It is a feeling that
the court's conceptions of legitimate expectations are very different from
one's own. And this is likely to be true, partly because of differences
between the reference groups of judges and clients, and partly because
of the nature of one important mechanism relied upon by the court
to insure conformity to institutionalized expectations.

The mechanism I refer to is the doctrine of *stare decisis.* . . .
[pp. 82–83]

A related aspect of *stare decisis* also contributes to the law's lack of
receptivity to new claims. This is the persistence, to some extent, of the
doctrine that only those *interests* will be recognized that were previously
recognized. That is to say, new needs for which court protection is
sought may be dismissed by the court with the deadly sentence, 'Plaintiff
has failed to state a cause of action,' which means that he has failed
to demonstrate that any court in the past has even been willing to
listen to evidence on such a violation of an expectation.

The central condition responsible for such dismissal seems to be that
the court's *manifest* function is to apply an already-existing law; the
latent function of resolving disputes *efficiently* is seldom recognized.

Two additional mechanisms by which the court's output of justice
may be kept in fairly close balance with community sentiments should,
however, be noted. One is the jury system. Although nominally only a
'trier of facts' when facts are in dispute, the jury probably tries a good
many things besides facts behind its closed doors. Without overt changes
in the legal doctrines, then, justice—according to the community's views
—may nonetheless be served, although, to be sure, in a mysterious and
somewhat 'chancy' way.

A second such mechanism is the system of communication internal
to the legal system itself. I include in this both law schools and the
extensive commentaries and criticism of judicial opinions in law journals.
It is commonly supposed, for example, that it was an academic article
by Brandeis and Warren in the *Harvard Law Review* that was responsible
for judicial recognition of a new tort, invasion of privacy.[34] To the
unknown degree to which the journals are considered by the bench and
bar, the legal system may be kept in fairly close touch with prevailing
community sentiments—depending also, of course, on the degree to
which academic jurists are themselves in touch with them.

The fact remains, however, that 'the law' is for many people something to be avoided if at all possible. There is not a very good market
for the law's output of justice; and—the other side of the same coin—

---

[33] R. K. Merton, *Social Theory and Social Structure* (1949), p. 74.
[34] 4 Harvard L.R. 193–220.

the law is not widely regarded as the place to take one's conflicts, except as a last resort.

A deeper reason for this than any I have so far considered may be related to the fact that, almost by definition, 50 per cent. of the people involved in litigation must have their expectations violated. Someone has to lose.

While the adversary system may work tolerably well as a transmission belt for inputs of facts and policy considerations, it can hardly work very well in persuading a litigant that his cause is being considered on its merits and with respect, except possibly by his own lawyer, who by definition is not in control of the situation.

Furthermore, there are two related characteristics of the law that contribute to making its output of ' justice ' unpalatable. One is the fact that the legal system tends to have written into it the assumption that in any dispute one side is right and the other side is wrong. The adversary system is built on this assumption and helps to reinforce it; and the court is ordinarily empowered only to decide a winner and a loser—not to find a way to help the loser adjust to his loss, or to avoid in the future the action that led to the loss, or to alter the conditions that led to the loser's behaving as he did.

The second difficulty is related to this. An assumption implicit in the operation of the law is that once rights and obligations have been authoritatively stated, individuals have only one mode of adaptation available to them: acceptance. The assumption, in other words, is that *learning* is the only response to a deprivation.

In fact, of course, there is good reason to believe that learning—that is, a reorganization of the individual's personality system so as smoothly to adapt to the new reality—is not even a very likely response, except under special conditions, such as those summarized by Leonard Cottrell [35] or those suggested by Parsons.[36]

The legal system does not include the machinery for insuring the amount of permissiveness, support, denial of reciprocity, and conditional reward required to make the court experience a learning experience. To the contrary, the obscure and complicated legal procedures remain a baffling barrier to the litigant's understanding of what happened to him, except to the degree to which his attorney informally plays the role of therapist. In consequence, the major impact may be frustration, with little to prevent the frustration from leaving a permanent residue of hostility.

It is interesting in this connexion, moreover, that a device that under certain conditions *could* help the losing litigant to adjust to his loss—and even, conceivably, to change his expectations and behavior—does not in fact function toward that end, and so far as I can discern is not even intended to do so. I refer to the written opinion delivered by appellate courts, setting forth the reason for the decision. An explanation of the decision addressed to the litigants might contribute to consensus in the long run; but the legal tradition seems to be rather to address the explanation to other lawyers—who, again, may or may not attempt to translate it for their clients in a way that might gain their acceptance of it. . . .   [pp. 84–87]

[35] The Adjustment of the Individual to his Age and Sex Roles in eds. Newcomb and Harth, *Readings In Social Psychology*, pp. 370–373.
[36] *The Social System* (1951), Chap. 7.

It is the central suggestion of this paper that a frame of reference such as that essayed here might not only help to overcome the barriers of sociolegal stereotypes, but also point the way to areas of sociolegal cooperation that would enrich both sociology and the administration of justice.   [p. 90]

P. SELZNICK

The Sociology of Law
(1959) [37]

. . . The sociology of law may be regarded as an attempt to marshal what we know about the natural elements of social life and to bring that knowledge to bear on a consciously sustained enterprise, governed by special objectives and ideals. Thus understood, legal sociology follows a pattern similar to that of industrial sociology, political sociology, and educational sociology. With some prophetic license, we can detect in all these efforts three basic stages of development.

The primitive, or missionary, stage is that of communicating a per-spective, bringing to a hitherto isolated area an appreciation of basic and quite general sociological truths, such as the significance of group mem-bership for individual behavior. This early phase characteristically includes much theoretical discussion and analysis of everyday experience. There may also be some organized research, but what there is is mostly demonstrative in function, more valuable for its educational effect than for anything else. In law, such demonstrative research has not been particularly important, in part because of the role played by fact-guided judicial decisions and by the writings of men with rich experience in legal affairs. Although most of the theoretical work in this field has been done by European social scientists, the task of communicating an elementary, not-very-sophisticated sociological perspective has been accomplished largely by American legal scholars who were influenced by European thought, and by some of the more articulate appellate judges.

The second stage belongs to the sociological craftsman. It is a muscle-flexing period marked by intellectual self-confidence, a zeal for detail, and an earnest desire to be of service. At this stage the sociologist seeks more than the communication of a general perspective. He wants to explore the area in depth, to help to solve its problems, and to bring to bear quite specific sociological techniques and ideas. There are a number of signs that the sociology of law is about to enter this stage of develop-ment.

The third stage, as I envision it, is one of true intellectual autonomy and maturity. This stage is entered when the sociologist goes beyond (without repudiating) the role of technician or engineer and addresses himself to the larger objectives and guiding principles of the particular human enterprise he has elected to study. He reasserts the moral impulse that marked the first stage of sociological interest and influence. But the third stage is of a higher, more sophisticated level than the first because the second stage has provided a sounder basis for critical analysis. . . .

In a broad sense, there is no real problem of articulating sociological

[37] From Chap. 4, pp. 115–127, of *Sociology Today*, edited by Robert K. Merton, Leonard Broom, and Leonard S. Cottrell, Jr.

inquiry to the needs of legal development. *Sociology can contribute
most to law by tending its own garden.* Truly sound knowledge regarding basic human relations and institutions will inevitably find its way into
legal doctrine. Truths so well founded that no reasonable, educated
man can deny them need no special means of communication beyond the
ordinary channels of education. It is well to remember that, although
the law is abstract, its decision-making institutions deal with a concrete
and practical world. Recognition of basic truths about that world
cannot be long denied. Moreover, the legal order is becoming increasingly broad in scope, touching more and more elements of society.
This means that sociological research addressed to the important
characteristics of society, and to the basic changes in it, will automatically
have legal relevance. This relevance, of course, goes beyond bare
description. It includes making the law sensitive to the values that are
at stake as new circumstances alter our institutions.

If this be true, if sociologists have only to mind their own business,
why a special concern for sociology of law? Perhaps the most obvious
answer is that two-way communication can bring to legal analysis more
rapid and direct benefits from sociological research. But as soon as this
communication begins, we see that the real problem and the real opportunity stem from the incomplete and tentative character of our knowledge.
There are very few incontrovertible sociological truths. Most of what we
know is tentative, not only in the sense that all scientific conclusions are
tentative, but also in the sense that our research in many vital areas is
still primitive and pioneering. Yet legal scholars are interested in this
work, and properly so, because the very least it does is to challenge
older images of man and society and offer new guides for the assessment
of experience. This kind of knowledge, however, cannot be absorbed
directly; it must be tested within the specific areas of legal interest; it
must withstand the common-sense critiques of the practical lawyer. Such
communication cannot take place effectively unless sociological inquiry
is made directly relevant to legal problems.

But the sociology of law has an additional, and more profound,
rationale than the communication of specific sociological knowledge
regarding nonlegal phenomena. The law is itself a social phenomenon,
an important agency of social control. The study of the law for
itself, as a part of the natural order, is very much the sociologist's
business. From this standpoint the sociology of law can contribute both
to the science of society itself and to the self-knowledge of legal practitioners. Since self-knowledge and moral development are so intimately
related, it is plain that here lies sociology's most important special
contribution. This is the distinctive office of the third, most advanced
stage of legal sociology.

Stage II and its Problems

In the second stage of development of legal sociology, as I have
suggested, the main effort is to apply sociological analysis to particular
problems of legal doctrine and legal institutions.

The present outcropping of interest in law on the part of sociologists
has been stimulated by a number of related developments. Probably
most important is the rising self-confidence among sociologists—
confidence in the ability of the field to cast new light on particular
areas and to help in the solution of practical problems. Another

stimulus has been the development and refinement of research methods, involving not merely statistical sophistication but the identification of characteristic social factors of proven researchability. This means that at least one brand of empiricism has been available for active service, ready to form the basis of large and quickly organized research operations.

Interest in law has also been encouraged by new work in the sociology of administration. These studies have restated some older problems regarding the interplay of formal systems of social control and the spontaneous behaviour of men and groups. Some of us who have worked in that field have discovered that in studying formal organizations we were also studying legal systems. It is clear that what we were learning about the functions of formal rules, the interdependence of authority and consent, and similar matters was not really new from the larger perspective of legal sociology. It is also painfully evident that some sociologists are prone to repeat mistakes of the past by overemphasizing the informal and spontaneous and deprecating the significance and the peculiar problems of a legal order.

Finally, recent years have seen a fresh approach to the relation between custom and law; today we regard the law as a more creative agency than earlier sociologists believed it to be. This new perspective has been largely stimulated and sustained by recent history in the field of race relations, especially by the Supreme Court's extension of the constitutional concept of equal protection of the laws.[38]

These developments promise a new and fruitful period of research and analysis. But we should take a close look at the characteristic avenues by which sociologists will enter the field. Perhaps we should speak of these as temptations, the better to mark out the probable risks and pitfalls.

An obvious temptation (although also an opportunity) is to offer research technique as the peculiar contribution of the sociologist. By technique, of course, I mean the apparatus of survey and experimental research, not the more common-sense historical and reportorial data-gathering that has been the main standby of sociological classics. It seems obvious to me that quantitative research can and must play an important role in legal sociology. Any continuing program of study in that field could easily keep a staff of survey technicians busy on fruitful projects. The subjective meaning of specific rules, such as the lawyer-client privilege, for clients as well as members of the bar; the social composition of the bench and of juror panels; the self-images of lawyers, their career lines and other matters affecting professional integrity; the quasi-legal claims and expectations of various classes of citizens—these and a host of other specific studies depend for their execution on sophisticated survey technique.

But a serious risk is entailed and should not be overlooked. If we emphasize technique, we inevitably design projects that are congenial to the skills at hand. To be sure, such projects often have a market value in that they promise information that seems to be of immediate practical use to a client. Yet we know from experience that technique-stimulated research is seldom effectively guided by significant theoretical concerns or even by matters of the greatest long-run importance to the client

[38] [For a discussion of this see *ante*, 121.]

himself. Attempts to apply small-group theory to the study of juries may seem an exception, but in fact they are not. The study of small groups, beyond certain first principles, is one of the more weakly developed areas in sociology; if this work is pushed to the forefront in legal sociology, it will be less for the sound knowledge it can offer than for the opportunity it presents to apply sophisticated research technique.

Another approach involves a similar risk, although it also begins from a posture of strength. Here one emphasizes the fund of sociological ideas, rather than the availability of research methods. The plan is to draw upon this sociological armory in order to illuminate particular problems in the legal field, whether of doctrine or of institutional functioning. . . . The effect upon legal doctrines and institutions of a number of sociological phenomena, including socialization, value systems, stratification, collective behavior, and demographic trends, would be studied. But the main objective of this pedagogical device is to impress upon the student the force of sociological concepts and principles; it is not offered as a substitute for the autonomous, research-oriented organization of a field of inquiry. We cannot indiscriminately apply all our sociological ideas to legal studies; we must have a theoretical ground for supposing that some notions will be more important than others.

An indifferent appreciation of the entire sociological armory encourages intellectually low-level research, for two reasons. On the one hand, there is a natural tendency to choose those sociological concepts or factors that are easiest to handle; since it is all sociology anyway, if no theoretical ground exists for choosing the more difficult problems this solution will seem quite respectable. Yet the net result may be fact-gathering of a quite trivial nature. On the other hand, this same indifference may result in choosing problems of immediate interest to a client, whether or not the studies entail any advance in our general knowledge.

The alternative to these approaches is more painful. It involves a double intellectual commitment, to problems of greatest theoretical concern in sociology and to problems that are truly important to the legal order itself. In sociology, the roughly defined area we call " social organization " remains a challenging frontier. In this field we attempt to identify the essential characteristics of different types of society, to locate the key human relationships that give a social order its distinctive qualities, to discover how major groups interact and what stable arrangements result. Most of the truly great names in sociology have been identified with broad studies of this sort. At the same time, these problems are the hardest to handle and are most frequently shunned.

From the legal side, the important problems also suggest an emphasis on studies of social organization. For example, what are the limits of law as an instrument of social control? What are the capabilities of courts, as we know them and as they could be? How much does society require of these agencies? How much can legitimately be demanded? Roscoe Pound stated this problem more than a generation ago, and offered some answers.[39] But research has been wanting. This

---

[39] Roscoe Pound, " The Limits of Effective Legal Action," Int. J. Ethics, 27 (1917), 150–67.

is the kind of problem that can be approached in many ways, but it surely demands both a broad theoretical perspective and an emphasis on societal needs and institutional potentialities. Thus an assessment of demands upon the legal system depends on what is going on within major groups and in the relations among them. Whether modern economic institutions can autonomously safeguard their members against arbitrary treatment and undue loss of liberty depends on the nature of participation and the dynamics of internal control. The sociological answer to this question inevitably affects the role of the courts. The potential achievements and vulnerabilities of both legal and nonlegal institutions are a proper and even urgent subject for sociological inquiry. . . .

Stage III and its Problems

As we approach a more advanced stage of development, all the classic problems of legal philosophy emerge again. For at this point we should be ready to explore the meaning of legality itself,[40] to assess its moral authority, and to clarify the role of social science in creating a society based on justice.

In a consideration of these matters, the central fact is the role of reason in the legal order. Legality as we know it is based on a combination of sovereign will and objective reason. The word *reason* has an old-fashioned ring to it, but its long life is not yet over. Reason is an authoritative ideal, and the bearers of reason have, inevitably, a creative legal role. We see this, not only in the idea and practice of grounded judicial decision-making, but in the vast body of critical literature produced by legal scholars. Whatever the lawyer's commitment to legal positivism, to the belief that law is what the legislatures and the courts enunciate and enforce, there is at least an implicit recognition that not all law is on the same level. Some law is inferior because it contains the wrong mixture of arbitrary sovereign will, including majority will, and right reason. This is especially true of judge-made law, but legislatures can also make inferior laws. An inferior legality is manifested in the disposition of judges to give a narrow construction to statutes that depart from common-law principles, and in the ease with which judicial conclusions are modified or reversed. An inherent legality is doubtless much influenced by the derivation of a rule—whether from immediate political pressures or from a larger evolution consonant with underlying principles of legal order. I think that the quality of legality, and gradations in it, will be a primary preoccupation of the sociology of law in the future, as it has been in the past. In this work, moreover, we shall have to study the relation between reason and social consensus, for we shall not be satisfied with the assumption that community sentiment, as it bears on law, is basically nonrational.

Because reason is legally authoritative, scholarship has a direct significance for law that it does not have for other fields. This is indicated by the special role of law-review articles and legal treatises cited as authority by the courts. This work usually involves a critical restatement of common-law doctrine, but it also can and does locate new rights. The restatement aspect does give this work a special status, but there is no fundamental difference between sociological learning

---

40 [A beginning has been made. See note 64 *ante*, 350.]

made legally relevant and the kind of analytical writing found in the law reviews. In any case, like any other inquiry, legal reasoning cannot but accept the authority of scientifically validated conclusions regarding the nature of man and his institutions. Therefore, inevitably, sociology and every other social science have a part in the legal order.

The underlying role of reason explains why legal scholarship and the sociology of law are mainly preoccupied with common law, and therefore with judicial behavior, rather than with legislation. It is true that somewhat more emphasis in legal training is now placed on legislation, reflecting the great growth of the legislative process. It is also true that the interpretation of statutes plays a large role in the judicial process. But it is and will undoubtedly remain true that the main access to the law by legal analysts is through the judiciary. More important for legal sociology, legal doctrine is a vital part of common law but of much less importance in legislation.

A concern for the role of reason must bring with it a certain disaffection with what has come to be known as legal realism. The hard-headed effort to base our notion of law on actual behavior is certainly congenial to a sociological orientation. But human behavior is a very subtle mixture of self-restraint and impulse, idealism and self-interest, behavior guided by a long-range end-in-view and behavior compelled by day-to-day pressures. We cannot accept as more than a passing polemical formula the aphorism that the law is what the judges say it is. Taken literally, this settles nothing, for if a consistency is found in judicial behavior, searching out the underlying premises of a normative system and upholding the essential ingredients of legality, then all nonpositivist interpretations of law are still available and the problems they raise are with us still.

The ideal of reason presumes that there are principles of criticism of positive law. It also presumes, as Lon Fuller has pointed out,[41] that there are principles of criticism of "living" law. Little is gained in any ultimate sense by looking beyond positive law to actual normative behavior. We must go on to seek out the foundations in reason for choosing among human norms those that are to be given the sanction of law. This will bring us, I cannot doubt, to an acceptance of some version of a doctrine of natural law, although it may not, and perhaps should not, be called that, given its historical associations. A modern naturalist perspective may be preferable, despite the still-unsettled question of whether an objective basis of normative order can be discovered, and despite the large differences between positivism and pragmatism, affecting the ideal of reason in law, regarding the subjective component of valuation and the role of will in judgment. But whatever the philosophical auspices, the search for principles on criticism based on social naturalism must go on. Law based on reason and nature summons man to his potentialities but sees those potentialities as something that science can identify; law based on reason and nature locates the weaknesses of the human spirit, such as pride, apathy, and self-abasement, and works to offset them. The natural order, as it concerns man, is compact of potentiality and vulnerability, and it is

---

[41] Lon L. Fuller, "American Legal Realism," Univ. of Pa. Law Rev., 82 (1934), 453 *et seq.*

our long-run task to see how these characteristics of man work them-selves out in the structure and dynamics of social institutions.

[pp. 115–127]

J. STONE

Law and the Social Sciences
(1966)

. . . Sociological jurisprudence, like any other outcropping of human thought, was itself a creature of a time and place, and its earlier scope and tenor were in part conditioned by this. Before World War I, when its work developed in the United States, the beginnings of social legislation and of a positive federal attitude towards economic institu-tions and their stability and progress were still struggling for legitimation in face of various social and economic ideologies, traditional common-law hostility to statutes, jealousy for states' rights, and the conceptualism and logicism shared with the followers of Austin in England and of the Pandectists on the European continent. The social evils to which statutes held unconstitutional were often a serious response, accelerated with accelerating industrial and economic change; so did the invocations of the federal commerce power against economic ills and abuses.

Stating the matter more generally, the maladjustment and inade-quacies of the law for its contemporary tasks gave to early sociological jurisprudence an overwhelmingly activist drive which, even when it expressed itself in general terms, was in fact directed at *ad hoc* remedies for all the particular defaults of the legal order. A great deal of the work in this area even to the present day is still of this nature. And, of course, thus regarded such a program is inexhaustible, and its non-fulfillment even in a century of work is certain. In this sense the program was over-ambitious, and was thus still open to the charge of failure even after it had contributed to massive changes in the law and in attitudes towards it. As with engineers of other kinds, and especially the traffic engineer of a modern city, Pound's " social engineer " was certain to be a busy man, far behind in his work, however many and mighty the projects already completed.

Finally, it seems clearer now than it was in 1946 [42] that movements of thought and action touching the relations of law and society, insofar as they move into more fruitful contact with other social sciences, must come to place more stress on the importance of cognition of the social and economic order in its complex unity. And this even when they are bent upon an approach to diagnosis and remedy of specific evils through legal action. Economic thought has come to approach the problems of human distress due to economic fluctuations through control of key points in an *understood* economic ordering, itself institutionally framed within the more comprehensive social order. Contemporary sociological thought, well illustrated as we shall shortly see in the aspirations of Parsons' later thought, seeks a framework of thought receptive of social data which will allow us to see " the social system " as an integrated equilibration of the multitude of operative systems of values and institu-tions embraced within it. Whatever the difficulties of the Parsonian

---

[42] [When Stone's *The Province and Function of Law* was published]

efforts in this direction, we believe that some corresponding change of horizons is likely in sociological jurisprudence, as many of the more elementary and glaring legal maladjustments which provoked the activism of its initial program become corrected.

The change may indeed already have begun. We are, for example, no longer perplexed by the question of interfering with liberty of contract, when gross inequality of bargaining power makes abuse of liberty likely. It has been handled in an *ad hoc* way by legislating for specific relations like landlord and tenant or lender and borrower. We are, on the other hand, increasingly perplexed by such comparatively new and diffuse problems as that of the use of trade union pressure against non-members, pressure of capital concentrations against competitors and consumers, the steady growth of juvenile and urban delinquency, the creeping paralysis of traffic congestion in the spreading metropolis, chronic delays in the administration of justice, the adjustment of capital-labor relations and of habits of leisure and systems of education to the age of automation.

These are the more characteristic kinds of areas demanding legal action for the future of the Western democracies. No doubt some problems will continue to be thrown up for which the *ad hoc* approach of early sociological jurisprudence, making direct assault on the points where legal maladjustment is immediately manifest, is apt. But the sociological jurist of the future will also have to approach his characteristic problems through a vast effort at understanding the wider social context, seeking by the light of available social knowledge the key points of the systems of action from which adjustment can be effectively made. Nor indeed, is this likely development at too great odds with some aspects of the past aspirations of sociological jurisprudence. For a number of these, such as the demand that the necessary expertise for pre-legislative tasks be made available on a stable institutionalized base, are as relevant to the broad tasks of cognition as they are to the *ad hoc* tasks of legal activism. So is the search, which has already produced crisis after crisis in the tasks of practitioners and courts, for more basic and meaningful categories of thought, for instance, in the law of damages for personal injuries, of liability for dangerous chattels and operations, of anti-trust law, of the law of economic association, and a score of others. And the impressive contemporary work of Willard Hurst in social and economic legal history is in important part a search for categories of thought, drawn from empirical historical data, which will serve to put into the order of reason the interplay of legal and non-legal phenomena in the dimension of time. . . .   [pp. 26–28]

I believe it to be of capital importance that the social sciences, and above all those bearing on problems of legal ordering, should not commit themselves *wholly and exclusively* to building over-all systems of thought, leaving it more or less to chance whether in the testing and elucidation of the theoretical principles involved the practical and sometimes gravely urgent problems of contemporary society are ever reached . . . The drive to over-all cognition and theory-building represents a salutary trend in the social sciences, and promises in the long run great improvements in man's self-control and social control. There are, however, at least two compelling reasons why we dare not commit *all* our best expertise to the building and testing of over-all theories; and why indeed, those who guide research activity should take steps to avoid this excessive commitment.

One reason is that the advancement of cognition itself requires a continual checking of over-all theory by reliable empirical data collected and verified out of the matrix and even unconsciously of that theory. This is even more so in the social sciences where for a variety of reasons the exact empirical testing of hypotheses by experimentation tailored to the hypotheses is possible only to a much lesser extent than in natural sciences. The flow of data and hypotheses from particular problem areas still at a distance from the reach of theory is a correspondingly precious source of confirmation, correction, and supplementation which should not be allowed to dry up.

The other reason, no less compelling, proceeds from the view which I take (but which not all my colleagues may share) concerning the responsibility of the social scientist (including the jurisprudent) towards the tasks of legal ordering. And it would be compelling even if in terms of the first reason the extension of knowledge were not involved. I have already briefly mentioned this second reason in my first essay. It is that in relation to legal ordering we are entitled to expect the assistance of social scientists in the alleviation of practical evils and the handling of practical problems. And we are entitled to this, not only in the long run but (so far as it *can* be made available) here and now. For generally some action-response must be made by citizens, lawyers, judges, and administrations in the here and now to these evils and these problems; and the response ought to be as adequate as our generation's state of knowledge can make it. We have already noted and welcomed the tendency for sociological jurisprudence to take a wider and more theoretical view of its subject-matter than it did in its pioneering decades from the turn of the century. We wish also now to insist, however, that sociological jurisprudence (under whatever name) should also strive to maintain its earlier courage and vigor in tackling the numerous situations of obvious conflict, distress, confusion and injustice which are thrown up constantly and urgently for practical handling. We must enable and even encourage scholars to address themselves to these without making them feel that they have wandered from the main roads of scholarship, or that their activity is any less respectable or important than the building or criticism or testing of over-all theoretical systems. . . .　　　　　　　　　　　　　[pp. 44–45]

7

AMERICAN REALISM

The " Revolt against Formalism " [1]

IN the nineteenth and at the beginning of the present century, *laissez-faire* was the dominant creed in America. This creed was associated, in the intellectual sphere, with a certain attachment to what has been called " formalism " in philosophy and the social sciences. This was marked by a reverence for the role of logic and mathematics and *a priori* reasoning as applied to philosophy, economics and jurisprudence, with but little urge to link these empirically to the facts of life. Yet empirical science and technology were increasingly dominating American society and with this development arose an intellectual movement in favour of treating philosophy and the social sciences, and even logic itself, as empirical studies not rooted in abstract formalism. In America this movement was associated with such figures as William James and Dewey in philosophy and logic, Veblen in economics, Beard and Robinson in historical studies, and Mr. Justice Holmes in jurisprudence.[2] It is important to note that this movement was especially hostile to the so-called British empirical school derived from Hume, and to which Bentham, Austin and Mill adhered. For while it is true that these thinkers were positivist and anti-metaphysical, they were for the anti-formalists, not empirical enough, since they were associated with *a priori* reasoning not based on actual study of the facts,[3] such as Mill's formal logic and his reliance

[1] See the admirable account of this development in Morton G. White's *Social Thought in America: The Revolt Against Formalism.*
[2] For characteristic features of " formalism " in modern law, and its sociological foundation, see especially, Max Weber, *Law and Economy in Society* (1954), (ed. M. Rheinstein), Chap. XI. Weber states the postulates of the formal rationality of modern law to be as follows :–
  (1) Every decision of a concrete case consists in the application of an abstract rule of law to a concrete fact situation.
  (2) By means of legal logic abstract rules of positive law can be made to yield a decision for every concrete fact situation.
  (3) Positive law constitutes a " gapless " system of rules or must at least be treated as if it were such a system.
  (4) Every instance of social conduct can and must be conceived as constituting either obedience to, or violation, or application, of rules of law. (See *ibid.,* pp. li, 64.)
[3] Emphasis on fact is to be found in many spheres of human activity at different periods. Thus, naturalism and realism in art and literature were familiar phenomena in the course of the nineteenth century, and have been associated in this instance with the rise of science and bourgeois standards of living (see M. Praz, *Hero in Eclipse* (1956)). But the inevitable reaction in favour of non-representational art occurred sooner than the corresponding intellectual development.

399

on an abstract "economic man." Bentham's hedonic calculus of pleasures and pains, and the analytical approach to jurisprudence derived from Austin. Nor, unlike the sociologists of Pound's persuasion, were they interested to borrow from Bentham such abstract analyses of society as his doctrine of conflicting human interests. What these writers in their various fields were concerned to emphasise was the need to enlarge knowledge empirically, and to relate it to the solution of the practical problems of man in society at the present day.[4] Hence pragmatism attempted to link truth with practical success in solving problems, and in its more developed form of instrumentalism, Dewey further emphasised the empirical approach by treating knowledge as a kind of experience arising out of human activity creating a problem, and which is attained when the problem is solved. Again Veblen emphasised the importance of studying institutions empirically and especially the connection between economic institutions and other aspects of culture. The new historians stressed the economic forces in social life and the need to study history as a pragmatic means of controlling man's future. All of these currents of thought played a vital role in the gradual movement of the United States from a highly individualist to a form of collectivist society in the course of the last fifty years.[5]

MR. JUSTICE HOLMES [6]

Both in his writings and in his long tenure as a Justice of the Supreme Court, Holmes played a fundamental part in bringing about a changed attitude to law. His emphasis on the fact that the life of the law was experience [7] as well as logic,[8] and his view of law as predictions of what courts will decide,[9] stressed the empirical and pragmatic aspect of law.[10] For him, too, legal history was to be studied

---

[4] This movement has been described as the American counterpart to Marxism and the historical schools in England, which tried to apply evolutionary ideas to social thinking: see M. Lerner, *America as a Civilisation* (1958), pp. 722–724. It was undoubtedly influenced in some aspects by Marxist thinking: *cf.* Morton G. White, *op cit.*, Chap. VIII.

[5] For a revealing account of the specifically American features of this movement, see W. H. Whyte, *The Organisation Man* (1957).

[6] Recent historians of pragmatism have doubted whether Holmes's prediction theory of law was ever seriously influenced by the writings of James or Peirce, indeed whether he understood the full impact of their philosophical theories. See Thayer, *Meaning and Actions* (1968), p. viii and *cf.* Fisch, in ed. Moore and Robin, *Studies in the Philosophy of Peirce*, pp. 3–32. Thayer points out, however, that Holmes found more interest in and sympathy for Dewey's outlook than in that of James or Peirce.

[7] For a discussion of what Holmes meant by experience, see Wiener, *Evolution and the Founders of Pragmatism* (1949), Chap. 8.

[8] *The Common Law* (1881), p. 1.   [9] See *post*, 423.

[10] Holmes was always somewhat ambivalent in his attitude towards theory. Despite his doubt that " there is any more exalted form of life than that of a great abstract thinker " (*ibid.*, p. 224), he preferred to leave " twisting the tail of the Cosmos " to his friend James. " Anything that will discourage men from

primarily as a first step towards a deliberate reconsideration of the worth of rules developed historically. "It is revolting to have no better reason for a rule than that so it was laid down in the time of Henry IV." [11] Also law must be strictly distinguished from morals, for the lawyer is concerned with what the law *is*, not with what it *ought* to be.[12] Yet here may be discerned something of a paradox, for Holmes also never tired of asserting how "policy" governed legal development, especially in the form of the "inarticulate" convictions of those engaged in creating law. The answer to this is that Holmes felt that the development of law could be justified scientifically, for the "true science of law . . . consists in the establishment of its postulates from within upon accurately measured social desires instead of tradition." [13] In this respect Holmes apparently relied more on practical than on pure science, the lawyer trained in economics and statistics,[14] though he nowhere clearly indicated how an objectively sound "policy" was to be attained. However, this was far more likely to be achieved when the real basis of legal rules was openly avowed rather than remaining inarticulate or suppressed. Holmes, it would seem, accepted the possibility of scientific valuation in law, but he did not go so far as Dewey in the view that the *choice* between different values can also be verified scientifically.[15] For Holmes, the arbiter of this choice could, in the last resort, only be naked force.[16]

believing general propositions I welcome only less than anything that will encourage them to make them " (*Holmes-Laski Letters*, I, 579), sums up his attitude. In law he reiterated that general propositions do not decide cases and stressed the practical aspects of law "as a business" (*Collected Legal Papers*, pp. 170–171), at the same time advising reliance on a science which will measure " the relative worth of our different social ends " (p. 226). "Very likely it may be that with all the help that statistics and every modern appliance can bring us there never will be a commonwealth in which science is everywhere supreme. But it is an ideal, and without ideals what is life worth? " (p. 242). But he also noted that: "We have too little theory in the law " and that " the world is governed today (more) by Kant than by Bonaparte " (*The Path of the Law*, 10 Harv.L.R. 457, 478).

11 *Collected Legal Papers*, p. 187. This aphorism was referred to approvingly in *U.S.* v. *Dege*, 364 U.S. 51 (1960), where it was held that a husband and wife could be indicted for conspiracy, notwithstanding the medieval doctrine that they are one person.

12 Here Holmes was at one with the Austinians. He also stressed that moral ideas in law were or should be limited to *external* standards.

13 *Ibid.*, pp. 225–226.

14 Of whom Brandeis later provided the prototype. On the "Brandeis brief," see A. T. Mason, *Brandeis and the Modern State*, Chap. VI, and *post*, 424. This technique has not so far been admitted in Canada : see *Saumur* v. *Quebec* [1954] 4 D.L.R. 641, 646. Nor has survey evidence. See *R.* v. *Murphy* (1969) 4 D.L.R. 3d. 289, on which see McDonald (1970) 8 Osgoode Hall L.J. 573.

15 See Morton G. White, *op. cit.*, Chap. XIII.

16 " I believe that force, mitigated so far as may be by good manners, is the *ultima ratio* ": *Pollock-Holmes Letters*, II, p. 36. *Cf. Holmes-Laski Letters*, I, p. 385: " As it seems to me that all society has rested on the death of men and must rest on that or on the prevention of the lives of a good many, I naturally shrink from the moral tone."

THE AMERICAN LEGAL SYSTEM

Holmes' view of law as " prediction " placed both litigation and the professional lawyers in the centre of the legal stage. His emphasis on what courts may do, rather than on abstract logical deduction from general rules, and on the inarticulate ideological premises which may underlie the decisions of courts,[17] focused attention on the empirical factors which constitute a legal system. There was, indeed, much in the American system which made this new approach seem especially acceptable to American lawyers.[18] For not only was the old Austinian analysis based on sovereignty singularly ill-adapted to the complexities of the federal constitution, but the function of the Supreme Court acting as a censor of legislation and deciding what were effectively political issues; the divergence of legal rules and decisions in different states, and even in the same state or court (having regard to a far laxer rule of precedent in America than in England); the large extent to which American courts were manifestly engaged in the process of generating new law [19]; and the vast congeries of courts involving a numerous judiciary, many of whom were elected politicians, and of very varying calibre; all these matters seemed to lend force to Holmes' vigorous insistence on a fresh and more empirical attitude to the legal process. And for those who were progressively minded Holmes' reliance on practical social science seemed to point the way to future progress, and his dissenting judgments, especially in the famous *Lochner* [20] and *Adams* [21] cases, were

---

[17] See *The Common Law*, pp. 35–36. It is important however not to allow such premises to rest merely on assumption or mythology. For example, it has long been supposed that English judges have shown a long-standing and regular bias against trade unions in the field of industrial litigation, but a recent scrutiny of the relevant case law seems to provide little, or at any rate inconclusive evidence for this view. See O'Higgins and Partington, " Industrial Conflict : Judicial Attitudes " (1969) 32 M.L.R. 53. *Cf., ante,* 37.

[18] The pragmatist movement also took root in Italy for a short period about the turn of the century. Among its protagonists, Mario Calderoni, who was trained in law, is particularly interesting for the jurist. He believed, for example, that the principle of responsibility considered by judges in punishing the criminal had its foundation in the fact that man's behaviour derives from the foresight of the consequences of his acts. This is not unreminiscent of Holmes. Pragmatism encountered strong opposition in Italy from idealistic philosophers like Croce and Gentile. See Gullace, *The Pragmatist Movement in Italy* (1962) 23 *Journal of the History of Ideas* 91.

[19] Focusing attention on the decade following 1958, and limiting his scope to the law of torts, Keeton shows how appellate courts throughout the United States virtually rewrote this area of the law in the space of ten years. See *Venturing To Do Justice* (1968). See also Jaffe, *English and American Judges as Lawmakers* (1970), *post*, 724.

[20] *Post*, 432.

[21] 250 U.S. 616 (1919). Propounding his doctrine that free speech should not be encroached upon in the absence of the threat of a " clear and present danger," Holmes J. pleaded for " free trade in ideas " and argued pragmatically that the constitution was an " experiment." *Cf.* James' search for what he called the " cash value " of ideas.

thought to point the way to a more rational and scientific application of the constitution to the actual social needs of a highly industrialised modern society.

THE " REALIST " MOVEMENT IN LAW

The general intellectual movement in favour of " realism " as against formalism perhaps reached its heyday by the end of the 1920s. Much of the characteristic tendencies of the sociological school, especially its reliance on interrelated social sciences, can be seen as reflections of Holmes' views on law. Yet its basic approach was a good deal more philosophical and abstract than accorded with thoroughgoing realism. Again, legal writers occasionally could be found who to some extent echoed Holmes' view of law as being what courts may decide. Indeed, Gray went so far as to assert that even a statute is not law until a court interprets it. But Gray, and also Salmond, for whom law was law because the courts in fact observe it,[22] remained analytical jurists, with little interest in the social foundations of law, and its relation to other social disciplines.[23] Thus, despite Holmes' great influence both as part of the general movement and as the outstanding American jurist and judge of his day, it was not until towards the end of his career that a positive legal movement under the designation of " legal realism " began to manifest itself.

The character, aims and tendencies of this movement can be adequately gleaned from the passages taken hereafter from the writings of Professor Llewellyn, one of its foremost protagonists. The following brief remarks will be concerned in the main with appraisal and criticism, but something must first be said of the views of another distinguished exponent of realism, the late Judge Jerome Frank.

Fact-sceptics and Rule-sceptics

Frank insists that there are really two [24] groups of realists, " rule-sceptics," as he calls them, who regard legal uncertainty as residing

---

22 Salmond defined law as the rules recognised and acted upon by courts of justice: see *Jurisprudence*, 11th ed., p. 17. *Cf.* Pollock and Maitland, *The History of English Law*, Vol. 1, p. xcv: " . . . law may be taken for every purpose, save that of strictly philosophical enquiry, to be the sum of the rules administered by courts of justice."

23 Although the Harvard case-method of legal education has also been associated with the rise of legal realism and pragmatism (especially in its emphasis on litigation and judge-made law) it must be borne in mind that its protagonists favoured the traditional approach. Of Langdell, dean of the Harvard Law School in the latter years of the nineteenth century and a high priest of this traditional method, Holmes once said: " To my mind he represents the powers of darkness. He is all for logic and hates any reference to anything outside of it ": *Pollock-Holmes Letters*, I, p. 17. But *cf. Canadian Jurisprudence* (ed. McWhinney), p. 12. Twining (1967) 30 M.L.R. 514, 526, contrasts the educational objectives of Langdell and Llewellyn.

24 It has been suggested that there are in fact *three* categories of sceptics. In his *American Legal Realism* (1968), Rumble detects " opinion-skepticism " in the

principally in the " paper " rules of law and who seek to discover
uniformities in actual judicial behaviour, and " fact-sceptics," who
think that the unpredictability of court decisions resides primarily in
the elusiveness of facts.[25] The former, he suggests, make the mistake
of concentrating on appellate courts, whereas it is to the activities
of trial courts that attention needs most to be directed.[26] No doubt
there is force in this contention, for it is familiar enough to find that
nice points of law often dissolve away before decisions " on the
facts," quite apart from the fact that the majority of cases involve no
disputed law at all. Also, the facts may affect the actual decision as
to the law, since courts often " wrench " the law in order to make it
fit what they conceive to be the merits of a case, not always with
adequate regard to the wider implications of their decision. But at
the same time it is difficult not to feel that Frank makes an over-
elaborated case about what in essence has never been far from the
thoughts of the legal profession, *viz.*, that you can never anticipate
with certainty which way a court or jury will jump on issues of fact,
and that innumerable factors combine to promote such uncertainty and

writings of a number of the Realists, notably Llewellyn, Felix Cohen and Bingham. The idea is better known in Judge Hutcheson's phrase as the " judicial
hunch " (see, 14 Cornell L.Q. 274). Though somewhat exaggerated and not a
little naive, there is some truth in the belief that judicial reasoning is *ex post
facto* decision making, mere rationalisation " intended to make the decision
seem plausible, legally decent, legally right . . . legally inevitable " (Llewellyn,
Jurisprudence, p. 58). Whilst " opinion-skepticism " is an undoubted under-
current in Realist thought (in spite of the cogent criticisms of the Realist
sympathiser, E. S. Robinson), to endow the idea with a separate label is to
inflate its importance and invite similar divisive speculations. Scepticism was
the Realists' one common point of departure and there are as many forms
of scepticism as there are sceptics. But this does not detract from Rumble's
point that there is greater judicial reluctance to discuss the policy behind
decisions than is found in regard to other officials—the reluctance is even
greater in this country. Is restraint a judicial virtue? (See pp. 79–83 ; 93–95,
102–103.)

[25] Frank never defined precisely " fact skepticism." Cahn, a great admirer of
Frank, described it as " an integral doctrine with three associated prongs ":
" it criticises our capacity to ascertain the transactions of the past, it distrusts
our capacity to predict fact-findings and value judgments of the future ; and,
finally, it discloses the importance of the personal element in all processes of
choice and decision." (Preface to Frank, *Courts on Trial*, Athenean edition
(1963), p. ix.) Both Cahn (*Confronting Injustice*, pp. 321–322) and Rumble
stress the relationship of fact-skepticism to Frank, the law-reformer. If a
tribunal decides on the basis of facts other than the actual facts (are facts
finite?), then improvements must be made to the fact-finding process. Rumble
believes this to be the theme of *Courts on Trial* (1949), whilst the earlier,
and better-known, *Law And The Modern Mind* (1930) concentrates on the
unpredictability of the tribunal's reaction to found facts, whatever the *real*
facts. But can the thinking process really be compartmentalised in this way,
and do not one's reactions to possible found facts often colour those facts
which one will find? (*American Legal Realism*, pp. 109–111.)

[26] See particularly Frank's searching criticisms of the American trial systems in
Courts on Trial (1949). See J. Frank, *Cardozo and the Upper-Court Myth*
(1948) 13 *Law and Contemporary Problems* 369.

to render it ineradicable.[27] In stressing this thesis, Frank effectively
makes the points that the textbook approach, which treats the
law as no more than a collection of abstract rules, is grossly misleading, and that much of legal uncertainty is inherent and not due to
deliberate mystification. But it must be said that Frank adds little
to his contentions by a curious affection for an implausible application of psycho-analysis,[28] whereby he seeks to attribute the search
for legal certainty to the need for a Father-figure,[29] the infallible
judge, nor by his reliance on the principle of indeterminacy in modern
physics, as showing the impossibility of attaining certainty in the legal
sphere.[30]

Achievements of the Realists

The earlier realists, including Holmes, were much concerned to
promote a new and more experimental and constructive attitude to
social life and thought, but avoided making any specific proposals
as a programme to be realised. Dewey, for instance, praised Holmes
on this very ground, because he had " no social panaceas to dole out,
no fixed social programme, no code of fixed ends to be realised." [31]
The later legal realists, and, more particularly, their descendants,
the jurimetricians and behaviouralists,[32] have been true to this
attitude by concentrating on developing actual techniques for helping the practitioner to understand and anticipate the trends of
judicial decisions. Much emphasis is placed on the need for detailed
social and factual studies on the actual working of the law in

---

[27] Lundstedt (*Legal Thinking Revised*, p. 394) describes Frank's *Law and the
Modern Mind* as " more amusing than indicative of fruitful thought." For a
more sympathetic appraisal of Judge Frank's contribution, see E. Cahn in (1957)
66 Yale L.J. 824 and in *Confronting Justice* (1967), pp. 265–324, where this and
all Cahn's other writings on Frank are reprinted.

[28] A phenomenon very familiar in present-day America: see, *e.g.*, M. Cowley,
Literary Situation in America, pp. 134–135. The influence of Gestalt psychology
upon Frank's writings should also be noted. See *Courts on Trial*, Chap. XII.
Judges decide cases by responding to the *whole* situation, hence their " hunches."

[29] Ironically enough, in a country usually regarded as matriarchal, and where
children are not considered to have an exceptionally well-developed bump of
parental reverence. E. and R. Sterba, *Beethoven and his Nephew* (1957), pp. 95,
303–305, give a similar Freudian explanation for the falsely idealised biographies
of " great men."   And what of Jung's " collective unconscious " as explaining
the belief in natural law? Frank did not test his belief empirically, but that
has been done, indirectly, by Ladinsky and Silver, *Popular Democracy* (1967)
Wis.L.R. 128. They comment: " Public acquiescence to judicial actions in the
realm of policy-making hardly seems to be a function of the ' priestly ' image
promulgated by Lerner or Frank . . . public support seems more a matter of
acquiescence or ignorance . . . of respect for the judiciary as one kind of
government official rather than as a distinctive office embodying unique functions
and status " (pp. 167–168).

[30] *Cf. ante*, 5.

[31] *Characters and Events*, I, pp. 100–101. All the " anti-formalists " were primarily
concerned with *method* rather than with a specific programme of reforms, and
herein lay their weakness: see Morton G. White, *op. cit.*, Chap. XII.

[32] *Post*, 415 and 419.

particular fields, and of the interaction of social practices and activities with courts, lawyers and others concerned to develop and apply legal rules. Whereas the early realists employed the social sciences as an appendage, using them to no profound effect,[33] the modern inventors of the realist tradition have become sophisticated in the techniques of the political scientist and sociologist. There is little to distinguish modern realism from modern sociological jurisprudence, for, as was suggested in the last chapter,[34] both have become subsumed in the all-embracing sociology of law. Perhaps, one way to distinguish the two movements at the moment is to see the sociological jurist as concerned with systems and classifications, with broad and *a priori* theories and often still with legal principles, whilst latter-day realists are principally engaged in accumulating knowledge as an aid to improved legal techniques.[35] The Chicago Jury Project, referred to in the chapter on sociological jurisprudence, is probably better seen as a product of realism.[36]

Certainly we may applaud the desire to avail ourselves of whatever other disciplines may teach the lawyer in the improvement of his techniques. And in many spheres where law touches deep social problems there is an obvious need for creatively informed rather than a technically traditionalist approach. This can be readily seen in such fields as monopolies, labour law, or juvenile delinquency.[37] Yet the English lawyer, in reading the realists' own assessments of their achievements, finds it difficult to avoid feeling that nothing very startlingly fresh has emerged from all these detailed studies, beyond what the reasonably progressive and socially-minded lawyer might already have accepted as axiomatic. Nor does he find very encouraging Llewellyn's own conclusion that " almost nothing the newer jurisprudence has yet found, and little that it seems likely to find within the next few decades, will prove in any manner *new*, to the best lawyers." [38]

Moreover, there is a great deal of traditional law, such as the rules for the formation and dissolution of contracts, which hardly seems to lend itself to any very profound sociological re-examination

---

[33] *Cf.* comments on Frank; *ante*, 405.

[34] *Ante*, 348.

[35] And law is expected to draw freely on such information, techniques or insights as may be elicited from other social sciences. See Rose, " The Social Scientist as an Expert Witness in Court Cases " in ed. Lazarsfeld, Sewell and Wilensky, *The Uses of Sociology* (1968), p. 100. This has, of course, led to the development of the Brandeis brief, *post*, 424. See also Haward, " A Psychologist's Contribution to Legal Procedure " (1964) 27 M.L.R. 656.

[36] *Post*, 465.

[37] See the development of two new series of publications in this country, *Law and Society* and *Law In Context*, both of which adopt this approach to such problems as road accidents, race relations and employment and torts and compensation.   [38] *Post*, 449.

or reassessment on the basis of new techniques, and these represent legal spheres with which the ordinary lawyer still remains very much concerned in his daily practice. From this point of view it is not easy to see how the better type of modern textbook can be radically reconstituted in the light of fresh techniques so as better to serve the modern lawyer. Yet it must be said that the realists have done good work in emphasising both the essentially flexible attitude of the judiciary towards developing precedent, even within the four corners of a rigid doctrine of precedent, and the operation of concealed factors in judicial law-making, and if they have exaggerated the intrinsic unpredictability [39] of law from the rules alone (and not every-one, even among practitioners, would say that they have), they have also shown that courts will always retain some freedom of movement which cannot be reduced to a merely mechanical application of past decisions to new sets of facts.[40] Also it should be borne in mind that the realists do not reject technical legal analysis, but merely emphasise that this is not in itself enough, if we wish to understand how the law works, or how it may best be developed or improved. And if so far little has been achieved in finding any far-reaching sub-stitute for the habitual legal technique which has served lawyers for centuries, realists have played their part in bringing about a changed outlook and attitude towards the legal system and the function of the law and the legal profession in society, which has made itself felt in all but the most traditionalist of the law schools of the common law world.

LLEWELLYN ON INSTITUTIONS AND " LAW-JOBS " [41]

The functional approach to law adopted by Llewellyn is well brought out by his treatment of law as an institution. For Llewellyn an institution is an organised activity which is built around doing a job or a " cluster " of jobs. In the case of a major institution, its " job-cluster " is fundamental to the continuance of the society or group in which it operates. The institution of law in our society is an

---

[39] *Cf.* the later writings of Llewellyn, particularly *The Common Law Tradition*, where decisions are said to be " reckonable " in eight out of ten cases provided the lawyer is taught how to read a case, to get its " situation-sense." See *post*, 409.

[40] The fallacious belief in a complete system of rules which can meet in advance all cases of doubt also underlies much philosophic confusion. Thus there is a feeling that a rule which leaves gaps is not really a rule at all, though the demand for foolproof rules cannot be met. " A rule is properly formulated if it does its work in the context it was meant for. Our error is to ask for perfect and complete rules ": D. Pole, *The Later Philosophy of Wittgenstein* (1958), p. 33.

[41] I would like to express my indebtedness in this section to an unpublished article by Professor W. L. Twining. See also his articles in (1967) 30 M.L.R. 514; (1968) 31 M.L.R. 165 and his *Karl Llewellyn Papers* (1968).

extremely complex one, consisting not only of a body of rules organised around concepts and permeated by a large number of principles. In addition there are certain elaborated techniques such as the use of precedent, and over and above all these matters is an ideology, consisting of a body of far-reaching values and ideals which, though to a large extent implicit rather than expressly avowed, may, nevertheless, form an immensely influential part of the institution of law as a whole. Apart from all these, there is also a host of practices, some very flexible, and others quite rigid, which determine how certain things within the legal system may or may not be done. All such matters control in various ways the activities of what Llewellyn calls the "men-of-law."

An institution has jobs to do, and the important thing is to see that these jobs are well and effectively carried out. A functioning institution is something which is rooted in the life of the community and has to be constantly tested by the needs of that community; and moreover, the results of its working have to be open to inquiry. Much of Llewellyn's interest has been centred upon what he calls the ways in which in various types of community the "law-jobs" are actually carried out.

"Law-jobs" [42] are Llewellyn's way of describing the basic functions of the law, which, for him, are two-fold: "to make group survival possible," but, additionally, to "quest" for justice, efficiency and a richer life. To this end he lists "law-jobs" as the disposition of "trouble-cases" (his study of the Cheyenne [43] was focused on this function of law, which Llewellyn believed was common to all systems at whatever stage of development); "preventive channeling," the reorientation of conduct and expectations to avoid trouble; [44] the provision of private law activity by individuals and groups, such as the autonomy inherent in a law of contract; and "the say," the constitutional provision of procedures to resolve conflict, much in the manner of Hart's "rules of adjudication." [45] The first three jobs describe "bare bones" law, but out of them may emerge, though Llewellyn gives no indication how, the additional "questing" phase of the legal order. For Llewellyn the problem was thus finding the best ways to handle

---

[42] See his account in 49 Yale L.J. 1355 and in Llewellyn and Hoebel, *The Cheyenne Way* (1941), Pt. III.

[43] Llewellyn and Hoebel, *The Cheyenne Way* (1941), the theme of which was to demonstrate that primitive law can be understood in terms of the functions common to it and to advanced systems. And see *post*, 568.

[44] So one of the keys to the Uniform Commercial Code, of which Llewellyn towards the end of his life was a prime mover, is the facilitating of commercial practices through custom, usage and agreement.

[45] *Ante*, 169. See *The Concept of Law* (1961), pp. 94–96.

" legal tools to law-job ends." [46] This brings one to his notion of a
" craft " as a minor institution. A craft in this sense consists of a kind
of " know-how " among a body of specialists who are engaged in performing certain of the jobs within the framework of an institution.
It consists of an organised and continuous body of skills developed
by specialists and handed down from generation to generation by a
process of education and practical example. The practice of the law
is the practice of a set of crafts, and of these one of the most
important is what is frequently called juristic method.

The Common Law Tradition

In Llewellyn's book, *The Common Law Tradition,* Llewellyn
develops this idea of a craft in considerable detail, as applied to the
juristic method of the common law. This book may be described
as a kind of handbook of the craft both of judging and of advocacy
within the framework of the common law tradition, though applied
especially to appellate cases. There is a certain irony in the thesis
of this book, coming from one who has long been identified, though
not altogether correctly, with the notion of the large measure of unpredictability in the decisions of the court. The aim of the book is to
deal with what it describes as a " crisis of confidence within the Bar,"
concerning especially the question whether there is a reasonable
degree of " reckonability " in the work of U.S. appellate courts.
Llewellyn begins by pointing out that the profession in America is
exceedingly worried because it is believed that the courts have moved
away from a basis of stable decision-making, in favour of deciding
cases on the basis of their sentiments, and then simply seeking for
ex post facto justification in their judgments.[47]

On the contrary, argues Llewellyn, there is a large measure of
predictability in case-law, and this he attributes to the general craft
of decision-making in the common law tradition. Llewellyn
examines in detail what he calls " a cluster of factors " which tend to
have a major steadying influence in producing stability in the work
of the courts. These include [48] such matters as " law-conditioned
officials "; known doctrinal techniques; the limiting of issues; the
adversary arguments of counsel; and so on. But especially, in this
book, Llewellyn emphasises the importance of what he calls the

---

[46] Llewellyn set this to verse. See his *Semi-Ballade on the Glorious Quest,* in
Jurisprudence (1962), p. 214.

[47] *Cf.* his address to the Conference of Chief Justices in 1959, in *Jurisprudence*
(1962), p. 215. *Cf. ante,* 403, n. 24.

[48] See *op. cit.,* p. 19. Rumble, *op. cit.,* pp. 51–53 has a useful discussion of these
steadying factors. He stresses Llewellyn's emphasis of the role a judge is expected
to play in the American judicial system as the most important of the fourteen
factors. (See *The Common Law Tradition,* pp. 46–47.)

general "period style" employed by the courts. This cluster remains a hypothesis. Llewellyn makes no attempt to test empirically any of his steadying factors. He gives no indication of how an assessment could be made of the relative weight of each, nor, indeed, how each can be used for predictive purposes. Here we have the essential breach between realism and behaviouralism, for behaviouralists would have done just this.[49] Llewellyn's discussion of "period style" is, nonetheless, of particular interest. In the common law, says Llewellyn, the practice of the courts has fluctuated between two types of style which he names the Grand Style and the Formal Style. The Grand Style is based essentially on an appeal to reason, and does not involve a slavish following of precedent; regard is paid to the reputation of the judge deciding the earlier case, and principle is consulted in order to ensure that precedent is not a mere verbal tool, but a generalisation which yields patent sense as well as order. Policy, under this style, comes in for explicit examination. Under the so-called Formal Style, on the other hand, the underlying notion is that the rules of law decide the cases; policy is for the legislature, not for the courts, and therefore this approach is authoritarian, formal and logical.[50]

Llewellyn does not assert that these styles are ever found in their absolute purity at any given moment; there tends rather to be a movement from one period to another between these two opposite poles. Thus, the Grand Style he regards as characteristic of the creative period of American law in the early part of the nineteenth century; thereafter there was a rapid move in the latter half of that century in America towards an increasingly Formal Style. Llewellyn argues that in recent times the American appellate courts have been moving steadily back towards the earlier type of Grand Style, and it is this tendency which has misled the legal profession into thinking that there is a higher measure of unpredictability in their decisions than there was in the previous more formal period.[51] This Llewellyn attributes to a misconception as to the ways in which the court uses precedent and the tremendous "leeways" which are afforded by the system of precedent, whatever particular period style may be in operation. Under any style of precedent there are multiple techniques by which opposite or conflicting results may be reached, and

---

[49] See the comments in Becker, *Political Behaviouralism and Modern Jurisprudence: A Working Theory and Study in Judicial Decision-Making* (1964), pp. 63–64.

[50] See *post*, 454.

[51] The Supreme Court under Chief Justice Warren is thought to have exemplified this approach. See the excellent critique of this in Bickel, *The Supreme Court and the Idea of Progress* (1970). On appellate courts, generally, see Keeton's account of creativity in the law of torts in roughly the same period (*Venturing to do Justice* (1968)).

the only question really is whether the court will employ a style which will produce a more effective and just outcome, and one more adapted to the social needs of the period, or will try to immunise itself to some degree against the changing pattern of the society in which the court has its being.

There are, however, two rather curious and unexpected features of this latest book of Llewellyn which do deserve some comment here. According to Llewellyn, it is a feature of the Grand Style, which he warmly approves, that the courts proceed to arrive at decisions in relation to what he calls " Situation-sense." It is exceedingly difficult to grasp exactly what the author has in mind by this concept. No doubt he was particularly concerned with the importance of not dealing so much with a unique situation, but a situation seen as a " type," and, therefore, providing a rule or principle for the future. Under the Grand Style, Llewellyn seems to be saying that insight and wisdom is developed whereby the judges will achieve a kind of objective criterion, though not one which can be specifically formulated, and so arrive at a wide measure of agreement as to what are the appropriate legal solutions both worthy of approval by the community and likely, in fact, to be approved by the community. This may or may not be true in relation to particular periods or particular legal systems, but it seems a very far cry from the scientific realism which has so long been regarded as one of the animating influences of the realist movement. It savours, indeed, far more of Savigny than of social science. Moreover, Llewellyn does not seem to face up to the fact that in many communities, certainly including his own, there may be vital issues involving conflicts of values between different groups and interests in the community; how, then, can there be any objective core of insight which can produce decisions appropriate to reconcile all this welter of confusion? It may well be that a more honest decision will be produced by a judge who approaches the question in the spirit of the Grand Style rather than looking at the matter through the spectacles of formalism. All the same, Llewellyn seems unduly optimistic when he claims that what he calls " the law of the singing reason " will tend to produce a rule yielding regularity, " reckonability " and justice all together.[52] It is fair to add, however, that Llewellyn does not put his case higher than saying that the Grand Style is likely to produce a greater proportion of such decisions than any other style.

The second rather curious feature of this book is that the author

[52] Note also the " law of fitness and flavor." " The work of the job in hand, and even more of the job at large, must fit and fit into the body and flavor of the law " (*Common Law Tradition*, p. 222). This " law " counters any activist tendencies. But on " activism " *cf.* Twining (1971) 87 L.Q.R. 398, 400–401.

confines his evidence almost exclusively to the material which
appears from the actual decisions of appellate courts. True, he
recognises that these do not disclose the whole truth of what he calls
" the facts of life," but he does insist that these provide adequate
material for revealing the techniques of the courts, especially if one
employs his chosen procedure, not of examining cases according to
their subject-matter, but in the order they happen to be reported in
the volumes of report relating to particular courts. But he insists
we must learn to read these cases, not for what they decide, but for
their " flavor." Do not look, he urges, to " what was held " but look
to " what was bothering and helping the court." In a sense, therefore, the wheel seems to have gone full circle, for we now find
Llewellyn virtually ignoring subjective factors; concentrating entirely
on the actual decisions of the court as opposed to extrinsic factors;
and, nevertheless, urging that far from being irrational and uncertain,
if one understands the proper technique of reading opinions, it is
possible to show that there is an exceptionally high measure of
" reckonability " in American appellate decisions. Despite all this,
Llewellyn is far from having renounced any of his earlier enthusiasms.
In fact he argues strongly that his latest book is still as much based
upon the realistic technique of the past as any of his previous contributions. The fervour of the movement has not disappeared; all
that is changed is the field of operations. It may have been necessary
before to spend a good deal of time attacking opposing views; now
the important thing is to get down to the actual study of the material,
and the opinions in court judgments are just as important a form of
material as any other. With this view, at any rate, even the most
orthodox common lawyer is hardly likely to dissent.

It is a little disarming to find that what started as a rather
revolutionary movement has ended up fundamentally as an appeal
for a common-sense approach to law. What Llewellyn claims to have
attempted and to some extent achieved is to establish a jurisprudence
which may serve the needs of the ordinary student of law, the
ordinary practitioner and the ordinary judge. In this process, a
good many myths have to be eliminated, and, in particular, both the
myth that certainty can be achieved under a legal system, or its
opposite, that predictability is unattainable.[53] On the contrary, urges

---

[53] That Llewellyn regards rules as playing a very significant role in the formulation
and development of law is sufficiently testified by his activity as one of the
chief draftsmen of the new Uniform Commercial Code which is being rapidly
adopted in the majority of the States of the Union. This Code has embodied to
a noteworthy degree the approach of what Llewellyn has called the " Grand
Style," and so providing a fabric of rules which will give the court the opportunity to apply " Situation-sense " to shape the deciding rule and to enable
the court to re-test the rules in the light of reason as it evolves from the
situation. Moreover, the Code's first canon of construction is: " This Act shall

Llewellyn, in this latest work, the common law system produces, in his view, a remarkably high measure of predictability so that a skilled lawyer proceeding on the basis discussed in his latest book ought, in Llewellyn's view, to average correct predictions in eight out of ten cases. Here, again, is reassurance enough for the orthodox.

SCIENTIFIC AND NORMATIVE LAWS

Is it a valid criticism of the realists that they ignore the purely normative character of legal rules and seek to replace these by scientific statements laying down uniformities of human conduct?[54] Legal rules are norms of conduct which are in themselves neither true nor false.[55] Yet the realist seems to be seeking to prove their truth or falsity in relation to the criteria of actual human behaviour. This is not an easy point to deal with, especially as it concerns a logical distinction of the kind to which the realist, with his addiction to brute fact, remains profoundly indifferent. On the whole, however, I do not think this criticism is really fundamental, for this reason. The realist does not in effect deny the normative character of legal rules. What he says is that these norms do not provide a certain clue to the actual behaviour of courts, legal officials or those engaged in legal transactions.[56] If we are to understand the actual working of law in human society it is not enough simply to peruse a collection of the relevant legal norms for these tell us but little about actual " legal behaviour," in the sense of how legal business is in fact transacted. Of course, a follower of Kelsen might say that this is outside the field of true legal science, but he cannot and indeed would not deny that it is a legitimate field of inquiry in itself. The Kelsenite, therefore, concentrates on his norms, the realist on his facts of society, each regarding the other's activity patronisingly as a peripheral study on the fringe of his own central sphere. Yet, it may be suggested, both equally represent essential aspects of the legal process if an overall picture is to be taken of law, which is both an intellectual conception and a function of human society.

be liberally construed and applied to promote its underlying purposes and policies." See Mentschikoff (Llewellyn's widow) (1964) 27 M.L.R. 107, 108 : " The extent to which [the U.C.C.] reflects Llewellyn's philosophy of law and his sense of commercial wisdom and need is startling."

54 This criticism is more valid in relation to Frank and some of the earlier writings of Llewellyn, but there is no doubt that later Realism as exemplified by mature Llewellyn took cognisance of the normative character of legal rules. See, for example, Llewellyn, *The Normative, The Legal, and the Law Jobs*, 49 Yale L.J. 1355, and in *The Common Law Tradition, post*, 450.   55 *Ante*, 8.

56 Admittedly the realist predilection, following Holmes, to treat rules of law as *predictions* of what the court may do, seems to go counter to this. But this is because the realist is here thinking of the viewpoint of the lawyer advising his client, rather than of the norm prescribed by the judge, or laid down for his guidance ; *cf.* Salmond, *Jurisprudence* ed. Fitzgerald (1966), pp. 40–41.

WHERE STANDS REALISM TODAY?

I have already indicated that the broader movement of realism showed signs of having passed its peak by the early 1930s, though in the sphere of jurisprudence its message not only continued but ushered in a distinctive movement which is by no means yet extinguished. But in law, as in other intellectual spheres, there are signs of a reaction, connected with the feeling that empiricism and positivism are not enough, and that some new *mystique* must be found to underpin the *ethos* of man and human society. Lawyers are once again to be found engaged in the search for some philosophical, ethical or religious natural law basis for human law,[57] inspired by the desire to arrive at some absolute scheme of values which can be held to support and enshrine their own sense of what is right and wrong, just or unjust. No doubt this trend receives encouragement from the wish to counteract the materialist convictions of the Communist world, though it is perhaps a little ironic at the present time, when technological superiority is becoming accepted as the ultimate value in the so-called uncommitted countries, that it should be thought helpful to overthrow social technology in favour of a scheme of absolute values, which may seem all but meaningless to those beyond the main stream of Western culture. For the moment, at any rate, if rather less confidence is felt in the West in the capacity of science and positivism to produce the Brave New World of its dreams, it remains equally unpersuaded that its future must necessarily unfold on Orwellian lines, or that only by embracing some new (or old) mystical faith can our human institutions be revitalised. This, however, is not to deny that a very real struggle is in progress in Western society between individual values and collective forces, in which the former run some danger of being submerged.[58] But it should be remembered that if Western industrialism has created this dilemma, it is, nevertheless, from the secular renaissance in the West that individualism has its roots, and that it was in the religious mists of the Middle Ages that collectivism attained its fullest expression.

In 1961, Professor Yntema, himself a leading realist, attempted

---

[57] See the writings of Fuller, *ante*, 138 and 243; Jerome Hall (1958) 7 Buffalo L.R. 351 and *Studies in Jurisprudence, post*, pp. 136–142; Northrop, *The Complexity of Ethical and Legal Experience* (1959), and of Goodhart, *English Law and Moral Law* (1953). See also the searching article by Rostow, "Realistic Jurisprudence" in *The Sovereign Prerogative* (1962), p. 18 who points to the paradox in this neglect of values and the image of the Realists as a law reform lobby.

[58] See W. H. Whyte, *The Organisation Man* (1957), who sums up the American dilemma in these words: ". . . the peace of mind offered by organisation remains a surrender, and no less so for being offered in benevolence. That is the problem" (p. 404). For a nostalgic salute to the "integrated society" of the Middle Ages, see Tannenbaum, *A Philosophy of Labor* (1951).

to assess the present and future of the movement.[59] After stressing both the importance and influence of legal realism upon American law, lawyers and law schools, he still conceded that a major defect of the movement had been neglect of the more humanistic side of law, particularly revealed both in its neglect of the comparative and historical aspects of law, and a tendency to place over-emphasis upon current " local practice." The result of this has been a certain loss of perspective, and in particular, a failure to distinguish between what is trivial or ephemeral on the one hand, and what is of wider import on the other. His suggestion for the future is not to abandon the critical achievements of realism, but to develop these on more constructive lines. This, he states, would involve a more humanistic conception of legal science, with due attention being paid both to the systematic analysis of legal theory and of historical and comparative research.

At all events, whatever may be the future of legal realism as a movement, it remains true that its impact has been such that things can never seem to be quite the same again.

Moreover it has indirectly engendered two movements, themselves closely related *viz.*, Jurimetrics and Behaviouralism. Like legal realism, neither of these movements has made much headway in this country, but the impact of each in the United States makes it impossible to ignore them. In one sense, they take over where realism left off, for, whilst the realists had some inspired ideas, developed a number of theoretical models, and urged us to exploit the social and technological sciences, these newer movements are firmly established within the mainstream of the social sciences and use techniques associated with them freely and to valuable effect. But because of their technical jargon, their neologisms and empirical analyses, looking frighteningly like higher mathematics, they are forbidding to the average English, and it is assumed, American lawyer. There follows some comment on the approach and value of each movement.

JURIMETRICS

This term was introduced into legal vocabulary by Lee Loevinger nearly a quarter of a century ago.[60] It signifies the scientific investigation of legal problems, especially by the use of electronic

---

[59] See H. E. Yntema " American Legal Realism in Retrospect " (1960–1961), 14 Vanderbilt L.R. 317.

[60] "Jurimetrics—the Next Step Forward " (1949) 33 Minn.L.R. 455 and *post*, 474. Although the impact of this movement in this country has not so far been great, useful work is being done by Colin Tapper who has introduced the subject in two articles (1963) 26 M.L.R. 121, and 8 J.S.P.T.L. 261. In the United States there are a number of specialist journals on the subject, the best being *Jurimetrics Journal* (formerly *Modern Uses of Logic in Law*).

computers and by symbolic logic. The cybernetic revolution was bound in time to leave its mark on legal material. For, on the one hand, the vast range and huge accumulations of material relevant to the legal process (a problem magnified in the United States) seemed to demand some kind of mechanical and mathematical approach, if only towards information storage and retrieval [61]; and, on the other, the complexity of modern statutory provisions with concomitant amendments and statutory instruments seemed to require more than traditional methods to enshrine and expound their meaning. Symbolic logic could perhaps provide a useful tool to this end.[62] But the current activities of computers in the legal field are much wider than this. It has, for example, been suggested [63] that computers are ideal aids to estate planning. The computer will eliminate arithmetical errors and data transposition oversights which can distort the data relied upon in making major decisions; and it can also organise data into meaningful categories. Further, the system can be programmed to organise and administer an estate through the two often alternative hypothetical probates of the " deceased " dying before his spouse or after. The computer may further assist in the litigation process by organising documents so as to assist information flow. Whilst documents can be classified without such sophisticated aids, as all lawyers know, it can be time-consuming and expensive and can lead to error: electronic data processing can eliminate all these deficiencies.[64]

More controversial types of question in the realm of behavioural research have also been undertaken. Thus experiments have been designed with computers to investigate such questions as the different ways in which the judge and a jury may decide the same case; the effect that the formulation of the legal rule as to insanity may have on jury verdicts; the reliability and credibility of testimony; and, more especially, the particularly realist preoccupation with the prediction of judicial decisions.[65] Work has also been done on the question how far patterns of consistency or regularity may be shown to exist in relation to a large number of judicial decisions in a particular legal field. It has even been suggested that the day may

[61] See the speech of Lord Bowden (273 H.L. col. 719–721) and *post*, 479.

[62] A particularly valuable introduction to symbolic logic is Kayton (1964) 33 Geo. Wash.L.R. 287. He stresses, by use of a helpful example, how symbolic logic may enable us to see which of a number of witnesses' contradictory accounts is the correct one. This may prove a fertile field for symbolic logicians and lawyers to explore together. See also Allen, in ed. Bigelow, *Computers and the Law* (1969), p. 167.

[63] By Paffendorf, *idem*, p. 70.

[64] See Shuman and Bagley, *idem*, p. 66. A number of other examples are given in this publication, prepared by the Standing Committee on Law and Technology of the American Bar Association.

[65] See the fuller discussion of this, *post*, 419.

come when defendants will be given the choice of trial with the aid of a computer.[66] Computers, it is postulated, would ensure uniformity and a fair application of the law. It is easy to throw up one's hands in horror, but is the "inscrutable" jury such a rational institution? You can at least programme a computer with biases acceptable to the community, or at least to a majority of it, but juries, and judges for that matter, retain their own caprices.

These developments have not occurred without vigorous resistance, especially on the part of those who believe that there are dangerous ideological and political implications in allowing even a proportion of legal inquiries to be conducted by machines rather than by individual judges or administrators. Those who have put forward the case for this new kind of experimental jurisprudence have attempted to disarm the critics by placing at the forefront of their expositions its limited scope and purpose. Thus it is urged that the aim of jurimetrics is not to eliminate reason or philosophy from jurisprudence or to find a substitute for necessary values which are an intrinsic part of law-making. All that this particular type of investigation is concerned with is those matters which are capable of being subjected to quantitative or probability assessments, and which can produce results capable of being scientifically verified or tested. All the same, these disavowals have not served to remove fears as to many dangers of a totalitarian kind which some have found to be inherent in any attempt at producing some kind of "machine-made justice." Many of these dangers have been strenuously put forward, such as those which might arise from the conceptual rigidity of computers, or a built-in bias which may result from a particular texture of analysis and interpretation involved in the use of computers and programming dependent on computers. Also, it has been argued that the development of solutions by mechanical or mathematical means may tend to cause officials and lawyers to avoid responsibility for hard decisions, in return for ready-made answers based on computers.

Nor, it must be admitted, has anxiety been allayed by the tendency of one or two of the exponents of this form of study to make rather more sweeping claims. For instance, one of the leading exponents of this approach, Frederick K. Beutel, in his work *Experimental Jurisprudence*, published in 1957, while conceding that for the present problems involving moral and social value-judgments cannot be effectively subjected to the technique of experimental jurisprudence, nevertheless, casts his eye towards a distant future when methods of scientific prediction may be so developed that they may take over the direction and control of what " some now call human values and that

[66] By Reed Lawlor (1967) 13 *Practical Lawyer* 3, p. 10.

this power may be turned to scientific purposes." [67] Here we do seem to be approaching that nightmare totalitarian régime adumbrated by Orwell and Aldous Huxley. Under such conditions, new scientific methods will be called for,[68] and it will be necessary for the overwhelming mass of people to hand over matters which they cannot understand to able scientists who can alone understand and be entrusted with the new types of governmental and legal devices. But the lesson here is that lawyers must not abdicate responsibility. As the distinguished political scientist, Harold Lasswell, has written: " whoever controls information (enlightenment) is likely to control public order." [69] If the computer revolution is to be conquered for popular government and wrenched from the possibility of scientific bureaucracy this can be done best by lawyers. This has already been seen to an extent in the way in which lawyers have reacted to the data bank's invasion of privacy.[70] Lawyers must continue to appraise the impact of computers on society. Whether they use them or not, government and every sort of commercial organisation, including, of course, their clients, will certainly do so.[71]

However, it may be that both the hopes and apprehensions arising out of the new science of jurimetrics are equally exaggerated. On the one hand, there may well be considerable scope for developing certain mechanical aspects relating to legal problems, particularly in

[67] p. 51.
[68] The leading works on this topic are *Jurimetrics*, a symposium edited by Hans W. Baade (1963); and Frederick K. Beutel, *Experimental Jurisprudence* (1957). The first of these works is especially valuable as containing not only an introduction into the general methodology of this new science, but also a number of examples of the type of work and experiments undertaken in this sphere, as well as some contributions from writers who attack the whole approach of the new science in view of its, as they think, totalitarian implications. The book also contains a short contribution by a Soviet jurist, indicating the way Soviet Jurisprudence is developing this new science in such spheres as legal reference; codification; legal teaching; and the assembly of legal and sociological information relating to such problems as delinquency and so on. It is interesting to note that this particular writer rejects the notion of these new techniques taking over man's creative labour, as being " frivolous." The reader may or may not be reassured by this assertion that " the most perfect machine will never be able to replace the creative effort of responsibility of man in any decision on a public matter, *i.e.* the legal regulation of social relations. There should be no illusions on that score" (p. 70). The non-mathematical legal reader may be somewhat dismayed by the mathematical appearance of some of the contributions in this volume, but should not allow himself to be deterred by this, as there is much in the volume of interest even to those not versed in mathematics, symbolic logic, or modern computer theory.
[69] See 21 Rutgers L.R. 645, 676. Enlightenment is one of Lasswell's eight value categories which the legal process is expected to maximise. See the discussion of Lasswell, *ante*, 349.
[70] See Westin, *Privacy and Freedom* (1967), and Warner and Stone, *The Data Bank Society* (1970).
[71] See Parts III and IV of *Computers and the Law*, *op. cit.* One administrative activity of particular concern to lawyers has been the use to which computers have been put since *Baker* v. *Carr*, 369 U.S. 186 (1962) to draw up plans for reapporting legislative areas.

relation to the searching out and organising of legal material, which can be done far more effectively by the aid of modern devices rather than by the traditional form of research. At the same time it seems unlikely that the more creative and discretionary aspects of the legal process can ever be adequately applied by computers or any other mechanical or mathematical device, however subtly programmed, since everything must depend in such matters on the actual form of the programming, which itself will have to be done by persons highly expert in the nature of the problems involved. Consequently, there seems no reason to believe that an electronic computer can ever provide a more satisfactory means of dispensing justice than a judge or jury. The creative side of law, therefore, seems likely to remain with the legal experts, though whether this will afford as much comfort to the ordinary citizen as to the experts themselves is perhaps not quite so certain as lawyers may care to think.

JUDICIAL BEHAVIOURALISM

This is the younger of the two movements, developing only in the last decade. It is difficult to assess as its proponents have reached no agreement on methods or aims, nor is there anything resembling a consistent theory. It is impossible to talk of a school of behaviouralists.[72]

The roots of behaviouralism are two-fold: realism, and to a lesser extent, sociological jurisprudence; and political science. From the former is taken the *faith* that judicial behaviour is predictable[73] and the *aim* of developing means of predicting decisions. From political science, on the other hand, is taken such techniques as scaling and small group psychology.

Why did behaviouralism develop? In what way is it different from legal realism? According to Glendon Schubert, the leading researcher in this field, the realists failed to achieve what they promised. "Legal research remains today at the primitive level of development, as a science, that generally characterised political science one or two generations ago. By and large, legal method is no more in phase with modern science than it was in the days of Austin." He pin-points two deficiencies in Realist thought, one in their theory, the other in their methods. "Science requires both theoretical models from which operationalized hypotheses can be

---

[72] The best introductions to the movement are Schubert's preface to section 5 of his own reader, *Judicial Behaviour* (1964), *post*, 481, and the symposium in 79 Harv. L.R. 1551, with contributions by different writers in the field and a critical overview by Lon Fuller. See also Stone, *Law and Social Sciences* (1966), pp. 50 *et seq.*

[73] More from Llewellyn than Frank. See, for example, Llewellyn's criticism of Frank's emphasis on unpredictability in *Jurisprudence*, p. 101 (written in 1931) and his own demonstration of " reckonability " in *The Common Law Tradition*.

inferred and methods for testing such hypotheses with data derived from empirical observations. The realists, with rare exceptions . . . had neither theory nor methods." [74] Schubert is careful to refer to "rare exceptions," though it is minor Realists, such as Herman Oliphant,[75] and not the major figures usually discussed who are excepted from his criticism. One might go further and suggest that, for example, Llewellyn's cluster of steadying factors *could* be the type of theoretical model that Schubert has in mind, though it is doubtful if Llewellyn so intended it. Nor did Llewellyn tell us how to use his "model," nor how to differentiate the effect of different factors. But even if the Realists developed models, they did not draw hypotheses from them, and certainly there was no attempt at empirical verification of any such hypothesis. This is not to say that they did not undertake research. They did, but their research was philosophical rather than scientific. Llewellyn's *Common Law Tradition* is an analysis of appellate decisions in explanation of the judicial process, an attempt to answer the question of what *rules* the courts apply. This is valuable research but it is not Schubert's *genre* of research.

The behaviouralists start with two advantages: the heritage of Realist questioning and their own technical expertise as social scientists. Their work tends to concentrate on multiple courts and majority decisions.[76] They thus limit themselves to contentious appellate decisions, the very tip of the iceberg.[77] There have been attempts to correlate attitudes and backgrounds with voting records, and to trace the development of blocs, the emergence of leadership and interaction and bargaining problems. And there has been a certain amount of prediction. Lawlor, for example, predicted that *Gideon* v. *Wainright* would overrule *Betts* v. *Brady*.[78] But, unlike

---

[74] See Schubert (1966) 34 Geo.Wash.L.R. 593, 600–601. See also *Judicial Behaviour, op. cit.*, pp. 1–18, and Becker, *Political Behaviouralism and Modern Jurisprudence*, Part II. A particularly good recent article tracing the relationship between behaviouralism and realism is Ingersoll (1966) 76 *Ethics* 253. See also Stone, *op. cit.*, pp. 69–71. It is one of the themes of Stone's perceptive essay that the behaviouralists' "lack of depth of knowledge of legal processes and the traditional body of juristic thought makes the risk of error and naïveté substantial" (p. 70).

[75] See Rumble's account of Oliphant's model, *op. cit.*, pp. 159–161, and comments at pp. 171–173. See also the writings of Felix Cohen and his functional model with its declaration of war on empirically unverifiable concepts (*The Legal Conscience* (1960)).

[76] By excluding unanimous decisions a veil is drawn over the divergences that may lie behind such decisions. The approach also, of course, gives undue weight to dissenting judgments. It should also be noted that judges can use the threat to dissent as a bargaining counter to secure a modification in the majority opinion. See, further, Fuller, 79 Harv.L.Rep. 1604, 1609–1611.

[77] *Cf.* the views of Frank, *ante*, 404.

[78] See *post*, 491. Note the distinction that Lawlor draws between traditional and personal *stare decisis*. Another leading behaviouralist, Kort, using similar mathematical analysis, failed to predict this overruling (see in ed. Schubert, *Judicial*

the Realists, they have not been concerned to help the practitioner and, accordingly find prediction after the event (what Nagel has termed *post diction* [79]) equally satisfying, though others will find their sense of values lamentable.

Since methods and research show great diversity it is proposed to comment briefly upon the approach of Schubert,[80] though references will be made to other writers. His concern has been with motivations behind judicial decisions, particularly with *attitude*. It is his thesis that judges do not agree or disagree because they reason in similar or different ways, but because they have similar or dissimilar attitudes. This seems to ignore their common training and environment, the " taught tradition " and institutional factors such as *stare decisis*. Schubert's method of discovering a judge's attitudes is similarly suspect. By looking at their previous decisions he believes he can elicit their reactions to fact-patterns and draws the hypothesis that a recurrence of fact-pattern will stimulate a similar response. But this is to reduce the judge to little more than a conveyor belt to which materials are fed and identical products emerge. It is also to adopt an over-mechanical concept of causation: a judge may be a Catholic of Irish ancestry and may have consistently decided labour disputes in favour of trade unions, but neither Schubert nor any other behaviouralist has shown that he so decided *because* of his religion or ethnic origin. Furthermore, the facts on which Schubert concentrates are not the " facts " at all; they are a distillation he finds in the judicial opinion. These are not the facts of the case, but those which the judge found significant. To find the actual fact sources, the behaviouralist should learn from Frank [81] and look at the briefs, oral arguments, minutes of case conferences, *etc.* There are, it is true, other methods of eliciting a judge's attitudes, sending him a questionnaire [82] or reading his articles, lectures, letters to the press,[83] or, presumably, " bugging " his house, but there is no reason to believe that any would be more successful, if, that is, his attitudes would tell us anything anyway. Further, as both Fuller [84] and Stone [85] point out, the behaviouralists put consistency at a

---

Behaviour, p. 477, at p. 490) because Lawlor claims, he limited himself to traditional *stare decisis*.

[79] In " Predicting Court Cases Quantitatively " (1965) 63 Michigan L.R. 1411, 1422.

[80] Schubert's writings are voluminous, but the following selection gives an insight into his methods and beliefs: *Quantitative Analysis of Judicial Behaviour* (1959); his introduction to Part 5 of *Judicial Behaviour, A Reader in Theory and Research* (1964) (part of which is extracted, *post*, 481); *Behavioural Jurisprudence* (1968) 2 *Law and Society Review* 407.

[81] See *post*, 434.

[82] A technique in fact tried by Nagel. See " Off-the-Bench Judicial Attitudes " in ed. Schubert, *Judicial Decision-Making* (1963).

[83] See Becker, *Political Behaviouralism and Modern Jurisprudence* (1964); pp. 22–26.

[84] See 79 Harv.L.R. 1604, 1616.

[85] See *Social Dimensions of Law and Justice*, p. 693.

premium as if the judicial process were a formalised game of "snap."
Stone quotes a Japanese scholar foreseeing with zest "the day . . .
when the courts will use [an electronic machine] in arriving at their
decisions." [86] Will the role of the behaviouralists seeking to explain
what judges will decide if they act consistently with past decisions
merge with that of the appellate judge whose concern is *justice*?

It must not be thought that attitude correlation is the only or,
indeed, the main approach of the behaviouralists. Another common
method employed is to relate social background to decision-making,
for example, the question whether prior judicial experience as a
first instance judge makes an appellate judge more likely to favour
judicial restraint or *stare decisis*. Schmidhauser [87] tested the *a priori*
assertion that there was, indeed, such a correlation by looking at a
large number of Supreme Court decisions where precedent was
overruled, and then establishing a propensity to overrule score for
each judge. On scaling them he found that judges with lower court
experience had a greater propensity to overrule than judges without
such experience. He also found that, contrary to expectations, dissenting judges had the lowest propensity to overrule, and drew the
conclusion that the stereotype of a dissenter was a "tenacious
advocate of traditional doctrine." Both these conclusions are interesting and valuable, but limited. Schmidhauser does not demonstrate
any causal link, any more than Schubert did. He produces instead
statistical evidence demonstrating the likelihood that a particular
background variable will produce a particular type of judge. Can
his conclusion be generalised? Is there not a danger in this, if not
in behaviouralism generally, of losing sight of the normative character
of law?

Schmidhauser, at least, produced results which were by no means
obvious. Yet much behaviouralist work is just that. They test
scientifically hypotheses that any experienced lawyer's hunch would
verify. Llewellyn believed he could predict decisions with an 80 per
cent. success rate. Schubert estimates 90 per cent. success. Is the
behaviouralists' effort worth while for this additional margin of success? We must bear in mind, also, that Schubert limits himself to
majority decisions and to limited areas of the law where policy is
paramount, such as civil liberties. Little or no work has been done
in commercial law or probate: the more traditional approach of
Llewellyn is not so limited.

This can only be an interim report, for judicial behaviouralism is
a growth science in its early infancy. At this stage it seems full of

---

[86] *Idem*, pp. 603–694, and *Law and the Social Sciences*, pp. 82–83.
[87] See "The Justices of the Supreme Court: A Collective Portrait" in (1959) 3
Midwest J.of Polit.Sci., pp. 1–57.

exaggeration, of false hope, rather as early Realism did. Just as the Realists saw just about every explanation for a decision but the legal rule, so the behaviouralists try to relate decisions to variables of fact, attitude or background ignoring why judges are there at all. If early Realists developed the gastronomic theory of law, then behaviouralists are in danger of developing the A-C/D-C theory of decision-making.[88] Like many sciences in formative stages, a good deal of sophistication is lacking. Two examples may be given. With their political science background they may be forgiven for thinking that judges are policy-makers and nothing else. But just as it would be wrong to ignore the political element in decision-making, it is equally heinous to see judges as politicians and nothing else. Perhaps future behaviouralists will rescue the "ought" of law and notice its underlying rationale. Secondly, as social scientists they cannot really think that judges are either black or white. To date, behaviouralism has built itself upon a crude psychology of judges, ignoring reasons for their voting and failing to calibrate the various shades of grey separating the black from the white. Future researchers must correct this error.

O. W. HOLMES

The Path of the Law

(1897) [89]

Take the fundamental question, What constitutes the law? You will find some text writers telling you that it is something different from what is decided by the courts of Massachusetts or England, that it is a system of reason, that it is a deduction from principles of ethics or admitted axioms or what not, which may or may not coincide with the decisions. But if we take the view of our friend the bad man we shall find that he does not care two straws for the axioms or deductions, but that he does want to know what the Massachusetts or English courts are likely

------

[88] No one has suggested that the electrical system of a court-room affects decision-making. Indeed, Fuller is ironically critical of the conservative nature of the extra-curial influences chosen by the researchers. "They do not ask whether the judge is for or against vivisection, cremation, nominalism or organic farming. They do not inquire whether his preferred drink is rye with ginger ale or a vodka martini with a discreet slice of lemon peel. Instead they ask such unimaginative questions as whether he is a Republican or a Democrat, whether he grew up in the city or in the country, and the like" (see 79 Harv.L.R. 1604, 1608–1609).

[89] [From (1897) 10 Harv.L.R. 457–478, copyright 1897, by the Harvard Law Review Association; reprinted in O. W. Holmes, *Collected Papers*, to which page references are given here. This extract has been described by Llewellyn as the "internationally-cited goblin-painting of realism" (*The Common Law Tradition*, p. 511).]

to do in fact. I am much of his mind. The prophecies of what the courts [90] will do in fact, and nothing more pretentious, are what I mean by the law.[91]   [pp. 172–173]

MULLER v. THE STATE OF OREGON

United States Supreme Court
203 U.S. 412 (1908)

While the general liberty to contract in regard to one's business and the sale of one's labor is protected by the Fourteenth Amendment that liberty is subject to proper restrictions under the police power of the State.

The statute of Oregon of 1903 providing that no female shall work in certain establishments more than ten hours a day is not unconstitutional so far as respects laundries.

BREWER J. . . . It may not be amiss, in the present case, before examining the constitutional question, to notice the course of legislation as well as expressions of opinion from other than judicial sources. In the brief filed by Mr. Louis D. Brandeis, for the defendant in error, is a very copious collection of all these matters, an epitome of which is found in the margin.[92] . . .

---

[90] [Even if "courts" here is wide enough to cover administrative or other tribunals, there are many classes of matters which in a modern state remain largely in the field of administration and negotiation, and are hardly ever the subject of litigation, *e.g.*, the subject-matter of the greater part of such statutes as the Electricity Act, 1947, the Transport Act, 1947, or the Television Act, 1964. This no doubt accounts for Llewellyn's expansion of the idea to cover "officials." (But see his Foreword to the revised edition (1951) of *The Bramble Bush*, pp. 8–9.) But it remains true that even in such cases negotiations may be conducted and decisions reached with one eye on what a court might conceivably decide. Nor is this a form of prediction which interests only "the bad man" in Holmes' sense.]

[91] [The idea of law as a kind of quasi-scientific prediction is by no means so modern and unorthodox as may be thought, for we find Sir Frederick Pollock putting forward ideas of this kind as long ago as in 1882. In a paper called "The Science of Case-law," Pollock remarks that a lawyer in advising on a new case follows a similar procedure to that of a man of science. Moreover, when a prediction is made, as to how a court will decide, this does not merely mean that a notion is formed of the probable opinion of a court of last resort, but the prediction is made with reference to an ideal standard, for even the final court itself will be guided by an ideal standard of scientific fitness and harmony. This ideal standard is objective in the sense that it derives from the legal habit of mind engendered among the legal experts, though it also has a fictional character in so far as it postulates a perfect and uniform system of law. Nor, says Pollock, does the uncertainty of legal prediction affect its scientific quality, for scientific prediction even in the strict sense is only approximate. The science of case-law may be much rougher than that of exact science; but on the other hand the science of politics is even rougher than that of case-law. (See Sir F. Pollock, *Jurisprudence and Legal Essays*, ed. A. L. Goodhart, pp. 176–182.) See now *Incorporated Council of Law Reporting* v. *Att.-Gen.* [1971] 3 W.L.R. 853, 865, 874. For the strikingly similar sentiments of Jhering, see Zweigert and Siehr (1971) 19 Am.J.Comp.L. 215, 228.]

[92] [After referring to the legislation of many states and countries the note proceeds:] Then follow extracts from over ninety reports of committees, bureaus of statistics, commissioners of hygiene, inspectors of factories, both in this country and in Europe, to the effect that long hours of labor are dangerous for women, primarily because of their special physical organization. The matter is discussed in these reports in different aspects, but all agree as to the danger. It would of course take too much space to give these reports in

The legislation and opinions referred to in the margin may not be, technically speaking, authorities, and in them is little or no discussion of the constitutional question presented to us for determination, yet they are significant of a widespread belief that woman's physical structure, and the functions she performs in consequence thereof, justify special legislation restricting or qualifying the conditions under which she should be permitted to toil. Constitutional questions, it is true, are not settled by even a consensus of present public opinion, for it is the peculiar value of a written constitution that it places in unchanging form limitations upon legislative action, and thus gives a permanence and stability to popular government which otherwise would be lacking. At the same time, when a question of fact is debated and debatable, and the extent to which a special constitutional limitation goes is affected by the truth in respect to that fact, a widespread and long continued belief concerning it is worthy of consideration. We take judicial cognizance of all matters of general knowledge.

It is undoubtedly true, as more than once declared by this court, that the general right to contract in relation to one's business is part of the liberty of the individual, protected by the Fourteenth Amendment to the Federal Constitution; yet it is equally well settled that this liberty is not absolute and extending to all contracts, and that a State may, without conflicting with the provisions of the Fourteenth Amendment, restrict in many respects the individual's power of contract.

That woman's physical structure and the performance of maternal functions place her at a disadvantage in the struggle for subsistence is obvious. This is especially true when the burdens of motherhood are upon her. Even when they are not, by abundant testimony of the medical fraternity continuance for a long time on her feet at work, repeating this from day to day, tends to injurious effects upon the body, and as healthy mothers are essential to vigorous offspring, the physical well-being of woman becomes an object of public interest and care in order to preserve the strength and vigor of the race.

Still again, history discloses the fact that woman has always been dependent upon man. He established his control at the outset by superior physical strength, and this control in various forms, with diminishing intensity, has continued to the present. As minors, though not to the same extent, she has been looked upon in the courts as needing especial care that her rights may be preserved. Education was long denied her, and while now the doors of the school room are opened and her opportunities for acquiring knowledge are great, yet even with that and the consequent increase of capacity for business affairs it is still true

detail. Following them are extracts from similar reports discussing the general benefits of short hours from an economic aspect of the question. In many of these reports individual instances are given tending to support the general conclusion. Perhaps the general scope and character of all these reports may be summed up in what an inspector for Hanover says: " The reasons for the reduction of the working day to ten hours—(*a*) the physical organization of women, (*b*) her maternal functions, (*c*) the rearing and education of the children, (*d*) the maintenance of the home—are all so important and so far reaching that the need for such reduction need hardly be discussed." [This is the origin of the Brandeis brief: *cf. ante*, 401. Schubert has remarked that " the Brandeis brief came to be accepted by the Supreme Court long before its academic equivalent came to have any substantial impact upon research and instruction in constitutional law " (*Judicial Behaviour*, p. 2).]

that in the struggle for subsistence she is not an equal competitor with her brother. Though limitations upon personal and contractual rights may be removed by legislation, there is that in her disposition and habits of life which will operate against a full assertion of those rights. She will still be where some legislation to protect her seems necessary to secure a real equality of right. Doubtless there are individual exceptions, and there are many respects in which she has an advantage over him; but looking at it from the viewpoint of the effort to maintain an independent position in life, she is not upon an equality. Differentiated by these matters from the other sex, she is properly placed in a class by herself, and legislation designed for her protection may be sustained, even when like legislation is not necessary for men and could not be sustained. It is impossible to close one's eyes to the fact that she still looks to her brother and depends upon him. Even though all restrictions on political, personal and contractual rights were taken away, and she stood, so far as statutes are concerned, upon an absolutely equal plane with him, it would still be true that she is so constituted that she will rest upon and look to him for protection; that her physical structure and a proper discharge of her maternal functions—having in view not merely her own health, but the well-being of the race—justify legislation to protect her from the greed as well as the passion of man. The limitations which this statute places upon her contractual powers, upon her right to agree with her employer as to the time she shall labor, are not imposed solely for her benefit, but also largely for the benefit of all. Many words cannot make this plainer. The two sexes differ in structure of body, in the functions to be performed by each, in the amount of physical strength, in the capacity for long-continued labor, particularly when done standing, the influence of vigorous health upon the future well-being of the race, the self-reliance which enables one to assert full rights, and in the capacity to maintain the struggle for subsistence. This difference justifies a difference in legislation and upholds that which is designed to compensate for some of the burdens which rest upon her.

We have not referred in this discussion to the denial of the elective franchise in the State of Oregon, for while it may disclose a lack of political equality in all things with her brother, that is not of itself decisive. The reason runs deeper, and rests in the inherent difference between the two sexes, and in the different functions in life which they perform.[93]   [pp. 419–423]

[93] [It is thought by some that the Brandeis brief has lost its impact today, and controversy rages over the relevance and acceptability of the brief. For example, in *Brown* v. *Board of Education, ante,* 121, a brief was submitted which referred to the psychological evils of segregation in schools (it has subsequently been published in (1953), 37 Minn.L.R. 427). The judgment of Warren C.J. however, relegates this brief to a footnote, and refers to it *en passant* as "modern authority" before proceeding to deal with the question on wider moral grounds (347 U.S. 483, 494, n. 11). Cahn has argued (30 N.Y.U.L.R. 150, 153–154, 160–161) that the court was not influenced by the brief. "It is fair to suspect the impact of the Brandeis brief is no longer so great as when the device was novel and judges were more readily impressed by the paraphernalia of science or pseudo-science. In the last two decades [he was writing in 1955], many Brandeis briefs have been conspicuously vulnerable in respect of statistical method, rationality of inferences from assembled data, adequacy of sampling, and failure to allow for—or to disclose—negative instances. Perhaps (he argues) their quality will improve with a more critical attitude on the judges' part " (p. 154). The desegregation brief conveyed little more than literary

W. JAMES

Pragmatism

(1907)

Pragmatism represents a perfectly familiar attitude in philosophy, the empiricist attitude, but it represents it, as it seems to me, both in a more radical and in a less objectionable form than it has even yet assumed.[94] A pragmatist turns his back resolutely and once for all upon a lot of inveterate habits dear to professional philosophers. He turns away from abstraction and insufficiency, from verbal solutions, from bad *a priori* reasons, from fixed principles, closed systems, and pretended absolutes and origins. He turns towards concreteness and adequacy, towards facts, towards action and towards power. That means the empiricist temper regnant and the rationalist temper sincerely given up. It means the open air and possibilities of nature, as against dogma, artificiality, and the pretence of finality in truth. [p. 51]

At the same time it does not stand for any special results. It is a method only.[95]

When the first mathematical, logical, and natural uniformities, the first *laws*, were discovered, men were so carried away by the clearness, beauty and simplification that resulted, that they believed themselves to have deciphered authentically the eternal thoughts of the Almighty. . . .

. . . But as the sciences have developed farther, the notion has gained ground that most, perhaps all, of our laws are only approximations. The laws themselves, moreover, have grown so numerous that there is no counting them; and so many rival formulations are proposed in all the branches of science that investigators have become accustomed to the notion that no theory is absolutely a transcript of reality, but that any one of them may from some point of view be useful. Their great use is to summarize old facts and to lead to new ones. They are only a man-made language, a conceptual shorthand, as someone calls them, in which we write our reports of nature; and languages, as is well known, tolerate much choice of expression and many dialects . . .

. . . Riding now on the front of this wave of scientific logic Messrs. Schiller and Dewey appear with their pragmatistic account of what truth

psychology. Should constitutional rights " rest on such flimsy foundations as some of the scientific demonstrations in these records? " Cahn is worried about the difficulty of drawing the line between " objective science " and " advocacy." Clark (one of those responsible for the desegregation brief) sees in Cahn's article " the basic circuitous plea that the law and the courts . . . should be isolated in Olympian grandeur from other intellectual and scientific activities of man " (5 Vill.L.R. 224); a remark with a good deal of truth. Clark makes the significant point that *Plessy* v. *Ferguson* had been challenged many times before, but *Brown* v. *Board of Education* was the first time that the aid of social scientists had been enlisted and it was the first taste of success. *Post hoc propter hoc*? Is this not a somewhat over-simplistic explanation of social change?

One explanation of the waning of interest in the Brandeis brief is that it is easier to employ to justify the *status quo*, to show, for example, that the legislature was justified in enacting a piece of legislation, than to show that legislation is inherently evil and should be struck down. (*Cf.* Paul Freund, *Supreme Court and Supreme Law*, pp. 49–50).]

[94] [" There is absolutely nothing new in the pragmatic method " (*ibid.*, p. 50). *Cf.* Llewellyn on legal realism, *post*, 449. See also Kolakowski, *Positivist Philosophy* (1972), Chap. 7.]

[95] [*Cf.* Llewellyn, *post*, 441.]

everywhere signifies. Everywhere, these teachers say, ' truth ' in our ideas
and beliefs means the same thing that it means in science. It means, they
say, nothing but this, *that ideas (which themselves are but parts of our
experience) become true just in so far as they help us to get into satisfactory relation with other parts of our experience*, to summarize them
and get about among them by conceptual short-cuts instead of following
the interminable succession of particular phenomena. Any idea upon
which we can ride, so to speak ; any idea that will carry us prosperously
from any one part of our experience to any other part, linking things
satisfactorily, working securely, simplifying, saving labor ; is true for
just so much, true in so far forth, true *instrumentally*.   [pp. 56–58]

Pragmatism, on the other hand, asks its usual question. " Grant an
idea or belief to be true," it says, " what concrete difference will its being
true make in any one's actual life? How will the truth be realized?
What experiences will be different from those which would obtain if the
belief were false? What, in short, is the truth's cash-value in experiential
terms?"

The moment pragmatism asks this question, it sees the answer: *True
ideas are those that we can assimilate, validate, corroborate and verify.
False ideas are those that we can not.* That is the practical difference it
makes to us to have true ideas; that, therefore, is the meaning of truth,
for it is all that truth is known-as.[96]   [pp. 200–201]

J. DEWEY

Logical Method and Law
(1924) [97]

. . . Logic is ultimately an empirical and concrete discipline. Men first
employ certain ways of investigating, and of collecting, recording and
using data in reaching conclusions, in making decisions; they draw
inferences and make their checks and tests in various ways. These
different ways constitute the empirical raw material of logical theory.
The latter thus comes into existence without any conscious thought of
logic, just as forms of speech take place without conscious reference to
rules of syntax or of rhetorical propriety. But it is gradually learned that
some methods which are used work better than others. Some yield conclusions that do not stand the test of further situations; they produce
conflicts and confusion; decisions dependent upon them have to be
retracted or revised. Other methods are found to yield conclusions which
are available in subsequent inquiries as well as confirmed by them. There
first occurs a kind of natural selection of the methods which afford the
better type of conclusion, better for subsequent usage, just as happens in
the development of rules for conducting any art. Afterwards the methods
are themselves studied critically. Successful ones are not only selected
and collated, but the causes of their effective operation are discovered.
Thus logical theory becomes scientific.

The bearing of the conception of logic which is here advanced upon
legal thinking and decisions may be brought out by examining the

96 [*Truth* thus becomes a value-judgment to be tested by its results or consequences,
   rather as the utilitarian judges moral worth.]
97 [From 10 *Cornell Law Quarterly* 17.]

apparent disparity which exists between actual legal development and the strict requirements of logical theory. Justice Holmes has generalized the situation by saying that " the whole outline of the law is the resultant of a conflict at every point between logic and good sense—the one striving to work fiction out to consistent results, the other restraining and at last overcoming that effort when the results become too manifestly unjust." [98] This statement he substantiates by a thorough examination of the development of certain legal notions. Upon its surface, such a statement implies a different view of the nature of logic than that stated. It implies that logic is not the method *of* good sense, that it has as it were a substance and life of its own which conflicts with the requirements of good decisions with respect to concrete subject-matters. The difference, however, is largely verbal. What Justice Holmes terms logic is formal consistency, consistency of concepts with one another irrespective of the consequences of their application to concrete matters-of-fact. We might state the fact by saying that concepts once developed have a kind of intrinsic inertia on their own account; once developed the law of habit applies to them. It is practically economical to use a concept ready at hand rather than to take time and trouble and effort to change it or to devise a new one. The use of prior ready-made and familiar concepts also give rise to a sense of stability, of guarantee against sudden and arbitrary changes of the rules which determine the consequences which legally attend acts. It is the nature of any concept, as it is of any habit to change more slowly than do the concrete circumstances with reference to which it is employed. Experience shows that the relative fixity of concepts affords men with a specious sense of protection, of assurance against the troublesome flux of events. Thus Justice Holmes says, " The language of judicial decision is mainly the language of logic. And the logical method and form flatter that longing for certainty and for repose which is in every human mind. But certainty generally is an illusion." [99] From the view of logical method here set forth, however, the undoubted facts which Justice Holmes has in mind do not concern logic but rather certain tendencies of the human creatures who use logic; tendencies which a sound logic will guard against. For they spring from the momentum of habit once forced, and express the effect of habit upon our feelings of ease and stability—feelings which have little to do with the actual facts of the case.

However, this is only part of the story. The rest of the story is brought to light in some other passages of Justice Holmes. " The actual life of the law has not been logic: it has been experience. The felt necessities of the times, the prevalent moral and political theories, intuitions of public policy, avowed or unconscious, even the prejudices which judges share with their fellow-men, have had a good deal more to do than the syllogism in determining the rules by which men should be governed." [1] In other words, Justice Holmes is thinking of logic as equivalent with the syllogism, as he is quite entitled to do in accord with the orthodox tradition. From the standpoint of the syllogism as the logical model which was made current by scholasticism there *is* an antithesis between experience and logic, between logic and good

[98] Collected Legal Papers, p. 50.
[99] *Ibid.*, p. 181.
[1] The Common Law, p. 1.

sense. For the philosophy embodied in the formal theory of the syllo
gism asserted that thought or reason has fixed forms of its own, anterior
to and independent of concrete subject-matters, and to which the latter
have to be adapted whether or no. This defines the negative aspect of
this discussion; and it shows by contrast the need of another kind of
logic which shall reduce the influence of habit, and shall facilitate the
use of good sense regarding matters of social consequence.

In other words, there are different logics in use. One of these, the
one which has had greatest historic currency and exercised greatest
influence on legal decisions, is that of the syllogism. To this logic the
strictures of Justice Holmes apply in full force. For it purports to be a
logic of rigid demonstration, not of search and discovery. It claims to
be a logic of fixed forms, rather than of methods of reaching intelligent
decisions in concrete situations, or of methods employed in adjusting
disputed issues on behalf of the public and enduring interest. Those
ignorant of formal logic, the logic of the abstract relations of ready-made
conceptions to one another, have at least heard of the standard syllogism:
All men are mortal; Socrates is a man; therefore, he is mortal. This is
offered as the model of all proof or demonstration. It implies that what
we need and must procure is first a fixed general *principle*, the so-called
major premise, such as " all men are mortal," then in the second place,
a fact which belongs intrinsically and obviously to a class of things to
which the general principle applies: Socrates is a man. Then the conclusion automatically follows: Socrates is mortal. According to this
model every demonstrative or strictly logical conclusion " subsumes " a
particular under an appropriate universal. It implies the prior and given
existence of particulars and universals.

It thus implies that for every possible case which may arise, there is
a fixed antecedent rule already at hand; that the case in question is
either simple and unambiguous, or is resolvable by direct inspection
into a collection of simple and indubitable facts, such as " Socrates is
a man." It thus tends, when it is accepted, to produce and confirm what
Professor Pound has called mechanical jurisprudence; it flatters that
longing for certainty of which Justice Holmes speaks; it reinforces those
inert factors in human nature which make men hug as long as possible
any idea which has once gained lodgment in the mind.

In a certain sense it is foolish to criticise the model supplied by the
syllogism. The statements made about men and Socrates are obviously
true, and the connection between them is undoubted. The trouble is
that while the syllogism sets forth the *results* of thinking, it has nothing
to do with the *operation* of thinking. Take the case of Socrates being
tried before the Athenian citizens, and the thinking which had to be
done to reach a decision. Certainly the issue was not whether Socrates
was mortal; the point was whether this mortality would or should
occur at a specified date and in a specified way. Now that is just what
does not and cannot follow from a general principle or a major premise.
Again to quote Justice Holmes, " General propositions do not decide
concrete cases." No concrete proposition, that is to say one with material
dated in time and placed in space, follows from any general statements
or from any connection between them.

If we trust to an experimental logic, we find that general principles
emerge as statements of generic ways in which it has been found helpful
to treat concrete cases. The real force of the proposition that all men

are mortal is found in the expectancy tables of insurance companies, which with their accompanying rates show how it is prudent and socially useful to deal with human mortality. The "universal" stated in the major premise is not outside of and antecedent to particular cases; neither is it a selection of something found in a variety of cases. It is an indication of a single way of treating cases for certain purposes or consequences in spite of their diversity. Hence its meaning and worth are subject to inquiry and revision in view of what happens, what the consequences are, when it is used as a method of treatment. . . .

[pp. 19–23]

B. RUSSELL

Dewey's New Logic [2]
(1939)

. . . let us consider the general problem of the relation of knowledge to the biological aspects of life. It is of course obvious that knowledge, broadly speaking, is one of the means to biological success; it is tempting to say, generally, that knowledge leads to success and error leads to failure; going a step further, the pragmatist may say that "knowledge" means "belief leading to success" and "error" means "belief leading to failure." To this view, however, there are many objections, both logical and sociological.

First, we must define "success" and "failure." If we wish to remain in the sphere of biology, we must define "success" as "leaving many descendants." In that sense, as every one knows, the most civilized are the least successful, and therefore, by definition, the most ignorant. Again: the man who, wishing to commit suicide, takes salt under the impression that it is arsenic, may afterwards beget ten children; in that case, the belief which saved his life was "true" in the biological sense. This consequence is absurd and shows that the biological definition is inadequate.

Instead of the objective biological test of success, we must adopt a subjective test: "success" means "achieving desired ends." But this change in the definition of "success" weakens the position. When you see a man eating salt, you cannot tell whether he is acting on knowledge or error until you have ascertained whether he wishes to commit suicide. To ascertain this, you must discover whether the belief that he wishes to commit suicide will lead to your own success. This involves an endless regress. . . .

The pragmatist may say, in reply, that the success which is a test of truth is social, not individual [3]: a belief is "true" when the success of the human race is helped by the existence of the belief. This, however, is hopelessly vague. What is "the success of the human race"? It is a

---

[2] [Dewey has himself summed up his doctrine in the well-known epigram: "Knowledge is successful practice."]

[3] [James himself rejected material success—what he called "the Bitch Goddess, Success"—as the goal of life, in favour of the harmonising of a man's inner life with his outward experience. But this came to be translated into "adjustment," which in the hands of personnel experts soon emerged as the means of making one's life effective in a world of business and money values. See M. Lerner, *America as a Civilisation* (1958), pp. 689, 693–694.]

concept for the politician, not for the logician. Moreover, mankind may profit by the errors of the wicked. We must say, therefore: "A belief is 'true' if the consequences of its being believed by all whose acts are affected by it are better, for mankind as a whole, than the consequences of its being disbelieved." Or, what comes to much the same thing: "A belief is 'true' if an ideally virtuous man will act on it." Any such view presupposes that we can know ethics before we know anything, and is therefore logically absurd. . . .

. . . The pragmatist's position, if I am not mistaken, is a product of a limited scepticism supplemented by a surprising dogmatism. Our beliefs are obviously not always right, and often call for emendation rather than total rejection. Many questions of the highest emotional interest cannot be answered by means of any of the old conceptions of "truth," while many of the questions that can be answered, such as "is this red?" are so uninteresting that the pragmatist ignores them. But in spite of his scepticism, he is confident that he can know whether the consequences of entertaining a belief are such as to satisfy desire. This knowledge is surely far more difficult to secure than the knowledge that the pragmatist begins by questioning, and will have to be obtained, if at all, not by the pragmatist's method, which would lead to an endless regress, but by that very method of observation which, in simpler cases, he has rejected as inadequate.[4]   [pp. 152–154]

LOCHNER v. NEW YORK

United States Supreme Court
198 U. S. 45 (1905)

. . . The statute necessarily interferes with the right of contract between the employer and employés, concerning the number of hours in which the latter may labor in the bakery of the employer. The general right to make a contract in relation to his business is part of the liberty of the individual protected by the Fourteenth Amendment of the Federal Constitution. *Allgeyer* v. *Louisiana*, 165 U. S. 578. Under that provision no State can deprive any person of life, liberty or property without due process of law. The right to purchase or to sell labor is part of the liberty protected by this amendment, unless there are circumstances which exclude the right. There are, however, certain powers, existing in the sovereignty of each State in the Union, somewhat vaguely termed police powers, the exact description and limitation of which have not been attempted by the courts. Those powers, broadly stated and without, at present, any attempt at a more specific limitation, relate to the safety, health, morals and general welfare of the public. Both property and liberty are held on such reasonable conditions as may be imposed by the governing power of the State in the exercise of those powers, and with such conditions the Fourteenth Amendment was not designed to interfere.

The State, therefore, has power to prevent the individual from making

---

4 [In his *A History of Western Philosophy*, Russell summed up the main difference between Dewey and himself: "He judges a belief by its effects, whereas I judge it by its causes where a past occurrence is concerned" (1961 edition, p. 780).]

certain kinds of contracts, and in regard to them the Federal Constitution offers no protection. If the contract be one which the State, in the legitimate exercise of its police power, has the right to prohibit, it is not prevented from prohibiting it by the Fourteenth Amendment. Contracts in violation of a statute, either of the Federal or state government, or a contract to let one's property for immoral purposes, or to do any other unlawful act, could obtain no protection from the Federal Constitution, as coming under the liberty of person or of free contract. Therefore, when the State, by its legislature, in the assumed exercise of its police powers, has passed an act which seriously limits the right to labor or the right of contract in regard to their means of livelihood between persons who are *sui juris* (both employer and employé), it becomes of great importance to determine which shall prevail—the right of the individual to labor for such time as he may choose, or the right of the State to prevent the individual from laboring or from entering into any contract to labor, beyond a certain time prescribed by the State.[5]

[pp. 53–54]

Mr. Justice *Holmes* dissenting.

. . . This case is decided upon an economic theory which a large part of the country does not entertain. If it were a question whether I agreed with that theory, I should desire to study it further and long before making up my mind. But I do not conceive that to be my duty, because I strongly believe that my agreement or disagreement has nothing to do with the right of a majority to embody their opinions in law. It is settled by various decisions of this court that state constitutions and state laws may regulate life in many ways which we as legislators might think as injudicious or if you like as tyrannical as this, and which equally with this interfere with the liberty to contract. Sunday laws and usury laws are ancient examples. A more modern one is the prohibition of lotteries. The liberty of the citizen to do as he likes so long as he does not interfere with the liberty of others to do the same, which has been a shibboleth for some well-known writers, is interfered with by school laws, by the Post Office, by every state or municipal institution which takes his money for purposes thought desirable, whether he likes it or not. The Fourteenth Amendment does not enact Mr. Herbert Spencer's Social Statics.[6] The other day we sustained the Massachusetts vaccination law. *Jacobson* v. *Massachusetts,* 197 U. S. 11. United States and state statutes and decisions cutting down the liberty to contract by way

---

[5] [From the majority opinion which declared the statute unconstitutional; *per* Peckham J.]

[6] [In his celebrated book, *Social Statics*, in 1850, Spencer even argued that the individual should be allowed to make avoidable fatal mistakes because in this way the inefficient and the stupid would be eliminated and the human species improved. The state should therefore not interfere to control medicine or protect individuals from " quacks." All measures which tended to put ignorance upon a par with wisdom would inevitably check the growth of wisdom. (See Kardiner and Preble, *They Studied Man* (1961), pp. 52–53.) *Cf. ante*, 225. See Macrae's remarks: "*Social Statics* and *The Man Versus the State* were treated by businessmen, lawyers, administrators and legislators—in that order of decreasing conviction—as truly embodying the fundamental laws of nature and society. Yet the period of his triumph was short. He already saw before his death the steady flowing of the collectivist tide in England. . . . He might have been cheered had he lived to see his influence continue in the United States " (see Introduction to *The Man Versus The State* (1969), pp. 48–49).]

of combination are familiar to this court. *Northern Securities Co.* v. *United States*, 193 U. S. 197. Two years ago we upheld the prohibition of sales of stock on margins or for future delivery in the constitution of California. *Otis* v. *Parker*, 187 U. S. 606. The decision sustaining an eight hour law for miners is still recent. *Holden* v. *Hardy*, 169 U. S. 366. Some of these laws embody convictions or prejudices which judges are likely to share. Some may not. But a constitution is not intended to embody a particular economic theory, whether of paternalism and the organic relation of the citizen to the State or of *laissez faire*. It is made for people of fundamentally differing views, and the accident of our finding certain opinions natural and familiar or novel and even shocking ought not to conclude our judgment upon the question whether statutes embodying them conflict with the Constitution of the United States.

General propositions do not decide concrete cases. The decision will depend on a judgment or intuition more subtle than any articulate major premise.[7] But I think that the proposition just stated, if it is accepted, will carry us far toward the end. Every opinion tends to become a law. I think that the word liberty in the Fourteenth Amendment is perverted when it is held to prevent the natural outcome of a dominant opinion, unless it can be said that a rational and fair man necessarily would admit that the statute proposed would infringe fundamental principles as they have been understood by the traditions of our people and our law. It does not need research to show that no such sweeping condemnation can be passed upon the statute before us. A reasonable man might think it a proper measure on the score of health. Men whom I certainly could not pronounce unreasonable would uphold it as a first instalment of a general regulation of the hours of work. Whether in the latter aspect it would be open to the charge of inequality I think it unnecessary to discuss.[8]   [pp. 75–76]

J. FRANK

Law and the Modern Mind

(English ed., 1949)[9]

Actually, these so-called realists have but one common bond, a negative characteristic already noted: skepticism as to some of the conventional legal theories, a skepticism stimulated by a zeal to reform, in the interest of justice, some court-house ways. Despite the lack of any homogeneity in their positive views, these "constructive skeptics," roughly speaking, do divide into two groups; however, there are marked differences, ignored by the critics, between the two groups.

---

[7] [Holmes J.'s dissent is a vigorous attack on personal narrow policy, but Holmes himself was an enthusiastic advocate of orientation of the law to considerations of *public* policy and the use of scientific means to establish this. See Morton White, *op. cit.*, pp. 104–105.]

[8] [Note the parallel line of thought in Dewey and Tufts, *Ethics*, published three years after Holmes' dissent, particularly their concern that present standards and ideals were formed in the past and were inapplicable to 1908, and their advocacy of "a larger application of scientific method to the problems of human welfare and progress." See Morton White, *op. cit.*, pp. 103–106. Holmes was firmly entrenched in the mainstream of the philosophical and intellectual thought of his period.]   [9] [From the Preface.]

The first group, of whom Llewellyn is perhaps the outstanding representative, I would call "rule skeptics." They aim at greater legal certainty. That is, they consider it socially desirable that lawyers should be able to predict to their clients the decisions in most lawsuits not yet commenced. They feel that, in too many instances, the layman cannot act with assurance as to how, if his acts become involved in a suit, the court will decide. As these skeptics see it, the trouble is that the formal legal rules enunciated in courts' opinions—sometimes called "paper rules"—too often prove unreliable as guides in the prediction of decisions. They believe that they can discover, behind the "paper rules," some "real rules" descriptive of uniformities or regularities in actual judicial behavior, and that those "real rules" will serve as more reliable prediction-instruments, yielding a large measure of workable predictability of the outcome of future suits. In this undertaking, the rule skeptics concentrate almost exclusively on upper-court opinions. They do not ask themselves whether their own or any other prediction-device will render it possible for a lawyer or layman to prophesy, before an ordinary suit is instituted or comes to trial in a trial court, how it will be decided. In other words, these rule skeptics seek means for making accurate guesses, not about decisions of trial courts, but about decisions of upper courts when trial-court decisions are appealed. These skeptics cold-shoulder the trial courts. Yet, in most instances, these skeptics do not inform their readers that they are writing chiefly of upper courts.

The second group I would call "fact skeptics." They, too, engaging in "rule skepticism," peer behind the "paper rules." Together with the rule skeptics, they have stimulated interest in factors, influencing upper-court decisions, of which, often, the opinions of those courts give no hint. But the fact skeptics go much further. Their primary interest is in the trial courts. No matter how precise or definite may be the formal legal rules, say these fact skeptics, no matter what the discoverable uniformities behind these formal rules, nevertheless it is impossible, and will always be impossible, because of the elusiveness of the facts on which decisions turn, to predict future decisions in most (not all) lawsuits, not yet begun or not yet tried. The fact skeptics, thinking that therefore the pursuit of greatly increased legal certainty is, for the most part, futile—and that its pursuit, indeed, may well work injustice—aim rather at increased judicial justice. This group of fact skeptics includes, among others, Dean Leon Green, Max Radin, Thurman Arnold,[10] William O. Douglas (now Mr. Justice Douglas), and perhaps E. M. Morgan.

Within each of these groups there is diversity of opinion as to many ideas. But I think it can be said that, generally, most of the rule skeptics, restricting themselves to the upper-court level, live in an artificial two-dimensional legal world, while the legal world of the fact skeptics is three-dimensional. Obviously, many events occurring in the fact skeptics'

---

10 [But Arnold was a critic of Frank and realism generally. For Arnold the law was an important symbol, an ideal of government. "The ideal of a judiciary which discovers its principles through the enlightened application of established precedents dramatizes that most important conception that there is a rule of law above men" (24 U.Chi.L.R. 634). The Realist had seen this but had regarded it as a defect in the law. But "the escape of the law from reality constitutes . . . its greatest strength." (*The Symbols of Government* (1935), p. 44).]

three-dimensional cosmos are out of sight, and therefore out of mind, in the rule skeptics' cosmos.

The critical anti-skeptics also live in the artificial upper-court world. Naturally, they have found less fault with the rule skeptics than with the fact skeptics. The critics, for instance, said that Llewellyn was a bit wild yet not wholly unsound, but that men like Dean Green grossly exaggerated the extent of legal uncertainty (i.e., the unpredictability of decisions). To my mind, the critics shoe the wrong foot: Both the rule skeptics and the critics grossly exaggerate the extent of legal certainty, because their own writings deal only with the prediction of upper-court decisions. The rule skeptics are, indeed, but the left-wing adherents of a tradition. It is from the tradition itself that the fact skeptics revolted.

As a reading of this book will disclose, I am one of the fact skeptics. The point there made may be summarized thus: If one accepts as correct the conventional description of how courts reach their decisions, then a decision of any lawsuit results from the application of a legal rule or rules to the facts of the suit. That sounds rather simple, and apparently renders it fairly easy to prophesy the decision, even of a case not yet commenced or tried, especially when as often happens, the applicable rule is definite and precise (for instance, the rule about driving on the right side of the road). But, particularly when pivotal testimony at the trial is oral and conflicting, as it is in most lawsuits, the trial court's " finding " of the facts involves a multitude of elusive factors: First, the trial judge in a non-jury trial or the jury in a jury trial must learn about the facts from the witnesses ; and witnesses, being humanly fallible, frequently make mistakes in observation of what they saw and heard, or in their recollections of what they observed, or in their courtroom reports of those recollections. Second, the trial judges or juries,[11] also human, may have prejudices—often unconscious, unknown even to themselves—for or against some of the witnesses, or the parties to the suit, or the lawyers.[12]

Those prejudices, when they are racial, religious, political, or economic, may sometimes be surmised by others. But there are some hidden, unconscious biases of trial judges or jurors—such as, for example, plus or minus reactions to women, or unmarried women, or red-haired women, or brunettes, or men with deep voices or high-pitched voices, or fidgety men, or men who wear thick eyeglasses, or those who have pronounced gestures or nervous tics—biases of which no one can be aware. Concealed and highly idiosyncratic, such biases—peculiar to each individual judge or juror—cannot be formulated as uniformities or squeezed into regularized " behavior patterns." In that respect, neither judges nor jurors are standardized.

---

[11] [Research since Frank wrote has shown that jury verdicts are not as unpredictable as he suggested. There is, for instance, a high coincidence between jury verdicts and the decision a judge would have arrived at without a jury. See Kalven and Zeisel, *The American Jury, post,* 465.]

[12] [*Cf.* C. P. Harvey, Q.C., *The Advocate's Devil.* Speaking of surgical cases, Mr. Harvey remarks that it is almost an even chance that any judge will approach a case of this sort with subconscious bias based on his own experience in hospital or a nursing home. " In one such case not long ago . . . efforts were made . . . to discover . . . whether the judge was still in possession of his own appendix. There is much to be said for such cases being tried by juries " (p. 50).]

The chief obstacle to prophesying a trial-court decision is, then, the inability, thanks to these inscrutable factors, to foresee what a particular trial judge or jury will believe to be the facts. Consider, particularly, the perplexity of a lawyer asked to guess the outcome of a suit not yet commenced: He must guess whether some of the witnesses will persuasively lie, or will honestly but persuasively give inaccurate testimony; as, usually, he does not even know the trial judge or jury who will try the case, he must also guess the reactions—to the witnesses, the parties and the lawyers—of an unknown trial judge or jury.

These difficulties have been overlooked by most of those (the rule skeptics included) who write on the subject of legal certainty or the prediction of decisions. They often call their writings " jurisprudence "; but, as they almost never consider juries and jury trials, one might chide them for forgetting " juriesprudence."

Moreover, most of them overlook another feature, not revealed in the conventional description of how courts decide cases, a feature unusually baffling: According to the conventional description, judging in a trial court is made up of two components which, initially distinct, are logically combined to produce a decision. Those components, it is said, are (1) the determination of the facts and (2) the determination of what rules should be applied to those facts. In reality, however, those components often are not distinct but intertwine in the thought processes of the trial judge or jury. The decision is frequently an undifferentiated composite which precedes any analysis or breakdown into facts and rules. Many a time, for all anyone can tell, a trial judge makes no such analysis or breakdown when rendering his decision unaccompanied by an explanation. But even when he publishes an explanation, it may be misdescriptive of the way in which the decision was reached. . . .

Shutting their eyes to the actualities of trials, most of the lawyers who write for other lawyers or for laymen about the courts are victims of the Upper-Court Myth. They have deluded themselves and, alas, many non-lawyers, with two correlated false beliefs: (1) They believe that the major cause of legal uncertainty is uncertainty in the rules, so that if the legal rules—or the " real rules " behind the " paper rules "—are entirely clear and crisp, the doubts about future decisions largely vanish. (2) They believe that, on appeals, most mistakes made by trial courts can be rectified by the upper courts. In truth, as noted above, the major cause of legal uncertainty is fact-uncertainty—the unknowability, before the decision, of what the trial court will " find " as the facts, and the unknowability after the decision of the way in which it " found " those facts. If a trial court mistakenly takes as true the oral testimony of an honest but inaccurate witness or a lying witness, seldom can an upper court detect this mistake; it therefore usually adopts the facts as found by the trial court. It does so because the trial court saw and heard the witnesses testify, while the upper court has before it only a lifeless printed report of the testimony, a report that does not contain the witnesses' demeanor, which is often significantly revealing. . . .

With this perspective, we get new light on the doctrine of following the precedents. . . . That doctrine . . . may have less practical importance to the ordinary man than its more ardent advocates accord it. Yet no sane informed person will deny that, within appropriate limits, judicial adherence to precedents possesses such great value that to abandon it would be unthinkable. . . .

However, even when properly and conscientiously utilized, the practice of following the precedents cannot guarantee the stability and certainty it seems to promise to some of those who confine their scrutiny to upper-court decisions. For, in an upper court, ordinarily no fact-finding problem exists, as the facts are beyond dispute, having already been found by the trial court. The usual questions for the upper court are, then, these: Do the facts of the case now before the court sufficiently resemble those of an earlier case so that the rule of that case is applicable? If there is such a resemblance, should that rule now be applied or should it be modified or abandoned? Although able lawyers cannot always guess how an upper court will answer those questions, the educated guesses of those lawyers are good in the majority of instances. When, in a trial court, the parties to a suit agree on the facts, so that the facts are undisputed, that court faces only those same questions; and again, usually, able lawyers can guess the answers.

But, to repeat, in most cases in the trial courts the parties do dispute about the facts, and the testimony concerning the facts is oral and conflicting. In any such case, what does it mean to say that the facts of a case are substantially similar to those of an earlier case? It means, at most, merely that the trial court regards the facts of the two cases as about the same. Since, however, no one knows what the trial court will find as the facts, no one can guess what precedent ought to be or will be followed either by the trial court or, if an appeal occurs, by the upper court. This weakness of the precedent doctrine becomes more obvious when one takes into account the "composite" factor, the intertwining of rules and facts in the trial court's decision.

This weakness will also infect any substitute precedent system, based on "real rules" which the rule skeptics may discover, by way of anthropology—i.e., the mores, customs, folkways—or psychology, or statistics, or studies of the political, economic, and social backgrounds of judges, or otherwise. For no rule can be hermetically sealed against the intrusion of false or inaccurate oral testimony which the trial judge or jury may believe.[13]   [pp. vii–xiv]

E. CAHN

Confronting Injustice

(1967)

. . . *The Challenge to the Law.* Wherever we look at the law, fact-skepticism has a leading role to perform. Consider, for example, the

---

13 [One aspect of Frank, often neglected, is that of Frank—the law reformer. He made a number of constructive proposals which taken together would go some way towards reducing fact-uncertainty. Rumble, *op. cit.*, pp. 126–130 gives a useful summary of some of Frank's ideas. His views on legal education are particularly pertinent. Reading only appeal court opinions was like "future horticulturists studying solely cut flowers." Instead, students should observe at first hand the operations of trial and appellate courts, the actions of legislatures and administrative agencies. Law schools ought to conduct legal clinics (*cf.* the development in the United States of neighbourhood lawyers, 80 Harv.L.R. 805–850). Case-books should contain the complete record of the whole case. See *Courts on Trial*, Chap. 16.]

application of the Fourteenth Amendment. It would seem very curious if the fundamental human fabric of the world's most powerful nation were to be determined by what a few senators of varying intellectual caliber may have intended—or hinted they intended—during the remote and unattractive year of 1868. Curious it would be; curious enough to be insupportable, I should think. We were rescued from any such tyranny of the dead, at least in respect of desegregation, by the way the Supreme Court treated the strictly historical arguments in *Brown* v. *Board of Education.* It was fact-skepticism that emancipated us. The Supreme Court declared that if 1868 aspired to rule the 1950's, 1868 ought to have been less ambiguous. With this profitable example to work with, the legal profession's next question may be: how many other despotisms of past over present can we undertake to subvert by the same technique; how many more historical bonds can fact-skepticism loosen, then dissolve?

Yet it is wise to remember that the shackles of the anticipated future can be tighter than those of the conceived past. Our entire juristic order—civil, criminal and administrative—is permeated with uncritical assumptions about future deterrence. The law takes property, liberty and even life under the supposed warrant of deterrence. What the judges call " public policy " they deduce in large part from inarticulate premises of deterrence. Deterrence shapes the rules of tort liability; deterrence attempts to vouch for censorship and sedition laws. In short, cool, self-possessed deterrence has its roster of victims no less than hot vindictiveness.

Fact-skepticism challenges us to make a detailed and radical re-examination of the entire rationale of deterrence. Does this or that assumed deterrent really deter? What other, uncalculated effects does it have? If in many instances it does deter, then how far dare the community go in penalising one person to influence the behavior of others?

Let me mention a single practical application among many. Fact-skepticism, in and of itself would provide two severally sufficient reasons for ending that rational infamy of ours, capital punishment: first, because capital punishment is not demonstrated to deter in fact; second, because under our system there is substantial danger of convicting and executing the wrong person. Jerome Frank concurred that each of these reasons is more than sufficient for abolishing the death penalty.

The Challenge to Political Theory and Cultural Anthropology. Here I suggest that fact-skepticism calls for a thoroughly candid review of what is taken for granted in phrases like " the rule of law," " representative government," " popular mandate," and " the consent of the governed." Let the timorous have no misgivings: our fabric of government is so superior to Russia's that we can easily afford to turn the full force of fact-skepticism on it. For example, Cold War or no Cold War, no American needs to deny or disparage the important human and personal factors that animate every variety of so-called " constitutionalism," including our own. One of the best features of fact-skepticism is that it warns men away from false supports and treacherous comforts. In this way, it impels them toward truth, which remains their faithful ally.

The Challenge to Philosophy in General and Pragmatism and Analytic Empiricism in Particular. A few years before the publication of *Courts on Trial,* a professor of philosophy and historian of American pragmatism declared that Holmes's analysis was " the only systematic application of pragmatism that has yet been made." If then fact-skepticism should edify the legal profession, how much more should it excite philosophers, ethicists and all who are concerned with the meaning of language and the foundations of moral responsibility! Surely they will wish to consider how deeply and how far fact-skepticism may affect Pierce's doctrine that the meaning of a concept is to be found in its conceived consequences and James's doctrine that " the true " is the long-run expedient in our way of thinking. In basic respects, are not these also prediction-theories? In so far as they are, it seems fair to analogize them to Holmes's. Since their subject matter is so very general, they may prove even more vulnerable to the prongs of fact-skepticism. Pragmatists and instrumentalists in every profession will appreciate the force and imminence of the challenge.

Now we approach fact-skepticism's ultimate contribution. Let us suppose along with Jerome Frank and Carl Becker that accurate knowledge of the past is generally elusive. Let us suppose along with Jerome Frank and William James that our abstract concept is often like the iron claw of a toy crane in an amusement arcade: while it may succeed in grasping the ordinary, humdrum objects in the cage, it will continually miss the things that are interesting, deviant or eccentric. Further, let us grant—for grant we must—that though occasionally we may be able to foretell certain direct and immediate consequences of a proposed statute or decision, we cannot pretend to prophesy the spreading network of eventual, indirect, mediate, oblique consequences. As Judge Learned Hand has said, " Such prophecies infest law of every sort, the more deeply as it is far reaching; and it is an illusion to suppose that there are formulas or statistics that will help in making them." No substitutes for critical judgment, no escapes from personal responsibility, no formulas? Yet prophecies and the making of prophecies " infest " not only the law but the totality of human experience. Surely then our account has reached its climax, which is:

The Challenge to American Society. If fact-skepticism can accomplish its full work of emancipation, perhaps we shall at last be free to realize the pristine American dream. In the years when our nation began, there was a sort of axiomatic expectation that this " new order of the ages," this unprecedented experiment in republican government would develop a wholly superior breed of human beings. On American shores men would flourish as never before, and gain new personal stature. Here nature and society would invite them to unfold their individual talents, to discover themselves—as it were, to reach out and push back the cultural frontiers. Eventually this democratic republic of ours would exhibit a new kind of political community composed in large part of moral aristocrats.

Today most of us would acknowledge that what was then a charming vision has become a matter of arresting urgency. It is no longer merely desirable, it is virtually indispensable that American society produce a multitude of superior human beings, men and women of understanding judgment and moral rectitude, of expansive horizons and humane sensibilities who can feel the full pathos of individual misfortunes and predicaments, yet venture to act on occasion as though the world were plastic.

By insisting on the personal element in all processes of decision, fact-skepticism underscores our state of need. It admonishes that the best and wisest propositions of social ethics, politics and law will not preserve us if the men who apply them to concrete transactions are themselves Philistines and mediocrities, even affable mediocrities. Nothing earthly can preserve us without sharply improved human qualities of leadership and citizenship.

Here, at this critical juncture the fact-skeptic may be heard speaking a message of (perhaps) unexpected but entirely reasonable optimism. Once he has shown that the grip of the past is loose and the grip of the future even looser, he may fairly contend that we enjoy considerable new elbowroom in the realm of the present. He relishes the present with a special confidence. His very questionings and doubtings have earned him the right to declare that men possess an enormously wider and more diverse register of individual and social choices than they have ever exercised. He may go on to explain that fact-skepticism is as suspicious of alleged impossibilities as it is of pseudoscientific nostrums. He may add—rather firmly—that one approved way to lift the heart is to exert the intellect. Who knows?—he will ask—while his congeners sit and fret in the darkness, some powerful source of enlightenment may be dangling there, within easy reach. This was the vital pattern of Jerome Frank's faith. He incessantly prodded and encouraged all our social institutions to produce *qualitative* men, and thus he paid a supreme tribute to the ideal of human dignity. . . .   [pp. 288–291]

K. LLEWELLYN

Some Realism About Realism

(1931) [14]

Real Realists

What, then, *are* the characteristics of these fermenters? One thing is clear. There is no school of realists. There is no likelihood that there will be such a school. There is no group with an official or accepted, or even with an emerging creed. There is no abnegation of independent striking out. We hope that there may never be. New recruits acquire tools and stimulus, not masters, nor over-mastering ideas. Old recruits diverge in interests from each other. They are related, says Frank, only in their negations, and in their skepticisms, and in their curiosity. [15]

There is, however, a *movement* in thought and work about law. The movement, the method of attack, is wider than the number of its adherents. It includes some or much work of many men who would

---

[14] [From (1931) 44 Harv.L.R. 1222, copyright 1931, by the Harvard Law Review Association. Now reprinted in K. Llewellyn, *Jurisprudence* (1962) at p. 42, with a few textual amendments, which have been embodied in those portions of the text quoted in this volume.]

[5] Names for them vary. I call them realists (so do Frank, Radin, and often, Yntema; Bingham also recognises the term. And I find it used in the same sense in the work of Cook, Douglas, Frankfurter)—stressing the interest in the actuality of what happens, and the distrust of formula. Cook prefers to speak of scientific approach to law, Oliphant of objective method—stressing much the same features. Clark speaks of fact-research, Corbin of what courts do. " Functional approach " stresses the interest in, and valuation by, effects. Dickinson speaks of the skeptical movement.

scorn ascription to its banner.   Individual men, then.   Men more or less interstimulated—but no more than all of them have been stimulated by the orthodox tradition, or by that ferment at the opening of the century in which Dean Pound took a leading part.   Individual men, working and thinking over law and its place in society.   Their differences in point of view, in interest, in emphasis, in field of work, are huge.   They differ among themselves well-nigh as much as any of them differs from, say, Langdell.   Their number grows.   Their work finds acceptance.

What one does find as he observes them is twofold.   First (and to be expected) certain points of departure are common to them all.   Second (and this, when one can find neither school nor striking likenesses among individuals, is startling) a cross-relevance, a complementing, an interlocking of their varied results " as if they were guided by an invisible hand."   A third thing may be mentioned in passing: a fighting faith in their methods of attack on legal problems ; but in these last years the battle with the facts has proved so much more exciting than any battle traditionalism that the fighting faith had come (until the spring offensive of 1931 against the realists) to manifest itself chiefly in enthusiastic labor to get on.

But as with a description of an economic order, tone and color of description must vary with the point of view of the reporter.   No other one of the men would set the picture up as I shall.   Such a report must thus be individual.   Each man, of necessity, orients the whole to his own main interest of the moment—as I shall orient the whole to mine: the workings of case-law in appellate courts.   Maps of the United States prepared respectively by a political geographer and a student of climate would show some resemblance ; each would show a coherent picture ; but neither's map would give much satisfaction to the other.   So here. I speak for myself of that movement which in its sum is realism ; I do not speak of " the realists "; still less do I speak *for* the participants or any of them.   And I shall endeavor to keep in mind as I go that the justification for grouping these men together lies not in that they are *alike* in belief or work, but in that from certain common points of departure they have branched into lines of work which seem to be building themselves into a whole, a whole planned by none, foreseen by none, and (it may well be) not yet adequately grasped by any.

The common points of departure are several.

(1) The conception of law in flux, of moving law, and of judicial creation of law.

(2) The conception of law as a means to social ends and not as an end in itself ; so that any part needs constantly to be examined for its purpose, and for its effect, and to be judged in the light of both and of their relation to each other.

(3) The conception of society in flux, and in flux typically faster than the law, so that the probability is always given that any portion of law needs reëxamination to determine how far its fits the society it purports to serve.

(4) The *temporary* divorce of Is and Ought for purposes of study.[16]   By this I mean that whereas value judgments must always be appealed to in

16 [The influence of Weber's *wertfrei* social science is apparent.   But, on the possibility of developing a value-free sociology as a myth see Gouldner, 9 *Social Problems*, 199–213.]

order to set objectives for inquiry, yet during the inquiry itself into what Is, the observation, the description, and the establishment of relations between the things described are to remain *as largely as possible* uncontaminated by the desires of the observer or by what he wishes might be or thinks ought (ethically) to be. More particularly, this involves during the study of what courts are doing the effort to disregard the question what they ought to do. Such divorce of Is and Ought is, of course, not conceived as permanent. To men who begin with a suspicion that change is needed, a permanent divorce would be impossible. The argument is simply that no judgment of what Ought to be done in the future with respect to any part of law can be intelligently made without knowing objectively, as far as possible, what that part of law is now doing. And realists believe that experience shows the intrusion of Ought-spectacles *during the investigation of the facts* to make it very difficult to see what is being done. On the Ought side this means an insistence on informed evaluations instead of armchair speculations. Its full implications on the side of Is-investigation can be appreciated only when one follows the contributions to objective description in business law and practice made by realists whose social philosophy rejects many of the accepted foundations of the existing economic order. (*E.g.*, Handler *re* trade-marks and advertising; Klaus *re* marketing and banking; Llewellyn *re* sales; Moore *re* banking; Patterson *re* risk-bearing.) [17]

(5) Distrust of traditional legal rules and concepts insofar as they purport to *describe* what either courts or people are actually doing.[18] Hence the constant emphasis on rules as " generalized predictions of what courts will do." This is much more widespread as yet than its counterpart: the careful severance of rules *for* doing (precepts) from rules *of* doing (practices).

(6) Hand in hand with this distrust of traditional rules (on the

---

[17] [This starting-point is at once the most controversial and difficult of Llewellyn's credo. It is not accepted by all Realists (see, *e.g.* Yntema (1960–61), 14 Vand. L.R. 317, 323–325). Together with point (5), it was the principal bone of contention with Pound, though Stone believes the controversy to have been illusory. (*Social Dimensions*, pp. 64–67). " It is certainly now clear," he writes, " that [Llewellyn] was asking *not for the observer to ignore the actor's ideals, but for the observer to put aside his own*, so that accurate observation and description should not be interfered with." (*ibid.*, pp. 64–65). And, in an article he wrote in 1939 (" One ' Realist's ' View of Natural Law for Judges," in *Jurisprudence*, p. 111), Llewellyn confirms that lawyers are concerned with values " applicable to a given going society," though from the point of view of the jurist this " ought " becomes an " is." See, further, on this question, Friedrich, 74 *Ethics* 201. Llewellyn's view of natural law has the relativist ring of Stammler about it. He distinguishes a lawyer's natural law from a philosopher's. The latter is concerned with the right ordering of any human society, the lawyer with principles " applicable to a given going society." A lawyer's natural law is an effort to bring the philosopher's Natural Law to bear in lawyer-like actual regulation " on legal problems in a particular society. It afford[s] a concrete guide to the making of proper positive law."]

[18] [The so-called Free-Law School on the Continent is to be distinguished from the Realists, since the former did not so much distrust rules, but asserted that there are many gaps in the law which the courts may fill by exercising a free discretion. This did not prevent there being a large area where the rules as formulated exercised a substantially effective control. See H. Kantorowicz (1934) Yale L.J. 1240. *Cf.* Frank, *Law and the Modern Mind*, pp. 301–306. For a recent appraisal of the Free-Law School see, Foulkes (1969), 55 *Archiv für Rechts-und-sozialphilosophie* 367.]

descriptive side) goes a distrust of the theory that traditional prescriptive rule-formulations are *the* heavily operative factor in producing court decisions. This involves the tentative exploration of the theory of rationalization for what light it can give in the study of opinions. It will be noted that " distrust " in this and the preceding point is not at all equivalent to " negation in any given instance."

(7) The belief in the worthwhileness of grouping cases and legal situations into narrower categories than has been the practice in the past.[19] This is connected with the distrust of verbally simple rules—which so often cover dissimilar and non-simple fact situations (dissimilarity being tested partly by the way cases come out, and partly by the observer's judgment as to how they ought to come out[20]; but a realist tries to indicate explicitly which criterion he is applying in any particular instance).[21]

(8) An insistence on evaluation of any part of law in terms of its effects, and an insistence on the worthwhileness of trying to find these effects.

(9) Insistence on *sustained and programmatic attack* on the problems of law along any of these lines. None of the ideas set forth in this list is new. Each can be matched from somewhere ; each can be matched

19 [The quest for narrower, more significant, categories is always a sound *first* approach to wide categories which are not giving satisfaction-in-use. But, of course, once satisfactory narrower categories have been found and tested, the eternal quest recurs, for wider synthesis—but one which really stands up in use. With this advice in mind, the framers of the Uniform Commercial Code often substitute narrower categories for a broad one, but the reverse is also occasionally true. For example, trust receipts, chattel mortgages, *etc.* are replaced by the umbrella, " security." See Twining, O'Donovan, Paliwala in Jolowicz, *The Division and Classification of the Law* 10, 24.]

20 [A striking illustration of this comes out in the writings of Willard Hurst. See particularly his study of the Wisconsin lumber industry, *Law and Economic Growth* (1964), and see the comment in Stone, 1 Israel L.R. 173, 192.]

21 [See the recent interest in this problem in ed. Jolowicz, *The Division and Classification of the Law* (1970). Jolowicz's thesis is that " developments both in social life and in the law itself have deprived many of the conventional headings of their factual frames of reference and so have rendered them inadequate as instruments for use in a critical survey of the law " (p. 6). A tile falls from a roof, bad workmanship is responsible but the occupier could not reasonably have detected this. A person is injured. He will probably recover damages in an action in nuisance. Not so, if he had stepped inside the garden gate (Occupiers' Liability Act 1957, s. 2 (4) (b)). *Cf.* the discussion of *Read* v. *Lyons*, *post*, 810. Jolowicz advocates factual classification and enlisting the help of social scientists and economists. The limitations of " fact-based " classification are sketched by Twining, O'Donovan and Paliwala, *op. cit.* They favour multidimensional classification, being of the opinion that a single, perfect scheme of classification is illusory. To identify the range of possibilities they would enlist the help of a computer. Fact-based classification is rejected because it is difficult to elucidate what is a fact (an accident is a fact, arson a legal concept, but what of the proverbial " agreement " or " alien "?). Furthermore, the concept " fact-based " gives no guidance in choice of levels of abstraction (*cf.* Stone, *post*, 774). Is Ursula an animal or a black female poodle puppy? And a black female poodle puppy can be classified by colour, sex, species or age. There may be an over-emphasis on the borderline case in this line of thought. Fact-based classification is clearly desirable and feasible in many contexts (*vide*, the examples given above). But one lesson is driven home in both these articles : legal classification requires the help of others than lawyers. Other valuable essays in this collection are those by Narain (p. 34), who argues for a value-based classification, a thesis not unlike Lasswell and McDougal's (*cf. ante*, 349), and by McClintock and Hadden (p. 48), who urge a functional analysis of law geared to its respective roles in the social control system.]

from recent orthodox work in law. New twists and combinations do appear here and there. What is as novel as it is vital is for a goodly number of men to pick up ideas which have been expressed and dropped, used for an hour and dropped, played with from time to time and dropped—to pick up such ideas and set about *consistently, persistently, insistently to carry them through.* Grant that the idea or point of view is familiar—the results of steady, sustained, systematic work with it are not familiar. Not hit-or-miss stuff, not the insight which flashes and is forgotten, but sustained effort to force an old insight into its full bearing, to exploit it to the point where it laps over upon an apparently inconsistent insight, to explore their bearing on each other by the test of fact. This urge, in law, is quite new enough over the last decades to excuse a touch of frenzy among the locust-eaters.[22]

The first, second, third and fifth of the above items, while common to the workers of the newer movement, are not peculiar to them. But the other items (4, 6, 7, 8 and 9) are to me the characteristic marks of the movement. Men or work fitting those specifications are to me "realistic" whatever label they may wear. Such, and none other, are the perfect fauna of this new land. Not all the work cited below fits my peculiar definition in all points. All such work fits most of the points.

Bound, as all "innovators" are, by prior thinking, these innovating "realists" brought their batteries to bear in first instance on the work of appellate courts. Still wholly within the tradition of our law, they strove to improve on that tradition.

(a) An early and fruitful line of attack borrowed from psychology the concept of *rationalization* already mentioned. To recanvass the opinions, viewing them no longer as mirroring the process of deciding cases, but rather as trained lawyers' arguments made by the judges (after the decision has been reached), intended to make the decision seem plausible, legally decent, legally right, to make it seem, indeed, legally inevitable—this was to open up new vision. It was assumed that the deductive logic of opinions need by no means be either a *description* of the process of decision, or an *explanation* of how the decision was reached. Indeed over-enthusiasm has at times assumed that the logic of the opinion *could* be neither; and similar over-enthusiasm, perceiving case after case in which the opinion is clearly almost valueless as an indication of how that case came to decision, has worked at times almost as if the opinion were equally valueless in predicting what a later court will do.

But the line of inquiry via rationalization has come close to demonstrating that in any case doubtful enough to make litigation respectable the available authoritative premises—*i.e.*, premises legitimate and impeccable under the traditional legal techniques—are at least two, and that the two are mutually contradictory as applied to the case in hand. Which opens the question of what made the court select the one available premise rather than the other. And which raises the greatest of doubts as to *how far* that supposed certainty in decision which derives merely or even chiefly from the presence of accepted rules really goes.

(b) A second line of attack has been to discriminate among rules with

---

[22] Since everyone who reads the manuscript in this sad age finds this allusion blind, but I still like it, I insert the passage: ". . . Preaching in the wilderness of Judea, And saying, Repent ye . . . And the same John had his raiment of camel's hair, and a leathern girdle about his loins; *and his meat was locusts* and wild honey." Matthew III, 1, 2, 4.

reference to their relative significance. Too much is written and thought about "law" and "rules," lump-wise. Which part of law? Which rule? Iron rules of policy, and rules "in the absence of agreement"; rules which keep a case from the jury, and rules as to the etiquette of instructions necessary to make a verdict stick—if one can get it; rules "of pure decision" for hospital cases, and rules which counsellors rely on in their counselling; rules which affect many (and which many, and how?) and rules which affect few. Such discriminations affect the traditional law curriculum, the traditional organisation of law books and, above all, the orientation of study: to drive into the most important fields of ignorance.[23]

(c) A further line of attack on the apparent conflict and uncertainty among the decisions in appellate courts has been to seek more understandable statement of them by grouping the facts in new—and typically but not always narrower—categories. The search is for correlations of fact-situation and outcome which (aided by common sense) may reveal *when* courts seize on one rather than another of the available competing premises. One may even stumble on the trail of *why* they do. Perhaps, *e.g.*, third party beneficiary difficulties simply fail to get applied to promises to make provision for dependents; perhaps the pre-existing duty rule goes by the board when the agreement is one for a marriage-settlement. Perhaps, indeed, contracts in what we may broadly call family relations do not work out in general as they do in business. If so, the rules—viewed as statements of the course of judicial behavior—as *predictions* of what will happen—need to be restated. Sometimes it is a question of carving out hitherto unnoticed exceptions. But sometimes the results force the worker to reclassify an area altogether. Typically, as stated, the classes of situations which result are narrower, much narrower than the traditional classes. The process is in essence the orthodox technique of making distinctions, and reformulating—but undertaken systematically; exploited consciously, instead of being reserved until facts which refuse to be twisted by "interpretation" force action. The departure from orthodox procedure lies chiefly in distrust of, instead of search for, the widest sweep of generalization words permit. Not that such sweeping generalizations are not desired—*if they can be made so as to state what judges do or ought to do.*

All of these three earliest lines of attack converge to a single conclusion: *there is less possibility of accurate prediction of what courts will do than the traditional rules would lead us to suppose* (and what possibility there is must be found in good measure outside these same traditional rules).   [pp. 1233–1241]

---

[23] [A striking example of the way in which the practice of officials may govern the operation of an important branch of law, is provided by the procedure in relation to tax law in this country. Many of the rules applied in this sphere are unofficially laid down by the Revenue Department, which sometimes sees fit to publicise their practices and sometimes not. The experienced practitioner in these matters needs to have ample knowledge of such practices and to weigh them carefully in tendering advice to his clients. Nevertheless it is still the somewhat unrealistic practice of textbook writers in such a field to pay little or no attention to the existence and content of operative practices of this kind. In the field of social welfare law certain secrets were recently published after pressure had been exerted by such groups as the Child Poverty Action Group. But this is a field into which lawyers have hardly entered (there is no legal aid before tribunals), so textbooks are not unrealistic: they do not exist.]

K. LLEWELLYN

Using the Newer Jurisprudence

(1940) [24]

What has been said can perhaps be summed up thus: the fact that judges and officials are not wholly free and must not be wholly free, divides on analysis and closer examination into two facts. The one fact is concerned with the control, the restraint, the holding down, of judges and officials; the other fact is concerned with the allowing to them of a limited degree and a limited kind of leeway, and the putting on them of a duty to exercise their uttermost skill and judgment within that leeway. Both of these facts must be seen, and both must be reckoned with, by any Jurisprudence which aims to cover the plain facts and the settled policies of our legal system. For there are two kinds of judicial or other official freedom which come in question, and the two kinds are very different. It is a fact in our legal system that judges are by no means free to be *arbitrary*, and our vital need that they shall not be free to be *arbitrary* has been caught into these rationales or doctrines about "laws and not men", and about "rules determining cases". But it is also a fact that our legal system does adjust to the individual case *and* to changes in our conditions and institutions; and that fact means that judges and other officials are free to some real degree to be *just* and *wise*, and that we have a vital need that judges and other officials shall continue to be to some real degree free to be *wise* and *just*. That fact happens, however, *not* to have been caught into an equally familiar, equally sharp, or equally precious rationale or doctrine. Yet it needs to be; it is no less a vital part of our legal system and of our judges' duty. There is the law, which we know as impersonal, and think of as clear; there is the right outcome, which we feel as also impersonal, and think of as hard to find, but capable of being found, and the office of the judge is to fulfil the demands of *both*, together.

Here one sees as under a miscroscope the essence of method and accomplishment of the newer Jurisprudence. The method is to take accepted doctrine, and check its words against its results, in the particular as in the large. The method is to attempt to take a fresh look, and a sustained, careful look, at what goes on. The method is then to try to keep all the relevant results in mind at once, to see whether Tuesday's results check with Monday's, and Wednesday's with either; and to be content with no formulation which does not account for *all* of the results. That is the first part of the method. The second part of the method, if the accepted doctrine does not seem to wholly square with all of the results, is to attempt another fresh look, from some other angles: If a doctrine does not do all that it purports to do, then why do people cling to it so hard? If a doctrine does not, in and by itself do all that it purports to do, then *what else* is at work helping the doctrine out? For there is something else at work, helping all doctrines out. There is the tradition of the judge's craft, stabilizing the work of our judges, and guiding it; and there are the ideals of that craft, which also stabilize and guide. Is this *something else* something wholly ineffable or spiritual or personal, so much so as to yield nothing at all to careful study, so much

---

[24] [40 Col.L.R. 581. Now reprinted in K. Llewellyn, *Jurisprudence* (1962), p. 128.]

so as to lay no foundation for more effective doctrine which can get closer to really doing what the doctrine we have is supposed to be doing? The idea underlying modern Jurisprudence is that harder and more intensive study of what goes on, and harder and above all more sustained study of the wisdoms and part-wisdoms in the books, checking them again and again against what goes on, can lay the foundation for more solid doctrine. On the particular matter of judging, the newer Jurisprudence is persuaded that the older, by putting on the doctrines of law more weight than those doctrines do bear or can bear alone, had put too little weight on the *art and craft of the judge's office*. One studies that art and craft by studying particular officers at work in their office, and seeking for the similarities in their attitudes and behavior. This has been misconceived, as being a delving into vagaries of individuals ; what it is, is a search for predictabilities and proper lines of work in the judge's office, which transcend individuality. These can be dug out only by case study.[25]   [pp. 586–588]

. . . For any lawyer is aware that whereas we have clear and established practice, and even rules, to tell, for instance, *how* to distinguish a precedent, and *how* to give even bold dictum full weight by quotation and citation of what " this court has declared ", as " a true expression of the principle ", we yet have no unambiguous rules at all to tell *when* to do the one or the other or anything between or different. And the same holds as to, say " remedial " and " strict " construction of statutes. Pound's line of initial approach to the matter is thoroughly sound: the necessary basis for better doctrine does lie in the laying out of new and more effective lines of descriptive study of the actual work of the courts with our rules of law, and within the frame of action, which those rules mark out. For it is by careful and accurate description of what the courts are doing that we can see wherein existing doctrine fails to *guide* them effectively in being wise, and fails to hold down their freedom to be " arbitrary ". Yet any attempted description will for the next decade need repeated testing in detail on particular series of cases in particular courts, so as to check up on just how good and accurate a description it may be ; and above all, so as to bring out for study what else and more there may be which also needs description and comparison. Only so can the basis be laid for clearer and more unambiguous doctrine on how judges are to go about the judge's job. To date, we have left much more of this to mere untutored and unguided experience than a system of Law has any business to.

The philosophy of this can be stated briefly: Legal doctrine cannot wisely attempt to achieve what is impossible of achievement. To make courts either stand still or ignore the justice of the case in hand is impossible. (It is also undesirable.) Doctrine which purports to cut down all freedom of the judge or other official is therefore unserviceable doctrine. In practice, it leads to the production and use of *de facto* leeways which *de jure* are left unmentioned ; and *de facto* but unmentioned leeways are both confusing and not subject to easy control. But to merely see this and then insist that judges—and other officials—are

25 [" Every body of law contains both a core of stability and a line of change—England stresses the element of precedent, that is tradition, Americans stress the dynamism by which lawyers are able to fashion new law out of new social experience ": M. Lerner, *op. cit.*, p. 427.]

in fact as free to move as the *rules of law now leave* them whenever they really *want* to move; or to insist that they *ought* to use all the freedom which the rules of law now leave them—either of these things is to make doctrine fit only for the super judges, the Mansfields and Marshalls, and not for the McWhirtles and McWhortles who, though good and solid men, do yet need guidance and may sometimes need control. To see what we have, in the way of either control or guidance, is a job for realistic observation, observation of fact, of detailed fact, observation which cuts beneath formula, sustained observation. To see just what is needed, in control of freedom to be arbitrary, while leaving the necessary freedom to be just, is a job for such observation plus legal statesmanship. To formulate for practical use rules and principles which can help materially in accomplishing the desired gain in both certainty and justice, is a job for legal engineering. The task is not chimerical, because we know that there can be training for the art of advocacy; the Greeks accomplished that, and so did the Scholastics. We know, too, that there can be training for counselling; the offices " break men in ", year by year. *Some* of the art of advocacy, *some* of the art of counselling, can be reduced to helpful rules and principles. Judging, too, is a craft and art of law. Well, then?

The " Well, then?" is a challenge, not a performance. The newer Jurisprudence is yet far from having worked out with clarity the relation, in the judges' actual work, of the ideal and ideological elements in our legal system to the words of the rules of law, or the relation of either of these to the going institutional practices of courts and judges. That is a plain next problem for study. The newer Jurisprudence can claim to have gotten it into the clear, to be seen as a problem. That is not too much. But what there is of it, is good.

Another problem, on which a beginning has been made, is the examination of the three major aspects of the judge, and of their relations to one another in his work. He is a *human being*, and in our system he is an American. He is a *lawyer*, and in our system he is a common-lawyer. He is a *judge*, and in our system a common-law judge of the modern American type—which is very different not only from being a Continental or English judge, but also from being merely an American, or merely a lawyer, or merely an American lawyer. Some of the older Jurisprudence is written as if a judge were practically nothing but a mechanical lawyer on a bench; some of the newer reads almost as if he were nothing but a human American in a black robe. Neither of these points of view is to be simply scorned, because there are facts under each; but no such point of view, *alone*, has value as more than a reminder that certain very real factors in the picture are never to be forgotten.[26]   [pp. 595–596]

Indeed it is a fair generalization that almost nothing the newer Jurisprudence has yet found, and little that it seems likely to find within the next few decades, will prove in any manner *new*, to the *best* lawyers. It will be, as it has been, a putting together of different pieces of what the

---

[26] [The widespread use of elected judges and the quasi-political function of the Supreme Court have created a greater interest in the ideology and other attitudes of particular members of the judiciary than is usual in other common law countries where such discussion is generally avoided at any rate during a judge's lifetime.]

best lawyers know—different pieces which even the best lawyers do not commonly put together and *compare*—so as to make the resulting Whole give other lawyers and especially new lawyers, a clearer and more usable picture of how the various crafts of the lawyer are best carried on: counselling, advocacy, judging, and administration.[27]   [p. 600]

Indeed when one takes as the central theme this problem of guidance to the judge—or to the legislator—or to the administrator—one finds every line of work in modern Jurisprudence falling into an organization as clear as that of spokes around a common hub, building themselves together into a common wheel. Any one of these lines may be pursued in a single paper or by a single writer, in utter independence of the others, in complete " narrow " specialization of effort, in seeming variety of direction among the different jobs; yet each in its own way works to and from the common center, each contributes toward the total central task which calls for use of all of them together. Let me illustrate by a number of lines of modern work which would seem to be at war, if any of them should be misestimated as being what it is not, namely as being an effort to stake out an exclusively valid approach to the *whole* field of Jurisprudence. None of these lines is to be soundly conceived as denying the worthwhileness, utility, necessity, of other, complementary lines of work. What each does is to insist that its own line has sufficient value, actual or potential, to warrant careful and sustained labor on its exploration. The older writers—such men as Bentham, Savigny, Jhering— seem sometimes to have written as if work in Jurisprudence had no point unless it could at the moment of its doing be brought into its right relation with a whole and rounded view of all of law and all law's work. The current writers, even along with the impatience they sometimes display with one another or with a tough-minded and sometimes tough-hided profession, do show a gratifying intellectual patience in this: that they are willing to work hard over one small piece of the picture, just as being one needed piece, in an effort to get *that piece* into better shape for synthesis tomorrow, and perhaps by someone else who may happen to take synthesis as his line of labor.   [pp. 604–605]

KARL LLEWELLYN

The Common Law Tradition
(1960)

Reckonability of Result

Theory of Rules

Before we again pick up the forecasting problem, let us make quick audit of this last assertion: Are the lines of inquiry we have been exploring indeed available to ordinary lawyers? Or do these leads or

---

[27] [The reader will note that a far more modest assessment of the prospects for realism seems to emerge from this article than in the earlier one quoted, *ante*, 441. See also Llewellyn's valedictory assessment of realism in an appendix to his final work, *The Common Law Tradition*, pp. 508–520. In this he stresses that " realism was never a philosophy ": it was, rather, a " method " and the " only tenet involved is that the method is a good one." " *Realism* is *not* a philosophy, but a *technology*. That is why it is eternal " (p. 510).]

devices go dumb or incoherent in the absence of some peculiar psychological or other technical training, or in the absence of some elaborate and inaccessible data, or in the absence of some intransmissible native knack? I submit that the signs to be looked for, though wholly unstandardized, are nonetheless as gross and unmistakable as road signs, and that there are obvious and valuable procedures of interpretation and use which are wellnigh as simple and communicable as the driving of a nail. Road signs *can* secrete themselves behind hedges, *can* break or fade, *can* be misleading; and nails *can* be hammered on the thumb; but for daily living the signs suffice to guide most folk and the process to rough-carpenter boards into some utility. I submit that the average lawyer has only to shift his focus for a few hours from " *what* was held " in a series of opinions to what those opinions suggest or show about *what was bothering and what was helping the court* as it decided. If he will take that as his subject matter, I submit that the average lawyer can provide himself, and rather speedily, with the kit of coarse tools we have been discussing and with evidence, too, of his own ability to use that kit to immediate advantage.

Is the effort worth while? Leave intellectual curiosity on one side, and the fun that comes from sudden novel cross-lighting of scenes otherwise too familiar for notice. Look, if you will, to bald practicality: does this proposed way of reading opinions, this proposed focus on the *How* of the court's deciding, substantially increase the reader's forecasting power, as contrasted with a forecasting based merely on a search for the prevailing doctrine, or with a forecasting based chiefly on feel, hunch, or guess, or with a forecasting based on some unanalyzed cross-play of those two? For the ordinary lawyer I submit that there can be no question as to the gain in predictive power. Spend a single thoughtful weekend with a couple of recent volumes of reports from your own supreme court, read this way, and you can never again, with fervor or despair, make that remark about never knowing where an appellate court will hang its hat. Spend five such weekends, and you will be getting a workable idea of the local geography of hat-racks.

Neither can there be question for most of the better appellate lawyers, that these approaches, based as they are on the best practice, make conscious and clear, and thus available even on bad days, values which in the absence of a good day may otherwise fail to come to bear. I speak not, naturally, of the genius or near-genius whose intuition regularly and almost on contact with a case strikes for the jugular, for that point and aspect which will catch and move the court; such a man has little need for these cruder forms of intellectual apparatus. For all except such, however, the point is clinched by certain propositions from the theory of rules:

The Function of Rules is Guidance

Rules Are Not to Control, but to Guide Decision

This is a fundamental truth which is inherent in the duty of a court to introduce into its work some touch of reason and some feeling for sense and fairness, in terms of the type-situation. Where the rule rates high in wisdom and is also technically clear and neat, the guidance is indeed so cogent as, in effect, to be almost equivalent to control or dictation; so, also, when the measure is technically well designed and the rule is a legislative product of unmistakable policy and is too fresh off the griddle for modifying circumstance to have supervened. But in such case the near-control is not because those rules are rules of law, but because of the particular kind of rule of law they happen—rather unusually—to be. So that it is of the essence to distinguish among rules of law, both in regard to what may be expected of them and in regard to what should be. This leads into two further companion propositions:

The Law of Compatibility

If application of the seemingly apposite rule is compatible with sense, then the use in the deciding of *both* sense and the rule narrows the spread of possible decision and significantly increases the reckonability not only of the upshot but also of the direction which will be taken by the ground on which the decision will be rested. To know this both limits the field of doubt and sharpens the eyes of inquiry.

The Law of Incompatibility

If application of the seemingly apposite rule is incompatible with sense, then reckonability of either upshot or direction of the " ground " of decision depends on factors apart from rule, sense, or both. To know this is to escape futile upset and to recognize instead the presence of danger and the need for exploration " outside " the simpler areas of inquiry.

The third of these theorems turns on the court's felt double duty to law and to justice, and is aptly driven home by Fuller's figure [28]: If you pen an animal in an enclosure too close for comfort, you can be sure it will try hard to get out, but to predict whether it will succeed (much more: how it will, if it does) calls for knowledge of more factors than just the " desire " and the " corral."

The second theorem above derives in one part from simple logic. The form of words in which a rule is normally cast is very likely, thanks to the looseness of language, to be subject to a range of readings which not only rove in scope from the perverse literalistic all the way to the semifigurative, but also swing through various compass points according to diverse definitions or flavors of the constituent terms. In such a situation an additional requirement that the " application " satisfy sense as well as the rule must materially, even hugely, cut down on both reach and region of the answers which are admissible. Even if sense falls not well within the worded rule (as, *McIntosh* does within *apple*), but in the dubious-penumbra (as, *rotting fruit* in regard to *barreled apples*), the employment of the combined criteria will have the narrowing and directive effect propounded by the theorem. This is an outgrowth less of logic than of the curious nature of our case law rules and concepts, which (we keep forgetting) are in essence Platonic; somethings whose reality and essence exist " out there " somewhere, felt more than grasped, indicated rather than bounded or gripped by any form of words at all, so that " the same rule " can be found and recognized in or under seven divergent and only *more or less* coextensive formulations. In our law, " the " rule rephrases of itself, almost, to adjust a notch or three, a compass point or four, to the call of sense, in what even when almost

[28] Fuller, American Legal Realism, 82 U.Pa.L.R. 429, 437 (1934).

automatic is nonetheless highly *creative* " application." [29] Such readjust-
ments alone, without adding in those which call for heavy puzzling, are
enough to lift study of sense as viewed and felt by the particular court
into the class of indispensable aids for sound forecasting.

From the combination of these companion theorems it flows almost
as a corollary that probability in prediction will vary with the technical
excellence of the rule itself—i.e., of its tailoring to purpose—and that
ease in such forecast will also increase with any increase in the accessibility of the sense concerned, the simplest access being by way of
sense which speaks in and from the rule itself. Thus, for instance, in
Mansfield's phrasing of the effects of negotiability, *taking* the paper
" fairly " and " in current course of trade " was a major feature of what
produced the protection. This criterion, so long as it remained vivid,
provided a sane and rather certain guide through troubled circumstance.
The disappearance of this " reason " aspect—culminating in the N.I.L.
focus not on process, but on form and status: the *holder* in due course—
led into a definitional type of discussion and decision which sought to
cut doctrine loose from life: What is " Value "? What is " Notice "?
What is " Good Faith "?—all without reference, direct or indirect, to
function, and so without recurrent check-up by reason. The result was
confusion—this on the point of prediction; and much unhappy law—
this on the point of sense-in-outcome. The N.I.L. cured neither, and on
this point worsened the latter.[30]. . .   [pp. 178–181]

Such rules . . . not only draw decision into relatively reckonable
channels, they also serve as an indexing machinery which leaves reason
and purpose fresh and vigorous even while applications are bringing
light into some areas of the penumbra.

Note that no explicit purpose clause or preamble is requisite—
though one can be useful; it is enough that the phrasing of the rule
reveals the reason. Note also that . . . the . . . rule chosen for illustration
marks out the sphere of the rule's application with clarity, though
elastically. For the marking of scope can be handled without recourse
to metes and bounds; a functional category, if both well designed and well
labeled, will indicate scope quite as neatly as it does reason. The metes
and bounds school of rule theory has sometimes been slow to grasp
this fact, a slowness which descends not only from the conveyancer's
approach to any legal document but from that individious misreading
of statutes which was too common during the Formal period.[31] Yet it
must be clear on meditation that given a reasonable judicial attitude
toward statutes, given, for instance, today's general attitude of willingness

---

[29] Levi's sequences [in *An Introduction to Legal Reasoning*, pp. 33–57] are superb
illustrations, especially *re* the Mann Act.

[30] Confusion in the old days bulked in the " Value " controversy, with some
slopping over into " Good Faith." The N.I.L. attempted to dispose of both
aspects by substantially removing the need for either, even in transactions
wholly out of current course. The courts' groping after sense continued, however. Hence, the " legal " issue of the lasting controversy just moved over into
the area of " notice " (neatly escaping the statute's planing off of " value " and
" good faith "), where the same sense-urges remain busy, and where the annotations have come in consequence to drown the investigator. Compare sub *Miller*
v. *Race*, 1 Burr. 452 (K.B. 1758), *ante*, page 410. The blinder and less informed
of the New York City bar, the bankers in general, and history-ignorance, duly
forced a rather simple clarification of the matter to be deleted from the Uniform
Commercial Code.

[31] [On the Formal period, see *ante*, 410.]

to further any perceptible and reasonable statutory purpose—given that, a functional category can under the law of compatibility count on very reasonable definiteness of application. Especially, if function in both rule and category are clear, the rule draftsman acquires a consoling insurance against those two inevitabilities: the situation overlooked and the unforeseen change of conditions. In a statutory rule intended as most statutes are—and as all rules of case law are—for lasting service, such insurance comes cheap at the price of using a zone rather than a surveyor's line to border the rule. Indeed the metes and bounds boys have a bent for forgetting how commonly the sharp-edged style of rule clashes with cases where it does not make sense, and so backs court and customer up against the law of incompatibility.[32]

Thus we come not only to a general gain in forecasting technique from the lines of opinion-reading here put forward, but to a perception that one particular kind of rule of law, if it be once found and phrased, will have peculiar power, and so to a fourth theorem from the theory of rules:

The Law of the Singing Reason

A rule which wears both a right situation-reason and a clear scope-criterion on its face yields regularity, reckonability, and justice all together. We may add that such a rule is a staff and a comfort to any court, as well as to any counselor.

There will be more to say about the rule with a singing reason; here we have to note that in this imperfect day such rules are not the rule. For the most part the courts and the rest of us must still make do with some strain, too often great strain, between authority and sense. This means, of course, that even a full resurgence of the Grand Style[33] of decision would leave us far short of the ideal in either reckonability or satisfaction. For effects must depend in great part upon material. It is true that fine craftsmanship can sometimes work magic with stuff and tools which make the angels weep; but even fine craftsmanship can do this only sometimes—and unpredictably—and the conditional sales sequences[34] remind us that if the work is centered too largely and too long on tolerability or decency merely of the immediate outcome, then the rule- and concept-stuff is likely to get out of hand, losing touch at last with both manageability and reason. It is indeed also true, as will be insisted in due course, that unremitting labor in the Grand Style does mean daily, weekly cumulative output of rules ever sharper in form, ever sounder in substance; but that, measured against the mountained inept or obsolescent stockpile, is still a task for generations. This last is no reason for any court to slacken or put off the effort; but it is good ground for not expecting too much, too often, too soon.

---

[32] Above, page 180. It is fascinating to observe the detailed worries of the New York Law Revision Commission, whose whole history and practice have been built in terms of exact and detailed minor reforms, with each imaginable contingency given accurate advance coverage, as they wrestled with the completely variant drafting philosophy of the Uniform Commercial Code in the 1952 draft. There open-ended drafting, with room for courts to move in and readjust over the decades, had been a basic piece of the planning. Some of this is suggested in N.Y.L.R.C. Report Relating to the Uniform Commercial Code, 1956, pp. 15–20; but to get the picture one must explore the full two volumes of Studies (1955).

[33] [On the Grand Style, see *ante*, 410.]   [34] Above, pages 124 f.

The Juice in the Orthodox Ideology

Meantime, when taken in conjunction with the Style of Reason and with the fact that the rule-stuff of the Grand Style was commonly draped with some canniness upon the needs of life, the law of the singing reason goes a long way to clear up what would else be almost an impasse in intellectual history: How, in contrast to the facts of legal life, could the idea (not the ideal) of decision " by the Law," decision independent of the persons of judges, either spring up or, especially, maintain itself across the centuries? I know that ideals and needs can sometimes and somehow bring forth mirages, mirages embraced with passion, of what " must be " in fact; and I know that man has felt deep need that the Law should in its work be firm and right, all but sacred, unspoiled and unspotted by the meddling or meanness of law's ministers. Yet it seems hard to believe that performance so regularly and openly subject to check-up, so close to daily living, so challenging to scrutiny, could easily become completely misdescribed, or could continue through the generations completely misdescribed, especially when, as with us, the largest segment of the ministers are themselves much more lay than priestly, and are scattered in substantial independence rather than guilded together into any such tight pike-hedge as would permit them to defend a pseudo mystery from exposure and pillory. Horse sense thus seems to urge that we can hardly be faced with a complete misdescription. And pondering goes on to suggest another thing about the standard or orthodox or conventional picture of how it is " the Law " which does— and should do—the deciding of appellate cases. It suggests that that conventional picture was in fact, in the days of the Grand Style, close enough to accuracy to serve as a very respectable description of what was going on.

One must not in these matters chase fireflies into the marshes of absurdity. The essence of the idea that appealed cases are decided " *by* the Law " (and I mean not merely " under law," or " according to " law," which, especially when " justice " is used to mean (more or less) adjudication," I see as a formula almost of issue-evasion) [35]—the essence is not that men, the Voices of the Law, shall play no part in the deciding. Neither is it the essence of the accompanying idea of " certainty " of such decisions that outcomes shall be so manifest beforehand that only fools could litigate and that advocacy must be empty ritual or theatre. Such misreadings or imputations are either the lampoons of adversary dialectic or else the crass thoughtlessness of the silly. In contrast, the ideas themselves include in " the Law," along with the rules of law, all the rest of the doctrinal environment in a fashion which adversary dialectic dares not face and of which the ignoramus is unaware. It is enough to mention here the general conceptual frame, the vibrant though almost unspoken ideals, the force-fields in doctrine and attitude which strain toward or against movement in any contemplated direction, the going techniques and going organization of the work of Law-Government. The ideas thus as of course embrace in " the Law " the skills and the traditions of the crafts of law, the ways of seeing, thinking, feeling, doing, and duty in and into which the craftsmen—the body of craftsmen —have been reared.[36] Implicit, moreover, in the ideas—including that

[35] See Pound, most recently, in 2 *Jurisprudence* 349 *et seq.* (1959).
[36] On this Pound has written excitingly. See my On Reading and Using the Newer Jurisprudence, 40 Columb.L.R. 581, 585, 589, 594, etc. (1940).

of "certainty" of decision—is a subliminal recognition that "the Law" holds room for men and for desires and for needs and for strivings of many, many kinds; that it holds room, nay rooms, already *partly* bodied forth in urges and tendencies within "the Law" itself—any one of which drives, within the all-pervading leeways, may meet another, clash, join issue, and produce a case in the appellate court. What is then needed is men—a bench—right-minded, learned, careful, wise, to find and voice from among the still fluid materials of the legal sun the answer which will satisfy, and which will render semisolid one more point, as a basis for a further growth. And the *certainty* in question is that certainty *after the event* which makes ordinary men and lawyers *recognize as soon as they see the result* that however hard it has been to reach, it is the right result.[37] Then men feel that it has *therefore* really been close to inevitable. Even most losers, as the strife subsides, may be hoped to look back with something of such understanding. In such a world there is no lack of office for the court, nor for the great creator on the bench; no lack of room, either, for litigants and lawyers. And the consequent "certainty" of outcome is the truest certainty legal work can have, a certainty reached not by deduction but by dynamics, moving in step with human need yet along and out of the lines laid out by history of the Law and of the culture; the certainty, then, not of logical conclusion from a static *universal*, but of that *reasonable regularity* which is law's proper interplay with life.

With such a scene to describe, and with the current legal rules and concepts well enough rough-fitted in the main both to lawyer's use and to the preindustrial layman's need, the orthodox image of decision "by the Law," in high degree decision forecastable and in equal degree independent of the person of the officer, could stand up, I repeat, as a rather true reflection of lawyers' day-to-day experience, and could then merit extra status and prestige by embodying at the same time an ideal valid and cherished: "Thus, it *ought* also to be."

Again, in the heyday of the Formal Style, the phrasing of the image, and no less the ideal of independence of the person, both measurably fit the facts. The meaning has then indeed become very different, what had been life-closeness has drifted away from life, what had been a moving harmony of law and justice builds instead into increasing tension. But the words, just as words, have much accuracy still; nor at any time can the ideal die that the work of an appellate court must somehow reflect and serve a something beyond and above, righter and steadier than, the individuals who happen to be sitting.

One change which occurred was, however, fateful. "The Law," as seen and understood in the Formal period, tended in lawyers' minds more and more to coincide until it substantially coalesced with "the law" as discussed by lawyers in court: the *mere rules* of law. And in action, the whole drive of the Formal Style was toward making sure, so far as might be, that it should be just those phrased rules which did do the deciding.

Hence as the formula traveled down the decades it traveled with its

---

[37] I have tried to express this in *Law and the Modern Mind*, 31 Columb.L.R. 82, 87–90 (1931). Nelles, *Towards Legal Understanding*, I, 34 Columb.L.R. 862 (1934), II, *ibid.* 1041, builds a beautiful background on the growth and success of this tradition of seeing and thinking in our legal history.

substance thinning and paling like Alice's Cheshire Cat, till what was left by, say, 1909 was a formula which had come to fly in the face of the current facts of work in court. To understand, despite such now flagrant misdescription, the stubborn grip of the formula on men's minds, one must remember not only the lasting validity of the ideal expressed, but the tradition, the long tradition, in which the same words had been a workably accurate depiction, and had acquired a sort of unchallengeable holiness of phrase. Such a tradition makes it easy to center one's noticing, one's attentiveness, at need one's argument, differ-entially on those cases which do fit the formula; such a tradition smooths the way to acceptance of the justification as if it were a report on the how of the deciding; if one did not look too hard, too closely, or too often, one thus used to be able to live with the illusion that the old " theory " was true—even in that horrible watered-down version of " the law " as meaning chiefly or exclusively the rules of law—except in odd cases or except where particular judges or courts had for some reason slipped off their job.

Yet ineptitudes or deficiencies in Formal description or Formal ideals for work need not at all jibe with equivalent defects in operation. Good work can be and has been done with creaking theory. More, the ideal of order is as valid an ideal as is that of dispassionate judging; when the premise is sound and the case fairly within it, those ideals are hard to rival; indeed, they have their standing even when they cannot claim to dominate, but only to counsel with other ideals as peers. The picture, when the work is in the hands of a good craftsman, is admirably presented by the elder Andrews of New York, or, later, by the elder Sanborn, or by Holmes in most of his non-Constitutional opinions. I do not see how anyone can doubt that Holmes enjoyed the method, the clean line, the finish of a Formal opinion; or that he enjoyed also, when he could come upon it, a premise which carried for the unthinking or untutored a touch of surprise. Job after job moves with a slightly remote, deftly articulated clarity to its seemingly foreordained conclusion. . . .

[pp. 182–187]

What held for operation, even sometimes among the best, held more among the lesser, encouraged as it was by the unhappy theory.

But today persistence in the old delusion no longer seems feasible. It is that impossibility which has engendered the crisis of faith to which repeated reference has been made. The fact itself is whiskered like Uncle Sam; it has been available on all hands for more than three score years and ten. By the '90's German-speaking judges of repute had begun to remark on what they thought to be a pattern, in their own work, of " the right solution first, the right reasoning to follow." Holmes published one of his most pungent discussions on the subject in 1897.[38] Seventeen years later World War I broke upon a Europe that had already seen the " free-law " fracas, Ehrlich's *Judicial Logic* and Gény's magnificent *Méthode*. Our own discussions of the '20's have been noted.[39] In 1930, Jerome Frank gathered portions of the relevant comment into his queer *Law and the Modern Mind*. The ensuing storm of protest did not really blow itself out; it just in due course vanished, leaving the basic facts clear.

---

[38] *The Path of the Law*, 10 Harv.L.R. 457 (1897), especially at 467. But that paper suggested no " pattern " of this kind as a normality.
[39] Above, pages 13 f.

But *what* facts have been left clear? That the *rules of law, alone,*
do not, because they cannot, decide any appealed case *which has been
worth both an appeal and a response.* Substantially, the mere bare
rules of law do today manage alone to decide that obnoxious but
persistent body of appeals in which in fact the applicable rules are
both firmly and reasonably settled—often enough re-examined, retested,
restated, and reaffirmed within the past few years—and in which the
facts of the case fall so obviously inside the core of the rule that
reasonable judges do not have to ponder. Again, there is that other
body of cases which falls outside any firm rule core but yet so plainly
within the urge or flavor or force-field of a rule or concept of law that
its extension either is obviously imperative or just happens so naturally
as to go unnoticed. There a touch of the older, wiser meaning of
"The Law" moves into action. Moreover, if what has been said
above holds true, then wherever the sense of the situation can be
expected to speak clearly to the court and to be understood, there,
in these days, another great portion of the older finer meaning of
"The Law" will also come to bear, testing, redirecting, reshaping
the very rules of law, along forefeelable lines of creation, and with
foreseeable results in the particular case. Still more: to the extent
that rules with singing reasons emerge and propagate and fight down
the less usable and less viable varieties of rule, "The Law"-at-work
expands, and we slowly approach complete regeneration of the truth
of an orthodoxy always lovely, and whose truth and standing faded
only because form and literalism were allowed to dry its pith. The
happy day is far ahead; but I count it a signal contribution of that
vital method of analysis known as legal realism that its hard-eyed and
sustained inquiries could, as they have, come to clean grips with a
moribund and misleading orthodoxy and come out then neither with
dismay nor with idle defense of emptiness nor yet with shallow cynicism,
but with recognition, appreciation, and practical furtherance of a
renascence still overlooked but gloriously green and strong.

Hence it is obvious that the factual material here gathered is not
set out with any purpose of showing that the rules of our law (those
of the singing reason excepted) are only in most restricted measure to be
relied on as " in themselves " deciding appellate cases. That fact is
manifest. My purposes are very different. I hope, and hope hard, that
the present material may make permanently untenable any notion that
creativeness—choice or creation of effective policy by appellate judges
—is limited to the crucial case, the unusual case, the borderline case,
the queer case, the tough and exhausting case, the case that calls for
lasting conscious worry. My material aims to put beyond challenge
that such creativeness is instead everyday stuff, almost every-case stuff,
and need not be conscious at all.

But by the same token, the same material aims to show and then
to hammer home that the creation moves in the main with steadiness,
that it answers carefully *and regularly* to the body of doctrine as that
body has been received and as it is to be handed on; that the creation
nevertheless and simultaneously, but in full consonance with that high
responsibility to The Law, answers also to the appellate court's duty
to justice and adjustment. I should hope to see the material persuade,
for example, of a thing like this (which I see no means of *proving*):
that in 80 per cent or better of the instances in which a court draws a

solving rule from prior (unheld) language, or from a pair of "see's" and a "cf.," or from "the tendency of our cases," the court is not merely reaching for authority or color to justify the decision in hand, but is also seeking and finding comfort in the conviction that the decision and the rule announced fit with the feel of the body of our law —that they go with the grain rather than across or against it, that they fit into the net force-field and relieve instead of tautening the tensions and stresses. I feel something of the same as I watch opinions turn to neighbouring jurisdictions for light or for further buttressing—especially when they pick up quotations packed with a combination of authority and situation-sense; even the "weight of authority" can sometimes have a tincture of this. . . . [pp. 189–191]

Ideal, Myth, Symbol, Sham, Hypocrisy

It is all very well to proclaim that despite much doctrine which is either delusion or myth, or else plain fraud, the appellate courts are still managing somehow to work out some reasonable steadiness of outcome, even some doctrinal steadiness and continuity; that is all very well, but does not the continuance of any such theory-contrary-to-proved-and-known-fact threaten the institution at its very heart? First, in the souls of its key officers; second, in that public faith without which even effective practical work in justice must be and remain empty? Here, surely, is an aspect of the crisis of confidence which can be coped with by no mere reference to "adequate performance"—performance, that is, which even though it may have somehow held up thus far, this long, may yet be termite-eaten.

This is a problem faced by every institution, not merely nor in any special manner by the appellate courts or by Law-Government at large. It is a problem to which there is no easy answer. For in all the work of man one major road to getting needed things done right has always been, it always must be, the building of a faith that the work can be done as it should be done, that almost any right craftsman can indeed come close to adequacy; and in order for such a faith to maintain itself it seems to be well-nigh necessary for the ordinary individual craftsman to believe, as well, that the ideal-picture is in fact approached most of the time by many or most of his brethren, even if not by himself. In this aspect a complete misdescription can have value. It can have value not only as an ideal and a symbol, but as providing stimulus and spur by the very fact of its inaccuracy. The evil, the corrosion "inside" the craft, comes not from misdepiction as such but from a waning of faith in the ideal and in effort toward the ideal; if the explicit or implicit goals come to be seen as worthless or futile, if tools and measures come to be used callously or selfishly (or in cynical routine) without regard to what the institution is for—that is what deadens. Such a waning of faith and effort may of course result in misdepiction of fact by the received theories; it may also itself result from such misdepiction. But it has no need to. For mere knowledge that gears do slip, that theories do need constant help from the skilled hand, that baling wire and chewing gum are often the only means to save "the book" or to save the game itself—this has never meant death, it has instead meant life for any institution whose craftsmen still had sap and feeling for their office. It does not follow that ideals and symbols can with regular impunity kick into loggerheads with life and fact; what does

follow is that misdescription by an idealized and dear-held theory-and-
symbol can rise even to the obtrusive without need to cause excessive
strain. In our particular case, the theory that the Rules of law do
decide the appeal, and that they ought to, has come to produce its strain
inside the system of the appellate courts; but, inside, that strain is
rendered quite tolerable by the understanding that what is essential
to the ideal and the symbol and the fact is reasonable consonance not
with the letter of the standard misdescription, but with its essential
intent: that the judges are not to move on their own, that they are to
answer to the Law (which is so much more than the Rules of law)
and also, if they can, to sense and justice. A clearer and cleaner
descriptive theory would indeed ease the situation, but, inside, its lack
has meant not cynicism, only a slowing and slurring of the work.

It is on the outside that the discrepancy of theory has done its
ravening. Here, too, the problem is that of every institution. Here,
too, there is a defending buffer between misdescription and any quick
disaster. Even severely misdescriptive theory can commonly be tolerated
by the pure or ordinary lay outsider. Partly, he sees and understands
too little, in detail, to take in the full degree of misdepiction; his faith in
his institutions is commonly rather tough; he is likely to think what
he does take in to be atypical; his normal reaction is to witch-hunt for
the evil persons who must be responsible for the distortion: "Throw the
rascals out." This, especially, if the times at large are bearable, and if
the institution in question is not beating the particular layman's toes
into pulp. Hence, since the Depression, laymen at large seem to me to
have survived with some comfort the rather patent fact that in the teeth
of those laymen's notions about what has been and should be, our
supreme courts are doing a good deal of law-making, and are handing
down decisions by no means forecastable from the Rules of law alone.
Public discussion of such matters seems to me to have had as little
direct effect as the blasts of Bentham against the "hypocrisy" of the
English courts of his day, or as attacks on waste and occasional corruption in the armed services, or as the successive revelations of gear-
slipping and stench in the government of Chicago or New York. Faith
in lasting symbols and ideals embodied in basic institutions tends to
straighten after the buffets of the wind unless times or toes are pinching
beyond endurance.

Thus the infiltration of corrosive cynicism into the appellate scene
seems to me to have been by way of a series of processes much more
indirect than any mere detection of error and pretense in the orthodox
ideology. It starts, as I see it, with politically-minded or incompetent
magistrates' or trial courts, and with favoritism, corruption, negligence,
or abuse of patronage among policing or administrative personnel. The
people who start and spread the gangrene are not the pure or general
public, but those of the public (criminals, politicians, businessmen of
great, small, or no legitimacy, gamblers, racketeers, mere parasites) who
have an "in," and their lawyers, and such official personnel as answer
to their whistle or as build political power on the less holy of alliances.
The situation reminds a little of an army living in and off a mildly
honest country, whose higher officers are on and at the job, but whose
company officers, noncoms, and more influential privates are to a third
or more sliders, grafters, and fixers dedicated to the main chance, with a
point of view and lingo that attribute to the whole and even to the

honest craftsmen their own perversities of angle and of action. It is against that general type of situation that the bar at large are led by the orthodox ideology and by their misunderstanding of appellate facts into " seeing " sham, hypocrisy, and irresponsible intrusion of the person even in the solid and healthy work of the solid and healthy core which remains to us despite any main-chancing in our law-governmental system. It is against that general type of situation that the business or union leader—not only uncorrected but actively mis-guided by his lawyer—measures trial court action, and takes a supreme court or Supreme Court dissent to unmask some covert, highly personalized, general vagary of decision. Over a good half century this " inside " or subpriest or noncom-and-subaltern " knowledge " of " the dirt " has been eating not only inside its own smaller public, but out into the greater public, and also, as indicated above, into the self-confidence of the appellate bench itself. With a typical blind self-inconsistency such a cynicized insider can recognize and respect the personal integrity in office of every individual appellate judge he personally knows, and yet be sure that the appellate bench at large is infected by dereliction which moves through the arbitrary or partisan to the almost corrupt. For when one is not of those high priests who see the formula in terms of its essential intent, and correct it daily, almost automatically, in their daily work, then observation of the discrepancy between the symbol and supposed pattern and the " dirty " fact *must* seem a sign of sham, of hypocrisy deliberate—even of fraud.

The only cure for such misbeliefs and for their evil consequences lies in complete recasting of the orthodox ideology which is their source.

One aspect of such recasting seems to me to offer itself, inside the court or out, rather freely and simply. That is, on the case law side, the open quest for situation-sense and situation-rightness as one main key to wise decision, the other main key being a recurrent accounting at once to the authorities as received and to the need for the ever sounder, ever clearer phrasing of guidance for the future. This is developed at length hereinafter; the concept is simple, and elementary legal education has really supplied all needed illustration; the only difficulty lies in getting a man to realize that what has all along been happening in great and striking cases has been happening (and needs to happen) also from week to week and day to day. Indeed, inside the court, established habits of work already hold enough of give and leeway to keep the most conscious of creative activity in the case law area from taking on any disruptive sense of sham or deceit.

But as things now stand, work with the resistant language of statutory authority seems to me much tougher on the temper of judicial steel, and on that of the bar's understanding and confidence. The problem is suggested below, in the section on Statutes (pp. 371 *et seq.*). Here I wish merely to insist that the art of extracting meaning from fixed language, or of putting meaning into it, can afford almost as wide a range of adjustment to need and situation-sense as do the techniques of case law, and deserves equally careful cultivation. It is to such cultivation that we must turn to keep out of appellate judicial work a feeling of tension, torsion, or hypocrisy when sense is being made out of statutes; for the given language is not to be ignored.

An Approach to the Crisis

What is the utter barebones for viable appellate judicial work is first
fourfold and then threefold: (1) Uprightness; (2) a modicum of judgment—neither wild men nor fools must dominate the bench; (3) a
modicum of reckonability of result; and (4) that reckonability must
in some material degree transcend the persons of the personnel. That is
the fourfold aspect, one of objective substance. The threefold is this,
one of subjective attitude: not only (1) must these things be there and at
work, to the knowledge and in the feelings of the judges, but (2) the
general public and, perhaps especially, all but unreasonable litigants,
must *feel* their presence, and (3) the bar must *know* them to be there.
The present crisis has afflicted in first instance the bar, but it has for
at least a decade, perhaps for more than two, been seeping through
the bar out into a much wider public which for lack of wherewithal to do
constructive or remedial thinking is helpless and a bit pitiable in its
trouble.

I am also persuaded, as has been indicated earlier, that there is
among our appellate judges themselves an almost tangible unease about
their work, that for some years now a certain olden inner sureness
of operation and of office has been leaking away. Partly I suspect
this to follow directly from the troubles of the bar. If your rooters
and only knowledgeable public exude a taint of dissatisfaction and
bafflement about your work, *and you can find no reason for it,* you get
bothered; and your quondam quiet self-confidence may suffer, too.
And indirectly, the troubles of the bar afflict you further. I have
spoken earlier of the time-burden imposed by the rank proliferation
of footless appeals; but even worse is the slackening of high-class
help from brief and oral argument, insofar as either baffled and
worried or lightheartedly gambling counsel pile the points high, wide,
and hit-or-miss because they have lost understanding of the process and
so lack confidence in the simple, the clear, the focused. Finally, I
trace the unease to the waning of the conscious, clean-cut traditions
of the appellate judges' craft, among the very craftsmen. Next door, by
1910 or 1920, the crutch of the casebook had drained most of conscious
working philosophy out of law teaching, and we have been struggling
for three decades to get back enough of such to keep curricula from
either drying up or coming apart at the seams. Even earlier, the shift
away from apprenticeship had, at least in the cities, choked off reliable
transmission of most of the old-time conscious working philosophy in
the crafts of advocacy and of counseling.

I think the appellate judges have also been feeling such an ebb.
I think that as appellate judging began to move out of the Formal
Style into that which flourishes around us, with little conscious working
philosophy of the craft at hand except the withered pseudo orthodoxy
of " It's the rules "—I think the appellate judges, for the most part, did
what men were doing in the other crafts of law: they stopped, pretty
much, thinking about it, in general, they buckled down instead to
doing it, here, now, right, and tomorrow again right, talking and
sweating much more over what than over how—and slowly losing all
contact whatever with the history of the traditions of their craft. And
my guess is—indeed, I think we can show it—that when self-examination
did set in—as with a nontypical person like Cardozo—it was substantially from a fresh start. Certainly there has as yet been a failure of

the great appellate judges, as also of the articulate appellate judges who are not yet great, to get together into any pooling of their craft-wisdom. It is a failure as striking as that we find among the great advocates or counselors of the past seventy-five years: what has been laid up, phrased, arranged, illustrated, and opened to a rising generation, of the communicable skills and wisdom of John G. Johnson, Rufus Choate, David Dudley Field, Elihu Root, Newton Baker, John W. Davis? Certainly, when one turns to the judges whose writings address themselves to building and communicating a workable working philoso-phy for the newcomer or the still worried old-timer, their writings, too, during the present century in this country look about like a crop of a couple of dozen alfalfa plants scattered over a ten-acre field—though the last few years have seen a gratifying upturn in hardheaded offerings.[40] It is all right to have a pure heart and to work your head off trying to get the job done as it should be done; but when your rooters stop rooting, your constituents lose ardor, and even the general public begin to mutter—and when the muttering attacks the doing of the very things which your conscience tells you that you *must* do, and which cause

[40] The mere existence of the Conference of Chief Justices offers both a where-withal and a stimulus for renewal. Meantime we have an emerging body of publication which is patently at work to cut from the general to the particular. The immediate post-Cardozo articles (Hutcheson apart) tended to offer an almost carefully vague wave of a wand toward change which once in a blue moon might be necessary. No gears meshed. More recently the judicial speaker has tended much more to get down to how, in particular. Judge Wilson (An Outlet for My Soul, 37 J.Am.Jud.Soc. 109 (1953)) was talking to a bar convention, but he went into the intangibles of his office. Later papers move, if anything, even more into the down-to-earth, hardheaded wrestling with daily problems: Justice Schaefer (then Chief), Precedent and Policy (1955), Ernst Freund Lecture, Uni-versity of Chicago Law School; Judge Breitel, Judicial Legislation, N.Y.L.J., December 8–12, 1958; Chief Justice Weintraub, Judicial Legislation, ibid., March 19, 1959; and the forthcoming paper of Judge Breitel on statutes. In Regard to Statutes, noted below, page 372. Judge Traynor (Some Open Questions on the Work of State Appellate Courts, 24 U.Chi.L.R. 211 (1957) got down further, and in a stubborn, lovely fashion, more closely to tomorrow's cases than did Cardozo at any point, if you read in terms of exactly how to do tomor-row's job. Let me say that I think my brother Traynor's major worry, the finding of a *pattern* to tell reversible from nonreversible error, is probably a full generation ahead of him and me. But he is *at it*, and being at it is what pushes the job along. E.g., without Traynor's worrying, how would I ever have picked up, to throw into the pool, the Illinois Supreme Court's explicit practice, in criminal cases, of offering as a criterion " whether there has been a miscarriage of justice "? That criterion is plainly inadequate; but it is no less obviously an admirable *first* step into the problem. It poses the major issue clearly. (Compare *ante*, p. 455.)
    The striking thing, may I repeat, as contrasted with the tenuous Cardozo-echoes of two generations back, is *bite* in the current approach from the judiciary. Their interest is in *how* to handle *tomorrow's* case. Characteristic is the advice by Kenison, C.J. (N.H.), to appellate advocates on how to " reach " the court they address: Some Aspects of Appellate Arguments, 1 N.H.B.J. 5 (1959).
    Useful, very, from outside, is such a study as Merryman's The Authority of Authority, 6 Stan.L.R. 613 (1954). I wish Merryman might have centred his study on the guts-conclusion from page 627: " Actually the application of authorities to cases to arrive at decisions is not nearly as simple or mechanical a process as the layman thinks it should be."
    Merryman's concentration on purported " authority " makes his net result as much out-of-line as it is useful; there are other factors which need medita-tion. Nevertheless, this is the kind of basic job, in research, which breaks down smugness and which opens up, for the sensitive: an entering wedge.

you at once your most trying turmoil and your greatest sense of right achievement—then I suggest that if you are to escape unease, you need at hand a working philosophy which for yourself is conscious, which is close and firm in its grasp of the working facts, and which is comforting because it offers a clear target, a craftsman's rifle, and a telescopic sight. That working philosophy needs also to be persuasive to your rooters and aids, the bar, and to the consumer of all law: the general citizen, in his infinite diversity.

Such a working philosophy—though at hand, lies disregarded.

The current crisis of confidence in the appellate courts is thus, as I see it, miles apart from that at the turn of the century, when widespread worry went to the wisdom and judgment of the bench (with the normal backwash into doubts about uprightness; in those days it was "The Interests own 'em! "). Today, for the State courts, neither worry nor attack goes particularly to the content of results, except as losing litigants (and specialized law professors) may grumble. The worry is instead over *reckonability* of results. Results are conceived to be *hopelessly* unpredictable. It is not mere uncertainty that festers, it is the feeling of hopeless helplessness. That hopeless helplessness wars with an old and not unreasonable tradition that it should not be; that it is wrong for such a thing to be. I am not maundering about "certainty" and womb-yearning or about law "the solid" as a father-substitute or similar unnecessary tripe. I am dealing with the sound and right feeling of the American lawyer and the American law-consumer that the work of his appellate tribunals has no business to be hopelessly unreckonable. If it is, then something is wrong; and the easiest thing to see as wrong is that the judges, the court, must be no longer under rein: they have the bit in their teeth and are using their own heads, or they have even slipped the bridle altogether. The reign of law makes a bitter, nasty pun.

As was said at the outset, it is to this crisis that this book and its material are addressed. The material shows, and I assert it shows beyond possibility of refutation, that *the crisis lies wholly in the second, the threefold, the subjective, the attitude area* (above, p. 462). On the objective side of how the work in being done, each one of the elements is open to huge betterment, of course, and needs the same, and needs it plenty; but not a single one of them is absent, and each stands well above the barebones level. Nor do I think that any other craft of our law, *taken as a whole and taken in the light of what is offered the craftsmen to work with,* is coming as close to turning out a proper job as is our appellate bench.[41]

If then the continuity-of-doctrine and the "sense or reason" aspects of our factual material here are to serve their purpose, they must address themselves to reckonability of appellate judicial results in first instance, and in second instance to the depersonizing of appellate judicial work. I have spoken above and shall speak again of the continuity-with-doctrine phase. The material also shows beyond contradiction that

---

[41] For a guess, this is the most controversial single unprovable judgment expressed in this book. But it is a careful one. And it is one which I should take aesthetic and even sadistic pleasure in debating. Pound was arguing the same, with much less current basis, as his conciliatory papers of 1914, Justice According to Law, I, 13 Columb.L.Rev. 696 (1913) II, 14 *ibid.* 1 (1914), III, *ibid.* 103.

the appellate courts are, day by day, drawing on reason and situation-sense to help out, to piece out, to guide, commonly to govern their choice and use of authorities and of authority techniques, with constant impact on the decisions, with a constant consequent reshaping also of the doctrinal materials used. But knowing these things is not in itself enough to allow, generally, of forecast, or of a working approach to forecast, of the outcome of appeals. Forecasting, prediction, reckoning, must for the purpose in hand be do-able, it must be done, by the ordinary lawyer. Well, then? [pp. 191–199]

H. KALVEN and H. ZEISEL

The American Jury

(1966) [42]

Reasons for Judge-Jury Disagreement—A Summary View

... How much disagreement is there between judge and jury in criminal cases? And, what are the reasons or sources of this disagreement?

We begin with the content of the reason code. ... The coding operation involved assigning highly specific reasons to the individual instances of disagreement. As the coding developed, it became possible to group the individual reasons into narrow sub-categories and those into larger categories. In the final stage of the coding process the reasons were subsumed into five generic categories.

It may prove helpful to run quickly through the evolution of this over-all framework. We will begin with excerpts from the raw, detailed reason code, in the hope that they will give some preliminary sense of the variety of the items that move the jury. In its original form the coding resulted in 227 specific items, which resolved themselves into the five ultimate categories. We list below, as illustrations, two sub-groups of the code: that for the *individual defendant*, with thirty items, and that for the sentiment the *defendant has been punished enough*, which has nine items. We would emphasize again that the development of the code was an evolutionary process. We perfected it as we coded, and we refined it further as we wrote up the materials. Coding was in no way a mere clerical operation, but rather it was close to the very heart of the study.

---

[42] [*The American Jury* is the culmination of the work of the Chicago Jury Project, perhaps the finest product of Realist orientation towards institution-focused research. See the comments in (1967) Criminal L.R., pp. 553 *et seq.* The methodology of the survey is described in Chaps. 2 and 3. Trial judges were asked to report, for cases tried before them, how the jury decided the case, and how they would have decided it, had it been tried before them without a jury. The judge was also asked to give descriptive and evaluative material about the case, the parties and counsel. The sample was limited to, what the authors describe as, " residue of self-selected judges " (p. 35), since no judge could be forced to co-operate. Whilst the authors essayed other methods, they concluded that this was the most practical approach. One could not, for example, have each case tried twice, once before a judge and jury and once by a judge alone. Nor could one bug a jury room. The Supreme Court had earlier outlawed this research practice. For the problems of jury research, generally, see Cornish, *The Jury* (1971), pp. 20–25.]

Sentiments About the Individual Defendant

- **Personal Characteristics of Defendant**
Youth
Old age
Woman
Attractive woman
Mother
War widow
Cripple, ill health
Sympathy in general

- **Social Status**
Poor, underprivileged
From influential family

- **Family**
Wife in court
Family in court
Children in court
Pregnant wife in court
Large family responsibility

- **Special Circumstances**
Model prisoner
Rendered valuable service to the government
Kind to victim
In no position to repeat crime
Long interval since last conviction

- **Court Appearance**
Favorable impression
Repentant
Crying, collapsed
—defendant
—witness for defendant

- **Occupational Record**
Soldier, veteran
Policeman, sheriff
Clergy
Student, football player
Long employment record
Prosecutor, political office

Defendant Sufficiently Punished

- **Directly Through His Act**
Had been in jail awaiting trial long enough
Only defendant was hurt
Loses parole anyway

- **Indirectly Through His Act**
Relative or friend killed or hurt
Punished by conscience

- **Independently**
Financial misfortunes
Other misfortunes

Spouse already fined for same act

Defendant afterwards beaten

So much for illustrations of the individual reason items. At the end of the coding process they seemed to fall into these categories:

- Evidence factors
- Facts only the judge knew
- Disparity of counsel
- Jury sentiments about the individual defendant
- Jury sentiments about the law

Since these labels are not self-explanatory, a brief description of each is provided. It should be stressed that, in each instance, the category locates a generic source of disagreement, without regard to whether it is the judge or the jury who is the more lenient.

Evidence factors. Although the traditional view of the jury is that it is largely concerned with issues of fact, it turns out to be surprisingly difficult to give a thumbnail sketch of evidence as a category of judge-jury disagreement. At times the jury may evaluate specific items of evidence differently; at other times the jury might simply require a higher degree of proof. Frequently evidentiary disagreement, in our usage, refers simply to the closeness of the case, which liberated the jury to respond to non-evidentiary factors. Under these special circumstances, issues of evidence, as we were able to handle them, are properly speaking not so much a cause for disagreement as a condition for it.[43]

Facts only the judge knew. Here the concern is with the occasional circumstance that, during or prior to the trial, an important fact will become available to the judge but not to the jury, such as whether the defendant had a prior specific criminal record or not. Whenever the judge notes such special knowledge on his part in a disagreement case, it has been taken as a reason for his disagreement. The rationale is that judge and jury were, in fact, trying different cases, and had the jury known what the judge knew, it would have agreed with him.[44]

Disparity of counsel. It was possible to collect data systematically on how evenly counsel for prosecution and for defense were matched. This category covers the instances in which the superiority of either defense or prosecution counsel was given as one of the reasons for the jury's disagreement with the judge.

Jury sentiments about the individual defendant. The type of defendant involved in a criminal case can vary across the entire spectrum of human personality and background, from the crippled war veteran who evokes intense sympathy to the loud mouth who alienates the jury. In this category are included all reasons for judge-jury disagreement attributable to the personal characteristics of the defendant.

Jury sentiments about the law. This category includes particular instances of "jury equity," reasons for disagreement that imply criticism of either the law or the legal result. For example, the jury may regard a particular set of facts inappropriately classified as rape, because it perceives what might be called contributory negligence on the part of the victim. A similar notion may operate in fraud cases in which the victim first hoped for an improper gain. Thus, a broader concept, contributory fault of the victim, evolves as a defense to a crime. This general category of jury sentiments about the law includes roughly a dozen sub-categories of such jury sentiments.[45]

There must remain, of course, a certain blandness and ambiguity about the major categories for the present. Since the purpose here

[43] There is something awkward about the classification of evidence itself as a source of disagreement where it serves as *the condition* for the jury's response to a sentiment, but, as will become apparent, in the close case where there is a sentiment both evidence and sentiment are assigned equal weight in producing the disagreement. Thus we resolve the problem of distinguishing the necessary condition from what is perhaps the sufficient condition somewhat arbitrarily.

[44] Logically this category would include cases where the jury had information not possessed by the judge, but such an occurrence would seem to be extremely rare.

[45] It may be of interest at this point to preview the elements of the Sentiments on the Law category. The four major sentiments are: The Boundaries of Self-Defense, Contributory Fault of the Victim, De Minimis, and Unpopular Laws, followed by seven lesser sentiments: Defendant Has Been Punished Enough, Punishment Threatened Is Too Severe, Preferential Treatment, Improper Police Methods, Inadvertent Conduct, Insanity and Intoxication, and Crime in a Subculture. A separate chapter has been devoted to each of these eleven themes; see Chapters 16 through 26, and also Chapter 27.

is only to provide an over-all summary view of the explanations for
judge-jury disagreement, these sketches will have to suffice. At this
point the categories simply provide a handy device for summarizing
the data. . . .

To say that the reason code fell into these five major categories is
to make more than a point about coding technique. It is to state a
theory. In its most general and also its least exciting form, the theory
is that all disagreement between judge and jury arises because of
disparity of counsel, facts that only the judge knew, jury sentiments
about the defendant, jury sentiments about the law, and evidentiary
factors, operating alone or in combination with each other; and as a
corollary, that the judge is less likely to be influenced by these factors
than is the jury. There is some gain in emphasis if we invert the
statement: unless at least one of these factors is present in a case, the
jury and the judge will not disagree.[46]. . .[47]   [pp. 104–109]

. . . [The American Realists] emphasized the translation of rules of law
into patterns of official behavior and took a skeptical view of the public
reasons offered by courts for their decisions. Their quest was for a
law in action as contrasted to a law on the books, and for latent or
hidden reasons. A fair description of our study is that it is an effort
to trace the law in action, to see how juries, the final arbiters of so
much criminal law, really decide cases.

What emerges perhaps as something of a surprise is that this reality
has so legal a texture. When the jury deviates from the official rules and
writes its own law, the categories of thought are familiar. For the
largest part the hidden reasons of the jury are reasons which can stand
public scrutiny; not infrequently the jury's rule turns out to be the law
in another jurisdiction. The realist emphasis seemed often to lend
itself to a kind of inside dopester jurisprudence in which the real reasons
for decisions would be very different from the surface reasons, and
probably rather nasty. Insofar as this study can be said to be a venture
in realism, it suggests that the ideas embodied in the formal rules and
doctrines of law are close to the policies that actually motivate decision-
makers in the real world.   [p. 497]

[46] This is not to say that the factors have no effect on the judge, but only that
they have a differential impact on the two deciders.

[47] [Space prevents the extracting of detailed statistics but, in brief, these showed
that, in the authors' words, " the jury spins close to the legal base line." There
is a high coincidence between jury verdicts and the decision a judge would have
arrived at sitting alone. In criminal cases there was agreement in 75·4 per cent.
of cases; in civil in 78 per cent. of cases. But judges classified only 30 per cent.
of cases of disagreement as arbitrary decision-making, " without merit." And
even here, comment the authors, jury lawlessness is only a quest for justice
giving " recognition to values which fall outside official rules." (See, further,
Cornish, *op. cit.*, pp. 179–180.) The then Lord Chief Justice of England
was asked to provide figures for England for comparative purposes. Lord
Parker pointed out, not surprisingly, that none were kept, but " as a matter
of impression " he surmised that it was rare for a jury to convict where a
judge would acquit (and such cases resulted often from a judge's legalistic
attitude towards, for example, corroboration of a sexual offence), and that jury
acquittals, where a judge would have convicted varied between 3 per cent.–10 per
cent. There are too few civil trials by jury in England for statistics to be
meaningful. Lord Parker's figures suggest that English juries dissent less often
than their American counterparts. Two reasons are suggested for this: greater
conformity of sentiment between judge and jury and stricter control of the
trial process in England.]

UNDERHILL MOORE and GILBERT SUSSMANN
The Lawyer's Law [48]
(1932)

. . . The lawyer advises as to the probable forms of the judicial behavior of courts. His clients are those against whom governmental intervention is sought, those who are seeking intervention in their own behalf, and those with enough foresight to wish to mold the present and the future in anticipation of the necessity of seeking or avoiding intervention in the future. . . .

. . . Only one among the many groups in the community engages the lawyer's professional attention. The likely behavior of judicial officers of the government is the burden of his advice. Seldom does he advise or assist in his client's contacts with the discipline committee of a church or club or with the arbitrations of a trade association. If he advises during his client's business negotiations, only rarely does his advice include more than a statement of what judicial behavior would be probable were the negotiations to take this course or that.

The professional work of the marketing expert compels him to take into account many factors besides the wares of his client and their distribution, the argument in advertisements, and skill in face to face contacts. For this reason he does not devise for his clients plans for selling ice cream on Hudson River ferryboats during the winter nor for selling golf clubs to the blind. Neither does he advise that slate roofing will be bought by nomadic groups or that attempts to sell uniforms for army or police in communities in which there is no organized government will succeed. . . . But the lawyer's work is commonly done in but one region, the outstanding elements of whose material and non-material culture appear to him to be relatively stable. He does not face the problem of securing favorable decisions from Abyssinian tribunals, from informal gatherings of Polynesian savages, as well as from the courts of his own country. In formulating his advice, therefore, he passes over unnoticed most of the cultural factors in his situations; and those which he does take into account are given no systematic consideration.

Like the practitioners of other professions, the lawyer has invented saws, adages, proverbs, and maxims to guide him in judging and advising how contacts with the courts will eventuate. These saws and maxims have been elaborated into a bulky professional literature which attempts to describe the way courts behave in the great variety of situations in which the individual is in contact with them. Thus on one side of its equations appears the behavior of judicial officers.

On the other side appears the behavior of parties, their witnesses, and counsel. Among all the variables present in his situations, the lawyer has chosen the behavior of the parties with which to equate the behavior of the courts. The obviousness of the variablity of the behavior of the parties and the great significance which in his cultural inheritance is attributed to the behavior of a human personality doubtless accounts for the choice. Consequently the primary statements of the lawyer's literature are written in the form of sequences of behavior. After the parties behave in this manner the court behaves in that manner.

These sequences are descriptions of the behavior of parties and the

[48] [From 41 Yale L.J. 566.]

behavior of courts in cases which have arisen in the past. A few sequences are descriptions of the behavior in a large group of very similar cases. But most of the situations in which individuals come in contact with judicial officers present eccentric behavior not only deviating from the usual and regular course but also deviating in its own peculiar manner and degree. In order to avoid the unwieldy bundle of particularities which would result from according a separate description to each of these situations, they are thrown into large groups and the common factors of the behavior in each group abstracted and a mere fragment of the behavior of the parties described. But this course is by no means always followed. Often a sequence is derived from one or a very few of these cases.

The sequences which are derived from a large group of very similar cases the lawyer has incorporated in propositions in which he ascribes a causal relation between the behavior of the parties and the decision of the court. But he has not clearly distinguished between causal relation attributed as a result of observation, causal relation hypothetically attributed because of belief that observation would justify it, and causal relation attributed because of faith in its existence. Consequently the sequences derived from one or a very few cases and those derived from the large groups of situations in which the eccentric behavior of the parties is only more or less similar are also regarded as disclosing a causal relation between behavior of parties and decision. Thus propositions which are verified hypotheses and propositions which are unverified hypotheses are, without distinction, regarded as rules of law which indicate not only how a court has, does and will behave, but also how a court must behave. Taken together these rules of law give a complete account of how a court decides in any and every situation.

It will be noted that no mention is made of statutes, ordinances, and regulations in describing how the lawyer derives the sequences in his rules of law because they are not derived from the models of behavior for parties, for court or for both set forth in statutes, ordinances, and regulations. The traditional attitude of the lawyer is that until these models have been refined by courts the weight to be accorded them in accounting for judicial behavior is too uncertain for them to be incorporated in his rules of law. In consequence he has no systematic procedure for dealing with them.

In formulating his professional advice, however, the lawyer's rules of law are not his exclusive or even principal reliance. In addition he takes into account every factor in the situation which he can differentiate from its context and on the basis of them and of his rules of law he makes an intuitional judgment of the form which judicial behavior will take.

The activities of the lawyer have for the most part been limited to advising how a court will act, *viz.*, whether it will intervene at all and if it does the model of behavior which will be prescribed. This limitation has resulted in the lawyer only casually observing whether or not the parties conform to the model. He has not attempted a systematic study of the degree by which the subsequent behavior of the parties conforms to the model. Neither has his professional work required him to study the effect, if any, of the form which the behavior of the parties takes after the decision, upon the behavior of persons who are not parties. Nor has it required him to observe and study the effect of his rules of law and of decisions and statutes upon the behavior of the community. In short, the study of judicial behavior and of statutes as devices for social control or for any purpose other than to aid in forecasting future judicial behavior does not come within his province. . . .

Some report should now be given of the lawyer's traditional ways of thinking. He takes no account of the fact that intuitional judgments are the bases for his advice. On the contrary his opinions are taken to be forecasts dictated by his rules of law. His rules of law do not appear to be unverified hypotheses. There is a failure to observe that the attribution in them of causal relation between decisions and the behavior of the parties is the product of either methodless empiricism or dogmatism. Since rules of law are taken to state an established causal relation and are not seen as hypotheses, the problems for research have appeared to be not the verification of rules of law but rather their historicity, their logical consistency with one another and their logical elaboration in postulate systems. For the same reason in the teaching of law the objective is seen as the imparting of knowledge of decisions and of the rules which the lawyer derives from them; the material, documents; and the method, exegesis.

In this way of thinking a judicial officer of the government appears to be a person without biological and cultural inheritance whose behavior is not the product of the factors regarded as significant in accounting for the behavior of human beings. This person's behavior seems to be fully accounted for by the law of the lawyer. Hence, the art or science of judicial behavior is a field of knowledge complete and self-sufficient, wholly independent of all others and coordinate with them. It is inadmissable to view hypothetically the behavior of a judicial officer as a response given in an inclusive situation. It is unnecessary in a study of such behavior to set up as a control a study of the like behavior of other persons.

In this way of thinking no account has been taken of the fact that in any situation which includes human behavior, past decisions are only one among many factors; that in any situation, whether or not decisions are one of the factors, it is a matter of tentative choice what factors are attempted to be correlated; that in choosing factors to be correlated there is no necessity for selecting the two factors of judicial behavior and behavior of parties; that any study which attempts to correlate but two factors is unlikely to supply even an index; and that the correlation of decisions and any other factor in the situation may profitably be studied by statistical method.

Another aspect of the lawyer's way of thought must be stated. He has come to share the layman's view that the lawyer's rules of law and the decisions from which they are derived, as well as statutes, are dominant factors in accounting for the behavior of the community. He often refers to them as "law," thereby implicitly attributing a causal relation between them and the behavior of the community of the same sort that he attributes in his rules of law between the behavior of parties and the decision of a court. This manner of speaking has led him and others to confuse lawyer's rules of law for the behavior of the court with rules of "law" for the behavior of the community applicable to every situation of daily life and regularly observed by everyone.

Such is the lawyer's traditional way of thinking of his problems, his data and his methods. To be sure it is grossly inadequate and filled with misleading notions. But for him it is a by-product of his professional work, seriously regarded on ceremonial occasions only, and never permitted to limit his field of vision to less than the whole situation upon which he gives an intuitional judgment. However, to the lawyer's rational account can be attributed his failure to recognize that his judgments are intuitional and given in inclusive situations of many biological and cultural factors, his failure to attempt an analysis of the process of his judgments and his failure even to begin systematically to take into account the factors in the situation.

II

When a lawyer advises his client of the probable form which, under the circumstances, the decision of a trial or appellate court will take, his forecast, it has already been observed, is an intuition of experience. This is equally true of forecasts as to rulings upon motions, objections to evidence, instructions, *etc.*, which the lawyer makes for his own guidance. In making his forecast, he takes into account every factor in the situation which he is able to differentiate, compares them with similar factors in other situations which he has experienced, estimates their similarities and dissimilarities, weights the results as best he may, and integrates them in his judgment. Since the lawyer's advice is a forecast of the probable form of judicial decision in a developing, inclusive situation he should frankly recognize that he is stating probabilities and adopt a method which provides for the systematic consideration of the factors in his situations and thus makes for the greatest available precision in stating probabilities.

A judicial ruling or decision is an event. The event which is the ruling should be distinguished from the opinion and also from the other concurring and following events, such as the behavior of the litigants and of others subsequent to the decision, which are thought of as its " consequences." Though the events regarded as consequences are, more often than not, more important than the ruling they are not events within the field of law. Nor is the form of the opinion a matter of professional forecasting.

The forecast of a particular event is a statement of the probability of its occurrence. A statement of the probability of its future occurrence is based upon the frequency of its past concurrence with other particular events. All the events in experience are conceived of as an inclusive situation organized with reference to a critical particular event, the concurrence of which with other events is the subject of inquiry. The number of such inclusive situations is as great as the number of critical events. Whatever the choice of critical events the problem of forecasting the concurrence of events in any one inclusive situation is no different from the problem of forecasting the concurrence of events in any other. Thus the forecasting of a particular ruling is no different from the forecasting of any particular event of behavior, as for example, the behavior of the discipline committee of a club or the decision upon an application for admission to the Yale Law School. This is true despite the fact that the ruling has official prestige and important consequences and despite the common belief that particular rulings must and do conform to statutes and prior decisions.

The statement of the probability of concurrence is the product of observation and statistical method. It would be impossible to observe the concurrence of the critical event with all the events in an inclusive situation. Inevitably a limited number of events is selected for observation. The selection is tentative and based upon the hypothesis that observation of the concurrence of the critical event with the selected events will indicate, sufficiently for the purpose in hand, the probability of the concurrence of the critical event under inquiry with all the events in the inclusive situation.

If there are a sufficiently large number of situations in which a critical event of the type selected for inquiry concurred with events identical with or, according to some relevant standard, similar to the selected events in the situation in hand, it may be possible by observing the frequency of each of the critical events to state the probabilities as to the form of the critical event in the situation at hand. For example, by observing the frequency of each of the several forms of the critical events of type E, *i.e.*, $E,^1$ $E,^2$ $E,^3$ $E,^4$ $E,^5$ which have in other similar situations concurred with $A,^1$ $B,^2$ $C,^3$ $D,^4$ it may be possible to state the probability that in the situation at hand, in which the selected events are also $A,^1$ $B,^2$ $C,^3$ $D,^4$ the precise form of the critical event will be $E.^5$ If in an idle moment it were imagined that there were a sufficiently large number of situations organized with reference to each event of behavior which is supposed to be regulated by the government and if it were further imagined that there were estimates of the frequency of the concurrence of each of the diverse forms of these events with each combination of forms of the selected events, then one would be conceiving the abstraction, a law regulating every event of behavior, and be imagining the actualization of the possibility of its statement.

But the critical events in the form of which the lawyer is interested comprise, it has been observed, a much more limited group than those in which the government is supposed to be interested. His group of critical events is confined to the behavior of courts. Lawyer's law, therefore, is much more limited than a law imagined to impinge upon everyone all the while. Among the lawyer's situations or cases there may be some in which the selected events are so similar in form to the events present in a large group of similar situations, in all of which the critical event is judicial behavior, to permit him to state the probabilities of the form of the critical event in the situation in hand from observation of the frequency of the concurrence of each form of the critical event in those situations. Thus *under certain circumstances* the lawyer is able to forecast the admission to probate of a will, duly attested and executed by a decedent who was of sound and disposing mind, or the entry of a default judgment after the failure to answer a summons and complaint within the prescribed time.

But in many instances, among the lawyer's cases, the situations in which the selected events are identical with or, according to some relevant standard, similar to the selected events in the situation in hand and in which the critical event is judicial behavior are so few in number that observation of the frequency of the concurrence of each form of the critical event in those situations will not indicate a useful probability of the form which the critical event will take in the situation in hand. These are the usual instances in which the case before the lawyer is not foreclosed by a number of recent cases from his own jurisdiction.

In dealing with such situations, therefore, he cannot proceed by the method which has been abstracted for stating probabilities of the form of the critical event but his procedure must be a variation of that method. Since there will not be a large enough number of situations like the situation in hand to permit the making of a sufficiently useful statement of probabilities, it will be necessary to include within the group situations in which the forms of the selected events differ from those in the situation in hand. It will no longer be possible to define the group and thereby earmark the situations to be included in terms of the form of the selected events. The situations within the group are chosen as follows. From the possible alternative forms of the prospective critical event in the situation in hand are chosen, on the basis of experiential judgment, the several forms which the critical event is likely to take. Any situation in which there is actualized any one of these likely possibilities is included. Since at least two likely possibilities will always be present, the group will include situations in which there are actualized at least two and perhaps more possibilities. It will be noted, also, that such a grouping permits the inclusion of situations having selected events differing in form from those in other situations within the group as well as from those in the situation in hand. On the basis of the similarity of the selected events the situations thus included will be classified in subgroups. Observation of the frequency of the actualization of each likely possibility will thus require observation of its concurrence with the selected events in each of the subgroups. Such observation will disclose that there is, at most but one, if there be any, subgroup of situations in which the selected events are identical with or, with reference to a relevant standard, similar to the selected events in the situation in hand. To enable the utilization of the data as to the frequency of the concurrence of each likely possibility with each combination of selected events, the selected events in the situation in hand must, with reference to some relevant standard, be compared with the selected events in the situations in each of the subgroups to determine the degree by which they deviate from each other.

The determination of the probabilities as to the form of the critical event is thus the result of the integration of two steps: (1) observation of the frequency of concurrence of each likely possibility with the various subgroupings of selected events and (2) measurement of the degree of deviation between the selected events in the situation in hand and those in the situations in the various subgroupings. The probabilities are the function of two variables, frequency of concurrence, and degree of deviation.[49] . . . [pp. 566–574]

LEE LOEVINGER

Jurimetrics—The Next Step Forward

(1949) [50]

It is one of the greatest anomalies of modern times that the law, which exists as a public guide to conduct, has become such a recondite

---

49 [Schubert, a leading behaviouralist, has written of Moore and Sussmann that they were "at least a quarter of a century ahead of [their] time and . . . writing for the wrong profession to boot" (*Judicial Behaviour*, p. 13). This essay thus provides a valuable bridge between Realism and Behaviouralism.]

50 [From 33 Minn.L.R. 455.]

mystery that it is incomprehensible to the public and scarcely intelligible to its own votaries. The rules which are supposed to be the guides to action of men living in society have become the secret cult of a group of priestly professionals. The mystic ritual of this cult is announced to the public, if at all, only in a bewildering jargon. Daily the law becomes more complex, citizens become more confused, and society becomes less cohesive. Of course, people do not respect that which they can neither understand nor see in effective operation. So the lawmongers bemoan the lack of respect for law. Now the lawyers are even bewailing the lack of respect for lawyers.

Many remedies are proposed: We must have better law enforcement—that is, more policemen to make the people obey the laws they do not understand. We must have a great moral renascence—presumably some sort of mystical process which will enable people intuitively to apprehend the mysteries of law. We need better education—catch 'em young, and teach them to respect the law while they're still credulous and uncritical. We ought to pass a new law to make people respect the old laws—ignorance of the law is no excuse, even for lawyers. We need better " public relations " between the lawyers and the public— which simply means that the lawyers want to advertise like everybody else. There is a school of support for every proposal except the one that it is the law itself which needs to be changed. . . . [p. 455]

Because jurisprudence has set the pattern for legal thinking, and because jurisprudence has been concerned with trying to answer meaningless questions by futile speculation, the law has proceeded very largely on *a priori* grounds and has adapted itself to social needs only under great pressure and very slowly. The lawyers have, in fact, so bemused themselves with words and theories that they have not even yet developed anything like a rational system for performing their principal function of deciding particular controversies. Most decisions are presented behind a verbal facade that is cast in the syllogistic form. But it requires little sophistication to demonstrate that the logical form has little to do with judicial decisions. [p. 470]

The terms which apply to [a] case are selected only after the result has been decided. But the choice of legal terms to describe an act is certainly not a " logical " operation. Where it is not purely arbitrary, it is, at most, intuitive. Thus, by present methods, the determination of every genuine legal issue is made at the sub-verbal (and usually subconscious) level, where formal " logic " can neither exist nor exert influence.

Recognition of the fact that lawsuits are not decided by logic is not new. Bentham suggested as much, and Holmes said it. More recently, Frank, Arnold and others have elaborated the point. But here the modern movement has bogged down. Frank insists that uncertainty is inherent in the legal process, and that the grasping for certainty in general principles is simply an expression of infantile emotional attitudes which have persisted into adulthood.[51] Arnold finds the explanation of the inconsistencies and absurdities of the law in the fact that all our social institutions are mere symbols of our dreams and aspirations.[52] But all this is merely a continuation of the ancient quest for the

[51] Jerome Frank, *Law and the Modern Mind* (1930) [and *ante*, 405.]
[52] T. W. Arnold, *The Symbols of Government* (1935).

philosopher's stone. The new school seeks it in some scientific, rather than some moral, explanation or principle, but the fallacy is the same. This is simply a new jurisprudence with a new vocabulary. The argument seeks to substitute a modern analysis for an ancient one, but the traditional techniques are still in use. It is all armchair speculation. . . .

[p. 472]

. . . The only important area of human activity which has developed no significant new methods in the last twenty centuries is law. . . .

. . . If we would increase our knowledge and have some chance of arriving at an intelligent solution to our problems, it is essential that we adopt scientific methods of inquiry. . . .   [p. 473]

In every field in which human knowledge has advanced, the story has been the same. Intuitive concepts and accidental practices seem adequate to primitive man. By repetition, they become habitual, then habit deepens into tradition, and finally tradition becomes unchallengeable truth. One day some skeptical mind suggests that perhaps the current version of truth is only tradition, perhaps tradition is only ossified habit, and, in any event, the adequacy of both beliefs and practices to contemporary situations should be tested by investigation. Immediately all the traditional objections are made: you can't experiment in this field; investigation is old stuff, our ancestors have made all the investigations necessary; since people are involved you can't be objective; this cold-blooded proposal is immoral because it disregards values; and anyway there are no practical methods of making the investigation. Note that exactly the same arguments, with slight changes of phraseology, apply equally well whether the subject matter is astronomy (how can you put a star in a test tube?), physics (Democritus knew all about atoms), physiology (you can't study men as though they were animals), psychology (if you don't take account of man's soul you destroy all our values), or, the most recent child of science, cybernetics (don't be silly—how can you make a machine that will think?). Note also that in every case in which we have disregarded these objections, we have been able to formulate meaningful problems, institute effective techniques, gather valid data, and finally not only enlarge our useful knowledge but increase our control over both the environment and ourselves.

The next step forward in the long path of man's progress must be from jurisprudence (which is mere speculation about law) to *jurimetrics* [53] —which is the scientific investigation of legal problems. In the field of social control (which is law) we must at least begin to use the same approach and the same methods that have enabled us to progress toward greater knowledge and control in every other field. The greatest problem facing mankind at this midpoint of the twentieth century is the inadequacy of socio-legal methods inherited from primitive ancestors to control a society which, in all other aspects is based upon the powerful techniques of a sophisticated science. The inescapable fact is that jurisprudence bears the same relation to a modern science of jurimetrics as astrology does to astronomy, alchemy to chemistry, or

[53] Of course it is not important what term is used to indicate the scientific discipline suggested. It is important that it have a distinctive name, as well as a general program. The name suggested here seems, to the author, as good as any, since it seems to indicate the nature of the subject matter, and corresponds to other similar terms, such as biometrics and econometrics.

phrenology to psychology. It is based upon speculation, supposition and superstition; it is concerned with meaningless questions; and, after more than two thousand years, jurisprudence has not yet offered a useful answer to any question or a workable technique for attacking any problem.

The utter futility of jurisprudence (as anything more pretentious than classroom or barroom entertainment) can be illustrated by a typical philosophical supposition. Suppose that all the legal scholars and lawyers in the United States (or in the world) were to be gathered in a single great conclave the day after tomorrow and presented with the questions of jurisprudence: What is law? What is the basis of law? What is the end and purpose of law? Define Justice, et cetera et cetera. Now suppose—this is a great feat of imagination—that all these lawyers should agree unanimously on answers to all of these questions. We would, at long last, then have authoritative definitions of concepts like law, justice, and perhaps even of crime, contract, property and tort. (It is too much to suppose that even this imaginary conclave should agree on what constitutes a divorce in the United States.) What would be the result? I venture to suggest it would be nothing at all. If the results of these deliberations were published in some Super-Restatement of the Law, they would, no doubt, be cited by judges (together with Coke, Blackstone and appropriate cases) in rendering opinions. But, as has already been pointed out, they would not materially influence the result in any particular case, and, most assuredly, would furnish neither better methods nor better answers for any present problems.

Let us continue this supposition one step further. Suppose—what is certainly not impossible—that half a dozen or a dozen competent young lawyers and professors should decide to address themselves seriously to jurimetrics. After a year or so of work in the field, they decide to meet together for the purpose of discussing the problems and results of jurimetrics. A time and place are arranged and an agenda drawn up. What are the questions with which jurimetrics is likely to be concerned? It is certainly impossible to predict, in advance of work in the field, exactly what form the problems will take. Still, the general form and probable subject matter of many of the questions which jurimetrics, at least in its earlier stages, will attempt to investigate can be anticipated. It is reasonable to suppose that the agenda might be something like this:

The Problems of Jurimetrics
. . . .

The Behavior of Judges

What statistical measures will most conveniently summarize the behavior of individual judges in various categories of cases? How can we institute and maintain the basic records for such measures?

How, within the framework of existing rules, can we investigate the behavior of juries, measure their reaction to evidence and instructions, and discover the determinant considerations in reaching verdicts?

On the basis of inquiries relating to the behavior of witnesses, can we construct any objective criteria for weighing testimony?

How can we adapt the generally recognized scientific measures of probability to the problems of legal "proof"?

On the basis of data relating to the behavior of persons engaged in the judging process, are there any observable differences between the behavior of judges-in-court, administrative "judges," and legislators? If we can discover such differences, how can they best be expressed qualitatively and quantitatively?

The Behavior of Legislators

What practical measures can be instituted for investigating and recording in summary form the patterns of legislative behavior?

Can reliable patterns of the kind presupposed in the radical-conservative-reactionary terms of popular speech be discovered? If so, are there similar behavior patterns among " judges "? What are the measures of such patterns?

To what extent does the behavior of legislators in legislature X during period Y, indicate the influence of precedent, evidence, personal interest and other factors? . . .

The contrast between the questions of jurimetrics and the problems of jurisprudence is patent. Perhaps the most striking difference is that the problems of jurisprudence are broad, general, and therefore limited in number, while the questions of jurimetrics are relatively narrow and specific, and so are much more numerous. But this is a superficial distinction. The profound differentiation lies in two facts. First, the problems of jurisprudence are basically meaningless, since they can only be debated but never decided nor even investigated; whereas the questions of jurimetrics are meaningful since they are capable of being investigated, and ultimately answered, even though we may not know the answers now. Second, the problems of jurisprudence are not truly significant problems, since even if they were " solved," in the only sense in which they could be " solved "—by the giving of authoritative definitions, the " solutions " would have no practical consequences in our lives. On the other hand, all of the questions of jurimetrics are genuinely significant, since even a partial or tentative answer to any one is likely to have far-reaching consequences for society and for the individual. In this sense, jurimetrics is eminently " practical " in its approach, as contrasted with the philosophical speculations of jurisprudence.

There are, of course, other differences between the two disciplines, some of which may not be apparent at this time. Certainly one of the most important is that the problems of jurisprudence are formally " static " problems which presuppose the existence of one final authoritative answer, while the questions of jurimetrics are " dynamic " in form in that they allow for changing answers as our knowledge increases. Indeed, in jurimetrics the questions themselves change as the body of knowledge grows, since the problems are constantly reformulated in terms of prior data. Further, it will be noticed that while legal theoreticians, like the traditional economists, have been concerned up to the present time exclusively with microlegal phenomena—theories about the application of law to individuals—jurimetrics takes a broader outlook to include also an inquiry into macrolegal phenomena—the effect of law upon the community. While we can never disregard the problems of the application of law to individuals, experience in many fields indicates that the macrocosmic approach is more likely to be a fruitful one in the early stages of scientific investigation. Even today the science of physics is able to formulate its macroscopic laws with much greater accuracy than its microscopic laws, and—if the Heisenberg principle is correct—there is an absolute limit to the precision of observation and prediction on the submolecular level.

Perhaps the greatest advantage of jurimetrics over jurisprudence, at least from the viewpoint of the public, is that it will establish within the law itself an institutional method for growth and change. It is true that lawyers and jurists are fond of making speeches and writing papers lauding the marvelous vitality of the common law institutions in adapting themselves to social change. It is also true that such praise comes almost exclusively from within the profession and almost always as a defense against the attacks of non-lawyers upon the immobility and inflexibility of the law. Regardless of the forensic facade with which it may be decorated, it is too obvious to admit of controversy that the present method of the law has the effect of making change as slow and as slight as possible, as well as of making law a completely closed system which will admit new knowledge only when it is smuggled in disguised as a "precedent." As in Jhering's juristic heaven, new facts and ideas can gain admission to the house of law today only by smashing their heads through the solid walls. Jurimetrics promises to cut windows in the house of law, so that those inside can see out, and to cut doors, so that those outside can get in. Significantly, jurimetrics is oriented neither to change nor permanence as such. It seeks knowledge, and is prepared to retain, discard or modify principles as the data may, in any case, demand. . . .

[pp. 483–490]

LORD BOWDEN

House of Lords Debate on Computers for Research
(1966) [54]

. . . I think that the effect of computers on economics, on medicine and on the social sciences will be vastly greater in the next few years than it has been hitherto on engineering and science. But since we are speaking in this House, I would suggest to your Lordships another, and even more important, application of computers: the application of computers to the law. The problems of the law as I see them—and I speak as a complete layman—are made vexatiously worse than they should be because of the enormous amount of data with which the wretched lawyer is confronted, the tremendous spate of new legislation which no man can read; and the extraordinary complexity of the phraseology which is used in Acts. I remembered, and will remind your Lordships of, the Rent Bill which we recently voted upon. As one of your Lordships subsequently said, it was an extraordinarily bad example of legislation by reference; it was, in fact, quite incomprehensible without the assistance of a large number of other documents which did not come with the Bill. This seems to be an inevitable part of legislation as we know it today; and it is necessary for any practising lawyer to have at his elbow a substantial library to which he has access immediately and with the contents of which he is extremely familiar, so that he can

[54] [Hansard H.L. Vol. 273, cols. 688–757, March 2, 1966.]

find the leading cases on the law as well as the appropriate legislation fairly quickly.

A computer is capable of doing this. A modern computer can have a memory much larger than the largest law library in this country. Furthermore, it can gain access to any part of it extremely quickly. So it is perfectly possible for a large computer to provide a lawyer with a list of appropriate references, Acts of Parliament, or, if you like, leading cases, if the information is in the machine and appropriate questions are posed to it.

But this is only the beginning of the potential application of the machine. The noble and learned Lord who sits on the Woolsack [55] has many times told us of the extreme complexity of the task of his law reformers and of the grave problems with which they are confronted in discovering what the law is, and whether the law is itself consistent: in other words, whether the citizen is enjoined by one section of it to do something which he is forbidden expressly to do by another Act of Parliament. It is difficult enough if one is drawing up a quite simple contract which is full of various conditional clauses to make certain that it is of itself entirely self-consistent. But when one considers the mass of the law, it seems to me that this task is virtually impossible.

On the other hand, the processes through which a lawyer must go are based always on arguments: "If so and so, then something else must follow. If something else has been done, then something else must not follow." In other words, the processes are logical; they are based on reasoning—at least, we hope they are—and they are based upon the facts of the case and the law as it is known. The processes of logical reasoning are precisely things which a computer can do with extraordinary speed. A modern machine is a million times as fast as a man and will do the work at perhaps one ten-thousandth of the cost. I therefore hope that the noble and learned Lord who sits upon the Woolsack will perhaps persuade his Committee of law reformers to see how far the task upon which these people are engaged can be facilitated by the use of a modern computer.

The word "jurimetrics" has already been coined by the Bar of New York State to describe this process.[56] All the statute law of the State of Philadelphia has already been recorded in the memory of a large computer machine over there. I think the idea has great potential. The work is just beginning. The tasks will be vexatious; they will be difficult; they will be time-consuming. I can assure any man who tries to do it that there will be moments of despair when he will decide that the prospect is hopeless; but I can also assure him that this is the common lot of people who use computers, and in the end these machines' extreme speed and fantastic ability to reason and to process data will come to his aid. I feel certain that this is the kind of enterprise in which the application of this vastly powerful technique to an ancient and traditional society will be extremely advantageous. . . .   [cols. 719–721]

[55] [The Lord Chancellor, then Lord Gardiner.]
[56] [It was, in fact, coined by Lee Loevinger, see *ante*, 474.]

GLENDON SCHUBERT

Mathematical Prediction of Judicial Behavior

(1964) [57]

. . . Instead of giving up in the face of the complexities presented by judicial (or any other kind of human) discretion, the behavioralists have sought to understand and to explain judicial discretion. This has led them to undertake the kind of empirical research that is exemplified in the three middle chapters of this book. These three chapters discuss judicial decision-making from the points of view of cultural anthropology, political sociology, and social psychology. In terms of predicating judicial decision-making, each of these approaches represents a different level of analysis, at a different degree of proximity from the decision-making event.

Social psychology, with its focus upon the attitudes of individual decision-makers, is most proximate to the empirical behaviors of judicial voting and opinion-writing. One can understand and explain—at least, at a first level of initial comprehension—everything about judicial decision-making on the basis of attitudinal similarities and differences of the individuals in the decision-making group. Of course, this requires a very comprehensive analysis of individual attitudes, including both attitudes toward the issues of public policy that individuals are asked to resolve and their attitudes toward each other, and toward all other participants in the decision-making process. Both legal norms and legal facts are viewed as functions of attitudes toward the public policy issues in a case. An individual judge's *perception* of the question to be decided—and such a perception, although idiosyncratic to the individual in a physiological sense, is a function of social interaction—is the psychological equivalent of the " objective " norm of the legalists; and this perception identifies for the individual decision-maker the criterion (attitudinal scale) for the evaluation he is to make in his decision. His perception of " the facts " is intricately interrelated with his perception of the criterion scale for substantive evaluation. The facts consist of the subset of items, relating to the set of real-life events associated with the case, which the individual judge selects; and his selection is based upon either or both of two reasons. If a judge's attitude toward an issue is both extreme and intense, he may include a fact among his subset, even though he might—if asked independently—rate as low the probability that such a fact corresponds to a relevant historical event in the case under consideration. This is because he believes the issue to be so important and the event to occur so frequently that, even though there might be some doubt about its occurrence in this particular case, the instant case will " do " as a vehicle for getting at the issue.

Conversely, even if a judge rates as high the probability that an item corresponds to empirical reality, he may exclude it from his subset of facts, because of his attitude toward the related issue; such items are " immaterial " or " irrelevant." The facts that a judge perceives to be most important are those with which he associates a high probability for validity, *and* which he identifies with an attitudinal scale upon which

[57] [From Schubert, *Judicial Behavior, A Reader in Theory and Research* (1964); the introduction to Part 5.]

his own position is extreme. Hence, individual perceptions of " the facts "
may vary widely in a given case, because such perceptions are *joint*
functions of validity estimations and substantive attitudes. At the same
time, individual perceptions of " the law "—which we have defined as
the selection of the relevant attitudinal scale or scales—will be influenced
by fact-recognition. Since norm-recognition and fact-recognition are, in
part, mutually interdependent, the perception of legal norms and legal
facts is a very complicated psychological process, which is further
complicated by its dependence upon the individual's social interaction.

As Chapter IV demonstrates, it is now possible to describe in some
detail how judicial attitudes affect judicial decision-making. Future
research may extend our present primitive knowledge of judicial perception of legal norms and facts as a socio-psychological process. From the
point of view of predicting judicial decision-making, the attitudinal
approach takes the position that, given complete knowledge of the
attitudes of a set of judges toward the issue or issues that they purport
to resolve in a case, the analyst predicts the behavior of the judges on
the basis of the imputed differentials in their attitudes. In short, the
judges are expected to behave consistently with their beliefs, and the
decision of the court is a linear function of the decisions of its individual
members. With the incomplete knowledge of judicial attitudes that can
be attained empirically, an analyst cannot expect to predict judicial
behavior without some error; so his predictions are stated and evaluated
in terms of probability criteria. Since judicial attitudes bear the most
proximate relationship to judicial decisions, it is reasonable to expect
that more accurate predictions will result from the use of attitudinal
data than from the meta-variables discussed in Chapters II and III.

Nevertheless, the attitudinal approach (which deals with the question:
how do judges differ in their attitudes?) constitutes only one level of
analysis; for—*ex hypothesi*—even if we could complete a perfect description *and prediction* of judicial decision-making on the basis of
individual judicial attitudes, we still would be left with the question:
what explains judicial attitudes? Chapter III provides an explanation, on
another level, of judicial decision-making, since this chapter deals with
the question: why do judges differ in their attitudes? For present purposes, we need only to summarize briefly the kind of answer that the
materials of Chapter III suggest. Judges differ in their attitudes because
they have come to accept some beliefs, and reject others, as the result
of their life-experience. What a judge believes depends upon his political,
religious, and ethnic affiliations; his wife; his economic security and his
social status; the kind of education he has received, both formally and
informally, and the kind of legal career that he has followed prior to
becoming a judge. His affiliations, marital and socio-economic status,
education, and career will in turn be largely influenced by where he was
born, and to whom, and when. From the point of view of predicting
judicial decision-making, it is not assumed that judicial decisions are a
direct function of judicial attributes. Decisions are a direct function of
attitudes, and attitudes are a direct function by attributes; thus, decisions
are affected by attributes only through the mediation of intervening
attitudinal variables. Therefore, we should expect that predictions of
judicial behavior, based upon attribute variables and data, will be less
successful than predictions based directly upon attitudinal variables and
data.

There is still a third level of possible analysis. Why and how does it matter where a judge was born, and to whom, and when? Why and how, in other words, are judicial attributes determined by cultural differences? Clearly, cultural variation is important both within a given political system (e.g., why do judges who are Southern, Democratic, and Baptist differ, in their attitude toward the " legality " of interracial marriage, from judges who are Northern, Democratic, and Jewish?) and between political systems. The analysis of cultural influences, in both primitive and complex political systems, is directed toward an attempt to understand and to explain how and why different judges come to acquire different attributes. Clearly, cultural variables are even further removed from the making of choices by judges, and the relationship of the macro-variables (posited by both cultural anthropology and structural-functional theory) to judicial decision-making is relatively remote, as Table I indicates. Consequently, we ought to expect that predictions of judicial behavior, based upon such cultural-systemic macro-variables, will be least successful.

It follows that attempts to predict judicial behavior have the highest probability of being successful if they are based directly upon attitudinal variables and data. It does not necessarily follow, however, that all analysts who have worked with attitudinal data have recognized that this is what they were doing. When they began, some persons who are considered judicial behavioralists were, and some indeed remain, committed to an empirical orientation toward research; and most of these persons have had little interest in theory. Several of them have been attracted by the legal-fact model of judicial decision-making, and they have designed research involving predictions of certain aspects of judicial behavior, notably decisional outcomes. Such persons have not worked with attitudinal variables, because they have not conceptualized their work in socio-psychological terms; but they have worked with attitudinal data, since an examination of their work makes it clear that the relationship they were investigating was judicial perceptions of facts. This explains why it has been possible for them to experience some success in making specific predictions of decisions, even though they designed and discuss their research in terms of a non-behavioral model. They might well have worked much more effectively and efficiently, if they had chosen to work directly with both attitudinal theory and variables as well as with attitudinal data.

Attempts have been made thus far to predict three aspects of judicial behavior on the basis of mathematical models of decision-making processes. One form of prediction is the specification of individual voting behavior; apparently, few attempts have been made to specify individual opinion behavior.[58] Evidently, it has seemed more complicated to make predictions of opinion behavior than of voting behavior. Two examples of predictions of individual voting behavior will be found in Section C of this chapter.

When group decisions are predicted as functions of specified individual behaviors, this is a most rigorous form of prediction, since it requires that one make simultaneously correct predictions for each individual

[58] See, however, Schubert, " Attitudinal Dimensions of Judicial Opinions and Votes : the Case of Robert Jackson " (unpublished ms.) [now published as *Dispassionate Justice* (1969)].

TABLE I

PREDICTION BETWEEN CLASSES OF VARIABLES

Classes of variable:

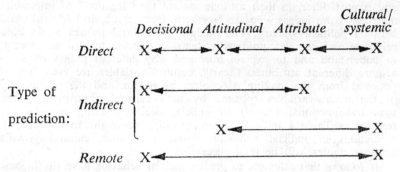

		Decisional	*Attitudinal*	*Attribute*	*Cultural/ systemic*
	Direct	X ⟷	X ⟷	X ⟷	X
Type of	*Indirect*	X ⟶		X	
prediction:			X ⟷		X
	Remote	X ⟷			X

member of the group. It is also possible, however, to predict other aspects of group behavior in addition to collective voting in specified decisions. For example, group relationships can be measured in terms of members' acceptance of each other's opinion,[59] of their statements (in opinions) of deference toward each other, or of their agreement in voting, or of their contiguity in psychological space. Usually, predictions stated in terms of statistical criteria require less rigor than predictions stated in terms of specific actions in a set of particular cases, because most statistical criteria make some allowance for error variance while determinate predictions for individual items do not—although the latter may, of course, be evaluated in terms of statistical criteria.

It is also possible to predict decisions as outcomes, such as pro or con a stipulated value, or (in the case of appellate courts) as affirmances or reversals of lower courts. If the outcome set consists of only two nominal categories, an analyst who knows little more than how to use a table of random numbers ought to be correct in half of his predictions of outcomes, providing that he makes enough predictions. Moreover, such gross predictions can in effect capitalize upon what would appear, in more explicit prediction of individual behaviors, to be multiple errors. For example, if one predicts a 5–4 outcome in a specified direction on the basis of a cumulative scale, it is required that a *particular* subset of four judges dissent; and if the case is so decided that a judge who was predicted to be in the majority subset dissents, and a judge who was predicted to be in the dissenting subset votes with the majority, then the prediction has erred in regard to two of the nine votes, even though the case was decided by a 5–4 vote and the effect of the outcome was in the direction specified. Such errors cancel each other out, in effect, when *only* the direction of outcomes is predicted; so the criterion level for successful prediction ought to be fairly high. Moreover, interest in such predictions, even when they appear to be quite successful, ought to focus upon the theoretical implications of the outcome of the experiment.

[59] S. Sidney Ulmer, "Leadership in the Michigan Supreme Court," in Schubert (Ed.), *Judicial Decision-Making* (New York: The Free Press of Glencoe, 1963), Chap. 1.

The fact that predictions succeeded is of no particular importance; we want to know why they succeeded, and how they can contribute to our understanding of judicial decision-making behavior. . . .   [pp. 445–448]

REED C. LAWLOR

What Computers Can Do: Analysis and Prediction of Judicial Decisions
(1963) [60]

Can Scientific Method be Applied to Law?

The ultimate successful use of computers in prediction of decisions depends on the extent to which scientific methods are applicable to law. Loevinger has pointed out many of the tasks, limitations, problems and benefits that arise when one attempts to apply scientific methods to the legal decision process.[61]

Heretofore the applicability of scientific methods to law has been hampered by the large amount of data available and the slow, laborious process heretofore required for its analysis. The development of extensive uses of scientific methods in the field of law has awaited the availability of computers.

For at least half a century, lawyers have debated the question whether scientific methods are useful in law. Roscoe Pound has said:

> Scientific methods need to be applied to law in order to meet the demands for full justice, that is, for solutions that go to the root of controversies; the demand for equal justice, that is, a like adjustment of like relations under like conditions; and the demand for exact justice, that is, justice whose operations within reasonable limits may be predicted in advance of action. In other words, the marks of a scientific law are conformity to reason, uniformity, and certainty.[62]

Justice Holmes went so far as to suggest that science might some day be used to evaluate the social ends of law:

> Gentlemen, I have tried to show by examples something of the interest of science as applied to the law, and to point out some possible improvement in our way of approaching practical questions in the same sphere. To the latter attempt, no doubt, many will hardly be ready to yield me their assent. . . . I have had in mind an ultimate dependence [of law] upon science because it is finally for science to determine, so far as it can, the relative worth of our different social ends; and, as I have tried to hint, it is our estimate of the proportion between these, now often blind and unconscious, that leads us to insist upon and to enlarge the sphere of one principle and to allow another gradually to dwindle into atrophy. Very likely it may be that, with all the help that statistics and every modern appliance can bring us, there will be a commonwealth

[60] [From 49 *American Bar Association Journal* 337, reprinted in Schubert, *Judicial Behavior* (1964), p. 492, to which page references relate.]
[61] Loevinger, " The Element of Predictability in Judicial Decision Making," *Proceedings 1st National Law and Electronics Conference* 249 (1960).
[62] Pound, " Mechanical Jurisprudence," 6 *Colum. L.Rev.* 604 (1908).

in which science is everywhere supreme.[63] [Today Justice Holmes's "appliances" include computers.]

Wiener has pointed out, correctly, that law is not an exact science [64] and has reiterated that the quest for certainty is doomed to failure.[65] But there is no such thing as an exact science. . . . But just as mathematical methods can be used to describe and analyze and predict experiences of physical and social science, they can also be used in law.

It is not certainty we seek in the law; it is less uncertainty. Scientific methods and computers can aid us in reducing the uncertainty.

Scientific Methods Seek to Predict Events

The ultimate goal of all scientific methods is reliable prediction of future events. As variable as it is, even the weather is becoming less unpredictable. Reliable prediction is also one of the ultimate goals of law. Successful prediction in law depends on understanding the law, understanding the facts and understanding people, especially judges. People are not completely unpredictable, especially when they are functioning as judges. Even if, as some seem to believe, the use of computers in aiding in the prediction of judicial decisions be futile, great benefits may flow from the effort. . . .

Even if logic has not been the life of the law, the law would have little life without it. Computers may give the law a new life which logic alone failed to supply. Computers may help us understand the nature of the law more fully. . . .

The development of a successful method for predicting decisions requires something more than the application of syllogistic principles to oversimplified statements of the law. The logic needed is modern mathematical logic, not merely the logic of the Aristotelian syllogisms.

Modern logic can be employed to relate the output of a court to its input. In a legal proceeding a pro or con decision constitutes the output, and facts constitute the input. With modern logic, logical equations can express the decisions (output) as a function of fact patterns (input), irrespective of the type of reasoning that is used to lead a judge from input to output.[66] Even if the judge's personal inclinations are unknown,

---

[63] Holmes, *Collected Legal Papers* 242 (1920). See also, 231.

[64] Wiener, *Briefing and Arguing Federal Appeals* 146 (1961).

[65] Wiener, "Decision Prediction by Computers: Nonsense Cubed—and Worse," 48 *A.B.A.J.* 1023 ; November, 1962.

[66] Lawlor, "Mathematical Aids to Prediction of Court Decisions," *Proceedings 2d National Law and Electronics Conference* (1962). See also, "Computer Aids to Legal Decision-Making," *M.U.L.L.* (1963).

Typical polarized facts of the kinds which the justices of the Supreme Court have indicated that they rely upon in reaching their decisions include the following: The petitioner was charged with a crime subject to capital punishment. The petitioner was young and immature. The petitioner was either illiterate or had a subnormal education or had only limited contact with the culture in which he was tried. The accused was an indigent. The petitioner was interrogated in the absence of counsel after arrest and before arraignment. The petitioner was arraigned at a time when he lacked assistance of counsel. The petitioner had no assistance of counsel at the trial or at the hearing on the plea of guilty. The petitioner's request for assignment of counsel was denied. The petitioner did not waive right to counsel explicitly at a time when he understood his rights and needs. Hearsay and other incompetent evidence was admitted by the trial court. The case arose in Alabama.

they are implicit in the equations. It is difficult, but not impossible, to derive the equations from decided cases. Usually alternative solutions are possible. Although what judges do may be more important than what they say, the *ratio decidendi* and dicta can be used to aid the analyst in expressing the decision as a fairly reliable mathematical (logical) function of the facts.

Everyone agrees that decisions depend upon circumstances. Usually we think of circumstances as being the facts of the case. Those who believe in the gastronomic theory of justice would add the temporary gastronomic condition of the judge to the circumstances and might even consider it the principal controlling circumstance. Prediction methods can be successful only to the extent that decisions are controlled by circumstances that are observable and measurable. The unobservable and unmeasurable circumstances cannot be taken into account except to the extent that it is recognized that they create a degree of uncertainty in the outcome. The measurement and description of uncertainty and the isolation of its causes are among the objects of statistical science.

It is not easy to know all the important circumstances of a case. But whatever they are, modern logic paves the way for expressing decisions as mathematical functions of those circumstances. Computers can apply those decision equations more rapidly and reliably than a person can.

The doctrine of precedent, or rule of *stare decisis,* is one form of judicial logic. Lawyers have different concepts about what *stare decisis* is, what it should be and whether it should control decisions. Since none better is available, we shall use the term *stare decisis* to describe certain rules of precedent that appear to describe the judicial process. We are free to do this, since at least one authority states that the literature of legal philosophy is almost totally lacking in any systematic treatment of the doctrine of precedent and *stare decisis.*[67]

There are at least three easily identified kinds or grades of rules of precedent. Under traditional, strict *stare decisis,* a court (regardless of its personnel) is bound by the prior decisions of courts of equal or higher level (regardless of their personnel). . . .

Most judges in the United States usually follow traditional *stare decisis,* at least when considering decisions of courts directly in line above them. But at the pinnacle of our judicial system—in our courts of last resort such as at the level of the United States Supreme Court—judges do not always feel constrained by traditional *stare decisis.* In spite of this, there is a strong suggestion that in the large majority of cases, individual judges are usually consistent with themselves and often cite their own prior decisions to support their position. This rule of precedent might be called " personal *stare decisis* ". . . . The term " personal *stare decisis* " is not a contradiction in terms; it is a practical handle for describing a practical situation. Even when a judge applies the rule of traditional *stare decisis* strictly, this forms part of his own personal *stare decisis.* Accordingly, in the United States any system of successful prediction of legal decisions that is to be effective must involve not only a study of earlier decisions, but also a study of the judges who rendered them. It requires the determination of the personal *stare decisis* or logic

---

[67] Wasserstrom, *The Judicial Decision: Toward a Theory of Legal Justification* 40 (1961).

of each judge, at least at the pinnacle level. And any rule that can be found for predicting the decisions for one judge is not necessarily applicable to the decisions of another judge.

"Traditional *stare decisis*" can be expressed succinctly by the equation:

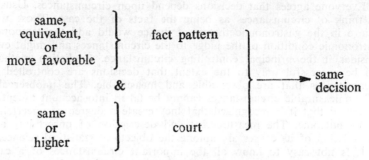

FIGURE 1.   TRADITIONAL STARE DECISIS

But "personal *stare decisis*" is expressed by the equation:

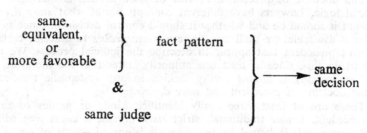

FIGURE 2.   PERSONAL STARE DECISIS

Panels of judges of appeal courts often apply a third principle that is very similar to traditional *stare decisis*. Individual subpanels of judges often feel bound by the prior decisions of subpanels of judges who are currently serving on the same court.[68] This might be called local *stare*

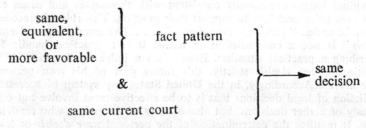

FIGURE 3.   LOCAL STARE DECISIS

[68] Cardozo, *The Nature of the Judicial Process* 171 (1947).

decisis. This rule, which may not always be subsumed under traditional *stare decisis,* can be expressed within the limits of controlling precedent by the equation depicted in Figure 3.

In all three of these equations the expression " more favorable fact pattern " means a fact pattern which is more favorable to the same kind of decision, that is, pro or con, or whatever it is to be called, as the fact pattern of the prior case or cases. Reference to a more favorable fact pattern is often omitted from explanations of *stare decisis.* . . .

One of the syndromes of personal *stare decisis* at the pinnacles of our legal systems exists in the frequent appearance of dissenting opinions of individual justices, especially where justices cite their own prior dissenting opinions in support of their current dissenting opinions. Under American law, it sometimes seems that many judges assume that they are entitled to their own opinions, especially if they are not required to account to a higher court.

Prediction is Impossible without Stare Decisis

Even if they are man-made, the principles of *stare decisis* are akin to the all embracing assumption of uniformity of natural science.[69] Without such a principle to guide us, prediction of legal decisions is impossible.

It has been said that *stare decisis* (probably traditional and local *stare decisis* taken together) governs decisions in over 95 per cent of the cases that come before the courts. It has been calculated that courts cite prior decisions of their own jurisdictions approvingly 95 per cent of the time.[70] Accordingly, it is reasonable to adopt the principles of *stare decisis* in programming a computer.

If individual judges are not consistent with themselves, there is little that modern science can do to aid in the analysis of the decisions of the judge, and his decisions are then unpredictable. But if a judge is consistent and the fact patterns to which he has responded can be ascertained, his voting behavior in a large number of related cases can be summarized in a mathematical equation and this equation can be used to " predict " future decisions in response to many new fact patterns. The same rule applies to an entire multi-judge court, but to a more limited extent. . . .

To the extent that individual judges are consistent, computers can be employed to make predictions with a corresponding degree of consistency. The reliability of prediction techniques requires study and measurement.

Kort,[71] Nagel[72] and Lawlor[73] have all developed methods for

---

[69] Pollock, " The Science of Case Law," *Essays in Jurisprudence and Ethics* 239 (1882). Also, *Jurisprudence and Legal Essays* 170 (1961).

[70] Nagel, " Sociometric Relations Among American Courts," 43 *SW.Soc.Sci.Q.* 136 (1962).

[71] Kort, " Predicting Supreme Court Decisions Mathematically: A Quantitative Analysis of the ' Right-to-Counsel ' Cases," 51 *Am.Pol.Sci.Rev.* 1 (1957). Kort, " Content Analysis of Judicial Opinions and Rules of Law," 4 International Yearbook of Political Behavior Research, *Judicial Decision-Making* (1963). Kort, " Simultaneous Equations and Boolean Algebra in the Analysis of Judicial Decisions," 28 *Law & Contemp.Prob.* [143–163].

[72] Nagel, " Weighting Variables in Judicial Prediction," *M.U.L.L.* 93 (September, 1960). Nagel " Using Simple Calculations to Predict Judicial Decisions," 4 *Am.Behav.Sci.* 28 (1960).   [73] *Supra,* notes 6 and 66.

analyzing cases with the view to predicting decisions. All depend on content, or fact, analysis of decisions. All three have directed their attention to the United States Supreme Court as a whole. In addition, Lawlor has applied his techniques to individual justices. All three make use of computers. The history of attempts to apply mathematical methods to prediction of decisions has been set forth elsewhere.[74] Loevinger has recognized that the hope of successful prediction in law lies in the development of effective methods of content analysis.[75]

In Kort's methods, weights are found for individual facts apparently relied on by the court in reaching its decision. The sum of these weights then gives the weight of the facts in a case. Kort found that when the weight of all the facts in a case exceeds a discoverable threshold value the case usually goes one way, but when it falls below it usually goes the other way. Nagel's method also employs a weighting technique.

Kort's and Nagel's techniques may be likened to the placing of weights on the scale of justice. The threshold is represented by a weight placed in one pan. It measures the burden of proof. The weights of the facts are placed in the other pan. Usually only when the total weight of the claimant's case outweighs the threshold weight can the claimant win. A lawyer whose facts don't weigh enough had better take another look at the facts of his case. The picture of justice holding a balance is no longer just fiction.

Lawlor's methods have used modern (symbolic) logic along with the principles of " traditional *stare decisis* " and " personal *stare decisis.*" While the principles of local *stare decisis* are also applicable, this has not been done yet. The mathematical analysis has been simplified by polarizing all the facts in the same direction, that is, by describing facts so that every fact, if present, tends to support a particular type of decision, such as a pro decision.[76] Though Lawlor's methods are of general application wherever decisions depend on patterns of definable facts, they have been applied so far only to a single field of law: the right-to-counsel cases of the United States Supreme Court. This field was selected for the first experiments because others—Kort and Schubert—have been testing their methods in this same field.

Still another method of analysis that is partially applicable to prediction has been developed by Schubert. His method utilizes a scalogram or Guttman scaling technique.[77] This technique was developed during World War II to measure the relative attitudes of servicemen to varying situations of the same general kind. Using this technique, Schubert showed that Supreme Court justices can be arranged along a scale in a predetermined order, and that knowledge of how one justice will vote can be employed to predict how all of the remaining justices on one, but only one, side of that one judge will probably vote. These methods have been tested in several fields of law. Though the scaling is imperfect, there is a strong indication that the methods are sound. What Schubert says in effect is that the votes of the justices are like dominoes. If you push over the vote of one judge, you know how the votes of almost all the other judges on one side will fall.

---

[74] *Supra*, notes 61 and 66.   [75] Loevinger, *supra*, note 61 at 273.
[76] *Supra*, note 66, second paragraph.
[77] Schubert, *Quantitative Analysis of Judicial Behavior* 269 (1959).

Finding Operable Facts is a Difficult Task

One of the most difficult aspects of content analysis lies in the identification and description of the facts that operate to control the decisions of the judges. These facts are ascertained from the published decisions. Sometimes, however, the description of the facts may seem objectionable. For example, in one case in its unanimous decision, the United States Supreme Court clearly indicated that the law of the State of Alabama was a peculiar fact of the case.[78] Therefore, this fact must be taken into account. Any criticism [79] that the truth or falsity of the statement, " the case arose in Alabama ", is to be considered a factor in analysis is not a valid criticism of the methods of prediction, but is in fact an unjustified criticism of the Court. This apparent stigma has now been removed by the Court itself in a subsequent unanimous decision.[80] Actually in any comprehensive study the state of origin is an important fact that must be taken into account.[81]

An analysis of the right-to-counsel cases discloses that for thirty years (the first right-to-counsel case [82] was decided in 1932) every justice has behaved consistently in accordance with his own personal *stare decisis* described broadly by equation (2) above. In other words, not even one United States Supreme Court justice was ever inconsistent with himself in this field of law so far as the decisions he rendered on the merit of the cases are concerned. Whether any judge was ever inconsistent in what he *said* rather than what he *did* has not been investigated.

Lawlor has also tested his methods by assuming that the Court obeys equation (1), the rule of traditional *stare decisis*, as well as by assuming that the individual judges obey equation (2), the rule of personal *stare decisis*. Contradictions between results obtained by these two methods are inevitable. Contradictions may signal when the court will overrule its prior decisions.

It is a fundamental principle of the behavior of a committee—and the Supreme Court is a committee—that is governed by a majority rule, that if the same questions arise time after time, the committee will eventually reverse its position if the individual committee members have a wide variety of individual but self-consistent attitudes and the membership of the committee changes from time to time. The fact that the Supreme Court sometimes overrules prior cases is not necessarily a reflection of changing conditions. It is primarily a reflection of the fact that the personnel of the Court has changed. In theory at least, so long as individual judges are consistent and are guided by their own individual theories of justice or evaluations of facts, it is inevitable that the Court will overrule earlier decisions, even some in which it has previously overruled even still earlier decisions.

Techniques are applied to Right-to-Counsel Case

The United States Supreme Court has asked counsel to brief the question as to whether its prior decision in *Betts* v. *Brady* should be reconsidered.[83]

[78] *Hamilton* v. *Alabama*, 368 U.S. 52 (1962).　　　　　　[79] *Supra*, note 65.
[80] *Carnley* v. *Cochran*, 369 U.S. 506 (1962).
[81] *Betts* v. *Brady*, 316 U.S. 455 (1942).
[82] *Powell* v. *Alabama*, 287 U.S. 45 (1932).
[83] *Gideon* v. *Cochran*, 135 So. 2d 746 (Fla.). In granting certiorari the Court requested briefs on this questions, 370 U.S. 908, 82 S.Ct. 1259.

A case on all fours is not before the Court. But it is interesting to feed into a computer the same fact pattern as that which was recognized in *Betts* v. *Brady* and to analyze this fact pattern with equations that have been developed by trial and error for the recent Court. The results of the analysis are prepared by the computer in the form of a letter. A slightly edited and shortened version of such a letter follows [84]:

> Dear Mr. Lawyer
> As you requested, an analysis has been made of the hypothetical right-to-counsel case that you presented entitled . . .

> ### *Like Betts* v. *Brady*

> This analysis was performed on an IBM 7090 computer. The program that was used was previously tested and developed on the IBM 7090 at Western Data Processing Center located at UCLA. Edgar A. Jones, Professor of Law at UCLA and Chairman of the UCLA Committee for Interdisciplinary Studies of Law and the Administration of Justice, sponsored the use of the Western Data Processing Computer for this purpose.
> In the case that you presented, you stated that the following facts are present . . .

>> 4 The petitioner was charged with a crime subject to five to ten years imprisonment.

>> 6 The petitioner was either illiterate or had a subnormal education or had only limited contact with the culture in which he was tried.

>> 11 The petitioner was arraigned at a time when he lacked assistance of counsel.

>> 12 The petitioner had no assistance of counsel between arraignment and the trial or between arraignment and the hearing on the plea of guilty.

>> 13 The petitioner had no assistance of counsel at the trial or the hearing on the plea of guilty.

>> 14 The petitioner had no assistance of counsel at the time of sentencing.

>> 17 The petitioner's request for assignment of counsel was denied.

>> 19 The petitioner did not waive right to counsel explicitly at a time when he understood his rights and needs.

>> 40 The accused was an indigent.

>> 42 The petitioner did not express nonchalance and indifference at the time he pleaded guilty,

> and that other facts found in previous right-to-counsel cases are absent.
> You have also stated that you are interested in the probable votes of the following justices . . .

> > Black
> > Frankfurter
> > Douglas
> > Clark

---

[84] This letter, which has been edited only slightly, was not stored in the computer and merely retrieved. It was composed by the computer to describe its solution to the problem presented.

Warren
Harlan
Brennan
Whittaker
Stewart

The computer analyzed the hypothetical case that you presented by four different methods, and then composed this report to you automatically from stock words, phrases, and sentences that had previously been stored in the computer.

First Method

In this method the computer locates pro-precedent cases and con-precedent cases. For this purpose a cited case is considered a pro-precedent case if and only if it meets the following requirements . . .

1. All of the facts of the cited case are present in your case.
2. No other facts are present in the cited case.
3. At least one justice voted pro on the cited case.

Also, for this purpose, a case is considered a con-precedent case, if and only if it meets the following requirements . . .

1. All of the facts of your case are present in the cited case.
2. No other facts are present in your case.
3. At least one justice voted con on the cited case.

Each of the following pro-precedent cases was identified by the computer. The justices who voted -pro- in the respective cases are indicated . . .

Betts v. *Brady*, 316 U.S. 455 (1942)
Black
Douglas
Murphy

Each of the following con-precedent cases was identified by the computer. The justices who voted -con- in the respective cases are indicated . . .

Betts v. *Brady*, 316 U.S. 455 (1942)
Stone
Roberts
Reed
Frankfurter
Byrnes
Jackson

Hudson v. *North Carolina*, 363 U.S. 697 (1960)
Clark
Whittaker

Second Method

The following table summarizes results obtained by comparing the facts in your case with the facts in right-to-counsel cases that have previously been decided. In this summary

A=The number of facts in your case that are also present in the cited case.

B=The number of facts that are absent from your case but are present in the cited case.

C=The number of facts that are present in your case but are absent from the cited case.

Only the facts listed in the questionnaire that you completed are considered, and facts are considered to be present if they were accepted by the majority in the case cited.

A	B	C		Case
4	8	6	1	*Powell* v. *Alabama*, 287 U.S. 45 (1932)
1	3	9	2	*Avery* v. *Alabama*, 308 U.S. 444 (1940)
9	5	1	3	*Smith* v. *Ogrady*, 312 U.S. 329 (1941)
10	0	0	4	*Betts* v. *Brady*, 316 U.S. 455 (1942)
7	4	3	5	*Williams* v. *Kaiser*, 323 U.S. 471 (1945)
7	4	3	6	*Tomkins* v. *Missouri*, 323 U.S. 485 (1945)

. . .

. . .

A	B	C		Case
10	3	0	35	*Hudson* v. *North Carolina*, 363 U.S. 697 (1960)
9	5	1	36	*McNeal* v. *Culver*, 365 U.S. 109 (1961)
8	3	2	37	*Reynolds* v. *Cochran*, 365 U.S. 525 (1961)
3	2	7	38	*Hamilton* v. *Alabama*, 368 U.S. 52 (1962)
8	1	2	39	*Chewning* v. *Cunningham*, 368 U.S. 443 (1962)
7	4	3	40	*Carnley* v. *Cochran*, 369 U.S. 506 (1962)

THIRD METHOD

A logic formula has been developed that describes the past behavior of the court as a whole in right-to-counsel cases. This formula takes into account certain distinctions that have been made by the court and also certain equivalences of facts that appear to be inherent in the decisions, if a simple rule is to apply.

Based upon this formula, the computer has calculated that the court as a whole will consider your case a -con- case.

FOURTH METHOD

Additional logic formulae have been developed for describing the manner in which individual justices have voted in the past when presented with various fact patterns.

In these formulae too account has been taken of distinctions that appear in the cases and also certain equivalences that appear to be inherent in the decisions, if simple rules are to apply. Additionally, account has been taken of some pertinent dicta in the decisions in which the individual justices have participated. Based upon these formulae, it is anticipated that the individual justices in whose votes you have shown an interest, will treat your case as a -pro- case or a -con- case, as indicated in the following table . . .

Pro   —Black
    Con—Frankfurter
Pro   —Douglas
    Con—Clark
Pro   —Warren

```
Pro    —Harlan
Pro    —Brennan
Con—Whittaker
Con—Stewart
```

It is therefore anticipated that the vote of the Supreme Court on the case that you presented would be . . .

```
Pro votes    5
Con votes    4
```

REMARKS

It is possible, of course, that the results obtained by different methods will be contradictory. Only time will tell how reliable various methods may be. They can succeed only if courts and individual justices follow consistent voting patterns and only if these voting patterns can be discovered and then described in mathematical terms.

You appreciate, of course, that this work is in an embryonic stage and that reliability of the methods depends very largely upon the analysis of prior decisions by lawyers and very largely upon your ability to predict what facts will be accepted by the court and the individual justices as a basis for decision.

Thank you for co-operating in this experiment. Your suggestions, criticisms and questions will be welcomed.

Betts v. Brady appears doomed

Since the letter is largely self-explanatory, little explanation will be given here. Notice that the computer analyzed the case with four different techniques. In the first technique precedents are cited. Notice how pro precedents and con precedents have been defined and that a case can be a con precedent for certain judges while being a pro precedent for others. The facts referred to in these definitions are all polarized in a pro direction.

In the second technique a comparison is made between the new case and every old case, merely listing the number of facts that are the same and the facts that are different. This technique is undergoing improvement. Only a few comparisons are presented here. That the case analyzed in the letter is on all fours with *Betts* v. *Brady* is indicated by the O's in columns B and C opposite the citation.

An interesting contradiction appears between the results of techniques 3 and 4. These techniques use one of the sets of equations that has been found to describe past decisions accurately. These equations had been chosen from the many possible equations as being descriptive of the past behavior of the individual justices as well as of the Court as a whole. The methods of developing such equations and selecting those to use for prediction purposes are still undergoing development.

Assuming traditional *stare decisis*, the computer calculated that the decision of the Court as a whole in this new case would be con. But if personal *stare decisis* is assumed, the computer calculates that five of the individual justices would vote pro, thus overruling the prior decision of the Court as a whole on the same set of facts. Other equations indicate that Justice Stewart could vote pro and that Justice Harlan could vote con without being inconsistent. If we assume that the predicted votes of Justices Warren, Black, Brennan, Clark and Douglas are correct, and we assume that the average attitude of Justices Goldberg, Harlan, Stewart and White would be about the same in this case as that of all the justices who have decided the right-to-counsel cases, the odds appear to be at least six to one that the present Court would overrule *Betts* v. *Brady* if a case on all fours were presented today. Eventually it is hoped to develop a system for automatically computing prediction of judicial decisions in probabilistic terms instead of calculating just black-and-white answers.

While the fact pattern of *Gideon* v. *Cochran* is not the same as *Betts* v. *Brady*, calculations based on the facts that appear in the briefs in *Gideon* v. *Cochran* indicate that the odds are at least about twenty to one that the petitioner will prevail regardless of whether *Betts* v. *Brady* is overruled. In making this kind of calculation it has been necessary to make some untested assumptions as to what facts alleged in the briefs will be used by the Court. . . .

In the future, lawyers who consider the interest of their clients paramount will not hesitate to employ computers to aid them in solving the problems of their clients to the extent that computer techniques are applicable at the time. And judges who are called upon to decide important cases may raise their eyebrows at attorneys who do not make use of computer facilities in their review and analysis of the law. As scientific methods for analyzing the law are further developed, justice may become less blind and we may approach Pound's standards of full, equal and exact justice and Holmes's dream of a scientific evaluation of the social values of legal decisions. . . .[85]   [pp. 494–505]

---

[85] [*Betts* v. *Brady* was in fact overruled shortly after this article was written in *Gideon* v. *Wainwright* 372 U.S. 335 (1963). An entertaining account of this case is Lewis, *Gideon's Trumpet* (1964).]

8

THE SCANDINAVIAN REALISTS

DESPITE the unfortunate ignorance in the common law world both of
the working of the legal systems in the Scandinavian countries, and of
their legal literature, common lawyers have, nevertheless, slowly become aware in recent years of a significant movement in legal thought
in those northern territories. Understanding of this movement has
gradually increased as a number of works by Scandinavian jurists has
been published in English which has contributed to our enlightenment. Further, the excellent annual series, *Scandinavian Studies in
Law,* has done much to foster interest in Scandinavian legal science.
As our knowledge of the methods and concepts of Scandinavian law
increases, the writings of these jurists become more meaningful.
The relative insularity of the Scandinavian countries, geographical
isolation, immunity from international commerce, together with early
national formulations of law, meant that Roman law had little
impact on their civilisation. In their substantive law and, though
less so, in their legal science, they remained outside the main legal
families of the world.[1] Even today, their law is less codified than
the rest of Europe and, as a result, more judge-orientated. This comes
out particularly in the writings of Ross[2] though, to a lesser
extent, in those of Olivecrona.[3] The Scandinavian penchant for
social welfare is apparent in the writings of Lundstedt,[4] though he
himself would never have admitted that his philosophy was tarnished
by ideology. Perhaps, above all, the jurists' rejection of metaphysics
comes out in the rather down-to-earth Scandinavian, particularly
Swedish, approach to crime and its treatment.

The movement appears to look to the late Professor Hägerström[5] as its spiritual father, but the protagonists now best
known in this country are Olivecrona, Lundstedt and Ross. Their
writings have aroused more than a mild interest here, perhaps because

---

[1] On which see David and Brierley, *Major Legal Systems of the World* (1968),
pp. 41–45, 89, 96. There is no doubt in the mind of Sundberg that the
Scandinavian systems are heavily influenced by Civil law (*Scandinavian Studies in
Law* (1969), p. 179).

[2] *Post,* 555.

[3] *Post,* 522.

[4] *Post,* 544.

[5] See the English translation, by C. D. Broad, of his *Inquiries into the Nature of
Law and Morals,* published in 1953. And see *post,* 515.

they seem to be in line with the empirical traditions in English philosophy and jurisprudence, and also to have some affinities to the sociological approach which has grown in influence in England during the last generation.[6] This chapter will seek to appraise certain of the views of these three writers, though it should be pointed out that Lundstedt's are a good deal more extreme than those of the other two. Lundstedt's posthumously published reflections [7]—extremely polemical in style, and generating a great deal more heat than English lawyers are accustomed to in so dry a field as legal theory—have only comparatively recently been vouchsafed to us, but unfortunately in an English version which is a model neither of clarity nor of literary form.

AXEL HÄGERSTRÖM (1868–1939)

"*No one of* [*Lundstedt, Olivecrona and Ross*] *is wholly self-contained. To understand them, or effectively criticise them, one must constantly return to Hägerström. They presume the substantial truth of his subtle and detailed analysis.*" [8]

A few comments on Hägerström's approach will, therefore, help to set the jurists in perspective.[9]

Hägerström was not a lawyer, but a philosopher whose attention was directed to law and ethics as particularly fertile sources of metaphysics. Hägerström's aim was to destroy transcendental metaphysics, and, where better to start than law. "All metaphysical concepts are sham concepts," mere word-play. Yet, legal thinking abounds with them: rights and duties, property, the will of the state etc. The fallacy had to be explained, an objective theory of knowledge had to be erected. Legal philosophy for Hägerström as, indeed, it became for his followers, is a sociology of law without empirical investigation, but built instead upon conceptual, historical and psychological analysis. Much of his writing is, accordingly, a critique of the errors of juristic thought. Austin, with his command theory and such concepts as the " will of the state," [10] and Kelsen's

---

6 Hägerström may have come under the influence of British empiricist philosophy through his acquaintance with Neo-Kantians like Lange. See Passmore (1961) 36 *Philosophy*, 143, 144.
7 *Legal Thinking Revised* (1956).
8 *Per* J. Passmore (1961) 36 *Philosophy* 143. The debt to Hägerström is less evident in the writings of Ross than the other two, but is marked nonetheless. For a recent attempt to trace Scandinavian Realism back earlier than Hägerström to early legal thinking in Denmark, see K. Illum, 12 *Scandinavian Studies in Law* 51, 57, where the writings of Ørsted (1778–1860) are cited as evidence of the realist trend.
9 See, further, Olivecrona, *Scandinavian Studies in Law*, Vol. 3, p. 125 and *Law as Fact* (2nd ed.), pp. 174–177, 227–233; Passmore, *op. cit.*; Broad, 26 *Philosophy* 99.
10 *Op. cit.*, note 5, pp. 20–35.

neo-Kantian reduction of the dualism of existence and validity into the category of *Sollen,* into, that is, metaphysics, come in for particular censure.[11] So, too, do factual explanations of the concept of a right.[12]

A short discussion of this will demonstrate Hägerström's method. He first reviews the attempts that have been made to discover the empirical basis of a right. He dismisses each as unsuccessful: "the factual basis which we are seeking cannot be found . . . either in *protection guaranteed* [13] or *commands issued* [14] by an external authority." He concludes that there are no such facts. The "idea" has nothing to do with reality: its content is some kind of supernatural power with regard to things and persons. Hägerström next sought a psychological explanation, and found it in the feeling of strength and power associated with the conviction of possessing a right: "one fights better if one believes that one has right on one's side." [15] Hägerström takes this discussion no further. But it is clear from his writings that, though rights may not exist, they are useful tools of thought. It is at this point that the jurists take up the analysis. Ross, for example, in *Tu-Tu,*[16] accepts implicitly Hägerström's analysis and shows how statements about rights made in a legal context may have realistic, meaningful content.

Hägerström also investigated the historical bases of the idea of a right. To this end he made extensive studies of Greek and, more particularly, Roman law and history.[17] His studies were conceived to demonstrate that the framework of the *jus civile* was a system of rules for the acquisition and exercise of supernatural powers. He was puzzled why, for example, the buyer claimed the *res mancipi* as his before the ceremony of *mancipatio* [18] was over. Hägerström's

[11] *Op. cit.,* note 5, p. 257. On the dualism see Ross, *On Law and Justice,* p. 11, and Kelsen, *ante,* 270.

[12] See MacCormack, *Juridical Review* (1971), 59. Sundby (1968) 13 Nat.L.Forum 72 deals with contemporary Scandinavian analyses of "right," but is useful in relating this to Hägerström.

[13] The state only steps in if the right of property is violated, so right of property (*cf.* novel disseisin) is a prerequisite of protection. Can a *sine qua non* of protection be identical with the fact of protection? See Olivecrona, 3 *Scand. Studies in Law* at p. 128.

[14] Can powers, for example to sell or transfer be explained in this way? Hägerström thinks not.

[15] *Op. cit.,* note 5, p. 5. This has unhappy implications for peace, both in society and the international arena, something of which the Scandinavians are well aware.

[16] *Post,* 556. On the relationship between Hägerström and *Tu-Tu,* see Olivecrona, *op. cit.,* pp. 177 *et seq.*

[17] See, *Der römische Obligationsbegriff* (2 Vols. 1927, 1941), parts of which are translated in *Inquiries into the Nature of Law and Morals.* The work as a whole has never been translated. His writings met a hostile reception from Roman scholars, see Olivecrona, *op. cit.,* pp. 231–233. See also MacCormack's articles on Hägerström and Roman law (1969), 4 *Irish Jurist* 153 and 37 *Tijdschrift voor Rechtsgeschiedenis* 439.

[18] See Nicholas, *Roman Law* (1962), p. 63.

explanation was that the buyer's statement was not true; that, in effect, he used the formal words to make the *res mancipi* his property: the words and gestures had a magical effect, the act was a ritual. He believed, and there is an element of truth in his belief, that modern law is equally a ritualistic exercise. One thinks of the legal oath, the black cap, the wedding ring or the coronation ceremony. But, as Pollock wrote,[19] ritual is to law as a bottle is to liquor: you cannot drink the bottle, but equally you cannot cope with liquor without the bottle. There is a danger in assimilating legal with ritual symbols, for ritual can only be understood if the *beliefs* underlying it are investigated, but legal symbols perform a *function* and are not concerned with beliefs.[20] The plausibility of the magical interpretation of symbols anyway rests on assumptions embedded in the anthropology of Tyler and Frazer's *Golden Bough*, and has been shown by modern research to be baseless.[21] The influence of Hägerström's thesis is nonetheless apparent in Olivecrona's analysis of legal language, in his discussion of what he calls " performatives," legal words which are used to produce certain desired results, usually a change in legal relationships.[22] Thus, " I do " said, during a marriage ceremony, influences people to regard a man and a woman in a different light from the way it treated them prior to the ceremony. In Olivecrona's words: " it is the language of magic." [23]

Two examples have been used to show Hägerström's influence. Others may be briefly noted: Hägerström's emphasis on law as rules about force comes out in the writings of both Olivecrona and Ross,[24] and Olivecrona's concept of " independent imperatives " [25] must be understood against the background of Hägerström's thoughts on the derivation of duties. These will be discussed in those contexts.[26]

LAW AS FACT

The Scandinavian Realists, as they are now frequently described, resemble many other modern schools in their positivist outlook and in their desire to eliminate all metaphysics. For them law can be explained purely in terms of observable facts, and the study of such facts, which is the science of law, is, therefore, a true science like any other concerned with facts and events in the realm of causality.[27]

---

19 Quoted in Passmore, 36 *Philosophy* 143, 156. *Cf. ante*, 353.
20 See MacCormack (1969) 4 *Irish Jurist* 153, 167.
21 *Idem*, p. 154 and 37 *Tijdschrift voor Rechtsgeschiedenis* 439.
22 See his *Legal Language and Reality* (in Essays in Honor of Pound ed. Newman), p. 151, and *post*, 530; and *Law as Fact* (2nd ed.), Chaps. 8 and 9.
23 *Legal Language and Reality*, p. 175.
24 *Post*, 527 and 551.
25 *Post*, 523.
26 On which see Passmore, *op. cit.*, p. 143 and *post*, 523, n. 7.
27 *Cf. ante*, 6.

Thus, all such notions as the binding force or validity of law, the existence of legal rights and duties, the notion of property and so forth are dismissed as mere fantasies of the mind,[28] with no actual existence other than in an imaginary metaphysical world of their own. If then those notions are dismissed as mere metaphysical will-o'-the-wisps, what is left for the legal scientist? Apparently nothing but predictions as to judicial behaviour, apart from various kinds of psychological pressures which, for various reasons not necessarily material, do in fact, human nature being what it is, exert an influence on human conduct, and given certain conditions promote that regularity of behaviour which we associate with a legal system. Does this mean that the normative element of legal rules is thus entirely eliminated? Not altogether, for Olivecrona propounds the view that rules of law are what he terms " independent imperatives," that is propositions in imperative form (as opposed to statements of fact) but not issuing, like commands, from particular persons.[29] It would seem, however, that Olivecrona attaches little importance to this analysis, since for him laws " exist " only in the sense that words are to be found written on pieces of paper, or intermittently stored or present in human minds or memories, and the real significance of these words is merely in the factual circumstance that these words are a link in the chain of physical causation, producing certain courses of behaviour on the part of human beings.[30] Lundstedt, on the other hand, is a good deal more thorough-going. Thus, Lundstedt rejects everything normative, which he apparently identifies with the metaphysical. For him this is something completely beyond the realm of experience and, therefore, non-existent. Legal rules are no more than " labels " which, torn from their context of legal machinery, are merely meaningless scraps of paper. In that context these " labels " may influence action, though the causal connection is extremely complicated.[31] It may be " quite practical " to speak of

---

[28] Bentham had long before propounded a similar view: see *Of Laws in General* (ed. Hart (1970)), pp. 251–253.

[29] *Cf. ante*, 161 and see *post*, 523 and 538.

[30] Olivecrona thus adopts the causal theory of language. See Waismann, *The Principles of Linguistic Philosophy* (1965), Chap. VI. Olivecrona distinguishes two types of legal language: technical (or hollow) and performative. The former is passive, describing a state of affairs. Thus, in the statement: " X is the owner of Blackacre," " owner " has no counterpart in the sensible world but it is a " signal " " invested with a social function because people have learnt to react to [it] in a particular manner " (Arnholm, *Scandinavian Studies in Law*, Vol. 6, p. 9). The latter is used to produce certain desired results; it is Hägerström's magic (*cf. ante*, 500). On this see *post*, 530, and *Law as Fact* (2nd ed.), Chaps. 8 and 9.

[31] Lundstedt also asserts (p. 316 *et seq.*) that legal rules are really no more than procedures for achieving a particular purpose (*i.e.*, achieving social welfare, *vide* p. 317) in exactly the same sense as engineers or sailors have recognised procedures for constructing buildings or conducting navigation. These latter, he

legal rules in common parlance (though there is really no *need* to do so) and there is no reason why ordinary practising lawyers should not use this form of words. But legal writers concerned with *actual* and not imaginary connections should refrain from arguing that, *because* of a certain rule, a legal duty is imposed. For this is to support a metaphysical or normative link which no amount of observation can establish as a physical fact.[32]

Thus, as Professor Campbell has admirably stated, while " Kelsen . . . offered an account of law stated purely in terms of *Sollen*, Lundstedt . . . tried to present an account purely in terms of *Sein*." [33] We may take leave to doubt, however, whether Lundstedt is not thereby throwing the baby out with the bath water. For what is being propounded is in effect the rejection of all conceptual thinking as a mere metaphysical fantasy.[34]

ROSS'S THEORY OF LAW

The most balanced view among the Scandinavian trio referred to here seems to be that of Professor Ross.[35] Ross emphasises the normative character of legal propositions but prefers the term " directives " or quasi-commands [36] to Olivecrona's " independent imperatives." But

avers, we do not call " rules," and there is no need to speak of " rules " at all. But this is a false analogy, since legal rules are normative, whereas the latter are purely *instrumental, i.e.,* they tell us how *in fact* we must act if we want to achieve a certain effect. Where the latter are also normative, we *do* describe them as rules, *e.g.,* rules governing sport, navigation, the use of highways, etc. *Cf.* R. M. Hare, *The Language of Morals,* Chaps. 6, 9 and 10. See, also, Olivecrona, 18 Rutgers L.R. 794, 798–799, where it is pointed out that Lundstedt is trying to assert five different things when he denies that there are legal rules. One of these is of special interest since it shows how close Lundstedt came to some of the American Realists *viz.* the actual regularity in the activity of the judge is caused by a great many factors besides the content of legislative acts, such as his sense of duty, his ambition to fulfil his task properly, social pressure etc. (*cf.* Lundstedt, *op. cit.,* pp. 319–320).

32 See Lundstedt, *op. cit.,* p. 301 *et seq.*
33 See (1958) 21 M.L.R., p. 566.
34 *Cf.* Jerome Hall, *op. cit.,* pp. 378–380. This attitude is also probably connected with the fallacy that meaning equals " naming," so that as such words as law, state, right, property, are not names corresponding to physical entities, they are meaningless. This ignores the *functional* use of many words, something which neither Olivecrona nor Ross overlooked: *cf. ante,* 39 and see *post,* 530 and 556.
35 See *On Law and Justice* (1958) and *Directives and Norms* (1968). For a criticism of the views expressed in the earlier work, see Arnholm (1957), 1 *Scandinavian Studies in Law* 11. Some useful comments on the later work are found in Mac-Cormack, *Judicial Review* (1970), 33.
36 In *On Law and Justice,* Ross explains his preference for " directive " over " independent imperatives." Bearing in mind that these were directed to judges (*cf. post,* 503), the choice of language reflected their range of application. One cannot command a judge or other legal authority. The shift in *Directives and Norms* to quasi-commands may partly be explained by Ross's widening of the concept (as explained, *post,* 503), and also by his analysis of the logic of imperatives (*i.e.,* deontic logic): rules of law are but one species of the genus directive; they are impersonal and heteronomous. Ross draws a useful diagrammatic summary of the types of directive in *Directives and Norms,* p. 60.

Ross points out that a distinction must be drawn between two kinds of legal knowledge, *viz.*, the law actually in force (for instance, a rule contained in a statute), and sentences in a textbook where the law in force is stated. Only the former are prescriptive; the latter, so far as they intend to afford knowledge of what is actually the law, consist of assertions or descriptions. They are propositions not *of* law, but *about* the law. The doctrinal study of law, that is the study of the rules of an actual legal system, is normative in the sense that it is *about* norms, but it actually consists of assertions.[37] These assertions state or purport to state what is "valid law" and one of the first problems of jurisprudence is to elucidate this concept.

"Valid Law"

Ross does not seek, as Lundstedt does, to reduce all law to sociological phenomena. On the contrary his conclusion is the more reasonable one that "valid law" means an abstract set of normative ideas which serve as a scheme of interpretation for the phenomena of law in action (*e.g.*, the actual physical activities involved in a transaction of sale).[38]

But from here Ross moved to a position which, as formulated in *On Law and Justice*, was narrow and less tenable. As such it was criticised in earlier editions of this book.[39] Ross formerly held that the validity of law could properly be considered only from one point of view, *viz.*, as a scheme of interpretation enabling us to comprehend, and within such limits as are practicable, to predict the activities of judges. Accordingly, he asserted that a legal norm such as a statutory rule was primarily a directive not to the population at large, but to the judge. In his more recent *Directives and Norms*, he has shifted his ground somewhat and countered some of this criticism. He now differentiates a logical and psychological point of view. Legal rules are rules about the exercise of force and as such are directed to officials. Their observance is based on "the experience of validity." A statutory prohibition against murder is *implied* in

---

37 In *Directives and Norms*, Ross distinguishes indicative and directive speech. (Note how he now investigates language by investigating speech, and see on this Hare, 78 *Mind* 464.) He warns that whilst directives may be in the imperative mood, or make use of deontics (*e.g.*, ought, duty), they may also be expressed in the indicative and give the false impression that they are descriptions of fact (*e.g.*, "whoever kills another man is imprisoned for five years to life"). See also Kelsen's distinction between norms and normative statements (*ante*, 274, n. 23) and see the discussion of Bentham, *ante*, 158. Of course in a system where textbook writers are authoritative (*cf. post*, 712), a statement in a textbook may very well be normative. Ross does not deny this. See *On Law and Justice*, p. 46.
38 *Ibid.*, p. 18.
39 See Lloyd, *Introduction to jurisprudence* (2nd ed.), pp. 294–296.

the rule directing the courts and other administrative agencies to deal with any case of murder brought before them in the requisite manner. Logically, then, the rule of substantive law, or primary rule, has no independent existence. But, and here lies the new emphasis, " from a psychological point of view . . . there do exist two sets of norms." For " rules addressed to citizens are felt psychologically to be independent entities which are grounds for the reactions of the authorities." It follows, therefore, that these primary rules must be seen as " actually existing norms, in so far as they are followed with regularity and experienced as being binding." [40] What Ross now suggests, therefore, is that there is " no need " to describe two sets of directives, one to the population at large and the other to the courts, for the former can be understood from the latter. " To know these (secondary) rules is to know everything about the existence and content of law." [41] This may be so, but it is still to miss a whole dimension of laws. It cannot really be supposed that laws are made to measure the behaviour of officials : law is a means of social control and as such is aimed at the public generally. It is also to pass over the reasons why the behaviour posited in the primary directive is generally obeyed. As Ross remarked in *On Law and Justice*, " the more effectively a rule is complied with in extra-judicial life, the more difficult it is to ascertain whether the rule possesses validity, because the courts have that much less opportunity to manifest their reactions." [42]

Ross now recognises the social dimensions of law. What he is saying in *Directives and Norms* is that, as a matter of juristic precision, it is possible to reduce all laws to directions to officials. But, he is admitting that this is not how society functions. A reference to the psychological existence of two sets of directives is a recognition that the behaviour and feelings of *all* members of society are the " social facts " required to determine the existence of rules of law. Ross thus now accepts what he earlier scorned in Olivecrona as " psychological realism," [43] for Olivecrona has never given officials the pre-eminence that Ross formerly did. But, when Ross refers to " all members of society," it must be noted that he qualifies this by limiting his norm to those to whom it applies. " Thus the directive that shops are to be closed at a certain hour relates only to those members of society who are shopkeepers." [44] But how is such a rule to be distinguished from a rule which is valid for society generally even though it regulates the behaviour of a limited class?

[40] *Directives and Norms*, pp. 90–92, and see *post*, 555.
[41] *Idem*, p. 91, *post*, 555.
[42] p. 36.
[43] *On Law and Justice*, p. 71.
[44] *Directives and Norms*, p. 83, *post*, 550.

This is a problem not solved by Ross. To suggest, as he might, that the distinguishing criterion is enforceability by the courts and other agencies is to return to the analysis of *On Law and Justice*; hardly a satisfactory solution.

Neither in *On Law and Justice* nor in *Directives and Norms* has Ross limited himself to a purely behaviouristic interpretation of judicial or social activity. With reference to the judge, Ross has insisted that " a behaviouralist interpretation . . . achieves nothing," [45] but one must take into consideration his " ideological " or " spiritual " life.[46] Analysis which began to look close to an American Realist position [47] thus comes to resemble the elucidation of an " internal attitude " which we associate with Hart.[48] As with Hart, the external aspect of law is described as the outwardly observable and regular compliance with a pattern of action. But this is not sufficient: there must also be a feeling of compulsion to observe the behaviour prescribed, what he describes as an " experience of validity." But, though, Ross's " verbal reactions of disapproval " look very like Hart's " critical reflective attitudes," their " internal aspects " do not coincide. Hart's criticism of Ross, voiced in a review of *On Law and Justice* still stands, for the type of distinction upon which Hart insists is one used to divide " two radically different types of statement for which an opportunity is afforded whenever a social group conducts its affairs by rules." [49] Ross has not reached this conclusion in spite of an analysis which seeks an understanding of directives through speech.

What must puzzle an English lawyer is why Ross is so insistent on approaching the interpretation of the concept of valid law from the viewpoint of a jurist formulating statements as to what he conceives to be the law—a viewpoint which is, admittedly, far more significant in Continental than in English practice—that he allows this completely to overshadow, if not to obliterate, every other possible approach. For, even if this particular approach could be shown to exist in the minds of textbook writers, it is not one which is likely to be matched in the minds of other categories of persons, such as legislators, legal practitioners, officials, businessmen and so forth.

[45] *Idem*, p. 88.

[46] *On Law and Justice*, p. 37, and see *post*, 553.

[47] *Idem*, p. 73. Ross, however, attributes a " behaviouristic " realism to Holmes on the ground that he refers to predictions of what courts *do*, and claims greater virtue for his own interpretation involving a synthesis of psychological and behaviouristic views (*i.e.*, both the external conduct of the judge and his normative ideology). But what Holmes was emphasising was what judges *do*, as contrasted with what they *say*, not with what they *think*, and here Holmes and Ross seem to be on common ground (*cf. ante*, 400).

[48] *Ante*, 169.

[49] (1959) *Cambridge Law Journal* 233, 237.

THE "VERIFIABILITY" PRINCIPLE

It would seem that these writers, if not directly influenced by, are much in line with, the so-called logical positivists of the Vienna Circle, who took the view that meaning is given by factual verifiability, and that therefore any proposition which is not verifiable in this way is accordingly meaningless, at any rate apart from a purely emotional significance. Hence all non-empirical statements—apart from logic and mathematics which were allowed an uneasy existence as tautologies or analytical statements—such as those of metaphysics or ethics, were dismissed as "nonsense." [50] But as has been remarked, the word "nonsense" is itself a highly metaphysical concept,[51] and it came to be realised that this just would not do, not the least reason being that the proposition about verifiability turned out itself to be metaphysical and therefore "nonsense," on the logical positivist interpretation.[52] It is a pity that the Scandinavian writers seem to have neglected the later works of Wittgenstein, in which he exposes the errors, which he earlier shared with others, in attributing a single function to language, to which all propositions must conform in order to make sense at all. In his teaching at Cambridge in the 1930s, and by his posthumously published writings,[53] Wittgenstein was at pains to remove this illusion and to demonstrate the infinitely varied uses of language, and the different types of meaning which may be secreted in different usages. This approach was employed mainly as a solvent of various perennial philosophical problems, but for the present purpose it may be invoked in order to reveal the fallacy in some of the earlier realist thinking. For the normative use of language is as perfectly legitimate as the empirical, and serves to direct our attention to a class of propositions which are not used as statements of empirical fact, but as guides to human conduct framed in imperative form.[54] It is this class of proposition that is the proper subject-matter (*inter alia*) of ethics and theology, as well as of jurisprudence. That such propositions may be related to empirical facts does not imply that the latter can be substituted for the former. For to do this

---

[50] The best-known statement in English of the logical positivist viewpoint is contained in A. J. Ayer, *Language, Truth and Logic*, 2nd ed., 1946. For useful historical accounts, see J. O. Urmson, *Philosophical Analysis* (1956), pp. 102–129; G. J. Warnock, *English Philosophy Since 1900* (1958), Chaps. 4 and 6: J. Passmore, *A Hundred Years of Philosophy* (1968), Chaps. 16–18. The uneasy existence accorded mathematics may be explained by the fact that the early members of the Circle were scientists or mathematicians.

[51] J. O. Urmson, *op. cit.*, p. 101.

[52] *Ibid.*, pp. 168–178.

[53] See especially *Philosophical Investigations* (1953). For a brief exposition, G. J. Warnock, *op. cit.*, Chap. 6. For a fuller, and extremely lucid, account, see Pears, *Wittgenstein* (1971) Part II.

[54] *Cf. ante*, 8.

is to overlook the fundamental distinction between " ought " and " is," and to engage in what Moore has stigmatised as the " naturalistic fallacy." [55] This does not mean, however, as the Scandinavian writers have apparently thought, that we must thereby acknowledge a special realm of existence for " ought " statements, distinct from that of empirical statements, at any rate unless we recognise that the word " exist " may be used in divers senses, as, for instance, when Kelsen equates it with validity.[56] What is involved here is a particular use of language, and this use can only be understood, as Wittgenstein demonstrated, by examining the actual ways in which this usage is effected. Indeed the more extreme of the Realists hardly seem to have faced up to the implications of their desire to banish all conceptual thinking as meaningless, since, as Jerome Hall has pointed out, this must affect the use of " ideas " in every sphere of thought, and in particular in the realm of legal theory itself. Thus they seem to be faced with the same dilemma as that which confounded the logical positivists, namely, how to answer the question why their own theory, which can only exist in the realm of ideas, and is, therefore, in that sense, metaphysical, is not also " nonsense." [57]

However, it must be recorded that recent Realist writings demonstrate a healthy and sophisticated appreciation of the problems and uses of legal language. Both Olivecrona and Ross in their later writings stress the multiple uses of language. In the words of Mac-Cormack: " The multiple function of language and the psychological realities of beliefs and feelings are the main elements in the explanation offered by Olivecrona and Ross of legal rules and their validity and of legal rights." [58] Some of this comes out in the discussion in the text and may be seen in the extracts which follow.[59] In particular, two points may be stressed. They do not conceive of their task as that of laying bare the existing meaning of some word or expression, but rather of shaping concepts to direct our lives. <u>Legal enactments are directives, geared to influence men's behaviour.</u>[60] Secondly, both have emphasised the <u>different types of legal language</u>: thus Ross distinguishes different categories of speech: the indicative, the directive and the emotive, and shows how legal regulation makes use of all three.[61] And, Olivecrona differentiates two types of legal language:

---

55 See *ante*, 9.
56 *Cf. ante*, 8 and 270.
57 See Jerome Hall, *op. cit.*, pp. 378–380.
58 (1970) *Juridical Review* 33, 38.
59 *Post*, 530 and 556.
60 The influence of Von Wright, particularly his *Norm and Action* (1963) should be noted.
61 *Directives and Norms*, p. 34.

the technical and the performative,[62] one passive, one creative. Both of these writers emphasise that legal rights and duties and property do not stand for any objects in the sensible world, yet that sentences in which these words occur do have certain functions. Thus, the lessons of the later Wittgenstein and of J. L. Austin are not lost on Olivecrona or Ross, even if their earlier writings, and certainly those of Lundstedt, betray a certain naïveté.

ORIGIN OF LAW

It is characteristic of the realist approach that in discussing the origin of law Olivecrona states that though the making of new " imperatives " presupposes a legal system already in being, we cannot trace law to its ultimate historical origin, since however far back we go there is always some social organisation in existence.[63] Thus, for him the origin of law is purely a question of factual and historical origins, of the growth " out of customary, magico-religious rules found in ancient societies." [64] But the jurist, except as a legal historian, is more concerned with the source of legal validity either of particular rules or of the legal system itself, rather than of the historical origin of law in the mists of time. It is this question that Olivecrona rejects as metaphysical, and therefore as meaningless, and thereby seeks to deprive us of a form of conceptual thought and of linguistic usage, the normative, which mankind (including, it is suspected, even the Scandinavians themselves) has found to be so utterly indispensable that it would be singular to discover that it is meaningless and had no distinctive usage in human life and affairs.[65]

---

[62] The expression is that of J. L. Austin (see his *How to do Things with Words*). On Austin, see Passmore, *op. cit.*, note 50, pp. 450–458.

[63] *Law as Fact* (1st ed., 1939), pp. 72–74. It should be noted that the so-called second edition published in 1971 is not a second edition at all, but a reworking of certain of the themes of the first. The second edition is an altogether " bigger " book, surveying what Olivecrona regards as the common roots of positivism and natural law and using historical analysis, both Roman and Nordic, to explain law. The particular passage referred to in the note will not be found in the 1971 edition, but the problem of " establishing a constitution " is discussed at pp. 96–105, where the problems of disentangling law from religion are delineated in a Roman context. See also 18 Rutgers L.R. 794, 807, where he suggests that natural law concepts (*e.g.*, the will of the people or the word of the Founding Fathers) are at the root of all law. But, even this suggests that some social organisation is in existence. It was, for example, received ideals and beliefs inherited from their countries of emigration which endowed certain people (*viz.*, the Founding Fathers) with authority to rule.

[64] *Law as Fact* (2nd ed.), p. 103.

[65] *Cf.* P. Winch, *Idea of a Social Science* (1958), p. 15: " Our idea of what belongs to the realm of reality is given for us in the language that we use. The concepts we have settle for us the form of the experience we have of the world." In this sense, Wittgenstein speaks of language as " forms of life," *Philosophical Investigations*, p. 226.

"REDUCTIONISM" AND LEGAL CONCEPTS

It should be added that the Scandinavians also are involved in another fallacy once associated with logical positivism, that of assuming that concepts can always be reduced by analysis to a series of factual propositions to which they are equivalent, and for which they can be substituted.[66] Hence it was thought at one time that all the so-called fictional entities of philosophy (such as the " physical " table we see and which had been stigmatised as a mere " logical construction ") could be spirited away by this process. Unfortunately it later became apparent that this form of reductionism would not even work in regard to such simple everyday concepts as " England " or " France," for instance, in such a sentence as " England declared war in 1939." [67] So, too, it will be found that no amount of conversion into factual statements will altogether eliminate the hard core of such concepts as rights and property, for the very good reason that such reduction ignores the normative factor.[68] Hence, quite apart from the practical inconvenience of doing without this vital form of legal shorthand (for who would prefer to propound a whole interlocking array of legal rules, or even perhaps the whole legal system, in order to avoid speaking of " rights " or " property "?), no amount of factual analysis is capable of providing a total substitute for this form of speech. This, indeed, is another aspect of Moore's so-called " naturalistic fallacy." [69]

FEATURES OF LAW

Despite the rejection of metaphysics, Olivecrona still engages in a search for the characteristic features of law. For him these are to be discerned in certain factual circumstances. Thus they are connected with a *de facto* organisation of persons, the state, which is ready to apply the laws and which possesses a monopoly of force for this purpose. Legislation operates by reason of the legislators occupying key positions, which enable them to bring psychological pressures upon the population as a whole. These pressures largely derive from the use of certain " formalities " in the act of legislation, which play a vital causal role in producing the psychological reaction essential

---

[66] *Cf.* J. O. Urmson, *op. cit.,* Chap. 10. A good example of this approach is in Ross, " *Tu-Tu*," *post,* 556.

[67] See this example worked out, in Urmson, *op. cit.,* pp. 151–152. But for a criticism, see B. Russell, *My Philosophical Development,* pp. 221–225.

[68] *Cf.* Wisdom's view that we cannot pass by deductive argument from one *type* of statement to another. Here he quotes Butler's saying: " Everything is what it is. and not another thing." See the discussion in D. Pole, *The Later Philosophy of Wittgenstein* (1958), pp. 116–120

[69] *Ante,* 9. There is also the point that as much of the law is uncertain or even unpredictable, no one can say, at any given moment, precisely what set of legal consequences are to be substituted for the concept of a right.

to compliance.[70] What Olivecrona is thus mainly concerned to show is that there is nothing mystical about the working of a legal system, and that there is no need to rely on fictitious entities or concepts such as the state, or the binding validity of law. Here again, however, like Lundstedt, he seems to confuse the two notions of normative and metaphysical. It may be that Olivecrona's description of psychological pressures is correct, though it is put forward, somewhat ironically for an empiricist, merely as an *a priori* assertion, without any factual evidence or proof that it may not be a gross over-simplification of the actual working of what Lundstedt never tires of describing as the immensely complex legal machinery. Thus, even if we may agree with Olivecrona's view of the necessity of force as the ultimate background to law, we may hesitate without evidence to accept his rather naïve explanation as to the way it influences human conduct.[71] Again his notion of the state as an "organisation" of persons hardly seems to avoid all suspicion of conceptual thinking. Also his insistence on "formality" in law seems more appropriate to a modern democratic state than to an autocratic system, as, for instance, one based on the will of the Roman Emperor,[72] an oriental despot, or a primitive chieftain.

LAW AND MORALS

Without going as far as Hobbes, who argued that law and morals were identical,[73] the Scandinavians [74] have sought to reverse the general notion of moral standards as being embodied in law by the idea that it is moral ideas that are themselves largely determined by law. Admittedly there are some moral feelings which are natural

---

[70] *Law as Fact* (1st ed.), Chap. 2, and see also (2nd ed.), pp. 93–96. But, how do people become acquainted with legislation? Very few actually witness the " formalities " of law-making. With this problem in mind Olivecrona has introduced what he calls " a secondary imperative sign," *viz.*, publication in an official gazette (something unknown in common law countries) and through intermediate reliable sources, the press and media. " Its psychological significance depends on the public's taking it for granted that a text which is said to be a law has really passed through the constitutional formalities " (see 18 Rutgers L.R. 794, 806). See Ross's criticism of this as " psychological realism " (*On Law and Justice*, pp. 71–74).

[71] *Law as Fact* (1st ed.), p. 143 *et seq.*

[72] Under the Dominate the will of the emperor was law however expressed, as he was not bound by any particular forms: see Jolowicz, *Historical Introduction to Roman Law*, pp. 478–479. And *cf.* the role of " formalities " under parliamentary sovereignty, *ante*, 232 *et seq.*

[73] *Cf. ante*, 179. See also the determinist view of Savigny and the historical school, *post*, 562 and its de-mysticised restatement in Ehrlich (*ante*, 340), and the classical Marxist viewpoint upturned in the Soviet concept of " parental law " (*post*, 632, n. 8 and 687). The writings of Olivecrona are also in striking contrast

---

For footnote 74, see page 511.

phenomena, such as love and compassion,[75] but these are insufficiently strong to produce the restraints necessary for civilised life. Law is, therefore, the primary factor in influencing moral standards, especially by its use of force. It is the regular use of force and the propaganda associated with it that establish moral standards. For instance, the general attitude to other persons' property is unthinkable independently of law and legal machinery, and if sanctions were removed man's morals would undergo a profound change.[76] Or, as Lundstedt prefers to put it, social life is not guided by an innate sense of justice but on the contrary it is the feelings of justice which are guided by the laws in force.[77]

Of course, to ask which came first historically, law or moral standards, is rather like inquiring which came first, the chicken or the egg. No doubt laws have frequently created fresh moral standards,[78] and in the case of some fundamental parts of the moral code, such as those relating to murder or theft, legal prohibitions go back to so early a period that it is difficult to disentangle legal, moral and religious decrees.[79] Nonetheless, if we view society at any particular stage of its development, we do find a moral sense urging particular standards of conduct as right or just, even though the law may take a contrary or neutral view. It is just this severance between law and morals that the empiricists since Hume have been desirous of emphasising.[80] True, as Olivecrona might urge, the development of moral standards is unthinkable (at any rate in civilised society) save in a context of an existing legal system, with force regularly applied to maintain at least a basic standard of social conduct, but this is very different from asserting that every change or improvement in

to those of the American sociologist, W. G. Sumner, whose philosophy was summed up in his classic *Folkways* (1906) in the telling phrase: "Legislation cannot make mores." Of course, few today accept this extreme conservative thesis. But the Scandinavian philosophy goes to the opposite extreme: not only can legislation make mores, but it is the prime mover in any change of sentiment or morality. It is this that is being criticised in this section.

[74] But Ross parts company with them here: see *On Law and Justice,* pp. 59–64.

[75] Cf. Jhering's four levers of social motion, *Law as a Means to an End,* ante, 339.

[76] *Law as Fact* (1st ed.), pp. 136–140.

[77] *Op. cit.,* p. 53.

[78] See the problems encountered in "Westernisation" programmes. In Turkey, for example, wholesale introduction of Western commercial law moulded commercial behaviour successfully, but the introduction of Western family law affected personal relationships but little (see Lipstein (1956) 6 *Annales de la Faculté Droit d'Istanbul* 10). Similarly, the attempt to impose a minimum age of marriage amongst Yemenite Jews in Israel foundered. (See Dror, 33 Tulane L.R. 749: there is an extract in Aubert, *Sociology of Law* (1969), p. 90.) Note the tenacity of "living law" (*cf. Ehrlich, ante,* 340, n. 18) in family relationships.

[79] Cf. *post,* 567.

[80] See *ante,* 47.

moral standards primarily derives from law, and not the other way
round. For instance, when we contemplate modern society we see
that improvements of a moral order, such as penal reform, often
derive not so much from society as a whole, and certainly not from
the impetus of its existing legal system, but from the energies of
an enlightened minority, which brings relentless pressure on the
recalcitrant majority. The force behind such movements may be of
various kinds, moral, religious or rational. Olivecrona would attribute law reform to enlightened self-interest,[81] and doubtless when
society is induced to change the law it is because it is persuaded to
believe that to do so is in its own best interest. But the moral force
initiating the reform may be quite selfless, as in the case of the great
penal reformers, and indeed some reforms may even, at least at first,
be thought socially harmful, though morally desirable, as, for instance,
in the case of the more lenient treatment of certain types of
offenders.[82]

LEGAL IDEOLOGY—THE METHOD OF JUSTICE V. SOCIAL WELFARE

For Lundstedt, all other jurists save himself, his mentor Hägerström
and perhaps his fellow realist Olivecrona have followed the road of
legal ideology, or the method of justice.[83] This means that they have
relied in one way or another on a material objective law, underlying
the actual legal system, and depending on the common sense of justice
to develop the law and to fill the gaps in the legal system. This is
condemned both as metaphysical nonsense, and as an attempt to
invoke natural law or justice to supply an objective valuation in what,
for the Realists, can only be purely subjective, since for them value
judgments depend purely on individual feelings and emotions, and are
incapable of scientific objectivity. Lundstedt directs an impassioned
onslaught on many of those modern thinkers whose thought might, by
the uninitiated, be believed to resemble his own, as, for instance, the
utilitarians, the sociological jurists, and the American Realists. For
Lundstedt, jurisprudence must be a *natural* science, based on observation of facts and actual connections, and not on personal evaluations
or metaphysical entities. Yet science has not so far progressed sufficiently in this field to enable us to establish or demarcate these
conections with precision. Hence the need for what he calls

---

81 *Op. cit.*, p. 167.
82 *e.g.*, the gradual abolition of capital punishment for offences against property,
   which was believed by many at the time to threaten society at its foundations.
   For an amusing and well-documented account of the "prophets of doom"
   ideology, see E. S. Turner, *Roads to Ruin* (1950).
83 Lundstedt was one of the intellectual leaders of the Swedish Labour party, so
   presumably also had an ideology, even if he was not aware of it.

" constructive " jurisprudence, which has to work practically on the hypothesis of certain social evaluations, such as that legal activities are indispensable for the existence of society, and that their aim must be to produce the most frictionless functioning of the legal machinery.[84] How then does this differ, for instance, from the Benthamite or the Pound approach? According to Lundstedt, because he proceeds not on an ideological basis, as, for instance, by seeking for " justice," but on arguments based solely on social realities, that is, on people as they are actually constituted. The " social welfare " method [85] which he propounds is, therefore, so he asserts, quite distinct from such common ideas as the needs of society or of social policy, as it means nothing but what is *actually considered* useful to men in society, with the way of life and aspirations that they have at a particular time. This implies the encouragement in the best possible way of what people in general *actually* strive to attain, and not what they ought to strive for. As knowledge increases legal activities may eventually be able to be based on a legal science which has a more or less complete knowledge of the facts, and which can establish social valuations on this foundation.[86]

One may, indeed, ask whether this outlook does not itself involve a number of personal valuations which are no less vulnerable than those of anyone else, on Lundstedt's view, *e.g.*, why should we aim at social welfare at all? But apart from this, Lundstedt's devotion to *actual* aspirations presumably adds up to the dominant views of the bulk of society, and seems to leave but little, if any, scope for the reforming impulses of a minority in advance of the sluggish opinions of the mass, or, indeed, scope for the possibility of moral pluralism. Thus, for Lundstedt, criminal law exists not so much to deter criminals but to foster the moral instincts against crime, and it does this by the regular enforcement of sanctions. Hence he dismisses the " ridiculous idea " of improving the criminal morally or socially, for the object of the penalty is to " break down the criminal." [87]

Moreover, although Lundstedt castigates Pound's jural postulates severely as " nothing more than phrases heaped upon phrases without the possibility of finding any line of thought," [88] and even if we may

---

[84] Lundstedt, *op. cit.*, pp. 131–136.

[85] For an attack on what he calls " the chimera of social welfare," see A. Ross, *On Law and Justice*, pp. 295–296; *cf.* pp. 360–363.

[86] *Legal Thinking Revised*, p. 128.

[87] *Ibid.*, pp. 219, 226. This outlook would seem to lead logically to the execution of irretrievable criminals, and though Lundstedt was apparently a believer in liberal democracy, there is a disagreeable flavour of Nazi totalitarianism in arguments such as these. Lundstedt's attitude stemmed from a belief that " guilt " is yet another metaphysical concept like " justice," and, to boot, a dangerous one since it interferes with punishment.

[88] *Ibid.*, p. 349.

admit some force in his criticism that these postulates, such as they are, are not pre-legal, but derive any meaning they may have from existing law, it is difficult to see why Lundstedt's own hypotheses as to the basis of the legal system are not equally *a priori*, drawn as they are (so far as appears) not from sociological research, but from personal reflection and individual evaluations. If it is true that Pound discusses law " in complete abstraction from our experience of it," [89] might this criticism not equally apply to the formulation of the " social welfare " method? It must be borne in mind that, in any event, in natural and any other science, hypotheses are only valuable in so far as they can be and are tested against verifiable observations.[90] In both instances the test of these various hypotheses seems still to come, and the reader may remain for the time being equally impressed (or unimpressed) before either set of unverified dogmatic hypotheses.[91]

SCANDINAVIAN AND AMERICAN REALISM

It has already been shown that the Scandinavian Realists share with the sociological jurists [92] a weakness for *a priori* assertions, while at the same time insisting on the need for basing the law on the needs of social life. But the Scandinavians link this attitude with varying degrees of hostility to all conceptual thinking, which they stigmatise as metaphysical or ideological. The American Realists, on the other hand, are not much interested in general theorising about law, and although they may share with the Scandinavians the feeling that rules do not decide cases, they do not altogether reject the normative aspect of legal rules.[93] What they are mainly interested in is the practical working of the judicial process, whereas the Scandinavians are more concerned with the theoretical operation of the legal system as a whole. Moreover, although the Scandinavians are the most extreme of empiricists, it is the Americans who primarily stress the need for factual studies in working out proper solutions for legal problems, and the Scandinavians who appear to rely mainly on argument of an

---

[89] *Ibid.*, p. 350.
[90] *Cf. ante*, 22.
[91] The same may be said of Ross's theory of " disinterested attitudes " (see *On Law and Justice*, pp. 364–369) which does not seem to rest on any form of sociological or psychological research.
[92] " While Pound was interested in general movements of thought and in grand generalisations, the Realists (American) advanced in pointed elucidations." J. Hall, in 44 Virg.L.R. (1958), p. 323.
[93] Perhaps this is why Lundstedt declares that Holmes' view of law, as predictions of what courts will do, " has no bearing on legal science, though it may stimulate a legal ideologist to reflection " (*op. cit.*, p. 391). But see also his list of criticisms (p. 393), all of which seem to turn on an alleged failure to analyse or understand certain basic conceptions. Even the last of these, the lack of a " positive method " based on social welfare, seems to argue against the pragmatical attitude of the Americans, in favour of a unified approach which is regarded as justifiable *a priori*.

a priori kind to justify particular legal solutions or developments.[94]
Altogether it may be said that the Scandinavian movement, for all its
positivism, remains essentially in the European philosophical tradition, whereas the American bears many of the characteristics of
English empiricism.

AXEL HÄGERSTRÖM

Inquiries into the Nature of Law and Morals
(1953) [95]

*What idea has one in one's mind in making a declaration of intention
in the sphere of private law, in so far as one is thinking of coming into
existence of rights and duties in connexion with it?*

In answering the above question it is convenient first to enquire what
is understood by 'rights' and 'duties' in a *law* within the sphere of
private law. Certainly such a law expresses in an imperative form the
idea of 'rights' and 'duties'. Such a law is undoubtedly of decisive
importance in giving effect to a 'declaration of intention' in accordance
with the content of the declaration. This is true also of customary law,
which is also regarded as determining 'rights' and 'duties' as something
which ought to happen, although in this case there are no propositions
expressed in a certain form.

In order to answer the latter question it is necessary to enquire what
the 'legislator' has in view when he brings about the occurrence of a
certain pronouncement concerning 'rights' and 'duties', which has the
character of a law.[96] This is the same as to enquire what he knows
concerning the consequence of such a pronouncement. It is plain that
what he knows, from his knowledge of the effectiveness of the legal
system, no matter what may be the cause of that effectiveness, is the
following. He knows that what is described, either in laws within the
sphere of private law or by some other method with the same content,
as the rights and duties arising in certain situations, will in fact come into
existence in the actual world. It will come into existence there in such
a way that the 'possessor of the right' in most cases receives the
advantages to which he is 'entitled' as against the person who is 'under
the obligation', and that conversely the latter party in most cases acts
as he is 'under an obligation' to act. This effect of legislation within the
sphere of private law on the whole always happens. If the 'possessor of
the right' needed *generally* to have recourse to a legal action, and if the
person who is 'under the obligation' needed *generally* to be compelled
by that means, it would be impossible to maintain the system of actions-
at-law itself.

---

[94] But for a discussion of investigations inspired by the sociological method, see
T. Eckhoff, "Sociology of Law in Scandinavia," in *Scandinavian Studies in Law*
(1960), Vol. 4, p. 29.

[95] [The date of the translation, by C. D. Broad.]

[96] What is to be understood by the word "legislator" [is] explained [by Häger-
ström] pp. 311 *et seq.*

But the 'legislator' also knows something further. He knows that anyone who fulfils the requirements of procedural law, especially as regards establishing the facts presupposed in the substantive law, will in general get a judgment against the defendant, which will in the last resort be enforced. Here it is a matter of complete indifference whether the facts in question *really* existed or not. Although in law 'rights' and 'duties' are attached to the *existence* of certain facts, anyone who can fulfil the requirements of the courts, especially as regards proofs, enjoys advantages which are at least equivalent to those which should accrue to the person who is described as 'possessing a right'. This, of course, does not prevent a person, whose case is supported by the actual facts to which he appeals, from getting satisfaction through a lawsuit. But in the lawsuit the question is simply whether or not the legal requirements in regard to the facts are satisfied. It may happen that the defendant has already satisfied the plaintiff's demands. If so, this operates only in the following way. The fulfilment, in regard to just this fact, of the requirements of the courts in the matter of proof concerning relevant facts, causes the plaintiff to lose his case.

But this makes plain what the idea of 'rights' and 'duties', which is expressed in the imperative form in every law within the sphere of private law, is really about, in so far as the 'legislator' had in mind something which he really knew would be actualized by means of the law. It is always a thought of the above-mentioned actual order of things; *i.e.,* the idea that, when certain facts exist, a person will as a rule enjoy certain advantages as against a certain other person or persons. But it is also an idea of something else, *viz.,* that legal proof in court, of the facts which the law regards as relevant, gives to a person of power, ultimately backed by compulsion, of getting at least an equivalent for the advantages which, according to the law, he should enjoy if the facts are as stated. It is evident, however, that the law becomes ineffective, *if* the person whom it designates as the possessor of a right against another person or persons neither receives the advantages in question gratuitously nor is able to fulfil the requirements of the courts. In that case the right amounts to nothing. This is of course presupposed in the law. On the other hand, the law has an effect, which does not agree with its text, if a person can in a lawsuit fulfil the legal requirements of proof without the alleged facts really existing. But even this effect follows from the law's own content. For even laws within the sphere of private law necessarily refer to legal processes, and give effective rules for them.

All this, however, holds only on the assumption that the 'legislator', in giving an imperative expression to certain ideas of 'rights' and 'duties', has in mind what he really can *know* to be the consequences of doing so. Another question is this. Does the legislator *believe* that he is *merely* bringing about such actual conditions; and does he therefore mean by 'rights' and 'duties' *only* what has been alleged above? But the following at least is now clear. Suppose that a private individual makes a 'declaration of intention' within the sphere of private law, with the object of bringing about the legal consequences corresponding to it, and that he believes that it will have this effect through actual law or through custom having the force of law. Such a person, in giving expression in imperative form to the idea of certain rights and duties coming into existence, has the following belief. He believes himself to know (and he therefore always has in view of making his declaration) that an actual situation of the kind contemplated will come into existence in accordance with the ideas thus imperatively expressed. He must therefore, like the legislator himself, mean by the ' rights ' and ' duties ', which he says will come into being, just such a factual situation. It is only necessary to make the following reservation here. A private individual cannot be sure that just *his* case may not be one of the exceptional cases in which recourse to the courts is necessary, either because of the recalcitrance or the impotence of the party who is under the obligation, or because of difference of opinion about the meaning of the declaration, or for some other reason. So the most that can be said here is that he means such a *de facto* set of order of things as would ensure, *either* that what is called a ' right ' will in fact be obtained from the party who is under the ' obligation ', *or* that the party who owns the ' right ' would acquire a power of the kind described through a process of law. But, just as with the legislator, so here with the ' declaration of intention ' within the sphere of private law, the question remains whether there is not something *further* in what is understood by ' rights ' and ' duties '.

Before entering upon this question, we must investigate what the judge understands by ' rights ' and ' duties ', when he makes a decision on the basis of law or custom. Suppose he decides in the plaintiff's favour by recognizing that a certain ' right ' belongs to the latter. He cannot possibly mean by this that the plaintiff *actually* will obtain, if necessary by legal compulsion, so far as possible an equivalent for the advantages which belong to him, according to law or custom, if the facts appealed to in the case are as alleged. For the plaintiff will obtain this equivalent only *through* the judge's decision. So the judge cannot make the actuality of the plaintiff's obtaining this equivalent the ground for his decision. Suppose that the judge, as is natural, understands by a ' right ' what the legislator understands by it according to the view stated above, *viz.*, a certain actual state of affairs, to which there corresponds as an alternative a power, backed by compulsion, as described above. Then he can merely proclaim that the plaintiff ought to have the disputed ' right ', and, no doubt, in such a way that the opposing party ' ought ' to be subjected to a certain compulsion. If he uses the expression ' is entitled ', he is merely expressing the *idea* of a right, not his *knowledge* of its existence. But he causes it to be realized *through* such an utterance in accordance with the ideal content of the law.

Here, for the sake of clearness, we raise the following question. What investigation does a judge, in a case in private law, make the basis of his decision? We ask first what it is that he investigates in view of the law or custom in the sphere of private law. This question will be treated, however, only from the point of view of a judge who understands the following by what the law (or custom having the force of law) calls a ' right ' or a ' duty '. He is assumed to understand by this something which *can* occur in the actual world, *i.e.*, a certain social state of affairs, which includes, as an alternative, a power conditioned by the rules of procedure in the courts. Here again the first question to be asked is whether he applies the legal ' ought ' to the actual case. The answer is a decided No! For the law's utterance ' It *shall* be so! ' is merely a phrase, which does not express any kind of idea, but serves as a psychological means of compulsion in certain cases. But it is only from ideas that any logical conclusion can be drawn. On the other hand, the ideal content of the law is of course used in the case in question. And it is only for *psychological* associative reasons, and not for *logical* ones, that the result which he reaches by this application presents itself to him as an ought.

Next we can raise the following question. 'Rights' and 'duties', founded on law or on custom having the force of law, cover two alternatives, *viz.*, (i) a direct action by one party for the benefit of the other, in accordance with the law or custom, or (ii) a power conditioned by the rules of procedure, of one party to set the law in motion against the other, whereby an equivalent can be obtained for the latter's neglect to perform the action. This power is either expressly stated in the law or tacitly understood in the custom to belong to the plaintiff, on condition that he can establish the facts which he alleges in his suit. But with *which* of these alternatives is the judge concerned, in so far as he seeks to realize the ideal content of the law in the case before him? Suppose that there is no doubt about the facts. Suppose, further, that the plaintiff asserts, and the defendant does not deny, that the defendant has not so far fulfilled, by his own free actions, the legal conditions which (in the plaintiff's opinion) are contemplated by the law as applied to the present case. Suppose, finally, that the defendant denies that the meaning of the law is what the plaintiff asserts it to be, though he does not contest the facts alleged by the plaintiff. On these suppositions, the judge of course investigates the case only from the point of view of the second alternative, *viz.*, the legal position as regards the law administered by the courts. He can do nothing concerning the first alternative. Supposing that the plaintiff has the law on his side, the judge would be talking nonsense if he decided that the plaintiff has a right in the former sense. The ideal content of the law cannot be realized in that way.

But take the case now that plaintiff and defendant agree on the meaning of the law as applied to the present case, and that the judge accepts their interpretation, but, that they disagree as to the facts relevant to the case, even, *e.g.* as to whether the defendant has not already fulfilled his obligations to the plaintiff. Then the judge would investigate the case according to the rules of the courts concerning evidence and the burden of proof. This implies that, here too, if the plaintiff wins, it can only be the second alternative that comes into the question; there can be no question of adjudging to the plaintiff a right in the sense of something that exists prior to the suit.

So the conclusion is as follows. Whether the dispute is concerned with the ideal content of the law or custom or with facts, a judge whose conception of 'rights' and 'duties' is determined by what he knows can be actualized in the physical world, he can never take account in his decision of 'rights' existing prior to the legal process. It is plain that it is here assumed that the case at issue really is of such a kind that it really could be decided exactly in accordance with established rules of law or custom. If this is not so, the judge himself functions as a legislator for the case. But we are not concerned with that.

We come now to our original question. Does not the 'legislator' in the sphere of private law, and also the private individual who makes a 'declaration of intention' within that sphere, after all really mean by 'rights' and 'duties' something more than a certain actual social

state of affairs? It does seem as if commonsense draws a distinction
between having a 'right' and *enjoying* it, and between *being* under an
'obligation' and that obligation being fulfilled even under compulsion.
Still more does it seem to distinguish between having a 'right' and
being able to win in a lawsuit in consequence of the rules of evidence
and the rules concerning the burden of proof. This difference shows
itself also in the common view of a lawsuit as a means of actualizing
in the physical world 'rights' and 'duties' which existed before the
suit was undertaken. Here it is held that the possibility of suing is
something which belongs to the person who has the 'right' as a
consequence or a function of his right in the primary sense. In the
same way, it is held that the subjection of the person who is under an
'obligation' to the compulsion of the court is a consequence of his
'obligation' in the primary sense. If the notion of a 'right' includes
as one alternative under it the possibility, under certain circumstances,
of acquiring by process of law an equivalent to the advantage to
which one is entitled; and if the notion of a 'duty' includes under it as
one alternative being subject to compulsion by the courts; then it is
clear that these cannot be a *consequence* of the existence of a 'right'
or a 'duty' respectively. For, in that case, neither could exist without
that which is said to be an effect of it. But an effect is always something other than its cause. But what does a 'right' or a 'duty' mean,
if empowerment by the courts or subjection to them, as the case may be,
is regarded as a consequence of its existence? It is plain that it
would by no means follow from the existence of a 'right' that there
is a power to compel by process of law the party who is under an
'obligation,' unless the notion of the 'right' included that power, and
unless the notion of being under an 'obligation' included being subject
to this power. But the power and the subjection would here exist quite
independently of any occurrence in actual life. It is clear that it need
not manifest itself even as an actual power given by the courts. For,
according to the commonsense view, one can have a 'right' without
the conditions required for obtaining such a power being fulfilled.
It may be, *e.g.* that one cannot prove the existence of the facts required,
when the burden of proof rests with oneself. Compare the state of
affairs here with the situation which arises if 'right' and 'duty' have
the meaning previously suggested. According to that view, they are
related to actual circumstances in the following way. A 'right' means
that he who possesses it either (i) will obtain from the party who is
under the corresponding 'obligation' the advantage to which he is
'entitled', or (ii) will acquire from the courts a power of compulsion,
provided that he fulfils their requirements, particularly in the matter
of proving the facts which the law explicitly states or which custom
tacitly implies as conferring the 'right'.[97] It is then clear that there is
nothing whatever left of 'rights' or 'duties,' if *neither* of the two
alternatives is fulfilled. It is true, no doubt, that it always holds good
that, *if* this or that condition were fulfilled in the actual world, the
'right' or the 'duty' would become something actual. Such a connexion is expressed imperatively in a law, and is thought of by anyone
who relies upon custom, as that which ought to happen. But it is
also part of the idea thus presented, to which the ought is attached,

[97] Similar remarks apply, *mutatis mutandis,* to the person who is under an
obligation.

that, if the conditions for exerting compulsion by process of law are not fulfilled and yet the action demanded is not performed, then the ' right ' comes to nothing. But, according to the usual way of looking at it, as soon as the facts exist which are connected in law or custom with the occurrence of a ' right ' or a ' duty ' within the sphere of private law, the ' right ' or the ' duty ' in question becomes a reality, even if the person who has the ' right ' neither actually enjoys the advantage attaching to it without recourse to the courts nor is able to fulfil the conditions required in order to obtain an equivalent by process of law.

It is, therefore, clear that the ' legislator ' in the sphere of private law *also* thinks that the effect of a legal enactment concerning ' rights ' and ' duties ' is the coming into existence of a power (and a state of subjection to that power) which falls outside the physical world. As regards juridical ' obligation ' in particular, this is supposed to be present in the ' obliged ' party, be it noted, quite regardless of whether he does or *can* fulfil it, and even of whether he actually feels any obligation whatever to perform the action which is said to be his ' duty '. The actual enjoyment of the advantages, to which one is said to be ' entitled ' as against the person who is under the ' obligation ', now becomes a mere exercise of the supernatural ' right ' which one has. This ' exercise ' issues from the ' right '; but the latter exists independently, even if it cannot be exercised because of natural obstacles. Conversely, the action which is ' obligatory ' is merely a fulfilment of the duty which exists independently of it. The authority who applies the law thus comes to be in the position that he can actually declare that the plaintiff *has* a certain right and the defendant a certain duty; and he can make this declaration, *as a true statement*, the basis for decisions concerning executive coercion. Even if the ' legislator ' *also* under-stands by ' rights ' and ' duties ' a certain social state of affairs which he aims at realizing, as we have shown to be the case, yet the idea of ' rights ' and ' duties ' as supernatural powers and bonds is present and active throughout. The latter is connected with the former point of view in such a way that the contemplated social state of affairs is regarded as a consequence of the existence of these rights and duties. And the very names ' rights ' and ' duties ' are based on this. But in this way legislation is supposed to be armed with a power of acting directly in the supernatural world, and by means of such action producing effects in the physical world.

Moreover, if the idea of ' rights ' and ' duties ', which is expressed in a legal imperative in the sphere of private law, has this supernatural meaning, then a person who makes a ' declaration of intention ' within that sphere, in the knowledge that it will be effective through law or custom having the force of law, will have the same idea of ' rights ' and ' duties.' He too will think of the social state of affairs, which is to arise, as a mere consequence of supernatural relationships of power.

Before going further in this matter, we would point out that the supposed supernatural power or obligation, as the case may be, is a logical absurdity. It is held to refer to a reality which is elevated above the physical world. Yet, on the other hand, every ' right ' is supposed to have as its *object* an advantage which belongs to the physical world, and every ' duty ' is supposed to have as its object a certain way of acting in that world.

K. OLIVECRONA

Law as Fact

(1st ed., 1939)

The Binding Force of Law

If we discard the superstitious idea that the law emanates from a god, it is obvious that every rule of law is a creation of men. The rules have always been established through legislation, or in some other way, by ordinary people of flesh and blood. In other words, they are produced by natural causes. On the other hand, they have natural effects in that they exert a pressure on the members of the community. The rules of law are a natural cause—among others—of the actions of the judges in cases of litigation as well as of the behaviour in general of people in relation to each other. The law-givers and other people who are in a position to lay down rules of law may actually influence the conduct of the members of the community. But that is certainly all they can do.[98]

We can never escape the conclusion that the law is a link in the chain of cause and effect.[99] It has, therefore, a place among the facts of the world of time and space. But then it cannot at the same time belong also to another world. The law cannot on the one hand be a fact (which it undoubtedly is) with natural causes and natural effects and on the other hand something outside the chain of causes and effects. To maintain the contrary involves pure superstition. The meaning must be—if there is any real meaning at all—that the law is endowed with a supernatural power.[1] Otherwise the words are empty, being used according to a secular habit without a real thought behind them.

Every attempt to maintain scientifically that law is binding in another sense than that of actually exerting a pressure on the population, necessarily leads to absurdities and contradictions. Here, therefore, is the dividing-line between realism and metaphysics, between scientific method and mysticism in the explanation of the law. The " binding force " of the law is a reality merely as an idea in human minds. There is nothing in the outside world which corresponds to this idea.[2]   [pp. 16–17]

---

[98] [An interesting outcome of the stress upon law as a means of exerting influence on human behaviour by affecting the motives of individuals, has been to direct attention to the various ways in which legislation may be made effective by being translated into changes in social behaviour. One difficulty is that modern laws are so complex that they are not suited to affect directly any people outside official circles, and therefore the influence upon the formation of motives must tend to be indirect rather than direct. For an attempt to explore the various levels at which this may occur, see an article by P. Stjernquist in *Legal Essays to Castberg* (1963) at p. 153.]

[99] [Olivecrona does not here seek to deny the distinction between a physical law of nature and a normative rule, but makes the point that the latter may itself operate as a physical cause of the conduct of human beings. But other Scandinavian realists, such as Lundstedt, go much further in attempting to eliminate the normative element of law altogether as a metaphysical fiction. *Cf.* *ante*, 501.]

[1] [*Cf.* the influence of Hägerström, *ante*, 499.]

[2] [But this does not exclude the normative *form* of the legal proposition. On the fallacy of regarding meaning as a kind of naming of objects, see *ante*, 56. See, further, *Law as Fact* (2nd ed., 1971), pp. 110–112.]

The Content of a Rule of Law

Thus the content of a rule of law of this type[3] is an idea of an imaginary action by a judge in an imaginary situation. We might add at once, however, that a rule of law is never intended to be regarded in isolation. It is always connected with other rules and its meaning does not emerge unless this connexion is observed. The rule about condemning the murderer to death is not only related to the law of procedure where the actions leading up to the judgment are pictured. Many more rules come into play. The accused must have attained a certain age, he must have been of sound mind when he committed the crime, and so on. Thus the picture of the imagined situation in which judgment should be given is very rich in detail. Many rules must be put together in order to make complete the picture of the situation and of the action desired.

With this qualification the content of the rules of law may be defined as *ideas of imaginary actions by people* (e.g. judges) *in imaginary situations.* The application of the law consists in taking these imaginary actions as models for actual conduct when the corresponding situations arise in real life.[4]   [p. 29]

A Rule of Law is not a Command in the Proper Sense[5]

The imperative theory has been so thoroughly criticised by previous authors that there is no need to discuss it at length here. We have only to confront the theory with obvious social facts. Its innermost meaning is to range law among the facts of the actual world. The commands, if there be any commands, are of course natural facts.[6] The theory, therefore, has the aim we pursue in this treatise. Only, the facts are misinterpreted when the rules of law are said to be commands in the proper sense of the word.

A command presupposes one person who commands and another to whom the command is addressed. In true appreciation of this fact, the imperative theory has endeavoured to point out from whom the "commands" emanate. Generally this has not been said to be any single individual. It would be hard indeed to maintain that the immense bulk of rules contained in the law of a modern state are the commands of any single human being. Such a being would undoubtedly require superhuman qualities. It is for this reason that the commands are ascribed to the *state*.

It is, however, impossible to maintain that the "state" properly speaking, could issue commands. The state is an organisation. But an

---

[3] [*e.g.*, that a murderer should be condemned to death.]

[4] [Later Olivecrona writings are not so judge-orientated. See, for example, *Legal Language and Reality*, p. 180 and *post*, 532, where the content of a rule is now its effect on everybody, not just judges.]

[5] [See further *Law as Fact* (2nd ed., 1971), pp. 120–126, and, particularly, his discussion of what Hare calls "the constative fallacy," the temptation to reduce imperatives to indicatives (pp. 125–126).]

[6] [This may be so in Austin's case, since he looked to the *fact* of habitual obedience as the ultimate source of law, as well as accepting the view that it was the mental state of the commander that gave an expression the characteristic of a *command* (*cf. ante*, 161). But another view is that stress is here laid simply on the imperative *form* of the legal proposition, and Olivecrona himself seems to favour this view (*post*, 523).]

organisation cannot, as such, be said to command. If this is maintained, the expression is at best a loose one for the fact that commands are given by individuals active within the organisation. Only in this sense is the statement at all reasonable. [pp. 35–36]

The Rules of Law as "Independent Imperatives"

Though not real commands, the rules of law, as has already been said, are given in the imperative form. The ideas about certain actions in certain situations, which form the contents of the rules, are not narratively described in the rules. The text of the law does not say that the law-givers or some other persons actually have conceived such and such imaginations in their minds. This would be absurd. The ideas are *imperatively* expressed. Whatever words are used, the meaning of a rule is always: this action *shall* be performed under such and such circumstances, this right *shall* arise from such and such facts, this official *shall* have this or that power, etc.

Now, does not this mean that the rules are, after all, commands? No, it does not. The term "command" may, of course, be used by everybody according to his own pleasure, provided that the meaning is made clear. What is important is not the terminological question. But different *things* must be kept apart if the real nature of the law is to be made clear. Such imperative statements as are found e.g. in the law, must be carefully distinguished from commands in the proper sense. They are something else. The imperative theory has neglected this distinction. For this reason it has been driven to unrealistic constructions in order to make the realities of the law fit in with the assumption that the rules are commands in the proper sense of the word.

A command in the proper sense implies a personal relationship. The command is given by one person to another by words or gestures meant to influence the will. Now the same kind of words is also used in many connexions where no personal relations whatever exist between the person who commands and the receiver of the command. The words can nevertheless have a similar, if not identical, effect. They function independently of any person who commands. We may in this case speak of "*independent imperatives*," in order to get a convenient term.

As an example of independent imperatives may be cited the Decalogue. It cannot be said that Moses is commanding us to do this or that. Nor is this supposed to be so. The words are said to be the commands of God. In reality the Decalogue is a bundle of imperative sentences, formulated several thousand years ago and carried through the centuries by oral tradition and in writing. They are nobody's commands, though they have the form of language that is characteristic of a command.

The rules of law are of a similar character.[7] [pp. 42–43]

---

[7] [*Cf., post*, 539. See also Passmore's account of Hägerström on the origin of "duties." When we take an act to be our duty, we believe it is objectively our duty, quite irrespective of the fact that someone has commanded it. The reason for this, according to Hägerström, is that in our early years we are commanded by parents, teachers, etc. We come to do things not because we are commanded to do them by a particular person, but because the action comes to be regarded as commanded by its very nature. See (1961) 36 *Philosophy* 143.]

Ordinary Legislation

From the traditional standpoint the act of legislating implies something inexplicable, though this is not always clearly realised. It is, however, inexplicable how the draft, or bill, can be lifted into another sphere of reality through being promulgated as a law. The draft is only a set of fictive articles, put before the legislative authorities for their consideration. The promulgated law, on the other hand, contains " binding " rules, i.e. it has a supernatural force. Thus the draft has undergone a profound change through the act of promulgation. The law is in essence something entirely different from the bill. And this change has been brought about by a vote in an assembly, or by the signing of a paper by a person in a prominent position.

This mysticism, and the scholasticism which follows in its wake, obviously has its origin in the idea of the binding force of the law. Once this idea is discarded as superstitious, there is nothing inexplicable about the act of legislating. It may be difficult to give a full explanation of its effect, since the matter is rather complicated, but the explanation will deal with facts only.

Legislating has an *actual* effect of supreme importance to the community. The draft had no significance for social life beyond that of being an object of discussion and formal proceedings. It was not a wheel in the machinery of the state. But the law is. The officials take it as a model for their actions and are virtually compelled to do so. The general public must take it into consideration as a barrier against some activities and a furtherance of others. The actual pressure of the law is there as soon as the draft has been promulgated.

The effect of the act of law-giving is in no way of a mystical character. It is only a question here of cause and effect in the natural world, on the *psychological* level.[8] The purpose of the law-givers is to influence the actions of men, but this can only be done through influencing their minds. How the influence works on the individual mind is a question for psychology. For the purpose of this treatise we need only point out the general conditions which make law-giving possible as an effective instrument of governing society, the basic elements in the structure of society which are a prerequisite to the functioning of the law-giving apparatus.

Under ordinary circumstances legislation takes place in accordance with the rules of the constitution. Its effect results in the first place from the general reverence in which the constitution is held and the habitual obedience to its rules. We find an attitude of this kind at least in every civilised country of the Western type (and no others need be considered here, for the sake of brevity). Everywhere there exists a set of ideas concerning the government of the country, ideas which are conceived as " binding " and implicitly obeyed. According to them certain persons are appointed to wield supreme power as kings, ministers, or members of parliament, etc. From this their actual power obtains. The general attitude towards the constitution places them in key-positions, enabling them to put pressure on their fellow-citizens and generally to direct their actions in some respects.

---

[8] [*Cf.* De Jouvenel, *Sovereignty*, on the extent to which men are ruled by " compulsive images " (pp. 296–298).]

I do not want here to inquire into the causes which have led to this attitude, or the causes which have brought those particular persons into power. That is a question for history and social psychology to answer. Here it is enough to point to the actual situation as it undoubtedly exists in every country where it is not temporarily suspended during a revolution. The attitude is not, of course, endowed with any intrinsic self-supporting stability. It must be sustained through an unremitting psychological pressure on the members of the community. For the holders of the key-positions to maintain themselves in their places it is above all necessary that they actually use the power conferred on them through the psychological situation in the country, and use it with a certain determination.[9]

The attitude towards the constitution has a double significance. First, it causes people positively to accept duly promulgated laws as " binding " upon everybody and take them without reflection or opposition as patterns for their conduct. Secondly, the power to legislate is monopolised by those who are designated as law-givers in the constitution. The minds of the people are so to speak shut off in every other direction. Nobody else can secure attention or obedience in the field reserved for the law-givers by the constitution. To put up a competition with them in this field is in most cases meaningless.

Thus, the effect of the attitude towards the constitution is first, that the constitutional law-givers gain access to a psychological mechanism, through which they can influence the life of the country ; secondly, that only they gain access to this mechanism and that everybody else is debarred from using it or building up another of the same kind.[10] I use

---

[9] [Even if it be admitted that law has to be explained in terms of facts, it may still be necessary, as the sociologist Durkheim has pointed out, to distinguish between social facts and psychological facts. The individual has not only a psychic life of his own but is born into a social world, and while we may have recourse to psychology to explain the features of the individual's psychic life, in the realm with which sociology is concerned the " facts " of social life may appear on quite a different level of abstraction from that of individual psychology.

This may be seen, particularly in the sphere of legal sociology. If we consider for a moment the features of a legal trial, the facts which may be of sociological significance will be such matters as the existence of particular kinds of legal institutions and of various legal procedures. In operating these no doubt the feelings of particular individuals involved may vary both in kind and degree, but it is not these individual sentiments that are the matter of immediate concern to the sociologist. What interests him is the common framework of institutions into which a person is born and which persists, not so much as a psychical but as a social system. In other words, he is interested not in the actors as such but with the various roles which are played by them. This does not mean of course that the sociologist is in no sense concerned with individual feelings, for statistical information as to these may have an important social bearing.

It may be said then, that one of the important points overlooked by Olivecrona's approach is that law exists not just as a set of ideas in the consciousness of individual citizens, but that it exists and persists as a social institution, and that if we are to seek a factual substratum to law, it should be sought not so much in the psychic reactions of individuals, but in the social character of institutions. *Cf.* E. E. Evans-Pritchard, *Social Anthropology* (1951), p. 45; J. Beattie, *Other Cultures* (1964), pp. 26–28, 73.]

[10] [Thus for Olivecrona the " legality " of a revolution is established when the revolutionaries have effectively seized hold of this mechanism and used its pressures to remove the reverence for the old régime in favour of their own. *Cf.* Austin's theory of habitual obedience. The latter looks at it from the point

the term " mechanism " on purpose as being, in my opinion, the appropriate one, since the reactions of people in this respect generally follow very definite lines and may be foretold with great accuracy. The attitude of the public is—under normal circumstances—so rigid and uniform that the psychological effect of the act of legislating takes place smoothly, without any special effort on the part of the law-givers. We are so familiar with this situation that it seems to be a part of the order of the universe like the rising and the setting of the sun. Therefore, we do not reflect on the simple fact that the effect of legislation is conditioned by the psychological attitude which we ourselves and the millions of other people maintain. Because of this attitude the law-givers can play on our minds as on a musical instrument.

Besides the attitude of mind among the general public, another basic condition is required for the process of legislating to be effective. This is organisation. There must be a body of persons, ready to apply the laws, if necessary with force, since it would be clearly impossible to govern a community only by directly influencing the minds of the great masses through law-giving. We shall have to return to this matter later on. The organisation that wields force, the state organisation, is largely composed of persons who are trained automatically to execute the laws which are promulgated in the constitutional form, irrespective of their own opinion of their advisability.[11] The organisation is therefore like a vast machinery, so regularly and certainly does it function. The law-givers sit in the centre of the machinery as before a switchboard, from where they direct the different wheels.

The real significance of the act of legislating is now apparent. The draft is not lifted into another sphere of reality but is simply made the object of certain formalities which have a peculiar effect of a psychological nature. The formalities are the essential thing. The legislative act consists in nothing but these. The same statements as those contained in a law, if made by the same persons without observing the constitutional form, are of no avail.[12]   [pp. 51–56]

The actual use of Force in the State Organisation

In every community force is consistently applied through the officials of the state, more particularly in three forms:—police measures against disturbances, infliction of punishment and execution of civil judgments. In all three cases physical violence or coercion is the ultimate expedient. It is used not only to disperse dangerous mobs if need be and to keep the peace generally. It is also an unavoidable instrument in the regular application of criminal and civil law. In criminal law, actual violence against the person of the criminal is used in the form of the death penalty and imprisonment. Even in civil law physical violence is sometimes used

of view of the obedient citizen transferring his allegiance; the former, from the point of view of the legislator, bringing the citizens into an appropriately receptive state of mind.]

11 [This ignores the discretion which it is impossible to eliminate and which all officials have. For the attitude of the Court of Appeal to police discretion over enforcement of gaming laws see *R. v. Commissioner of Police ex p. Blackburn* [1968] 2 Q.B. 118 and on arrest generally see La Fave, *Arrest: The Decision to take a Suspect into Custody* (1965).]

12 [This is not necessarily so; *cf.* note 72, *ante*, 510. Custom as a source of law has proved a problem to Olivecrona.]

against a person, as e.g. when a tenant is ejected from the premises by means of force and when imprisonment for debt takes place. Generally, however, violence against a person is not needed in civil matters. Nevertheless, it must not be forgotten that physical force is the basis of execution in these cases too. Thus the goods of the debtor are seized by force if he does not deliver them peacefully when they are required in order to pay his debt. Physical force is resorted to in administrative law, also, when necessary. In the whole field therefore, the provisions of the law are ultimately carried out by physical force or violence.[13]

Actual violence is, however, kept very much in the background. The more this is done, the smoother and more undisturbed is the working of the legal machinery. In this respect many modern states have been successful to an extent which is something of a miracle, considering the nature of man.[14] Under suitable conditions the use of violence in the proper sense is so much reduced that it passes almost unnoticed.

Such a state of things is apt to create the belief that violence is alien to the law or of secondary importance. This is, however, a fatal illusion. One essential condition for reducing the application of violence to this extent is that there is to hand an organised force of overwhelming strength in comparison to that of any possible opponents. This is generally the case in every state organised on modern lines. Resistance is therefore known to be useless. Those who are engaged in applying force in criminal and civil matters of the ordinary kind are few in number, it is true. But they are thoroughly organised and they are in each case concerned with only a single individual, or a few individuals.

[pp. 124–125]

Law chiefly consists of Rules about Force

Thus the traditional ways of defining the relations between law and force must be discarded. It is impossible to maintain that law in a realistic sense is guaranteed or protected by force. The real situation is that law—the body of rules summed up as law—consists chiefly of rules *about* force,[15] rules which contain patterns of conduct for the exercise of force.

It must be kept in mind, of course, that at the same time the rules contain patterns of conduct for the private citizens. But these patterns, or rules, are only another aspect of the rules about the use of force, and those rules are the deciding factor. The citizens have to make their behaviour conform to them. Rules about " rights " and " duties " which are not also rules for the use of overwhelming force are of little avail in actual life. Rather than accept the traditional classification of rules as primary and secondary I should therefore like to call the rules about force primary rules and the rules for the conduct of private citizens secondary rules.[16] This would not be quite exact, however. In reality the rules of civil and criminal law are at one and the same time rules for the private citizens as well as for the use of force by the officials. It is only a question of different aspects of the same rules. But we are justified in

[13] [See also *Law as Fact* (2nd ed., 1971), pp. 271–273.]

[14] [Olivecrona's is essentially a Hobbesian view of man and society. See *ante*, 178 and Lloyd, *The Idea of Law*, Chap. 1.]

[15] [See, too, A. Ross, *On Law and Justice* (1958), pp. 52–58.]

[16] [*Cf.* Kelsen's view, *ante*, 275.]

defining law as rules about force, since everything turns upon the regular use of force.[17]

Outside civil and criminal law, in administrative law, there is a vast amount of rules which are not directly concerned with the use of force (e.g. rules about education, health, communications etc.). Sometimes force is necessary even in this field, though on the whole the rules are applied by the officials in other ways. But all these rules presuppose an organised force behind them and they presuppose that force is used according to the rules of civil and criminal law. However important they may be in our time, they must therefore be regarded as an addition to that central body of rules which consists of the rules about force. It might be added that the constitution consists of rules which indirectly concern the use of force, in that they regulate the laying down of rules of civil and criminal law.	[pp. 134–135]

Our Moral Standards and the Law

In so far as thoughts of unlawful acts enter the mind and appear attractive, they are more effectively counteracted by the involuntary moral impulse than by cold calculations about the risks. An unconditional: " You shall not! " rings in our ears. " This is low! It is detestable!" Such independent imperatives and expressions of value beat down the tendencies to unlawfulness. And these ideas and the feelings which accompany them are to a very large extent—though not, of course, exclusively,—a consequence of the " administration of justice " through regular infliction of punishment and extraction of damages.

It might, however, be suggested that the relations between the law and the moral ideas are the very opposite to this—i.e. that the moral ideas are the primary factor and that the law is inspired by them. In fact this is the position generally taken up by jurisprudence and legal philosophy. The principal rules of law are represented as being based on " justice ". This means either that they are founded on an abstract norm, existing by itself *in nubibus*, or that the law is founded on our *ideas* about justice. Both these ways of stating the case are incorrect.

It is hardly necessary specifically to refute the contention that the law is based on abstract justice. This view is too openly superstitious. The only question which need be discussed is whether the *ideas* of justice are the primary factor in regard to the law or whether they are fashioned by the law. . . .

. . . The first question is how the moral standards of every single individual are fashioned and what is the influence of the use of force according to the rules of law in this respect. Everybody grows up in a community where a legal machinery has existed since times immemorial.

17 [Schulz, *Principles of Roman Law*, pp. 20–24, 158, 196–197, points out that much of a society's organisation may consist of non-legal customs, and instances, in Roman law, restraints on *patria potestas* and testation, marriage customs, etc. The realist view is to equate these with law as kinds of psychological pressures which are all causally effective. Olivecrona, however, also relies on the sanctionist criterion of organised force as differentiating legal from other norms and denies that law can be based on the state, which itself presupposes the law (pp. 40–41). Elsewhere, he asserts that the specific feature of legal rules is their relation to a state organisation, which, by a monopoly of force, can establish new imperatives and ensure general obedience. See his essay on " Law as Fact," in *Interpretations of Modern Legal Philosophy* (1947), p. 555.]

The question concerns the influence of this machinery and its rules on our moral ideas. The second question concerns the part played by moral ideas in the formation of new rules added to the already existing body of rules of law. To begin with, the first question only will be discussed.

With regard to this question it seems obvious that it must be answered in the sense indicated above. Our upbringing makes this unavoidable. The character is necessarily formed under the influence of our surroundings, especially in earlier years. The society where we live puts its stamp on our ideas. But among the forces working within society the law is without doubt one of the foremost. The law certainly cannot be a projection of some innate moral convictions in the child or adolescent, since it existed long before he was born. When he grows up and becomes acquainted with the conditions of life he is subjected to its influence. The first indelible impressions in early youth concerning the relations to other people are directly or indirectly derived from the law. But the effect is not only to create a fear of the sanctions and cause the individual to adjust himself so as to be able to live without fear. The rules also have a positive moral effect in that they cause a deposit of moral ideas in the mind.

The rules of law are independent imperatives. In that form they are communicated to young and old. You shall not steal!—of this type are the rules concerning our behaviour. Now these imperatives are (so to speak) absorbed by the mind. We take them up and make them an integral part of our mental equipment. A firm psychological connexion is established between the idea of certain actions and certain imperative expressions, forbidding the actions or ordering them to be done. The idea of committing e.g. theft is coupled with the idea of an imperative: you shall not! Then we have a moral command with " binding force ". We speak of a moral command when an independent imperative has been completely objectivated and therefore is regarded as binding without reference to an authority in the outer world. The chief imperatives of the law are generally transformed in that way. Only when this is the case is the law really firmly established.

A moral influence of the law is required for its effectivity only in respect of a limited number of fundamental rules, and only in these cases is such an influence possible. For the rest it is enough that the idea of a moral obligation to abide by the law as such is sustained and that it is not damaged by unreasonable laws or arbitrary jurisdiction.

Several things explain how the rules of law can thus be absorbed by the whole people. The suggestive effect of the imperatives is enormous when there is power behind them—here the majestic power of the state, working relentlessly according to the rules about sanctions. This power is surrounded by august ceremonies and met with a traditional and deep-rooted reverence. All this combines to make a profound impression on the mind, causing us to take the fundamental "commands" of the law to heart as objectively binding. We do it all the more readily since we understand, at least instinctively, the necessity of these rules for the maintenance of peace and security.

The absorption of the imperatives cannot, of course, be effected under all circumstances. On the contrary, it is possible only under specific conditions, which ought to be thoroughly studied. Broadly speaking the first requirement is that the rules appear as reasonable to most people, i.e. as furthering ends which are generally recognised as desirable. Otherwise the rules will have no moral effect or may even arouse moral indignation. Also it is necessary that the application of sanctions is regular and fairly impartial.

It seems impossible not to admit that those are, in brief words, the relations between the law and the moral standards of the individual. The law is the primary factor. The individual is caught in its grip from the earliest stage in life and his moral ideas are developed under its influence. The law—including the regular use of force according to the rules—is not, of course, an isolated factor. There is never a single cause for such a complicated thing as our moral ideas. The causes are necessarily manifold. Above all, the use of force must be associated with propaganda, preparing the minds for the reception of the imperatives, and there must be a direct inculcation of the imperatives through parents, teachers, superiors etc. What is suggested here is merely that the use of force is one of the chief factors in the moulding of our moral standards, and not the other way round.[18]   [pp. 151–156]

K. OLIVECRONA

Legal Language and Reality

(1962) [19]

Understanding the Legal Language

The purpose of all legal enactments, judicial pronouncements, contracts, and other legal acts is to influence men's behavior and direct them in certain ways. The legal language must be viewed primarily as a means to this end. It is an instrument of social control and social intercourse. We may call it a *directive* language in contrast to a *reporting* language. It is advisable to lay stress on this distinction; for our inveterate habit of regarding language as primarily a means of describing facts easily leads to misinterpretations. . . .

Legal performatives.

Let us start from another example of Austin's.[20] At the launching of a new ship the wife of the president of the shipping company smashes a bottle of champagne against the bow of the ship in saying: " I name this ship the Queen Elizabeth." Everybody then agrees that the ship carries the name of " Queen Elizabeth." But suppose, Austin continues, that at the last moment a low fellow rushes forward, snatches

---

18 [For a recent discussion of Olivecrona on law and morals, see Merrills (1969) 19 U. Toronto L.J. 46. The criticism is voiced that Olivecrona's account distorts the view of law by failing to consider what Hart has called (see *ante,* 169) the internal aspect of rules of law. Morality is instrumental in achieving acceptance of the rules of law from this internal point of view. This is overlooked by Olivecrona. It may be suggested, however, that both Olivecrona and his critic have adopted over-simplistic models of law and morality, and that the relationship between them is more interactional. Olivecrona has not discussed this question in the second edition of *Law As Fact.*]

19 [From *Essays In Honor of Pound* ed. Newman (1962), p. 151.]

20 " Philosophical Papers," pp. 222, 226 f. [The Austin is J. L. Austin, the twentieth century philosopher, not John Austin.]

the bottle, and smashes it against the ship's side shouting: " I name this ship Generalissimo Stalin." The christening ceremony would then be held to have misfired, and the ship would not really carry the name of " Generalissimo Stalin."

What is the difference? In both cases, a performative sentence is pronounced with reference to the ship. In the first case, this is thought to be done in the proper way. If the president's wife, with customary ceremony, has pronounced the sentence giving the ship a name, everybody falls into line and calls the ship by this name. In the other case, this does not happen. The christening of the ship by a person not appointed to the task is regarded as an outrage and people pay no heed to it.

The difference, therefore, lies in the effect of the performative sentence on other minds. People are prepared to accept, without the slightest reflection, and to use the name given to the ship by the president's wife. This disposition follows from the prevalence of a certain custom with regard to the naming of ships. The custom has its roots in practical considerations: it is convenient to have names for ships which are universally employed. Attempts of name-giving outside the rules of the custom are disregarded and even met with hostility.

The example is instructive. In simple form, we have here before us some valuable tools for social control and intercourse: an " appointment " of a person to perform an act, a ceremony intended to draw attention to the act and elate the feelings of the onlookers, and a performative sentence that is the very core of the act. The effect of the act is psychological; it depends on people being conditioned to respond in a uniform way to the act, namely, to use a certain form of speech with regard to the ship. The whole thing fulfills a social function which is held to be useful.

Evidently it would be useless to discuss whether the ship really has the name or not. The name is not, objectively speaking, attached to the ship, even if some letters to that effect are painted on its sides. What happens is only that people use the name with reference to the ship.

We now turn to the act of marriage. For this act there are ancient and new ceremonies, centering upon a few performative words which purport to make the parties man and wife. What happens? The psychological effect is instantaneous, uniform, and far-reaching. Everybody falls into line and regards the newly wedded couple as man and wife, using these words. They are thereby socially classified in a new way. This entails a great many consequences of an ethical, religious, social, and legal kind. Certain ethical rules are now held to apply to the couple. They are treated socially according to customs referring to married people. In the legal sphere, a number of rules apply to them.

No mystical, supersensible bond is formed by the act of marriage. We need not, for that reason, discuss whether it is a reality or not to be married; it surely is. But the reality is not supersensible. It consists in a certain kind of place in the social context, depending on people's uniform reaction to the marriage ceremony. Take this reaction away and the performative words are inane. We are all conditioned to respond to the act in certain ways, and we do it. Thus, when people are known to, or supposed to, have gone through the ceremony in the proper way, then the couple is, so to speak, embedded in social surroundings giving them a certain position and requiring them to conform to certain rules. At the basis of it all are considerations as to the importance of stability in family relationships.

If the act is to call forth these effects, observance of the customary, or prescribed form is essential. If the performative words of the act are pronounced at the theater, or in jest, or in any connection except by the right person in the proper circumstances, no real marriage is held to be concluded. The act is said to be void. This expression is derived from the magical origin of acts. It means that the act lacks the force of producing the effect intended by the words. What actually happens is, of course, that pronouncements made outside the proper context are disregarded. This is the reverse side of our inclination to respond in a certain way to the right ceremony.

We have now talked about the psychological effects of the act of marriage. But what about its legal effects? Are they not something else?

Legal effects are spoken of in two different senses, which must be kept apart:

(i) Legal effects are the effects implied in the rules of law with regard to personal relations and property. Strictly speaking, the word " effect " is inappropriate in this connection. No legal effects in this sense are *caused* by the act of marriage. What takes place is an alteration in the actual situation to which the legal rules refer. A new fact has been added to the situation; and this fact entails the applicability of a number of rules referring to " married " persons. This is the whole thing. The so-called effects are nothing but the contents of rules. The legal situation has been changed through the act of marriage in that this act is relevant according to a complex of rules; the rules applying to the couple are now different from what they were before the act.

(ii) Legal effects mean effects that take place through the action of the courts or other state agencies. A man is, for instance, sent to prison for not supporting his wife and children.

The effects of this latter sort are actual effects. They are dependent on the psychological effectiveness of the legal rules; they take place because the state organs feel bound by the rules and therefore apply them carefully. All real effects of the act of marriage are therefore ultimately psychological effects.

On similar lines all sorts of legal acts may be analyzed: promises, conveyances, appointments, creations of juridical persons, promulgations of laws, and so on. They have the common feature of being more or less standardized performatives. Their consequences are of a double nature. First, they have immediate, psychological effects. The promisor feels himself bound; the promisee feels entitled to expect the promisor to act accordingly; contrary behavior is apt to provoke hostile reactions. Secondly, the acts correspond to certain requirements in the law; they are relevant in one way or another for actions by the state organs. Since the state organs regularly apply the rules, the promisor is likely to be exposed to a sanction if he breaks his promise; his awareness of this fortifies the immediate psychological effect of the promise on him.

It is a general rule that these performative sentences must be pronounced in special connections in order to have a psychological effect. This is easy to understand. Anybody can utter any performative sentences at will; but social consequences cannot be attached to irregular pronouncements. It is absolutely necessary to sort out and qualify such performative utterances as are to be instruments of social control and intercourse. This is done through the reference to a certain form and to certain circumstances. People are taught to respond only to pronouncements made in such contexts. In ancient times the legal acts were in general highly formal. The exact ceremony had to be performed and the exact words had to be uttered; among the Romans, as we know from Gaius, the slightest irregularity originally made the act void: the magic did not work. Gradually, the formal requirements have been mitigated. For large areas no form at all is prescribed in the law; even if made quite informally, a promise may be held to be legally valid. Nevertheless, the words as such are never thought to be relevant from a legal point of view; the situation in which they are pronounced must be of an appropriate character, even if this situation can only be vaguely described, or rather, perhaps, felt to be the right one.

The discussion has referred to the performatives currently used within the legal system. Performatives without any connection with law or social custom would generally be regarded as a senseless play of words. But there are important borderline cases, when performatives are used outside the rules of law or custom but with the intention of bringing about a more or less radical change in the legal situation. This is the case of the colonels who have put the previous dictator to flight and now announce that they have assumed power. Ostensibly, this phrase reports a fact. But the real intention is to impress people so that they believe the new rulers to have the power and therefore transfer their attitude of obeisance to them. Everything depends on the psychological effects of the announcement. If it is not met with sufficient resistance, power will come to the *Putsch* men, or else the strong words will be lost in the tumult.   [pp. 177–181]

K. OLIVECRONA

Law As Fact
(2nd ed. 1971)

The Nature of Legal Rules

. . .

Rules of Enacted Law

Enacting and proclaiming a text as a law according to the constitution is used as a means of exerting influence on the minds of people and thereby on their behaviour. The purpose is to restrain certain kinds of activity and to promote others. What else could be the meaning of legislation?

To achieve its purpose the text must be able to call forth certain ideas concerning human conduct in the mind of a reader; a pattern of behaviour has to be placed before his eyes. But something more is needed. It is not enough that people form abstract ideas of certain actions. If I simply imagine the situation of two drivers going in opposite directions, each of them keeping to the right, I have no rule in mind. A rule says that people shall behave in accordance with a pattern. A traffic rule, for instance, says that drivers shall keep to the

right on the roads. In a typical rule of enacted law expression is given
to an idea of a pattern of conduct in such a way as to impress people
with the feeling that the pattern ought to be followed when occasion
arises.

Consequently, we can discern two elements in such a legal rule.
On the one hand we have an imagined pattern of conduct, on the
other hand the particular form in which expression is given to it. We
shall now study these two elements separately.

The Pattern of Behaviour

A committee charged with the task of drafting a set of regulations
proceeds roughly in the following way. After making an inquiry into
the existing situation and forming an opinion on its defects, the committee draws a mental picture of a new state of things. This implies
devising certain patterns of conduct to be observed in certain circumstances. Next comes the question of supplying a motive for people to
behave in accordance with those patterns. This is usually done by
attaching unpleasant consequences to contrary behaviour.

In the simple case of traffic regulations the committee seeks to
visualize a desirable order on the roads in which drivers and pedestrians
consistently act in certain definite ways in various situations so as to
make the traffic flow smoothly with as little danger to the participants
as possible. On the basis of these considerations a series of patterns of
conduct for drivers and pedestrians are worked out. These patterns
are put forward in the text which, after due procedure, becomes a law.

The pattern of conduct is the *ideational element*, or the *ideatum*,
of a rule. It makes up the content of the rule as opposed to the form of
expression.

In order to supply a motive for people to conform to the patterns of
conduct in the traffic regulations penalties are attached to deviations
from these patterns. This implies setting up patterns of conduct for
other people: the police, the public prosecutors, and the judges. (For
the sake of brevity, the jury may be disregarded.) For the judge the
ideatum of such a rule consists in a certain action on his part taken
in a certain situation: according to the rules of procedure, a person
has been legally charged with causing a collision through turning to the
left without making a sign, and it has been convincingly shown that
he has really done so; in this situation the judge metes out a penalty.

The content of legal rules like these, therefore, is an idea of a certain
conduct as being observed in a certain situation. For the driver it is
the idea of his making a sign when he is going to make a turn on a
road; for the judge it is the idea of his pronouncing, in due form, a
decree concerning a penalty to be exacted from a driver who has been
shown not to have made a sign when this was required by the first rule.

From this it appears that two elements can be distinguished in the
ideatum of a rule. On the one hand, there is the situation of the driver
on the road when he is going to make the turn and the situation of the
judge when he is to make his decision. On the other hand, we have
a certain action to be taken by a person in this situation: for the
driver to make a sign, for the judge to give a sentence of a certain
kind. The first element may be called the *requisitum* because it
represents the requirements that should be present when the action

is to be taken. The other element, the action itself, may be called the *agendum*. To apply a rule means acting according to the *agendum* in a situation corresponding to the *requisitum*.

In the example, the rules are as little complicated as one could think. Yet, even here neither the *requisitum* nor the *agendum* is as simple as may be supposed at first sight. This is especially true of the rule for the judge. To get a full picture of the *requisitum* it is not enough to know the traffic regulations alone. In addition, a great many rules of procedure and evidence have to be taken into consideration. One must know the constitution of the courts: how they are to hold their sessions, how an indictment is to be made, how evidence is to be produced, and so on. All these rules and many more are needed for the description of the situation in which sentence is to be given. As regards the *agendum* of the judge, many rules besides the traffic regulations have also to be taken into account. The driver must for instance be old enough to be liable to punishment. In many cases both the *requisitum* and the *agendum* will be infinitely complicated.

There is, indeed, no case where a single legal provision can be regarded in isolation by the judge or by any other person called upon to decide what sort of action conforms to the law in a given situation. Each provision is like a piece in a puzzle. Many pieces have to be put together before one can say whether an actual situation corresponds to any legal *requisitum* and, if this is the case, what sort of *agendum* is applicable. The *requisitum* and the *agendum* of the respective legal provisions are the material out of which the final *requisitum* and *agendum* are built. In many cases the purpose of the pieces is to contribute to determining the *requisitum* or the *agendum* laid down in a number of other rules. An example of this is a provision offering a definition of words used in the law. In a law on the sale of goods such terms as ' current price ', ' promptly ', etc., may be defined. These definitions form part of the *requisitum* of several rules. Other definitions may refer to words used to express the *agendum* of a rule.

The composition of the *ideatum* of legal rules raises many questions. . . . For the present it is sufficient to point out that every legal rule must be conceived as a means of directing human behaviour. Therefore, a rule must depict a situation in which an action is to be performed. Only two remarks should be added here:

(i) In the example from the traffic regulations the assumption was made that the legal text expressed separate rules for the people on the roads and for the authorities charged with the application of sanctions. In many cases, especially in criminal law, we find only rules of the latter kind. The law says, for instance, that larceny is to be punished in this or that way. This is a rule for the courts. But the rule for the courts is used as a means of directing the behaviour of the general public; it is not necessary to give a separate rule stating that larceny must not be committed.

(ii) Considerable complications arise out of the use of the fundamental legal concepts, such as the concepts of rights and duties, in expressing legal rules. On the face of it, such rules are concerned with the creation, alteration, transference, and extinction of rights and duties. We may assume that their ultimate purpose is to direct human behaviour. But how this is done is an intricate problem that needs elaborate treatment. . . .

The Form of Expression

The form of expression is determined by the purpose of legislation: to direct the conduct of people. But the text is not an expression of a wish on the part of the lawgiving authorities that people should behave in this or that way. Nor does it contain advice to people as to what is prudent to do in order to gain certain advantages and avoid unpleasant consequences. It is quite true, of course, that one can draw inferences in this respect from the contents of a law; but the meaning of the law is not to say that you ought to do so-and-so if you want to reap such and such benefits, or that you ought to abstain from certain kinds of actions if you do not want to expose yourself to sanctions. The law says directly that you *shall* do this or that, you *shall not* do such and such. The traffic regulations do not tell people that it will be expedient to keep to the right. They say that you shall keep to the right. The form of expression is therefore the imperative.

It is characteristic of the imperative that it does not refer to any values for the addressee. The imperative is unconditional. It may refer to a hypothetical situation: if this or that happens, do such and such. But no advantage is given as the reason why one should act in the way prescribed. In this sense the imperative is unconditional.

Often a 'shall' or some word to the same effect is employed in the formulation of a rule. ('The seller shall effect delivery of the goods as required by the contract and the law.') But this is not necessary. The indicative mood may as well be used. The essential thing is that the law as a whole is put forward in an imperative sense. The text is published in a form known to be effective in making people feel obliged to behave in accordance with the patterns enunciated. It is only a matter of style if the patterns of behaviour are expressed in the indicative form or as imperatives. Different traditions exist in this respect. . . .

Now if laws consist of imperatives, it seems natural to reason in the following way. An imperative is a command. But a command presupposes someone who issues it. Therefore one has to seek for a commanding authority. This can only be some supreme power in society. The question will therefore be how that power is to be conceived.

So we seem to be back at the will-theory again. But then all the difficulties previously exhibited will arise. As was shown, it is impossible to find any power in society, existing independently of a working law, whose commands could be the law; and the legislative process does not result in the issuing of commands by the lawgivers.

We are apparently faced by a dilemma. On the one hand, the imperative character of the laws is evident. They say what people shall or shall not do. On the other hand, no commanding authority can be said to exist and no commands are given through legislation. . . .

[pp. 115–119]

The Imperantum

Besides the *ideatum*—the behaviour put before the mind of the recipient—a command contains another element. This is something conveying the impression that the behaviour in question shall be observed. For the sake of brevity this element may be called *imperantum*.[21]

When the imperative mood is used, it serves as an *imperantum*. It is a way of speaking calculated to incite another person to an action or to inhibit an action by him. The imperative mood, however, is no exclusive form for giving a verbal command. An *imperantum* may as well be adjoined to a sentence in the indicative mood. If I say to a child: 'You shut the door', this is a command if the words are uttered in a certain way with the intention of causing the child to shut the door. Though the indicative mood is used, the sentence does not serve to convey information. It is a suggestive sentence. The *imperantum* is the tone and bearing of the speaker. In some languages the imperative mood does not even differ from an infinitive. The way of using the words decides whether a phrase is an imperative or a constative sentence.

Even when the imperative mood is employed, the expression and the carriage of the speaker are of great importance. They belong to the *imperantum* and serve to strengthen the effect of the imperative mood. Indeed, no mere words as such constitute a command. Even a sentence in the imperative mood must be pronounced in a certain way if it is to be a real command. The *imperantum* may be more or less striking. Sometimes it includes a forceful display of personality; at other times it is hardly noticeable, and the command becomes similar to a courteous request.

To make commands effective on a large scale the recipients have to be inured to receiving commands from the speaker. Preparation on the part of the recipients is therefore of the utmost importance if lines of command are to function reliably. In every hierarchical organization the subordinates are trained to respond to commands from above, and sanctions are enforced in case of disobedience. The extreme form of such training is military drill, which tends to make obedience instant and automatic.

The amount of personal effort needed to ensure obedience is chiefly dependent on the degree of preparation in the recipient. If he is well conditioned to respond to commands from a person who is supposed to be his superior, no special effort at all is required; it may be sufficient to put before his eyes what he is to do. The contention that 'authority' or 'right to command' is needed for a command to be effective stems from the experience that some preparation in the recipient is generally required. But the legal or moral relationship expressed by words like 'authority' and 'right' is substituted for the actual psychological factors that cause one man's behaviour to be directed through the commands of another.

The *imperantum* is aimed at the volitional side of the recipient's mind, not at the intellectual side. The idea of the behaviour to be observed is aroused by the ideational element in the command. The echo of the *imperantum* in the mind of the addressee is 'I must' or something similar. But no idea besides the mental image of the words themselves is evoked. Nothing is signified by the 'must' or its equivalents.

[21] The use of the home-made latin words '*ideatum*' and '*imperantum*' may be excused on account of their practicability.

In its simplest form the *imperantum* is the form of language, the manner of speaking, and the bearing of the speaker. Such forms of the *imperantum* are spontaneous. Other forms are conventional or standardized. The officer's uniform and the word signifying his grade belong to the *imperantum* in his case. In a business firm an executive's title and the designation of his place in the organization are elements in the *imperantum*. Innumerable contrivances are used to build up an *imperantum* according to the needs of the circumstances. They serve to make it a matter of course that persons in certain positions should follow orders from persons in other positions.

Among the means of standardization the most important are perhaps the formalities that are to be used in making certain pronouncements. The distinction between private utterances and official orders depends on the circumstances in which the pronouncements are made and on the form that is employed. To be an official order, an utterance has to be made in a special context and in a certain way. The same distinction is maintained in business life; a bank clerk is acting ' on behalf of the bank ' only when certain formalities are observed.

Nowadays forms are far less rigorous than in ancient times. There is so much informality that we are inclined to think that formalities are no longer of any importance. This is, however, a mistake. The formalities have become looser, but they are as prevalent as ever. Forms are necessary in every society as a means of signalling what pronouncements are to be taken as guides to action and, above all, taken as legally relevant.

Independent Imperatives

A face-to-face command implies a personal relationship between two individuals. But imperative phrases are widely used outside such relationships. The sentence: ' You shall speak the truth ' may be uttered as a command; but it may be uttered in giving instructions concerning right behaviour.

Such imperative phrases may conveniently be called independent imperatives since they are independent of the personal relationship characteristic of a command. They are similar to commands in the proper sense in that they serve as means of inculcating a certain behaviour in a categorical way. For this reason it seems legitimate to classify them as a kind of imperative side by side with commands.[22]

No clean-cut distinction can be made between commands and independent imperatives. The personal relationship pertaining to a command may be more or less close. As the distance between the persons grows, the commands assume the character of independent imperatives. A mediating form is that which obtains when a person or a god is represented in imagination as issuing commands.

Habits of language make us prone to think of ' imperatives ' as identical with commands in the strict sense of the word. There even

---

[22] On the concept of independent imperatives *cf.* I. Tammelo in 49 *Archiv für Rechts- und Wirtschaftsphilosophie* (1963) 257 *et seq.*; J. Stone, *Legal System and Lawyers' Reasoning* (1964) 93. Alf Ross adopts the concept though he prefers to use the more general term ' directive ' (*On Law and Justice*, 1958, 8). Recently the independent imperatives have been discussed in a clarifying way by Enrico Pattaro in a long article in the *Rivista trimestrale di diritto e procedura civile* 1968.

seems to be some psychological difficulty in conceiving imperatives without referring them to an *imperator* addressing somebody else. The matter is, however, very simple. Imperative sentences may be put forward in many ways and disseminated through many channels. No *imperator* is needed. The addressee may be an audience of millions.

The category of independent imperatives is very large. It comprises ethical sentences as well as legislative enactments. But why should only verbal pronouncement be included in this category? It seems correct to include a number of mute signs, as for instance traffic lights. Even a fence around a garden or the lock to one's door may be said to have the function of an independent imperative. Usually neither the fence nor the lock is a physical obstacle of importance to an intruder. But both of them are signs to stop and keep hands off. If one looks at things in this way, independent imperatives of divergent kinds will be encountered at almost every step.[23]

Rules of Law Independent Imperatives

The imperative theory as found in classical natural law doctrine and continued by great teachers of law until our day was led astray by the tenet that the rules of law were imperatives in the sense of declarations of will by an *imperator*. When a divine law was held to exist, this law was the will of God. Human law was the will of the sovereign, the people, or the state, as explained in many different ways.

Every attempt to identify the lawgiving will with a real human will necessarily failed. The will was a mythical will, created in imagination to meet the requirements of preconceived ideas.

The clue to the riddle of the nature of the rules called legal is the concept of independent imperatives. The imperative character of those rules is evident. But an imperative is no declaration of will. It is a mode of expression used in a suggestive way in order to influence the behaviour of people. The rules of law form a vast complex of such expressions containing patterns of conduct that are more or less universally followed within a group of people. Their efficacy depends on a set of relatively firm attitudes among the people which in their turn have manifold and deep-seated causes. . . .

But what is the *imperantum*? Of what does it consist?

It cannot be taken for granted that the *imperantum* is the same in all cases. Enacted law, ancient customary law, and judge-made law have to be considered separately with regard to the question of the *imperantum*.

Rules of enacted law are independent imperatives that have passed through a series of formal acts. The *imperantum* is the whole setting in which the enactment takes place: the working constitution, the organization functioning according to its rules, the familiar designations of parliamentary bodies and state officials, etc. Once a constitution has been firmly established, the people respond automatically by accepting as binding the texts proclaimed as laws through the act of promulgation. Thanks to this attitude among the addressees the *imperantum* becomes effective.

The fulcrum is the act of promulgation. It is immediately decisive

---

[23] Cf. E. Bucher, *Das subjektive Rechts als Normsetzungsbefugnis* (1965) 69.

for the officials charged with the publication of new laws. Other officials rely on the publication being conscientiously performed according to constitutional rules, so that only texts that have been rightly promulgated—but all such texts—are printed in the official collection of laws. Only very rarely do courts or other state authorities have occasion to ascertain for themselves whether a text has been promulgated in proper form.

The general public knows nothing of such formalities as promulgation. The texts reach them under the official appellation of law and that is enough. The appellation of law, when presumed to be correctly applied, carries with it the implication that the rules of conduct contained in the text are binding on everybody.

As regards ancient customary law, nothing can be said of general application concerning the *imperantum*. Conditions have differed widely. An example may suffice to illustrate how we have to conceive the *imperantum* in remote, primitive times.

In my own country it is recorded in the oldest sources that the law was authoritatively preserved in the memory of wise men ('men of young memory') before the time when it was written down. The 'lawman' (*lagman*) had to recite the law at the *ting*, the assembly of free men. The text was rhythmical and alliterative, which made it impressive (the language was beautiful) and easily remembered. Probably the men acclaimed the recitation by the clang of arms. This procedure corresponded to the modern act of promulgation, though it had to be often repeated. The law was what the lawman had said it to be. Those who were present had to repeat it to their homefolk. This presupposes that they had learnt the law by heart. To do so must have been highly important to every freeman; it was an essential part of his education. One can imagine how long, dark winter evenings in the huts were spent in teaching the young people the law with an occasional saga as a reward for good results. At the *ting* one had occasion to refresh one's memory, fill up gaps, and correct errors.

The law was couched in strongly imperative language. But the *imperantum* was not made up solely by the imperative form of speech. To it also belonged the solemnity of the *ting* (held on holy ground), the position of the lawman, the acclamation by the assembly, the authority of parents, etc., in short everything that contributed to create the feeling that these rules were sacred and should be unconditional guides for conduct.

Judge-made law is not identical with the pronouncements of the courts. Each decision is a decision on an individual case. It differs from the act of legislation in that it is not a proclamation of general rules. According to the traditional view, the courts are the authoritative interpreters of the law. For that reason it is supposed to be possible to infer the contents of the law from the decisions of the courts: since the decision in the case A versus B has been based on the rule X, this rule belongs to the law of the land.

To be valid, such inferences are supposed to be made according to certain traditional rules. *Obiter dicta* are not to serve as a basis for inferences. Courts of different degrees possess different grades of authority. Some decisions are entirely rejected as a basis for inferences concerning the law, etc.

Inferences from decisions can actually be drawn by lawyers and laymen alike. But the practical importance of the inferences varies with the status of the persons drawing them. When a court, on the basis of previous decisions, declares that rule X belongs to the law, this is generally accepted. Rule X is then firmly established as a rule of law. The opinions expressed by renowned writers may have the same effect. Between themselves these authorities, practically speaking, decide what is to be regarded as the law and therefore applied by the courts in the future.

In actual fact, however, the 'inferences' are not real inferences. From the pronouncement of a court nothing can be inferred concerning the content of a pre-existing law. One may perhaps conclude that the court was of the opinion that there was a pre-existing law of this or that content. Not even this, however, is necessarily true. A modern judge may very well be conscious of the fact that he is not merely applying a pre-existing law in making this particular decision.

When a court accepts or rejects a previous ruling of a court as a guide for its own action, it really draws no inference. It makes a decision. It decides to regard this ruling as representing the law, or, from a more modern point of view, it decides that this is the most reasonable solution to the legal problem raised by the case before it. The decision usually entails that the rule which the court has embraced will be placed, in the opinion of lawyers, within the body of rules designated as 'the law'. Likewise, a writer on law decides to accept or reject the rulings of courts as representing the law. Depending on his renown, and possibly on his arguments, his decision will be followed by legal opinion. The law will be what he declares it to be.

These decisions by courts and writers are the nearest counterpart in the field of judge-made law, to promulgation in the field of legislation. The body of texts officially designated as enacted laws is exactly defined through a series of acts of promulgation. General opinion relies, without hesitation or doubt, on this formal criterion. (Exceptions, as for instance the situation after an abrupt change in the system of government, may here be disregarded.) The decisions to accept or reject rulings of courts as expressing the law are not formalized in the same way. Therefore the body of rules regarded as belonging to judge-made law is not as exactly circumscribed. Its compass can only be more or less vaguely defined and is often the subject of controversy.

Particular Imperatives

In the general discussion of the nature of legal rules a certain objection against the imperative theory has played an important part. Conceding that rules prescribing some conduct may be viewed as imperatives, it has been pointed out that there are other rules besides the rules of conduct, such as the rules concerning the acquisition, import, transference, and loss of rights. The right of ownership is acquired in certain ways; it is transferred through such and such acts; and it may be lost in other ways. It has been suggested that the rules governing these legal questions are not imperatives because they do not say that you shall behave in this or that way. Instead, they regulate the legal effects of so-called operative facts. The case is the same with rules regulating the acquisition, import, and loss of legal qualities, such as being king or president, judge or member of the Diet, married or guardian of a minor. It will seem that such rules are not imperatives.[24]

The importance of the objection is evident since a very considerable part of legal rules is of this kind: most of private law and large sections of public law. If valid, the objection would also be an argument against the view here expounded of legal rules as independent imperatives.

The objection rests on the assumption that imperatives are necessarily imperatives of conduct. What else but a conduct could be imperatively prescribed? But if imperatives are always directed towards the conduct of an addressee, it is really difficult to fit the legal rules about rights and legal qualities into the category of imperatives.

The basic assumption, however, is unfounded. It may seem obvious that imperatives must always refer to other people's conduct. But our actual language does not conform to this preconceived idea. If I hand over a watch to my son saying: 'This shall be your property', I am using an imperative form of speech. But I am not commanding him to do anything. The imperative is directed towards his acquiring the ownership of the watch.

This sort of language may, upon reflection, seem strange. But it is a fact that we have it; and it is a most important part of our legal language. We constantly use it in legal transactions. It is employed in legislation in laying down that a person shall acquire ownership of a piece of land through certain formalities; that he shall lose it when certain things happen, etc.

These imperatives are obviously of a peculiar kind. In a previous work I called them 'imperatives of existence' because they refer to the coming into existence of rights and legal qualities.[25] The choice of expression was not a particularly happy one. It is much better to adopt the term 'performatory' or 'performative' expressions introduced by J. L. Austin.

The imperatives in question will here be called *performatory imperatives*. Their meaning is that something should come to pass: a right should be created or transferred; a person should acquire a legal quality. This effect is held to be brought about through these imperatives. . . .

[pp. 126–134]

A. V. LUNDSTEDT

Legal Thinking Revised

(1956)

The Method of Justice

Regarding the justice-judgment, the matter is somewhat complicated by the fact that very often a *claim* is said to be just. This contains a tautology, in so far as the claim—quite naturally used by jurisprudence as a legal ideological factor—is considered to be based on (material) law and everything based on that must obviously be just. But not seldom jurisprudence finds itself in such a position

---

[24] This objection is clearly stated by Larenz, *Methodenlehre der Rechtswissenschaft* (1960) 152 *et seq.*
[25] *Judgments in civil cases* (Swedish 1943) 69.

that it is forced to decide whether a certain claim is to be regarded as present, i.e. really to be a claim and consequently based on (material) law, or not. This question is answered in the positive if it can be proved that it is *just* that a claim of the type in question arises. Consequently natural justice is considered *partly* to form the basis for the whole system or body of rules of law already known, *partly* in a certain case at hand to make the basis for the rule of law not yet clearly known which is to be applied in a case of the kind under consideration. Here appears the *true external, so to speak, character of justice : to be the result of a balancing against each other of the interests of the parties*, that of the defendant to be free from punishment or any other legal reaction, and that of the plaintiff of sentencing or adjudging the defendant to this or that legal reaction. This weighing of interests—or more properly, this balancing against each other of the reasons for the interests of each of the parties—is characteristic for all shades of jurisprudence and not only for the jurisprudence of interests. This balancing is only a consequence of the belief in natural justice as the ultimate substratum for law. The 'weighing' or 'balancing' against each other of the reasons for the interests of the parties illustrates better than anything else that we have in front of us nothing but a question of *evaluation*.[26]   [p. 51]

. . . The principal argument in *my* criticism of legal ideology—this argument being completely sufficient in itself—is *that* the entire substratum for legal ideology, the so-called material law and its basis natural justice, lacks the character of reality ; *that*, accordingly, even legal rights, legal obligations, legal relationships and the like lack such a character ; *that* the common sense of justice (the feelings or sentiments of justice) far from being able to support the 'material law' on the contrary, receives its entire bearing through the maintenance of law, i.e. legal machinery, which takes the common sense of justice (= the feelings of justice) into its service and directs it in grooves and furrows advantageous to the society and its economy, and *that* consequently legal ideology does not perceive and *cannot* perceive those realities appertaining to the legal machinery such as they are, but places them right on their head.[27]

[p. 53]

. . . What would happen to human beings if legal activities were discontinued? Little imagination is necessary in order to understand that this would mean the collapse of society and thus the destruction of the human beings therein, to the extent that they could not find refuge in any other society where legal activities were perhaps still exercised and, consequently, a social order was still functioning. Thus the following view seems well grounded: Legal activities are actually indispensable for the existence of society and thus for the people in a society. If this is

---

[26] [Lundstedt argues here that any attempt to develop law on the basis of the common sense of justice is to assume that natural justice represents a kind of "material law" underlying the actual legal system. This he dismisses as a non-existent metaphysical (or ideological—he uses these words as virtually synonymous) construction. For Lundstedt everything that is not physical fact is pure fantasy; thus all concepts, such as rights and duties, are dismissed as unrealistic. This applies to legal rules themselves—they are mere labels, an "unreal superstructure" on the legal machinery. Lundstedt denies the normative character of legal rules, as he equates "normative" with metaphysical. See *op. cit.*, Pt. III, but *cf. ante*, 501.]

[27] [*Cf. ante*, 512.]

taken into consideration, then no other interest as the incentive for legal activities can be discovered, which is not determined by ideological or otherwise false conceptions, than exactly the following: *Legal activities are indispensable for the existence of society.* If this statement cannot be refuted by the presentation of another interest, which is not dependent on false conceptions, in the exercise of legal activities, it must be accepted. For my own part I regard it as precluded that another interest of this kind could possibly be found. In the literature with which I am familiar it has never been possible to trace such an interest.[28]   [pp. 131–132]

Method of Social Welfare

With the method of social welfare as a principle or, perhaps better, as a guiding motive for legal activities, I mean in the first place the encouragement in the best possible way of that—according to what everybody standing above a certain minimum degree of culture is able to understand —which *people in general actually strive to attain.* This consists in such things as suitable and well-tasting food, appropriate and becoming clothes, according to one's own or the general taste, dwellings furnished in the best and most comfortable way, security of life, limb, and 'property', the greatest possible freedom of action and movement, therein also including limitation of the amount of work a person may be required to do within a specified period of time, possibilities for education etc.— in brief, all conceivable material comfort as well as the protection of spiritual interests. I do not take any standpoint at all as to the question of what man *ought* to aim to strive for, not at all to the question, if on the whole he *ought* to propose any goal for his labor, hardships and troubles. Every type of valuation in such a respect is absolutely detached from what I insert in my thesis of social welfare.[29] I do not even seek to determine anything at all in the respect of whether it is of value for man to protect his possibilities of life and perhaps develop them, or whether it would instead be better to destroy them, or as it is said in Scandinavia 'put a torpedo under the Ark'. In such a respect I only establish as a *fact* what can be observed in general, namely, that the overwhelming majority of human beings (in Sweden as well as in all

[28] [Thus Lundstedt would base tort liability not on justice, guilt, fault, or any other "metaphysical" concept but simply on what is necessary for the maintenance of the general security of society. As liability cannot be based on "fault," *all* liability is strict, but how strict in particular cases depends on the social purpose of the rule. What a man "ought" to have done or known depends not on what is morally just but on what is socially desirable. To some extent this view coincides with modern tort law, with its emphasis on objective standards and its substitution of social for moral blameworthiness. Lundstedt also argues that in criminal law *mens rea* is relevant not to guilt but to the harmful consequences for society if people were exposed to the criminal law for non-intentional acts. See *op. cit.*, pp. 224–240, 252–268. Presumably therefore on Lundstedt's view, if social security requires the execution of insane killers or sexual offenders, it would be a mere metaphysical aberration to preserve their life. For a critical discussion of Lundstedt's theories as applied to tort, see J. Hellner, in *Scandinavian Studies in Law* (1958), pp. 158–172.]

[29] [In this way Lundstedt seeks to differentiate his sociological approach from others, such as Pound's, which are based on value-judgments, *i.e.*, what people *ought* to do. Lundstedt wishes to concentrate on fact alone. Yet Pound's "interests" are also based on actual human desires and his scheme of values purport to be statements of values actually accepted.]

other countries of a comparable cultural development) *wish to live and develop their lives' possibilities.*

Starting from this state of affairs I have sought to show that—as far as those, which exercise influence on the organization and administration of society directly or indirectly, are freed from conceptions of legal-ideological interests—there is nothing else to be determined for the developing of legal machinery than the consideration of what is required, in order that the actual aspirations of men just indicated may be realized to the most practicable extent. As far as persons in general have these aspirations, as far as they are not controlled by the Indian principle of contemplation, for example (i.e. the lapsing into Nirvana, the absolute nothing as the final end) or, perhaps, brought to the verge of despair by an inclination for positive activity directed towards destroying society—so far nothing but the aspirations just hinted at can be found out which has the power to arouse and maintain an interest so strong and so general that it can in process of time be decisive for legislation and the interpretation of law. It is obvious that the interest in legislation and the administration of law is indissolubly united with these aspirations. Without both of these legal activities no order would be conceivable, only chaos which in its turn would make the aspirations of mankind impossible. [pp. 140–141]

A. ROSS

On Law and Justice
(1958)

Analysis of the Concept " Valid Law "

Let us imagine that two persons are playing chess,[30] while a third person looks on.

If the onlooker knows nothing about chess he will not understand what is going on. From his knowledge of other games he will probably conclude that it is some sort of game. But he will not be able to understand the individual moves or to see any connection between them. Still less will he have any notion of the problems involved in any particular disposition of the pieces on the board. . . . [p. 11]

. . . Human social life . . . acquires the character of community life from the very fact that a large number (not all) of individual actions are relevant and have significance in relation to a set of common conceptions of rules. They constitute a significant whole, bearing the same relation to one another as move and countermove. Here, too, there is mutual interplay, motivated by and acquiring its significance from the common rules of the social " game." And it is the consciousness of these rules which makes it possible to understand and in some measure to predict the course of events.

I will now examine more closely what a rule of chess actually is, and in what way it is possible to establish what the rules are which govern the game of chess.

I have in mind here the primary rules of chess, those which deter-

---

[30] [*Cf.* the " language games " of Wittgenstein, *ante*, 39.]

mine the arrangement of the pieces, the moves, "taking," and the like, and not rules of chess theory.

As to the latter a few remarks will suffice. Like other technological rules they obviously are of the nature of hypothetical theoretical pronouncements. They assume the existence of the primary rules of chess and indicate the consequences which different openings and gambits will lead to in the game, judged in relation to the chance of winning. Like other technological rules their directive force is conditioned by an interest —in this example the interest in the winning of the game. If a player does not have this interest, then the theory of the game is without importance to him.

The primary rules of chess, on the other hand, are directives. Although they are formulated as assertions about the "ability" or "power" of the pieces to move and "take," it is clear that they are intended to indicate how the game is to be played. They aim directly, that is, unqualified by any underlying objective, to motivate the player; they tell him, as it were: This is how it is played.

These directives are felt by each player to be socially binding; that is to say, a player not only feels himself spontaneously motivated (" bound ") to a certain method of action but is at the same time certain that a breach of the rules will call forth a reaction (protest) on the part of his opponent. And in this way they are clearly distinguished from the rules of skill contained in the theory. A stupid move can arouse astonishment, but not a protest.

On the other hand, the rules of chess are not tinged with morality; this is the result of the fact that normally no one really wants to break them. The wish to cheat at a game must be due to the fact that a player has an aim other than merely to win according to the rules of the game; for example, he may want to be admired or to win a sum of money which is at stake. This latter aim is often present at a game of cards, and it is well known that the demand for honourable play here takes on a moral value.

How is it possible then to establish which rules (directives) govern the game of chess?

One could perhaps think of approaching the problem from the behaviourist angle—limiting oneself to what can be established by external observation of the actions and then finding certain regularities. But in this way an insight into the rules of the game would never be achieved. It would never be possible to distinguish actual custom, or even regularities conditioned by the theory of the game, from the rules of chess proper. Even after watching a thousand games it would still be possible to believe that it is against the rules to open with a rook's pawn.[31]

The simplest thing, perhaps, would be to go by certain authoritative rulings, for example, rulings given at chess congresses, or information contained in recognised textbooks on chess. But even this might not be sufficient, since it is not certain that such declarations are adhered to in practice. Sometimes games are played in fact in many varying ways. Even in a classic game like chess variations of this kind can occur (for example, the rule about "taking" *en passant* is not always adhered to).

---

[31] [See also, *post*, 550. For a discussion of the relevance of games as a model see Hughes (1968), 77 Yale L.J. 475 reprinted in ed. Hughes, *Law, Reason and Justice* (1969), pp. 101, 104–107.]

This problem of what rules govern "chess" must therefore, strictly speaking, be understood to refer to the rules which govern an actual game between two specific persons. It is their actions, and theirs alone, which are bound up in a significant whole and governed for both of them by the rules.

Thus we cannot but adopt an introspective method. The problem is to discover which rules are actually felt by the players to be socially binding, in the sense indicated above. The first criterion is that they are in fact effective in the game and are outwardly visible as such. But in order to decide whether rules that are observed are more than just customary usage or motivated by technical reasons, it is necessary to ask the players by what rules they feel themselves bound.

Accordingly we can say: a rule of chess "is valid" means that within a given fellowship (which fundamentally comprises the two players of an actual game) this rule is effectively adhered to, because the players feel themselves to be socially bound by the directive contained in the rule. The concept of validity (in chess) involves two elements. The one refers to the actual effectiveness of the rule which can be established by outside observation. The other refers to the way in which the rule is felt to be motivating, that is, socially binding.

There is a certain ambiguity in the concept "rule of chess." The rules of chess have no reality and do not exist apart from the experience of the players, that is, their ideas of certain patterns of behaviour and, associated therewith, the emotional experience of the compulsion to obey. It is possible to abstract the meaning of an assertion purely as a thought content ("2 and 2 make 4") from the apprehension of the same by a given person at a given time ; and in just the same way it is also possible to abstract the meaning of a directive ("the king has the power of moving one square in any direction") from the concrete experience of the directive. The concept "rule of chess" must therefore in any accurate analysis be divided into two: the experienced ideas of certain patterns of behaviour (with the accompanying emotion) and the abstract content of those ideas, the norms of chess.

Thus the norms of chess are the abstract idea content (of a directive nature) which make it possible, as a scheme of interpretation, to understand the phenomena of chess (the actions of the moves and the experienced patterns of action) as a coherent whole of meaning and motivation, a game of chess ; and, along with other factors, within certain limits to predict the course of the game.

The phenomena of chess and the norms of chess are not mutually independent, each of them having their own reality ; they are different sides of the same thing. No biological-physical action is as such regarded as a move of chess. It acquires this quality only by being interpreted in relation to the norms of chess. And conversely, no directive idea content has as such the character of a valid norm of chess. It acquires this quality only by the fact that it can, along with others, be effectively applied as a scheme of interpretation for the phenomena of chess. The phenomena of chess become phenomena of chess only when placed in relation to the norms of chess and vice versa.

The purpose of this discussion of chess has undoubtedly become clear by now. It is a pointer toward the statement that the concept "valid norm of chess " may function as the model for the concept " valid law " which is the real object of our preliminary considerations.

The law too may be regarded as consisting partly of legal phenomena and partly of legal norms in mutual correlation.

Observing the law as it functions in society we find that a large number of human actions are interpreted as a coherent whole of meaning and motivation by means of legal norms as the scheme of interpretation. A purchases a house from B. It turns out that the house is full of termites. A asks B for a reduction in the purchase price, but B will not agree. A brings an action against B, and the judge in accordance with the law of contract orders B to pay to A a certain sum of money within a given time. B does not do this. A has the sheriff levy upon the personal property of B which is then sold in auction. This sequence of events comprises a whole series of human actions, from the establishment of the law of contract to the auction. A biological-physical consideration of these actions cannot reveal any causal connection between them. Such connections lie within each single individual. But we interrupt them with the aid of the reference scheme " valid law " as legal phenomena constituting a coherent whole of meaning and motivation. Each one of these actions acquires its legal character only when this is done. A's purchase of the house happens by word of mouth or with the aid of written characters. But these become a " purchase " only when seen in relation to the legal norms. The various actions are mutually motivating just like the moves in chess. The judge, for example, is motivated by A's and B's parts in the deal (and the further circumstances in connection with it, the condition of the house), and by the precedents establishing the law of contract. The whole proceeding has the character of a " game," only according to norms which are far more complicated than the norms of the game of chess.

On the basis of what has been said, the following hypothesis is advanced: The concept " valid (Illinois, California, common) law " can be explained and defined in principle in the same manner as the concept " valid (for any two players) norm of chess." That is to say, " valid law " means the abstract set of normative ideas which serve as a scheme of interpretation for the phenomena of law in action, which again means that these norms are effectively followed, and followed because they are experienced and felt to be socially binding.[32]

This conclusion may perhaps be thought commonplace, and it may seem that a vast apparatus of reasoning has been employed to this end. This might be true if the problems were approached by a person with no preconceived notions. But it would not be true for an historical approach. By far the greater part of all writers on jurisprudence up to the present have maintained that the concept " valid law " cannot be explained without recourse to the metaphysical. The law according to this view is not merely an empirical phenomenon. When we say that a rule of law is " valid " we refer not only to something factual, that can be observed, but also to a " validity " of a metaphysical character. This validity is alleged to be a pure concept of reason of divine origin or existing *a priori* (independent of experience) in the rational nature of man. And eminent writers on jurisprudence who deny such spiritual metaphysics have never-

---

[32] By the judge and other legal authorities applying the law. [This is no longer Ross's view as to the range of directives. See *ante*, 503 and *post*, 555.]

theless been of the opinion that the " validity " of the law can only be explained by means of specific postulates.

Seen in this light our preliminary conclusion will, I trust, not be called commonplace. This analysis of a simple model is calculated to raise doubts as to the necessity of metaphysical explanations of the concept of law. Who would ever think of tracing the valid norms of chess back to an *a priori* validity, a pure idea of chess, bestowed upon man by God or deduced by man's eternal reason? The thought is ridiculous, because we do not take chess as seriously as law—because stronger emotions are bound up with the concepts of law. But this is no reason for believing that logical analysis should adopt a fundamentally different attitude in each of the two cases. [pp. 13–18]

A. ROSS

Directives and Norms
(1968)

A norm is to be defined as a directive which corresponds in a particular way to certain social facts

. . . It is not possible to define the concept 'norm' (in a way useful to the social sciences) so that it denotes either simply a kind of meaning content (which includes all or only some directives), or simply a set of social facts. Both approaches must founder as too one-sided. We must then further conclude that a definition is required which integrates both aspects of the matter in the concept 'norm'. On this basis, I put forward the following definition: *a norm is a directive which stands in relation of correspondence to social facts,* the nature of the relation to be specified subsequently. The only directives which can stand in the required relation are the impersonal directives with the exclusion of the autonomous moral directives; that is, those directives which have been called . . . 'quasi-commands' and 'constitutive rules based on mutual agreement'.

Before I undertake the task of specifying what relation of correspondence is relevant, I want to stress the fundamental adequacy of the definition. The norm is said to be a directive, in the sense of a meaning content; to this extent the definition is adequate with regard to the use according to which a norm can be *followed* or *complied with,* felt to be *binding,* and *logically* related to other norms so that they together constitute a *system of norms.* But according to the definition a directive is a norm only if it corresponds to certain social facts, in a way to be specified. To say that a norm 'exists' means, then, that these facts exist; and to this extent the adequacy of the definition is secured with regard to that use of 'norm' which requires that norms can exist, and that statements to this effect form part of the description of societies.

Now, in undertaking the task of specifying how directives are related to social facts, I assume provisionally that we are concerned only with generally formulated directives, or rules.[33] It is, then, barely questionable that the fundamental condition for the existence of a norm must be that

---

[33] [*Cf. Directives and Norms* (1968), para. 22.]

in the majority of cases the pattern of behaviour presented in the direc-
tive (s → b) is followed by the members of the society. If a rule is not
effective in this sense, then it would be misleading to say that it 'exists',
if such a statement is meant to be part of a description of social facts.

That a pattern of behaviour is on the whole *followed* does not mean
that every member of the society generally acts in the same way in
given circumstances. Usually the description of *s* is so qualified that the
norm will concern only certain categories of the members of the society.
Thus the directive that shops are to be closed at a certain hour relates
only to those members of society who are shopkeepers.

That the pattern is *on the whole* followed involves a certain vagueness
which makes it difficult to decide in some circumstances whether or not
a norm exists.

This condition, however, is not of itself sufficient to provide an
adequate definition. For it is necessary for the establishment of a norm
that it be followed not only with external regularity, that is with observable conformity to the rule, but also with the consciousness of following
a rule and being bound to do so.[34] If this requirement is not met (I shall
subsequently return to the question of what it implies) then many patterns
of social behaviour which differ essentially from those traditionally called
norms would be included under the concept. I have in mind the following
types of observable regularities of behaviour:

Patterns Biologically or Physically Based

Man's biological make-up and the general economy of nature effect
conformity of behaviour in many ways. Most of us sleep during the
night and are awake in daytime; we turn on the light when it becomes
dark and wear more clothes when it is cold; we carry an umbrella or
a raincoat if it looks like rain.

Technical Patterns

As we have mentioned earlier, some directives are offered as advice
or directions for the most efficient performance of certain tasks and
achievement of certain goals. When faced with similar tasks, people will
to a great extent act uniformly and follow directions which are warranted
by technology and tradition. This is especially true of professional
undertakings. Bricklayers are trained in the time-honoured methods of
building a wall or a chimney, gardeners learn how to graft and plant
cuttings, tailors are taught the traditions of their profession.

Folkways (habits which lack binding force)

Because of uniform interests and traditions uniform habits grow up
in the life of a people. In certain circles, under certain circumstances, it
is usual to celebrate Christmas with a Christmas tree and gifts; to eat at
set hours; to dance at the local inn on Saturday night; to get engaged
before being married; to wear a wedding ring; to serve mustard with
boiled cod; to have children baptized and confirmed. These patterns,

---

[34] H. L. A. Hart, *The Concept of Law* (1961), pp. 54–56. [And see *ante*, 169.]

without changing their substance, may become customs of a normative
character merely by being deeply established.

These three and perhaps other classes of behaviour patterns are
characterized by external conformity or regularity, without being internalized, that is, without being experienced as binding. This much, I
believe, commonly agreed. But agreement comes to an end when the
question is raised of what is meant by calling a pattern of behaviour
' binding '.[35] Two answers have commonly been given. Some writers have
attached importance to the condition that the rule of action is experienced internally as *valid* (' binding ' means arousing a feeling of obligation). Others have regarded as the decisive feature the external fact
that violation of a rule is regularly met by a reaction (sanction) on the
part of other members of society, the individual agent feeling himself
in a position of coercion: either he follows the rule, or runs the serious
risk of being exposed to punishment of some kind (' binding ' means
' *coercing* ').

On the former account, the criterion of a pattern of behaviour's
having binding force lies in mental experiences and reactions either of the
agent himself or of a spectator. A person who is in situation *s* (that is, a
situation in which behaviour *b* is expected, in accordance with the
supposed pattern) feels a special prompting or impulse to act according
to the pattern. This impulse does not appear as a manifestation of his
needs and interests; it may, indeed, conflict with these. Even though
there exist no external hindrances to acting in violation of the pattern,
and although his interests prompt him to act differently, the agent, under
the influence of this impulse, does not feel free to do so. He feels himself
to be subject to a peculiar kind of ' compulsion ', but not a compulsion in
the usual sense of a pressure stemming from the threat of sanctions—a
threat of having inflicted on him some evil, which provides an incentive
to act based on his interests and fears. The ' compulsion ' that constitutes
' binding force ' resembles the compulsion which arises out of the
threat of sanctions in so far as the agent does not feel free, but rather
feels under pressure to act in a way which conflicts with the way he
would *like* to act. But it differs from external compulsion in that the
impulse which prevents him from following his desires is not itself
experienced as a manifestation of any need or interest; that is, it is not
rooted in the fear of some evil or the desire for some good. For this
reason, the compelling impulse has a stamp of unintelligibility and
mystery, as if it did not arise from his own nature but was a dictate
coming to him from outside.

This peculiar experience of being bound is manifested verbally in
deontic words and phrases. Asked why he is acting against his own
interest the agent will give answers such as ' because it is my *duty* to
do so ', ' because it is the *right* thing to do ', ' because I *ought* to do it
whether I like it or not '. . . .

What the agent experiences immediately, a witness may experience
by imagining himself in the agent's place. For him the impulse manifests
itself as the *expectation* that the pattern in question will be followed.
This ' expectation ' is not, however, theoretical (like that expressed in
' rain is to be expected later in the day ') but constitutes a *demand* (a

---

[35] [*Cf.* Olivecrona, *ante*, 521.]

deontic term).[36] It shows itself verbally as an expression of *approval* or *disapproval* according to whether the demand is satisfied: he did *right*, or *wrong*, he *ought* not to have acted in that way. Verbal reactions of disapproval are often accompanied by adverse feelings, ranging from cool reserve to anger and indignation; and these emotions may be so strong that they lead to acts of violence, such as lynching. Although reactions of this kind are, we may suppose, produced mainly by the violation of the interests of the one who reacts, they may also be disinterested and caused by pure moral indignation. It is another question whether moral indignation can always be assumed to conceal hidden motives of self-interest (e.g., envy).[37]

I shall call any experience of obligation, rightness, wrongness, approval, or disapproval, the *experience of validity*. It must be made clear that this term designates certain psychological phenomena; 'validity' is nothing but the peculiar characteristic of these experiences. When I speak of the 'experience of validity', then, I am not referring to a recognition of 'validity' in the sense . . . of a property inherent in moral principles, which cognitivists claim to exist and non-cognitivists deny. But it is not accidental that the word 'validity' is used to characterize these psychological experiences; for it is just the false interpretation of these experiences which has given rise to the idea of an objective quality of validity accessible to cognition.

According to the rival account of the 'binding' character of a behaviour pattern, what distinguishes a binding norm from non-binding conformity, or internal regularity from external conformity, is a set of observable facts: if the pattern of behaviour is violated, there regularly follows a reaction on the part of the society. This reaction comes either from individuals acting spontaneously or from the institutionalized organs of society created for this purpose (the police, the courts, and executive authorities). This is Geiger's view. According to him, as we have seen, $s \to b$ expresses an existing norm if the pattern $s_1 \to r$ is regularly followed, where s_1 stands for s & $\sim b$ ($s \to b$ is violated) and r signifies a reaction which has the character of a sanction. A norm exists, on this view, if compliance with its directed pattern of behaviour is guaranteed by *threat of coercion*. The experience of the norm as 'binding' is the internal reflection of this external fact.[38]

To some extent the two views lead to the same results. For the emotional and perhaps physical reactions of disapproval will in themselves constitute a sanction. The crucial question must then be one of approach: can the existence of a system of sanctions and, hence, of a normative system, be discovered merely by external observation of behaviour?

The answer is that it cannot. Not any disagreeable reaction is a sanction. The notion of a sanction is intimately connected with the feeling of disapproval. A merely external record of behaviour must lead

---

36 [*Cf.* Bentham, *ante*, 158.]

37 Cf. Svend Ranulf, *The Jealousy of the Gods and Criminal Law at Athens*, vol. I-II (1933–4); *Moral Indignation and Middle Class Psychology* (1938).

38 'That a norm is binding means: it is probable that either people comply with it or that violation of it calls forth an adverse reaction'. Theodor Geiger, *Vorstudien zu einer Soziologie des Rechts* (1947), p. 165, cf. pp. 26, 32 ff., 47, 157 *et seq.*

to unacceptable results, by abstracting from the meaning of the reaction and its mental background. A person who earns a certain income is regularly met with the requirement to pay a certain sum to the Inland Revenue. Why do we not interpret this demand as a sanction (a fine) which shows the existence of a norm forbidding the earning of such an income?[39] Why are customs duties not considered to be sanctions against imports, or the coercive measures taken with regard to the insane interpreted as sanctions against becoming insane? These and similar questions are not answerable on behaviouristic premisses; and this proves that a behaviouristic account of what it is for a norm to exist cannot be sustained.

The inadequacy of the account is especially obvious in the case of legal norms. Since legal sanctions are applied according to the decisions of the courts, the existence of a legal norm would have to be derived from an observed regularity in court decisions. But external observation is not sufficient for establishing such a regularity. For a long period of time a judge may display a certain typical reaction; he may, for example, regularly impose penalties for criminal abortion. But the pattern of reaction may change suddenly, if a new law has been passed. Nor can regularity be ascertained by recourse to the observation of a more general pattern of behaviour, viz., ' obeying the legislator '. For it is not possible, from the observation of behaviour alone, to identify the ' legislator ' who is being obeyed. External observation alone might lead us to believe that it is certain individuals who are obeyed, that is, those persons named as members of the legislature. But one day there is a general election and the composition of the legislature changes. And so we go on, perhaps right up to the constitution; but even the constitution may be changed. A behaviourist interpretation, then achieves nothing. For the *change* in the judge's behaviour can be understood and predicted only by taking into account ideological facts, that is, only by assuming the existence of those feelings of validity, or ideology, which motivate the judge's decisions. Only on the hypothesis of the allegiance which the judge feels toward the constitution, its institutions and the traditionally recognized sources of law, is it possible to interpret changing judicial reactions as a coherent whole—as regularities constituted by an ideology. . . .[40]

The future behaviour of the courts, as we have seen, cannot be

[39] [Cf. *ante*, 276.]

[40] [The argument of Ross that the validity of a legal norm is to be construed in purely factual terms as referring solely to the probability of some factual consequence, may be open to the following objection. If, for example, one takes the concept implied in the word " punishable," Ross argues that this can only be explained in terms of a probability of a person being punished in the event of certain conduct occurring, in accordance with established legal procedures. But surely the notion of " punishability," refers not so much to the probability of a person being effectively punished, but to the existence of a norm which prescribes punishment in relation to a given act. For instance, under the Motor Insurers' Bureau Agreement with the Ministry of Transport, a person injured in a traffic accident who has an unsatisfied judgment against the driver, can enforce that judgment against the Bureau. It would seem, however, that this liability, though almost invariably accepted, is not one of fixed law (see *Fire Insurance Ltd.* v. *Greene* [1964] 3 W.L.R. 319) yet on Ross's theory, we are still obliged to treat it as a legal norm. *Cf.* U. Scarpelli, *Contributo alla Semantica del Linguaggo Normativo* (1959), pp. 87–88.]

predicted on the basis of past decisions alone. Judicial regularity is not external, habitual and static, but rather internal, ideological and dynamic.

There is another reason why the sanction theory will not do. As we have seen, according to that theory, the criterion for the existence of the norm $s \to b$ is that the pattern $s_1 \to r$ is regularly followed. But in this case, what kind of regularity is it supposed to be? Does the formula $s_1 \to r$ itself signify a mere habit without binding force, or a pattern of behaviour which itself has a normative character? The latter must be the case: People are *expected* to disapprove of contraventions of a norm. That $s_1 \to r$ is binding is especially obvious when r is taken to be the reaction of the courts to violations of legal norms. Geiger agrees with this. If, however, $s_1 \to r$ is itself a norm, that is, a pattern of behaviour which is binding, then the theory entails the existence of a third norm, $s_2 \to r$ according to which sanctions are to be applied against whoever violates the second norm $(s_1 \to r)$ which itself demands the application of sanctions against whoever violates the first norm $(s \to b)$—and so *ad infinitum*. Any norm requires as its basis an infinite chain of norms. A pattern of behaviour is said to be a norm, to be binding, only if it is backed up by sanctions. But the coercive measures themselves are taken in accordance with norms which have also to be backed up by sanctions applied in accordance with norms—and so on to infinity. A model which thus implies an infinite regress cannot be adequate as a description of reality.

I have dwelt at length on Geiger's theory of sanctions, because we have to understand why it is unsound before we can see what social facts are referred to when we speak of the existence of a legal norm, or its being in force. The opinion is widely held that what constitutes the existence of a legal norm is the fact of the physical power behind the law, a power that will be exercised against offenders by the police, the courts and executive agencies. It is said that the law consists of rules which will be maintained, if the need arises, by means of physically coercive force—the use of violence. On this view, a law like the one which requires a buyer to pay the stipulated price depends in turn upon another rule which requires coercive sanctions to be used against the buyer who refuses to comply voluntarily. What is the nature of these secondary sanction-demanding norms? If it is said that they are themselves legal rules we land in the infinite regress mentioned already: secondary rules presuppose third level rules which presuppose fourth level rules, etc.[41] If it is said, on the other hand, that the secondary rules are not themselves legal rules, we have on our hands the paradox that the rules which govern the judge's exercise of his office are not legal rules. In addition to these complications, the theory has the unfortunate consequence that large parts of what is normally considered the law are denied to be of a legal nature and are excluded from the province of the law. For it is a fact that there can be no enforcement of much of constitutional law, administrative law, and procedural law, in so far as these concern the competence and obligations of the highest organs of the state. Such is the case especially where there exists no judicial review of legislation.[42]

These complications and unacceptable consequences disappear, if we

41 [Cf. Bentham, *ante*, 157 and see comment in note 51, p. 268.]
42 *On Law and Justice*, pp. 52 *et seq.*

take the position that legal rules are not rules *maintained by* the exercise of coercion but rules *about* its exercise; they are rules which are in general not enforced but followed voluntarily, that is, in virtue of the feeling of validity which endows the rules with binding force. Legal rules are directed at those in authority, the organs of the state, and their source of effectiveness is the allegiance of officials toward the constitution and the institutions derived from it, together with the non-violent sanctions of disapproval and criticism which are implied in this attitude. Legal rules govern the structure and functioning of the legal machinery. By ' legal machinery ' I mean the whole set of institutions and agencies through which the *actes juridiques* and the factual actions we ascribe to the state are undertaken. It includes the legislature, the courts, and the administrative apparatus, to which belong the agencies of enforcement (especially the police and the military). To know these rules is to know everything about the existence and content of the law. For example, if one knows that the courts are directed by these laws to imprison whoever is guilty of manslaughter, then, since imprisonment is a reaction of disapproval and, consequently, a sanction, one knows that it is forbidden to commit manslaughter. This last norm is implied in the first one directed to the courts; logically therefore, it has no independent existence. The upshot is that, in describing a legal order, there is no need to employ a double set of norms, one demanding of citizens a certain type of behaviour (e.g. not to commit manslaughter), and the other prescribing for the agencies of the legal machinery under what conditions coercive sanctions are to be applied (e.g., if manslaughter has been committed). At times, those drafting statutes employ the device of formulating a legal rule as a directive to the courts, leaving it to the citizen to infer what conduct is required of him. The criminal code is drawn in exactly this way. Nowhere is it stated in so many words that manslaughter is prohibited. The prescription against this and other crimes is, rather, inferred from the appropriate rules of the criminal code which are directed to the judge. The Danish Criminal Code, section 237, thus simply states that ' he who kills another man shall be sentenced for manslaughter to imprisonment from 5 years and into lifetime '. More commonly, however, another device is employed. *Primary* rules (or substantive law) state how citizens are obliged to behave. It is impossible to infer from these rules alone how a judge is to decide in the case of a violation. According to the circumstances of the case, the judge may specify as a sentence some punishment (whose kind and severity is left unspecified by the primary law), or enjoin some performance or payment for damages. For this reason a set of *secondary* rules (the law of sanctions) is required to specify what sanctions may be exacted of those who violate the substantive law, and to make more precise the conditions under which various sanctions may be applied. Such rules are directed to the judge, instructing him how to decide different types of case. They are often expressed in terms of the *legal effects* that arise out of violations of substantive law; for example, when it is said that the legal effect of overdue delivery is to give the buyer a right to claim damages. This rule in fact amounts to a directive to the judge, requiring him to hold for the plaintiff when he sues in appropriate circumstances.

Are we to conclude from this that there are two sets of legal norms, one addressed to the citizens stating their obligations, and another addressed to judges, directing them to decide certain cases in certain ways?

From a logical point of view, we must answer in the negative: there exists only one set of rules, namely, the so called 'secondary' rules which prescribe how cases are to be decided, which, that is, basically prescribe the conditions under which violent coercion is to be exercised. For we have seen that primary norms, logically speaking, contain nothing not already implied in secondary norms, whereas the converse does not hold.[43]

From a psychological point of view, however, there do exist two sets of norms. Rules addressed to citizens are felt psychologically to be independent entities which are grounds for the reactions of the authorities. If we apply our definition of the existence of a norm, primary rules must be recognized as actually existing norms, in so far as they are followed with regularity and experienced as being binding. It is immaterial to the question of the existence of these rules that they are, in addition, sanctioned by the threat of coercion and consequently obeyed from mixed motives, both interested (fear of sanctions) and disinterested (respect for law and order). Confusion on this point might lead to the mistaken objection that our logical thesis that there exists only one set of norms implies that the law is obeyed solely from fear of sanctions.[44]

[pp. 82–92]

A. ROSS

Tû-tû

(1956) [45]

... We find the following phrases, for example, in legal language as used in statutes and the administration of justice:

1. *If a loan is granted, there comes into being a claim;*
2. *If a claim exists, then payment shall be made on the day it falls due,*

which is only a roundabout way of saying:

3. *If a loan is granted, then payment shall be made on the day it falls due.*

That "claim" mentioned in (1) and (2), but not in (3), is obviously, like "*tû-tû*", not a real thing; it is nothing at all, merely a word, an empty word devoid of all semantic reference. Similarly, our assertion to the effect that the borrower becomes "pledged" corresponds to the allegorical tribe's assertion that the person who kills totem animals becomes "*tû-tû*".[46]

We too, then, express ourselves as though something had come into being between the conditioning fact (juristic fact) and the conditioned legal consequence, namely, a claim, a right, which like an intervening vehicle or causal connecting link promotes an effect or provides the basis

---

[43] *Op. cit.*, pp. 45–46, *cf.* pp. 66–69.

[44] *Op. cit.*, pp. 68 *et seq.*

[45] [From *Scandinavian Studies In Law* (1956), Vol. 1, p. 139, also in 70 Harv.L.R. 812.]

[46] [Earlier in this article Ross has explained that amongst the Noisulli Islanders the belief is held that (*inter alia*) if a man encounters his mother-in-law he is "Tu-Tu" and if he does not undergo purification a terrible calamity will befall the whole community.]

for a legal consequence. Nor, really, can we wholly deny that this terminology is associated for us with more or less indefinite ideas that a right is a power of an incorporeal nature, a kind of inner, invisible dominion over the object of the right, a power manifested in, but nevertheless different from, the exercise of force (judgement and execution) by means of which the factual and apparent use and enjoyment of the rights is effectuated.

In this way, it must be admitted, our terminology and our ideas bear a considerable structural resemblance to primitive magic thought concerning the invocation of supernatural powers which in their turn are converted into factual effects. Nor can we deny the possibility that this resemblance is in reality rooted in a tradition, which, bound up with language and its power over thought, is an age-old legacy from the infancy of our civilization.[47] But after these admissions have been made, there still remains the important question, whether sound, rational grounds may be adduced in favour of the retention of a " *tû-tû* " presentation of legal rules, i.e. a form of circumlocution in which between the juristic fact and the legal consequence there are inserted imaginary rights. If this question is to be answered in the affirmative, the ban on the mention of rights must be lifted. Now I do maintain that this question must be answered in the affirmative, and shall proceed to show why, taking as my point of departure the concept of ownership.

The legal rules concerning ownership could, without doubt, be expressed without the use of this term. In that case a large number of rules would have to be formulated, directly linking the individual legal consequences to the individual legal facts. For example:

> if a person has lawfully acquired a thing by purchase, judgement for recovery shall be given in favour of the purchaser against other persons retaining the thing in their possession;
>
> if a person has inherited a thing, judgement for damages shall be given in favour of the heir against other persons who culpably damage the thing;
>
> if a person by prescription has acquired a thing and raised a loan that is not repaid at the proper time, the creditor shall be given judgement for satisfaction out of the thing;
>
> if a person has occupied a *res nullius* and by legacy bequeathed it to another person, judgement shall be given in favour of the legatee against the testator's estate for the surrender of the thing;
>
> if a person has acquired a thing by means of execution as a creditor and the object is subsequently appropriated by another person, the latter shall be punished for theft,

and so on, bearing in mind, of course, that in each case the formula might be far more complicated.

An account along these lines, would however, be so unwieldy as to be practically worthless. It is the task of legal thinking to conceptualize the legal rules in such a way that they are reduced to systematic order

---

[47] In his book *Der römische Obligationsbegriff* (1927), vol. I, Axel Hägerström has cited weighty arguments in support of the magical origin of Roman legal conceptions. Modern research in sociology and history of religion also points in the same direction; see in this connection, Alf Ross, *Towards a Realistic Jurisprudence* (1946), Chap. IX, pp. 2–5, and *Max Weber on Law in Economy and Society* ed. by Max Rheinstein (1954), p. 106. [And see ante, 499.]

and by this means to give account of the law in force which is as plain and convenient as possible. This can be achieved with the aid of the following technique of presentation.

On looking at a large number of legal rules on the lines indicated it will be found that it is possible to select from among them a certain group that can be arranged in the following way:

$$
\begin{array}{llll}
F_1\!\!-\!\!C_1 & F_2\!\!-\!\!C_1 & F_3\!\!-\!\!C_1 \ldots F_p\!\!-\!\!C_1 \\
F_1\!\!-\!\!C_2 & F_2\!\!-\!\!C_2 & F_3\!\!-\!\!C_2 \ldots F_p\!\!-\!\!C_2 \\
F_1\!\!-\!\!C_3 & F_2\!\!-\!\!C_3 & F_3\!\!-\!\!C_3 \ldots F_p\!\!-\!\!C_3 \\
\quad . & \quad . & \quad . \\
\quad . & \quad . & \quad . \\
F_1\!\!-\!\!C_n & F_2\!\!-\!\!C_n & F_3\!\!-\!\!C_n \ldots F_p\!\!-\!\!C_n
\end{array}
$$

(Read: the conditioning fact F_1 is connected with the legal consequence C_1 etc.) This means that each single one of a certain totality of conditioning facts $(F_1\!-\!F_p)$ is connected with each single one of a certain group of legal consequences $(C_1\!-\!C_n)$; or, that it is true of each single F that it is connected with the same group of legal consequences $(C_1 + C_2 \ldots + C_n)$, or, that a *cumulative plurality of legal consequences is connected to a disjunctive plurality of conditioning facts.*

These $n \times p$ individual legal rules can be stated more simply and more manageably in the figure:

$$
\left.\begin{array}{c} F_1 \\ F_2 \\ F_3 \\ . \\ . \\ . \\ F_p \end{array}\right\} \rightarrow O \left\{\begin{array}{c} C_1 \\ C_2 \\ C_3 \\ . \\ . \\ . \\ C_n \end{array}\right.
$$

where O (ownership) merely stands for the systematic connection that F_1 as well as $F_2, F_3 \ldots F_p$ entail the totality of legal consequences C_1, $C_2, C_3 \ldots C_n$. As a technique of presentation this is expressed then by stating in one series of rules the facts that "create ownership", and in another series the legal consequences that "ownership" entails.

It will be clear from this that the "ownership" inserted between the conditioning facts and the conditioned consequences is in reality a meaningless word—a word without any semantic reference whatever, serving solely as a tool of presentation. We talk as if "ownership" were a causal link between F and C, an effect occasioned or "created" by every F, and which in its turn is the cause of a totality of legal consequences. We say, for example, that:

(1) If A has lawfully purchased an object (F_2), ownership of the object is thereby created for him.

(2) If A is the owner of an object, he has (among other things) the right of recovery (C_1).

It is clear, however, that $(1)+(2)$ is only a rephrasing of one of the presupposed norms $(F_2\!-\!C_1)$, namely, that purchase as a conditioning fact entails the possibility of recovery as a legal consequence. The notion that between purchase and access to recovery something was

" created " that can be designated as " ownership " is nonsense. Nothing is " created " as the result of A and B exchanging a few sentences legally interpreted as " contract of purchase ". All that has occurred is that the judge will now take this fact into consideration and give judgement for the purchaser in an action for recovery. . . .[48]   [pp. 144–148]

F. CASTBERG

Problems of Legal Philosophy
(1957)

The Normative Character of Law [49]

It is common to the above-mentioned opponents of the normativistic conception of law that they all choose to regard the law quite realistically. They understand the law partly as an expression of probability, based on the factual regularity in social life, partly as a psycho-physical fact characterized, among other things, by an irrational experience of an idea of validity.

If one seriously tries to carry through the conception of law as the expression of a sociological probability (Lundstedt), it turns out that precisely what is typical of law and of legal thinking disappears. The rule of law—the legal proposition—is not a proposition stating that a certain future course of events is probable. It is not that which is its characteristic feature. And neither the judge nor the juridical theoretician can confine himself to ascertaining the ideas of validity that attach themselves to the rule, and the probability of its being enforced. Practical legal life, especially, is unthinkable without the conception of law as a binding norm. A layman, who in a certain situation asks the question of what is existing law, may perhaps content himself with trying to foresee the probable social reactions that his actions—whether he acts in one way or another—will produce. But the judge can scarcely do that. He cannot confine himself to trying to calculate the consequence for himself of his deciding the case in such or such a way. At most, it is conceivable that a calculation of the chances for a judgment to be

[48] [Ross describes words like ownership as " without meaning, *i.e.*, without any semantic reference, and serve a purpose only as a technique of presentation " (p. 149). But *cf. ante*, 56 as to this theory of meaning. Also, is it possible within the context of a legal system to eliminate a corporation by reducing it to a set of rules relating to individuals? This is something like the well-known and ineffectual " bracket-theory." That a corporation has rights and duties distinct from those of individuals is a perfectly meaningful assertion in law. Nor, it should be noted, does this entail the existence *de facto*, of a corporate " entity." Ross's view that legal concepts have no semantic reference is also less tenable when one gives the notion of semantic reference a rather wider ambit. For instance if we say that Jones is the owner of that motor-car, does this not have a semantic reference in the fact that it will normally be associated with certain attitudes and behaviour both of Jones himself in relation to the motor-car, and also to attitudes and behaviour of other persons in relation to that article? (*Cf.* U. Scarpelli, *op. cit.*, p. 91). For further criticisms, see A. W. B. Simpson, " The Analysis of Legal Concepts," in (1964) 80 L.Q.R. 534.]

[49] [It should not be thought that all Scandinavian jurists are associated with the realist viewpoint. What follows is an attack on the anti-normative view of law, by a Norwegian writer.]

affirmed in a higher instance, be made the basis of a decision in the lower instance. But in any case, a court which itself passes judgment in the last instance cannot resort to such a calculation.

In reality, of course, one does not reason in that way at all, when legal questions are to be decided. Legal thinking does not consist of an examination of more or less probable motivation processes on the part of the persons acting in the judicial machinery. But it consists of more or less certain conclusions from ideas with normative contents. In order to comprehend these ideas—the legal norms—we certainly take our point of departure in psycho-physical realities, such as statutes, regular modes of action in connection with ideas of validity, etc. But the norms are not identical with any single psychic or physical reality of this kind. Solely by means of mental operations which have the character of logical [50] inferences from norms, can the " science of law " answer the question that society necessarily must put to it, namely: what is right and what is wrong in the endless number of conflicts which are provoked by all social life.

One may call this view of the law and of legal thinking metaphysical. I doubt if that is correct. But even if it were,—if the notions of " norm," " legal duty " and " validity " really must be regarded as metaphysical notions, it would be a mistaken " realism " to try to eliminate these notions from juridical thinking. For without these notions, all juridical thinking is impossible. That is something which the legal and philosophical examination of the notions cannot avoid ascertaining. . . .

The fact that normative statements can be correct or incorrect and form the foundations for logical operations is a necessary assumption for all the cultural life of human beings. This assumption is here just as fundamentally necessary as is, in theoretical understanding, the assumption that our statements about reality can be true or false and that they can form the foundation for inferences according to the laws of logic.[51]   [pp. 31–33]

---

50 [For the nature of these so-called " logical " inferences, see *post*, 730.]
51 [Normative propositions are part of our language with a logic of their own; as such they are related to actual human conduct just as much as, though in a different way from, factual propositions.]

9

HISTORICAL AND ANTHROPOLOGICAL JURISPRUDENCE

THE ROMANTIC REACTION

Two principal movements emerged as a reaction to the natural law thinking of the eighteenth century. One was the school of legal positivism which has already been discussed [1]; the other, by way of contrast, relied upon a mystic sense of unity and organic growth in human affairs. The Romantic Movement was itself part of an ample surge of the human mind against the classical and rationalistic standards of the eighteenth century in favour of feeling and imagination, and this impact was naturally felt especially in the realm of art and literature. Its influence in the sphere of thought was, however, equally pervasive. The impulses stirring in both fields emerged strikingly in the figure of Rousseau, whose romantic writings revealed not only a new literary style but also a belief in the mysterious entity of the collective will.[2] An even profounder attachment to the organic roots of society was evinced by Edmund Burke, who, by emphasising the national foundations of the mysterious forces which move society, gave the organic approach its link with nationalism that became so prominent a feature during the nineteenth century.

HEGEL AND SAVIGNY

But it was in Germany that this new movement was to find the most fertile soil. The Germans have been described as "the people of the romantic counter-revolution against the rationalism of the Enlightenment—of . . . the mystical uprising against intellectual clarity." [3] To one of the main apostles of this development, Hegel, brief reference only can be made.[4] It suffices here to say that his doctrine of the state as a living organism, an end-in-itself, whose constitution is determined by the political consciousness of the People (*Volk*),[5] and

---

[1] *Ante*, 153.
[2] Cf. *ante*, 182.
[3] E. Heller, *The Ironic German* (1958), pp. 156–157. See also P. Geyl, *Debates with Historians*, pp. 4–8.
[4] On Hegel, see *post*, 630. Savigny was also much influenced by Hugo and Schelling.
[5] "No doubt, this strange *Volk* [*i.e.*, the German], which has haunted the souls of its sons with the uncontrollable persistence of a ghost, has denied itself the 'present' not only for the sake of its 'becoming' and its messianic future, but also in its archaic faithfulness to the mythological past": E. Heller, *ibid*.

whose destiny lies in the hands of History, conceived as a mysterious teleological force, was allied to a fervent Teutonic nationalism,[6] which set its stamp on the organic theory of law and the state. It was this nationalistic organic view of legal development which provided the climate of thought for the historical school as developed by Savigny.[7] Not much in the way of genuine historical perspective could be discerned in the writings of Rousseau, with his imaginary speculations on the noble savage [8] and the original state of nature and the social contract, any more than in Hegel, with his faith in a mystical World-Spirit marching inexorably towards Germanic supremacy. If the roots of a more truly historical attitude are to be traced, these will be found rather in the earlier writings of Vico and Montesquieu.

THE *Volksgeist*

Savigny, however, sought to link a genuine and serious study of the course of development of Roman law from ancient times up till its existing state as the foundation of the civil law of contemporary Europe, with a belief in the organic nature of law as a product of the spirit (*Volksgeist*) [9] of a particular People (or perhaps nation or race, for the German word *Volk* is characteristically ambiguous). This led him to regard custom as the fundamental and natural form of law, and to view schemes of codification with hostility,[10] and even to treat legislation itself with considerable reserve, unless sufficiently rooted in the popular consciousness. His views on these and kindred matters can best be studied in the extracts from one of his principal works which are quoted hereafter.[11] It will suffice here to draw attention

---

[6] For Hegel history involved the unfolding of the idea of freedom. In the early oriental empires only the despot was free; under Rome, there was freedom for some but not for all; only in the modern Germanic state (whose epitome was, curiously enough, that of Prussia) would the freedom of *all* be realised. See Hegel, *Philosophy of History.*

[7] See H. Kantorowicz, " Savigny and the Historical School of Law," (1937) 53 L.Q.R. 326.

[8] Of Rousseau's noble savage Burrow has written: " [it] has very much the air of a rococo toy, part of the furniture of a *fête champêtre*, rather than of a tool of social understanding " (*Evolution and Society*, p. 5).

[9] This term was introduced by Puchta, whose name must be coupled with Savigny as one of the founders of the historical school.

[10] Curiously enough, Hegel himself believed in codes and was unsympathetic to the historical school of Savigny. See Hegel, *Philosophy of Right* (transl. T. M. Knox), pp. 135–136, 357–358; and *cf.* Vinogradoff, *Outlines of Historical Jurisprudence,* I, 128. Savigny's hostility was qualified rather than absolute. He believed, as against Thibaut, that attempts to codify were premature, and would be an obstacle to the natural development of law through the *Volksgeist*. But codification would be a proper course of action when experts (jurists, historians, linguists, and, perhaps, judges) discovered, and were able to announce, *that* law which resided in the collective consciousness. Codification *was* then desirable. Savigny, it should be noted, was the Prussian Minister of Legislation.

[11] *Post,* 576.

to certain difficulties which seem never to have been adequately faced by the protagonists of this movement, and then to refer to later developments in the approach to the nature and function of customary law.

What is Meant by a " People " ?

The writers of this persuasion seem to assume that every " People " is in some way an identifiable entity, with a corporate conviction or will of its own. This approach later crystallised in Gierke's theory of the " real " personality of corporate bodies, and his desire to establish the superiority of Germanic law, as against Roman law, in countenancing this view.[12] We are thus, in the first place, required to accept that collective groups possess some kind of metaphysical personality distinct from the members comprised in the group, a view which recalls the old fallacy that words are names of " things," and that there must be a distinct entity denoted by every word.[13] But, more than this, it is implied that the notion of a " people " is a perfectly definite one that can be applied to specific groups which possess this mysterious collective consciousness. This appears to postulate a degree of unity of thought and action in particular nations, races, or the inhabitants of political units, of which there is little evidence in human history.[14] And it seems to ignore the role and effects of conquest by war; the position of enslaved and servile populations; and the control of nations and empires by ruling minorities, and the manner in which these latter may impose new patterns on their subjects (whether in the spirit of a " creative minority " in Toynbee's sense,[15] or of a " power *élite* " in that of Professor C. W. Mills [16] is immaterial). Nor does this theory deal adequately with the introduction of alien law and custom by peaceful penetration, as in the case of a Western code being adopted in such a country as modern Japan. Savigny was much exercised by the remarkable phenomenon of the so-called " Reception of Roman Law " into Germany in the sixteenth century, which he regarded as " the greatest and most remarkable action of a common customary law in the beginning of the modern age." [17] His explanation of this, however, as having been adopted into the popular consciousness of the German People is hardly convincing, and is

---

[12] See his celebrated *Das deutsche Genossenschaftsrecht, passim.*
[13] Cf. *ante,* 56. And see Lloyd, *Unincorporated Associations* (1938), Chap. 1.
[14] See also the point made by Stone (*Social Dimensions,* pp. 162–163) that the consciousness of people can no longer be regarded as an inviolable inner spirit since it is a prey to mass-suggestion by propaganda and mass media, and these are usually concentrated in an élite.
[15] See *A Study of History,* Vol. III, pp. 239 *et seq.* and Vol. XII, p. 305.
[16] See C. Wright Mills, *The Power Elite* (1956). More generally see T. B. Bottomore, *Elites and Society* (1964). See also the Marxist view of society, *post,* 632.
[17] *System of Modern Roman Law* (transl. W. Holloway), p. 63.

really little more than a legal fiction.[18] That "to probe the spirit of the German *Volk* Savigny went straight back to Roman law" is perhaps the strangest of paradoxes in Savigny's thought.[19]

LEGISLATION AND *Juristenrecht*

It must be admitted that the historical school had at least, if in a most confusing manner, grasped the important truth that law is not an abstract set of rules simply imposed on society, but is an integral part of that society, having deep roots in the social and economic habits and attitudes of its past and present members. Moreover, equally acceptable is the view that judges and lawyers generally, as forming part of the society in which they live and have their being, reflect many, if not all, the basic habits and attitudes of their society, so that the development of the law, so far as it rests in their hands, will probably conform in a broad and general way to the patterns of behaviour which are widely approved or at least accepted in that society. But this is far from saying that the judge, in reaching a decision or framing a rule, is acting as a mere organ of the people's consciousness. A great deal of law, for one thing, is highly technical, and a legal profession, like any other compact body, develops an impetus of its own which may lead it in many directions, and by no means only in that one which would be approved or even understood by the popular consciousness. " Could it be pretended (remarks Sir Carleton Allen) that a pious faith in the sanctity of seisin burns in the bosom of the Commonwealth suffusing all its members with a healthy glow? "[20] Again, the judge, though he may be representative of his country and age, nevertheless has a creative function in developing the law, which cannot be exercised by merely imagining how society as a whole would decide the question before him, even assuming society is capable of forming any view at all.[21] And to assert that in some inexplicable and metaphysical manner the judge's thought somehow " connects " on each occasion with the People's mind is the merest subterfuge. Even Savigny recognises that owing to the complexity of developed law the precise details of decisions are a specifically juristic task beyond the scope of the popular consciousness. But the gap is not bridged by simply postulating an automatic correlation between

---

18 But *cf.* the interesting modern example of the reception of the common law into Nigeria: see A. N. Allott, in " Nigerian Law, Some Recent Developments," I.C.L.Q. (1965), Supp.Pub. No. 10, p. 31 and Allott, *Essays in African Law* (1969).

19 See Dawson, *The Oracles of the Law* (1968), pp. 451–452.

20 *Law in the Making*, 7th ed., p. 114.

21 Cf. Lloyd, *Public Policy* (1953), Chap. 7. Judges do, however, fashion such concepts as that of the " reasonable man " to create the appearance that they are deciding cases in accordance with common morality. See, on this, Atiyah, *Accidents, Compensation the Law* (1970), pp. 96–99.

lawyers' law and popular consciousness (or perhaps one should say, in more modern phraseology, *sub*-consciousness). Nor can this be laid down even as a *desideratum*, for on many issues public opinion may be non-existent, hopelessly divided or unascertainable, and on some matters at least the judge must be expected to set a higher standard than one which is in fact observed or accepted by the mass of the community.[22] This is to say nothing of the view, already discussed, that law is itself the moulder of custom rather than the reverse.[23]

As for legislation, Savigny seemed greatly to underrate its significance for modern society.[24] A progressive society, as Maine later pointed out, has to keep adapting the law to fresh social and economic conditions,[25] and legislation has proved in modern times the essential means of attaining this end, however imperfectly. And with this objective, those who exercise the legislative authority have frequently while paying heed if not lip-service to public opinion, to provide a lead in many directions where the public is confused or undecided, and even in some cases where there may be widespread hostility to a proposed reform.[26] Certainly if the legislator had been obliged to wait upon the public mind to give clear guidance as to each future step, the history of law reform during the last century would have been deprived of many of its most signal achievements.

SIR HENRY MAINE

In England the historical approach, divested of its mystical adherence to the *Volksgeist*, made important advances in the pioneering hands of Sir Henry Maine.[27] Maine opposed to rationalising theories of natural law and the utilitarian schools,[28] a serious endeavour to study

---

[22] Lloyd, *Public Policy, op. cit.*, pp. 126–127.

[23] Savigny admitted it was impossible to avoid some statutory legislation, but said this should only be when " higher political progress " demanded a change in the law, or to resolve doubts, or where a positive provision is required (*e.g.*, the period for prescription).   [24] *Ante*, 510.

[25] *Post*, 836. Maine did not admire judicial legislation in English law, and favoured codification. But he was essentially an " evolutionist."

[26] Cf. the controversy regarding the recommendations of the Wolfenden Committee on *Prostitution and Homosexuality* (1957), Cmnd. 247, and its subsequent implementation in the Sexual Offences Act 1967, or that surrounding the passing of the two Race Relations Acts, on which see Lester and Bindman, *Race and Law* (1972), Chap. 3.

[27] Maine's background, life and some of his ideas are traced in a new biography by George Feaver, *From Status to Contract* (1969). An appraisal of Maine, in the context of Victorian evolutionary sociology has recently been made by J. W. Burrow, *Evolution and Society* (1966), reprinted with a new preface in 1970 (Chap. 5 is devoted to Maine).

[28] Maine was not, however, opposed to the principles of Utilitarianism, merely its exposition in the writings of Bentham and Mill. He was opposed to their deductive method, their lack of scientific analysis. His opposition to natural law and, more significantly its social contract manifestations, was based on what he regarded as their unhistorical nature. See, further, Burrow, *op. cit.*, p. 28.

the nature and development of early law both in its actual historical context, and also as illuminated by the study of undeveloped societies in the contemporary world. In practice this meant for Maine principally the early law of Greece, Rome and the Old Testament, supplemented by the native law of India. Insufficient research into these, as well as a failure to distinguish clearly between different stages in the development of early law and custom, led Maine into some intuitive generalisations, which though brilliantly formulated and expounded, find little support among present-day legal historians and anthropologists. This applies particularly to his notion of early law passing through three consecutive phases of royal judgments, aristocracies as repositories of custom, and finally an Age of Codes.[29]

The Idea of Custom

In the nineteenth century, both students of legal history and the anthropologists who studied surviving primitive societies [30] were too ready to assume that law and custom were really quite distinct conceptions, the former being characteristic of more or less developed societies, the latter alone being encountered in early or tribal society. Moreover, custom was conceived as absolutely rigid, complete conformity being enforced by the overwhelming power of group sentiment, amply fortified by religion and magic.[31] In this stage of human affairs it was thought impossible to differentiate between legal, moral, or religious rules, since all these were completely interwoven into a single texture of customary behaviour.[32]

Malinowski

With the twentieth century came a great increase in field research among tribal peoples and a more profound understanding of the working of customary rules in an undeveloped society. This has led to a consensus of informed opinion that tribal peoples do possess a system of law in a genuine sense,[33] that this system, which varies

---

29 See *post*, 581. See also the point made by Burrow (*op. cit.*, p. 178) that Maine's "method of comparative philology proved a blind alley; historical explanation continued to do duty to analytic ones, while Maine's emphasis on common racial origins narrowed his horizon without validating his method." Maine's reasons for investigating India, but not other undeveloped societies was common Aryan origins of its peoples and of those of Europe.

30 The tendency today is to refer to such societies more neutrally, as, for example, "tribal" or "stateless" or "segmentary lineage" societies. "Tribal" or "stateless" will be used normally in this chapter, and throughout the book, but "primitive law" and "primitive societies" will be retained where the reference is to classical anthropology, where this terminology was consistently used. *Cf.*, *e.g.*, the terminology used by Maine and Malinowski with that used by Gluckman or Bohannan.

31 See such writers as Durkheim, Hobhouse and Frazer.

32 Maine, *Ancient Law*, Chap. 1. *Cf. Early Law and Custom*, p. 5.

33 *Cf. ante*, 41.

greatly among different peoples and at different stages of development, is both flexible and capable of developing, and that breaches of the law may occur frequently and are attended by more or less established sanctions. Moreover, although religion may be reckoned as one of the sources of law in tribal societies and legal rules may in some cases derive much of their authenticity from religious beliefs, it is quite possible to differentiate between the religious and secular rules of a stateless society.[34]

Though, not always, as comes out in an account given by the notable contemporary social anthropologist, Max Gluckman. He shows that the Barotse *Kuta*, in judging the whole man, delves into the long history of the " multiplex " relations of the parties and, in doing so, may take into consideration the extent to which the parties have fulfilled or broken moral obligations, rules of etiquette, ritual prescriptions and the like. And Gluckman admits to an inability to describe the Barotse judicial process "without using the word 'law' to cover these kinds of rules and conventions, as well as the rules which the judges enforce more specifically." [35]

One of the leaders of this new approach was Malinowski, who conducted prolonged field-studies into the habits and mode of life of the Trobriand Islanders.[36] These studies led Malinowski to the view that the basis of primitive law was "reciprocity," a notion bearing some resemblance to Duguit's "social solidarity." [37] Thus, by means of a primitive "stop-list," a failure to comply with a man's economic obligation (*e.g.*, to make a customary payment), would result in the economic support of the community being withheld from the defaulter, who would thus be left helpless and alone. But it is now generally thought that Malinowski gave a too idealised picture of the Trobrianders, and exaggerated the force of reciprocity as against that of more directly coercive sanctions. Malinowski recognised that customary law was often breached in Trobriand society, but his views seemed to change at different periods as to the extent to which sanctions might be employed against defaulters.[38]

---

[34] See A. S. Diamond, *Primitive Law*, 2nd ed. Also Hoebel, *Law of Primitive Man* (1954), pp. 257–260; and Gluckman, *Judicial Process among the Barotse* (1967), pp. 264–267. The latter two writers consider Diamond goes too far in his criticism of Maine, by seeking to make a clear separation between the social phenomena of law and religion in early society. See also J. Stone, *Social Dimensions of Law and Justice*, pp. 134–135.

[35] *The Ideas of Barotse Jurisprudence*, Chap. 1, at p. 17. *Cf.* the Soviet concept of parental law, one of the features of which is also a judging of the whole man. A Soviet court too might ask " whether a particular person had behaved as a reasonable incumbent of a specified social position." *Cf.* Berman, *post*, 687.

[36] See especially, *Crime and Custom in Savage Society* (1926) and his lengthy introduction to Hogbin, *Law and Order in Polynesia* (1934).

[37] *Cf. ante*, 105.

[38] See Schapera, in ed. Firth, *Man and Culture* (1957), p. 139.

It appears that the Trobrianders are peculiar in having highly organised tribal institutions coupled with a remarkably undeveloped legal machinery for handling disputes,[39] but all the same, even among them there is a good deal of "socially approved force," [40] which Malinowski seemingly under-estimated, though he did acknowledge that the ultimate sanction of compulsion or even death might be inflicted when the life of the community was endangered. In his later writings Malinowski came down finally in favour of the view that law, even in early society, rests ultimately on coercive sanctions, though its actual working may owe much to the feeling or need for reciprocity.[41] At the present day most leading anthropologists place great emphasis on the role of sanctions in tribal society, though these may be more or less organised, and may be invoked by society itself or left to the wronged individual or group, subject only to legal regulation.[42] Radcliffe-Brown points out that the blood-feud may be strictly regulated, and that it indicates not an absence of law but of centralised government. The main object of sanctions, however, is not so much the punishment of the offender as restoring the *status quo ante,* that is, the maintenance of society as a working system, for social solidarity has been breached and must be restored.[43]

Hence, the point stressed by Bohannan,[44] among others, that litigants must concur in the settlement suggested by the elders if the case is to be considered thoroughly successful, a goal which contemporary Soviet jurisprudence also puts at a premium.

---

[39] Hoebel, *op. cit.,* p. 206.   [40] Schapera, *op. cit.,* p. 154.

[41] See his *Freedom and Civilisation* (1947). As Seagle points out (*Quest for Law,* p. 34) " not all primitive peoples exchange fish for vegetables."

[42] Controlled sanctions, which partake of a régime of legality, will also be supplemented by unorganised or " diffuse " sanctions which do not involve any institutional behaviour or action by specific individuals or groups. Thus ostracism and house-burning may operate as important types of diffuse social sanctions, and even the belief in witchcraft and sorcery may have a similar effect as deterring anti-social conduct which may be thought likely to result in reprisals by witchcraft. (See J. Beattie, *Other Cultures* (1964), p. 172.) For the difficulty of establishing the received conceptual pattern of the common law in such a matter as the meaning ascribed to *mens rea,* in a society where a belief in witchcraft still remains an integral part of the outlook of a society, see R. B. Seidman, " Witchcraft and Mens Rea: A Problem of Society under Radical Society Changes," in (1965) 28 M.L.R. 46.

[43] See J. Beattie, in *New Outline of Modern Knowledge* (1956), pp. 267–269. For further comments on the character and role of sanctions and the process of enforcement in tribal societies, see Gluckman, *Politics, Law and Ritual in Tribal Society* (1965), pp. 196–198, 202–207.

[44] See *Justice and Judgment Among the Tiv* (1957). See also the point made by Gluckman in his *The Ideas of Barotse Jurisprudence* (p. 9) that a dominant value of the Lozi society, and it may well be a characteristic of tightly knit, well-integrated societies, is that " villages should not break up and that kin should remain united." A good example of this ideology is brought out by Llewellyn and Hoebel when they describe the case of Pawnee, a Cheyenne deviant who on a horse-stealing expedition is beaten and left for dead by an enforcement agency but who, on finding his way back to his camp, is welcomed, treated handsomely and rehabilitated by a tribal chief (*The Cheyenne Way* (1941), pp. 6–9).

RECENT DEVELOPMENTS IN THE STUDY OF TRIBAL LAW

At the present day more and more attention is being paid to the actual working of legal rules in particular tribal societies.[45] Thus Hoebel has sought to show how the basic jural postulates [46] (in Pound's sense) differ in different primitive societies; how these are rooted in the social, economic and environmental conditions of these societies; and how each society has a pattern of legal norms directed to maintaining a stable society in the light of those postulates. For this purpose Hoebel examines a number of specific societies in different stages of development, from the extremely primitive Eskimos to the Ashanti monarchy. The conclusion he reaches is that all societies to a greater or less extent have legal rules enforced by legally controlled sanctions (what Olivecrona would call, " rules about force," [47]), even if, in the least developed stage, these latter may do no more than control the right to inflict force without revenge or the blood-feud ensuing, so long as the proper procedure is followed. Where, however, a society is less well integrated, wrongful retaliation may in fact occur; what this means is that the law has broken down, and a blood-feud may result until the situation can be restored. Nor must we look for a " court " as the necessary mark of legal process, for though something of this kind may be found in more developed societies, in others we may have to be satisfied with some kind of " proceeding " following an established order.[48]

More recently still, one of the most interesting studies has been that of Gluckman on the judicial process among the Barotse. His conclusion, based on a detailed study of cases, is that this judicial process corresponds with more than it differs from the judicial process in Western society,[49] though it must be admitted that he is here dealing with a society which is sufficiently developed to possess what are in effect established judicial tribunals.[50] Like Hoebel, Gluckman also emphasises the flexibility of law in tribal societies, and the process by which new rules are constantly being created and old ones reinterpreted.[51]

---

[45] A useful guide to some of the work being done today is the reader by Paul Bohannan, *Law and Warfare* (1967): a particularly lucid introduction to the problems of legal anthropology is an article in that volume by Redfield (p. 3), taken from (1964) 33 U.Cinc.L.R. 1–22. See also the volume of cross-cultural case studies edited by Laura Nader, *Law in Culture and Society* (1969).

[46] For one example (the Ifugao), see *ante*, 380.

[47] *Ante*, 527.

[48] Hoebel, *op. cit., passim*, and *post*, 584.   [49] *Op. cit.*, p. 357.

[50] See, *e.g.*, F. Huxley, *Affable Savages* (1956), who describes the Urubus of Brazil as a tribe without any system of law enforcement; the only sanction is shaming into conformity, apart from supernatural retribution (see pp. 106–111, 161–162; on the blood-feud, pp. 127–128).

[51] *Ibid.*, especially Chaps. 5 and 6. In African territories where English law has been introduced, the principle was established that customary law was generally

This problem continues to exercise Gluckman and, in his latest writings,[52] he has attempted to posit what he regards as the minimum requirements of procedure to characterise a particular conflict resolution as a judicial process. He requires, for instance, the examination and assessment of evidence [53] and thus rejects such ordered proceedings as the Eskimo song-contest [54] and "drumming the scandal" among the Tiv [55] as not legal. There is a danger that, in searching for "adequate" categories, Gluckman may be guilty of cultural solipsism, of taking his Barotse, which, as already pointed out, have more contact with Western "civilisation," as the norm and rejecting as pre-legal proceedings which do not meet their standards. The pitfall is one into which Austin, of course, fell, though his study even of English law was far from empirical.

Legal anthropology has come a long way since Malinowski.[56] He defined law so diffusely that his definition became almost a definition of custom. More recent theoretical writings, as exemplified by that from Bohannan extracted below,[57] are agreed that law only exists when there are legal institutions for handling conflict. But in developed societies conflict is frequently channelled into non-legal institutions, the family or professional associations. The relationship between social and legal institutions may thus be the key. Custom, in the sense of familial obligation or a code of ethics crystallised by a profession, plays a role in developed Western societies. It plays a bigger role in tribal societies, where, according to Durkheim, consciences are uniform and strong. Law grows with societal complexity,[58] with the decline in the importance of bodies of kindred, with the growth in power of central organisation. Law has grown in England in this century as other bonds of obligation (*e.g.,* religion) and other groups of allegiance (*e.g.,* the family) have declined. What begins as "custom" becomes redefined in legal institutions and is then turned upon the social conflicts which custom cannot resolve. In many of

applicable save in so far as it was not repugnant to natural justice, equity and good conscience. (See "The Common Law in West Africa," by W. C. Akow Daniels (1964) I.C.L.Q. 574.) The principles of natural justice, however, do not mean simply the view that English law would take of a given situation, but have to be adjudged in relation to the social conditions prevailing in the territory in question: see *Dawodu* v. *Danmole* [1962] 1 W.L.R. 1053. See Gower, *Independent Africa, The Challenge to the Legal Profession*, p. 94. For a different problem of culture conflict, see *Mohammed* v. *Knott* [1969] 1 Q.B. 1.
52 See "The Ideas in Barotse Jurisprudence" (1965), *Politics, Law and Ritual in Tribal Society* (1965), and his new edition of *The Judicial Process among the Barotse*, containing a long reappraisal in the light of criticism of the book.
53 See *Politics, Law and Ritual in Tribal Society*, Chap. V.
54 See Hoebel, *The Law of Primitive Man* (1954), pp. 93–99.
55 See Bohannan, *Justice and Judgment among the Tiv* (1957), for example at pp. 142–144.
56 See Bohannan's comment on the disastrous influence of *Crime and Custom in Savage Society, post,* 621.
57 *Post,* 619.   58 *Post,* 622.

the tribal societies studied by legal anthropologists custom is sufficient for the needs of that society. It is all too easy to assume that because we need law that so must "less happy peoples." Yet too much anthropology has started from a Western framework into which the mechanics of tribal societies have been fitted. Gluckman's attempt to use the "reasonable man"[59] concept in a Barotse context is one example of this, Llewellyn and Hoebel's explanation of Cheyenne law in Western pigeon-holes[60] another. Does it really help us under-stand the legal and pre-legal processes of less developed societies to introduce a Hohfeldian pattern of jural relations as Hoebel did?[61] A more fruitful approach, it is thought, is to study simpler societies with fewer pre-conceived ideas (it would be fantasy rather than idealism to believe one could abolish them). To start with an Austinian sovereign in mind is to dismiss many societies as pre-legal, including, as Austin himself found, the international system. To expect to find a formalised sanction, or a regularised code of evidence may prove similarly stultifying. However, there is increasing recog-nition[62] that we may learn more about law in developed societies by studying its equivalent in simpler societies. Function is more import-ant than form.

CUSTOM IN DEVELOPED SYSTEMS

As law develops and becomes more complex the creative role of custom may be expected to diminish. Hence, though many basic insti-tutions of a legal system may have a customary origin this is more a matter of historical perspective than of present creative force. Yet the creative role of custom is not entirely extinguished. For apart from local custom and usages imported into contracts, it may also play a part in developing the law affecting particular sections of the community as, for instance, in regard to commercial transactions.[63] For law, if it is to be progressive, must in such cases seek to mould itself on the framework of customary practices and expectations. In this sense the view of Savigny contains important insights, which were later developed more fruitfully by sociological writers such as Ehrlich.[64]

[59] See *post*, 595.
[60] See the comment in Hall, "Methods of Sociological Research in Comparative Law in Hazard and Wagner," *Legal Thought in the United States of America under Contemporary Pressures* (1970), p. 156.   [61] See *post*, 585.
[62] In, for example, Barkun's *Law without Sanctions* (1968) or Fallers's *Law without Precedent* (1969).
[63] For an account of how trade customs as a source of commercial law have dis-appeared in the face of the written contract, see Devlin, *Samples of Law Making* (1962), Chap. 2.
[64] See *Fundamental Principles of the Sociology of Law* (transl. Moll), (1936), especially Chaps. 20 and 21. *Cf. ante*, 355. See also Fuller (1969) 14 *Am.J. of Jurisprudence* 1 and *post*, 598.

Roman Law

For the Romans as for present day civilians, law was primarily statute law and its development consisted in statutory interpretation.[65] Hence customary law on the whole played a subordinate part, though many institutions, such as *patria potestas,* were recognised as having a customary basis. There was no general customary law recognised throughout the empire, though much of the *jus gentium* was rooted in the customs of the Mediterranean mercantile communities. It was not until post-classical times that general custom (*usus*) was recognised as a source of law and then, on the theory of Julian, that as statutes only bound due to the *consensus utentium,* so, too, what was accepted by the people without writing was equally binding. And though it could not prevail against a statute, a statute could somewhat inconsistently be abrogated by desuetude. Local custom, too, was recognised as valid, though Roman law failed to produce detailed rules comparable to those of the common law for ascertaining the existence of custom and determining its validity. It is also noteworthy that the Romans regarded the rules applied by legal decisions as a kind of customary law,[66] and this approach finds echoes in the views of many later civilians.[67] Prior to the age of codification, although the civilians engaged in much learned debate as to the position of custom in the civil law,[68] they did not always distinguish between custom in the sense of the usages of the community, and in its more specialised meaning of *Juristenrecht,* which denotes rather the practice of the courts or the legal profession, than of the people as a whole, though no doubt these mutually react upon each other. At the present day in civil law systems, the codes have ensured the relegation of custom to a very subordinate role, apart from the introduction of mercantile usages into commerical contracts.[69]

The Common Law

In its medieval origins much of the common law was undoubtedly customary, and Professor Plucknett has shown how flexible was medieval custom and how capable of being adapted to new social needs. In this period legislation and judicial precedent were merely regarded as the means of creating new customs.[70] But as the royal courts and the common law consolidated themselves and triumphed over communal jurisdiction the creative role of custom in the strict sense diminished, and the mass of legal refinements spun out by the

---

[65] Jolowicz, *Historical Introduction to Roman Law,* 2nd ed., p. 99. But *cf.* Schulz, *Principles of Roman Law,* p. 13.
[66] Schulz, *op. cit.,* pp. 14–18.
[67] Jolowicz, *Roman Foundations of Modern Law,* pp. 36–37.
[68] See *ibid.,* pp. 21–23.
[69] *Post,* 610.   [70] See *Legislation of Edward I,* Chap. 1.

courts became rather a matter of creative judicial development than of the adoption of the actual practices of the community. So that, although the habit persisted, from Bracton to Blackstone, of referring to the common law as custom, the " common custom of the realm," [71] this was, as it still remains, in essence *Juristenrecht*, law developed by what Bentham called " Judge and Co.," [72] and if bearing some relation to popular sentiment, by no means derived from pre-existing customs or usages. Thus the judges may be conceived as interpreting or giving effect to popular sentiment in the development of the doctrine of the reasonable man in the law of negligence, though hardly in their exposition of the rule in *Shelley's Case*. And, as in most legal systems, custom no doubt plays a part in establishing an acceptable basis for the fundamental social institutions, such as family law, the ownership of property, the laws of inheritance, and so forth.

But the modern common law can find but a subordinate place for custom as a source of specific legal rules. Much of the present-day learning on custom relates purely to local customs, and here the common law has laid down a series of tests for ascertaining the validity of such customs. One of these stipulates that the custom shall have existed from time immemorial (quaintly defined as, since the year 1189),[73] and so has left little scope for this type of law as the centuries have rolled on. Other tests have had a less important effect. The doctrine that the custom must not be contrary to the fundamental principles of the common law, has been rarely invoked.[74] And the need for the *opinio necessitatis*, that is, that the custom shall be treated as legally compulsory, has excited a good deal more interest among speculative civilians than among hard-headed common lawyers.[75] On the other hand, the rule that a custom, to be valid, must not be unreasonable, has retained a certain importance as enabling the courts to exercise a considerable measure of control

---

[71] Blackstone's description of the common law : see *Commentaries*, I, 67.

[72] See Austin, *Lectures on Jurisprudence*, II, p. 645. *Cf. post*, 783. The distinction between the role of the people and the judiciary in creating customary law is brought out by Braybrooke (50 Mich.L.R. 71), who emphasises that customary law is really *Juristenrecht*.

[73] This was settled upon by analogy with the limitation period fixed by the Statute of Westminster of 1275, for bringing writs of right. And see *Simpson* v. *Wells* (1872) L.R. 2 Q.B. 214. On the effect of discontinuance within legal memory, see *Mercer* v. *Denne* [1904] 2 Ch. 534; and on the effect of a right being granted by licence (*precario*), see *Mills* v. *Colchester Corporation* (1867) L.R. 2 C.P. 476. See also *Iveagh* v. *Martin* [1961] 1 Q.B. 232. Plucknett (*A Concise History of the Common Law*, p. 312) emphasises that the requirement of antiquity is a modern invention designed to curb " a dangerous anomaly." *Cf.* for international law, *North Sea Continental Shelf Cases* I.C.J.Rep. 1969, p. 343.

[74] For an example, see *post*, 618.

[75] See Jolowicz, *Roman Foundations of Modern Law*, pp. 26–28. For a criticism of this doctrine, see A. Ross, *On Law and Justice* (1958), p. 93. For its application to international law see Nelson, (1972), 35 M.L.R. 52, commenting upon *North Sea Continental Shelf Cases, op. cit.*, at p. 43.

over what local customs are admissible.[76] Whether this rule entails
the acceptance of the Austinian view that custom is not law until
accepted by the courts [77] remains a matter of controversy, but hardly
one of practical significance. It is curious, however, that even at the
present day it still remains unsettled whether reasonableness is to be
judged by the standards of the year 1189 (to which the legal origin
of the custom is to be traced) or by those standards which now prevail.[78] Common sense, if not common law, would seem to point to
the latter solution, but this does not necessarily imply that the court
treats custom as invalid until accepted by it, for it may be said
that a custom is lawful and binding provided it is reasonable by
contemporary standards.[79]

A custom, to prevail, must be merely local as regards both a
defined district and as regards the class of persons concerned.[80] For
if it were completely general it would either take effect as a rule of
the common law or would derogate from it, and this no general
custom is allowed to do. An exception has long been acknowledged
in the case of the custom of merchants, and it is in this manner that
our mercantile law has been developed. Lord Mansfield was able
to incorporate much of the law merchant into the common law by
adopting the customs of the mercantile community. How far, however, the power still exists to modify the general law by new mercantile custom remains uncertain. It is accepted that the courts can
still recognise new categories of negotiable instruments pursuant to
the custom of merchants [81] for otherwise, it is said, the law merchant
would be fixed or stereotyped and incapable of expansion.[82] But the
last exercise of this power was in 1898,[83] and in any event it hardly
establishes the power at the present day to create an entirely new rule,
as opposed to merely extending such an established institution as
negotiability to a new category of documents. Moreover, once such
a new rule has been created, it seems very doubtful whether it can
subsequently be changed. On the whole, the common law is distinctly

---

[76] See the numerous cases cited in Appendix I, in C. K. Allen, *op. cit.*, p. 614 *et
seq.* Ross (*op. cit.*, p. 97) describes the conditions governing this admissibility as
embodying an " ideology, whose function is to conceal the judge's freedom and
law-creative activity." See also Dias (1970) C.L.J. 75, 81–83.
[77] *Cf. ante*, 217.
[78] Contrast *Bryant* v. *Foot* (1868) L.R. 3 Q.B. 497, and *Lawrence* v. *Hitch, ibid.*,
521.
[79] Cf. the effect of public policy on contracts.
[80] *Blundell* v. *Catterall* (1821) 5 B. & A. 268; *Earl of Coventry* v. *Wills* (1863) 12
W.R. 127. On the rather different approach to custom in Scots Law, see " Custom
as a Source of Law in Scotland " by J. T. Cameron, (1964) 27 M.L.R. 306.
[81] *Goodwin* v. *Roberts* (1875) L.R. 10 Ex. 337; and see *post*, 616.
[82] *Ibid.*, p. 346.
[83] *Bechuanaland Exploration Company* v. *London Trading Bank* [1898] 2 Q.B. 658;
and see *Edelstein* v. *Schuler* [1902] 2 K.B. 144.

hostile at the present day to any attempt to modify the general law by reason of new or changed mercantile custom,[84] a rigidity of attitude, be it admitted, which may have contributed to driving business men away from the commercial court and into arbitration.

General mercantile custom of the kind just discussed must be carefully distinguished from commercial usages imported into particular contracts, for these do not operate of their own force but have to be implied as a term in the contract in question.[85] In fact such usages are of far greater significance at the present day than local customs, and may even have the result of gradually effecting a general change in the law. For though, unlike a decision on local custom, a customary term may have to be proved anew in relation to every contract litigated upon, eventually the usage may become so notorious

---

[84] See *Diamond Alkali Export Corporation* v. *Fl. Bourgeois* [1921] 3 K.B. 443; *Wilson Holgate* v. *Belgian Grain Co.* [1920] 2 K.B. 1; *Comptoir d'Achat* v. *Belgian Grain Co.* [1949] A.C. 293, and Devlin, *Samples of Law Making*, Chap. 2. The rule in *Edie* v. *East India Company* (1761) 2 Burr. 1216, that once a custom of the law merchant had been judicially recognised no effect can be given to a later contrary custom, is no longer accepted (see *Anglo-African Shipping* v. *Mortner* (1962) 1 Lloyd's Rep. 610, 616, and *Tehran-Europe* v. *S.T. Belton* (*Tractors*) *Ltd.* [1968] 3 W.L.R. at pp. 214 and 217).

[85] Thus the usage must not be inconsistent with the express terms of the contract: *Re Sutro and Heilbut* [1917] 2 K.B. 348; *Affréteurs Réunis* v. *Walford* [1919] A.C. 801. A usage will also not be imported into a contract unless it is reasonable. (See *Tucker* v. *Linger* (1883) 8 App.Cas. 508). The general position governing usages has been recently explained in these terms:—" Usage " is apt to be used confusingly in the authorities in two senses, (i) a practice, and (ii) a practice which the court will recognise. " Usage " as a practice which the court will recognise is a mixed question of fact and law. For the practice to amount to such a recognised usage, it must be certain, in the sense that the practice is clearly established; it must be notorious, in the sense that it is so well known in the market in which it is alleged to exist that those who conduct business in that market contract with usage as an implied term, and it must be reasonable. The burden lies on those alleging usage to establish it. . . . The practice that has to be established consists of a continuity of acts, and those acts have to be established by persons familiar with them, although they may be sufficiently established by such persons without a detailed recital of instances. Practice is not a matter of opinion of even the most highly qualified expert as to what is desirable that the practice should be. However, evidence of those versed in a market, may be admissible and valuable in identifying those features of any transaction that attract usage and in discounting other features which for such purpose are merely incidental and if there is a conflict of evidence about this it is subject to being resolved like other conflicts of evidence. Arrangements or compromises to the same effect as the alleged usage do not establish usage; they contradict it. They may be the precursors of usage, but usage presupposes that arrangements and compromises are no longer required. It is, in my view, clearly not necessary that a practice should be challenged and enforced before it can become a usage as, otherwise a practice so obviously universally accepted and acted on as not to be challenged could never be a usage. However, enforcement would be valuable and might be conclusive in establishing usage. What is necessary is that for a practice to be recognised usage it should be established as a practice having binding effect. A party to a contract is bound by usages applicable to it as certain, notorious and reasonable, although not known to him. If the practice, though certain and notorious is unreasonable it follows that it cannot constitute a usage which the court will enforce as a usage. Nevertheless if a party knows of such a practice and agrees to it, then though unreasonable, he is bound by it (*per* Ungoed-Thomas J. in *Cunliffe-Owen* v. *Teather* [1967] 3 All E.R. 561, at pp. 572–573).

as to enable the court to take judicial notice of it without further proof.[86] Thus a usage may, unless expressly excluded, determine the content of a specific class of commercial contract. Also it must be borne in mind that even in the absence of a usage in the strict sense, the general practice in a particular class of trade may induce a court to imply a term on the ordinary basis that it is necessary to the commercial efficacy of the contract.[87] There are, indeed, more ways than one in which commercial practice may indirectly be given a quasi-legislative effect.[88]

C. VON SAVIGNY

System of Modern Roman Law [89]
(1840)

In the general consciousness of a people lives positive law and hence we have to call it people's law (*Volksrecht*). It is by no means to be thought that it was the particular members of the people by whose arbitrary will, law was brought forth; in that case the will of individuals might perhaps have selected the same law, perhaps however and more probably very varied laws. Rather is it the spirit of a people living and working in common in all the individuals, which gives birth to positive law, which therefore is to the consciousness of each individual not accidentally but necessarily one and the same. Since therefore we acknowledge an invisible origin of positive law we must as to that origin, renounce documentary proof: but this defect is common to our and every other view of that origin, since we discover in all peoples who have ever presented themselves within the limits of authentic history an already existing positive law of which the original generation must lie beyond those limits. There are not wanting proofs of another sort and suitable to the special nature of the subject-matter. Such a proof lies in the universal, uniform recognition of positive law and in the feeling of inner necessity with which its conception is accompanied. This feeling expresses itself most definitely in the primeval assertion of the divine origin of law or statutes; a more manifest opposition to the idea of its arising from accident or the human will is not to be conceived. A second proof lies in the analogy of other peculiarities of peoples which have in like manner an origin invisible and reaching beyond authentic history, for example, social life and above all speech. In this is found the same independence of accident and free individual choice, the same generation from the activity of the spirit of the people working in common in each individual; in speech too

---

[86] See *Re Matthews* (1875) 1 Ch.D. 501, 506. *Cf. Angu* v. *Atta* (1916) Gold Coast Privy Council Judgments 1874–1928, p. 43, regarding the proof of *native* customary law.

[87] See, *e.g.*, the cases on the need for obtaining import or export licences, such as *Sethia* v. *Partabmull* [1950] 1 All E.R. 51.

[88] Another instance is that of standard form contracts, which have become extremely common, and not only in relation to commercial contracts. See on these H.B. Sales, "Standard Form Contracts," in (1953) 16 M.L.R. 318.

[89] English translation by W. Holloway (1867).

from its sensible nature, all this is more evident and recognizable than in law. Indeed the individual nature of a particular people is determined and recognized solely by those common directions and activities of which speech as the most evident obtains the first place.

The form however in which law lives in the common consciousness of a people is not that of abstract rules but as the living intuition of the institutions of law in their organic connexion, so that whenever the necessity arises for the rule to be conceived in its logical form, this must be first formed by a scientific procedure from that total intuition. That form reveals itself in the symbolical acts which display in visible shape the essence of the jural relation and in which the primitive laws express themselves more intelligibly and thoroughly than in written laws.

In this view of the origin of positive law, we have at present kept out of sight the progress of the life of a people in time. If we now look also at this operation upon law we must above all ascribe to it an establishing force. The longer the convictions of law live in a people, the more deeply they become rooted in it. Moreover law will develop itself by use and what originally was present as a mere germ will by practice assume a definite shape to the consciousness. However in this way the changing of law is also generated. For as in the life of single men, no glimpse of complete passiveness can be perceived, but a continual organic development, so is it with the life of peoples and with each single element of which that concrete life is composed. Thus we find in speech a constant gradual shaping and development and in like manner in law. This gradual formation is subject to the same law of generation from inner power and necessity, independent of accident and individual will, as its original arising was. But the people experiences in this natural process of development, not merely a change in general, but it experiences it in a settled, regular series of events and of these each has its peculiar relation to the expression of the spirit of the people in which the law is generated. This appears in the clearest and strongest manner in the youth of a people for then the connexion is more intimate, the consciousness of it is more generally diffused and is less obscured by the variety of individual cultivation. Moreover in the same degree in which the cultivation of individuals becomes heterogeneous and predominant and in which a sharper division of employments, of acquirements, and of ranks produced by these, enters, the generation of law which rests upon the common consciousness becomes more difficult; and this mode of generation would disappear altogether if new organs for that purpose were not formed by the influence of these self-same new circumstances; these organs are legislation and the science of law of which the nature will be immediately explained.[90]

90 [In a negative sense, it is doubtless true that if a system of law is not in any genuine way a product of a people's way of life, as where it has been simply transplanted from an alien culture, it will enjoy little respect on the part of either the rulers or the ruled, and will be all too easily disregarded or ignored: see, in relation to present-day Korea, P. C. Hahn, "The Rule of What Law? A Korean Conundrum" (1966) 6 Journal of I.C.J., p. 278. See also Lipstein, "The Reception of Western Law in a Country of a Different Social and Economic Background" (1957–1958) 8–9 *Revista del Instituto de Derecho Comparado* 69, where the strength of the *Volksgeist* in a family context is shown to be particularly resilient.]

This new development of law may have an entirely different relation to the originally existing law. New institutions of law may be generated by it, the existing law transformed or it may be entirely swept away if it has become foreign to the thought and need of the age.

People (*Volk*)

The generation of law has been preliminarily posited in the people as the active, personal subject. The nature of this subject will now be more accurately defined. If in the examination of the jural relation, we remove by abstraction, all its special content, there remains over as a common nature, the united life of a plurality of men, regulated in a defined manner. We might naturally be led to stop short at this abstract conception of a plurality and regard law as its discovery, without which the external freedom of no individual could subsist, but such an accidental meeting of an undefined multitude is a conception both arbitrary and entirely wanting in truth: and even if they found themselves so met together, the capacity for producing law would be entirely wanting since with a need the power of at once supplying it, is not given. In fact we find so far as history informs us upon the matter, that wherever men live together, they stand in an intellectual communion which reveals as well as establishes and develops itself by the use of speech. In this natural whole is the seat of the generation of law and in the common intelligence of the nation penetrating individuals, is found the power of satisfying the necessity above recognized.

The boundaries however of individual nations are certainly undefined and wavering and this state of doubt also shows itself in the unity or variety of the law engendered in them. Thus as to kindred races it may appear uncertain whether they are to be regarded as one people or as several: in like manner we also frequently find in their law not an entire consonance, probably however an affinity.

Even where the unity of a people is undoubted,[91] within its limits are often found inner circles which are included in a special connexion side by side with the general union of the people, as cities and villages, guilds and corporations of every sort which altogether form popular divisions of the whole. In these circles again a special generation of law may have its seat as particular law, side by side with the general law of the nation which by that particular law is on many sides completed or altered.[92]

When we regard the people as a natural unity and merely as the subject of positive law, we ought not to think only of the individuals comprised in that people at any particular time; that unity rather runs through generations constantly replacing one another, and thus it unites the present with the past and the future. This constant preservation of law is effected by tradition and this is conditioned by, and based upon, the not sudden but ever gradual change of generations. The independence of the life of individuals, here asserted of law, appertains first to the unchanged continuation of the rules of law: it is secondly too the foundation of the

---

[91] [Savigny nowhere faces up to the questions, What is a People? and, what are the criteria for determining its degree of unity, natural or artificial ? Later writers put a greater emphasis on *racial* unity, but again the meaning of race was either evaded or deliberately obscured.]

[92] Thus arose in Rome, the ancient customary law of individual *gentes*.

gradual formation of law and in this connexion we must ascribe to it a special importance.

This view in which the individual people is regarded as the generator and subject of positive or practical law may appear too confined to some who might be inclined to ascribe that generation rather to the general spirit of humanity than to that of a particular people. On closer examination these two views do not appear conflicting. What works in an individual people is merely the general human spirit which reveals itself in that people in a particular manner. The generation of law is a fact and one common to the whole. This is conceivable only of those, between whom a communion of thought and action is not only possible but actual. Since then such a communion exists only within the limits of an individual people so here also can practical law alone be created, although in its production, the expression of a generative principle common to men in general, is perceived, but not the peculiar will of individual peoples, of which perhaps no single trace might be found in other peoples. For this product of the people's mind is sometimes entirely peculiar to a single people, though sometimes equally present in several peoples.   [pp. 12–17]

Customary law

This name may easily mislead us into the following course of thinking. When anything whatever needed to be done in a jural relation, it was originally quite indifferent what was done; accident and arbitrary will anyhow settled the decision. If the same case presented itself a second time, it was easier to repeat the same decision than to deliberate upon a new one and with each fresh repetition, this procedure of necessity appeared more convenient and more natural. Thus after a while such a rule would become law as had originally no greater claim to prevail than an opposite rule and the cause of origin of this law was custom alone. If one looks at the true bases of positive law, at the actual substance of it, he will see that in that view, cause and effect are exactly reversed. That basis has its existence, its reality in the common consciousness of the people. This existence is an invisible thing; by what means can we recognize it? We do so when it reveals itself in external act when it steps forth in usage, manners, custom; in the uniformity of a continuing and therefore lasting manner of action we recognize the belief of the people as its common root and one diametrically opposite to bare chance. Custom therefore is the badge and not a ground of origin of positive law. However this error which converts custom into a ground of origin has also an ingredient of truth which must now be reduced to its proper dimensions. Besides those bases universally recognized in the consciousness of a people and undoubted, there are many determinations as to details which have in themselves a less certain existence; they may obtain such an existence, by being through constant practice brought more definitely to the consciousness of the people itself . . .

Legislation

. . . If we enquire first as to the contents of written law, they are already determined by the mode of derivation of the law-giving power; the already present people's law supplies those contents or what is the same thing, written law is the organ of people's law. If one were to doubt that, one must conceive the lawgiver as standing apart from the nation; he however rather stands in its centre, so that he concentrates in himself their spirit, feelings, needs, so that we have to regard him as the true representative of the spirit of the people. It is also entirely erroneous to regard this position of the legislator, as dependent upon the different arrangement of the legislative power in this or that constitution. Whether a prince makes the law or a senate or a larger collection of people formed by election or perhaps the agreement of several such powers is furnished for legislation, the essential relation of the legislator to the people's law is not at all changed and it is again owing to the error of the conception censured above, if some believe that real people's law is only contained in the laws made by selected representatives. . . .

The influence of legislation upon the progress of law is more important than upon its original formation. If through changed manners, views, needs, a change in the existing law becomes necessary or if in the progress of time entirely new legal institutions are necessary, these new elements may indeed be introduced into the existing law by the same innate invisible power which originally generated the law. It is however precisely here that the influence of legislation may become most obviously beneficial, nay indispensable. Since those operative principles only enter gradually, there of necessity arises an interval of uncertain law and this uncertainty is brought to an end by the expression of the law.[93] . . . Lastly into the history of every people, enter stages of development and conditions which are no longer propitious to the creation of law by the general consciousness of a people. In this case this activity, in all cases indispensable, will in great measure of itself devolve upon legislation. . . .

Juristic law

It is a natural consequence of the development of nations that as culture progresses, special activities and acquirements should separate and thus form separate occupations for the different classes. Thus also law, originally the common property of the collective people, by the more extended relations of active life is developed in so special a manner that it can no longer be mastered by the knowledge uniformly spread among the people. Then is formed a special order of persons skilled in law who as an actual part of the people, in this order of thought represent the whole. The law is in the particular consciousness of this order, merely a continuation and special unfolding of the people's law. It leads henceforth a double life; in outline it continues to live in the common consciousness of the people, the more minute cultivation and handling of it, is the special calling of the order of jurists. . . .

Relation Between Sources of Law

From the previous exposition it follows that originally all positive law is people's law and that side by side with this spontaneous generation, comes legislation (often even in early times) enlarging and propping it

---

93 [The modern reader may well ask himself how such social legislation as Factories Acts, Public Health Acts, Town Planning Acts, etc., could ever come into being by the process here envisaged. The answer is that in an age of *laissez-faire* their exclusion would be regarded as wholly laudable.]

up. Then by the progressive development of the people, legal science is added; thus in legislation and the science of law, two organs are furnished to people's law, each of which simultaneously leads its independent life. If lastly in later times, the law-forming energy departs from the people as a whole, it continues to live in these organs. Then since the largest and most important parts of the old people's law have been incorporated into legislation and legal science, that law shows itself very little in its original shape but merely appears through their medium. Thus it may happen that people's law may be almost hidden by legislation and legal science in which it lives on, and that the true origin of existing positive law, may be easily forgotten and misunderstood. Legislation especially, in its external influence has such a preponderance, that the delusion easily arises that it is the sole true ground of origin of law and that all others must be considered in the subordinate position of a mere supplement or adjunct to it. Law however is never in a healthy condition, unless these law-forming powers work harmoniously together, none of them isolating itself from the others: and since legislation and legal science are the continuous product of individual consciousness and reflexion, it is also of importance that correct views of the origin of positive law, and of the true connexion of the powers co-operating in that production, should obtain and assert the mastery. [pp. 28–42]

SIR HENRY MAINE

Ancient Law
(ed. Sir F. Pollock)

Themistes [94]

The earliest notions connected with the conception, now so fully developed, of a law or rule of life, are those contained in the Homeric words " Themis " and " Themistes." " Themis," it is well known, appears in the later Greek pantheon as the Goddess of Justice, but this is a modern and much developed idea, and it is in a very different sense that Themis is described in the Iliad as the assessor of Zeus. It is now clearly seen by all trustworthy observers of the primitive condition of mankind that, in the infancy of the race, men could only account for sustained or periodically recurring action by supposing a personal agent. Thus, the wind blowing was a person and of course a divine person; the sun rising, culminating, and setting was a person and a divine person; the earth yielding her increase was a person and divine. As, then, in the physical world, so in the moral. When a king decided a dispute by a sentence, the judgment was assumed to be the result of direct inspiration.[95] . . .

Even in the Homeric poems we can see that these ideas are transient. Parities of circumstance were probably commoner in the simple mechanism of ancient society than they are now, and in the succession of similar cases awards are likely to follow and resemble each other. Here

[94] [For a detailed criticism of Maine's theory of early law, see A. S. Diamond, *Primitive Law*, 2nd. ed. (1950).]
[95] [But see Maine's *Early Law and Custom*, p. 163, where he admits that such judgments are doubtless drawn from pre-existing custom.]

we have the germ or rudiment of a custom, a conception posterior to
that of Themistes or judgments. However strongly we, with our modern
associations, may be inclined to lay down *a priori* that the notion of a
Custom must precede that of a judicial sentence, and that a judgment
must affirm a custom or punish its breach, it seems quite certain that the
historical order of the ideas is that in which I have placed them.[96] . . .

Customary Law

The important point for the jurist is that aristocracies were universally
the depositaries and administrators of law. They seem to have succeeded
to the prerogatives of the king, with the important difference, however,
that they do not appear to have pretended to direct inspiration for each
sentence. The connection of ideas which caused the judgments of the
patriarchal chieftain to be attributed to superhuman dictation still shows
itself here and there in the claim of a divine origin for the entire body of
rules, or for certain parts of it, but the progress of thought no longer
permits the solution of particular disputes to be explained by supposing
an extra-human interposition. What the juristical oligarchy now claims
is to monopolise the *knowledge* of the laws, to have the exclusive possession of the principles by which quarrels are decided. We have in fact
arrived at the epoch of Customary Law. Customs or Observances now
exist as a substantive aggregate, and are assumed to be precisely known
to the aristocratic order or caste. Our authorities leave us no doubt that
the trust lodged with the oligarchy was sometimes abused, but it certainly
ought not to be regarded as a mere usurpation or engine of tyranny.
Before the invention of writing, and during the infancy of the art, an
aristocracy invested with judicial privileges formed the only expedient by
which accurate preservation of the customs of the race or tribe could be
at all approximated to. Their genuineness was, so far as possible, insured by confiding them to the recollection of a limited portion of the
community.

The epoch of Customary Law, and of its custody by a privileged
order, is a very remarkable one. The condition of jurisprudence which
it implies has left traces which may still be detected in legal and popular
phraseology. The law, thus known exclusively to a privileged minority,
whether a caste, an aristocracy, a priestly tribe, or a sacerdotal college,
is true unwritten law. Except this, there is no such thing as unwritten
law in the world. English case-law is sometimes spoken of as unwritten,
and there are some English theorists who assure us that if a code of
English jurisprudence were prepared we should be turning unwritten law
into written—a conversion, as they insist, if not of doubtful policy, at all
events of the greatest seriousness. Now, it is quite true that there was
once a period at which the English common law might reasonably have
been termed unwritten. The elder English judges did really pretend to
knowledge of rules, principles, and distinctions which were not entirely
revealed to the bar and to the lay-public. Whether all the law which they
claimed to monopolise was really unwritten, is exceedingly questionable;
but at all events, on the assumption that there was once a large mass of
civil and criminal rules known exclusively to the judges, it presently ceased

[96] [This notion of custom may be compared with the Roman and modern civilian
    idea of case-law as creative of a kind of customary law: cf. *ante*, 572, and
    Jolowicz, *Roman Foundations of Modern Law*, pp. 36–37.]

to be unwritten law. As soon as the Courts at Westminster Hall began to base their judgments on cases recorded, whether in the year-books or elsewhere, the law which they administered became written law. At the present moment a rule of English law has first to be disentangled from the recorded facts of adjudged printed precedents, then thrown into a form of words varying with the taste, precision, and knowledge of the particular judge, and then applied to the circumstances of the case for adjudication. But at no stage of this process has it any characteristic which distinguishes it from written law. It is written case-law, and only different from code-law because it is written in a different way.

From the period of Customary Law we come to another sharply defined epoch in the history of jurisprudence. We arrive at the era of Codes, those ancient codes of which the Twelve Tables of Rome were the most famous specimen. In Greece, in Italy, on the Hellenised sea-board of Western Asia, these codes all made their appearance at periods much the same everywhere, not, I mean, at periods identical in point of time, but similar in point of the relative progress of each community. Everywhere, in the countries I have named, laws engraven on tablets and published to the people take the place of usages deposited with the recollection of a privileged oligarchy. It must not for a moment be supposed that the refined considerations now urged in favour of what is called codification had any part or place in the change I have described. The ancient codes were doubtless originally suggested by the discovery and diffusion of the art of writing. It is true that the aristocracies seem to have abused their monopoly of legal knowledge; and at all events their exclusive possession of the law was a formidable impediment to the success of those popular movements which began to be universal in the western world. But, though democratic sentiment may have added to their popularity, the codes were certainly in the main a direct result of the invention of writing. Inscribed tablets were seen to be a better depository of law, and a better security for its accurate preservation, than the memory of a number of persons however strengthened by habitual exercise. [pp. 10–13]

Law and Progressive Societies

The movement of the progressive [97] societies has been uniform in one respect. Through all its course it has been distinguished by the gradual dissolution of family dependency, and the growth of individual obligation in its place. The Individual is steadily substituted for the Family, as the unit of which civil laws take account. The advance has been accomplished at varying rates of celerity, and there are societies not absolutely stationary in which the collapse of the ancient organisation can only be perceived by careful study of the phenomena they present. But, whatever its pace, the change has not been subject to reaction or recoil, and apparent retardations will be found to have been occasioned through the absorption of archaic ideas and customs from some entirely foreign source. Nor is it difficult to see what is the tie between man and man which replaces by degrees those forms of reciprocity in rights and duties which

[97] [Maine regarded these as exceptional. " The natural condition of mankind (if that word ' natural ' is used) is not the progressive condition. It is the condition not of changeableness but of unchangeableness. The immobility of society is the rule ; its mobility is the exception " (*Popular Government*, p. 170).]

have their origin in the Family. It is Contract. Starting, as from one
terminus of history, from a condition of society in which all the relations
of Persons are summed up in the relations of Family, we seem to have
steadily moved towards a phase of social order in which all these relations
arise from the free agreement of Individuals. . . .

The word Status may be usefully employed to construct a formula
expressing the law of progress thus indicated, which, whatever be its
values, seems to me to be sufficiently ascertained. All the forms of Status
taken notice of in the Law of Persons were derived from, and to some
extent are still coloured by, the powers and privileges anciently residing
in the Family. If then we employ Status, agreeably with the usage of
the best writers, to signify these personal conditions only, and avoid
applying the term to such conditions as are the immediate or remote
result of agreement, we may say that the movement of the progressive
societies has hitherto [98] been a movement *from Status to Contract.*

[pp. 180–182]

E. A. HOEBEL

The Law of Primitive Man
(1954)

The Functions of Law

Law performs certain functions essential to the maintenance of all but
the most simple societies.

The first is to define relationships among the members of a society,
to assert what activities are permitted and what are ruled out, so as to
maintain at least minimal integration between the activities of individuals
and groups within the society.

The second is derived from the necessity of taming naked force and
directing force to the maintenance of order. It is the allocation of
authority and the determination of who may exercise physical coercion
as a socially recognized privilege-right, along with the selection of the

---

[98] [It is to be noted that Maine qualifies this celebrated dictum by the word
" hitherto." Certainly since his day the movement has been away from freedom
of contract towards an increasingly collectivist society, though not one which
can be readily brought within the category of status as understood in earlier
ages. Cf. Friedmann, *Law in a Changing Society*, Chap. 4. What Maine,
however, meant by status was the sum total of an individual's rights, obligations and disabilities conferred or imposed irrespective of his own volition. Most
of the examples relied upon to suggest that the trend of progressive society noted
by Maine has now been reversed do not fall within the category of status in
this sense, but are rather examples of imperative norms of the law of contract,
whether imposed by the law itself, or by the imposition of " standard form "
contracts (see O. Kahn-Freund, " A Note on Status and Contract in British
Labour Law " (1967) 30 M.L.R. 635. See also G. Sawer, *Law in Society*,
pp. 65–69). Strong support is expressed by Gluckman for Maine's emphasis
on status in the law of tribal society. In such society most of the transactions
involving the exchange of goods and services do not occur between strangers.
Men and women hold land and other property, and exchange goods and services,
as members of a hierarchy of political groups and as kinsfolk. People are
linked in transactions with one another because of pre-existing relationships of
status between them (see M. Gluckman, *Politics, Law and Ritual In Tribal
Society* (1965), pp. 17–18, 44–49, and in *Ideas and Procedures in African
Customary Law* (1965), pp. 253, 263.]

most effective forms of physical sanction to achieve the social ends that the law serves.

The third is the disposition of trouble cases as they arise.

The fourth is to redefine relations between individuals and groups as the conditions of life change. It is to maintain adaptability.[99]

Purposive definition of personal relations is the primary law-job. Other aspects of culture likewise work to this end, and, indeed, the law derives its working principles (jural postulates) from postulates previously developed in the nonlegal spheres of action. However, the law's important contribution to the basic organization of society as a whole is that the law specifically and explicitly defines relations. It sets the expectancies of man to man and group to group so that each knows the focus and the limitations of its demand-rights on others, its duties to others, its privilege-rights and powers as against others, and its immunities and liabilities to the contemplated or attempted acts of others.[1] This is the " bare-bones job," as Karl Llewellyn likes to call it. It is the ordering of the fundamentals of living together.

No culture has a specific starting point in time; yet in the operation of the first function it is as though men were getting together and saying to each other, "Look here! Let's have a little organization here or we'll never get anywhere with this mess! Let's have a clear understanding of who's who, what we are to do, and how we are going to do it!" In its essence it is what the social-contract theorists recognized as the foundation of social order.

The second function of the law—the allocation of authority to exercise coercive physical force—is something almost peculiar to things legal.

Custom has regularity, and so does law. Custom defines relationships, and so does law. Custom is sanctioned, and so is law. But the sanctions of law may involve physical coercion. Law is distinguished from mere custom in that it endows certain selected individuals with the privilege-right of applying the sanction of physical coercion, if need be. The legal, let it be repeated, has teeth that can bite. But the biting, if it is to be legal and not mere gangsterism, can be done only by those persons to whom the law has allocated the privilege-right for the affair at hand.

We have seen that in primitive law authority is a shifting, temporary thing. Authority to enforce a norm resides (for private wrongs) with the wronged individual and his immediate kinsmen—but only for the duration of time necessary to follow through the procedural steps that lead to redress or punishment of the culprit. In primitive law the tendency is to allocate authority to the party who is directly injured. This is done in part out of convenience, for it is easier to let the wronged party assume the responsibility for legal action. It is also done because the primitive

---

[99] Cf. K. N. Llewellyn, " The Normative, the Legal, and the Law-jobs: The Problem of Juristic Method," *Yale Law Journal*, 49:1355–1400 (1940). See also Llewellyn and Hoebel, *The Cheyenne Way*, Chap. xi. [*Cf. ante*, 408.]

[1] [Hoebel is following Hohfeld's terminology; cf. *ante*, 248. The use of contemporary technical terms when describing primitive societies is criticised by Sawer, as this in itself tends to give tribal law the appearance of a degree of definition which it does not have, and thereby begs the very question to be decided, *i.e.*, to what extent legal institutions and concepts in our sense are reproduced in undeveloped forms of society; see G. Sawer, *Law in Society*, pp. 43–47.]

kinship group, having a more vital sense of entity, is naturally charged
with a heavier emotional effect. In any event, when the community qua
community acknowledges the exercise of force by a wronged person or
his kinship group as correct and proper in a given situation, and so
restrains the wrongdoer from striking back, then law prevails and order
triumphs over violence.

We have also found in our studies of primitive societies that in a
limited number of situations authority is directly exercised by the community on its own behalf. It takes the form of lynch law in some instances where clear procedures have not been set up in advance, as in
the Comanche treatment of excessive sorcery and Shoshone treatment
of cannibalism. Lynch law among primitives, however, is not a back-
sliding from, or detouring around, established formal law as it is with us.
It is a first fitful step toward the emergence of criminal law in a situation
in which the exercise of legal power has not yet been refined and allocated
to specific persons. It is a blunt crude tool wielded by the gang hand
of an outraged public.

Yet lynch law is rare among primitives. Even the simplest of them
have crystallized standards as to what constitutes criminal behavior,
and the exercise of public authority is delegated to official functionaries—
the chieftain, the council of chiefs, and the council of elders.

Power may sometimes be personal, as is the power of the bully in the
society of small boys, and as was to some extent the power of William
the Conqueror. But personal tyranny is a rare thing among primitives.
Brute force of the individual does not prevail. Chiefs must have followers.
Followers always impose limitations on their leaders. Enduring power
is always institutionalized power. It is *transpersonalized*. It resides in
the office, in the social status, rather than in the man. The constitutional
structures of the several tribes examined in this book have all clearly
revealed how political and legal authority are in each instance delimited
and circumscribed.

This point is emphasized only to dispel any residue of the hoary
political philosophies that assumed without basis in fact that primitive
societies existed under the rule of fang and claw.

However, the personal still obtrudes. An " office " although culturally
defined is, after all, exercised by an individual. And who that individual
is at any moment certainly makes a difference. There is leeway in the
exercise or non-exercise of power just as there are limits. A man may be
skilled in finding the evidence and the truth in the cases he must judge
and in formulating the norms to fit the case in hand—or he may be all
thumbs. He may be one who thirsts for power and who will wield all
he can while grasping for more. Or he may shrink from it. Power
defined through allocation of legal authority is by its nature transpersonalized, yet by the nature of men it can never be wholly deperson-
alized. A Franklin Roosevelt is not a Warren Harding.   [pp. 275–278]

The third function of law calls for little additional comment, for the
disposition of trouble cases has been our main methodological interest
and has already been the subject of a large part of this book. Some
trouble cases pose absolutely new problems for solution. In these cases
the first and second functions may predominate. Yet this is not the
situation in the instance of most legal clashes in which the problem is
not the formulation of law to cover a new situation but rather the appli-

cation of pre-existing law. These cases are disposed of in accordance
with legal norms already set before the issue in question arises. The
job is to clean the case up, to suppress or penalize the illegal behavior
and to bring the relations of the disputants back into balance, so that
life may resume its normal course. This type of law-work has frequently
been compared to work of the medical practitioner. It is family doctor
stuff, essential to keeping the social body on its feet. In more homely
terms, Llewellyn has called it, " garage-repair work on the general order
of the group when that general order misses fire, or grinds gears, or even
threatens a total breakdown." [2] It is not ordinarily concerned with
grand design, as is the first law-job. Nor is it concerned with redesign
as is the fourth. It works to clean up all the little social messes (and the
occasional big ones) that recurrently arise between the members of the
society from day to day.

Most of the trouble cases do not, in a civilized society, of themselves
loom large on the social scene, although in a small community even one
can lead directly to a social explosion if not successfully cleaned up.
Indeed, in a primitive society the individual case always holds the threat
of a little civil war if procedure breaks down, for from its inception it
sets kin group against kin group—and if it comes to fighting, the number
of kinsmen who will be involved is almost always immediately enlarged.
The fight may engulf a large part of the tribe in internecine throat-cutting.
Relatively speaking, each run-of-the-mill trouble case in primitive law
imposes a more pressing demand for settlement upon the legal system
than is the case with us.

While system and integration are essential, flexibility and constant
revision are no less so. Law is a dynamic process in which few solutions
can be permanent. Hence, the fourth function of law: the redefinition
of relations and the reorientation of expectancies.

Initiative with scope to work means new problems for the law. New
inventions, new ideas, new behaviors keep creeping in. Especially do
new behaviors creep in, nay, sweep in, when two unlike societies come
newly into close contact. Then the law is called upon to decide what principles shall be applied to conflicts of claims rooted in disparate cultures. Do
the new claims fit comfortably to the old postulates? [3] Must the newly
realized ways of behaving be wholly rejected and legally suppressed
because they are out of harmony with the old values? Or can they be
modified here and altered there to gain legal acceptance? Or can the
more difficult operation of altering or even junking old postulates to
accommodate a new way be faced? Or can fictions be framed that can
lull the mind into acceptance of the disparate new without the wrench
of acknowledged junking of the old? What *is* it that is wanted? The
known and habitual, or the promise of the new and untested? Men
may neglect to turn the law to the answer of such questions. But they
do not for long. Trouble cases generated by the new keep marching
in. And the fourth law-job presses for attention.

[2] Llewellyn, " The Normative, the Legal, and the Law-jobs," p. 1375 and see
ante, 408.
[3] [This refers to the basic jural postulates of the particular society: cf. *ante*, 379
and 380.]

Recapitulation of just one Cheyenne case will throw the process into focus. The acquisition of horses greatly altered all Plains Indian cultures. One important Cheyenne basic postulate ran,[4] "Except for land and tribal fetishes, all material goods are private property, but they should be generously shared with others." When it came to horses, this led some men to expect that they could freely borrow horses without even the courtesy of asking. For horse owners this got to the point of becoming a serious nuisance, as in the cases of Pawnee and Wolf Lies Down.[5] Wolf Lies Down put his trouble case to the members of the Elk Soldier Society. They got his horse back for him with a handsome free-will offering of additional "damages" from the defendant to boot. The trouble case was neatly disposed of. But the Elk Soldiers did not stop there. There was some preventive channeling of future behavior to be done. Hence the "Now we shall make a new rule. There shall be no more borrowing of horses without asking. If any man takes another's goods without asking, we will go over and get them back for him. More than that, if the taker tries to keep them, we will give him a whipping." Here was the fourth function of law being performed. The lines for future conduct re horses were made clear.

Work under Function IV [6] represents social planning brought into focus by the case of the instant and with an eye to the future.

The problem of reorienting conduct and redirecting it through the law when new issues emerge is always tied to the bare-bones demand of basic organization and the minimal maintenance of order and regularity. It may also shade over into work colored by a greater or lesser desire to achieve more than a minimum of smoothness in social relations. When this becomes an important aspect of law-work, a special aspect of law-ways activity may be recognized: the creation of techniques that efficiently and effectively solve the problems posed to all the other law-jobs so that the basic values of the society are realized through the law and not frustrated by it.

The doing of it has been called by Llewellyn "Juristic Method." [7] It is the method not only of getting the law-jobs done but doing them with a sure touch for the net effect that results in smoothness in the doing and a harmonious wedding of what is aspired to by men and what is achieved through the law. It is the work not just of the craftsman but of the master craftsman—the kind of man the Polynesians call *Tui Thonga,* Great Adept.

Skill in juristic method may be the unique quality of a great judge or chief who judges for his people. In which case you may have a single man, or occasional men, cropping up to soften hard-shell legalism. Or it may become an institutional quality of a whole system in which a tradition of method is to keep one eye on the ultimate social goals of men and another on the working machinery to see that it is steering toward those goals. For juristic method, while it works on the immediate grievance to see that "justice" receives its due, also looks beyond to discern as far as possible the ultimate effect of the social policy that

---

4 [As formulated by Hoebel, and for Hoebel's formulation of Ifugao postulates, see *ante,* 380.]
5 [See pp. 146–149 of Hoebel's book.]
6 [See *ante,* 587.]
7 [Cf. *ante,* 407.]

the *ratio decidendi* will produce. It weighs and balances the "rights" of the individual in *this particular case* against the need for order per se and the far-running needs of the group as a whole. It recognizes that regularity exists not only for the sake of regularity, which is no *Ding an sich*, but as a means to social and individual existence. But it also knows that absolute regularity is impossible in social physiology. It seeks as best it may to keep the working law flexible enough to allow leeway at the points where leeway will not cause the social fabric to part at the seams, and at the same time it seeks to maintain sufficient stiffness in the fibre of the law so that it will not lose its binding effect. . . .

Admittedly it would be hard, if not impossible, to scale a society on a measure of juristic method. Yet, grossly perceived, it can be seen to exist among primitives, often in large degree, and I venture to state in larger degree than in the archaic law of some of the Mediterranean civilizations, and in England after the Common Law had hardened and before Equity had been created to counteract its unreasonable effects.

If ever Sir Henry Maine fixed an erroneous notion on modern legal historians, it was the idea that primitive law, once formulated, is stiff and ritualistic (and by implication weak in juristic method).[8] The sample of case materials that has been set forth in this book has surely shown a large amount of flexible action in haggling (viewed dimly) and argument (viewed generously) over substance and penalty. In most primitive trouble cases the situation is surprisingly fluid, but flowing within channels that are built by the pre-existing law and moving to a reasonably predictable settlement. The channels, however, shift and bend like the course of a meandering river across the bed of a flat flood plain, though flowing ever in a given direction. Men are at work on the law.

The very fact that the bulk of the substance and procedure of primitive law emerges through case action involving claim and counterclaim, pleading and counterpleading, tends to keep legal behavior relatively close to the prevailing social values. Which way a new issue will go will depend not alone upon the facts but also upon the skill of the litigants in framing the issue and arguing the relevance of their respective positions to the prevailing social ideas of right conduct and group well-being—or upon persuasiveness in argument that a new orientation of values is in order to meet changed conditions, even though the tough man and his kinsman, though "wrong," may sometimes make his position stick with naked force. Thus, the wise claimant argues his case not in terms of "this is good for me" but rather by maintaining "this is what we all want and should do." If he is a primitive advocate, it is more likely than not that he will also insist, if he can, that this is the way it has been from time immemorial. But the past certainly has no inflexible grip on primitive law.

Fiction [9] is one of the great devices of juristic method by means of which men fit new legal norms into old principles so as to reorient conduct without the need to junk long-standing postulates. Except for the universal practice of adoption, whereby outsiders are identified *as if* they are actually kinsmen, primitive men do not have to rely too heavily

---

[8] Maine, *Ancient Law*, esp. chaps. ii and iv.
[9] "Any assumption which conceals, or affects to conceal, the fact that a rule of law has undergone alteration, its letter remaining unchanged, its operation being modified." Maine, *Ancient Law*, p. 25 [and see *post*, 837].

on the subterfuge of fiction to achieve legal change. Nevertheless, when the need is there many tribes have had recourse to its use.

An outstanding example may be found in adoptive marriage among the patrilineal groups of Indonesia. The important value for these people is to maintain the unbroken continuity of the paternal lineage. To do this, a family without sons adopts their daughter's husband as a " son " with the effect that her children remain within their clan and their inheritance will remain within their line.[10]   [pp. 279–284]

Thus far . . . we have been concerned with the functions of law in their universal aspects. Do these lead to universal principles of content ? Yes, but among the highly diversified cultures of the primitive world they are few and very generalized for the most part.

The one assumption of overwhelming importance underlying all primitive legal and social systems is the postulation of magico-religious forces as being superior to men, and also that spirit beings have emotional intelligence similar to man's. Its effect on the law systems was shown in the previous chapter to be variable. It is strongest in its consequences among those peoples whose religion emphasizes the role of ancestral spirits, and where the anger of spirits is believed to jeopardize the well-being of the entire society. The sins that arouse such anger are almost certainly taken up by the law as crimes. Almost universally, excessive abuse of personal control of supernatural powers (sorcery out of hand) is treated as a crime. On the other hand, appeal to the supernatural to solve problems of evidence through use of oracles, divination, conditional curse or oath is a very nearly universal legal device.

Homicide within the society is, under one set of conditions or another, legally prohibited everywhere. Likewise, it is universally recognized as a privilege-right under certain circumstances, either in self-defense against illegal, extreme assault (including sorcery) or as a sanction for certain illegal acts.

Virtually every society assumes the relative social inferiority of women (the Ifugao are one exception) and allows male relatives and husbands demand-rights and privilege-rights, powers and immunities, in relation to their female relatives and wives that do not find their equivalents on behalf of the women as against the males. Thus it appears to be universal on the primitive level (and general on the civilized level) that the husband may kill the adulterous wife caught *in flagrante delicto*. For the wife to enjoy such a privilege-right is most rare.

Law universally supports the principle of relative exclusiveness in marital rights. Adultery seems always to be punishable under the law, although just what constitutes adultery will be variable as marriage and kinship forms vary. The right to life and the right to wife are legal fundamentals. All legal systems, primitive and civilized, assume the importance of the kinship group, and all support it as a medium of inheritance of property rights.

All legal systems give cognizance to the existence of rights to private property in some goods; but among primitives land is legally treated as belonging directly or ultimately to the tribe or the kinship group; it is rarely sustained legally as an object of private property.[10a]

10 Ter Haar, *Adat Law in Indonesia*, pp. 175–176.
10a [*Cf.* M. Mead, *ante*, 146.]

When the law-jobs get done, these norms inevitably become the common denominator of legal culture. But the functions of law, whatever the norms they may give rise to in any particular society, are what constitute the crucial universal elements of the law. Any one or half-hundred societies may select one rule of law and not another—the range is wide— but none can ignore the law-jobs. In the last analysis, that the law-jobs get done is more important than how they are done. Their minimal doing is an imperative of social existence. Their doing with juristic finesse is an achievement of high skill. [pp. 285–287]

M. GLUCKMAN

Judicial Process among the Barotse
(revised ed. 1967)

Law and " Regularities"

For the Lozi [11] *mulao* is law and order wherever it occurs. It includes regularities in rainfall and seasons, movements of the sun and moon, night and day, growth of crops, human physiology; and it also covers all regularities in human conduct, personal, tribal, and general.[12] [p. 230]

Sources of Law

In the judicial process we see the law as a body of rules applied to a set of facts which have been proved in evidence. The judges, in the above terms, state that such and such legal rules will be enforced in this dispute: by their very statement they make those rules legal. They extract these particular rules from all the rules ' accepted by all normal members of the society as defining right and reasonable ways in which persons ought to behave in relation to each other and to things.' In this selection they should be guided by certain criteria and rules. For the body of the law in Loziland consists of rules of varying type and origin. These are the various material ' sources of the law' as commonly defined in Western jurisprudence. In Lozi, as in Western, jurisprudence these sources are customs, judicial precedents, legislation, equity, the laws of natural morality and of nations, and good morals and public policy. A further source, not usually listed by jurisprudents, is natural necessities—the laws or regularities operating in the environment and in human beings and criminals. [p. 231]

When the court comes to give its decision, the judges cannot consult accumulated and sifted statutes or precedents, or other records. The judges remember and cite those precedents which seem to accord with their moral judgment, and even incidents which never came to trial for the very reason that they exhibited moral behaviour. Moreover, in the same way as the absence of detailed previous precedents does not restrict the judges' moral discretion, so this absence appears to prevent all of them feeling that their decision on the case under trial establishes an absolute precedent for the future.[13] [p. 234]

[11] [A peoples of Barotseland: see *op. cit.*, p. 1.]
[12] [For a more complete taxonomy of *Mulao* see Gluckman, *The Ideas in Barotse Jurisprudence*, p. 20.]
[13] [*Cf.* Gluckman, *Politics, Law and Ritual in Tribal Society*, pp. 183–190.]

Though they are well aware that changes have been made, and cite and date certain of these changes, they probably tend in the absence of written records to give a greater antiquity to some rules than these rightfully have. Indeed, since the form of judgment is often the bare affirmation that 'this is our law—we know it of old', the judges can confer antiquity on comparatively recent innovations. They could, indeed, enforce new usages, dating from the arrival of the British, as established custom. The law as a whole is 'received tradition', present in the minds of the judges and drawn from living relations about them: hence it has an inherent mutability which reflects changes in social life and in the individuals who participate in that life.

Because the Lozi courts are applying an unwritten law, they cannot make a thorough survey of its various sources. Indeed, I have never seen a *kuta* [14] refer to written records of Ordinances, of their own rules, or of past decisions. Statutes, including those few well-known parts of British legislation which Lozi courts enforce, are not numerous and cover limited spheres of action. Their own edicts are stated in simple sentences: they reduce British prolixity to similar simplicity. Judicial precedents tend to be regarded as illustrating the application or enforcement of custom, rather than as a separate source of law. In Loziland custom is still the main part of 'the common law'. This necessarily affects the manner of its enforcements in adjudication, where it forms a source on which the judges draw.   [p. 236]

Custom

Lozi themselves think of tribal customs as a part of law and a source of legal rulings in somewhat this fashion. Customs (*mikwa*) are by no means the same thing as laws (*milao*). Since the Lozi themselves are dominant in Barotse courts the distinction between law and custom, and the treatment of custom as a source of law, emerges most clearly in reference to the customs of subject and foreign tribes. The *kuta* will not enforce other tribes' customs where it considers these conflict with Lozi law. . . . Moreover, they recognize explicitly that 'the law of the *kuta*' enforces observance of some customs, but not of all. . . .' The Lozi speak of 'laws' and 'customs' separately, though they may use the words interchangeably.   [p. 237]

The Lozi themselves are a comparatively homogeneous people, and the judges are drawn from and related by kinship throughout the populace, which is not cut by class divisions. Hence judges do not call for evidence on what Lozi custom is. At least I never heard of this, and when I suggested it as a possible need they laughed at me. Judges know what Lozi custom is. There is no fiction of judicial ignorance, and judicial notice is unrestricted: it embraces every aspect of life.
                                              [pp. 238–239]

Morality

'Morality' serves as a source of Lozi judicial decision first in that it bridges the all-important gap between the law and evidence of the facts. This gap can only be partially crossed by formal logic: morality selects from the evidence those premises of fact which provide the foundations on which the bridge of judgment unites facts to law. The parties' plead-

14 [A kind of native council or court: see Gluckman, p. 9.]

ings, in which they state both their cases and their view of what is the applicable law begins the process, because every rule of law is a value-judgment. I know of no concept of Lozi law which has not a high ethical implication. Furthermore . . . the very description of the facts is similarly impregnated with judgments of approval and disapproval. Even false evidence tries to make action appear reasonable in terms of common values. Therefore to apply law in any way at all to facts involves a process of moral selection from the evidence which is likely to condition the whole judicial process. Secondly, as we have just seen, moral considerations guide the selection of appropriate rules of laws and precedents for application. Thus morality operates in almost all disputes between kin, and between lords and underlings, as general equity, 'a liberal and humane interpretation of law in general, so far as that is possible without actual antagonism to the law itself' (C. K. Allen).

Thirdly, exhortations of morality are used to awaken the consciences of litigants to accept judgments, which are sermons on parental, filial, and brotherly love. It is important in this process that the litigants themselves have the same norms as judges, and indeed even lie in terms of those norms.   [p. 259]

Law and Custom

I suggested in introducing this chapter, that certain false problems had crept into the analysis of primitive law because of a tendency to regard it as something quite different from developed law. One of these false problems is the attempt to find a distinction between law and custom, as if they are in some sense antithetical concepts. Law can only be posed in antithesis to non-law. Custom has the regularity of law but is a different kind of social fact. As we have seen, the judges may use even the least important of customs as a check on the varied flow of social life. Therefore the jurisprudential conception of custom as one source of law, in the sense of judicial decision, and also as a part of the whole *corpus juris,* can be applied without distortion to the Lozi data. Lozi judges draw on custom to give their verdicts. They state this explicitly. In doing so they also clearly speak of customs as forming, with statutes and other rules, part of the whole body of law of their nation—the Lozi *corpus juris.* This is likely to be true of all simple societies which have courts.   [pp. 261–262]

Judicial logic thus operates within a social and cultural milieu, and to a large extent applies and develops the law along historical and customary lines. But since custom is not consulted in written records, many customs are those, if not of today, at most of yesterday. Therefore customs still have creative energy for Lozi law. They possess this energy in two ways. Cardozo concluded of Anglo-American law that

undoubtedly the creative energy of custom in the development of common law is less today than it was in bygone times. . . . It is, however, not so much in the making of new rules as in the application of old ones that the creative energy of custom most often manifests itself today. General standards of right and duty are established. Custom must determine whether there has been adherence or departure.[15]

15 *Nature of the Judicial Process,* pp. 59 and 62.

Custom in the first sense still produces new rulings of the Lozi *kuta*, as on rights of kinsmen to each other's help and property. Custom in the second manner is at work in every case in present-day situations, determining how the judges will define and specify, and apply, basic concepts by customary and reasonable standards—law itself, right and duty, liability, the motivations of upright incumbents of all social positions. As Cardozo said, this application of customary usage and standards by the criteria of what a reasonable person would do, leads to consideration of what he has called ' the method of sociology in the judicial process '. This raises a new and fundamental problem: the nature and operational value of legal concepts themselves.[16]   [pp. 289–290]

'Certainty' and 'Uncertainty' in Law

Lozi law thus exists both as a body of rules to which people ought to conform and which the courts ought to enforce, and as a series of specific judgments on particular disputes, which are the law for those disputes. These are law in general (*corpus juris*) and law in action (*adjudication*). The two not only may diverge, as obviously where a judge gives a partial or other bad decision; but they cannot coincide because they are quite different kinds of social phenomena. Lozi law in general is partly a body of very general principles relating general and flexible concepts (e.g. ' you cannot sue your host if a fishbone sticks in your throat '—*volenti non fit injuria*), and partly a body of general statements about the relationships of social positions (e.g. if you leave the village you lose rights in its land; a son must respect and care for his father). These are general relations between general concepts which are applicable to many different situations. They are contained in a variety of sources: statutes, precedents, customary practice, usage, good morals, equity—I need not repeat the full list. Law in action applies the law in general to diverse actual situations, and draws on all these sources, but does so usually by emphasizing the moral decision. The judges also draw on presumptions about standardized usages, both of conduct and misconduct, in evaluating the evidence. In these processes they manipulate the general principles and the particular rules and usages of law in an attempt to achieve justice. Sometimes they cannot do so because statutory or customary rules apply too precisely. But since their main task is to specify a series of flexible concepts (ranging from ' law ' itself to ' leaves the village '), for the particular dispute, they introduce through these concepts and their interconnections equitable argument to assess reasonable performance of duties and reasonable exercise of rights. The varied flexibility of the key concepts of Lozi law and ethics is one of their attributes as instruments of argument. It enables the law to cover various situations and to develop so that it can accommodate social change. In this way the law in general is channelled through law in action to cover the infinite variety of situations in social life. Each legal ruling is unique to its situation of dispute: it is stated in terms of fixed principles.

The Lozi judicial process is thus centrally the specification of general concepts, with moral implications, in order to apply them to specific circumstances so as to defend established and emergent values of right-doing. These concepts can be arranged in a hierarchy in which the

---

[16] [*Cf.* Gluckman, *Politics, Law and Ritual in Tribal Society*, pp. 198–202.]

most important—law itself, right, duty, and wrong—are widest in their generality, and have multiple referents. Other more limited elastic concepts refer to human motivations and these operate in the context of similarly more limited concepts of social positions. General and flexible standards of reasonableness, rightness, and customariness pervade the hierarchy. This series of concepts operates in actual life through other concepts of twofold flexibility, which define the process of trial and judgment on evidence. This is the logical process by which Lozi law is made the final enforcing agency to relate ideals to the actualities of social life. The 'certainty' of law resides in the 'uncertainty' of its basic concepts. I hope my flexible use of 'certainty' here does not negate entirely the value, or the resolution, of this paradox.   [pp. 325–326]

The Reasonable Man

It is perhaps now reasonable time that I gave the Lozi phrase for 'a reasonable man'. It is clear from the texts and from my discussion of the preceding cases that in practice judges do not often use such a phrase explicitly, but that the reasonable man is usually implicitly present when they contrast reported behaviour with the norms of behaviour of particular positions. One *general* phrase in Lozi is *mutu yangana*: *mutu*=person, and *ngana*=mind, wisdom, intelligence, intellect, reason, sense, commonsense. From the many contexts in which I have heard *mutu yangana* used, I consider it is best translated as 'a man of sense', with the meaning that Jane Austen brought out in *Sense and Sensibility*. . . . It includes the idea of 'having sound principles'. This is made clearer in the more common general Lozi phrase used in contexts where people are being judged: *mutu yalukile*, of which 'an upright man' is probably the best English rendering. '—*Lukile*' is an adjective from the verbal root *kuluka*, 'to go straight', 'to stand upright'. 'Straightforwardness', 'uprightness', 'decency', 'principle', 'virtue', are therefore the qualities which the Lozi demand of people. This demand includes both sense or reasonabless (*ngana*) and uprightness (*kuluka*). . . .

That *mutu yalukile*, an upright man, embraces both sense and uprightness is apparent if we recall the cross-examinations and judgments in cases cited. In 'The Case of the Biassed Father'[17] the village headman would have behaved sensibly and uprightly if he had been impartial in settling the dispute between his sons and his nephews, as would SAYWA in 'The Case of the Violent Councillor' had he not backed his own children. Reference to any of the praises or reprimands bestowed by judges emphasizes this partial identification. However, the identification is only partial, and *mutu yangana* and *mutu yalukile* are distinguished. For though the judges assess behaviour, in considering evidence, by the standard of the upright man, and urge this standard on litigants, the law only demands 'reasonable' behaviour—the standard of 'the sensible man'. Hence the upright man does not have mistresses, but the law only requires that a man should not neglect his wives while he pursues mistresses, and allows him mistresses if they be not married to others. . . .

---

17 [The cases referred to by Gluckman are described in detail in the book.]

Lozi judges do not make continual explicit use of the general phrase for a reasonable man because in most cases they are giving judgments on the behaviour of persons occupying specific social positions in multiplex relations—they are chiefly concerned with relationships of status. Therefore the judges more often work explicitly with the phrases, 'a good husband', 'a sensible induna', and so on. Indeed, they often use the term for the social position without using the qualificative. This in itself states the norms of customary behaviour and reasonable fulfilment of obligations. The emphatic use of terms defining social position is very common in praising people. For example, Lozi rarely speak of a woman as an industrious gardener without adding, ' *Kimusali* ' (' she's a wife '), or, ' *Kimwana* ' ('she's a child '), since gardening is so important a duty of women. Similarly, when it became known how much Nyambe, the son of NAWALA Mutondo, had brought back from Johannesburg for his kin, people said of him: ' *Kimwana, uezize* '—' he's a child, he has done [what he ought to have done] '. This phrase, ' *Uezize* ', (' he [or she] has done ') is often used on its own of a man who has fulfilled his obligations, beyond reasonable demands. Similarly, Lozi say, 'He's a chief—an induna—a headman—a subject,' for political positions; 'He's a fisherman—a herdsman—a servant,' for employees; 'He's a magician—a smith—a potter—a carver,' for specialists; and so forth.

Judges also use this common practice of reference, and in doing so they are setting up the differentiated standard of the reasonable and perhaps even upright incumbent of a particular social position. Recall what ALULEYA said to one nephew in ' The Case of the Biassed Father ': ' You, B, I see you are really a man, because you said, " My brothers, do not leave home." And you went to your father to adjust matters. You should have persisted more, but your behaviour when you returned to Loziland shows you are really a man.' ' A man ' here means one who tries to see that a family dispute is argued out and settled.

Again, in ' The Case of the Man who Helped his Mother-in-Law Cross a Ford ' a judge praised a girl who said she could not live with her husband after he saw her two maternal uncles' wives naked and slept with one of them. He told her husband: ' I support your wife; she is a good girl, a true woman [wife]. If our children were the same, we would have children.' Here the girl is praised because she recognizes her duties to her maternal uncles, so she is ' a child ', and these conflict with her duties as a woman and wife of their wives' seducer, so she is ' a woman '.

This usage is not, of course, peculiar to the Lozi. We have it in phrases such as, ' he's a man—a gentleman—a sportsman—a king ', and so on. In both cultures it implies approbation of a person showing the qualities and conforming to the norms demanded of a certain social position; or in the negative—as ' *hasimulena yo* ', ' he is not a chief ', —it states disapprobation of a person who has failed to show these qualities, or has exhibited contrary qualities, and has violated the appropriate norms. Note how in ' The Case of the Eloping Wife ' the judges said of her insults to her father: ' Now your father has no child ' . . . ' Find another father.' But this sort of phrase, common though it be in everyday usage presumably everywhere, is of great sociological importance because it covers the whole social process of judging people against norms, and it is therefore very significant when it is used in the judicial process, as among the Lozi. It is their ' reasonable person ' differentiated by sex and in manifold social positions.

In addition to these phrases for the reasonable incumbent of a social position, the Lozi also apply the verb ' *kuutwahala* ', ' to be understandable ', ' to be obvious ', ' to be reasonable ', to the whole of evidence or to particular actions. *Kuutwahala* is a derivative of *kuutwa*, to hear or understand, which is also used frequently by judges. *Kukolwahala*, to be credible, from *kukolwa* (to believe) is similarly used. *-Lukile*, right, is also applied to actions and to evidence; but I did not record this use of *-ngana*, sensible, without a noun of social position. Again, the Lozi do not always use these phrases explicitly—at least they do not appear often in my necessarily abbreviated records and I do not recall their frequent use. Unfortunately, while I was in the field I was not yet on the look-out for them. But I noted their appearance sufficiently often to be able to cite them as established legal concepts, and to say that they are always implicitly present in the judges' statement of norms against the recapitulation of witnessed or reported actions. These phrases too are commonly used outside the courts.

The judges therefore use in this aspect of their work a process and standards that are common throughout the society. They are setting up minimum standards which people ought to observe, if they are not to be punished, for various social positions. These are not always ideal standards, for Lozi ethics demands fulfilment of obligations beyond the basic reasonable norm, and generous refusal to insist on rights. The concept of ' reasonable ' measures the range of allowed departure from the highest standards of duty and absolute conformity to norm, and the minimum adherence which is insisted on. Professors Llewellyn and Hoebel drew attention to this important problem in their *The Cheyenne Way: Conflict and Case Law in Primitive Jurisprudence*, when they wrote: ' . . . one phenomenon of law, as of institutions in general, which has received altogether too little attention save in relation to bills of rights and the due process clause, is the two *ranges of leeway* of man's conduct which are a part of any legal or social system— the range of permissible leeway and the range of actively protected leeway '.[18] Curiously, though Professor Llewellyn is a jurist, he did not suggest taking over the legal concept of ' reasonable standards ' to handle this problem, though I hope I have already shown how these standards among the Lozi cover both ' the range of permissible leeway, and the range of actively protected leeway '. Indeed, it seems to me that ' the reasonable man ' should become as important in sociology and social anthropology as are concepts like the ideal type, the average man, and the deviant. If ' the reasonable man ' is more precisely the man who conforms reasonably to the customs and standards of his social position, clearly he corresponds closely with the concept of ' the *rôle* of a particular *status* ', which has become so important in current anthropology and sociology.[19] The rôle of a status—for which I prefer the term (social) position to avoid the plural ' statuses '—is that series of actions which a person ought to perform, and which his fellows are entitled to

[18] Norman: University of Oklahoma Press (1941), at p. 23.
[19] See *e.g.*, Linton R., *The Study of Man*, New York and London: Appleton —Century (1936), pp. 114 ff. and Parsons T., and Shils E. (editors), *Towards a General Theory of Action*, Cambridge: Harvard University Press (1951), passim.

expect from him. Professors Parsons and Shils thus speak of the expectations of the rôle. . . . This qualification is important, for it sets those standards of conformity in meeting the demands of one's rôle which courts will enforce for a particular situation. The situations which confront people vary greatly, particularly at times when major social changes are occurring. Many rôles, defined in general terms such as ' a husband must care for his wife ', remain constant; but in all the variety of actual, and even changing, situations, the concept of ' reasonableness ' enables judgments to be passed on actions in terms of new as well as of established standards. . . .   [pp. 125–129]

L. L. FULLER

Human Interaction and the Law
(1969) [20]

This neglect of the phenomenon called customary law has, I think, done great damage to our thinking about law generally. Even if we accept the rather casual analysis of the subject offered by the treatises, it still remains true that a proper understanding of customary law is of capital importance in the world of today. In the first place, much of international law, and perhaps the most vital part of it, is essentially customary law. Upon the successful functioning of that body of law world peace may depend. In the second place, much of the world today is still governed internally by customary law. The newly emerging nations (notably in India, Africa, and the Pacific) are now engaged in a hazardous transition from systems of customary law to systems of enacted law. The stakes in this transition—for them and for us— are very high indeed. So the mere fact that we do not see ourselves as regulating our conduct toward fellow countrymen by customary law does not mean that it is of no importance to us as world citizens.

The thesis I am going to advance here is, however, something more radical than a mere insistence that customary law is still of considerable importance in the world of today. I am going to argue that we cannot understand " ordinary " law (that is, officially declared or enacted law) unless we first obtain an understanding of what is called customary law.[21]

In preparing my exposition I have to confess that at this point I encountered a great frustration. This arises from the term " customary law " itself. This is the term found in the titles and the indices, and if you want to compare what I have to say with what others have said, this is the heading you will have to look under. At the same time the expression " customary law " is a most unfortunate one that obscures, almost beyond redemption, the nature of the phenomenon it purports to designate. Instead of serving as a neutral pointer, it prejudges its subject; it asserts that the force and meaning of what we call " customary law " lie in mere habit or usage.

Against this view I shall argue that the phenomenon called customary law can best be described as *a language of interaction*. To interact meaningfully men require a social setting in which the moves of the participating players will fall generally within some predictable pattern.

[20] [From (1969) 14 Am. J. of Jurisprudence 1.]
[21] [This thesis is also presented by Barkun in *Law Without Sanctions* (1968).]

To engage in effective social behavior men need the support of inter-meshing anticipations that will let them know what their opposite numbers will do, or that will at least enable them to gauge the general scope of the repertory from which responses to their actions will be drawn. We sometimes speak of customary law as offering an unwritten "code of conduct." The word "code" is appropriate here because what is involved is not simply a negation, a prohibition of certain disapproved actions, but also the obverse side of this negation, the meaning it confers on foreseeable and approved actions, which then furnish a point of orientation for ongoing interactive responses. Profes-sors Parsons and Shils have spoken of the function, in social action, of "complementary expectations"[22]; the term "complementary expecta-tions" indicates accurately the function I am here ascribing to the law that develops out of human interaction, a form of law that we are forced—by the dictionaries and title headings—to call "customary law.". . .   [pp. 2-3]

The first of these objections[23] is that customary law in primitive societies may lay down rules that have nothing to do with human interaction. There may be offenses against deities and spirits; a man may be punished, even by death, for an act committed out of the pres-ence of other persons where that act violates some taboo. The answer to this is, I suggest, that animistic views of nature may vastly extend the significance one man's acts may have for his fellows. . . . The extent to which one man's beliefs and acts will be seen as affecting his fellows will depend upon the degree to which men see themselves as parts, one of another, and upon their beliefs about the intangible forces that unite them. Within the extended family the distinction between other-regarding and self-regarding acts will assume an aspect very different from what it has in our own society, composed, as that society is, largely of strangers with a strong disbelief in the supernatural.

A further objection to the conception of customary law as a language of interaction may be stated in these terms: Any such conception is much too rationalistic and attributes to customary law a functional aptness, a neatness of purpose, that is far from the realities of primitive practice. Customary law is filled with ritualistic routines and pointless ceremonies; these may cater to a certain instinct for drama, but they can hardly be said to serve effective communication or the development of stable expectations that will organize and facilitate interaction.

In answer I would assert, on the contrary, that a significant function of ritual is precisely that of communication, of labelling acts so that there can be no mistake as to their meaning. . . . Certainly among a people who have no state-kept official records to show who is married to whom, the elaborate wedding ceremonies found in some customary systems can be said to serve a purpose of communication and clarification.

To illustrate the points I have been making with regard to ritualism, and, more generally, with regard to the communicative function of customary practices, I should like to refer briefly to a development that appears to be occurring in the diplomatic relations of Russia and the United States. Here we may be witnessing something like customary

[22] Talcott Parsons and Edward Shils, *Toward a General Theory of Action* (1951), p. 64.
[23] [*i.e.*, to treating customary law as a language of interaction.]

law in the making. Between these two countries there seems to have arisen a kind of reciprocity with respect to the forced withdrawal of diplomatic representatives. The American government, for example, believes that a member of the Russian embassy is engaged in espionage, or, perhaps I should say, it believes him to be *over*engaged in espionage; it declares him *persona non grata* and requires his departure from this country. The expected response, based on past experience, is that Russia will acquiesce in this demand, but will at once counter with a demand for the withdrawal from Russia of an American diplomatic agent of equal rank. Conversely, if the Russians expel an American emissary, the United States will react by shipping back one of Russia's envoys.

Here we have, for the time being at least, a quite stable set of interactional expectancies; within the field covered by this practice each country is able to anticipate with considerable confidence the reactions of its opposite number. This means that its decisions can be guided by a tolerably accurate advance estimate of costs. We know that if we throw one of their men out, they will throw out one of ours.

It should be noticed that the practice is routinized and contains (at least latently) ritualistic and symbolic qualities. Suppose, for example, that the American authorities were confronted with this dilemma: the Russians have declared *persona non grata* a high-ranking member of the American embassy in Moscow, and it turns out to be difficult to find an appropriate counterpart for return to Russia. We may suppose, for example, that the Soviet representatives of equal rank with the expelled American are persons Washington would like very much to see remain in this country. In this predicament it could cross the minds of those responsible for the decision that they might, in order to preserve a proper balance, return to Russia five men of a lower rank than the expelled American, or perhaps even that the expulsion of ten filing clerks would be the most apt response.

Now I suggest that any responsible public official would reflect a long time before embracing such an alternative. Its danger would lie in the damage it would inflict on the neat symbolism of a one-to-one ratio, in the confusion it might introduce into the accepted meaning of the acts involved. This is a case where both sides would probably be well-advised to stick with the familiar ritual since a departure from it might forfeit the achieved gains of a stable interactional pattern.

The illustration just discussed may seem badly chosen because it represents, one might say, a very impoverished kind of customary law, a law that confers, not a reciprocity of benefits, but a reciprocity in expressions of hostility. But much of the customary law of primitive peoples, it should be recalled, serves exactly the same function. Open and unrestricted hostilities between tribes often become in time subject to tacit and formalized restraints and may, in the end, survive only as a ritualistic mock battle.[24] Furthermore, in the diplomatic practice I have described here there may be present a richer reciprocity than appears on the surface. At the time of the *Pueblo* incident it was suggested that Russia and the United States may share an interest in being moderately

---

[24] There is thus less paradox than might at first appear in the title of Paul Bohannan's anthology, *Law and Warfare—Studies in the Anthropology of Conflict* (1967).

and discreetly spied on by one another. We don't want the Russians to pry out our military secrets, but we want them to know, on the basis of information they will trust, that we are not planning to mount a surprise attack on them. This shared interest may furnish part of the background of the ritualistic and patterned exchange of diplomatic discourtesies that seems to be developing between the two countries. . . .

[pp. 5–8]

. . . How much of what is called customary law really deserves the epithet " law " ? Anthropologists have devoted some attention to this question [25] and have arrived at divergent responses to it, including one which asserts that the question is itself misconceived, since you cannot apply a conception interwoven with notions of explicit enactment to a social context where rules of conduct come into existence without the aid of a lawmaker. Among those who take the question seriously the answer proposed by Hoebel has perhaps attracted the most attention; it will repay us to consider it for a moment. Hoebel suggests that in dealing with stateless or primitive societies

. . . law may be defined in these terms: A social norm is legal if its neglect or infraction is regularly met, in threat or in fact, by the application of physical force by an individual or group possessing the socially recognized privilege of so acting.[26]

There are, I suggest, a number of difficulties with this solution. First, it seems to define "law" by an imperfection. If the function of law is to produce an ordered relationship among the members of a society, what shall we say of a system that works so smoothly that there is never any occasion to resort to force or the threat of force to effectuate its norms? Does its very success forfeit for such a system the right to be called by the prestigious name of "law"?

Again, can it always be known in advance whether the infraction of some particular norm will be visited with forceful reprisal? The seriousness of the breach of any rule is always in some measure a function of context. One might be inclined to hazard a guess that few societies would regularly punish with violence infractions of the rules of etiquette. Suppose, however, that a peacemaking conference is held by delegations representing two tribes on the verge of war; a member of one delegation uses an insulting nickname in addressing his opposite number; the result is a bloody and disastrous war. Is it likely that his fellow tribesmen would be content to visit on the offender some moderate measure of social censure? If this illustration seems contrived, it may be observed that in our free society it is an accepted legal principle that a man incurs no liability for expressing to another a low opinion of his intelligence and integrity. If a lawyer trying a case in court were to take advantage of this freedom in addressing the judge, he might very well find himself escorted forcibly from the courtroom to serve a jail sentence for contempt.

Perhaps the basic objection to Hoebel's proposal is that it ignores the *systematic* quality of primitive law. The law of the tribe or extended family is *not* simply a chart of do's and don't's; it is a program for

[25] References to most of the literature on this subject will be found in Max Gluckman, *The Judicial Process among the Barotse of Northern Rhodesia*, 2nd ed. (1967), chs. V and IX.
[26] E. Adamson Hoebel, *The Law of Primitive Man* (1954), p. 28.

living together. Some parts of the program may achieve articulation
as distinct " norms " imposing specially defined " sanctions." But the
basic logic of customary law will continue to inhere in the system as a
whole. Lévi-Strauss may seem at times to drive this quality of primitive
social orders to the point of caricature,[27] but if so, his efforts have
provided a wholesome antidote to the tendency to assume that any
customary system can be reduced to a kind of code book of numbered
paragraphs, each paragraph standing forth as a little law complete in
itself.

A recent controversy among anthropologists is worthy of consideration in this connection. In his famous book, *The Judicial Process
among the Barotse of Northern Rhodesia*, Max Gluckman suggested
that a key element of Barotse legal reasoning lay in the concept of
" the reasonable man." The fact that this concept also plays a role
in more " advanced " systems argued, so Gluckman concluded, for a
certain unity in legal reasoning everywhere. This conclusion was rather
emphatically rejected by a number of his professional colleagues.[28]

Perhaps it may help to clarify the issues by considering a rule of
law, familiar to every reader, that is at least customary in origin. I refer
to " the rule of the road " by which (over most of the world) one
passes the oncoming vehicle on the right. Now it would seem redundant
and even absurd to introduce into this context anything like the concept
of the reasonable man; I pass on the right, not because I am a reasonable
man, but because it is the rule. But suppose a situation is encountered
in which the presuppositions underlying the rule no longer hold. For
example, one is driving in a parking lot, without marked lanes, where
other vehicles are coming and going, backing and turning. Or, driving
on a regular highway, one encounters an approaching vehicle careening
back and forth across the road apparently out of control. In situations
like these what is demanded is plainly something like the judgment and
concern of " the reasonable man "; in such a context the rule of the
road can furnish at most a kind of presumptive guide as to what to do
when other factors in the situation offer no clear solution.

Primitive society, like vehicular traffic, is run by a system of interlocking roles. When one man steps out of his role, or a situation
arises in which a familiar role forfeits some or all of its meaning, then
adjustments will have to be made. There can be no formula to guide
these adjustments beyond that of " reasonableness "—exercised in the
light of the demands of the system as a whole. . . .   [pp. 10–12]

. . . If we permit ourselves to think of " contract law " as the " law "
that the parties themselves bring into existence by their agreement, the
transition from customary law to contract law becomes a very easy one
indeed. The difficulty then becomes, not that of subsuming the two
kinds of law under one rubric, but of knowing how to draw a clear
line of division between them. We may say of course (using the jargon
I have inflicted on the reader here) that in the one case the relevant
interactional expectancies are created by words; in the other, by actions.

But this is too simple a view of the matter. Where words are used,
they have to be interpreted. When the contract falls within some general

---

27 See Claude Lévi-Strauss, *The Savage Mind* (1962, English trans. 1966).
28 *Op. cit. supra* note 9, pp. 82–162, 387–398. (Gluckman's answer to critics on this
point will be found in the second reference.) [And see *ante*, 595.]

area of repetitive dealings, there will usually exist a body of "standard practice" in the light of which verbal ambiguities will be resolved. Here, in effect, interactional regularities in the world outside the contract are written into the contract in the process of interpretation. In commercial law generally it is often difficult to know whether to say that by entering a particular field of practice the parties became subject to a governing body of customary law or to say that they have by tacit agreement incorporated standard practice into the terms of their contract.

The meaning of a contract may not only be determined by the area of practice within which the contract falls, but by the interactions of the parties themselves after entering their agreement. If the performance of a contract takes place over a period of time, the parties will often evidence by their conduct what courts sometimes call a "practical construction" of their agreement; this interpretation by deeds may have control over the meaning that would ordinarily be attributed to the words of the contract itself. If the discrepancy between the parties' acts and the words of their agreement becomes too great to permit the courts to speak of a "practical construction," they may hold that the contract has been tacitly modified or even rescinded by the manner in which the parties have conducted themselves toward one another since entering the agreement.

Generally we may say that in the actual carrying out of a complex agreement between friendly parties, the written contract often furnishes a kind of framework for an ongoing relationship, rather than a precise definition of that relationship. For that definition we may have to look to a kind of two-party customary law implicit in the parties' actions, rather than to the verbal formulations of the contract; if this is true of contracts that are eventually brought to court, it must be much more commonly so in situations where the parties make out without resort to litigation.

If the words of a contract have to be interpreted in their interactional context, or in the light of the actions taken under them by the parties, the actions that bring customary law into existence also have to be interpreted sometimes almost as if they were words. This problem of interpretation is at once the most crucial and most neglected problem of customary law; intrinsically difficult, it is made more so by inept theories about the nature of customary law, such as those explaining it as an expression of "the force of habit" that "prevails in the early history of the race."

The central problem of "interpretation" in customary law is that of knowing when to read into an act, or a pattern of repetitive acts, an obligatory sense like that which may attach to a promise explicitly spelled out in words. All are agreed that a person, a tribe, or a nation does not incur an obligation—"legal" or "moral"—simply because a repetitive pattern can be discerned in his or its actions. All would probably also agree that the actions which create customary law must be such as enter into *inter*actions, though a complication ensues when we recall that under some circumstances inaction can take on the qualities of action, as when it becomes appropriate to call it "acquiescence" or "forbearance." Beyond this we encounter almost a vacuum of ideas.

Into this vacuum there is projected at least one articulate attempt at formulating a test. This is found in the doctrine of *opinio necessitatis*. According to this principle (which still enjoys some esteem in

international law) customary law arises out of repetitive actions when
and only when such actions are motivated by a sense of obligation, in
other words, when people behave as they do, not because they want to,
or because they act unreflectively, but because they believe they have
to act as they do. This seems a curiously inept solution. In clear
cases of established customary law, it becomes a tautology; in situations
where customary law is in the process of being born, it defaults. . . .

[pp. 14–16]

The familiar phenomenon of the spread of customary law from
one social context to another suggests a further distinction between
customary law and contract law that deserves critical examination here.
It may be said that a contract binds only the parties to it, while customary
law normally extends its rules over a large and at times somewhat
unclearly defined community. The first observation is that while this
spread of customary law is a common occurrence it is by no means
inevitable. Something that can be called two-party customary law can
and does exist; it is, again, only linguistic prejudice that makes us
hesitant about this employment of the word " law."

Where customary law does in fact spread we must not be misled
as to the process by which this extension takes place. It has sometimes been thought of as if it involved a kind of inarticulate expression
of group will; the members of *Group B* perceive that the rules governing
Group A would furnish an apt law for them; they therefore take over
those rules by an act of tacit collective adoption. This kind of
explanation abstracts from the interactional processes underlying
customary law and ignores their ever-present communicative aspect.
Take, for example, a practice in the field of international relations,
that of offering a twenty-one-gun salute to visiting heads of state. By a
process of imitation this practice seems now to have become fairly
general among the nations. One may say loosely that its appeal lies
in the appropriateness of a resounding boom of cannon as a way of
signalizing the arrival of a distinguished visitor. But why twenty-one
guns, instead of sixteen or twenty-five? It is apparent that once the
pattern of twenty-one became familiar, any departure from it could
generate misapprehension; spectators would spend their time, not in
enjoying the grandeur of cannon roar, but in counting booms, attributing
all sorts of meanings—intended and unintended—to any departure
from the last allocation. Generally we may say that where *A* and *B*
have become familiar with a practice obtaining between *C* and *D*, *A*
is likely to adopt this pattern in his actions toward *B*, not simply
or necessarily because it has any special aptness for their situation, but
because he knows *B* will understand the meaning of his behavior and
will know how to react to it.

As for the proposition that a contract binds only those who made
it, who actively and knowingly assented to its terms, a mere glance at
modern contracting practice is sufficient to reveal how unreal and purely
formal this proposition can become. Only a tiny fraction of the
" contracts " signed today are actually negotiated or represent anything
like an explicit accommodation of the parties' respective interests. Even
contracts drafted by lawyers, and in theory specially fitted to the parties'
situation, are apt to be full of traditional or " standard " clauses borrowed
from other contracts and from general practice. These clauses are
employed for a great variety of reasons—because the lawyer is in a

hurry, or because he knows from the precedents how courts will construe them, or because the interests at stake are insufficient to justify the fee that would be appropriate to a more careful, specially tailored phrasing.

But the realities of contracting practice are much farther removed from the picture of a " meeting of minds " than is suggested by a mere reference to standard clauses. In fact, the overwhelming majority of contracts are embodied in printed forms, prepared by one party to serve his interests and imposed on the other on a take-it-or-leave-it basis. . . .

There remains for discussion one further distinction that can be made between contract law and customary law. This lies in the notion that a contract comes into effect at once, or when the parties stipulate it shall, while custom becomes law only through a usage observed to have persisted over a considerable period.

This is, again, too simple a view of the matter. The notion that customary law comes into effect gradually and only over a considerable period of time comes about, in part because of mistaken implications read into the word " customary," and in part because it is true that normally it takes some time for reciprocal interactional expectancies to " jell." But there are circumstances in which customary law (or a phenomenon for which we have no other name) can develop almost overnight. . . . [pp. 16–18]

As for the notion that a contract binds at once, and before any action has been taken under it, this is again a misleading simplification, especially when the matter is viewed historically. . . .

It appears likely that in all legal systems the enforcement of the executory bilateral contract is a development that comes quite late.[29] . . . with the development of something like a market economy. . . . [p. 19]

I have treated both customary law and contract law as inter-actional phenomena. I have viewed them as arising out of interaction and as serving to order and facilitate interaction. Can anything like this be asserted of enacted law, as typified, for example, by the statute? Can we regard enacted law itself as dependent on the development of " stable interactional expectancies " between lawgiver and subject? Does enacted law also serve the purpose of ordering and facilitating the interactions of citizens with one another? . . .

Let us test the question whether enacted law serves to put in order and facilitate human interaction by inquiring how this conception applies to some actual branches of the law . . . consider the law embraced under the following headings: contract, agency, marriage and divorce, property (both private and public), and the rules of court procedure. . . . they facilitate human interaction as traffic is facilitated by the laying out of roads and the installation of direction signs. To say that these branches of law would be unnecessary if men were more disposed to act morally is like saying that language could be dispensed with if only men were intelligent enough to communicate without it. The fact that the branches of law just listed include restraints as well as enabling provisions detracts in no sense from their facilitative quality;

[29] [It developed in English law only in the seventeenth century. See Milsom, *Historical Foundations of the Common Law* (1969) Chap. 12.]

there is no more paradox here than there is in the proposition that highway traffic can be expedited by signs that read, " NO LEFT TURN," " STOP, THEN ENTER."

An interactional theory of law can hardly claim acceptance, however, simply because it seems apt when applied to certain branches of the law, such as contracts, property, agency, and marital rights. The law of crimes, for example, presents a quite different test, for here an interactional view encounters an environment much less congenial to its premises. There would, for example, be something ludicrous about explaining the rule against murder as being intended to facilitate human interaction by removing from men's confrontations the fear that they may kill one another. Murder, we are likely to say, is prohibited because it is wrong, not because the threat of it can detract from the potential richness of man's relations with his fellows.

Viewed from a historical perspective, however, the matter assumes a very different aspect. Students of primitive society have seen the very inception of the concept of law itself in limitations on the blood feud. A member of *Family A* kills a member of *Family B*. In a primitive society the natural response to this act is for the members of *Family B* to seek revenge against *Family A*. If no limits are set to this revenge, there may ensue a war to the death between the two families. There has, accordingly, grown up in many primitive societies a rule that blood revenge on the part of *Family B* must, in the case supposed, be limited to one killing, though the injured family is regarded as being entitled as of right to this degree of counterkill. A later development will normally prohibit blood revenge and require instead compensation in the form of " blood money " for the life of the man whose life was taken. Here, plainly, the law of murder serves to regulate interaction and, if you will, to facilitate interaction on a level more profitable for all concerned than killing and counterkilling.

Today the law against murder appears on the surface to have become entirely divorced from its interactional origins; it is seen as projecting its imperative, " thou shalt not kill," over the members of society generally and without regard to their interrelations. But what has in fact happened is that interactional issues that were one central have, as the result of legal and moral progress, been pushed to the periphery, where they remain as lively as ever. The most obvious example is offered by the plea of self-defense; a man is still legally privileged to kill an aggressor if this is necessary to save his own life. But how shall we interpret " necessary " in this context? How far can we expect a man to run some risk to his own life in order to avoid taking the life of another? Again, there is the question of reducing the degree of the offense when a man kills in " hot blood," as when he comes upon another making love to his wife. Finally, there are the disputed issues of killing to prevent a felony or to stop a fleeing felon. In all these much-debated cases the rule against homicide may be modified, or punishment reduced, by a reference to the question: what can reasonably be expected of a man in these interactional situations?

. . . There are, certainly, some manifestations of law which cannot readily be forced into this frame of thought. Perhaps the most significant of these lies in that portion of the criminal law relating to what have been called " crimes without victims." . . .

It is no accident . . . that it is in this area . . . that the grossest failures of law have everywhere occurred. . . .

We should begin by asking ourselves why the law fails so notably in this general area of "crimes without victims." The usual answer is that you cannot enforce morality by law. But this is not so. Keeping promises may be a moral obligation, yet the law can and does successfully force people to keep their promises. Not only that, but the legal enforcement of promises, far from weakening the moral sense of obligation, tends to strengthen it. Suppose, for example, a situation where men associated in some business enterprise are discussing whether they ought to perform a disadvantageous contract. Those who believe they are morally bound to do so are in a position to remind their less principled associates that if the contract is broken they will all be brought to court and will subject themselves, not only to the cost, but also to the opprobrium of an adverse judgment. There are areas of human concern, then, where the cliché that you can't make men act morally by law does not hold. These are, I believe, precisely the areas where the law's sanctions reinforce interactional expectancies and facilitate a respect for them.

In dealing with primitive systems a distinction is sometimes taken between wrongs and sins.[30] A wrong is an act that inflicts a palpable damage on the fabric of social relations; a sin is thought to work a more diffuse harm by spreading a kind of corruption. Typically in primitive societies wrongs and sins are dealt with by different standards and different procedures, formalized "due process" being not uncommonly relaxed in the case of sins. While I would not recommend a resort to sorcery or ostracism as a way of dealing with modern sins, I think we might profitably borrow from primitive society some of the wisdom displayed in the basic distinction between wrongs and sins. Perhaps we might also add to that wisdom the insight that the best way for the law to deal with at least some modern sins is to leave them alone. . . .   [pp. 20–23]

It is time now to turn to what may seem the more basic question: Does enacted law itself depend for its existence on the development of "stable interactional expectancies" between lawgiver and subject? . . .

The law does not tell a man what he should do to accomplish specific ends set by the lawgiver; it furnishes him with base lines against which to organize his life with his fellows. A transgression of these base lines may entail serious consequences for the citizen—he may be hanged for it—but the establishment of the base lines is not an exercise in managerial direction. Law provides a framework for the citizen within which to live his own life, though, to be sure, there are circumstances under which that framework can seem so uncomfortably lax or so perversely constrictive that its human object may believe that straightforward managerial direction would be preferable.

If we accept the view that the central purpose of law is to furnish base lines for human interaction, it then becomes apparent why the existence of enacted law as an effectively functioning system depends upon the establishment of stable interactional expectancies between lawgiver and subject. On the one hand, the lawgiver must be able to

---

[30] E.g., Henry Maine, *Ancient Law*, 10th ed. (1884), pp. 359–361.

anticipate that the citizenry as a whole will accept as law and generally observe the body of rules he has promulgated. On the other hand, the legal subject must be able to anticipate that government will itself abide by its own declared rules when it comes to judge his actions, as in deciding, for example, whether he has committed a crime or claims property under a valid deed. A gross failure in the realization of either of these anticipations—of government toward citizen and of citizen toward government—can have the result that the most carefully drafted code will fail to become a functioning system of law. . . .   [p. 24]

. . . The first observation is that this form of law [30a] is at home completely across the spectrum of social contexts, from the most intimate to those of open hostility. That the family cannot easily organize itself by a process of explicit bargaining does not mean there will not grow up within it reciprocal expectancies of the sort that, on a more formal level, would be called "customary law." Indeed, the family could not function without these tacit guidelines to interaction; if every interaction had to be oriented afresh and *ad hoc*, no group like the family could succeed in the discharge of its shared tasks. At the mid-range, it should be observed that the most active and conspicuous development of customary law in modern times lies precisely in the field of commercial dealings. Finally, while enemies may have difficulty in bargaining with words, they can, and often do, profitably half-bargain with deeds. Paradoxically the tacit restraints of customary law between enemies are more likely to develop during active warfare than during a hostile stalemate of relations; fighting one another is itself in this sense a "social" relation since it involves communication.

That customary law is, as I have expressed it, "at home" across the entire spectrum of social contexts does not mean that it retains the same qualities wherever it appears. On the contrary, it can change drastically in nature as it moves from one end of the spectrum to the other. At the terminal point of intimacy customary law has to do, not primarily with prescribed acts and performances, but with roles and functions. The internal operations of a family, kinship group, or even tribe, may demand, not simply formal compliance with rules, but an allocation of authority, and a sense of trusteeship on the part of those who make decisions and give directions. In the middle area, typified by arm's length commercial dealings, customary law abstracts from qualities and dispositions of the person and concentrates its attention on ascribing appropriate and clearly defined consequences to outward conduct. Finally, as we enter the area of hostile relations, a decided change in the general "flavor" of customary law takes place. Here the prime desideratum is to achieve—through acts, of course, not words—the clear communication of messages of a rather limited and negative import; accordingly there is a heavy concentration on symbolism and ritual.

The influence of social context should be borne in mind, I suggest, in weighing against one another the sometimes conflicting views of anthropologists as to the nature of customary law. It is interesting in this connection to compare two works that have become classics: Malinowski, *Crime and Custom in Savage Society* (1926), and Gluckman, *The Judicial Process Among the Barotse of Northern Rhodesia* (1955, 2d ed. 1967).

30a [*i.e.* customary law.]

Malinowski sees the central principle of customary law in a reciprocity of benefits conferred; he even suggests, in one incautious moment, that the sanction which insures compliance with the rules of customary law lies in a tacit threat that if a man does not make his contribution, others may withhold theirs. Though Gluckman is for the most part careful in limiting his generalizations to the particular society he studied, he seems to see as a central concept of customary law generally that of " the reasonable man." " The reasonable man," for Gluckman, is the man who knows his station and its responsibilities and who responds aptly to the shifting demands of group life. Simplifying somewhat we may say that the central figure for Malinowski is essentially a trader, albeit one who trades on terms largely set by tradition rather than by negotiation. For Gluckman it is the conscientious tribesman with a sense of trusteeship for the welfare of the group.

When we observe, however, the internal economic and kinship organizations of the two societies studied, it becomes apparent why the two scholars should arrive at such divergent conceptions of the model of man implicit in customary law. Malinowski begins his account by observing that the human objects of his study, who live dispersed on different islands, are " keen on trade and exchange." The first concrete situation he discusses involves two village communities on the same island at some distance from each other, the one being located on the coast, the other inland. Under a " standing arrangement " between the two, the coastal village regularly supplies the inland village with fish, receiving in return vegetables. The " trade " between the two is not, of course, the product of explicit bargaining, and indeed at times each of the villages will seek, not to give short measure, but to put the other to shame by outproducing it.

Among Gluckman's Barotse, on the other hand, economic production and consumption are organized largely on a kinship basis. The cases before the *kuta* studied by Gluckman were chiefly cases that might be described as involving the internal affairs of an extended family, though those affairs included some property disputes. Something of the range of the cases studied is suggested by sampling of the titles Gluckman assigns to them: " The Case of the Cross-Cousin Adultery," " The Case of the Wife's Granary," " The Case of the Urinating Husband," " The Case of the Headman's Fishdams (or) the ' Dog-in-the-Manger ' Headman." The atmosphere of the arguments and decisions, reported so vividly by Gluckman, reminds one of what might be expected in a court of domestic relations, mediating the tangled affairs of the family and, occasionally and reluctantly, exercising a power to put them straight by judicial fiat.

The two systems of customary law studied by Malinowski and Gluckman operated, it is plain, in quite different social contexts, though this does not mean that a Malinowski might not find elements of reciprocity or exchange among the Barotse, or that a Gluckman could not find apt occasion to apply the concept of " the reasonable man " among the Trobrianders. I would suggest generally that if we seek to discover constancies among the different systems of customary law we shall find them in the interactional processes by which those systems come into being, rather than in the specific product that emerges, which must of necessity reflect history and context. . . . [pp. 31–33]

R. DAVID and J. BRIERLEY

Major Legal Systems in the World To-day
(1968) [31]

Custom

The Idea of Custom

According to one concept of the sources of law, custom plays a preponderant role in all legal systems [32]; and in developing or applying the law, legislators, judges and authors are, as a matter of fact, more or less consciously guided by the opinion and custom of the community. According to this notion, the role of custom as a source of law is analogous to that attributed by Marxist thinking to the material conditions of production; they are the infra-structure upon which the law is built.[33] The positivist school, on the contrary, has attempted to dismiss the role of custom altogether; according to this view, custom now occupies only a minimal place in a codified law which in the future is to be identified with the will of the legislators. While this position is not realistic, that of the sociological school which gives the expression "source of law" an unusual sense exaggerates the role of custom in the other direction. Custom is not the fundamental and primal element of law that the sociological school would like it to be; it is but one of the elements leading to the just solution. In modern societies, this element is far from having the primordial importance of legislation. But it is also far from being as insignificant as the doctrine of legislative positivism would have it.

In theory, French and German jurists have different attitudes to custom. French jurists are tempted to see in it a somewhat outdated source of law which, since the incontestable predominance of legislation has been recognized, is insignificant. German jurists, on the other hand, are inclined to represent legislation and custom as two sources of law on the same level.[34] Their attitude derives from the Historical School which, in the 19th century, taught them to see law as a product of popular conscience. This theoretical difference is however of no practical consequence. The fact is that in France and Germany one behaves as though legislation had become almost the exclusive source of law; but in both, the reality is something else. Custom has a much more important place than appearances would seem to allow.

The Practical Role of Custom

Legislation itself, in order to be understood, often has to appeal to custom for the necessary clarification of the ideas of the legislators. Without such recourse it cannot be said for example when a person has committed a fault, whether a certain mark constitutes a signature, whether the person committing an infraction may plead attenuating

---

[31] [This book is a translation and adaptation of David, *Les Grands Systèmes de Droit Contemporains* (1964).]
[32] Lévy-Bruhl (H.): *Sociologie du droit* (1961).
[33] [See *post*, 655.]
[34] The same position was adopted, in the beginning, by the Greek Civil Code of 1946, but *cf.* Zepos (P. J.): "Quinze années d'application du Code civil hellénique," Rev. int. dr. comparé, 1962, pp. 281–308.

circumstances, whether an object is a family keepsake, or whether there is the moral impossibility of procuring written proof of an obligation. Any effort made to eliminate the role of custom in these respects will result in a conceptualism or in a casuistry contrary to the spirit of the law of Romano-Germanic countries; an attempt to suppress the enormous role which custom, *secundum legem*, has thus acquired seems futile.

On the other hand, the role of custom *praeter legem* has greatly diminished with the progress of codification and the acknowledged primacy of legislation in the democratic regimes of modern political societies. Today, jurists of the Romano-Germanic family seek at any price to cite legislative texts in support of their reasoning. Under these conditions, custom *praeter legem* is relegated to a very secondary role.

In the same way the role of custom *adversus legem* is very restrained, in appearance at least, even though it is not denied in principle by the doctrine. The courts, it is clear, do not like to set themselves up against the legislative power.

In truth, any analysis of custom is falsified by the dogma of legislative positivism which, linked to the progress of democratic ideas, has prevailed since the 19th century. Jurists, converted to this doctrine which codification [35] appeared to make evident and incontestable, only considered custom *secundum legem* as possible. Consequently, they have made every effort to present customs which in reality were *praeter* or *adversus legem* as customs *secundum legem* helping to "interpret" legislation. Apart from very rare exceptions, custom has thus lost in their eyes its character as an autonomous source of law. It hardly seemed worth discussing; the only problem remaining was that of the interpretation of legislation.

A more exact view of custom can be obtained if, by resuming the traditional approach, one ceases to confuse law (*droit*) and legislation (*loi*). If legislation is not identified with law, but thought of simply as a means—the main one today—of arriving at a knowledge of law, there is nothing to prevent acknowledgement of the usefulness of sources other than legislative texts. Among these other sources, custom will figure very largely so natural and, one may say, so inevitable is it to consider men's behaviour in order to establish, objectively, what is considered socially just. Custom, however, has no intrinsic value, at least in theory; it is only worth retaining to the extent that it serves to indicate the just solution. The jurist must not therefore apply it automatically; he must bring his criticism to bear on it and, in particular, ask whether it is reasonable. [pp. 101–103]

Custom and Rules of Socialist Human Intercourse

Custom

. . . Custom only remains important in the U.S.S.R. to the extent that it is useful or necessary for the interpretation or the application of enacted law (*consuetudo secundum legem*), or in those very few instances where the law itself refers to custom or usage and abandons certain matters to this kind of regulation. References to custom are thus found

---

[35] [In France the law of 30 Ventôse, An.xii (March 31, 1804) abolished all general or local customs, but some still survive in the *Code Civil*. See Gutteridge, *Comparative Law*, p. 80.]

in the R.S.F.S.R. agrarian code (arts. 8, 77) and in the commercial
shipping code of the U.S.S.R. (arts. 89, 90).

This secondary importance of custom in the Soviet legal system is
not at all surprising. Particular mention should nonetheless be made
of it because it indicates a complete rejection of what, up until now,
has been the general rule in Russia. But the complete rejection of
custom by Soviet law has nothing to do with the phenomenon which,
in countries of the Romano-Germanic system, brought about the
substitution of an essentially enacted law, founded on codes, for the
previous customary law. This latter transformation was essentially one
of techniques and not, as a general rule, in either its object or result,
a change in the substantive solutions of customary law. In the U.S.S.R.,
on the other hand, a complete change in the substance of the law
accompanied the change in technique. It was intended, in a truly *social*
revolution, that citizens become accustomed to live in a completely
different manner and according to new rules.

The Rules of Socialist Human Intercourse

The decline of custom in the U.S.S.R. is however only provisional.
The ideal of Marxism-Leninism is to build a society in which there
is no longer any law and where social relations will be ruled only by
custom.[36] Custom, therefore, although rejected today, is called upon
to play a future role of the very highest importance when the communist
goal has been attained and law will be needed no longer. This future
assured to custom appears already in certain expressions of Soviet law
or doctrine which make reference to rules of human intercourse in the
socialist community. Article 130 of the Soviet constitution states: " It is
the duty of every citizen of the U.S.S.R. to observe the Constitution
of the U.S.S.R., to fulfil the law, to maintain labour discipline, honestly to
perform public duties and to respect the rules of socialist human intercourse."

Writers, both in the U.S.S.R. and outside, have wondered what
significance should be attached to this expression and what consequences should be drawn from it. For some the reference to the rules
of socialist human intercourse appeared to be a formula susceptible of
replacing the bourgeois legal notion of public order and good morals.
Others have seen in it the basis for a kind of custom *praeter legem*
through which certain obligations might be imposed on citizens (such
as that of bringing help or assistance to one's neighbour in certain
circumstances) apart from those instances where such obligations result
from a legislative text. Thought of in either of these ways, the words
of article 130 of the Constitution have received little application outside of
cases where further consequences have been specified more concretely
by other legal texts.

In fact however the formula of article 130 has quite another
meaning; and it is deformed when any attempt is made to charge it
with juridical content and therefore to attribute it significance within
the framework of the legal order. The " rules of socialist human
intercourse " to which the article refers are not—and are not intended
to be—law. The expression can only be really understood by considering the future era of communist society: law will disappear and only the

36 [See *post*, 674.]

rules of living in a communist society will remain to govern men's behavior. At the present time the words of article 130 have only a very limited significance; they are however the basis for certain experiments in new social structures [37] in the U.S.S.R. The rules of human intercourse in a socialist community are the basis for all the administrative activities of the country in which citizens can, from now on, voluntarily co-operate such as enrolling in the militia or in various social services. These activities presage the total reality of human intercourse in the communist society of tomorrow.   [pp. 202–204]

T. F. T. PLUCKNETT

Legislation of Edward I
Custom in the Medieval Period

We naturally contrast statute law with common law, and legislation with custom, for the common law is indubitably the custom of the realm. Here we must beware of the modern conception of custom as immemorial and immutable. True and living custom was neither the one nor the other, as the middle ages well knew. How old must a usage be before it can be dignified with the name and acquire the legal validity of custom ? There was much speculation. Thus the civilian Azo regards ten or twenty years' usage as a ' long custom '; thirty years make a ' very long ', *longissima*, custom; forty years make it ' age-old ', *longaeva*. Canonists adopted much the same calculus of age, but with a strong preference for forty years as the qualifying age.[38] Both civilians and canonists showed a marked hostility to custom, which accorded ill with their authoritarian principles.

If customs could come into existence so unceremoniously, then one might expect to find that they were, in fact, instruments for legal change rather than the fossilized remains of a remote past which modern legal theory has made them. Confirmation for this view comes from two different quarters. In the first place there is historical material of the sort collected in a very suggestive note by Julius Goebel in his remarkable study of *Felony and Misdemeanor*.[39] This material seems to show that in the dark ages virtual legislation might spread outwards from the great monasteries. Ancient charters had given them the right to their ' customs '; and those customs were not confined to the regulation of the domestic and internal affairs of the community, but overflowed to the surrounding country-side which the monastery owned and governed. An examination of them shows that they contained novelties which we are bound to regard as virtually legislation. As Professor Goebel remarks, with trans-Atlantic tartness, ' such a custom may have been a folkway, but it was the way of the folk in power '. In the second place, not only

[37] [See, for example, the experiments in regulating the family described by Berman in *Justice In The U.S.S.R.* (1963) Chap. 14.]
[38] See the valuable collection of texts reprinted in Wehrlé, *De la coutume dans le droit canonique* (which also includes civilian material). It has been pointed out in another connexion that Bracton can describe four days as *longum tempus, longum intervallum*—Pollock and Maitland, *History of English Law*, ii. 141, n. 1. Life was short in those days.
[39] Julius Goebel, *Felony and Misdemeanor*, i. 229–32, n. 80.

did this sort of thing happen, but medieval theorists also knew that it happened. The civilians and canonists of the thirteenth and fourteenth centuries had a proper reverence for the ancient Digest, Code, and Institutes, but that did not prevent them from watching with keen interest the living law around them. Their observations of the contemporary scene convinced them that customs were born, and made, and changed. Particularly, they were forced to admit that much change was effected by means of judicial decision.[40]

Now to frame a theory of judicial decision as a source of law was, for them, a singularly difficult task. At the very outset there were the decisive words of the Code that judgment must be according to law, and not according to precedent.[41] This obstacle was insuperable; but it could be circumvented. If one precedent by itself was inadmissible, two precedents were rather different, and could be regarded as constituting evidence of a custom. So we soon come to the triumphant maxim: 'Twice makes a custom.'[42]

Once again, then, we are reminded of the ease with which custom may come into being, as well as of the frailty of the distinction between precedent and proof of custom. It is easy to demonstrate, if demonstration be needed, that the common law of England is just such a custom, alive and vigorous, growing and changing. Both king and people desired amendments from time to time, and achieved them. The theorists were laying it down that custom derived its force from the consent of the prince *or* of the people, and this unresolved disjunctive is full of significance.[43] Some customs may well have been genuine folkways, but we may properly allow a large place (as does Professor Goebel) to the folk in power. In short, we must recognize the possibility that much of the common law may be ultimately of legislative origin. On rare occasions some memory or tradition of this lingered on. Thus a remarkable charter printed by Sir Frank Stenton asserts that our common-law rule of the partition of land among daughters when there is no son was due to a *statutum decretum* of the time of Stephen.[44] A chronicler alleges that Geoffrey FitzPeter, instigated by the servants of the devil, procured a decree which

---

40 [Marc Bloch has emphasised how in the early Middle Ages, custom was one of the most flexible ever known, for it was not fixed in writing or dealt with by a trained profession, but was largely dependent on human memory. Moreover, change was apt to be produced because whenever an act was repeated three or four times it was likely to become a precedent. When for instance a shortage of wine occurred in the royal cellars in the ninth century, the monks of Saint-Denis were asked to supply 200 hogshead. Thereafter this provision was claimed in every successive year as a right, and it required an imperial charter eventually to abolish this customary right. (See M. Bloch, *Feudal Society*, p. 114).]

41 Cod. 7. 45. 13: 'non exemplis, sed legibus judicandum sit'.

42 Gratian, c. 25, C. 25, q. 2: 'binus actus inducit consuetudineum'. Hostiensis rejects the requirement of ten precedents (which some had proposed on the ground that ten sheep made a flock as defined in Dig. 47. 14. 3). By about 1259 'twice makes a custom' appears in such popular books as Pierre de Fontaines, *Conseil à un Ami*, 492.

43 Hostiensis, *Summa Decretalium* (1517), f. 25, *qualiter consuetudo probari debet*. St. Thomas Aquinas, *Summa Theologica* Ia IIae, q. 97.3 add 3, places the consent of a 'free' people above that of the prince; but the civilians came to realize that the conception of the people as a source of law was incompatible with their imperialist dogma: Walter Ullmann, *The Medieval Idea of Law*, 63–4.

44 Stenton, *The First Century of English Feudalism*, 39, 259.

forbade the devise of land,[45] while Bracton preserves for us the memory of those sleepless nights during which the terms of the assize of novel disseisin were being thrashed out.[46] Chroniclers have even preserved the actual text of some of Henry II's innovating decrees. Otherwise, we should never have known of some of these momentous measures, for very soon they were completely dissolved in the swift-moving stream of the common law and lost to memory, as far as the general public, and even lawyers, were concerned.

It is important to realize that this state of affairs is not peculiar to the twelfth or earlier centuries, but is equally the situation in the thirteenth century. Long ago Maitland collected documents from various rolls which were legislative in effect although not statutory in form.[47] Outside official circles these texts were unknown, and soon they were forgotten even by the official successors of the judges to whom they had been originally addressed. For the future, therefore, they took effect not as royal edicts but simply as common law.[48] Notable examples which have been printed are an order of 1219 which had the effect of substituting jury trial for the ordeals in criminal cases,[49] and an order of 1256 which curtailed the powers of tenants in chief to alienate.[50] Of these, the former became simply a part of common-law procedure; the latter was merged in the mass of rules which constituted the royal feudal prerogative. Nor can we close the list with Henry III, for Edward I himself often issued informal writs of a legislative character. Sometimes imperfect copies of them enjoyed a limited currency among the legal profession, but often the texts were entirely lost until modern research brought them to light. Of this latter kind there is an interesting example in a decree upon the very technical matter of average contribution in maritime law.[51]

Indeed, there is evidence which compels us to admit that legislation of the highest importance could be effected under Edward I without even the slight formalities which accompanied the instances just mentioned— as far as we know, without any surviving document to witness it. One of the most striking examples is to be seen in the position of executors. In Maitland's words, 'a change as momentous as any that a statute could make, was made without statute and very quietly' when for the first time the courts of Edward I gave actions of debt for and against executors.[52] This step was of the utmost gravity. It abruptly closed the development of the English heir along the lines of the Roman *haeres*. By recognizing the executor as an institution of English law for the purpose of dealing with the decedent's chattels although preserving the descent of land to the heir, it cut our law of property permanently into two separate portions, and so it has remained until the present century. It would be difficult to deny that this change was as grave as anything to be found printed in the *Statutes of the Realm;* yet it has seemingly left no trace on roll or in chronicle. Strange as all this seems to us, it is

---

[45] Dugdale, *Monasticon*, iv. 147, cap. 18; Pollock and Maitland, *History of English Law*, ii. 327.
[46] 'Multis vigilis excogitatam et inventam'—Bracton, f. 164b.
[47] Pollock and Maitland, i. 180, n. 4.
[48] Cf. Plucknett, *Statutes and their Interpretation*, p. 135.
[49] *Patent Rolls* (1216–25), 186; *Law Quarterly Review*, xxvii. 352.
[50] *Close Rolls of Henry III* (1254–6), 429; *Law Quarterly Review*, xii. 299.
[51] Sayles, *Select Cases in King's Bench* (Selden Society), i. 156–7.
[52] Pollock and Maitland, ii. 347.

highly probable that a contemporary theorist, if he were asked to analyse the situation, would find the problem tolerably simple. He would remark that the common law is the custom of the realm; that the king's court has declared that custom (as it is well entitled to do); that it is not very significant whether the new custom contradicts the old, for the essentials are that the custom should be in itself reasonable, and fortified with the consent (tacit consent sometimes is good enough) of either the prince or the people. On those grounds the matter is simple—the common law has got a new rule, and that is all.   [pp. 6–10]

These later developments are so familiar that it is necessary to make a conscious effort in order to get back to the atmosphere of Edward I's age. We have to forget sovereignty and parliament, and keep our minds fixed firmly upon the common law, thinking of it as a living and changing organism, deriving its binding force from the fact that king and people willingly accepted it, until such time as they should change it. We must remember too that change was easy [53] and might be effected in very informal ways. Although many changes have left no trace whatever, and others have left traces which are discoverable only by prolonged excavation in the Public Record Office, and although yet others were announced in a few exceptional documents which were both written and published, nevertheless all three types are essentially the same (in so far as the reign of Edward I is concerned) for all these procedures were merely incidents in the life of the custom, going on inside it, part of its natural functions, and in no sense the injection of a foreign substance from outside.
                                                                    [p. 15]

GOODWIN v. ROBARTS
(1875) L.R. 10 Ex. 337

COCKBURN C.J. . . .

The substance of Mr. Benjamin's argument is, that, because the scrip does not correspond with any of the forms of the securities for money which have been hitherto held to be negotiable by the law merchant, and does not contain a direct promise to pay money, but only a promise to give security for money, it is not a security to which, by the law merchant, the character of negotiability can attach.

Having given the fullest consideration to this argument, we are of opinion that it cannot prevail. It is founded on the view that the law merchant thus referred to is fixed and stereotyped, and incapable of being expanded and enlarged so as to meet the wants and requirements of trade in the varying circumstances of commerce. It is true that the law merchant is sometimes spoken of as a fixed body of law, forming part of the common law, and as it were coeval with it. But as a matter of legal history, this view is altogether incorrect. The law merchant thus spoken of with reference to bills of exchange and other negotiable securities, though forming part of the general body of the lex mercatoria, is of comparatively recent origin. It is neither more nor less than the usages of merchants and traders in the different departments of trade, ratified by the decisions of Courts of law, which, upon such usages being proved before them, have adopted them as settled law with a view to the

---

[53] A change for the better needs no consents—Bracton, f. 1*b*.

interests of trade and the public convenience, the Court proceeding herein
on the well-known principle of law that, with reference to transactions
in the different departments of trade, Courts of law, in giving effect to
the contracts and dealings of the parties, will assume that the latter have
dealt with one another on the footing of any custom or usage prevailing
generally in the particular department. By this process, what before was
usage only, unsanctioned by legal decisions, has become engrafted upon,
or, incorporated into, the common law, and may thus be said to form
part of it. "When a general usage has been judicially ascertained and
established," says Lord Campbell, in *Brandao* v. *Barnett*[54] " it becomes
a part of the law merchant, which Courts of justice are bound to know
and recognise." [p. 346]

It thus appears that all these instruments which are said to have
derived their negotiability from the law merchant had their origin, and
that at no very remote period, in mercantile usage, and were adopted
into the law by our Courts as being in conformity with the usages of
trade; of which, if it were needed, a further confirmation might be found
in the fact that, according to the old form of declaring on bills of
exchange, the declaration always was founded on the custom of merchants.

Usage, adopted by the Courts, having been thus the origin of the
whole of the so-called law merchant as to negotiable securities, what is
there to prevent our acting upon the principle acted upon by our predecessors, and followed in the precedents they have left to us? Why is it
to be said that a new usage which has sprung up under altered circumstances, is to be less admissible than the usages of past times? Why is
the door to be now shut to the admission and adoption of usage in a
matter altogether of cognate character, as though the law had been
finally stereotyped and settled by some positive and peremptory enactment? It is true that this scrip purports, on the face of it, to be a
security not for money, but for the delivery of a bond; nevertheless
we think that substantially and in effect it is a security for money, which,
till the bond shall be delivered, stands in the place of that document,
which, when delivered, will be beyond doubt the representative of the
sum it is intended to secure. Suppose the possible case that the borrowing government, after receiving one or two instalments, were to determine to proceed no further with its loan, and to pay back to the lenders
the amount they had already advanced; the scrip with its receipts would
be the security to the holders for the amount. The usage of the money
market has solved the question whether scrip should be considered
security for, and the representative of, money, by treating it as such.

The universality of a usage voluntarily adopted between buyers and
sellers is conclusive proof of its being in accordance with public convenience; and there can be no doubt that by holding this species of
security to be incapable of being transferred by delivery, and as requiring
some more cumbrous method of assignment, we should materially hamper
the transactions of the money market with respect to it, and cause great
public inconvenience. [pp. 352–353]

We must by no means be understood as saying that mercantile usage,
however extensive, should be allowed to prevail if contrary to positive
law, including in the latter such usages as having been made the subject

[54] 12 Cl. & F., at p. 805.

of legal decision, and having been sanctioned and adopted by the Courts, have become, by such adoption, part of the common law. To give effect to a usage which involves a defiance or disregard of the law would be obviously contrary to a fundamental principle. And we quite agree that this would apply quite as strongly to an attempt to set up a new usage against one which has become settled and adopted by the common law as to one in conflict with the more ancient rules of the common law itself.   [p. 357]

If we could see our way to the conclusion that, in holding the scrip in question to pass by delivery, and to be available to bearer, we were giving effect to a usage incompatible either with the common law or with the law merchant as incorporated into and embodied in it, our decision would be a very different one from that which we are about to pronounce. But so far from this being the case, we are, on the contrary, in our opinion, only acting on an established principle of that law in giving legal effect to a usage, now become universal, to treat this form of security, being on the face of it expressly made transferable to bearer, as the representative of money, and as such, being made to bearer, as assignable by delivery.   [pp. 357–358]

JOHNSON v. CLARKE

[1908] 1 Ch. 303

PARKER J.[55] . . .

I think it may be inferred from the history of fines that our common lawyers never doubted the personal capacity of a married woman to act of her own free will. There was, however, no doubt a presumption that, except when acting in auter droit, she never did exercise free will, such presumption being based on the common law theory of marriage. In allowing the presumption to be rebutted in exceptional cases the common lawyers did not in any way contradict their own principles. They merely allowed what was really only presumption of fact to be rebutted under exceptional circumstances, at the same time taking care that the evidence rebutting the presumption was as cogent as possible. They found such evidence in the result of an examination before the King's justices entered on the records of the King's Courts. It became, therefore, possible for a married woman to dispose of her real estate notwithstanding the common law presumption arising out of the common law theory of marriage. It is possibly due to the comparative unimportance of personal property in early times that no similar method of disposition was evolved in the case of a married woman's interests in personalty.

Contemporaneously with the development of the fine as a method of alienating land, there grew up in various manors and townships other customary forms of alienation, these also involving in the case of married women a separate examination directed to ascertain and establish, with-

---

55 [At common law a married woman could alienate her property with the concurrence of her husband, if separately examined by justices; otherwise it was presumed that the act was without her free will. *Held*: a custom of burgage tenure allowing alienation without a separate examination was bad. The artificiality of the approach is signalised by the fact that equity admittedly did not insist on this requirement in regard to separate property.]

out the possibility of a doubt, that in alienating her interests in real estate she was acting of her own free will. Judging by the history of the fine, it is quite clear that such customary forms of alienation would not seem unreasonable to the common lawyer, provided the examination were such as to be sufficiently cogent evidence of the fact sought to be established, namely, that, notwithstanding the presumption of the common law, the married woman was exercising that free will which is necessary to all voluntary alienations. Customs for a wife to dispose of her realty by deed or surrender, with her husband's concurrence and after separate examination, have always therefore been deemed good customs. I do not, however, think that this fact, any more than the history of the fine, can properly be adduced as evidence that a custom for a married woman to dispose of her realty by deed with her husband's concurrence, but without any form of separate examination, is a good custom. I am, on the contrary, of opinion that a lawyer, conversant with the principles of our common law, would consider such a custom as in reality a custom for a married woman to dispose of her realty without any such exercise of free will as is necessary to all voluntary alienations at common law. For the common law theory of marriage would prevail in the local area in which the custom was alleged as in the realm generally; the results of a marriage in such area would be the same, and there, as elsewhere, the words of the writ, "Cui ipsa in vita sua contradicere non potuit," would be equally applicable. [pp. 315–316]

I have come to the conclusion, therefore, that the alleged custom cannot be upheld, because it is unreasonable, as conflicting with the general principle of the common law that an exercise of free will was essential to alienations and contracts, and that a married woman was not in a position to exercise such free will. Such a custom would, in other words, be against "common right." [p. 318]

PAUL BOHANNAN

The Differing Realms of The Law
(1965) [56]

Double Institutionalization

Law must be distinguished from traditions and fashions and more specifically, it must be differentiated from norm and from custom. A norm is a rule, more or less overt, which expresses " ought " aspects of relationships between human beings. Custom is a body of such norms —including regular deviations and compromises with norms—that is actually followed in practice much of the time.

All social institutions are marked by " customs " and these " customs " exhibit most of the stigmata cited by any definition of law. But there is one salient difference. Whereas custom continues to inhere in, and only in, these institutions which it governs (and which in turn govern it), law is specifically recreated, by agents of society, in a narrower and recognizable context—that is, in the context of the institutions that are legal in character and, to some degree at least, discrete from all others.

[56] [In 67 *American Anthropologist*, No. 6, part II, pp. 33–42; extract taken from reprint in *Law and Warfare* ed. Bohannan (1967).]

Just as custom includes norms, but is both greater and more precise than norms, so law includes custom, but is both greater and more precise. Law has the additional characteristic that it must be what Kantorowicz calls "justiciable," [57] by which he means that the rules must be capable of reinterpretation, and actually must be reinterpreted, by one of the legal institutions of society so that the conflicts within nonlegal institutions can be adjusted by an "authority" outside themselves.

It is widely recognized that many peoples of the world can state more or less precise "rules" which are, in fact, the norms in accordance with which they think they ought to judge their conduct. In all societies there are allowable lapses from such rules, and in most there are more or less precise rules (sometimes legal ones) for breaking rules.

In order to make the distinction between law and other rules, it has been necessary to introduce furtively the word "institution." I use the word in Malinowski's sense. [58]

A legal institution is one by means of which the people of a society settle disputes that arise between one another and counteract any gross and flagrant abuses of the rules (as we have considered them above) of at least some of the other institutions of society. Every ongoing society has legal institutions in this sense, as well as a wide variety of nonlegal institutions.

In carrying out the task of settling difficulties in the nonlegal institutions, legal institutions face three kinds of tasks: (1) There must be specific ways in which difficulties can be disengaged from the institutions in which they arose and which they now threaten and then be engaged within the processes of the legal institution. (2) There must be ways in which the trouble can now be handled within the framework of the legal institution, and (3) There must be ways in which the new solutions which thus emerge can be re-engaged within the processes of the nonlegal institutions from which they emerged. It is seldom that any framework save a political one can supply these requirements.

There are, thus, at least two aspects of legal institutions that are not shared with other institutions of society. Legal institutions—and often they alone—must have some regularized way to interfere in the malfunctioning (and, perhaps, the functioning as well) of the nonlegal institutions in order to disengage the trouble-case. There must, secondly, be two kinds of rules in the legal institutions—those that govern the activities of the legal institution itself (called "adjectival law" by Austin, and "procedure" by most modern lawyers), and those that are substitutes or modifications or restatements of the rules of the nonlegal institution that has been invaded (called "substantive law").[59]

Listed above are only the minimal aspects that are all shared by all known legal institutions. . . .

Seen in this light, a fairly simple distinction can be made between law and custom. Customs are norms or rules (more or less strict, and with greater or less support of moral, ethical, or even physical coercion) about the ways in which people must behave if social institutions are to perform their tasks and society is to endure. All institutions (including legal institutions) develop customs. Some customs, in some societies, are

57 [In *The Definition of Law* (1958), p. 76 and see *ante*, 68.]
58 *The Dynamics of Culture Change.*
59 [*Cf.* Hart's classification of primary and secondary rules, *ante*, 168.]

*re*institutionalized at another level: they are restated for the more precise purposes of legal institutions. When this happens, therefore, law may be regarded as a custom that has been restated in order to make it amenable to the activities of the legal institutions. In this sense, it is one of the most characteristic attributes of legal institutions that some of these " laws " are about the legal institutions themselves, although most are about the other institutions of society—the familial, economic, political, ritual, or whatever.

One of the reddest herrings ever dragged into the working of orderly jurisprudence was Malinowski's little book called *Crime and Custom in Savage Society*. . . . It has had an undue and all but disastrous influence on the rapprochement between anthropology and jurisprudence. Malinowski's idea was a good one; he claimed that law is " a body of binding obligations regarded as right by one party and acknowledged as the duty by the other, kept in force by the specific mechanism of reciprocity and publicity inherent in the structure of . . . society." His error was in equating what he had defined with the law. It is not law that is " kept in force by . . . reciprocity and publicity." It is custom, as we have defined it here. Law is, rather, " a body of binding obligations regarded as right by one party and acknowledged as the duty by the other " *which has been reinstitutionalized within the legal institution so that society can continue to function in an orderly manner on the basis of rules so maintained*. In short, reciprocity is the basis of custom; but the law rests on the basis of this double institutionalization. Central in it is that some of the customs of some of the institutions of society are restated in such a way that they can be " applied " by an institution designed (or, at very least, utilized) specifically for that purpose.

One of the best ways to perceive the doubly institutionalized norms, or " laws," is to break up the law into smaller components, capable of attaching to persons (either human individuals or corporate groups) and so to work in terms of " rights " and their reciprocal duties or " obligations." In terms of rights and duties, the relationships between law and custom, law and morals, law and anything else, can be seen in a new light. Whether in the realm of kinship or contract, citizenship or property rights, the relationships between people can be reduced to a series of prescriptions with the obligations and the correlative rights that emanate from these presumptions. In fact, if it is not carried too far and unduly formalized, thinking in terms of rights and obligations of persons (or role players) is a convenient and fruitful way of investigating much of the custom of many institutions.[60] Legal rights are only those rights that attach to norms that have been doubly institutionalized; they provide a means for seeing the legal institutions from the standpoint of the persons engaged in them.

The phenomenon of double institutionalization of norms and therefore of legal rights has been recognized for a long time, but analysis of it has been only partially successful. Kantorowicz, for example, has had to create the concept of " justiciability " of the law. It would be better to say that legal rights have their material origins (either overtly or covertly) in the customs of nonlegal institutions but must be *overtly restated* for the specific purpose of enabling the legal institutions to perform their task.

[60] See Hohfeld, *ante*, 248; Hoebel, *ante*, 584.

A legal right (and, with it, a law) is the restatement, for the purpose of maintaining peaceful and just operation of the institutions of society, of some, but never all, of the recognized claims of the persons within those institutions; the restatement must be made in such a way that these claims can be more or less assured by the total community or its representatives. Only so can the moral, religious, political, and economic implications of law be fully explored.

Law is never a mere reflection of custom, however. Rather, law is always out of phase with society, specifically because of the duality of the statement and restatement of rights. Indeed, the more highly developed the legal institutions, the greater the lack of phase, which not only results from the constant reorientation of the primary institutions, but also is magnified by the very dynamic of the legal institutions themselves.[61]

Thus, it is the very nature of law, and its capacity to " do something about " the primary social institutions, that creates the lack of phase. Moreover, even if one could assume perfect legal institutionalization, change within the primary institutions would soon jar the system out of phase again. What is less obvious is that if there were ever to be perfect phase between law and society, then society could never repair itself, grow and change, flourish or wane. It is the fertile dilemma of law that it must always be out of step with society, but that people must always (because they work better with fewer contradictions, if for no other reason) attempt to reduce the lack of phase. Custom must either grow to fit the law or it must actively reject it; law must either grow to fit the custom, or it must ignore or suppress it. It is in these very interstices that social growth and social decay take place.

Social catastrophe and social indignation are sources of much law and resultant changes in custom. With technical and moral change, new situations appear that must be " legalized." This truth has particular and somewhat different applications to developed and to less highly developed legal systems. On the one hand, in developed municipal systems of law in which means for institutionalizing behavior on a legal level are already traditionally concentrated in political decision-making groups such as legislatures, nonlegal social institutions sometimes take a very long time to catch up with the law. On the other hand, in less developed legal systems, it may be that little or no popular demand is made on the legal institutions, and therefore little real contact exists or can be made to exist between them and the primary institutions.[62] Law can, as we have seen in another context, become one of the major innovators of society, the more effective the greater a people's dependence on it. . . .   [pp. 45–50]

R. SCHWARTZ and J. MILLER

Legal Evolution and Societal Complexity
(1964) [63]

. . . The evolution of legal organization . . . warrants attention for several reasons. As the mechanism through which substantive law is

---

[61] *Legal Systems and Lawyers' Reasonings* (1964), Chap. 1, part 1.
[62] *Social Dimensions of Law And Justice* (1965) Chap. 2, s. 17.
[63] [From 70 *American Journal of Sociology* 159.]

formulated, invoked, and administered, legal organization is of primary importance for understanding the process by which legal norms are evolved and implemented. Moreover, legal organization seems to develop with a degree of regularity that in itself invites attention and explanation. The present study suggests that elements of legal organization emerge in a sequence, such that each constitutes a necessary condition for the next. A second type of regularity appears in the relationship between changes in legal organization and other aspects of social organization, notably the division of labor.

By exploring such regularities intensively, it may be possible to learn more about the dynamics of institutional differentiation. Legal organization is a particularly promising subject from this point of view. It tends toward a unified, easily identifiable structure in any given society. Its form and procedures are likely to be explicitly stated. Its central function, legitimation, promotes crossculturally recurrent instances of conflict with, and adaptation to, other institutional systems such as religion, polity, economy, and family. Before these relationships can be adequately explored, however, certain gross regularities of development should be noted and it is with these that the present paper is primarily concerned.

This article reports preliminary findings from cross-cultural research that show a rather startling consistency in the pattern of legal evolution. In a sample of fifty-one societies, compensatory damages and mediation of disputes were found in every society having specialized legal counsel. In addition, a large majority (85 per cent) of societies that develop specialized police also employ damages and mediation. These findings suggest a variety of explanations. It may be necessary, for instance, for a society to accept the principles of mediation and compensation before formalized agencies of adjudication and control can be evolved. Alternatively or concurrently, non-legal changes may explain the results. A formalized means for exchange, some degree of specialization, and writing appear almost universally to follow certain of these legal developments and to precede others. If such sequences are inevitable, they suggest theoretically interesting causative relationships and provide a possible basis for assigning priorities in stimulating the evolution of complex legal institutions in the contemporary world.

. . . Several characteristics of a fully developed legal system were isolated for purposes of study. These included counsel, mediation, and police. These three characteristics, which will constitute the focus of the present paper,[64] are defined as follows:

counsel: regular use of specialized non-kin advocates in the settlement of disputes

mediation: regular use of non-kin third party intervention in dispute settlement

police: specialized armed force used partially or wholly for norm enforcement.

[64] The original study also included damages, imprisonment, and execution. These were dropped from the present analysis, even though this unfortunately limited the scale to three items, to permit focus on statuses rather than sanction. Data on damages will be introduced, however, where relevant to the discussion of restitution.

These three items, all referring to specialized roles relevant to dispute resolution, were found to fall in a near-perfect Guttman scale.[65] . . .

FINDINGS

In the fifty-one societies studied, as indicated in Table 1, four scale types emerged. Eleven societies showed none of the three characteristics; eighteen had only mediation; eleven had only mediation and police; and seven had mediation, police, and specialized counsel. Two societies departed from these patterns: the Crow and the Thonga had police, but showed no evidence of mediation. While these deviant cases merit detailed study, they reduce the reproducibility of the scale by less than 2 per cent, leaving the coefficient at the extraordinarily high level of better than ·98. Each characteristic of legal organization may now be discussed in terms of the sociolegal conditions in which it is found.

TABLE 1

SCALE OF LEGAL CHARACTERISTICS

Society	Counsel	Police	Mediation	Errors	Legal Scale Type	Freeman-Winch [66] Scale Type
Cambodians	x	x	x	......	3	*
Czechs	x	x	x	......	3	6
Elizabethan English	x	x	x	......	3	6
Imperial Romans	x	x	x	......	3	6
Indonesians	x	x	x	......	3	*
Syrians	x	x	x	......	3	*
Ukrainians	x	x	x	......	3	6
Ashanti	......	x	x	......	2	5
Cheyenne	......	x	x	......	2	*
Creek	......	x	x	......	2	5
Cuna	......	x	x	......	2	4
Crow	......	x	......	1	2	0
Hopi	......	x	x	......	2	5
Iranians	......	x	x	......	2	6
Koreans	......	x	x	......	2	6
Lapps	......	x	x	......	2	6
Maori	......	x	x	......	2	4
Riffians	......	x	x	......	2	6
Thonga	......	x	......	1	2	2
Vietnamese	......	x	x	......	2	6
Andamanese	......	......	x	......	1	0
Azande	......	......	x	......	1	0
Balinese	......	......	x	......	1	4

[65] [Guttman scaling, or linear cumulative scaling, is a method for measuring differences in, and the consistency of, the attitudes of a group of persons, or, as here, cultural patterns of different societies, toward a single shared value or institution.]

[66] [Freeman and Winch studied a sample of 48 societies. The asterisks refer to societies not studied by them. See (1957) 62 Amer.J. of Sociol. 461–466.]

TABLE 1—*continued*

Society	Counsel	Police	Mediation	Errors	Legal Scale Type	Freeman-Winch Scale Type
Cayapa................			x	......	1	2
Chagga................			x	......	1	4
Formosan aborigines....			x	......	1	0
Hottentot..............			x	......	1	0
Ifugao			x	......	1	0
Lakher................			x	......	1	2
Lepcha................			x	......	1	3
Menomini			x	......	1	0
Mbundu................			x	......	1	3
Navaho			x	......	1	5
Ossett................			x	......	1	1
Siwans			x	......	1	1
Trobrianders..........			x	......	1	*
Tupinamba			x	......	1	0
Venda................			x	......	1	5
Woleaians			x	......	1	0
Yakut................			x	......	1	1
Aranda................					0	0
Buka.................					0	0
Chukchee..............					0	0
Comanche.............					0	*
Copper Eskimo........					0	0
Jivaro					0	0
Kababish..............					0	1
Kazak................					0	0
Siriono					0	0
Yaruro					0	0
Yurok................					0	1

MEDIATION

Societies that lack mediation, constituting less than a third of the entire sample, appear to be the simplest societies. None of them has writing or any substantial degree of specialization. Only three of the thirteen (Yurok, Kababish, and Thonga) use money, whereas almost three-fourths of the societies with mediation have a symbolic means of exchange. We can only speculate at present on the reasons why mediation is absent in these societies. Data on size, . . . indicate that the maximum community size of societies without mediation is substantially smaller than that of societies with mediation. Because of their small size, mediationless societies may have fewer disputes and thus have less opportunity to evolve regularized patterns of dispute settlement. Moreover, smaller societies may be better able to develop mores and informal controls which tend to prevent the occurrence of disputes. Also, the usually desperate struggle for existence of such societies may strengthen the common goal of survival and thus produce a lessening of intragroup hostility.

The lack of money and substantial property may also help to explain the absence of mediation in these societies. There is much evidence to support the hypothesis that property provides something to quarrel about. In addition, it seems to provide something to mediate with as well. Where private property is extremely limited, one would be less likely to find a concept of damages, that is, property payments in lieu of other sanctions. The development of a concept of damages should greatly increase the range of alternative settlements. This in turn might be expected to create a place for the mediator as a person charged with locating a settlement point satisfactory to the parties and the society.

TABLE 2

DAMAGES IN RELATION TO LEGAL FUNCTIONARIES

		No Mediation	Mediation Only	Mediation and Police	Mediation, Police, and Counsel	Total
Damages	..	7	17	10	7	41
No damages	..	6*	3	1	0	10
Total	..	13	20	11	7	51

* Includes Thonga, who have neither mediation nor damages, but have police.

This hypothesis derives support from the data in Table 2. The concept of damages occurs in all but four of the thirty-eight societies that have mediation and thus appears to be virtually a precondition for mediation. It should be noted, however, that damages are also found in several (seven of thirteen) of the societies that lack mediation. The relationship that emerges is one of damages as a necessary but not sufficient condition for mediation. At present it is impossible to ascertain whether the absence of mediation in societies having the damage concept results from a simple time lag or whether some other factor, not considered in this study, distinguishes these societies from those that have developed mediation.

POLICE

Twenty societies in the sample had police—that is, a specialized armed force available for norm enforcement. As noted, all of these but the Crow and Thonga had the concept of damages and some kind of mediation as well. Nevertheless, the occurrence of twenty societies with mediation but without police makes it clear that mediation is not inevitably accompanied by the systematic enforcement of decisions. The separability of these two characteristics is graphically illustrated in ethnographic reports. A striking instance is found among the Albanian tribesmen whose elaborately developed code for settling disputes, Lek's Kanun, was used for centuries as a basis for mediation. But in the absence of mutual agreements by the disputants, feuds often began immediately after adjudication and continued unhampered by any constituted police.[67]

[67] M. Hasluck, *The Unwritten Law in Albania* (1954).

From the data it is possible to determine some of the characteristics of societies that develop police. Eighteen of the twenty in our sample are economically advanced enough to use money. They also have a substantial degree of specialization, with full-time priests and teachers found in all but three (Cheyenne, Thonga, and Crow), and full-time governmental officials, not mere relatives of the chief, present in all but four (Cuna, Maori, Thonga, and Crow).

Superficially at least, these findings seem directly contradictory to Durkheim's major thesis in *The Division of Labor in Society*. He hypothesized that penal law—the effort of the organized society to punish offenses against itself—occurs in societies with the simplest division of labor. As indicated, however, our data show that police are found only in association with a substantial degree of division of labor. Even the practice of governmental punishment for wrongs against the society (as noted by Freeman and Winch) does not appear in simpler societies. By contrast, restitutive sanctions—damages and mediation— which Durkheim believed to be associated with an increasing division of labor, are found in many societies that lack even rudimentary specialization. Thus Durkheim's hypothesis seems the reverse of the empirical situation in the range of societies studied here.[68]

COUNSEL

Seven societies in the sample employ specialized advocates in the settlement of disputes. As noted, all of these societies also use mediation. There are, however, another thirty-one societies that have mediation but do not employ specialized counsel. It is a striking feature of the data that damages and mediation are characteristic of the simplest (as well as the most complex) societies, while legal counsel are found only

---

[68] A basic difficulty in testing Durkheim's thesis arises from his manner of formulating it. His principal interest, as we understand it, was to show the relationship between division of labor and type of sanction (using type of solidarity as the intervening variable). However, in distinguishing systems of law, he added the criterion of organization. The difficulty is that he was very broad in his criterion of organization required for penal law, but quite narrow in describing the kind of organization needed for non-penal law. For the former, the "assembly of the whole people" sufficed (*op. cit.*, p. 76); for the latter, on the other hand, he suggested the following criteria: "restitutive law creates organs which are more and more specialized: consular tribunals, councils of arbitration, administrative tribunals of every sort. Even in its most general part, that which pertains to civil law, it is exercised only through particular functionaries: magistrates, lawyers, etc., who have become apt in this role because of very special training" (p. 113). In thus suggesting that restitutive law exists only with highly complex organizational forms, Durkheim virtually insured that his thesis would be proven—that restitutive law would be found only in complex societies.

Such a "proof," however, would miss the major point of his argument. In testing the main hypothesis it would seem preferable, therefore, to specify a common and minimal organizational criterion, such as public support. Then the key question might be phrased: Is there a tendency toward restitutive rather than repressive sanctions which develops as an increasing function of the division of labor? Although our present data are not conclusive, the finding of damages and mediation in societies with minimal division of labor implies a negative answer. This suggests that the restitutive principle is not contingent on social heterogeneity or that heterogeneity is not contingent on the division of labor. [Nor is Hart's model of a primitive system (see *ante*, 169) consistent with these findings, for damages and mediation would be the result of the introduction of secondary rules.]

in the most complex. The societies with counsel also have, without exception, not only damages, mediation, and police but, in addition, all of the complexity characteristics identified by Freeman and Winch.

It is not surprising that mediation is not universally associated with counsel. In many mediation systems the parties are expected to speak for themselves. The mediator tends to perform a variety of functions, questioning disputants as well as deciding on the facts and interpreting the law. Such a system is found even in complex societies, such as Imperial China. There the prefect acted as counsel, judge, and jury, using a whip to wring the truth from the parties who were assumed a priori to be lying.[69] To serve as counsel in that setting would have been painful as well as superfluous. Even where specialized counsel emerge, their role tends to be ambiguous. In ancient Greece, for instance, counsel acted principally as advisors on strategy. Upon appearance in court they sought to conceal the fact that they were specialists in legal matters, presenting themselves merely as friends of the parties or even on occasion assuming the identity of the parties themselves.[70]

At all events, lawyers are here found only in quite urbanized societies, all of which are based upon fully developed agricultural economies. The data suggest at least two possible explanations. First, all of the sample societies with counsel have a substantial division of labor, including priests, teachers, police, and government officials. This implies an economic base strong enough to support a variety of secondary and tertiary occupations as well as an understanding of the advantages of specialization. Eleven societies in the sample, however, have all of these specialized statuses but lack specialized counsel. What distinguishes the societies that develop counsel? Literacy would seem to be an important factor. Only five of the twelve literate societies in the sample do not have counsel. Writing, of course, makes possible the formulation of a legal code with its advantages of forewarning the violator and promoting uniformity in judicial administration. The need to interpret a legal code provides a niche for specialized counsel, especially where a substantial segment of the population is illiterate.

CONCLUSIONS

These data, taken as a whole, lend support to the belief that an evolutionary sequence occurs in the development of legal institutions. Alternative interpretations are, to be sure, not precluded. The scale analysis might fail to discern short-lived occurrences of items. For instance, counsel might regularly develop as a variation in simple societies even before police, only to drop out rapidly enough so that the sample picks up no such instances. Even though this is a possibility in principle, no cases of this kind have come to the authors' attention.

Another and more realistic possibility is that the sequence noted in this sample does not occur in societies in a state of rapid transition. Developing societies undergoing intensive cultural contact might provide an economic and social basis for specialized lawyers, even in the absence of police or dispute mediation. Until such societies are included in the

[69] S. Van der Sprenkel, *Legal Institutions In Manchu China* (1962).
[70] A. H. Chroust, "The Legal Profession In Ancient Athens" (1954) 29 *Notre Dame Lawyer* 339–389.

sample, these findings must be limited to relatively isolated, slowly changing societies.

The study also raises but does not answer questions concerning the evolution of an international legal order. It would be foolhardy to generalize from the primitive world directly to the international scene and to assume that the same sequences must occur here as there. There is no certainty that subtribal units can be analogized to nations, because the latter tend to be so much more powerful, independent, and relatively deficient in common culture and interests. In other ways, the individual nations are farther along the path of legal development than subtribal units because all of them have their own domestic systems of mediation, police, and counsel. This state of affairs might well provide a basis for short-circuiting an evolutionary tendency operative in primitive societies. Then too, the emergent world order appears to lack the incentive of common interest against a hostile environment that gave primitive societies a motive for legal control. Even though the survival value of a legal system may be fully as great for today's world as for primitive societies, the existence of multiple units in the latter case permitted selection for survival of those societies that had developed the adaptive characteristic. The same principle cannot be expected to operate where the existence of " one world " permits no opportunity for variation and consequent selection.

Nonetheless, it is worth speculating that some of the same forces may operate in both situations.[71] We have seen that damages and mediation almost always precede police in the primitive world. This sequence could result from the need to build certain cultural foundations in the community before a central regime of control, as reflected in a police force, can develop. Hypothetically, this cultural foundation might include a determination to avoid disputes, an appreciation of the value of third-party intervention, and the development of a set of norms both for preventive purposes and as a basis for allocating blame and punishment when disputes arise. Compensation by damages and the use of mediators might well contribute to the development of such a cultural foundation, as well as reflecting its growth. If so, their occurrence prior to specialized police would be understandable. This raises the question as to whether the same kind of cultural foundation is not a necessary condition for the establishment of an effective world police force and whether, in the interest of that objective, it might not be appropriate to stress the principles of compensatory damages and mediation as preconditions for the growth of a world rule of law.[72]   [pp. 160–169]

---

[71] For an interesting attempt to develop a general theory of legal control, applicable both to discrete societies and to the international order, see Kenneth S. Carlston, *Law and Organization in World Society* (1962). [Note, however, that the thesis presented by Schwartz and Miller deals with the evolution of legal institutions and not a whole legal order. The generalisation about the growth of international legal order may not, therefore, be warranted.]

[72] [Do societies evolve in one progressive line? (*cf*. Maine, *ante*, 581) Schwartz and Miller seem to rule out any form of cyclical development whereby society experiments with one form, then another. On this, see Friedman and Ladinsky (1967) 67 Colum.L.R. 50. Contemporary examples are the English attitude towards industrial relations and the United States re-criminalisation of the juvenile court, as exemplified by *Re Gault*, 387 U.S. 1 (1967.]

10

MARXIST THEORY OF LAW AND SOCIALIST LEGALITY

HEGEL'S LOGICAL DIALECTIC

Hegel aimed to replace the rationalist individualism of the eighteenth century by a new kind of Reason personified in a mystical World-Spirit governing the course of human history. For this purpose he devised a new logical dialectic according to which two contradictory propositions, instead of excluding each other by virtue of the law of contradiction, could produce, in the form of thesis and anti-thesis, a solution by way of synthesis on a higher level. This involved a double confusion. For, in the first place, values were treated as inherent in reality, thereby ignoring Hume's principle that "ought" cannot be derived from "is." [1] Moreover, secondly, Hegel applied his doctrine not merely to logic but to opposite forces in nature or society, though such forces have nothing to do with a *logical* contradiction. In this way he applied the dialectic method to his philosophy of history, which envisaged the progressive realisation of Reason in the form of the World-Spirit, [2] manifesting itself on the road to perfection, by means of continuing conflicts each in turn being resolved in a higher synthesis. For Hegel the highest synthesis attainable on earth was the state conceived as an absolute value or end-in-itself, [3] and more particularly the German State, which Hegel envisaged as developing out of contemporary history. [4] Hence followed the deification of the state at the expense of individual values, for the individual could only attain his higher destiny as a cog in the state-machine to which he was relentlessly subordinated. [5] Also,

---

[1] See *ante*, 31. See also H. Kelsen, *What is Justice?* (1957), pp. 169–170.

[2] Hegel substituted for the familiar idealist notion of a higher reality beyond the actual world, the doctrine of a higher reality in the shape of what a thing is capable of *becoming* when it has realised its full potentialities. This has some resemblance to Aristotle, *cf. ante*, 90.

[3] Thus the state for Hegel represented the highest fulfilment of the human will, and embodied in itself a separate fully rational will distinct from the will of the individuals comprised in and submerged by this new entity. *Cf. post*, 654.

[4] Holmes J. once remarked to Pollock that Hegel "has not succeeded in convincing me that the King of Prussia was God in his day": *Pollock-Holmes Letters*, I, 188. It is fair to point out that by the German World Hegel meant, in effect, modern western civilisation, though at the same time, in sympathy with contemporary German romanticism, he does attribute to the Germans a special inborn quality of the German *Volk*. (See Plamenatz, *Man and Society* (1963), pp. 207–208).

[5] Hegel's dialectical process nonetheless left intact social institutions such as the family and civil society.

for Hegel, although spirit rather than matter represented the true reality and governed the world, the conflict of spirit or ideas could manifest itself at the national level, so that national warfare might prove the means to progress. It is not difficult to see how such a doctrine, espoused either in its original form or as developed or expounded by later writers, could lead naturally to the totalitarianism and aggressive wars all too familiar in the present century.[6]

MARX'S DIALECTICAL MATERIALISM

Marx accepted Hegel's dialectic while, as a thoroughgoing materialist, rejecting his attempt to relate it to a spiritual principle underlying the world and history. On the contrary, for Marx, nothing existed except the material world and thus the dialectic process as applied to humanity had to be interpreted in material terms.[7] For Marx the means of economic production was thus decisive in determining the general character of the social, political and spiritual processes of life. The means of production is basic too, it is the " infra-

---

[6] Though Hegel is not as illiberal as he is sometimes presented, he does play down the individual. By insisting so much that man owes everything to the community he belongs to, and above all to the State, there is a suggestion that he also owes absolute obedience: see Plamenatz, *op. cit.*, pp. 243, 262–263.

[7] Thus Marx declared that, by substituting for the idealist element the realities of the industrial system, he had turned Hegel's dialectic " right way up." For an admirable discussion, see G. H. Sabine, *History of Political Theory*, 3rd ed., Chap. 33. On the relation of the Marxist economic interpretation of history, law and society to later sociological theory, including jurisprudence, see M. G. White, *Social Thought in America* (1952), Chap. 8; and *cf. ante*, 399. An important attempt on Marxist lines to elaborate a more subtle interpretation of the interplay between legal institutions and the economic order of society was put forward by the distinguished Austrian jurist, Karl Renner. While accepting that legal institutions gradually take shape within the context of the economic forms of life prevailing in a given society, he argued that a certain rigidity inherent in the forms of law would result in the formal structure and concepts of the legal system being carried over into a society which was evolving new social and economic relationships. This would result in a certain tension arising between the form and structure of the law on the one hand and its social function on the other. But such, for Renner, is the adaptability of law and legal concepts in a mature system of law, that while the forms of the old structure are still retained, the inner content of the law is gradually transformed by the dexterity with which those who operate the legal system contrive to ferment new wine in old bottles.

Renner concentrated particularly on the concept of ownership, and the subtle and striking way in which the traditional concept of ownership had none the less undergone an inner transformation as new types of social economy have been developed. Thus, Renner sought to show, with much detailed elaboration, the way the law, under the guise of the concept of private ownership, gradually transformed ownership into an institution of public law. Once such an inner transformation of a traditional concept has taken place, it can then be put to new social and economic functions, so that though the law may itself result from the social and economic forces within society, it becomes itself an active agent in reshaping those social conditions. The relationship of economics to law is thus revealed not as a simple one-way causation, but rather a subtle interplay of mutual action and reaction. (See Karl Renner, *Institutions of Private Law and Their Social Function* (English translation with Introduction by O. Kahn-Freund) and also G. Sawer, *Law in Society*, pp. 178–181).

structure " of society; and law, like other cultural features of a society, is no more than the " superstructure," an ideological reflection of the underlying economic realities.[8] Historical evolution was seen as working through the resolution of material contradictions inherent in society. Of all these the most fundamental was the clash of class interests,[9] the class warfare based on economic conflict, which Marx saw, following the confusion of Hegel's method, as a logical contradiction. The struggle between classes was linked with the rise of the institution of private property; as for the state, it arose as an engine of compulsion to protect the class of property owners against the property-less class. On Hegelian principles this clash was bound to become more acute, particularly with the rise of capitalism, with its division of society (as Marx believed) into a capitalist class destined to become richer and richer, and a proletariat condemned to increasing poverty.[10] Only a revolution could resolve this conflict, and so produce a new Hegelian synthesis, which Marx envisaged as a Communistic society without private property or organised coercion in the form of the state or law. Hence Marx's viewpoint was essentially that of a prophet foretelling, like the prophets of old, of the doom and destruction of the existing order, and its ultimate

[8] According to Marx, the mode of production determines all non-economic phenomena. Marx consistently maintained that base and superstructure stand to each other as a cause to an effect, the former always dominating the latter. Engels, however, after Marx's death, revised this interpretation of the relationship between base and superstructure. He argued that there is causal interaction between economic base and superstructure. " It is not that the economic position is the *cause and alone active*, while everything else has a passive effect. There is, rather, interaction on the basis of the economic necessity, which ultimately always asserts itself." (letter to Sparkenburg, 1894 in Marx and Engels *Correspondence* 1846–1895, p. 475). Engels' rejection of Marxian economic determinism and political fatalism is of great importance to Soviet jurisprudence, particularly in its Stalinist manifestations, where the creation of Socialist society through legal machinery is stressed. Stalin himself referred to the superstructure as " an exceedingly active force, actively assisting its base to take shape and consolidate itself, and doing everything it can to help the new system finish off and eliminate the old base and the old classes " (*Marxism and Linguistics*, p. 10). The concept of parental law (see Berman, *post*, 687) would not be possible without Engels' reinterpretation of the relationship between base and superstructure, nor would it be possible for Soviet jurists to urge the use of law to produce social change (see, for example, Kechekyan (1956) 6 *Transactions of the Third World Congress of Sociology*). See, further, Jaworskyj, *Soviet Political Thought* (1961), pp. 26–30. Golinsky's comment that " neither Marx nor Engels ever sensed the reciprocal effect of the superstructure upon the base " (*Soviet Law and Govt.*, Vol. 1, No. 1, pp. 13, 15) is an *ex post facto* justification of Soviet practice and a good example of the need to square practice with ideology, but it is not accurate.

[9] " No credit is due to me for discovering the existence of classes in modern society, nor yet the struggle between them," wrote Marx in 1852, quoted in Bottomore and Rubel, *Selected Writings in Sociology and Social Philosophy* (Pelican, 1963), p. 19. Early formulations are those of Ferguson and Millar, eighteenth century Scottish historians.

[10] The views of Marx and Engels were heavily coloured by industrial conditions in the mid-Victorian era. The development of social welfare legislation since those days emphasises the danger of seeking to deduce universal laws or principles from what may prove only local or temporary circumstances.

replacement by a new Utopian society, where equality and justice would flourish without the need for any coercive order. " Nothing (says Kelsen) can show more clearly the futility of the dialectic method than the fact that it enables Hegel to praise the state as a god, and Marx to curse it as a devil." [11]

THE TWO ASPECTS OF MARXISM

Much of the difficulty in assessing the contribution of Marxism and its role in contemporary ideology, is due to the fact that it contains two very different strands, though these are often closely interwoven. On the one hand, Marxism involved and set the trend towards the close exploration of the actual conditions, especially economic, which exist in a given society, and which control or at least influence the political, social and legal organisation of that society in a given period. This approach, which itself was much influenced by earlier socialist thinkers such as Saint-Simon,[12] has been one of the formative factors in the development of modern social science. Such an approach, is, or at least can be expected to be, scientific in spirit and relativist, in the sense that it concentrates on facts, especially material facts, and attempts to eschew value-judgments. On the other hand, Marxism involved not merely a scientific attitude, but also a political doctrine,[13] which was closely linked with Hegelianism, in its philosophical aspect, to which was added a revolutionary bent, envisaging the creation of a just society. From Hegel was derived the idealist and absolutist doctrine that world history is conditioned by some kind of necessity to take a certain course, or to put it another way, that history is in some mystical manner ethically conditioned to produce an ideal society. This ushered in the prophetic aspect of Marxism, to which Marx's own sense of political urgency added a further distinguishing attribute. For Marx, though the course of world history cannot be fundamentally changed by men's actions, it can in some way be either delayed or speeded up, and furthermore the inherent contradictions and injustices prevailing in a given society can only be swiftly exorcised by a social and economic revolution. Hence the fundamental difference between the political

[11] Kelsen, *op. cit.*, p. 172.
[12] On Saint-Simon see Bowle, *Politics and Opinion in the Nineteenth Century* (1954), Chap. 4. For his influence upon Marx, largely through German Saint-Simonians such as Ludwig Gall and Moses Hess, see Bottomore and Rubel, *Selected Writings In Sociology and Social Philosophy* (Penguin edition 1963), pp. 24–26, 43, and Plamenatz, *German Marxism and Russian Communism* (1954), pp. 16–17, 153–155, 308–314. The influence of Hess on Marx is discussed by S. Hook, *From Hegel to Marx* (1962), Chap. 6.
[13] Marx became a socialist *before*, not after, having conceived his sociological theory of history. This is clear from the publication of his early writings. See Bottomore and Rubel, *op. cit.*, pp. 40–42.

outlook of Hegel and Marx. For Hegel everything that occurred was part of the morally ordained world order, and therefore whatever is, is right, whereas for Marx, it was the moral system of the future to which he looked forward with prophetic zeal. In the present he saw only injustice, though on the horizon, in the future, was to dawn a new order where right would ultimately prevail.

"Withering Away" of State and Law

The contradictions inherent in capitalist society were thus inevitably to provoke a revolution, which in its turn would produce the dawn of a new era. The successful revolution would put an end to the old bourgeois state and law. With the end of an economy based on capitalism and class conflict the state would become superfluous, and in Engel's celebrated phrase, both the state and its product of coercive law would become unnecessary and would "wither away." The coercive régime of law would thus be replaced by an "administration of things," since some administrative regulation would remain necessary to regulate society in an orderly way. But in a society without class conflict and clash of interests, where everyone would spontaneously accept a minimum of orderly regulation, it was apparently thought that there would be little scope for conflict and therefore no need for a system of coercive law as a means of enforcing such regulation.[14] If this attitude may seem to us somewhat naive, it should be remembered that it is not perhaps so far removed from concepts of some of the English and continental philosophical radicals, liberals and socialists of the nineteenth century.[15] Both the utilitarian belief in the possible attainment of a society in which there would be little need for legal interventionism to achieve social order, and the belief in the liberal doctrine of *laisser-faire*, by which the greater part of social order would be effectively established by contracts freely entered into by individuals given virtually unlimited freedom under the law to express their own individual wills, are after all, different only in degree from the utopian vision of the ultimate attainment of a society free of all law and coercion whatsoever.

Some of the more fervent prophets of the new order did indeed envisage the instantaneous accomplishment of the disappearance of the state and of the law with the successful outcome of the revolution. Lenin, however, adopted a more hard-headed and realistic approach, by recognising that even a successful revolution could not

14 See Plamenatz, *Man and Society* (1963), pp. 376–386.
15 *Cf. ibid.*, pp. 45–48, 108–109. Rousseau still accepted the need for coercive law even in a just society, based on his principles. For similar contemporary trends see the writings of Paul Goodman, discussed in T. Roszak, *The Making of a Counter Culture* (1968), Chap. 6. See further R. Dahrendorf, *Essays In the Theory of Society* (1968), pp. 151–178.

result in the immediate elimination of all the apparatus of the state and the panoply of the law. It would take time for a totally classless society to emerge, and though therefore Lenin did not abandon the Marxist conception of the ultimate withering away of the state when such a society has been attained, he still recognised the need, during an interim period when class conflict had still to be eliminated, and the surviving elements of the bourgeoisie extruded, for the apparatus of the state and coercive law to be retained.[16] There must be an interim period, a period of transition between the old and the new, during which socialism would be built as a transition to a purely Communist order. During this stage the class struggle would still not have ceased, since resistance to the consequences of the revolution would continue. The institutions of law and the state would, therefore, remain necessary, but it would be a new kind of law representing not the dominance of the minority over the majority, but of the majority—the " dictatorship of the proletariat "—over the minority of anti-revolutionaries, wreckers and saboteurs. Thus would come into being a new form of " revolutionary legality " embodying the right of the new ruling class to use the coercive power of the state to suppress their opponents and create a new régime. This, at any rate, was the interpretation placed on the early years after the Russian revolution by such commentators as Vyshinsky,[17] with a characteristically naive readiness to identify the Communist party leaders with the mass of the proletariat. Yet, as time has gone on, and the new order in the Soviet Union has consolidated itself, it has become increasingly apparent that the so-called " transitional period " is likely to be of indefinite duration, and the vision of the ultimate new Communist Jerusalem has continued to recede, in much the same way as the Second Coming and the end of the world, at first viewed as imminent by the primitive Christians, eventually paled into remote and indeterminate future events. During the reign of Stalin it thus became established doctrine that the " withering away " of the state would ultimately come not by a weakening but by an intensification of state authority. Only with the annihilation of " capitalist encirclement " could this aim be achieved, but when it was attained there would be no need for law or punishment, for people would be so accustomed to observe the fundamental rules of community life that they would fulfil these without constraint.[18] Thus are we presented with the

---

[16] See *post*, 657.

[17] See Vyshinsky, *Law of the Soviet State*, pp. 38–62.

[18] *Ibid.*, pp. 46–50. *Cf.* Prof. Hall's remarks on Plato: " . . . in a perfect society everyone understands and conforms to the Natural Law. . . . For these persons, positive laws are not only unnecessary, it would be superfluous, indeed, indefensible, to attempt to subject them to such laws " (*Studies in Jurisprudence and Criminal Theory* (1958), p. 68).

ideal of perfect conformity, where total indoctrination can go no
further. Like most Utopians from Plato onwards,[19] the Marxist
delights in a vision of unconditional yielding to what he considers
to be the just society.

LAW IN THE SOVIET STATE

Revolutionary Legality

In the early days after the Revolution the traditional form of legal
thinking was still viewed with much suspicion. Thus for Pashukanis,
since law was merely an instrument of capitalist oppression, all true
law was private law, and private law was no more than a means
whereby, " under the guise of civil relations between equals, those in
control of the means of production exercise their power over the
others." [20] Carrying the argument from the western legal ideology of
laisser-faire to what seemed to him its logical conclusion, Pashukanis,
in the spirit of Maine,[21] saw contract as the foundation of all law.
Thus labour law was nothing more than a series of employment
contracts; family law derived from a contractual view of marriage;
and even criminal law rested on a kind of bargain between the state
and the citizen, whereby equivalent punishments were meted out
for particular acts regardless of social-economic implications; again,
the constitutional basis of government by consent derived from the
concept of " social contract." But, under a guise of superficial
equality, Pashukanis saw all law as nothing but a cloak for bourgeois
class interests, and for him law was necessarily a capitalist institution.
In an embryonic form it might be found in feudal or slave societies,
but only under capitalism could it achieve its highest development.[22]

To speak of " proletarian law " is therefore a contradiction in
terms. The disappearance of the economic market must inevitably
lead to the ultimate disappearance of the legal element in human
relations. In a socialist community, on the other hand, private law
disappeared, since everything done was to be in the interests of the
community. The private law sector was thus to be swallowed up in
the public sector, which was conceived as purely administrative,
consisting not of fixed rules, but of guides to the exercise of administrative and judicial discretion.

In fact this early ideal was never fully achieved. During the

---

[19] *Cf. ante*, 89.
[20] Friedmann, *Legal Theory*, 5th ed., p. 371.
[21] See *ante*, 584.
[22] See, further, on Pashukanis, Fuller (1949) 47 Mich.L.R. 1157 and for an account
of the rehabilitation of Pashukanis see Kamenka and Tay (1970), *Problems of
Communism*, Part 1, p. 72.

period of the New Economic Policy,[23] introduced by Lenin as a temporary mixed system, neither capitalism nor socialism, to meet the harsh economic realities of the early 1920's, it was recognised that there had to be some restoration of bourgeois law to accommodate the situation. Some element of socialist law was however recognised, for example, by putting the emphasis in criminal law on " measures of social defence " rather than on crime and punishment as such, and in the celebrated article 1 of the Civil Code, which provided that civil rights were to be protected by law except where exercised in contradiction to their social-economic purpose. The NEP was followed by the period of the Plan, which it was thought at first would replace law. The Plan would not be an instrument of coercion, but an expression of the rational foresight of the planners, with the whole people participating freely. Society could be administered without coercion, in the absence of class conflicts, and any occasional clashes would not warrant an elaborate system of law and justice. Such relics of law as would survive during this transitional period would be so subordinated to political and economic needs, that they could not be expected to crystallise into the shape of a legal system. There would be a phase of what was called " revolutionary legality," where law, though it had not yet withered away, would be gradually disappearing and would be totally subordinated to social and economic need. Despite this, even Pashukanis conceded that the coercive power of the state must remain in order to prepare conditions for the ultimate withering away of the power of government. True this might be regarded as involving a contradiction, but such a contradiction did no more than reflect the Marxian dialectic.[23a]

Socialist Legality

Despite all these high sounding manifestos, and their undoubted influence in displacing or weakening many aspects of traditional law, the fact remains that throughout this early period law still continued to function in an attenuated way, courts of law remained in operation, and legal proceedings, both civil and criminal, were decided by the courts. 1936, however, proved to be the watershed between the revolutionary concept of law, and a new conception of a more permanent and stable form of socialist law. In that year the official doctrine was propounded, that although the Marxian concept still remained desirable and could be expected ultimately to be achieved when the whole world had attained a classless situation, for the time being, while Soviet socialism existed solely on a national basis,

[23] A good account is G. F. Hudson, *Fifty Years of Communism* (1968), Chap. 9. For the impact on Soviet law see Berman, *Justice in the U.S.S.R.,* pp. 33–37.
[23a] *Cf.* Stalin, *post,* 666.

surrounded by capitalist powers, there would remain the need for the protection of the state and for the concept of stable law. So far as the Soviet Union was concerned, the socialist society had been achieved and the transitional period to socialism could be regarded as terminated, since there was no longer any class warfare in that society, all hostile elements having been eliminated. This, however, was not to be regarded as ushering in a withering away of the state and the law, but on the contrary there were to be established legal institutions on a socialist basis. Thus was inaugurated what was deemed to be the first stage of the classless society, based on the dogma that each man was to receive according to his work, though this might be expected ultimately to develop at some date beyond the foreseeable future, into the final stage of communism in which each would receive according to his need.

The principal exponent of the new doctrine of stable socialist law was Vyshinsky, who strenuously attacked the former view of Pashukanis, arguing that, far from reaching its highest development under capitalism, such an economy in fact led to the decay of law and legality, and that only under socialism would law attain its highest achievement. The lesson had been well learned that without a legal order the régime could not effectively control either social relationships or the economic organisation which was required for the new technological age. The need for stability was thus manifested throughout the whole of the legal system. Emphasis on crime and punishment, based on personal guilt, rather than on " social defence," was reinstated, and in family law divorce once again became a matter for judicial proceedings.[24] A law of contract, governed by the principles of the Civil Code, was reinstated, and in the law of personal injuries, the concept of "fault" once again became the basis of liability. At the same time it was recognised that there was a sphere for coercion outside the scope of law, in all those areas where the stability of the régime was still regarded as at risk. In Professor Berman's words, it was assumed that politics were beyond law, and law extended only to those areas of society in which the political factor had been stabilised. "Where the stability of the régime is threatened, law goes out of the window."[25] There was thus the coexistence of law and terror, not made easier by the fact that the border line between these two was constantly shifting. For example, the theft of state property, which might be regarded as a matter to be dealt with by the ordinary process of law, could easily become

---

[24] In 1944. The pendulum has swung the other way again and the introduction in 1968 of new Fundamental Principles has liberalised divorce law. See Gorkin, 7 Sov.Law and Government, No. 3, p. 29 and Stone (1969) 18 I.C.L.Q. 392.
[25] *Op. cit.,* p. 57.

transferred to the realm of counter-revolutionary crime, and thus fall under the aegis of the secret police.

After Stalin's death, in 1953, there were numerous attacks launched on the violations of socialist legality which had occurred under his régime.[26] These have produced some liberalisation of the area of socialist legality on the one hand, as well as a reduction, though not an elimination, of the sphere given over to police repression. Today, as is shown in the extract from Strogovich,[26a] socialist legality has assumed a new importance. Law is seen as a primary instrument in the development of a communist Utopia: socialist legality requires absolute unquestioning observance of these legal norms, and a searching examination of the causes of the gap between legal norm and social behaviour.

SOME CONCEPTS OF SOVIET LAW [26b]

Thus, on the one hand, we find that while Soviet law still embraces such traditional legal categories as contract, the overall control that the state exercises in the sphere of economic production and planning has radically changed the nature of this relationship. Contracts are still needed, for example, to regulate transactions between state corporations, and special tribunals have been created to enforce these. Yet in so doing, these tribunals must have regard to the economic policy of the government and its sanctions are not merely damages but administrative actions, such as the making of adverse reports to a higher administrative authority. " This reveals (Friedmann points out) [27] a characteristic feature of a fully socialised law. The institution of contract is taken over from capitalist systems and preserved but for different purposes. It is predominantly a means of ensuring efficiency in the carrying out of the national plan. Therefore public and private law sanctions, criminal and civil law, are mixed and the court fulfils administrative as well as judicial functions."

Nor, in the view of experienced commentators, have the recent post-Stalin political developments had much effect in bringing Soviet legal ideas into line with the concepts of traditional jurisprudence. It is more a " change of climate " than a change in the legal system as such. Thus, it must be understood that the Soviet Constitution of 1936 is in no sense the " supreme law " of the land. " It is, rather, a solemn declaration of general policies and an approximate scheme of government authorities, whose procedure, however, is not neces-

[26] The most famous was Khrushchev's denunciation at the 20th Congress of the Communist Party in 1956.
[26a] *Post*, 680. See also *post*, 678 and *post*, 643 *et seq.*
[26b] Concepts of Soviet law are a synthesis of western and socialist ideologies.
[27] *Legal Theory*, 4th ed., p. 338 (omitted in 5th ed.).

sarily bound by the constitutional provisions. . . . A constitutional provision may be set aside by an administrative decree and the newly enacted rule is incorporated into the Constitution only at a later date. . . . The Soviet jurists are fully aware of the indefinite relationship of their constitution, legislation and decrees. They seek to blur the distinction between the authority of a constitutional provision, a legislative enactment, and an administrative decree. . . . In fact, the most recent act prevails regardless of whether it is called law, resolution or anything else, and without regard to the name of the central government agency which issued it, the real sovereign power [28] resides outside the official government. The decision is made somewhere at Party-top level and then made public as an act of one or another government authority." [29]

The differences between western law and law on the Soviet pattern may perhaps best be brought out in those spheres where in the context of comparable bodies or codes of law, fundamental differences nonetheless emerge which derive from the opposing ideological assumptions upon which those bodies of law are based. A few significant illustrations may be given. There is still a certain amount of private housing in the Soviet Union, and the civil code regulates its use, as it does all housing. Although many of its provisions as to recovery of possession, and the passing of property resemble those to be found in western law, there are a number of significant differences. Thus a man is regarded as needing only one house, and this of a limited size, and, therefore, the citizen is allowed to retain only one dwelling house in his personal [30] ownership, and its maximum size is severely delimited. Any other house which he may own must be sold, given away, or otherwise alienated by the owner within one year. It is expressly forbidden for the citizen to retain ownership of a house and to use it to derive unearned income. Any attempt to do so renders the house liable to confiscation without compensation. Again, communal control is illustrated by the provision that if a citizen mismanages a house by allowing it to become dilapidated, then the executive committee of the local soviet

[28] It will be realised how difficult it is to apply the notion of Austinian sovereignty or indeed, of Kelsen's hierarchy of logically self-consistent norms, to these conditions. Yet it remains unprofitable simply to deny that there is in the Soviet Union anything deserving of the description of a " legal order."

[29] V. Gsovski, address to International Congress of Jurists held in Athens, *Report* (1956), p. 31. See also pp. 34–36, for a detailed reference to features of the Soviet system which involve fundamental departures from the distinction, in western jurisprudence, between judicial activity and administration.

[30] " Private ownership has been so named in order to show that it must only be used for the satisfaction of the personal needs of the individual enjoying such right, and for the purpose for which such property is intended, and not in order to draw profit from it or to use it for speculative ends " (David and Brierley, *Major Legal Systems of the World* (1968), p. 215).

of workers' deputies may set the owner a period for its repair, and failure to comply may result in confiscation of the house without compensation.[31]

Reference has already been made to the difference in the economic function of the law of contract in the western system of law, and under a system of law following the Soviet pattern, where contract has become an instrument consciously employed for the development of the whole economy. This distinction is strikingly brought out by the fact that in East European law there is frequently imposed upon state or social institutions a legal duty to conclude a contract, a principle which is of primary importance in socialist legal systems. The principal way in which this arises is where the contract is deemed necessary for the implementation of an overriding economic plan, but such a duty may arise even outside the realm of such a plan, for example, in the case of production contracts on the part of a state enterprise, where that enterprise is bound to make contracts with individual producers on the basis of its own planned production. This duty to make a contract has been recognised not merely as a duty arising in administrative law, violation of which may result in payment of a penalty to the state, but also as a civil law duty for which the remedy of damages is available to the injured party. It is true that in western legal systems, very exceptionally, a duty to make a contract may arise, particularly in the case of certain monopoly positions, such as duties imposed on public carriers, and such duties may, but generally do not, have sanctions attached to them. For example, no action will lie for damages against the Post Office for refusal or failure to supply a telephone line to a would-be subscriber. And even the imposition of compulsory third-party insurance, which is fairly universal at present in the western world, does not impose a duty upon any insurance company to accept the proposal of a particular motor car owner.[32]

There seems also to be some social significance in the difference between western tort law, which allows damages to be recovered not merely for financial loss, but also for pain and suffering, and for disfigurement or injury not involving loss of earning capacity, and Soviet law which allows claims only for proved financial loss.[33]

---

[31] See B. Rudden, " Soviet Housing and the New Civil Code," (1966) 15 I.C.L.Q. 231. See also J. N. Hazard, *Communists and their Law* (1969), pp. 204 *et seq.* For the regulation of state housing, see pp. 333–336.

[32] See S. Szaszy, " The Duty to Conclude a Contract In East European Law," (1964) 13 I.C.L.Q. 1470: for other aspects of contract law in East European systems, see Szubert, " Contract of Employment in Polish Labour Law," (1962) 25 M.L.R. 36.

[33] See E. L. Johnson, " Compensation for Victims of Criminal Offences in English and Soviet Law " (1964) C.L.P. 144. In the field of personal injuries Soviet law has moved steadily away from an earlier emphasis on strict liability towards

A further interesting contrast is provided by a comparison between the law of industrial property in western and Soviet law. Whereas under western law the patentee is given a proprietary monopoly, in the socialist countries he is merely given the right of utilisation of his patent, but not the right of industrial production or trade distribution. Further, the East European patentee has the negative right of preventing others using his patent without recompense, but cannot prevent its use for payment. The socialist countries have also supplemented the ordinary law of patents by a law of inventions under which an inventor may request from the state a mere recognition of his invention, as a result of which a certificate of authorship will be issued to him, and at the same time render him entitled to certain special payments for which a scale is laid down by law. In certain cases disputes as to the value of an invention can be determined by a court of law. Some such states have even gone further, and introduced a law of discoveries by which is meant the establishment of hitherto unknown objective laws, properties or phenomena of the material world. Legal protection takes the form of the protection of authorship symbolised by a State Diploma, and the payment of a premium by the state. It is clear that such novel provisions, while affording no evidence of a withering away of state law, nevertheless show a concern for the social as against the individual aspects of property, which is undoubtedly characteristic of the present state of legal development in socialist countries.[34]

Law, then, in the Soviet view, is merely an aspect of government which is regarded as identical with the system of social control as a whole, dominating every aspect of social life. This should not, however, blind us to the fact that the Soviet system does work through law, and that it has produced a legal order which embodies the basic principles of the Revolution, and has given this institutional form.[35] But the *role* of law must not be confused with the *rule* of law, for, as Professor Berman remarks, " under a total state, a highly developed legal system is, in the long run, a necessity—and the rule of law is an impossibility." [36]

---

fault as a means of enforcing the duty to take care, and thus act as a moral teacher. Social insurance exists, but the social insurance agency has the right to sue the wrongdoer for any benefits it has paid. (See J. N. Hazard, *op. cit.*, pp. 385–389.) More recently, strict liability has been reintroduced, especially in the field of motor vehicles, as a means of securing an exceptionally high degree of care. This follows the pattern of western European codes (*ibid.*, p. 416).

34 See A. Vida, " The Law of Industrial Property in Peoples' Democracies and the Soviet Union," in (1962) 12 I.C.L.Q. 898; J. N. Hazard, *op. cit.*, Chap. 11.
35 H. J. Berman, " Soviet Law and Government," in (1958) 21 M.L.R. 19.
36 *Ibid.*, p. 26.

CONTEMPORARY LEGAL THOUGHT IN THE SOVIET UNION

The Soviet Union has now begun its "expanded construction of communism." Under Khrushchev it was argued that the State no longer needed to get stronger and that the dictatorship of the proletariat had ceased to be necessary. The new Soviet concept is of an "All-People's State," [37] a society based on voluntary social co-operation rather than force, persuasion rather than coercion. The consequences of this are brought out in the 1961 Party Programme. The importance of the Party as an élite, as *the* social organisation is stressed, as is the intention to democratise public administration and, in so doing, eliminate bureaucracy.[38] Vyshinsky's jurisprudence, still dominant after Stalin's death, was denounced in the same year (Pashukanis [39] was gradually and partially rehabilitated). Stalin's laws were attacked for lacking legality and jurists for falling under the "cult of personality." [40]

The 1961 Party Programme thus inaugurates a new era of legal thought. Characteristic of this era is the support given to law and legality during the transitional period to Communism, emphasis upon a strict observance of socialist legality, the need to abolish crime and its causes, and the increased role given to social organisations, people's patrols,[41] and comrades courts,[42] as a means of increasing participation in justice. Much of this comes out in Strogovich's "Problems of Methodology in Jurisprudence " [43]: the attack on Vyshinsky who "impoverished jurisprudence and introduced elements of a peculiar pragmatism " [44]; the explanation that norms of Soviet law express the will of the Soviet people and the policies of the Communist party and that they are guaranteed by consciousness, social influence, education and persuasion and, finally, compulsion; and the insistence on a "rigorous and undeviating adherence to and execution of Soviet laws by authorities and citizens." [45] Ioffe and Shargorodsky [46] ask why should socialism need law more than

---

[37] With the fall of Khrushchev this concept has mysteriously and unaccountably disappeared, though nothing has been substituted in its place.

[38] See P. Romashkin, "Problems of the Development of the State and Law in The Draft Program of the C.P.S.U." in *Soviet Law and Government*, Vol. 1, No. 1, p. 3.

[39] On which see Kamenka and Tay (1970) *Problems of Communism*, Part I, p. 72.

[40] A good example is "For Complete Elimination of the Harmful Consequences of the Personality Cult in Soviet Jurisprudence " in *Soviet Law and Government*, Vol. 1, No. 1, p. 24.

[41] On which see Berman, *Justice in the U.S.S.R.*, pp. 286–288.

[42] *Idem*, pp. 288–291. On developments in Eastern Europe, see W. E. Butler in 1972 *Current Legal Problems*.

[43] See *Soviet Law and Government*, Vol. IV, No. 2, p. 13.

[44] *Idem*, p. 17. Vyshinsky is not referred to specifically, but it is clear that he is the object of attack.

[45] *Idem*, p. 20.

[46] See *Soviet Law and Government*, Vol. II, No. 2, p. 3.

capitalism, and conclude that under capitalism law is a stabiliser, but that in a socialist society law is needed to build the society, to develop productive forces. But, like Strogovich, they realise that law by itself is not enough. " Merely to enact the very best of legal norms is inadequate. Only adherence to socialist legality can assure a situation in which regulation by legal norms is actually implemented in life." [47] The need to publicise law is another preoccupation in Soviet jurisprudence.[48] Thus, Golunsky [49] has stressed that legal norms must be formulated in such a manner that the " goal pursued by the establishment of any norm is clear to the very broadest strata of the population." [50]

With this emphasis on socialist legality it may be asked how trials of writers [51] and demonstrators, so much in the public gaze, are justified by Soviet jurists. As far as trials of writers are concerned Soviet critics of the trials apparently accept that socialist legality was observed. The problem is that the laws under which the prosecutions take place are articulated so as to be broad in ambit and vague in definition. The judicial role is to decide the case " on the basis of law in conformity with socialist legal consciousness." [52] Socialist legality is *one* element of socialist legal consciousness. Observance of the statute does not assist any judge, Soviet or English, where there are gaps which need fixing. The soviet answer is to seek an objective standard laid down by the Party: Party policy is, in fact, one of the authoritative sources where law is deficient.[53]

The 1961 Party Programme left open the question of the role of law upon the attainment of Communism.[54] It is clear from Soviet jurists that Soviet law is " a most important lever . . . in establishing the material and technical base for Communism " [55] and that " its role is also important in the field of ideological education of the Soviet people, builders of the new, Communist society." [56] Less clear is whether law will atrophy when Communism emerges. Ioffe

[47] *Idem*, p. 8.
[48] See Berman, *op. cit.*, pp. 299–302.
[49] In *Soviet Law and Government*, Vol. 1, No. 1, p. 13.
[50] *Idem*, p. 18.
[51] The most notable being that of Sinyavsky and Daniel, on which see ed. Hayward, *On Trial* (1967). See also P. Litvinov, *The Demonstration in Pushkin Square* (1969).
[52] See S. Weiner, " Socialist Legality on Trial " in *Problems of Communism* (1968), Part 4, p. 6.
[53] See, further, Weiner at p. 12.
[54] See the account in Romashkin, *Soviet Law and Government*, Vol. 1, No. 1, p. 3, 5 *et seq.* At p. 9 he quotes Khrushchev: " How can anyone conceive of an organised human society without norms and rules of intercourse obligatory for all its members! . . . The life of people in such a society would become simply unbearable and be like Babel."
[55] *Per* Ioffe and Shargorodsky, *Soviet Law and Government*, Vol. II, No. 2, p. 3.
[56] *Idem*.

and Shargorodsky see the need for "normative regulation." "Communism is," according to these leading jurists, "a highly organised society of free and conscious working persons in which society is self-administered, work for the good of society becomes an inner need for all, a conscious necessity." [57] But "Communist society, like no other, will stand in need of unified planning of the economy and organised allocation of labour and regulation of working time." [58] Nonetheless, in "Communist society there will be no law, as there will be no state and state compulsion." [59] It is recognised that there will be "occasional excesses by individuals" but such violations of norms of social behaviour will be met by "measures" applied by "public opinion, the strength of the group, social influence." [60] Khrushchev had promised Communism by 1980. Today, it still remains on the distant horizon.

THE THREE STRANDS OF SOCIALIST LAW

In his book *Justice in the U.S.S.R.*,[61] Professor Berman has illuminatingly explained how the present state of law in that country can only be adequately understood if regard is had to the three principal strands from which it is derived. In the first place, there is the Marxist heritage. This has transmitted a number of distinctive features to the present state of Soviet law. It is Marxism that gives that law its collectivist character, so that legal problems are deliberately treated as social problems. Again, the dialectical character of Soviet law is brought out in its readiness to accept contradictions and inconsistencies as part of the dynamic need to adapt to continuing social and economic changes.[62] The Marxist theory is also evident in the recognition of extra-legal means of social control. Where the social order is threatened law must give way to force; hence the precarious character of all Soviet law.

This brings us to the second main strand in present day Soviet law, namely its specifically Russian character, derived from historic Russian conceptions of man and society. If we hark back to the core of truth in Savigny, there is a national culture whose roots lie deep in Russian history, and whose influence can be felt even after the vast revolutionary changes in that society which have been wrought during the last fifty years. This of course is not a peculiarity of the Russian scene, as similar historical and cultural influences

[57] *Idem*, p. 6.
[58] *Idem*.
[59] *Idem*, p. 7.
[60] *Idem*.
[61] (2nd edition, 1963.)
[62] *Cf.* Stalin, *post*, 666.

could be found to give distinctive features to the legal systems of other
states which are now swayed by Marxist ideology in one form or
another, such as Poland, Yugoslavia [63] or China.[64]

In this context Professor Berman concentrates particularly on the
subjectivism of Russian thought in connection with crime, and its
close link with the concept of sin, and the regeneration of the sinner.
Despite the earlier attempts, shortly after the revolution, to reject
such traditional approaches in favour of a social and collectivist
approach to crime, and the rejection of " guilt " in favour of measures
of social defence, Russian law never really came to terms with this
approach, and later developments have shown a marked reversal in
favour of subjective standards. Thus, in the case of criminal negligence the court will have regard not just to an objective criterion,
but will seek to explore the subjective qualities of the accused,
such as whether the given personality, with his individual capacities,
development and qualifications, could have foreseen the consequences
which occurred. An example given is that of a person accused of
criminal negligence in the management of a store, where the defence
was that the manager had been promoted to a position for which
she was not qualified, as she was barely literate. This defence was
sustained by the highest court, on the ground that to be convicted it
must be shown that the accused in the concrete situation, and guided
by his own knowledge and abilities, could avoid the loss which had
occurred.[65] Again, reference is made to a provision of the criminal
code which enables an accused person to be acquitted, even though
he committed the criminal act, if at the time of the verdict he personally no longer constitutes a social danger.[66] In the result, there
is a curious mixture of what seems by western standards excessive
harshness in the sphere of crimes which are regarded as having an
ideological or political significance, and at the same time excessive
leniency towards ordinary individual crimes involving persons or
personal property, a degree of leniency which manifested itself in
the pre-revolutionary Russian law in the punishment of murder. On
the other hand, where the Soviet state suddenly decides that a certain

---

[63] See *post*, 649.
[64] See *post*, 651. For a full discussion of the " common core " in the family of
Marxist socialist legal systems, see J. N. Hazard, *Communists and their Law*
(1969), Chap. 19. This common core is attributed to a number of facts, but to
none more than " the degree of involvement of all elements of society and
of its institutions in the operation of a fully state-owned and planned economy "
(p. 523). Hazard concludes that " there are universals found in all the fourteen
Marxian socialist states which provide reason to conclude that the legal
systems of those states, in spite of a wealth of differences, a vocabulary and
even a ' grammar ' inspired by the Romanist systems, constitute a distinctive
legal family " (*ibid.*, pp. 527–528). Hazard's thesis has been subjected to severe
criticism. See, for example, Ehrenzweig, 58 Calif.L.R. 1005 and Berman (1971)
Problems of Communism, Part 5, p. 24.
[65] p. 256.   [66] pp. 306–307.

type of crime has become a serious social evil, then the sanctions against it may be suddenly increased to what would be regarded in the west as involving an excessive degree of severity.

Professor Berman also reminds us that until the nineteenth century the law played a relatively minor role in Russian society, but with the westernisation of Russia, there was a great deal of conscious borrowing from western legal sources. The attempt to build up a Russian legal system in the western image constituted a challenge. But non-legal social and personal values which have been traditionally developed in Russian life over the centuries still retained their influence.

The attempt to develop a specifically Soviet legal system which may achieve some kind of synthesis between western conceptions of the supremacy and rationality of law, while nevertheless not renouncing many of the traditional non-legal values of the Russian people, viewed historically, has meant that Russian law, while still sometimes paying lip service to the western idea of the completeness of law, acknowledges and accepts that whole spheres of activity remain outside the law. Hence, especially in the field of politics, including any offence which may be regarded as of political significance, reliance may still be placed on non-rational, non-legal factors. A curious amalgam of violence on the one hand and of moral unity, actual or induced, on the other, will then prevail unquestioningly over merely juristic canons of substantive law or procedure.

This overriding and traditional acceptance of a large sphere of life which is outside the realm of law has also been influential in producing the third strand of legal thinking, which has served to produce the distinctive attributes of modern Soviet law. This third element is what Professor Berman designates as " parental law." The traditional role of western law, which Roscoe Pound has described as that of de-limiting and recognising existing interests in society, and giving effect to such interests in a rational and orderly way, is based on the philosophy that those who are subject to law know their own interests as independent adults and are capable of asserting these. Law may have an educative function, as is brought out clearly in some modern legislation of the type of the Race Relations Acts,[67] but this role is still regarded as secondary to the fundamental role of organising interests and resolving conflicts between them.

In the Soviet system, on the contrary, the educational role of the

---

[67] On the English Race Relations Acts as educators, see ed. Abbott, *The Prevention of Racial Discrimination In Britain* (1971), Chap. 9 and Lester and Bindman, *Race and Law* (1972) Chap. 2.

law has become central to the administration of justice. The centre
of gravity has thus shifted from the concept of the citizen who knows
what he wants, and is simply demanding the recognition of his
just claims or interests, to a new conception of members of a society,
which is still immature, but which is moving to a higher phase of
development. The law, the courts and the judges must therefore all
play an educational role in guiding this more dependent kind of
citizen into a true understanding of social needs and of the individual's
role in society, and the law is therefore seen as a means of training
people to fulfil their responsibilities.[68] As Professor Berman points out,
this form of parental law, though clearly having a background in
socialist thought, nevertheless has deep roots in Russian history.
This is not to say, of course, that it is unique to Russia or similarly
organised semi-communist states. The gradually developing collectivist tradition in the western type of welfare state has also placed
emphasis on the educational role of the law, but such an approach
still remains, in western tradition, strongly offset by the concept of
the individual standing forth independently and claiming recognition
of what he conceives to be his just interests and his legal rights.
Hence the strong emphasis laid in modern western law on legally
recognised individual human rights, which must necessarily diminish
the parental and educative role of the law. The relatively insignificant
role of such individual rights in Soviet ideology, has allowed far
greater scope for the trend towards the parental function of law. As
an illustration of the influence of this type of approach and its effect
on what by western standards would be regarded as individual
human rights, we may consider the case of the People's Courts and
the so-called Anti-Parasite Laws.

The use of popular tribunals as an instrument of law enforcement
involves an attempt to bring the official law of the state into closer
contact with the minds and hearts of the people, and thereby to
enshrine what are regarded as officially established values into the
consciousness of ordinary citizens. At the same time the use of such
procedures is thought of as a means of reintegrating the offender
into the collective, and the use of the collective to administer such
procedures is regarded as having educational value for all the
participants, both judges and offenders.

The anti-parasite laws provide a striking illustration of the belief
in the educative function of law. These provided for resettlement in
specially designated localities for a number of years of persons found

---

[68] The so-called " duty to rescue," *i.e.*, a duty of the citizen to rescue those in
peril, is perhaps referable to this approach, though such a duty has as yet been
confined in U.S.S.R. to criminal law. In some East European systems, however,
a civil law duty is also established. (See J. N. Hazard, *op. cit.*, pp. 410–415.)

to be avoiding socially useful work and leading to an anti-social parasitic way of life. A noteworthy feature of these laws is that an offender might be sentenced not only by the regular courts in a summary procedure, and then without the usual guarantees of criminal trial and the right of appeal, but also by general meetings in factories or collective farms, with a possibility of review by the local municipal council.[69]

Such developments emphasise not only the way in which the coercive force of law is used by its extension to the most intimate social relations, to fortify and develop group consciousness along the lines of officially accepted norms of morality, but also to preserve loyalty to the state itself. At the same time, the flexibility of the rules, and the informality of the procedures, will be regarded by the western standards of law as totally incompatible with that system of legally guaranteed individual rights available not only against other citizens, but also against all legal authorities and against the state itself.[70]

YUGOSLAVIA

The developments of socialism in Yugoslavia make an interesting comparison. The Yugoslavs regard the Soviets as revisionists: they deplore, particularly, the development of State capitalism and growth of bureaucracy with its concomitant caste opposed to the true interests of the proletariat. The Yugoslav goal is to place the means of production at the people's disposal and for the power of the state and law to disappear. The ideals of the U.S.S.R. and Yugoslavia are thus the same, but the Yugoslavs regard Soviet delay in implementing the ideal as a repudiation of it.[71]

Thus the Yugoslav Constitution [72] embodies a decentralised state and puts a premium on local autonomy and on workers' participation in the economic management of the country. In each enterprise there is a workers' council which controls profits and

[69] See pp. 291–298. The governing statute is reproduced at pp. 291–294. More recently the anti-parasite laws have fallen into disrepute and have been replaced by more traditional legal process (see J. N. Hazard, *op. cit.*, pp. 122 *et seq.*)

[70] Berman has returned to this theme a number of times since. The most recent examples are (1972) 21 I.C.L.Q. 81 and 20 *Problems of Communism*, Part 5, p. 24. In the latter he quotes the interesting statistic that the three leading Soviet law journals published, between 1958 and 1970, about 400 articles on the educational role of law or some aspect of it (p. 30). Berman suggests that Hazard indirectly refers to this aspect of Soviet law when in his *Communists and Their Law* (1969), he speaks of " mobilisation for total social involvement " and the creation of the " new socialist man."

[71] For a short statement of Yugoslav criticism of the Soviet method, see David and Brierley, *Major Legal Systems of the World*, pp. 240–242.

[72] The 1963 Constitution is reproduced in Jan F. Triska, *Constitutions of the Communist Party-States* (1968), p. 477. On decentralisation, see Hazard, *Communists and their Law* (1969), pp. 51–57.

manages it,[73] assuming greater powers in these respects than any equivalent workers' organisations in the U.S.S.R.

Workers' self-management, as the Yugoslav approach has come to be called, has been accompanied by the elusive jurisprudential concept of " social property." [74] Social property is neither state property nor private property although it partakes in some measure of both. Authoritative definitions of social property stress its Marxian origins. For example, Edward Kardelj has written: " Marx explicitly states that the socialisation of the means of production does not mean the abolition of personal property but the abolition of class property. . . . But, social property means, in fact, the personal appropriation of the product of society on the basis of one's own labour." [75] Kardelj postulates that Marx's main concern was to restore the means of production to the workers. State capitalism, the system the Yugoslavs believe is operated in the U.S.S.R., is but the first stage of this process. Social property is the ultimate expression of this goal, in the Yugoslav view, because administration of the instruments and means of production is vested more directly in the hands of the workers.

The Yugoslav concept of social property has been criticised by the Soviets as " petty-bourgeois anarcho-syndicalism," [76] " an anarchic system of atomised self-governing co-operatives which would inevitably fall under the influence of market forces." [77] Nonetheless, the growing move towards decentralisation in the Soviet Union [78] can be seen as a response to Yugoslav developments and the acceptance that the Yugoslav system is worth consideration. Further, other East European states have fostered enterprise autonomy: notably Hungary and Czechoslavakia [79] during the so-called " Prague Spring." Social property is probably best explained, not as a property concept at all, but rather as a means of administration, a means to an end, the goal being the abolition of private property. In this case it is a negative, transitory concept.

Ultimately, the Yugoslavs believe, the development of social self-government will bring in its wake an end to law and state. Kardelj [80] wrote in 1961: " The functions of the State as an instrument of compulsion will be diminishing in the proportion in which the producers themselves and the overall social-economic relations will be

---

73 On which see Clegg, *A New Approach To Industrial Democracy* (1963); Singleton and Topham, *Workers' Control In Yugoslavia.*
74 On which see *The Basic Principles of the Constitution*, Part III and Chloros, *Yugoslav Civil Law* (1970), Chaps. XII, XIII.
75 *Idem*, p. 166.   76 Quoted in Chloros, at p. 164.
77 *The Times*, September 29, 1968, quoting from *Izvestia.*
78 See *Soviet Statutes and Decisions* (1966), No. 3, p. 52.
79 See Ota Sik, *Plan and Market Under Socialism* (1967).
80 Quoted in Chloros, *op. cit.*, p. 152, n. 5.

enabling people increasingly to govern themselves while requiring the form of State authority to regulate their mutual relations in lesser and lesser measure." Instead of law social control will be exercised by " an aggregate of adjusted moral principles and rules, a system which will find its support predominantly in the conscience of developed and free socialist citizens and in the automatic reaction of society against the acts of individuals who might want, not to destroy the whole system, because that will then no longer be possible, but only to violate certain rules of social behaviour." [81]

CHINA

Our knowledge of law and legal institutions in China is not great.[82] The Chinese have never had a legal tradition at least as that term is understood in the West. Legality has no roots in Chinese civilisation, law being regarded as the sign of an imperfect society. Confucius, the fount of traditional Chinese wisdom, believed that societal cohesion was furthered by example and established morality, not by regulation and punishment.[83] A distinction was drawn in Chinese culture between *Li* and *Fa*: *Fa*, law, is an unpleasant necessity; *Li*, an ethical system of proper behaviour is the more worthy and more useful method of social control. The dichotomy of *Fa* and *Li* is by no means ignored in contemporary Chinese jurisprudence, where Maoism can be seen as an inheritance of the concept of *Li* and where *Fa* is seen as a necessary instrument to strike at counterrevolutionary elements in Chinese society, such as landlords, nascent capitalists and other rotten elements.[84]

Since the Communist take-over, Chinese society has passed through a number of phases and law accordingly has had a number of vicissitudes. The pattern bears striking resemblance to Soviet legal history. In early days revolutionary legality was the by-word. There was extensive Party and government control over law. Justice was dispensed by ad hoc revolutionary people's tribunals. Cohen [85] quotes a newspaper report of 1951 to illustrate the crudity of political control in the formative era of Chinese Communism. A large public meeting had been convened for the accusation of counterrevolutionaries. The Minister of Public Security " suggested " that 220 criminals be sentenced to death. The Mayor followed him, asking the crowd what

---

[81] *Per* Professor Dordević, a leading jurist, quoted *idem*.
[82] For accounts and materials, see Van der Sprenkel, *Legal Institutions in Manchu China* (1962) and J. A. Cohen, *The Criminal Process In The People's Republic of China 1949–1963* (1968).
[83] On the Confucian attitude to law, see Schwartz in Cohen, *idem*, pp. 62–70.
[84] *Cf.* Victor Li, *post*, 693, where external and internal models are contrasted, the former corresponding roughly to *Fa*, the later to *Li*.
[85] In 82 Harv.L.R. 967, 977.

should be done to these " vicious despots, bandits, traitors and special agents." " Shoot them!" the audience shouted. " Right, they should be shot," the Mayor replied. " Following this meeting we shall hand over the cases to the Military court . . . for conviction. Tomorrow, conviction; the next day execution." The crowd responded with wild applause and loud cheers. But, as in the case of the Soviet Union, early revolutionary fervour succumbed, about 1954, to outside pressures for respectability and to the need for stability and predictaability. The Party strategists looked ahead to a period of " socialist construction " based on the Stalinist model. This " called for a regularised, sophisticated judicial system that would, at least in principle, preside over the law enforcement apparatus." [86] The 1954 Constitution resembles Stalin's 1936 Constitution. Not least remarkable is Article 78 of the Chinese Constitution: " people's courts shall conduct adjudication independently and shall be subject only to the law." [87] The essentially bourgeois ideal of judicial independence is thus articulated in the constitutions of both major Communist powers.

For a time judicial decision making was " insulated from direct interference by other government agencies but with the question of Party interference in individual cases unsettled in both theory and practice." [88] The Procuracy, for example, was given a major role in exercising supervision of the judicial process. Soviet materials were used as guides.[89] The virtues of legality were preached. But this came to an end with the Anti-Rightist Movement of 1957–58.[90] The courts were humbled. Their powers were emasculated. Nonjudicial agencies began to handle cases: the public security force regained the unfettered capacity to impose serious sanctions such as " rehabilitation through labour " and " controlled production." [91] " The judiciary was subjected to ideological indoctrination. It was argued that law could not be a sufficient guidance to the courts as this was not yet complete, could not keep pace with rapid social changes and could not differentiate local circumstances. " Only the Party could provide the courts with up-to-date, comprehensive

---

86 *Idem*, p. 978.
87 *Cf.* Soviet Constitution 1936, Art. 112.
88 See Cohen, 82 Harv.L.R. 967, 1002.
89 Cohen, *idem*, quotes the case of a railroad worker, Hung, whose trial for counterrevolutionary activity was interrupted by the court secretary who noted that both the criminal code of the R.S.F.S.R. and a leading Soviet text on criminal law stated that circulation was an essential element in the crime of defamation. Hung was acquitted of counterrevolutionary activity (he had written on a piece of paper: " Mao Tse-Tung is Dead ") and defamation. He was criticised for his " backward opinion." See 82 Harv.L.R. 967, 968–987.
90 For the effect of which on the legal system, see Cohen, *The Criminal Process, op. cit.*, pp. 14–15. See also *idem*, pp. 468–473 for Chinese materials on the role of the defence lawyer at this time
91 See Cohen, *op. cit.*, p. 990.

leadership demanded by their work." [92] To one commentator it was clear that " the Party ha[d] in effect supplanted the judiciary as the instrument of law." [93] The Soviets have been forthright in their condemnation of Chinese violations of " socialist legality." In 1964 *Izvestia* declared: " Things have come to a strange pass when the secretary of a district Party committee ousts the judge, sits at the bench himself, and starts to decide cases." [94] But the Chinese revolution is thirty-two years younger than its Soviet counterpart, and such violations of legality were commonplace in the Soviet Union until the 1950's. Occasional excesses must not blind us to the fact that courts remained. Cohen's point that " resort to familiar institutions designated ' courts ' in order to carry out revolutionary measures minimises the shock of change, enhances the legitimacy of a new regime and produces a powerful instrument for educating the populace about the new values, goals and policies," [95] is well-taken, and abundantly evidenced by Soviet as well as Chinese experience.

Of more recent developments in China we know even less. In particular little has filtered through of the impact of the " Cultural Revolution " [96] of the late 1960's upon law and lawyers. Victor Li [97] believes the early stages of this were characterised by a " drastic decline in the position of the formal legal system." [98] The Red Guards took over legal work. The very need for law was called in question. Strengthening the legal system meant adopting wholesale feudal, capitalist, and revisionist legal systems. But " as the Cultural Revolution ran its course, a gradual effort was made to restore order. . . . Sometime round late 1967 or early 1968, the desire to smash the political-legal system began to give way to an attempt to strengthen this system and to rebuild it according to correct Maoist principles." [99] The central authorities even began to use law to re-assert their authority.

The present position of law and legal institutions in China cannot be ascertained with certainty. There are indications that law is being strengthened once again: a new constitution is, for example, in the pipe-line. But, nevertheless, non-judicial tribunals do adjudicate and impose sanctions. The Cultural Revolution certainly has not

---

[92] *Idem*, p. 992. *Cf. ante*, 644.
[93] See F. Schurmann, *Ideology and Organisation In Communist China* (1966), p. 180.
[94] Quoted in Cohen, *op. cit.*, p. 971.
[95] *Idem*, pp. 1001–1002. *Cf.* Berman's comments on " parental law," *ante*, 647, and *post*, 687.
[96] See Joan Robinson, *The Cultural Revolution In China* (1969).
[97] (1970) *China Quarterly*, Part 4, p. 66. And *post*, 693.
[98] *Post*, 696.
[99] *Post*, 700.

strengthened legality; the injection of revolutionary fervour, the emphasis upon re-education and the "deification" of the Party Chairman, Mao Tse-Tung, demonstrate the Chinese belief in forms of social control other than law: *Li* has once again re-asserted itself.

HEGEL

Philosophy of Right
(Translated T. M. Knox)

The Idea of the State

The state in and by itself is the ethical whole, the actualization of freedom; and it is an absolute end of reason that freedom should be actual. The state is mind on earth and consciously realizing itself there. In nature, on the other hand, mind actualizes itself only as its own other, as mind asleep. Only when it is present in consciousness, when it knows itself as a really existent object, is it the state. In considering freedom, the starting-point must be not individuality, the single self-consciousness, but only the essence of self-consciousness; for whether man knows it or not, this essence is externally realized as a self-subsistent power in which single individuals are only moments. The march of God in the world, that is what the state is. The basis of the state is the power of reason actualizing itself as will. In considering the Idea of the state, we must not have our eyes on particular states or on particular institutions. Instead we must consider the Idea, this actual God, by itself. On some principle or other, any state may be shown to be bad, this or that defect may be found in it; and yet, at any rate if one of the mature states of our epoch is in question, it has in it the moments essential to the existence of the state. But since it is easier to find defects than to understand the affirmative, we may readily fall into the mistake of looking at isolated aspects of the state and so forgetting its inward organic life. The state is no ideal work of art; it stands on earth and so in the sphere of caprice, chance, and error, and bad behaviour may disfigure it in many respects. But the ugliest of men, or a criminal, or an invalid, or a cripple, is still always a living man. The affirmative, life, subsists despite his defects, and it is this affirmative factor which is our theme here.

The Particular State

The state in its actuality is essentially an individual state, and beyond that a particular state. Individuality is to be distinguished from particularity. The former is a moment in the very Idea of the state, while the latter belongs to history. States as such are independent of one another, and therefore their relation to one another can only be an external one, so that there must be a third thing standing above them to bind them together. Now this third thing is the mind which gives itself actuality in world-history and is the absolute judge of states. Several states may form an alliance to be a sort of court with juris-diction over others, there may be confederations of states, like the Holy Alliance for example, but these are always relative only and restricted, like 'perpetual peace'. The one and only absolute judge, which makes itself authoritative against the particular and at all times, is the absolute mind which manifests itself in the history of the world as the universal and as the genus there operative.   [p. 279]

K. MARX

Preface to Contribution to Critique of Political Economy
(1859) [1]

I was led by my studies to the conclusion that legal relations as well as forms of State could neither be understood by themselves, nor explained by the so-called general progress of the human mind, but that they are rooted in the material conditions of life, which are summed up by Hegel after the fashion of the English and French writers of the eighteenth century under the name *civil society*, and that the anatomy of civil society is to be sought in political economy. The study of the latter which I had begun in Paris, I continued in Brussels where I had emigrated on account of an expulsion order issued by M. Guizot. The general conclusion at which I arrived and which, once reached, continued to serve as the guiding thread in my studies, may be formulated briefly as follows: In the social production which men carry on they enter into definite relations that are indispensable and independent of their will; these relations of production correspond to a definite stage of development of their material powers of production. The totality of these relations of production constitutes the economic structure of society—the real foundation, on which legal and political superstructures arise and to which definite forms of social consciousness correspond. The mode of production of material life determines the general character of the social, political, and spiritual processes of life. It is not the consciousness of men that determines their being, but, on the contrary, their social being determines their consciousness. At a certain stage of their development, the material forces of production in society come in conflict with the existing relations of production, or—what is but a legal expression for the same thing—with the property relations within which they had been at work before. From forms of development of the forces of production these relations turn into their fetters. Then occurs a period of social revolution. With the change of the economic foundation the entire immense superstructure is more or less rapidly transformed. In considering such transformations, the distinction should always be made between the material transformation of the economic conditions of production which can be determined with the precision of natural science, and the legal, political, religious, aesthetic or philosophical—in short, ideological—forms in which men become conscious of this conflict and fight it out. Just as our opinion of an individual is not based on what he thinks of himself, so can we not judge of such a period of transformation by its own consciousness; on the contrary, this consciousness must rather be explained from the contradictions of material life, from

---

[1] [This passage and that from *German Ideology* are translated by T. B. Bottomore, and taken from Bottomore and Rubel, *Karl Marx, Selected Writings In Sociology and Social Philosophy* (1961).]

the existing conflict between the social forces of production and the relations of production. No social order ever disappears before all the productive forces for which there is room in it have been developed; and new, higher relations of production never appear before the material conditions of their existence have matured in the womb of the old society. Therefore, mankind always sets itself only such problems as it can solve; since, on closer examination, it will always be found that the problem itself arises only when the material conditions necessary for its solution already exist or are at least in the process of formation. In broad outline we can designate the Asiatic, the ancient, the feudal, and the modern bourgeois modes of production as progressive epochs in the economic formation of society. The bourgeois relations of production are the last antagonistic form of the social process of production; not in the sense of individual antagonisms, but of conflict arising from conditions surrounding the life of individuals in society. At the same time the productive forces developing in the womb of bourgeois society create the material conditions for the solution of that antagonism. With this social formation, therefore, the prehistory of human society comes to an end.   [pp. 67–69]

K. MARX

German Ideology
(1845–1846)

Since the State is the form in which the individuals of a ruling class assert their common interests, and in which the whole civil society of an epoch is epitomized, it follows that the State acts as an intermediary for all community institutions, and that these institutions receive a political form. Hence the illusion that law is based on will, and indeed on will divorced from its real basis—on *free* will. Similarly, law is in its turn reduced to the actual laws.

Civil law develops concurrently with private property out of the disintegration of the natural community. Among the Romans the development of private property and civil law had no further industrial and commercial consequences, because their whole mode of production remained unchanged. Among modern peoples, where the feudal community was disintegrated by industry and trade, a new phase began with the rise of private property and civil law, which was capable of further development. The first town which carried on an extensive trade in the Middle Ages, Amalfi, also developed at the same time maritime law. As soon as industry and trade developed private property further, first in Italy and later in other countries, the perfected Roman civil law was at once taken up again and raised to authority. When, subsequently, the bourgeoisie had acquired so much power that the princes took up their interests in order to overthrow the feudal nobility by means of the bourgeoisie, there began in all countries—in France in the sixteenth century—the real development of law, which in all countries except England proceeded on the basis of the Roman Code. Even in England, Roman legal principles had to be introduced for the further development of civil law (especially in the case of personal movable property). It should not be forgotten that law has not, any more than religion, an independent history. [pp. 228–229]

ENGELS

Anti-Dühring

(Quoted and translated in M. Oakshott, *Social and Political Doctrines of Contemporary Europe*)

The State

The state, therefore, has not existed from all eternity. There have been societies which managed without it, which had no conception of the state and state power. At a certain stage of economic development, which was necessarily bound up with the cleavage of society into classes, the state became a necessity owing to this cleavage. We are now rapidly approaching a stage in the development of production at which the existence of these classes has not only ceased to be a necessity, but is becoming a positive hindrance to production. They will fall as inevitably as they arose at an earlier stage. Along with them, the state will inevitably fall. The society that organizes production anew on the basis of the free and equal association of the producers will put the whole state machine where it will then belong: in the museum of antiquities, side by side with the spinning-wheel and the bronze axe. [pp. 129–130]

"Withering Away" of the State

The proletarian seizes the state power and transforms the means of production in the first instance into state property. But in doing this, it puts an end to itself as the proletariat, it puts an end to all class differences and class antagonisms, it puts an end also to the state as the state. Former society, moving in class antagonisms, had need of the state, that is, an organization of the exploiting class, at each period for the maintenance of its external conditions of production; that is, therefore, for the forcible holding down of the exploited class in the conditions of oppression (slavery, villeinage or serfdom, wage-labour) determined by the existing mode of production. The state was the official representative of society as a whole, its embodiment in a visible corporation; but it was this only in so far as it was the state of that class which itself, in its epoch, represented society as a whole: in ancient times, the state of the slave-owning citizens; in the Middle Ages, of the feudal nobility; in our epoch, of the bourgeoisie. When ultimately it becomes really representative of society as a whole, it makes itself superfluous. As soon as there is no longer any class of society to be held in subjection; as soon as, along with class domination and the struggle for individual existence based on the former anarchy of production, the collisions and excesses arising from these have also been abolished, there is nothing more to be repressed, which would make a special repressive force, a state, necessary. The first act in which the state really comes forward as the representative of society as a whole—the taking possession of the means of production in the name of society—is at the same time its last independent act as a state. The interference of the state power in social relations becomes superfluous in one sphere after another, and then ceases of itself. The government of persons is replaced by the administration of things and the direction of the process of production. The state is not " abolished ", *it withers away.* It is from this standpoint that we must appraise the phrase " free people's state "—both its justification at times for agitational purposes, and its ultimate scientific inadequacy—and also the demand of the so-called anarchists that the state should be abolished overnight. [pp. 130–131]

freedom & the existence

LENIN

of the state are , for Marxists

State and Revolution

(1917)

mutually exclusive .

(Quoted and translated in M. Oakshott, *op. cit.*)

It may be said without fear of error that of this argument of Engels', which is so singularly rich in ideas, only one point has become an integral part of socialist thought among modern Socialist Parties, namely, that according to Marx the state " withers away "—as distinct from the anarchist doctrine of the " abolition of the state ". To emasculate Marxism in such a manner is to reduce it to opportunism for such an " interpretation " only leaves the hazy conception of a slow, even, gradual change, of absence of leaps and storms, of absence of revolution. The current, widespread, mass, if one may say so, conception of the " withering away " of the state undoubtedly means the slurring over, if not the repudiation, of revolution.

Such an " interpretation " is the crudest distortion of Marxism, advantageous only to the bourgeoisie; in point of theory, it is based on a disregard for the most important circumstances and considerations pointed out, for example, in the " summary " of Engels' argument we have just quoted in full.

In the first place, Engels at the very outset of his argument says that, in assuming state power, the proletariat by that " puts an end to the state . . . as the state ". It is not " good form " to ponder over what this means. Generally, it is either ignored altogether, or it is considered to be a piece of " Hegelian weakness " on Engels' part. As a matter of fact, however, these words briefly express the experience of one of the great proletarian revolutions, the Paris Commune of 1871. As a matter of fact, Engels speaks here of the " abolition " of the *bourgeois* state by the proletarian revolution, while the words about its withering away refer to the remnants of the *proletarian* state *after* the socialist revolution. According to Engels the bourgeois state does not " wither away ", but is " *put an end to* " by the proletariat in the course of the revolution. What withers away after the revolution is the proletarian state or senior-state.

Secondly, the state is a " special repressive force ". Engels gives this splendid and extremely profound definition here with complete lucidity. And from it follows that the " special repressive force " for the suppression of the proletariat by the bourgeoisie, for the suppression of the millions of toilers by a handful of the rich, must be superseded by a " special repressive force " for the suppression of the bourgeoisie by the proletariat (the dictatorship of the proletariat). This is precisely what is meant by putting an end to "the state as the state". This is precisely the "act" of taking possession of the means of production in the name of society. And it is obvious that such a substitution of one (proletarian) "special repressive force" for another (bourgeois) "special repressive force" cannot possibly take place in the form of "withering away".

Thirdly, in regard to the state "withering away", and the even more expressive and colourful "ceasing of itself", Engels refers quite clearly and definitely to the period *after the state* has "taken possession of the means of production in the name of society", that is, *after* the socialist revolution. We all know that the political form of the "state" at that time is the most complete democracy. But it never enters the head of any of the opportunists who shamelessly distort Marxism that Engels here speaks of *democracy* "withering away", or "ceasing of itself". This seems very strange at first sight; but it is "unintelligible" only to those who have not pondered over the fact that democracy is *also* a state and that, consequently, democracy will also disappear when the state disappears. Revolution alone can "put an end" to the bourgeois state. The state in general, i.e. most complete democracy, can only "wither away".

Fourthly, after formulating his famous proposition that "the state withers away", Engels at once explains concretely that this proposition is directed equally against the opportunists and the anarchists. In doing this, however, Engels puts in the forefront the conclusion deduced from the proposition, the "state withers away", which is directed against the opportunists.

One can wager that out of every 10,000 persons who have read or heard about the "withering away" of the state, 9,990 do not know, or do not remember, that Engels did not direct the conclusions he deduced from this proposition against the anarchists *alone*. Of the remaining ten, probably nine do not know the meaning of "free people's state" or why an attack on this watchword contains an attack on the opportunists. . . . The conclusion drawn against the anarchists has been repeated thousands of times, vulgarized, dinned into people's heads in the crudest fashion and has acquired the strength of a prejudice; whereas the conclusion drawn against the opportunists has been hushed up and "forgotten"! . . .

Fifthly, this very same work of Engels', of which everyone remembers the argument about the "withering away" of the state, also contains a disquisition on the significance of violent revolution. Engels' historical analysis of its role becomes a veritable panegyric on violent revolution. This "no one remembers"; it is not good form in modern Socialist Parties to talk or even think about the importance of this idea, and it plays no part whatever in their daily propaganda and agitation among the masses. And yet, it is inseparably bound up with the "withering away" of the state into one harmonious whole. . . .[2]   [pp. 131–133]

[2] [For an account of the evolution of Lenin's thought on state and law, see E. H. Carr, *The Bolshevik Revolution*, Part I (Penguin, 1966), pp. 238–256.]

E. B. PASHUKANIS

Theory of Law and Marxism [3]
(1924)

The Tasks of the General Theory of Law

. . . As Marx pointed out in his *Critique of the Gotha Program*, the transition epoch is characterized by the fact that human relations will perforce be closed in for a certain period of time by "the narrow horizon of bourgeois law." What Marx conceived this narrow horizon of bourgeois law to comprise, it is interesting to analyze. He takes as a premise a social order wherein the means of production belong to all society, and wherein producers do not exchange their products—consequently he is taking a stage higher than the New Economic policy through which we are living. The bond of the market is replaced entirely by an organized bond, and accordingly "labor consumed in the manufacture of product is not manifested in the shape of value (as a supposed property of the products themselves) since here—in contrast to capitalist society—the labor of the individual is part of the collective labor directly and not indirectly." [4] But even if the market and the barter of the market were completely eliminated, the new communist society must for a certain time "bear upon itself in all relationships—economic, moral, and intellectual—the sharply defined imprint of the distinguishing attributes of the old society from whose innermost parts it came to light" (Marx). This is stated in the principle of distribution whereby "each producer personally obtains precisely what he furnishes to society (after the making of certain deductions)." Marx emphasizes that—regardless of radical changes of content and form—"the principle here dominant is the same principle as that which prevails in the barter of goods equivalents: a definite quantum of labor in one form is exchanged for the same quantum of labor in another form." Insofar as the relationships of the individual producer and society continue to retain the form of an equivalent exchange, they continue to that extent to preserve the form of law as well—for "by its very nature, law is merely the application of a like scale." However, the natural differences of individual capacities are not here taken into consideration, wherefore "by its content, this law—like law of every sort—is the law of inequality." Marx says nothing as to the necessity of state authority whose coercion would guarantee the fulfillment of these norms of the "unequal" law which preserves its "bourgeois limitedness"—but this is perfectly obvious. Lenin drew the inference that "as regards the distribution of products *of consumption*, bourgeois law, of course, presupposes inevitably the *bourgeois state* as well, since law is nothing without a mechanism capable of *compelling* the observance of legal norms; the result is that not only does bourgeois law remain for a certain time under communism, but so does the bourgeois state as well—without a bourgeoisie!" [5] Once the form of an equivalent relationship is provided, this means that a form of law is provided—a form of public (that is to say, state) authority—which is thereby enabled to

3 [From Babb and Hazard, *Soviet Legal Philosophy* (1951), p. 111.]
4 Marx, *Critique of the Gotha Program* (Russian ed., 1919), p. 15.
5 Lenin, *The State and Revolution* (Russian ed.), p. 93.

remain in force for a certain time, even in conditions where the division into classes no longer exists. The dying out of law—and therewith of the state—will be complete, according to the view of Marx, only when " labor, having ceased to be a means of life, shall itself become the primary demand of life "—when the all-sided development of individuals shall be accompanied by an expansion of production forces, and everyone shall labor voluntarily, according to his capacities—or in the words of Lenin—" shall not make deductions after the fashion of Shylock so as not to work an extra half hour more than someone else ": in a word, when *an end shall finally have been put to the form of the equivalent relationship*.

Accordingly, Marx conceived of the transition to expanded communism, not as a transition to new forms of law, but as the dying out of the juridic form in general—as liberation from this heritage of the bourgeois epoch which was destined to outlive the bourgeoisie itself. At the same time, Marx points out the basic conditions of the existence of the legal form—a condition rooted in economics itself: the unification of labor exertions upon the principle of an equivalent exchange —that is to say, he opens up the profound inner connection between the form of law and the form of goods. Society, which according to the condition of its production forces *is constrained* to preserve a relationship of equivalency between expenditures of labor and compensation therefor in a form which is reminiscent (although only remotely reminiscent) of the exchange of goods values, *will be constrained* to preserve also the form of law. It is only if we start from this basic element that we can understand why a whole series of other social relationships takes on juridic form. On the contrary, to reason that courts and statutes will remain for ever and aye, for the reason that certain crimes against personality and so forth will not disappear under the maximum of economic security, is to take elements which are derivative and of minor importance for the principal and basic elements. For even bourgeois advanced criminalistics are convinced theoretically that the struggle against criminality may itself be regarded as per se a task of medical pedagogy for whose solution the jurist—with his " bodies of crimes," his codes, his concept of " guilt," his " unqualified or qualified criminal responsibility," and his subtle distinctions between participation, complicity, and instigation—is entirely superfluous. And if this theoretical conviction has not as yet led to the abolition of criminal codes and criminal courts, this is so only because the overcoming of the form of law is associated not only with going beyond the framework of bourgeois society but also with a radical deliverance from all the survivals of that society.

A critique of bourgeois jurisprudence from the viewpoint of scientific socialism must take as a model the critique of bourgeois political economy furnished by Marx, and to this end should first and foremost repair to the enemy's territory—that is to say, it should not cast to one side the generalizations and abstractions worked out by bourgeois jurists who started from the demands of their time and their class but, having subjected these abstract categories to analysis, open up their genuine significance: that is to say, show the history which is responsible for the legal form. . . .   [pp. 122–124]

Goods and Subject

Only with the complete development of bourgeois relationships does the law acquire an abstract character. Each man becomes a man in general; labor of every sort is reduced to socially beneficial labor in general,[6] and every subject becomes an abstract juridic subject. At the same time the norm, too, takes on the logically perfect form of an abstract general statute. The juridic subject is, therefore, the abstract goods-possessor elevated to the heavens. His will—understood in the juridic sense—has its real basis in the wish to alienate as it acquires, and to acquire as it alienates. In order for this wish to be realized, it is essential that the wishes of goods-producers go out to meet each other. This relationship is expressed juridically as a contract or accord of independent wills, and contract is therefore one of the central concepts in the law. In more grandiloquent phraseology, it becomes a constituent part of the idea of law. In a logical system of juridic concepts, contract is only one of the species of commercial agreement in general—that is to say, one of the means of effecting a concrete manifestation of one's will —with the aid of which the subject exerts an influence taking effect upon the legal sphere round about him. History and reality, on the contrary, demonstrate that the concept of commercial agreement grew out of contract. Aside from contract, the very concepts of subject and will in the juridic sense exist only as lifeless abstractions. In contract these concepts acquire their genuine movement, and simultaneously in the act of exchange the juridic form acquires its material foundation in its purest and simplest form. The act of exchange accordingly, concentrates and focuses within itself the elements most essential for both political economy and for law as well. In exchange, according to the words of Marx, " the will relationship (or the juridic relationship) is furnished by the economic relationship itself." Once it has arisen, the idea of a contract seeks to acquire universal significance. Goods-possessors were, of course, owners before they " acknowledged " each other as such—but they were owners in another organic and extra-juridic sense. " Mutual acknowledgment " signifies nothing but an attempt to interpret, with the aid of the abstract formula of contract, the organic forms of appropriation resting on labor, seizure, and so on which a society of goods-producers, as it is emerging, finds ready-prepared. *Per se* the relationship of man to a thing is completely lacking in juridic significance of any sort. This is the feeling of jurists when they try to conceive of the institute of private property as a relationship between subjects—that is to say, between people. They construe the relationship, however, in a purely formal manner—and their construction is moreover negative, being universal prohibition, resting upon all except the owner, against using and disposing of the thing. While this conception is suitable for the practical purposes of dogmatic jurisprudence, it is completely unsuited to theoretical analysis. In these abstract prohibitions, the concept of

[6] " With its cult of the abstract man—particularly in its bourgeois development, in protestantism, deism, and so forth—Christianity is the form of religion most in conformity with the society of goods-producers, among whom the chief social prerequisite of production consists in the fact that for them the products of labor are goods—that is to say, values—and that they treat their private works as identical, each with the other, in this uniform shape, as homogeneous human labor." I Marx, *Das Kapital* (Russian ed., 1923), p. 46.

Reasonable man

property loses every sort of living meaning and repudiates its own prejuridic history.

If, however, the organic " natural " relationship of man to a thing—that is to say, the appropriation of the thing—genetically constitutes the starting point of development, then the conversion of this relationship into a juridic relationship was accomplished under the influence of the demands—called into being by the circulation of boons—that is to say, chiefly by purchase and sale. Hauriou [7] directs attention to the fact that originally maritime trade and trade by caravans created no demand for a guarantee of property. The distance which separated the persons participating in the exchange afforded the best guarantee against all claims of whatsoever sort. The formation of a constant market makes solution of the problem as to the law of disposing of goods—and consequently as to a law of property—indispensable. The title of property in ancient Roman law—*mancipatio per aes et libram*—shows that it was conceived simultaneously with the phenomenon of internal exchange. In the same way, transmission by inheritance became established as a title of property only as and from the time when civil turnover manifested an interest in such transfer.

In exchange—in the words of Marx—" solely by the will of another, one goods-possessor . . . can appropriate the goods of another, alienating his own goods." This is precisely the meaning which the representatives of the natural-law doctrine tried to express when they strove to find a basis for property in some primordial contract. They were correct: not, of course, in the sense that any such contract ever had a place in history, but in the sense that natural or organic forms of appropriation acquire juridic " reason " in mutual acts of acquisition and alienation. In the act of alienation, the effectuation of the right of property—as an abstraction—becomes a reality. Every other sort of application of a thing is associated with a concrete species of using it as a means of consumption or as a means of production. When a thing is functioning as an exchange value, it becomes an impersonal thing—a pure object of the law—and he who is disposing it becomes a subject—a pure juridic subject. The explanation of the contradiction between feudal property and bourgeois property must be sought in a different relationship to turnover. In the eyes of the bourgeois world, the chief fault of feudal property is not in its origin (seizure and violence) but in its immobility—in the fact that it was incapable of becoming an object of mutual guarantees as it passed from hand to hand in acts of alienation and acquisition. Feudal property, or the property associated with the feudal order, violates the abstract principle of bourgeois society—" the equal possibility of attaining inequality." Hauriou, one of the most penetrating bourgeois jurists, rightly puts mutuality into the foreground as the most effective guarantee of property, as well as one which is realized with a minimum measure of external violence. This mutuality—guaranteed by the laws of the market—gives property the character of an " eternal " institution. By way of contrast, the purely political guarantee, provided by the mechanism of state constraint, is nothing more than a defense of a given personnel of proprietors—that is to say, it is nothing more than an element possessing no significance of principle.

[7] [On Hauriou, see Jennings, in ed. Jennings, *The Modern Theories of Law* (1933), pp. 68–85.]

In history, the struggle of classes has led more than once to a new distribution of property—to the expropriation of usurers and owners of latifundia.[8] But these shocks—however unpleasant for the groups and classes which suffered—did not shake the fundamental bulwark of private property itself: the economic association of properties through exchange. The very people who had risen up against property on one day had to affirm property on the day following when they met in the market as independent producers. Such was the course of all the non-proletarian revolutions. Such was the logical deduction from the ideal of the anarchists who—casting away the external indicia of bourgeois law (state coercion and statutes)—preserve its inward essence: the free contract between independent producers.[9]

Thus it is only the development of the market that in the first instance creates the possibility and the necessity of turning man who is appropriating things by way of labor (or plunder) into a juridic owner. Between these phases there is no impassable boundary. "The natural" imperceptibly passes over into the juridic, precisely as armed robbery merges in the closest fashion with trade. . . .   [pp. 169–172]

Law and Morality

It must, therefore, be borne in mind that morality, law, and state are forms of bourgeois society. The fact that the proletariat may be compelled to use them by no means signifies that they can develop further in the direction of being filled with a socialist content. They have no capacity adequate to hold a socialist content and are bound to die out to the extent that it is brought into being. Nevertheless, in the present transition period, the proletariat must necessarily utilize in its class interest these forms which have been inherited from bourgeois society and thereby exhaust them completely. To this end, the proletariat must first and foremost have a notion of the historical origin of these forms which is perfectly clear and free from ideological haziness. Its attitude must be one of sober criticism not only as regards the bourgeois state and bourgeois morality, but also as regards its own state and its own proletarian morality—that is to say, it must comprehend the historical necessity alike of their existence and of their disappearance.[10]
                                                                    [p. 201]

Law and Breach of Law

. . . The origin of criminal law is historically associated with the custom of blood vengeance. There is no doubt that these phenomena are close

---

8 " It may in justice be said that, over a period of two thousand years, private property has been maintained by the violation of property." Engels, *The Origin of the Family, Private Property and the State* (20th German ed.) p. 112.

9 Thus, for example, Proudhon declares: " I desire a contract but not statutes. In order that I may be free, the entire social edifice must be rebuilt on the principles of mutual contract " (10 *Idées Générales de la Révolution* 138): at a later point, however (p. 293), he is compelled to add: " the norm in accordance with which a contract is to be carried out will not rest upon justice alone, but likewise upon the general will of the persons entering upon life in common—a will which compels the fulfillment of the contract, albeit by force."

10 Does this mean that " there will be no morality in society of the future?" Of course not, if morality is understood in a broad sense as the development of the loftiest forms of humanity and the conversion of man into a generic being (to use the expression of Marx).

to each other genetically. But vengeance becomes *completely vengeance* only because it entails a money fine for causing death as well as punishment: that is to say, even here the subsequent stages of development— as is frequently to be seen in the history of mankind—explain the intimations implicit in the preceding forms. If, however, we approach the same phenomenon from the opposite end, we shall see therein nothing but a struggle for existence: that is to say a purely biological fact. For the criminal law theorists whose vision is fixed on a later epoch, blood vengeance coincides with *jus talionis*—that is to say, with the principle of equal retribution, whereunder the vengeance for the insult taken by the person insulted or by his clan (*gens*) eliminates the possibility of further vengeance. In reality . . . the most ancient type of blood vengeance was not at all of this character. Conflicts between clans (*gentes*) are transmitted from generation to generation. The insult—even though it is carried into vengeance—remains itself as a basis for a new vengeance. The insulted person and his kind become the insulters, and so on from one generation to another—not infrequently until the hostile clans are completely exterminated.

Vengeance begins to be regulated by custom, and is converted into requital according to the rule of *jus talionis*: "an eye for an eye and a tooth for a tooth," only when—side by side with vengeance—a system of composition arrangements or money redemption begins to grow strong. The idea of an equivalent—this first purely legal idea—has always the same form of goods as its source. Crime may be regarded as a special variety of turnover in which the exchange—that is to say, the contractual—relationship is established ex post facto: that is to say, after the willful action of one of the parties. The ratio between the crime and the requital is nothing more than the same exchange ratio. Accordingly Aristotle—speaking of equalization in exchange as a species of justice—divides it into two sub-species: equalization in voluntary actions and equalization in involuntary actions, and to the former category he somehow or other refers economic relationships: purchase and sale, bailment, and so on, while to the latter he refers crimes of various sorts which entail punishment as some kind of equivalent. The definition of crime as a contract concluded against one's will also belongs to Aristotle. Punishment comes out as an equivalent balancing the damage sustained by the injured party. Grotius, as everyone knows, accepted the same idea. However naïve these conceptions may appear at first glance, there is latent in them far more of a flair for the form of law than in the eclectic theories of contemporary jurists.

The examples of vengeance and punishment enable us to observe with extraordinary distinctness unnoted transitions whereby the organic and the biological are associated with the juridic. This merging is intensified by the fact that man is in no condition to renounce the interpretation of the phenomena of animal life to which he is accustomed —that is to say, the juridic or ethical interpretation. In the actions of animals he involuntarily finds the meaning put into them strictly speaking, by subsequent development—that is to say, by the historical development of man.

In reality, the act of self-defense is one of the most natural manifestations of animal life. It makes no difference whether we encounter it as an individual reaction of a particular animal or whether it is self-defense by the collective. Scholars who have observed the life of bees assert that if a bee tries to penetrate into an alien hive so as to steal honey, the bees who guard the entrance at once throw themselves upon the intruder and begin to sting it; and if it penetrates into the hive, they kill it forthwith as soon as they find it there. No less rare in the animal world are cases when the reaction is separated by a certain interval of time from the circumstances which evoke it. The animal does not respond immediately to the attack, but defers his response to a more convenient time. Self-defense here becomes vengeance in the true sense of the word. And inasmuch as defense is indissolubly connected for modern man with equal requital, it is not surprising that Ferri, for example, is ready to recognize the presence of the juridic instinct in animals.

In reality the juridic idea—that is to say, the idea of an equivalent —becomes perfectly distinct and attains objective realization only at that stage of economic development where this form becomes customary as equalization or leveling in exchange: that is to say, at all events in human society and not in the world of animals. It is not at all necessary to the achievement of this result that vengeance be completely ousted by redemption. And it is precisely in the case where redemption is rejected as something shameful (and this view is long dominant among primitive peoples), and the realization of personal vengeance is recognized as a sacred obligation, that the act of vengeance itself takes on a new coloration which it did not possess when there was as yet no alternative. Specifically, the idea of the only adequate means of requital is put into it. Refusal of redemption in the form of money, as it were, emphasizes that the blood which is spilled is the sole equivalent for the blood which has previously been spilled. Vengeance ceases to be a purely biological phenomenon, and becomes a juridic institute insofar as it is brought into some particular association with the form of equivalent exchange: exchange according to value. . . .   [pp. 207–209]

J. STALIN

Political Report of the Central (Party) Committee to the XVI Congress [11] [12]

(1930)

It may be said that such a formulation of the problem is " contradictory." But surely we have a " contradiction " of the same kind with the problem of the state? We are for the withering away of the state, while at the same time we stand for strengthening the dictatorship of the proletariat which represents the most potent and mighty authority of all the state authorities that have existed down to this time. The highest development of state authority to the end of making ready the conditions *for* the withering away of state authority: there you have the Marxist formula. Is this " contradictory "? Yes, it is " contradictory." But it is a living, vital contradiction and it completely reflects Marxist dialectics.

[11] [12] Stalin, *Collected Works* (Moscow, 1949), p. 369.
[12] [From Babb and Hazard, *Soviet Legal Philosophy* (1951), p. 235. This statement of Stalin's was characteristic of the early days of Stalinist authoritarianism. See also the report of the Georgia Conference, *post*, 667.]

GEORGIAN CONFERENCE ON LAW
(1930) [13]

CHAIRMAN BOLOTNIKOV:

Comrades, permit me to declare open the Joint Conference of the Georgian Society of Marxist Theorists of State . . . and of the representatives of the Georgian Institute of the Soviet Construction and Law. . . .

[The purpose of the Conference is:] (1) to determine the dislocation, that is, the distribution of forces on the legal front in Soviet Georgia, and (2) to account for the Marxist forces operating here in the legal sector.

. . . Keeping our objective in mind, we shall be able to reveal our own forces and also the forces of our adversaries. At the very beginning I should make the point clear that the various theories to be criticized here are anti-Marxist and hence ideologically harmful. Consequently, we are using the term " adversary " in its literal sense.

We consider the authors of the books to be criticized here to be fully devoted to the Soviet authority; however, while bitterly struggling for the Marxist-Leninist world outlook in all social spheres, we should and will struggle against all manifestations alien to Marxism —against all idealistic and pseudoscientific concepts—regardless of their source.

. . . .

GEGENAV:

The theory of law is a class ideology. As rightly stated by Engels, juridical world outlook is the classic world outlook of the bourgeois society, and the religious outlook was the classic world outlook of the feudal society. Consequently, in the present epoch of intensified class struggle our class enemies are, naturally, in a favorable position in the field of the theory of law, because this field of ideology has not yet been adequately subjected to Marxist criticism. Hence, Stuchka's thesis that the revolution of law is merely beginning is to a considerable degree valid even at the present time.

---

[13] From *Protiv Idealizma v Pravovoi Mysli Sovetskoi Gruzii* [Against Idealism in the Legal Thought of the Soviet Georgia], Stenographic notes from the discussion of A. I. Gegenav's paper " Legal Thought in the Soviet Georgia," ed. A. A. Bolotnikov (Eku-Tiflis, 1931). [The translation is from Jaworskyj, *Soviet Political Thought* (1961) to which work page references refer.]

   " Georgian Conference on Law " consists of excerpts from the Joint Conference of the Georgian Society of the Marxist Theorists of State and the representatives of The Georgian Institute of Soviet Construction and Law. The Conference took place on October 25–26, 1930. A similar conference was conducted in the Ukraine in 1930. These two were followed by the First All-Union Congress of Marxist Legal Theorists, which met in Moscow, January 7–14, 1931.

   . . . These conferences were called at the initiative of the political authority, which sought either to persuade or coerce Soviet writers to adopt the Party line. Initially, many participants in these conferences assumed that they were attending an academic forum for the purpose of impassioned discussions. They soon discovered, however, that the conferences were intended to serve as a " battleground " for the " proletariat's struggle against its class enemies." The discussions that followed were conducted " in the spirit of bolshevik criticism and self-criticism." They were filled with passion, drama, and threats. It is hoped that the following excerpts from the Georgian Conference will give the reader some insight into the atmosphere that prevailed during these discussions.

[Gegenav continues to trace law to its " bourgeois origin "; he then turns to criticizing Surladze's *Force and Law* (1925), in which the author succumbed to the influence of " the pluralist ontology of Husserl." Gegenav then subjects Vacheishvili's *Kelsen's Theory of Law and State* (1929) to criticism.]

This book is characteristic of the developments taking place in the field of the theory of law in Georgia. . . . Professor Vacheishvili presents Kelsen uncritically and without objecting to his theories. I think that such a presentation of Kelsen can be considered to be nothing but the popularization of Kelsen's views, and his views belong to the arsenal of the bourgeois philosophy of law. In fact, this book . . . is an apology of Kelsenianism. . . .

DZHAPARIDZE : . . .

As you know Pashukanis was regarded as the most serious and the most consistent theorist of Marxist law until now. But what do we see now? Against him are a whole number of Marxists—Liberman, Reztsov, and especially Stalgevich, who denounce Pashukanis for his subjectivism which has nothing in common with Marxism. At the same time, Stalgevich denounces Dotsenko for his idealism of the purest type —and so it goes on endlessly. Such is the present condition of the Marxist theory of law. . . . Naturally, Marxist thought in the sphere of law has barely started and it is obvious that its development will require a more business-like and calmer atmosphere. . . .

VACHEISHVILI : . . .

I maintain that the bourgeois theory of law is more elaborate at present than the Soviet Marxist theory of law. Anyone who follows bourgeois legal ideology and compares it with the Marxist will agree with me. This is so because the Marxist theory of law is only now in the process of being formulated. Undoubtedly, the founders of Marxism provided the main principles of this system, but as yet we lack a finite system of law. What I am saying is also being agreed to by such representatives of the Marxist theory of law as Pashukanis and Stalgevich. Marx brilliantly developed the political economy and sociological conceptions, but he did not exhaust all the theoretical problems of law and state. Someone may object to what I am saying: " Please, Marx offers plenty in his *Capital* and in *A Critique of Political Economy*." Naturally he does; he has shown us the way to construct the Marxist theory of law. I fully agree with this, but this does not mean that we already have a finite system of law. One who sees what is going on in Russian Marxist literature must agree that the Marxist theory of law is in a stage of being formulated at present. The works of Pashukanis, Stalgevich, Dotsenko, Razumovskii, and others are the best proof of this. One must follow and study Russian Marxist literature. I have studied it to the best of my abilities, and I do believe that the Marxist theory of law does not constitute a finite conception. . . .

. . . If Pashukanis, one of the finest jurists in the Marxist camp, is being denounced at present as a thinker who deviates from the Marxist concept of law and who presumably fails to understand the Marxist theory, then what could be said of me—I do not even claim to be thoroughly familiar with the Marxist theory.

Now I turn to . . . the work on Kelsen. In 1929 I had the misfortune to have written a book on him. It was written in the Georgian language. Its name is: *Kelsen's Theory of Law and State*. Why did I select Kelsen? It may appear that I entertained certain sympathies with Kelsen, but that is not true. I do not have any sympathies for Kelsen. I selected him as the most vivid illustration of the trend known as normativism.

Why have I been interested in normativism? Normativism is the best example of the results to which the juridical, or normative, method leads. My book on Kelsen is not simply a presentation of Kelsen or, as Comrade Gegenav said, a popularization of Kelsen. . . . Had Comrade Gegenav read it, and especially had he read the fifth chapter carefully, he would have noticed that there is no popularization of Kelsen. I presented there a comparative evaluation of the sociological and normative methods. I have insisted upon the use of the sociological method during my entire theoretical career and in all my books. . . .

LISOVSKII: . . .

Comrade Naneishvili does not pretend to be a Marxist—this is very good. However, this does not give him the right to assert that it is impossible to deduce a picture of the superstructure from the notion of the basis. He gave us the following example: " A house is being built; I see its foundation but I don't know what its superstructure will be." I don't know what an architect would say on this subject but I think that he would say the following: seeing the foundation of a building, I cannot describe all the details of its superstructure but I can say whether it will be a factory or an apartment house; I can say whether it will be a one-floor or a multistory structure, whether it will be made from bricks or concrete. (*A voice from the audience*: Because there is a blueprint.)

In the field of sociology, Marxists regard the fact that the superstructure is fully dependent upon the basis as self-evident, therefore, that it is possible to define the superstructure in terms of its basis. I may not be a musician, but I can determine the character of the music of a society once its [economic] basis has been pointed out to me. (*A voice from the audience*: Correct!)
. . . .

NANEISHVILI:

[In response to the denunciation that he succumbed to Kelsen's normative theory of law, which is " a typical fascist ideology of the decaying bourgeoisie."] . . . You spoke the whole time of Kelsen, but you are not familiar with him. You don't know that, speaking of the origin of law, Kelsen published a work—*Wesen der Demokratie*—in which he acknowledges the fact that law is undoubtedly a product of class struggle.

And if you don't believe me, tomorrow I will bring for you the brochure. What I want to say is that you are accusing me of such things that I cannot even speak about, because what you have found in my book is not written there. You are, indeed, a clever man, and you have made the audience laugh, but laughing is not enough! A book must be understood, and you have failed. (*Talakhadze*: But I quoted from it!) Quoting is not enough. Anyone who is literate can quote, but this is not sufficient to understanding the complex problems. I want to tell you one thing: if you want to chase us out of the Institute, then tell us—we'll go.

However, if you want us to collaborate with you . . . , then give us an opportunity to hear *our own* phrases . . . and not the phrases that you attribute to us. For, using your approach, it is easy to destroy not only me but Kant, Hegel, and even Marx himself. If you criticize Marx, not on the basis of what he has said but according to what you attribute to him, then, you must admit, it will be easy to take him apart (*Talakhadze:* Would you perhaps quote any phrase from Marx that could be easily criticized?) You know quite well that the atmosphere of yesterday's discussions is quite different from that of today. Yesterday I listened to papers that were correct in all respects. I factually believed that you invited us here to learn something from a pure academic discussion of various points of view. But, strictly speaking, this has not been the case—you have failed to accomplish this, Comrade Talakhadze. I appreciated yesterday's lecture by Comrade Lisovskii. But today's personal attack upon me by Comrade Talakhadze I consider to be inadmissible in an academic forum. (*Applause.*)

TALAKHADZE:
Then it is doubtful that you will learn anything at all, if you adopt such a view.
. . . .

TUMANOV:
. . . We Marxists assert that law is carried out in practice by means of coercion and violence, because all law is a class law, and the law of the class without coercion is not a law. . . .
. . . . I would like to make Comrade Vacheishvili understand that in our country of proletarian dictatorship, in the epoch of an intensified class struggle . . . , a calm, academic presentation of the view of our enemies is unsuitable. . . . Indeed, we should be familiar with the views of our enemies. . . . But you, [Comrade Vacheishvili] a participant in this struggle, must yourself declare on whose side you are: with Kelsen or with us.
. . . .

BARIGYAN:
From the Marxist point of view, everything is historical. Historical is not only the content but also the form. We are frequently being told that Marxism is merely one of the many possible points of view. But this is pure relativism. We are not merely defending Marxism but we consider it to be the only correct and scientific world outlook.

CHAIRMAN BOLOTNIKOV:
[Concluding remarks] . . . We hope that the honorable professors will pay attention to our comradely advice. We have no desire to threaten anyone. But we think that our criticism will definitely exert an influence upon them—that it will impel them to acknowledge unequivocally their theoretical errors and to tell us to what extent they adhere to the views subjected to criticism here. If the criticized authors . . . are ready " to die for the last letter of their works," they will remain our enemies, and henceforth we'll be struggling against them mercilessly, resolutely, and everywhere. However, if they admit their errors, if they do not insist stubbornly and dogmatically upon their anti-Marxist positions, we are ready to help them. We are modest people, and

although we do not intend in any way to lecture professors, we believe
that we are capable of helping some of them to rid themselves of Adam's
weakness.

With your permission, the Conference is closed. [pp. 281–285]

A. VYSHINSKII

A " New " Approach to Socialist Law [14] [15]

(1938)

In asserting that law is nothing but a form of capitalist relationships
and that law can develop only under the conditions of capitalism
(when law supposedly attains its highest development), the wreckers
who have been busying themselves on our legal front were striving
toward a single objective: to prove that law is not necessary to the
Soviet state and that law is superfluous, as a survival of capitalism,
under the conditions of socialism. In reducing Soviet law to bourgeois
law and in claiming that there is no ground for the further development
of law under socialism, the wreckers aimed at liquidating Soviet law
and the science of Soviet law. This is the basic significance of their
activity as provocateurs and wreckers. Proceeding along this path,
they outdid themselves in discovering all sorts of motives, concepts, and
"theories" that would facilitate their achieving their criminal purpose.
To this is credited the intensified propaganda of the withering away of
the law, which we have mentioned above. To this are credited also
such distortions as the reduction of law at one time to economics and
at another to policy. In each case alike, we destroy the specific character
of law as the aggregate of the rules of conduct, customs, and the
rules of community living established by the state and coercively
protected by state authority. In reducing law to economics—as Stuchka
did when he asserted that law is coincident with production relationships
—these gentlemen have toppled down into the morass of economic
materialism. . . .

. . . During recent years more than a little has been done to purify
our science from distortions of every sort, contrary to Marxism and
Leninism alike. This work of purification must be continued further,
inasmuch as traces of these perversions are still in evidence here and
there. Relapses, too, are occasionally noted in this sphere. Our aim
must be that at the present time the science of Soviet law and state
direct its basic attention to the working out of the problem of the content of Soviet socialist law as an expression of the will of the working
class that has triumphed and of the entire Soviet people. Our task is
now to provide a positive definition of our Soviet socialist law. The
first attempt to furnish such a definition of law was made by the
Institute of Law of the Academy of Sciences, which considered and

[14] [From M. Jaworskyj, *Soviet Political Thought* (1967), p. 324.]
[15] *From* " Osnovnye Zadachi Nauki Sovetskogo Sotsialisticheskogo Prava " [The
Fundamental Tasks of the Science of Soviet Socialist Law], *Sotsialisticheskaya
Zakonnost*, No. 8 (1938), pp. 12–17.
These are excerpts from Vyshinsky's address at the First Congress on the
Problems of the Science of Soviet State and Law, held in 1938. An English
translation of the whole address is available in Babb and Hazard (eds.), *Soviet
Legal Philosophy* (Cambridge, Mass., 1951).

adopted propositions that I presented. That attempt was made—and I emphasize the fact that it is only a first approximation of a definition —in Proposition 24, which says, " Law is the aggregate of the rules of conduct expressing the will of the dominant class and established in legal order, as well as of customs and rules of community life, confirmed by state authority, the application of which is guaranteed by the coercive force of the state to the end of safeguarding, making secure, and developing social relationships and arrangements advantageous and agreeable to the dominant class." [16]

Law is neither a system of social relationships nor a form of production relationships. Law is the aggregate of rules of conduct, or norms, yet not of norms alone, but also of customs and rules of community living confirmed by state authority and coercively protected by that authority.

Our definition has nothing in common with normativist definitions; normativism starts from the completely incorrect notion of law as " social solidarity " (Duguit) or as a norm (Kelsen), which is a final integration of the content of law (and with no reference to the social relationships which actually define that content). The error of the normativists is that when they define law as an aggregate of norms they confine themselves to that element, conceiving of the legal norms themselves as something closed in and explained by themselves. Duguit's definition of law as social solidarity contradicts reality, history, and the facts. Law was never an expression of social solidarity. It was always an expression of dominance, an expression of struggle and contradictions, and not an expression of solidarity. Kelsen starts from an objective law that stands above all phenomena and defines all the phenomena of social life. According to him, the state itself is nothing but " the unity of the internal significance of legal propositions," merely the personification of objective legal order—nothing but a norm or an order. The vice in the definitions of Duguit, Kelsen, and other normativists is that they have furnished a definition of a norm which is itself idealistic and abstract and merely the definition of dogmatic jurisprudence. They do not see in law an expression of the will of the classes dominant in society. They do not see in law the expression of the class interests dominant in a given society. They do not see that statute and law draw their content from the definite economic or production conditions dominant in society. In the last analysis, production and exchange define the entire character of social relationships. Law is the regulator of those relationships. Our definition starts from the relationships of dominance and subordination expressed in the law. We consider that our definition is in complete accord with Marxist-Leninist methodology. Of course, incompleteness and inaccuracy are possible in our definition —wherefore that definition must be considered and verified from every side and in the most attentive and critical manner. . . .

. . . The problem of the will of the Soviet people as the source of our socialist law possesses extraordinary interest. Our law is the will of our people elevated to the rank of a statute. In capitalist society, allusions to the will of the people served as a screen that veiled the exploiting nature of the bourgeois state. Under the conditions of our

16 The proposition is set out in its final form to conform with the resolution of the Council.

country the matter is different in principle: <u>there has been formulated among us a single and indestructible will of the Soviet people, which is manifested in the unparalleled unanimity with which the people vote in the elections for the Supreme Soviet of the U.S.S.R.</u> and the Supreme Soviets of the Union and Autonomous Republics for the bloc of Communist and non-Party candidates. Our Soviet people consist of the working class, the peasant class, and the toiling intellectuals. Our statutes express the will of our people, which is ruling and which is creating new history under the guidance of the working class. Among us, the will of the working class merges with the will of all the people. This provides the basis for speaking of our Soviet socialist law as an expression of the will of the whole people.[17]   [pp. 324–326]

S. A. GOLUNSKII *and* M. S. STROGOVICH

The Theory of State and Law [18]
(1940)

Law and Custom

. . . Side by side with norms of law and morality, there is still another line of norms—not identical with either law or morality—operating in society and likewise regulating human relations: customs. *A custom is a rule of conduct observed in society by virtue of immemorial habit —because it has been applied many times over a long period.* Such rules become integrated in the way people live, and are confirmed in human consciousness. With law and morality they regulate the social relations of people.

There is a similarity between custom and moral norms in that neither is guaranteed by the coercive force of the state and each is therefore observed in society by virtue of habit, traditions, and established practices, and without direct intervention by the state. On the other hand, custom is differentiated from morality as follows: a moral rule— the moral view of human beings—is always bound up with an appraisal of conduct or behavior as good or bad; the appraisal of conduct as immoral means that it is bad—antisocial—inconsistent with what is required of people in their relationships with each other; whereas custom, as distinguished from morality, has no necessary connection with such appraisal of conduct or behavior. Custom is applied because the rule of conduct embraced in the custom has been constantly applied and has become part of the way people live—has become a habit and not because such rule is good or bad. Thus the rule accepted in society for people to greet each other when they meet—taking off their hats, and to wear clothes cut after the general style, is a custom. In other words, custom includes every sort of rule of human conduct historically formed and confirmed by constant application. In many cases, however, the infraction of a custom may be a violation of morality as well: as where one refuses to proffer his hand in order to offend another who has given no cause for such refusal.

[17] [On the contradictions inherent in this paragraph see H. Kelsen, *The Communist Theory of Law* (1955), pp. 129–132.]
[18] [From Babb and Hazard, *Soviet Legal Philosophy* (1951), p. 351.]

Historically, customs came before law. During the primordial social order, when there was neither state nor law, it was custom that constituted the basic form of regulation of social relationships. Later certain customs began to be enforced with authority by the state and sustained by its coercive force—becoming thereby legal norms. When a custom is thus invested with authority by the state and so becomes a legal norm, it is termed a legal custom. Such legal customs, taken in the aggregate, are termed *customary law*.

The part played by customs differs with different conditions, depending on their specific content. Frequently customs formed and established over the ages constitute a menacing form of conservatism, retarding the development of production relationships and of culture: such were the customs which were created before the revolution among the peasantry (being conditioned by squire and capitalist oppression) in connection with the system of individual, tiny, scattered peasant farms, and spread by reason of the peasantry being cast into obscurity and beaten down under tsarism. These customs were themselves strongly felt, even under soviet authority, until the collectivization of agriculture changed the entire complexion of the soviet village and reorganized agriculture upon socialist foundations. When collectivization was being put into operation, the kulaks, in their resistance to soviet authority, reposed great reliance on obsolete customs among the peasants and made use of them for counterrevolutionary agitation. In such cases socialist law came out against custom—abrogated custom—and put in its place a different norm—a different rule of conduct—whose fulfillment the coercive force of the state guarantees. Law not only eliminates obsolete customs, which have lost their meaning in the changed social relationships, but also promotes the creation of new customs.

In socialist society a system of *socialist customs* has formed and is growing stable. These customs are grounded on socialist law but have not become legal customs for the reason that they are not linked with constraint on the part of the state. Thus the rules applied under socialist competition in enterprises and institutions, and the new family relationships between husband and wife or parents and children, have taken on all the features of customs among us, established rules of conduct, already being carried out by force of habit and with no constraint of any sort exerted by the state. It is true that, in this field, socialist customs are very closely interwoven with social morality; but where we have new family relationships or production and professional discipline formed on new foundations and firmly rooted, we are undoubtedly face-to-face with customs, basically socialist customs.

In communist society—when capitalist encirclement shall have been destroyed and the state and law shall have withered away—it is custom (side by side with morality) that will regulate socialist relationships in place of law. Of communist society, Lenin said that in that society "people will gradually get the habit of observing the elementary rules of life together—rules known for ages and commonplace for thousands of years in all the copybooks—of observing them without violence, without constraint, without subordination—*without the special mechanism for constraint which is called the state.*" These rules observed by force of habit will also be the customs of communist society. . . .

[pp. 381–383]

Conditions under which Socialist Law will Wither Away

The same causes that are responsible for the *withering away of the state* are responsible for the withering away of law: in communist society the rules of life in common will be observed without the constraint exerted by a state mechanism, solely by virtue of the conscious discipline of the communist social order, respect for each other and for their common interests, and established habits which have become part of the mode of living. Communist morality and communist customs will stand in the place of law. Governing things and production processes will take the place of governing people. This requires, over and above all else, that the communist social order be brought to realization, with its inherent principle: " from each according to his capacities, to each according to his needs," when neither compulsory regulation of the distribution of production nor watchfulness to see that no one receives more than his due will any longer be necessary. Next, it is essential—if law is to wither away—that people become habituated to observance of the rules of life together: fulfilling them voluntarily and unconstrainedly. And finally—even if these conditions are both present—law, like the state, can wither away only when socialism shall have triumphed in all—or at least in the principal—countries, and capitalist encirclement shall have been destroyed. So long as such encirclement continues to exist, the state is preserved—and so is law, as the aggregate of rules of conduct whose observance is guaranteed by the state's coercive power. So long, therefore, as the state is preserved, the most important task will be—as it has been—that socialist law and legality be strengthened as mighty instruments for safeguarding communist arrangements, for the communist education of citizens, and for the struggle against hostile encroachments on the part of capitalist encirclement.　　　[pp. 399–400]

O. S. IOFFE and M. D. SHARGORODSKII

The Significance of General Definitions in the Study of Problems of Law and Socialist Legality

(1963) [19]

. . . With the transition from the state of the proletarian dictatorship to the Soviet state [20] of the entire people, the rule of the working class is replaced by the political rule of the entire people. New goals are advanced before this state, goals which stem from the entry of our society into the period of the comprehensive building of communism. It is precisely in conjunction with the fulfillment of these tasks that a unity of the entire people is established and cemented, which eliminates the need to preserve the proletarian dictatorship. But the final goals of the socialist state of the entire people remain the same as under the proletarian dictatorship. It poses as its goal the building of communism, and its organizing activity, directed by the Communist Party, is subordinated to this goal. Nor may one leave out of consideration the fact that, in the international arena, the Soviet state of the entire people, like the other socialist states, opposes states of the exploitative type, and

[19] [From a translation in *Soviet Law And Government*, Vol. 2, No. 2, p. 3.]
[20] [On which see *ante*, 643.]

it does so as the spokesman for the will of the working masses. Thus, although it is a state of the entire people, our state can, and actually does, receive a definite class evaluation—in terms of its goals, by comparison with social forms preceding the new organization of society established and being established in the U.S.S.R., and also as a type of state opposed to exploitative types of state.

Analogous reasoning is applicable to socialist law. The socialist law of the period of the proletarian dictatorship was an expression of the will of the dominant, i.e., the working, class. However, it was always emphasized, and correctly, that the will of the working class coincides with the will of the entire working population, and that Soviet socialist law expresses the will of the working class and of the entire Soviet people. Statements of this kind were based upon recognition of the indubitable proposition that, under socialism, there is not, and cannot be, a dominant will of any single portion of society imposed upon another portion. The will of the working class was characterized as dominant in the sense that inasmuch as the working class exercises political rule, it is entirely natural that its will acquires dominant significance.

From the standpoint of the object of rule (the social relationships actually existing) and the final goals for the attainment of which it is exercised (the communist transformation of society), the will of the entire people embodied in Soviet socialist law at the present stage of its development is of the same type as the will that found expression in the socialist law of the period of the proletarian dictatorship. Being the will of the entire people, it retains the same social content and the same social direction.

Therefore, it may be stated that the general definition of the essence of law as the expression of the will of specific, politically dominant classes, seen through the prism of dominance over social relationships, with consideration of the existence of different and opposed legal systems, is also entirely applicable to the concept of socialist law in general. But if this law is, in essence, the will of the dominant class—in form the totality of the norms protected by the state, and in function the regulator of social relationships—then one may define the general concept of law in accordance therewith: law is the state will of the politically dominant class expressed in the totality of norms protected by the state as the class regulator of social relationships. . . .

Communist society is a society to which state compulsion is foreign, in which law does not exist, and social relationships are not regulated by law. But does it follow that the withering away of law in the period of transition to communism means the withering away of normative regulation in general? Can we conceive of communist society as a society in which normative regulation is replaced by the unregulated creative solution of problems of behavior? It seems to us that such prognoses are untenable and scientifically unjustified. Communism is a highly organized society of free and conscious working persons in which society is self-administered, work for the good of society becomes an inner need for all, a conscious necessity, and the abilities of each will be applied with the greatest benefit for the people.

The need for normative regulation of the relations existing in communist society derives from the very nature of that society. "Communist society is not an alliance of self-contained economic organisms, isolated from each other. No, communist society, like no other, will stand in

need of unified planning of the economy and organized allocation
of labor and regulation of working time. The need for this stems
from the need for the development of the productive forces, from the
profound interconnection of various branches of the economy, from
the interests of steady technical progress, from the communist principles
of distribution and use." [21]

Thus, the economic life of communist society will inevitably produce
a need for normative regulation, inasmuch as planned economy, technical
progress and, in general, the economic life of society at so high a level
of its development are impossible without such regulation. There can
be no doubt that the technology operative under communist society will
inevitably require the observance of general rules of behavior elaborated
on the basis of the experience and collective reason of society as a
whole and of experts in the various fields of science, technology, etc.

On the other hand, as has been pointed out repeatedly, we are not
utopians and do not rule out the possibility of occasional excesses
by individuals even under the conditions of communist society. The
psychological characteristics of individuals, particularly under conditions
in which the social causes of crime (both internal and external, both
immanent and foreign to the given social system) may, in exceptional
cases, induce violation of the elementary rules of the human community,
known for ages and established over millennia. Society will not ignore,
and will be incapable of ignoring such violations; it will inevitably have
to establish common standards of behavior.

The transition to communist society does not at all mean that all
compulsion will be completely eliminated and that there will be a complete cessation of the normative regulation of social relationships. Communism is a society that will have neither state nor law, but compulsion
is not something that must necessarily be a function of the state, nor
must normative regulation be a matter of law. Lenin repeatedly called
attention to the fact that compulsion exists in all human groups. In
communist society there will be no law, as there will be no state and
state compulsion. The difference between legal measures and the measures
to be applied to persons violating the norms of social behavior under
communism consists in the fact that they will rest not upon state
compulsion but solely upon public opinion, the strength of the group,
social influence. [22]

In socialist society, regulation by norms and, in particular, by law,
is of vastly greater significance than in the socio-economic formations
previously existing. This is an entirely legitimate process resulting from
the fact that whereas, in capitalist society, social relationships develop
in elemental fashion, under the conditions of socialism they are regulated
consciously and in a planned manner. Moreover, conscious influence on
the course of social development becomes the stronger, the more advanced
the development of the process of transition " from the realm of
necessity to the realm of freedom." Thus, for example, whereas in
capitalist society the number of commodities of a particular type produced, and their prices, are regulated by the spontaneous laws of the
market, under the conditions of socialist society they are established

[21] [From a speech of N. Khrushchev on the Communist Party Programme.]
[22] [From an article by Karapetian and Razin entitled *On Investigating the Development of Soviet Statehood*, published in Russian in 1961.]

by norms, although in both instances they are, in the final analysis, determined objectively by the law of value. That is why regulation by law is especially important in socialist society, inasmuch as, if it does accord with the objective laws of social development, properly understood, it serves to promote this development. Contrariwise, the errors sometimes committed in the organization of the legal regulation of social relationships have a negative influence upon the course of social development.

Thus, for example, for a number of years prior to 1953 the prices paid for collective farm products turned over under the requirement of compulsory deliveries failed, in a very great number of cases, to correspond to the expenditures of the collective farms in producing these products. There was no consideration of the cost of production in the collective farms, and the prices fixed for these products were completely unrelated to production costs.

It was noted at the March 1962 Plenum of the C.P.S.U. Central Committee that much harm was being done by the economically unjustified approach taken in a number of areas to determining farm produce procurement quotas, and that no indices had been developed to make it possible objectively to evaluate the functioning of the collective and state farms. All of this impeded the development of agricultural production for many years.

It must also be noted that the law of planned, proportional development of the economy does not function automatically: it is realized consciously by socialist society in the plans of economic development. These plans are developed by the Communist Party and the socialist state on the basis of scientific cognition of the objective laws of development of socialist society.

Moreover, in capitalist society (as in the exploitative socio-economic societies preceding capitalism), law as a whole is directed toward reinforcing and sanctifying the existing social relationships of dominance and subordination, and its basic task consists of protecting the existing system. Therefore it is the prohibitive (coercive) aspect of law—sanctions, punishment, and their objective properties—that comes to the forefront.

In socialist society, law is directed for the first time not only to changing the existing social relationships but to transforming them. Therefore it is important to establish not only how the norms of socialist law should influence specific relations subject to regulation, but also how they help in the solution of the fundamental task of building a communist society.

The only question posed in the process of lawmaking to reinforce existing relationships is the method of regulation. But it is also necessary to investigate both the possibility and the need for selecting not only the method of regulation, but, within given limits, the very course of development. It is quite obvious that, when the latter problem is dealt with, the limits of choice prove to be considerably broader, and the task consists of selecting the optimum variant of legal regulation.

Thus, the social relationships of socialist society in the period of the comprehensive construction of communism must, for objective reasons, be regulated by the norms of law, and this regulation is more important under the conditions of socialism than at any previous time. However, merely to enact the very best of legal norms is inadequate. Only adherence to socialist legality can assure a situation in which regulation by legal norms is actually implemented in life and social relationships and truly regulated in accordance with these norms, and the goals posed in the process of lawmaking are thereby attained.

That is why the party poses the task of assuring rigorous adherence to socialist legality, the uprooting of all violations of law and order, the elimination of crime, and the abolition of all causes giving rise to it. . . . [pp. 6–8]

M. S. STROGOVICH

Problems of Methodology in Jurisprudence
(1965) [23]

. . . As in any other science, there is but one method for cognition in jurisprudence—the scientific method of the materialist dialectic, which alone is correct—and it does not share its dominance with any other scientific methods, the more so as the others serve, each in its special field, a more complete and rounded study of state and law and facilitate realization of the method of the materialist dialectic. Therefore, Soviet jurisprudence firmly excludes that which in bourgeois jurisprudence is sometimes termed "methodological pluralism," a diversity of methods of cognition enjoying equal status and significance.

Jurisprudence is a complex set of scientific disciplines. It includes so broad, general, and synthesizing a field as the theory of state and law or, to be more exact, the general theory of state and law, which studies the general principles, the general regularities, the general properties of state and law. It also includes the concrete branch legal sciences which study individual branches of law, individual spheres of state activity and legal regulation: public law, administrative law, civil law, criminal law, procedural law, etc.

Jurisprudence and all its branches are related to philosophy. In each of them the study of state and law presents problems whose solution is impossible without a correct methodological approach, without the proper application of philosophical principles. If these things are not present, serious errors are inevitable.

The following example may be cited. Marxist-Leninist epistemology understands truth as objective truth—as the correspondence of the concept of an object to the object itself, i.e., as an adequate reflection in thought of the object as it exists outside that thought and independent of it. In jurisprudence the problem of objective truth is posed in various fields, on different planes, and most sharply and urgently in the field of procedure, as the requirement that a court, in undertaking to solve cases within its competence, must establish facts in complete and exact correspondence with reality. Lacking this, socialist justice is impossible. However, until recently, the notion was widespread in the legal literature that it is impossible to demand of a court that it disclose the whole and actual truth, since a court is not a scientific laboratory, but a state organ engaged in practical activity, and in settling a case it suffices if the facts established by the court are probable even if it proved impossible to establish them with certainty. Therefore, for an individual to be

[23] [From translation in *Soviet Law and Government*. Vol. 4, No. 4, p. 13.]

found guilty of having committed a crime, and for criminal punishment to be applied to him, it suffices if the individual's guilt is probable to a high degree. Clearly, this is a profoundly erroneous viewpoint that can only stimulate and justify violations of legality by the courts; it is false above all in the epistemological, methodological sense, and it sins against Marxist-Leninist epistemology. . . .   [p. 14]
. . . Soviet socialist law is the totality of norms, of rules of behavior, established or sanctioned by the laws and other acts of the Soviet state. The norms of Soviet law express the will of the Soviet people and the policies of the Communist Party.[24] The norms of Soviet law demand unswerving adherence, which is guaranteed by the consciousness of Soviet people, by social influence and measures of education and persuasion, and, if this proves inadequate, by measures of state compulsion.
For Marxist jurisprudence the norms of law are not arbitrary formulations of the lawmaker, not abstract legal forms that may be filled with any content whatever, not the "imperative propositions" of logic detached from actual social reality, as they are often depicted in bourgeois jurisprudence. The norms of law are the expression of particular social regularities and social relations. In the past, chiefly in the 1920's, there prevailed in the Soviet legal literature the entirely correct view that law was the mode of expression and mediation of social relations. It was precisely this viewpoint that found expression in the writings of such distinguished Soviet legal scholars as P. I. Stuchka and E. B. Pashukanis. True, these authors offered differing interpretations of the mediation of social relations by law, and they sometimes erred in their solution of the problem, but the very posing of the problem and the direction of the investigation were correct. In subsequent years this way of putting the problem was pushed into the background, and law came to be interpreted primarily as a means of effectuating various political measures. This impoverished jurisprudence and introduced elements of a peculiar pragmatism into it.
Of course, Soviet law is always a means of bringing the policy of the Soviet government and the Communist Party to realization, but this is accomplished solely by the framing and effectuation of legal norms, laws, that express the objective regularities of the development of socialist society.
Thus, the development of the socialist state and law are characterized by a number of specific regularities: expansion of democratic legal principles, forms and institutions, enhancement of the role of socialist legality and its reinforcement in all spheres of state and social life, expansion of the sphere of social influence and reduction of the sphere of application of state compulsion to assure observance of the norms of law, etc. . . .   [pp. 16–17]
. . . The purpose of studying the norms of existing socialist law is not only its improvement but its consistent effectuation and the proper application of legal norms to the activity of state agencies and public organizations and the citizenry. The consolidation, strengthening, and maintenance of socialist legality in all spheres of state and social life have always been, and are today, an important task of Soviet jurisprudence. Soviet socialist legality is the rigorous and undeviating adherence to and execution of Soviet laws by all state agencies, public

---

[24] [*Cf. ante*, 643.]

organizations, persons in authority, and citizens. The principle of socialist legality does not admit of violation of the law, deviation from the law or getting around the law—under no circumstances and not for any reason. If a law has become outdated or does not justify itself in practice, it should be repealed and replaced by a new one. But so long as a law has not been repealed it should be carried out unswervingly, and no one has the right to disregard it, to bypass it because he does not agree with it, or for any other reasons. It is necessary to train people, citizens, officials, and civic activists in the spirit of profound respect for Soviet law and intolerance of any and all violations of the law.[24]

This constitutes the basis of the task facing Soviet jurisprudence: to investigate the existing legislation, to disclose the sense and content of the laws, and to interpret the laws in such a way as to facilitate their proper application, their effectuation in life, in practice. Often such invest-igation and study of existing law are characterized as formalism, a formal approach, " juridifying," etc. . . . If such research rests on scientific grounds, it expresses the aid that jurisprudence offers in guaranteeing and reinforcing socialist legality in various spheres of state and social life.

Socialist law rests upon the principles of socialist democracy and humanism, and is permeated by these principles. This finds its expression both in the character and the orientation of Marxist-Leninist juris-prudence. . . . [p. 20]

V. A. TUMANOV

Contemporary Anti-Marxism and the Theory of Law
(1969) [25]

. . . The leitmotif of bourgeois Marxology of law comes down to holding that Marxism, in the final analysis, underestimated law and ascribed to it a place of little significance, or at best not of primary importance, in the system of social institutions and values. From this premise, two principal conclusions are drawn in one form or another. The first is that in a socialist society built on the foundation of Marxist theory, the law is also given a role of little significance because of the spirit of this theory. The second is that it is precisely the ideology of the West that is the major and most reliable defender of law.

Two lines of argument enjoy greatest popularity in attempts to demonstrate the " underestimation of the role of law " in the theory of Marx and Engels:

(a) The conclusion of Marxist theory on the withering away of the state and law in the communist society of the future is interpreted to mean that Marx and Engels regarded the law as, at best, an inevitable but happily transient evil. Stoyanovitch asserts that Marx was the first major thinker " who put law in the dock." [26] In the conclusions of his book *Marxisme et Droit*, he writes: " I conclude my speech in defense of the law faced with the hostility that Marxist doctrine has demonstrated

24 [A good example of this in practice is brought out in 10 *Sov. L. and G.* 241 " The Staff Legal Adviser."]
25 [Translation from *Soviet Law and Government*, Vol. 8, No. 1, p. 3. Tumanov heads a section of the Institute of State and Law, U.S.S.R. Academy of Sciences.]
26 Stoyanovitch, *Marxisme et Droit*, pp. 333–334.

toward the law." [27] The authors of a book published in the United States, *Law: Its Nature, Functions and Limits,* hold that both positive and negative answers have been given, in the course of the development of social thought, to the question: "Is law necessary?" They assert that a negative answer has been given by, among others, "communist legal theorists." In this connection they adduce a long list of extracts (the book is organized fundamentally as a reader) from the writings of Lenin and the works of P. I. Stuchka, E. B. Pashukanis, S. A. Golunskii, and M. S. Strogovich, which speak of the withering away of law in the communist society of the future. [28]

By this logic everyone who might utter such a phrase as the axiom, "man is mortal," could be called a misanthrope. For the thesis that law will wither away is an evaluation of law from the standpoint of historical perspective, and not of its role in a developed class-structured society organized as a state. For that matter, Marxism speaks of the future withering away of the state. However, bourgeois critics not only do not call Marxism an enemy of the state but, on the contrary, accuse it of "étatisme."

Attention must also be given to the fact that when bourgeois authors accuse the theory and practice of socialism of underestimating law and of lacking respect for it, what is meant by law is not the totality of laws and other normative enactments, but a considerably broader notion, including law in the subjective meaning of the word (i.e., the rights and freedoms of citizens), the principle of legality, the degree of implementation of legal principles in the life of society, etc. They imagine that the "withering away of law" is a matter of the elimination precisely of these elements, above all, human rights and freedom. Here their logic overreaches itself because Marxism, in speaking of the withering away of law, refers not to the disappearance of the rules of the life of society and the rights and freedoms of man, but to the withering away of state compulsion as the specific characteristic that gives social norms their legal character.

(b) Another line of argument amounts to a highly peculiar interpretation of the Marxist postulate of the primacy of the economic structure of society, which determines all other superstructural phenomena, including the law. From this proposition the conclusion is drawn that, for Marx, law was something "second-rate," not having a significance of its own, an appendage dependent upon economics but not having fundamental meaning in defining the destinies and paths of development of society. Moreover, as a "plaster cast" taken of the economy, law loses the character of a spiritual value, which also demeans its worth as a means for attaining justice and other social ideals. An American, Professor S. Stumpf, speaking of the Marxist interpretation of the relationship between law and the economy, has recourse to a very strange comparison of law with the tail of an animal that follows it automatically. [29] However banal and worn-out is the accusation against Marxism of "vulgar economism," one must not underestimate the possible propaganda effect this may have, because in the eyes of many

[27] *Ibid.,* p. 391.
[28] See C. Howard and R. Summers, *Law, Its Nature, Functions and Limits* (Prentice-Hall, 1965), pp. 23–27.
[29] See S. Stumpf, *Morality and the Law* (Nashville, 1966), p. 63.

readers abroad the concept "economics" often has a very specific meaning that is associated with notions of capitalist business in its most unpleasant aspects.

In reality, from the fact that law cannot be explained in isolation from the socio-economic structure of society, Marxism has never drawn the conclusion that law is determined only by economics and is a plaster cast of it. Marxism has repeatedly directed attention to the fact that if law were determined solely by economics and in the absence of intermediate factors, it would be impossible to explain why the forms in which law expressed similar economic conditions often manifested great differences. On the other hand, relationships that differ in their socio-economic essence may prove similar in the manner in which they are regulated by law. A variety of factors leave a very significant imprint upon the law: political conditions, the dominant ideology, religion in certain epochs, national psychology, historical traditions, and the like. Moreover, in a developed society, the state, in its lawmaking activity, has to reckon with the prevailing system of law as it has taken shape. Marx gave special emphasis (and this action was later repeatedly developed by Lenin) to the fact that law is conditioned by the level of culture attained in a society.

Marxism has never confined itself to evaluating a given type of law or functioning legal system from the standpoint of its correspondence (or non-correspondence) to the economic system in society. Marx and Engels not only did not deny but, on the contrary, emphasized that the bourgeois law of their day corresponded to the new capitalist mode of production and was in that sense necessary, albeit transient. At the same time, they criticized this law for its injustice to the majority of the working population, for its formalism, for its disregard of moral principles in favor of cash on the line, and for elevating to a universal sociological law the notion that everyone has his price. In essence this is simply an axiological critique of bourgeois law; it is the very value-system approach that bourgeois authors accuse "economic materialism" of neglecting. In the Marxist view, law does not lose its character as an important social value just because it is associated with the socio-economic system of society. As a value, law resists a regime of arbitrary rule and lawlessness. While over the centuries the content with which law has been imbued has not always answered the needs of progress, the fact is that without law it is impossible to establish the principles of democracy, equality, and freedom.

It is not without interest to recall that many years ago G. V. Plekhanov criticized the view of a German jurist, Post, who asserted that law is purely the product of necessity, in which it is vain to seek any basis of ideals whatever. In criticizing this proposition, Plekhanov commented that the nature of any legal system depends upon the modes of production and the interrelationships among human beings created by these modes. In this sense law does not and cannot have any basis of ideals, because its basis is always real. But the real basis of any given system of law does not rule out an idealist attitude toward it on the part of members of the given society.

We should like to emphasize once again that any distortion of the Marxist theory of law is inevitably projected onto the socialist system so as to emphasize over and over again its alleged "legal imperfections."

H. Berman, an American Sovietologist specializing in law, has been developing for a number of years a model according to which the existence of law under socialism contradicts the spirit, if not the letter, of Marxism, the very existence of " socialist law " being an innovation in Marxist theory.   In propounding this thesis, Berman at first merely ignored Marx's well-known postulates propounded in the Critique of the Gotha Programme and developed by Lenin in State and Revolution and other works.   Later, after his concept had been subjected to criticism in the Soviet literature, Berman attempted to interpret these propositions as though they refer not to the new socialist type of law but only to the retention of bourgeois law in the transition period.[30]

When speaking of " bourgeois law " under socialism, Marx and Engels place the concept " bourgeois law " in quotes because they are not referring to bourgeois law, strictly speaking, as Berman assumes, but merely to the fact that the new law is not yet free of one of the characteristic features of legal regulation in the preceding social system, to wit, the application of a uniform standard to unequal relationships. When this is done, however, " bourgeois law " is no longer bourgeois in its class content and social goals, for while distribution occurs by the application of a uniform standard to unequal relationships, this occurs on the basis of new relations of production and the abolition of private ownership of the instruments and means of production. Berman says that the classical Marxist writers did not employ the term " socialist law." However, in this connection, as in many others, philological organization is a poor guide in clarifying the essence of the question. Does Berman seriously suppose that, when they employed such concepts as " the state system of communist society " or " the proletarian state," the founders of Marxism conceived of a new state without a new law?

The Hungarian jurist I. Szabo comments with complete justification: " In their writings, Marx and Engels gave comparatively less attention to questions of law in the new state arising as the result of the socialist revolution than to the question of that state as such. Nevertheless, there is ample basis to judge the views of Marx and Engels on socialist law from their statements on the socialist state." The majority of the goals which, in the opinion of Marx and Engels, the new state must begin to implement the morning after the socialist revolution are impossible to achieve without the help of law. . . .   [pp. 8–13]

Marx and Bourgeois Schools of Law

Let us take note of yet another device that has gained wide popularity in the bourgeois legal literature. Many Western authors are possessed by an almost morbid passion to seek out signs of similarity between the Marxist conception of law and those of bourgeois scholars, and thus to assimilate Marxism in them, as it were. If one were to compare the conclusion in this regard by various Western authors, a very strange and absurd picture emerges, for Marxism then looks like a variant of all the most important bourgeois legal schools: a variant of natural law (Kelsen, Stumpf), of the sociological jurisprudence of Kelsen, of the historical school of law (Ross, Jaeger), of the jurisprudence of interest (Fechner), of naturalist organic conceptions (Bourdeau), etc.

30 " A Reply to V. A. Tumanov," *Soviet Law and Government*, Vol. IV, No. 3.

The treatment of the socialist theory of law as a variant of legal positivism is particularly widespread.

One's attention is drawn to the fact that Western authors are particularly inclined to picture Marxism as highly similar to that bourgeois theory which the writer in question looks at most critically. Kelsen, for example, engaged in long arguments against natural law and the sociology of law which, in his view, interfered with an objective, "pure" knowledge of law. It is not remarkable that in his hands Marxism, too, sometimes looks like the natural law approach and sometimes like juridical sociologism in the spirit of the bourgeois schools. The proponents of "a revived natural law" see the principal task of Western legal thought in overcoming positivist notions; hence the practice of approximating Marxist concepts to positivism and even normativism. Thus, all the arguments directed against the theory being criticized are transferred, in the reader's eyes, mutatis mutandis, to Marxism.

All these parallels and comparisons are generally made on the basis of the most superficial analogies. Let us illustrate this with the constructs of those authors who regard Marxism as similar to the historical school of law. A. Ross, the Danish legal theorist, noted for his anti-communist prejudice, writes: "Marx's attitude to the problem of the social conditioning of the law and the possibility of legal politics is fundamentally the same as that of the historical school: law is not created arbitrarily, but is a necessary product of evolution. The legislator in reality is powerless. He is the mouthpiece of necessity. This agreement between Marxism and the historical school is the simple result of the fact that the two ideologies are twigs on the same branch—romantic, historicist fate philosophy." True, Ross is compelled to admit that the economic structure, which in Marx is the basis of the law, is fundamentally different from "the spirit of a people," which is the basis of the historical school. However, he deals with this obstacle, too, quite easily by declaring that, in the Marxist conception, the "consciousness of the ruling class" takes the place of the "national spirit." [31]

H. Jaeger, in a specialized piece of research, "Savigny and Marx," argues that because Savigny was teaching at the University of Berlin while Marx was studying there, the former played a significant role in the genesis of the Marxist doctrine. One might agree with this if the reference were to Marx's struggle against the reactionary views of the historical school. This struggle actually was a feature of the genesis of the Marxist doctrine. We are all familiar with Marx's article "The Philosophical Manifesto of the Historical School of Law," which condemned the reactionary concept of that school. [32] However, Jaeger has something entirely different in mind. In his opinion, Marx, beguiled by Hegelianism, broke with his former teacher, Savigny, and subjected the historical school to criticism because Hegel's attitude toward it was hostile. But in a later period, particularly during the writing of Capital, when Marx had created his own doctrine as the result of his criticism of Hegelianism, he again felt the influence of the views of Savigny and returned in many respects to the thinking of his former teacher. [33] "It

[31] A. Ross, *On Law and Justice* (University of California Press, 1959), p. 350.
[32] Marx and Engels, *Soch.*, Vol. 1, pp. 85–92.
[33] See H. Jaeger, "Savigny et Marx," *Archives de philosophie du droit*, 1967, Vol. XII, pp. 65–89. [See further, McLellan, *Marx before Marxism* (1972), pp. 106–108.]

may be noted that the jurist Savigny and the economist Marx were in agreement on the fundamental matter that law is no more than a reflection of the life of society. . . . Savigny and Marx are one in recognizing that the relationship between law and social life and the economy is a cause-and-effect relationship," writes Jaeger.

Jaeger asks us not to confine ourselves to superficial phenomena in comparing the views of Marx and Savigny. But do not his, and Ross', treatment of Marxism and the historical school of law as closely resembling each other, merely on the grounds that both theories regard law as a derivative of the life of society, lie at " the surface of phenomena "? If one goes a bit deeper, it immediately appears that Marxism and the historical school have utterly differing notions of the relationship between them, not to speak of the fact that the socio-political trends of the two theories are in diametrical opposition. Thus, what we are confronted with is not a scientific generalization but an unscientific abstraction that ignores the essence of the question. Were we to adopt the method offered by Ross and Jaeger, we could, without difficulty, list as resembling each other not only Marxism but the historical school of Jhering, Hauriou, Durkheim and a good dozen or more other bourgeois writers, since they all agree that law is the product of evolution and a reflection of the life of society. Moreover, Marxism never spoke, as did the historical school, of the helplessness of the law-giver in general, but emphasized that the law-giver cannot abolish the objective regularities of the development of society, although the law-giver may act in a direction that is opposed to the course of social development.

The tendency to treat the Marxist theory of law as similar to bourgeois schools has, in some measure, the purpose of maintaining the prestige of bourgeois legal thought, picturing itself as long familiar with what Marxism arrived at. Simultaneously, this serves to deny the originality of Marxist theory. In a number of cases these comparisons are associated with the notion of " intellectual convergence," i.e., with attempts to link Marxism to the bourgeois schools (for example, the attempt to build a link between existentialism and Marxism). In this connection, the socialist literature correctly emphasizes that the tendency, now fashionable in the West, to find points of similarity between Marxist theory and bourgeois concepts is inadmissible for Marxism. Marxism rejects peaceful coexistence in the realm of ideology. . . .

[pp. 15–18]

FUNDAMENTAL PRINCIPLES OF LEGISLATION OF THE USSR AND
UNION REPUBLICS ON MARRIAGE AND THE FAMILY

(1968) [34]

Article 1. Tasks of Soviet legislation on marriage and the family. The tasks of Soviet legislation on marriage and the family shall be:

the further strengthening of the Soviet family based on the principles of communist morality;

the building of family relations [based] on a voluntary marital union of a woman and a man and on feelings of mutual love, friendship,

[34] [Translation from Soviet Statutes and Decisions, Vol. IV, No. 4 (1968), p. 110.]

and respect for all members of the family free from material calculations;

the bringing up of children by families in organic combination with their social upbringing in the spirit of devotion to the Motherland, of a communist attitude toward work, and of participation by the children in the building of a communist society;

protecting the interests of mothers and children in all possible ways and assuring a happy childhood to each child;

the final elimination from family relations of harmful survivals and customs of the past;

the fostering of a feeling of responsibility toward the family.[35]

H. BERMAN

Justice in the U.S.S.R.
(1963)

Law of a New Type

. . . We have explained Soviet law,[36] in the first instance, as a Marxian socialist response to the social and economic problems which have confronted the Soviet regime. To this analytical dimension we have added a historical dimension, explaining Soviet law in terms of inherited traditions and experiences as they have imposed themselves on the habits and memories of both the rulers and the people. Yet Soviet law cannot be fully explained either by the logic of socialism or by the experience of Russian history or by both together. Many of its most important features are neither uniquely socialist nor uniquely Russian but are rather a product of a social philosophy which—though entirely congenial to both socialism and the Russian heritage—is to be found in other non-socialist countries as well. We are compelled, therefore, to approach our subject once more, from a quite different angle.

To understand a legal system it is necessary to distinguish between the official law proclaimed by the state and the unofficial law which exists in the minds of men and in the various groups to which they belong. Each of us has his own conceptions of rights, duties, privileges, powers, immunities—his own law-consciousness. And within each of the communities in which we live—the family, school, church, factory,

---

[35] [The first Constitution (1924) of the Union of Societ Socialist Republics gave the central (or federal) government the power to establish " fundamental principles " of civil and criminal legislation and of court organisation and procedure, leaving the detailed codification of these matters to the individual republics. The present (1936) U.S.S.R. Constitution originally vested jurisdiction over criminal and civil codes exclusively in the central government, contemplating the abandonment of the dual system of fundamental principles and republican codes. Although several drafts of all-union codes were prepared, they never were adopted, and in 1957 the Constitution was amended to restore the pre-1936 situation. Since 1958, the U.S.S.R. has enacted fundamental principles of criminal law, criminal procedure, correctional-labour legislation, civil law, civil procedure, court organisation, family law, public health, labour law, water law, and land law. The provisions of the Fundamental Principles are binding throughout the territory of the U.S.S.R.; the republican codes and statutes enacted in pursuance thereof may and do elaborate these provisions in greater and divergent detail, but in the event of an inconsistency, the all-union enactment shall prevail.]

[36] [See *The Three Strands of Socialist Law,* discussed *ante,* 645.]

commercial enterprise, profession, neighborhood, city, region, nation—there is likewise an unofficial and largely unwritten pattern of obligations and sanctions. The official law of the state, with its authoritative technical language and its professional practitioners, cannot do violence to the unofficial law-consciousness of the people without creating serious tensions in society. At the same time, official law is more than a reflection of popular law-consciousness; it also shapes it, directly or indirectly.[37]

This distinction between official and unofficial law is essential to a full understanding of the peculiar blending of Marxist theory and Russian history into a "new type" of law. It was the prophecy of classical Marxism that once class domination is eliminated, and once the economy is publicly integrated and rationalized, it will not be necessary to put conflicting claims through the wringer of legal reasoning, judicial conscience, and precedents. Marx and Engels foresaw a classless society in which disputes would be settled by the spontaneous, unofficial social pressure of the whole community, by the group sense of right and wrong or at least of expediency. They saw a precedent for this in the condition of certain primitive peoples who have no positive law, no state, but instead punish aberrational behavior through informal, spontaneous group sanctions. As among primitive societies at the beginning of history, so in classless society at the end of history, they said in effect, control will exist only in the habits and standards of the whole people, in the *mores* of the good society. This moral consciousness implicit in the Marxist utopia is something broader than law-consciousness. Nevertheless the two go together. Both are psychological rather than official. One is the feeling of what one *ought* to do, the feeling of being morally bound; the other is the feeling of what one *has* to do, the *feeling* of being *legally* bound.

The idea of a society without law goes down hard in a culture such as that of the West, where positive law tends not to be treated as merely one particular means of social control but rather to be identified with social control altogether, so that every social norm, or at least every norm tolerated by the state, is assimilated to positive law. There is no case which does not fall under *some* rule. But in Russia, where both law-consciousness and positive law remained rudimentary through the centuries, where whole spheres of life were left outside the realm of law, the Marxist vision found an echo in the hearts and minds of the people. The Russian revolutionaries were not primarily interested in creating, ultimately, a new legal order, in the external, positive sense; they were interested rather in creating, ultimately, a new sense of justice, as between man and man. They seized on the Marxist promise that, with the elimination of the bourgeoisie and the abolition of all survivals of capitalism, the community would come to be regulated like a family, like a kinship society, by customary standards, by unofficial law, rather than by positive law. This corresponded to the historic Russian ideal of the regeneration of man and to the Russian conception of a society based on love and

[37] See L. I. Petrazhitskii, *Teoriia prava i gosudarstva v sviazi s teoriei nravstvennosti* (The Theory of Law and State in Connection with the Theory of Character; Saint Petersburg, 1909). Petrazhitskii gave the name "intuitive" law to the "law in the minds of men." See H. W. Babb, "Petrazhitskii: Science of Legal Policy and Theory of Law," *Boston University Law Review*, XVII (1937) p. 793. [*Cf.*, also, the theory of Ehrlich, *ante*, 355.]

on service, a society with a mission. Only now such a society was to spring from the materialist conception of history, from class struggle and the end of class struggle, rather than from Christian faith in the Kingdom of God. Dostoevsky's vision of the transformation of the State into the Church was replaced by Lenin's vision of the transformation of the State into the Party. . . .   [pp. 279–281]

Law as a Teacher and Parent

Of course every system of law educates the moral and legal conceptions of those who are subject to it. In the *Digest* of Justinian it is explicitly recognized that the task of law is the moral improvement of the people. Thurman Arnold describes the judicial trial as a " series of object lessons and examples." "It is the way in which society is trained in right ways of thought and action, not by compulsion, but by parables which it interprets and follows voluntarily." [38] Justice Brandeis was a leading exponent of the view that the courts should recognize the importance of their educational function.

Nevertheless, the educational role of law has not been traditionally regarded as central. Law has been conceived primarily as a means of delimiting interests, of preventing interference by one person in the domain of another, of enforcing rights and obligations established by the voluntary acts of the parties insofar as that is compatible with the social welfare. It has been assumed that the persons who are the subjects of law, the litigants or potential litigants, know their own interests and are capable of asserting them, that they are independent adults whose law-consciousness has already been formed. In some cases this goes so far, under our adversary procedure, as to enable the judge to sit back as an umpire while the opposing lawyers do battle with each other. The subject of law in our system, "legal man," has been the rugged individualist, who stands or falls by his own claim or defense and is presumed to have intended the natural and probable consequences of his acts. To educate his legal conceptions is no mean task. It requires a very good judge even to attempt it. At best he will succeed in educating only indirectly, secondarily, by seeing that justice is done.

In the Soviet system, on the contrary, the educational role of law has from the beginning been made central to the concept of justice itself. [39] Law still has the functions of delimiting interests, of preventing

---

[38] Thurman Arnold, *The Symbols of Government* (New Haven, 1935), p. 129.

[39] Lenin stated as the most important task of the new Soviet courts that of "*securing the strictest carrying out of the discipline and self-discipline of the toilers. We would be ridiculous utopians if we imagined that* such a task could be realized on the next day after the fall of the power of the bourgeoisie, that is, in the first stage of transition from capitalism to socialism, or (that it could be realized) without compulsion. *Without compulsion such a task is completely unrealizable. The Soviet courts must be an* organ of the proletarian state, realizing such compulsion. *And on them is imposed the huge task of educating the population to labor discipline.*" (*Works* (4th Russian ed.), XXVII, 191.) The educational role of the courts continued to be emphasised. The changes in the mid-1930's only affected this idea insofar as they gave new dignity to the concept of law, which was now to survive into socialism and even communism. Of course law has never been considered the only or even the most important Soviet instrument of education, but since the mid-1930's its

interference, of enforcing the will and intent of the parties—but the center of gravity has shifted. The subject of law, legal man, is treated less as an independent possessor of rights and duties, who knows what he wants, than as a dependent member of the collective group, a youth, whom the law must not only protect against the consequences of his own ignorance but must also guide and train and discipline. The law now steps in on a lower level, on what in the past has been a prelegal level. It is concerned with the relationships of the parties apart from the voluntary acts by which their alleged rights and duties were established; it is concerned with the whole situation, and above all, with the thoughts and desires and attitudes of the people involved, their moral and legal conceptions, their law-consciousness. Soviet law thus seeks not simply to delimit and segregate and define, but also to unite and organize and educate. The result is the creation of entirely new legal values within a framework of language and doctrine which otherwise appears conventional and orthodox.

It is apparent that the Soviet emphasis on the educational role of law presupposes a new conception of man. The Soviet citizen is considered to be a member of a growing, unfinished, still immature society, which is moving toward a new and higher phase of development. As a subject of law, or a litigant in court, he is like a child or youth to be trained, guided, disciplined, protected. The judge plays the part of a parent or guardian; indeed, the whole legal system is parental.

It should be understood that the words "parental" and "educational" as used in this context are morally inconclusive. The parent or guardian or teacher may be cruel or benevolent, angry or calm, bad or good. He may dislike the child. But he is responsible for the child's upbringing. To speak of "parental law" is therefore not so much to describe the state which proclaims and applies the law as to describe the assumptions which are made regarding the nature of the citizen and his relationship to the state. To say that under Soviet law the state has extended the range of its interests and its powers is not enough. The state has sought in law a means of training people to fulfill the responsibilities now imposed on them—and it has made this function of law central to the whole legal system.

"Parental law" may be implicit in the actual practice of socialism as such. It surely has deep roots in Russian history. Yet it is essential to isolate the parental features of Soviet law from both its socialist and its Russian background, for parental law is not restricted to socialism or to Russia. According to Karl Llewellyn, "our own law moves steadily in a parental direction." [40] . . .   [pp. 282–284]

prestige has been considerably enhanced. At the same time there has developed a much greater respect for the educational value of traditional legal institutions— of criminal sanctions, for example. Law now educates by its very dignity and authority.

[40] Karl N. Llewellyn, "Lectures on Jurisprudence" (mimeographed; 1948). Llewellyn contrasts the "adversary" with the "parental" system, drawing for his definition of "parental" on the law of the New Mexican Pueblo Indians, the medieval Inquisition, and the Soviet trials of major political offenders. He lists the following characteristics of the parental system: (1) the court may dig up evidence for the defendant. (2) The court may make a prior investigation of facts. (3) The objective of the trial is reintegration of the offender with the Entirety; confession and repentance are normal preliminaries to a treatment viewed primarily as reeducational ("making an example," elimination of the

. . . The extension of official law, juristic law, to domains once left to the informal processes of family life, the school and church, the local community, work associations, business associations, and the

offender, are out of key with the procedure, an extreme measure of panic; love for the Entirety and for the erring member is the proper emotional and intellectual keynote. (4) Criminal and civil offenses tend to merge, though reparation and restitution aspects are readily seen as involving private rights which need to be respected. (5) It is natural and right to draw into the case any past misconduct, even though previously punished, and the defendant's attitude as well as his actions; prior good conduct can weigh in mitigation (the wrong was a mere lapse) or in severity (knowledge and experience entail extra responsibility); not the offense alone but the whole man is in question.

Llewellyn here focuses on the parental role of the court, particularly in its procedural aspects. Roscoe Pound uses the word "socialization" to describe the dominant tendency of American legal development in the twentieth century, focusing on the changes in substantive law. There is a close connection between Pound's "socialization" (which is not necessarily connected with socialism in the Soviet sense of a planned economy) and Llewellyn's "parentalism." Pound lists the following changes: (1) growing limitations on an owner's use of his own property, and notably on the antisocial exercise of rights; (2) growing limitations on freedom of contract; (3) growing limitations on an owner's freedom of disposition of his own property; (4) growing limitations on the power of a creditor or an injured party to exact satisfaction; (5) liability without fault merging into the insurance principle of liability, making enterprises and ultimately the community as a whole responsible for agencies employed for their benefit; (6) increased assertion of public rights in basic natural resources ("the change of *res communes* and *res nullius* into *res publicae*"); (7) growing intervention of society through law to protect dependent persons, whether physically or economically dependent; (8) tendency to hold that public funds should respond for injuries to individuals by public agencies; (9) replacement of a purely contentious conception of litigation by one of adjustment of interests; (10) reading of the obligation of contract as subject to the overriding requirement of reasonableness, of which, despite current confusion of grounds, the doctrine of frustration seems to be an example; (11) increased legal recognition of groups and persons in stable relations to each other as legal units instead of exclusive recognition of individuals and juristic persons as their analogues (the collective labor contract, and the "common rule" of an industry, and the labor union itself are examples); (12) the tendency to relax the rule as to trespassers (Roscoe Pound, *Outlines of Lectures on Jurisprudence* [5th ed.; Cambridge: Harvard University Press, 1943], pp. 43–48).

The idea of parental law and the idea of socialized law (in Pound's sense) are brought together in Petrazhitskii's phrase, "the socialization of the psyche."

Obviously many of the features of parental law exist in all legal systems. The reason that a new term such as parental law is needed is to indicate a shift in the center of gravity of the legal system. Any particular rule or institution of the Soviet legal system may be found in some other system; the ensemble, however, is different.

One difficulty with the word "parental" is that it may connote the idea of kinship in a literal sense. Of course the state does not literally reproduce the litigants in a parental system of law. "Parental" is used here in a broader and more figurative sense. The state, through law, plays the role of guardian, and the individual before the law is like a ward.

Any absolutism tends toward parentalism. Parental law should not, however, be identified with the absolute state as such. In many ways a more appropriate analogy may be made to the Church in its Roman Catholic, Anglican, or Eastern Orthodox forms. The priest is called father; the very word pope (*papa*) means father.

The Soviet writers do not use the phrase "parental law." However, there is great stress in Soviet legal literature on the educational role of Soviet law, and here the word "educational" (*vospitatel'naia*) has a very wide connotation, implying rearing or upbringing. Whatever the particular word used, the crux of the matter is the focus on the role of law in the upbringing of people.

like, has posed a crucial problem for twentieth-century man. Together with the extension of legal controls we are witnessing a withering of the inner strength of these associations. Here are relationships which are so close-knit as to require more spontaneous responses, relationships which are so delicate and so intimate as to demand more mobility and flexibility than law traditionally allows. We are in danger that the life will go out of them, as they become subjected to the formal and time-consuming processes and definitions of law. " The letter killeth, but the spirit giveth life " is a saying which takes on new meaning as our social order becomes more and more legalized.

The significance of Soviet legal development lies in just this conscious extension of law to the most intimate social relations. The Soviet rulers have abandoned the original Marxist theory that the abolition of class struggle will render law unnecessary, that a society without exploitation can live on informal, indefinite, unofficial social practices and standards. They have not officially abandoned their dream of such a time; but classless socialist law itself is now conceived as a means of producing it. In other words, the Soviets take their stand in the future, at the end of time, when life will be regulated by the norms and imperatives of social custom, as written in the conscience of mankind. Looking backward into the present from this end-time, they seek by the use of norms and imperatives of official law to form, in an official sense, the functions of the various social groups and associations to which their citizens belong. They attempt to use law to strengthen those groups and associations by appealing to the con-science of their members in terms of their legal rights and duties, thereby identifying conscience, group consciousness, and loyalty to the state. They thus attempt to preserve the inner strength, the inner mobility and flexibility, of relationships of family, commerce, labor, and so forth—by the formal definitions and processes of law itself. In this way they apparently seek to check the social disintegration, depersonalization, and disenchantment which are produced by a mechan-ized, industrial, mass-production society. Of course law is not the sole means, or even the primary means, by which they strive to achieve this end. Informal influences, including both political and administrative pressures, play a more important part in shaping day-to-day decisions than does the official legal system. Yet law is one of the major instru-ments which the Communist Party uses to create the kind of society it wants.

Soviet law cannot be understood unless it is recognized that the whole Soviet society is itself conceived to be a single great family, a gigantic school, a church, a labor union, a business enterprise. The state stands at its head, as the parent, the teacher, the priest, the chairman, the director. As the state, it acts officially through the legal system, but its purpose in so acting is to make its citizens into obedient children, good students, ardent believers, hard workers, successful managers.

This, indeed, is the essential characteristic of the law of a total state. . . .   [pp. 364–366]

VICTOR H. LI
The Role of Law in Communist China
(1970) [41]

Two Models of Law

During the past 20 years, the Chinese Communists have made use
of two different models of the relationship of law to the moulding
and controlling of conduct, each having its own rationale and objectives. Depending on the period, one model or the other has been
dominant, but on the whole, they have existed side by side in a
combination of harmony and competition.

The first model (for convenience, I will call it the " external
model ") is based upon the establishment of a formal, detailed and
usually written set of rules, that is, a legal code which defines
permissible and impermissible conduct. A governmental organization
enforces compliance with these rules, resolves ambiguities and settles
disputes. This organization in turn has regulations of its own that
specify the manner in which it should operate, and that provide means
for members of the public to obtain redress against improper official
actions. Generally, the rules of law tend to be complicated and
difficult to understand. Not only must they deal with the almost
infinite variety of human conduct, but they must also contend with
human ingenuity trying to get around the established rules. The legal
system used to enforce these rules also tends to be large and complex.
Consequently, trained specialists are required to manage the legal
bureaucracy and to act as legal advisors to the public.

This model of law is similar to and derives mainly from the
western legal concepts that were introduced into China at the beginning
of this century, and reinfused into Chinese life with the adoption of
Soviet legal institutions, methods and thinking after Liberation in
1949. To a lesser degree, this model also is influenced by traditional
Chinese legal practices. Some of the early legalist philosophers (*fa chia*)
had similar attitudes towards the role and function of law.[42] More
important, in spite of the Confucian disdain for formal coercive law,
China has had for many centuries an active and complex legal system,
complete with codes, courts, and the like.[43] Thus, as part of their
cultural heritage, the Communists possessed some familiarity with the
formal legal system and with centralized bureaucratic government.

The adoption of the external model of law provides many advantages for the Chinese. For one thing, it makes the Chinese legal system
more recognizable, and consequently more acceptable, to the west
and to the Soviet Union. This is an important consideration, given

---

[41] [From *China Quarterly* (1970), Part 4, p. 66.]

[42] T'ung-tsu Ch'ü, *Law and Society in Traditional China* (The Hague: Mouton,
1961); *The Book of Lord Shang*, J. J. L. Duyvendak, trans. (London: Arthur
Probsthain, 1928); *The Complete Works of Han Fei*, W. K. Liao, trans.
(London: Arthur Probsthain, 1939 and 1959).

[43] See generally, Derk Bodde and Clarence Morris, *Law in Imperial China:
Exemplified by 190 Ch'ing Dynasty Cases* (Cambridge, Mass.: Harvard Uni-
versity Press, 1967); T'ung-tsu Ch'ü, *Local Government Under the Ch'ing*
(Cambridge, Mass.: Harvard University Press, 1962); Sybille van der Sprenkel,
Legal Institutions in Manchu China (London: Athlone Press, 1962).

China's past difficulties with western criticism of the Chinese legal system and with extra-territoriality. In addition, the external model provides a clear and rationalized system of government and administration to nation-builders who are seeking clarity and rationality. It also strengthens central control. Through the establishment of legal rules and procedures, higher-level authorities not only can provide guidance for lower-level officials, but also can restrict the scope of their discretionary powers. Through the medium of law, the public can know when an official is acting improperly and can inform the higher-level authorities through the various complaint and appeal procedures. The legal system also is an effective means of controlling the public. In addition to maintaining a degree of public order, law can be used to publicize and to enforce new social policies, as well as to monitor the implementation of and response to these policies.

The second model of law (I will call it the "internal model") is quite different. Proper modes of behaviour are taught not through written laws, but rather through a lengthy and continuing educational process whereby a person first learns and then internalizes the socially accepted values and norms. Compliance is obtained not through fear of governmental punishment, but from a genuine understanding and acceptance of the proper rules of conduct. Where such self-control fails, social pressure arises spontaneously to correct and to control the deviant. The coercive power of the state is used for enforcement only in the most serious cases in which the deviant is particularly recalcitrant or depraved. Since each individual is deeply involved in the legal process, law must be very simple and must be capable of being applied without the help of skilled specialists. And, since enforcement is handled to a large extent by the community at large, the role of the state in legal administration is limited and the size of the legal bureaucracy is small.

This model seems to include many traditional Chinese ideas and practices. Especially striking is its similarity to the concept of *li*.[44] Both rely heavily upon persuasion and education rather than force, and upon the use of social pressure rather than governmental power. Both also stress the importance of internalizing the rules of conduct and point out the ineffectiveness of using fear of punishment to make people behave. Indeed, if one substitutes the term "socialist morality" for "Confucian morality" and the term "comrade" for "*chü tzu*," one can use some of the Chinese classics to describe this model of law.

While the traditional influences certainly are present, other factors are no less important. Communist Chinese ideology, for example, calls for the participation and involvement of the masses in all aspects of government, including law.[45] Some degree of decision-making and sanctioning power also is granted to the masses, or at least to a

---

[44] See B. Schwartz, in ed. Katz, *Government Under Law and the Individual* (1957), reprinted in J. Cohen, *The Criminal Process in the People's Republic of China, 1949–1963: An Introduction* (1968), for an enlightening description of the meanings and functions of *fa* and *li*. [And *ante*, 651.]

[45] See generally, James R. Townsend, *Political Participation in Communist China* (Berkeley and Los Angeles: University of California Press, 1967). For a discussion of the relation of the mass line to legal work, see Stanley Lubman, "Mao and Mediation: Politics and Dispute Resolution in Communist China," *California Law Review*, No. 55 (November 1967), p. 1284.

local social group. Ideological commitment to the mass line is reinforced by some practical considerations. To begin with, internalization of the socially accepted values and norms is a more effective means of controlling conduct than the use of coercive force, and self-policing is much cheaper than the employment of a vast state police apparatus. In addition, because of problems such as the size and variety of Chinese society, the difficulties of communication and the limited amount of available resources, Peking can exercise direct and strict control over local administration only in the most important matters. For most routine items, including much of the administration of the legal system, it is more efficient and effective to permit a substantial degree of local autonomy. Furthermore, the Communists have a distrust of and a dislike for bureaucrats and bureaucratism. This is due in part to a reaction against the isolation and abuses of power by the traditional and Nationalist power-holders, and in part to a fear that an entrenched bureaucracy will not heed Party direction. As a result, the Party uses the masses to act as a check on official actions and as a counter-balance to official power.

Other aspects of the internal model also reflect a combination of traditional and non-traditional influences. For example, the traditional practice of having members of the community handle most of the work of dispute settlement and control of deviant conduct prepared the way for the contemporary belief that legal administration does not require the services of skilled specialists. This traditional influence is reinforced by the Communists' own experiences. In the border and liberated areas which they occupied before 1949, there was little functional specialization in the government or the legal system. Cadres tended to be jacks-of-all-trades. This worked fairly well since the areas were small, the societies they contained were simple and the cadres and the masses were highly motivated by the concerns of revolution and war. In addition, almost no legal specialists were available, even if the Communists had wanted to use them. This personnel problem was not alleviated after Liberation, even though the law schools and the practitioners remaining from the Nationalist regime provided a small supply of legally trained persons. Consequently, legal theory and practice had to be adjusted to enable generalists to operate the legal system.

There are a number of areas where the external and internal models of law conflict or, at least, pull in opposite directions. For example, the internal model stresses local initiative and decision-making power, and tolerates considerable variations in norms, methods and results from area to area. This runs counter to the external model's desire for clarity and certainty and emphasis on strong central government. The external model's reliance upon a professional bureaucracy and skilled specialists to administer the legal system in an efficient and rationalized manner conflicts with the internal model's commitment to simplicity and mass participation. The internal model also lacks the clear appeal procedures and channels of the external model, and therefore must find very different means to protect the individual from arbitrary actions by officials or by members of his peer group.

While the two models are quite dissimilar, some of their differences are more apparent in theory than in practice. Often the two models complement each other, with the external model handling serious matters and the internal model dealing with more routine affairs. Furthermore, the existence of the internal model usually does not preclude the simultaneous existence of the internal model. In general, a person does not learn what he can and cannot do by studying or referring to the legal codes. Most notions concerning proper and improper conduct are learned as part of the socialization process, a process whose concepts and practices greatly resemble those of the internal model.

By the same token, over a period of time the internal model tends to evolve into the external model. In the ideal internal model, general patterns of proper conduct are truly internalized so that one " knows " what to do in each case. In many instances, however, this general understanding consists of or soon turns into a list of specific precepts. These may be called *li*, rules of propriety and morality, or any other legal or non-legal name, but in due course they come to have much the same effect as the rules of law in the external model. Both the precepts and the rules of law tell one what to do in a particular situation; failure to comply results in sure and unpleasant consequences, although in the internal model, these may be social or economic sanctions rather than 40 blows of the heavy bamboo. In a similar manner, the informal style of the internal model tends to ossify and to become rigid and formalized. With continued development and refinement, the legal system increases in complexity, and legal specialists are needed more and more to operate the system. At the same time, despite the emphasis on self-policing and community action, the legal bureaucracy tends to grow and the state comes to play a larger role in legal work.   [pp. 72–76]

. . . .

The Cultural Revolution and the two models of law

It is difficult to write with assurance about the Cultural Revolution, since many of the events of that period are still unclear. Nevertheless, in the area of political-legal work several broad patterns of development can be seen, although there are variations, which are sometimes considerable, from one part of the country to another. To a large extent, these patterns reflect the continuing interplay of the external and the internal models of law.

The initial stage of the Cultural Revolution was characterized by a further drastic decline in the position of the formal legal system. Beginning in the summer of 1966, many Red Guard groups entered into, and in some instances even took over, political-legal work. They conducted investigations of their political enemies, carried out arrests, and through a variety of tribunals and mass meetings, adjudicated cases and imposed sanctions.[46] The Red Guards sometimes worked in conjunction with the public security and the court, but often acted independently without reference to the formal legal organs.[47] This

---

[46] " Report on an Investigation into the Facts of the Persecution of the Aug. 1 Combat Corps," *Kang pa-i*, 15 October, 1967, in *SCMP*, No. 4096 (10 January, 1968), p. 1.

[47] See " Resolutely Defending the Dictatorship of the Proletariat, Checking the Evil Wind of Fighting, Smashing and Looting," *Pei-ching kung-jen*, 17 May, 1967, in *SCMP*, No. 3966 (23 June, 1967), p. 13 ; " Brief Introduction to the Three Big

by-passing of the formal legal system had occurred in past campaigns, of course, but never to such an extent nor in a manner so disorganized and so free from central control.

The Cultural Revolution differed from past campaigns in one major respect: whereas the entire political-legal system was criticized again, the public security for the first time became the primary target of the attacks. These attacks came from several different directions. At the central level, the leaders of the Cultural Revolution accused the public security of being the stronghold of the anti-Mao group. Lin Piao said:

> Public security work had been under the control of P'eng Chen, Lo Jui-ch'ing, Lu Ting-i and Yang Shang-k'un—especially under P'eng Chen and Lo Jui-ch'ing—for seventeen years. They did not of course carry out all things according to Mao Tse-tung's thought. . . . The thought of Chairman Mao has not yet established its dominance and absolute authority in the public security and judicial systems.[48]

Hsieh Fu-chih, the Vice-Premier and Minister of Public Security admitted:

> Our great leader Chairman Mao has told me on eight to ten occasions that thoroughgoing revolution must be carried out in the public security organs, procuratorates, and law courts, because the things copied from the Kuomintang and the Soviet revisionists have deep-rooted influence and P'eng Chen and Lo Jui-ch'ing had controlled them for more than ten years.[49]

Chiang Ch'ing told of how she and Chairman Mao were shadowed, how their letters were censored, and how listening devices were installed in their residence. She demanded that "the public security organs, procuratorates and law courts must be completely smashed." [50] The distrust of the entire public security system was reflected in one of Chairman Mao's "latest instructions" which provided:

> Public security organs are a knife in the hands of the proletariat. If properly grasped, they can be used to attack the enemy and protect the people; if not, they can easily be used against us. If they are taken away by the enemy, there will be even greater danger. Hence public security work can only be under the direct leadership of the Party Committee and *cannot be under the vertical leadership* of the relevant government department.[51]

Factions in Shenyang," *Liao-lien chan-pao*, 6 September, 1967, in *SCMP*, No. 4091 (13 January, 1968), p. 7; " US Agents Sentenced in Peking," New China News Agency (NCNA) (Peking), 27 September, 1967, in *SCMP*, No. 4031 (29 September, 1967), p. 18.

[48] " Chairman Mao and Central Committee Leaders on Public Security Organs, Procuratorates and Law Courts," *Fan P'eng Lo hei-hsien*, No. 2 (July 1968), in *Survey of China Mainland Magazines (SCMM)* (Hong Kong: U.S. Consulate General), No. 625 (3 September, 1968), p. 15.

[49] *Ibid*. p. 16.

[50] *Ibid*.

[51] " Chairman Mao's Latest Instructions," *Wen-ko t'ung-hsin*, No. 1 (6 October 1967), in *SCMP*, No. 4060 (15 November 1967), p. 1. Emphasis added.

Some of the attacks on the public security on the local level followed similar lines. Red Guard groups recognized very early in the Cultural Revolution that the support of the public security was needed if the "reactionary powerholders" were to be overthrown. One successful Red Guard group in Heilungkiang felt that they could "instruct the rest of China how to do it," and suggested that " (b)efore seizing the power of the leadership of the provincial Party Committee, the newspapers and radio, as the voice of the proletariat revolution, and the Public Security Bureau, as an organ of the dictatorship, should first be seized." [52] In many areas, however, the public security sided with the existing powerholders against the Red Guards or, at least, in trying to preserve public order and to prevent violence, inhibited the actions of the Red Guards. The public security was attacked for this reactionary stance. The attacks quickly expanded to accusing the public security of always having been reactionary and of having been the tool by which leftist revolutionaries had been suppressed for more than 10 years.[53] This organ was also criticized for having been too lenient with class enemies. Following the Liu-P'eng-Lo line that class struggle was over, the public security adopted the erroneous position that "everyone is equal before the law," and thus failed to distinguish between the enemy and the people. Therefore, it became not a weapon of the working class in the class struggle, but rather a means by which reactionary persons could be protected.[54]

In addition to attacks on its political position, the public security was also criticized for having a bad work style. Many of these criticisms repeat the charges which were levelled against the judiciary and the external model of law in 1952 and 1957. For example, the public security was accused of not respecting the masses and of failing to implement the mass line.[55] That is, as the public security cadres developed more professional expertise, they began to feel that the participation of the masses in public security work only contributed confusion and inefficiency. They believed instead that "cases must be handled by a small number of technically proficient experts, and the masses of the people can do nothing in this respect." [56] This reliance

[52] "Experience of Heilungkiang Red Rebels in Seizing Power," NCNA, February 10, 1967, in *SCMP*, No. 3880 (15 February 1967), p. 1.

[53] See, for example, "Consolidate the Victory of the Struggle Launched by Revolutionaries to Seize Power," *JMJP*, 13 February 1967, in *SCMP*, No. 3999 (28 February 1967), p. 1; "Down With Chiang Hua," *Wen-ko t'ung-hsin*, No. 16 (July 1968), in *SCMP*, No. 4230 (1 August 1968), p. 1. See also, "Another Criminal Proof of ' Canton Repudiate T'ao Joint Committee's ' Attempt to Seize Power From the Army," *San chün lien wei chan-pao*, No. 10 (13 September 1968), in *SCMP*, No. 4275 (10 October 1968), p. 1. Hsieh Fu-chih estimated that fully 80 per cent. of the *hsien*-level public security organs supported the conservatives. "Comrade Hsieh Fu-chih's Important Speech," *Chiu P'eng Lo chan-pao*, No. 3 (February 1968), in *SCMP*, No. 4139 (15 March 1968), p. 5.

[54] "Completely Smash the Feudal, Capitalist and Revisionist Legal Systems," *Fan P'eng Lo hei-hsien*, No. 2 (July 1968), in *SCMM*, No. 625 (3 September 1968), p. 23; "Down with P'eng Chen, the Sworn Enemy of Proletarian Dictatorship," *JMJP*, 15 October 1967, in *SCMP*, No. 4051 (31 October 1967), p. 1.

[55] "Suppression of the Masses Is Bourgeois Dictatorship," *Wen hui pao*, 5 June 1968, in *SCMP*, No. 4210 (3 July 1968), p. 1.

[56] *Ibid.*, p. 4. See also, Ts'ui Min *et al.*, "Overthrow the Rule of the Bourgeois ' Scholar Tyrants,' " *JMJP*, 6 June 1966, in *SCMP*, No. 3722 (21 June 1966), p. 12, in which Peking Law School's emphasis on professional proficiency rather than Chairman Mao's thought was criticized.

upon specialists and upon specialized techniques separated the public security from the people and rendered it difficult or impossible for the Party and the masses to supervise public security work. It also made public security cadres feel that they were somehow "special" and superior to the common people. All these factors contributed to the formation of an independent kingdom mentality within the public security.

Reminiscent of some of the criticisms made against the retained KMT judges in the early 1950s, the personal style of the cadres was again attacked. "The capitalist roaders of the judicial organs also worshipped things of foreign and ancient origin. They abolished the revolutionary work style, and advocated that lawyers should attend court in European dress and pointed shoes, and assume the airs of bourgeois lords." [57]

More generally, the entire external model of law came under criticism.[58] The development of political-legal organs and the push for "strengthening the legal system" were called attempts to adopt wholesale the feudal, capitalist and revisionist legal systems. Legal procedure once again was charged with causing undue confusion and with being a ruse by which justice could be thwarted. The use of lawyers was also denounced, since this led only to endless battles of words rather than to concrete results.

The very role of and need for law were called into question. To begin with, since the Liu-P'eng-Lo group controlled the political-legal system, many if not most of the laws could be presumed to further the reactionary cause and to provide legal barriers behind which traitors could hide. Through the ruse of requiring strict adherence to law, this group "attempted to fetter with law the instruments of dictatorship hand and foot, and prevent the masses of the people from daring to interfere with counter-revolutionary activities." [59] On a deeper level, the "bourgeois" position that law should be the ultimate guide for action was strongly criticized. Under this theory, the masses would take orders not from the Party, but from the law. The masses also would look to the law rather than to Chairman Mao's thoughts for guidance and inspiration.[60] There was a renewed demand for fewer laws, not more laws, and even a call for "lawlessness." [61]

The transformation of the political-legal organs was accomplished in part by a revolt of the leftist elements within these organs and in part by the entry of revolutionary mass organizations into political-legal work. The most important factor, however, was the decision "to impose military control on all organs of dictatorship"—that is, on all political-legal organs.[62] Three-way alliances were formed, consisting of

---

[57] "Completely Smash the Feudal, Capitalist and Revisionist Legal Systems," p. 25, above, n. 54.
[58] *Ibid.*   [59] *Ibid.*
[60] *Ibid.*
[61] "In Praise of 'Lawlessness,'" *JMJP*, 31 January 1967, in *SCMP*, No. 3879 (14 February 1967), p. 13.
[62] "Vice Premier Hsieh Fu-chih's Talk at the Supreme People's Court" (excerpts), *Hung tien hsün*, No. 3 (27 March 1968), in *SCMP*, No. 4157 (11 April 1968), p. 4. In the same talk, Hsieh rejected the suggestion that the Supreme Court be merged with the Ministry of Public Security, but left the question open with respect to the procuracy. He also called for a reduction in the staffs of the political-legal organs.

members of the People's Liberation Army (PLA), revolutionary cadres, and the masses. In the public security, military control committees of the PLA were placed over each organ.[63] In addition, many public security cadres were purged and replaced with demobilized PLA men.[64] In some areas, PLA soldiers were stationed within the public security organs.[65]

As the Cultural Revolution ran its course, a gradual effort was made to restore order and to re-establish lines of communication and control. Sometime around late 1967 or early 1968, the desire to smash the political-legal system began to give way to an attempt to strengthen this system and to rebuild it according to correct Maoist principles.[66] Political-legal cadres were barred from joining mass organizations or from participating in political demonstrations, and were ordered to be strictly subordinate to the local revolutionary committee.[67] Mass organizations were urged to support the public security in its work, but they were also warned by Chou En-lai not to interfere in its internal rectification.[68]

At the same time, the central authorities tried to make use of law to re-establish their control. The term " according to law " appeared once again in many directives,[69] and strict compliance with central regulations was urged.[70] The mass line was also toned down somewhat on the theory that to let the masses decide everything would be " tailism " and would indicate a lack of leadership.

It is difficult to assess the present position of the political-legal system. The formal legal organs continue to operate, but they appear to share their powers with a variety of informal bodies. For example, one can find reports making it clear that the court still functions, but one can also find reports describing how other non-judicial tribunals

---

[63] See, for example, " PLA's Great Role in Seizure of Power in Shansi Reviewed," NCNA, 28 February 1967, in *SCMP*, No. 3891 (3 March 1967), p. 11.

[64] " Important Speeches by Central Leaders on March 15 " (Chinese source unknown), in *SCMP*, No. 4181 (20 May 1968), p. 1 ; " Important Speeches by Central Leaders on March 18." Red Guard tabloid dated 13 April 1968, and produced by the " Red Rebel Corps " of Yingte Middle School, Kwangtung, in *SCMP*, No. 4182 (21 May 1968), p. 1.

[65] " Comrade Hsiao Ssu-ming Commander of X Army and Vice Chairman of Tientsin Municipal Revolutionary Committee, Relays Speeches Made by Central Leaders at Reception," *Wen-ko t'ung-hsün*, No. 14 (April 1968), in *SCMP*, No. 4172 (7 May 1968), p. 17.

[66] " Shanghai Revolutionary Committee Adopts Resolution Strengthening Dictatorship of the Proletariat," NCNA, 8 June 1967, in *SCMP*, No. 3958 (13 June 1967), p. 1 ; " Vice Premier Hsieh Fu-chih's Talk at the Supreme Court," above, n. 62.

[67] " The Premier's Speech," *Hung-ch'i t'ung-hsin*, No. 1 (Mid-June 1968), in *SCMP*, No. 4212 (8 July 1968), p. 1 ; " Accusations by Victimized Passengers of No. 606 Special Train," *Liu-ling-liu tz'u t'e-pieh lieh-ch'e shih-chien chuan-k'an* (12 July 1968), in *SCMP*, No. 4230 (1 August 1968), p. 12.

[68] " Premier Chou's Talk with Five Representatives of Proletariat Revolutionary Rebels of Canton," *Kuang-yin hung-ch'i* 29 October 1967, in *SCMP*, No. 4091 (3 January 1968), p. 1. A related item appears in *SCMM*, No. 611 (22 January 1968), p. 12.

[69] In the " six articles on the public security " (*kung-an liu t'iao*), the term " according to law " appears five times.

[70] See, for example, " Opinions Concerning Cleaning Up of Teachers' Ranks," *Tung-fang-hung tien hsün*, No. 2 (July 1968), in *SCMP*, No. 4227 (29 July 1968), p. 4.

adjudicate cases and impose sanctions.[71] The most far-reaching change appears to have been the replacement of a large number of cadres who had considerable professional expertise and departmental ties, with a new group of cadres who have little experience in political-legal work or little loyalty to the political-legal system. Perhaps harking back to the early years after Liberation, there will be another period where functional lines are blurred and where the work style is loose and informal.   [pp. 104–109]

[71] On the court continuing to function, see, for example, "Current News," *Kung-jen chan-pao*, 1 December 1967, in *SCMP*, No. 4122 (20 February 1968), p. 6. On non-judicial organs adjudicating cases, see, for example, "A Serious Statement," *Hsüeh-an chuan-k'an* (8 December 1967), in *SCMP*, No. 4117 (13 February 1968), p. 1.

11

THE JUDICIAL PROCESS

MODERN legal theory has been much concerned, especially in America, to explore the inner workings of the judicial system.[1] The earlier attitude, and one which the newer jurisprudence has not altogether dispelled, is to regard the judiciary as the priests of the law, the repositories of its ancient rules and traditions; decisions are thus distilled in a mysterious way by the judge *in scrinio pectoris sui*; moreover he never creates new law but only declares fresh applications of the ancient rule.[2] *Eppur si muove!* Despite this doctrine the course of legal development has gone on and the legal system has been gradually remoulded, albeit often haltingly and inadequately, to meet new social needs. In the meantime judicial orthodoxy still clings as its sheet-anchor to the assumption that it is for the judge to apply the law as it is and not to make new law, and the hieratic tradition may be seen to survive, both in the treatment of the American Supreme Court Judges as High-Priests and Guardians of the Constitution, and in the common law reverence for judicial as against mere juristic utterance.

STARE DECISIS

To follow past decisions is a natural and indeed a necessary procedure in our everyday affairs. To take the same course as has been taken previously, or as has usually been adopted in the past, not only confers the advantage of the accumulated experience of the past but also saves the effort of having to think out a problem anew each time it arises. Accordingly, in almost any form of organisation, precedents have to be established as guides to future conduct, and this applies not merely to legal systems but to all rule or norm-creating bodies, whether clubs, government departments, schools, business firms or churches. There

---

[1] This chapter concentrates on the judicial process. However, particularly in the United States, effort has been expended in showing how parallel judgment processes work. A useful reader, in which judicial, legislative, executive and administrative processes are detailed and compared, is Auerbach *et al., The Legal Process* (1961). Such " grand theory " is in its infancy in this country; the writings of Vickers (*The Art of Judgment* (1965), *Value Systems and Social Process* (1968)) being distinguished exceptions. His analysis of various reports (*Buchanan* on road traffic, *Robbins* on universities, the Royal Commission on capital punishment) demonstrating their reasoning, analysis and structure is compelling reading. See, for example, *The Art of Judgment* (1965), Chap. 3.

[2] But on the medieval attitude towards the power of the court to create new " customs," see *ante*, 613.

is, however, an inevitable danger that this tendency to follow past precedents may lead to stereotyped procedures and so stultify progress, and much of the working success of any organisation may depend on its ability to apply precedents creatively.[3] The infinite variability of the facts in human situations comes to the assistance of mankind not only by rendering it impossible to apply past rulings purely mechanically, but by providing scope for the gradual moulding of the rules to meet fresh situations as they arise. There is a constant inter-action between rules and the factual situations which they govern, for a too rigid observance of the rules may stereotype the very structure and activities of society itself, whereas a freer approach will allow a richer interplay of social forces.[4]

Whilst restraint in exercising the judicial power to overrule precedents makes for stability, abstention can defeat this very stability, for a practice of rigid adherence to precedent will eventually produce an accumulation of outmoded rules which are likely to be blurred by artificial distinctions.[5]

Precedent has thus always been the life-blood of legal systems, whether primitive,[6] archaic or modern. It is, of course, particularly prominent in the common law, but barely less so in the modern civil law. The special features of the present-day common law system of precedent may, perhaps, be summarised as (i) a particular emphasis on judicial decisions as the core of the legal system; (ii) a very subordinate role conceded to juristic writings, as against decisions of the courts, in the exposition of the law; (iii) the treatment of certain judi-

---

[3] It has been suggested that " vagueness is not incompatible with precision. . . . A painter with a limited palette can achieve more precise representations by thinning and combining his colours than a mosaic worker can achieve with his limited variety of tiles, and the skilful superimposing of vagueness has similar advantages over the fitting together of precise technical terms." (Quine, *Word and Object* (1960), p. 127.) See also Christie, 48 Minn.L.R. 885.

[4] A rigid social system need not necessarily be based upon the rigidity of the laws. In ancient China positive law was reduced to a minimum, and the judicial authorities were regarded as having the paternalistic function of resolving each case on its merits with a view to preserving social harmony, rather than enforcing predetermined legal standards of justice. The rigidities of Chinese society were due to bureaucracy and the institutions of family life rather than to legalism. (See J. Needham, *Science and Civilisation in China*, Vol. II, Chap. 18.) The Confucian distinction is between *Li* (propriety) and *Fa* (law), between, what Victor Li has called, the internal and external models of social control (see *ante*, 651 and 693). See also Schwartz, " On Attitudes Toward Law In China " in ed., Katz, *Government under Law and the Individual* (1957), pp. 27–39 and Bozeman, *The Future of Law in a Multicultural World* (1971), pp. 140–160.

[5] See Keeton, *Venturing to do Justice* (1969), p. 15 who points out that : " Courts refusing to overrule precedents outright are virtually forced to accomplish reform by devising a labyrinth of rules with dubious and unpredictable implications. Thus, overpowering demands of justice encourage such courts to make casuistic distinctions that produce doubt rather than certainty, irregularity rather than even-handedness and vacillation rather than constancy." *Cf.* Llewellyn's contention that a formal style does not make for predictability (*ante*, 410).

[6] *Cf.* Gluckman, *Judicial Process among the Barotse*, pp. 253–258.

cial decisions as binding on other judges; and (iv) the form of judicial judgments and the mode of reporting these. Something on all these points will emerge from the brief ensuing discussion of the rule of *stare decisis* in the common law and in other systems.

The Common Law Approach

What is regarded today as the characteristic attitude of the common law in treating judicial decisions as binding in themselves on future courts is in fact quite a modern feature, being hardly older than the nineteenth century. The earlier view was far closer to the modern civilian attitude, for it regarded decisions as expressions of opinion as to the state of the law whose weight depended on the judge or judges who pronounced them, but which were not actually authoritative in the sense of compelling the judges to follow those opinions, even if they were thought to be wrong.[7] Indeed, the modern common law doctrine could hardly have arisen until there was in existence an established hierarchy of courts and an efficient system of law reporting.[8] As to the latter, the reports of Burrows and of Durnford and East laid the foundations in the latter half of the eighteenth century for the systematised series of the modern period, but it was not till well into the nineteenth century, with the great procedural reforms of that era, that an established hierarchical structure was conferred on the judicial system. Lord du Parcq has reminded us how an appeal from Lord Eldon's decisions sitting as Lord Chancellor in the Court of Chancery, to the House of Lords, usually meant an appeal to Lord Eldon himself and " two mutes," thus designating the lay peer and stray bishop who were rounded up for this purpose to make a quorum.[9]

Even at the present day a certain informality casts its shadow over the English system of reporting, for that system knows nothing of an official series, despite the immense weight it accords to judicial

---

[7] See *per* Vaughan C.J. in *Bole* v. *Horton* (1673) Vaughan's Rep., p. 382; Hale, *Hist. Com. Law*, Chap. IV, p. 63 (ed. 1739).

[8] Lord Holt's protest, in 1704, is well known: " . . . . these scrambling reports . . . will make us appear to posterity for a parcel of blockheads ": *Slater* v. *May*, 2 Ld.Raym. 1072. Of Espinasse, Pollock C.B. once said that " he heard only half of what went on in court, and reported the other half." (See E. S. P. Haynes, *The Lawyer*, p. 204). It has recently been demonstrated that the report we have relied upon for so important a case as *Slade's* is in fact " a polished redaction of [Coke's] own speeches for the plaintiff " and that this " created the impression that [Coke's] own successful arguments had the force of judicial resolutions," *per* Baker (1971) C.L.J. 51, 53. This raises the question of how reliable private reports are, for this revelation may be but the tip of the iceberg. In a system where precedent is relied upon less, as in France, the need for an efficient system of law-reporting has, nonetheless, been emphasised. See Dawson, *The Oracles of the Law* (1968), pp. 385–386.

[9] (1949) 1 *Current Legal Problems*, pp. 3–4.

utterances.[10] Nor does a case need to be in a regular report to demand the attention of the court, for any unreported decision, if vouched for by a member of the Bar, enjoys an authority no less than if it had been reported, provided the court is satisfied that it is sufficiently informed as to the facts of the case and what was decided thereon. On the other hand, cases, even if fully reported, if not certified by a barrister, are relegated to an uneasy limbo: strictly, they should not be read to a subsequent court at all, but this rule, though occasionally reaffirmed,[11] is in practice often waived or conveniently overlooked.

When an overall view is taken of the existing rules of *stare decisis* in English law, it is evident that there is room for a good deal more flexibility than might be supposed.[12] Thus courts of co-ordinate jurisdiction [13] are not bound by each other's decisions (though for this purpose the so-called Divisional Court enjoys a somewhat ill-defined pre-eminence [14]), and obviously a decision of a lower court can only persuade but not bind its superior.[15] And the ruling by the House

10 But note the *preference* expressed for the *Law Reports* over the *Law Times* series in *Duke of Buccleuch* v. *I.R.C.* [1967] 1 A.C. 506, 527–528 *per* Lord Reid. The *Law Reports* contained a revised judgment deleting a particular passage which Lord Reid would also have deleted. But Lord Reid also pointed to the dangers of a multiplicity of reports: the I.R.C. had relied upon the unrevised report and had been misled as a result.

11 See *Birtwhistle* v. *Tweedale* [1954] 1 W.L.R. 190.

12 A tribunal, such as the Lands Tribunal, is not entitled simply to follow its own previous decisions but is bound to consider each case as it arises on its merits: see *Merchandise Transport Ltd.* v. *British Transport Commission* [1962] 2 Q.B. 173 and *West Midland Baptist Association* v. *Birmingham Corp.* [1968] 2 Q.B. 188. So is the Restrictive Trade Practices Court. See Stevens and Yamey, the *Restrictive Trade Practices Court*, Chap. 6. An excellent illustration of flexibility is the reasoning of the House of Lords in *Conway* v. *Rimmer* [1968] A.C. 910, where at least eight reasons were found why *Duncan* v. *Cammell Laird* [1942] A.C. 624 should not govern. See *post*, 755.

13 But a judge should not reject a decision of a court of co-ordinate jurisdiction unless convinced that the earlier decision is wrong: see *Island Tug Ltd.* v. *S.S. Makedonia* [1958] 1 Q.B. 365.

14 See, *e.g.*, *Police Authority for Huddersfield* v. *Watson* [1947] K.B. 842, 848. However, the basis of Lord Goddard's reasoning has since been removed, as he founded his argument upon the ground that there was no appeal from the Divisional Court (in criminal matters). This state of affairs was rectified in 1960 by the Administration of Justice Act, s. 1.

15 The doctrine *communis error facit jus* is of very uncertain operation. But it is clear that, as the bonds of *stare decisis* are gradually loosened, there has been a diminution in the force of this doctrine. It is a concept totally alien to continental jurisprudence. Recent cases suggest that the courts are now prepared to draw a line between areas of law where the litigants can be said to have relied upon a previous line of decisions (see, *e.g.*, *Re Darnley's Will Trusts* [1970] 1 W.L.R. 405, a conveyancing practice crystallised by the profession) and those where the law refuses to accept that they can have done so (*e.g.*, *R.* v. *Bow Road Domestic Proceedings Court, ex parte Adedigba* [1968] 2 All E.R. 89, a decision on jurisdiction in affiliation or *Ross Smith* v. *Ross Smith* [1962] A.C. 280 where the court, by a three to two majority, narrowed a jurisdictional limitation of nullity proceedings). See also the reasoning of Widgery L.J. in *R.* v. *Newsome and Browne* [1970] 2 Q.B. 711 that the cases in issue were recent (not of long-standing) and could, therefore, be disposed of more easily (though the criminal division of the Court of Appeal does not anyway apply *stare decisis* very rigorously). See also *Button* v. *D.P.P.* [1966] A.C.

of Lords in 1898 that it is bound by its own decisions has now been replaced by the recognition that that tribunal, while treating its former decisions as normally binding, may depart from a previous decision when it appears right to do so.[16] But this direction has made little difference to House of Lords practice. It is clear that their lordships had found little difficulty in circumventing undesirable precedents in the years before 1966.[17] It is equally apparent that the decisive step of overruling *in as many words* a previous decision of the House is too traumatic for many of the law Lords to contemplate. In five years there has been no direct application of the newly acquired power. Dogma has changed: little else. When the opportunity presented itself in *Conway* v. *Rimmer* [18] to overrule *Duncan* v. *Cammell Laird*,[19] at least eight reasons were adduced why *Duncan* should not govern. Only Lord Morris was bold enough to suggest that *Duncan* should be overruled.[20]

As for the civil Court of Appeal, which still adheres to the doctrine that it is finally bound by its own decisions, both the development of the so-called *per incuriam* rule, as well as an increasing readiness to distinguish earlier decisions viewed with disfavour, has effected a considerable mitigation.[21] Lord Denning is already on record as favouring the adoption, as regards the Court of Appeal's own decisions, of the ruling recently accepted by the House of Lords. Though he has not yet succeeded in carrying his brethren with him, his view may well eventually prevail, possibly with some encouragement from the House of Lords itself.[22] Never-

---

612; *West Midland Baptist Association* v. *Birmingham Corporation, op. cit.,* at pp. 214–215. For the very different American attitude, see Karlen, *Appellate Courts in the U.S.A. and England* (1963) pp. 66–68.   [16] See *post,* 754.
[17] See Cross, 82 L.Q.R. 203 for an illuminating discussion of some of the methods used.   [18] See *post,* 755.   [19] [1942] A.C. 624.
[20] Clark (1969) 32 M.L.R. 142, 144 would add Lord Upjohn, but Lord Upjohn clearly states he is not with the "departers" and his view was "apart altogether" from the 1966 Statement. The view that only Lord Morris was prepared to overrule *Duncan* is supported by Stone, 69 Colum.L.R. 1162, 1171. Recent decisions show the presence of earlier tensions. Thus, in *Cassells* v. *Broome* [1972] 1 All E.R. 801 and *Jones* v. *Secretary of State for Social Services* [1972] 2 W.L.R. 210 the Lords emphasised that the power to depart from a previous decision would be exercised sparingly and cautiously. The majority in *Jones* thought that the *ratio* of an earlier Lords' case was wrong, yet only a minority of three (in both *Cassells* and *Jones* a full court of seven sat) was prepared to overrule it. It was deemed generally inappropriate to use the new weapon in cases of statutory construction, unless the existing decision was causing administrative difficulties or individual injustice. In *Cassells,* it was said that the object of the 1966 Statement was not to tear up the doctrine of precedent nor to encourage a tendency periodically to chop and change the law. In *British Railways Board* v. *Herrington* [1972] 1 All E.R. 749, however, the formulation of an occupier's duty to a trespasser in *Addie* v. *Dumbreck* [1929] A.C. 358 was not followed; it was held to be restrictive and inadequate to changed social conditions.   [21] *Post,* 763.
[22] There are now at least six occasions since the House of Lords Practice Statement on which Lord Denning has expressed dissatisfaction with the practice crystallised in *Young* v. *Bristol Aeroplane Co.* (*post,* 763). In *Eastwood* v. *Herrod* [1968]

theless, the basic flexibility of the system is preserved, not so much by the formal limitations on the rule of *stare decisis*, but by the relative freedom with which courts may and often do determine the scope and limits of past precedents and whether to apply them to the fresh circumstances which have arisen, or to distinguish these from the facts and circumstances held to be material in previous cases. In this way, within certain limits, there remains a certain room for manoeuvre, without which no legal system would be workable. For only a totally static society could tolerate a completely rigid system of law.[23]

Rules of Law or Rules of Practice

From the point of view of legal theory there has been much speculation as to the authority of Lord Gardiner's statement. The statement was not part of a judicial judgment. Not being issued in a curial capacity the statement can have no legal force. It follows that if rules of precedent have legal force, then a rule modifying them would itself have to have legal force. The whole juridical status of precedent is thus called in question, and not for the first time.

One means of escape from this logical conundrum is to say that rules of precedent are not rules of law but rules of practice.

2 Q.B. 923, he preferred "a way round the strict doctrine of precedent" to "the endless task of distinguishing the indistinguishable and reconciling the irreconcilable" which makes "confusion worse confounded." He invited the cynic to "comment on this process if he likes" (p. 934). In *Boys* v. *Chaplin* [1968] 1 All E.R. 283, he held (Diplock L.J. was in agreement, and Lord Upjohn did not dissent) that an interlocutory order by a Court of Appeal consisting of two lords justices was not binding on the Court of Appeal, and the *ratio decidendi* of the order need not be followed by a subsequent Court of Appeal if it was wrong; and foresaw "the time . . . when we [may] have to reconsider the self-imposed limitation stated in *Young's* case" (pp. 288–289). Subsequently, in *Gallie* v. *Lee* [1969] 2 Ch. 17 (see *post*, 764) and *Hanning* v. *Maitland (No. 2)* [1970] 1 Q.B. 580, he expressed the view that the Court of Appeal was no longer absolutely bound by its own decisions: in *Gallie* he provoked hostile reaction from Russell L.J. (see *post*, 765) and sympathy, though not support, from Salmon L.J. (see *post*, 765). In *Broome* v. *Cassells* [1971] 2 Q.B. 354, he had the support of Salmon and Phillimore L.JJ. in his repudiation of a House of Lords' decision which the Court of Appeal held had been decided *per incuriam* by the House of Lords which was then bound by its own decisions and which, said the Court of Appeal, had not even been discussed (though this is not strictly accurate (see McGregor (1971) 34 M.L.R. 520)). The Court of Appeal's approach was severely censured in the Lords, see *Cassells* v. *Broome* [1972] 1 All E.R. 80]. Lord Dilhorne stated two grounds on which the Court of Appeal can justifiably refuse to follow a Lords' decision: *viz.*, where what was said was *obiter*, and where there are two clearly inconsistent Lords' decisions. But, otherwise, the judicial system only works if someone is allowed to have the last word and the last word is loyally accepted (p. 854).

Most recently, in *Barrington* v. *Lee* [1971] 3 All E.R. 1231, 1238, Lord Denning was disposed to overrule a decision of the Court of Appeal which had stood for barely six months.

[23] For a detailed study of the present English case law on *stare decisis*, see R. Cross, *Precedent in English Law*, Chaps. 3 and 4.

Gardiner's pronouncement is often in fact characterised as a Practice Statement. The question as to how a Statement with no legal force could modify rules of precedent would thus be avoided. Glanville Williams [24] has adopted such an approach. He has argued that the binding force of *Tramways* [25] ruling cannot be derived from the binding force of that case as a precedent until we know that the House of Lords was bound by its own decisions. So, he argued, in 1957, the House of Lords was free to overrule its own decisions, including *Tramways*. In view of this the operation of rules of precedent cannot derive from the fact that rules of precedent are legal rules. Consequently, he argued, that such binding force as rules of precedent have, must be based rather on their standing as " rules of practice." It may be readily conceded that Williams' case is logically unanswerable. But, as Stone, [26] has pointed out, this does not dispose of the matter. " Whether this is really a solution still depends on the assumption that ' rules of law ' and ' rules of practice ' are mutually exclusive categories," [27] or denying that a " rule of practice " may not itself also be a " rule of law." What, therefore, characterises a " rule of practice " and are all rules of practice functionally similar? Can a statement, even assuming it was issued in a curial capacity, have binding effect as a " rule of practice," any more than as a " rule of law "?

It is difficult to see, employing Williams' own logic, how the binding force of a rule of practice can be based on some earlier practice, any more than the binding force of a rule of precedent can be based on an earlier precedent laying down such a rule. As Stone suggests the vicious circle can only be broken by positing the characteristics of " practice " that make the rule so observed binding, rather as we can indicate what features of " customary " behaviour make the rules observed binding in the general law. " We might . . . say that the hierarchical rules of precedent are binding rules of law, not because some court on some occasion announced them, but rather because of ' observed regularities of behaviour conforming to " the practice " . . . a steady manifestation of an *opinio necessitatis* by the legislature in all of this.' [28] But if we do we must recognise courts which vindicate them by acts of reversal, deference of lower courts to these reversals, and also long-standing acquiescence by the legislature in all of this." [28] But if we do we must recognise that the " rule of practice *here involved* is also a ' rule of law.' "

---

[24] See *Salmond on Jurisprudence* (11th ed., 1957), pp. 187–188. This passage is omitted from the 12th edition, edited by Professor Fitzgerald.

[25] [1898] A.C. 375.

[26] See 69 Colum.L.R. 1162, 1162–1168, 1189–1202 (1969).

[27] At p. 1165. Stone compares this logical status with *legal* status.

[28] *Idem.*

A distinction can be drawn between *descriptive* rules of practice and *prescriptive* rules of practice. There are, for example, " rules of practice " whereby judges prevent the introduction of evidence which, though legally admissible, might excessively prejudice a party. Failure to do this will not, however, be a basis for reversal on appeal. Such a " rule of practice " is descriptive of past and expected future behaviour, but is not prescriptive for the future. Thus, in *Connelly* v. *D.P.P.*,[29] the House of Lords could disapprove of the rule of practice [30] that a count for murder could not be joined with one for robbery, both having arisen from the same facts. Lord Devlin explicitly stated that the " rule of practice " was not a " rule of law." The Lords' disapproval of the practice did not, therefore, require the appeal to be allowed, as it would have done had the rule been a " rule of law." [31]

In referring, however, to rules of precedent as " rules of practice," one has in mind something less vague and imprecise. For with precedent it is the practice, the behaviour of conforming, reversing, submitting etc., what Hart [32] has referred to as a " critical reflective attitude," which takes the nature of precedent beyond the merely descriptive, so that the rules become prescriptive for judicial behaviour. If this is so (and ignoring the fact that *Tramways* was the culmination of a long process and not one innovatory step [33]) then the rule in *Tramways* became such with the conduct of other judges and lawyers between 1898 and 1966. " The rule which, immediately on its enunciation in 1898, faced the difficulties described by Glanville Williams, might by 1966, by reason of that practice, have become a rule both *descriptive* of past practice, and also *prescriptive* of a rule of law binding in the future." [34] Similarly, the 1966 Statement *in itself* has no binding effect, but would acquire such when a " degree of conformity to it, and the *opinio necessitatis* grounding this, became manifest in the behaviour of courts." [35] The significance of the Gardiner pronouncement must, therefore, be sought in observing and interpreting the differences, if any, in court behaviour before and after the Statement. As has been suggested,[36] and as a glance at *Conway* v. *Rimmer* [37] will readily confirm, the leeways of precedent

[29] [1964] A.C. 1254.
[30] In accordance with *R.* v. *Jones* [1918] 1 K.B. 416.
[31] But the Lords announced that the challenged " rule " should not have effect " as a rigid rule " in the future. For the relation of this to the doctrine of prospective overruling see *post,* 727.
[32] See *ante,* 169.
[33] Earlier cases are *Att.-Gen.* v. *Windsor* (1860) 8 H.L.C. 369; *Beamish* v. *Beamish* (1861) 9 H.L.C. 274.
[34] *Per* Stone, *op. cit.,* p. 1168.
[35] *Idem.*
[36] *Ante,* 706.
[37] *Post,* 755.

were sufficiently flexible before 1966 (and still are) for the Lords
to develop the law in a creative manner, without recourse to their
new weapon.[38]

The Civil Law

In the classical Roman system the *judex*, to whom the trial of a case
was submitted, was a layman; legal development therefore rested not
in the hands of professional judges but of the jurists. But Maine's
generalisation that the Roman law was the product not of the bench
but of the bar [39] is very far from the mark, for the class of jurists did
not act as advocates and were advisers not merely to parties to litigation, but also to the *judices* and magistrates, as well as being active
on the council of the Emperor.[40] The Emperor himself also gave
decisions in judicial proceedings (*decreta*), and these were treated as
authentic interpretations of the law, though in cases where a new
principle was involved it was regarded as a question of construction
whether the imperial decision was intended to lay down a general
rule or merely to provide for the particular case.[41] The decline of
the Roman system was strongly marked by the mechanical Law of
Citations of A.D. 426, for, as Buckland has remarked, "in law opinions
should be estimated by *weight*, not number." [42]

In the modern civil law it must not be thought that there is to be
found complete unity of theory and practice, though broadly speaking
these systems concur in denying absolute authority to judicial precedent and in attaching a good deal more weight to juristic writings. In
some ways the civil law of France is highly individual and rooted in
French historical traditions,[43] but as one of the outstanding and best
known of the modern civil law systems it may usefully serve as our

---

38 Another interesting consideration of this problem is contained in Roy Stone,
"Logic and law, The Precedence of Precedents" (1967) 51 Minn.L.R. 655. He
believes that the Practice Statement is an example of the "Cretan liar" paradox
(Epimenides in stating that "All Cretans are liars" must have been making a
false statement since he was a Cretan), that it has cast unjustifiable doubt on
the legal authority of *Tramways*, the pronouncement of which on precedent
is a rule of law "analogous to a rule of interpretation," that *Tramways*
preserves the internal logic of the system. The Practice Statement reversal
is thus contradictory in the same way that the "Cretan liar" paradox is.
However, it is difficult to see why the *Tramways* pronouncement does not itself
suffer from the same logical pit-fall as the "Cretan liar" or, indeed, Gardiner's
Practice Statement. *Cf. Hicks* (1971) C.L.J. 275, 283.
39 *Ancient Law* (ed. Pollock), p. 32.
40 See Jolowicz, *Hist. Intro. to Roman Law*, p. 372.
41 *Ibid.*, p. 382.
42 *Textbook of Roman Law*, 3rd ed., p. 34. This law named 5 jurists as primary
authorities, and then provided mechanical rules for deciding where there was
disagreement between them. For details, see Jolowicz, *op. cit.*, pp. 472–473.
43 On which see Dawson, *The Oracles of the Law*, Chap. IV.

example of their general approach.[44] One important feature of these systems since the nineteenth century is that they are usually, though not invariably, based on a series of codes, so that the fabric of the law is regarded as primarily statutory, the judiciary's task being limited to applying the provisions of the code itself, together with later amendments. But the original theory that the French Napoleonic code was the sole source of law, exemplified by the provision prohibiting the judge from pronouncing by way of general disposition,[45] was soon seen to be impracticable, and for long now the decisions of the courts (*la jurisprudence*) have been acknowledged to play a major role in the development of the law.[46] Moreover, since Gény propounded the judicial role in terms of a " *libre recherche scientifique*," [47] the creative function of the judiciary has been widely accepted. And yet " debate still continues . . . on the issue whether *jurisprudence* is a source of law." [48] Gény's opinion, for long the authoritative one, held that " the rules originating in court decisions had none of the attributes of legal rules," they could merely " propel the formation of custom, whose force derived from the comment of those whose ' interests ' the rules affected." [49] But who were the " users of custom " and how was their consent to be obtained? An attempt to answer this has recently been made by Professor Maury,[50] who has suggested that the " interested " parties will be men of law whose professional judgment " will impose itself " on those affected by the rule. This novel twist to the old concept of *Juristenrecht* [51] has not proved uncontroversial, as will be seen in one of

---

[44] For German attitude see Cohn, *Manual of German Law*, Vol. 1, pp. 4–6 and, more fully, Dawson, *op. cit.*, Chaps. III (historical) and VI (on the modern case-law revolution); for the Italian see Cappelletti *et al.*, *The Italian Legal System: An Introduction* (1967), pp. 270–273 ; for the Spanish see Brown, 5 I.C.L.Q. 364, 367–372. General surveys are found in David and Brierley, *Major Legal Systems* (1968) at, *inter alia*, pp. 73–85, 103–111, 316–321 ; Merryman, *The Civil Law Tradition* (1969), Chaps. IV–VI.

[45] But this provision (in Art. 5) must be read together with Art. 4, which provides that a judge who refuses to decide a matter under the pretext of the silence, obscurity or insufficiency of the law is guilty of a denial of justice. The status and role of the French judge was fixed during the Revolution when the judiciary was the enemy. The germ of Article 5 was developed by the Constituent Assembly in 1790 as one of two measures aimed at subjugating the judiciary. (Art. 5 is backed by provisions in the Penal Code (Art. 127) which prescribe civic degradation for judges " who intermeddle in the exercise of legislative power." See Dawson, *op. cit.*, pp. 375–382.) The other curbing measure was the insistence that judges give reasons for their decisions (decisions had, and still have, to be *motivé*).

[46] *Cf.* D. Lloyd, " Codifying English Law," in (1949) 2 *Current Legal Problems*, 155.

[47] See F. Gény, *Méthode d'Interprétation en Droit Privé*, (2nd ed., 1932). And see now an American translation published by West Publishing Company for the Louisiana Law Institute (1963).

[48] *Per* Dawson, *op. cit.*, p. 422. He quotes Esmein's opinion expressed in 1952 that this debate is " never closed."

[49] *Idem*, p. 417.

[50] See *post*, 751.

[51] *Ante*, 564.

the extracts from Dawson. It shows the wide gap between common and civil law approaches. Certain other differences call for emphasis.

Thus, firstly, precedents even of superior courts are not recognised as automatically binding subsequently either on themselves or on inferior tribunals. This distinction has tended to diminish, and it is now generally agreed that a decision of the *Cour de Cassation* is to all intents and purposes regarded as authoritative for the future. Yet deviation is not in itself a ground for quashing a decision of a lower court and there have been famous occasions when lower courts, often encouraged by writers of *doctrine*, have resisted innovations of the *Cour de Cassation*.[52] At the same time it must be realised that the judicial system under the civil law is far less centralised than that of the common law and judges are far more numerous; in particular there are normally several regional appellate courts of co-ordinate jurisdiction. And although decisions are reported in official series on a scale comparable to that of common law jurisdictions, the judgments of the courts consist usually of a very pithy enunciation (in France embodied in a series of staccato sentences each prefaced by the words " *attendu que . . .*") of the reasons for the decision, without any citation or discussion of authorities.[53] It is here that the importance of juristic opinion comes to the fore, for this (*la doctrine*) is to be found not only in treatises, but in learned annotations appended to reported cases, which partake partly of the nature of the sort of discussion to be found in the lengthy and argumentative judgments of common law judges, and partly of the nature of contributions to learned periodicals. Again, textbooks,

---

[52] Examples may be found in Dawson, *op. cit.*, p. 404.

[53] In French judgments, individual precedents are not cited as they are in this country. Indeed, the *Cour de Cassation* will quash the decision of a lower court if the only reason given for it is an earlier judgment even of the *Cour de Cassation* itself: such a decision will not be *motivé*. See Dawson, *op. cit.*, p. 405 note 13, though he points out that the cases cited which point to this conclusion " were *not* quashed because they did quote the borrowed reasons "; this was additional to the main ground of review. However, decisions are cited. Dawson, *idem*, pp. 405–406, estimates previous cases will be cited once in a hundred lower court judgments selected at random. He concludes: " decisions of the Court of Cassation operate as precedents controlling lower courts to a far greater degree than formal opinions acknowledged " (p. 405). He also notes, with interest, the keeping by the *Cour de Cassation* since 1947 of a card index of summaries of all decisions rendered by that body so that " when a case presents a question of principle or its solution would be susceptible of causing a contrariety of decision " a plenary session must be summoned. German judicial opinions are expressed at much greater length and with frequent references to text-writers and previous case-law. Dawson writes (p. 494): " judicial opinions themselves still read at times like small treatises, with full and careful formulations of doctrine and rounded propositions of law that can all too readily be extracted from context."

while citing cases at least as frequently as do English treatises, contain but little discussion of their actual content, or of judicial judgments in particular cases.

It is interesting to note how American law, while basically proceeding from the common law viewpoint, has taken on some features of the civil law approach.[54] Thus not only is *stare decisis* applied far less rigidly,[55] the Supreme Court in particular not regarding itself as finally bound by its own decisions,[56] but growing weight (going a good deal beyond existing English practice) is accorded to leading textbooks, and to compilations such as the American *Restatement of the Law*. There are, of course, compelling reasons to be found in the Supreme Court's constitutional functions as well as in the comparative rigidity of that constitution, for the refusal of the Court to regard itself as bound by its predecessors' opinions,[57] but apart from this

[54] Interesting discussions on the contrast between appellate procedure and practice in England and in the United States will be found in the writings of Delmar Karlen. He emphasises that American appellate courts see their role in wider terms than their English counterparts and tend to concentrate on questions of law and policy rather than the actual issues of litigation. Furthermore, legislative inactivity forces judges to become the lawmakers (*cf.* Jaffe, *post,* 724). Although *stare decisis* is less rigid, the additional bulk of case-law in the U.S.A. means less freedom of choice for the judges, such that, although a rule is never beyond challenge, there is frequently an authority if one searches for it. There is thus the danger of overlooking important cases, which gives great scope to a *per incuriam* doctrine (see 78 L.Q.R. 370, and *Appellate Courts in the U.S.A. and England* (1963), pp. 154–155). In his latest book, Karlen has related the more flexible doctrine of *stare decisis* to the delay and congestion in American courts. The fact that any decision may be reconsidered at any time affects the attitudes of the profession and the judiciary. He is critical of the American attitude towards citation of cases ("Dozens of decisions are cited to American courts where one would do in England," p. 68). He believes the Supreme Court must shoulder its share of the blame ("They have weakened . . . *stare decisis* and, by increasing the uncertainty of litigation, have increased its volume," pp. 85–86). Further, their "grand style" has encouraged the belief that if one delays the trial long enough, "something may turn up," some new defence may be created and an otherwise guilty defendant escape. The doctrine of prospective overruling (*post,* 727) has mitigated this danger somewhat (see Karlen, *Judicial Administration—The American Experience* (1970), particularly Chap. 3).

[55] In Canada the doctrine of *stare decisis* is stricter, but the Supreme Court has recently decided it was no longer bound by its own decisions. Laskin, *The British Tradition In Canadian Law* (1969) opines that it departed from its own decisions "but without the blare of trumpets before it abandoned in word (but cautious word) and covert deed . . . its acceptance of *stare decisis* in respect of its own decisions" (pp. 66–67). But, he also suggests that precedent in the Ontario Court of Appeal is even stricter than its English counterpart. He cites *R.* v. *De Clercq* [1966] 1 O.R. 674 and *London Assurance Co.* v. *Jonassen* (1968) 66 D.L.R. (2d) 692, 695. See also MacGuigan (1967), 45 Can. Bar Rev. 627, 652 *et seq.*

[56] Roberts J. once stated that this brings "adjudications of this tribunal into the same class as a restricted railroad ticket, good for this day and train only": *Smith* v. *Allwright* 321 U.S. 649, 669 (1944).

[57] It has been pointed out by the U.S. Supreme Court that a constitutional precedent is less subject to the strict rule of *stare decisis* than a precedent which may be altered by legislation (*Glidden* v. *Zdanok,* 370 U.S. 530, 543 (1962)). It is the very fact that constitutional amendment is a laborious and cumbersome process which has led the court to establish this firm principle (See J. S. Williams, "Stability and Change in Constitutional Law," in (1963) Vanderbilt L.R., 221).

the influence may be detected of a judicial system containing numerous regional courts of separate or co-ordinate jurisdiction and which, like the civil law system, by its very structure, excludes a sharply defined and rigid rule of *stare decisis*. Moreover such a system leads naturally to the approach where judicial opinions are weighed not only with respect to their position in the hierarchy of courts from which they were uttered, but also with regard to the stature enjoyed, in the view of the profession, by the judges responsible for those opinions. The differing laws of the various state jurisdictions have also had the result that American textbooks tend more and more to resemble those of civilian countries in concentrating rather on statements of principle than on a discussion of particular cases. At least since the days of Pollock this has been the partial aim of serious legal writers in England, but the central and authoritative role conceded to actual decisions still necessitates a detailed setting forth of particular cases and judicial utterances, which makes even the best text to a large extent a repertory of case-law. Yet this is not altogether a disadvantage, preserving as it does the traditional common law attachment to concrete problems, rather than to abstract formulations. In this it resembles the classical Roman law itself, for the jurists were nothing if not practical men of business, whose preoccupations were concrete cases rather than general rules.[58]

CRITIQUE

The rule of *stare decisis* may be defended on a number of grounds,[59] but is usually justified on the basis that it is conducive to legal certainty. So Lord Eldon said that it was "better that the law should be certain than that every judge should speculate upon improvements."[60] But when judicial utterances (and if *stare decisis* rests upon judicial practice,[61] this is our best evidence) are weighed the rationale of certainty seems to be more one of the ability of legal advisers to rely upon previous statements of the law. This was implicit in Lord Halsbury's judgment in *Tramways*[62] and was stressed by Lord Gardiner in his pronouncement.[63] If reliance is the underlying rationale of *stare decisis,* then this could be achieved, within a looser system of precedent, by the adoption of prospective

---

[58] Though these were often not so much actual cases, but those discussed in an imaginary way in lawyers' chambers: see Buckland and McNair, *Roman Law and Common Law*, 2nd ed., p. 9.

[59] See Wasserstrom, *The Judicial Decision* (1961), pp. 60–83; Hodgson, *Consequences of Utilitarianism* (1967), pp. 142–149.

[60] In *Sheddon* v. *Goodrich*, 8 Ves. 481, 497; (1803) 32 E.R. 441, 447.

[61] *Cf. ante,* 707.

[62] *Post,* 754.

[63] *Post,* 755.

overruling.[64] But there are few signs that English courts will reject that last relic of the declaratory theory of precedent, retrospective overruling. Even were they to do this, there would still remain uncertainty as to *which* rule would be applied in a case. There would still remain the ability of the courts to refine away unpopular cases by subtle distinctions. There would still be uncertainty as to the open texture of rules, such as the category of due care in negligence.[65] Certainty may, as Frank [66] often reminded us, be an illusory target.

There are signs that *stare decisis* is becoming more flexible.[67] A rigid doctrine is inimical to the scientific development of the law, since bad decisions stand out like signposts directing the law into wrong paths and so impeding a rational approach. One cannot help but reflect here what would have been the effect on English (and Scottish law) if the majority decision of three to two had been the other way in *Donoghue* v. *Stevenson*.[68] But House of Lords' decisions are no longer irreversible. And, with the creation of the Law Commissions, Parliament has become a more active law-reforming body. Nevertheless, a hierarchy of courts, and a Court of Appeal fettered by its own decisions, allow less flexibility and freedom of movement than the more elastic civilian systems. Perhaps the difference in approach is most marked in the happily-declining English doctrine of *communis error facit jus*.[69] It has been suggested that it is not better to be *consistently wrong* than *ultimately right*.[70] For, as Paton asks, " Should we carry our natural love of equality as our attribute of justice so far as to treat twenty plaintiffs unjustly because one case laid down an unjust rule?" [71] In France decisions dated by social change are not followed. In England there are now ways of despatching such decisions. But it may be, to quote Paton again, that " what is more important than the machinery is the quality of the men who control it." [71]

Ratio Decidendi

Any legal system which uses precedents, whether these are regarded as technically binding or not, will have necessarily to consider in what

---

[64] *Post*, 727.
[65] So Stone refers to categories such as this as " categories of illusory reference," under which a court exercises a creative choice under the cloak of logical analysis. See *Legal System and Lawyers' Reasonings* (1964), Chap. 7, and *post*, 772.
[66] *Ante*, 434.
[67] See *ante*, 706.
[68] [1932] A.C. 562.
[69] *Ante*, n. 15.
[70] Paton, quoting Isaacs J. in *Australian Agricultural Co.* v. *Federated Engine Drivers* (1913) 17 C.L.R. 261, 278 (*Jurisprudence* (3rd ed.), p. 193).
[71] *Idem*, p. 194.

way they are relevant to future cases. For this purpose it is generally accepted that this relevancy is to be found in the fact that decisions involve some principle of general application. How is this principle to be ascertained ? This appears to be a matter of first importance, at least in such a system as English law, where a decision may be treated as absolutely binding on future courts, for these courts ought to be able to determine in some way what it is that binds them.

Traditional theory on this matter has generally been content to regard the binding part of a decision as the legal principle formulated by the court in relation to the matter actually decided.[72] But as Dr. Goodhart has pointed out [73] this will not always do, for in some cases the court may have decided a case without enunciating any rule at all, and in other instances its formulation of principle may be too wide or too narrow. The first of these objections hardly seems very significant, since, though in older cases judgments are sometimes very brief or non-existent (often due to the inadequate mode of reporting), present-day judgments tend to grow longer and increasingly elaborate. On the other hand, no illustration is needed to prove the point that judges, however cautious they may be by training and disposition, sometimes state rules in terms wider than needed for the disposal of the matter in hand. This situation is well recognised in the orthodox theory, which confines the *ratio decidendi* (or binding principle of the case) to the formulation of the applicable rule in the case so far as it is *necessary* to the matter which is being decided, the remainder being mere *obiter dicta*.[74] This still leaves open the question how such necessity is to be ascertained, though it has long been accepted that a case only binds as to " like facts." [75] But what are *like* facts for this purpose ? If, for instance, a court decides that there is a duty of care owed in relation to a loaded gun, and lays down a principle of liability for dangerous things, is the vital fact here that the article was a gun, so that the decision is limited (so far as the *ratio*

---

[72] See the illuminating essay by Montrose, *Ratio Decidendi and the House of Lords* which shows the classical view to have the support of the Court of Appeal of Northern Ireland and South African courts. (*Precedent In English Law and other Essays* (1968), pp. 151–157).

[73] See " The *Ratio Decidendi* of a Case," in *Essays in Jurisprudence and the Common Law* (1931), pp. 5–8.

[74] But as to the weight to be accorded to some dicta, " A battery of howitzers off the target is more impressive than a pop-gun on it ". (*Per* Ungoed-Thomas J., in *Re Grosvenor Hotel, London (No. 2)* [1964] 2 All E.R. 674 at p. 680). But in *Re Grosvenor Hotel, London* [1964] 3 W.L.R. 992, at p. 1025, Salmon L.J. observed : " This is undoubtedly true, but a battery of howitzers off target sometimes does great damage to what is intended to be preserved."

[75] When a court explicitly states that its decision is limited to the particular facts before it, this is an indication that the ordinary reasoning by analogy is to be excluded, or at least severely limited. Even here, however, there must remain some scope for later interpretations.

goes) to guns alone, or is it also binding as to all or some other objects which might equally be regarded as dangerous? [76]

Dr. Goodhart suggests that the better way to approach this problem is to elucidate the *ratio* of a case from the facts themselves rather than from the principle enunciated by the court. The only facts which are material are those treated as such by the judge deciding the case, and Dr. Goodhart accordingly propounds detailed rules by which it may subsequently be ascertained which facts the judge has found to be material.[77] Nor, as some critics have imagined, are the statement of the rule of law or the reason given for it by the judge, to be ignored. On the contrary, " these are of peculiar importance, for they may furnish us with a guide for determining which facts [the judge] considered material and which immaterial." [78] But it is only the decision in the case based on the facts treated by the judge as material which constitutes the binding *ratio.* The judge who decides the case is the sole master of what facts are or are not to be deemed material, and any later court, having discharged the task, as best it may, of ascertaining what facts the earlier court found to be material, is compelled to accept such finding, even if it should later appear that the judge had obviously based himself on a mistaken or non-existent fact.[79] It has been sometimes thought, though erroneously, that this theory is similar to that of the American Realists, who emphasise that what judges do rather than what they say, is what matters, and that the *ratio* of a case is rather what later courts construct out of it than the precise formulations or findings of the judge who decided the case.[80] But Dr. Goodhart differs strongly from this appreciation, since he claims that later courts are bound, in ascertaining the *ratio,* by the findings of the original judge as to what facts were material. True it is that later courts may have to " interpret " the earlier judgment to glean what facts really were found to be material, but this, says Dr. Goodhart, is very different from " constructing " a principle out of earlier cases.[81]

The advantage of this theory over the traditional one must either derive from its stating more accurately how the courts do in fact proceed to elicit the *ratio* of a case, or in its providing a more certain or satisfactory procedure for ascertaining the *ratio* in doubtful cases. It seems open to question, however, whether this theory qualifies on

[76] *Cf.* H. H. Levi, *An Introduction to Legal Reasoning* (1950), pp. 6–19. See also C. Perelman's concept of " essential categories " (*The Idea of Justice and the Problem of Argument,* pp. 16–19).
[77] *Cf.* Dawson, *post,* 748.
[78] A. L. Goodhart, in (1959) 22 M.L.R., at p. 119.
[79] See *post,* 771.
[80] *Cf. ante,* 407.
[81] *Op. cit.,* p. 123.

either of these counts. Dr. Goodhart says he believes that most English courts do follow his method in doubtful cases,[82] but there seems little or no evidence to support this. Moreover is the guidance offered by his theory really helpful in doubtful cases ? For instance, one of Dr. Goodhart's rules for determining the material facts as seen by the court, is that all facts " implicitly " treated as immaterial are to be so considered.[83] But whether we call this interpretation or construction, the door is obviously wide open here for varying opinions as to what was really material fact in the particular case. On the other hand, while in practice affording little more guidance than the traditional approach, this theory does seem to involve an undue degree of rigidity in trying to tie later judges down slavishly to the attitude adopted by the original judge to the materiality of a particular fact.[84]

Nor does the formula sometimes used to the effect that it is only the underlying principle which binds, afford much help. Indeed, it has been called " grossly misleading," for failing to distinguish between the specific points which may be decided by a case from the more general propositions which may lay behind those points.[85] It may often happen that a specific issue will be determined, though the general proposition underlying the decision may be later held to be unacceptable. For instance, in *London County Territorial Association* v. *Nichols* [86] the decision that a Territorial Army Association is not bound by the Rent Acts, is beyond question, but the underlying general proposition that a body which is an " emanation " of the Crown will share the Crown's immunity from statute law, has since been severely criticised and rejected.[87]

Professor Julius Stone has referred to the essential fallacy in the idea that there is only one *ratio decidendi* implicit or explicit in a particular case. On the contrary, he argues that there is " a range of alternative *rationes decidendi* competing *inter se* to govern future situations and as among these, only future decisions will show which is binding." [88] Stone goes on to point out that the area of judicial choice is much restricted both by the nature of the *ratio decidendi* as well as by other factors. Thus the judge is required to give scrupulous

82 *Ibid.*, p. 124.
83 See *post*, 768.
84 See R. N. Gooderson, " Ratio Decidendi and Rules of Law " (1952) 30 Can.B.R. 892.
85 See D. P. Derham, " Precedent and the Decision of Particular Questions," (1963) 79 L.Q.R. 49.
86 [1949] 1 K.B. 35.
87 *B.B.C.* v. *Johns* [1965] Ch. 32.
88 " The Ratio of the Ratio Decidendi " (1959) 22 M.L.R. 597, at p. 608 ; see *post*, 772 and also *Legal System and Lawyers' Reasonings* (1964) Chap. 7, particularly pp. 267–274 and 69 Colum.L.R. 1162, 1171 *et seq.*

heed to the alternatives presented by the authoritative legal materials, including especially past decisions. It is in choosing between such alternative principles that the interest shifts to the elements of technique, skill, experience and plain wisdom with which such choices are made. It may be added that these are the matters upon which Llewellyn places special stress in his book *The Common Law Tradition*, where he notes no less than sixty-four techniques for handling precedent.[89]

Lord Denning has urged that there has been a noteworthy change of attitude on the part of the House of Lords, which no longer regards the reasoning of previous cases as sacrosanct. He cites such decisions as *Public Trustee* v. *I.R.C.*[90] and *Scruttons* v. *Midland Silicones Ltd.*[91] as showing that the House will not treat as absolutely binding any line of reasoning in a previous case which was not necessary to the decision, but will regard itself as at liberty to depart from it if convinced that it was wrong.[92] This seems to imply that what was " necessary to the decision," on the strict view of the common law rule of precedent, may be approached more freely if the later court thinks that the earlier reasoning was wrong. For if " necessary to the decision " means no more than drawing the line between what is ratio and what is dictum, then there would be nothing novel at all in this new approach adumbrated by Lord Denning himself.[93] However, the reference by Lord Denning to *Scruttons* v. *Midland Silicones* suggests that he intended the latter court to be the arbiter of what was " necessary to the decision."

Certainly, in the years before the Gardiner pronouncement on precedent, the House of Lords was adopting a freer attitude towards its earlier decisions than was previously manifested. A striking illustration was *Scruttons* v. *Midland Silicones*, which refused to treat the earlier decision of *Elder, Dempster* v. *Paterson*[94] as laying down any general principles, particularly having regard to the obscurity of the judgments in that case and the apparent conflict of opinions which they displayed. Lord Reid indicated that there

[handwritten margin note:] Is this not the same as the American Realists — the M. of L decided what was the ratio & what was dicta

---

[89] See *The Common Law Tradition, ante*, 450 and pp. 77 *et seq.*
[90] [1960] A.C. 398.
[91] [1962] A.C. 446.
[92] See also his dissenting opinion in *London Transport Executive* v. *Betts* [1958] A.C. 213, at p. 247: " . . . . when a particular precedent—even of your Lordships' House—comes into conflict with a fundamental principle, also of your Lordships' House, then the fundamental principle must prevail. This must at least be true when the particular precedent leads to absurdity or injustice, and the fundamental principle to consistency and fairness."
[93] See *Penn-Texas Corporation* v. *Murat Anstalt (No. 2)* [1964] 2 Q.B. 647, followed by Lord Denning in *Hanning* v. *Maitland (No. 2)* [1970] 1 Q.B. 580, 587.
[94] [1924] A.C 522.

were three cases where limits might be placed on a prior decision of the House of Lords, *viz.*; (1) where the earlier decision was " obscure "; (2) where the decision was out of line with other authorities or established principles; (3) where the rule laid down was wider than necessary for the decision.[95] Statements such as those of Lord Denning and Lord Reid demonstrate the lengths to which judges went to avoid inconvenient precedents. It is thought, however, that, at least as far as the House of Lords is concerned, such sophistry is no longer necessary.

It may be suggested that the judges do not and are never likely to tie themselves rigidly to any precise method of elucidating the *ratio* of a case.[96] The courts will inevitably approach different cases in different ways, some with greater and some with a lesser measure of freedom. It is this freedom to manoeuvre which is really enshrined in the traditional theory. For though that theory may appear to place an undue stress upon the actual formulation of the rule by the original court, it is qualified by the need for later courts to decide how far that formulation was or was not " necessary " for the purposes of the decision.[97] For this purpose the later court will scrutinise both the facts of the earlier case as far as these appear in the judgment or elsewhere, and the language used by the judge. In interpreting these the later court is likely to be influenced by many variable factors, such as the age of the earlier case; who were the judges composing the court; the arguments which were put forward and examined by it; and its own sense of the needs of the situation and how far it is felt desirable to extend or limit the express formulations of the earlier deci-

---

[95] For a general comment, see G. Dworkin, " Stare Decisis in the House of Lords," (1962) 25 M.L.R. 163 at pp. 171–174.

[96] Thus in a doubtful case a court may take refuge in saying the *ratio* not being clear, it is not part of a tribunal's duty to spell out with difficulty a *ratio decidendi* in order to be bound by it (*G.W.R.* v. *S.S. Mostyn* [1928] A.C. 57, 73); or that it is always dangerous to take one or two observations out of a long judgment and treat them as if they gave the *ratio decidendi* (*Cheater* v. *Cater* [1918] 1 K.B. 247, 252).

[97] The traditional theory is, however, sometimes formulated as " the principle of law which the judge considered necessary to the particular case before him " (Paton, *Text Book of Jurisprudence*, 3rd ed., p. 180). Undoubtedly there are judgments which support this view (see, *e.g.*, Devlin J. in *Behrens* v. *Bertram Mills Circus Ltd.* [1957] 2 Q.B. 1, 23). But this over-rigid statement takes insufficient account of the practice by which courts freely " distinguish " earlier cases. Nor does such an artificial test as that proposed by Wambaugh (*viz.*, reverse the proposition under examination and if the reversal would not affect the decision of the case, then the proposition is *obiter*) help much in practice, since it ignores the " open texture " (*post*, 382) of words. Thus, if a rule of liability is laid down regarding dangerous things in a case concerning guns, this test will not help us to decide whether the binding rule governs only guns, or dangerous articles generally. On Wambaugh see Cross, *Precedent in English Law* (2nd ed.) pp. 51–61.

sion.[98] It may, therefore be that Dr. Goodhart's remark [99] that " few attempts have been made to state any rules by which these general principles can be determined " reveals both the wisdom of the judges in declining to make *stare decisis* more rigid than need be and so tie their hands unnecessarily, and the recognition by juristic writers that the whole process is too indeterminate to be reduced to specific rules.

JUDGE-MADE LAW

It can hardly be a matter of serious dispute at the present day that, within certain narrow but not clearly defined limits, new law is created by the judiciary.[1] Attention centres primarily not so much on the *fact* of judicial legislation but rather on the ways in which this occurs, and the motives, attitudes and reasoning which underlie the development of the law by this means, the constitutional and technical hazards of judicial law-making.[2] Thus it is realised that in a sense whenever a court applies an established rule or principle to a new situation or set of facts (or withholds it from these new facts) new law is being created. But this process is inevitably a very gradual and piece-meal one, a step-by-step progression, graphically described in Holmes' phrase of legislating " interstitially," [3] that is, within the interstices of the existing fabric of the law. Sometimes indeed, a court may take a bolder step, by laying down a new rule or principle which itself contains the potentiality of creative expansion and development. Even here new law is virtually never created completely *in vacuo,* for the court will strive to follow such analogies as are to be derived from established legal principle and to root its decision so far as may be in the past rulings. Thus was the decision come to in such a leading case as *Rylands* v. *Fletcher*; similarly a court may,

---

[98] An admirable recent illustration will be found in the way the C.A. virtually resiled in *Fisher* v. *Taylor's Stores* [1956] 2 Q.B. 78 from the effect of its own previous inconvenient decision in *Atkinson* v. *Bettison* [1955] 1 W.L.R. 1127. See also *Craddock* v. *Hampshire C.C.* [1958] 1 W.L.R. 202, and the comment thereon by R. E. Megarry in (1958) 74 L.Q.R., p. 350 and *Hanning* v. *Maitland (No.* 2) *op. cit.,* where the disastrous *consequences* of *Nowotnik* v. *Nowotnik* [1967] P. 83 weighed heavily with the later court.

[99] (1959) 22 M.L.R. 118.

[1] The most trenchant demolition of the long-prevailing myth is Frank, *Law and the Modern Mind* (1930), pp. 45–55. See also Ross in ed. Hughes, *Law, Reason and Justice* (1969), pp. 217–234, who distinguishes the underlying fiction from fiction in its creative sense, as it was used by Maine (*post,* 836). To understand, what Ross calls, theoretical legal fictions, one must see the judicial role in terms of myth and cultic rites.

[2] Jaffe, *English and American Judges as Law Makers* (1969), pp. 34–35 raises a number of questions which typify those upon which concentration is now focused. By what warrant, and in what senses, is the judiciary authorised to make law? What, if any, are the effective limits upon the exercise of judicial power? What problems flow from its being an *ad hoc* decisional process? Can the judiciary be trusted to move in the right direction? See *post,* 724.

[3] *Southern Pacific Co.* v. *Jenson* 244 U.S. 205, 221 (1917).

as in *Donoghue* v. *Stevenson*, find itself obliged to choose between conflicting lines of past cases, and may settle for a comparatively bold generalisation in favour of one of those choices, while striking out for it a wider field than may have seemed implicit in the earlier decisions.

Nor is it only in the common law field that new law is created judicially, for as we shall see the same process is at work in the sphere of statutory construction.[4] Modern English legislative theory and practice seeks to fetter the judge by very detailed drafting,[5] which attempts however unsuccessfully to envisage all the situations which the legislator intends to be covered, and by the doctrine that the courts must apply only the words of the statute, and cannot apply them by analogy to new cases not explicitly covered by these words. Yet this approach is of little avail to restrain a court which is mindful to apply what it regards as the real sense or meaning of the statute. Moreover, there are even modern English statutes which resemble the Continental type of legislation, by laying down no more than broad general principles or conceptual ideas, and leaving the courts to expound their meaning and scope.[6]

It is the traditional framework within which a judge operates, and the fact that his whole professional training and background tend to induce caution, that nearly everywhere cause courts to " soft-pedal " the creative side of their activities. This is particularly apparent when a court is being pressed too hard or too far in favour of what it regards as a novel proposition; in such a case it will be very apt to say that however unsatisfactory the law may be, the court merely applies and cannot change the law, which remains the exclusive province of the legislature. Nor indeed, even if one acknowledges the creative side of the judicial process, can one ignore the element of fundamental truth which resides in such an asseveration, for the constricted framework within which judicial legislation functions renders it different in kind from ordinary legislation. The legislature—apart from any constitutional limitations—is legally, if not *de facto*, free to make innovations as it sees fit and deal in an abstract way

---

4 *Cf. post*, 733.

5 An outstanding example of the reverse, of complete discretion being conferred upon the judiciary is s. 22 of Administration of Justice Act 1969. The Winn Committee on Personal Injuries Litigation, 1969 (Cmnd. 3703) had recommended that interest should accrue on damages in personal injuries litigation from the date of the issue of the writ. The Committee suggested percentages, but the Act, implementing the Report, omitted to prescribe any percentages, leaving it to the judges to fill in what percentages were deemed appropriate. The Court of Appeal was thus obliged in *Jefford* v. *Gee* [1970] 2 Q.B. 130 to legislate in a blatant manner. Had they followed the Winn Report, it would almost have been a case of legislation by committee.

6 A constitution of the American type gives the court even greater freedom. See E. H. Levi, *An Intro. to Legal Reasoning* (1950), pp. 5–6; *post*, 806.

with all future cases; a court, on the other hand, is limited to the actual issues and the parties before it, and is to an extent restricted by the scope of legal aid, and operates within a traditional framework and subject to the force of professional opinion [7] of what is good law, and the possibility of being reversed on appeal. It is, therefore, hardly surprising that courts are fairly reluctant to avow their own creative function, so limited does it appear to any particular court in any individual case. Even in a legal system where the legislative power of the judiciary is explicitly conceded, as with the provision of the Swiss Civil Code to the effect that the judge may, in the last resort, fill gaps in the law by applying the rule he would have laid down if acting as legislator,[8] it is significant that this provision has been hardly ever acted upon, the courts preferring to develop new law by interpretation of well-tried and established legal principles.

However, this has not been the German experience. " The German Pandectists, like lawmakers in other countries had failed to see the problems raised by large concentrations of economic power and new forms of industrial organisation." [9] Further, there was legislative impotence in the face of post-war economic catastrophe. The result was that the courts, spurred on by jurists like Oertmann, filled the gaps. They did this by, what Hedemann has called, " the flight into general clauses." Of these the most notable were Articles 242 [10] and 826,[11] which gave enormous scope for judicial participation, the opportunity being grasped with open hands. There was, of course, continuing and increasing resort to general clauses under the Nazis, though Dawson believes that this was " in large part a working out of ideas that had germinated before 1933." [12]

Yet within the severely constricted field of judicial law-making there is scope for a broader or narrower approach according to whether the courts are endeavouring consciously to develop the law relatively freely to meet new social and economic conditions,[13] or

---

[7] In France recent juristic thought, notably that of Maury, has stressed that it is acceptance of newly-made *jurisprudence* by professional opinion that makes the law, so created, law. See Dawson, *post*, 751.

[8] Art. 1 ; *post*, 839.

[9] Dawson, *op. cit.*, p. 464.

[10] " The obligor is bound to carry out his performance in the manner required by good faith with regard to prevailing usage."

[11] " Whoever causes injury to another intentionally in a manner offending good morals is bound to repair the injury."

[12] *Op. cit.*, p. 478. Examples of the use of general clauses both before 1933 and after are found in Dawson, *op. cit.*, pp. 461–479, and Schlesinger, *Comparative Law* (3rd ed., 1970), pp. 498 *et seq.*

[13] For recent illustrations of this see *Chic Fashions* v. *Jones* [1968] 2 Q.B. 299 ; *Porter* v. *Porter* [1969] 3 All E.R. 640, where Sachs L.J. referred to a county court registrar's decision to refuse a wife maintenance who had committed adultery as " decades, if not generations out of date " (p. 643), *Re W.* [1971] 2

whether, in a spirit of conservatism, the aim is to tie legal development pretty literally to the precise enunciations of previous judges.
The contrast here is sometimes expressed as between judicial valour
and judicial timidity,[14] and certainly we may contrast the bold vision
of Lord Mansfield with the outlook of some of his contemporaries, or
the black-letter law of Baron Parke with the wide judicial sweep of
Blackburn J.; nor are similar contrasts lacking at the present day.
Yet even the highest measure of judicial valour must nevertheless
heed the restraints to which I have previously referred, though it may
find room even within those narrow limits for much useful creative
work, as witness for instance the effect of the great case of *Donoghue*
v. *Stevenson*. It is sometimes said that at the present day there is
little or no scope for the judicial creation of fresh common law
principles.[15] Obviously in a highly developed system such as our
own the scope for this becomes much diminished, but it may be
suggested that the spark of potential creativity is never wholly extinguished.

English and American Judges as Lawmakers

In the view of a leading American authority the English common
law has suffered a menopause.[16] " There have been great judges in
England " but he fears " the great English judge [is] a relic of the
past." " Are," he asks, " these gods dead today, the victims of
their irrelevance? Or have they moved to America where a new
Pantheon is flourishing? "[17] Although he somewhat overstates the
decline in English judicial law-making,[18] there is no doubt that it
palls in comparison with that in the United States. The last fifteen
years have been Llewellyn's " grand style " personified. Keeton[19]

All E.R. 49 and *J. v. C.* [1970] A.C. 668 (increasing recognition of welfare of a
child in adoption and guardianship proceedings and increasing acceptance of
medical and psychological evidence, on which see Michaels, 83 L.Q.R. 547,
Adedigba [1968] 2 Q.B. 572; *Mohammed* v. *Knott* [1969] 1 Q.B. 1. Note also
B.R.B. v. *Herrington* [1972] 1 All E.R. 749, particularly the judgment of Lord
Pearson (pp. 785–786). See also Veitch on a similar trend in African countries
(1971) 34 M.L.R. 42).
14 *Cf.* the respective judgments of Denning and Asquith L.JJ. in *Candler v. Crane,
Christmas and Co.* [1951] 2 K.B. 164.
15 See *per* Devlin J. in (1956) 9 *Current Legal Problems*, pp. 11–15.
16 Jaffe, *English and American Judges as Lawmakers* (1969), p. 2.   17 *Idem*, p. 1.
18 He is critical, for example, of English judicial impotence in the face of executive
authority, yet contents himself with citing *Arlidge* [1915] A.C. 120; *Liversidge*
v. *Anderson* [1942] A.C. 206 and *Duncan* v. *Cammell Laird* [1942] A.C. 624.
He relegates *Ridge* v. *Baldwin* [1964] A.C. 40 to a footnote and ignores *Padfield*
v. *Minister of Agriculture* [1968] A.C. 997; *Anisminic* v. *Foreign Compensation
Commission* [1969] 2 A.C. 147; *Lain's Case* [1967] 2 Q.B. 864; *Re H. K.* [1967]
2 Q.B. 617 among others. Indeed, control of executive action is one of the
growth areas of English law. And this is only to confront Jaffe with his own
terms of reference, to ignore creativity in torts, labour law, family law, conflict
of laws and other areas. A recent example of creativity is *Herrington*, *op. cit.*,
n. 13.   19 *Venturing to do Justice* (1969).

has shown how the law of torts has been revolutionised in a single decade, and the "activist" Warren Court has been subjected to innumerable studies.[20] It is impossible to list, and invidious to choose between, the areas in which the Supreme Court has left its mark. But most noticeably it has fought for the underprivileged, those for whom the "power élite" does not fight, nor legislative pressure groups stir.[21]

How is this difference in judicial role to be explained? Jaffe makes a number of constructive suggestions. "The judicial performance must be judged as a part of the total legal performance." [22] Judicial activism is not so necessary where the legislature takes an interest in law reform and social development. In this country we have the Law Commission and an active, centralised Parliament: in the United States law reform proposals are often generated by a commission but state legislatures suffer from inertia and lack of time. In England legislature and judiciary to some extent act in partnership: in the United States the judiciary is a one-man firm. The fact that many Congressional chairmen are senior conservatives from southern states adds to the imbalance by providing bottlenecks in the legislative process, no doubt just as the House of Lords did when, according to Jaffe, the common law was fertile.[23]

Another explanation of this difference of emphasis goes back to the differences in legal education in the two countries [24]: the writing of the law review, the study of other disciplines, the emphasis in a country of fifty jurisdictions on a comparative approach. Jaffe especially emphasises the law review: "it is characteristic of this writing that it seeks to go beyond a mere statement of the law. The writer . . . seeks to impose upon the material . . . his views of what the law should be. . . . The courts grow more and more hospitable to this body of writing. In torts, in conflict of laws, in labour law, to take examples, notable judicial reorientation is going forward as a co-operative enterprise of judiciary and professariat. . . . From the very beginning of his education the lawyer and judge-to-be is indoctrinated in a concept of law as adaptation." [25] It is, of course,

---

[20] The most interesting is Alexander Bickel's *The Supreme Court and the Idea of Progress* (1970), on which see Skelly Wright, 84 Harv.L.R. 769.

[21] Apart from the desegregation cases (*ante*, 121), see the legislative reapportionment cases, *Baker* v. *Carr*, 369 U.S. 186 and *Reynolds* v. *Sims*, 377 U.S. 533, and those which protect the accused, *Miranda* v. *Arizona*, 384 U.S. 436 (1966), *Gideon* v. *Wainwright*, 372 U.S. 335 (1963), and succour the indigent, *Goldberg* v. *Kelly*, 391 U.S. 254 (1970). The point is made forcefully by Denenberg [1971] C.L.J. 134, 141–144.   [22] *Op. cit.*, p. 5.

[23] See Buchanan and Tullock, *The Calculus of Consent* (1962), on log-rolling.

[24] See Jaffe, *op. cit.*, Chap. V.

[25] *Idem*, p. 107. Twining (87 L.Q.R. 398, 399) is critical of Jaffe's model of English legal education, but Jaffe portrays an accurate picture of contemporary legal education in both countries. Twining's comments on the imprecision of some of Jaffe's concepts, "activism," "conservative," etc., are nearer the mark.

from this background that the Brandeis brief developed, itself a spur to judicial activism.

Thirdly, the different emphasis may be explained by the different image [26] we accord our respective judiciaries. Lord Radcliffe summed up what for many is the archetypal image of the English judge when he described him as "objective, impartial, erudite and experienced declaimer of the law that is." [27] Perhaps, it is these qualities which make judges natural choices to chair tribunals of investigation, like that which inquired into the siting of London's third airport. But Radcliffe continues: "we cannot run the risk of finding the archetypal image of the judge confused in men's minds with the very different image of the legislator." [28] This may explain Lord Reid's reluctance in *Myers* v. *D.P.P.* and *Pettitt* v. *Pettitt* to develop respectively new exceptions to the hearsay rule and new matrimonial property concepts.[29] Most American judges, on the other hand, are elected and stand for re-election on their record [30]; they are politicians and in their hands is the interpretation of a Constitution, many of the key phrases of which have rough edges. American judges also are less fettered by the bonds of *stare decisis*.[31]

This may go some way towards explaining the difference in role. But Jaffe is equally concerned to extrapolate the advantages and hazards of judicial lawmaking. Of the advantages he cites empiricism and the ability to feel the way step by step, to test from case to case the consequences of a particular decision. But, there are limits to what a judge can do. He can declare desegregation of schools "with all deliberate speed." Yet he cannot desegregate. Ten years after *Brown*,[32] only 2·3 per cent. of Southern Negro children were attending desegregated schools.[33] A judge cannot administer "bussing," or institute social security laws or even a law of contributory negligence.[34] And he always stands the risk of being accused of being too radical or too conservative. Some American states may recall a judge, others his decision where it conflicts with legislative policy. So long as judicial decisions are retroactive they may, unlike most statutes, defeat reasonable expectations. But, since Cardozo's *Sunburst* judgment, American courts have experimented with prospective lawmaking.[35] But, even if reasonable

---

26 In *The Path of the Law from 1967* (1968), p. 14.
27 *Idem.*
28 *Idem.*
29 See 12 J.S.P.T.L. 22 (1972).
30 On which Karlen, *Judicial Administration—The American Experience* (1970), pp. 25–32.
31 *Ante*, 713.
32 *Ante*, 121.
33 See (1967) 77 Yale L.J. 321, 322. More recent progress is described in 84 Harv. L.R. 32–46, particularly p. 35 note 21.
34 Bickel (1964) 64 Colum.L.R. 193, 218; Keeton, *op. cit.*, pp. 45 *et seq.*
35 *Post*, 727.

expectations are not often disturbed, <u>there is little doubt that public opinion and morality are often flouted by decisions of the Supreme Court</u>. Additional protection of criminal defendants comes " curiously at a time when the public [was] more and more aroused by the apparent increase in violent crime.[36] If the softening up on obscenity (the introduction of " the redeeming social value test ") did not meet with much public approval,[37] the decision holding a non-sectarian and non-compulsory prayer in state schools to be prohibited because it offended the prohibition of " an establishment of religion " was openly defied in some States.[38]

If this gives the impression of " oligarchic usurpation " then Jaffe reassures us that there are constraints and obstacles to unfettered power. "<u>Not only the will of those who are judged but of those who judge has been trained to accept the authority of the law.</u>"[39] "<u>Law-conditioned officials</u>" <u>work within a network of substantive rules,</u>[40] accept certain principles (*e.g.*, the primacy of <u>legislative intent</u>), and decisions must be rationalised.[41]

Prospective Overruling

One criticism which has been maintained against the process of judge-made law is that it operates retrospectively. Thus a decision which overrules, or in some way modifies, an earlier precedent is generally assumed to be applicable in all subsequent cases which come before the courts, even though those cases involve acts done, or transactions entered into, on the basis of the previous decision. It is, therefore, argued that because a decision involving a change in the law will upset such earlier transactions, injustice will thereby be created.[42] Moreover, the effect of overruling a decision which has stood for many years tends to discourage courts from reviewing such a decision, even when they are of opinion that it was wrongly decided.

That precedents operate in this retrospective fashion seems clearly related to the old-fashioned theory of the common lawyers, that

---

[36] Jaffe, *op. cit.*, p. 100.

[37] An account of this may be found in Clor, *Obscenity and Public Morality* (1969). Even Rembar, who acted as devil's advocate, was forced to conclude that " the current uses of the new freedom are not all to the good " (*The End of Obscenity* (1969)).

[38] See Dolbeare and Hammond, *The School Prayer Decisions: From Court Policy to Local Practice* (1971). See also (1971) 23 *Journal of Legal Education* 106–150.

[39] Jaffe, *op. cit.*, p. 35.

[40] *Cf.* Llewellyn, *The Common Law Tradition, ante,* 409.

[41] Further difficulties of judicial legislation are considered by Wechsler, *post,* 800.

[42] Thus, one of the justifications posited by Lord Halsbury in *Tramways, post,* 754, and Lord Gardiner in his Practice Direction, *post,* 755 is that reliance has been placed on previous decisions. See Wasserstrom, *The Judicial Decision* (1961) pp. 66–69. See also *ante,* 714.

decisions of the courts merely declare pre-existing law.[43] A decision that an earlier case was wrongly decided, must, therefore, be deemed to have been in operation even before the later decision was laid down. This is pure fiction, and it is hardly surprising that at least in a jurisdiction where the old declaratory theory is now totally discredited, fresh thought has been given to the question whether precedents must necessarily be given a retrospective effect. In 1932, the United States Supreme Court recognised for the first time that the effect of overruling an earlier established principle need not necessarily be given a retrospective effect in all cases.[44] What the court held in that case, in overruling a previous decision, was that the ruling in that decision should still apply both to the case then before the Supreme Court, as well as to all other similar transactions which had been entered into in reliance upon the earlier decision, but that the new rule would apply to all other cases arising in the future. This approach has been confirmed in the more recent decision of *Linkletter* v. *Walker*.[45] Although this development has been acknowledged in some quarters as a liberalising move, and therefore to be welcomed, it has not passed without some criticism. Thus one commentator, while welcoming the development in a general way, recognises that it opens up as many difficulties as it solves, and that it must probably be confined to relatively few situations, and those of exceptional importance.[46]

It is recognised that the courts, in applying this doctrine, may have to distinguish carefully between different kinds of cases, and the degree in each in which it is prepared to give scope to the new doctrine of overruling only in prospect. It may, for instance, be necessary to treat criminal cases differently from civil cases, and again, different categories of civil cases may call for different treatment, according to the degree to which certainty is regarded as more important than ultimate justice. It is argued that a new and considerable measure of uncertainty might be injected into the judicial process in this way, since there is no guarantee that courts in future cases will necessarily abide by the indication that in such cases the court will apply the new rule as laid down prospectively in an earlier decision. It has also been suggested, perhaps a little naively, that if a rule is to be applied only to future cases, prospective

---

[43] See Blackstone, *Commentaries*, Vol. 1, pp. 69–70 for the orthodox view. *Cf.* Frank's caustic comment: "They no more make or invent new law than Columbus made or invented America." (*Law and the Modern Mind*, p. 32).

[44] See *Great Northern Ry.* v. *Sunburst Oil and Refining Company* 287 U.S. 358 (1932) (Cardozo J.).

[45] 381 U.S. 618 (1965), on which see Mishkin, 79 Harv.L.R. 56.

[46] Friedmann, *Legal Theory* (5th ed.), pp. 507–511. For a full account of the problems of prospective overruling, see J. Stone, *Social Dimensions of Law and Justice*, pp. 658–677 and Keeton, *Venturing to do Justice*, pp. 33–53.

plaintiffs will have little incentive in bringing an action where it is sought to persuade the court that an earlier ruling is incorrect.[47]

Although English courts have not so far given consideration to this potential new power,[48] it is noteworthy that one eminent English judge, in referring to the American doctrine, and admitting that it may be open to some criticism, has nevertheless suggested that it is a development which deserves consideration in this country. " It is a logical corollary to the recognition more readily accorded in the U.S.A. than here at present that the Courts do change the law." [49] Lord Diplock points out that the doctrine is open to the criticism that the actual party to the judgment is treated differently from others who have already acted in the same way as he has, but this differentiation will not arise if the court, as in the *Sunburst Case*, still applies the old rule to transactions entered into in reliance on the earlier decision.[50]

JUDICIAL REASONING

If, within certain limits, courts have a free choice to decide which way decisions are to go, what is it, if anything, that governs or controls that choice? Certainly not mere logical deduction or inference [51] in the sense of syllogistic reasoning, for legal rules, ideas, and concepts are expressed in words, whose uncertain sphere of operation precludes the statement of legal reasoning in the rigidly defined terms by which conclusions may be logically deduced from stated premises.[52] Nor is

[47] For this reason a number of American decisions, in overruling prospectively, nevertheless applied the new rule retroactively to the claim before the court. It was argued that such decisions encouraged socially beneficial attacks upon outmoded doctrine, in many cases the doctrine of charitable immunity. See the criticism of this approach in Keeton, *op. cit.*, pp. 35–36.

[48] Though Friedmann, *idem*, pp. 510–511, believes that in *Hedley Byrne* v. *Heller* [1964] A.C. 465, the House of Lords " found another way of doing virtually the same thing." He points out that the Lords could have limited themselves to pointing to the exclusion of liability clause in the defendants' statement but " chose instead to enunciate . . . a future principle of responsibility." In this light it is interesting that some of the earliest criticism of prospective overruling was based on the belief that it rendered the decision *obiter dictum*. Cross, *Precedent In English Law* (2nd ed.), pp. 220–221 suggests that, as yet, the House of Lords has ventured to overrule with prospective effect no rules of law, but in *Connelly* v. *D.P.P.* [1964] A.C. 1254 they overruled a rule of practice with this effect. *Cf. ante*, 709. See now Lord Simon's suggestion that the doctrine should be seriously considered, preferably by Parliament (*Jones* v. *Secretary of State for Social Services* [1972] 1 All E.R. 145, 198).

[49] See Diplock L.J., *The Courts as Legislators* (Holdsworth Club Lecture 1965), pp. 17–18. Of course, prospective law-making is familiar and acceptable: every case of first impression involves the exercise of such power.

[50] The doctrine has recently been acknowledged, at least in constitutional cases, in India. (See 84 L.Q.R. 173).

[51] For the various types of inferences drawn by courts, see W. A. Wilson " A Note on Fact and Law," (1963) 26 M.L.R., 609. See also Ryle, *The Concept of Mind* (1949), pp. 121–122: " a law is used as, so to speak, an inference-ticket," and Gottlieb, *The Logic of Choice* (1968), for an examination of the concept of rule and rationality with regard to legal reasoning. [52] But *cf.* Castberg, *post*, 802.

this surprising, for not only do legal rules and concepts depend for their usefulness on their very indefiniteness and flexibility,[53] but as Holmes remarked in one of his most striking phrases, " the life of the law has been not logic but experience." [54]

Ordinary language, in which law is necessarily expressed (for how otherwise could its contact with real life be maintained ?) is not an instrument of mathematical precision but possesses what has been happily described as an " open texture." [55] Some part of the meaning of words is given by ordinary usage, but this does not carry one far in those peripheral problems which law courts have to solve in applying words, and legal rules expressed in words. We all know what a highway is, but does it for the purpose of a particular rule, include a pavement or a forecourt? Is a flying-boat a " ship " ? [56] Does the rule of negligence impose a duty regarding oral utterances? [57] Such questions do not call so much for logical answers as for *decisions*. Rules of law are not linguistic or logical rules but to a great extent *rules for deciding*.[58]

Does this mean that questions for legal decision are really questions of words, whose decision is essentially arbitrary, in the sense that the decision in any particular case might just as well have gone one way as another ? The reply to this may be left to Professor Wisdom.[59] As he points out, such a view is to " distort and denigrate legal discussion," [60] for it ignores the way that rational persuasion proceeds, by setting a problem in a certain context of like and

[53] *Cf.* Gluckman, *Judicial Process among the Barotse*, p. 291 *et seq.*
[54] *Common Law*, p. 1. It has recently been suggested that this " striking phrase " is but the progeny of Jhering's more tortuous passage : " Life is not here to be a servant of concepts, but concepts are here to serve life. What will come to pass in the future is not postulated by logic but by life, by trade and commerce, and by human instinct for justice." This is quoted by Zweigert and Siehr in (1971) 19 Am.J.C.L. 215, 226. Holmes *had* read this passage. See de Howe, *Holmes, The Proving Years*, Vol. II, p. 152.
[55] See F. Waismann, on " Verifiability " in *Logic and Language* (ed. A. G. N. Flew), 1, p. 119. *Cf.* the discussion between Hart and Fuller, on the " core " and " penumbra " of meaning, in (1958) 71 Harv.L.R. 593 *et seq.* See also H. L. A. Hart, *Concept of Law*, Chap. 7. Gottlieb, *op. cit.*, Chap. 8 supports Fuller's advocacy of the role of purpose in the application of rules. He believes that purpose can be used to *preclude* the application of a rule in situations which seem to fall squarely within its language when such application would lead to results entirely alien to its purpose (p. 109). An example would be a statute which prohibited " vehicles " from parks : would the mounting on a pedestal of a truck used in the war fall within the ban? One might object that it would be an eyesore, but aesthetic appearance is not the object of the statute. Unfortunately, the difficulty with " purpose " as a test is its elusiveness and indeterminateness. See Hart, *idem*, p. 125. See also Summers, in ed. Summers, *More Essays In Legal Philosophy* (1971), 101, 117–119.
[56] *Cf. Polpen* v. *Commercial Union* [1943] K.B. 161. Or see the similar reasoning of Anscombe, *Intention* (1954), pp. 58–64.
[57] See *Hedley Byrne Ltd.* v. *Heller* [1964] A.C. 465.
[58] *Cf.* A. G. N. Flew, *op. cit.*, pp. 3–4.　　　　　　[59] *Post*, 798.
[60] See Wisdom, in *Polemic* no. 4, 1946, and in *Philosophy and Psychoanalysis* (1953), p. 249.

different cases, and showing how certain factors or reasons may be brought to bear in order to satisfy us that one course rather than any other or others is desirable or " right." The mistake here is to expect a chain of deduction or demonstrative reasoning, for this is not how ordinary rational argument works. It is rather a question of presenting a succession of cumulative reasons which severally co-operate in favour of saying what the reasoner desires to urge: " the legs of a chair, not the links of a chain." [61] But this is really the very opposite of the " arbitrary," which suggests a purely haphazard, irrational and fortuitous conclusion though, as Hughes points out, this is not to suggest that the real explanation of the decision, its *motivation*, may not be contained in its reasoning.[62] The essence of legal reasoning is in all essentials, save that the lawyer engages in a more searching inquiry for *precise* reasons for his decisions, comparable to the process of reasoning in ordinary life, whether concerned with ethical or practical problems.[63] Thus when we decide that something is good or desirable, beautiful or ugly, we mean to express a judgment. This may be intended as a mere expression of a subjective emotion, but more often it involves implicitly or explicitly the idea that we can give reasons in support of that judgment. So too, if a practical decision is called for, such as the choice of a profession or of a candidate by a selection committee, the choice *may* be purely arbitrary, but more likely will be based on a weighing of reasons why one rather than another choice is to be made. Such a choice is not *logical* in the sense of being deductively inferred from given premises, but it has a kind of logic

---

[61] *Post*, 798. *Cf.* Hart in Arist. Proc., Suppl. Vol. 29, pp. 257–264, who cites *Re Makein* [1955] Ch. 194 as an interesting illustration. Others which may be offered are *Staton* v. *National Coal Board* [1957] 1 W.L.R. 893, and *Lister* v. *Romford Ice Co.* [1957] A.C. 555.

[62] See Hughes, in ed. Hughes, *Law, Reason and Justice* (1969), p. 101. Levi has commented that " the function of articulated judicial reasoning is to help protect the court's power by giving some assurance that private views are not masquerading behind public view " (in ed. Hook, *Law and Philosophy* (1964), p. 281). On this see Ch. Perelman, 3 Israel L.R. 1, 3–4.

[63] The lawyer's reasoning is also fortified by highly developed procedures and techniques, covering such matters as fact-finding and recording and analysing previous decisions. See also G. Gottlieb, *The Logic of Choice* (1968). Gottlieb argues for, and explores the character of a form of reasoning in the fields of both law and ethics, which can be regarded as rational, without being either deductive or inductive. A further conclusion is that a court's commitment to follow principle whenever it can find one to guide it, rather than to follow its own inclinations, is precisely what is meant by the commitment to apply the rules of a system and to apply them impartially. According to Gottlieb, the distinction between rule and discretion is misleading; for courts are never strictly bound by rules, while on the other hand courts are not entirely free to choose between competing purposes and interests, since pre-existing constitutional or other commitments may be available to guide them in the application of rules. The system of legal rules is not therefore in any meaningful sense a " closed " system.

of its own, being based on rational considerations which differentiate it sharply from mere arbitrary assertion.[64]

Legal rulings then, not being statements of fact or logical inferences, cannot be treated as in themselves true or false, for such a criterion is inapplicable to decisions involving choice between alternatives. They can however be properly regarded as right or wrong, or good or bad, in the sense that they either are or are not based upon cumulative reasons which are found to be acceptable.[65] Of course the notion of " acceptability " necessarily involves the need for some agreement as to what are ultimately to be the valid criteria for resolving a dispute, for if there were no such common or widely approved grounds it would be impracticable to settle any dispute whatever.[66] In practice, however, broad agreement of this kind does generally exist in law as in everyday problems, and this is a factor of human social life based on experience, and without which no community could survive or indeed come into existence at all. This does not mean that these so-called ultimate criteria are absolutes in a natural law sense, but simply that it is senseless to ask for justification of criteria which are *ex hypothesi* to be treated as ultimate for a particular purpose and within a particular community. And though their origin may be in some instances ethical, they may equally derive from practical experience, custom, or tradition.

Moreover courts, like ordinary people, may and generally do employ differing criteria, reflecting varying attitudes towards the solution of the problems with which they are called upon to deal. Cardozo's celebrated discussion of the four methods of the judicial process [67] is really concerned to draw attention to such varying criteria as commonly underlie judicial reasoning. Thus custom, tradition, historical development, sociological utilitarianism, and ethics all play their part. As for what Cardozo describes as the method of philosophy, or following along the line of logical progression, what is here involved is not logical deduction in the strict sense but the rational

---

64 For an attempt to elaborate a new kind of logic relevant both to legal problems and to everyday reasoning, see Toulmin, *Uses of Argument* (1958). It should be pointed out however, that many of Toulmin's strictures on ordinary logic and his proposed substitutes are highly controversial, and therefore must be treated with reserve by non-specialists.

65 *Cf.* Weldon, *Vocabulary of Politics*, p. 44. As Popper has remarked, arguments cannot determine decisions, but this does not mean that we cannot be helped by such arguments; on the contrary, it is most helpful to analyse the consequences likely to result from different alternatives between which we have to choose (*The Open Society and its Enemies.* Vol. II, p. 232). *Cf.* Ladd, in ed. Friedrich, *Rational Decision* (1964), 126, 128, where the emphasis is on " rational decisions " rather than correct ones.

66 *Cf.* Toulmin, *Reason in Ethics*, Chap. 14.

67 *Post*, 784.

use of *analogy*, whereby a case is compared with like and unlike, so as to determine the " proper " scope of a legal rule. No analogy is compelling in a purely logical sense as leading to a *necessary* conclusion; but as a practical matter human beings do reason by analogy, and find this in many instances a useful way of arriving at normative or practical decisions.[68] Here again, even in what Cardozo characterises as the logical method, the basis of this approach is primarily human experience of the efficiency and utility of analogical reasoning.[69]

STATUTORY CONSTRUCTION [70]

At the present day one of the most important of judicial functions is the construction of statutes. It is from this point of view that one may discern the widest divergence between common law and continental practice. The former proceeds on the basis that the common law itself represents the basic fabric of the law, into which statutes are interwoven.[71] Hence the practice of drafting statutes in the fullest detail, and the broad assumptions that a statute deals only with those cases which fall within its actual wording, and that there is no judicial power to " fill gaps " in a statute by arguments based on analogy,[72] although, as we have seen, this is the acknowledged way in which the

[68] For a discussion of the working of argument by analogy in legal decisions, see E. H. Levi, *Introduction to Legal Reasoning* (1950). Levi suggests that " the avoidance of explicit policy determination by referring to prior and selected examples " appears as a substitution of the idea of equality for a head-on examination of " issues of policy " (in ed. Hook, at p. 273). This is in part an answer to Wechsler's insistence that a judge who makes changes in the law must " take seriously the duty of reworking the pattern of the law " (*post*, 800). *Cf. post*, 806 and in ed. Hook, *Law and Philosophy* (1964), p. 263 *et seq.* As F. Schmidt remarks, " Like to like is probably the value norm most firmly rooted in the democratic society of today " (*Scandinavian Studies in Law* (1957), I, p. 195). See also Ch. Perelman, *The Idea of Justice* (1963), pp. 51–8.

[69] See also Stone, who has argued in detail that the fallacy that decisions can be reached by logical inference to the exclusion of considerations of social needs, policies and personal evaluations, is brought about in many instances by what he calls " categories of illusory reference." For Stone, these serve as devices which permit a court to exercise creative choices, though under the guise of a logical analysis which is in fact illusory. (See J. Stone, *Legal System and Lawyers' Reasonings* (1964), Chap. 7 and (1969) 69 Colum.L.R. 1162, 1176–1182.)

[70] The word " construction," although generally treated as equivalent to " interpretation " in English legal practice, seems preferable at least as applied to those cases where a court has to do more than extract a meaning from the use of particular words. See *per* Devlin J. in (1958) 4 S.P.T.L. Journal, p. 208; and Ekelöf in *Scandinavian Studies in Law* (1958), p. 88.

[71] *Cf.* Kahn-Freund's remark that our matrimonial property law " rests on a number of *statutes*, but here is a case in which statutory law has become part of the legal mores to such an extent that the courts do not even bother to mention the legislative basis upon which their decisions rest. The principle of separation of property . . . is a living refutation of that outdated antithesis of principles of the common law as against mere provisions of statutes which you still sometimes find in the more old-fashioned books " (*Matrimonial Property*, The Josef Unger memorial lecture, 1971, p. 10). See also Scarman, *post*, 741, n. 14.

[72] *Cf. Hancock* v. *Lablache* (1878) 3 C.P.D. 197, and *Baylis* v. *Blackwell* [1952] K.B. 154.

common law itself may be developed by the courts.   Continental
theory, on the other hand, treats statutes (usually, but not necessarily,
in codified form) as the basis of the law, but these tend to be drafted
in a very general and abstract way, the task being left to the courts
to fill in the details of the statutory provisions by reference to a presumed legislative intention.   Moreover, it is generally accepted that
gaps in a statute may be filled by analogical reasoning, on the footing
that the legislature might be presumed to have desired to cover such
cases if it had had these in contemplation.

It would seem, therefore, that the English approach is primarily
based on ascertaining the plain meaning of the words used, whereas
that of the civil law is directed to ascertaining the intention of the
legislature.[73]   This distinction may appear to explain why continental
courts have recourse freely to *travaux préparatoires* or legislative
material, whereas English courts resolutely refuse to have regard to
such matters.[74]   In fact the reality is a good deal less simple than this,
and there is rather less difference between the two approaches than
may appear at first sight.

No doubt the orthodox English theory starts from the assumption
that a literal interpretation would be followed save where this leads
to a result so manifestly unreasonable as to constrain the court to
seek some other solution.[75]   In such a case the court is to have regard
to the intention of the legislature.[76]

Chief Justice Tindal called this the " only rule." [77]   Much ink has
been spilt in trying to answer what legislative intent is.   Radin in

---

[73] On which see Merryman, *The Civil Law Tradition* (1969), Chaps. IV–VIII, where
this is explained in terms of the growth of state positivism leading to a state
monopoly on law-making.   [74] See *post*, 833 (and particularly 834, n. 58), 850.

[75] *Cf.* Bowen L.J. in *L.N.W. Ry.* v. *Evans* [1893] 1 Ch. 16, 27: " These canons do
not override the language of a statute where the language is clear: they are only
guides to enable us to understand what is inferential. In each case the Act . . .
is all-powerful, and when its meaning is unequivocally expressed the necessity
for rules of construction disappear and reaches its vanishing point."

[76] *Cf.* Salmond, *Jurisprudence*, 12th ed., pp. 131–140. Nevertheless English law
insists on relating this intention (if any) to the date when the legislation was
passed; see *Att.-Gen.* v. *Prince Augustus* [1957] A.C. 436; *Kingston Wharves* v.
Reynolds [1959] A.C. 187.   But this will not prevent a statute being applied to
future circumstances, different though these may be from the situation at the
date of the Act, where the language of the statute is apt to cover new situations
not foreseeable at the date of the statute. See, *e.g.*, *Re Scremby Corn Rents*
[1960] 1 W.L.R. 648. Thus the word " carriage " in an old statute may be held
applicable to a motor-vehicle, even though such a vehicle was unthought of at
the date of the statute. It has been pointed out that the error of substituting
" authors' intention for meaning of language " is that it ignores the fact that
a written work once created acquires a meaning which, though dependent on
men's usage, is still independent of its creator's motives; and interpretation is
precisely a search for this meaning. Succeeding generations, therefore, to whom
a statute may apply, can only reasonably be held bound by the meaning of its
words *to them* (see J. Stone, *Law and the Social Sciences* (1966), p. 60).

[77] In *Sussex Peerage Claim* (1844), 11 Cl. and F. 85. Lord Simon describes 5
avenues of approach to this in *Borough of Ealing* v. *Race Relations Board*
[1972] 2 W.L.R. 71, 82.

1929 [78] suggested it was a fiction. " The least reflection makes clear that the lawmaker . . . does not exist. . . . A legislator certainly has no intention whatever in connection with words which some two or three drafted, which a considerable number rejected, and in regard to which the majority might have had, and often demonstrably did have, different ideas and beliefs." [79] Nor was it relevant for, " when the legislature has uttered the words of a statute, it is *functus officio*." [80] Interpretation was a distinct job. It followed that preliminary materials had no relevance.

Landis's [81] reply attempted to distinguish two ideas in the concept " intent." It was " a confusing word, carrying within it both the teleological concept of purpose and the more immediate concept of meaning." [82] Meaning was discoverable: purpose was not. He deprecated the exclusionary rules for, if intent as meaning was to be found anywhere, it was in legislative records.

To Payne,[83] writing in 1956, statutory construction was an act of partnership. There being no *référé legislatif* [84] the interpreter was called upon to use his discretion. The legislator delegated to the interpreter the task of determining the particular application of a general rule, rather as it delegated power to make subordinate legislation to a local authority. Just as the latter was circumscribed by the *ultra vires* doctrine, so the former must exercise *discretio*, but not *arbitrium*. In Glanville Williams's words: " a judge has a discretion to include a flying-boat within a rule as to ships or vessels; he has no discretion to include a motor car within such a rule." [85] Parliament often uses general words intentionally in the belief that judges are the most adept in filling in the details. Neither cruelty nor collusion was ever defined by Parliament and the divorce judges left unfettered were able to develop these doctrines to fit changing social conditions.

The most important contribution to this debate has come from MacCallum.[86] His essay is an outstanding example of the new analytical jurisprudence,[87] and no summary can do justice to his sustained conceptual thinking. But, broadly, his theme is that three

---

[78] 44 Harv.L.R. 863.
[79] *Idem*, p. 870.
[80] *Idem*, p. 871.
[81] 44 Harv.L.R. 886.
[82] *Idem*, p. 888.
[83] C.L.P. 96.
[84] On which see Strömholm, 10 Scand. Studies in Law 178.
[85] (1945) 61 L.Q.R. 303. *Cf.* the oft-quoted U.S. Supreme Court ruling that an aeroplane was not a " motor vehicle " within the meaning of a Federal Statute (*McBoyle* v. *U.S.* 283 U.S. 25 (1931)).
[86] In ed. Summers, *Essays In Legal Philosophy* (1968), 237 (originally in (1966) 75 Yale L.J. 754).
[87] On which see Summers, *ante*, 260.

distinct, yet rarely distinguished, questions may be asked of legislative intent: does it exist? Is it discernible? Is it relevant? The complexity of the first two questions leads him to conclude: does enough hang on such appeals [to legislative intent] to make their continuance worth while even in the face of the difficulties exposed? "Is it worth our while in terms of the ideological and practical importance of such appeals, to seek institutional changes strengthening the analogies between these appeals and appeals to intentions elsewhere in law and in life generally? . . . Legislatures and institutional environments in which they operate are, in a sense, our creatures and can be altered." [88] Perhaps the most constructive part of his article is where he essays a number of models of legislative intent for "one may seek to bring the appeals [to legislative intent] closer to the conditions under which we attribute intentions to corporations, to principals *via* the intentions of their agents, or, above all, to individual men." [89]

But the search for legislative intent goes on. This has led the courts to develop a number of conventions as a means of searching out intent. There is inherent in these the customary broad and narrow approach. The latter is dominant: hence the need felt to develop conventions or rules. These may be classified as grammatical rules, such as the *ejusdem generis* rule,[90] or the rule *expressio unius exclusio alterius*,[91] and various presumptions, such as those restricting the construction of statutes which interfere with existing rights affecting the liberty of the subject, or which are penal in effect.[92] But although the books are full of instances where

[88] *Op. cit.*, p. 272.

[89] *Idem*, pp. 273–273. The models are set out at pp. 262–271.

[90] For recent examples, see *Chandris* v. *Moller* [1951] 1 K.B. 240, 246; *Culley* v. *Harrison* [1956] 2 Q.B. 71; and *Brownsea Haven Properties* v. *Poole Corpn.* [1958] Ch. 574. It should not be thought that this rule involves a purely rational process. The legislature intends other *like* instances to be covered by their general categorising clause, but what is a "like" case may involve considerations of policy. In *Cleveland* v. *U.S.*, 329 U.S. 14 (1946), a Mormon polygamist was indicted under the Mann Act of 1910 for transporting plural wives across state lines. The Act used the clause "prostitution, debauchery or any other immoral purpose." The Court convicted, holding polygamy to be an immoral purpose, as contrary to Christianity. It is thought that this interpretation went far beyond Congressional intention in passing, what was known as, the "White Slave Traffic Act."

[91] *R.* v. *Palfrey and Sadler* [1970] 2 All E.R. 12, where Winn L.J. pointed out that *alterius* meant "other of two" and that, in such a case, choice of one excluded the other. But "except in that special case, the maxim had no effect in logic or law" (p. 16).

[92] For recent cases regarding the interpretation of penal statutes, see *Inland Revenue Commissioners* v. *Hinchy* [1960] A.C. 748; and *Re H.P.C. Productions Ltd.* [1962] Ch. 466. Concerning the presumption against the retrospective effect of

such rules have been ostensibly applied, they are very apt to dissolve away like chaff before the wind whenever the court feels at all strongly that another interpretation is to be preferred.[93] In such cases the court may invoke the so-called rule in *Heydon's Case*,[94] or the " mischief " rule, which affords a platform for a broader approach. As for the notion that the court has no power to fill " gaps " in legislation, very respectable authority will be found in support of this, yet if one looks at the way courts actually construe statutes it becomes apparent that courts are frequently engaged in doing just this very thing,[95] and indeed few statutes would prove workable if there were not some judicial freedom in this respect. Yet all the reasons for judicial caution to which reference has already been made, operate here with redoubled force, and tend both to limit the degree to which courts will allow such constructions to be pushed, and also the extent to which they are willing openly to avow that they are really exercising a kind of supplementary legislative function.

Nor does the refusal of English courts to make use of legislative material[96] turn so much on a fundamental difference of principle, but rather on the distinction between actual legislative practice under common law and civilian systems. For whether one accepts the " plain meaning " approach or that of a presumed and largely fictitious legislative intention, there is no reason in principle why courts should not avail themselves of whatever relevant material can be found in explanation or exposition of the meaning of statutes. Even the most literal approach must have regard to the context[97] in which

legislation, see *A.-G.* v. *Vernazza* [1960] A.C. 965, and *Carson* v. *Carson* [1964] 1 W.L.R. 511 and *Herridge* v. *Herridge* [1966] 1 All E.R. 93; *Williams* v. *Williams* [1971] 2 All E.R. 764; *Powys* v. *Powys* [1971] 2 All E.R. 116. As regards the presumption concerning international law, see *Collco* v. *Inland Revenue Commissioners* [1962] A.C. 1, and *Post Office* v. *Estuary Radio* [1968] 2 Q.B. 740. For statutes which encroach upon existing rights, see *Allen* v. *Thorne Industries* [1968] 1 Q.B. 487.

93 See, *e.g.*, *Liversidge* v. *Anderson* [1942] A.C. 206; *Minns* v. *Moore* [1950] 1 K.B. 241. Thus courts have had little difficulty in construing statutory offences as involving absolute prohibitions, despite their penal character. *Cf. Sweet* v. *Parsley* [1970] A.C. 132; *Warner* v. *Metropolitan Police Commissioner* [1969] 2 A.C. 256; *R.* v. *Ball and Laughlin* (1966) 50 Cr.App.R. 266 (on which see now *R.* v. *Gosney* [1971] 3 W.L.R. 343) and *Rowlands* v. *Hamilton* [1971] 1 W.L.R. 647 (on which see Goodhart (1971) 87 L.Q.R. 289).

94 See *post*, 823.

95 See, *e.g.*, such cases as *Rees* v. *Hughes* [1946] K.B. 517; *Cunliffe* v. *Goodman* [1949] 2 All E.R. 946; *Chandris* v. *Moller* [1951] 1 K.B. 240; *Wagg* v. *Law Society* [1957] Ch. 405; *Baker* v. *Sims* [1959] 1 Q.B. 114; *Lucy* v. *Henleys* [1970] 1 Q.B. 393; *Eddis* v. *Chichester Constable* [1969] 2 Ch. 345 (noted by Jackson (1969) 32 M.L.R. 691).

96 The earliest clear instance of this refusal appears to be *Millar* v. *Taylor* (1769) 4 Burr. 2303.

97 So, for example, the whole or any part of an Act may be relied on to arrive at the true meaning of a particular phrase (*Att.-Gen.* v. *Prince Ernest August of Hanover*), where Lord Simonds said that context " in its widest sense " could

the words appear, and it is purely arbitrary whether that context is confined to the four corners of the statute itself, or may be derived from all the surrounding circumstances out of which that statute arose. English discussion of this question often hinges upon the undesirability of the courts having to read the debates in Hansard, in order to find out the meaning of a statute.[98] Yet though continental practice does not forbid courts to peruse parliamentary debates for this purpose, they are generally regarded as having little bearing on the meaning of the language used. " Very few judges will take the trouble to look these debates up in the official reports." [99] What the courts are really concerned to study are the various reports and comments of expert committees [1] and of the Minister charged with the progress of the bill, which take place at various stages prior to and in the course of the legislative process.[2] The bill itself will probably be drafted in a very general form, so that recourse will have to be had to the various expositions of its provisions and the discussion of disputed points, in order to obtain guidance as to how the bill, when enacted, should be applied. This legislative material is often, as in Sweden, published in a semi-official publication, and its contents are regarded as directives to the courts (though not all are

include not only the statute, but its preamble (*cf. J.* v. *C.* [1970] A.C. 668, 697–8, 710), the existing state of the law, other statutes *in pari materia*, and the mischief which the statute intended to remedy. (See also *D.P.P.* v. *Schildkamp* [1971] A.C. 1, 10, 20, 28.) Where a statute is giving effect to an international treaty, it may be construed in light of that (*Post Office* v. *Estuary Radio* [1968] 2 Q.B. 740). As far as marginal notes are concerned, Sachs L.J. in *Gosling* v. *Gosling* [1968] P. 1, 26, refused to be influenced by them. (See also *Limb* v. *B.T. Docks* [1971] 1 All E.R. 828, 839.) Since *Schildkamp, supra*, it seems punctuation will be taken account of (*per* Ld. Reid, p. 10). It used to be thought that recourse to the short note or headings was not permissible, but this may need re-examination in the light of the general relaxation in exclusionary rules in *Hanover* and *Schildkamp*.

98 Thus the laxer U.S. practice (which allows such material to be used) has been criticised for the abuses it is said sometimes to engender. So Frankfurter J. (Some Reflections on the Reading of Statutes, 47 Colum.L.R. 527, 543) quipped " only when legislative history is doubtful do you go to the statute " and Curtis, another critic, referred to " fumbling about in oceans of legal process for the shoddiest unenacted expressions of intention " (quoted in Law Commission, Law Com. 21, p. 33). But, for an example of a statute where reference to the parliamentary history could throw considerable light on Parliament's intention, see Hickling, 29 M.L.R. 32. *Cf.* also the observations of Lord Reid, quoted *post*, 755.

99 F. Schmidt in *Scandinavian Studies in Law* (1957), I, p. 170. In France the practice of consulting legislative materials is resorted to less than it was in pre-Gény positivist days. Today, the practice is to consult *travaux préparatoires* only where there is obscurity or ambiguity in the text. See Law Com. No. 21, para. 58.

1 In the uniform Commercial Code of the United States, each section is followed by a comment which is not part of the official Code but is used as a valuable aid to construction in litigation, and these comments have frequently been cited by the courts in their judgments on the construction of the Code.

2 For an illuminating discussion, see Ekelöf in *Scandinavian Studies in Law* (1958), II, p. 77 *et seq.* and Strömholm in *Scandinavian Studies in Law* (1966), p. 175 *et seq.*

of equal weight), which are less authoritative than the statute itself, but still an instrument for influencing judicial opinion, though a court is free to reject it. The draftsman himself is also expected to draft the bill with an eye on these directives, and Supreme Court judges are often themselves expert draftsmen, having at various times in their careers been engaged in advising upon the preparation and drafting of parliamentary bills. In Sweden, indeed, " they have been appointed to their office because of their capacity for that kind of work rather than because of their experience as judges." [3] More-over, at least in the smaller continental countries, one or more of the judges dealing with a case may have been concerned in the drafting of a relevant statute, and will be expected to advise the court expertly on this matter, or it may be known which judges or lawyers were so concerned, and these may quite properly be consulted.[4] Continental lawyers see nothing odd in the attitude of those medieval English judges who reproved counsel by telling him: " Do not gloss the statute for we made it and understand better than you what it means." [5] It is, therefore, from the rigidly maintained distinction, characteristic of the modern, but not the ancient common law, between the judicial and the legislative function, as well as from the very different course of legislative proceedings in England and on the Continent, that these contrary attitudes towards *travaux préparatoires* spring.

A good deal of criticism has been levelled in recent years against the way English courts seem to swing from one type of statutory construction to another, one day interpreting a statute very narrowly, and another day favouring a broad approach. Is there room for a more systematic and rational approach ? One suggestion put forward by Friedmann [6] and more recently by Lord Evershed, is that statutes might be classified into categories, such as social purpose statutes, and technical statutes, and that different principles of construction might prevail in relation to each category. But it appears doubtful whether such categorisation is really practicable. At least it seems generally agreed that the various specific rules and presumptions of interpretation are pretty valueless and should be scrapped, for they

[3] F. Schmidt, *op. cit.*, pp. 178–179.
[4] Ekelöf, *op. cit.*, pp. 92–93.
[5] *Cf.* Plucknett, *Statutes and their Interpretation*, p. 49. But note the approach of Edmund Davies L.J. in *Lucy* v. *Henleys* [1970] 1 Q.B. 393 in referring to the report of which he was the chairman which led to the Limitation Act 1963, the interpretation of which was in doubt. He noted that the problem under review had not been contemplated by the committee and added: " I take leave to doubt that such an unhappy outcome was envisaged by the sponsors of the Bill." But he commented: " Unfortunately that is an irrelevant consideration ... the law is found in statutes, not reports " (pp. 405–407).
[6] *Post*, 825.

largely cancel one another out. As Paton remarks, " the rules hunt in pairs," [7] and one may share a continental lawyer's " difficulty in understanding how English jurists can obtain any guidance from such a standard work as *Maxwell on the Interpretation of Statutes.*" [8] Lord Evershed, after referring to the old doctrine of the " equity " of a statute, whereby the courts had a certain latitude in stretching it to cover cases not expressly dealt with, makes the interesting suggestion that it might be as well to revive this doctrine and confer on the judiciary the function of rendering an Act just and workable and of giving effect to sensible solutions, unless the terms of the Act itself precluded this.[9] Such a change would doubtless entail a fundamental reversal of the present form of legislative drafting. Draftsmen and courts are at present engaged in a battle of wits, the draftsman seeking to anticipate the restrictive interpretations of the courts by inserting the most elaborately detailed provisions to ensure that particular situations are covered, which often has the unfortunate result of excluding from the effect of the statute equally relevant situations which were not actually thought of at the time.

Another approach, urged by a Swedish jurist, is that statutes should be drafted solely by reference to obvious cases. The courts should then determine the sphere of application of a statute by reference to the underlying purpose of those obvious cases, and should extend the statute to analogous cases, where this would further the purpose of the statute ascertained in this way.[10] In fact such a procedure is often in practice adopted by continental courts, even where the court itself, with traditional conservatism, purports to " subsume " a case under the actual principle or wording of a statutory provision. But such a method, at least in this explicit form, cuts right across the traditional English form of drafting and of statutory construction.[11]

An attempt to broaden the approach to statutory interpretation was made in New Zealand by the Acts Interpretation Act 1924,

---

[7] *Jurisprudence*, 3rd ed., p. 218.

[8] Ekelöf, *op. cit.*, p. 77.

[9] " Impact of Statute on Law of England " (Proc. of Brit. Academy, Vol. 42, pp. 261–262). See also Lord Evershed, " The Changing Role of the Judiciary in the Development of Law " (1961) 61 Col.L.R., p. 761. Lord Evershed puts in a plea that the rules of statutory interpretation should be reconsidered and formulated afresh, and that there should be a recession from the extreme elaboration of statutory form, and a return to a statement of the parliamentary intention so as to give some scope to a principle of interpretation designed to give rational and coherent effect to the statute (p. 789).

[10] Ekelöf, *op. cit.*, p. 79 *et seq.*, who calls this the " teleological " method. But see the criticisms of a fellow-Scandinavian, in Schmidt, *op. cit.*, p. 157 *et seq.*

[11] See, however, the most interesting discussion of the scope and method of judicial construction of statutes, *per* Lord Denning in *Escoigne Properties* v. *I.R.C.* [1958] A.C. 546, at pp. 565–566.

which lays down that " every Act shall be deemed remedial, and shall accordingly receive such fair, large and liberal construction and interpretation as will best ensure the attainment of the object of the Act according to its true intent, meaning and spirit." It is not altogether clear how frequently this provision is expressly cited to or relied upon by the courts, but it does appear to have exerted a silent influence upon professional and judicial attitudes in regard to this matter.[12]

An important contribution to the subject of the interpretation of statutes has recently been made by a joint report of the two Law Commissions.[13] On the general approach to interpretation, it is the opinion of the Law Commissions that to place undue emphasis on the literal meaning of the words of a provision is to assume an unattainable perfection in draftsmanship. The rule in *Heydon's Case,* while not without merits, is somewhat outdated, because it assumes that statute is subsidiary or supplemental to the common law, whereas in modern conditions many statutes mark a fresh point of departure rather than a mere addition to, and qualification of the principles of the common law.[14] Also, the inability of courts to refer to legislative material makes exhortations to consider the policy of a statute somewhat ineffective. Doubtless it is for this reason that general provisions such as that contained in the New Zealand Act of 1924 have had comparatively little direct effect.[15]

The Commissions recognise that presumptions of intent do have a role to play in emphasising that legislation is made within the framework of a society with particular social and economic values

---

[12] For a discussion of this cardinal rule of statutory interpretation see Burrows (1969) 3 N.Z.U.L.R. 253, where it is suggested that this section " merely abolishes the distinction between penal and remedial statutes which existed at common law " (p. 277). " But . . . there can be no suggestion that the New Zealand courts are entitled to go any further, or be any more liberal, than are the English Courts in interpreting ' remedial ' legislation " (p. 255). The section is currently in vogue as it enables a court to interpret a provision " as to conform to its ideas of what is socially necessary " (p. 278). However, judicial opinion is agreed that " its comforting philosophy offers no panacea " until legislative intent has been ascertained [*per* Haslam J. in *Nunns* v. *Licensing Control Commission* [1967] N.Z.L.R. 76, 78] and that it is really " of limited assistance in the interpretation of statutes in which the true intent cannot be clearly ascertained from the text and historical and circumstantial context " (*per* Turner J. in *Gifford* v. *Police* [1965] N.Z.L.R. 484, 500).

[13] Law Commission and Scottish Law Commission (Law Com. 21, Scot.Law Com. 11), *The Interpretation of Statutes* (1969).

[14] *Cf.* Scarman, *Law Reform—The New Pattern* (1968), pp. 45 *et seq.* where the traditional attitude exemplified by *Heydon* is described as " seeing the common law [as] the seamless fabric covering all the activities of man; the statute [as] the tailor's stitch in time, to patch the fabric where gaps or other defects appear in the course of wear " (p. 46).

[15] See Burrows (1969) 3 N.Z.U.L.R. 253, 258–259, who comments that since " travaux préparatoires " and reports of parliamentary debates are inadmissible " the court is left only with the pre-existing law, the defects in it and the courts' reference as to the kind of remedy Parliament must have intended to provide for those defects," in other words the rule in *Heydon's Case.*

which, it can legitimately be assumed in the absence of evidence to the contrary, the legislature intended to respect. But, it is pointed out that a judge is hardly bound effectively by such presumptions for a number of reasons, in particular, because many presumptions are of imprecise scope, and there is no accepted test for solving a conflict between differing presumptions. Nor is it thought that a way out of the difficulty could be found by some kind of statutory classification of legislation [16] with appropriate presumptions. This is rejected as being impracticable, since any comprehensive statutory directives would either have to be so generalised as to afford little guidance to the courts, or so detailed that they would lead to intolerable complexity and rigidity of the law.[17]

Turning to the vexed issue of reference to legislative material, the Commissions agree that a case can be made out for excluding reports of Parliamentary proceedings for the interpretation of statutes, but on the other hand they favour the admission of specially prepared material which might be used in ascertaining the context in which statutory provisions are to be read. It is recognised, however, that there would be considerable practical difficulties in initiating such a system generally, and, for the time being, the Commissions confine themselves to a limited recommendation that any relevant report of a Royal Commission, or any law reform commission body such as themselves, upon which legislation was based, might be considered by the courts in ascertaining the meaning of any provision of an Act. This would mean that, for instance, a report of the Law Commission itself, or of the Law Reform Committee, which has resulted in legislation, could be referred to by the courts for the purposes of interpretation.[18] The Commissions consider also that, in connection with codification, an explanatory statement and illustrative commentary on the code could provide authoritative, though not compelling guidance on the code's interpretation, which would be particularly valuable, especially in the early years of the operation of the code. The Commissions also recommend that the courts should, in interpreting a statute, be entitled to refer to the terms of any relevant treaty or international agreement which is referred to in the statute.

---

[16] *Cf. ante,* 739.

[17] The Commissions do, however, favour laying down statutory presumptions in three difficult areas of interpretation *viz.,* mens rea in criminal offences, civil liability for breach of statutory duty, and implementation of international treaty obligations. See paras. 35, 38, 78.

[18] There have been several recent attempts (all unsuccessful) to introduce provisions into particular Bills (*viz.,* Theft Bill, Animals Bill, Matrimonial Proceedings and Property Bill, all three of which were based on reports of committees of law reform) to allow reference, for the purposes of construction, to the Reports, upon which the legislation was based. See *post,* 834, n. 58.

Lastly, the Commissions seek to clarify and extend the general concept underlying the rule in *Heydon's Case*, by proposing that the courts should favour a construction which would promote the general legislative purpose underlying the provision in question, fortified, as this would be, by the enlarged power given to the courts to refer to certain relevant legislative material.

Useful though the implementation of these recommendations might be, the Commissions would probably be the first to acknowledge that their influence would be likely to be somewhat marginal on the general impact of statute law. A further valuable innovation would result from the proposal, made by Sir Leslie Scarman,[19] the Chairman of the Law Commission, that there should be something in the nature of a Ministry of Justice, whose function would be to scrutinise all proposed legislation emanating from any government or other source, and to have the function of insuring that such legislation is both adequately expressed to achieve the maximum degree of possible clarity, and at the same time properly integrated into the existing body of law. It seems unlikely, however, that any great progress in such matters will be attained so long as governments regard the passage of the maximum quantity of legislation which can be enacted within the available parliamentary time as an overriding consideration, totally overshadowing the need for clarity and good drafting. The fault at the present time certainly lies not with the highly expert parliamentary draftsmen, but with those who are responsible for operating the parliamentary machine.

EQUITY

One judicial attitude, which is given especial prominence, is the equitable. This is sometimes contrasted with justice according to law, as when Aristotle treats it as a *corrective* of legal justice.[20] From this viewpoint it may be regarded as merely another name for natural law or justice, but its narrower and more specific role is when it functions as an integral part of the legal process.[21] This it may some-

---

[19] *Law Reform—The New Pattern* (1968) Lecture 2 and see *post*, 848.
[20] *Post*, 835. In some if not all periods, equity has been linked with natural law; cf. *ante*, 74 *et seq.*
[21] In the fourteenth century the law of England had still not crystallised into a body of clearly established substantive rules. There was however a belief in an overriding justice beyond human control, though for various mechanical reasons, such as the corruption or intimidation of a jury, justice might not have been attained in particular cases. The appeal to equity in this period therefore, was an appeal to the royal fount of justice, to the " head office," to see that justice prevailed where the ordinary legal mechanisms had for some reason failed to achieve this result. By the sixteenth century however, when the substantive rules of the common law had crystallised into, in many cases, a rigid form, the need was felt for a dispensing power in regard to the positive law whose rules, when correctly applied, might still produce an unjust result. For historical reasons

times do as a distinct portion of the legal system separate from and to some extent confronting and modifying the ordinary set of legal norms. When this occurs, as in England, it has naturally tended to suggest that equity is something distinct from law and derivable from some other source than the common and statute law of the realm. But whether equity operates in this distinctive manner through a separate tribunal, or as an integral part of the legal system itself, its character remains essentially the same, for in either case it is not really something outside the legal system but it emanates from the overall system and operates within it. It is this which gives it its practical significance, in contrast to the rhetorical flourishes of natural law.

Two aspects of equitable justice may be discerned, one generally associated with its earlier, the other with its later phase. In the first instance we find equity regarded as a means of mitigating the strict rigour of the legal rule. As Aristotle points out, the very generality of a legal rule will inevitably involve injustice in particular cases, if applied rigidly. Hence equity temporises, tempering the wind to the shorn lamb, by individualising the treatment of the particular case.[22] At first this might be purely an exercise of individual discretion,[23] as where a common law judge told a medieval litigant that he must wait seven years if he wished to enforce an oppressive but lawful penalty clause.[24] Such a process might well be open to the gibe that it would vary according to the length of the foot of whoever chanced to be exercising the discretionary power, but with time it tends to create new legal norms and remedies, such as the institution of the

this appeal to a higher justice was made to the Lord Chancellor as the Keeper of the King's Conscience, who administered equity as a means of avoiding injustice in cases which might result from a strict application of the positive law. (See the illuminating discussion in S. F. C. Milsom, *Historical Foundations of the Common Law* (1969), Chap. 4.)

[22] *Post*, 835. *Cf.* the role of the jury as discussed by Devlin J. in *Trial by Jury*, pp. 154–157; the author cites Lord Goddard as saying that a " jury can always be trusted to do justice where it might be impossible to bring a case strictly within the M'Naghten Rules." See also Cornish, *The Jury* (Pelican, 1971), pp. 179–180. It is the view of Kalven and Zeisel (*The American Jury, ante*, 468 n. 47) that a prime cause of the limited judge-jury disagreement stems from the jury's desire to temper the strict application of the law by equity (Chaps. 15–18, 20, 21).

[23] C. K. Allen argues that equity is a separate *source* of law since it involves the application of the judge's " trained sense of *discretionary* justice." (See *Law in the Making*, 7th ed., p. 415.) But it is difficult to see why the prior training, which presumably affects all judicial decisions, makes equity a distinct source of law. Moreover discretion is most commonly provided for these days by statute, *e.g.*, in such enactments as the Inheritance (Family Provisions) Act 1938, the Law Reform (Contributory Negligence) Act 1945, the Divorce Reform Act 1969 and the Legal Aid Act 1964.

[24] Cited by C. K. Allen, *Law in the Making*, 7th ed., p. 402.

trust in English law, and the form of " bonitary " ownership [25] developed by the praetor in Roman law.

The second aspect of equity really grows out of the first, when it comes to be recognised that what is needed is not merely a discretionary power to mitigate the asperities of the law in individual instances, but a more generally humane and liberal approach to the interpretation and development of the legal norms themselves, so that the rules themselves might reflect the spirit of what the Romans called " humanitas." [26] Many examples of this process at work may be discovered in the later Roman law,[27] as for instance the interpretation of documents according to their intent rather than their form, and the rule of restitution in cases of unjust enrichment. And the modern civil law has in turn exploited this approach mainly by means of the so-called *clausulae generales.*[28] The characteristic of this approach is that it generally succeeds in permeating the whole legal system, and it is, perhaps, because English equity developed early on purely separatist lines, and so created a distinct set of equitable norms, in many instances administered even more rigidly than the rules of law, whose rigour they were devised initially to mitigate,[29] of the discretionary element in equitable remedies even at the present that this general equitable attitude had received little express recognition in modern English law.[30] On the other hand English law still preserves the earlier individualising attitude of equity, in its retention day.

---

[25] By this means, for instance, such persons as a widow were enabled to claim to participate in a deceased's estate, though excluded by the strict civil law: see H. F. Jolowicz, *Historical Introduction to Roman Law,* 2nd ed., p. 97.

[26] *Cf.* F. Schulz, *Roman Legal Science,* pp. 297–299. See also Newman, 17 I.C.L.Q. 807, 809.

[27] In classical Roman law equity was mainly located in the special rules of the praetorian edict, though this was not referred to as *aequitas.* These rules were strictly administered and thus resembled particular English equity as developed in the Court of Chancery in the seventeenth and eighteenth centuries. See Buckland and McNair, *Roman Law and Common Law,* 2nd ed., pp. xviii–xix; Jolowicz, *op. cit.,* pp. 95–99, 520–522. Jolowicz points out that, as with the later English equity, the praetorian system worked together with the civil law and they were not antagonistic to one another (*ibid.,* p. 214).

[28] *Cf. ante,* 723.

[29] Hence Buckley J.'s well-known dictum that " this court is not a court of conscience ": *Re Telescriptor Ltd.* [1903] 2 Ch. 174, 195. There seems to be doubt as to the authenticity of Harman J.'s alleged dictum that " equity is not to be presumed to be of an age past child-bearing "; see Megarry, *Miscellany-at-Law,* p. 142. The most recent attempt of equity to give birth is the much controverted right of a deserted wife to retain the matrimonial home; but the H.L. has now held that no such right against third parties exists at all: see *National Provincial Bank* v. *Ainsworth* [1965] A.C. 1175. The legislature subsequently created a new carefully-regulated right by the Matrimonial Homes Act 1967.

[30] Equity has had a more dynamic role in modern American law, where it has been used as an instrument of economic power, *e.g.,* the use of the injunction as a means of controlling strikes. See M. Lerner, *America as a Civilization* (1958), pp. 430–431. For a comparison of the role of equity in English and American law see Newman, *op. cit.,* at pp. 815–830.

This is not to say that the equitable approach does not in fact manifest itself in less overt and more disguised ways throughout the modern English legal system. Thus it may be discerned in the broader approach to statutory construction, and in much of our modern law of negligence.[31] But its limitations may be equally remarked in the over-rigid and mechanical construction of documents sometimes emanating from our courts,[32] as well as in the difficulty occasionally encountered in adjusting the law to meet new situations.[33] Accordingly, what is sometimes felt to be lacking in English law as at present administered, is a more pervasive spirit of equity informing every aspect of the judicial process, and to this Lord Denning has drawn attention in his cogent plea for a new equity.[34]

JOHN P. DAWSON

The Oracles of the Law
(1968)

La Doctrine

. . . The analytical note is a great invention. It is hard to imagine what French law would be without it. It is not a peculiarly French invention, for similar notes are appended to some of the reports in other European countries—Germany and Italy, for example. In France many of the notes are not written by law professors but by lawyers, even by judges. They appear as footnotes to reports of recent cases in several series that are published by private enterprise and commonly used by lawyers. They therefore have a far greater impact on the legal profession than do modern American law reviews, though they perform the same function as a forum for free criticism and exchange of views. Being comments on the cases reported, they address themselves to specific issues, to all the nuances in the facts, to the motives for decision whether expressed or veiled, and to the possibilities of reconciling results with those in earlier cases, by distinctions or otherwise. The analytical note is also expected to assemble all the resources of doctrine, to criticize and evaluate it in its bearing on the specific problem. It is an extremely flexible instrument, expressing the skill, learning, and insight of individual authors but requiring them to address themselves to the interests and needs of practitioners as well as to those of their academic colleagues.[35]

---

31 Consider, too, the observations of Lord Simonds in *National Bank of Greece* v. *Metliss* [1958] A.C. 509, at p. 515.
32 *e.g.*, in *Re Diplock* [1944] A.C. 341.
33 Consider such cases as *Armstrong* v. *Strain* [1952] 1 T.L.R. 82; and *Re Miller's Agreement* [1947] Ch. 615, discussed by Denning L.J. in " The Need for a New Equity " (1952) 5 *Current Legal Problems*, pp. 4–5. A more recent illustration is provided by *Byrne* v. *Kinematograph Renters Ltd.* [1958] 1 W.L.R. 762; see the comment on this by D. Lloyd in (1958) 21 M.L.R. 661 *et seq.*
34 *Post*, 840.
35 Meynial, I 196–97 makes some of these points and many others of interest.

The gradual rapprochement between *jurisprudence* and *doctrine* which began in this way, during the last three decades of the nineteenth century, must have elevated each in the eyes of the other. Carefully prepared analytical notes in the standard law reports spread among the legal profession the ideas and influence of academic authors. On the other hand, it must have made an impression on the academic world that a distinguished professor, Labbé, devoted his efforts for 30 years to the thoughtful and respectful analysis of hundreds of reported cases, on topics ranging over most of French private law. He and others like him discovered for themselves and revealed to their colleagues the depth, richness, and complexity of the gloss the courts had laid on the codes. This gloss was the law that the state applied, through the agency, the judiciary, that the state had empowered to apply it. At the turn of the century a leading historian-law professor, Esmein, revealed how attitudes had changed. He called on his colleagues for a new effort. In the teaching he received in his own youth, he said, some professors had gone so far as to discuss court decisions, but he urged that they should do this for a broader purpose than merely to establish support for their own " systems." In research and writing, he declared, the academic profession had as one of its primary tasks the study of *jurisprudence* for its own sake, showing its history and often irregular growth, its own internal order and consistency: " It is [*jurisprudence*] that is the true expression of the civil law, this is the real and positive law. . . . It is this, just as much as the Code itself, that must be studied directly and scientifically." [36]

To study court decisions was one thing, but to admit they made law was another. The problem that has tortured French lawyers ever since had emerged by 1900. The nature of the problem had been discerned by Gény, in his important work, published in 1899. His main object was to free interpreters of the Code from the limitations inherent in the exegetical method. In arguing for " free scientific research " he used as perhaps his most cogent arguments the great changes made through court decisions, changes that the older authors had ascribed to the legislator. Did this mean that courts had " a praetorian power," that their decisions had any of the attributes of law or could hamper the freedom of the interpreter? Emphatically not. Any such suggestions, however ingeniously or seductively made, would violate the principle of separation of powers and would confer on courts a legislative power which was clearly denied them by basic French legislation. The only way that judicial decisions could produce new law would be through translation into rules of custom.[37] And so this great emancipator, on the eve of the twentieth century, reverted to the views of the medieval glossators, summed up in the maxim *non exemplis sed legibus iudicandum.* . . .

[pp. 398–400]

---

[36] A. Esmein, " La Jurisprudence et la Doctrine," introducing the first number of the Revue Trimestrielle du Droit Civil, 1902, 1, esp. 10–12.

[37] Gény, Méthode d'Interprétation et Sources, I 209–11, II 33–53. These views were reaffirmed in the Epilogue added by the author to the second edition of 1919: II 259–67. [*Cf. ante,* 711].

The Working Methods of French Case-Law

. . . The Spartan economy of high court opinions extends not only to issues of law; the facts too are brusquely treated.[38] This is much less true of lower courts. Indeed the lower one descends in the judicial hierarchy the fuller, in general, will be the disclosure of facts. But the Court of Cassation serves as the nation's model. Its controls over the growth of doctrine are powerful enough to fix the spotlight on its work in most discussions of French case law. To readers trained in our own tradition, the extreme parsimony of its statements of facts is even more striking than the brevity of its propositions of law. It is not only striking but in a way more important, for it raises issues that are central not only to workable case-law technique but to conceptions of the kind of law that judges are qualified to make.

If American lawyers were to ask themselves why an ample disclosure of essential facts is an essential requirement of a judicial opinion, a short answer might be that the opinion would be almost meaningless without it.[39] A theory of precedent means, of course, that the reasons given in each case are thought to carry a commitment for the future. But our training is that absolutely everything said in the course of a judicial decision must be understood as relevant to the decision of the particular case. Broad statements are clues to attitudes and therefore have considerable interests. They may later be swept out of their context and applied very widely. But this process is always subject to challenge. A lawyer or a court in a later case, testing the proposition against new facts, can call the statement merely dictum. This postaudit in the light of new facts and new experience is a corrective we find indispensable. It seems almost axiomatic that if the postaudit is to be effective the facts to which the court responded must be fully disclosed, until by repeated testing in different contexts the meaning of the proposition and most of its consequences have been made more clear.

The point can be illustrated by a comment made in 1948 by a distinguished French author, Georges Ripert. He was discussing the new rules of tort liability manufactured by the Court of Cassation, primarily though not exclusively directed to persons owning or controlling motor vehicles. His comment was: "It is one of the inconveniences of the creation of law by the courts that sometimes a rule is established because of particular considerations of a given case but must then be applied in cases in which one would prefer that it was not." [40] The implications

---

38 In part this is due, no doubt, to the lack of any independent fact-finding power in the Court of Cassation and the assigning in general of fact-finding to the " sovereign " powers of lower courts. These restrictions on the high court have been said to give " greater strength to its decisions ; the rule of law is laid down in pure form, abstracted from considerations of facts." Ancel, " Case Law in France," J. Comp. Leg. & Int'l L. (3d ser.), XVI 1, 15 (1934).

39 [It is thought that English lawyers would adopt the same approach.]

40 Dalloz 1948.J.485, 486, quoted by von Mehren, The Civil Law System, 413. In the analytical note in which this comment appeared Professor Ripert was discussing the question whether an owner of a motor vehicle was liable jointly with a user to whom he had transferred custody, and under the same strict tests. Actually his principal complaint was against the *chambre civile* of the Court of Cassation, which " does not have the habit of modifying its *jurisprudence*, even when a new case discloses the inconveniences of the solution that it has previously adopted. It thinks, with reason, that a variation would be an evil worse than an occasional injustice." Paraphrased, the complaint of Professor Ripert seemed to be that the *chambre civile* followed its own precedents too rigorously.

of this statement would certainly not be acceptable generally to French courts and authors. It attributes a force to judge-made rules that is denied in theory and rejected in practice, as I will suggest in a moment. But in a system in which case-law techniques were well understood and highly developed it is difficult to imagine how such a statement could even be made. The carryover of rules from old case to new need not be automatic. All that is needed is the distinction, elementary for us, between decision and dictum. This distinction is much more than a useful technique. It expresses a limitation that we take for granted on the powers of judges in law-creation. No matter how uncompromisingly it had been asserted, a proposition used in a prior decision carries no compulsion for a later decision unless on postaudit the similarities between the cases seem to exclude any rational distinction. Even then, the proposition can be retracted; the earlier case can be overruled.

Without this reserved power to retract or revise, the duty to follow past decisions would present a major dilemma. Plainly the significance of any particular case will depend on the combined effect of the reasons given and the facts that in a sense adhere to them. It may be possible, though surely it is difficult, to give reasons phrased so narrowly that they could not apply under any conceivable circumstances to any other future case. The requirement of a reasoned opinion implies that the reasons given do carry beyond the particular case, to cases that have not yet arisen, that have not been briefed or analyzed or even clearly foreseen, that may involve persons not yet born. The " neutral " principles that have been advocated in decisions interpreting our Constitution would require an even more deliberate projection of ideas; unless principles could be discovered that would govern a wide range of comparable cases a court would be expected to discard a solution to which it was otherwise predisposed.[41] This affirmative duty to dispose in advance of cases that have not yet arisen is certainly not accepted in all the areas regulated by our judge-made law. At times there is great virtue in avoiding commitments, in framing reasons as narrowly as possible. The main point is, in any event, that cases not yet litigated cannot be finally and conclusively "prejudged" (as the Romans put it long ago). No matter what care and imagination have been enlisted in the effort, the reasons stated will take on new aspects when sights are adjusted from the angles given by another, new case. The commitment entailed in the adoption of reasons is not final and cannot be.

A shorter way to say this is that courts are *not* legislatures. The function of courts is to decide cases. It is only in modern England that the habit has developed of reading judicial opinions as though they were statutes. It has been only in England likewise that appellate court judges (the House of Lords and the Court of Appeal) declared themselves incapable of overruling themselves, though the House of Lords has now overruled itself on this issue. There has no doubt been some connection between the literalism with which judges' sayings are read in England and the self-imposed impotence to retract them, though it would be hard to distinguish cause and effect. The result was that English high court judges conferred on themselves a power

---

[41] Herbert Wechsler, "Toward Neutral Principles of Constitutional Law," in Principles, Politics, and Fundamental Law (Cambridge, Mass., 1961), 1 [and see extract, *post*, 800].

to make irrevocable pronouncements, a power that a supposedly omnipotent Parliament does not claim for itself. It may not reassure our
French colleagues to know that the source of this power and the reasons
given in England to explain it were at all times as unintelligible in the
United States as they have been in France. It is no wonder that
French authors have recoiled from a theory that conceded to judges
such extensive law-making powers, even though judge-made dogma
was not so immutable in England as theory asserted and elaborate
casuistical techniques open tortuous paths of escape for the nimble.

The hostility still shown in France toward the whole conception of
judicial precedent may be due in part to dismay inspired by the
English example. Yet the great freeze in England is less than a century
old; and before it set in, very different views prevailed, much closer
to our own. The extreme to which the English doctrine of precedent
has been carried during the last seventy years has helped, I believe, to
perpetuate in Europe a basic misunderstanding, by obscuring the
primary purpose of a system of precedent. That purpose is to restrict,
not to enlarge, the powers of judges. The feature of our system that
French critics think obnoxious is that the reasons given in each
particular case are treated as commitments, in some degree binding in
later cases. When the reasons must be published, as they now must be
in France, they can be cited and used by counsel, as they constantly
are in France. If any compulsion is felt to treat like cases alike, the
likelihood of these comparisons should induce care in formulating the
reasons in each case as it comes along. A theory of precedent can
thus limit power in a double sense: the court is constrained not only
by the reasons expressed in earlier cases but by the need in the case
before it to define with care the commitment it is making to the
future. These constraints can become effective only if courts are conceived to have a duty to do more than decide the particular case by
finding and applying an appropriate rule. They can be effective only
if courts accept a responsibility to the legal system as a whole, to
maintain its order and consistency while constantly engaged in new
creation. So far as time and insight permit, we expect each individual
court opinion to weave itself into the seamless web.

It is this sense of responsibility for the ordering of their own
creations that seems to me to be missing in the opinions of French
courts, especially the Court of Cassation. The initial handicap that the
Court of Cassation has imposed on itself is its flat refusal to refer
explicitly to its own past decisions, though this refusal is in itself
symptomatic. Without explicit references it would be difficult even to
make a good start on the task of reconciling the solution reached in
any particular case with those of earlier cases. Also, the one-sentence
format of the court's opinions, with its wearisome repetition of whereas
clauses, is severely constricting, though its survival too is symptomatic.
More basic is the extremely cryptic and laconic style with which the
court expresses both facts and law. Propositions of law are drafted with
utmost care and precision but they hang suspended in space, for no
effort is made to reconcile them with very different propositions asserted
in other, nearly related cases or to explain why they would not apply
if the facts of the case were somewhat different. Where the court is
inching its way forward in a new and unexplored area, as in the modern
extensions of tort liability, the economy with which its doctrines are

phrased enables it to avoid any premature generalization; as one shrewd observer has put it, the court in such cases " keeps its secrets " well.[42] But much of the time, as in the 1925 case of the simulated gift, the propositions used are gross over-generalizations—sufficient to dispose of the pending case but demonstrably false if the facts are slightly changed. The reports are filled with subordinate propositions that have been formulated by the courts, in rich and wonderful variety. These propositions can be emitted or amended freely because they are not felt to carry commitment, though perhaps it could be said that they do not carry commitment because they are emitted so freely. The judges are very careful to prove their compliance with the formal sources of law, code or statute. Doctrines of lowlier origin, such as those produced by judicial opinions, merely serve to dispose of the particular case. They are at most a form of argumentation. They do not make law and cannot make law, for this was the mandate of the Revolution.

Modern French law has thus been transformed by a kind of case law, administered by the courts with a primitive case-law technique. How the courts acquired their " praetorian power " is still a puzzling problem for theorists. Far more important, and never discussed, is the destructive effect of history on the working methods of French case law. But working methods reflect convictions and have important consequences.

The central *conviction*, which still lies deep, is that judges cannot be lawmakers; from this the conclusion seems to follow that they have no responsibility for shaping, restating and ordering the doctrine that they themselves produce. If the premise in this argument were more carefully defined, one could accept it, but however it may be phrased the conclusion does not follow.

Of the many *consequences* two are at this point most important:

(1) If one will grant, as some might not, that order is desirable and that codes alone cannot produce it, the reasoned opinion is a powerful instrument by which judges can help to organize the results of their own work. If they abstain from the effort to the degree that they have in France, the legal system as a whole is deprived of a key resource.

(2) An effective case-law technique employed by judges through the medium of the reasoned opinion, with the responsibilities that it should entail, has the purpose and should have the effect of limiting the powers of judges. Its absence in France has resulted from a desire to limit the power of judges, but it has produced instead a much greater freedom for judges than we would consider tolerable.   [pp. 411–415]

The Enigma of Judge-Made Law

. . . Debate still continues . . . on the issue whether *jurisprudence* is a source of law; as one writer has put it, in France this debate is " never closed." [43] One of the most influential contributions has come from Professor Maury, writing in 1950.[44] He started by restating the basic French doctrine of separation of powers and the Code prohibition

[42] Lawson, Negligence in the Civil Law, 235.
[43] Esmein, Rev. Trim., 1952, 17, 19.
[44] " Études sur la Jurisprudence en Tant que Source du Droit," Études Offertes à Georges Ripert (Paris, 1950), 28.

of law-making by judges, but concluded that this prohibition " condemns only the Anglo-Saxon system of precedent." He then quoted
the question asked by a colleague who aimed to show that *jurisprudence*
gained nothing through becoming *constante*—how can the mere repetition of decisions on the same issue give them an authority that each
single decision could not have? This authority had been explained by
another colleague as a tacit delegation from the legislature, through its
silence and inaction.[45] This, Maury said, was a fiction, since most of the
members of the legislature are ignorant of the course of judicial
decision and a majority vote to impose correctives is difficult to
mobilize; besides, there was a serious question whether legislative
power could be delegated in this way. He also rejected a thesis that
had been advanced the year before. It explained all the rules in force
in any social milieu as the product of the power that effectively
controlled each social group; they became legal rules when they were
enforced by public officials, like judges or administrators, who were
agents of society and were invested with a share of its power. This
conception is reminiscent of a proposition once advanced tentatively
in the United States: law is what officials do in fact.[46] But Maury
concluded that power unregulated by law was repugnant, and there
remained also the more specific question—how could one explain the
lawmaking power of a single decision or ascertain its effect on the
future? For his own solution, however, Maury proceeded to borrow
the central idea embedded in this proposal: the judge, he said, does
have power in fact, regularly and lawfully conferred on him: " by his
occupation and in the exercise of his function he enjoys a certain power
of his own which he can use and does use in reality, to exceed at times
the limits of his competence." The power, existing merely as pure fact,
cannot create a legal rule unless it secures the consent of those " interested." Those " interested " will be, not the mass of persons potentially
subject to the judge-made rule but " the judges themselves, the men of
law, the jurists who in some degree will represent this mass and whose
technical opinion will impose itself " on those affected by the rule.
Adhesion or consensus will often come promptly but at times the
practicing bar, the jurists and lower courts will resist. Then the judicially
created rule does not become law until there has developed " a belief
in the obligatory character of the rule, a recognition of its validity
expressed by acceptance or resignation, or in any case by the absence
of opposition."

Subsequent discussions have circled around the medieval themes that
have thus been arrayed in modern dress. Maury described his own view
as " pleuralistic." [47] Other academic jurists were attracted by a thesis that
gave them, as well as the practicing bar and lower courts, a share in
producing the " common adhesion " that validated judge-made custom.[48]

---

45 V. Waline, " Le Pouvoir Normatif de la Jurisprudence," Études en Honneur de
   Georges Scelle (Paris, 1950), II 613.
46 Karl Llewellyn, The Bramble Bush (New York, 1951), 8–10, giving in a foreword
   amplification of the thought that he had intended to express in 1930.
47 Études Ripert, note 44 above, at 28, 50.
48 Le Balle, Cours d'Institutions Judiciaires, 110–13 ; G. Marty & P. Raynaud, Droit
   Civil (Paris, 1956), 204–05. Henri Mazeaud, Cours d'Institutions Judiciaires et
   Droit Civil (Paris, 1957–1958), 124–25, merely calls the rules originating in

By providing a broader base of consent it has relieved the anxiety of some who are still reluctant to take the final step and declare that court decisions are a " formal source." [49] Those who follow Maury's view do not go all the way in reviving medieval conceptions. They do not assert, as did the medieval Italians, that the *communis opinio doctorum* is enough in itself to make law. They mainly rely, as did Maury, on some isolated but dramatic instances in which the resistance of lower courts, supported by the jurists, has induced the Court of Cassation to overrule itself.[50] Even in Belgium, where lower courts are held under tighter rein by the Belgian Court of Cassation, Maury's analysis has received at least nominal support.[51] . . .   [pp. 422–424]

. . . Professor Dupeyroux, writing in 1960, declared that he could see no way to refute the Maury thesis but he used it for the opposite purpose, of sounding the tocsin against the " imperialism " of judges.[52] The rules enforced by judicial decision, he said, do not merely " resemble " law; they merge (*se confondent*) with the law, they are as binding on the population and almost as binding on judges as code or statute could be, they in effect displace the Code in areas that it already regulates, and they have the quality of generality that is the principal mark of the legislative norm. It is useless and unrealistic to deny that courts have engaged in legislation; and, since a complete separation of governmental powers is not realizable in any case, judicial legislation can occur without *necessarily* encroaching on the governmental sphere assigned to the legislature. Then comes the surprise. The conclusion is that French courts have in fact encroached—grossly, flagrantly, abusively. This is because the legislature itself has grossly and flagrantly defaulted. Judges have (improperly) filled great gaps where legislation was silent, as in the area of governmental liability that is assigned to the *Conseil d'Etat*. Worse than this, judges have acted directly contrary to law and

jurisprudence " un véritable droit coutumier," though going on to suggest that the differences between French and " Anglo-Saxon " countries were much less significant than had often been asserted.

[49] Fragistas, Mélanges Maury (1960), II 139, 149–53, though this author seems to part company from Maury in reserving to the population as a whole a power to invalidate the " custom " originating in judge-made rules where it runs contrary to the " popular sentiment of right."

But P. Robier, " L'Ordre Juridique et la Théorie des Sources du Droit," Études Ripert, 9, 12–13, and G. Holleaux in Revue Internationale de Droit Comparé, 1961, 869, seem content to make the break and declare that jurisprudence is a " veritable formal source " through the authority conferred by law on the Court of Cassation. René David, Les Grands Systèmes de Droit Contemporains (Paris, 1964), is still more emphatic, though his views may be suspect in France since they are based on knowledge of how our case law actually works. [David is now translated as David and Brierley. *Major Legal Systems of the World* (1968).]

[50] Especially the great cases of stolen cars, whose owners were finally held not to have them in their " guard " when being driven by the thieves. Boulanger, Rev. Trim., 1961, 417, 432.

[51] R. Warlomont, " L'Autorité du Précédent Judiciaire," Annales de Droit et de Sciences Politiques, 1951, 69, 80–81.

[52] O. Dupeyroux, " La Jurisprudence, Source Abusive du Droit," Mélanges Maury (1960), II 349. Despite his declared inability to refute Maury, Professor Dupeyroux in footnotes (pp. 355–56) expressed some distrust of the notion of professional consensus, describing it as " undemonstrated and undemonstrable." The end of resistance by practitioners and lower courts he considered to be usually a helpless submission to the overriding powers of the Court of Cassation. These points seem worth elaboration in something more than brief footnotes.

the legislature has been unable to contain them. This has been especially true in the judicial work of the *Conseil d'Etat*, but the indictment extends to the ordinary judiciary as well. These developments mark the decadence of democracy. France is governed by technicians and bureaucrats, making political decisions under the forms of adjudication but accountable to no one. In their audacity they have even had support from legal theorists and practitioners. They have made *jurisprudence* an " abusive source " of law, erasing the prudent precautions set up by the revolutionary assemblies. The author reminded his readers of the passionate words of Robespierre who declared in 1790: " the word *jurisprudence* of the courts . . . must be effaced from our language." [53]

[pp. 425–426]

LONDON STREET TRAMWAYS CO. v. LONDON COUNTY COUNCIL

[1898] A.C. 375

LORD HALSBURY L.C. . . . .

My Lords, it is totally impossible, as it appears to me, to disregard the whole current of authority upon this subject, and to suppose that what some people call an " extraordinary case," an " unusual case," a case somewhat different from the common, in the opinion of each litigant in turn, is sufficient to justify the rehearing and rearguing before the final Court of Appeal of a question which has been already decided. Of course I do not deny that cases of individual hardship may arise, and there may be a current of opinion in the profession that such and such a judgment was erroneous; but what is that occasional interference with what is perhaps abstract justice as compared with the inconvenience— the disastrous inconvenience—of having each question subject to being reargued and the dealings of mankind rendered doubtful by reason of different decisions, so that in truth and in fact there would be no real final Court of Appeal? My Lords, " interest rei publicae " that there should be " finis litium " at some time, and there could be no " finis litium " if it were possible to suggest in each case that it might be reargued, because it is " not an ordinary case," whatever that may mean. Under these circumstances I am of opinion that we ought not to allow this question to be reargued. [54] . . .

[p. 380]

LORDS MACNAGHTEN, MORRIS, and JAMES OF HEREFORD concurred.

PRACTICE DIRECTION

[1966] 3 All E.R. 77

Before judgments were given in the House of Lords on July 26, 1966, Lord Gardiner L.C., made the following statement on behalf of himself and the Lords of Appeal in Ordinary:

[53] The reference to Robespierre appears in Mélanges Maury, II 349, 352–53. The encroachments by judges on the legislator are attacked, pp. 367–77.

[54] [It has been suggested, with justification, that this case was " all but " an issue of *res judicata* and that Lord Halsbury's judgment may have been taken as authority for more than he intended. See Stevens, 28 M.L.R. 509, 514n. See also Cross, *Precedent in English Law* (2nd ed.), p. 106.]

Their Lordships regard the use of precedent as an indispensable foundation upon which to decide what is the law and its application to individual cases. It provides at least some degree of certainty upon which individuals can rely in the conduct of their affairs, as well as a basis for orderly development of legal rules.

Their lordships nevertheless recognise that too rigid adherence to precedent may lead to injustice in a particular case and also unduly restrict proper development of the law. They propose therefore to modify their present practice and, while treating former decisions of this House as normally binding, to depart from a previous decision when it appears right to do so.

In this connection they will bear in mind the danger of disturbing retrospectively the basis on which contracts, settlements of property and fiscal arrangements have been entered into and also the especial need for certainty as to the criminal law.

This announcement is not intended to affect the use of precedent elsewhere than in this House.[55]

CONWAY v. RIMMER

[1968] A.C. 910 [56]

LORD REID

. . . If the commonly accepted interpretation of the decision of this House in *Duncan* v. *Cammell, Laird & Co. Ltd.*[57] is to remain authoritative the question admits of only one answer—the Minister's statement is final and conclusive. Normally I would be very slow to question the authority of a unanimous decision of this House only 25 years old which was carefully considered and obviously intended to lay down a general rule. But this decision has several abnormal features.

Lord Simon thought that on this matter the law in Scotland was the same as the law in England and he clearly intended to lay down a rule applicable to the whole of the United Kingdom. But in *Glasgow Corporation* v. *Central Land Board* [58] this House held that that was not so, with the result that today on this question the law is different in the two countries. There are many chapters of the law where for historical and other reasons it is quite proper that the law should be different in the two countries. But here we are dealing purely with public policy—with the proper relation between the powers of the executive and the powers of the courts—and I can see no rational justification for the law on this matter being different in the two countries.

---

[55] [For its effect on the Court of Appeal, see *ante*, 706, note 22 (first series).]

[56] [The facts of *Conway* v. *Rimmer* were that a former probationary police constable was suing his former superintendent for malicious prosecution (he had been prosecuted for larceny of an electric torch, a charge which the judge had not left to the jury). In the course of discovery, the defendant disclosed a list of documents in his possession, which included four reports made by him about the plaintiff during his period of probation and a report by him to his Chief Constable for transmission to the D.P.P. in connection with the larceny charge. The Home Secretary objected to the production of all five documents on the ground that each fell within a class of document the production of which would be injurious to the public interest.]

[57] [1942] A.C. 624.

[58] 1956 H.L.(S.C.) 1.

Secondly, events have proved that the rule supposed to have
been laid down in *Duncan's* case is far from satisfactory. In the large
number of cases in England and elsewhere which have been cited in
argument much dissatisfaction has been expressed and I have not
observed even one expression of whole-hearted approval. Moreover
a statement made by the Lord Chancellor in 1956 on behalf of the
Government, to which I shall return later, makes it clear that that
Government did not regard it as consonant with public policy to
maintain the rule to the full extent which existing authorities had held
to be justifiable.

I have no doubt that the case of *Duncan* v. *Cammell, Laird & Co.
Ltd.* was rightly decided. The plaintiff sought discovery of documents
relating to the submarine *Thetis* including a contract for the hull and
machinery and plans and specifications. The First Lord of the Admiralty
had stated that " it would be injurious to the public interest that any
of the said documents should be disclosed to any person." Any of
these documents might well have given valuable information, or at
least clues, to the skilled eye of an agent of a foreign power. But Lord
Simon L.C. took the opportunity to deal with the whole question of
the right of the Crown to prevent production of documents in a
litigation. Yet a study of his speech leaves me with a strong impression
that throughout he had primarily in mind cases where discovery or
disclosure would involve a danger of real prejudice to the national
interest. I find it difficult to believe that his speech would have been
the same if the case had related, as the present case does, to discovery
of routine reports on a probationer constable. . . .

　　. . . At the end [59] he said that a Minister
　　" ought not to take the responsibility of withholding production
　　except in cases where the public interest would otherwise be
　　damnified, for example, where disclosure would be injurious to
　　national defence, or to good diplomatic relations, or where the
　　practice of keeping a class of documents secret is necessary for the
　　proper functioning of the public service."

I find it difficult to believe that he would have put these three examples
on the same level if he had intended the third to cover such minor
matters as a routine report by a relatively junior officer.

　　. . . It is universally recognised that here there are two kinds of
public interest which may clash. There is the public interest that harm
shall not be done to the nation or the public service by disclosure of
certain documents, and there is the public interest that the administration of justice shall not be frustrated by the withholding of documents
which must be produced if justice is to be done. There are many cases
where the nature of the injury which would or might be done to the
nation or the public service is of so grave a character that no other
interest, public or private, can be allowed to prevail over it. With
regard to such cases it would be proper to say, as Lord Simon did,
that to order production of the document in question would put the
interest of the state in jeopardy. But there are many other cases where
the possible injury to the public service is much less and there one
would think that it would be proper to balance the public interests
involved. I do not believe that Lord Simon really meant that the

[59] [*Op. cit.*, p. 642.]

smallest probability of injury to the public service must always out-
weigh the gravest frustration of the administration of justice.[60] . . .
                                                              [pp. 938–940]
    . . . It appears to me that the present position is so unsatisfactory
that this House must re-examine the whole question in light of all the
authorities.

    Two questions will arise: first, whether the court is to have any
right to question the finality of a Minister's certificate and, secondly,
if it has such a right, how and in what circumstances that right is to
be exercised and made effective.

    A Minister's certificate may be given on one or other of two
grounds: either because it would be against the public interest to
disclose the contents of the particular document or documents in
question, or because the document belongs to a class of documents
which ought to be withheld, whether or not there is anything in the
particular document in question disclosure of which would be against the
public interest. It does not appear that any serious difficulties have
arisen or are likely to arise with regard to the first class. However wide
the power of the court may be held to be, cases would be very rare
in which it could be proper to question the view of the responsible
Minister that it would be contrary to the public interest to make public
the contents of a particular document. A question might arise whether
it would be possible to separate those parts of a document of which
disclosure would be innocuous from those parts which ought not to be
made public, but I need not pursue that question now. In the present
case your Lordships are directly concerned with the second class of
documents. . . .   [pp. 943–944]
    I do not doubt that it is proper to prevent the use of any document,
wherever it comes from, if disclosure of its contents would really
injure the national interest, and I do not doubt that it is proper to
prevent any witness, whoever he may be, from disclosing facts which
in the national interest ought not to be disclosed. Moreover, it is the
duty of the court to do this without the intervention of any Minister
if possible serious injury to the national interest is readily apparent.
But in this field it is more than ever necessary that in a doubtful case
the alleged public interest in concealment should be balanced against
the public interest that the administration of justice should not be
frustrated. If the Minister, who has no duty to balance these conflicting
public interests, says no more than that in his opinion the public
interest requires concealment, and if that is to be accepted as conclusive
in this field as well as with regard to documents in his possession, it
seems to me not only that very serious injustice may be done to the
parties, but also that the due administration of justice may be gravely
impaired for quite inadequate reasons. . . .
    In my judgment, in considering what it is " proper " for a court
to do we must have regard to the need, shown by 25 years' experience
since *Duncan's* case, that the courts should balance the public interest
in the proper administration of justice against the public interest in
withholding any evidence which a Minister considers ought to be
withheld. . . .

[60] [A rare articulated example of Poundian balancing of interests (on which see
ante, 370) in an English judgment.]

I would therefore propose that the House ought now to decide that courts have and are entitled to exercise a power and duty to hold a balance between the public interest, as expressed by a Minister, to withhold certain documents or other evidence, and the public interest in ensuring the proper administration of justice. That does not mean that a court would reject a Minister's view: full weight must be given to it in every case, and if the Minister's reasons are of a character which judicial experience is not competent to weigh, then the Minister's view must prevail. But experience has shown that reasons given for withholding whole classes of documents are often not of that character. For example a court is perfectly well able to assess the likelihood that, if the writer of a certain class of document knew that there was a chance that his report might be produced in legal proceedings, he would make a less full and candid report than he would otherwise have done.

I do not doubt that there are certain classes of documents which ought not to be disclosed whatever their content may be. Virtually everyone agrees that Cabinet minutes and the like ought not to be disclosed until such time as they are only of historical interest. But I do not think that many people would give as the reason that premature disclosure would prevent candour in the Cabinet. To my mind the most important reason is that such disclosure would create or fan ill-informed or captious public or political criticism. The business of government is difficult enough as it is, and no government could contemplate with equanimity the inner workings of the government machine being exposed to the gaze of those ready to criticise without adequate knowledge of the background and perhaps with some axe to grind. And that must, in my view, also apply to all documents concerned with policy making within departments including, it may be, minutes and the like by quite junior officials and correspondence with outside bodies. Further it may be that deliberations about a particular case require protection as much as deliberations about policy. I do not think that it is possible to limit such documents by any definition. But there seems to me to be a wide difference between such documents and routine reports. There may be special reasons for withholding some kinds of routine documents, but I think that the proper test to be applied is to ask, in the language of Lord Simon in *Duncan's* case, whether the withholding of a document because it belongs to a particular class is really "necessary for the proper functioning of the public service." . . .   [pp. 950–952]

It appears to me to be most improbable that any harm would be done by disclosure of the probationary reports on the appellant or of the report from the police training centre. . . .   [p. 954]

LORD MORRIS OF BORTH-Y-GEST

My Lords, stated in its most direct form the question—one of far-reaching importance—which is raised in this case is whether the final decision as to the production in litigation of relevant documents is to rest with the courts or with the executive. I have no doubt that the conclusion should be that the decision rests with the courts. . . .
                [p. 954]

. . . My Lords, it seems to me that that decision was binding upon the Court of Appeal in the present case. Your Lordships have, however, a freedom which was not possessed by the Court of Appeal.

Though precedent is an indispensable foundation upon which to decide what is the law, there may be times when a departure from precedent is in the interests of justice and the proper development of the law. I have come to the conclusion that it is now right to depart from the decision in *Duncan's* case.[61] [p. 958]

. . . My Lords, I have embarked upon a survey of the decisions prior to *Duncan's* case because I would have a measure of reluctance in disturbing a decision given in 1942 if it had been a re-statement of clear principles which for long had been widely accepted. It seems to me, however, that there was much authority which would have warranted an entirely different statement of principle in *Duncan's* case, though doubtless in that particular case without leading to any different result. This circumstance, when coupled with the fact that it is clear that the law in Scotland differs from that proclaimed in *Duncan's* case, affords ample warrant, in my view, to justify a new appraisement of the position. It can also be said that though courts have since 1942 been obliged to follow *Duncan's* case they have often expressed disquiet in doing so. The case of *Ellis* v. *Home Office* [62] may be mentioned as an example of this. Furthermore, the statements made by Viscount Kilmuir L.C. in 1956 and 1962, which we were invited to consider, show that the Government, being aware of complaints concerning the previous practice, decided to make the modifications of it which were announced in the two statements.

In my view, it should now be made clear that whenever an objection is made to the production of a relevant document it is for the court to decide whether or not to uphold the objection. The inherent power of the court must include a power to ask for a clarification or an amplification of an objection to production though the court will be careful not to impose a requirement which could only be met by divulging the very matters to which the objection related. The power of the court must also include a power to examine documents privately, a power, I think, which in practice should be sparingly exercised but one which could operate as a safeguard for the executive in cases where a court is inclined to make an order for production, though an objection is being pressed. I see no difference in principle between the consideration of what have been called the contents cases and the class cases. The principle which the courts will follow is that relevant documents normally liable to production will be withheld if the public interest requires that they should be withheld. In many cases it will be plain that documents are within a class of documents which by their very nature ought not to be disclosed. Indeed, in the majority of cases I apprehend that a decision as to an objection will present no difficulty. The cases of difficulty will be those in which it will appear that if there is non-disclosure some injustice may result and that if there is disclosure the public interest may to some extent be affected prejudicially. The courts can and will recognise that a view honestly put forward by a Minister as to the public interest will be based upon special knowledge and will be put forward by one who is charged with a special responsibility. . . . [pp. 970–971]

---

[61] [This is the only clear statement in *Conway* v. *Rimmer* to the effect that *Duncan* v. *Cammell Laird* would be overruled in the spirit of the Practice Direction (*ante,* 754).]
[62] [1953] 2 Q.B. 135.

LORD HODSON.

. . . The present case raises the question whether the time has come to reconsider that decision. Attention has been drawn to various considerations which have exercised the minds of the court since the decision was given and in particular your Lordships' attention was drawn to an answer given by the Lord Chancellor (Viscount Kilmuir) in answer to a question in this House which showed the difficulty and, furthermore, the undesirability of maintaining the rule in its full rigour. It was, inter alia, proposed that in some classes of documents, such as those concerned with claims for negligence against the Crown, privilege should in future not be claimed. Likewise, in cases where statements are made by witnesses to the police in civil cases it was proposed that these should be produced. These proposals have, as your Lordships understand, been accepted and followed.

It is in the case of documents for which protection is claimed on the ground of their class, irrespective of their contents, on what may be called the " candour " ground that the principal difficulty arises, for it is not to be disputed that there are classes of documents which from their very character ought to be withheld from production if protection is properly claimed on grounds of state. I have in mind those enumerated by Salmon L.J. in *In re Grosvenor Hotel, London (No. 2)* [63] such as Cabinet minutes, dispatches from ambassadors abroad and minutes of discussions between heads of departments. The expression " class," however, covers not only such documents which pass at a high level and which require absolute protection, but also those communications not readily distinguishable from those passing in the ordinary course of business conducted by commercial organisations and carrying only a qualified privilege.

The class of documents with which this appeal is concerned is not on the highest level from the point of view of the public interest, looked at as state documents, although in another aspect of the public interest, looked at as material upon which justice is required to be done, they may well be highly significant. They are documents in the possession or control of the respondent, Thomas Rimmer, a one-time superintendent of police in the Cheshire Constabulary, who is being sued in an action for malicious prosecution by the appellant who was at material times a probationary police constable in the Cheshire Constabulary. . . .

[pp. 973–974]

The principle to be applied in every case is that documents otherwise relevant and liable to production must not be produced if the public interest requires that they should be withheld. . . .

Their Lordships applied that test to the documents in the case which included the contract for the hull and machinery of the submarine *Thetis*, letters written before the disaster, which befell her, relating to the vessel's trim, reports as to the condition of the *Thetis* when raised, a large number of plans and specifications relating to various parts of the vessel and a notebook of the foreman painter employed by the respondents. They did not, however, analyse the documents in order to determine under which of the two heads (contents or class) they fell to be included and found it sufficient to lay down the law in the wide terms stated and apply it to the documents as a whole. In those

63 [1965] Ch. 1210, 1258–9.

circumstances I agree with the majority of the Court of Appeal in holding that the decision in *Duncan* v. *Cammell, Laird* was binding and conclusive.

Nevertheless, your Lordships are free to reconsider the matter if it is considered right so to do. Certainly several cases have arisen in recent years in which the courts have shown themselves repelled by the idea that all public departments' communications should be held back at the discretion of the Minister in whose hand the documents might be. One would have supposed that the qualified privilege which protects non-malicious communications in the ordinary case should be sufficient just as much where government departments are concerned as where the affairs of ordinary citizens are concerned under the control of business which may perhaps employ a vast number of people. . . .

[p. 976]

. . . In deciding whether *Duncan* v. *Cammell, Laird* is open to reconsideration it is worth remembering that the conclusion was reached under a misapprehension as to the corresponding law of Scotland. The Scottish cases show that although seldom exercised the residual power of the court to inspect and if necessary order production of documents is claimed. By a misapprehension, however, in *Duncan's* case the protection in Crown privilege cases in both countries was held to be absolute. This misapprehension no longer prevails since the decision of this House in *Glasgow Corporation* v. *Central Land Board.*[64]

The Attorney-General, while seeking to maintain the generality and width of the rule in *Duncan's* case, does however, concede that objection on behalf of the Crown to production of a document can be overridden if shown (a) not to have been taken in good faith; (b) to have been actuated by some irrelevant or improper consideration, for example, the production might expose a want of efficiency in the administration of a department or lay it open to claims for compensation; or (c) to have proceeded upon a false factual premise, for example, that a document belonged to a class to which it did not in truth belong. Once the concession is made, I find it difficult to see how the court could reach any conclusion on these matters without inspection of the document in question. This, indeed, is conceded by the Crown and goes a long way towards a concession that the ultimate control should be with the court. . . .

[pp. 977–978]

. . . The plans of warships, as in *Duncan's* case, and documents exemplified by Cabinet minutes are to be treated, I think, as cases to which Crown privilege can be properly applied as a class without the necessity of the documents being considered individually. The documents in this case, class documents though they be, are in a different category, seeking protection not as state documents of political or strategic importance but as requiring protection on the ground that "candour" must be ensured.[65] . . .

[p. 979]

LORD UPJOHN.

My Lords, there can be no doubt that the basic principle to be applied in cases where the Crown claims privilege from production of documents is to be found in the following passage in Lord Simon's speech in the case of *Duncan* v. *Cammell, Laird & Co. Ltd.* when he said:

[64] 1956 S.C.(H.L.) 1.   [65] [The speech omitted is that of Lord Pearce.]

"The principle to be applied in every case is that documents otherwise relevant and liable to production must not be produced if the public interest requires that they should be withheld. This test may be found to be satisfied either (a) by having regard to the contents of the particular document, or (b) by the fact that the document belongs to a class which, on grounds of public interest, must as a class be withheld from production." [66]

This case is concerned only with class documents, for privilege is claimed only on that ground in respect of four documents which are no more than reports on the progress of the appellant, a probationer constable, and in respect of one which is concerned with a report upon the appellant for submission to the Director of Public Prosecutions. The first question is whether the affidavit of the Home Secretary claiming privilege for these documents is final and conclusive and must be accepted as such by the courts as the majority of the Court of Appeal held, following Lord Simon's view which was summarised in the sentence:

"Although an objection validly taken to production, on the ground that this would be injurious to the public interest, is conclusive, it is important to remember that the decision ruling out such documents is the decision of the judge."

He then points out, however, that the judge must so rule.

My Lords, apart altogether from our recent liberation from some of the chains of precedent, which for my part I think should only be exercised rarely and sparingly, I do not think that the *Cammell, Laird* case governs this case for a number of reasons.

First, it is now quite clear that per incuriam the House misunderstood the law of Scotland as now explained and enunciated in *Glasgow Corporation* v. *Central Land Board.*[67] While the law of England and that of Scotland may differ in many respects it is really essential, in the interests of justice to Her Majesty's subjects in both parts of the United Kingdom, that the rules relating to Crown privilege should be the same. This factor alone entitled your Lordships to review the matter de novo.

Secondly, I do not think that the observations of Lord Simon were intended to bind or did bind the courts to reach the conclusion that in every case (save where honesty or bona fides were challenged) the affidavit of the Minister claiming privilege is conclusive, and I put this on two grounds. In the first place, although it was not so stated in express terms in Lord Simon's speech I am of opinion that the claim of privilege in that case was based and rightly based on a "contents" basis. The late Mr. A. V. Alexander (as he then was) based his claim at all events in part upon the advice of his technical advisers; at a time of total war when the very latest design of submarine founders on her trials the slightest escape to the public of the most innocent details may be a source of danger to the state; and it matters not that some details may have been disclosed at an earlier inquiry; the greater publicity of an action may afford enemy agents an opportunity they missed earlier. So I think Lord Simon's remarks were, in relation to class

[66] [1942] A.C. 624, 636.
[67] 1956 S.C.(H.L.) 1.

documents, strictly obiter. But in the second place, whether I am right or wrong in that, I do not think for one moment that Lord Simon had in mind a type of document, such as routine reports on a probationer constable, when he made his general observations on the law. I agree entirely with the cogent arguments advanced by my noble and learned friend, Lord Reid, in his speech, for thinking that Lord Simon never intended that the claim of the Minister should be conclusive in such cases; so on that ground, too, the documents in this case being so different from those in *Cammell, Laird,* I think it is open to your Lordships to review the matter.

Thirdly, I think there is a broader ground upon which your Lordships can re-examine this matter. The privilege which is claimed is, and I now quote again from the passage in Lord Simon's speech with which I started, on the ground that documents " liable to production must not be produced if the public interest requires that they should be withheld." . . . [pp. 989–991]

YOUNG v. BRISTOL AEROPLANE CO.

[1944] K.B. 718

LORD GREENE M.R. . . .

In considering the question whether or not this court is bound by its previous decisions and those of courts of co-ordinate jurisdiction, it is necessary to distinguish four classes of case. The first is that with which we are now concerned, namely, cases where this court finds itself confronted with one or more decisions of its own or of a court of co-ordinate jurisdiction which cover the question before it and there is no conflicting decisions of this court or of a court of co-ordinate jurisdiction. The second is where there is such a conflicting decision. The third is where this court comes to the conclusion that a previous decision, although not expressly overruled, cannot stand with a subsequent decision of the House of Lords. The fourth (a special case) is where this court comes to the conclusion that a previous decision was given per incuriam. In the second and third classes of case it is beyond question that the previous decision is open to examination. In the second class, the court is unquestionably entitled to choose between the two conflicting decisions. In the third class of case the court is merely giving effect to what it considers to have been a decision of the House of Lords by which it is bound. The fourth class requires more detailed examination and we will refer to it again later in this judgment. . . . [pp. 725–726]

Where the court has construed a statute or a rule having the force of a statute its decision stands on the same footing as any other decision on a question of law, but where the court is satisfied that an earlier decision was given in ignorance of the terms of a statute or a rule having the force of a statute the position is very different. It cannot, in our opinion, be right to say that in such a case the court is entitled to disregard the statutory provision and is bound to follow a decision of its own given when that provision was not present to its mind. Cases of this description are examples of decisions given per incuriam. We do not think that it would be right to say that there may not be other cases of decisions given per incuriam in which this court might properly consider itself entitled not to follow an earlier decision of its own. Such cases would obviously be of the rarest occurrence and must be dealt with in accordance with their special facts. Two classes of decisions per incuriam fall outside the scope of our inquiry, namely, those where the court has acted in ignorance of a previous decision of its own or of a court of co-ordinate jurisdiction which covers the case before it—in such a case a subsequent court must decide which of the two decisions it ought to follow; and those where it has acted in ignorance of a decision of the House of Lords which covers the point—in such a case a subsequent court is bound by the decision of the House of Lords.

On a careful examination of the whole matter we have come to the clear conclusion that this court is bound to follow previous decisions of its own [68] as well as those of courts of co-ordinate jurisdiction. The only exceptions to this rule (two of them apparent only) are those already mentioned which for convenience we here summarize: (1.) The court is entitled and bound to decide which of two conflicting decisions of its own it will follow. (2.) The court is bound to refuse to follow a decision of its own which, though not expressly overruled, cannot, in its opinion, stand with a decision of the House of Lords.[69] (3.) The court is not bound to follow a decision of its own if it is satisfied that the decision was given per incuriam.[70]   [pp. 729–730]

GALLIE v. LEE

[1969] 2 Ch. 17

LORD DENNING M.R.

. . . My brethren think that we are not at liberty to adopt this principle.[71] It is contrary, they say, to previous authorities in this court. I do not agree. There is no case against it save the *Carlisle* [72] case and that is inconsistent with many others. It can, therefore, be disregarded. But even if there were authorities against it, they are only to be found in this court, and are not in the House of Lords. We are, of course, bound by the decisions of the House, but I do not think we are bound by prior decisions of our own, or at any rate, not absolutely bound. We are not fettered as it was once thought. It was a self-imposed limitation: and we who imposed it can also remove it.[73] The House

---

68 [Although a full court has no more authority than an ordinary court, one is occasionally convened. See Blom-Cooper and Drewry (1971) 34 M.L.R. 364. Nor does it matter that the case was not fully argued previously: *Morelle Ltd.* v. *Wakeling* [1955] 2 Q.B. 379, on which see *Joscelyne* v. *Nissen* [1970] 2 W.L.R. 509, 520–521 *per* Russell L.J.]

69 [The Divisional Court has applied this doctrine in relation to previous decisions of the C.A.: *R.* v. *Northumberland Compensation Tribunal* [1951] 1 K.B. 711.]

70 [In *Broome* v. *Cassells* [1971] 2 Q.B. 354 this doctrine was extended to cover decisions of the House of Lords given *per incuriam*. *Cf.* Lord Diplock's statement that this only applies " to the right of an appellate court to decline to follow one of its own previous decisions " (*Cassells* v. *Broome*)].

71 [*viz.*, that signing a document having legal consequences without reading that document and relying on the word of another as to its class and contents did not found the defence of *non est factum* against a building society which had acted on the faith of the document being the deed of the signer. Russell and Salmon L.JJ. agreed that *non est factum* had not been made out, but for different reasons.]

72 [*i.e., Carlisle and Cumberland Banking Co.* v. *Bragg* [1911] 1 K.B. 489.]

73 [For this argument see *ante*, 707. But unlike the House of Lords, the Court of Appeal is not the final court of appeal and the Court of Appeal can only

of Lords have done it. So why should not we do likewise? We should be just as free, no more and no less, to depart from a prior precedent of our own, as in like case is the House of Lords or a judge of first instance. It is very, very rarely that we will go against a previous decision of our own, but if it is clearly shown to be erroneous, we should be able to put it right. . . .   [p. 37]

RUSSELL L.J.

. . . I add that I do not support the suggestion that this court is free to override its own decisions, now that the House of Lords has given itself ability to override its own decisions. I am a firm believer in a system by which citizens and their advisers can have as much certainty as possible in the ordering of their affairs. Litigation is an activity that does not markedly contribute to the happiness of mankind, though it is sometimes unavoidable. An abandonment of the principle that this court follows its own decisions on the law would I think lead to greater uncertainty and tend to produce more litigation. In the case of decisions of the House of Lords error, or what is later considered to be error, could only previously be corrected by statute: and the other demands on parliamentary time made this possibility so remote that the decision of the House of Lords not necessarily to be bound by a previous decision was justifiable at the expense of some loss of certainty. But the availability of the House of Lords to correct error in the Court of Appeal makes it in my view unnecessary for this court to depart from its existing discipline.[74] . . .   [pp. 41–42]

SALMON L.J.

. . . I am, however, convinced that so long as this court considers itself absolutely bound by its own decisions I have no power to adopt the Master of the Rolls' conclusions; I must accept the law as stated in the authorities to which I have referred in spite of the fact that it results too often in inconsistency, injustice, and an affront to common-sense. The dicta to the effect that this court is absolutely bound by its own decisions are very strong: see, for example *Young* v. *Bristol Aeroplane Co.* [1944] 1 K.B. 718; [1946] A.C. 163, 169; *Bonsor* v. *Musicians' Union* [1956] A.C. 104, but no stronger than those by virtue of which the House of Lords until recently treated itself as similarly bound by its own decisions. The point about the authority of this court has never been decided by the House of Lords. In the nature of things it is not a point that could ever come before the House for decision.[75] Nor does it depend upon any statutory or common law rule. This practice of ours apparently rests solely upon a concept of judicial comity laid down many years ago and automatically followed ever since: see *The Vera Cruz (No. 2)* (1884) 9 P.D. 96 *per* Lord Brett,

---

change its " practice " on precedent if the House of Lords allows it to do so, that is, does not overrule Court of Appeal decisions on the basis that the Court of Appeal decided the case otherwise than in accordance with a previous Court of Appeal decision.]

[74] [There also exists the so-called " leap-frog " appeal instituted in the Administration of Justice Act 1969 (see ss. 12–16) which opens the possibility of an appeal from a first instance court direct to the House of Lords in certain specified circumstances.]

[75] [*Cf.* the comment in note 73 *ante*, 764.]

at p. 98. Surely today judicial comity would be amply satisfied if we were to adopt the same principle in relation to our decisions as the House of Lords has recently laid down for itself by a pronouncement of the whole House. It may be that one day we shall make a similar pronouncement. I can see no valid reasons why we should not do so and many why we should. But that day is not yet. It is, I think, only by a pronouncement of the whole court that we could effectively alter a practice which is so deeply rooted. In the meantime I find myself reluctantly obliged to accept the old authorities, however much I disagree with them. My only consolation is that in spite of the present unsatisfactory state of this branch of the law, it enables us, on the facts of this case, to reach a decision which accords with reason and justice.[76]   [p. 49]

A. L. GOODHART

The Ratio Decidendi of a Case [77]

Having, as a first step, determined all the facts of the case as seen by the judge, it is then necessary to discover which of these facts he has found material for his judgment. This is far more difficult than the first step, for the judge may fail to label his facts. It is only the strong judge, one who is clear in his own mind as to the grounds for this decision,[78] who invariably says, " on facts *A* and *B* and on them alone I reach conclusion *X* ". Too often the cautious judge will include in his opinion facts which are not essential to his judgment, leaving it for future generations to determine whether or not these facts constitute a part of the *ratio decidendi* The following guides may, however, be followed in distinguishing between material and immaterial facts.

(1) As was stated above in discussing the principle of a case in which there is no opinion, the facts of person, time, place, kind, and amount are presumably immaterial. This is true to an even greater extent when there is an opinion, for if these facts are held to be material particular emphasis will naturally be placed upon them.

(2) All facts which the court specifically states are immaterial must be considered immaterial. In *People* v. *Vandewater* [79] the defendant, who was charged with maintaining a public nuisance, kept an illicit drinking place. There was proof that the house was actually disorderly as persons became intoxicated on the premises and left them in that condition. The majority of the New York Court of Appeals, speaking by Lehman, J., held that the fact that acts of annoyance and disturbance had occurred was immaterial. The learned judge said [80]:

---

[76] [*Gallie* v. *Lee* was affirmed *sub nom. Saunders* v. *Anglia Building Society* [1970] 3 All E.R. 961.]

[77] [From *Essays in Jurisprudence and the Common Law* (1931), p. 1 ; reprinted from (1930) 40 Yale L.J. 161.]

[78] It was Jessel, M.R., who said, " I may be wrong, but I never have any doubts ". An astounding example of an uncertain judgment is Lord Hatherley's opinion in *River Wear Commissioners* v. *Adamson* (1877), 2 App.Cas. 743, 752. Of this Atkin, L.J., said, in *The Mostyn*, [1927] P. 25, that he was unable to determine whether Lord Hatherley, " was concurring in the appeal being allowed, or the appeal being dismissed, or whether he was concurring in the opinion given by Lord Cairns ".

[79] 250 N.Y. 83.

[80] At p. 96. Italics mine.

It is the disorderly *character* of the illicit drinking place which constitutes the offense to the public decency. That offense arises from the nature of the acts habitually done upon the premises and the injury to the morals and health of the community which must naturally flow therefrom, apart from the annoyance or disturbance of those persons who might be in the neighbourhood.

This case strikingly illustrates the distinction between the view that a case is authority for a proposition based on all its facts, and the view that it is authority for a proposition based on those facts only which were seen by the court as material. If we adopt the first view, then the majority judgment is only a *dictum*, not binding in any future case in which the facts do not show actual disorder. Under the second view the court has specifically stated that the fact of disorder is immaterial. The case is, therefore, a binding precedent in all future cases in which either orderly or disorderly illicit drinking places are kept. The case can be analyzed as follows:

Facts of the case

Fact I.   *D* maintained an illicit drinking place.
Fact II.   This illicit place was noisy and disorderly.
Conclusion.   *D* is guilty of maintaining a nuisance.

Material facts as seen by the court

Fact I.   *D* maintained an illicit drinking place.
Conclusion.   *D* is guilty of maintaining a nuisance.

By specifically holding that fact II was immaterial, the court succeeded in creating a broad principle instead of a narrow one.

(3) All facts which the court impliedly treats as immaterial must be considered immaterial. The difficulty in these cases is to determine whether a court has or has not considered the fact immaterial. Evidence of this implication is found when the court, after having stated the facts generally, then proceeds to choose a smaller number of facts on which it bases its conclusion. The omitted facts are presumably held to be immaterial. In *Rylands* v. *Fletcher* [81] the defendant employed an independent contractor to make a reservoir on his land. Owing to the contractor's negligence in not filling up some disused mining shafts, the water escaped and flooded the plaintiff's mine. The defendant was held liable. Is it the principle of the case that a man who builds a reservoir on his land is liable for the negligence of an independent contractor? Why then is the case invariably cited as laying down the broader doctrine of "absolute liability"? The answer is found in the opinions. After stating the facts as above, the judges thereafter ignored the fact of the contractor's negligence, and based their conclusions on the fact that an artificial reservoir had been constructed. The negligence of the contractor was, therefore, impliedly held to be an immaterial fact. The case can be analyzed as follows:

Facts of the case

Fact I.   *D* had a reservoir built on his land.
Fact II.   The contractor who built it was negligent.
Fact III.   Water escaped and injured *P*.
Conclusion.   *D* is liable to *P*.

[81] (1868) L.R. 3 H.L. 330.

Material facts as seen by the court

Fact I.   *D* had a reservoir built on his land.

Fact III.   Water escaped and injured *P*.

Conclusion.   *D* is liable to *P*.

By the omission of fact II, the doctrine of "absolute liability" was established.

It is obvious from the above cases that it is essential to determine what facts have been held to be immaterial, for the principle of a case depends as much on exclusion as it does on inclusion. It is under these circumstances that the reasons given by the judge in his opinion, or his statement of the rule of law which he is following, are of peculiar importance, for they may furnish us with a guide for determining which facts he considered material and which immaterial. His reason may be incorrect and his statement of the law too wide, but they will indicate to us on what facts he reached his conclusion.   [pp. 15–18]

(4) All facts which are specifically stated to be material must be considered material. Such specific statements are usually found in cases in which the judges are afraid of laying down too broad a principle. Thus in *Heaven* v. *Pender*[82] the plaintiff, a workman employed to paint a ship, was injured owing to a defective staging supplied by the defendant dock owner to the shipowner. Brett, M.R., held that the defendant was liable on the ground that,[83]

> whenever one person is by circumstances placed in such a position with regard to another that every one of ordinary sense who did think would at once recognize that if he did not use ordinary care and skill in his own conduct with regard to those circumstances he would cause danger of injury to the person or property of the other, a duty arises to use ordinary care and skill to avoid such danger.

Cotton and Bowen, L.JJ., agreed with the Master of the Rolls that the defendant was liable, but the material facts on which they based their judgment were [84] that (*a*) the plaintiff was on the staging for business in which the dock owner was interested, and (*b*) he "must be considered as invited by the dock owner to use the dock and all appliances provided by the dock owner as incident to the use of the dock". The principle of the case cannot, therefore, be extended beyond the limitation of these material facts.

(5) If the opinion does not distinguish between material and immaterial facts, then all the facts set forth in the opinion must be considered material with the exception of those that on their face are immaterial. There is a presumption against wide principles of law, and the smaller the number of material facts in a case the wider will the principle be. Thus if a case like *Hambrook* v. *Stokes Bros.*,[85] in which a mother died owing to shock at seeing a motor accident which threatened her child, is decided on the fact that a bystander may recover for injury due to shock, we have a broad principle of law.[86] If the additional fact that the

---

[82] (1883) 11 Q.B.D. 503.

[83] At p. 509.

[84] At p. 515.

[85] [1925] 1 K.B. 141.

[86] See the judgment of Atkin, L.J., at p. 152.

bystander was a mother is held to be material we then get a narrow principle of law.[87] Therefore, unless a fact is expressly or impliedly held to be immaterial it must be considered material.

(6) Thus far we have been discussing the method of determining the principle of a case in which there is only a single opinion, or in which all the opinions are in agreement. How do we determine the principle of a case in which there are several opinions which agree as to the result but differ in the material facts on which they are based? In such an event the principle of the case is limited to the sum of all the facts held to be material by the various judges. A case involves facts A, B and C, and the defendant is held liable. The first judge finds that fact A is the only material fact, the second that B is material, the third that C is material. The principle of the case is, therefore, that on the material facts A, B and C the defendant is liable. If, however, two of the three judges had been in agreement that fact A was the only material one, and that the others were immaterial, then the case would be a precedent on this point, even though the third judge had held that facts B and C were the material ones. The method of determining the principle of a case in which there are several opinions is thus the same as that used when there is only one. Care must be taken by the student, however, to see that the material facts of each opinion are stated and analyzed accurately, for sometimes judges think that they are in agreement on the facts when they only concur in the result.[88]

Having established the material and the immaterial facts of the case as seen by the court, we can then proceed to state the principle of the case. It is found in the conclusion reached by the judges on the basis of the material facts and on the exclusion of the immaterial ones. In a certain case the court finds that facts A, B and C exist. It then excludes fact A as immaterial, and on facts B and C it reaches conclusion X. What is the *ratio decidendi* of this case? There are two principles: (*a*) in any future case in which the facts are A, B and C, the court must reach conclusion X, and (*b*) in any future case in which the facts are B and C the court must reach conclusion X. In the second case the absence of fact A does not affect the result, for fact A has been held to be immaterial. The court, therefore, creates a principle when it determines which are the material and which are the immaterial facts on which it bases its decision.

It follows that a conclusion based on a fact, the existence of which has not been determined by the court, cannot establish a principle. We then have what is called a *dictum*. If, therefore, a judge in the course of his opinion suggests a hypothetical fact, and then states what conclusion he would reach if that fact existed, he is not creating a principle. The difficulty which is sometimes found in determining whether a statement is a *dictum* or not, is due to uncertainty as to whether the judge is treating a fact as hypothetical or real. When a judge says, " In this case as the facts are so and so I reach conclusion X ", this is not a *dictum*, even though the judge has been incorrect in his statement of the facts. But if the judge says, " If the facts in this case were so and so then I

---

[87] See the judgment of Bankes, L.J., at p. 146.
[88] *Cf.* the various judgments in *Great Western Ry. Co.* v. *Owners of S.S. Mostyn* [1928] A.C. 57. See note in (1928) 44 L.Q.R. 138 on this point.

would reach conclusion X ", this is a *dictum*, even though the facts are as given. The second point frequently arises when a case involves two different sets of facts. Having determined the first set of facts and reached a conclusion on them, the judge may not desire to take up the time necessarily involved in determining the second set. Any views he may express as to the undetermined second set are therefore *dicta*. If, however, the judge does determine both sets, as he is at liberty to do, and reaches a conclusion on both, then the case creates two principles and neither is a *dictum*. Thus the famous case of *National Sailors' and Firemen's Union* v. *Reed* [89] in which Astbury, J., declared the General Strike of 1926 to be illegal, involved two sets of facts, and the learned judge reached a conclusion on each.[90] It is submitted that it is incorrect to say that either one of the conclusions involved a *dictum* because the one preceded the other or because the one was based on broad grounds and the other on narrow ones.[91] On the other hand, if in a case the judge holds that a certain fact prevents a cause of action from arising, then his further finding that there would have been a cause of action except for this fact is an *obiter dictum*. By excluding the preventive fact the situation becomes hypothetical, and the conclusion based on such hypothetical facts can only be a *dictum*.[92]

Having established the principle of a case, and excluded all *dicta*, the final step is to determine whether or not it is a binding precedent for some succeeding case in which the facts are prima facie similar. This involves a double analysis. We must first state the material facts in the precedent case and then attempt to find the material ones in the second one. If these are identical, then the first case is a binding precedent for the second, and the court must reach the same conclusion as it did in the first one. If the first case lacks any material fact or contains any additional ones not found in the second, then it is not a direct precedent.[93] Thus in *Nichols* v. *Marsland* [94] the material facts were similar to those in *Rylands* v. *Fletcher* [95] except for the additional fact that the water escaped owing to a violent storm. If the court had found that this addi-

---

[89] [1926] 1 Ch. 536.

[90] The first set of facts included the fact of the General Strike. The second set excluded the General Strike, but included the fact that the internal rules of the union were violated.

[91] For conflicting views on this point see note by a learned writer in (1926) 42 L.Q.R. 289, and also note in 42 L.Q.R. 296.

[92] In *Lynn* v. *Bamber* [1930] 2 K.B. 72, McCardie, J., held that unconcealed fraud was a good reply to a plea of the Statutes of Limitation. As, however, he found that there was no fraud in the case before him, it is submitted that his statement as to the Statutes of Limitation was a *dictum*. On this point see note in (1930) 46 L.Q.R. 261.

[93] It may, however, carry great weight as an analogy. Thus if it has been held in a case that a legatee who has murdered his testator cannot take under the will, this will be an analogy of some weight in a future case in which the legatee has committed manslaughter. It is important to note that when a case is used merely as an analogy, and not as a direct binding precedent, the reasoning of the court by which it reached its judgment carries greater weight than the conclusion itself. The second court, being free to reach its own conclusion, will only adopt the reasoning of the first court if it considers it to be correct and desirable. In such analogous precedents the *ratio decidendi* of the case can with some truth be described as the reason of the case.

[94] (1875) L.R. 10 Ex. 255.

[95] (1868) L.R. 3 H.L. 330.

tional fact was not a material one, then the rule in *Rylands* v. *Fletcher* would have applied. As it found, however, that it was a material one, it was able to reach a different conclusion.

Before summarizing the rules suggested above, two possible criticisms must be considered. It may be said that a doctrine which finds the principle of a case in its material facts leaves us with hardly any general legal principles, for facts are infinitely various. It is true that facts are infinitely various, but the material facts which are usually found in a particular legal relationship are strictly limited. Thus the fact that there must be consideration in a simple contract is a single material fact although the kinds of consideration are unlimited. Again, if *A* builds a reservoir on Blackacre and *B* builds one on Whiteacre, the owners, builders, reservoirs, and fields are different. But the material fact that a person has built a reservoir on his land is in each case the same. Of course a court can always avoid a precedent by finding that an additional fact is material, but if it does so without reason the result leads to confusion in the law. Such an argument assumes, moreover, that courts are disingenuous and arbitrary. Whatever may have been true in the past, it is clear that at the present day English courts do not attempt to circumvent the law in this way.

The second criticism can be stated as follows: If we are bound by the facts as seen by the judge, may not this enable him deliberately or by inadvertence to decide a case which was not before him by basing his decision upon facts stated by him to be real and material but actually non-existent? Can this conclusion in such a case be anything more than a *dictum*? Can a judge, by making a mistake, give himself authority to decide what is in effect a hypothetical case? The answer to this interesting question is that the whole doctrine of precedent is based on the theory that as a general rule judges do not make mistakes either of fact or of law. In an exceptional case a judge may in error base his conclusion on a non-existent fact, but it is better to suffer this mistake, which may prove of benefit to the law as a whole, however painful its results may have been to the individual litigant, than to throw doubt on every precedent on which our law is based.

CONCLUSION

The rules for finding the principle of a case can, therefore, be summarized as follows:

(1) The principle of a case is not found in the reasons given in the opinion.

(2) The principle is not found in the rule of law set forth in the opinion.

(3) The principle is not necessarily found by a consideration of all the ascertainable facts of the case, and the judge's decision.

(4) The principle of the case is found by taking account (*a*) of the facts treated by the judge as material, and (*b*) his decision as based on them.

(5) In finding the principle it is also necessary to establish what facts were held to be immaterial by the judge, for the principle may depend as much on exclusion as it does on inclusion. . . .   [pp. 20–25]

J. STONE

The Ratio of the Ratio Decidendi
(1959) [96]

The Term " Ratio Decidendi ": Distinction Between Descriptive and Prescriptive Senses

Should we not, in the first place, try scrupulously to respect the distinction between that use of the term *ratio decidendi* which describes the process of reasoning by which decision was reached (the " descriptive " *ratio decidendi*), and that which identifies and delimits *the* reasoning which a later court is bound to follow (the " prescriptive " or " binding " *ratio decidendi*)?

Descriptively the phrase imports merely an explanation of the court's reasoning to its conclusion, based on sociological, historical and even psychological inquiry. The finding from such an inquiry is true or untrue *as a matter of fact*; it could not be refuted merely by showing that logically the same decision could have been reached by different reasoning, or by showing that *as a matter of law* the actual reasoning was fallacious, unpersuasive or even downright improper and impermissible. This descriptive *ratio decidendi* may, of course, itself be sought at various levels; it may for instance be limited to the level of verbal behaviour of the judge, or it may seek to embrace the level of his total behaviour.[97] Prescriptively used, on the other hand, the phrase *ratio decidendi* refers to a normative judgment requiring us to choose a particular *ratio decidendi* as legally required to be drawn from the prior case, that is, as the binding *ratio decidendi*.

The relation between the ambits of the descriptive and prescriptive *rationes* is normally at least one of overlapping. The degree of overlapping, and how near it may approach coincidence, depend, *inter alia*, on which of the competing methods of discovering the prescriptive *ratio decidendi* is assumed to be correct.[98] The range of the prescriptive *ratio decidendi*, in particular, does not *of necessity* fall within that of the descriptive. For instance, in that version of the prescriptive *ratio* which stresses the proposition of law enunciated by the court as a basis of its holding, the prescriptive *ratio decidendi* would necessarily coincide

---

[96] [From 22 M.L.R. 597. Stone has returned to this subject a number of times. See, for example, *Legal System and Lawyers' Reasonings* (1964), Chap. 7 and (1969) 69 Colum.L.Rev. 1162, 1176–1182.]

[97] To avoid further complicating issues already too complex, and in order to give Professor Goodhart's theory its most favourable ground, I have consciously limited the later remarks here on the descriptive *ratio decidendi* to the former level, to motives of decision express or implicit through verbal behaviour, as distinct from the actual psychological motivation leading the court to decision. Cases may, of course, occur in which the reasons express or implicit in the court's judgment do not correspond with the actual motivations. Many American realists in their time proposed not only that description should normally proceed at the deeper level, but that increased knowledge of this level was so important and neglected that all efforts should be concentrated on it, and the search for the prescriptive *ratio decidendi* if necessary abandoned, or at least suspended.

[98] And, of course, on the level of description which is being attempted.

with or at least be included within the descriptive.[99] On the other hand, in a version (such as Professor Goodhart's) which rests on the relation between the "material facts" and the holding, and for which the court's enunciated propositions of law are relevant only insofar as they imply a view of what facts are "material," the position is different. Insofar as the later court, looking at the whole report of the precedent case, may select as "material" (in the precedent court's view) facts different from those which could be inferred to be so from that court's enounced propositions of law, the prescriptive *ratio* might turn out to differ from the descriptive.

The present distinction between descriptive and prescriptive *rationes* may clarify the difference between Professor Goodhart,[1] Mr. Simpson,[2] and Professor Montrose,[3] as to whether it can be useful or proper to use the term "*ratio decidendi*" to refer to the original court's actual reasoning in reaching its holding, without reference to the question whether that reasoning is binding in a later case. The present answer to this would be that no harm can come of this, provided that we are careful to indicate by some such adjective as "descriptive" or "actual," that one is not intending by the use of the phrase to say anything about *the binding force* of the reasons. A fuller analysis would then require us to add that this "descriptive" or "actual" *ratio* is, on one version of the prescriptive *ratio decidendi*, deemed to be binding insofar as it is a basis of the actual decision. (Beyond that it remains (also on that version) merely descriptive, or in common parlance *obiter*.)

Approaches to the Operation of the "System" of Stare Decisis

Related to the distinction between the descriptive *ratio decidendi* and prescriptive *ratio decidendi*, are two approaches to the behaviour of courts as this bears on the problem of the *ratio decidendi*. One approach is that of the observer who seeks to describe and explain *as a matter of fact* how present decisions are related to prior decisions. The other approach seeks to establish from the behaviour of courts themselves, perhaps supplemented by assumed first principles, the limits within which, *as a matter of law*, a prior decision prescribes a binding rule for later decisions. It seeks (to use Professor Goodhart's term) to establish a "system" by which we can test what ground of decision of an earlier case is legally binding on the court in a later case.

That the present writer's account of the working of precedent has been directed essentially to description and explanation is obvious. It is quite explicit from the beginning to the end of the relevant chapter. At the beginning it was asked:

> "What are the features of our system of precedent which can give an appearance of stability and continuity and nevertheless permit constant change to take place, new propositions to be established, old ones discarded in whole or in part, and permit

[99] This would be subject to only apparent qualification, for instance, insofar as the legal proposition enunciated is wider than necessary to base the holding on the instant facts.
[1] A. L. Goodhart, "The *Ratio Decidendi* of a Case" (1959) 22 M.L.R. at 121–122.
[2] A. W. B. Simpson, same title (1958) 21 M.L.R. 155–156.
[3] J. L. Montrose, same title (1957) 20 M.L.R. 587–588 [and in *Precedent and Other Essays* (1968), pp. 151–157].

all this to proceed seemingly on the basis of logical deduction from pre-existing premises." [4]

And, at the end of the chapter, it was said that the "main purpose" had been:

"to display the devices and techniques whereby English judges can live and work by the creative light of (what Holmes had called) 'good sense' (as opposed to logic), even while they render homage to the authoritative premiss and the syllogistic deduction. It was to display how they are able to promote legal flux under the very banner and in the very stronghold of *stare decisis*; how, in Holmes' words, 'knowing too much to sacrifice good sense to the syllogism,' they are able to present the growth of the law as 'logical in form,' even while they make the creative choice before which logic stops short." [5]

Which of these attitudes is adopted by a particular inquiry is generally a matter of taste, or direction of intellectual interest. But it may also involve much more than that. To engage for example on an inquiry concerning *the* method, or even *the best* method, of discovering from the report of a single case what is "THE *ratio decidendi*" of that case, may also be an intellectually impermissible activity, unless at least two assumptions can be made. One of these is that there is normally ONE *ratio decidendi*, AND ONE ONLY, which explains the holding on the facts, and is as such binding. The other is that such a *ratio decidendi*, assumed to exist, can be delimited from examination of the particular case itself. Professor Goodhart's paper of 1931 (originally published 1930), [6] both by its general thesis and by its detailed argument, indulges both of these assumptions. It is, indeed, a model of their indulgence.

Acceptability of the Underlying Assumptions of Professor Goodhart's View

It is believed that the assumptions just stated will not bear examination, and the reasons for this belief may here be expanded as follows.

If the *ratio* of a case is deemed to turn on the facts in relation to the holding, and nine facts (a)–(j) are to be found in the report, there may (so far as logical possibilities are concerned) be as many rival *rationes decidendi* as there are possible combinations of distinguishable facts in it. What is more, each of these "facts" is usually itself capable of being stated at various levels of generality, all of which embrace "the fact" in question in the precedent decision, but each of which may yield a different result in the different fact-situation of a later case. The range of "facts" of *Donoghue* v. *Stevenson*, standing alone, might be oversimplified into a list somewhat as follows, each fact being itself stated at alternative levels. [7]

---

4 J. Stone, *The Province of Function of Law* (1946), 168.
5 *Ibid.*, at 206.
6 In (1930) 40 Yale L.J. 161–183 [and *ante*, 766].
7 [This might be done with many other cases: see, for example, the approach adopted in *Conway* v. *Rimmer* to the material facts of *Duncan* v. *Cammell Laird, ante*, 755.]

(a) *Fact as to the Agent of Harm.* Dead snails, *or* any snails, *or* any noxious physical foreign body, *or* any noxious foreign element, physical or not, *or* any noxious element.

(b) *Fact as to Vehicle of Harm.* An opaque bottle of ginger beer, *or* an opaque bottle of beverage, *or* any bottle of beverage, *or* any container of commodities for human consumption, *or* any containers of any chattels for human use, *or* any chattel whatsoever, *or* any thing (including land or buildings).

(c) *Fact as to Defendant's Identity.* A manufacturer of goods nationally distributed through dispersed retailers, *or* any manufacturer, *or* any person working on the object for reward, *or* any person working on the object, *or* anyone dealing with the object.

(d) *Fact as to Potential Danger from Vehicle of Harm.* Object likely to become dangerous by negligence, *or* whether or not so.

(e) *Fact as to Injury to Plaintiff.* Physical personal injury, *or* nervous or physical personal injury, *or* any injury.

(f) *Fact as to Plaintiff's Identity.* A Scots widow, *or* a Scotswoman *or* a woman, *or* any adult, *or* any human being, *or* any legal person.

(g) *Fact as to Plaintiff's Relation to Vehicle of Harm.* Donee of purchaser, from retailer who bought directly from the defendant, *or* the purchaser from such retailer, *or* the purchaser from anyone, *or* any person related to such purchaser or other person, *or* any person into whose hands the object rightfully comes, *or* any person into whose hands it comes at all.

(h) *Fact as to Discoverability of Agent of Harm.* The noxious element being not discoverable by inspection of any intermediate party, *or* not so discoverable without destroying the saleability of the commodity, *or* not so discoverable by any such party who had a duty to inspect, *or* not so discoverable by any such party who could reasonably be expected *by the defendant* to inspect, *or* not discoverable by any such party who could reasonably be expected *by the court or a jury* to inspect.

(j) *Fact as to Time of Litigation.* The facts complained of were litigated in 1932, *or* any time before 1932, *or* after 1932, *or* at any time.

Let us first consider the question of " materiality " *apart from any view on that matter " explicitly " or " implicitly " manifest in the precedent court's opinion.* As to none of these facts (a)–(j), and as to none of the several alternative levels of statement of each of them, could it be said on the basis of the report of *Donoghue* v. *Stevenson* alone that it was on its face not " material " (in the logical sense) to the holding in that case. Even as to the time of litigation, as to which we are most tempted to say that this at least must be " immaterial " on the face of it, we must be careful to avoid a *petitio principii.* Are we really prepared to assert with dogmatism that *Donoghue* v. *Stevenson* should have been, and would in fact have been, so decided in 1800? If not, it follows that *logically, i.e.,* apart from any special indication that should be drawn from the precedent court's own attitude, the " *ratio* " of *Donoghue* v. *Stevenson* did not compel later courts to impose liability in any case where only some of the above possible " material " facts, and some levels of statement of them, were found. And another way of saying this is that (apart still from such special indication) a *ratio decidendi* drawn from a case by the "material facts" method can only be prescriptive or binding for a later case whose facts are "on all fours" *in every respect*. And since the *italicised* words must be taken seriously, this reduces the range of binding *ratio decidendi* to vanishing point. Outside this range, the question always is whether in the later court's view the presence in the instant case of *some* of the facts (a)–(j), at some of their alternative levels or generalised statement, is more relevant to its present decision, than is the absence of *the rest of them*. And this is not a question of the "materiality" of facts to the decision in the precedent case imposing itself on the later court. It is rather a question of the analogical relevance of the prior holding to the later case, requiring the later court to choose between possibilities presented by the precedent case.

At this point then, before we begin searching for the precedent court's assertion as to which facts and levels of statement of them are "material," it is correct to say that the questions: What single principle does a particular case establish? What is *the ratio decidendi* of this case as at the time of its decision? are strictly nonsensical. It can only be answered by saying that there is no such single principle or *ratio* that can in terms of the "material facts" test be binding in a later case.

Does it then overcome this difficulty to define "materiality" as Professor Goodhart in effect does, in terms of the precedent court's explicit or implicit assertion as to which of facts (a)–(j) are material? Or to insist that the question, What are "material facts" by which we determine the prescriptive *ratio* of a case? is always to be determined *according to the view of the precedent court*, and not according to the view of the later court or observer. (Indeed, in defending his position in 1959 [8] this distinction becomes almost its central bastion.) Yet there will often be the gravest doubt as to what facts the precedent court "explicitly or implicitly" "determined" to be material. There will often be inconsistent indications from what is expressed or implicit, even in a one judge court. Such inconsistencies as between the concurring judgments in appellate courts are notoriously also a constant and fruitful source of legal uncertainty and change. The more important the issue and the instance of appeal the more likely are there to be multiple judgments and therefore multiple versions of the *ratio decidendi* and this by any test. And there are other chronic sources of competing versions and indeterminacies later to be mentioned.

Professor Goodhart recognises some of these difficulties in distinguishing which of facts (a)–(j) are "material," and in particular that this would involve some guesswork on the part of later courts in applying his system. In his latest exposition he urges that they nevertheless do not affect his "system" since they are due to "the subject-matter itself, and not to the system which is applied to it." [9] On the most favourable understanding of this, it appears to mean that the difficulties spring from deficiencies in articulation of the precedent court or in the report, or other characteristics which are of a more or less "accidental" nature. Even to this it would have to be said that the "accident-proneness" in the subject-matter makes the difficulties serious and constant.

Yet these are not the most crucial difficulties with Professor Goodhart's system. The crucial ones arise rather from the several alternative levels of statement of each "material fact" of the precedent case, ranging from the full unique concreteness of that actual case, through a series of widening generalisations. In this series only the unique concreteness is *firmly* anchored to the precedent court's view that a given Fact A is "material"; and *ex hypothesi* that level of unique concreteness can scarcely figure as a part of the binding *ratio* for other cases. By the same token the reach of the *ratio*, even after each "material fact" seen by the original court is identified, will vary with the level of generalisation at which "the fact" is stated. How then is the "correct" level of statement of Fact A to be ascertained by the later court?

Is this question too to be referred back entirely to the "explicit" or "implicit" view of the precedent court, as to which is the "material" level of statement of each "material" fact? Are we to say that merely because the House in *Donoghue* v. *Stevenson* might have stated the material fact as to the agent and vehicle of harm in terms of bottles of beverage, this concludes one way or another a later case as to cartons of butter, or the wheels of automobiles? Is it reasonable to assume that courts using language appropriate to the case before them do, or could, address themselves in their choice of language to all the levels of generality at which each "material" fact (a)–(j) of the concrete case is capable of statement, not to speak of the possible combinations and variations of these facts, and the implications of all these for as yet unforseen future cases? Yet unless it is reasonable so to say it would reduce judgment in later cases to a kind of lottery (turning on the chance of words used) to say that the later holding is controlled by that level of generalised statement of the assumed "material fact" which is explicit in the precedent court's judgment. And to admit also that level which might be "implicit" in the former judgment would in most cases be merely to impute to the precedent court a choice of levels of generalised statement (and therefore of the reach of the *ratio* in the instant case) which must in reality be made by the instant later court.

If, on the other hand, Professor Goodhart's reference of the question of "materiality" back to the precedent court does not extend to the question, Which level of generalised statement of the "material fact" is determinative of the *ratio*? the *impasse* of his system would become, if possible, even clearer, because more patent. Each "material fact" of a case would then have to be recognised as capable of statement in an often numerous range of more or less generalised versions, the range of the *ratio* varying with each version. Since this is so the extraction of the *ratio decidendi* in the course of later judgment could never have the flavour of discovering the single correct *ratio decidendi* of the earlier case, by merely identifying *nunc pro tunc* the "facts" deemed "material" by the precedent court as at the instant of the precedent decision. And this is quite additional to the difficulties, already mentioned, of so identifying these "material facts."

We here approach the very core of the difference between Professor Goodhart and the present writer concerning "the *ratio decidendi* of a case." However it be as to the interesting ancillary points of debate between Professor Montrose and Mr. Simpson on matters collateral to this writer's position, both of them are agreed (and, it is believed, correctly) on two matters.[10] One is that Professor Goodhart's " system " of discovering the *ratio decidendi* neither *describes* adequately the actual process by which case law is built up, nor can it be the answer to the question, How do we discover " the *ratio decidendi* of a single case " ? They are also agreed, and correct in believing, that this writer shares their conclusions on these two matters. If there has been doubt on this it is hoped that the present restatement will dispel it. For this restatement is intended to spell out and supplement the main gist of the treatment in *The Province and Function of Law*. This is, that there is not (despite Professor Goodhart's theory) any one *ratio decidendi* which is necessary to explain a particular decision, and is discoverable from that decision. . . . [pp. 600–607]

Judicial Choices and the Ratio of the Ratio

It seems appropriate at this point to place the areas within which the exercise of judicial choice is compelled by the indeterminate nature of the *ratio decidendi*, along with other areas of such required judicial choice. Such a stocktaking, as it were, of the bearing of modern juristic thought on " the rule of *stare decisis*," may afford some at least of the answer to Lord Wright's question how the " perpetual process of change " in the common law (and above all its movement on appellate levels) is to be reconciled with " the rule of *stare decisis*." The main areas of judicial choice listed below, which thus call for recognition, will quickly be seen to occupy a number of the principal " control centres " in the operation of a system of precedent. A brief summation of each follows.

(a) Choices Unavoidably Arising from the Nature of Terms Used in Substantive Rules, or from Interrelations of Rules.

(b) Choices Unavoidably Arising from Competing Methods of Seeking " the *Ratio Decidendi* of a Case."

(c) Choices Unavoidably Arising from the Competing Versions of the *Ratio Decidendi* of a Particular Case, when the " Material Facts " Method is Applied even to a Single Judge Decision.

(d) Additional Choices Arising from the Competing Versions of the *Ratio Decidendi* of a Particular Case (by any Test) when Several Judgments are Given.

(e) The Multiplication of Available Choices Arising from the Interplay of the Above.

Choices unavoidably arising from the terms used in substantive rules and their interrelations: categories of illusory reference

The common law is at least as rich as any other in the use of terms which leave open for the court a substantial choice as to the result to be reached in a particular case. Some years ago it was sought to identify and illustrate the main kinds of categories, whether consisting of supposed distinctions, or of particular terms used in rules, principles, standards or conceptions, which allow freedom of choice to courts despite seeming to require a particular result to be reached. One is the

---

[10] See esp. A. W. B. Simpson, *op. cit.* (1958) 21 M.L.R. 159–160; J. L. Montrose, in (1957) 20 M.L.R. 587, 593–594.

category of meaningless reference, of which most examples resolve themselves into the legal distinction without the factual difference. Though
the court may seem to treat such a legal distinction as determinative
of the case, its decision can still obviously not be determined by it.
Another is the category of concealed multiple reference, where a single
verbal term represents a number of different though related legal notions,
each with a different set of legal consequences, and where the courts,
operating under the appearance of a single rule, can still exercise freedom to reach the results they think appropriate by shifting from one
legal notion to the other.

Even more ubiquitous and important, throughout the legal system
and its operation, are the legal categories of competing reference, and
the single category with competing versions of reference. No source
of litigation on matters of law is more central on the appellate level
than the availability of alternative starting points for logical arguments,
both of which converge in their conclusions on the instant facts, to make
available opposite conclusions. When this occurs, apart from questions
of hierarchy of authority, the court is not only free to choose between the
alternatives unembarrassed by legal compulsion; it is obliged to do so.
Nor is even the circuitous argument without its importance in a going
system of law, though the legal category of circuitous reference (as
might be expected from the sophistication of lawyers) usually has its
circuity concealed. Some theories of quasi-contractual recovery and of
frustration of contract, which have had their influence, are examples.
Nor should it be necessary at this stage to do more than recall the wide
ramifications, throughout the common law, of categories of indeterminate
reference, such as that of reasonableness or fairness, in allowing courts
to reach variable conclusions in the particular case, within a wide
range of legal possibilities. This type of legal category is particularly
illuminating since its effect is openly to invite the court to inject into
the living body of the older law insights arising from the court's knowledge of contemporary social relations and the contemporary environment.
But the fact that the invitation is here openly given, should not prevent
us from seeing that this injection also takes place within the areas of
required judicial choice which the other types of illusory reference also
provide.[11]

Choices unavoidably arising from competing methods of ascertaining the supposed ratio decidendi of a case

It may be, as Professor Goodhart has again argued so earnestly,
that his own purported method for finding the *ratio decidendi*, namely
" to find the material facts as seen by the judge and his conclusion
based on them," [12] may often yield different results from other methods
(variously described) which focus on " the reasons given for decisions "
by judges, or on the rule of law " enunciated " by the court.[13] Indeed, it

[11] See, for fuller treatment, J. Stone, *The Province and Function of Law* (1946),
c. 7 [see now *Legal System and Lawyers' Reasonings* (1964) ch. 7]. For an
attempt to represent the logical structure of the fallacies of legal reasoning,
discussed in that chapter, by use of symbolic logic, see I. Tammelo, "Sketch
for a Symbolic Juristic Logic " (1956) 8 *Journal of Legal Education*, 277, at
300–302. See also U. Klug, *Juristische Logik* (2nd ed., 1958), 144.
[12] *Ibid.*, at 119.
[13] *Ibid.*, at 118.

seems to have been a main point of his original article,[14] as well as of the issue he has currently taken with Mr. Simpson, that the different tests may well yield different *rationes* and therefore opposed results in later cases.

Insofar as this main point was accepted,[15] we would then be confronted with the indubitable fact that British courts continue, more than a generation after the "correct method" was presented to them, to use also, more or less cogently, the other "methods" which are liable to produce other results. It was indeed precisely the neglect even of any attempt to apply the Professor Goodhart's "material facts" test by the Court of Appeal of Northern Ireland[16] in relation to the House of Lords case of *Geo. Wimpey & Co., Ltd.* v. *B.O.A.C.*,[17] that led Professor Montrose to write the stimulating article which initiated the present exchanges. Whatever weight be attached to Professor Goodhart's view that "most English courts" follow "the method" to which he is seeking to give a "guide," it seems clear both that judicial practice does not consistently do so, and that no rule of law compels them to do so. It follows that insofar as different methods are thought to be capable of yielding different *rationes*, there is here one constantly important source of judicial choices at the very heart of the notion of *stare decisis*. And this would be additional to the choices which (in the present view) necessarily and in any case arises from the competing versions of "the material facts" of any particular case, considered under the next head.

Choices unavoidably arising from the competing versions of the ratio decidendi of a particular case

Additional to the areas of choice just examined, and even more important, are those which arise for any court which may seriously attempt to rely wholly on Professor Goodhart's test of "the material facts as seen by the judge and his conclusion based on them," in seeking the *ratio decidendi* of a previous case. It but rarely if ever occurs that the previous decision has explicitly stated: "Out of the facts (a)–(j) appearing in this case the material facts as I see them solely basing my conclusion are A, B and C." Yet unless it does this (at least

---

14 Repr. in *Essays in Jurisprudence and the Common Law* (1931), 1–26.
15 Mr. Simpson points out that the court's application of the enunciated proposition of law in the instant case implies a holding as to what are "the material facts," and thus amounts in the end to the same test as Professor Goodhart's. If the latter be taken on its own claims, *i.e.*, as yielding one single *ratio* from within the precedent case, Professor Goodhart might perhaps seem correct in insisting that "the material facts" as he would find them in the report as a whole, may not be the same as might be drawn from the court's application of the enunciated proposition of law. This would arise, in the present view, because of the different available levels of statement of each particular "material fact," because the notion "fact" itself is a notion of multiple versions. (See *supra*, pp. 603–604.) Merely because the precedent enunciated proposition of law referred to snails in bottles would not prevent a later court, operating on the "material facts" test, from holding that the "material fact" did not concern snails or bottles as such, but only as examples of a wider range of noxious agents and vehicles embracing these.

Yet, since the multiple versions of each "fact" arising from different levels of statement also prevent Professor Goodhart's test from yielding any single *ratio* (see *supra*, pp. 605–606), this clarification seems also to boomerang on Professor Goodhart's own positions, leaving the particular controversy rather in the air.
16 In *Walsh* v. *Curry* [1955] N.I. 112.   17 [1955] A.C. 169.

in effect) there is no logically valid method whereby a later court, looking only at that single case, can decide with certainty that the facts A, B and C are "material," while facts D–J are not. For, in mere logic (as has been seen) it is possible to draw as many general propositions from a given decision as there are possible combinations of distinguishable facts in it. But merely looking at the facts it is impossible *logically* to say which are to be taken as the basis for the *ratio decidendi*. The question—What single principle does a particular case establish? has for these reasons been said (and correctly so) to be "strictly non-sensical, that is, inherently incapable of being answered." [18]

Moreover, as has also been seen, the *ratio decidendi* to be drawn by the later court on this "material facts" test would have still a greater number of competing versions, by virtue of the truth that each "fact" itself can be stated at different levels of generality, ranging from a supposed "snail in an opaque bottle" to "a noxious agent." The guess-work component involved in most cases in separating out the "material" from the other facts, would be vastly compounded by further guesswork concerning each of the facts guessed to be "material." I mean by "further guesswork," guesswork as to the *level of generality at which each of these facts was "material."* For many such levels of statement will equally embrace the fact appearing in the report; but the breadth of the *ratio decidendi* would have to be dependent on the level of generality of meaning which the later court thinks the precedent court "explicitly or implicitly" had its eye on.[19]

Choices unavoidably arising from multiplicity of judgments in many appellate cases

The articles of Professors Paton and Sawer,[20] and more recently of Professor Montrose,[21] have well stressed the problematical impact of the role of concurring or dissenting judgments on any simple theory of how to discover "the *ratio decidendi* of a case." It may still be important to bring out again the fuller context of these important contributions. The duties of later judicial choice here arising are a special and most important area of the operation of the single legal category ("the assumed *ratio decidendi* of the case") with several, and possibly numerous, competing versions, none of them authoritative, all of them more or less persuasive.

What is so important to observe is that the *ratio* with the several competing versions, far from being marginal in the system of *stare decisis*, is one of its main products. The structure and *modus operandi* of our courts, especially at the appellate level where points of law which are under stress come to be reviewed, seem to be geared so as to increase the range of competing versions available in rough proportion to the importance of the point of law. The large discretion left to a single judge for discussion of his reasons, and for *obiter dicta*, the separate opinions habitually given by the members of appellate courts and of the House of Lords, whether concurring or dissenting, may all be

[18] *Cf. The Province and Function of Law* (1946), 187.
[19] See *supra*, pp. 603 *et seq.*, for fuller demonstration of these positions.
[20] G. W. Paton and G. Sawer, "*Ratio Decidendi* and *Obiter Dictum*" (1947) 63 L.Q.R. 461.
[21] J. L. Montrose, "*Ratio Decidendi* and the House of Lords" (1957) 20 M.L.R. 124.

productive of numerous versions of the legal category under examination. Even where all the decisions concur for the instant facts, the differing versions are liable to be brought into bitter competition by the slightly different state of facts of a future case. It is essentially from this feature of House of Lords decisions that there derives its wide freedom of action, despite the rule that it is bound by its prior decisions.[22] For since no sanctity attaches to one set of concurring reasons as against another, one may be preferred to another, or even used merely to neutralise it, leaving the field clear. This technique of distinguishing is often regarded as in the nature of an evasion of the system of precedent. It is respectfully submitted that, on the contrary, it affords a deep insight into its essential nature. "Competing versions" of a legal category are a normal feature of the authoritative materials; and wherever they exist, a set of facts will sooner or later arise which stands between the competing versions, and can only be dealt with by a fresh creative decision. The system of separate speeches merely sets this aspect into relief.[23]

The vast further multiplication of available choices arising from the interplay of the above

Each area of required judicial choice arising in the above several ways imports room for action of a later court uncoerced by a supposed single *ratio decidendi* of the earlier case. Each such area may later present itself in a particular case. And while all of them may not necessarily be present in every important appellate case, more than one of them may be, and indeed, often are, present together. When this occurs the effect of the interaction of the two areas will be to increase the area of judicial choice, not merely in arithmetical but in geometrical proportions, by dint of the range of combinations and variations of the series of choices available in each area.

The duty of choice in the interpretation of a precedent containing in its language a "category of illusory reference" (as above described) will be further expanded if later courts resort to competing versions of the method of determining its *ratio*. And even if later courts all choose one method of determining its *ratio*, the choices might still be greatly expanded because the later courts, despite their similarity of method, still reach (as we have seen they may) competing versions of the *ratio decidendi* of that particular precedent. And, of course, there will often be superadded to such situations, especially where the precedent is a leading case decided at a high appellate level, the range of choices and of further combinations and variations of them, arising from varied rules "enunciated," or "material facts" explicitly or implicitly found, as a basis of the respective decisions in a multiplicity of appellate judgments in the single case. [pp. 610–615]

22 [See now *ante*, 705.]
23 *Cf. The Province and Function of Law* (1946), 179–181. [In *Saunders* v. *Anglia Building Society* [1970] 3 All E.R. 961, Lord Reid referred to the dangers of only one speech in the House of Lords: "Then statements in it have often tended to be treated as definitions and it is not the function of a court . . . to frame definitions" (p. 964). See also similar statements to this effect in *British Railways Board* v. *Herrington* [1972] 1 All E.R. 749, 761 (Lord Morris), 769–770 (Lord Wilberforce) and in *Cassells* v. *Broome* [1972] 1 All E.R. 801 *per* Lords Reid and Hailsham. It may be that the single judgment technique of civilian countries hampers the flexible development of the law in those countries.]

J. AUSTIN

Lectures on Jurisprudence

(ed. Campbell)

Judge-made Law [24]

. . I must here observe that I am not objecting to Lord Mansfield for assuming the office of a legislator. I by no means disapprove of what Mr. Bentham has chosen to call by the disrespectful, and therefore, as I conceive, injudicious, name of judge-made law. For I consider it injudicious to call by any name indicative of disrespect what appears to me highly beneficial and even absolutely necessary. I cannot understand how any person who has considered the subject can suppose that society could possibly have gone on if judges had not legislated, or that there is any danger whatever in allowing them that power which they have in fact exercised, to make up for the negligence or the incapacity of the avowed legislator. That part of the law of every country which was made by judges has been far better made than that part which consists of statutes enacted by the legislature. Notwithstanding my great admiration for Mr. Bentham, I cannot but think that, instead of blaming judges for having legislated, he should blame them for the timid, narrow, and piecemeal manner in which they have legislated, and for legislating under cover of vague and indeterminate phrases, such as Lord Mansfield employed in the above example, and which would be censurable in any legislator.[25]   [pp. 218–219]

The judiciary law made by the tribunals, is, in effect, the joint product of the legal profession, or rather of the most experienced and most skilful part of it: the joint product of the tribunals themselves, and of the private lawyers who by their cunning in the law have gotten the ear of the judicial legislators. In the somewhat disrespectful language of Mr. Bentham, it is not the product of judge only, but it is the joint product of Judge and Co. So great is the influence of the general opinion of the profession, that it frequently forces upon the Courts the adoption of a rule of law, by a sort of moral necessity. When the illations or anticipations of lawyers as to what the Courts would probably decide if the case came before them, has been often acted upon, so many interests are adjusted to it, that the Courts are compelled to make it law. What a howl would be set up (and not unjustly) if the Courts were to disregard the established practice of conveyancers; although, until sanctioned by judicial decisions, it is not strictly law. Being constantly acted upon, and engaging a vast variety of incidents in its favour, it performs the functions of a law, and will probably become law as the particular cases arise. . . .

Independently of the checks which I have just mentioned, judges are

[24] [*Cf. ante*, 176.]

[25] [" In this country where the rules of judge-made law hold a place of almost paramount importance in our legal system, it can hardly be said that Parliament is the author of those rules. . . . In truth, Parliament has no effective power of preventing their being made, and to alter them is a task which often baffles the patience and skill of those who can best command Parliamentary support." (See *Student's Austin's Jurisprudence* (1909), ed. R. Campbell, at p. 99, a passage omitted in the longer work.)]

naturally determined to abide by old rules, or to form new ones, by consequence from, or analogy to, the old.

They are naturally determined by two causes.

1. A regard for the interests and expectations which have grown up under established rules: or under consequences and analogies deducible from them.

2. A perception of consequence and analogy: which determines the understanding, independently of any other consideration.

The truth is, that too great a respect for established rules, and too great a regard for consequence and analogy, has generally been shewn by the authors of judiciary law. Where the introduction of a new rule would interfere with interests and expectations which have grown out of established ones, it is clearly incumbent on the Judge *stare decisis*; since it is not in his power to indemnify the injured parties. But it is much to be regretted that Judges of capacity, experience and weight, have not seized every opportunity of introducing a new rule (a rule beneficial for the future), wherever its introduction would have no such effect. This is the reproach I should be inclined to make against Lord Eldon.

A striking example of this backwardness of Judges to innovate, is to be found in the origin of the distinction between law and equity; which arose because the Judges of the Common Law Courts would not do what they ought to have done, namely to model their rules of law and of procedure to the growing exigencies of society, instead of stupidly and sulkily adhering to the old and barbarous usages. Equity, when it arose, has remained equally barbarous from the same cause: the rule *aequitas sequitur legem* has been too much regarded; a rule which, if followed literally, would leave nothing for the Courts of Equity to perform.

Owing to the causes to which I now have adverted, and to others which I pass in silence, there is more of stability and coherency in judiciary law, than might, at the first blush, be imagined. [pp. 644–647]

CARDOZO

Nature of the Judicial Process

The Method of Philosophy

The work of deciding cases goes on every day in hundreds of courts throughout the land. Any judge, one might suppose, would find it easy to describe the process which he had followed a thousand times and more. Nothing could be farther from the truth. Let some intelligent layman ask him to explain: he will not go very far before taking refuge in the excuse that the language of craftsmen is unintelligible to those untutored in the craft. Such an excuse may cover with a semblance of respectability an otherwise ignominious retreat. It will hardly serve to still the pricks of curiosity and conscience. In moments of introspection, when there is no longer a necessity of putting off with a show of wisdom the uninitiated interlocutor, the troublesome problem will recur, and press for a solution. What is it that I do when I decide a case? To what sources of information do I appeal for guidance? In what proportions do I permit them to contribute to the result? In what proportions ought they to contribute? If a precedent is applicable, when do I refuse to follow it? If no precedent is applicable, how do I reach the rule that will make a precedent for the future? If I am seeking logical consistency,[26] the symmetry of the legal structure, how far shall I seek it? At what point shall the quest be halted by some discrepant custom, by some consideration of the social welfare, by my own or the common standards of justice and morals? Into that strange compound which is brewed daily in the cauldron of the courts, all these ingredients enter in varying proportions. I am not concerned to inquire whether judges ought to be allowed to brew such a compound at all. I take judge-made law as one of the existing realities of life. There before us, is the brew. Not a judge on the bench but has had a hand in the making. The elements have not come together by chance. *Some* principle, however unavowed and inarticulate and subconscious, has regulated the infusion. It may not have been the same principle for all judges at any time, nor the same principle for any judge at all times. But a choice there has been, not a submission to the decree of Fate; and the considerations and motives determining the choice, even if often obscure, do not utterly resist analysis. In such attempt at analysis as I shall make, there will be need to distinguish between the conscious and the subconscious. I do not mean that even those considerations and motives which I shall class under the first head are always in consciousness distinctly, so that they will be recognized and named at sight. Not infrequently they hover near the surface. They may, however, with comparative readiness be isolated and tagged and when thus labeled, are quickly acknowledged as guiding principles of conduct. More subtle are the forces so far beneath the surface that they cannot reasonably be classified as other than subconscious. It is often through these subconscious forces that judges are kept consistent with themselves, and inconsistent with one another. We are reminded by William James in a telling page of his lectures on Pragmatism that every one of us has in truth an underlying philosophy of life, even those of us to whom the names and the notions of philosophy are unknown or anathema. There is in each of us a stream of tendency, whether you choose to call it philosophy or not, which gives coherence and direction to thought and action. Judges cannot escape that current any more than other mortals. . . . [pp. 9–12]

. . . I have put first among the principles of selection to guide our choice of paths, the rule of analogy or the method of philosophy. In putting it first, I do not mean to rate it as most important. On the contrary, it is often sacrificed to others. I have put it first because it has, I think, a certain presumption in its favour. Give a mass of particulars, a congeries of judgments on related topics, the principle that unifies and rationalizes them has a tendency, and a legitimate one, to project and extend itself to new cases within the limits of its capacity to unify and rationalize. It has the primacy that comes from natural and orderly and logical succession. Homage is due to it over every competing principle that is unable by appeal to history or tradition or policy or justice to make out a better right. All sorts of deflecting forces may appear to contest its sway and absorb its power. At least, it is the heir presumptive. A pretender to the title will have to fight his way. [pp. 31–32]

[26] [Logic is here used as equivalent to argument by analogy; *cf. ante*, 733, *post*, 810.]

. . . Example, if not better than precept, may at least prove to be easier. We may get some sense of the class of questions to which a method is adapted when we have studied the class of questions to which it has been applied. Let me give some haphazard illustrations of conclusions adopted by our law through the development of legal conceptions to logical conclusions.[27] A agrees to sell a chattel to B. Before title passes, the chattel is destroyed. The loss falls on the seller who has sued at law for the price. A agrees to sell a house and lot. Before title passes, the house is destroyed. The seller sues in equity for specific performance. The loss falls upon the buyer. That is probably the prevailing view, though its wisdom has been sharply criticized. These variant conclusions are not dictated by variant considerations of policy or justice. They are projections of a principle to its logical outcome, or the outcome supposed to be logical. Equity treats that as done which ought to be done. Contracts for the sale of land, unlike most contracts for the sale of chattels, are within the jurisdiction of equity. The vendee is in equity the owner from the beginning. Therefore, the burdens as well as the benefits of ownership shall be his. Let me take as another illustration of my meaning the cases which define the rights of assignees of choses in action. In the discussion of these cases, you will find much conflict of opinion about fundamental conceptions. Some tell us that the assignee has a legal ownership. Others say that his right is purely equitable. Given, however, the fundamental conception, all agree in deducing its consequences by methods in which the preponderating element is the method of philosophy. We may find kindred illustrations in the law of trusts and contracts and in many other fields. It would be wearisome to accumulate them. . . .   [pp. 38–40]

The Methods of History, Tradition and Sociology

The method of philosophy comes in competition, however, with other tendencies which find their outlet in other methods. One of these is the historical method, or the method of evolution. The tendency of a principle to expand itself to the limit of its logic may be counteracted by the tendency to confine itself within the limits of its history. I do not mean that even then the two methods are always in opposition. A classification which treats them as distinct is, doubtless, subject to the reproach that it involves a certain overlapping of the lines and principles of division. Very often, the effect of history is to make the path of logic clear. Growth may be logical whether it is shaped by the principle of consistency with the past or by that of consistency with some pre-established norm, some general conception, " some in-dwelling, and creative principle." [28] The directive force of the precedent may be found either in the events that made it what it is, or in some principle which

---

27 [This approach is sometimes called " the jurisprudence of concepts." *Cf.* the problem of liability for injury inflicted negligently on a child while still *in utero*. " Logic " might suggest that no duty can be owed to a " non-existent " person, but see *Montreal Tramways* v. *Leveille* [1933] 4 D.L.R. 337; *Smith* v. *Brennan*, 31 N.J. 353 (1960). For French position see *Minister of Education* v. *Dame Saulzc*, The Review (I.C.J.), March, 1969, pp. 43–45. In recent English cases doubt over establishing the duty of care has led judges to sanction settlements out of court. See *S.* v. *Distillers Co.* [1970] 1 W.L.R. 114.]

28 Bryce, *Studies in History and Jurisprudence*, II, p. 609.

enables us to say of it that it is what it ought to be. Development may involve either an investigation of origins or an effort of pure reason. Both methods have their logic. For the moment, however, it will be convenient to identify the method of history with the one, and to confine the method of logic or philosophy to the other. Some conceptions of the law owe their existing form almost exclusively to history. They are not to be understood except as historical growths. In the development of such principles, history is likely to predominate over logic or pure reason. Other conceptions, though they have, of course, a history, have taken form and shape to a larger extent under the influence of reason or of comparative jurisprudence. They are part of the *jus gentium*. In the development of such principles logic is likely to predominate over history. An illustration is the conception of juristic or corporate personality with the long train of consequences which that conception has engendered. . . . [pp. 51–53]

. . . If history and philosophy do not serve to fix the direction of a principle, custom may step in. [p. 58]

. . . It is, however, not so much in the making of new rules as in the application of old ones that the creative energy of custom most often manifests itself today. General standards of right and duty are established. Caution must determine whether there has been adherence or departure. My partner has the powers that are usual in the trade. They may be so well known that the courts will notice them judicially. Such for illustration is the power of a member of a trading firm to make or indorse negotiable paper in the course of the firm's business. They may be such that the court will require evidence of their existence. The master in the discharge of his duty to protect the servant against harm must exercise the degree of care that is commonly exercised in like circumstance by men of ordinary prudence. The triers of the facts in determining whether that standard has been attained, must consult the habits of life, the everyday beliefs and practices, of the men and women about them. Innumerable, also, are the cases where the course of dealing to be followed is defined by the customs, or, more properly speaking, the usages of a particular trade or market or profession. The constant assumption runs throughout the law that the natural and spontaneous evolutions of habit fix the limits of right and wrong. A slight extension of custom identifies it with customary morality, the prevailing standard of right conduct, the *mores* of the time. This is the point of contact between the method of tradition and the method of sociology. They have their roots in the same soil. Each method maintains the interaction between conduct and order, between life and law. Life casts the moulds of conduct, which will some day become fixed as law. Law preserves the moulds, which have taken form and shape from life. . . . [pp. 62–64]

. . . From history and philosophy and custom, we pass, therefore, to the force which in our day and generation is becoming the greatest of them all, the power of social justice which finds its outlet and expression in the method of sociology.

The final cause of law is the welfare of society. The rule that misses its aim cannot permanently justify its existence. " Ethical considerations can no more be excluded from the administration of justice which is the end and purpose of all civil laws than one can exclude the vital air from

his room and live." [29] Logic and history and custom have their place.
We will shape the law to conform to them when we may; but only within
bounds. The end which the law serves will dominate them all. There is
an old legend that on one occasion God prayed, and his prayer was " Be
it my will that my justice be ruled by my mercy." That is a prayer
which we all need to utter at times when the demon of formalism tempts
the intellect with the lure of scientific order. I do not mean, of course,
that judges are commissioned to set aside existing rules at pleasure in
favor of any other set of rules which they may hold to be expedient or wise. I mean that when they are called upon to say how far
existing rules are to be extended or restricted, they must let the welfare
of society fix the path, its direction and its distance. We are not to forget,
said Sir George Jessel, in an often quoted judgment, that there is this
paramount public policy, that we are not lightly to interfere with freedom
of contract.[30] So in this field, there may be a paramount public policy,
one that will prevail over temporary inconvenience or occasional hardship,
not lightly to sacrifice certainty and uniformity and order and coherence.
All these elements must be considered. They are to be given such weight
as sound judgment dictates. They are constituents of that social welfare
which it is our business to discover. In a given instance we may find
that they are constituents of preponderating value. In others, we may
find that their value is subordinate. We must appraise them as best we
can. . . .   [pp. 65–67]

    . . . Social welfare is a broad term. I use it to cover many concepts
more or less allied. It may mean what is commonly spoken of as public
policy, the good of the collective body. In such cases, its demands are
often those of mere expediency or prudence. It may mean on the other
hand the social gain that is wrought by adherence to the standards of
right conduct, which find expression in the *mores* of the community.
In such cases, its demands are those of religion or of ethics or of the
social sense of justice, whether formulated in creed or system, or immanent in the common mind. One does not readily find a single term to
cover these and kindred aims which shade off into one another by imperceptible gradations. Perhaps we might fall back with Kohler and
Brutt and Berolzheimer on the indefinable, but comprehensive something
known as Kultur if recent history had not discredited it and threatened
odium for those that use it. I have chosen in its stead a term which, if
not precise enough for the philosopher, will at least be found sufficiently
definite and inclusive to suit the purposes of the judge. . . .[31]
                                                              [pp. 71–73]

---

[29] Dillon, *Law and Jurisprudence of England and America*, p. 18.
[30] *Printing etc. Registering Co.* v. *Sampson* (1875) L.R. 19 Eq., 462, 465.
[31] [The extent to which moral, social and economic factors and policy considera-
    tions are operative in judicial decisions is becoming increasingly apparent in many
    of the recent decisions of the House of Lords. Reference has already been made
    to the striking decision in *Shaw* v. *Director of Public Prosecutions* (see *ante*,
    69), and in *Overseas Tankship* v. *Morts Dock* [1961] A.C. 388 much stress
    was laid upon the alleged injustice of the earlier *Re Polemis* rule, which was not
    followed. Lord Simonds said that, " It does not seem consonant with current
    ideas of justice or morality that, for an act of negligence, however slight or
    venial, which results in some trivial or foreseeable damage, the actor should be
    liable for all consequences however unforeseeable and however grave, so long
    as they can be said to be ' direct '." [1961] A.C. at p. 422.
        And who can doubt the strong policy element in such recent decisions as

GLANVILLE WILLIAMS

Language and the Law [32]

. . . The opinion is steadily growing that semantics is an important prolegomenon to the study of philosophy and of the so-called 'inexact' sciences, such as psychology and the social sciences. In the past philosophers have tended to mistake the structure of discourse for the structure of the universe, and a training in semantics helps to prevent this error. In psychology and the social sciences it is coming to be recognized that one of the greatest difficulties is the difficulty of statement, and that many disputes are due to the imperfections of language. Lawyers, perhaps, are not in such need of having the imperfection of language impressed upon them; for every case on construction is an object-lesson in it. Still, even they are not immune from error, as I shall seek to show. Jurisprudence, too, is in my opinion badly in need of semantic analysis. It is ridden with disputes, and many of them turn out on examination to be disputes not as to matters of fact or value-judgment but purely as to the use of words. A student of jurisprudence who comes to the subject armed with an understanding of what is a verbal dispute, will find that his knowledge enables him to pare off the unprofitable matter from his subject. It helps him, in Locke's words, to clear the ground a little, and to remove some of the rubbish that lies in the way of knowledge.   [pp. 72–73]

. . . Some words, though not equivocal in the sense of having two or more distinct definitions, are yet obviously vague in their meaning, as for example 'about', 'near', 'more or less'. Such words, which ought generally to find no place in legal documents, give considerable trouble when they do occur. What I am concerned to demonstrate in this section is that not merely some but all words are capable of occasioning difficulty in their application. . . .   [p. 181]

. . . The difficulty of using such words as these does not press upon the ordinary man because it usually does not matter to him whether, for instance, he calls a number of stones a 'heap' or not. All that matters is that he should make his meaning clear enough for the purpose on hand. Suppose that a housewife is following a cookery book which tells her to add a pinch of mustard to a particular dish. She cannot tell how many grains make a pinch, but she can guess what is meant by a pinch and if she puts too much, or too little, her palate will in due course discover her error.

With law it is different, for in law we make sharp consequences hang upon these words of gradation. The question whether a man is left in

Hedley Byrne Ltd. v. Heller [1964] A.C. 465; Gollins v. Gollins [1964] A.C. 644; Williams v. Williams [1964] A.C. 698; Rookes v. Barnard [1964] A.C. 1129; Rondel v. Worsley [1969] 1 A.C. 191, and Dorset Yacht Co. Ltd. v. Home Office [1970] A.C. 1004. For an interesting assessment of the policy element in English judicial decisions, and the difficulties created by the Restrictive Trade Practices Act, 1956, in requiring a court to arrive at economic evaluations and predictions, see R. B. Stevens, "Justiciability: The Restrictive Practices Court Re-examined," [1964] P.L. 221. An interesting suggestion made recently is that behaviouralists (on which see *ante*, 419) should turn their attention to discovering the likelihood of judges in given circumstances deciding a case by the different methods outlined by Cardozo. See Schwartz in ed. Grossman and Tanenhaus, *Frontiers of Judicial Research* (1969), pp. 489, 490–492.]
[32] [From (1945) 61 L.Q.R.]

freedom or detained in a mental institution depends on whether he is judicially classified as sane or insane,[33] as also does the question whether his dispositions of property are upheld or not.[34] Whether a man is punished or acquitted may turn simply and solely upon whether an attempt to commit a crime was sufficiently ' proximate ', or upon whether a statement that he falsely swore was ' material ' to a judicial proceeding; and in a murder case it may be literally a question of life or death whether the accused intended to hurt by means of an act ' intrinsically likely to kill '.[35] Well may a convict echo the words of the poet—

' Oh, the little more, and how much it is !
And the little less, and what worlds away ! '

In tort we have one rule for reservoirs, another for duck-ponds; and the Court somehow has to draw the line between the two. A libel is in ' permanent ' form and a slander in ' transient ' form; but permanency is a matter of degree. In the law of negligence and nuisance the defendant pays full damages or nothing according as the Court puts his conduct at the ' reasonable ' or ' unreasonable ' end of what is in fact a continuous gradation. So also with remoteness of damage. The law of vicarious liability abounds in such puzzles; thus (*a*) the employer of an independent contractor is not liable for him merely because he is employed to do an ordinarily hazardous act, but is liable for him if he is employed to do an extra-hazardous act[36]; (*b*) the distinction between a servant and an independent contractor rests on the infinitely variable matter of control; (*c*) the master of a servant who exceeds his authority is responsible for some excess, but not for excessive excess[37] and (*d*) the master of a vanman who deviates from his route and negligently injures a pedestrian is liable if the deviation is a slight one but not if the deviation is such that every yard he goes is a yard away from his employment and not to it[38]—no precise angle being laid down. A contract to be valid must be ' certain in its terms ', and certainty of meaning is, as it is the object of these pages to show, a question of degree. The ' lodger ' shades off into the ' lessee of a flat '; yet somehow the Courts must draw a line between them, because the relative law is different. In some parts of the law, such as copyright and charities, we must distinguish between a thing that concerns ' the public or a portion of the public ' and a thing that concerns ' private individuals ', this resulting in innumerable perplexities.

Judges refuse to be frightened by these difficulties. They are not intimidated from saying that the case is on one side or the other of the line merely because they discover that the line is difficult to draw. Thus

---

33 See, *e.g.*, Lunacy Act, 1890, ss. 4, 28, and Sch. 2, Form 8.
34 ' The difficulty to be grappled with arises from the circumstance that the question is almost always one of degree. There is no difficulty in the case of a raving madman or a drivelling idiot in saying that he is not a person capable of disposing of property. But between such an extreme case and that of a man of perfectly sound and vigorous understanding, there is every shade of intellect, every degree of mental capacity. There is no possibility of mistaking midnight for noon; but at what precise moment twilight becomes darkness is hard to determine '; *per* Lord Cranworth L.C. in *Boyse* v. *Rossborough* (1857) 6 H.L.C. 2 at 45, quoted by Hannen J. in *Boughton* v. *Knight* (1873) L.R. 3 P. & D. 64 at 67.
35 The terminology is that of Kenny (*Outlines of Criminal Law*, 15th ed., 155); but the word ' intrinsically ' seems to be meaningless in this context.
36 *Honeywill & Stein* v. *Larkin Bros.* [1934] 1 K.B. 191.
37 *Poland* v. *Parr* [1927] 1 K.B. 236 at 243.   38 Pollock, *Torts*, 14th ed., 70–1.

in one of the cases working out the limits of the rule against remoteness, where a limitation was upheld as not infringing the rule, Lord Nottingham said: ' It hath been urged at the bar, where will you stop if you do not stop at *Child and Bayly's Case* ? I answer, I will stop everywhere when any inconvenience appears, no where before '.[39] Blackburn J. observed of the rule in *Hadley* v. *Baxendale*: ' It is a vague rule, and as Bramwell B. said, it is something like having to draw a line between night and day; there is a great duration of twilight when it is neither night nor day; but on the question now before the Court, though you cannot draw the precise line, you can say on which side of the line the case is '.[40] ' Courts of Justice ', said Chitty J., ' ought not to be puzzled by such old scholastic questions as to where a horse's tail begins and where it ceases. You are obliged to say, " This is a horse's tail ", at some time.' [41] Similarly Lord Coleridge C.J.: ' The Attorney-General has asked where we are to draw the line. The answer is that it is not necessary to draw it at any precise point. It is enough for us to say that the present case is on the right side of any reasonable line that could be drawn '.[42] And Lindley M.R.: ' It is urged that it is difficult to draw the line. I admit that it is extremely difficult. . . . It is always a question of degree. It may be asked. What is the difference between one cart and two, and so on ? You cannot draw the line in that way. Nothing is more common in life than to be unable to draw the line between two things. Who can draw the line between plants and animals ? And yet, who has any difficulty in saying that an oak tree is a plant and not an animal? ' [43]

So also, judges are not always deterred in framing new legal rules by the consideration that they may be hard to apply. In the words of Bowen L.J.: ' It is not a valid objection to a legal doctrine that it will not be always easy to know whether the doctrine is to be applied in a particular case. The law has to face such embarrassments '.[44] In the *Pollock-Holmes Letters* Holmes writes: ' People in the law as elsewhere hate to recognize that most questions—I think I might say all legal questions—are questions of degree.[45] I have just sent back an opinion of one of our JJ. with a criticism of an argument in it of the " where are you going to draw the line " type—as if all decisions were not a series of points tending to fix a point in a line '.[46]   [pp. 183–185]

I have already pointed a number of legal morals in the course of this section, but some general conclusions of legal interest remain to be drawn.

---

[39] *Duke of Norfolk's Case* (1681) 2 Swans. 454 at 468; 3 Chan.Cas. 14 at 36.
[40] *Hobbs* v. *L. & S.W. Ry.* (1875) L.R. 10 Q.B. 111 at 121. Cp. Scrutton L.J. in *The San Onofre* [1922] P. 243 at 253.
[41] *Lavery* v. *Pursell* (1888) 39 Ch.D. 508 at 517. See also Pollock C.B. in *White* v. *Bluett* (1853) 23 L.J.Ex. 36 at 37: ' By the argument a principle is pressed to an absurdity, as a bubble is blown until it bursts.'
[42] *Mayor of Southport* v. *Morriss* [1893] 1 Q.B. 359 at 361.
[43] *Att.-Gen.* v. *Brighton & Hove Co-operative Supply Assn.* [1900] 1 Ch. 276 at 282. Cp. *per* FitzGibbon L.J. in *Gregg* v. *Fraser* [1906] 1 Ir.R. 545 at 578–9; ' This is in each case a pure question on the construction of a written document, whether the case lies on the one side or on the other of a definite *line* in the mathematical sense—a line without breadth—every case must lie on one side of that line or on the other . . . and " line balls " are barred.'
[44] *Dashwood* v. *Magniac* [1891] 3 Ch. 306 at 364.
[45] *Cf.* Wilson, 32 M.L.R. 361 (1969).
[46] Pollock-Holmes Letters (Cambridge, 1942), ii, 28.

(1) In the first place, the theory here advanced destroys completely and for ever the illusion that the law can be completely certain. Since the law has to be expressed in words, and words have a penumbra of uncertainty, marginal cases are bound to occur. Certainty in law is thus seen to be a matter of degree. (2) Correlatively, the theory destroys the illusion that the function of a judge is simply to administer the law.[47] If marginal cases must occur, the function of the judge in adjudicating upon them must be legislative. The distinction between the mechanical administration of fixed rules and free judicial discretion is thus a matter of degree, not the sharp distinction that it is sometimes assumed to be. This is not to say that judges have an unlimited legislative power. A judge has a discretion to include a flying-boat within a rule as to ships or vessels; he has no discretion to include a motor car within such a rule. . . .   [pp. 302–303]

H. L. A. HART

Problems of the Philosophy of Law
(1967) [48]

Problems of Legal Reasoning

There are . . . two preliminary issues of peculiar concern to philosophers and logicians which demand attention in any serious attempt to characterize the forms of legal reasonings.

Deductive Reasoning

It has been contended that the application of legal rules to particular cases cannot be regarded as a syllogism or any other kind of deductive inference, on the grounds that neither general legal rules nor particular statements of law (such as those ascribing rights or duties to individuals) can be characterized as either true or false and thus cannot be logically related either among themselves or to statements of fact; hence, they cannot figure as premises or conclusions of a deductive argument. This view depends on a restrictive definition, in terms of truth and falsehood, of the notion of a valid deductive inference and of logical relations such as consistency and contradiction. This would exclude from the scope of deductive inference not only legal rules or statements of law but also commands and many other sentential forms which are commonly regarded as susceptible of logical relations and as constituents of valid deductive arguments. Although considerable technical complexities are involved, several more general definitions of the idea of valid deductive inference that render the notion applicable to inferences the constituents of which are not characterized as either true or false have now been worked out by logicians. In what follows, as in most of contemporary jurisprudential literature, the general acceptability of this more generalized definition of valid inference is assumed.

---

47 The illusion has, of course, been destroyed many times, notably by Dickinson, ' The Law behind Law ' (1929) 29 Col. L. Rev. 113, 285. But it has extraordinary vitality. One still sees discussions among international lawyers upon the respective merits of legal tribunals and tribunals deciding *ex aequo et bono*, without any express statement by either side that the distinction is one of degree.

48 [From Encyclopaedia of Philosophy ed. Edwards, vol. 6, p. 264.]

Inductive reasoning

Considerable obscurity surrounds the claim made by more conventional jurisprudential writers that inductive reasoning is involved in the judicial use of precedents. Reference to induction is usually made in this connection to point a contrast with the allegedly deductive reasoning involved in the application of legislative rules to particular cases. "Instead of starting with a general rule the judge must turn to the relevant cases, discover the general rule implicit in them. . . . The outstanding difference between the two methods is the source of the major premise—the deductive method assumes it whereas the inductive sets out to discover it from particular instances" (G. W. Paton, *A Textbook of Jurisprudence*, 2d ed., Oxford, 1951, pp. 171–172).

It is of course true that courts constantly refer to past cases both to discover rules and to justify their acceptance of them as valid. The past cases are said to be "authority" for the rules "extracted" from them. Plainly, one necessary condition must be satisfied if past cases are in this way to justify logically the acceptance of a rule: the past case must be an instance of the rule in the sense that the decision in the case could be deduced from a statement of the rule together with a statement of the facts of the case. The reasoning insofar as the satisfaction of this necessary condition is concerned is in fact an inverse application of deductive reasoning. But this condition is, of course, only one necessary condition and not a sufficient condition of the court's acceptance of a rule on the basis of past cases, since for any given precedent there are logically an indefinite number of alternative general rules which can satisfy the condition. The selection, therefore, of one rule from among these alternatives as the rule for which the precedent is taken to be authority must depend on the use of other criteria limiting the choice, and these other criteria are not matters of logic but substantive matters which may vary from system to system or from time to time in the same system. Thus, some theories of the judicial use of precedent insist that the rule for which a precedent is authority must be indicated either explicitly or implicitly by the court through its choice of facts to be treated as "material" to a case. Other theories insist that the rule for which a precedent is authority is the rule which a later court considering the precedent would select from the logically possible alternatives after weighing the usual moral and social factors.

Although many legal writers still speak of the extraction of general rules from precedents, some would claim that the reasoning involved in their use of precedents is essentially reasoning from case to case "by example": A court decides the present case in the same way as a past case if the latter "sufficiently" resembles the former in "relevant" respects, and thus makes use of the past case as a precedent without first extracting from it and formulating any general rule. Nevertheless, the more conventional accounts, according to which courts use past cases to discover and justify their acceptance of general rules, are sufficiently widespread and plausible to make the use of the term "induction" in this connection worth discussing.

The use of "induction" to refer to the inverse application of deduction involved in finding that a past case is the instance of a general rule may be misleading: it suggests stronger analogies than exist with the modes of probabilistic inference used in the sciences when general propositions of fact or statements about unobserved particulars are inferred from or regarded as confirmed by observed particulars. "Induction" may also invite confusion with the form of deductive inference known as perfect induction, or with real or alleged methods of discovering generalizations sometimes referred to as intuitive induction.

It is, however, true that the inverse application of deduction involved in the use of precedents is also an important part of scientific procedure, where it is known as hypothetic inference or hypotheticodeductive reasoning. Hence, there are certain interesting analogies between the interplay of observation and theory involved in the progressive refining of a scientific hypothesis to avoid its falsification by contrary instances and the way in which a court may refine a general rule both to make it consistent with a wide range of different cases and to avoid a formulation which would have unjust or undesirable consequences.

Notwithstanding these analogies, the crucial difference remains between the search for general propositions of fact rendered probable by confirming instances but still falsifiable by future experience, and rules to be used in the decision of cases. An empirical science of the judicial process is of course possible: it would consist of factual generalization about the decisions of courts and might be an important predictive tool. However, it is important to distinguish the general propositions of such an empirical science from the rules formulated and used by courts.

Descriptive and Prescriptive Theories

The claim that logic plays only a subordinate part in the decision of cases is sometimes intended as a corrective to misleading descriptions of the judicial process, but sometimes it is intended as a criticism of the methods used by courts, which are stigmatized as " excessively logical," " formal," " mechanical," or " automatic." Descriptions of the methods actually used by courts must be distinguished from prescriptions of alternative methods and must be separately assessed. It is, however, notable that in many discussions of legal reasoning these two are often confused, perhaps because the effort to correct conventional misdescriptions of the judicial process and the effort to correct the process itself have been inspired by the realization of the same important but often neglected fact: the relative indeterminacy of legal rules and precedents. This indeterminacy springs from the fact that it is impossible in framing general rules to anticipate and provide for every possible combination of circumstances which the future may bring. For any rule, however precisely formulated, there will always be some factual situations in which the question whether the situations fall within the scope of the general classificatory terms of the rule cannot be settled by appeal to linguistic rules or conventions or to canons of statutory interpretation, or even by reference to the manifest or assumed purposes of the legislature. In such cases the rules may be found either vague or ambiguous. A similar indeterminacy may arise when two rules apply to a given factual situation and also where rules are expressly framed in such unspecific terms as " reasonable " or " material." Such cases can be resolved only by methods whose rationality cannot lie in the logical relations of conclusions to premises. Similarly, because precedents can logically be subsumed under an indefinite number of general rules, the identification of *the* rule for which a precedent is an authority cannot be settled by an appeal to logic.

These criticisms of traditional descriptions of the judicial process are in general well taken. It is true that both jurists and judges, particularly in jurisdictions in which the separation of powers is respected, have frequently suppressed or minimized the indeterminacy of legal rules or precedents when giving an account of the use of them in the process of decision. On the other hand, another complaint often made by the same writers, that there is an excess of logic or formalism in the judicial process, is less easy to understand and to substantiate. What the critics intend to stigmatize by these terms is the failure of courts, when applying legal rules or precedents, to take advantage of the relative indeterminacy of the rules or precedents to give effect to social aims, policies, and values. Courts, according to these critics, instead of exploiting the fact that the meaning of a statutory rule is indeterminate at certain points, have taken the meaning to be determinate simply because in some different legal context similar wording has been interpreted in a certain way or because a given interpretation is the " ordinary " meaning of the words used.

This failure to recognize the indeterminacy of legal rule (often wrongly ascribed to analytical jurisprudence and stigmatized as conceptualism) has sometimes been defended on the ground that it maximizes certainty and the predictability of decisions. It has also sometimes been welcomed as furthering an ideal of a legal system in which there are a minimum number of independent rules and categories of classification.

The vice of such methods of applying rules is that their adoption prejudges what is to be done in ranges of different cases whose composition cannot be exhaustively known beforehand: rigid classification and divisions are set up which ignore differences and similarities of social and moral importance. This is the burden of the complaint that there is an excessive use of logic in the judicial process. But the expression "an excessive use of logic " is unhappy, for when social values and distinctions of importance are ignored in the interpretation of legal rules and the classification of particulars, the decision reached is not more logical than decisions which give due recognition to these factors: logic does not determine the interpretation of words or the scope of classifications. What is true is that in a system in which such rigid modes of interpretation are common, there will be more occasions when a judge can treat himself as confronted with a rule whose meaning has been predetermined.

Methods of discovery and standards of appraisal

In considering both descriptive and prescriptive theories of judicial reasoning, it is important to distinguish (1) assertions made concerning the usual processes or habits of thought by which judges actually reach their decisions, (2) recommendations concerning the processes to be followed, and (3) the standards by which judicial decisions are to be appraised. The first of these concerns matters of descriptive psychology, and to the extent that assertions in this field go beyond the descriptions of examined instances, they are empirical generalizations or laws of psychology; the second concerns the art or craft of legal judgment, and generalizations in this field are principles of judicial technology; the third relates to the assessment or justification of decisions.

These distinctions are important because it has sometimes been argued that since judges frequently arrive at decisions without going through any process of calculation or inference in which legal rules or precedents figure, the claim that deduction from legal rules plays any part in decision is mistaken. This argument is confused, for in general the issue is not one regarding the manner in which judges do, or should, come to their decisions; rather it concerns the standards they respect in justifying decisions, however reached. The presence or absence of logic in the appraisal of decisions may be a reality whether the decisions are reached by calculation or by an intuitive leap.

Clear cases and indeterminate rules

When the various issues identified above are distinguished, two sets of questions emerge. The first of these concerns the decisions of courts in " clear " cases where no doubts are felt about the meaning and applicability of a single legal rule, and the second concerns decisions where the indeterminacy of the relevant legal rules and precedents is acknowledged.

Clear cases

Even where courts acknowledge that an antecedent legal rule uniquely determines a particular result, some theorists have claimed that this cannot be the case, that <u>courts always " have a choice</u>," and that assertions to the contrary can only be ex post facto rationalizations. Often this skepticism springs from the confusion of the questions of methods of discovery with standards of appraisal noted above. Sometimes, however, it is supported by references to the facts that even if courts fail to apply a clearly applicable rule using a determinate result, this is not a punishable offense, and that the decision given is still authoritative and, if made by a supreme tribunal, final. Hence, it is argued that although courts may show a certain degree of regularity in decision, they are never bound to do so: <u>they always are free to decide otherwise than they do</u>. These last arguments rest on a confusion of finality with infallibility in decisions and on a disputable interpretation of the notion of " being bound " to respect legal rules.

Yet skepticism of this character, however unacceptable, does serve to emphasize that it is a matter of some difficulty to give any exhaustive account of what makes a " clear case " clear or makes a general rule obviously and uniquely applicable to a particular case. Rules cannot claim their own instances, and fact situations do not await the judge neatly labeled with the rule applicable to them. Rules cannot provide for their own application, and even in the clearest case a human being must apply them. The clear cases are those in which there is general agreement that they fall within the scope of a rule, and it is tempting to ascribe such agreements simply to the fact that there are necessarily such agreements in the use of the shared conventions of language. But this would be an oversimplification because it does not allow for the special conventions of the legal use of words, which may diverge from their common use, or for the way in which the meanings of words may be clearly controlled by reference to the purpose of a statutory enactment which itself may be either explicitly stated or generally agreed. A full exploration of these questions is the subject matter of the study of the interpretation of statute.

Indeterminate rules

The decisions of cases which cannot be exhibited as deductions from determinate legal rules have often been described as arbitrary. Although much empirical study of the judicial process remains to be done, it is obvious that this description and the dichotomy of logical deduction and arbitrary decision, if taken as exhaustive, is misleading. Judges do not generally, when legal rules fail to determine a unique result, intrude their personal preferences or blindly choose among alternatives; and when words like " choice " and " discretion," or phrases such as " creative activity " and " interstitial legislation " are used to describe decisions, these do not mean that courts do decide arbitrarily without elaborating reasons for their decisions—and still less that any legal system authorizes decisions of this kind.

It is of crucial importance that cases for decision do not arise in a vacuum but in the course of the operation of a working body of rules, an operation in which a multiplicity of diverse considerations are continuously recognized as good reasons for a decision. These include a wide variety of individual and social interests, social and political aims, and standards of morality and justice; and they may be formulated in general terms as principles, policies, and standards. In some cases only one such consideration may be relevant, and it may determine decision as unambiguously as a determinate legal rule. But in many cases this is not so, and judges marshal in support of their decisions a plurality of such considerations which they regard as jointly sufficient to support their decision, although each separately would not be. Frequently these considerations conflict, and courts are forced to balance or weigh them and to determine priorities among them. The same considerations (and the same need for weighing them when they conflict) enter into the use of precedents when courts must choose between alternative rules which can be extracted from them, or when courts consider whether a present case sufficiently resembles a past case in relevant respects.

Perhaps most modern writers would agree up to this point with this account of judicial decision where legal rules are indeterminate, but beyond this point there is a divergence. Some theorists claim that notwithstanding the heterogeneous and often conflicting character of the factors which are relevant to decision, it is still meaningful to speak of a decision as *the* uniquely correct decision in any case and of the duty of the judge to discover it. They would claim that a judicial choice or preference does not become rational because it is deferred until after the judge has considered the factors that weigh for and against it.

Other theorists would repudiate the idea that in such cases there is always a decision which is uniquely correct, although they of course agree that many decisions can be clearly ruled out as incorrect. They would claim that all that courts do and can do at the end of the process of coolly and impartially considering the relevant considerations is to choose one alternative which they find the most strongly supported, and that it is perfectly proper for them to concede that another equally skilled and impartial judge might choose the other alternative. The theoretical issues are not different from those which arise at many points in the philosophical discussions of moral argument. It may well be that terms like "choice," "discretion," and "judicial legislation" fail to do justice to the phenomenology of considered decision: its felt involuntarily or even inevitable character which often marks the termination of deliberation on conflicting considerations. Very often the decision to include a new case in the scope of a rule or to exclude it is guided by the sense that this is the "natural" continuation of a line of decisions or carries out the "spirit" of a rule. It is also true that if there were not also considerable agreement in judgment among lawyers who approach decisions in these ways, we should not attach significance and value to them or think of such decisions as reached through a rational process. Yet however it may be in moral argument, in the law it seems difficult to substantiate the claim that a judge confronted with a set of conflicting considerations must always assume that there is a single uniquely correct resolution of the conflict and attempt to demonstrate that he has discovered it. . . .   [pp. 268–271]

J. WISDOM

Gods [49]

In courts of law it sometimes happens that opposing counsel are agreed as to the facts and are not trying to settle a question of further fact, are not trying to settle whether the man who admittedly had quarrelled with the deceased did or did not murder him, but are concerned with whether Mr. A. who admittedly handed his long-trusted clerk signed blank cheques did or did not exercise reasonable care, whether a ledger is or is not a document,[50] whether a certain body was or was not a public authority.

In such cases we notice that the process of argument is not a *chain* of demonstrative reasoning. It is a presenting and representing of those features of the case which *severally co-operate* in favour of the conclusion, in favour of saying what the reasoner wishes said, in favour of calling the situation by the name by which he wishes to call it. The reasons are like the legs of a chair, not the links of a chain. Consequently although the discussion is *a priori* and the steps are not a matter of experience, the procedure resembles scientific argument in that the reasoning is not *vertically* extensive but *horizontally* extensive—it is a matter of the cumulative effect of several independent premises, not of the repeated transformation of one or two. And because the premises

---

49 [From 1944 Proc.Arist.Soc., and reprinted in J. Wisdom, *Philosophy and Psycho-Analysis* (1953). See also Stone, *Legal System and Lawyers' Reasonings* (1964), pp. 325–337.]

50 *The Times*, March 2nd, 1945. See also the excellent articles by Dr. Glanville L. Williams in the *Law Quarterly Review*, ' Language and the Law '. The author, having set out how arbitrary are many legal decisions, needs now to set out how far from arbitrary they are—if his readers are ready for the next phase in the dialectic process.

are severally inconclusive the process of deciding the issue becomes a matter of weighing the cumulative effect of one group of severally inconclusive items against the cumulative effect of another group of severally inconclusive items, and thus lends itself to description in terms of conflicting ' probabilities '. This encourages the feeling that the issue is one of fact—that it is a matter of guessing from the premises at a further fact, at what is to come. But this is a muddle. *The dispute does not cease to be a* priori *because it is a matter of the cumulative effect of severally inconclusive premises.* The logic of the dispute is not that of a chain of deductive reasoning as in a mathematic calculation. But nor is it a matter of collecting from several inconclusive items of information an expectation as to something further, as when a doctor from a patient's symptoms guesses at what is wrong, or a detective from many clues guesses the criminal. It has its own sort of logic and its own sort of end —the solution of the question at issue is a decision, a ruling by the judge. But it is not an arbitrary decision though the rational connections are neither quite like those in vertical deductions nor like those in inductions in which from many signs we guess at what is to come; and though the decision manifests itself in the application of a name it is no more merely the application of a name than is the pinning on of a medal merely the pinning on of a bit of metal. Whether a lion with stripes is a tiger or a lion is, if you like, merely a matter of the application of a name. Whether Mr. So-and-So of whose conduct we have so complete a record did or did not exercise reasonable care is not merely a matter of the application of a name or, if we choose to say it is, then we must remember that with this name a game is lost and won and a game with very heavy stakes. With the judges' choice of a name for the facts goes an attitude, and the declaration, the ruling, is an examination evincing that attitude. But *it is an exclamation which not only has a purpose but also has a logic,* a logic surprisingly like that of ' futile ', ' deplorable ', ' graceful ', ' grand ', ' divine '. . . .[51]

[pp. 157–158]

---

[51] [For a suggestion that a new model of reasoning can be constructed, based to some extent on the ancient tradition of rhetorical argument, whereby conclusions may be arrived at which are worthy of reliance, even though not susceptible of stringent proof in the strict logical sense, See Ch. Perelman, *The Idea of Justice and the Problem of Argument* (1963). After a full exploration of this approach, Stone has argued forcibly that too much should not be expected from this new type of rhetorical logic. He points out how much of legal reasoning depends not just on inferences from established legal propositions, but on the use of ideals and established techniques, such as the common law approach to *stare decisis.* Moreover, in a society with conflicting standards and values it is not easy to predicate, as Perelman appears to do, that fundamental propositions from which the law may proceed to its conclusions, can generally be found to command a general consensus. At the most therefore, it would seem that the new rhetoric does not differ very much from the traditional common law approach whereby " good grounds " are sought for justifying particular decisions, such grounds being deployed as cumulatively persuasive rather than logically conclusive. The new terminology seems unlikely to provide more than a new conceptual framework for constructing legal arguments, rather than a novel technique differing in substance from the traditional methods of generations of lawyers both in common law and civil law countries. (See Julius Stone, " Reasons and Reasoning in Judicial and Juristic Arguments," in *Legal Essays to Castberg* (1963), p. 170).]

H. WECHSLER

Toward Neutral Principles of Constitutional Law
(1959) [52]

The main constituent of the judicial process is precisely that it must be genuinely principled, resting with respect to every step that is involved in reaching judgment on analysis and reasons quite transcending the immediate result that is achieved. To be sure, the courts decide, or should decide, only the case they have before them. But must they not decide on grounds of adequate neutrality and generality, tested not only by the instant application but by others that the principles imply? Is it not the very essence of judicial method to insist upon attending to such other cases, preferably those involving an opposing interest, in evaluating any principle avowed?

Here too I do not think that I am stating any novel or momentous insight. But now, as Holmes said long ago in speaking of " the unrest which seems to wonder vaguely whether law and order pay," we " need education in the obvious." [53] We need it more particularly now respecting constitutional interpretation, since it has become a commonplace to grant what many for so long denied: that courts in constitutional determinations face issues that are inescapably " political "— . . . —in that they involve a choice among competing values [54] or desires, a choice reflected in the legislative or executive action in question, which the court must either condemn or condone. . . . What is crucial, I submit, is not the nature of the question but the nature of the answer that may validly be given by the courts. No legislature or executive is obligated by the nature of its function to support its choice of values by the type of reasoned explanation that I have suggested is intrinsic to judicial action—however much we may admire such a reasoned exposition when we find it in those other realms.

Does not the special duty of the courts to judge by neutral principles addressed to all the issues make it inapposite to contend, as Judge Hand does, that no court can review the legislative choice—by any standard other than a fixed " historical meaning " of constitutional provisions [55]—without becoming " a third legislative chamber "? [56] Is there not, in short, a vital difference between legislative freedom to appraise the gains and losses in projected measures and the kind of principled appraisal, in respect of values that can reasonably be asserted to have constitutional dimension, that alone is in the province of the courts? Does not the difference yield a middle ground between a judicial House of Lords and the abandonment of any limitation on the other branches—a middle ground consisting of judicial action that embodies what are surely the main qualities of law, its generality and its neutrality? This must, it seems to me, have been in Mr. Justice Jackson's mind when in his chapter on the Supreme Court " as a political institution "

---

52 [From *Principles, Politics and Fundamental Law* (1961), p. 3, a collection to which page references refer. It is originally found in (1959) 73 Harv.L.R. 1.]
53 Holmes, *Law and the Court,* in Collected Legal Papers 291, 292 (1920).
54 [Golding has questioned the possibility of speaking of principled judicial decision-making when more than one value is at stake. See in ed. Summers, *Essays In Legal Philosophy* (1968), pp. 208, 224–227.]
55 Hand, *op. cit. supra* note 3, at 65.
56 *Id.* at 42.

he wrote [57] in words that I find stirring, " Liberty is not the mere absence of restraint, it is not a spontaneous product of majority rule, it is not achieved merely by lifting underprivileged classes to power, nor is it the inevitable by-product of technological expansion. It is achieved only by a rule of law." Is it not also what Mr. Justice Frankfurter must mean in calling upon judges for " allegiance to nothing except the effort, amid tangled words and limited insights, to find the path through precedent, through policy, through history, to the best judgment that fallible creatures can reach in that most difficult of all tasks: the achievement of justice between man and man, between man and state, through reason called law "? [58]

You will not understand my emphasis upon the role of reason and of principle in the judicial, as distinguished from the legislative or executive, appraisal of conflicting values to imply that I depreciate the duty of fidelity to the text of the Constitution, when its words may be decisive—though I would certainly remind you of the caution stated by Chief Justice Hughes: " Behind the words of the constitutional provisions are postulates which limit and control." [59] Nor will you take me to deny that history has weight in the elucidation of the text, though it is surely subtle business to appraise it as a guide. Nor will you even think that I deem precedent without importance, for we surely must agree with Holmes that " imitation of the past, until we have a clear reason for change, no more needs justification than appetite." [60] But after all, it was Chief Justice Taney who declared his willingness " that it be regarded hereafter as the law of this court, that its opinion upon the construction of the Constitution is always open to discussion when it is supposed to have been founded in error, and that its judicial authority should hereafter depend altogether on the force of the reasoning by which it is supported." [61] Would any of us have it otherwise, given the nature of the problems that confront the courts?

At all events, is not the relative compulsion of the language of the Constitution, of history and precedent—where they do not combine to make an answer clear—itself a matter to be judged, so far as possible, by neutral principles—by standards that transcend the case at hand? I know, of course, that it is common to distinguish, as Judge Hand did, clauses like " due process," cast " in such sweeping terms that their history does not elucidate their contents," [62] from other provisions of the Bill of Rights addressed to more specific problems. But the contrast, as it seems to me, often implies an overstatement of the specificity or the immutability these other clauses really have—at least when problems under them arise. . . .   [pp. 21–24]

. . . The courts have both the title and the duty when a case is properly before them to review the actions of the other branches in the light of constitutional provisions, even though the action involves value choices, as invariably action does. In doing so, however, they

---

[57] Jackson, The Supreme Court in the American System of Government 76 (1955).
[58] Frankfurter, *Chief Justices I Have Known*, in Of Law and Men 138 (Elman ed. 1956).
[59] Principality of Monaco v. Mississippi, 292 U.S. 313, 322 (1934).
[60] Holmes, *Holdsworth's English Law*, in Collected Legal Papers 285, 290 (1920).
[61] Passenger Cases, 48 U.S. (7 How.) 283, 470 (1849).
[62] Hand, *op. cit. supra* note 3, at 30.

are bound to function otherwise than as a naked power organ; they participate as courts of law. This calls for facing how determinations of this kind can be asserted to have any legal quality. The answer, I suggest, inheres primarily in that they are—or are obliged to be— entirely principled. A principled decision, in the sense I have in mind, is one that rests on reasons with respect to all the issues in the case, reasons that in their generality and their neutrality transcend any immediate result that is involved. When no sufficient reasons of this kind can be assigned for overturning value choices of the other branches of the Government or of a state, those choices must, of course, survive. Otherwise, as Holmes said in his first opinion for the Court, " a constitution, instead of embodying only relatively fundamental rules of right, as generally understood by all English-speaking communities, would become the partisan of a particular set of ethical or economical opinions. . . ." [63]

The virtue or demerit of a judgment turns, therefore, entirely on the reasons that support it and their adequacy to maintain any choice of values it decrees, or, it is vital that we add, to maintain the rejection of a claim that any given choice should be decreed. The critic's role, as T. R. Powell showed throughout so many fruitful years, is the sustained, disinterested, merciless examination of the reasons that the courts advance, measured by standards of the kind I have attempted to describe. I wish that more of us today could imitate his dedication to that task. . . . [64]   [pp. 27–28]

F. CASTBERG

Problems of Legal Philosophy
(1957)

Logical conclusions as means to the understanding of general norms

Just as the logical conclusion is the necessary means of proceeding from the general, normative statement to the individual judicial decision, it is also a necessary means of knowing the contents of the general legal norms themselves. . . .

The deductive operations of the mind—the conclusions from general to special—are, for the rest, not the only way of gaining an understanding of the norms that are to be regarded as expressions of existing law. We also apply in our legal thinking norms that we have found by a more or less conscious generalization of positively determined rules of law. We argue—by a kind of induction—from the validity of certain special norms to the validity of a more general norm, of which these special norms may be regarded as applications. Or we skip this conclusion from the special to the general norm, and argue by analogy directly from the special norm to another special norm concerning a " nearly-related " circumstance. This so-called analogical conclusion is, as is known, a constantly recurring figure of thought in juridical arguments. In many cases, the justification of such an analogical conclusion is evident. From a regulation

---

[63] Otis v. Parker, 187 U.S. 606, 609 (1903).
[64] [Wechsler subsequently returned to this theme in ed. Hook, *Law and Philosophy* (1964), p. 290.]

which prohibits the bringing of dogs into railway-trains, one may, for instance, conclude with certainty [65] that the bringing of bears is also prohibited !—In other cases, it is just as obvious that one must argue antithetically and not analogically. The analogical conclusion may be forbidden by a valid, positive, legal norm, as is the case in certain legal systems in the field of penal law. Its use may also in many cases be out of the question, even if it is not positively forbidden. From a rule stating that lectures are suspended on Sundays, one cannot analogically conclude that they are also suspended on week-days. Here, on the contrary, the antithetical conclusion is indubitable.

Thus logic has its necessary position in all understanding and application of existing law. It would have no sensible meaning at all to have a legal order, if the legal norms that the legal order consists of could not form points of departure for conclusions as to what is to be regarded as binding in special and individual cases. Human beings take for granted that the norm-syllogism is a justified form of logical argument. The fact that they take this for granted and arrange themselves accordingly, is the condition of all regulated social life.[66]

Logic has its place in legal thinking. But it has not undivided power. It is far from being the case that all legal questions may be solved by logical conclusions alone. I shall deal with this in the next paragraph.

The Insufficiency of Logic in Legal Thinking

The fluid limits of the notions

The notions of which general, legal statements are composed are always more or less indefinite. In life there are no sharp transitions. But legal notions impose limitations in view of the needs of human society. Thus in law a limit is drawn between acts that are inadvertent and acts which are not, between the use of property which is customary and that which is not. And the limit becomes decisive in the question of right and duty, for instance the question of whether damages are to be paid or not. But the need of notional limitation in law does not prevent the fact that doubt often must prevail as to where the limit is really drawn. Even if the law defines the notions it uses, new doubts will present themselves in the limitation of the notions employed by the definition.

Thus the logical subsumption under the statements of the law is not in all cases self-evident. And this does not only apply to such normative statements that in their applications explicitly assume a valuation. As an example may be mentioned a prohibition of " undue " competition, or a rule stating that certain agreements are invalid, because it would be contrary to " integrity or good faith " to appeal to them. That the field

---

[65] [But this is not a matter of *logical* certainty, in the sense that the conclusion is a *necessary* one.]

[66] [The syllogistic mode of reasoning is obviously relevant to cases of legal inference where there is no dispute as to the validity of the inference. For instance, where a statute prohibits a motor-vehicle proceeding at more than 30 m.p.h. along a highway, the court by finding that in the particular instance before it a motor vehicle was driven at a speed in excess of 30 m.p.h. will draw the inference that an offence has been committed under this provision. Any reference to logical reasoning in cases of this sort, however, can be said to be " trivial " in the sense that the procedure is only strictly available where it is unnecessary, *i.e.,* where the scope of the premises is not in dispute.]

of operation of such rules is indefinite and not automatically given, needs no further proof. But rules which do not straightforwardly refer to a concrete valuation in this way, will also raise numerous questions concerning the limitation of the notions and consequently of the field of operation of the rules. A law regulates, for instance, the sale of milk. Does the notion of milk here comprise cream as well? Para. 96 of the Norwegian Constitution prohibits, among other things, punishment except after a judgment. Does the notion of punishment here comprise also detention of work-shy persons in an establishment for compulsory labour? From the norm-statements themselves it does not immediately appear how questions like these are to be answered.

The different possibilities of subsumption

It may thus be established that the notions employed in general normative statements, always have fluid limits. One must go still further. The immediate conclusion from the general legal statement to a statement of a special case never gives more than a more or less strong presumption that the conclusion is the correct one according to the system of law to which the general statement belongs. . . .

Nevertheless, the syllogistic conclusion is an important instrument of thought in the investigation of reality. For we generalize our observation in a common statement long before we have observed all the individual phenomena comprised by the statement. In this way we form an hypothesis. Any new instance that turns up we bring under our common statement, thus drawing a conclusion, and we must afterwards ascertain by verification whether the conclusion led us to a result that agrees with our experience of reality. . . .

The case of the norm-logic syllogism is similar. We take our point of departure in a general, normative statement, and subsume the special case under the general statement; the result we arrive at in this way, we subject to a subsequent test, where, incidentally, new norm-logic arguments are brought to application. These operations of the mind may present themselves more or less clearly to the reasoning person. As usual, one forms one's opinion much more by instinct than by circumstantial, clearly formulated mental operations of this kind. Nevertheless, it is according to this schema that legal arguments are carried out.

The test of the result of the subsumption that corresponds to the verification of an hypothesis, is quite different from the examination of an actual circumstance. For it is not here a question of ascertaining that an event takes place or that a factual quality is present. But the result of the norm-conclusion must be accepted or rejected according as it harmonises or disagrees with other valid statements of normative contents. The verification is carried out by new logical subsumptions. A certain interpretation of a rule of law, is for instance, rejected, because it definitely disagrees with certain interests, which the rules of the law are designed to further and which must be regarded as guides to the interpretation.

Even if the wording of the law linguistically leads to a certain result, it is not therefore certain that precisely this subsumption is the correct one. It is a well-known phenomenon that the lawyer at times has to set aside the letter of the law in favour of its " reasonable " meaning. The conclusion at which one arrives by an automatic subsumption under the words of the law, is tested, in other words, by means of guiding propositions, which serve as bases of logical deductions. . . .   [pp. 60–65]

The sliding scale from certain to uncertain understanding of the law

One may imagine an infinite series of legal statements, where the extremities are the undoubtedly correct [67] and the undoubtedly incorrect statements, and where the intermediate statements represent all degrees of certainty. There will then be statements the correctness of which is indubitable, and statements the incorrectness of which is indubitable. There will be statements the correctness or incorrectness of which is doubtful to a higher and a lower degree. And in the central point of the series, there will be such statements as cannot be asserted to be either correct or incorrect; in other words, there are equally strong arguments for one solution as for the other.

This idea may also be expressed thus: our statements of legal relationship represent a sliding scale from certainty of correctness to complete uncertainty and further to certainty of incorrectness. We are not here concerned with degrees of correctness. One can no more speak of degrees of correctness in connection with normative statements, than one can speak of degrees of truth in the understanding of reality. But one may speak of degrees in the certainty with which a normative statement may be set forth as correct. And one may speak of degrees in the probability with which a statement of reality agrees with reality.[68]

In legal thinking itself, one is familiar with the idea of a sliding scale. The conception of the continuity of reality and imperceptible transitions from greater to lesser interests are conceptions with which lawyers are quite familiar. Thus the law accords certain claims to a buyer if goods are supplied that have " essential " defects. All the possible defects of an article, however, represent a scale from undoubtedly essential to undoubtedly unessential ones. Somewhere the lawyer must draw the line. But in the borderline cases, the subsumption will be doubtful.

The current conception of a sliding scale in subsumptional questions of this kind has an application in all legal thinking. Even the most precise formulation of a provision of law cannot prevent a case arising one day in which the subsumption must give occasion to doubt. The stand one takes to subsumptional questions in such a doubtful case has a lower degree of certainty than the stand one may take to the normal questions of subsumption, so to speak, in the application of such a clearly-defined provision of law. It is exactly the fact that clearly-defined provisions of law create relatively few subsumptional doubts, which—from the point of view of legal security—gives these provisions their superiority to legal " standards ", " general clauses ", in short: indefinite commands of law.

But it thus applies to all conceivable legal statements that they may be imagined to be arranged in a sliding scale according to the degree of certitude with which they may be regarded as correct or incorrect. Even

---

[67] [What does " correct " mean here? By what standard is it judged, *e.g.*, absolutely, or by what a court may or will decide ?]
[68] " The view, occasionally held, that probability is concerned with degrees of truth, arises out of a confusion between certainty and truth." *J. M. Keynes*: A Treatise on Probability (1921), p. 15, note 1.

statements about a general legal proposition as being valid law also represent every degree of certainty and uncertainty. About a proposition in a law that has been recently passed, we decide with a high degree of certainty that it expresses existing law. About a proposition in an old and rarely applied decree, the same assertion is perhaps very doubtful. Of a proposition in a law that has been newly repealed, we may lay down with certainty that it gives no adequate expression for what is existing law to-day.

In every domain, the logic of legal thinking is ruled by the principle of the sliding scale. [pp. 84–86]

Practical consequences

Legal statements may thus represent all degrees of certainty, and it must be the task of legal science to achieve results that represent the highest possible degree of certitude. The generalizing, " constructive " science of law seeks the logical connection between the legal norms, as it tries to attain to propositions of law that are as comprehensive as possible and under which newly arising cases may be subsumed. The sociologico-teleologically directed science of law aims at understanding the social functions of the law and at drawing conclusions from statements about the ends of the law. And no juridical method can disregard the demand that the law shall function justly.

A comprehensive exposition of all these circumstances may in many cases lead to results that may be characterized as undoubtedly correct. Even if no generalization is logically necessary,—even if the values that the law is to further may be found to be unmeasurable, and though the notion of justice may raise problems even of a metaphysical nature, the result of the juridical operations of the mind may nevertheless at times have such a character that there is no reasonable cause for doubt.[69]

Even the most comprehensive juridical investigation, however, cannot —as it has been demonstrated—lead to certain results in all cases. Often the results we arrive at must give rise to stronger or weaker doubts.

[p. 87]

E. H. LEVI
An Introduction to Legal Reasoning
(1949)

The basic pattern of legal reasoning is reasoning by example. It is reasoning from case to case. It is a three-step process described by the doctrine of precedent in which a proposition descriptive of the first case is made into a rule of law and then applied to a next similar situation. The steps are these: similarity is seen between cases; next the rule of law inherent in the first case is announced; then the rule of law is made applicable to the second case. This is a method of reasoning necessary for the law, but it has characteristics which under other circumstances might be considered imperfections.

These characteristics become evident if the legal process is approached as though it were a method of applying general rules of law to diverse facts—in short, as though the doctrine of precedent meant that general rules, once properly determined, remained unchanged, and then were

[69] [Surely this is a very different thing from a logically necessary conclusion?]

applied, albeit imperfectly, in later cases. If this were the doctrine, it would be disturbing to find that the rules change from case to case and are remade with each case. Yet this change in the rules is the indispensable dynamic quality of law. It occurs because the scope of a rule of law, and therefore its meaning, depends upon a determination of what facts will be considered similar to those present when the rule was first announced. The finding of similarity or difference is the key step in the legal process.

The determination of similarity or difference is the function of each judge. Where case law is considered, and there is no statute, he is not bound by the statement of the rule of law made by the prior judge even in the controlling case. The statement is mere dictum, and this means that the judge in the present case may find irrelevant the existence or absence of facts which prior judges thought important.[69a] It is not what the prior judge intended that is of any importance; rather it is what the present judge, attempting to see the law as a fairly consistent whole, thinks should be the determining classification. In arriving at his result he will ignore what the past thought important; he will emphasize facts which prior judges would have thought made no difference. It is not alone that he could not see the law through the eyes of another, for he could at least try to do so. It is rather that the doctrine of dictum forces him to make his own decision.

Thus it cannot be said that the legal process is the application of known rules to diverse facts. Yet it is a system of rules; the rules are discovered in the process of determining similarity or difference. But if attention is directed toward the finding of similarity or difference, other peculiarities appear. The problem for the law is: When will it be just to treat different cases as though they were the same? A working legal system must therefore be willing to pick out key similarities and to reason from them to the justice of applying a common classification. The existence of some facts in common brings into play the general rule. If this is really reasoning, then by common standards, thought of in terms of closed systems, it is imperfect unless some overall rule has announced that this common and ascertainable similarity is to be decisive. But no such fixed prior rule exists. It could be suggested that reasoning is not involved at all; that is, that no new insight is arrived at through a comparison of cases. But reasoning appears to be involved; the conclusion is arrived at through a process and was not immediately apparent. It seems better to say there is reasoning, but it is imperfect.

Therefore it appears that the kind of reasoning involved in the legal process is one in which the classification changes as the classification is made. The rules change as the rules are applied. More important, the rules arise out of a process which, while comparing fact situations, creates the rules and then applies them. But this kind of reasoning is open to the charge that it is classifying things as equal when they are somewhat different, justifying the classification by rules made up as the reasoning or classification proceeds. In a sense all reasoning is of this type, but there is an additional requirement which compels the legal process to be this way. Not only do new situations arise, but in addition people's wants change. The categories used in the legal process must be left

69a [*Cf. ante*, 716.]

ambiguous in order to permit the infusion of new ideas. And this is true even where legislation or a constitution is involved. The words used by the legislature or the constitutional convention must come to have new meanings. Furthermore, agreement on any other basis would be impossible. In this manner the laws come to express the ideas of the community and even when written in general terms, in statute or constitution, are molded for the specific case.

But attention must be paid to the process. A controversy as to whether the law is certain, unchanging, and expressed in rules, or uncertain, changing, and only a technique for deciding specific cases misses the point. It is both. Nor is it helpful to dispose of the process as a wonderful mystery possibly reflecting a higher law, by which the law can remain the same and yet change. The law forum is the most explicit demonstration of the mechanism required for a moving classification system. The folklore of law may choose to ignore the imperfections in legal reasoning, but the law forum itself has taken care of them.

What does the law forum require? It requires presentation of competing examples. The forum protects the parties and the community by making sure that the competing analogies are before the court. The rule which will be created arises out of a process in which if different things are to be treated as similar, at least the differences have been urged.[70] In this sense the parties as well as the court participate in the law making. In this sense, also, lawyers represent more than the litigants.

Reasonably by example in the law is a key to many things.[71] It indicates in part the hold which the law process has over the litigants. They have participated in the law making. They are bound by something they helped to make. Moreover, the examples or analogies urged by the parties bring into the law the common ideas of the society. The ideas have their day in court, and they will have their day again. This is what makes the hearing fair, rather than any idea that the judge is completely impartial, for of course he cannot be completely so. Moreover, the hearing in a sense compels at least vicarious participation by all the citizens, for the rule which is made, even though ambiguous, will be law as to them.

Reasoning by example shows the decisive role which the common ideas of the society and the distinctions made by experts can have in shaping the law. The movement of common or expert concepts into the law may be followed. The concept is suggested in arguing difference or similarity in a brief, but it wins no approval from the court. The idea achieves standing in the society. It is suggested again to a court. The court this time reinterprets the prior case and in doing so adopts the rejected idea. In subsequent cases, the idea is given further definition and is tied to other ideas which have been accepted by courts. It is now

---

[70] The reasoning may take this form: A falls more appropriately in B than in C. It does so because A is more like D which is of B than it is like E which is of C. Since A is in B and B is in G (legal concept), then A is in G. But perhaps C is in G also. If so, then B is in a decisively different segment of G, because B is like H which is in G and has a different result than C.

[71] [For a recent illustration of analogous reasoning which was accepted by only one of the three members of the C.A., see *John Carter* v. *Hanson Haulage Ltd.* [1965] 2 W.L.R. 553.]

no longer the idea which was commonly held in the society. It becomes modified in subsequent cases. Ideas first rejected but which gradually have won acceptance now push what has become a legal category out of the system or convert it into something which may be its opposite. The process is one in which the ideas of the community and of the social sciences, whether correct or not, as they win acceptance in the community, control legal decisions. Erroneous ideas, of course, have played an enormous part in shaping the law. An idea, adopted by a court, is in a superior position to influence conduct and opinion in the community; judges, after all, are rulers. And the adoption of an idea by a court reflects the power structure in the community. But reasoning by example will operate to change the idea after it has been adopted.

Moreover, reasoning by example brings into focus important similarity and difference in the interpretation of case law, statutes, and the constitution of a nation. There is a striking similarity. It is only folklore which holds that a statute if clearly written can be completely unambiguous and applied as intended to a specific case. Fortunately or otherwise, ambiguity is inevitable in both statute and constitution as well as with case law. Hence reasoning by example operates with all three. But there are important differences. What a court says is dictum, but what a legislature says is a statute. The reference of the reasoning changes. Interpretation of intention when dealing with a statute is the way of describing the attempt to compare cases on the basis of the standard thought to be common at the time the legislation was passed. While this is the attempt, it may not initially accomplish any different result than if the standard of the judge had been explicitly used. Nevertheless, the remarks of the judge are directed toward describing a category set up by the legislature. These remarks are different from ordinary dicta. They set the course of the statute, and later reasoning in subsequent cases is tied to them. As a consequence, courts are less free in applying a statute than in dealing with case law. The current rationale for this is the notion that the legislature has acquiesced by legislative silence in the prior, even though erroneous, interpretation of the court. But the change in reasoning where legislation is concerned seems an inevitable consequence of the division of function between court and legislature, and, paradoxically, a recognition also of the impossibility of determining legislative intent. The impairment of a court's freedom in interpreting legislation is reflected in frequent appeals to the constitution as a necessary justification for overruling cases even though these cases are thought to have interpreted the legislation erroneously.

Under the United States experience, contrary to what has sometimes been believed when a written constitution of a nation is involved, the court has greater freedom than it has with the application of a statute or case law. In case law, when a judge determines what the controlling similarity between the present and prior case is, the case is decided. The judge does not feel free to ignore the results of a great number of cases which he cannot explain under a remade rule. And in interpreting legislation, when the prior interpretation, even though erroneous, is determined after a comparison of facts to cover the case, the case is decided. But this is not true with a constitution. The constitution sets up the conflicting ideals of the community in certain ambiguous categories. These categories bring along with them satellite concepts covering the

areas of ambiguity.   It is with a set of these satellite concepts that reasoning by example must work.   But no satellite concept, no matter how well
developed, can prevent the court from shifting its course, not only by
realigning cases which impose certain restrictions, but by going beyond
realignment back to the overall ambiguous category written into the
document.   The constitution, in other words, permits the court to be
inconsistent.   The freedom is concealed either as a search for the intention of the framers or as a proper understanding of a living instrument,
and sometimes as both.   But this does not mean that reasoning by
example has any less validity in this field.[72]   [pp. 1–6]

D. LLOYD

Reason and Logic in the Common Law [73]

An inquiry into the relation of logic to law does not substantially differ
from an investigation of the role logic plays in real life.   In the sense of
a formal method of reasoning whereby deductions are rigorously and
necessarily inferred from general premises it is conceded even by the
logicians themselves [74] that logic has but little application to real life.[75]
The reason for this is not far to seek.   Logic in the formal sense is
concerned with what has been termed the ' grammar ' [76] or deductive
implications of propositions of complete generality and abstractness,
such as ' all men are mortal ', or in symbolic logic, of the type ' p implies
q '.   In the realm of reality, however, abstract generalities impinge but
little upon human affairs.   This is not to say that such generalisations do
not play a part in the psychological approach to many subjects of human
discussion, and it is perhaps from this angle that such considerations most
frequently intrude themselves.   Nevertheless, real life is concerned mainly
with deduction from particular facts, and viewed practically there are no
generalisations which do not have to be hedged round with endless
qualifications.   As a distinguished modern philosopher has put it, ' In

---

[72] [See further as to the effect of a written constitution, E. Levi, *op. cit.*, pp. 41
et seq. See also a recent restatement of his views in ed. Hook, *Law and
Philosophy* (1964), pp. 263–282.]

[73] [(1948) 64 L.Q.R. 468; for a criticism, see Jensen, *Nature of Legal Argument*
(1957), Chap. 1; and a reply thereto by D. L. in (1958) 7 I.C.L.Q. 618,
619–620. For an interesting account of the historical role of the conceptual
mode of reasoning of the common law, and its influence both for good and ill
on the substance of that law, see Milsom, " Reason in the Development of the
Common Law " (1965) 81 L.Q.R. 496.]

[74] ' We live even more by intuition than by logic ' (G. G. Coulton, *Medieval
Panorama*, p. 648).

[75] See, *e.g.* Keynes, *Formal Logic*, 4th ed., pp. 6–7. Cf. Stebbing, *Modern Introduction to Logic* (' Logic is concerned not with what is actual but with what is
possible ', p. 474). Professor Morris Cohen, who urges the application of logic
to human affairs states the case no higher than this : ' Logic is an exploration of
the field of most general abstract possibility. This may make logical information
very thin; but it is not therefore devoid of significance. Not only does it rule
out impossibilities but it reveals the possibility of hypotheses other than those
usually taken for granted; and in this respect it frees the mind and contributes
not only to the fixed form but to the living growth of science ', *A Preface to Logic*,
1946, p. 7; cf. pp. 188–92.

[76] See *e.g.*, Wittgenstein, *Tractatus Logico-Philosophicus*, p. 55; Carnap, *Logical
Syntax of Language*, pp. 1–8.

fact, there is hardly a question to be asked which should not be fenced round with qualifications as to how much, and as to what pattern of circumstances. Aristotelian logic, apart from the guardianship of mathematics, is the fertile matrix of fallacies. It deals with propositional forms only adapted for the expression of high abstractions, the sort of abstractions usual in current conversation where the presupposed background is ignored '.[77] It is therefore hardly surprising that ' in any contact between life and logic, it is not logic that is successful '.[78]

Now law is certainly concerned with the elucidation of general propositions and their application to particular cases, and to this extent we may perhaps accept Maitland's dictum when he observed that ' law was the point where life and logic meet '.[79] Still it requires but little reflection to realise that no court can, or indeed ought to construe such propositions as pure generalities unrelated to the facts of life into which they must be integrated. Every proposition, however general in form, must in law be viewed in the light of what Professor Whitehead has called its ' pattern of circumstances '. In this way emerges the fact, so often noted,[80] that in law, as in real life, there is always an element of choice. When a logician determines the implications of the proposition, ' all men are mortal ' he proceeds on the footing that each word has a definite circumscribed ambit which is quite inflexible. When, on the other hand, a judge seeks to apply to the facts before him a rule of law which asserts that ' the person who for his own purposes brings on his lands and collects and keeps there anything likely to do mischief if it escapes, must keep it in at his peril ',[81] there is not one word in this sweeping generalisation which is not capable, as subsequent litigants have discovered, of infinite refinement and qualification.[82] It can hardly be contested therefore that the lawyer is never faced with anything in the nature of logical compulsion and that attempts to state judicial decisions in the form of a syllogism or in any other form of high abstraction [83] are both misconceived and misleading. No doubt once a particular decision has been arrived at, it can always be expressed in this form, but to do so may well be very misleading for two reasons: (a) It suggests wrongly that the decision was

---

[77] A. N. Whitehead, *Adventures of Ideas*, Chap. 9, § 5.

[78] H. J. Laski, *Studies in the Problem of Sovereignty*, p. 201.

[79] Introduction to Year Books of Edward II, *Selden Society Series*, Vol. 1, 411.

[80] Professor Goodhart has pointed out that this has been recognised at least since 1782, when it was discussed by Paley (see *Modern Theories of Law*, p. 13).

[81] The so-called rule in *Rylands* v. *Fletcher*, as formulated by Blackburn, J. (L.R. 1 Ex. at pp. 279–80).

[82] ' Numerous cases may be found in which the courts, faced with unanswerable arguments based on logical deduction from existing categories, have in effect declined to accept the deduction . . . ' (Stone, *Province and Function of Law*, 1947, pp. 201–2). But from the point of view of strict logic there are no such *unanswerable* arguments to be deduced from legal propositions: not only is there no *legal* compulsion to follow logic but there is, in such propositions, no *logical* compulsion either. In law, unlike formal logic, there are no ' universals ' or ' absolute words '. Cf. Frank, *Law and the Modern Mind*, pp. 67–8.

[83] Modern logicians have, of course, developed the science of logic far beyond the bounds of the old Aristotelian syllogism. But though modern symbolic logic has been fruitfully applied to the foundations of mathematics, its application to more mundane affairs has yet to emerge. For this reason the syllogism is still referred to in this article as the typical formal logical process, or at any rate the only one likely to be encountered for the present in judicial reasoning. See M. R. Cohen, *op. cit.*, pp. vii, 36, 82; Dewey in 10 Cornell L.Q. 17; and for symbolic logic generally, Stebbing, *op. cit.*, pp. 163 *et seq.* [Cf. *ante*, 428.]

arrived at as a matter of necessary logical implication; (b) it tends to imply that further consequences can be deduced as a matter of logic and that such deductions also follow as a matter of law.[84]

Law then is not so much concerned with logic or reason in the formal sense but rather with 'reasonableness', and if no more than this is implied in the assertion of the coincidence of law and reason, then it may be truly said that, though the Common Law has sometimes fallen short of Coke's famous dictum, it has at least striven to attain that objective. What is 'reasonable' in given circumstances may permit of endless differences of opinion, but none the less it undoubtedly represents one of the most vitalising notions which have animated the growth of the Common Law. The whole modern law of negligence, which bids fair ultimately to take over most if not all of the law of tort, enshrines this basic viewpoint. Of course, in English law, a judge is severely limited in applying rules of 'reason' in this sense by the wealth of binding precedents which he must perforce follow, but it is when he comes to 'distinguish' those previous cases that he still often retains ample scope for applying his sense of 'reasonableness'. It may, in a given case, be conceded that X is liable in set of circumstances 'A', but what the judge will usually have to decide, without an exact precedent to guide him, is whether X is also liable if 'A' obtains, plus or minus circumstance 'B'. In deciding such issues English courts (which are not always ready to admit the extent to which their choice is free) sometimes employ language to indicate that they are making logical deductions when they are in fact doing no more than applying their sense of reasonableness. This is far from saying that reasonableness is a matter of purely subjective impulse[85]: subjective sentiment no doubt cannot be divorced entirely from the judicial role, but what is reasonable refers rather to that pattern of sentiment which inheres in a particular community or some section of it. The judge as a member of the community is bound to share more or less in its common notions, and indeed we often find judges expressing sympathy with such sentiments when they find themselves reluctantly constrained by an earlier precedent to decide a case in conflict with what must seem reasonable to the common man.[86]

84 Cf. the question examined by logicians as to whether we learn anything new by means of syllogistic inference (Stebbing, *op. cit.*, pp. 217–8). Professor Cohen points out that the usual argument that there can be nothing in the conclusion which is not 'contained' in the premises, involves 'an uncritical spatial metaphor' (*op. cit.*, p. 13), and ignores the psychological element. 'We must distinguish between *novelty*, the psychological factor, and the logical connection between premises and conclusions' (p. 185). Mr. Justice Cardozo's description of logical method as 'the derivation of a consequence from a rule or a principle or a precedent which, accepted as a datum, contains implicitly within itself the germ of the conclusion' (*Nature of the Judicial Process*, p. 49), seems to be little more than a fiction as applied to the legal process.

85 Though, no doubt, the American 'realist school' exaggerates the extent to which the 'personal equation' enters into judicial decisions, the view may be ventured that it has done well to stress that this is a factor to be reckoned with. It has, of course, never been ignored by legal practitioners, but hitherto there had been something in the nature of a conspiracy of silence on the subject among jurists. Cf. Frank, *op. cit.*, Part 1, Chap. 12.

86 Thus in *Howard* v. *Walker* [1947] 2 All E.R. 197, on the possible right of action of a person injured by tripping over a defective paving on another's land, Lord Goddard C.J., said: 'It may be that the law is not entirely satisfactory on this point. No doubt, it is difficult for a layman to understand why, if he is walking

It is here rather than in the realm of pure logic that questions of 'consistency' arise. The fact that a plaintiff injured in an explosion when outside the defendants' premises can recover damages, though were he injured when on the other side of the fence he would be without remedy, does not result in any inconsistency which infringes the rules of logic. There is nothing essentially 'illogical' (as was argued by counsel in *Read* v. *Lyons* [87]) in a plaintiff being able to recover in the one case and not the other, and there can be no logical compulsion inherent in a rule of law which constrains liability to be imposed in case 'A' if it is imposed in case 'B'. The language of logic as applied to such a situation is entirely misleading. What it is really sought to assert is that the sentiment of the community would feel it fundamentally 'unreasonable' that the plaintiff should recover in the one case and not the other, and that the courts should accede to this sentiment. This argument is of course a perfectly legitimate one which the courts are entitled to examine in the light of every other factor which they consider relevant to the 'reasonableness' of the general rule. One of these factors, for example, may be their view of the general undesirability of imposing strict liability on factory owners who are carrying out a process for the public benefit, and there is of course an endless variety of considerations which might or might not influence a particular decision. The role of the advocate is naturally to persuade, and it may be more effective psychologically to clothe an argument based on sentiment in the unassailable garb of logic. The language of logic tends to be employed as 'an instrument of persuasion',[88] and advocates will, no doubt rightly, avail themselves in a difficult case of every instrument which lies to their hand. In this they are perhaps encouraged by the tendency of the judges themselves sometimes to wrap up their decisions in terms of logical inference.[89] To this extent such a case as *Read* v. *Lyons* may possibly serve as a healthy corrective.[90]

[pp. 473–477]

---

along a road and slips into an excavation at the side of it, he should be entitled to recover, whereas if he slips into the excavation as he is endeavouring to get on to the road, he is not, but I must take the law as I find it' (at p. 199).

[87] [1947] A.C. 146.

[88] Stone, *op. cit.*, p. 146. Yet logic is not in fact a method of producing certainty or conviction but 'the demonstration of the logical structure of the system studied'. M. R. Cohen, *op. cit.*, p. 15. 'The art of thinking must not be confused with logic', Stebbing, *op. cit.*, p. 493.

[89] There is perhaps much to be said here for the view that the judicial process of reasoning resembles that of the ordinary person who starts with a conclusion and afterwards tries to find premises which will substantiate it. Frank, *op. cit.*, p. 100. Some writers, *e.g.*, Wurzel, have gone so far as to suggest that though law is incapable of preserving a strictly logical form, the judges are bound to frame their decisions in pseudo-logical form, so as to avoid outraging public opinion and thereby diminishing the authority of the law! See *op. cit.*, pp. 229–31.

[90] [*Cf.* Pareto, *Mind and Society*, sect. 14: "Human beings have a very conspicuous tendency to paint a varnish of logic over their conduct." Thus there is no strictly logical basis upon which one can draw a distinction between injury caused by the ejected fragments of a machine as against injury caused by fragments of the object upon which the machine was working (*Close* v. *Steel Co. of Wales* [1962] A.C. 367); between careless statements and other forms of carelessness or between physical or merely pecuniary injury (*Hedley Byrne Ltd.* v. *Heller* [1964] A.C. 465); or between wages and sick pay drawn during a man's service as against the disability pension drawn after his discharge, for the purpose of assessing damages resulting from personal injury (*Browning* v. *War Office*

HOME OFFICE v. DORSET YACHT CO. LTD.

[1970] A.C. 1004

LORD DIPLOCK

The specific question of law raised in this appeal may therefore be stated as: Is any duty of care to prevent the escape of a Borstal trainee from custody owed by the Home Office to persons whose property would be likely to be damaged by the tortious acts of the Borstal trainee if he escaped? This is the first time that this specific question has been posed at a higher judicial level than that of a county court. Your Lordships in answering it will be performing a judicial function similar to that performed in *Donoghue* v. *Stevenson* [91] and more recently in *Hedley Byrne & Co. Ltd.* v. *Heller & Partners Ltd.*,[92] of deciding whether the English law of civil wrongs should be extended to impose legal liability to make reparation for the loss caused to another by conduct of a kind which has not hitherto been recognised by the courts as entailing any such liability.

This function, which judges hesitate to acknowledge as law-making, plays at most a minor role in the decisions of the great majority of cases, and little conscious thought has been given to analysing its methodology. Outstanding exceptions are to be found in the speeches of Lord Atkin in *Donoghue* v. *Stevenson* [91] and of Lord Devlin in *Hedley Byrne & Co. Ltd.* v. *Heller & Partners Ltd.*[92] It was because the former was the first authoritative attempt at such an analysis that it has had so seminal an effect on the modern development of the law of negligence.

It will be apparent that I agree with Lord Denning M.R.[93] that what we are concerned with in this appeal ' is . . . at bottom a matter of public policy which we, as judges, must resolve '. He cited in support Lord Pearce's dictum in *Hedley Byrne & Co. Ltd.* v. *Heller & Partners Ltd.*[94]

> ' How wide the sphere of the duty of care in negligence is to be laid depends ultimately on the courts' assessment of the demands of society for protection from the carelessness of others.'

The reference in this passage to ' the courts ' in the plural is significant for—

> ' As always in English law the first step in such an inquiry is to see how far the authorities have gone, for new categories in the law do not spring into existence overnight ';

per Lord Devlin.[95]

The justification of the courts' role in giving the effect of law to the judges' conception of the public interest in the field of negligence is based on the cumulative experience of the judiciary of the actual

[1963] 1 Q.B. 750). For a further discussion on the role of logic in legal reasoning see " Logic in the Law," by A. C. Guest, in *Oxford Essays in Jurisprudence*, at p. 176.]

[91] [1932] A.C. 562 ; [1932] All E.R.Rep. 1.

[92] [1963] 2 All E.R. 575 ; [1964] A.C. 465. [On which see Stevens (1964) 27 M.L.R. 121.]

[93] [1969] 2 All E.R. at 567 ; [1969] 2 Q.B. at 426. [In the Court of Appeal hearing of the instant case. See also Lord Denning M.R. in *Dutton* v. *Bognor Regis Building Society* [1972] 2 W.L.R. 299, 313.]

[94] [1963] 2 All E.R. at 615 ; [1964] A.C. at 536.

[95] [1963] 2 All E.R. at 608 ; [1964] A.C. at 525.

consequences of lack of care in particular instances. And the judicial development of the law of negligence rightly proceeds by seeking first to identify the relevant characteristics that are common to the kinds of conduct and relationship between the parties which are involved in the case for decision and the kinds of conduct and relationships which have been held in previous decisions of the courts to give rise to a duty of care.

The method adopted at this stage of the process is analytical and inductive. It starts with an analysis of the characteristics of the conduct and relationship involved in each of the decided cases. But the analyst must know what he is looking for; and this involves his approaching his analysis with some general conception of conduct and relationships which *ought* to give rise to a duty of care. The analysis leads to a proposition which can be stated in the form: ' In all the decisions that have been analysed a duty of care has been held to exist wherever the conduct and relationship possessed each of the characteristics A, B, C, D etc, and has not so far been found to exist when any of these characteristics were absent.'

For the second stage, which is deductive and analytical, that proposition is converted to: ' In all cases where the conduct and relationship possess each of the characteristics A, B, C, D etc., a duty of care arises.' The conduct and relationship involved in the case for decision is then analysed to ascertain whether they possess each of these characteristics. If they do the conclusion follows that a duty of care does arise in the case for decision.

But since ex hypothesi the kind of case which we are now considering offers a choice whether or not to extend the kinds of conduct or relationships which give rise to a duty of care, the conduct or relationship which is involved in it will lack at least one of the characteristics A, B, C or D etc. And the choice is exercised by making a policy decision whether or not a duty of care ought to exist if the characteristic which is lacking were absent or redefined in terms broad enough to include the case under consideration. The policy decision will be influenced by the same general conception of what ought to give rise to a duty of care as was used in approaching the analysis. The choice to extend is given effect to by redefining the characteristics in more general terms so as to exclude the necessity to conform to limitations imposed by the former definition which are considered to be inessential. The cases which are landmarks in the common law, such as *Lickbarrow* v. *Mason*,[96] *Rylands* v. *Fletcher*,[97] *Indermaur* v. *Dames*,[98] *Donoghue* v. *Stevenson*,[91] to mention but a few, are instances of cases where the cumulative experience of judges has led to a restatement in wide general terms of characteristics of conduct and relationships which give rise to legal liability.

Inherent in this methodology, however, is a practical limitation which is imposed by the sheer volume of reported cases. The initial selection of previous cases to be analysed will itself eliminate from the analysis those in which the conduct or relationship involved possessed characteristics which are obviously absent in the case for decision. The proposition

[96] (1787) 2 Term Rep. 63; [1775–1802] All E.R.Rep. 1.
[97] (1868) L.R. 3 H.L. 330; [1861–73] All E.R.Rep. 1.
[98] (1866) L.R. 1 C.P. 274; [1861–73] All E.R.Rep. 15.

used in the deductive stage is not a true universal. It needs to be qualified so as to read: 'In all cases where the conduct and relationship possess each of the characteristics A, B, C and D etc., *but do not possess any of the characteristics Z, Y or X etc., which were present in the cases eliminated from the analysis,* a duty of care arises'. But this qualification, being irrelevant to the decision of the particular case, is generally left unexpressed.

This was the reason for the warning by Lord Atkin in *Donoghue* v. *Stevenson* [99] itself when he said:

'. . . in the branch of the law which deals with civil wrongs, dependent in England at any rate entirely upon the application by judges of general principles also formulated by judges, it is of particular importance to guard against the danger of stating propositions of law in wider terms than is necessary, lest essential factors be omitted in the wider survey and the inherent adaptability of English law be unduly restricted. For this reason it is very necessary in considering reported cases in the law of torts that the actual decision alone should carry authority, proper weight, of course, being given to the dicta of the judges.'

The plaintiff's argument in the present appeal disregards this warning. It seeks to treat as a universal not the specific proposition of law in *Donoghue* v. *Stevenson* which was about a manufacturer's liability for damage caused by his dangerous products but the well-known aphorism used by Lord Atkin to describe [1] a 'general conception of relations giving rise to a duty of care':

'You must take reasonable care to avoid acts or omissions which you can reasonably foresee would be likely to injure your neighbour. Who, then, in law is my neighbour? The answer seems to be— persons who are closely and directly affected by my act that I ought reasonably to have them in contemplation . . . when I am directing my mind to the acts or omissions which are called in question.'

Used as a guide to characteristics which will be found to exist in conduct and relationships which give rise to a legal duty of care this aphorism marks a milestone in the modern development of the law of negligence. But misused as a universal it is manifestly false.

The branch of English law which deals with civil wrongs abounds with instances of acts and, more particularly, of omissions which give rise to no legal liability in the doer or omitter for loss or damage sustained by others as a consequence of the act or omission, however reasonably or probably that loss or damage might have been anticipated. The very parable of the good Samaritan [2] which was evoked by Lord Atkin in *Donoghue* v. *Stevenson* illustrates, in the conduct of the priest and of the Levite who passed by on the other side, an omission which was likely to have as its reasonable and probable consequence damage to the health of the victim of the thieves, but for which the priest and Levite would have incurred no civil liability in English law. Examples

[99] [1932] A.C. at 583, 584; [1932] All E.R.Rep. at 13.
[1] [1932] A.C. at 580; [1932] All E.R.Rep. at 11.
[2] Luke x, verse 30.

could be multiplied. You may cause loss to a tradesman by withdrawing your custom although the goods which he supplies are entirely satisfactory; you may damage your neighbour's land by intercepting the flow of percolating water to it even though the interception is of no advantage to yourself; you need not warn him of a risk of physical danger to which he is about to expose himself unless there is some special relationship between the two of you such as that of occupier of land and visitor; you may watch your neighbour's goods being ruined by a thunderstorm although the slightest effort on your part could protect them from the rain and you may do so with impunity unless there is some special relationship between you such as that of bailor and bailee.

In *Hedley Byrne & Co. Ltd.* v. *Heller & Partners Ltd.*, which marked a fresh development in the law of negligence, the conduct in question was careless words, not careless deeds. Lord Atkin's aphorism,[3] if it were of universal application, would have sufficed to dispose of this case, apart from the express disclaimer of liability. But your Lordships were unanimous in holding that the difference in the characteristics of the conduct in the two cases prevented the propositions of law in *Donoghue* v. *Stevenson* from being directly applicable. Your Lordships accordingly proceeded to analyse the previous decisions in which the conduct complained of had been careless words, from which you induced a proposition of law about liability for damage caused by careless words which differs from the proposition of law in *Donoghue* v. *Stevenson* about liability for damage caused by careless deeds.

In the present appeal, too, the conduct of the defendant which is called in question differs from the kind of conduct discussed in *Donoghue* v. *Stevenson* in at least two special characteristics. First, the actual damage sustained by the plaintiff was the direct consequence of a tortious act done with conscious volition by a third party responsible in law for his own acts and this act was interposed between the act of the defendant complained of and the sustention of damage by the plaintiff. Secondly, there are two separate 'neighbour relationships' of the defendant involved, a relationship with the plaintiff and a relationship with the third party. These are capable of giving rise to conflicting duties of care. This appeal, therefore, also raises the lawyer's question 'Am I my brother's keeper'? A question which may also receive a restricted reply. . . .   [pp. 1057–1061]

. . . From the previous decisions of the English courts, in particular those in *Ellis* v. *Home Office* and *D'Arcy* v. *Prison Comrs.*, which I accept as correct, it is possible to arrive by induction at an established proposition of law as respects one of those special relations: viz A is responsible for damage caused to the person or property of B by the tortious act of C (a person responsible in law for his own acts) where the relationship between A and C has the characteristics: (1) that A has the legal right to detain C in penal custody and to control his acts while in custody; (2) that A is actually exercising his legal right of custody of C at the time of C's tortious act; and (3) that A if he had taken reasonable care in the exercise of his right of custody could have prevented C from doing the tortious act which caused damage to the person or property of B; and where also the relationship between A

---

[3] [1932] A.C. at 580; [1932] All E.R. at 11.

and B has the characteristics; (4) that at the time of C's tortious act A has the legal right to control the situation of B or his property as respects physical proximity to C; and (5) that A can reasonably foresee that B is likely to sustain damage to his person or property if A does not take reasonable care to prevent C from doing tortious acts of the kind which he did.

Upon the facts which your Lordships are required to assume for the purposes of the present appeal the relationship between the defendant, A, and the Borstal trainees, C, did possess characteristics (1) and (3) but did not possess characteristic (2); while the relationship between the defendant, A, and the plaintiff, B, did possess characteristic (5) but did not possess characteristic (4). What your Lordships have to decide as respects each of the relationships is whether the missing characteristic is essential to the existence of the duty or whether the facts assumed for the purposes of this appeal disclose some other characteristic which if substituted for that which is missing would produce a new proposition of law which *ought* to be true.

As any proposition which relates to the duty of controlling another man to prevent his doing damage to a third deals with a category of civil wrongs of which the English courts have hitherto had little experience it would not be consistent with the methodology of the development of the law by judicial decision that any new proposition should be stated in wider terms than are necessary for the determination of the present appeal. Public policy may call for the immediate recognition of a new sub-category of relations which are the source of a duty of this nature additional to the sub-category described in the established proposition; but further experience of actual cases would be needed before the time became ripe for the coalescence of sub-categories into a broader category of relations giving rise to the duty, such as was effected with respect to the duty of care of a manufacturer of products in *Donoghue* v. *Stevenson*. Nevertheless, any new sub-category will form part of the English law of civil wrongs and must be consistent with its general principles. . . .   [pp. 1063–1064]

. . . The analogy between 'negligence' at common law and the careless exercise of statutory powers breaks down where the act or omission complained of is not of a kind which would itself give rise to a cause of action at common law if it were not authorised by the statute. To relinquish intentionally or inadvertently the custody and control of a person responsible at law for his own acts, is not an act or omission which independently of any statute, would give rise to a cause of action at common law against the custodian on the part of another person who subsequently sustained tortious damage at the hands of the person released. The instant case thus lacks a relevant characteristic which was present in the series of decisions from which the principle formulated in *Geddis* v. *Proprietors of Bann Reservoir* [4] was derived. Furthermore, there is present in the instant case a characteristic which was lacking in *Geddis* v. *Proprietors of Bann Reservoir*. There the only conflicting interests involved were those on the one hand of the statutory undertakers responsible for the act or omission complained of and on the other hand of the person who sustained damage as a consequence of it. In the instant case, it is the interest of the Borstal trainee himself which

4 (1878) 3 App.Cas. 430.

is most directly affected by any decision to release him and by any system of relaxed control while he is still in custody that is intended to develop his sense of personal responsibility and so afford him an opportunity to escape. Directly affected also are the interests of other members of the community of trainees subject to the common system of control; and indirectly affected by the system of control while under detention and of release under supervision is the general public interest in the reformation of young offenders and the prevention of crime.

These interests, unlike those of a person who sustains damage to his property or person by the tortious act or omission of another, do not fall within any category of property or rights recognised in English law as entitled to protection by a civil action for damages. The conflicting interests of the various categories of persons likely to be affected by an act or omission of the custodian of a Borstal trainee which has as its consequence his release or his escape are thus of different kinds for which in law there is no common basis for comparison. If the reasonable man when directing his mind to the act or omission which has this consequence ought to have in contemplation persons in all the categories directly affected and also the general public interest in the reformation of young offenders, there is no criterion by which a court can assess where the balance lies between the weight to be given to one interest and that to be given to another. The material relevant to the assessment of the reformative effect on trainees of release under supervision or of any relaxation of control while still under detention is not of a kind which can be satisfactorily elicited by the adversary procedure and rules of evidence adopted in English courts of law or of which judges (and juries) are suited by their training and experience to assess the probative value.

It is, I apprehend, for practical reasons of this kind that over the past century the public law concept of ultra vires has replaced the civil law concept of negligence as the test of the legality, and consequently of the actionability, of acts or omissions of government departments or public authorities done in the exercise of a discretion conferred on them by Parliament as to the means by which they are to achieve a particular public purpose. According to this concept Parliament has entrusted to the department or authority charged with the administration of the statute the exclusive right to determine the particular means within the limits laid down by the statute by which its purpose can best be fulfilled. It is not the function of the court, for which it would be ill-suited, to substitute its own view of the appropriate means for that of the department or authority by granting a remedy by way of a civil action at law to a private citizen adversely affected by the way in which the discretion has been exercised. Its function is confined in the first instance to deciding whether the act or omission complained of fell within the statutory limits imposed on the department's or authority's discretion. Only if it did not would the court have jurisdiction to determine whether or not the act or omission, not being justified by the statute, constituted an actionable infringement of the plaintiff's rights in civil law.

These considerations lead me to the conclusion that neither the intentional release of a Borstal trainee under supervision, nor the unintended escape of a Borstal trainee still under detention which was the consequence of the application of a system of relaxed control intentionally adopted by the Home Office as conducive to the reformation of trainees, can have been intended by Parliament to give rise to any cause of action on the part of any private citizen unless the system adopted was so unrelated to any purpose of reformation that no reasonable person could have reached a bona fide conclusion that it was conducive to that purpose. Only then would the decision to adopt it be ultra vires in public law.

A Parliamentary intention to leave to the discretion of the Home Office the decision as to what system of control should be adopted to prevent the escape of Borstal trainees must involve, from the very nature of the subject-matter of the decision, an intention that in the application of the system a wide discretion in the application of the system may be delegated by the Home Office to subordinate officers engaged in the administration of the Borstal system. But although the system of control, including the sub-delegation of discretion to subordinate officers, may itself be intra vires, an act or omission of a subordinate officer employed in the administration of the system may nevertheless be ultra vires if it falls outside the limits of the discretion delegated to him—*i.e.*, if it is done contrary to instructions which he has received from the Home Office.

In a civil action which calls in question an act or omission of a subordinate officer of the Home Office on the ground that he has been 'negligent' in his custody and control of a Borstal trainee who has caused damage to another person the initial inquiry should be whether or not the act or omission was ultra vires for one or other of these reasons. Where the act or omission is done in pursuance of the officer's instructions, the court may have to form its own view as to what is in the interests of Borstal trainees, but only to the limited extent of determining whether or not any reasonable person could bona fide come to the conclusion that the trainee causing the damage or other trainees in the same custody could be benefited in any way by the act or omission. This does not involve the court in attempting to substitute, for that of the Home Office, its own assessment of the comparative weight to be given to the benefit to the trainees and the detriment to persons likely to sustain damage. If on the other hand the officer's act or omission is done contrary to his instructions it is not protected by the public law doctrine of intra vires. Its actionability falls to be determined by the civil law principles of negligence, like the acts of the statutory undertakers in *Geddis* v. *Proprietors of Bann Reservoir*.

This, as it seems to me, is the way in which the courts should set about the task of reconciling the public interest in maintaining the freedom of the Home Office to decide on the system of custody and control of Borstal trainees which is most likely to conduce to their reformation and the prevention of crime, and the public interest that Borstal officers should not be allowed to be completely disregardful of the interests both of the trainees in their charge and of persons likely to be injured by their carelessness, without the law providing redress to those who in fact sustain injury.

Ellis v. *Home Office* and *D'Arcy* v. *Prison Comrs.* are decisions which are consistent with this principle as respects the initial inquiry. In neither of them was it sought to justify the alleged acts or omissions of the prison officers concerned as being done in compliance with instructions given to them by the appropriate authority (at that date the prison commissioners) or as being in the interests of the prisoner whose tortious act caused the damage or of any other inmates of the prison. If the test suggested were applied to acts and omissions alleged in those two cases they would in public law be ultra vires.

If this analogy to the principle of ultra vires in public law is applied as the relevant condition precedent to the liability of a custodian for damage caused by the tortious act of a person (the detainee) over whom he has a statutory right of custody, the characteristic of the relationship between the custodian and the detainee which was present in those two cases, *viz.,* that the custodian was actually exercising his right of custody at the time of the tortious act of the detainee, would not be essential. A cause of action is capable of arising from failure by the custodian to take reasonable care to prevent the detainee from escaping, if his escape was the consequence of an act or omission of the custodian falling outside the limits of the discretion delegated to him under the statute.

The practical effect of this would be that no liability in the Home Office for ' negligence ' could arise out of the escape from an ' open ' Borstal of a trainee who had been classified for training at a Borstal of this type by the appropriate officer to whom the function of classification had been delegated, on the ground that the officer had been negligent in so classifying him or in failing to reclassify him for removal to a ' closed ' Borstal. The decision as to classification would be one which lay within the officer's discretion. The court could not inquire into its propriety as it did in *Greenwell* v. *Prison Comrs.*[5] in order to determine whether he had given what the court considered to be sufficient weight to the interests of persons whose property the trainee would be likely to damage if he should escape. For this reason I think that *Greenwell* v. *Prison Comrs.* was wrongly decided by the county court judge. But to say this does not dispose of the present appeal for the allegations of negligence against the borstal officers are consistent with their having acted outside any discretion delegated to them and having disregarded their instructions as to the precautions they should take to prevent members of the working party of trainees from escaping from Brownsea Island. Whether they had or not could only be determined at the trial of the action. But this is only a condition precedent to the existence of any liability. Even if the acts and omissions of the Borstal officer alleged in the particulars of negligence were done in breach of their instructions and so were ultra vires in public law it does not follow that they were also done in breach of any duty of care owed by the officers to the respondents in civil law.

It is common knowledge, of which judicial notice may be taken, that Borstal training often fails to achieve its purpose of reformation, and that trainees when they have ceased to be detained in custody revert to crime and commit tortious damage to the person and property of others. But so do criminals who have never been apprehended and criminals who have been released from custody on completion of their sentences or earlier pursuant to a statutory power to do so. The risk of sustaining damage from the tortious acts of criminals is shared by the public at large. It has never been recognised at common law as giving rise to any cause of action against anyone but the criminal

[5] (1951) 101 L.J. 486.

himself. It would seem arbitrary and therefore unjust to single out for the special privilege of being able to recover compensation from the authorities responsible for the prevention of crime a person whose property was damaged by the tortious act of a criminal, merely because the damage to him happened to be caused by a criminal who had escaped from custody before completion of his sentence instead of by one who had been lawfully released or who had been put on probation or given a suspended sentence or who had never been previously apprehended at all. To give rise to a duty on the part of the custodian owed to a member of the public to take reasonable care to prevent a Borstal trainee from escaping from his custody before completion of the trainee's sentence there should be some relationship between the custodian and the person to whom the duty is owed which exposes that person to a particular risk of damage in consequence of that escape which is different in its incidence from the general risk of damage from criminal acts of others which he shares with all members of the public.

What distinguishes a Borstal trainee who has escaped from one who has been duly released from custody, is his liability to recapture, and the distinctive added risk which is a reasonably foreseeable consequence of a failure to exercise due care in preventing him from escaping is the likelihood that in order to elude pursuit immediately on the discovery of his absence the escaping trainee may steal or appropriate and damage property which is situated in the vicinity of the place of detention from which he has escaped.

So long as Parliament is content to leave the general risk of damage from criminal acts to lie where it falls without any remedy except against the criminal himself, the courts would be exceeding their limited function in developing the common law to meet changing conditions if they were to recognise a duty of care to prevent criminals escaping from penal custody owed to a wider category of members of the public than those whose property was exposed to an exceptional added risk by the adoption of a custodial system for young offenders which increased the likelihood of their escape unless due care was taken by those responsible for their custody.

I should therefore hold that any duty of a Borstal officer to use reasonable care to prevent a Borstal trainee from escaping from his custody was owed only to persons whom he could reasonably foresee had property situate in the vicinity of the place of detention of the detainee which the detainee was likely to steal or to appropriate and damage in the course of eluding immediate pursuit and recapture. Whether or not any person fell within this category would depend on the facts of the particular case including the previous criminal and escaping record of the individual trainee concerned and the nature of the place from which he escaped.

So to hold would be a rational extension of the relationship between the custodian and the person sustaining the damage which was accepted in *Ellis* v. *Home Office* and *D'Arcy* v. *Prison Comrs.* as giving rise to a duty of care on the part of the custodian to exercise reasonable care in controlling his detainee. In those two cases the custodian had a legal right to control the physical proximity of the person or property sustaining the damage to the detainee who caused it. The extended relationship substitutes for the right to control the knowledge which the custodian possessed or ought to have possessed that physical proximity in fact existed. . . .   [pp. 1066–1071]

HEYDON'S CASE
(1584) 3 *Co. Rep.* 7 *b*

. . . And after all the Barons openly argued in Court in the same term, *scil.* Pasch, 26 Eliz. and it was unanimously resolved by Sir Roger Manwood, Chief Baron, and the other Barons of the Exchequer, that the said lease made to Heydon of the said parcels, whereof Ware and Ware were seised for life by copy of court-roll, was void; for it was agreed by them, that the said copyhold estate was an estate for life, within the words and meaning of the said Act. And it was resolved by them, that for the sure and true interpretation of all statutes in general (be they penal or beneficial, restrictive or enlarging of the common law), four things are to be discerned and considered:—

1st. What was the common law before the making of the Act.

2nd. What was the mischief and defect for which the common law did not provide.

3rd. What remedy the Parliament hath resolved and appointed to cure the disease of the commonwealth.

And, 4th. The true reason of the remedy; and then the office of all the Judges is always to make such construction as shall suppress the mischief, and advance the remedy, and to suppress subtle inventions and evasions for continuance of the mischief, and *pro privato commodo,* and to add force and life to the cure and remedy, according to the true intent of the makers of the Act, *pro bono publico.* And it was said, that in this case the common law was, that religious and ecclesiastical persons might have made leases for as many years as they pleased, the mischief was that when they perceived their houses would be dissolved, they made long and unreasonable leases: now the stat of 31 H. 8. doth provide the remedy, and principally for such religious and ecclesiastical houses which should be dissolved after the Act (as the said college in our case was) that all leases of any land, whereof any estate or interest for life or years was then in being, should be void; and their reason was, that it was not necessary for them to make a new lease so long as a former had continuance, and therefore the intent of the Act was to avoid doubling of estates, and to have but one single estate in being at a time: for doubling of estates implies in itself deceit, and private respect, to prevent the intention of the Parliament. And if the copyhold estate for two lives, and the lease for eighty years shall stand together, here will be doubling of estates *simul & semel,* which will be against the true meaning of Parliament. . . .   [pp. 7b–8a]

SEAFORD COURT ESTATES LTD. v. *ASHER*
[1949] 2 K.B. 481
DENNING L.J. . . .

. . . Whenever a statute comes up for consideration it must be remembered that it is not within human powers to foresee the manifold sets of facts which may arise, and, even if it were, it is not possible to provide for them in terms free from all ambiguity. The English language is not an instrument of mathematical precision. Our literature would be much the poorer if it were. This is where the draftsmen of Acts of Parliament have often been unfairly criticized. A judge, believing himself to be fettered by the supposed rule that he must look to the language and nothing else, laments that the draftsmen have not provided for this or that, or have been guilty of some or other ambiguity. It would certainly save the judges trouble if Acts of Parliament were drafted with divine prescience and perfect clarity. In the absence of it, when a defect appears a judge cannot simply fold his hands and blame the draftsman. He must set to work on the constructive task of finding the intention of Parliament, and he must do this not only from the language of the statute, but also from a consideration of the social conditions which gave rise to it, and of the mischief which it was passed to remedy, and then he must supplement the written word so as to give " force and life " to the intention of the legislature. That was clearly laid down by the resolution of the judges in *Heydon's case*,[6] and it is the safest guide to-day. Good practical advice on the subject was given about the same time by Plowden in his second volume *Eyston* v. *Studd.*[7] Put into homely metaphor it is this: A judge should ask himself the question: if the makers of the Act had themselves come across this ruck in the texture of it, how would they have straightened it out? He must then do as they would have done. A judge must not alter the material of which it is woven, but he can and should iron out the creases. . . .[8]   [pp. 498–499]

MAGOR AND ST. MELLONS R.D.C. v. NEWPORT CORPN.
[1952] A.C. 189

LORD SIMONDS . . .

. . . My Lords, the criticism which I venture to make of the judgment of the learned Lord Justice [9] is not directed at the conclusion that he reached. It is after all a trite saying that on questions of construction different minds may come to different conclusions, and I am content to say that I agree with my noble and learned friend. But it is on the approach of the Lord Justice to what is a question of construction and nothing else that I think it desirable to make some comment; for at a time when so large a proportion of the cases that are brought before the courts depend on the construction of modern statutes it would not be right for this House to pass unnoticed the propositions which the learned Lord Justice lays down for the guidance of himself and, presumably, of others.

" We sit here," he says,[10] " to find out the intention of Parliament and of Ministers and carry it out, and we do this better by filling in

---

6 (1584) 3 Co.Rep. 7b.   7 (1574) 2 Plowden, 465.
8 [On Lord Denning and statutory interpretation see Montrose in *Precedent and other Essays* (1968) Chap. 9. Montrose distinguishes between linguistic and legislative gaps, formal and substantial. He believes that Denning L.J. had in mind the former sense, that gaps were gaps in the wording in the sense that actual words were ambiguous. This is supported by Denning's phrasing (" not alter the material . . . but iron out the creases ") and by his statement in *London Transport* v. *Betts* that " judges have no right to fill in gaps which they suppose to exist in an Act of Parliament, but must leave it to Parliament itself to do so " ([1958] A.C. 213, 247). Lord Denning reiterated what he said in *Seaford* in *Eddis* v. *Chichester Constable* [1969] 2 Ch. 345.]
9 [Lord Justice Denning.]   10 [1950] 2 All E.R. 1226, 1236.

the gaps and making sense of the enactment than by opening it up to destructive analysis." The first part of this passage appears to be an echo of what was said in *Heydon's Case* 300 years ago, and, so regarded, is not objectionable. But the way in which the learned Lord Justice summarizes the broad rules laid down by Sir Edward Coke in that case may well induce grave misconception of the function of the court. The part which is played in the judicial interpretation of a statute by reference to the circumstances of its passing is too well known to need restatement; it is sufficient to say that the general proposition that it is the duty of the court to find out the intention of Parliament—and not only of Parliament but of Ministers also—cannot by any means be supported. The duty of the court is to interpret the words that the legislature has used; those words may be ambiguous, but, even if they are, the power and duty of the court to travel outside them on a voyage of discovery are strictly limited: see, for instance, *Assam Railways & Trading Co. Ld.* v. *Inland Revenue Commissioners*,[11] and particularly the observations of Lord Wright.[12]

The second part of the passage that I have cited from the judgment of the learned Lord Justice is no doubt the logical sequel of the first. The court, having discovered the intention of Parliament and of Ministers too, must proceed to fill in the gaps. What the legislature has not written, the court must write. This proposition, which restates in a new form the view expressed by the Lord Justice in the earlier case of *Seaford Court Estates Ld.* v. *Asher*[13] (to which the Lord Justice himself refers), cannot be supported. It appears to me to be a naked usurpation of the legislative function under the thin disguise of interpretation. And it is the less justifiable when it is guesswork with what material the legislature would, if it had discovered the gap, have filled it in.[14] If a gap is disclosed, the remedy lies in an amending Act.   [pp. 190–191]

W. FRIEDMANN

Law and Social Change in Contemporary Britain
(1951)

Three Approaches to Statutory Interpretation [15]

Three types of legal approach to the interpretation of statutes may conveniently be distinguished, both in Continental and Anglo-American jurisprudence.

[11] [1935] A.C. 445.

[12] Ibid. 458.   [13] [1949] 2 K.B. 481, 498–9 [see *ante*, 823].

[14] [*Cf.* Lord Simonds' approach to gap-filling in *Shaw* v. *D.P.P.*, *ante*, 70, very much an example of legislative gap-filling. *Cf. ante*, 824, n. 8.]

[15] [The passages quoted here, are not reprinted in Prof. Friedmann's later published book entitled *Law in a Changing Society* (1959). However, on pp. 36–7 of that book, he indicates continuing adherence to the views previously expressed by him. The discussion in the new book, nevertheless, is mainly directed to showing how even when courts appear to be applying a literal interpretation, or approaching a question of interpretation in accordance with technical canons of construction, it is nonetheless frequently the case that value-judgments are involved in the decisions. (See especially, pp. 34–62.) In the second edition (1972), he notes that his approach has received " powerful confirmation " in *R.* v. *Drybones*, 9 D.L.R. (3rd) 473 (1970), a decision of the Canadian Supreme Court: the Bill of Rights " has the substantive weight of a constitutional document " (pp. 58–60).]

The Pseudo-logical or Textbook Approach

The first is the analytical and pseudo-logical approach. It is paramount in the current textbooks on the interpretation of statutes. In English jurisprudence the three main pillars of the traditional interpretation of statutes are the literal rule the golden rule, and the mischief rule. The literal rule says that, if the meaning of a section is plain, it must be applied regardless of the result. The golden rule says that where the ordinary sense of the words would lead to some absurdity or inconsistency, the literal interpretation must be modified accordingly. The mischief rule expresses both the oldest and the most modern approach. Derived from *Heydon's Case* decided in 1584, it directs the interpretation of a statute in accordance with its general policy and the evil which it was intended to remedy. The social purpose of the statute must be found out in the light of the previous law, the specific defect unprovided for by that law, the specific remedy decided on by Parliament, and the true reason of the reform. . . .   [pp. 239–240]

The Social Policy Approach

It is the vacillation between one type of interpretation and another, as applied to the increased tempo and urgency of modern social legislation, which has exasperated many legal critics. Dr. Jennings has given an illustration of the disastrous result to which these judicial vacillations rather than social prejudice have led in the case of public health legislation.[16] No less unfortunate has been the frequent obstruction of urgent and unobjectionable housing improvement schemes, through the judicial construction of the relevant orders and improvement schemes as ' quasi-judicial ' even where the schemes were subject to approval by higher authorities.[17] This had led a number of modern critics to suggest an alternative principle of interpretation which may be called the ' social objective ' principle. It has been advocated among others by Laski,[18] Jennings[19] and Llewelyn Davis.[20] Two arguments are adduced in support. Firstly, the critics say that the prevailing rules of statutory interpretation allow for diversity, vacillation and confusion. This is undoubtedly correct. Secondly, they allege that the prevailing tendency of courts is one of hostility to modern social reform legislation. This contention is more doubtful.

As distinct from the history of the United States Supreme Court, the cases in which British courts have used their judicial power deliberately to frustrate a social purpose are not frequent.[21] *Roberts* v. *Hopwood*[22] is probably the outstanding example. The recent tendency of British courts has undoubtedly been one of greater sympathy towards the social objectives of a statute. Outstanding examples are the interpretation of

---

16 ' Judicial Process at its Worst ' (1938) 1 M.L.R. 111.
17 Cf., in particular, *R.* v. *Electricity Commissioners* [1924] 1 K.B. 171, and *Estate and Trust Agencies* v. *Singapore Improvement Trust* [1937] A.C. 898. Recent decisions show a sharp reversal of this attitude.
18 Annexe 5 to Report of Committee on Ministers' Powers, 1932.
19 ' Courts and Administrative Law ' (1936) 49 Harv.L.R. 426.
20 (1936) 35 Col.L.R. 519.
21 [See D. Lloyd, " Ministers' Powers and the Courts," in (1948) 1 *Current Legal Problems* 89.]
22 [1925] A.C. 578.

the Road Traffic Act 1930, in favour of the third party whose compulsory insurance was the intention of the Act,[23] a recent decision of the Court of Appeal [24] which, refusing to surcharge Birmingham City Councillors for a wartime children's allowance scheme, expressed principles starkly contrasting with those of *Roberts* v. *Hopwood*, the protection of the minimum standards to which an indigent tenant must be held entitled in modern Britain,[25] the many recent refusals of the House of Lords and the Court of Appeal to hamper housing or town-planning policy by construing a ministerial decision as ' quasi-judicial ',[26] or the interpretation of the Statute of Westminster against the broad political purpose of granting full constitutional and political autonomy to the Dominions.[27]

Secondly, liberal as against social policy interpretation has not always been reactionary, as shown by the case of *Ellerman Lines* v. *Murray*.[28]

Thirdly, the social objective policy sometimes has to be balanced against other legal or constitutional principles. The much-debated decision, for example, by which the House of Lords in *Minister of Health* v. *Yaffé* [29] held that a clause in the Housing Act under which ' the order of the Minister when made shall have effect as if enacted in this Act ' did not preclude the power of the court to hold the Minister's order to be *ultra vires,* was, in some of the judgments, coupled with a bias in favour of the house-owner as against public authority.[30] But the predominant concern of the House was with the constitutional problem of delegated legislation.

Fourthly, there are numerous statutory clauses which have no apparent or obvious social objective, but may nevertheless in a concrete case give rise to profound differences of social and political philosophy. Such a case is *Nokes* v. *Doncaster Amalgamated Collieries*.[31] The section of the Company Act which gives the court power to transfer, by statutory amalgamation, all the property and liabilities of one company to another and which defines property as including ' property rights and powers of every description ' is on the face of it of a highly technical character, and has no obvious policy behind it. Yet the section gave rise to one of the most important modern public policy decisions in English law when the House of Lords had to decide whether ' property ' included the services of miners and other employees. By a majority of four it held that the principle of personal freedom of labour did not permit the compulsory transfer of employees' contracts in the course of amalgamation. Lord Romer, in his dissenting judgment, pointed out that it

---

[23] *Monk* v. *Warbey* [1935] 1 K.B. 75.
[24] *Re Decision of Walker* [1944] K.B. 644. [But see the more recent decisions of *Prescott* v. *Birmingham Corporation* [1955] Ch. 210; and *Taylor* v. *Munrow* [1960] 1 W.L.R. 151, which indicate a strong reversal of the trend indicated in the text above.]
[25] *Summers* v. *Salford Corporation* [1943] A.C. 283.
[26] Cf., in particular, *Johnson* v. *Minister of Health* [1947] 2 All E.R. 395, and *Franklin* v. *Minister of Town and Country Planning* [1948] A.C. 87.
[27] *British Coal Corporation* v. *The King* [1935] A.C. 500, and *Att.-Gen. for Alberta* v. *Att.-Gen. for Canada* [1947] A.C. 503.
[28] [1931] A.C. 126.
[29] [1931] A.C. 494.
[30] Cf. the judgment of Scrutton L.J. in the Court of Appeal and the dissenting judgment of Lord Russell in the House of Lords.
[31] [1940] A.C. 1014.

was futile to protect employees and workers in the relatively rare cases of amalgamation of companies while they were powerless in the far more frequent cases of changes of management or policy control through the acquisition of a controlling interest in a company, without change of legal identity.

Lastly, there are statutes with clauses so general and comprehensive that the definition of their policy is itself subject to the fluctuations of time and public opinion. This applies in particular to written constitutions, the problem of whose judicial interpretation in a democratic society—where the judiciary is neither compelled nor necessarily inclined to adjust its attitude to that of the current legislative or executive policy—has become increasingly complex and problematical, as shown by the history of the United States, Canada and Australia. The ' policy ' of a constitution designed to govern the life of a State, usually a Federal State, for many decades or even centuries, is itself a flexible conception. This gives rise to special problems of interpretation.

It follows that the ' social policy ' interpretation, while an essential corrective to the pseudo-analytical interpretation, can at best only give a partial answer to our problem.

The ' Free Intuition ' Approach

A third school, despairing of any reliable objective rules to guide the judge in the interpretation of codes and statutes, advocates the use of free and creative intuition by the judge. In some ways this line of thought represents a more radical development of the social objective theory. It arose from the same revolt—initiated on the Continent by Ihering and Gény—against *Buchstabenjurisprudenz*, the exaggerated reverence for literal interpretation which usually goes hand in hand with a conservative philosophy. But this theory does not necessarily stop there. Its extreme exponents advocate the power of the judge to alter a statute where the results of literal interpretation would be absurd or grossly unjust. Apart from Ehrlich, who advocated this approach as early as 1903, this school of thought found its most forceful exponents in Germany after the First World War, when a reactionary judiciary often enough defeated the purposes of republican legislation.[32] Some theoretical justification is lent to this view by the theory of the Vienna School of Jurisprudence which describes the judicial process as inherently creative, as being concerned with the making as well as the application of law. In American jurisprudence a counterpart is found in the views of some of the more extreme realists who discount legal principle and logical deductions altogether and see the solution in the free and creative handling of the concrete situations by adult and mature lawyers.[33]

---

[32] [Cf., Friedmann, *Legal Theory* (5th ed.), p. 85.]

[33] Mr. Justice Holmes, regarded by many realists as the personification of such a lawyer, was himself far from such an unorthodoxy except for certain over-popularised statements not borne out by his own judicial record. Radin seems close to the way of thinking described in the text when, despairing of the many delusive rules, he says that ' the sound sense of many judges will frequently penetrate this smoke screen and reach results that seem satisfactory, but it is often done half-consciously and almost surreptitiously ' (1930) 43 Harv.L.R. at p. 882.

The free intuition approach can however lead to very different results. In the hands of the Nazi regime it became a convenient way to dispense with legislative reform, while judges schooled in Nazi thinking or subject to rigid political pressure could distort existing statutes in the name of ' healthy instincts of the people '. There are obvious theoretical weaknesses in this approach. To admit that legal problems are infinite, that no codification or statutory regulation can preclude the element of choice or the weighing of social values and interests in the judicial process, does not mean that legal logic and rules are valueless. They are an important enough guide in the vast majority of routine cases. . . .

[pp. 246–250]

The Need for Differentiation

In a free society, there is no master solution which could resolve the judicial dilemma. Totalitarian societies direct the judge to decide in accordance with political principles laid down by his government, and they ensure his obedience by political and disciplinary pressure. The free judge has no such easy way out. His independence of changing legislative and executive trends is one of the few permanent essentials of democracy, yet he cannot isolate himself from the broad trend of political and social developments. Where judges have done so, as the majority of the United States Supreme Court have done between the middle of the 19th century and the early 1930's, the results have been socially disastrous.

The adult judge will have no illusions about the uncertainty of the situation and the frequent conflict of guiding principles. He must resolve such problems from case to case, yet a somewhat more differentiated guide and approach should be possible than has hitherto been assumed. The weakness of most theories of statutory interpretation lies in the assumption that all statutes are of the same type. A certain move towards differentiation has been made by Willis [34] in his distinction between social reform, penal and taxation statutes. It should however be carried further. . . .

[pp. 252–253]

. . . While there is no magic guide to the proper interpretation of statutes, a differentiation between various types of statutes should greatly assist an intelligent and rational approach to statutory construction. The main categories of statutes which ought to be distinguished for this purpose are: firstly, constitutional statutes; secondly, statutes implementing a specific social objective; thirdly, statutes carrying out specific legal reforms; fourthly, acts implementing international conventions; fifthly, penal statutes; sixthly, taxation statutes. This leaves a large proportion of predominantly technical acts in the interpretation of which a judge must be guided by the same principles as in the creative development of precedent.[35]

[p. 265]

---

[34] 16 Can.B.R., p. 23.

[35] [Cf. the attitude of Law Commissions, *ante*, 742. What Friedmann is arguing for has been done to some extent by positing different presumptions, *e.g.*, in a statute implementing an international convention there is a presumption that the government intends to carry out its international obligations (*Post Office* v. *Estuary Radio* [1968] 2 Q.B. 740).]

H. C. GUTTERIDGE

Comparative Law

2nd ed.

The Comparative Interpretation of Statute Law

. . . The first problem with which we are faced is that of endeavouring to form some estimate of the different techniques which are employed in the various legal systems for this purpose. This is no easy task for an English lawyer, because our law is for the most part free from the influence of the theories as to the nature of the interpretative function which are prevalent in the civil-law countries. It is true that English law is much richer than any of the continental systems in canons of construction, but these canons all centre on the duty of the judges to ascertain the intention of the legislator in making use of the particular word or phrase which is to be interpreted. Continental law, on the other hand, is replete with theories of various kinds. Some of these theories have not met with general acceptance, but they have combined in an assault on the grammatical and logical views of the interpretative function which has had a notable influence on judicial technique.

The extreme position taken up by the ' Free Law ' [36] school of thought has, it would seem, been abandoned. According to this theory a judge is invested with the widest powers in dealing with the language of a statute. He may disregard it if it is either incomplete or ambiguous or if he thinks that the wording is calculated to lead to injustice. If he exercises this prerogative he is under a duty to apply the rule which he conceives would have been formulated by the legislator if he had been aware of the consequences. This theory, which represents the swing of the pendulum away from the positive or rigid theories of the interpretative function, had a very brief life and has now been discarded.

More important are the theories which envisage the ' social purpose ' of a law as a guide to the intentions of the legislature. In Germany the controversy between the ' positivists ' and the ' rationalists ' ended in favour of those who hold that, where the meaning of a statute is ambiguous, the judge must adopt the interpretation which accords most closely with the social or economic purpose (*Zweck*) of the statute.[37] A similar concept has found its way into French law in the guise of the doctrine of the *but social*, and has received the powerful support of Gény and other writers.[38] It is not easy to ascertain the extent to which these theories are put into practice by the judges, though it is clear that they are often resorted to when the usual methods of logical interpretation

---

[36] Eugen Ehrlich, *Freie Rechtsfindung und freie Rechtswissenschaft* (1903); Kantoro-wicz (Gnaeus Flavius), *Der Kampf um die Rechtswissenschaft* (1906); Gény. *Méthode d'Interprétation*, vol. II (1919), p. 330. For a concise account of the ' Free Law ' movement [see Foulkes, 55 *Archiv. für Rechts-und-sozialphilosophie* 367 (1969).]

[37] See, generally, Savigny, *System des Römischen Rechts* (1840); Wach, *Handbuch des Zivilprozessrechts;* Ihering, *Zweck im Recht* (1877).

[38] Gény, *Méthode d'Interprétation, supra.* See also Planiol, *Traité Elémentaire de Droit Civil* (12th ed.), vol. I (1932), no. 224; Colin-Capitant, *Cours Elémentaire de Droit Civil Français* (6th ed.), vol. 1 (1930), no. 3. Bonnecase, ' The Problem of Legal Interpretation in France ', *Journal of C.L.* (3rd Ser.), vol. XII (1930), p. 79.

prove to be inconclusive.[39] But the intention of the legislator, which Lord Watson once described as ' a very slippery phrase ', is the basis of interpretation in all systems of law, and when the judge in a French or German court embarks on a voyage of discovery of the *but social* or *Zweck* he is, in reality, seeking to ascertain the intention of the legislator. The social or economic purpose of a modern statute must, of necessity, coincide, in most cases, with that intention. It must not be assumed that the legislator has acted capriciously or in an arbitrary manner. The perusal of any modern statute book will show that the overwhelming majority of laws relate to matters of social or economic rather than political importance. A judge on the continent of Europe is entitled . . . to carry his investigation into the intention of the legislator much further than would be permitted to any of his English colleagues, and it is unlikely that he will travel very far from the path thus marked out for him. It must be conceded, however, that the theory is supple, and it undoubtedly provides judges with loopholes by means of which they can escape from the necessity of giving effect to an interpretation of the normal type which would bring about a result which they regard as contrary to the highest standards of justice, more especially if the statute with which they are dealing is somewhat antiquated or does not cover the ground completely.[40] On the whole the theory finds its chief exponents in university lecture rooms, but it has been adopted authoritatively in certain instances, e.g. in the Swiss civil code, which provides that the judge shall apply its provisions in accordance with the spirit rather than the letter of the text,[41] and in the first Article of the Soviet civil code of 1922 which in terms subordinates the protection of civil rights to cases in which this is required by the economic and social purpose of the law.[42] The truth of the matter appears to be that judges of all jurisdictions display the like reluctance to put themselves in the place of the legislator unless they are obliged to do so for the purpose of avoiding an interpretation which might lead to an obvious miscarriage of justice. Even our English judges, fettered by rigid canons of construction, have, on occasion, shaken off their bonds, as in the case of the equitable interpretation of Section 4 of the Statute of Frauds which established the doctrine of part performance.[43] The continental judges have greater freedom of action where the phraseology of a statute is ambiguous, but this is due to differences in the technique of interpretation rather than to the influence of any theory upon which the interpretative function is founded.

This brings us to the next question, namely, whether there is a common basis on which the process of interpretation rests in all systems of

[39] See the authorities cited in the two preceding footnotes, and Dabin, *La Vie Juridique des Peuples (Belgique)*, p. 162. [See also, David and de Vries, *French Legal System*, pp. 93, *et seq.*]

[40] See Bonnecase, *loc. cit.* Dr. Walton (' Delictual Responsibility in Civil Law ', *L.Q.R.* vol. LXIX, p. 92) refers to this as a ground for the greater ' elasticity and power of development ' of French law as compared with English law. This may, however, be doubted. English commercial law has, for instance, proved itself to be more flexible than its French counterpart.

[41] Swiss civil code, Article 1 ; *Exposé des Motifs du Code Civil Suisse*, Berne (1902), p. 14 ; Williams, *Swiss Civil Code (Sources of Law)*, p. 42.

[42] Patouillet, *Les Codes de la Russie Soviétique*. [*Cf.* H. J. Berman, *Justice in the U.S.S.R.* (1963), pp. 36, 56.]

[43] See the opinion of Lord Hardwicke in *Attorney-General* v. *Day* (1749) 1 Ves-Sen. at p. 217.

law. This question does not admit of a ready answer. Up to a certain point the English judge and his continental colleague adopt methods which are identical because each of them will take the intention of the legislator into account as the dominant consideration. If the language of the statute is such as to make that intention clear the judge must accept it as it stands, even if the rule does not correspond to his own views of that which would be right and proper in the circumstances. Moreover, each of them must construe the statute as a whole and is entitled to disregard its language if a grammatical interpretation would lead to absurdity or repugnance.[44] But if it is entirely a question of ambiguity of language the English and continental methods of interpretation part company, and we come to the crux of the whole matter.

It is somewhat dangerous to generalise about a complicated question of this kind, but, as we are more immediately concerned with a bird's-eye view of the situation, it may, perhaps, be permissible to attempt a very brief summary of the attitude of the continental systems of law towards the function of judicial interpretation and to outline it in the following way. Statute law, whether in the form of a code or of an amending statute, may give rise to difficulties of interpretation in several ways. It may be imperfect in the sense that it omits to deal, or only deals in part, with the circumstances to which it is applicable *ex facie*. In this event the judge must determine whether the omission is deliberate, or whether it is due to some oversight on the part of the legislator. If it appears that the statute is silent because the legislator intentionally refrained from any expression of his will, the judge must disregard the statute and seek elsewhere for a rule of law to be applied to the matter. If the omission is inadvertent it becomes the duty of the judge to make good the deficiency, but in this case he may be assisted by the possibility of reasoning by analogy to other rules contained in the same code or statute.[45] Problems may also arise owing to the existence of two or more conflicting statutory rules, in which case *lex generalis* must give way to *lex specialis*,[46] and if there is an ' antinomy ', i.e. a deadlock, the rules must be regarded as cancelling one another.[47] A statutory rule may become obsolete by reason of some change in social or economic circumstances and can no longer be interpreted in the light of the *Zweck* or *but social* of the law, or it may be of such a nature that its enforcement would lead to absurdity or injustice. In all these cases the judge must disregard the rule.[48] Finally—and this is the normal case—a difficulty of interpretation may arise because the language of the statute is defective and its meaning is ambiguous. The judge may, in such a case, resort to the historical origins of the rule; he may consult the records of the legislature—including the parliamentary debates which preceded the enactment of the rule—for the purpose of ascertaining the intention of the legislator.

[44] See *Becke* v. *Smith* (1836) 2 M. and W. 191 ; *Grey* v. *Pearson* (1857) 6 H.L.C. 61. *Cf.* Gény, *op. cit.* at p. 252; Planiol, *op. cit.* vol. 1, § 216; Enneccerus, Kipp and Wolff, *Lehrbuch des Bürgerlichen Rechts*, vol. 1, § 51; and Venzi, *Diritto Civile Italiano* (5th ed.), p. 13.
[45] Schuster, *The Principles of German Civil Law* (1907), p. 11.
[46] [*Cf. Dean* v. *Wiesengrund* [1955] 2 Q.B. 120.]
[47] Enneccerus, Kipp and Wolff, *loc. cit.*
[48] *Ibid.,* § 54, 1.

An English judge is in this latter respect not so favourably situated as his continental colleague, owing to the more rigid delimitation of his powers. He must confine himself to what the legislator has said in the statute, and can only take the surrounding circumstances into account so far as they are matters of common knowledge. He must make the best of the text and give effect to any meaning which it bears which is not manifestly unjust or fantastic, even though the result may be to defeat the intentions of the legislator. He may not consult the reports of the debates on the measure in Parliament or any other record of the ministerial or parliamentary deliberations which have led to its enactment.[49] He must ignore the statements made to Parliament by ministers in charge of the draft bill and the reports thereon of parliamentary or governmental committees.[50] The statute simply means what it says in a literal sense and this is all that counts, even though the judge as an individual may be well aware that a reference to the preliminary stages of the parliamentary history of the statute would reveal the actual intention of the legislator beyond doubt.

This rule has been defended on the ground that the worst person to construe a statute is he who is responsible for its drafting because he is disposed to confuse what he intended with the effect of the language which he has employed. This may be so in certain cases, but it seems to be difficult to avoid the conclusion that this deliberate hoodwinking of the judiciary must often result in the distortion of the object of a statute where its meaning is ambiguous. . . .   [pp. 101–105]

. . . In France consultation of the preliminary proceedings leading up to legislation has long been a ' favourite instrument of judicial interpretation '.[51] The judges will in case of doubt consult not only ministerial statements and reports of parliamentary committees but also the reports of debates in the Chamber and the Senate.[52] The like use is made of these materials by the German courts in cases of doubt where light may be thrown in this way on the intentions of the legislator. Frequent resort is had, in particular, to the preliminary drafts of the German civil code and the reports of the various committees which carried out the work of revision.[53]   [p. 107]

ASSAM RAILWAYS v. *C.I.R.*
[1935] A.C. 445

LORD WRIGHT . . .

. . . The question, which is by no means free from difficulty, depends on the true construction of the words of the section, read in connection with the Income Tax Act as a whole and in accordance with the usual rules of construction.

---

[49] *Regina* v. *Hertford College* (1878) 3 Q.B.D. 693.

[50] *Davis* v. *Taff Vale Railway Co.* [1895] A.C. 542.

[51] Lambert, Pic and Garraud, ' The Sources and Interpretation of Labour Law in France ', *International Labour Review,* vol. XIV (1926), p. 24.

[52] [But *cf. ante,* 738.]

[53] See Enneccerus, Kipp and Wolff, *op. cit.* § 50; Schuster, *The Principles of German Civil Law* (1907), p. 11. The German law reports contain many instances of the employment of this method of interpretation. See *Reichsgerichtsentscheidungen,* vol. XXVII, pp. 3, 27; *ibid.* vol. LI, p. 274.

Mr. Latter sought to introduce into his argument certain recommendations from a Report of a Royal Commission on Income Tax in 1920; he argued that, as the Act of 1920 followed these recommendations, it should be presumed that the words of the section were intended to give effect to them and hence they could be used to show what was the intention of the Legislature in enacting the section. It would, perhaps, in this case be sufficient ground for rejecting, as your Lordships did, this contention and refusing to look at the Report, that it had not been used or referred to either before the Special Commissioners or before Finlay J., or the Court of Appeal. But on principle no such evidence for the purpose of showing the intention, that is the purpose or object, of an Act is admissible; the intention of the Legislature must be ascertained from the words of the statute with such extraneous assistance as is legitimate: as to this I agree with Farwell L.J. in *Rex* v. *West Riding of Yorkshire County Council* [54] where he says " I think that the true rule is expressed with accuracy by Lord Langdale in giving the judgment of the Privy Council in the *Gorham Case* [55] in Moore, 1852 edition, p. 462. 'We must endeavour to attain for ourselves the true meaning of the language employed'—in the Articles and Liturgy—'assisted only by the consideration of such external or historical facts as we may find necessary to enable us to understand the subject matter to which the instruments relate, and the meaning of the words employed.'" In this House, where the judgment of the Court of Appeal was reversed (*Attorney-General* v. *West Riding of Yorkshire County Council* [56]) no reference was made to this point. It is clear that the language of a Minister of the Crown in proposing in Parliament a measure which eventually becomes law is inadmissible and the Report of Commissioners is even more removed from value as evidence of intention, because it does not follow that their recommendations were accepted. Mr. Latter relied on certain observations of Lord Halsbury L.C. in *Eastman Photographic Materials Co.* v. *Comptroller-General of Patents, Designs, and Trade-Marks.* [57] The Lord Chancellor was there referring to the Report of a Commission that had sat to enquire into the working of the earlier Act, which had been superseded by the Act actually being construed by the House: but Lord Halsbury refers to the Report not directly to ascertain the intention of the words used in the Act, but because, as he says, " no more accurate source of information as to what the evil or defect which the Act of Parliament now under construction was intended to remedy could be imagined than the report of that commission." Lord Halsbury, it is clear, was treating the Report as extraneous matter to show what were the surrounding circumstances with reference to which the words were used so that the case came within the principle stated by Lord Langdale. The rule is in principle analogous to the rules laid down in the four resolutions of the Barons of the Exchequer recorded in *Heydon's Case.* . . . [58]   [pp. 457–459]

[54] [1906] 2 K.B. 676, 717.
[55] (1852) The Case of the Rev. G. C. Gorham against the Bishop of Exeter as heard and determined by the Judicial Committee of the Privy Council on appeal from the Arches Court of Canterbury, by Edmund F. Moore.
[56] [1907] A.C. 29.   [57] [1898] A.C. 571, 575.
[58] [The question of admissibility of legislative material has been the subject of recent Parliamentary debate. In the light of the Law Commission's recommendation (referred to *ante*, 742), a draft clause was appended to a proposed Matrimonial Proceedings and Property Bill (now the Act of 1970), empowering a judge to seek guidance from the Law Commission paper which was the source

ARISTOTLE

Nicomachean Ethics

(transl. Sir David Ross)

Equity, a corrective of legal justice [59]

Our next subject is equity and the equitable (τό ἐπιεικές), and their respective relations to justice and the just. For on examination they appear to be neither absolutely the same nor generically different; and while we sometimes praise what is equitable and the equitable man (so that we apply the name by way of praise even to instances of the other virtues, instead of 'good', meaning by ἐπιεικέστερον that a thing is better), at other times, when we reason it out, it seems strange if the equitable, being something different from the just, is yet praiseworthy; for either the just or the equitable is not good, if they are different; or, if both are good, they are the same.

of the proposed legislation. Lord Wilberforce, also took the initiative of proposing an amendment to the Animals Bill (now the Animals Act 1971) which would have allowed reference to the Law Commission paper on Civil Liability for Animals. The move was seen as a selective experiment. The controversy it aroused was totally unforeseeable and, it is thought, unjustified. It was mildly attacked in the House of Lords, and subjected to a tremendous broadside in the Commons. The legal profession was also opposed to the move (see, for example, Law Guardian, December 1969, pp. 11–13). It was suggested that certainty, perspicuity and brevity would all suffer; "the more words there are, the more words are there about which doubts may be entertained": that there would be more recourse to lawyers, that trials would be longer and more expensive and the opportunity for appeal greater. Opponents of the measure pointed out that the value of the Law Commission paper would diminish with the passage of the Bill through Parliament. To some there was even the constitutional objection that the admissibility of a Law Commission paper would undermine Parliamentary sovereignty by giving us rule by civil servants, that the Law Commission would be raised above the judges in authority. Many were worried about the availability of Law Commission papers: an amendment to place a copy of relevant reports in legislation was rejected, however, on the basis of cost and the legitimacy of making people buy both. But since the bar and the judiciary would both have access, the fears that solicitors in Penrith or Penzance would be handicapped seem exaggerated.

In favour of the experiment it was argued that the judiciary was in favour. "All it will do," said the Lord Chancellor (Lord Gardiner), "is to regularise what Lord Denning told us judges do." It is undoubtedly true that the strict "rule" is no longer universally followed. It was also emphasised that the clauses imposed no obligation to consult Law Commission material; merely a power so to do. It was stressed that consultation was a convenient process, a time-saver. Lord Wilberforce, proposing its adoption in the Animals Bill, pointed to the obscurity of the common law and the clarity and accessibility of the Law Commission's exploration of it. It was better, he urged, to read this than plough through law reports. But most significantly it is thought that admissibility of *travaux préparatoires* would enable the courts to get away from literalism to the underlying purposes of the legislator, to fill gaps, unscramble ambiguities, to get to the realisation that statutes are not a "stitch in time" but the real stuff of the law.

The opponents of the measure prevailed and *Assam* still represents the law. But see also *L.C.C.* v. *Central Land Board* [1958] 1 W.L.R. 1296, 1299; *Esgoigne* v. *I.R.C.* [1958] A.C. at 566; *Letang* v. *Cooper* [1964] 3 W.L.R. 573, 578 and *Post Office* v. *Estuary Radio* [1968] 2 Q.B. 749. See also the interesting comments of Lord Simon in *Borough of Ealing* v. *Race Relations Board* [1972] 2 W.L.R. 71, 82–85.]

[59] [For an admirable discussion of equity in Aristotle's writings, see E. Barker's edition of *The Politics*, pp. 367–372. See also J. W. Jones, *Law and Legal Theory of the Greeks*, pp. 64–65.]

These, then, are pretty much the considerations that give rise to the problem about the equitable; they are all in a sense correct and not opposed to one another; for the equitable, though it is better than one kind of justice, yet is just, and it is not as being a different class of thing that it is better than the just. The same thing, then, is just and equitable, and while both are good the equitable is superior. What creates the problem is that the equitable is just, but not the legally just but a correction of legal justice. The reason is that all law is universal but about some things it is not possible to make a universal statement which shall be correct. In those cases, then, in which it is necessary to speak universally, but not possible to do so correctly, the law takes the usual case, though it is not ignorant of the possibility of error. And it is none the less correct; for the error is not in the law nor in the legislator but in the nature of the thing, since the matter of practical affairs is of this kind from the start. When the law speaks universally, then, and a case arises on it which is not covered by the universal statement, then it is right, where the legislator fails us and has erred by over-simplicity, to correct the omission—to say what the legislator himself would have said had he been present, and would have put into his law if he had known. Hence the equitable is just, and better than one kind of justice—not better than absolute justice, but better than the error that arises from the absoluteness of the statement. And this is the nature of the equitable, a correction of law where it is defective owing to its universality. In fact this is the reason why all things are not determined by law, viz. that about some things it is impossible to lay down a law, so that a decree is needed. For when the thing is indefinite the rule also is indefinite, like the leaden rule used in making the Lesbian moulding; the rule adapts itself to the shape of the stone and is not rigid, and so too the decree is adapted to the facts.

It is plain, then, what the equitable is, and that it is just and is better than one kind of justice. It is evident also from this who the equitable man is; the man who chooses and does such acts, and is no stickler for his rights in a bad sense but tends to take less than his share though he has the law on his side, is equitable, and this state of character is equity, which is a sort of justice and not a different state of character.

[pp. 132–134] [60]

SIR HENRY MAINE

Ancient Law

(ed. Pollock)

Progressive Law

　　. . . I confine myself in what follows to the progressive societies. With respect to them it may be laid down that social necessities and social opinion are always more or less in advance of Law. We may come indefinitely near to the closing of the gap between them, but it has a perpetual tendency to reopen. Law is stable; the societies we are speak-

[For relevant passages from Aristotle's *Rhetoric*, see E. Barker's edition of *The Politics*, pp. 369–372. Aristotle explains how appeals to equity may be best made by an advocate pleading in the courts, and relates it to the "unwritten" law regarded as underlying and supplying the deficiencies of the body of enacted law. *Cf. ante*, 77.]

ing of are progressive. The greater or less happiness of a people depends on the degree of promptitude with which the gulf is narrowed.

A general proposition of some value may be advanced with respect to the agencies by which Law is brought into harmony with society. These instrumentalities seem to me to be three in number, Legal Fictions, Equity, and Legislation. Their historical order is that in which I have placed them. Sometimes two of them will be seen operating together, and there are legal systems which have escaped the influence of one or other of them. But I know of no instance in which the order of their appearance has been changed or inverted. . . .[61]   [p. 31]

H. F. JOLOWICZ
Historical Introduction to Roman Law
(2nd ed.)

. . . But all the lofty verbiage of Cicero and even the devotion to *aequitas* of a great lawyer like Servius Sulpicius naturally did not suffice to change the character of the ancient system at a single blow. Such a change needs, if it is to be successful, the elaboration of a technique which can only be achieved by several generations, and it was precisely this elaboration which was the work of the classical jurists. It is their mastery of technique which makes the classical lawyers superior to the Byzantines, whose desire to bring about an equitable result in every case, without a similar professional understanding, ends frequently in high-sounding phrases through which no principle capable of general application can be perceived.

An example of the increasing, but by no means perfect, flexibility of the classical law may be seen in its treatment of some of the effects of the *capitis deminutio minima*, resulting from adrogation. The old civil law rule was that the rights of the *adrogatus* passed (with the exception of some which were lost) to the *adrogator*, but that the *adrogator* was not liable for the debts. On the latter part of the rule, however, the civil law had already grafted an exception. Debts which the *adrogatus* owed as heir to some deceased person did pass to the *adrogator*, on the ground, it was said, that he became heir in place of the *adrogatus*. There can be little doubt that this exception was only allowed because the rule itself was practically inconvenient and unjust, but further than this the civil law did not go. Praetorian law, however, prevented injustice by allowing an action against the *adrogatus*, with the fiction that he had not suffered *capitis deminutio*, and (unless the action were defended by the adoptive father) allowing the goods which the *adrogatus* brought with him to be taken in execution.[62] It must not, however, be thought that all the undesirable results of *capitis deminutio* were dealt with thus satisfactorily. Usufruct, which was a highly personal right, was still lost by this " civil death ", although it is clear that the rule was inconvenient, and that testators were at pains to provide against the contingency by certain drafting devices.

Instances of this sort might be multiplied to any extent to show the

---

[61] [Kahn-Freund has suggested that in matrimonial property law the courts first tried equity but have now succumbed, contrary to Maine's " general proposition " to fiction. (See *Pettitt* v. *Pettitt* [1970] A.C. 777 and *Gissing* v. *Gissing* [1970] 3 W.L.R. 255.) Kahn-Freund advocates " jumping across the ' equity ' stage from fiction to legislation." ((1970) 33 M.L.R. 601, 630).]   [62] Gai. III. 83–84.

varying degrees in which the classical law succeeded in emancipating itself from the undesired results of ancient rules, but it is at least equally important to realise how much flexibility it attained by the use of what may be called rather standards than rules. New rules could then be deduced from these standards without impairing their usefulness for the settlement of future difficulties. Of these standards, *bona fides* supplies the most striking example. No one can exhaust the meaning of " good faith ", and the acceptance of a rule, that e.g. such and such conduct on the part of a seller does not conform to the standard of faith, does not mean that other kinds of dishonest conduct may be indulged in with impunity. There had, of course, been *bona fidei* actions before the end of the republic, but the great opportunities which this conception gave were only realised later. For instance, it was always usual in sales that the seller should, by express stipulation, make himself liable in case of eviction, but it was not until the classical period was well advanced that he was made liable even without any express promise, no doubt on the ground that it would be contrary to good faith if he attempted to escape such ordinary liability.

Dolus received a similarly wide extension of application, and could include any act which did not conform with the requirements of *bona fides*. Hence the delictal *actio doli* came to be available not only, as originally, in cases of actual trickery, but much more generally where the defendant's conduct in refusing what was asked of him was contrary to *bona fides* and caused loss to the plaintiff. Thus Ulpian [63] allowed it where the defendant had given the plaintiff permission to quarry a stone on his land, and after the plaintiff had expended money on doing so, refused permission to remove the stone.

A more primitive system would have been at a loss to deal with such a case. The land and the stone belonged to the defendant, and there was no contract to create a duty in him towards the plaintiff.   [pp. 423–425]

H. C. GUTTERIDGE

Comparative Law
(2nd ed.)

Aequitas

The continental codes contain many references to equity but do not define it.[64] An English writer is therefore on delicate ground when he seeks to discuss its nature and characteristics. It would, however, seem to be clear that *Équité* or *Billigkeit* are concepts of a somewhat vague character with an undefined sphere of application. The *Vocabulaire Juridique* defines *Équité* as follows: ' Conception d'une justice qui n'est pas inspirée par les règles du droit en vigueur et qui même peut être contraire à ces règles.' Von Tuhr regards *Billigkeit* as the yardstick which furnishes a standard of justice to be adopted by a judge when called upon to exercise his discretion.[65] Dusi draws a distinction between

---

[63] D. 4. 3. 34.
[64] *e.g.* Articles 565, 1135 of the *Code Civil*, Articles 315–19 of the *Bürgerliches Gesetzbuch*, and Article 4 of the Swiss civil code.
[65] *Op. cit.* vol. 1, p. 30; Article 4 of the Swiss civil code provides that, when the law expressly leaves a matter to the discretion of the judge, he must base his decision on principles of justice and equity.

legge and *equità*. The former, he says, represents a standard of justice applicable as a general rule to any given group of cases. *Equità*, on the other hand, ' è la giustizia del caso singolo' which means in effect that it is the standard which a judge must apply in an individual case if he comes to the conclusion that injustice would result from the application of the *legge* or general, or ordinary, rule to the facts of the dispute which it is his duty to determine.[66] Pothier takes a somewhat different view because he regards *Équité* as furnishing a basis for the declaration of rights and duties in general.[67] It would seem that the nearest equivalent to these concepts in our law is that of ' natural justice' which has been roughly handled in our courts but has survived, though possibly only in an attenuated form. But continental lawyers regard the concept of *aequitas* as something more than ' vague jurisprudence'[68] or ' well-meaning sloppiness of thought',[69] though they may not be in agreement as to its precise nature or as to the extent of its application. The part played by it in continental law is, however, a far more modest one than that which is assigned to equity, in the technical sense,[70] by our law. But its importance cannot be denied because it provides the main foundation on which the judges have based the process by means of which they can escape from a narrow or formalistic interpretation of the letter of the law and can give new life in a different guise to codified rules which have become outworn owing to changes in social conditions.

[p. 96]

FRENCH CIVIL CODE

Art. 1135. Agreements bind not only in respect of what is expressed therein, but also as regards all consequences which equity, usage or law give to the obligation according to its nature.

SWISS CIVIL CODE

Art. 1. The law must be applied in all cases which come within the letter or the spirit of any of its provisions.

Where no provision applies, the judge shall decide according to the existing customary law, and, failing which, according to the rules which he would lay down if he had himself to act as legislator.[71]

Herein he must be guided by approved legal doctrine and case-law.

Art. 4. Where the law expressly leaves a point to the discretion of the judge, or directs him to take circumstances into consideration, or to

---

[66] *Istituzioni di Diritto Civile*, vol. 1, p. 49.

[67] David, ' The Doctrine of Unjustified Enrichment ', *Cambridge L.J.* vol. v (1934), p. 205.

[68] *Baylis* v. *Bishop of London* [1913] 1 Ch. per Hamilton L.J. at p. 140.

[69] *Holt* v. *Markham* [1923] 1 K.B. per Scrutton L.J. at p. 513. *Contra*, see the expression of his views by Lord Wright in the *Fibrosa Case* [1943] A.C. at pp. 62 and 63 ; Winfield, *Province of the Law of Tort*, pp. 128 *et seq.; Local Government Board* v. *Arlidge* [1915] A.C. per Lord Shaw at p. 136;' *Robinson* v. *Fenner* [1913] 3 K.B. at p. 842.

[70] [*i.e.*, as constituting a distinct branch of English law; but on the role of equity in the broader sense in modern English law, *cf. ante*, 746.]

[71] [For the interpretation of this clause, see Williams, *Swiss Civil Code: Sources of Law* (1923), pp. 54–60.]

consider whether a ground alleged is material, he must base his decision on principles of justice and equity.[72]

LORD DENNING

The Need for a New Equity [73]

. . . I have considered the three ways of filling the gap which Maine suggested, fiction, equity and legislation. If they are exhausted where is a new means to be found? It is at this point that I begin to regret the fusion of law and equity. We have now no call upon natural justice. We have one system of courts and one system of law. We have a Lord Chancellor but we have no over-riding equity. The Courts of Chancery are no longer courts of equity. They have no jurisdiction to mitigate harshness or to soften rigidity. They are as fixed and immutable as the courts of law ever were.

Sir William Holdsworth said once that the separate systems of law and equity still live ' in the separate intellectual cast which they impose upon those who study and apply them '. If he meant by this to suggest that the Chancery lawyers have a greater reserve of natural justice than the common lawyers, I cannot agree with him. The Judicature Acts and Property Acts have had a very definite effect on the work of the Chancery Division. It has become much concerned with dealings in land, and devolution of estates. In those branches of the law certainty is, quite rightly, of paramount importance. It does not matter so much what the rule is, so long as it is certain. People who deal in property do not want to buy lawsuits or to inherit them. They want to know exactly what will happen if they use such and such words, and exactly how to provide for such and such a contingency. In this branch of the law words are the masters who must be obeyed. It was the same with the old real property law of the common lawyers with its shifting uses and contingent remainders and so forth. Our real property law was as devoid of moral concepts as mathematics. Rights and wrongs did not enter into it. Nor the redress of grievances. Only words and rules: and logical deductions from them. In those early days land was the most important kind of property; and the common lawyers were so absorbed in land problems that they approached other problems in the same frame of mind. They looked for certainty, and gave justice a second place. In their hands the law of contract and torts tended to become as technical and rigid as the law of property. In order to have a cause of action the plaintiff had to fit his complaint into one of the established forms of action, or else he had no remedy. It was only by the efforts of great judges like Holt and Mansfield, Blackburn and Willes that the common law managed to keep itself free from these restricting bonds.

The Judicature Acts have had a beneficial effect on the Queen's Bench Division. It is not so much concerned with the transfer of property as with the redress of grievances. It gives compensation for

---

72 [For the background to these and similar articles in civilian codes, see Ramos (1970) 44 Tulane L.R. 720.]
73 [From (1952) 5 *Current Legal Problems*, 1.]

wrongs done and injuries inflicted. In these branches of the law justice is at least as important as certainty, and probably more important. Moral concepts play a large part. The classic judgment of Lord Atkin in *Donoghue* v. *Stevenson* starts with the Christian precept 'Thou shalt love thy neighbour as thyself'. He says, 'The rule that you are to love your neighbour becomes in law, you must not injure your neighbour; and the lawyer's question, Who is my neighbour? receives a restricted reply'.[74] The truth is that the plain man can see well when a wrong has been done; and he looks to the courts of justice to afford a remedy for it. If the judges should say, 'We admit that a wrong has been done but cannot give you a remedy', that is a tacit admission that the law is failing to fulfil its function. It is failing to do justice. The common lawyers seek to avoid that reproach. New days bring new wrongs, or wrongs of a new kind, and the law must be developed so as to give redress for them.

The law, as I see it, has two great objects: to preserve order, and to do justice; and the two do not always coincide. Those whose training lies towards order, put certainty before justice; whereas those, whose training lies towards the redress of grievances, put justice before certainty. The right solution lies in keeping the proper balance between the two. But how is this to be done? The House of Lords are the persons to perform the task; and they have on occasion done it in notable fashion. Thus in the case of *Donoghue* v. *Stevenson* Lord Atkin, with the help of two great Scots lawyers, did justice by creating a new tort of negligence notwithstanding the protests of two great Chancery lawyers who wished for no change. Subsequent events have proved that Lord Atkin and his two Scots colleagues were right and that the fears of the Chancery dissentients were groundless. That case shows, however, the defects of our system. Just change the composition of the House of Lords by one member and the development of English law would have been retarded for generations. . . .

I repeat again: Where is the new equity to be found? Not in the judges, for they are forbidden to legislate. Not in the House of Lords. . . . It is, I think, to be found in the new spirit which is alive in our universities. There must rise up another Bentham to expose the fallacies and failings of the past and to point the way to a new age and a new equity. We stand at the threshold of a new Elizabethan era. Let us play a worthy part in it.[79]   [pp. 7–10]

---

[74] [1932] A.C. 562, at p. 580.

[79] [Lord Denning rejected the House of Lords as an instrument of producing what, he calls, the "new equity," as it was then bound by its own decisions. (*Cf.* Lord Denning in *Broome* v. *Cassells* [1971] 2 Q.B. 354). Although, since 1966, it has had the freedom to depart from previous decisions where these are thought to be wrong, it is a power used most sparingly (*cf. ante*, 755). Nevertheless, the House of Lords is a more creative body than it was twenty years ago. But, whereas, when Lord Denning wrote, the role of legislation was thought to be limited, the creation of the Law Commission and the prospect of codification may be said to have changed Lord Denning's perspective somewhat. The future development of English law seems to lie with that body and in legislation, not least codification. It exemplifies Lord Denning's ideal of "another Bentham," though (*pace* Bentham) there will always be an important, if subsidiary role, for "judge-made" law.]

SIR L. SCARMAN

Law Reform—The New Pattern
(1968)

The New Pattern

. . . Law reform is not exclusively a legal topic: it is also a social and moral problem. It is no longer possible to think of the law as an esoteric and technical discipline, whose values are safe in the hands of the Judges and the profession. Contemporary society requires that it be given the opportunity to test its laws by its own criteria; it insists that laws are either to serve the needs of society or to be rejected. In other words, our fellows in society require first to understand, and then to evaluate the laws that govern them. We demand, not only that the tables be brought down from the mountain and their meaning made clear, but that we have the liberty to smash and replace them. And so, to meet and overcome the challenge of law reform, we must call not only for the technical learning of the lawyer, but for a full understanding of, and sympathy with, the habits, feelings and values of ordinary men. Unless this challenge is met, law reform will be, in very truth, a barren exercise. A difficulty presents itself at the outset: it is that none of our existing institutions possesses, in itself, the blend of technical learning, social awareness, and power to get things done that are required. The courts have the technical learning most assuredly; the social awareness perhaps; but neither the opportunity nor the power to tackle the job systematically. The government, by its control of Parliament, has the power and the opportunity, but lacks the learning and, sometimes, the will. Parliament has the social awareness but, if one has to face realities, neither the learning nor the opportunity—though in theory sovereign, it is controlled not by itself, but by the government. And the government is, more often than not, overwhelmed by the tide of its own business.

If therefore law reform, in any worth-while sense, is to have a future in England, the ultimate problem can be seen to be one of the machinery of government. A revolution in our law making procedures is required. The revolution must ensure that those who have the power, that is to say, the government and Parliament, create for themselves the opportunity to use it; and recruit to their service the experience, learning and knowledge to enable them to use it wisely. In a constitutional context, this means that our legislative processes must be reformed: in a legal context, this means that use must be made of a far greater variety of disciplines and skills, legal and otherwise, than have so far been harnessed to the direct service of the law.　　　　　　　[pp. 7–8]

. . . At the instance of the executive, Parliament has made a take-over bid in a field of activity which has been for centuries the traditional reserve of the courts and the legal profession. The terms of the bid are to be found in the Law Commissions Act, 1965, to which I now turn.

The Act has established machinery for the purpose of promoting the reform of the law. It has set up two permanent Commissions: one known as the Law Commission, concerned with the law of England; the other known as the Scottish Law Commission, concerned with the law of Scotland. The Commissioners are to be lawyers. The Act provides that the English Commissioners shall be persons appearing to the Lord Chancellor to be suitably qualified by the holding of judicial office, or by experience as barristers or solicitors, or as teachers of law in a university. A similar provision covers the Scottish Commission. The two Commissions are required to act in consultation with each other. The function of each Commission is described by the Act as that of taking and keeping under review all the law, with a view to its systematic development and reform. An indication is given as to the broad objectives to be sought; for the Act makes specific mention of codification, the elimination of anomalies, the repeal of obsolete and unnecessary enactments, the reduction of the number of separate enactments, and generally the simplification and modernization of the law. This short summary of the targets set the two Commissions is significant for its emphasis on the state of the statute law. Codification, repeal, reduction of enactments—all these are guiding the attention of the Commissioners towards enacted law. When the Act describes the methods of work to be followed by the Commission, the emphasis on statute law is again clear. The English Commission (which is my concern) is to prepare and submit to the Lord Chancellor, from time to time, programmes for the examination of different branches of the law with a view to reform, and to make recommendations as to the agency by which those examinations are to be carried out. In undertaking such examinations the Commission, if it thinks reform is necessary, is to formulate proposals by means of draft Bills. If requested by the Lord Chancellor, it is to prepare comprehensive programmes for the consolidation and revision of the statutory law, and to prepare draft Bills to give effect to these programmes. It is to provide advice and information to government departments and other bodies concerned, at the instance of the government, with proposals for law reform. In the performance of its functions, the Commission is to obtain information as to the legal systems of other countries.

The programmes of the Commission, if approved by the Lord Chancellor, are to be laid before Parliament. Likewise, the Commission's proposals for reform, formulated according to an approved programme, are to be laid before Parliament whether or not the Lord Chancellor approves them. . . .   [pp. 9–11]

. . . The Commission has been called into being to advise the government and Parliament, first in the planning of law reform; secondly, in the formulation of detailed proposals for the reform of the law. The theory that underlies the Act is that law reform should be the province of the legislature; that the legislature requires specialist advice in the planning and formulation of law reform; and that this advice should be provided by a body independent of the executive and of Parliament. . . .

A plain implication of these provisions of the Act is that proposals for the reform of the law, though made to the legislature, ought to be kept outside the field of political controversy. They are to be carefully considered by an expert body before the introduction of legislation. The public is to be given an opportunity of debating them—also before the introduction of legislation. And, finally, when Parliament itself has to consider them, it should have the benefit of expert advice and prior public discussion.

Two further features of the Commission should be mentioned. It holds an initiative in the reform process, and it is more than a mere committee, whose existence may be terminated by the stroke of a Minister's pen. It is an institution, having a statutory existence. Neither the anger of a Minister nor the rebellion and resignation of Commissioners can destroy it. It exists until Parliament by enactment delivers the coup de grâce. These two features merit a little reflection. Prior to the Act, law reform usually began with an investigation undertaken either by an ad hoc body, set up with clearly defined terms of reference, or by a standing committee, to whose attention specific topics would be referred from time to time.   [pp. 11–13]

. . . I turn to the other side of the Commission's duty—its responsibility for the form and arrangement of the statute law. . . .

. . . A moment's reflection will reveal how vital to the success of the Commission's work is an intelligibly written and arranged statute book. The Commission can effect law reform only through the medium of enactment. If its enactments have to take their place in a disordered or unintelligible collection of the statute law, the state of the law will not really be improved. The Commission thus has a vital interest in improving the arrangement and drafting of the enacted law. Its statute law programme is to be seen as complementary to its programme for law reform. As the White Paper [80] which foreshadowed the Law Commission's Act said: 'English law should be capable of being recast in a form which is accessible, intelligible and in accordance with modern needs'. Put plainly, there really is no point in codifying the law of contract, unless the final result is to make the law more accessible and more intelligible. Let me take an illustration from our current work. As the law reform programme recognizes, the general principles of the law of contract are by now well established. By declaring its intention to codify this well established law, the Commission is challenging the value of reported judicial decisions as the receptacle of the law; it is suggesting that the law would be more accessible and more easily understood if it were found in an enacted code.

Consolidation and statute law revision are exceedingly technical exercises. Nevertheless, a proper understanding of the future of law reform requires that these two techniques be themselves properly understood. Consolidation is the process of modernizing statute law which it is desired to retain in force. It is a process to which Parliament has frequently resorted, long before the establishment of the Law Commission. . . .

. . . Government Departments and Parliament have always been alert to the need of consolidating statute law, but never before 1965 has there been set up any permanent body to plan the job.

Statute law revision is the process of repeal of obsolete or obsolescent or unnecessary statutory provisions. Again, there is nothing new about this process, save only that it is now to be a planned operation by a permanent body acting in an advisory capacity to Parliament. The modernization by way of consolidation of those parts of the enacted law which it is desired to retain in force, combined with the repeal of the obsolete, the obsolescent and the unnecessary, is designed to reduce the collection of our statutes, known as the statute book, to manageable proportions and intelligible form. It is to be seen as the

[80] Cmnd. 2573.

indispensable companion of the law reform programme. Thus, the Law Commission is engaged, not only in formulating proposals for improving the substance of the law, but in cleaning up the collection of statutes, so that its proposals, if enacted, may take their place in a well-arranged, well-drafted body of statute law. . . .   [pp. 18–21]

. . . Parliament's enactment of law reform proposals emanating from the Law Commission and other agencies was, of course, to be expected, and devoutly to be prayed for. The uncovenanted blessing that has followed the establishment of the two Commissions is their indirect effect upon the whole climate of legal thinking and our attitudes towards the systems of other countries. It is not too much to say that comparative legal studies have now come into their own as an essential prerequisite to sound reform. . . .

. . . A notable illustration of this attitude was given us by the House of Lords in July 1966. Here, in my opinion, credit should be given to the remarkable achievement of the Scottish Law Commission. In their first programme they boldly included ' Judicial Precedent ', and made the comment that it had never been expressly decided that the House of Lords was bound in a Scottish appeal by the rigid doctrine of *stare decisis*. They mentioned that this doctrine was applicable to English law. In July 1966 the Lord Chancellor announced that the House of Lords would no longer consider itself bound to follow an earlier decision of the House, if, in all the circumstances, it thought it right to depart from it.[81] In their second annual report the Scots described what happened and, in particular, quoted the Lord Chancellor's announcement that: ' Too rigid adherence to precedent may lead to injustice in a particular case, and also unduly restrict the proper development of the law.' The story speaks for itself. It is not too far-fetched to suggest that the very existence of the two Commissions, and the declared programme of the Scottish Law Commission, together with the steps they took to investigate the matter, had a persuasive effect upon their Lordships' House. . . .   [pp. 22–24]

The Problems

. . . There can be no doubt that the Commission is well constituted to do the technical work of law reform. The Commissioners are lawyers: they work full time, in close consultation with the legal profession, the universities and government departments. They are divorced from the World of Whitehall and Westminster, and they have the research facilities to study, not only English law, but the legal systems of other countries as well.

But is such a body fitted to handle any but the technical questions of law reform? Undoubtedly, many believe that one can draw a distinction between lawyers' law and other types of law.[82] To take one example, Lord Devlin in his address to the Law Society's National Conference in September 1966 drew a distinction between what he

[81] [*Ante*, 754.]
[82] [See Lord Reid's remarks in *Pettitt* v. *Pettitt* [1970] A.C. 777 and see Reid, " The Judge as Law Maker " in 12 J.S.P.T.L. 22, where family law is cited as an example of an area where " the ordinary man can form just as good an opinion as the lawyer " (p. 23).]

labelled, 'lawyers' law reform' and social or political law reform. When the law is changed in order to achieve a new social or political objective, this, he said, was not lawyers' law reform; but when social and political objectives are agreed and it is found that the law is defective in carrying them out, this, he said, was properly described as law reform. If Lord Devlin was arguing for the existence of a special world of lawyers' law, I would respectfully disagree. There is no cosy little world of lawyers' law in which learned men may frolic without raising socially controversial issues. . . .   [pp. 26–27]
. . . I challenge anyone to identify an issue of law reform so technical that it raises no social, political or economic issue. If there is any such thing, I doubt if it would be worth doing anything about it.

But I do not think that Lord Devlin was concerned to establish the existence of a cloud cuckoo land of technical lawyers' law. He was concerned with a vital question: how in the field of law reform to identify those questions upon which a lawyer may properly pass judgment, and those upon which judgment may be passed only after other interests have been consulted. In other words, he was seeking to chart the path of the lawyer through the shoals and rocks of controversy. He was accepting that the challenge of law reform is that it can only be successfully achieved by a combination of the lawyers' learning and the social awareness of the community.

The Law Commission's first programme reveals that the Commission accepts that its activities cannot be confined by the unreal boundaries of a so-called lawyers' law.   [p. 28]
. . . Given a careful approach, an open mind, and a true sense of the limits within which a specialist body has the right to pass a judgment or state a conclusion, the Law Commission should find no insuperable difficulty in the formulation of proposals for law reform in controversial areas of the law. An understanding of the limitations imposed upon it by its own expertise, and a proper use of the practices of consultation, social enquiry and research, should suffice to enable it to produce worth while proposals.

But I fear that this answer does not solve the fundamental problem of law reform. . . . It raises the problem of translating law reform proposals into enacted law. This is not merely a question of Parliamentary time, though this is important. There is here a more general, more basic difficulty. The truth is that neither Government nor Parliament have yet adjusted themselves to the new organ that they have planted in their own body—and there is a real danger that, against their own true will, they may reject their own planting. It would be a tragedy if law reform should falter through a failure of the political machine to adjust itself to the task of enacting law reform proposals.

The problem has several facets, of which Parliamentary time is only one. I propose to deal with them under two headings: time, and the passage of legislation. The problem of finding Parliamentary time does not arise from any lack of will for law reform. The government and Parliament have much else to do. The government has to govern, and Parliament has to discuss questions of economic and social policy, great and small, and foreign affairs: it remains, to its great credit, a busy forum for the airing of grievances of all sorts. But further, it has to find time to legislate. Such legislation may be of great volume and complexity, and much of it is far removed from law reform; it is likely to enjoy a continuing priority over measures of law reform. No wonder that Parliamentary time is a very scarce commodity. Yet time must be found for law reform. A timorous beginning has been made with the establishment of the Second Reading Committee in the House of Commons. This committee is designed to take non-controversial legislation off the floor of the House, thereby saving the House's time. The Misrepresentation Bill was handled by this committee. There are, however, limitations upon its effectiveness. Perhaps its greatest weakness is that it requires the consent of the Opposition, if a Bill is to be referred to it. Her Majesty's Opposition has the duty to oppose; in a sense, it is betraying its duty if it facilitates the legislative programme of the Government. There must be periods of Parliamentary activity in which an Opposition will obstruct the passage of non-controversial legislation for the legitimate purpose of denying the Government time for its legislative programme, if it can. This is no more than democracy in action.

Perhaps a more hopeful approach to the problem of time is to be found in the reform of the House of Lords. I agree with Lord Devlin, and others, who have advocated the use of the House of Lords for the introduction of law reform measures. Even in the unreformed House, there is a greater concentration of legal learning than one will find elsewhere. The House also contains already a great number of Peers having a wide experience outside the law. And, finally, the House of Lords does have the time. If the House is to be reformed, if some of its existing powers are to be diminished, I can see no reason why it should not be given an extended opportunity to handle the legislative problems of law reform.

But if Parliamentary time is found, it must be properly used. A law reform measure is, of necessity, a complex creature, which stands or falls as a whole. It needs careful explanation and cannot be allowed to become subject to ignorant or uninstructed amendment. How can one reconcile Parliamentary sovereignty with the restraint upon amendment that is needed if law reform is to avoid going down, in chaos, to defeat?

The Law Commission itself is not equipped or designed to guide the passage of its own proposals through Parliament. It is not a government department; it is, by its very nature, divorced from the executive and from the legislature. The best that it can do is to prepare its proposals in a form ready for enactment, i.e. as a draft Bill. But the Bill, when introduced, will need not only explanation but a pilot to steer it on its way. Our existing institutions,[82a] lacking as they do a Minister in the Commons with specific responsibility for law reform, fail to bridge the gap between the Law Commission and the legislative process. In the Commons, there are two Law Officers: they already carry heavy responsibilities, which require their full and unremitting attention. In the Lords, there is the Lord Chancellor—his office overwhelmed by a vast and varied load of duties. He is also under the disability of having to preside in the Chamber when he sits.

Other countries have faced this difficulty. Some have solved it by the establishment of a Ministry of Justice. Others bring their law

---

[82a] [This question was recently debated in the House of Lords. See Hansard, vol. 316, cols. 1273–1313.]

reform agency into a very close relationship with their legislature, and put on to the agency members of the legislature. An illustration of how this can be done may be found in New York. The New York Law Revision Commission was established in 1934. It is a body of lawyers with functions very similar to our Law Commission. But its membership includes four ex-officio members, the two chairmen of the Judiciary Committees of the Senate and the Assembly, and the two chairmen of the Codes Committees of both Houses. These four ex-officio members introduce the Bills drafted by the Commission. Each Bill, when introduced, is accompanied by two documents: a statutory note giving a short explanation of the Bill's purpose; and a longer document, called a recommendation, which argues the reasons for the Bill. Thus, New York has integrated its Law Reform Commission into the working machine of government, and has secured two priceless advantages: first, that those who formulate the proposal bear the responsibility for piloting it through the legislature: and second, that all members of the legislature called upon to enact the proposal are provided with documents explaining the Bill.

The other solution, to which I have referred, is the establishment of a Ministry of Justice. The Civil Law countries, by and large, leave law reform to a department of the Ministry of Justice. There is nothing necessarily inconsistent between a Ministry of Justice and the common law. Some Commonwealth countries already have such a Minister; and great common lawyers such as Benjamin Cardozo in New York, and Lord Haldane in England, have advocated the establishment of one. A Ministry of Justice could bridge the gap between the Law Commission and Parliament. It would have advantages over the New York solution, in that the Law Commission could be retained as a non-political, specialist advisory body. The Minister would be responsible in the Commons for piloting law reform legislation. He and the Lord Chancellor could, in their different Houses, watch for and prevent the ignorant or uninstructed amendment. Through his department he would be able to organize, in a way not yet attempted in this country, the legal services available to the government, so that the general pattern of legislation, i.e. its drafting and arrangement, could be made to conform to the legal requirements set for a coherent statute book. But, even if a department of Justice, under a Minister responsible to the Commons, is too much of a break with tradition to be immediately acceptable, why not a third law officer? He should be a lawyer but need not be a member of the Bar. Indeed, it would be an advantage if he were to be a solicitor. The Minister should have, I suggest, a specific responsibility for law reform.

But the presence of a third law officer, or another Minister in the Commons, does not provide the complete answer. Parliament itself must adjust its procedures to the requirements of law reform. Law reform is likely to take two forms—one, the short measure, and the second, the long measure. A good example of a short law reform measure was the Misrepresentation Bill introduced last year. The classical long law reform measure will be a codification—for example, a Contract Code when that is ready to be introduced. Present Parliamentary procedures can handle, reasonably effectively, the short measure, particularly if time is saved by referring it in the Commons to the

Second Reading Committee. But the real challenge will come when the codifications are introduced. They will, of course, stand no chance, unless there is a law officer, or Minister with legal qualifications, entrusted with the task of guiding them through the Commons. But Parliament cannot be expected to pass these measures as though it were signing a blank cheque. It owes it to the nation to satisfy itself that the proposed code is not only right in principle, but effective and workable in detail. The Law Commission will, of course, have said so; but Parliament cannot shift its own responsibility for the efficiency of its legislation on to any other body, even the Law Commission. I would suggest that the way in which the Highways Act 1959 was passed into law provides an answer. That Act was a consolidation with amendments. It emerged from the deliberations of a departmental committee, whose report was presented to Parliament in January 1959. After its second reading, it was referred to a Select Committee of the two Houses, which considered it in detail. Thereafter its passage through both Houses was not difficult. There is here a valuable analogy. In place of the Departmental Committee Report, there will be available to Parliament, when dealing with a major measure of law reform, a Report and draft Bill prepared by the Law Commission. A Bill introduced into either House, if based on the Law Commission's proposal and draft, could, after its second reading, be referred to a Joint Select Committee which could subject it to detailed and expert consideration, sufficient to satisfy Parliament that Parliament's responsibility for the effectiveness of its legislation had been discharged. Such a process of examination by a select Committee should effectively exclude the ignorant, the uninstructed or the wrecking amendment.

It will be clear from what I have said that the basic challenge to law reform—how to translate proposals into law—has not yet been met. I believe that it can be met only by certain adjustments in both government and Parliament. The government must be prepared to bridge the gap between the non-political Law Commission and the Parliamentary machine. Parliament must adjust its processes so that time may be made available for law reform. It must also ensure that measures of law reform shall receive from Parliament full consideration without becoming imperilled by foolish amendment. There are no insuperable difficulties here, provided there exists the will to overcome them. . . . [pp. 36–44]

The Future Shape of the Law

. . . Once one has moved into a world of enacted law, the guidance given by the old common law cases on the interpretation of statutes is not sufficient. The problem is not solved by affirming that the Judges must give effect to the words of the statute. Although it must always remain a salutary rule that the enacted words should be sovereign and, if clear, should be applied, this is only a beginning. Words are, of necessity, an imprecise means of communication. They are frequently reasonably capable of more than one meaning. Further, statute law, being an attempt to declare a policy (or policies) applicable to the future, cannot always cover every contingency. How are the courts to solve problems of ambiguity and the problems of the uncovered case?

There is, I think, advantage in seeing how these problems have been solved in civil law systems which are accustomed to find their law in a code. For example, in French law [83] the court, if the law be obscure or ambiguous, is required to discover the true will of the legislator. The court must look first to the language of the statute but, if that leaves them in doubt, they are entitled to assistance from the case law, the legislative history, academic writings and opinions of eminent jurists. The Court is also encouraged to reason by analogy, that is to say, to apply the principles stated in the statute, although their application be not directly required by any enacting words. In Germany [83] the practice is much the same. There are no fixed rules of interpretation and no relevant material is excluded from the consideration of the court. In Denmark [83] a Bill is accompanied by an explanatory statement, drafted so as to amplify ' for the Members of Parliament and the public the subject matter of the Bill . . . and account is to be taken of the fact that it is likely to be a guide to those who administer the Act, and to the Courts '. In Switzerland the civil code [84] requires that, in default of an applicable provision, the Judge will decide according to the customary law: and, in default of a custom, according to the rules which he would have established, had he been the legislator.

These methods are alien to the common law save only that it, like every civilized legal system, requires the court to begin with the enacted words of the statute. In particular, the common law denies to the court the use of legislative history or the reports of committees to explain the range and scope of enacting words, their purpose or object: per Lord Wright, *Assam Railways* v. *C.I.R.* [1935] A.C. 445 at p. 458.[85]

The two Law Commissions in their joint working paper [86] have suggested a solution. They recommend, first, that words must be read in their context: secondly, that the context must include all other enacted provisions of the statute: thirdly, that it should include the reports of Royal Commissions and similar committees, and any other explanatory material that might be made available by Parliament. Finally, they suggest that, if for any reason, the statute has failed to express an intention which covers the particular circumstances of the case, the court should be ready to argue by analogy from other provisions in the statute, so as to give effect to its intended purpose. It will be observed that the two Law Commissions have suggested that the legislator should prepare explanatory material, and that the courts should take this material into consideration in interpreting the enacted law. Thus, they have recognized the close relationship between making and interpreting statutes and the fundamental importance of improving communications between the makers and the interpreters.

If interpretation should develop along these lines, the courts will have to decide how to deal with the earlier case law, and the limits to be imposed upon argument by analogy. The legislator will have to decide how to make available the explanatory material.

To deal first with the problems of the court, it will be necessary to strike a balance between the earlier case law and the new code. The problem has been largely solved, I suggest, by the observations of Lord

[83] See Appendices A, B and D, Law Com. Published Working Paper (14).
[84] Swiss Civil Code, Art. I. [*Ante,* 839.]
[85] [*Ante,* 833.]
[86] Published Working Paper (14), pp. 50–53. [See *ante,* 741.]

Herschell in *Vagliano* v. *Bank of England*.[87] One may deduce from his speech the following rules:

(a) All pre-existing case law ceases to have the authority of precedent.
(b) The law is to be deduced from an examination of the language of the statute. It is improper to try to make the language comply with the old law.
(c) Given a 'special ground' (Lord Herschell), it is permissible to ascertain the meaning of the code by reference to old case law, e.g. for words of technical meaning.

This approach is again evident in the judgment of Lord Alverstone in *Wallis* v. *Pratt*,[88] and was approved by the Privy Council in *Robinson* v. *Canadian Pacific Railway Co*.[89] Neither Lord Herschell nor Lord Alverstone would prohibit reference to the earlier case law. Each would regard such reference as legitimate, but only as an aid to construction. Indeed, two benefits may be expected to flow from a study of the earlier case law: First, it is always helpful to see the law in action; the way in which a distinguished Judge has applied it to a comparable situation. Secondly, it would be quite inconsistent with the general policy of providing courts with as much assistance as possible, if, while letting them read Royal Commission Reports, one denied them the help of earlier case law, where it was relevant. If the courts follow Lord Herschell and Lord Alverstone, when dealing with codified law, the first of the court's problems will be solved.

The court's problem as to the limits to be imposed upon argument by analogy is more difficult. If it applies a statute to a factual situation, which the statute's provisions neither expressly nor by necessary implication cover, it is, in fact, making law. It is putting itself in the place of the legislator and drafting legislation. I doubt if either the Judges or the public would find this a welcome exercise of judicial power. Yet, the court has to reach a decision. It cannot content itself with a mere certificate that the law is defective, and leave it to Parliament to produce a remedy. If by a fair, large and liberal interpretation of the provisions of the statute, a solution cannot be reached, English courts would then, I expect, fall back on the common law, the customary law of the country. I would think this to be better than allowing the Judge to exercise his own discretion as to what the law ought to be. But perhaps the true safeguard, if the statute be silent but the particular case requires decision, is in the art and instinct of the Judge. If, as Felix Frankfurter has said, interpretation is an art and its answers will be found only in its exercise, let us acknowledge that there will be the occasional case where the soundness of the law must depend upon the good sense of the Judge.

The vital function that interpretation will come to play in a world of enacted law really makes the case for the provision by the legislator of written material to aid the courts and the legal profession. The dangers and difficulties here are many. First, there is a real danger of accumulating too much documentary material. Secondly, there is the danger that much material which is relevant will prove unreliable. Thirdly, there

---

[87] [1891] A.C. 107 p. 145.
[88] [1911] A.C. 394 p. 398.
[89] [1892] A.C. p. 481.

is the question, who is to prepare the explanatory material—the executive, Parliament, or some other body?

All these difficulties and dangers point to the necessity of restriction. One must limit the sheer volume of the material; there is a limit to what the country solicitor can read—or store on his shelves. One must ensure that the material which is made available is reliable and authoritative.

I do not convict myself of an unruly cynicism, I hope, if I suggest that Parliamentary debates and all the clutter of Hansard are an unsure guide to the purpose of a statute. Whether one thinks of the burden on the ordinary lawyer up and down the country, or the difficulty of discovering from Hansard any reliable guide to the meaning of statute law, one thing is clear: that we should be relieved of the necessity of having to go to that source to interpret the law. These considerations point to the requirement of a memorandum and commentary, more or less elaborate, according to the nature of the statute being explained, to be prepared by the government department or other body responsible for the statute, and subject to Parliamentary scrutiny.

Finally, assuming our law to rest upon enactment, as interpreted by the courts, how is it to be kept in good shape? Judicial interpretation must be relied upon in the first place. However strictly the Judges limit themselves to interpretation, they will, at the same time, be busying themselves with the adjustment of the law to the particular facts of the case they have to decide. Yet, since in a world of enacted law they may well feel their true task is interpretation, and not law making, it would not be right to expect them to correct or develop the main body of the statute law. Writing in 1861, John Stuart Mill, speaking of codification, used these words:

> If the laws of this country were, as surely they will soon be, revised, and put into connected form, the Commission of codification by which this is effected should remain as a permanent institution to watch over the work, protect it from deterioration, and make further improvements as often as required.

Here, I think, is the future task of the Law Commission, once the reform and codification of the general law has been effected. Its main duty should become that of keeping its own creation up to date. One can visualize the system working something like this. In their day-to-day work the Judges will do their best to interpret the law in a fair, large and liberal way. Where, notwithstanding their best endeavours, they are confronted with a particular case which reveals anomaly, defect or omission, they will make the weakness of the law known to the Commission. The Commission will prepare its report and proposal for submission to Parliament. The government and Parliament must co-operate by providing legislative time each session for the consideration of amendments to the statute law recommended by the Commission to correct anomaly or fill gaps.

It is interesting to observe that the State of Louisiana has established a system for keeping its codified law up to date. The state has established a Law Institute, one of whose objects, as defined by statute,[90] is:

---

90 Act 166 of 1938: R.S. (Louisiana) 24: 201–205.

To recommend the repeal of obsolete articles in the Civil Code and Code of Practice and to suggest needed amendments, additions and repeals.

The Law Commission, under its present Act of Parliament, is bound to consider all proposals for law reform submitted to it. Thus, we have in being already a Commission which could undertake the vital task of keeping the law in repair.

In these lectures I hope I have shown that the fundamental feature in law reform is the removal of the development and growth of the law from the more or less exclusive control of the legal profession, so as to become the continuing responsibility of the legislator. Magnificent as is the history of the common law, it is open to the criticism of having been far too exclusively the business of one profession. The lawyer has succeeded the priest in his control of the secrets of the law; and the shelves upon which those secrets have been concealed have been as inaccessible as the altars guarded by the priests in primitive times. Justification for the law reform, the outlines of which I have charted in these three lectures, is that if it be carried through with determination, the state of the law will assuredly become more accessible, more intelligible, and the responsibility of all of us. Society will have an opportunity, through its representative institutions, and after taking the professional advice of the lawyer, to form its own view as to the laws it requires, and to make sure that it gets them. Law reform will not succeed, unless society is prepared to concern itself with the creation and maintenance of sound and just laws. If society, or its representative institutions, are too busy on other problems to find time for reflecting on the law, then my advice would be to abandon the whole difficult business and leave it to the lawyers. But this is a counsel of despair, which Parliament by passing the Law Commissions Act of 1965 has shown it will not tolerate. The future is bright, if only we will seize our opportunities.   [pp. 56–64]

APPENDIX*

BENTHAM

Of Laws in General

This proposition stands in need of explanation: the truth of it depends upon the idea annexed to the word *sovereign*. The case is, that supposing the powers in the state to be thus distributed, there is no one person or body of persons in whose hands the sovereignty is reposed. Suppose two bodies of men, or for shortness' sake two men, the one possessing every power of the state, except that the other in case of a public accusation, preferred in such or such forms, has the power of judging him; including such power as may be necessary to carry the judgment into execution. It is plain the sovereignty would not be exclusively in either: it would be conjunctively in both. Yet in common speech it is probable that the first man would be styled *the* sovereign, or at least *a* sovereign: because his power would be constantly in exercise: the other's only occasionally, or perhaps never. Now then if the narrow sense were to be given to the word *sovereign*, it is plain that the proposition above mentioned concerning the impossibility of the sovereign's being judged by anyone, would not be true. A logician of the ordinary stamp (for nothing is more common than to be versed in the forms of dialectics without any clear notions of terminology) would find no difficulty in maintaining the contrary, and proving it by what to him might seem a demonstration. Taking advantage of the inexplicit notions annexed to the words *superior* and *inferior*, he would perhaps assume for his medium this proposition, that it is impossible for a man to be superior and inferior to another at the same time: or perhaps in different propositions he would use the same word *sovereign* in two different senses: at one time in its strict and proper sense; at another time in its popular and improper sense, according to the distinction above taken. Till men are sufficiently aware of the ambiguity of words, political discussions may be carried on continually, without profit and without end. It may occur, that the distribution of power above supposed is not an expedient one, or that it cannot be a lasting one. This may or may not be the case: but the expediency or the durability of such an arrangement are points with which we have nothing to do here. I consider here only what is possible: now it is possible: for every distribution as well as every limitation of power is possible that is conceivable. The power of the governor is constituted by the obedience of the governed: but the obedience of the governed is susceptible of every modification of which human conduct is susceptible: and the rules which mark it out, of every diversity which can be clearly described by words. Wheresoever one case can be distinguished from another, the same distinction may

---

* This appendix is Bentham's own note omitted from the extract from *Of Laws in General* at p. 197 (see fn. 32a). In the text Bentham is describing by what sanctions a sovereign can be bound. In this note he develops the germ of a doctrine of judicial review, showing that where sovereignty is divided, one part of the sovereign could be bound by another.

obtain in the disposition to obedience which may have established itself among the people. In the former case they may be disposed to pay it to one magistrate, in the latter to another: or in the former case they may be disposed to obey one of those magistrates, and in the latter nobody. Many are the commonplace phrases in use which would seem to assert the contrary: that an *imperium in imperio* is a monster in politics: that no man can serve two masters: that a house divided against itself cannot stand: and these phrases are made to pass for arguments. There is indeed something specious in them at first sight: and without due examination a man may be easily misled by them. Thus much is indeed true, that the same individual branch of power cannot be possessed, and that exclusively, by two persons at the same time. But any two branches of power may that are distinguishable: and any one branch of power may be shared amongst ever so many. What gives rise to the internal contests by which states are agitated or destroyed, is that two different men or bodies of men claim exclusively the same individual branch: which in governments that are not purely monarchical may ever be the case, and that on all sides with the best faith imaginable, while laws are wanting to decide the matter, or those which there are are ambiguous or obscure. The minuteness and refinement of which the distribution of powers in a state is susceptible depends upon the proficiency that is made in the anatomy of language, and the use that is made of the proficiency in the body of laws.

INDEX

Figures in heavier type are references to selected texts.

ADMINISTRATION AND LAW,
Kelsen's distinction, 296–297

AMERICA,
Declaration of Independence, 113n.
equity, 745n.
precedent doctrine, 713–714, 809–810
realist school, *see* REALISTS,
American.
Restatement of the Law of Torts,
344n., **363–365**
sociological school, 342–351
statutory construction, 738n., 826,
828

AMERICA, CONSTITUTION, **113–114**
binding effect of, 113
Fourteenth Amendment, **114–130,
136–138, 424–426, 432–434**
judicial interpretation of, 239n., 713n.,
722n., 809–810
judicial lawmaking, 402n., 410n.,
724–727
natural law, 82
natural rights, 114–130
problems of, 117n.
sovereignty in, 220, 230, 232

ANALOGY,
argument by, in judicial process,
732–733, 784–786, 802, 806–810

ANALYTICAL JURISPRUDENCE. *See*
SOVEREIGNTY, IMPERATIVE THEORY
AND ANALYTICAL POSITIVISM.

ANALYTICAL POSITIVISM. *See* POSITIVISM;
SOVEREIGNTY, IMPERATIVE THEORY
AND ANALYTICAL POSITIVISM.

AQUINAS,
authority of law, 223n., 614n.
customary law, 614n.
Maritain, 110
natural law, 78, 79, 82, **96–102**, 110,
111n., 143, 148n.

ARISTOTLE,
distributive justice, 344, 371n., 665
equity, 743, 744, **835–836**
Hegel's resemblance to, 630n.
natural law, 77, **90–92**, 94–95, 107n.
slavery and, 96
practice of virtue, 102

ARNOLD, T.,
definition of law, 39
judicial trial, 689n.
legalism, 38n.

ARNOLD, T.—*cont.*
natural law, 82
realists, 435

AURELIUS, MARCUS,
reason and law, 92n.

AUSTIN, J.,
aims, 176
American Realists, hostility of, 399–
400
Bentham, 155–159, 160, 176n., 217n.
Blackstone, 218n.
command theory of law, 8n., 66, 81,
160–177, **207–224**, 522n.
concepts of law, 264
constitutional law, 218–219, 223–224
criticisms of, 46, 66, 160–175, 265–266,
276, 498–499
customary law, 21, 42, 160, 217, 570,
573n., 574
defining law, 40, 44, 45, 59, 64n., 159,
207–211
equity, 784
evaluation of his work, 175–177
general and particular jurisprudence,
10, 12, 21, 22
human law and divine law, 218n.
international law, 44, 160, 208, 212,
216–217, 223, 284, 571
judge-made law, 176, **783–784**
jurisprudence,
nature of, **20–22**
philosophy or science? 11
Kelsen's theory compared, 277–278,
280, 291n.
morals and law, 48, 159, 164–166, 211–
220, 240, 247
natural law, 159, 208, 217
Olivecrona's theory compared, 525n.
primitive law, 20, 42, 169, 217
religion, 212n.
rules, 65
sanctions, 166–168, 210–211, 214, 217
sovereignty, 162–164, 170–171, 176n.,
220–224
definition of, 220–223, 232
limits on, 223–224, 232n.
status, 61

AUSTRALIAN CONSTITUTIONAL LAW,
sovereignty, 235–236

BARKUN, M., 7n., 42n., 167n., 288n.
571n.

857